THE BIBLICAL ILLUSTRATOR

ST. LUKE

VOL. II

THE

BIBLICAL ILLUSTRATOR

BY

JOSEPH S. EXELL

ST. LUKE

VOL. II

BAKER BOOK HOUSE
GRAND RAPIDS 6, MICHIGAN
1955

Library of Congress Catalog Card Number: 55-11086

PHOTOLITHOPRINTED BY CUSHING - MALLOY, INC.
ANN ARBOR, MICHIGAN, UNITED STATES OF AMERICA
1955

THE BIBLICAL ILLUSTRATOR.

ST. LUKE.

CHAPTER VIII.

VER. 1. He went throughout every city and village, preaching.—*Village preaching :*—I. WE HAVE HERE THE SUBJECT OF OUR LORD'S MINISTRY—"the glad tidings of the kingdom of God." In these words there is a manifest allusion to the predictions in which the prophets foretold the dispensation of grace and truth by Jesus Christ. The Greek word translated "kingdom" is of a more extensive meaning than the English one by which it is rendered, being equally adapted to express both the terms "reign" and "kingdom." The first relates to the time or duration of the sovereignty, the second to the place or country over which it extends. Yet although it is much oftener the time than the place that is alluded to in the Gospels, it is never in our common version translated "reign," but always "kingdom." The expression is thereby often rendered obscure and awkward, as for instance, when motion is applied to a kingdom; when it is spoken of as coming, approaching, being near at hand, and the like. The word is rightly translated "kingdom" when it refers to the state of perfect felicity to be enjoyed in the world to come; but it is not always thus rendered with the same propriety when it relates to the reign of Christ, by His truth and Spirit upon earth. If, therefore, it be asked, when did the reign of heaven properly begin? we answer, When that prediction in the Psalms was fulfilled—"Thou hast ascended up on high, Thou hast led captivity captive; Thou hast received gifts for men; yea, for the rebellious also, that the Lord God (the Holy Spirit) might dwell amongst them." To a limited extent Jesus reigned before His ascension. He pardoned sins, promulgated laws, and brought very many under the dominion of His truth and grace. But the plenitude of the Holy Spirit's miraculous gifts and sanctifying influences was reserved till Christ was glorified, to grace His inauguration as King of Zion; as monarchs when they are crowned, although they may have reigned some time before, on that great occasion bestow favours on their subjects, and elevate some to distinctions and honours. II. WE NOW PROCEED TO CONSIDER THE SCENE OF OUR LORD'S MINISTRY. He preached in Judæa, and Samaria; in Jerusalem, in Sychar; but His time was chiefly spent in the towns and villages of Galilee—a distant and despised province, which the inhabitants of Jerusalem and Judæa regarded with such contempt that it was asked, "Can any good thing come out of Nazareth?" One would think that had our Saviour intended that secular princes should rule in His Church, that the head of the State should by virtue of His office be also the head of the Church within His dominions, instead of spending so much of His time in Galilee, He would have converted Herod, and given him authority to settle all matters of doctrine and discipline for His subjects. 1. We have fully revealed to us and in our possession that truth by which Christ reigns, and accomplishes His gracious purposes. No new, additional revelation will be granted to the end of time. 2. We have Christ, enthroned in universal dominion, full of grace and power, present by His Spirit, with all His faithful servants, to make His truth effectual in the accomplishment of the purposes of eternal mercy. (*Essex Congregational Remembrancer.*) *Preaching everywhere :*—Three "commercials" entered the railway carriage at C——, and it was not long before all in the compartment were in conversation. Being one of the number, I took my part in the

1

discussions which were held upon various topics. As per usual, the weather was commented upon, the state of Ireland, and the dulness of trade. This last subject seemed to be the most fruitful, for each traveller had his own tale to tell. As the different towns were mentioned which were the markets for the goods "travelled in" by the three gentlemen, I mentioned various incidents in connection with most of them, and through constantly visiting these places displayed some acquaintance with nearly every one spoken of by the "commercials"; until one of them said, "Are you on the road?" "Yes," said I, "I have been on the road ever since I was nine years old." All looked surprised, and then another made the remark, "That was rather early to begin such a rough life!" This produced the following reply upon my part: "Oh, there is nothing like starting young—a good beginning is half the race." "May I ask what you travel for?" inquired a third. "I am on the road to heaven, and I travel for my Master; preaching everywhere for the salvation of souls." (*T. Spurgeon.*)

Vers. 2, 3. **And certain women.**—*Mary of Magdala:*—This woman has " suffered much at the hand of many" commentators; preachers, painters, and poets, ancient and modern. It is high time to do something to remove the foul stain which has so long rested on her fair fame. In the various notices of her history in the Gospels she exhibits " a character as pure and as devoted from the very first as any in the Gospel pages—a character not displaying merely the reflex action of a repentant spirit, but the faith which worketh by love." She was—I. A GREAT SUFFERER HEALED BY CHRIST (Luke viii. 2). II. A GREAT MINISTRANT TO CHRIST (Luke viii. 2, 3; Mark xv. 41). III. A FAITHFUL ADHERENT TO CHRIST. She follows Him to the last, and is one of the women who played such a prominent part in connection with the death, burial, and resurrection of the Saviour (Mark xv. 40; John xix. 25). IV. A SINCERE MOURNER FOR CHRIST (cf. Matt. xxvii. 61; Mark xv. 47; John xx. 1, 2, 11–18). V. AN HONOURED MESSENGER OF CHRIST (John xx. 17, 18; Mark xvi. 10). (*T. S. Dickson, M.A.*) *The ministry of women:*—We know very little about the women of this little group. Mary of Magdala has had a very hard fate. The Scripture record of her is very sweet and beautiful. Demoniacal possession was neither physical infirmity nor moral evil, however much it may have simulated sometimes the one or the other. Then as to Joanna, the wife of Chuza, Herod's steward, old Church tradition tells us that she was the consort of the nobleman whose son Christ healed at Capernaum. It does not seem very likely that Herod's steward would have been living in Capernaum, and the narrative before us rather seems to show that she herself was the recipient of healing from His hands. However that may be, Herod's court was not exactly the place to look for Christian disciples. But, you know, they of Cæsar's household surrounded with their love the apostle whom Nero murdered, and it is by no means an uncommon experience that the servants' hall knows and loves Christ, whom the lord in the saloon does not care about. And then as for Susanna, is it not a sweet fate to be known to all the world for evermore by one line only, which tells of her service to her Master. I. LOOK AT THE CENTRE FIGURE—THE PAUPER CHRIST—AS THE GREAT PATTERN AND MOTIVE FOR US OF THE LOVE THAT BECOMES POOR. 1. The noblest life that was ever lived on earth was the life of a poor man, of one who emptied Himself for our sakes. 2. Think of the love that stoops to be served. It is much to say, "The Son of Man came not to be ministered unto, but to minister"; but I do not know that it is not more to say that the Son of Man let this record be written, which tells us that " certain women ministered to Him of their substance." II. Look at the complement of this love—the love that stoops to be served, and that is THE LOVE THAT DELIGHTS TO SERVE. 1. There is the foundation—" Certain women which had been healed of their infirmities." Ah! there you come to it. The consciousness of redemption is the one master-touch that evokes the gratitude that aches to breathe itself in service. 2. Do we not minister to Him best when we do the thing that is nearest His heart, and help Him most in the purpose of His life and death? III. THE REMEMBRANCE AND RECORD OF THIS SERVICE. Just as a beam of light enables us to see all the motes dancing up and down that lay in its path, so the beam from Christ's life shoots athwart the society of His age, and all those little insignificant people come for a moment into the full lustre of the light. The eternity of work done for Christ. How many deeds of faithful love and noble devotion are all compressed into these words: "Which ministered unto Him." It is the old story of how life shrinks, and shrinks, and shrinks in the record. How many acres of green forest ferns in the long ago time went to make up a seam of coal as thick as a sixpence? Still there is the record, compressed, indeed, but existent. And how many names may drop out? Do you not think that these anonymous "many others which ministered" were just as dear to Jesus Christ as Mary and Joanna and Susanna? How strange it must be to those women now! So it will be to you all when you get up yonder. We shall have to say, "Lord, when saw I Thee?" &c. He will put a meaning and a majesty into it that we know nothing about at present. When we in our poor love have poorly ministered unto Him, who in His great love greatly died for us, then at the last the wonderful word will be fulfilled: "Verily I say unto you, He shall gird Himself and make them to sit down to meat, and will come forth and serve them." (*A. Maclaren, D.D.*)　　*Self-devotion of women :*—The reckless rapture of self-forgetfulness, that which dominates and inspires persons and nations, that which is sovereign over obstacle and difficulty, and peril and resistance, it has belonged to woman's heart from the beginning. In the early Pagan time, in the Christian development, in missions and in martyrdoms, it has been shown; in the mediæval age as well as in our own time; in Harriet Newel and Florence Nightingale; in Ann Haseltine as truly and as vividly as in any Hebrew Hadassah or in any French Joan of Arc. You remember the Prussian women after the battle of Jena, when Prussia seemed trampled into the bloody mire under the cannon of Napoleon and the feet of the horses and men in his victorious armies. Prussian women, never losing their courage, flung their ornaments of gold and jewellery into the treasury of the State, taking back the simple cross of Berlin iron, which is now the precious heirloom in so many Prussian families, bearing the inscription, "I have gold for iron." That is the glory of womanhood; that passion and self-forgetfulness, that supreme self-devotion with which she flings herself into the championship of a cause that is dear and sacred and trampled under foot. It is her crown of renown, it is her staff of power. (*Dr. Storrs.*)

Ver. 4. **He spake by a parable.**—*Nature and design of parables :*—I. WHAT IS A PARABLE? It is a mode of instruction founded on the resemblances or analogies between spiritual and natural objects or events. 1. The form of the parable is a direct or indirect statement of a fact, or a narrative of either some possible or real event, that had occurred once or frequently. The growth of the mustard-seed is a fact of constant occurrence. The parable of Scripture differs from ordinary figurative language, not in its nature, but in its subject. And it might perhaps be correctly defined—a figurative description of religious doctrine. 2. To pass to the substance of the parables. We find their themes mainly to be—the sublime truths of grace, redemption, and retribution; the soul, its responsibilities and its destiny; the Church, and its destiny. II. WHY DID THE LORD JESUS CHRIST TEACH BY PARABLES? 1. He designed to show the union between nature, human life, and the gospel. His presence among men was itself a manifestation of the Divine in the human, the invisible in the visible, the supernatural in the natural. The parable is a similar clothing of the unknown in the known, the heavenly in the earthly. 2. To unveil the mysteries of redemption. 3. To conceal the truth. "That, seeing, they might not see." He aimed again at avoiding a premature irritation of his enemies. Scribes, Pharisees, Sadducees, Herodians, elders and priests (proud, earthly, ignorant, bigoted, envious and murderous), were continually acting as spies around him. It was, therefore, indispensable that he should avoid giving them any ground of accusation before the Sanhedrim, the civil tribunal, or the people. (*E. N. Kirk, D.D.*)　　*Our Lord's parables :*—1. The design of the gospel is to convert men from sin, and save their souls from hell; this is the real purpose of God. 2. Let us move forward a step: It is so ordered in the Divine wisdom that human free-will can refuse to accept the gracious provisions of the gospel, and even finally reject them. 3. Of course, therefore, we perceive that the preaching of the gospel will instantly divide men into two classes, whose moral state must be determined by their attitude towards it. 4. Thus we reach another suggestion: The gospel rejected or perverted does not lose its power, but now goes right on in driving the soul into deeper rebellion and hardness. 5. It now becomes clear precisely what God does do in the process of darkening the understanding and blinding the mind of a rebellious man who will not consent to be renewed and saved. He goes on doing what he was doing before. Suppose two merchant-vessels out on the same sea, sailing before the same wind which comes prosperously on their quarter. Suddenly upon one of them a mutiny is organized; the captain is murdered, and the crew put in irons; then the captors turn on their course exactly, face in the opposite direction, and start for some desolate pirates' isle where they may beach their stolen cargo in safety. The same wind which drives the honest ship along now drives the wicked one too, and so it helps in the crime. But all it really does to help is—to keep blowing on. Once for all be it said, that God never does anything to harden a heart which would not soften it, if properly received. 6. So, finally, we learn that the responsibility of all heart-hardening under the gospel lies only upon the wilfulness of the man whose heart has been hardened. (*C. S. Robinson, D.D.*)

Vers. 4–15. **A Sower went out to sow his seed.**—*Parable of the Sower :*—I. By THE WAYSIDE. 1. The design intended in God's ordinance of preaching—what is it? We answer, your salvation. 2. The means of becoming interested in this salvation are also here declared. "Lest they should believe," says the parable, "and be saved." 3. A hindrance, with many, occurs at the very outset. No sooner is the Word of life spoken to them than—"then cometh the devil, and taketh away the word out of their hearts, lest they should believe and be saved." 4. The success or failure of this hindrance will be owing, not to Satan—though his power is fearfully great—but to yourselves. II. UPON A ROCK. A class of hearers in whom there is some appearance of believing the gospel. Further, their assent is not a cold and involuntary, but a warm and lively, approbation—"They receive the Word with joy." III. AMONG THORNS. A class of persons whose consciences appear to be touched, and, in a certain sense, permanently touched, by the solemn verities of the gospel. And a change has been wrought upon them, by what they have felt. IV. ON GOOD GROUND. The superiority of this class consists in—1. A difference of the soil. Here is "an honest and good heart." 2. A difference in the reception given to the seed sown; that is, to the Word of salvation. The honest and good heart, "having heard the Word, keeps it." 3. There is a difference in the growth also, where the seed falls upon an honest and good heart. It germinates, not hastily, as where neither root nor moisture are found; not irregularly, and amidst perpetual resistance, as where thorny cares, deceitful riches, and ensnaring pleasures choke it; but "with patience"—progressively, uniformly. 4. A difference in the fruit produced. (*J. Jowett, M.A.*) *The parable of the Sower :*—1. Are you a careless hearer? 2. Are you an unsteadfast hearer? 3. Are you a worldly-minded hearer? 4. Are you a faithful hearer? (1) Faithful hearers present to the sower an honest and good heart. (2) They hear and understand : they go along with the love of the Lord as He instructs them, even if they cannot comprehend all mysteries, or gain all knowledge. (3) They keep the Word : they think of it, meditate upon it. (4) Whoever has been the human sower, they regard the seed as what it is in truth, the Word of God which effectually worketh in him that believeth—they are very jealous for the Lord God of Hosts—watchful that no one speak lightly or jestingly of it—most watchful, in being very reverent towards it themselves. (5) And they are patient also, in the possession of the Word—patient in trials, because they have such a pledge of God's goodwill towards them—patient with others, as taught here in God's exceeding great patience towards them—patient in darkness, knowing and feeling that that Word is still, and will always be, a lantern unto their feet and a light unto their paths. (6) And finally, in this patience they bring forth fruit— each man according to his several ability—"some thirty-fold," &c. They are assured that God asks them, not merely for attention, but for fruit : not only for a deep root, but for much fruit : not for an unworldly heart alone, but for that glorious fruit of the Spirit which proves that the inner life of their souls has been begun, continued, and ended in God. (*Canon G. E. Jelf.*) *Parable of the Sower :*—This parable displays profound knowledge of human nature, of human character, and of human history. I. THOSE REPRESENTED BY THE SEED THAT FELL BY THE WAYSIDE ARE INFIDELS. Having the means and opportunities of knowing and practising Christianity, yet rejecting it wilfully and obstinately. II. THOSE REPRESENTED BY SEED SCATTERED ON ROCKY SOIL ARE THE INDOLENT AND TIMID. III. THOSE REPRESENTED BY SEED SPILLED AMONG THORNS ARE THOSE WHO ARE INFLUENCED BY THE STRONG AND ACTIVE PASSIONS. IV. THOSE REPRESENTED BY SEED SOWN ON GOOD SOIL ARE GOOD CHRISTIANS WHOSE IMPRESSIONS OF RELIGION BECOME DEEPER AND BRIGHTER IN DIFFERENT DEGREES. This class includes all sincere persevering Christians. 1. There must be a good and honest heart. 2. A disposition to hear the Word, to receive it without prejudice, and with a sincere resolution to profit by it. 3. Constancy. Retaining the knowledge acquired, and constantly making additions to it.　4. Bringing forth fruit with patience.　Our motives may be good, so also may be our intentions and aims; but to give these their full value they must be carried into action.　Actions, followed by habits, complete the character.　5. Fruit in different proportions.　Yet the lowest degree—thirtyfold—is not small.　(*J. Thomson, D.D.*)　*The Word of God as seed :*—God does not establish full-formed things.　He plants seeds which grow.　This is the uniform method of His procedure in every department, natural and spiritual.　A seed is the most wonderful thing in the world.　There is nothing else that contains so much in so little bulk. There is nothing else that concentrates within it such capacities and possibilities. It is the origin and end of organic life.　It forms the bridge of transition from the grain of sand to the living cell.　By means of it the naked rock is covered with verdure, and the desolate wilderness transformed into a garden.　The analogy between the Word of God and a seed is remarkably close and striking.　There are innumerable points of resemblance between them; but in this exposition I can only point out a few of the more obvious and impressive.　1. The first point of comparison is found in the life which they both possess.　A seed is a living thing.　And in this respect is it not a striking emblem of the Word of God ?　That Word is a living Word.　"The words that I speak unto you," says Jesus, "they are spirit and they are life."　It is not truth merely in a spoken or a written form.　It is more than knowledge.　It is a living power; it does not work mechanically, but vitally.　The words of Christ were the concentration and embodiment of His own life, just as truly as the seed is the concentration and embodiment of the life of the plant.　It is the highest of all life.　And just as in nature it has been proved that dead matter cannot originate life under any circumstances whatever, except by the introduction into it of a living seed, so without the instrumentality of the Word of God there can be no spiritual life.　The Spirit takes of the recorded things of Christ, and shows them to us.　Without the Word there would be nothing to know, or obey, or love; without the Spirit there would be no saving knowledge, no obedience, no love.　The Spirit operating upon the heart apart from the Word would be only to give a vague inclination without an object as its end and purpose. And therefore all religion that does not spring from the seed of God's Word is a dim abstraction of an unreal sentimentality.　It is aimless and powerless, the continual ploughing and harrowing of a field without putting any seed into it.　2. Another point of resemblance between the seed and the Word is the twofold nature of both.　A seed consists of two parts: the embryo, or germ, which is the essential principle of life, and the materials of nourishment by which, when the seed germinates, the young life may grow.　The seed is not all a living principle; its inner essential life reposes in a shrine so small that it can barely be seen.　You take away fold after fold of the minute seed, part after part of its structure, and, after all, you have removed only food and clothing.　The vital germ has eluded you; and even when you have come to the last microscopic cell, you know not how much of this cell itself is living principle, and how much mere provision for its wants.　There is the same dual combination in every spoken and written word of thought and form, of sound and sense.　As it was necessary that the Divine should appear in human nature in Christ, so it is necessary that we should have the Divine thought, the Divine life, in the literary form in which it is embodied in Scripture.　We could not apprehend it otherwise.　The living principle in the seed would not grow without its wrapping of nourishment and clothing; and the mind of God could not affect us unless it were revealed to us in our own human language, in the flowing images of time and sense with which we are familiar. When it is said that we are born again of incorruptible seed, of the Word of God that liveth and endureth for ever, it is not meant to be implied that the Word of God is itself the begetting principle.　It is only the mode in which the principle works, the vehicle by which the mysterious power embodied in it operates.　It is not the human language or thought, but the Divine life within it, that creates us anew.　And when it is further said that this living Word endureth for ever, we are taught thereby that while it is only the vehicle of God's begetting principle, it is no mere transient chaff, or husk, or nourishing material, like the perisperm of the natural seed, which has only a temporary purpose to serve, and then decays and passes away when it has served that purpose.　It is "no mere sacramental symbol lost in the using," but it lives by and with the Divine principle which it reveals and employs, and endures for ever.　And just as we see in the natural seed, owing to its twofold nature, an unbroken continuity of life, pausing here and unfolding itself there, casting off the chaff and the husks that have served their purpose that it may expand freely, the perisperm dying that the embryo may grow; so we see in the Word of God the same principle of identity running through the successive stages of its development—the same vital truth of redemption passing through various dispensations that have become old and are ready to perish, growing to more and more, casting off effete forms, and unfolding itself more clearly and fully in new forms better suited to the new needs. We see the germ that was planted in the first promise of the seed of the woman growing successively into the patriarchal and legal dispensations, and, when the leafage and fruitage of these dispensations waxed old and perished, taking a grander form in the gospel dispensation, and blossoming and fruiting with a new and Divine life in a new and regenerated world. 3. A third point of resemblance between the Word of God and a seed may be found in the small compass within which the living principle is enshrined in both. Nothing, as I have said, holds so much in so little bulk as a seed. It is the little ark that swims above a drowned world, with all the life of the world hidden within it. It is a miniature orb, embracing the whole mystery of animated nature. An atom, often not so large as a grain of sand, contains within it all the concentrated vitality of the largest forest trees. It is a most remarkable example of nature's packing; for a seed consists of a single or a double leaf, folded in such a way as to take up the smallest possible room. And in this respect the Word of God may be compared to a seed. It is truth in its seed-form. We have in the Scriptures the most concentrated form of heavenly teaching. Nothing is omitted; nothing is superfluous. It contains all that is necessary for the salvation of man. Nothing can be added to it or taken away from it. It is rounded and finished off—full-orbed and complete, as every seed must be. All is contained within the smallest compass, so as to be easiest of comprehension, easiest of being carried in the memory, and easiest of being reduced to practice. And the Word of God is so compacted in the seed-form, because it needs to be unfolded in the teaching and life of man. The soil was made for the revelation of the seed; and the seed was made to be revealed by the soil. As the seed cannot disclose what is in it unless it fall into appropriate soil, and be stimulated to growth by suitable conditions, so the Word of God cannot disclose all that it contains unless it grow in an understanding mind and in a loving heart; unless by meditation and prayer it can expand from the seed-form to the blade, and the ear, and the full corn in the ear. As wonderful as the unfolding of a beautiful flower from an almost invisible seed is the unfolding of the depth and fulness of meaning that is in the smallest precept of Scripture. For every new generation, the Word of God has new revelations and adaptations. The seed in the new soil and circumstances reveals new aspects of truth. The Word of God, like the great word of nature which is the illustration of it, holds in reserve for every succeeding age some new perception, some new disclosure of the Divine order and economy, revealing to no man, however studious and zealous, more than a part, and ever opening new vistas to reverent love and intelligence. 4. A fourth point of resemblance between the Word of God and a seed is the variety and beauty that may be recognized in both. Have you ever examined a seed under a magnifying glass? It is often seen to be very curiously formed, even by the naked eye; but the microscope reveals new beauties and marvels of construction in it. The other day, in my garden, I took up the withered head of a poppy, and poured out into the palm of my hand the contents of its curious seed-vessel. There was a little heap of very small round seeds that would take a long time to count. I looked at the handful with the aid of my pocket lens, and I saw, to my delight, that each was beautifully chased and embossed on the outside. For the shapes of beauty often displayed by seeds language has no terms. A whole volume might be filled with an account of them. Some have curious wing-like appendages, on which they float away in the air in search of a suitable growing-place; some are covered with silky down, and some with lace-like tunics, while many kinds have hard enamelled or embroidered surfaces; and their colouring is as varied and beautiful as their forms. In this, the minutest of God's works, this smallest and inmost shrine of life, His attention is acuminated, and His skill, as it were, concentrated; so that, above all others, these little things assure us that we are not living in a world left to itself, but in one that reveals at every step the "besetting God." And in this respect of beauty and variety, does not the Word of God compare with the seed? How wonderfully is the Bible constructed! It is fashioned in human imagery. Every kind of literary style is found in it. The same truth is conveyed in many forms, and always in the most appropriate dress. Proverb and allegory and parable, history, psalm and prophecy, song and incident, everything that can charm the imagination and quicken the intellect and satisfy the heart, is employed to make its doctrines and precepts interesting and impressive. 5. A fifth point of resemblance between the Word of God and a seed may be seen in the wonderful effects which they both produce. There is something almost creative in a seed. You take a seed to a desert, sow it there, and you change the barren sand, by its growth, into a fruitful field. That seed alters the whole character of a place, makes the climate more genial and the soil more fertile, and the very heavens more accommodating. The flow of streams, the nature of the winds, the sunshine, the dew, and the rainfall, the verdure of forest and field, all depend upon the effects which a little seed produces. Man himself has his well-being affected by the growth of a seed. The sowing of seed must ever be the first process towards a higher state of things. Man's natural life hangs upon the sowing of corn. His whole civilization springs from it. His capacity of improvement and capability of receiving spiritual instruction, and consequently all the revelations and experiences of the kingdom of heaven, are connected with the sowing of the seed of the meat that perisheth. And in all these respects, do not the effects produced by the Word of God resemble those of the natural seed? The Word of God is quick and powerful. It awakens an instinctive reverence which no other word inspires. When it enters the soul, it stirs up feelings that are peculiar to itself. It does not lie dormant in the intellect, but quickens the conscience. It does not affect our opinions or specula- tions merely, it affects our heart and life. We regulate our conduct and thought by scientific or literary truth, but such truth does not lord it supreme over our being: it is subordinate to us—it is our servant, and we use it for our own pur- poses. But the Word of God dominates our whole nature, and we must submit to it for its own sake. We cannot use or subordinate it to ourselves; we feel that it must use us, and that we must obey it. It has the power of transmutation in it. It has a spiritual quickening energy. It is the source of saving life to souls dead in trespasses and sins. It has taken its place in the heart of human culture. Nothing else has wrought such a mighty revolution in human ideas. It is a Divine seed which came from heaven, and has brought the kingdom of heaven down to men—made the desert to rejoice and blossom as the rose. The harvest which has sprung from it is everywhere visible in the Church and the world. It is increasing in beauty and fruitfulness every day. We are sent into the world to sow, and not to destroy—to sow the seed of heaven, and thus raise in it a heavenly produce foreign to it, impart to it a principle of spiritual life which, by its growth, will choke out old evils, and make all things new. And let us remember that we must give our own life in the sowing, as the plant gives its life in the seed. (*H. Macmillan, D.D.*)   *The Sower; or, the origin and authority of the gospel:*—The man who sows has an end in view. On that his heart is set. The sower wisely selects, in reference to established laws, the means which are adapted to this end. In other words, this parable presents to our view, as its groundwork—The nature of the gospel as a revelation; the contents of the gospel as an instrument of redemp- tion. I. CHRIST CAME TO REVEAL GOD. I understand revelation to be contrasted with—1. Speculation. The human mind is limited in its range of knowledge, and yet has an unlimited sphere opened to it. 2. Argument or reasoning. Here we need to discriminate. The Word of God is to be believed, because He affirms it; and He will hold His children responsible to recognize His voice. It only remains now to state, in regard to the nature of the gospel as a revelation, that it is a—3. Direct unveiling of truth—it is called a mystery hidden from ages. II. THE SON OF GOD CAME TO REVEAL GOD IN CHRIST. It is a revelation of God; but of God in Christ. It contains, then, as the instrument of redemption, or as the word of the kingdom—1. The ground, extent, and consequences of man's controversy with God. The Scriptures contain, also—2. The ground and terms of reconciliation. 3. The motives to reconciliation. (*E. N. Kirk, D.D.*)   *The four fields:*—1. On the hard field the seed can take no root. There are hearts like that hard field here to-day. They have been trampled hard by sin. The seed cannot grow there. I have heard of a man who had attended the Church for years, and who, when he was dying, told the clergyman that he had never heard one of his sermons. As soon as the sermon began, this man was accustomed to begin thinking of the result of his last week's trade, and planning for the week to come. So the good seed fell unheeded on the hard, trampled field, and the birds of the air carried it away. 2. The seed which fell on the shallow field took root, and grew up very fast. But there was no depth of soil, the seed was not well rooted, and so it quickly withered away, and brought no fruit. How many of these shallow fields we have amongst us! The people represented by them are ready enough to come to church, and to take an interest in religious matters. But their religion is like an ague, a hot fit succeeded by a cold one. There is a special danger for such people in the wild, excitable forms of so-called religion, so common in these days. They forsake the old paths and the sober truths of the gospel for some scene of hysterical excitement, where men would force the seed to grow rapidly in a hot atmosphere of passion ; and they mistake feelings for religion, and noisy display for real conviction. 3. Some seed fell on the thorny field, where the weeds grew thickly and choked it. Ah ! my brothers and sisters, how many Epistles and Gospels, how many lessons and sermons have been lost to you because your life is choked with weeds ! 4. And last of all, there is the good field, where the seed grows and bears abundant fruit. We cannot all bring forth the same fruit, or an equal amount. As one star differeth from another star in glory, so it is with God's people. There is the saint of high and holy life, whose word and teaching sway the multitude. And there is the simple old cottager, who spells out her Bible with dim eyes and painful labour, and finds her treasure there. But both alike are God's good fields, where the seed brings forth fruits. (*H. J. Wilmot-Buxton, M.A.*) *Parable of the Sower :*—I. THE SEED ITSELF. The seed is the Word of God—the word of prophecy ; the word of promise ; the word of sound doctrine ; the word of strong exhortation, and solemn warning, and high encouragement, which is given by inspiration of God. 1. A quickening seed. It brings the dead in sin to spiritual life. It is also productive of much consolation to those who are quickened thereby. 2. A holy seed. 3. An incorruptible seed. 4. A seed of fruitfulness in every good word and work to do God's will. 5. An abiding seed. II. THE DIFFERENT RECEPTIONS OF THIS SEED, AND THE CONSEQUENT DIFFERENT RESULTS. III. PRACTICAL OBSERVATIONS. 1. An important caution to all hearers to take heed how they hear, and to remember their awful responsibility. 2. Much matter of humiliation to the whole Church. There never has been, and never can or will be, any profitable hearing of the Word, unless the Holy Spirit change the heart and prepare the soil for the reception of the Divine seed. 3. Much matter of encouragement to every weak believer. If the work of the Holy Spirit is begun on the heart, the Word of truth may be heard with profit ; and it has been heard with profit by all who are separated from the world, and transformed by the renewing of their mind. 4. Finally, the parable sets forth matter of important instruction to the individuals on the way to Zion, relative to the subject-matter of preaching that shall be profitable for them to hear. (*W. Borrows, M.A.*) *Christ's classification of human hearts :*—According to the Bible, nothing determines the true worth of a man more clearly than the way in which he acts with regard to the Divine Word ; and the different manner of his treatment of it. The Lord places this before us most clearly, intelligibly, in this parable. 1. The indifferent. A very numerous class. Word sown upon, not in, heart ; and therefore is given up to any one who will take it away. To such persons life is a walk, not a journey. Unimportant to them whether they arrive at a definite goal ; they only ask for the invigorating air on the way, to delight themselves with the sight of the beauties around them, and in cheerful conversation with those about them. The enjoyment of life is their watchword ; they do not desire to live, that is to say, to work, but to enjoy. 2. The frivolous. The Divine Word does not take root in these. It takes root only in the heart softened and moistened with the tears of daily humiliation. 3. The impure. These have gone the way of humiliation ; but have not quite given place to the Saviour. They have reserved this and that sinful joy and pleasure, this and that so-called favourite sin and weakness. Their spiritual life is gradually choked in them, and at last is entirely quenched. 4. The pure. These have had their hearts purified and made beautiful and good, by faithfully laying hold of the beauty and goodness of the Saviour. In this state of preparation they hear and receive the Word, and bring forth fruit. They do not release themselves from this obligation, but follow it earnestly and strictly, yet without self-righteousness. They bring forth the fruit of love, the only ripe fruit. They bring forth patience in humble and constant endurance, amid inward and outward afflictions ; also in patience with the often scanty fruit, and especially in a mind which quietly and joyfully submits itself to God in all things. They bring forth fruit in different ways, partly because their soil is of different degrees of goodness, partly because their industry and faithfulness in preparing their soil are different. But none among them assumes superiority over the others ; they all love each other like brethren. These alone are the hearts which really belong to

Christ. (*R. Röthe, D.D.*)   *Parable of the Sower :*—I. THE HEEDLESS.   Hearing without attending.   All a matter of form.   II. THE HEARTLESS.   Interest easily enlisted ; feelings quickly touched.   Feelings so soon stirred are not likely to be deep, and principles quickly influenced are no safe guides.   "Ruined by adversity " is the epitaph of the heartless.   They may be good for a time, but they cannot be good long.   III. THE BREATHLESS.   This is the prevailing phase of modern worldliness.   It is an age of hurry.   Many persons would be excellent Christians if only they were not so many other things besides ; if they were not so engrossed in business, or absorbed in pleasures, or preoccupied by cares.   This will not do. If religion is to thrive at all, it must carry on simultaneously two processes ; it must strike root downward and bear fruit upward.   These are precisely the two things which the worldly man's religion can never do.   IV. THE GUILELESS.   Of these, if we may say it with reverence, it must have been a real pleasure to our Lord to speak. Not, indeed, that the good are all perfect, or all alike good.   No sameness in grace, any more than in nature.   We expect differences, even among guileless hearts.   It is characteristic of the guileless that they make no show for a long time ; they develop surely, but very slowly.   " Saved by patience " shall be written over them.   (*T. E. Marshall, M.A.*)   *The first parable :*—The first snowdrop, the first green leaf on naked hedges, the first few notes that sounding from bush or tree break the long, dreary silence—still more, the first smile that lights up an infant's face, its first gleam of intelligence, its first broken word, possess an interest and yield a pleasure peculiar to themselves.   With more interest still—did the world hold such treasures—would we look on the first stanzas of Homer's muse ; the first attempt of Archimedes' skill ; the first oration of Demosthenes ; the first sermon of Chrysostom ; the first sketch of Rubens ; though we could hope to see nothing in these but the dawn of talents, which, at maturity, produced their splendid works, and won them immortal fame.   What gives the interest to these things, gives a peculiar interest to this parable.   Others may be as instructive and as beautiful, but of all those parables that He strung like pearls on the thread of His discourses, this is the first Jesus ever spake.   As peculiarly befitting Him who came to sow saving truths broadcast on the world, no subject could form a more suitable introduction ; and with the Divine skill with which He chooses, Jesus handles the topic.   I. THE SOWER.   II. THE SEED.   1. There is life in seed.   Gospel truth is the incorruptible and immortal seed ; and though ornaments, polish, illustrations, eloquence in sermons, may help the end in view, as feathers do the arrow's flight, or their wings the thistle-downs, as they float, sailing through the air, to distant fields, it is to the truth of God's Word, blessed by God's Spirit, that sinners owe their conversion, and saints their quickening and comfort in the house of God.   2. There is force in seed.   What so worthy to be called the power as well as the wisdom of God as that Word which, lodged in the mind, and accompanied by the Divine blessing, fed by showers from heaven, rends hearts, harder than the rocks, in pieces ? (Jer. xxiii. 29).   3. There is a power of propagation in seed.   There is not a shore which shall not be sown with this seed ; not a land but shall yield harvests of glory to God and of souls for heaven.   III. THE SOIL.   1. Hearers represented by the wayside.   Some who carefully cultivate their fields, or their gardens, or their business, or their minds, take no pains whatever to cultivate their hearts.   2. Hearers represented by the stony ground.   What have we here ? the Word listened to with attention ; with more, much more than attention ; with such feelings as a man under sentence of death hears the news of his pardon, or men on a wreck, lashed to the mast, hanging on the shrouds, hear the cry, the joyful cry, "A boat ! a lifeboat ! "   Let us remember that convictions may be mistaken for conversion ; admiration of the servant for attachment to his Master ; an appreciation of the moral beauties of the gospel for an appreciation of its holiness ; the pleasures of emotion, or such gratification as taste enjoys in a beautiful discourse, for the pleasures of piety.   3. Those represented by the ground with thorns.   Dr. Johnson put the point well, when, on Garrick showing him his beautiful mansion and grounds, the great moralist and good man laid his hand kindly on the player's shoulder, and said, "Ah ! David, David, these are the things which make a death-bed terrible ! "   The equally dangerous and deadly influence of great poverty I may illustrate by a scene which I have not forgotten, nor can forget. Alone, in the garret of a dilapidated house, within a wretched room, stretched on a pallet of straw, covered only by some scanty, filthy rags, with no fire in the empty chimney, and the winter wind blowing in cold and fitful gusts through the broken, battered window, an old woman lay, feeble, wasted, grey.   She had passed the eleventh hour; the hand was creeping on to the twelfth. Had she been called? It was important to turn to the best account the few remaining sands of life; so I spoke to her of her soul, told her of a Saviour—urging her to prepare for that other world on whose awful border her spirit was hovering. She looked; she stared; and raising herself on her elbow, with chattering teeth, and ravenous look, muttered "I am cold and hungry." Promising help, I at the same time warned her that there was something worse than cold and hunger. Whereupon, stretching out a naked and skinny arm, with an answer which if it did not satisfy the reason touched the feelings, she said, "If you were as cold and as hungry as I am, you could think of nothing else." The cares of the world were choking the Word. 4. Those represented by the good ground. (1) They receive the Word. In their case it does not, so to speak, go in at the one ear and come out at the other. It does not fall on their minds to run off like water from a stone; it falls, but it is as seed into a furrow, to lodge itself in their hearts. They do not reject, but receive it. (2) They understand it—appreciate its value; feel its power; and "comprehend with all saints what is the breadth, and length, and depth, and height of the love of Christ, which passeth knowledge." (3) They keep the Word: as—in contra-distinction to soils that, puffed up by winter frosts, throw out, or others that starve their plants—good ground keeps the corn. With hearts where the tenderness of flesh is associated with the tenaciousness of stone, as granite keeps the letters of its inscription, so they "keep the Word." (4) They bring forth fruit. In the form of good works, of unselfish, gentle, and heavenly dispositions, of useful, noble, holy, and Christian lives, they bring forth fruit—some much; some little; but all some. (*Thomas Guthrie, D.D.*)   *Preachers and hearers :*—I. AN HONOURABLE OCCUPATION. 1. The work of the husbandman too often regarded with contempt. 2. The husbandman a type of Christ. 3. Christ the type of many true teachers, inasmuch as their life's morning is promising, and their evening dispiriting. II. AN HONOURABLE OCCUPATION MAY HAVE DISASTROUS RESULTS. 1. Unsuccessful results do not lessen the value of the seed. 2. Unsuccessful efforts should not be taken as the measure of the sower's capacity and faithfulness. 3. Unsuccessful efforts must then be studied in relation to the sphere of operations. 4. The best seed will do no good on some lands. 5. The most skilful workman cannot turn a rock into a fruitful garden. III. AN HONOURABLE OCCUPATION MUST HAVE BLESSED RESULTS. There will be patches of good ground in every farm. There are honest and good hearts in every community. No true teacher will have entire failure. (*W. Burrows, B.A.*) *The Divine Sower and His seed :*—Two things are clear at starting. 1. The seed is all of one kind—not a mixture, but the same throughout; many grains, but one, and only one quality. 2. It is absolutely and perfectly good; not only the same quality throughout, but that quality perfect, and so each and every grain complete in itself in all that constitutes the perfection of seed. I. THE SEED. Seed is a living reality; seed is the germ or origin from which the plant in its strength and beauty springs. Yet withal seed, living as it is, quick with life which should propagate itself to a thousand generations, is dependent for its germination and its fruitfulness on the soil which receives it when sowed. Now our Lord teaches us that seed, possessing, as we know it does, these qualities, is an apt emblem of the Word of God. II. THE SOWER. Jesus Christ Himself. As men do not always scatter their seed literally with their own hands, but use machinery, and yet it is in truth not the machine, but the man who sows it, by whom the seed is sowed, so, whenever His seed is sowed, He is the Sower, using the hands and mouths of men as His instruments, not giving up His office and work to them to discharge for Him, but Himself discharging His office and work by and through them. It is only a partial account of the ministry of His Church to say that He works upon men's souls by means of it; it is He in it who thus works, and works effectually. He it is, then, who went out as the Sower; He went out, and He has never turned back; He has never ceased of His sowing. But when did He go out? It has been well written— "He is said to go out by the act of taking flesh, clothed wherewith He went forth as a husbandman, putting on a garment suitable for rain, sun, and cold, albeit He was a King." And yet we cannot limit His going out to sow to the actual period of the world's history at which it pleased Him to put on that garment visibly before the eyes of men; for as it was His purpose from eternity to become Incarnate, so the power and virtue of His Incarnation reaches back as well as forward. III. SEED AND SOWER ARE ONE. Christ is the Sower, Christ is also the Seed; for He is the Word of God. He sows Himself. And He is the Life; He hath life in Himself; He quickeneth whom He will. (*C. S. Turner, M.A.*)   *The seed :*—In order to obtain the leading thought of the parable, and so get the key to all that follows, we must reverse the explanatory proposition, "The seed is the Word of God," and take it thus—"The Word of God is seed." The principle of germination is essentially Divine, and the germ idea is the distinctive characteristic of God's work. Man's sole method of increase is collection ; God ever multiplies by scattering. We fill our garners with the harvested grain, and call it wealth ; but its only end is destruction. God sends His sunshine to dry the ripening ear, and His wind to shake out the bursting seeds, and lo ! for every fallen grain an hundred like to itself, all instinct with the same reproductive energy. Man constructs his wondrous mechanisms and quickens them into life with the subtle forces which he wrests from nature and compels to his will. But they wear out or rust out in time, and never reproduce themselves after their kind. If he plant them, they will not grow ; if he break them and scatter their parts, they are utterly destroyed. Or he builds his mighty monuments and leaves them for time to crumble; and long centuries after we dig from the earth their imperishable remnants which have lain as they fell. Under God's law a tree shoots heavenward, more complex and marvellous than the grandest result of human ingenuity. Its fruit falls, and from its decay another tree springs into being ; a branch is cut and thrust into the ground, and that, too, becomes a tree ; a bud is slipped off and inserted in a growth of diverse character, but it becomes a limb, and bears fruit, and reproduces after its own kind. And even if God's monuments, the everlasting mountains, crumble away, they make soil which enters into living organisms, which die and are resolved into dust, which is upheaved by some terrible throe of nature, and lo ! a mountain again. Nothing ever produced by man can germinate. Nothing produced by God ever failed to do so, if placed in the proper conditions. Therefore, if the Bible be seed, it is God's Word. But if the Bible be God's Word, it must be seed; its distinctive character must be the germinative principle. It is the revelation to man of God's truth. But it cannot possibly be all that truth, nor even any part of that truth in its fullest development, because God's truth must be infinite, and this finite world could, therefore, never contain it. Being seed, however, it contains the germ of truth which, if subjected to the requisite conditions, will inevitably multiply itself in infinite series and ratio after its own kind. He who receives this seed as in good ground will, with absolute certainty, in due season bring forth as bounteous a harvest as his capacities may admit. He who receives God's revelation understandingly, becomes possessed of all its potential results of Divine knowledge, which, under proper intellectual and spiritual culture, will be developed to the full capacity of his intellectual and moral constitution in this life and in the life hereafter. (*Robert Wilson, M.D.*) *The Sower sowing His seed :*—I. THE SOWER IS CHRIST HIMSELF. He that sows the good seed is the Son of man. Are not ministers sowers ? 1. Christ sows His own field, which He hath dearly purchased with His precious blood : they sow not their own fields, but His, not being "lords of the heritage of God " (1 Pet. v. 3). 2. He sows His own seed : so in the text. The sower sowed His seed. They have no seed of their own, but fetched out of His garner. 3. They differ in the manner of sowing. He was the most skilful Sower that ever was. He knew exactly what grain every ground was fitted for. With Him were treasures of wisdom. We that have but drops from His fulness, are unskilful in comparison. He could speak to men's private and personal sins, as the woman at the well. He could answer to men's thoughts and reasonings ; we not so. 4. We differ in efficacy. We may sow and plant, and this is all. Suppose it be Paul, or Apollos himself, we can give no increase, nor make anything to grow. But He can sow, and give increase at His pleasure. He can warm it with the beams of grace, streaming from His own brightness (Mal. iv. 2). He is the Sun of Righteousness. He can blow upon His field with the prosperous winds of His gracious and quickening spirit (Isa. iii. 8 ; Cant. iv. 16). II. THE ACTION. This Sower goeth forth. Christ goeth forth to sow three ways. 1. In spirit, by inward inspirations and heavenly motions. And thus He sowed in the hearts of Adam, Noah, Abraham, and the prophets ; who were, with other holy men, immediately inspired and acted by the Holy Ghost (1 Pet. i. 21). So with the penmen of Scripture, and the apostles. 2. In person, according to His humanity He cometh out from the bosom of His Father, and comes into the field of the world by His happy Incarnation. 3. In the ministry of His servants He goeth forth, both the prophets and teachers before Him. III. THE INTENTION is, to sow His seed. 1. As seed is a small and contemptible thing, altogether unlikely to bring such a return and increase ; so the Word preached seems a weak and contemptible thing (1 Cor. i. 23). 2. As the seed in the barn or garner fructifies not, unless it be cast into the earth; so the Word, unless cast into the ears and hearts of men, is fruitless, regenerateth not, produceth no fruits of faith. 3. As the sower pricks not in his seed, nor sets it, but casts it all abroad, and knows not which of his seed will come up to increase, and which will rot and die under the clods; so the minister (God's seedsman) speaks not to one or two, but casts his seed abroad to all in general; neither knows he which and where the Word shall thrive to increase, and where not, but, where it doth increase, it riseth with great beauty and glory, as the grain of mustard seed becomes a tree in which the birds of heaven may build the'r nests. 4. As seed hath a natural heat, life, and virtue in it, by which it increaseth and begetteth more seeds like unto itself; so the Word cast into the good ground hath a supernatural heat in it, being as fire (Jer. v. 14), and a lively power to frame men like itself, to make them, of fleshly, spiritual; of blind, quick-sighted; of dead in sin, alive in grace. And as one grain quickened, brings sundry tillows, and many grains in each; so one Christian converted, and receiving this power in himself, gaineth many unto God, desiring that every one were as he is, except his bonds and sins. 5. As seed cast into the ground lives not, unless it die first; so the Word preached brings no fruit or life, unless it kill first and work mortification; yea, and by continual sense of frailty and acquaintance with the cross, it keeps under such natural pride and corrupt as resist the work of it. 6. As seed cast never so skilfully into the earth is not fruitful, unless God give it a body (1 Cor. xv. 38); so neither is the Word, unless God add His blessing (1 Cor. iii. 6). (*Thomas Taylor, D.D.*) *Plentiful sowing:*—Men do not perish, brethren, because there are not sufficient truths to save them. The seed-basket is ever full, and willing hands are ready to scatter the seed in all directions. What thousands of precious truths are uttered in men's hearing every sabbath day! It is estimated that eighty thousand sermons are preached in this country every week; and what hundreds of thousands more are circulated in the homes of the people by the press; and what constant utterance of saving truths by earnest men in Sabbath schools, in conversation, and by the couch of the afflicted! And yet does the upspringing of this holy seed appear in general righteousness, fidelity, and purity? Is the condition of society a manifestation of the truth supposed to be cherished in its inner life? Alas! no. The truth is but rarely sown in the heart. (*W. O. Lilley.*)

Ver. 5. **Some fell by the wayside.**—*The field-path:*—This first kind of soil is the only one of the four mentioned in which nothing came of the sowing. In this alone there is a combination of causes which renders any good result impossible. Three causes are shown: 1. Before the sowing the soil was incapable of receiving the seed, for it was beaten hard by constant traffic. 2. After the seed had fallen upon it men trod it under foot and crushed out its life. 3. That which remained upon the surface the birds devoured. The connection between the three is obvious. Had the soil not been trodden hard beforehand, neither would the after-treading have destroyed the seed, nor would the birds have found it lying ready. Hid in the bosom of the earth, it would have been safe from both. It is the picture of a thoroughly worldly man—not what would commonly be called a wicked man, not a man whose life is a scandal to the society in which he moves, by reason of the grossness of his vices, or the profane or ribald licence of his conversation, but simply one who may be in all outward and social respects without a speck or flaw in his character—nay, who may even be scrupulous in performing all such external acts of religion as the world is pleased to account marks of respectability and good taste, but who is withal simply incapable of receiving any wholesome impression from the ministry of the Word of God, because he has given up his whole heart and mind to worldly things, and heart and mind under their unopposed influence have become completely hardened. Such a man hears the Word. It is beautiful to him, it is pleasant to him, just as, and in no other way, than some history, or poem, or fiction, written by the hand, inspired by the genius of a fellow-man, is pleasant or beautiful. As the work of God's hand, the revelation of God's mind, he never for a moment recognizes it; as the voice of God's Spirit speaking to and bearing witness with His own spirit he never for a moment thinks of it or feels it. And this because there is drawn over his heart and mind and spirit—over all that part of his being in which exists most fully the image of God and the counterpart of the Divine mind—that hard, callous covering of worldliness which is the common road of all that is unprofitable and vain, but is like armour of proof against the entrance of aught that is good and holy into the soil beneath. (*C. S. Turner, M.A.*) *How to reclaim the indifferent :*—If the farmer wish to throw into one his separated fields, and make the old roadway part of his productive soil, he knows that the very causes of its hardness have added some fertilizing elements, and that only deep and thorough tillage is needed to accomplish his purpose. But he carefully chooses the time to put in the plough. He does not begin his work when the frost has bound the land in its icy fetters, nor when the drought and heat have reduced it to stony hardness. But meantime he is diligently removing the fences and clearing away, as opportunity may offer, the obstructions which have accumulated. And then some day, when he sees it softened by gentle showers, which the shading clouds have allowed to soak into its bosom, he ploughs deep and harrows thoroughly, and lo, the work is done! In the same way must we deal with this indifference to religion. If we attack such a man when his heart is cold and careless, or when some angry spirit of controversy warms him into resistance, we shall meet only disappointment. In fact, we are sure to be disappointed if we attack him at all. We must wait patiently and watch closely. We must gently and quietly remove as we may the barriers which most frequently we have ourselves erected about him. So long as we keep him fenced out from the companionship and familiar intercourse of pious people, we can make no impression upon him. It was not John the Baptist, but Jesus the Christ who was the friend of publicans and sinners. If we seek the society of such people, and show interest and pleasure in their company, at first they may be shy, but we shall soon see that pass. If we are careful not to obtrude our religion upon them they will always be careful not to make their irreligion offensive to us. And then some time, when the clouds of sorrow have overshadowed them, and the gentle rain of kindly sympathy has softened the hard crust of reserve, God gives us our opportunity, and we may drop the rich seed of His saving truth into the deep furrows which lie open in the mellowed soil. Who knows but that when the harvest season comes, we may trace the old roadway all through the burdened field by the line of heavier sheaves which it has ripened! (*R. Wilson, M.D.*) *The highway ground :*—I. THE KIND OF SOIL. 1. As an highway lieth careless, neglected, unbounded, common, not several, but is trodden and beaten with the feet of all sorts of passengers, so these hearers' hearts are not closed and made several for the seed of God's Word, and for heavenly things, but lie common and open to all tentations and suggestions of Satan, to the covetous and carnal desires of earthly things, which eat up heavenly; to vain wandering, idle cogitations and thoughts, all which make a thoroughfare and beaten path in the heart. 2. As in an highway if any seed fall, no man looks to cover it, no man respects it, as looking for no good at all of it, but leaves it to be trodden of beasts, and eaten up of birds : so with these hearers, when the Word is preached, they hear it carelessly, without all attention, or affection, they care not to understand it, never cover it by meditation, nor receive it further than by giving it the hearing; they expect no good from it ; let errors and lusts come and tread it down, let the devil by suggestions and tentations devour it up; they care neither to understand, nor receive, nor remember it. 3. As highway ground can neither receive nor cover the seed, or if it should, it is so hard and padded, that it cannot afford it the least rooting, at least to come unto fruit, the crop will never fill a man's hand : even so these hearers, like hard and paved earth, continually trodden and trampled with wandering thoughts, and fruitless cogitations, and tentations of the devil, hear the Word sometimes, but without heart, mind, affection. A little seed may lie on the superficies or top of their brain, or tongue, or may make a little show on the outside, but nothing of it gets within them, nor takes any root, and consequently yields no fruit of faith, of God's fear, of piety or Christian conversation. II. CAUSES OF UNFRUITFULNESS. 1. Inward. Their own disposition : they tread the seed under foot ; that is, despise and undervalue it. It is the careless hearer who understands not, nor attains. The careless hearer is the worst hearer of all, as this first ground is the worst ground of all. The other two are bad both, yet they gave the seed some cover, and receive it in; but these hold it out, and leave it where they found it. 2. Outward. The malice of the devil (see ver. 12). Where are three things to be considered : (1) The description of this malicious person, both by his name and by a similitude. (2) The exercise of his malice : "he cometh." 3. The end of his coming ; threefold : (1) To steal the Word. (2) To hinder faith. (3) To bereave men of salvation. (*Thomas Taylor, D.D.*) *Seed on the wayside ; or, the heedless hearer :*—This part of the parable is founded on the principle that attention is the first claim of the gospel. The gospel claims attention from us—I. AS TRUTH By a mental law, truth and the mind can have no connection but through the medium of attention. 1. The attention is voluntary. 2. Attention is under the law of habit. 3. An obligation rests on man to exercise and improve this power. For we know that some of the highest obligations of life involve a right exercise of attention. II. As a SYSTEM OF TRUTH HAVING PECULIAR DIFFICULTIES TO THE HUMAN MIND. For it includes—1. Spiritual facts as its basis and its end. The difficulties of life have been the occasion of making all the greatness the world has ever witnessed in men. 2. Painful truths; being a direct, unqualified attack upon cherished desires and confirmed habits. 3. The doctrines of the gospel are contested truths. And the contest, our Lord informs us, is first begun by another party before man takes it up. Some find insuperable difficulties in particular doctrines. Others are prejudiced against the principles for being so much better than those who profess to believe them. And he has taught another class in his school to look within themselves for illumination. III. As TRUTH OF SUPREME IMPORTANCE. 1. It is God's special revelation in human language. It is God's Word, addressed to all men, and to every man. Then, by everything sacred and decent, by every consideration of propriety and of duty, every human being should listen to the Word of God. And again we are bound to give such attention, because the Scriptures—2. Fully and strongly exhibit our duties; the chief of which are those we owe to God. They also fully exhibit our duty to man. 3. God here treats of life and death eternal. This is the sum. (*E. N. Kirk, D.D.*) *World-hardened:*—They hear the Word as a man hears in a dream. They do not attend to it. It is a mere sound that has no meaning in it to them. If you ask them, "What think ye of Christ?" they reply by saying that they have not thought at all. He is not personal to them at all. It is a common thing to meet men and women who have been church-goers all their lives, and who tell you with the blandest manner, when you speak to them about their souls, that they have never really given the matter any serious thought. No impression of truth has been made upon their hearts. They are indifferent to it all, though keenly alive to and intelligent concerning a score or a hundred earthly interests. They are sometimes called "gospel-hardened," but this is a great mistake. They are world-hardened. They are like the mill-owner who had given half the money required to build a stately church upon the services of which he attended, and who, when asked what he thought of the sermon of dedication, to which he had been outwardly listening, said: "The fact is, I did not hear what the pastor was saying. I could not help thinking all through the service, as I looked at the spacious proportions of this edifice, if it was a cotton mill how many spindles I could set up in it." The man was mill-hardened. A lady confessed to me once that, during the sermon, though she heard the words of it and understood the theme as I discussed it, she had been planning for a dinner party that she was to give during the week. Here was a heart society-hardened. I knew another man who acknowledged that during the sermon he had been mentally making a note of the men whom he noticed in the congregation, and arranged in his own mind how and when he would see them in order to induce them to take out policies in a great life insurance company, of which he had recently been made the local agent. Thus do men harden their hearts and become wayside hearers. (*G. F. Pentecost.*)

Ver. 6. **And some fell upon a rock.**—*The shallow soil:*—It is evident that there is a very considerable difference between the persons whose state is signified by the shallow soil and those who are represented by the hard field-path. By those the Word of God is not received at all—merely heard with the outward ears, and in no true sense understood; by these the Word is not only received, but received with joy. The persons now in question do not simply listen to the Word of God with pleasure and admiration, as the worldly man does, because of the outward graces in which its expression is clothed. No! their joy is a joy of the heart—they understand that which they hear, in a sense in which the worldly man understandeth it not. Its inner meaning—its spiritual beauty—is not hidden from them, as from him. They are able to discern and to appreciate it as a revelation of God, and the excellence, the purity, the righteousness, the loveliness of that which is revealed find in their hearts a powerful attraction. They listen to the gospel story and, far from only enjoying it as a beautiful story, they feel themselves drawn "with cords of a man, with bands of love," by Him of whose love and labour for them the story tells. Nor does the effect of the Word end there. They not only understand, they not only feel, but they act. The love of Christ constrains them—constrains them to break away from evil habits, to exercise self-denial, to follow in many ways that which they see to be good. What more, you may ask, could be expected or desired? Is not this the very result which the Divine Sower looks and longs for? Is not this proof which cannot be gainsaid that the Divine seed has taken good root, and is fulfilling the purpose of its sowing? How can this soil be classed as unfruitful when it is actually bearing so goodly a crop? Alas! the Sower Himself answers our questions. It is all good while it lasts; but it endures but for a time, and all trace of it is gone long before the reapers go forth to gather in the harvest. Then they find no more fruit here than on the path, and they carry no sheaves hence, for all its past promise, to add to the store in the Master's barn. (*C. S. Turner, M.A.*) *On stony ground :*—The wayside had suggested incapacity for fruitage, resulting from a misapplication of the moral and intellectual faculties, the consequence of which was indifference to sacred things. The stony ground illustrates another and equally disastrous condition of irreligion, produced by an entirely different cause. Here the soil is good. In fact, in such places it is often of superior quality, produced by the rotting of leaves and other refuse matter in the moisture which cannot soak into the ground, But it has no depth. The seed which falls on this rich warm mould is rapidly quickened and soon germinates, shooting up with a green luxuriance that gives promise of speedy and abundant returns. The roots are thrown out all along the surface, but they can take no firm hold on the soft and yielding material, and the tap-root, which ought to penetrate deep into the subsoil to give support to the plant and find a never-drying source of moisture, is bruised and turned aside by the underlying stones against which it strikes, while the very rapidity and luxuriance of growth soon exhausts the scanty materials which nourish it. The warm sunshine which ought to give life and vigour becomes a source of injury instead, and the wilted plant droops, dies, and is forgotten long before the harvest season comes. Now we know perfectly well that such ground is far from useless; that if the proper treatment be applied it is often the most profitable, for these are just the conditions which we select or produce artificially for forcing. We want rich and rapid growth, and we know how to obtain it. Every gardener knows what special care must be bestowed upon the hot-bed to prevent the loss of all his labour. The hot, damp, shallow soil receives greedily the proffered seed, and with a marvellous quickness develops the germ. But the most assiduous attention is demanded, for these hot-bed plants are far more delicate than those beside them from the same seed. They must he mulched and watered, the sunshine must be courted, but shaded off as it grows too warm, the cold air must be carefully excluded, but often discreetly admitted, and the least relaxation of all this diligence means destruction. A sash left open, a mat removed, a single watering forgotten, and the plants wither and droop. The very same soil, if deeply dug, thoroughly drained, and well fertilized, will become permanently strong and productive. Surely we are only too familiar with the application in all its various degrees. We see all about us people in every stage and character of irreligion who were once, to some extent at least, professedly pious. It is fearful to contemplate how many such there are, and how very difficult it is to reawaken them to any interest in religion. The facility with which great numbers of persons may be made to acknowledge the influence of religious emotion is familiar to us all, and a little observation will also make us familiar with the startling disproportion of those numbers to the comparatively few who persevere. Nothing could be further from the truth than to accuse such persons of hypocrisy, for emotional characters are almost always sincere. It is precisely because their minds are so receptive, their feelings so readily impressed by eloquent and earnest appeals, that we find them yielding so readily and accepting the assurance of God's love with a gladness as real as it is demonstrative. But they have no depth of character, and their very shallowness causes a rapid and luxuriant development of practical religion. The drunkard is suddenly reformed; the profane swearer becomes frequent in prayer; the brawler grows peaceable and patient under insult. But one after another the old evil habits of life get the better of them, and their last state is worse than the first, because religion has become to them an experimental failure; the glowing faith which believed conversion an accomplished fact has given way to disappointment, and the man has lost all confidence in the reformatory influence and efficacy of religious belief and effort. Now if we bear in mind this warning lesson of the Master, we shall always become watchful and careful when we see any unexpectedly prompt and promising yielding to religious influence or exhortation. Beware of the quick fertility of the stony ground. (*Robert Wilson, M.D.*) *Stony ground :*—I. THE KIND OF SOIL. A kind of bad hearers. compared to stones, or stony ground. 1. For the natural hardness, which cannot be broken nor softened. 2. For their coldness: not warmed with the heat of the sun of righteousness, nor the Spirit of God, but abide cold as stones. 3. For their heaviness: a stone will not easily be removed out of his place, his proper centre is the earth. 4. For their unprofitableness, and resistance of the fruits of the earth: for as stoniness of ground by the curse upon man's sin became very noisome to the fruits of the earth, so the stoniness of heart, a part of the curse, more hinders fruits of grace than any stony ground can hinder seed cast into it. 5. As stony ground and common stones are little esteemed, but rejected of men; so this stony ground is as little respected of God. Yet herein our hard hearts are worse than stones: they increase not their hardness; but ours is daily increased by wilfulness and perverseness. II. Now to the SUCCESS OF THE SEED in this stony ground: and first, the hopeful and commendable, in the beginning—" it sprung up." Which implies that of Matt. xiii. 20, "He which heareth the Word, and incontinently with joy receiveth it." Where we have four things considerable. 1. This bad ground receiveth the Word: wherein they go beyond the former hearers, who only heard the Word, but left it as soon as they heard it; let the devil, or any devouring bird eat it and take it from them, they care not. 2. This bad ground receives it "incontinently" (saith Matthew), when God speaks they will hear, and without delays or excuses willingly receive when God proffers. 3. These bad hearers, and stony ground receive it with joy. 4. This stony ground brings up the seed sown. (1) It rises to external obedience and reformation of many, perhaps most things. (2) The seed springeth up to an outward profession, as those that hope to be saved by it, and so to an outward fellowship and communion with the saints in the Word, sacraments, and many other godly exercises, both public and private. (3) It springeth up in the stony ground to a kind of faith, which hath in it not an enlightening only, but a taste of the heavenly gift and the powers of the world to come, by which they are partakers of the Holy Ghost; that is, something they have so like true sanctification that both themselves and others may think them truly sanctified. Some of the Israelites tasted of the fruits of the land of Canaan, and did thereby perceive what a good land it was and desired part in it, and conceived good hope of enjoying and possessing it, yet never enjoyed it, but perished in the wilderness. Learn hence how far a bad hearer may go in Christianity. A man may hear the Word with diligence, receive it with joy, believe with some assurance, grow up to high place in the profession of religion, bring forth fruits of commendable obedience, and all this while be bad ground and in damnable estate. Having spoken of the success of this seed cast into the stony ground, in the commendable hopes it gave in the beginning; now we proceed to the lamentable and doleful success in the conclusion with the reason of it, both in the words now read unto you. 1. "It withered away." 2. "Because it lacked moisture." First, of the withering of these glorious professors, then of the causes. This withering is a falling away, but not all at once, but by little and little, as a leaf loseth his greenness and flourish, and withers by degrees. For the word implieth the manner of their falling. Neither is it a falling away in part, or for a time, as the disciples and Peter in the time of Christ's passion; but a final falling away from all their graces, from which falls is no return or rising. Here consider four things: 1. How men wither away in grace. 2. The danger of withering. 3. Notes of a man withering. 4. The use and application of all. For answer to the first: Men, even great professors in the Church, wither four ways. 1. In judgment. 2. In affection. 3. In practice. 4. In the use of the means. The second is the danger of such withering: Which we shall clearly see in four particulars. 1. In respect of God they are most hateful, seeing they can find nothing more worthy forsaking than the good way, and esteem everything better worth keeping than God's image and graces. 2. In respect of the Church: They bring scandal to the weak, and the scorn of the wicked upon themselves and all professors. 3. In respect of the sin itself: None more dangerous. For first, relapses, we say, are far more dangerous than first diseases. Secondly, Satan returning, comes with seven more wicked spirits than himself, and so he is for ever held under the power of Satan. Thirdly, this sin is commonly punished with other sins, which is God's most fearful stroke, to which He seldom gives up His own. Fourthly, it is in the degrees of the sin against the Holy Ghost, and easily brings a man into that estate that there may be left no sacrifice for his sin. 4. In respect of the judgment that awaits and overtakes this sin. The judgment is certain. The third general thing proposed is: Notes of a man withering in grace. And these are six. 1. A resting in a common and general hope of a good estate, without desire or endeavour to seek marks of certainty or special assurance in himself. As a foolish tradesman hopes his estate is good enough, and bears his creditors in hand it is so ; but he is loath to cast up his books or come to a particular view of it. No surer argument of a man decaying. 2. An opinion of sufficiency, that he hath grace enough, he will seek no more because he pleaseth himself in his present measure ; and he that careth not to increase his stock wastes of the principal. And not to go forward is to go backward. 3. A comparing of a man's self with those that are of lower and inferior graces or means. 4. A shunning or slighting of God's ordinances ; a willing excommunicating himself from the assemblies when he list. That man's strength is abating who falls from his meals. He must eat that must live. And the plant that would not wither must draw moisture daily. Or, if using public means diligently he neglect private, he is on the withering hand. 5. Secret sins ordinarily committed, not bewailed, not reformed. 6. Hatred of God's children, and the way of just men, whether open or secret. What be the means to keep us from withering ? 1. Get sound judgment, to discern the truth from error. If we would not fall we must be grounded on the foundation of the prophets and apostles ; by private reading, meditating and conferring of the Scriptures, which notably begets and confirms soundness of judgment; and by prayer, which obtains the spirit who is called the spirit of judgment. The lamp fails without oil. 2. Sound persuasion of the truth thou professest ; that thou mayest not please thyself that thou hearest the truth from the mouth of the preacher; or hast it in thy Bible at home; no, nor content thyself that thou hast it in thy mouth or discourse, but that thou hast the experience of it in thine heart. 3. Sound affection and love to the truth upholds from withering in it, when the wise Christian esteems the pearl worth selling all to buy it. Love anything better than grace, thou art gone. Demas loves the world better, and easily forsakes the truth. How many lights in the beginning of their profession have been extinct by the world coming upon them. 4. Sound conscience ; to which is required—(1) sincerity ; (2) tenderness. Now the marks to know a hard heart are these : 1. When God's Word makes no impression or gets not within the heart to renew or reform the man, though sometimes it may scratch the outside and restrain him. 2. Neglect, or light overpassing the works of God's mercy or justice, upon himself or others. 3. Unfeelingness of hardness, and unwillingness to feel it ; no mislike of it, no desire to understand the danger of it. 4. For the maintaining their estate, credit, and favour in the world, or their lusts and pleasures, to oppose and dislike such doctrines, courses, and persons as have the word on their sides. 5. Out of resolution of following a man's own present course, whatsoever persuasion or doctrines he hears to the contrary, to fly occasions and companies which might touch or work upon his conscience. 6. Habits and customable sins, which make the heart as a pathway. A soft heart smites itself for once sinning and for small sinning. (*Thomas Taylor, D.D.*) *Seeds on stony places ; or, the cowardly hearer :*—Here is a case of great promise in the commencement. We should here take a distinct view of the nature of courage. The common notion of it is, indifference to danger. But that does not distinguish this noble principle from rashness. It properly refers to that quality of mind by which the higher sentiments overrule the dread of suffering. These sentiments are such as patriotism, philanthropy, integrity, sense of duty, and sense of right. The opposite state of mind is that which places the escaping from suffering above every consideration. And it is a person governed by that principle that is pointed out by this part of the parable. This habit of placing comfort before goodness equally facilitates the beginning and the ending of his religious life ; for —I. It prevents him from even understanding the theory of the gospel, and much more from truly accepting its provisions. Imagine a person awakened by the law of God to an apprehension of danger ; of guilt in his sight, and consequent exposure to the Divine wrath. If he would regard the testimony of God, he would find more in his case than the exposure to suffering. But such is the operation of selfishness in the human heart, that often where this sense of danger is irresistibly urged home, there is still such a magnifying of suffering as the great evil, that the attention shall be fully absorbed by that. The first consequence is—1. He neither sees that Christ comes to save him from sin ; nor that he is a sinner. 2. He misapprehends the atonement, or the ground of Christ's death. This must make a superficial Christian. 3. He fails also to see the work of the Holy Spirit, and his own obsolute dependence on that Spirit for renewal and sanctification. There lies in that heart the deep, dead, broad rock of impenitence and pride. Into its compact substance no root of conviction, of repentance, of faith, of love, ever penetrated. The very thing he has bargained for is an easy service. Christ gives peace ;

and it is peace he wants, and not trouble. He can accordingly sail in smooth seas, and live well in fair weather with his religion. But—II. HE CAN DO NO BETTER WITH THE PRACTICE OF THE GOSPEL THAN WITH ITS THEORY ; for—1. It requires him to struggle with sin in his own heart. The work to which Christ calls us is a progressive conquest over spiritual evils in ourselves. 2. His conflict with the world. Men of superficial religion are generally very much perplexed to know what the Scriptures mean by " the world," against which they speak so severely. (*E. N Kirk, D.D.*)

Ver. 7. And some fell among thorns.—*The thorn roots :*—These are not thoroughly worldly persons, who pay no heed at all to the Word of God ; nor yet are they persons who trust to their own feelings and impulses, and what are called religious impressions, for strength to stand in the evil day, and to endure tribulation for the sake of Christ ; but they are those who set themselves to accomplish the task which our Lord says is impossible, of serving God and Mammon, of making, as it has been said, the best of both worlds. They cannot seek God with their whole heart, because their heart is always occupied, in part at least, with some other object. God and the things of God are acknowledged by them as having a claim on their time and thoughts, but it is only the spare time, only the thoughts of (so to say) idle moments, that they can afford to give up in response to this claim. Whatever home the Word of God can find for itself in vacant spaces of mind and heart it is welcome to occupy ; whatever influence it can exercise within the narrow limits which other things do not fill, they do not grudge it ; but it can by no means be permitted to interfere with more pressing interests, or to assert anything like a free right of entry into all the concerns of life. It is not at all, I think, that, like those represented by the shallow soil, they grasp eagerly at the sweet and comforting portions of the Word's teaching, set aside all that is more stern and terrible, and so live really under the influence of that part of the Word which they have gladly received until they wake to the conviction that what they have received is only a part, and that the time has come when the choice lies between giving up the part received and receiving in addition the part set aside, and then have not sufficient earnestness to take the harder and better course, and so fall away altogether. Rather it would seem they do from the first recognize both sides of the teaching— the sweetness of the promises, and the awfulness of the threatenings ; but at the same time there is something which prevents them from fully appreciating either the one or the other ; something which hinders them from really using all their energies that they may avoid the threatened woe and attain the promised blessedness. And this something is the hold upon their hearts which is already established by cares, riches, pleasures, delights of the world. Thus they feel some desire to escape the future punishment of sin, but the desire of being free from present cares lies deeper, and if it comes to a question between voluntary endurance of cares here for the sake of happiness hereafter, and self indulgence now with the risk of misery in the future, they choose the latter, because they see the things temporal more clearly than the things eternal, and what they see most clearly they rank most highly. Thus also they wish to enjoy the glories of heaven, but they wish also to have all they can of the enjoyments of earth, and if they must forego one for the sake of ensuring the other, they will most readily forego that which they wish for most feebly, because its excellence and desirableness is least real to them, and this again will be the distant glory which is discerned by faith only, not the present enjoyment which forces itself upon the notice of their senses. (*C. S. Turner, M.A.*) Among thorns :—Here a new and startling thought is brought out, which leads our minds into a different and most suggestive channel. The Master's mind recurs to the great germ-principle, and teaches us that God's Word is not the only seed that is sown broadcast over the world ; that the controlling application of God's fundamental laws covers evil as well as good, and that all through this vast glebe of nature there are seeds which never fell from the hand of the Divine Husbandman, quick with the same mysterious germ of life, subject to the same law of germination and development under like conditions, and bound by the same inexorable necessity to reproduce themselves after their kind, but noxious in character, waging ceaseless and destructive warfare against the good, and promising an inevitable harvest of sorrow and death. Remembering, now, that all life is governed by this same law of the germ, we may go for our first illustration to what we call " animate nature," where the seed is found under the form of the egg. Walking by the waterside we find two eggs on the shore, so nearly similar in size, and shape, and colour, that an unpractised eye would scarcely distinguish one from the other. The same white, brittle shell, every section of which is some modification of the arch, equally the strongest form to resist external violence and the weakest against pressure from within. Break this shell and we find in each a similar living membrane, an air-chamber for the support of the young animal, a yolk for its nourishment suspended by twisted ligaments and protected by an envelope of glairy albumen, with the germ-vesicle containing potentially the future young as yet indistinguishable by any human power. We submit these almost exactly similar eggs to the requisite conditions of time and heat until the breaking shell reveals the developed young, and lo! the marvellous difference! From the one, a bird of pure and beautiful plumage, serviceable to man in its every part, an ornament to nature and fitted to walk the land, to float on the crested wave, or to cleave the light air with its sweeping pinions as it soars toward heaven. From the other a scaly monster of loathsome form and frightful aspect, fitted to live only in slime and mire, and destined only to destroy its fellow-creatures. These results, we know, will be invariable, nor can any power reverse or modify them. Thus we learn how exact are the analogies between moral and physical nature. Experience teaches us, further, how full is all soil of the seeds of noxious weeds, and the parable shows us how equally full is our moral nature of the germs of deadly sins and cares which choke out every growth of good. So true is this in the physical world, and so absolutely impossible is it to detect the germs of life prevailing everywhere, that science has even dreamed of spontaneous life as the only solution of the mystery. Prepare your ground, however carefully, for the seeding, it will be green with unwelcome growths long before your grain has sprouted. Let a drop of purest water remain exposed for a few hours, it will swarm with animalculæ and microscopic vegetables. Make anywhere an artificial pond, and in process of time it will contain fish and water-plants, but rarely of useful kinds. The air we breathe is full of the infinitesimal spores of deadly maladies, ready to germinate and produce their lethal fruit; but who ever heard of an atmosphere quick with the seeds of health? Under the same great law, then, the soul of man, his moral nature, the moral atmosphere in which he lives, must be full of those evil germs which bring forth the "thorns" of the parable. So evident has been this truth to all human experience, that men have believed in a dual source of life—the Ormuzd and Ahriman of the Persian mythology, the God and Demiurge of the Gnostic philosophy, the one the creator of evil, the other of the good. But whence come these seeds of evil? How is it that these germs of destruction so pervade all nature? Science has but recently demonstrated that they are not, in the physical world, of spontaneous origin. The water which so rapidly developes life becomes utterly lifeless when heated to boiling and absolutely excluded from the air. There is one series of processes familiar to us which gives the clue to all the rest, because it shows how God works in creation by the instrumentality of the law of germination. In the barren depths of ocean one of the lowest forms of animal life, the coral polyp, multiplies itself into unnumbered millions, exuding from its body the stony substance which slowly reaches to the surface and forms a reef. This catches the floating seaweed and the drifting pieces of wreck, which decay in the sunshine and form a soil. Some nut or fruit, protected by its hard covering, is borne by the waves from a far-off shore and cast upon the new-formed island, and sprouting there, in process of time produces a tree, which in turn produces others like itself. The falling leaves and rotting stems increase the depth of the soil. The wearied sea-birds seek shelter from the storm, and soon form a colony. Then other birds are driven there, and drop the seeds of their food, and man comes in his vessels and leaves behind him other germs of animal and vegetable life. Thus, in the course of centuries, a great and populous island comes into being. Were our opportunities and our faculties sufficient to the task, we could doubtless in the same way trace out the most mysterious of these phenomena, and learn how in thousands of simple, but unsuspected ways the seeds are carried and planted. The squirrel buries his winter store of nuts and acorns, only a small part of which are consumed; and in a few seasons the growth is entirely changed, and the grassy plain becomes a forest; the swift-winged pigeon is slain by the hawk miles away from his feeding ground, and the undigested seeds in his crop are scattered, and shoot into plants hitherto unknown there. But in the moral world there is another and a darker agency at work to disseminate the germs of evil, as it snatches away the seed which falls by the wayside; for we learn from the parable of the tares among the wheat that "an enemy hath done this." There is an evil being of great power and malignant purpose who fills man's heart with the deadly seeds of worldly cares and sorrows, and who well knows that the richest and mellowest soil is the best for his objects. (*Robert Wilson, M.D.*) *Among thorns :*—I. WHY LUSTS ARE COMPARED TO THORNS. Carnal lusts are fitly compared to thorns in five respects. 1. There are some flowers, and some show on thorns, small fruits, and many pricks; so whatever appearance these lusts make, no good fruit riseth of them, but many pricks and sorrows by them in the end. Thorns pierce the body, lusts the mind. 2. Thorns are everywhere armed, and ready to wound and tear him that, meddling with them, doth not carefully fence himself; so they that nourish the cares of the world, or addict themselves to pleasure or profits, pierce themselves through with many sorrows. 3. As a thorn held softly pricks not nor hurteth, but when it is held hard and crushed, it easily draweth blood; so a man may use this world, as not using it, without danger, and hold softly the profits and pleasures of this life; but grip them, and fasten on them, there is certain hurt. 4. Thorns and briars are the dens and receptacles of serpents and poisonful worms and creatures; so are these unmortified desires the harbours of infinite noisome sins, which shall creep as thick into the soul as the frogs into Pharaoh's lodgings. As Israel, not content with God's daily allowance, but out of a covetous and distrustful desire, against God's commandments, saved some of the manna till morning, but it was all full of worms, and stunk; so do fleshly minds, by nourishing unlawful lusts, turn manna into worms. 5. As thorns and briars are at last good for nothing but fuel for fire; so these thickets of lusts, and pursuit after the profits and pleasures of this life, are the proper fuel of the fire of the great day, and prepare the ground itself (which all worldlings are), without timely repentance, as fuel for the fire of hell, which is unquenchable. II. THESE BAD HEARERS ARE APTLY COMPARED TO THORNY GROUND. For as a thorny and weedy soil chokes and kills at length such seeds as come up hopefully; so a heart, stuffed with unmortified affections, at length resists and chokes the seed of God's Word, that it shall not prosper to the salvation of that hearer in the harvest; for—1. These thorns supplant the Word, and unroot it again, as thorns, to root themselves, undermine the seed below. 2. These thorny corruptions hinder the comfortable heat and shine of the sun from the heart, namely, the sweet beams and influence of the spirit of grace, which cannot come so sweetly and freely to the heart to cherish the growth and work begun, as thorns hinder the sun from plants. 3. Thorns draw away the moisture which should preserve the plants in their growth and greenness; even so these inward lusts draw the heart from means of moisture and grace; they sometimes give a man leave to hear, but as they prevail and take up the heart, there shall be little time allowed to remember, meditate, or apply that which is heard, and as small leave to bring things into practice. III. THORNS AND LUSTS OF ANY SORT, SUFFERED TO GROW IN THE HEART, DO SOON OVERGROW THE WORD OF GOD, AND SUFFER IT NOT TO PROSPER. For as the husbandman, who suffers thorns and weeds to choke his seed coming up, loseth his harvest; even so that man loseth his part in the gospel that cherisheth lusts and disordered desires in his heart, together with the gospel. Hence the Apostle James (chap. i. 21) telleth us that if we would hear the Word so as it may be ingrafted in us, we must first cast away, or put off as an old rag, "the superfluity of maliciousness and filthiness," that is, the abundance of carnal affections, looseness of life, pride, disdain, wrath, contention, earthly pleasures, vanity, evil speaking of Divine doctrine, &c.; and in the next verse shows that with these lusts men may be hearers of the Word, but never doers till they be weeded out; they will at length overgrow it. Reasons: 1. Ill weeds, we say, spring apace; good seeds or herbs not half so fast. We shall see a bramble grow more in seven months than an oak in seven years. So our text—the thorns grow up with the seed, but choke it by overgrowing. 2. Our grounds are fit and prepared to produce thorns rather than bring up the good seed. Our hearts are the natural mother to lusts, but a stepmother to seeds of grace. For there lies in our nature a sea of evil lusts lurking; our own original lust is a fountain, and an inordinate disposition to all evil. From which fountain issue innumerable streams of actual lusts, which are the innumerable motions of the soul, contrary to every commandment of God; all which, in their several armies and bands, issue out against God and His Word, as the Philistines still warred against Israel. Now, our ground being so apt to weeds, they will soon overgrow the Word, if but a little neglected. 3. A part of the curse on man's sin is that the earth should bring forth thorns and thistles. The earth should have brought them forth, if man had not sinned; but they should not have been so noisome and hurtful to man and the fruits of the earth. Even so it is a part of the curse of our sin that there should grow up such noisome lusts (as thorns) in the ground of our hearts, as do far more hinder the growth of grace in our hearts, and choke the seed of the Word sown in our souls, than all the weeds and thorns in the world can choke the seeds and fruits of the earth. Lusts are still remaining in the best, but not now as a curse, but only, as the Canaanites, to keep them humble. 4. The reign of lust cannot but thrust down the reign of the Word; for, first, that the Word may reign, it must be understood, but thorns hinder the light of the sun from the seed. One thorn is enough to darken the eye of the understanding. Secondly, that the Word may reign, it must first renew. But there can be no new creature, till the old man be put off, with his lusts (Eph. iv. 22, 23). Thirdly, that the Word may reign, it must be obeyed when it commands, and be expressed in the fruits of holiness. But lusts unsubdued oppose themselves, and hinder the motions when they should come into practice, and the Lord's plant becomes fruitful only on that condition, that the Father purge it (John xv.). Again, how can a man walk on cheerfully in his way that hath a thorn sticking in his foot? No less do these thorns cast men back in their way of obedience. These superfluities of lusts and inordinate desires are as dead branches, that must be lopped off before fruit can be expected. (*Thomas Taylor, D.D.*) *The seed among thorns; or, the fatal compromise:*—We are now introduced to another character, which we may denominate—the compromising. They strike hands with the gospel, but with the world at the same time. Some are willing to suffer for their soul's good, who are still unwilling to relinquish each rival to Christ. The case has these prominent features—there is, under the hearing of the gospel, a partial suppression of worldliness. But the worldly desires gain an ultimate victory over the gospel. I. THE PARTIAL SUPPRESSION OF WORLDLINESS IN HEARING THE WORD. 1. The attention of the mind is, for the time, diverted from the world. Human consciousness follows the will and sensibilities. It takes no cognisance of deep, underlying principles in the heart. They may be master-principles, giving to the character its every distinctive feature, and shaping the whole current of action; and yet, under particular circumstances, they shall be to the soul's consciousness, annihilated. This law of the mind is of the first magnitude; and yet human history is filled with the delusions which men practise on themselves by overlooking it. Now, men may have no consciousness that they are governed by a love of the world, and may readily embrace the hopes of the gospel, under an impression of their entire sincerity and earnestness in doing it, while at the same time their hearts cling to the created sources of enjoyment, with a tenacity strong as the desire of happiness and dread of misery can make it. The first reason of this temporary ascendancy of the gospel, and of their delusion in regard to its completeness, is the strong impression which is, for the time, made on the sensibilities. It may come in various forms. One is—a temporary disgust with the world. This has deceived thousands; for this very disgust derives its acuteness from the strength of that affection which is disappointed. The man who has calmly looked behind every mask the world wears, long recognized the hollowness of its pretensions, and the falseness of its promises, is the very farthest from any paroxysm of disgust. He has been accustomed to consider a thorn a thorn, and if by any inattention he leaned his hand upon it, and it pierced him, he only reproaches himself for his heedlessness, and walks thereafter more guardedly. But here are your romancers, whose gravest occupation in youth was the day-dream. They studied the world through their fancies and their favourite writers. And on some dark day a storm arises, and lightnings strike the cherished tree on which grew their heart's fondest hopes. In an instant its blossoms wither; its leaves are scattered; its shattered trunk alone remains. And to the heart's moanings there is no response but sullen thunder, howling wind, and roaring floods. Such has the world become in one day to some that most fondly cherished, most devoutly worshipped it. Now the love of the world, as a principle, may remain entirely unshaken by all this violence. 2. The gospel is taken up without reference to its opposition to the world. Men do regard themselves as religious who never formed one definite idea as to the peculiar spirit of the gospel and its unworldly features. There are thorns in the ground which will yet effectually choke every religious sentiment and purpose. II. THE ULTIMATE TRIUMPH OF THE WORLD OVER THE GOSPEL. "He also that received seed among the thorns is he that heareth the word; and the care of the world and the deceitfulness of riches choke the word; and he becometh unfruitful. I. The feebleness of the religious principle. It sprung from transient causes. If these causes had been made merely occasions it would have been well. But it remained a thing of impulse, and did not become a matter of principle. He should have struck the blow that would have emancipated him from the world. 2. The strength of the worldly principle. There is a care which becomes us, as endowed with forethought. The poor feel it, the rich feel from it. Itself a sin, it begets sin. It fills the mind with so many vain desires, perplexing thoughts, and wicked purposes, that God's Holy Word can find no permanent entertainment there. Then an innumerable host of interests, objects, and passions are included under the phrase—the lust of other things. But we have gone far enough to see this principle established—that the mastery of one worldly desire over the human heart will effectually neutralize all the power of the gospel. The evidence of it is in the fact that the prevalence of that desire proves the complete delusion of the soul on a vital point. And every indulgence of the desire strengthens the soul's aversion to God. (*E. N. Kirk, D.D.*)   *Thorns like flowers:*—Our thorns sometimes appear like flowers. Our worldly cares seem quite legitimate, our sins appear pleasant, our earthly graspings necessary; but there is not a single thing that hinders the reception and supremacy of the truth within us that will not become a thorn to pierce us. The rose of our sinful delights will wither, and we shall find that our hearts have nourished thorns. All these evil growths must be destroyed, brethren; the high towering thorns of pride that cast their shadow upon all tender springings of violet-like virtues; the creeping, entangling thorns of lusts; the glossy-leaved thorns of deceit so smooth to the eye and yet so stinging to the touch; the long, bare spiney thorns of malice; the short stubbed thorns of worldly worry, and the sharp-hooking thorns of covetousness—all must be rooted out of us if the truth is to spring up into the pleasant foliage of moral beauty and the sweet fruit of gracious deeds. (*W. O. Lilley.*)

Ver. 8. **And other fell on good ground.**—*The good ground:*—Here consider, as in the former—1. The soil, good ground: where first, how it comes to be good: secondly, how it is known to be good, namely, by hearing with honest and good hearts. 2. The success of the seed in it—fruitfulness. 1. For the measure, or plenty—an hundredfold. 2. For the continuance, or constancy—with patience. Of these in their order. And first, how the ground doth come to be good. Answer: It is called good, *non à priori*, because the Word finds it so; but *à posteriori*, because by the Word it is made so. Every man's heart by nature is a stiff ground, a barren and cursed earth (Eph. ii.). 2. But as stiff and bad ground becomes good by good husbandry and manuring, so do our hearts by the husbandry of the Good Husbandman. He alone changeth the heart. I. It is called a good heart in two respects. 1. As emptied of bad qualities. 2. As well qualified by grace. (1) It is emptied of bad qualities, being clean contrary to all the bad disposition of the three former kinds of ground. So as being contrary to all the other, it receives willingly, retains constantly, and perseveres fruitfully unto the end. (2) It is well qualified by grace, as in our text. (*a*) God hath made it of a cursed and barren earth, good ground. (*b*) It hears the Word beyond the other. The former heard it, but without desire, this hears with study to learn, and industry to understand. (*c*) It keepeth the Word in memory, mind, and practice; the other heard, but kept nothing, because there was no fit place to keep it in. (*d*) It brings fruit. In the other was some care to hear, but here is a care of fruitfulness. (*e*) It is careful to proceed in grace, to double and increase the measure of fruits, from thirty to sixty, and so to a hundredfold: but the other soon fall from their measure. (*f*) It hath obtained by grace an invincible fortitude against temptations and trials, so as no fears or forces shall remove them from the study of piety and fruits of grace; for they bring forth fruits with patience, as the other did not. II. So it is called an honest heart. As good is a general word, excluding evil qualities, and including good; so honest also is a general word, and put for the whole approved disposition of the soul, containing both civil and religious honesty. Here for our further direction in so weighty a business we will consider three things. 1. Means, whereby to attain a good and honest heart. 2. Marks, to know when it is so. 3. Motives to the attaining of such a heart. The means are generally two. 1. Let us see our defect in nature, that our hearts are not good by nature, but stiff and stubborn as the stiffest ground. 2. Let us therefore seek a supply by grace. This grace is twofold—1. Of action. 2. Of acceptation. The grace of action is threefold—1. Preparation. 2. Of new creation. 3. Of irrigation. But because all this grace of action is imperfect in this life, therefore that our hearts may become truly good and honest, there needs also the grace of acceptation. The best ground is good but in part, and no man can say his heart is clean, but much evil and guile will cleave unto it. Yet, where God hath begun a good work, and beholds a constant purpose of good, resolving against all sin, and to please Him in all things, He is pleased to behold only the work of His own finger, and to see us only in our Head, in whom He beholds us all fair and good, imputing His goodness to us, and covering our remainders of evil in Him. He esteems us according to that we are coming to, not by that we have attained. These are the means whereby our hearts become good. Now of the marks whereby they may be known so to be. These marks, because they are many, we will in general reduce them to seven heads, and consider this good heart. 1. In respect of God. 2. Christ. 3. The Spirit of God. 4. The ordinances of God. 5. Itself. 6. Good duties. 7. Sin and evil. In respect of God, it hath five excellent properties. First, It desires nearer union with God daily, and all things shall set it nearer unto God. For it knows that everything is so much the more good as it approacheth unto the chief good. Secondly, If it seek God it will " seek Him with the whole heart " (Psa. cxix. 10), which is a sound conformity of the inward and outward man, directed in the service of God according to the truth of the word. Thirdly, A good heart will only and wholly stand to God's approbation in that it doth or doth not. Fourthly, A good heart resteth and rejoiceth in God as in the best and only portion (Psa. lxxiii. 25). Fifthly, A good heart aims at the glory of God in all things. " In all his parts " (1 Cor. vi. 20)—in his body, because it is His, and in his spirit, because He is a Spirit. In respect of Christ it hath five other excellent qualities. First, It preferreth Christ before a thousand worlds (Phil. iii. 8). Secondly, A good heart rejoiceth more in Christ and His love than in worldly joys. Thirdly, A good heart, seeing that Christ hath given Himself wholly unto us, gives itself wholly to Him. Fourthly, A good heart prepares a room in it for Christ to dwell in (Eph. iii. 17). Fifthly, A good heart conforms itself to Christ, and will walk as He gave example. For it knows the Scripture hath set Him out, not as a Redeemer only, but as a pattern of good life and imitation. It looks unto the Spirit of God; in four kinds of notes. 1. In respect of spiritual assurance. 2. Spiritual worship. 3. Spiritual graces. 4. Spiritual growth. A good and honest heart looks to the ordinances of God, and so hath many excellent qualities. In two general respects—1. In respect of Christian religion itself. 2. In respect of the means by which it is upheld, and these are three—1. The Word and sacrament. 2. The Sabbaths and assemblies. 3. The pastors and ministers. A good and honest heart hath many marks in respect of itself—as the Scriptures ascribe many properties unto it without which it cannot be good. 1. Newness. 2. Softness. 3. Cleanness. 4. Singleness. 5. Fruitfulness. 6. Watchfulness. Marks of a good heart in respect of good duties. It considereth, first, that it is God's new workmanship created to good works (Eph. ii. 10). Marks of a good heart in respect of sin. It knoweth, first, that nothing is properly hated of God but sin, as being directly against His law and His image, who is a God hating iniquity ; and as God Himself is the chief and absolute good, so only sin is the chief and absolute evil. Hence—1. It sees the misery of sin, and groans under the burden. 2. It truly repents for sin. 3. It seeks pardon. 4. It feareth and watcheth all sin to come, as it hateth and shameth for all sin past. As nature shuns and fears all serpents, even little ones as well as great, so grace shuns all sins, and hates them, being the spawn of the Serpent. First, it knows all are hateful to God, all prejudicial to the soul, as one hole in a ship, or one swine in a garden, or one fly in the apothecary's box is enough to spoil all ; therefore it watcheth all. Secondly, Seeing small sins are commonly harbingers to greater, it dares not venture on the smallest. Thirdly, It knows that the way to avoid final defection, or backsliding, is to fear staying a little. Fourthly, It fears the show, the taste, the occasions, the first appearances of sin, lest from the broth, it easily fall to the flesh. Fifthly, It fears and hates his own sins more than all other men's, and not as it is said of Anthony, " He hated the tyrant, not tyranny." " I hate that I do " (Rom. vii. 15). Sixthly, It hates and fears his own inward sins as much as the outward ; wisely damming the fountain and well-head, and stocking up the root. Seventhly, It hates and fears the repetition of sin, and much more shakes off the habit of it, lest he should suddenly grow to expertness in the trade. Lastly, It hates and mourns for other men's sins, and stops them when he can (Psa. cxix. 136). " And now tell you weeping " (Phil. iii. 18). Yea, the sins of others against God more smite a good heart with sorrow than their own sins can an evil.   5. It retains and still renews a full purpose of not sinning, so as though it sin, the conscience can testify that it is carried against the settled purpose of it. (*Thomas Taylor, D.D.*)   *The seed in good ground; or, right reception of the gospel :*—I. WHAT IS THE RIGHT RECEPTION OF THE GOSPEL ?   The answer may be given in a word.   It is the reception of it into the mind and heart as the remedy for sin.   This involves—1. The recognition of sin.   An honest heart is one that acknowledges its wrong.   There is no honesty in any of us denying that we are sinful before God and sinners against Him.   2. The acceptance of the remedy offered.   II. WHAT, THEN, ARE THE RESULTS ?   I. The whole character is changed. 2. A change in the whole life.   If a brackish fountain has suddenly lost its bad qualities, the change will be discovered in the sweetness of the stream that flows from it.   III. There is, then, A GREAT RESPONSIBILITY in preaching, hearing, and possessing the Word of God.   Our responsibility is to God.   That a field has soils of various kinds, may be a matter of no interest to any one else; but to the frugal farmer it is a matter of great interest.   To the passing traveller it would occasion no anxiety to know whether all was hard as the wayside; or all a light soil on a broad undivided rock; whether thorns and thistles had intertwined their noxious roots over all its surface; or whether it would give bread to the sower, and return thirty, sixty, and a hundredfold to the reaper.   But to the industrious labourer this was a matter of the first moment.   (*E. N. Kirk, D.D.*)

Ver. 10. Unto you it is given to know the mysteries of the kingdom of God.— *The mysteries of the kingdom :*—A mystery, as the word is used in Scripture, is nothing more than an unknown thing.   It has no reference to anything obscure, or awful, or difficult to understand.   The most simple truth may be called a mystery so long as it is concealed.   That a Gentile could be converted to Christ was a mystery to the Jews—an unknown thing, not a thing difficult to be understood. Read the text, "Because it is given unto you to know the *secrets* of the kingdom of heaven, but to them it is not given," and the meaning is plain and complete. I .Let us endeavour TO DISTINGUISH THE TWO CLASSES,—on the one hand, those to whom it was given to know the mysteries of the kingdom; on the other, those to whom it was not so given.   Some have interpreted this passage as a judicial sentence of perpetual ignorance and unbelief.   I am more disposed to interpret it as a description of a hardened and obdurate state of mind—a wilful ignorance connected with gross stupidity. Because their hearts had waxed gross, and their ears were dull, and their eyes were closed—wilfully closed—the Lord left them to the mystery of the parables, but expounded the interpretation to His disciples in their more private intercourse. Jesus had spoken His parables from a ship on the Sea of Galilee to vast multitudes who collected to hear Him from the neighbouring towns and country.   We have, then, abundant illustration of the character of this multitude.   They came from the places in which He had done most of His mighty works—Capernaum, Chorazin, Bethsaida, and the neighbourhood.   In their synagogues Jesus had expounded the Holy Scriptures and showed their fulfilment in Himself.   But these people had seen His wonderful works as though they saw them not, and heard His words of wisdom and love as though they heard not.   The application is to you, and an affecting application it is.   Take heed how ye hear.   See that ye refuse not Him that speaketh from heaven.   The dreadful shadow of the second death had fallen upon the multitude, and no beams from the Light and Life of the world could dispel its gloom.   And oh, consider that the men of the neighbourhood where Jesus chiefly taught were those denied the interpretation of the parable.   Exalted to heaven by their privileges, they were debased and brought near to hell by the abuse of them.   Now let us look to those to whom Jesus gave the interpretation.   The inquiry is, What had they which the others had not?   If the disciples had not knowledge, they had the desire to obtain it, and the spirit to make it productive. 1. They had the desire to obtain it.   In learning the mysteries of the kingdom (as in everything else) the docile disposition and the acquisition of knowledge are inseparably connected.   What cared the multitude for the hard sayings of Jesus? Gratify their vain curiosity, amuse them with signs and wonders, feed them with loaves and fishes, and they are content.   But the disciples—that is, the learners— longed to know the whole meaning of the Saviour's lessons.   They heard the parables, and they sought the interpretation.   They felt that they lacked wisdom; they hungered and thirsted after the knowledge of righteousness, and with the docility of children they desired to learn the mysteries of the kingdom of heaven. To them it was given to know—to them, having the teachable disposition, the instruction was readily and freely afforded. Multitudes are still ignorant of the truths of the Gospel, even in the midst of this bright day of clear, evangelical, heavenly light; but the ignorance of every one of them amidst so many means of instruction is to be attributed to their own wilful indisposition to learn. To how many among us is the Bible enveloped in thick darkness! its great truths are still to them mysteries of the kingdom—secrets hidden from their view, as with a Pharisaic contempt, or a sinful dislike, they pass their wandering eyes over the words of the sacred page. They read, but understand not what they read. They have no interpreter. The Holy Spirit they have resisted and repelled. The avenues by which pure, Divine, holy truth might reach their hearts they have closed by the corruptions of the flesh and the cares of the world. But some of you have otherwise learned Christ. You were impelled by an ardent desire, and you went with humility, like children, to sit at the feet of Jesus to learn of Him. His words, read in the letter of Scripture, became much more than letter as you read them; they became spirit and life. You felt their spiritual quickening power. Imploring by earnest prayer the light of heaven, that light shone upon the Book of God, and you saw as you had never seen before, wonderful things out of His law. Thus to you much has been given. But—2. The disciples had a spirit to make their knowledge productive. They did not neglect or abuse the knowledge they had. The good seed in their hearts brought forth its own fruit in its season. How often have the elements of scriptural knowledge been abused, and how often have they been suffered to lie neglected in the heart! And abuse or neglect will always prevent a clear and believing perception of the mysteries of the kingdom. If this be so, no one ought to utter a word of complaint respecting his ignorance of the mysteries of the Gospel. Why do they remain hidden from him? The answer is at hand: because he is not faithful to the little light he already has obtained. Men often see not the doctrine, because the present duty, always plain, it disregarded by them. You may think you know little of the mysteries. But do you not know that you ought to seek more earnestly than you have sought? to practise more self-denial than you have yet practised? to do many things you have not done, and to refrain from doing much that you continue to do? It is no wonder that you should remain still in ignorance of many things, seeing you have already more light than you follow in the practical part of religion. II. LET US CONSIDER THE MEANS BY WHICH THESE MYSTERIES WERE REVEALED TO THOSE TO WHOM IT WAS GIVEN TO KNOW THEM. 1. A plain and easy way of giving the true knowledge is made apparent. We have the admonitions of Christ as well as His teaching. Our duty is not mysterious. We can seek wisdom, and seek it in the path of obedience. 2. The mysteries are revealed in their appropriateness to ourselves and their application to our wants: revealed to our hearts, according to our need. Show the man himself, a sinner ready to perish—the suitable Saviour for him is revealed by His paying the penalty of sin. 3. The mysteries are revealed in succession, as they prove useful, not to gratify curiosity. (*R. Halley, D.D.*) *The mysteries of the kingdom of heaven :*—God is always undoing mystery. He keeps no mystery for the sake of the mystery. He is never withholding, but always giving. His work in relation to us has been from the first an unfolding. He is the God that giveth truth. I say again, He does not put forth His will to hide, but ever and always to reveal. The mysteries of God are the things that the wise and prudent so often turn aside from—they take them as matters of course; and many besides the wise and prudent, many fools likewise, many who are wise in their own eyes—let me say all who are wise in their own conceits. "Of course, of course," they say; "we know all about that; but we want to understand this, and we want to know what that means; and we want to see how you can account for this, and whether or not you can put this and that and the next thing in your scheme," when all the time things are crying out in them and around them which they think are too common, too simple, puerile perhaps; "they do not interest us," they say. That which God requires of men is just to attend to the thing, whatever it is, that He requires of them, as revealed in their heart, in their feeling, in their sense, that they are not doing altogether right, that they are not being altogether right. And while they are speculating, perhaps, upon what they call the mysteries, what the theologian calls the mysteries, the thing that is a mystery to them is the thing that every simple child-heart can understand. When God calls His children it is that they respond as children in obedience—in obedience. The Lord in His parable is telling us something that perhaps has ceased to be looked upon as at all a mystery with us. Do you know what St. Paul so often calls the mystery that he has to reveal? It looks to us a simple thing enough. It was a very hard thing for many at that time to receive it, and now in other forms it is hard still for certain kinds of minds to receive it. It was just that God loved the Gentile as much as the Jew, that God was no respecter of persons, that He cares for the poor man as much as for the rich. That was the mystery. We think not very mysterious after the common use of the word, but the mystery is the simple truth, the fact of relationship that lies deepest and uppermost and everywhere throughout nature, making life worth living, and men worth being. That kind of mystery is a thing that it is so difficult somehow to wake up the minds of men to see. Try to show any man his duty and he will immediately begin to ask you questions about theories. To get man or woman to acknowledge —I do not mean by word of mouth, but by act of soul, by powerful emotion of the spirit, of themselves, of their will—to acknowledge, I say, that there is between their hearts and the infinite, all-pervading, unseen force of life, that there is a heart thinking about their hearts, and wanting to have them, that there is a father-love at the heart of things that is looking down and brooding over the hearts of His children, and drawing them to lift up the heart to God, and be in His presence a live thing opening door and window to the reception of that which He is continually trying to give—this is the mystery, the absolute simplicity of life to which it seems scarcely possible sometimes—I mean it sometimes seems scarcely possible —to wake up one's own flesh and blood to understand and feel, for we are all one family in Him in whom the whole family in heaven and earth are named. Some would think it a grand thing to be told they could increase their life twofold, tenfold, and live for hundreds of years. God knows if I would turn that leaf to gain that. I should simply scorn it. Whatever is true in any of these things, whatever is true is mine; but I do not want it except by growing to it in the natural progress of the law of Him who is the root of my being, and who has told me that I inherit with Jesus Christ that which my Father has to give. I would put my hand forth, I say, to take no glory of existence save what the natural process of His developing of an obedient child comes to me in its own free, simple form. If you want to attain anything in the shape of true moral, physical, spiritual progress, I say, be the simple disciple of Jesus Christ. That is what you are born men and women for, not to make money, but to know God; and to know Christ is the only way to know God. You may learn of the power of God, but the power of God is not God. God is love, and until we love with our whole souls we do not know God. We may know Him a little, less or more, in proportion as we are capable of loving; or rather, not as we are capable of it, but as we do it—we know God. And in this spirit let us look at the parable that our Lord had just spoken about as containing mystery. Well, God knows it is to me the deepest of all mysteries, even in the common sense of mystery, a thing that utterly perplexes me, and I just stop there and cannot understand it, and that is, the point when the heart of man, the child of God, stops turning its back upon Him, and begins to wheel round the other way; the point when the prodigal, who is the type of every one who goes away from God, and loves anything better than God. God, it seems to me, alone can see and know that, but that this turning takes place we know, and plenty of testimony could you have to the fact. And so in this parable about the seed sown. And looking at all the parables of Christ, what I find in them is this, that He is doing what He can just so to wake up the soul of man, and to cause this change to be begun in the soul of man. He does not speak the parables for the purpose of concealment. Neither does He speak them for the purpose of instructing the intellect and the understanding about things. That is not His work, though all that follows is. Ah, you would know something, friends—let me speak to my young friends present—you would know something of the glory of a life that is independent of outside things. If you just set yourselves to be the thing God meant you to be, set yourselves to obey Him whom the Father sent just to make you shine in the very light, the supernal light, that is all about at the root of everything, wisdom and knowledge, everything that the heart of man falsely worships, precious as it is, freely worships at your command, and if you would but be Divine as you are meant to be, if you will be earthy, if you will be poor creatures, if you will be what Dante calls "insects in whom the formative power is lacking, defective insects that cannot pass into the glorious butterfly"; he says—and I am speaking now of what one of the greatest of men said six hundred years ago—"Do you not know," he says, "that you are worms that are meant to go forth as the angelic butterfly?" "O foolish man," he says, "why do you seek low things? Why are you content to be unborn in the cocoon, or in the chrysalis of the worm?" The Lord speaks, I say, in all His parables to wake up that power of life in us that makes a man put everything aside and look up and feel that he has but to be, and he must be, he must be the thing that the Eternal Father made His child to be, else we are but the defective insect we may be born. So what do I find? Here is the story of sowing seed. It falls on different soils, and at last it comes on good soil, and the Lord does not say a word about anything that the soil can do. But He seeks to make us think it and feel it and weigh it in our minds, and speaks of something that we have got to do with it—the hard-trodden ground by the wayside and the poor soil on the rock, with the corn hanging its head, drying up with the drought, and the corn that would look over the tops of the thistles—that would say, "I am bad soil, but I cannot help it; the seed has fallen, but what have I got to do with it?" But there is good soil, and that soil knows that it has got to do with it, and that is just the difference. When the truth of God comes to a true heart—and God claims that the heart should be true, and if the heart is not true there is its condemnation already—when the word drops into the true heart, the true heart says, "I must keep that: I must mind what I am about, I must see to this thing or that," and so it grows and grows. There was one man I heard sometimes when I was a youth, and I cared more to hear him than all the rest put together. When I came out from hearing him perhaps I could not tell you a word he had said, but I knew I had something to mind; and you may make that a test whether you have been the true ground or not, when anything true has come to your consciousness as truth. The great trouble is, first, with those who never know that anything has anything to do with them. The time has not come, somehow. There may be good soil underneath, but the top is hard-trodden. There is something that seems to prevent any form of the truth getting down to the growing part of them. But when there is a sense of any call that you have not obeyed, made haste to obey it, that you may the sooner come forth into the light. Then there are some, you know, that are the picture of the different kinds of people. Well, I will not say it is wonderful, because it comes from the wonderful. Look how simple it is. There are those when they get moved with feeling begin to grow. They start very fast, you think, as though they would take heaven by storm, but the storm takes them; they are beaten down. They do not like to suffer. Well, we do not any of us like to suffer; but the question is, whether we will make the effort and even if foiled, make an effort again, to meet the future, or whether we shall let adverse powers, whatever they may be, beat us down to the dust, and we lie in the mud instead of soaring in the free air. What is it you want more than anything else? A good many of you think more about the cares of the world, the deceitfulness of riches; and the desires of other things enter in and choke the word—the word, the truth of God that you have got in you. There is something that you know is your duty. You may not love it very much. You have not seen the glory of it. It is to you like a rough diamond that does not shine. It is very dirty, perhaps. But you have got something in you that you know you ought to use. That is the thing the Lord speaks of; that is the thing that is come out of the heart of God into your heart, and the question is, are you caring about that more than anything else, or are you thinking, "Well, I mind it just enough no. be cast out. You know it is absurd to ask me to be perfect. I am not perfect. I cannot be perfect," and the person that says that has not tried enough to know the difficulty of it, but only takes it for granted. Mother, do you think as often about your Father as you think about your child? Oh, I do not want you to love your child less. God forbid. There are very mistakenly wicked things said of that kind. Mothers say, "I love my child too much." Foolish woman! you never loved your child enough. If you had loved your child aright he would have forced you to lift up your heart to your Father in heaven. You are loving yourself, not your child. No, we cannot love each other too much. Oh, friends, the absurdity of it, that we will give three-fourths to man, and give God a fourth. Are we seeking Him as the business of life, or are we making money the business of life, and thinking of God now and then, sometimes? I do not understand half ways of things. But the people that are in the condition of this corn growing amongst thorns, they are perhaps the last that will understand it to mean themselves; the strangeness of which is this, that a few more years and all the possibility of my having anything whatever to call my own—I shall have no hand to hold it, not to say no pocket to put it into. Then there is the ground that bears, some fifty, some sixty, and some a hundredfold. You get nothing except you look at that part. It is for yourself. But then perhaps you will say, "May some bring forth thirty, some sixty, and some a hundredfold?" Yes. "Does not that imply that the Lord is content to accept an inferior quantity? That some He will take though they only bring Him thirtyfold, and others when they bring Him sixty. But the hundredfold seems to be a maximum, and therefore it seems to imply that, well, perhaps we may bring thirtyfold and we shall be accepted. How low would it go, do you suppose? Twentyfold? Tenfold? How far down would it go?" Well, I think that the disposition that would be content to bring the thirtyfold would prefer to bring one seed or none at all. And I am certain of this, that if it be possible for you to bring forth forty, fifty, or sixtyfold, the Lord will not be content with your thirtyfold. And you will have something to go through yet. For observe this—"Every branch in Me that beareth fruit, He purgeth it." Why? Because it is bringing forth fruit, why should He be hard upon it? He wants more fruit, and the man who is content with himself anywhere, is just the man that the Lord is not content with. I will tell you your thirtyfold would do very well provided you are not content with it, and you want to make it more. Oh, what a hopeless thing, do you say; we can never get at that? That He will see to, if you see that you want it, and that you are acting as far as you can upon it. He will see to that. Do you think that your Father in heaven will be content to have you, His child, deformed, ugly, lame, worn as with famine, with dirty face and hands, clothed in rags? What kind of a father or mother would it be who would be content to have a child such? Ah, ne or she might be exulting unspeaking to have that poor miserable child in his or her arms, but would he be content to see it like that? Friends, do you want it? (*G. Macdonald, LL.D.*) *A right attitude essential to perceiving God's truths:*—An Eastern legend relates that somewhere in the deserts of Arabia there stood a mass of jagged rock, the surface of which was seamed and scarred by the elements; but whenever any one came to the rock in the *right way* he saw a door shape itself in the sides of the barren stone, through which he could enter in, and find a store of rich and precious treasures, which he could carry away with him. There are some things in God's universe that seem as barren and unattractive as bare and fissured rocks, but which contain an inwardness of warmth and sweetness inconceivable. The inner holies of God are fast concealed from those who will not come aright, with a heart of love and trust, but open to all who are willing to see and to hear. (*Christian Age.*)

Ver. 11. **The seed is the Word of God.**—*The seed:*—I. THE TRUTH TAUGHT, THE SEED SOWN BY JESUS CHRIST, THE GREAT SOWER. 1. The necessity of repentance. 2. The forgiving love and power of God. 3. The necessity of holiness; of obedience, submission, trust, unselfishness, and brotherly love. 4. Christ enjoined fidelity, and warned of judgment to come. 5. Christ taught the necessity of His death for our redemption; proclaimed Himself the one Mediator between God and man; declared our dependence upon Him for all spiritual life and strength; promised His Spirit to lead us into all truth, and His grace to enable us to endure to the end. II. THE APPROPRIATENESS OF THE ANALOGY BETWEEN THE SEED AND THE TRUTH. 1. Both contain the principle of life. 2. The development of the life in each depends upon conditions. The seed must be sown in congenial soil, and duly watered and nurtured; the truth must be received into an honest and good heart. (*A. F. Joscelyne, B.A.*) *Missionary sermon:*—I. WHAT IS THE SEED TO BE SOWN? The Word of God. II. THE SOIL UPON WHICH THIS SEED IS TO BE CAST. The field is the world. III. THE MANNER OR SPIRIT IN WHICH THE SEED IS TO BE SOWN. 1. With much prayer. 2. In simple faith upon God's promises. 3. In entire dependence upon the influences of the Holy Ghost. 4. In a spirit of love to Christ and the souls of men. 5. Not sparingly, but bountifully. (*J. Hatchard, A.M.*) *Use the Bible:*—Never were there so many Bibles in the world. The seed of eternal life is in our days plenteously sown. Why, then, has the crop failed so shamefully? The failure of a crop must be owing to one or more of these four causes. Either (1) the seed must be bad; or (2) the season must be bad; or (3) the land must be bad; or (4) the tillage must be bad. Now the failure of a crop of holiness cannot be owing to the first of these causes, for the seed is as good as ever. Nor is the failure owing to any peculiarly bad season. The influence of the Holy Ghost still falls, like mild showers, gently and plentifully on men's hearts, to soften and fit them for receiving the Word of God. The Sun of Righteousness still shines in the heavens, and from His golden throne, when the good wheat has sprung up and come to ear, He pours down warmth enough to ripen it and bring it to perfection.

Nor again is the failure of the seed due to the badness of the soil. Bad enough it is, to be sure, naturally; but we know how much the very worst soil may be bettered by care and labour. Man's heart is not worse than it was formerly. The scantiness of the crop, then, is owing to nothing but badness of tillage. (*A. W. Hare.*)　　*The seed gives life by means of death :*—Just so is it with all truth, and superlatively so is it with *the* Truth. How often does the discoverer reap his first harvest in derision and loss! How often does the pioneer of some beneficent enterprise lay its foundation in his own wealth, health, and peace! How often does the patriot pay the penalty of living a purer and nobler life than his self-seeking contemporaries! Above all, what a countless army of men, "valiant for the faith and truth upon the earth," have had to water the seed of Christ's gospel by their blood and tears! How often in this and that land, and in none more than in our own, have those gospel institutions, which are God's Tree of Life for the world, had to grow up like a weeping willow and suck their first nutriment from the graves of their martyr-slain! The blood of Scotland's proto-martyr, the noble Patrick Hamilton, and the memory of his dying prayer, "How long, O Lord, shall darkness cover this realm?" fomented the young Reformation life over a comparatively silent germinating period of more than twenty years. Knox, and with him Scotland, kindled at the pile of George Wishart. Andrew Melville caught the falling mantle of Knox. And as with the martyrs under Popery in that century, so with those under the "black prelacy" of the next. When Richard Cameron fell on Aird's Moss—as if in answer to his own prayer as the action began, "Lord, spare the green and take the ripe!"—all the more strenuously strove Cargill, till he, too, in the year following, sealed the truth with his blood. And more followed, and yet more, through that last and worst decade of the pitiless storm known, as by emphasis, "the killing time." Through those terrible years Peden dragged out a living death, and, as he thought of Cameron now at rest, often exclaimed, "O to be with Richie!" Young Renwick, too, caught up the torn flag, nobly saying, "They are but standard-bearers that have fallen; the Master lives." Thus one after another, on blood-drenched scaffold or on blood-soaked field, fell the precious seed-grain to rise in harvests manifold, till just at the darkest hour before the dawn, Renwick's martyrdom closed the red roll in 1688, the very year of the Revolution, and the seed so long "sown in tears" was reaped in joy." Marvel not at this. He who is at once the sower and the seed had Himself to die that we might live. (*T. Guthrie, D.D.*)　　*Vitality of latent seeds :*—Much interesting information has been furnished lately upon the vitality of buried seeds. It is astonishing how long many of them retain their germinating powers although lying so deep in the earth as to be beyond the reach of atmospheric influences. This is so—*e.g.*, with the seeds of gorse. A piece of land in Northamptonshire was converted from a furze fox-cover to pasture, a state in which it remained for thirty years or more; it was then deeply cultivated, and the following season a crop of gorse sprung up over the whole field. A gardener, in order to plant some rhododendrons last spring, turned over a quantity of peat soil, the bottom portion being brought to the surface. That bed is now covered with a thick crop of seedling foxgloves, the seed of which must have been lying there in a state of complete dormancy for probably half a century. In the same manner do seeds of truth often lie in the hearts of men. The sower forgets that he has scattered them, or mourns that they have not sprung up. The harvest may come, however, after many years have rolled away, for the seed contains the germ of a God-given life. Those who scatter the "Word of God" ought never to despair of results. (*Christian Journal.*) *Sowing the seed of the Word :*—Billy Dawson, that great natural orator, had a wonderful sermon on the "Sower and the Seed." With every stroke of the hand in imitation of the act of sowing, the speaker would drop some blessed passage of Scripture. The Methodist chapel in one of the midland counties not being big enough, the use of the Particular Baptist Chapel was secured. The minister of the chapel was upon the platform. Dawson gave this "sowing speech," and went along the platform scattering the seed and giving one passage of Scripture after another : "God so loved the world;" "Come unto Me, all ye that labour;" then there came another handful; "If any man sin, we have an Advocate with the Father, Jesus Christ the righteous, and He is the propitiation for our sins, and not for ours only, but also for the sins of the whole world." "There, it's out," he said, "and you can do what you like." When remonstrated with for this breach of ministerial propriety he said, "I did not think about the chapel, nor the parson; I thought about the seed." (*Handbook to Scripture Doctrines.*)

Ver. 12. **Then cometh the devil.**—*The devil's punctuality, power, and purpose :*—
I. First observe the evil one's PUNCTUALITY. No sooner does the seed fall than the
fowls devour it. Our text says "then," that is, there and then, "cometh the
devil." Mark renders it, "Satan cometh immediately." Whoever else may loiter,
Satan never does. No sooner does a camel fall dead in the wilderness than the
vultures appear. Not a bird was visible, nor did it seem possible that there could
be one within a radius of many miles, yet speedily there are specks in the sky, and
soon the devourers are gorging themselves with flesh : even thus do the spirits of
evil scent their prey from afar, and hasten to their destroying work. A little delay
might put the case beyond Satanic power, hence the promptitude of diabolic activity.
II. Notice his POWER. It is not said that he tries to do it, but that he actually does
so. He sees, he comes, and he conquers. His power is partly derived from his
natural sagacity. He is more than a match for preacher and hearer united if the
Holy Spirit be not there to baffle him. He has also acquired fresh cunning by long
practice in his accursed business. Moreover, he derives his chief power from the
man's condition of soul : it is easy for birds to pick up seed which lies exposed on
a trodden path. III. His PURPOSE. "Lest they should believe and be saved" Satan
takes away the Word out of their hearts. Here also is wisdom—wisdom hidden
within the enemy's cunning. If the gospel remains in contact with the heart its
tendency is to produce faith. (*C. H. Spurgeon.*)   *Inattentive hearers :*—I. WHAT
IS FAITH ? I answer, it is a firm persuasion of the truth of the gospel, accompanied
with a deep sense of its importance, and a cordial acceptance of its gracious
proposals ; and so producing the genuine fruits of love and obedience. We have
heard the gospel. Have we believed it ? Have we received it in the love of it ? and
are our hearts and lives influenced and governed by it ? II. To speak of THE SALVATION
PROMISED TO THEM THAT BELIEVE. 1. A salvation from moral evil. 2. A salvation
from natural evil. Not that good men are exempted from the common afflictions of
life. But they are converted into blessings for them, and they are provided with all
needful supports under their afflictions. 3. A deliverance also from penal evil. III.
THE CONNECTION BETWEEN FAITH AND SALVATION. It is necessary, in order to our being
saved, that we believe. Now this necessity arises out of the Divine appointment,
and the reason and nature of the thing. 1. It is the will of God, that those who are
saved should believe. 2. There is a fitness or suitableness in faith to the end of
its appointment, so that the necessity of it arises out of the nature of the thing
itself. No sober man who contemplates faith, accompanied with those dispositions
and affections necessary to constitute a real Christian, can pronounce it an unreasonable and useless thing. And how is that good to be possessed without a
temper of heart suited to the enjoyment of it ? And how is this temper to be
acquired but by believing ? Thus have we considered the nature of faith, described
the salvation promised to it, and shown the connection between the one and the
other. Let us now return to the argument in the text. Satan clearly perceiving
the influence of faith in the great business of salvation, and well knowing, too, that
faith comes by hearing, uses all his artifices to divert men's attention from the
Word, and to prevent its salutary effect upon their hearts. It now remains that we
make two or three reflections on the general subject of this discourse. 1. If Satan
takes the measures you have heard to prevent the success of the gospel, and to
confirm men in impenitence and unbelief, how truly is he denominated by our
Saviour "the wicked one," and how righteous is that sentence which will shortly
be executed upon him! 2. How much is it to be lamented that men will suffer
themselves to be deceived and ruined by the devices of this great adversary ! 3.
And lastly, Let us admire and adore the grace of God which defeats the designs of
Satan, and makes the Word effectual upon the hearts of multitudes, notwithstanding
all the opposition it meets with. (*S. Stennett, D.D.*)   *The fowls of the air :*—
Satan's power would be far less formidable if it extended to our circumstances only,
and did not reach to our mind. We have, however, the express testimony of the
Word of God that it does reach thus far ; and it is this district of Satanic power
which I purpose now to investigate. 1. With those faculties of mind, if there be
any, which are purely intellectual, which do not in any way determine or affect
moral character and conduct, it cannot be supposed that the great enemy of mankind busies himself at all. 2. Perhaps, however, there are fewer powers which are
purely intellectual than we are accustomed to imagine. The mind and heart of
man are very closely and subtly kneaded up together. Certain it is that there are
certain faculties which, more or less, belong to both elements, of which it is hard
to say whether they are more intellectual or moral. 3. One of these is memory.

The agency of the fowls in the parable is external; it is not in the soil itself, nor is it connected with the soil; and in like manner, the foe who removes the seed from the heart, that is, from the memory of man, is external.   In this parable you have the hosts or tribes of the air doing the work of the prince of the power of the air. 4. Thus, for all who recognize the words of Christ as being the very truth of God, it seems to be a settled point, resting upon the authority of the Master, that Satan exercises a certain power over the memory. 5. I turn with a sense of relief from this dark part of the subject to notice the immense power for good which the memory has under a guidance much greater than that of Satan—the guidance of the grace of God. 6. In conclusion, let the memories of the young be thoroughly charged with the Word of God.   (*Dean Goulburn.*)   *Transient piety :*—Beloved, how many professors fail in this respect. They follow the Lord by fits and starts; they go out from us because they are not of us; for if they had been of us, doubtless they would have continued with us. They leap into religion as the flying-fish leaps into the air; they fall back again into their sins, as the same fish returns to its element. They make a great flame for a time like the crackling of thorns, but lo! the flame has soon expired, for they are not like the miraculous bush which burned, God dwells not in them. (*C. H. Spurgeon.*)   *Lack of continuance :*—The great trial of our Christian life is at this point. Will we continue? Thousands of girls begin to practise at the piano; thousands make no small attainment; but only the scores continue, and become eminent. Half a college class, at some time or other, begin to collect a cabinet or herbarium, but only here and there one perseveres. After years have elapsed that one has become, perhaps, possessed of a wonderful treasury, and is, perhaps, also in the way of renown. All, or nearly all, of this is due to his gift of continuance. One day I was looking at a fruit-bearing passion-vine, covering half the side of a friend's house, vigorous, graceful. That friend showed me two or three little, tiny, frail-looking specimens of the same in a box. "Why," said she, "I keep the box full of seeds, but only a few of them germinate. They are so slow in germinating, too. It takes two or three months for one to make its appearance." How many persons there are who would never have any noble passion-vine climbing in beauty about their dwelling, simply because they have no grace of continuing to care for the plant in the slow months of its early life. (*A. L. Stone.*)

Ver. 14. And that which fell among thorns.—*Signs of excessive worldliness :*—I. To APPLY TESTS OF WORLDLINESS IS VERY NECESSARY. It is difficult to convince ourselves that we are too much engrossed in our worldly cares. If a man is intemperate, or profane, or fraudulent, it is easy for him to know his own sin; but worldliness comes to us so much under the guise of duty, that it is difficult to detect its real character. There is, also, the further difficulty, that it is so hard to fix the boundary between a necessary attention to business and a sinful absorption in it. II. One sign of excessive worldliness is, GREAT ANXIETY OF MIND IN OUR WORLDLY PURSUITS. A Christian should be diligent in business, and improve every lawful means of acquisition, but not as if his whole happiness were at stake. His real treasure is untouched, however the world may go with him. III. But the great test by which the Christian should judge, is THE EFFECT OF HIS WORLDLY BUSINESS UPON HIS RELIGIOUS DUTIES. Even when the duties of devotion are regularly performed, it may be with the world uppermost in our hearts. When the Bible is read, the eye may see its words, but the thoughts may be upon some plan for the day, so that we may read as we would with one at our side calling us away to something we love better. (*W. H. Lewis, D.D.*)   *Why cares and pleasures are associated together :*— No two persons are more unlike at first sight than the man of care and the man of pleasure. The man of care does not know what pleasure is; he is always fretting and chafing at something or other; everything goes wrong, or seems to go wrong, with him; he is always making the worst of things, looking at their dark side rather than their bright side. The man of pleasure, on the other hand, passes his whole existence in the sunshine. If, by chance, trouble comes in his way, he puts it from him, or closes his eyes against it; he is too much bent on enjoying himself to allow anything to annoy and disturb him. How comes it, then, that unlike, nay, opposite as such characters are, they are here set down side by side, and are represented as occupying precisely the same ground? How comes it that he who saunters leisurely through life, gathering freely as he goes of every pleasure, and he who drags himself heavily along, under the weight of many burdens, find themselves standing side by side at last, and coming to the same end? It is not difficult to find the reason. The cares of life and its pleasures are both of the nature of weeds—weeds of very different kind indeed, but each of them equally the natural product of the human heart; each requires only to be left to itself, and it will soon overrun the whole heart, and choke the good seed. And it will not make much difference, at the great harvest-day, whether the failure of the crop in us was owing to an undue growth of cares or of pleasures. (*H. Harris, B.D.*) *Good ground spoilt by neglect :*—The very same piece of ground stands for both the man of care and the man of pleasure. And what kind of ground is it? Strange to say, the ground itself seems to be very good ground; it is not the hard wayside, where the seed never once gets beneath the surface, but is trodden under foot by every passer-by, and picked up by the birds; it is not even like the rocky ground, where there is no depth of soil to support the root when the seed has sprung up and begun to grow. No, the ground of which we are now speaking stands the very next to the good ground, and seems to be of very much the same kind with it; and yet, whilst the one is bringing forth its thirty-folds, and sixtyfold, and hundredfold, ripe for the harvest, the other has not a single full ear; it yields no more than the rocky ground, no more, even, than the wayside. And yet, how is this? How comes it to be so near to the good ground, and yet so far removed from it? how comes it to promise so much, and to break its promise so entirely? We shall, perhaps, best answer this question by means of an example. We sometimes, then, see two pieces of allotment, or garden-ground, lying alongside each other, the one with a very plentiful crop, the other growing nothing but weeds. And how comes this? It cannot be owing to any natural difference in the two pieces of ground, for they lie within a few feet of one another, and are exposed to just the same amount of air, and rain, and sunshine. How comes it, then, that the produce of the two pieces of land is so very different? We shall have no difficulty in finding the answer. We shall say at once, it is quite plain that these two pieces of ground have been treated quite differently; one of them has been kept properly looked to, and the other has not. And this, too, is the very difference of which we are in search between the good ground and the ground choked with thorns in the parable; the soil itself is the same, or much the same, in each, only in the one case it has been properly attended to, and in the other it has been left to itself. And so, whilst on the good ground the seed has had nothing to hinder it from steadily grow-ing and ripening for the harvest, the seed on the other ground, after making a vigorous effort, has stopped short, and never got any further; the depth of earth which supports it has lent the same amount of nourishment to the weeds which have been allowed to grow up with it. As it has grown, so they have grown; and long before the time of the harvest has come, they have all run together, the good seed and the weeds, and have choked each other. (*Ibid.*) *Worldly amusements :*— I. On those amusements which are absolutely sinful, it is not necessary that we spend many words. II. There are innocent amusements in which a Christian may indulge, but with moderation. Still there must be a wise moderation. The love of pleasure, even where it confines itself to innocent modes of gratification, is an insinuating and mischievous passion. It may sow the seeds of indolence, create a distaste for the serious business of life, and so make a man's course profitless both to himself and to others. We may see this in the history of nations. A pleasure-loving has never been a noble and manly people. When the Athenians yielded to the fascinations of the theatre, and appropriated to its purposes the funds that had been designed for the defence of the State, they speedily forgot their ancient love of freedom; the glories of Marathon and Salamis were shadowed by the disaster of Chœroneia, and the invincible antagonists of Xerxes became the fawning slaves of Philip. Even the Romans, who had conquered the world, and had for ages boasted of their independence, were content to wear their chains, when their tyrants had learned the art of lulling them to sleep by the Siren-like strains of pleasure, and the voices that had once been raised to rebuke their oppressors, were heard only to clamour for the bloody games of the circus. These are lessons to us both as indi-viduals and as a nation. Changes in the moral character of both are for the most part accomplished noiselessly. III. There are doubtful pleasures, as to which it becomes the Christian to exercise careful discrimination. To point out some considerations which may serve to guide the exercise of this high Christian expediency, is what we propose here. 1. Regard must be paid to the actual rather than to the possible character of any amusement, and each one must be judged by what it is not by what it might be. 2. Regard must be had to the tendencies of an amusement. We admit freely that this is a test to be applied with great caution. It is not a fair objection to any recreation to point to isolated cases, in which indulgence has been followed by serious moral and spiritual evil. It cannot be questioned that a pleasure, though not sinful in its character, may, in its general influence, be unfriendly to spiritual earnestness. 3. Each man must have regard to his own individual temperament. So varied are our mental habits and tendencies, that we may pass unscathed through scenes which would inflict on others permanent and wide-spread injury. 4. Still more must every man respect his own conscience, and not exercise a liberty wider than it approves. 5. We must, in deference to the opinions, feelings, and spiritual interests of others, sometimes exercise a self-denial which our own consciences do not feel to be requisite for our own safety. (*J. G. Rogers, B.A.*)

Ver. 15. **But that on the good ground are they, which in an honest and good heart, having heard the Word, keep it.**—*The necessity of patience.*—The necessity of patience in the Christian course appeareth by these reasons: 1. The scope of the gospel is to make men fruitful Christians. But this can never be, without the persecution of the world (2 Tim. iii. 12). The shadow doth not more undividedly follow the body, than persecutions and trials follow the profession of the gospel. This necessity of suffering afflictions implies and infers a necessity of patience. 2. It is necessary in respect of the manuring and preparing to fruit. The best ground brings no fruit unless it endure the plough, the harrow, the cold, the frost: even so the Lord prepareth His children to fruits of grace, by patient enduring many trials. The walnut tree is made fruitful by beating, camomile by treading upon, the palm by pressing, and the Christian by suffering. 3. In respect of the producing of fruits, there is great need of patience: seeing there is no fruit of grace which Satan seeks not to kill in the very sprouting and first appearance; as the child in his birth (Rev. xii. 4). And the wicked world seeks to blast them with the east wind of reproaches, yea to nip and pinch them, out-face and destroy them, with strong and violent persecutions: so as without patience "enduring the cross, and despising the shame," this thirtyfold cannot be expected, much less an hundredfold. Thus Christ Himself brings forth to us all His blessed fruits, not without the greatest patience, proportioned to His greatest sufferings: and after the same manner must we also bring forth our fruits to Him. 4. It is necessary, in respect of the growth and ripening of fruits. The seed sown comes not up all at once, but by degrees; "first the blade, then the ear, then ripe fruit" (Mark iv. 28). So all our graces and fruits are small at first, and receive increase by little and little. 5. It is necessary in respect of things that might hinder the growth, if patience prevented not: as first, the smart of present afflictions; for every affliction is "grievous for the present" (Heb. xii. 11), the mention thereof oftentimes makes us shrink, and startle, and grow out of heart, because of the roughness of our way. But now "by patience we possess our souls," the present remedy of the disciple's greatest persecutions (Luke xxi. 17–19), whereas by impatience we lose ourselves, and lessen our fruits. Secondly, the common crosses which accompany our mortal life will make us weary enough, unless patience supply some strength, and under-shore us. Thirdly, inward temptations, and disquietness of conscience, the wounds of spirit, are so intolerable, that the violence of them often shakes off many fruits, and makes the Christian walk weakly many days. Now patience alone keeps the soul at peace and quietness, waiting for God unto succour or issue. It holds the heart in expectation of the accomplishment of God's promises, and our happiness in Christ. Fourthly, there are enemies without, which hazard our fruits. Fifthly, infirmities of brethren with whom we converse, were a great means to shake off our fruits (as Barnabas lost his sincerity for a time by Peter's dissimulation), if patience did not uphold to discern and "bear the infirmities of the weak" (Rom. xv. 1, 2). 6. Patience is necessary in respect of the harvest of fruits, the gathering and full reaping of all the seed sown. And thus the good ground brings forth "with patience," *i.e.*, with patient expectation of the full fruits; the first-fruits whereof are already attained (Rom. viii. 25). (*Thomas Taylor, D.D.*) *Effectual hearing:*—If you would hear the Word aright, be not only attentive, but retentive. Lay the Word up in your memories and hearts. "The seed on the good ground are they who, having heard the Word, keep it." The Greek word for "keep" signifies "to hold the Word fast, that it do not run from us." If the seed be not kept in the ground, but is presently washed away, it is sown to little purpose: so, if the Word preached be not kept in your memories and hearts, it is preached in vain. Many people have memories like leaky vessels—the Word goes out as fast as it comes in: how, then, can it profit? If a treasure be put into a chest and the chest not locked, it may easily be taken out: a bad memory is like a chest without a lock, the devil can easily take out all the treasure. Labour to keep in memory the truths you hear: the things we esteem we are not so apt to forget. (*T. Watson.*) *Meditation renders good impressions lasting :*—Gotthold had for some purpose taken from a cupboard a vial of rosewater, and, after using it, inconsiderately left it unstopped. Observing it some time after, he found that all the strength and sweetness of the perfume had evaporated. Here, thought he with himself, is a striking emblem of a heart fond of the world and open to the impression of outward objects. What good does it do to take such a heart to the house of God, and there fill it with the precious essence of the roses of paradise which are the truths of Scripture? What good to kindle in it a glow of devotion, if we afterwards neglect to close the outlet —by which I mean, to keep the Word in an honest and good heart. How vain to hear much, but to retain little, and to practise less. How vain to experience within us sacred and holy emotions, unless we are afterwards careful to close the heart by diligent reflection and prayer, and so keep it unspotted from the world. Neglect this, and the strength and spirit of devotion evaporates, and leaves only a lifeless form behind. (*Scriver.*) *Remarkable fertility :*—Paul Joanne ascribes amazing fertility to the soil of Mentone, and backs his assertions by a story which reads like a legend. He says that a stranger coming to pay a visit to his Mentonese friends stuck his walking-stick into the ground and forgot it. Coming back some days afterwards to seek his cane, he was surprised to find it putting forth leaves and young branches. He declares that the little tree has grown vastly, and is still to be seen in the Rue Saint Michel. We have not seen it, and are afraid that to inquire for it in the aforesaid Rue would raise a laugh at our expense. We may believe the story or not as we please; but it may serve as an emblem of the way in which those grow who are by grace planted in Christ. All dry and withered like a rod we are thrust into the sacred soil, and life comes to us at once, with bud and branch and speedy fruit. Aaron's rod that budded was not only a fair type of our Lord, but a cheering prophecy of ourselves. Whenever we feel dead and barren let us ask to be buried in Christ afresh, and straightway we shall glorify His name by bearing much fruit. (*C. H. Spurgeon.*) *The mystery of growth :*—In the growth of a grain of wheat are three miracles of wonders, viz., the power of absorbing fresh materials, the power of changing them into living vegetable substance, and the power of arranging the new materials according to a fixed pattern. Could we see this process through a powerful magnifying glass, so that the particles which are to be absorbed should seem as large as marbles, we should see millions of such marbles building themselves up into a green tree; some marching to one part, some to another; then changing themselves into tree substance, and, finally, all arranged into an exact pattern, so that no one can mistake the nature of the tree. Growth is a mystery. (*E. White.*) *With patience :*—Of all the characteristics of the good hearer, this, as it is the most valuable, is also the hardest to attain. To wait is even harder than to labour and to obey. Unless we are to have our harvest very soon, we have hardly the heart to sow. The husbandman has long patience—must have it—till he receives the early and the latter rain. So with us. To become a good hearer, *i.e.*, a good doer of the Word, is a task which requires long patience. We must suffer many a killing frost, many a darkening shower, many a burning sun, before the good seed cast into our hearts by that great Sower, who daily goes forth to sow, will gladden us with its increase. But the longer we wait the more precious will be the harvest—it is only ill weeds that spring up apace—and the sweeter the taste of the bread which has been so hardly earned, and so long in coming. (*S. Cox, D.D.*)

Ver. 16. No man, when he hath lighted a candle.—*The lighted lamp :*—The truth symbolized by this imagery is the self-revealing character of the real disciple of Christ. His teaching is reproductive as the seed corn, it is diffusive as the light. The lamp is lighted to fill the room with light, and for no other purpose. Similarly all Christian truth which comes to the individual is intended to be diffused in a manner calculated to strike the attention of all who come from darkness into this marvellous light. If we compare the analogous expressions in Matthew, we see how naturally our Lord's teaching glided off from this point into exhortations to transparent sincerity. For as the best lamp is one which gives most light, and casts the smallest shade, the best Christian is he who reflects most of Christ and least of self. (*F. E. Toyne.*) *The place and function of the lamp :*—We see at a glance that this parable throws some light on the social customs of the age and land in which it was spoken. It reminds us, for instance, that in Palestine, as indeed in ancient

Greece and Rome, when the darkness fell, little lamps, containing oil and a wick, were brought into the rooms of all classes of the people and placed on slender stands, commonly some two or three feet high, to give light to all who were in the house. Our Lord uttered this parable to teach us that no man is illuminated for his own sake, just as no lamp is lit for its own sake. Just as the lamp is lit that it may shine, so we are taught that we may teach. No truth is a private possession, just as no truth is of any private interpretation.

> " Heaven doth with us as we with torches do,
> Not light them for themselves; for if our virtues
> Did not go forth of us, 'twere all alike,
> As if we had them not."

No truth is, or can be, dangerous. All that we can learn, we may learn. All that we have learned we are bound to teach; all that we have received we are bound to give. To conceal from others any truth which we ourselves have been taught of God is to hide the lamp that has come to us under a bushel or under a couch, instead of setting it under a lampstand. (*S. Cox, D.D.*) *Difference between this and other versions of the parable :*—Whereas St. Mark, who wrote mainly for the Romans, speaks of a Roman measure, the *modius*, St. Luke, who wrote for the whole Gentile world, speaks simply of a " vessel," any vessel or measure used throughout the habitable globe. And whereas St. Matthew, writing mainly for Jews, speaks of the lamp as kindled that it may give light " unto all that are *in* the house," St. Luke speaks of it as kindled in order " that they who *enter* into the house " may see the light. For St. Matthew was himself a Jew, and wrote for those who, like himself, were already *in* the household of God; but St. Luke was a Gentile, and wrote for those who, like himself, had a great desire to *enter* into God's house and find themselves at home in it. He and they had, so to speak, long stood outside the Father's house, seeing and desiring the light that shone through its windows; but now Christ had called them into the house, had bidden them enter, had assured them that the house was built and the lamp lit *for them* as for the Jews, for all who would *come into* it, as well as for all who are already in it. (*Ibid.*) *The good done by being good :*—It is somewhat remarkable, and worthy of being remembered, of the late Dr. Charles Hodge, that the closing sentence of an unfinished autobiography—perhaps the last words which he wrote—speaking of a purpose which he formed to hold up a godly companion whom he greatly loved to his students as an example, he wrote: " I wanted to show them how much good could be done by simply being good." *Hiding the light :*—A young lady in a fashionable home had been brought to Christ, and had been enabled for some years, amid much opposition, to faithfully witness for Him. The attention she attracted was often painful to her; and once, when repulsed and wounded in an effort of this kind, she for a time lost heart, and felt she should have to give up being a *consecrated* Christian. Just at this time she was invited to visit friends whom she had never seen, and who knew but little of her; and she resolved, that while there she would not openly speak of her Saviour, or put herself in a position to be noticed as peculiarly religious. Her visit passed away; and not happily to herself, she was enabled to keep her resolution. Upon the day of her leaving for home, a most attractive and accomplished lady, a fashionable woman of society, while walking alone with her, suddenly asked her, " Where is your sister, and why did she not come here? I mean your *religious* sister, the one who is known as the 'religious Miss J.' It was because I heard that she was to be here that I, too, accepted an invitation to come and spend the holiday. I am tired of the empty, unsatisfying life I am leading, and have longed to talk with a real Christian." With shame and confusion the faithless witness was obliged to confess that she had no sister; that she was the one who had been sometimes called the " religious Miss J.," and that *shame* of the badge, that should have been borne gladly for her Saviour, had kept her silent. A precious opportunity to lead a weary soul to the Master had been lost. (*D. W. Whittle's Life, Warfare, and Victory.*)

Ver. 17. **For nothing is secret that shall not be made manifest.**—*The paradox :*— Nothing is secret that shall not be made manifest, &c., that is to say, " There is now absolutely no light or truth veiled from men which it is not the intention and purpose of God to uncover and reveal to them as soon as they are able to receive it; nor was there ever, at any time, anything hidden from them which it was not for their good to hide from them for the time, and which was not disclosed to them so soon as it was for their good that the disclosure should be made. We have in this axiom and paradox—1. The very charter of science. 2. A warrant for all honest inquiry. 3. A solid ground for hope. (*S. Cox, D.D.*) *Secret things made visible in due time:*—Dr. Draper, in his "History of the Conflict between Religion and Science," says: "A shadow never falls upon a wall without leaving thereupon a permanent trace, a trace which might be made visible by resorting to proper processes. The portraits of our friends or landscape views may be hidden on the sensitive surface from the eye, but they are ready to make their appearance as soon as proper developers are resorted to. Upon the walls of our apartments there exist the vestiges of all our acts, silhouettes of whatever we have done. I have seen landscapes and architectural views, taken in Mexico, developed, as artists say, months subsequently in New York, the images coming out after the long voyage in all their proper forms and in all their contrast of light and shade. The photo had forgotten nothing. It had signally preserved the contour of the everlasting mountains and the passing smoke of a bandit fire." (*Christian Journal.*)

Ver. 18. **Take heed, therefore, how ye hear.**—*How to hear the Word:*—Several classes of persons, to be met with in every congregation, should attend to this caution. I. In the first rank of these may be placed THE INDIFFERENT HEARER. II. Another class of persons who should give heed to the warning of the text are represented by THE CRITICAL HEARER. III. A third class of church-goers who derive little benefit from preaching, may be described as CAPTIOUS HEARERS. 1. Endeavour always to listen to the preaching of the gospel with a mind free from prejudice. Blind prepossessions and one-sided prejudices are like the trade winds, which, holding out in one course, render compass and rudder alike useless. When prejudice puts its hands before the eyes, that hand, small as it is, will be large enough to hide the sun. 2. Again. Sermons should be heard with a desire to profit by them. 3. Lastly. Sermons should be heard with humble dependence on God's Holy Spirit, to open the understanding and to touch the heart. Plead His own promise (Isa. lv. 10, 11). (*J. N. Norton, D.D.*) *The teaching of the Church:*— The Church teaches and is taught in turn; every Christian contributes to this mutual teaching, and has a share in it. Preaching can only have a strictly moral effect; it communicates to us thoughts and feelings, and therefore appeals to the thought and to the feeling. It provokes decisions, and therefore stimulates the will. It is accordingly the most moral means of grace, that which necessitates most the effective participation of our freedom. "Take heed, therefore, how ye hear." To give more weight to that exhortation, let us consider who He is who speaks to us; what He tells us; the kind of attention which the truth revealed by Him requires; and, lastly, what it costs to despise it. I. WHO SPEAKS TO YOU IN THE TEACHING WHICH YOU SEEK AT THE FOOT OF THE PULPIT OF TRUTH? Do you not know that it is God Himself? He speaks to you first by the Holy Book, which is the basis of all faithful preaching. Revelation must become real and present, passing through the impressions, the aspirations, the experiences, the secret sorrows of the human heart at every period. Certainly, our word must not be blindly received—it must be brought to the test of the infallible Word of God: for the pure gold of truth which we bring you by preaching is too often alloyed through human frailty. God condescends to speak through our unworthy mouths and to take us for His instruments also. Why, my brethren, do you so seldom perceive this? It is, in the first place, the fault of your preachers, who, too often being infatuated with themselves, interposing their personalities between you and the truth, care more for the fame of their name than for the triumph of Jesus Christ. Are you not constantly spreading under their feet that fatal net of vainglory? II. It is God who speaks to you; BUT WHAT DOES HE TELL YOU? That which is of the utmost consequence to you—that which is necessary for time and for eternity. God does not speak to amuse our intellect, or to send to our hearts a sweet and figurative emotion. He wants to restore us to the truth in every respect. He reveals us to ourselves by rooting out every illusion of our mind. He shows us, in the narrow path which proceeds from the cross, the way of returning to God and to be restored to our own. III. THE KIND OF ATTENTION REQUIRED. Shut up, as we are commonly, in the circle of visible things, it is difficult for us to lift our minds to the contemplation of invisible things. Our thoughts have been too much accustomed to creep; their heavy wings do no longer carry them, by a sudden flight, towards the celestial heights. Our preoccupations are for the world; this is the real disposition of our spirit—it has a great inclination for it. If we do not energetically react against that natural tendency, we shall be hurried by the stream of vanity far from truth. Attention is the prize of continued exertion—it supposes a firm resolution to remove every frivolous distraction. We must be watchful every moment to drive away those flocks of birds always ready to pick up the seed of eternal life as it falls on the soil. Yet attention is not sufficient, Christian truth claims a particular attention. It is not enough to bring great sagacity, a penetrating spirit, trained to study and fully determined to learn the truths which are presented. If it were only the question of a purely human knowledge, we should not require more. Religious truth has organs of its own, and by which it reveals itself to man. It addresses itself above all things to his heart and his conscience. There, in our moral being, is the inward eye, able to perceive the heavenly light; there is the sense of the Divine. Neither the understanding, nor the imagination, nor the reason, abandoned to itself, will ever receive a ray of it, because it may happen that we deny God and the invisible world, while we possess these faculties in a superior degree. Take heed, therefore, how ye hear. He only remembers it who tries to accomplish the Divine will, and who, from the always vague and movable impression, passes to positive acts. Besides, nothing is more sad, nothing, I should say, is more demoralizing, than to understand our duties and not perform them. To know the best and to do the worst is the perversion of perversions. Let us not take Christianity as Pharisees or as artists; let us take it seriously, as the rule of our life, a rule not only for the great days, but for the most ordinary course of existence. (*E. de Pressensé, D.D.*)　　*The art of hearing*:—For be ye well assured that this is an infallible sign that some excellent and notable good is toward you, when the devil is so busy to hinder your hearing of the Word, which of all other things he doth most envy unto you. Therefore as he pointed Adam to another tree, lest he should go to the tree of life (Gen. iii.), so, knowing the Word to be like unto the tree of life, he appointeth you to other business, to other exercises, to other works, and to other studies, lest you should hear it and be converted to God, whereby the tribute and revenue of his kingdom should be impaired; therefore mark how many forces he hath bent against one little Scripture, to frustrate this counsel of Christ, "Take heed how you hear." First, he labours all that he can to stay us from hearing; to effect this, he keeps us at taverns, at plays, in our shops, and appoints us some other business at the same time, that when the bell calls to the sermon, we say, like the churlish guests, We cannot come (Matt. xxii.). If he cannot stay us away with any business or exercise, then he casts fancies into our minds, and drowsiness into our heads, and sounds into our ears, and sets temptations before our eyes; that though we hear, yet we should not mark, like the birds which fly about the church. If he cannot stay our ears, nor slack our attention as he would, then he tickleth us to mislike something which was said, and by that make us reject all the rest. If we cannot mislike anything which is said, then he infecteth us with some prejudice of the preacher; he doth not as he teacheth, and therefore we less regard what he saith. If there be no fault in the man, nor in the doctrine, then, lest it would convert us, and reclaim us, he courseth all means to keep us from the consideration of it, until we have forgot it. To compass this, so soon as we have heard, he takes us to dinner, or to company, or to pastime, to remove our minds, that we should think no more of it. If it stay in our thoughts, and like us well, then he hath this trick; instead of applying the doctrine, which we should follow, he turns us to praise and extol the preacher. He made an excellent sermon! he hath a notable gift! I never heard any like him! He which can say so, hath heard enough; this is the repetition which you make of our sermons when you come home, and so to your business again till the next sermon come; a breath goeth from us, and a sound cometh to you, and so the matter is ended. The Jews did hear more than all the world beside, yet because they took no heed to that which they heard, therefore they crucified Him which came to save them, and became the cursedest people upon the earth, which were the blessedest nation before; therefore the A B C of a Christian is to learn the art of hearing. There is no seed which groweth so fast as God's seed, if it be sown well; therefore, that I may show you that method of hearing, which Christ commendeth here to His disciples, it is necessary to observe five things: first, the necessity of hearing; secondly, the fruit which cometh by hearing; thirdly, the kinds of hearers; fourthly, the danger of hearing amiss; fifthly, that manner of hearing, which will make you remember that which is said, and teach you more in a year than you have learned all your life. Is not this the cause why God doth not hear us, because we will not hear Him? Is not this the cause why ye are such doctors in the world, and such infants in the Church? Ye learned your trade in seven years, but you have not learned religion in all your years. Can you give any reason for it but this? You marked when your master taught you your trade, because you should live by it; but you marked not the preacher when he taught you religion, because you do not live by it. Come now to the danger by hearing amiss. Christ saith, " Take heed how you hear." An evil eye engendereth lust, and an evil tongue engendereth strife; but an evil ear maketh an heretic, and a schismatic, and an idolater. This careless hearing made God take away His Word from the Jews; therefore, you may hear the Word so as it may be taken from you, as the talent was from him that hid it (Matt. xxv.); for God will not leave His pearls with swine; but as He saith, " What hadst thou to do to take My words in thy mouth, seeing thou hatest to be reformed?" so He will say, "What hadst thou to do to take My Word in thy ear, seeing thou hatest to be reformed?" The greatest treasure in the world is most despised, the star which should lead us to Christ, the ladder which should mount us to heaven, the water that should cleanse our leprosy, the manna that should refresh our hunger, and the Book that we should meditate on day and night (Psa. i. 2), lieth in our windows, no man readeth it, no man regardeth it; the love of God, and the love of knowledge, and the love of salvation is so cold, that we will not read over one Book for it, for all we spend so many idle times while we live. If Samuel had thought that God had spoken to him, he would not have slept; but because he thought it was not God, but Eli, therefore he slept; so, because you remember not that it is God which speaks, therefore you mark not. But if you remember Christ's saying, " He which heareth you, heareth Me, and he which despiseth you, despiseth Me," you would hear the voice of the preacher, as you would hear the voice of God. Now, to show you how you should hear; when Peter and John would make the cripple attentive, they said unto him, " Look upon us " (Acts iii.); so many, to sharpen their attention, desire to stand before the preacher, that they may look him in the face. By this little help Peter showeth that we had need to use many helps to make us hear well. Christ in the beginning of this chapter sends us to the husbandman to learn to hear. As he prepareth the ground before he soweth his seed, lest his seed should be lost, so we should prepare our hearts before we hear, lest God's seed be lost. What a shame is this, to remember every clause in your lease, and every point in your father's will; nay, to remember an old tale so long as you live, though it be long since you heard it; and the lessons which ye hear now will be gone within this hour, that you may ask, What hath stolen my sermon from me? Therefore that you may not hear us in vain, as you have heard others, my exhortation to you is, to record when you are gone that which you have heard. (*H. Smith.*) *The heavenly thrift:*—First, he giveth us a stock, to prove our husbandry, and then if we thrive with that, he doth add more unto it, now a little, and then a little, until at last the inheritance come too. As they which try a vessel, first put water into it, to see whether it will hold water, then they commit wine into it; so, first, God giveth us one grace; if we use that well, then he giveth another, and another, and another; according to that, " He which is found faithful in a little, shall be made lord over much." Thou shalt have a love to hear, read, and meditate : after thou shalt have a little knowledge to judge and speak of God's Word, of the Spirit, and of doctrines; then thou shalt ascend to faith, which will bring thee unto peace of conscience; then thou shalt meet with good books, and God will send thee teachers to instruct thee, and encourage thee, like the angels which came to Christ when He hungered. Thus a traveller passeth from town unto town, until he come to his inn; so a Christian passeth from virtue to virtue, until he come to heaven, which is the journey that every man must endeavour to go till death. Christ saith not, It shall be taken from them which have, but from them which " seem to have." (*Ibid.*) *Hearing the Word:*—Those to whom the gospel is preached must take heed how they hear; take heed as to the act, matter, manner. 1. As to the act: Take heed *that* ye hear. This is implied, and necessarily supposed. 2. As to the object or matter: So take heed *what* ye hear. *How* with Luke is *what* with Mark. 3. As to the manner: *How.* This is principally intended, though the other be necessary. It is in vain to hear, in vain to hear that which is good, except we hear it well. The manner being principally intended, I shall principally insist on it. I need not go far for reasons; this chapter affords abundance. 1. Few hear well. There are not many good hearers; the most miscarry; therefore there is need to take heed. Of four sorts of hearers in the parable. three are naught.

but one good. 2. There are many enemies to oppose, and many impediments to hinder you in hearing. 3. The advantage or disadvantage (Mark iv. 24, 25). According as you measure to God in hearing, so will He measure to you in blessing or cursing. 4. The gospel, according as it is heard, is a great mercy or a great judgment, a blessing or a curse, therefore great reason to take heed. The abuse of the greatest mercy may curse it. 5. It is that by which you must be judged at the last day—Judge, &c., according to this gospel (Rom. ii. 16; John xii. 48). If we neglect, we shall never taste of Christ. The children of the kingdom shall be cast out. It will be with you in this nation, and this place, as with the Jews—He turned from them to the Gentiles. He will take Christ and the gospel from you and give it to others; and when the gospel is gone, then look for destruction and desolation. The Lord convince you of the sinfulness of this sin! 1. It is a high contempt of God, of Christ. Contempt is the highest degree of dishonour; God is jealous of this. 2. If you will not hear God now, God will not hear you in the time of distress, though you may make many prayers (Isa. i. 15). He will send you to the gods whom ye have served. 3. Consider the state of the damned, those who, for neglecting the light, are cast into outer darkness. Use II. Exhortation to this duty. It is a duty of Christ's enjoining, and to His disciples. To further the practice of it, I shall (1) remove impediments that hinder; (2) prescribe means to facilitate and direct. 1. The impediments are ignorance, contempt, distractions, prejudice, obduration, bad ends or principles. Distractions : Wanderings, rovings of mind, will, affections, senses, caused by the cares of the world and lusts of the flesh; carefulness of other things makes careless of the Word. It is hard to hit a moving object, a bird in flight; as well, to as much purpose, sow the waves in a tempest, or cast seed upon branches tossed with the wind, as preach to a distracted, wandering hearer; nothing fixes, sinks, abides; his soul is like a highway, every man or beast has free passage. The remedy is to fix your whole soul on God. Prejudice : An ill conceit of the gospel; the matter, or the manner of delivery, plainness, simplicity; or ministers, their persons, conversation, office, or execution of it. To remove it, consider there is no reason, no room for prejudice against the gospel; those that despise it never saw its glory, nor tasted its sweetness—"If our gospel be hid, it is hid to them that are lost" (2 Cor. iv. 3). Shall we think worse of the sun because a blind man speaks against it, because an owl cannot behold it? and for ministers, there is glory enough in the gospel to gild them, how mean soever. 2. Directions how to hear. (1) Get a punctual knowledge of the state of your souls in reference to God. The reason is this, we must take heed how we hear, that we may hear fruitfully, that the Word may be profitable. It is most profitable when it is seasonable. It cannot be seasonable to you (whatever it be in itself), except you be acquainted with your soul's condition. (2) Before you hear, endeavour to get your souls into a capacity of hearing fruitfully, to get spiritual advantage by hearing. Take pains with your hearts in private before ye come, make them tender, fit to receive impressions. Set them open, that Christ may come in. Make room, empty them of sin and vanity, that the Spirit may work freely, with liberty, without interruption. Get them melted in prayer, sublimated, raised by meditation. (3) Receive the Word, and every part of it, as concerning thee in particular. Get knowledge of your greatest wants, weakest graces, strongest lusts, worst distempers, coldest affections, difficultest encumbrances, that so you may know how to apply the Word. (4) Be not satisfied with anything in hearing, but the presence of God. That special presence, when operative, makes the Word effectual to the ends appointed. The presence of the Lord His glory filled the tabernacle under the law; and His presence is as abundant and glorious under the gospel. (5) Take heed of suppressing any good motions raised by the Word. Constant hearers have experience of some convictions of sin, and resolve to leave it and mind the soul. Nourish these, take heed of smothering them. They are the blessed issues of heaven; will you stifle, murder them in the conception, make them like an untimely birth? They are buds springing from the immortal seed; will you nip them? They are sprigs planted by the hand of Christ, which would grow into a tree of life; will ye pluck them up by the roots, expose them to the frosts, break them while young and tender? They are sparks kindled by the breath of God, heavenly fire; will you quench it? (6) Come with resolution to do whatever ye shall hear, to comply with the whole will of God without reserves. There must be no more respect of truths than respect of persons. Obedience is the sweetest harmony the Lord can hear on earth, the perfection of it is a consonancy to the Divine will; if every string, every act be not screwed up thereto, there can be no concert, nothing but discord, harsh and unpleasing in His ear. It is not enough to promise God to the half of the kingdom ; halting obedience will never come to heaven : all, or none. (7) Mix it with faith—" The word preached did not profit them, not being mixed with faith in them that heard it " (Heb. iv. 2). Faith is a necessary ingredient to all spiritual services. (8) Receive the truth in the love of it—"Because they received not the love of the truth," *i.e.*, truth in love, " that they might be saved " (2 Thess. ii. 10). He that would hear savingly, must hear it with love ; not out of fear, custom, not for by-ends, for credit, profit, preferment ; but out of love to the naked truth, for its own native loveliness, without extrinsical consideration ; as the truth is in Jesus, of Him, from Him. (*D. Clarkson, B.D.*) *On reading and hearing the Word of God :*—I. The dignity and excellence of the truths contained in the gospel appears in the fullest evidence when we reflect that they are the words of God, the dictates of that eternal wisdom from whence all light, all science is derived. II. Still, my brethren, you will neither read nor hear the Word of God with any fruit, unless you bring with you suitable dispositions. (*J. Archer.*) *On hearing the Word :*—Your mode of hearing, therefore, should correspond, on the one hand, to the character you sustain as rational and accountable creatures ; and, on the other, to the un-speakable importance of Divine realities. Hence we remark—I. That it becomes you to hear ATTENTIVELY, and WITH DISCRIMINATION AND JUDGMENT. II. That it becomes you to hear, on all occasions, WITH AN EARNEST DESIRE TO BE PERSONALLY BENEFITED. 1. Among those who appear in our sanctuaries, there are multitudes of merely formal attendants. 2. Among those who hear us, there are also frequently not a few actuated solely by motives of idle curiosity. 3. There are others who make it their entire business to sit in judgment upon the merits and defects of our addresses, both as to their style and as to their matter. 4. But, probably, the most numerous class of our hearers who stand in need of rectified habits, or, at least, that class which comprehends the greatest number of truly pious individuals, consists of those who hear for any but themselves. III. Always hear with the impression upon your minds, that THE OPPORTUNITY YOU ARE ENJOYING MAY BE THE LAST YOU WILL EVER BE FAVOURED WITH. IV. See to it that you always hear IN A DEVOTIONAL FRAME OF MIND. (*J. P. Dobson.*) *Directions for hearing sermons :*—I. DIRECTIONS FOR HEARING. 1. Hear the Word from right motives and for right ends. Multitudes go to church because their fathers went, their neighbours go, and they do not love to be singular. Many go, not to hear, but to see or to be seen. Some hear sermons to furnish their heads with knowledge, not to enrich their hearts with grace. 2. Our hearing should be preceded, accompanied, and followed by earnest prayers for the Divine blessing. 3. Hear the Word of God with pleasure and grati-tude. Compare your circumstances with those of your forefathers, who had no other instructor than nature's light ; and with those of the many dark places of the earth, full of the habitations of cruelty. 4. Cultivate an honest, impartial love to truth, and a meek, humble, candid, and teachable spirit. Nothing ought to be admitted as an article of faith, or a rule of life, which is not either expressly contained in, or, by just consequence, inferred from the sacred oracles. Meekness is the fruit of the Spirit. Apply, therefore, to Him to form in you, by His grace, that humble, teachable disposition, which is so necessary to render outward instruc-tion truly profitable. 5. Hear the Word with understanding and judgment. 6. Hear with attention, seriousness, and solemnity of spirit. Men are renewed and sanctified by the truth. But truth, not heard with serious attention, has no such salutary energy. 7. Let such a lively faith mix itself with your hearing as will produce affections suited to the truths you hear. A report, however interesting in its own nature, if not credited, can neither engage our affections nor influence our practice. 8. Wisely apply what you hear to your own case ; and for that end, endeavour to be well acquainted with the true state of your souls. II. DIRECTIONS AFTER HEARING. 1. Endeavour to remember what you have heard. A transient glance discovered some blemish on his face ; but the faint impression it made on his imagination quickly vanishes, and, not observing it dis-tinctly, he is at no pains to wipe it off. 2. Meditate, and expostulate with your hearts, upon what you have heard. Think not, when the minister has done preach-ing, that your work is over. 3. Converse with your fellow-Christians about what you have heard. 4. Reduce what you have heard to practice. 5. Often examine how you have heard and improved the Word. 6. If you have received any benefit by the Word, ascribe to God all the glory. (*J. Erskine, D.D.*) *How the Word is to be read and heard :*—I. SOME THINGS ARE TO GO BEFORE HEARING. 1. Preparation. (1) Getting the heart impressed with an awful sense of the majesty and holiness of that God into whose presence we are going, and whose word we are to hear (Psa. lxxxix. 6). (2) Banishing out of the heart worldly cares that are lawful at other times (Matt. xiii. 7). (3) Application of the blood of Christ to the soul for removing guilt, and doing away any controversy betwixt God and the soul (Amos iii. 3). (4) Purging the heart of carnal and corrupt lusts and affections (1 Pet. ii. 1, 2). (5) Stirring up in the heart spiritual desires (1 Pet. ii. 2). 2. Prayer. Pray (1) For assistance to the minister (2 Thess. iii. 1). (2) For a meal to ourselves (Psa. cxix. 18). (3) For an outpouring of the Spirit in His own ordinances. II. SOME THINGS ARE TO GO ALONG WITH HEARING. 1. Attending unto the Word diligently. This implies—(1) Waiting diligently upon the ordinances, so as people make it their business to catch opportunities of the Word, and let none slip which Providence will allow them to overtake. They that are only chance customers to ordinances, whose attendance is ruled by their own conveniences, without conscience of duty, causing them to take them only now and then as their fancy takes them, cannot expect good of them. (2) A fixing and bending of the ear and mind to what is spoken. Hence is that counsel of the wise man (Prov. ii. 1, 2). (3) A discerning of what they hear, so as to distinguish betwixt truth and error, the corn and the chaff (Mark iv. 24; Acts xvii. 11). (4) An endeavouring to know the mind of God in His Word, to hear with understanding. 2. Receiving the Word rightly. (1) With faith. A faith of assent. And a faith of application. (2) With love. A love of esteem, highly prizing it. A love of desire after it. A love of complacency in it. 3. Laying it up in our hearts. III. SOME THINGS ARE TO FOLLOW AFTER HEARING THE WORD. 1. Meditation on it in your hearts (Psa. i. 2). 2. Conferring of it on your discourse. 3. The main thing is practising it in your lives. (*T. Boston, D.D.*)

Hearers :—Jedediah Buxton, the famous peasant, who could multiply nine figures by nine in his head, was once taken to see Garrick act. When he went back to his own village, he was asked what he thought of the great actor and his doings. "Oh!" he said, "he did not know; he had only seen a little man strut about the stage, and repeat 7,956 words." Here was a want of the ability to appreciate what he saw, and the exercise of the reigning faculty to the exclusion of every other. Similarly our hearers, if destitute of the spiritual powers by which the gospel is discerned, fix their thoughts on our words, tones, gestures, or countenance. and make remarks upon us which from a spiritual point of view are utterly absurd. How futile are our endeavours without the Holy Spirit! (*C. H. Spurgeon.*) *Hearing :*—"I have an ear for other preachers," Sir John Cheke used to say, "but I have a heart for Latimer." Here is a very clear and main distinction. Too often men hear the word sounding its drums and trumpets outside their walls, and they are filled with admiration of the martial music, but their city gates are fast closed and vigilantly guarded, so that the truth has no admittance, but only the sound of it. Would to God we knew how to reach men's affections, for the heart is the target we aim at, and unless we hit it we miss altogether. (*Ibid.*) *Hearing carelessly :*— We crossed and recrossed the river several times by the ferry-boat at Basle. We had no object in the world but merely amusement and curiosity, to watch the simple machinery by which the same current is made to drift the boat in opposite directions from side to side. To other passengers it was a business, to us a sport. Our hearers use our ministry in much the same manner when they come to it out of the idlest curiosity, and listen to us as a means of spending a pleasant hour. That which should ferry them across to a better state of soul, they use as a mere pleasure-boat, to sail up and down in, making no progress after years of hearing. Alas! it may be sport to them, but it is death to us, because we know it will ere long be death to them. (*Ibid.*) *Uselessness of mere hearing :*—What a mistake to imagine that, by hearing first one preacher and then another, we can derive benefit to our souls! More is wanted than such hearing. A raven may fly from cage to cage, but it is not thereby changed into a dove. Go from room to room of the royal feast, and the sight of the tables will never stay thy hunger. Reader, the main thing is to have and hold the truth personally and inwardly; if this be not seen to, thou wilt die in thy sins, though ten thousand voices should direct thee to the way of salvation. Pity indeed is it that the bulk of hearers are hearers only, and are no more likely to go to heaven than the seats they sit on in the assembly of the saints. (*Ibid.*) *The ear's music room :*—Picture to yourselves the contrast between a great orchestra containing some hundred performers and instruments, and that small music-room built of ivory, no bigger than a cherrystone, which we call an ear, where there is ample accommodation for all of them to play together. The players, indeed, and their instruments, are not admitted. But what of that if their music be? Nay, if you only think of it, what we call a musical performance is, after all, but the last rehearsal. The true performance is within the ear's music-room, and each one of us has the whole orchestra to himself. When we thus realize the wondrous capabilities of the organ of hearing, I think we shall not fail to find an intellectual and æsthetical as well as a great moral admonition in the Divine words, " He that hath ears to hear, let him hear." (*Dr. Wilson.*)   *Right hearing:*—"I reckon that's very much o' what the Lord Jesus meant when He said, ' Take heed how ye hear.' Whatever it means, an' whatever it don't mean, it means this plain enough—Don't hear anyhow. You see that was the way with the ground that didn't prosper—it took the seed all anyhow. There was the wayside; it let the seed come just as it could, and o' course it all got trodden under foot, or was eaten up by the fowls, an' not a grain was left. An' then I daresay Brother Wayside went complainin' that he couldn't get any good under that preacher. There was the weedy ground, too, let it fall in anyhow among the thorns an' thistles, an' they grew up an' choked it. An' I shouldn't wonder but Sister Weedy-ground whispered to Brother Wayside very piously, that for her part she did wish they had a preacher that would stir them up. Then there was Mister Stoney-ground, who liked it very much, an' nodded to everybody over the nice sermon, but when the sun was up, that is, when dinner-time came, he could hardly remember the text. They all heard : but they were anyhow hearers. But there was dear old Father Good-ground, whenever he heard the Word it got in an' went down, an' took root, an' sprang up, an' bare fruit, an' brought forth a hundred-fold ; such wonderful crops o' love, an' joy, an' peace, that set all the folks a scratchin' their heads however he could manage it ! Yet it was no such great secret; he got ready beforehand, that was all. He prepared for the seed. He'd have been weedy-ground, too, only he had been down on his knees, an' pulled up the chokin' cares an' Saturday's worries; he had picked out the stones, an' had ploughed up the field, an' had given the seed a chance, that was all, an' so he got a harvest. You see there was the same sower, an' the same seed, an' yet it was only the ground that was got ready beforehand that got any good."—(*From " Daniel Quorm."*)   *On hearing the Word of God:*—That we may so hear, as to profit by hearing, it is required—1. That we hear with attention. 2. That we hear with impartiality. 3. That we hear with meekness. 4. That we hear the Word with an actual intention of practising what we hear. (*Bp. Smalridge.*)   *The pulpit and the pen:*—1. A critical spirit is a great hindrance to profitable hearing. 2. A formal spirit is a great hindrance to profitable hearing. 3. The preparation of the heart is necessary to profitable hearing. 4. A teachable spirit is needful for profitable hearing. 5. Attention is necessary to profitable hearing. (*J. Kelly.*) *Eloquent listening :*—There is such a thing. The really eloquent listener is the devout listener—one who has come up to church as to the house of God, to meet God there, to sit at His feet, to learn of Him, with a heart anxious to know His will that he may do it. When people rush from their late beds, or their studied toilets, or their newspapers, to the house of God, without a moment's preparation of serious thought, or reading of the Word, or prayer, what wonder that they find the services tedious and the sermon dull? The deaf might as well go to hear Beethoven's symphonies, or the blind to witness the glories of a sunset, as for such to go and hear a sermon with a reasonable expectation of finding it eloquent profitable, or interesting. (*Anon.*)   *Prepared hearing :*—There is a common consent among mankind that there should be some preparedness for worship. I see the visible signs of it here to-day. Before the Sabbath dawned you began to prepare clean linen and brighter garments than those of common days. It is but an outward and common matter ; still, within the shell there lieth a kernel. My counsel to you is — cleanse your hearts rather than your garments. (*C. H. Spurgeon.*)   *A weighty exhortation :*—To give more weight to this exhortation, let us consider — I. WHO IS HE WHO SPEAKS TO US ? God Himself. 1. By the Holy Book. 2. By our preaching, in the measure in which it is approved of Him. 3. By the Holy Spirit. II. WHAT DOES HE TELL US ? That which is of the utmost consequence to us, for time and for eternity—the central truth which sways all others. III. WHAT KIND OF ATTENTION DOES THE TRUTH REVEALED BY HIM REQUIRE? Mere attention is not sufficient. Christian truth claims a particular attention. It is not enough to bring great sagacity, a penetrating spirit, trained to study and fully determined to learn the truths which are presented. Religious truth has organs of its own, by which it reveals itself to man. Take heed, therefore, how ye hear. If your heart is not well prepared, if your conscience is not upright, you will certainly have sounds ringing in your ears: but those sounds, which bring to others an unspeakable joy, will for you be lost in the air where they vibrated. IV. WHAT IS THE COST OF DESPISING THE TRUTH? The Word of God does not return to Him without effect, it comes back to Him after having saved us or ruined us. (*E. de Pressensé, D.D.*) *The prepared hearer :*—The words of the text are necessary not only to give point to the parable of the sower, and to send it home to the hearts of the hearers, but also to prevent them from putting a disastrous misinterpretation upon the parable, from supposing that "the state of mind described as existing in different men, originated in some inherent necessity." I. THE HEARER SHOULD BE PREPARED AS WELL AS THE PREACHER. 1. He should have his body, so far as possible, in such a condition that it will not interfere with the free action of the mind. Some people break the Sabbath on a Saturday. 2. The mind should be prepared. Worldly cares and preoccupations should be bidden to stand aside. 3. Above all, the spirit should be prepared, be devout, humble, receptive. II. THE PREPARED HEARER WILL HEAR ATTENTIVELY, in the spirit of the words uttered by Cornelius to Peter (Acts x. 33). 1. There cannot have been proper attention when a man goes away crediting the preacher with something which he never dreamt of saying. 2. There cannot have been proper attention when a sermon, which cost its preacher considerable pains in the production, is forgotten in less than a week. 3. There cannot have been proper attention when the sermon leaves no lasting result in the hearts and lives of the hearers. "Faith cometh by hearing," as well as "hearing by the Word of God." III. THE PREPARED HEARER WILL NOT HEAR CENSORIOUSLY. I do not say that you should not hear critically in the true sense of that much-abused word. For true criticism is nothing more or less than judgment. But to bring a sound and healthy judgment to bear upon what we hear is one thing, to listen in a spirit of fault-finding is another. The man of censorious spirit; the man who thinks less of the sun than of his spots, can never hear to profit. Listen charitably and patiently. IV. THE PREPARED HEARER WILL CARRY AWAY SOMETHING VALUABLE FROM THE POOREST PREACHER AND THE FEEBLEST SERMON. As good George Herbert has it:

"God calleth preaching folly. Grudge thou not
To pick out treasures from an earthen pot.
The worst speak something good. If all lack sense,
God takes a text, and preacheth patience.
He that gets patience, and the blessing which
Preachers conclude with, hath not lost his pains." (*J. R. Bailey.*)

To him shall be given.—*The law of use :*—Hearing and doing should go together. Knowledge that is practical, blossoming out into character, shall keep on growing from knowledge to knowledge, more and more. But knowledge that never blossoms into character, shall by and by cease even to be knowledge. The tree that bears no fruit shall not be fruitless only; it shall rot and die. The idea is, that having is something quite other than mere passive possession—the upturned, nerveless palm of beggary. Having, real having, is eager, instant, active possession, the sinewy grip. Having is using. Anything not used is already the same as lost. It will be lost by and by. I. This law of use is PHYSICAL law. Exercise, to be sure, may be overdone, as in training for athletic contests. But, on the other hand, muscular force gains nothing by being husbanded. Having is using. And to him that hath, shall be given. He shall grow stronger and stronger. What is difficult, perhaps impossible to-day, shall be easy to-morrow. He that keeps on day by day lifting the calf, shall lift the bullock by and by. So, even in this lowest sphere, the law is inexorable. Having is using. Not using is losing. Idleness is paralysis. II. This law of use is COMMERCIAL law. Whoever indolently inherits an estate, never really comes into possession of it. Most of our famous merchants of to-day, of yesterday, are, or were, the architects of their own fortunes. Wealth goes down easily enough into the second generation, but not so easily into the third, and still less easily into the fourth. We take a tremendous risk in bequeathing fortunes to our children. Unless the children have been very carefully trained in the art of getting, they probably have not learned the art of keeping. III. This law of use is MENTAL law Even knowledge, like the manna of old, must needs be fresh. It will not keep. The successful teacher is always the diligent and eager learner. It is related of Thorwaldsen that when at last he finished a statue that satisfied him, he told his friends that his genius was leaving him. Having reached a point beyond which he could push no further, his instinct told him that he had already begun to fail. So it proved. The summit of his fame was no broad plateau, but a sharp Alpine ridge. The last step up had to be quickly followed by the first step down. It is so in everything. New triumphs must only dictate new struggles. If it be Alexander of Macedon, the Orontes must suggest the Euphrates, and the Euphrates the Indus. Always it must be on and on. Genius is essentially athletic, resolute, aggressive, persistent. Possession is grip, that tightens more and more. Ceasing to gain, we begin to lose. IV. This law of use is also MORAL law. Here lies the secret of character. There is no such thing as standing still. And character, at last, is not inheritance, nor happy accident, but hardest battle and victory. From country to city is like some great change in latitude, and soil, and climate. As in going to the tropics, so here also the senses are stormed and captured. Luxuries, once only imagined, as a Greenlander might imagine an orange-grove, are now always in sight. Gains, that once seemed fabulous, are now the common talk of the street, the office, and the club. Something is in the air that poisons the blood like malaria. The muscles relax. The will relaxes. And, before we think of it, there is the old story, the old sad story, of mere passive and pliant goodness brought to bitter grief and shame. Or else the danger is overcome, and the manhood of man escapes unhurt; like the three young Hebrews out of the furnace in Babylon, like Daniel out of the lions' den. If prayer be, what Tertullian has pictured it, the watch-cry of a soldier under arms, guarding the tent and standard of his General, then the habit of it ought to be growing on us. For the night is round about us, and, though the stars are out, our enemies are not asleep. If the Bible be what we say it is, then we should know it better and better. The longer we live, and the more we look beneath the surface of things, the more there is of mystery. So of all the virtues and graces. They will not take care of themselves. Self-denial and self-control, as against self-seeking and self-indulgence; absolute, chivalric integrity, as against the sharpness of the market; unshaken faith in God and man, in spite of all the mystery and meanness of life; the one simple purpose of loyal, steadfast stewardship and service in our day and generation; these neither come unasked, nor stay unurged. Easy things are of little worth. The spontaneities are mostly bad; mere weeds and briers. For the whole Church, in its organic life, the law is just the same. King David conquers out in every possible direction, north, east, and south. Solomon, settling down to the enjoyment of inherited dominion, loses the paternal conquests, bequeathing to his son a kingdom doomed already to dismemberment. So must the Church be always militant just so long as any body, or any thing, in this world remains unchristian. Such is the law: always the law, everywhere the law. Its law is not simple growth, as of the palm-tree, but conflict, as of armies. He that hath, to him shall be given; and he that hath not, from him shall be taken even that which he hath. Be it remembered, however, that every gain is a vital factor. Interest changes constantly to capital, and changes rapidly. The progression is swiftly geometrical. It is the beginning always that costs. The poor invalid, after long confinement, is borne out to the carriage for a morning drive. If it agrees with him, the half-hour to-day may be doubled to-morrow. In toil or trade no dollar comes so hard as the first one. The next two or ten come easier; and more and more easy all along. A solitary virtue in some human life, if such a thing were possible, would be a forlorn and dreary sight: like a shaft of granite in a sandy waste, or a single bird in a silent sky. Thank God, the virtues go together: like trees in a forest; like birds in white-winged flocks, filling the whole sky with song. First, the chief end of discipline is high personal character. Second, character is triumph over temptation. Third, the surest conservative of character is service. Finally, let me emphasize, by repeating the two great lessons of our text. The first is, that beginnings are difficult: all beginnings, but especially in character; difficult by reason of bad appetites and passions. The best habits are not the ones most easily formed. "He that hath!" It is a great thing to have. The second lesson is, that gains and losses grow always more rapid and easy. Character grows always steadily less and less conscious of its own determinations. Moses knew not that his face shone. Samson knew not that his strength was gone. Bad habit begins easily enough. Good habit begins with effort, as one would climb a steep mountain, or lift a heavy gate from its hinges. But it ends in second nature. And the dividing line is crossed as silently as the tide swings, coming in this instant, going out the next; as silently as the sun crosses the Equator, northward and southward, carrying summer with it, leaving winter behind it. (R. D.

Hitchcock, D.D.)   *The possession of appreciation:*—That which Shakespeare and Wordsworth had of the seeing eye and the understanding heart is shared by you and me if we can read their writings with any appreciation. Have so much of that, of what they had, and in that measure there is given to you what was given to them. To him that hath it shall be given. Only bring to nature and life something of mind as free as mind should be, and you shall find them not sparing of their gift. Not only in regard to literature, art, science, the end of which is thought, but in regard to thought and feeling, in which the practical interests of men and nations are involved, to have in one's self something which is real at all, or worth anything, is to be in the way of having much. *(J. Service, D.D.)*   *An incentive to culture:*—More or less in every sphere of thought and activity, the inducement which a man has to cultivate what nature has given him in the shape of power and faculty, is that the reward is great. Much is given to him that has. That inducement is strong here as it is nowhere else. Augustine, it is said, when he failed as a lawyer, took the infinite for his career. As far as the infinite is synonymous with religion it is a term for a career which is open to every man, and in which success is no question of chance but one of effort and endeavour. In regard to religion, as in regard to every other department of human life, there is, of course, a difference between man and man, between class and class, people and people, generation and generation. By nature one man has much of what you call religious feeling, another man little. That is a fact not to be ignored. But whatever a man has in this kind, be it little or much, there is this inducement to cultivate it, that as far as, by putting it into exercise and so really possessing himself of it, he can be said to have it, much is given to him in it and with it, much in proportion to what he already has. Every step forward and upward in the career of Augustine's—the infinite—the wider and greater is the prospect which for the soul is not prospect but property. *(Ibid.)*   **From him shall be taken even that which he seemeth to have.**—*True and false possession:*—Apparent arbitrariness in this utterance. Not so, however. It is the expression of a law which underlies all things. Similar words occur frequently in the Gospels, in connection not only with parable of sower, but also with those of talents, pounds, &c. Thus the universality of its application is indicated. I. WHAT IS THE NATURE OF TRUE POSSESSION? 1. It is something which is part of a man's very self. 2. It is something which he turns to account, and does not allow to fust in him unused. II. THERE IS A SEEMING POSSESSION WHICH IS FALSE. Does not conform to these two conditions. It is either external to the man, or unemployed by him. III. TRUE POSSESSIONS TRULY USED EVER INCREASE, WHILE UNTRUE POSSESSIONS VANISH. " Seemeth " because it was offered him ; " hath not " because he did not accept it. Apply to the highest possessions. Gospel privileges. Take heed how ye use them—how ye hear. *(Anon.)*   *The grand test of a religious life:*—The principle enunciated is one which applies to many other things besides religious lessons and spiritual gifts. We all of us know for instance that there is a learning which is no learning ; that there is a wisdom which is no wisdom ; that there is a strength which is no strength ; and a skill which is no skill. We know very well what is meant for instance by learning which is got up for a special occasion and is not part of a man's real knowledge, which has not, as it were, mixed itself up with his faculties, and of which he does not understand the fundamental principles, and cannot tell what are the relations of it to other kinds of knowledge, or what is the right application of it to ourselves. Such knowledge as that prepared for any particular purpose may be entirely possessed and enjoyed at the moment after it has been so prepared, and yet everybody knows how entirely it passes away and is forgotten. For although the man had it in one sense, in another he had it not. So again, for instance, those who know anything of the writings of Aristotle will remember how he describes the spurious kinds of courage. There is, he says, a courage which is merely born of ignorance, which a man feels when he is in great danger ; because he does not know what the danger is, he does not perceive its extent or how serious is his risk. That same man, when this danger was hidden from him, was perfectly calm and collected, yet if he knew what really was around him would very probably prove a mere coward, altogether unable to keep the balance of his mind. Just as we are told that sometimes men who have walked past precipices in the dark without the least sensation of fear, have turned sick and faint at heart when they have seen the danger they had incurred. So he says there is a courage which is born of knowledge, that courage which a man exercises when in danger because he knows precisely what are the limits and what the extent of that danger, knows exactly how he can deal with it, and consequently is able to keep himself perfectly calm and collected where others would be seriously afraid. Such courage is indeed real and genuine as far as it goes, and yet that very same man if he were put in circumstances where his knowledge would no longer apply, if he found himself in the greatest danger of which he knew nothing and the limits of which he could not estimate, might possibly be filled with an unreasonable panic, and lose his presence of mind when most he needed it. But true courage is that which rests upon real principle. It does not depend upon circumstances, but on a sense of duty which makes a man brave because he ought to be brave, and his master who put him there requires that no want of presence of mind, no disturbance of the balance of his intellect should interfere with the service which he has to do. The difference between them is that one man has courage really, and the other man while he has courage, yes, and as far as it goes, genuine courage, yet after all has it not. But our Lord is here of course applying this principle to the lessons which He Himself was teaching. " Take heed how ye hear!" He is applying it to religious instruction and spiritual gifts, and to the service of God. And it is not difficult if we turn to the Old Testament to find instances which will illustrate most clearly for us the application of this principle to human character. Thus when we read how Saul put away the wizards in Israel, plainly because he desired seriously to fulfill the will of God, we have no reason to doubt the sincerity of his desire. We have no reason to suppose it was hypocrisy, as we commonly use the word : that he desired to wear a religious character in the eyes of his fellows, and to obtain the approval of Samuel the prophet by doing the will of God. Yet we find afterwards this same Saul in his darkest need, when he cannot obtain counsel any longer from God, turns to the witch of Endor for advice, and thus falsifies all his previous services. Or to come down later still. Look at Ahab the king of Israel. He, we are told, after the slaughter of Naboth the Jezreelite, was reproved by Elijah the prophet in such stern language that he was struck, it may be with alarm, or it may be remorse, and showed every token of genuine repentance. He humbled himself and wept, and we are told that his repentance was accepted by God, and God Himself made an immediate acknowledgment of it, and therefore we know it could not have been merely a false exhibition of regret. But was Ahab really penitent ? Are we able to say afterwards that his life was changed? In the very next chapter we find that he imprisons Micaiah the prophet because he will not speak smooth things to him, and then comes down the final judgment of God on the wicked king. But once more to turn to the instances which would naturally strike every reader of the Old Testament as the most striking instance of all, let us look at the familiar history of the prophet Balaam, and when we read it what do we see ? Do we see a man who had no desire to obey God's will : a man who was simply a rebel against the truth that was revealed to him ? On the contrary, we know that he was a prophet to whom God's will was plainly shown, and we see that he was a wicked man, and that he died a wicked man's death. But have we any reason to say that his obedience to the Lord was entirely hypocritical ? So far from that we see plainly that he is resolute to do exactly that which he is bidden. He does not flinch for a moment from the path of strict obedience. Not even in the presence of the king who could advance him to honour, not even there does he fail to pronounce the blessing which God requires him to pronounce, yet was his obedience all genuine ? We can plainly see that his heart was set upon finding some way or other of reconciling obedience in the letter with disobedience in the spirit, and going to the very verge of what is forbidden. He is resolute to do what he is told, but he will go as near as he possibly can to what he is told not to do. All through he is hoping that some way may be found by which the service of God and the service of man may be reconciled, and though he does what he is told his wish is for self-indulgence. He has obedience and genuine obedience, and yet he has it not. It is worthless although it is there. And if we turn to the New Testament we may find similar illustrations which I need not describe at so much length. Such, for instance, was the character of the man who buried his lord's money in the earth. He had the talent which his lord had given him, and yet he had it not. Now, brethren, it is not difficult to see that all this applies also to ourselves, and to our own lives. We, too, if we choose to look can easily find many respects in which perhaps we really have and yet have not, and assuredly many in which we are in danger of coming under the censure of our Lord. Let us, for instance, speak of some of the doctrines which we all hold. Let us take the doctrine of the omnipresence of God, one of the fundamental truths of the Christian faith, and which no Christian doubts for a single moment, and one which, if we did not believe, we should never venture to call ourselves Christians at all. We believe that God is present everywhere, and that He sees everything we do, and that He knows everything we think. We believe that His is the last, the supreme, the decisive judgment upon all our lives. And now let me ask you, if we have this doctrine, may it not sometimes nevertheless be said that we have it not? Let me ask you how often it may be the case that things that you would do when other people are not by, you would be unwilling, ashamed, afraid to do in the presence of others. Can it be said we are real believers in the omnipresence of God if it has no effect whatever upon our lives? Let me turn now, brethren, not to other doctrines, but rather to characters and circumstances of life. Let me, for instance, compare for a moment two different men under different circumstances who yet, under many respects, shall seem to be precisely alike. I will suppose two men who come here to church and who take a part in the service and worship of God, who listen to His Word when read and hear the message which God's minister has to deliver. I will suppose these two men are both of them touched and moved, that they have heard words which in some way or other happen to suit their own particular case, and I will suppose their hearts are stirred within them, and they feel somehow as if they had learnt a fresh lesson and caught a new sight of God's truth, as if something was cleared up before them which had not before been plain to them; and they go away and feel, "I have been the better for coming here to church; that service has done me good," and with that with one man there it ends. It is a genuine feeling; there is no hypocrisy in it at all, but there it ends and there is no more of it. But the other man, once his conscience is awaked, inasmuch as he is always on the watch to do what his conscience bids him, finds that there is a difference to be made in his own personal life, he sees something that he ought to change, he perceives something that he ought to elevate and purify and make more heavenly; he perceives something that he ought to give up, and some characteristic which is not quite consistent with the true service of God, he says he must cleanse himself from everything of that sort, and accordingly it has made a real difference—slight perhaps—very slight, it is but the service of one afternoon, but it makes a real difference. Now here the two men have received both the same spiritual gifts, the same spiritual teaching, but the one man hath it and the other hath it not. To have the truths of God is to live in them and for them; to rise towards them, to grow in them, to learn somewhat more of God by them; it is to make them part of our lives constantly by day and by night, and unless we can make the doctrine of God ours in that sense, then we shall have to learn that they are not ours at all. (*Bp. Temple.*)

Vers. 19–21. **Then came to Him His mother and His brethren.** — *Spiritual relationship to Christ:*—It is the higher kinship of the soul. Christ did not set aside time relationships, but He opened up a far higher view, with which these were in analogy. Men know each other in various relationships; but very few men know themselves. Very few men know one another; but in the degree in which they do, they know each other at different points of the wide extension of man and his relations. A man may know his parentage and his home. That is primary knowledge, and very noble it is. He may know men by their co-operations and partnerships in the affairs of life—that, and only that. He may know men by some similar tastes and pursuits. Artists know artists; musicians know musicians; working men know working men; inventors know inventors. There is a line of sympathy that goes out from all these different points by which men interpret in other people something that they have in themselves. It is a knowledge which consists simply in the attempt to interpret in others something that we have felt in our own selves—to liken ourselves to those around about us. So a man may know his fellow-men in times of great excitement by partizan feeling, by party feeling, or by patriotism. The real relationship, the truest, the highest, while it does not disdain these lower relationships, regards them as external and transient. You may know men as parents, and not know them at all. You may know men as business factors and be utterly outside of them and ignorant of them. You may know men by tastes, by professions, by pursuits, and yet not know them interiorly. You may know men as your countrymen, and as faithful to law and order in times of great confusion; and yet that is exterior knowledge. It is juxtaposition, for the most part. Interiorly, how little does a man know his fellow-men until he has in himself the higher qualities, spiritual and intellectual, and until he interprets the like qualities that are in those around about him! Apply this to the relationship of men with Christ and with God. In the truest and highest sense, not until men rise into those qualities which constitute God can they be said to understand Him. We can understand Him when He thunders, because we can thunder in a small way; we can understand Him when He speaks of Himself as the Creator, because we are mechanicians in a certain way; when He sets His palace in order in the heavens above, when He fills the earth with His glory, when the firmament declares His glory and the earth His handiwork, we can understand all that well enough, because we ourselves are creators, re-arrangers of physical qualities and matter; and so we feel that we have an understanding of God; and we have. But our great wish is that we could understand Him according to our senses all the way through: "Why does He not speak to me? That is the way my children understand me. I wish God would bring Himself down within the scope of my eyes. Why does He not hear me? Why does He not come within the realm of my ear? Why does He not come where I can lay my hand upon Him—thrust it into His side, indeed?" We are always trying to come to a knowledge of God by bringing Him down to a level with our condition; then we think that we should understand Him; but the disciples did not. His brethren and His mother did not, and He was upon the line and level of their physical condition. They were just as far from Him, and just as far from satisfaction in regard to Him, as if they had never seen Him, or as if He had gone early from the cradle to the grave. And to-day men are seeking to know God by ratiocination. They are searching the origin of things, the germs of life, its unfoldings and its philosophy; and all of them are playing round about this great problem of the universe: "Is there a God? Where is He? Who is He? What is He?" The royal road to knowledge is goodness. He that loves, we are told in explicit language, knows God, though He cannot imagine the amplitude of such love. He that only knows the candle knows what the sun is a little bit; but the candle does not give him any conception of the magnitude and majesty and glory of the sun. He that loves here has one letter of the alphabet, as it were, but not the whole literature and philosophy of the Divine nature. This is the highway through which, and only through which, John declares that any man can come to an understanding of God. God is love; love is His constituent element, and no man can understand God that does not understand love. As no man can understand heroism except through the recipiency of, or sensibility to, heroism in himself; as no man can understand good taste except through the foregoing feeling of what is harmonious and beautiful; so it is in regard to the great discernments that reveal God to us. (*H. W. Beecher.*) *The affinity of the faithful :*—As this voice came to Christ while He was labouring, so many such voices come to us while we are labouring. One saith, Pleasure would speak with you; another saith, Profit would speak with you; another saith, Ease would speak with you; another saith, A deanery would speak with you; another saith, A bishopric would speak with you; another saith, The court would speak with you. Here is the rule now; if you live by it, then you are kin to Christ. As other kindreds go by birth and marriage, so this kindred goeth by faith and obedience. Hearers are but half kin, as it were in a far degree; but they which hear and do are called His mother, which is the nearest kindred of all. Therefore if you have the deed, then are you kin indeed; there is no promise made to hearers, nor to speakers, nor to readers; but all promises are made to believers or to doers. Again, by this you may learn how to choose your friends. As Christ counted none His kinsmen, but such as "hear the Word of God, and do it"; so we should make none our familiars, but such as Christ counteth His kinsmen. Again, you may see the difference between Christ and the world; Christ calleth the godly His kinsmen, be they never so poor, and we scorn to call the poor our kinsmen, be they never so honest; so proud is the servant above his Master. Again, by this you see how Christ is to be loved; for when He calleth us His mother, He shows us the way to love Him as a mother; for indeed He is the mother of His mother and His brethren too. Again, by this, all vaunting and boasting of kindred is cut off. Glory not in that thou hast a gentleman to thy father, glory not that thou hast a knight to thy brother, but glory that thou hast a Lord to thy brother. Again, by this you may know whether you be kin to Christ; as those priests were shut out of the temple which could not count their genealogy from Aaron, so they shall be shut out of heaven that cannot reckon their pedigree from Christ. Here are the arms now whereby you may show of what house you came. Lastly, by this you may know the devil's kinsmen, and therefore Christ saith, "You are of your father the devil" (John viii. 44), showing that the devil and the wicked are as near kin as

Christ and the faithful. (*H. Smith.*) *The two families—the natural and the spiritual:*—From these words of the Lord Jesus I learn that, without repudiating the family relations of earth, He institutes and proclaims the family relations of heaven. As a faithful minister of the gospel said once to a despotic sovereign, " There are two kings and two kingdoms in Scotland," explaining how Church and State may live and thrive on the same spot at the same time, giving and receiving help reciprocally, if each will consent to confine itself to its own sphere and exercise only its own functions; so the Scriptures intimate that two families pervade society, both having to a great extent the same persons as members, yet without jealousy or collision, getting and giving reciprocal support. Both families are of God. He has planned and constituted them. To Him they owe their origin, and from Him they receive their laws. A place has been assigned to the one in creation; to the other in redemption. The one is the grand Institute of Nature; the other the grand Institute of Grace. Both are good, each as far as it goes ; but the second is deeper, longer, broader, higher than the first. The first is the family for time ; the second is the family for eternity. I. CHRIST IN THE GOSPEL PERMITS THE NATURAL FAMILY, IN ALL ITS INTEGRITY, TO REMAIN UNDISTURBED. Jesus was Himself the member of a family. He received the benefits of that position, and fulfilled its duties. Honour all the pure affections of human nature, for they thrill in the Saviour's breast; loathe all the sins that stain it, for they crucified the Son of God. If you examine the natural affections and instincts of living creatures, you will find that one principle lies like a measuring rod along the whole—utility. These affections are inserted, and inserted such as they are, in the constitution of the creature, because of their usefulness. They are the instruments whereby the Maker works out His own design. Some living creatures, as fishes and certain species of birds, have no perceptible filial or parental affections at all. In their case the instinct is not needed, and therefore is not found. In others, including all the higher grades of the brute creation, the parental affection is developed in great intensity for a short period, and then altogether ceases. A mother that would have shed her blood for her offspring a month ago, when it was feeble, does not know it to-day, at least does not acknowledge it in the herd. The instinct, having served its purpose, is not left dangling after its work is done. Relative affections in human kind expatiate on a wider field, and are more enduring. Here we enter a region in which these affections find room to range ; they become, accordingly, manifold and strong. The roots go deeper down in the deeper, richer soil. A short-lived maternal love would not serve the purpose here ; and therefore a mother's love in this region is not short-lived. Christ was a perfect man. He was not only perfectly holy, but completely human. He took all our nature without its defects and defilements. He experienced filial and fraternal love. He loved His mother and His brethren with the true affection of a son and a brother. No disciple of Christ is permitted to break the bonds of kindred, and abjure the affections of consanguinity, on the plea of his Master's example or command. Superstition has always shown a tendency to exalt the spiritual relations by crushing the natural; it would build up, according to its own false conception, the family of God on the ruins of the family of man. God did not built up the family in order to pull it down again. As the ordinances of the earlier dispensation were a shadow, and so a prediction, of better things to come in Christ, the natural family is a type, and so a promise, of the spiritual and heavenly. II. CHRIST IN THE GOSPEL ESTABLISHES, ON THE SAME SPHERE, A NEW SPIRITUAL FAMILY. If any man be in Christ he is a new creature ; in the new creature a multitude of new affections spring and flow, but being on a higher level, they never run foul of the affections that expatiate on the lower sphere of temporal things. Mind, conscience, immortality, have been imparted to man, and these faculties have free scope for action ; but those operations of the higher nature do not in any measure impede the inhalation of air, the circulation of the blood, or any of the other processes which belong to us in common with inferior creatures. Now, as mind, acting in another sphere, comes not into collision with the functions of the body, so the new spiritual affections, which belong to us as Christians, do not interfere with the original affections which belong to us as men. There is a process in agriculture which presents an interesting parallel to the simultaneous and commingling growth of relations for time and relations for eternity in human hearts. A field is closely occupied all over with a growing crop which will soon reach maturity, and will be reaped in this season's harvest. The owner intends that another crop, totally different in kind, shall possess the ground in the following year ; but he does not

wait till the grain now growing has been reaped—he goes into the field and sows the seed of the new while the old is still growing and green. In some cases a method is adopted which is, from our present point of view, still more suggestive : the seed which shall complete its functions within the present season, and the seed which, springing this year, shall bear its fruit upwards, are mixed together in the same vessel and scattered together on the same ground. Nor does the one lie dormant for a season while the other monopolizes the soil ; both spring up at the same, or nearly the same time. The plant for the future germinates at once, but it does not reach maturity till the following year; the plant intended for the present season—the wheat or the barley—grows rapidly and ripens ere the winter come. Lowly, meekly at the roots of the waving grain springs the plant of the future ; it passes through its earlier stages while the tall stalks of the wheat are towering over its head. It springs although the grain is growing on the same spot, and springs better because the grain is growing there. The vigorous growth of another species all around it shelters its feeble infancy; and after the winter has passed, in another season, it starts afresh and comes forth in its own matured strength. Thus the affections and relations that belong to the future spring and grow under the shadow of the affections and relations that belong to the present. Those stars that studded the dark blue canopy of the sky were lovely ; often through the weary night did the lone watcher lift his. eyes and look upon them. They seemed to him a sort of company, and while he gazed on the bright glancing throng he felt himself for the moment somewhat less lonely. Yet you hear no complaint from that watcher's lips when those stars disappear ; for the cause of their disappearance is the break of day. Either the many fond individual companionships which cheer disciples in the night of their pilgrimage will remain with them, as bright particular stars in the day of eternity, or they will fade away before its dawning ; if they remain, their company in holiness will be a thousandfold more sweet ; if they disappear, it will not be that those joys have grown more dim, but that we do not observe them in the light of a more glorious day. Two practical lessons, one in the form of a warning, and the other in the form of an encouragement, depend from the subject visibly, and claim a notice at the close. 1. Reverting again, for a moment, to the analogy of seed for the future sown and springing under the shade of a crop that is growing for the present season, we may gather from nature a caution which is needful and profitable in the department of grace. When this season's crop, amidst which next season's seed was sown in spring, has been cut in harvest and carried home, I have seen the field in whole or in part destitute of the young plants which ought at that time to have covered its surface, the hope of future years. Sometimes after this season's harvest is reaped, no living plant remains in the ground. As you walk over it at the approach of winter, you see rotting stubble, the decaying remnants of one harvest, but no young plants, the promise of another year. Why ? Because the first crop has grown too rank in its robust maturity, and overlaid the second in its tender youth. The principle of this lesson applies to the business of life as well as the reciprocal affections of kindred. Beware! Open your hearts and take the warning in. Have you hope for pardon and eternal life in the son of God, the Saviour ? Then bear in mind that, under the shade of your city-traffic and your home-joys, a tender plant is growing, native of a softer clime—a plant whose growth is your life, whose decay your ruin, in the great day ; a plant that needs indeed the shelter of honest industry and pure family affections, but dies outright under the choking weight of their overgrowth ; and see to it that the profits and pleasures of time do not, by their excess, kill the hope for eternity. What is a man profited although he gain the whole world, if he lose his own soul ? 2. It is ever true, according to the symbolic prophecy of the Apocalypse, that the earth helps the woman—that the occupations and affinities and friendships of this life may and do cherish the growth of grace in the soul. (*W. Arnot.*) *On rightly seeking the Saviour* :—
I. THEY DESIRED TO SEE CHRIST. This their desire might proceed—1. From a proud and vainglorious principle, from which the best of men are not entirely free. They might want to make it known that they were related to Christ, a person so followed and talked of, who preached such heavenly doctrines, and performed such astonishing miracles. 2. From an undue, and, indeed, mercenary regard to the health of Christ's body and safety of His person. 3. From natural love, without any other design but to please themselves with the company and conversation of one with whom they were so nearly connected, and for whom they had so great regard. Religion is no enemy to natural affection. 4. There might also be a

mixture of spiritual affection. Yet, though the principle might be good, their conduct was reprovable, the application being unseasonable; and the check that Christ gave them should teach us, that no intrusion or solicitation should draw us from the work of the Lord. II. THOSE WHO DESIRE TO SEE CHRIST DO NOT ALWAYS TAKE RIGHT METHODS TO OBTAIN THEIR END. 1. Some, through an improper humility or servile dread, keep at a distance from Christ, even when they have earnest desires to see Him, which desires will never be answered without nearer approaches to Him. 2. Others seek Christ in duties and ordinances, in the streets and broadways, when they ought to see Him in their own closets. They seek Him abroad, but not at home, whereas the kingdom of Christ is within us, and where should the King be but in His kingdom? 3. Others, again, seek Christ out of the Church, who ought to seek Him in it. They "stand without." Let them come in, and seek Christ where He is to be found. (*B. Beddome, M.A.*) *The Lord's answer respecting His mother and brethren:*—On these words of our Lord we may remark—1. That they are not intended to cast a slur on His mother and brethren, or to undervalue the duties men owe to their relations. 2. That we must not allow our regard to our relations to interfere with our duty to God. 3. The sinfulness and folly of all superstitious regard to the Virgin Mary. 4. Nothing but personal obedience and faith can avail for safety. 5. The great love Jesus bears to His true disciples, and the high honour He bestows on them. (*James Foote, M.A.*) *Divine and human relationship:*—A little sad, wasn't it? that His mother and brethren were not sitting about Him. For, as another evangelist says, "He looked round on those that were about Him." His disciples, who were learning of Him, were nearest to Him naturally, and His mother and His brethren were outside. It is a sad thing for any of us to be called by His name, and not know Him. It is the business of our human being to know Christ, and nothing else is our business. You observe Christ is always talking about His Father in heaven. You would think He knew nothing else. Did He, then, repudiate the earthly mother, and the earthly brother and sister? No verily. But it is a profound, absolute fact that our relation to God is infinitely nearer than any relation by nature. (*George Macdonald.*) *The true relatives of Christ:*—Kinship with Christ is not a matter of genealogy or of Church position, or the men around Him would have had it; not of birth, nor of the will of the flesh, nor of the will of man. Kindred with Christ is a matter of nature, and nature can never be tested but by action. If a man is a partaker of the Divine nature that will show itself, and the will that will rule him will no longer be his own, but the will of his Father who is in heaven. (*W. Arthur, M.A.*) *Divine relationships:*—We have here two things, a character and a blessing. I. THE CHARACTER. "These which hear the Word of God and do it." II. THE BLESSING. "The same are my brother and sister and mother." (*Dean Vaughan.*) *Spiritual relationship* (An Epiphany Sermon):—Successive steps in Christ's revelation of Himself. 1. At twelve years' old, though He must be about His Father's business, yet He remained subject for the present. 2. At marriage-festival—"Woman, what have I to do with thee?" a clearer Epiphany, and yet—"Mine hour is not yet come." 3. His friends, His mother, seek Him. He utters words which show that in the higher spiritual relationship claimed for His disciples there is no room for sex; the tie of brotherhood and motherhood a faint type only of the close communion between the redeemed and the Redeemer. 4. At last, dying, He commends His mother to the disciple, "Behold *thy* mother," as if to show that the human relationship had ceased for Himself and her. Natural relationships are swallowed up, the spiritual eclipsing them. Results of acknowledging this fact: I. DISCOMFORT. II. CONSOLATION. III. PRACTICAL EFFECT ON OUR LIVES, viz., our future relationship will be decided not by our present earthly ones, but by our birth of God. (*C. Warren, M.A.*) *Christ and kinship with Him:*—I. THE SPIRITUALITY OF CHRIST'S MISSION AND HIS ABSORPTION IN IT. Affections, even the purest, must be sacrificed when they intrenched upon His liberty to do what He had come into the world to do. "To this end was I born, and for this cause came I into the world, that I should bear witness unto the truth." Think of the loneliness of Christ. While holding intercourse with His friends at Bethany, or surrounded by His disciples, or pressed upon by the crowd, He was yet alone, always alone—alone in His knowledge of the full meaning of His life's work, alone in the endurance of His bitterest pain, alone in the constancy and grandeur of His unfailing purpose. II. THE LARGE-HEARTEDNESS OF CHRIST. He had two great lessons to teach men—The Fatherhood of God, and the common brotherhood of man. How much larger our hearts would be, how much more generous our sympathies, if we shared more largely His Spirit of universal love. III. THE NATURE OF KINSHIP WITH HIM. We all hear, and we all may do the Word of God. We have, then, set before us in the text a privilege in which we all may share—a sacred relationship with Christ into which we all may enter. Application: 1. Is there anywhere any poor man sorely tried, buffeted by circumstances, self-despising and despised of others, but who desires with all his heart to do the will of God. Rise up, and be of good courage, for thou art Christ's brother. 2. Thou art perhaps a widow left alone and poor to struggle with the world; or a mother with the anxious care of a family upon thy shoulders; or a daughter whose life is passing away in some joyless home, and in devotion to an invalid parent whose petulance is thy daily cross. Be patient, and struggle on. Bear the cross, and do the duty, because it is God's will. And remember for thine encouragement in every hour of trial that thou art Christ's sister. 3. And O, aged mother's heart, bereft of thy children, and refusing to be comforted because they are not, think that the Lord of life and glory condescends to call Himself thy son. He will be the comfort and stay of thy declining days, the prop of thy feebleness, the companion of thy loneliness. (*J. R. Bailey.*) *The household of faith:*—I. THE CONNECTION WHICH IS HERE PROCLAIMED. 1. In regard to the connection, the first point is as to the parties between whom it subsists. On the one side, we have a personage of inconceivable greatness and power. Is it some glorious angel whom God made as a specimen of what the Creator can do? No. It is one who is above the angels, and concerning whom it is written, "Let all the angels of God worship Him." This is one to whom it can be said, "Thy throne, O God, is for ever and ever." It is the eternal Son, the heir and Lord of all. It is Jehovah Himself, God manifest in the flesh! On the other hand, we have a portion of the human family. We have a company of dependent and powerless beings, whose breath is in their nostrils, and who have nothing of their own. Between Him, so great, and them, so mean, there is now the affinity mentioned in the text. He, the blessed and only Potentate, discovers and recognizes in them His brother, His sister, His mother! 2. The next point we shall inquire into is the nature of the connection. (1) It is a close connection. There are many relations which belong to the constitution of human society. There are, for example, the relations of magistrate and subjects, master and servants, teacher and pupils, and so on. But the closest relation of all is the family relation. The family relation is fraught with intimacies which are known to no other. This is the relation which is declared in the text between Christ and His people. Christ and His people are embraced in the same family circle, the word being taken in its most limited acceptation. They are not remotely allied to Him. They are His nearest kindred. They are His brother, His sister, His mother. No tie of blood can be closer than that by which He and they are connected. (2) It is an endearing connection. Love wells out of it—reciprocal love. We see, then, that between Jesus and His followers there is a connection which is fitted to give rise to love—which is fitted, we may say, to give rise to it in no ordinary degree, and to produce a most peculiar and devoted attachment. (3) It is a connection that cannot be transferred. We are familiar with connections whose transference is easy, and is constantly taking place. There is the connection between master and servant. The master may be changed; and so may be the servant. There is the connection between bosom friends. He who is my friend now may become my foe in a little while, and I may get another friend in his room. Although I may change my friend, I cannot change my mother. Although I may change my servant, I cannot change my son. The connection between Christ and His people, then, is fixed. He cannot be supplanted in His relation to them, nor they in their relation to Him. (4) It is a connection that cannot be destroyed. Recent occurrences in the history of the world have strikingly shown that the connection between a sovereign and his subjects is perishable, and may be suddenly dissolved. But, happen what may, brother and sister will continue to be brother and sister, and a man's mother is his mother as long as she lives. Neither accidents nor efforts can sever the family tie. Death, indeed, may come, and, in one sense, put an end to it. But even death cannot prevail against the bond by which Christ and His disciples are united. He liveth for evermore, and so do they. 3. Our third point is the advantage with which the connection is fraught to Christ's people. The Lord is laid under obligations by it, which will redound to their benefit. A brother, a sister, a mother, have peculiar claims, which no relative, with a conscience and a heart, will disregard. (1) Is the disciple a brother? He has a claim upon the Saviour as such. One of the most emphatic declarations of Scripture tells of "a Friend that sticketh closer than a brother." When a man is in straits of any kind, who so likely as his brother to relieve him, if that brother be able? Now, then, let the Christian rejoice that he is the brother of the Lord. Let him remember it in trouble, and let him not be cast down. The Lord Himself remembers it, and says to him, "Call upon Me in the day of trouble, and I will deliver thee." (2) Does Christ declare that the disciple is His sister? A sister has claims even stronger than a brother. A sister is weak, and needs a guardian, and an arm to lean upon. A sister is timid, and needs a companion who has boldness and decision, that he may lead her forth, take her through the crowd, and encourage her by the way. A sister needs a prompt and powerful champion, that she may be defended from insult, and that her purity and honour may be cared for. And a sister turns to her kind and manly brother as the guardian, the bold companion, and the prompt and powerful champion that she needs. When Christ says that His disciple is His sister, He gives His people to understand that He is all this to them. And O how He cherishes and tends them ! (3) Christ says that His disciple is His mother. This also has great significance. It speaks to us of a son who devotes the vigorous labour of his prime to win a subsistence for his mother, and to make for her a comfortable and happy home. 4. A fourth point is the formation of the tie between Christ and His people. How is it constituted? How, then, is the rank of His mother and His brethren acquired? The question is answered in the following verse—" Whosoever shall do the will of My Father which is in heaven, the same is My brother, and sister, and mother." It is as much as to say to us all, " Do the will of My father in heaven, and ye shall become very dear to Me ; ye shall acquire the strong claims of the closest relationship." But what must we understand by the will of His Father? We have His own definition of the will of His Father, when He says, " This is the work of God, that ye believe on Him whom He hath sent." After Christ's ascension, the Apostle John announced the will of the Father, saying, " This is His commandment, that we should believe on the name of His Son Jesus Christ." And is this the way to become members of the family of Jesus? Is this the way to do, if we wish to be the brother, and sister, and mother of the Lord? This is the way. He comes to us in the Father's name, with gracious proposals, as the sinner's Friend. Let us bid Him welcome; let us accept His offers ; let us yield to His love. So shall we be His: and He shall be ours. " To as many as receive Him, to them gives He power to become the sons of God, even to them that believe in His name." It is by faith that we enter the family of Jesus. 5. Our last point is the evidence of the tie. For this we go again to the same verse :—" Whosoever shall do the will of My Father which is in heaven, the same is My brother, and sister, and mother." That which creates the tie, also manifests it. Take notice, says our Lord, take notice of the person that does My Father's will, and believes in Me ; take notice of My follower, My disciple! The same is My brother, and sister, and mother. There is a family likeness between Christ and His people. The doing of the Father's will is a family characteristic. It is a feature by which a member of the Church of the first-born may be infallibly discovered. Christ, the chief, the great Brother of the household, is the image of the Father. And of all the members of the blessed household it can be said that, " beholding as in a glass the glory of the Lord, they are changed into the same image, from glory to glory, even as by the Spirit of the Lord." One remark we must add here, lest the mother and the brethren of Jesus be discouraged. It is not our doctrine, it is not the doctrine of Scripture, or of the text, that those only who attain to a perfect fulfilment of the will of the Father can claim to be the kindred of the Lord. His meaning was, and the true doctrine is, that his brother, and sister, and mother, are they who have entered the school, who are learning the lesson, and have begun to practise the duty, of obedience to the will of the Father. II. The second branch of our subject relates to THE DELIGHT WHICH JESUS HAS IN THIS CONNECTION. The text is expressive of feelings of complacency and satisfaction. It was a burst of affection, the utterance of a loving and joyful heart, when He exclaimed, " Behold My mother and My brethren." To illustrate the delight which Jesus has in the affinity between Him and His people, it may be well to show what is His behaviour towards them. 1. He visits them. It happens sometimes in a family of humble rank, that one of the members rises far above the rest in point of circumstances and position. And it happens also, sometimes, in such cases, that the great and wealthy member of the family forgets his poor kinsmen, and seldom or never goes to see them. But Christ does not forget His people. He came and saw them often during the old dispensation. He has never been long away from them. One visit, most notable for the wonders of love it exhibited, was His advent in the flesh. It had been described beforehand, but the half was not told. "The Word was made flesh, and dwelt among us, and we beheld His glory." When He was departing, He said, "I will see you again." The family of Jesus, like other families, has its meetings; the members often assemble; and now and then, at stated periods, they hold high festival together. On such occasions He, the exalted Brother to whom all look up, is never away. Absentees there may be, but He is not one of them; His place is never empty. Are they in darkness? He visits them and gives them light. 2. He sends gifts to them. He, the Brother of great possessions, sends gifts to His lowly kindred. All power is His, both in heaven and in earth. Do they need gold? He sends them gold, tried in the fire. Do they need raiment? He furnishes them with white raiment, that they may be clothed—robes of righteousness, garments of salvation. Do they need meat and drink? He gives them bread of life, wine and milk, honey out of the rock. We have spoken of their family feasts, but these would be feasts of emptiness, were it not for His bounty. What shall we say more? To express everything in a word, He sends them the Holy Spirit. That heavenly gift is completely subject to His administration. 3. He dwells among them. It is customary for the members of a family to dwell together. They group with each other in the same abode. It may seem strange to say that Christ dwells with His friends, after we have said that He visits them. But both are true. In this case there is no real inconsistency. Just before His ascension He declared to His disciples, "Lo, I am with you alway, even to the end of the world." I am going away, yet will I never be absent. "In Salem is His tabernacle, and His dwelling-place in Zion." 4. He acknowledges them. "Behold My mother and My brethren." Behold these fishermen, these peasants, these obscure Galileans, who receive My doctrine. These are My relatives; see, this is the family to which I belong. And was not that a signal acknowledgment of kinsmanship that He gave in the case of the three children, when, before Nebuchadnezzar, and his princes and captains, and the vast Babylonian concourse, He walked in the midst of the furnace along with them? He promised that He would confess His brethren before His Father and before His holy angels. He is confessing them now in His continual intercession at God's right hand. (*A. Gray.*)

Vers. 22–25. **He went into a ship with His disciples.**—*The Saviour in the ship:*—1. We do not need to be literally at sea, or to feel waves literally breaking over our heads, to find out what absolute helplessness is. The greater number of us, at some time in our lives, have known what it was to touch the last limit of our strength. One of the commonest forms of this exhaustion of human strength is in the struggle with disease or death, approaching yourself or some one you love like a part of yourself. The powers that overmatch us, tire us out, and run us down, are various—time, hereditary maladies, sudden sickness, the superior strength of other people serving their own interests against us, that formless enemy, never so seen as to be struck, but often "preventing" us—that we call "bad luck"; everything that edges about our inclinations, thwarts our plans, baffles the brain and the will, and brings us up where we wish not to be. Most plainly it is a part of God's scheme of mercy to lead us, in our self-confidence and self-will, every one of us, to just that point, so that when we are obliged to stop trusting or calculating for ourselves we shall come willingly to Him. The heart, with all its external, traditional, or formal knowledge of the Saviour, may hold Him as if He were asleep in its own dark chamber. He wakes, to us, whenever we go to Him and call upon Him. And they are the reckless mariners on a deeper sea who put the waking off, on one pretence or another, till the ship is covered with the waves. 2. Observe that when, at last, the voyager comes sincerely and anxiously to that, and utters the prayer, Christ does not refuse him because he did not call sooner, or because when he prayed his prayer was not the purest and loftiest of prayers. Hardly any heart's prayer is that, when it is first agitated under the flashing conviction that it is all wrong. While its deep disorder is first discovered it can think only of being delivered. The life of God in the soul of man is always a growing thing, and so by necessity must be imperfect at the beginning. Every one that asketh receiveth more than he asketh. None of us know what to pray for as we ought. To him that crieth only in fear, and because the weather of this troublesome world is too much for him, the sea is smoothed. And whosoever so cometh, provided only it is to the Lord that he directs his supplication, shall in no wise be cast out. 3. But we should miss the full breadth of gospel teaching in this miracle of the quieted tempest if we saw nothing more in it than a mere figure or likeness of what goes on in an individual heart. The whole strain of the New Testament teaches us a profounder doctrine than this of the connection between the visible world of nature and the invisible world of God's spiritual kingdom. We needed to know what the Pagan, the Jew even, and many a student of science born and bred in Christendom has never really comprehended, that the Person of Jesus, Son of God and Son of Man, is the actual bone of a living unity between both these two great realms of God's creation; that He mediates between them and reconciles them. Scholars will never explore nature thoroughly, or right wisely, till they see this religious signification of every law, every force, and every particle of matter, and explore it by the light of faith. God is in everything or in nothing—in lumps of common clay, as Ruskin says, and in drops of water, as in the kindling of the day star, and in the lifting of the pillars of heaven. 4. Incomplete still would this enlarging view of the miracle be, if it did not further disclose to us the true practical use both of the gospel miracles themselves, and of every other gift and blessing of heaven, in leading us up in affectionate gratitude to Him who stands as the central figure among all these visible wonders, the impersonation of all spiritual beauty, the heart of all holy love, and the originator of all the peace-making powers which tranquilize and reconcile the turbulences of the world. "The men marvelled, saying, What manner of man is this!" It was not the mercy to men's imperilled or sick bodies that Christ had first in view when He loosened the bodily ordinances and let the streams of Divine energy flow in on mortal sufferers. "That ye might believe in Me"— this is the continual explanation—we might almost say the excuse, He offered for deeds that must necessarily be exceptional and temporary. (Bp. F. D. Huntington.) The miraculous stilling of the storm :—When we use the words "Lord, save us, we perish," we are really rehearsing two articles of our belief. 1. We are declaring that we believe there is a Lord—that in the visible world there is an invisible God with His over-ruling, and controlling, and appointing will. 2. We are also declaring that we believe this God is our Lord Jesus Christ. This it is which distinguishes Christian prayer from all other prayer. The story before us divides itself naturally into three parts: the voyage before the storm; the storm; the miraculous stilling of the storm. In each of these three parts we have one thing in common. We have man, in some way or other, encountering, or encountered by the outward and visible world. I. MAN SUBDUING NATURE. It was by the knowledge of the elements and the laws of nature that man learned thus to sail upon the deep; and in this fact you have represented for you the whole of the material progress of humanity —all the triumphs of science, all the glory and beauty of art, all that marvellous mastery that man obtains by his inventive and creative will over the secret powers of nature, as he unlocks them one by one, and compels her to tell him her deepest mysteries—all that man has done as he has advanced from horizon to horizon of discovery, finding still new worlds to conquer, until we stand amazed at our own progress and the infinity of it. II. NATURE SUBDUING MAN. Here we have the storm, in which the elements are man's masters and not his servants; and he that one minute before was the boasting lord of nature is its toy and sport. The very foam upon the crest of those billows is not more helpless in the grasp of the elements than the lord and the king of them; they toss him to and fro, as the wind drives the stubble in the autumn. This is the terrible aspect of nature. This is nature in her might, and in her majesty, and in her pitilessness, and in her capriciousness—when nature seems everything, and man, in her awful presence, dwindles and dwarfs into very nothingness. This is nature as she masters man. Is it, then, any wonder that, in the early struggles of mankind with this terrible visible power of the creature, men came to worship the creature—that they ascribed to every one of these powers a divinity; that in the voice of the wind, and in the roar of the sea, and in the raging of the fire, they saw the signs of a Divine presence, and they said to these elements: "Spare us," or "Save us, or else we perish"? And so all creation became peopled with gods—cruel gods, capricious gods, vengeful gods, gods whom men bribed with blood, gods whom, even while they bribed them, they could not love, and did not believe that they loved them. This is the first and most terrible form of creature worship; this was the idolatry of the heathen. But then, brethren, mark this; that such a worship as this could not continue long, because it is the worship of ignorance; it is the belief in the supernatural, only because it confuses the unknown with the supernatural. Even as science advanced must this faith melt away. Ever must the domain of the known push itself forward into the domain of the unknown. Ever does the man of science take one by one the gods of the man of superstition and break them upon their pedestals, and tell him this : " What you worship is no god. What you worship is no lord. It is not your lord; it is a servant of yours; and I class it in this or that rank of your servants." It is that last and most terrible aspect of nature, when she appears, not as many gods, or many wills, but as a great soulless piece of mechanism, of which we are only part—a terrible machinery in which we are, somehow or other, involved, and in the presence of which the sense of our freewill leaves us. III. THE MIRACULOUS AND THE SUPERNATURAL. We hear a prayer, and we see a miracle. In the face of the might of nature and the terror of her elements there rises up a Man in answer to man's cry—there is heard a Man's voice, which is yet the voice of God; and it rebukes the winds and the sea, and the elements of nature own their real Lord; and immediately there is a great calm. What is it, then, that we see ? We see a miracle, and a miracle that answers to prayer; we see the living spirits of living men, in the hour of their agony and their distress, appealing from nature to the God of nature; and we have recorded the answer of God to man's prayer. The answer is, that God is Lord both of man and of nature; and we say, therefore, that the miracle, and the miracle alone, sufficiently justifies the prayer. We say that the reason why men may pray is, and can only be, that they know and believe, that there is a will which rules the visible. If you have not this belief, then all prayer is an unreality and a miserable mockery. (*Bp. W. C. Magee.*)   *God's answers to man's prayers for help :*—If prayer were always followed by a miraculous answer, then prayer would be easy enough ; or, on the other hand, if there were no thought of an answer, then it might be possible, though not easy, to submit ourselves to the inevitable. But to pray, and not to receive an answer, and yet to believe that the very not receiving is an answer ; to cry, " Save, or we perish," and to seem about to perish ; to believe that in what seems perishing is really salvation ; to look for the living and watchful Christ, and to see what seems only the sleeping and regardless Christ, and yet to believe that the time will come when, at His word, there shall be a great calm—this is the patience, this is the faith of those who worship an incarnate Lord. And so we trace the history of Christ's Church, and so we strive to trace the history of our own lives. Comparatively easy it is to trace the Church's history along her voyage. The Church gives time for comparing events and testing faith ; and so, believing still in the presence of her living Lord, the litanies of His Church ring out, as they have ever rung, clearly and loudly, and high above the roar of the tempest and the rushing of the waters, still the prayer is heard, " Good Lord, deliver us " ; and still again and again, as the storm sweeps by, and the Church passes out into calmer waters, still comes the voice of thanksgiving, " He *hath* delivered us." Even in our shorter voyage are there none of us who can remember times when we have knelt in agony and wrestled in prayer with the Saviour, who seemed to have forgotten us, when the mighty storm of temptation and the billows of calamity seemed about to destroy us, and when we have cried to Him to save us, and He has seemed to sleep and to refuse to save ? But at the last we can remember how He did reveal Himself, not stilling the raging storm when we would have had Him still the terrible tempest, not sparing, it may be, the precious bark that we had rigged, and manned, and launched ourselves with trembling hopes and loving prayers, and watched with eyes tearless with agony, as we saw it about to sink before us ; and we have been led to see and believe that the living and loving Lord was answering even then our prayer, for the bark has at length entered that haven where we would be, and where the vexed waters of our voyage never awake a ripple on the calm depths of its eternal peace. (*Ibid.*)   *The miracle on the lake :*—1. This miracle proved Jesus to be both God and man, and therefore able to save us from our sins. 2. This miracle proves that the Redeemer never forgets His people, though He sometimes appears to do so. 3. This miracle proves that the Redeemer will certainly deliver His people at last. What should hinder Him ?—not want of power, for He is " the mighty God," as this history abundantly shows ; not want of knowledge, for He is infinitely wise to know how to save ; not want of will, for He loves them and delights to help them. 4. This miracle proves that Jesus is a Being whom it is impiety and ruin to resist, but duty and happiness to obey. (*James Foote, M.A.*)   *The storm on the lake :*—" They took Him even as He was " ! It was well. We need preparations. The Son of God needed none. Preparations are ours, not His ! He is always ready, and for every emergency—for a storm as well as a calm. We are all of us always crossing over. We have some plan, some pleasu·e, some expectation, something we are looking forward to to-morrow, or next week, or next year, or at the close of our toils. Something we have, all of us, always before us, and towards which we are crossing—something on " the other side " of the present, whatever that may be, but which, before we reach, we may have to pass through a storm. But if it is necessary to our safety that we have Jesus with us in crossing over, it is equally necessary to our calmness, our peace, our joy, that Jesus be awake in us. It is in the storms of life that the all-sufficiency of Jesus comes out. We have never half known Him till now. We heard so before; we have proved it now. (*F. Whitfield.*)　　*Christ rebuking the elements :—* Why did Christ " rebuke " the elements? The word appears to me the language of one who either sees moral guilt; or who, in His affection, is indignant at something which is hurting those He loves. The elements, in themselves, cannot, of course, do a moral thing. But is it possible that the prince of the power of the air had anything to do with that storm? Was there some latent fiendish malice in that sudden outbreak of nature upon Christ and His Church? But however this may be, there is another aspect in which we ought to see it. We know that to the second Adam there was given just what the first Adam forfeited—perfect dominion over all creation. Accordingly, Christ was careful, one after another, to assert and show His supremacy over the whole natural creation—over the fishes, as when He made them crowd at His word to a given spot; over the swine; over the fig tree; over the earth, opening at His will; over the seas, unlearning their usual law, and making a pavement for His feet. In this light the present hurricane was like a rebellion, or Christ treated it as such, that He might show His mastership. Hence that royal word, " He rebuked them," and hence the instant submission. But it might be, in His affection for His followers, as of one angry at what was disturbing their peace, He rebuked those troubled winds. For God is very jealous for His children's happiness; and whatever touches it, He is displeased at. You may be assured of this—if you are a child of God, and any person, or anything, ever comes near to injure or to distress you, God is grieved with that person or that thing—He will rebuke it. (*J. Vaughan, M.A.*)　　**And they launched forth.**—*Setting sail :—*I take these words simply as a motto, that I may speak to you of the duty of setting sail on the Christian voyage. 1. " The other side "—the heavenly shore—that is the true destination for every one of us. 2. Your whole nature, with its varied powers and capacities, is the vessel with its furniture, freight, and crew. 3. Christ the Captain. You have no right to sail in any direction you please. 4. It is to be feared that there are many, even in our religious assemblies, who have never yet taken Christ as their appointed Captain, and decisively set sail on the Christian voyage. Repentance and faith necessary. 5. And here, in passing, I would say a word to any who may have set out years ago on this voyage, and yet are now back again at their old moorings. The sky was bright, and you set sail " with flying colours." But by-and-by came the storm. You were not prepared for such gusts of temptation. You had not anticipated such hurricanes of trial. And so you allowed yourself to be driven back, by stress of weather, to the shore you had left. If you had only obeyed the commands of Christ, you might have weathered the storm, and been making progress even now towards the heavenly kingdom. 6. If you have not yet set sail, let me exhort you to do so at once. 7. If you have set sail under Christ, why should you not hoist His flag? (*T. C. Finlayson.*)　　*The soothing voice of Jesus :—*During a heavy storm in the Mediterranean Sea, which lasted two whole days and nights, I was unable to get any sleep, the rolling of the vessel was so terrific. Two men were washed from the wheel and the lifeboat broken. Whilst lying awake hour after hour I heard at intervals a voice calling out some words which I could not clearly distinguish amidst the roaring of the wind and waves, but which I took to be intended to cheer on the sailors in their perilous work. I afterwards found the voice was that of the night-watch, who on completing his round each half-hour shouted " All is well! " I thought of the voice of Jesus as it rises above the storm, encouraging the despondent, tempest-tossed mariner in his voyage to the better land. (*Richilde.*)　　*Christ for our Captain :—*Now, I want you to come and see Jesus lying there upon the deck of the ship. Ah, how tired He is! Look at that face, so white, with the lines so deeply graven, the hands stretched out in utter helplessness. He had spent the whole day in preaching; then He had gone away and spent the night in prayer; the next morning He ordained the twelve, and before there was any time for breakfast the multitude came back again. When His friends heard of this they said, " He is out of His mind." They always say that; whenever a man begins to be enthusiastic about the welfare of his neighbour they are sure to think he is mad.

But all the great and noble deeds done in this world have been wrought by those who have been branded as madmen, and until we go mad too I do not think we are likely to do much good among our fellows. The very word "enthusiasm" means God in the man. When Livingstone was in Central Africa he tells us that he met some Englishmen who had gone there to shoot big game, and that these fellows talked about their self-sacrifice in exposing themselves to the same perils with himself. Self-sacrifice! Oh! in some cases the word becomes damnable. We never hear of self-sacrifice except for Jesus Christ. When a man goes to the ends of the earth to collect beetles, or catch fish, or shoot big beasts, who ever hears of self-sacrifice? But the moment he sets out on this long journey in order to help his neighbour, he is at once said to be demented. It is only for Jesus Christ that people invent these excuses. People are always needed elsewhere when Christ wants them. A man often takes one day a week from business to look after his garden or to enjoy himself with his children; but if when you knocked at his office door and were told he was absent on that occasion—as he always devoted one day a week to the care of the poorest of the poor—you would say, "Dear me, how very extraordinary! There must be some little softening of the brain." No, no, sir! softening of the heart; and would to God you would catch the complaint and die of it. They said, "He is beside Himself." And then His mother came. I never rightly understood before why she came, but I see it now. Poor mother! She saw the pale face, she knew how tired He must be; and He has had nothing to eat, and so she desired to speak with Him; but He was not to be hindered in His work, and so the day is passed in unremitting toil, until at last His condition became such as to suggest that strong arms support Him down to the ship, and the moment He is laid upon the deck, and His head touches the hard coil of ropes which is His pillow, He is fast asleep. Perhaps you have never thought of Christ being worn out with hard work. There is a kind of notion that He renewed His bodily strength from the springs of His Divinity. No, no; that is one of the temptations of the devil that Jesus Christ had always to withstand. If the devil could only have persuaded the Master to have met him as the Son of God there would have been no shame in his defeat; but to meet and conquer him as Man, as bone of our bone and flesh of our flesh, that was the triumph of Christ. And so Jesus knew what it was to be utterly worn out. You sometimes have spent the day in work, so hard that you have hardly been able to drag one foot after another. Well, to-night you think to yourself, "Blessed Lord, I never thought before I had so much of Thy sympathy. I never knew before that Thou couldst say to me, 'I know all about it; I too have been worn out.'" There may be some mother here whose rest is often broken at night, whose day is filled with dreary toil until the brain throbs and the blood is as fire. Ah! Jesus can come to thee and say, "Dear heart, I know what it is. I, too, have been utterly spent." He is asleep on the deck of the ship. Come and gaze upon Him yet again. Are you troubled with sleeplessness, sir? I do not mean under a sermon, but at night when you go to rest? I am told it is an increasing complaint, and I know there are a great many remedies, some of them worse than the disease; but here is one which the Master Himself used. Why does He sleep so soundly? I pray you try His remedy—get thoroughly worn out in doing good. The next time, sir, that you cannot sleep, just you try the remedy. Call on that poor old man whom you know, who seemed ill when you saw him last, and whose rent you think is not paid; sit and talk and pray with him, and when you leave, give him five shillings, for advice gratis is not worth much, and if at night you do not sleep you shall have sweeter dreams, perchance, than those who do. The Master sleeps. We talk about the sleep of the just. There were only two men who ever slept the sleep of the just—Adam and Jesus Christ. We hear in poetry of infant slumbers, pure and light; but some of you mothers know that the little ones sometimes awake with shrieks and cries from fevered dreams. No, no; there were only two sleeps which were the sleep of the just, and what a contrast between them! See where God has cast the deep sleep upon Adam. Was there ever such a resting place? The mossy bank whereon he lies; trees that bend lovingly over him as if to screen him; winds that are hushed lest they disturb his rest; the birds trilling forth their sweetest songs, as if to mingle with his dreams; the flowers that pour their fragrance round about him—these were the surroundings of Adam; but look, I pray you, at the rude discomforts of my Lord. We have heard of the plank bed, and our heart has gone out in indignation as well as in pity on that matter, but here is the plank bed of our Master. How little Thou didst know of luxury and comfort! You poor folks, take this to your heart: you can say this, "Well, I know that Jesus Christ knows more about my lot than the rich folks." Oh, if I had had the ordering of that night, how different it would have been! Instead of the thin dress of the Galilean peasant, how I would have wrapped Him in robes so warm, how soft would have been His couch! I would have had the heavens hung with gold and crimson to curtain the couch of my Lord, and I would have charged the winds to sink down behind the purple hills lest they should ruffle with a breath the glassy surface of the lake that bore upon its bosom my sleeping Master. But it may not be. The wind is veering to the south-west, and there is going to be a dirty night. How the waves leap up and how the wind whistles and howls! Exactly. Think you that Christ is a fair-weather sailor? Think you that my Lord comes to see us only when we are in port, or to say "good-bye" when we weigh anchor and set out upon the voyage? Oh, no! that is not my Christ. My Christ never says "good-bye." He says, "Soul, I am going with thee." "But, Master, it is going to be a very dirty night." "Very well; if it is to be rough for thee, it will be rough for Me." I want a Christ to go to sea with me, to take life just as I find it. My Master! Thou art just the very Christ we want. Come, look once more. He is asleep in the hinder part of the ship. Then have I got more than His disciples. I have often said, "How glad would I have been to have looked into Thy face, to have drunk in the sweet music of Thy voice, to have felt the touch of Thine hand, to have had Thy shadow fall upon me, and to have told how I loved Thee." Yes, that would have been much, but I have done more than that. Do you not see how that bodily presence shut Him in and shut them out, made a great gulf between them as black and deep and dark as hell? He sleeps! Oh, how dreadful is the storm! how the waves toss and tumble and roll, and yet He sleeps! Oh, I should not like to have a sleeping Christ! Nay. "He that keepeth Israel doth neither slumber nor sleep." They watch that He may sleep, but my Master watches that I may rest. Now have I more than they. Look again. He is in the hinder part of the ship asleep. Why did He sleep? This was one reason—because He had nothing else to do. Well, I cannot but think that if you wanted to see John at his best it would be when he is running before a gale of wind, and Peter when taking in a reef, and Philip handling an oar. Jesus Christ was a carpenter. He was wonderfully clever at teaching people how to get to heaven, but what could He do on board ship? He could not help them at all, so He went to sleep. Oh, how the wind whistled! how the sea was tossed and tumbled! I seem to hear the hurly-burly of the storm. Here comes a wave leaping higher and higher, as if impatient for its prey, and His disciples would fain call upon Him to awake. Ah, how instinctively the heart turns to Jesus when trouble comes! I think nothing grieves Jesus Christ more than that we should keep Him out of the management of things. As soon as ever they get ashore I think I know what Peter said to his fellows. He would take them aside and say: "I have been thinking about last night, and I will tell you what I should like to do." "What is that?" says John. "Let us make Him Captain. You see we can take in a reef, He can quiet the waves; we can put the helm up, He can hush the winds. Master, come, be Captain; just tell us how to put the craft about; take the helm." Oh, blessed be His name! He does so love us when He can take the management. Dear friends, it hurts Jesus Christ when we shut Him out. Mother, there are those boys of thine. You have often asked the Lord to bless and save their souls, but thou art worrying thyself about what they are going to do in life. The Lord Jesus Christ knows how to help them a great deal better than thou dost. Ask Him to come in and guide thee and them. Sir, thy Master understands your business better than thou dost. Make Him the head of the firm, and say "Come in." I remember I had, some years ago, to preach a sermon, and two or three venerable doctors of Divinity were going to be present. Through thinking about them, perhaps, more than the sermon I began to get rather nervous. While I was sitting in my study working at the text, "Cast all thy care upon Him," and getting down very deep—I used to be rather an eloquent preacher, but, thank God! that has gone—all of a sudden, in the midst of my profound philosophical discourse, the door was burst open, and, looking up, I was about to say, "Now run away," but the father was a great deal stronger than the philosopher, and the words died away on my lips, for there stood a little three-year-old, with chubby cheeks, holding in her hand a broken toy, the face a picture of great sorrow, the lip quivering, the tears running down her cheeks, and the hands holding out the broken doll. And what think you I did? Why, thrust aside my philosophical discourse, and said, "Come here, little one; what is the matter?" The child's grief was too deep for words; she could only hold up the broken toy and give a great sob, which told its own story. I said, "I think we can manage this," and the philosophical discourse was forgotten, and I got the gum bottle, and when I had restored the plaything, and put it in her arms again, I felt that I had my reward. The tears were dried up, and the sunshine came back to the little face, and, lifting herself on tiptoe, she paid me with a kiss, and then another, and then she trotted away, and at the door she turned to look back and nod her head and let me see her thanks again. I tore up my philosophical discourse, and I said I will go down and tell the people that we are just poor little children, and that our griefs are broken toys, and that our Lord hath joy in stooping down and taking into His hand our poor little sorrows, and healing them and wiping our tears away, and watching the sunshine come back again. Oh, how sorry Jesus is when you shut Him out, when you do not open the door to Him! Oh, I beseech you take Him as your Captain, let Him take the helm, and say to Him, "Lord, what wilt Thou have me to do?" He sleeps. I can fancy John saying, "I wonder He can sleep on such a night as this." "Yes," says Peter; "we can hardly hear each other speak for the noise." Oh, how the wind howls, how the poor craft staggers and strains—now climbing the crest of a wave, now deep down in the trough of the sea! "I wonder the Master can sleep—how tired He must be! Master, awake!" Ah! He was wide awake then. His was a mother's love, not a father's love. Your Father can sleep in a thunderstorm, you can sleep when the south-west wind moans and howls about the house, and when the waggons go rumbling along on their way to the market, but let the little one at mother's side just make the feeblest beginning of a cry, and she is awakened in an instant. You, sir, sleep for ten minutes afterwards by the clock, you know you do. My Lord's love—oh, it is the daintiest and most delicate thing upon the face of the earth! The love that Jesus Christ hath for us is a mother's love; we have never to speak twice before He hears. The first time He is awake and listening, and there is a great calm. (*M. G. Pearse.*)

Ver. 25. **Where is your faith?** *Where is your faith?*—It is as much as if He had said, "You thought that I was sleeping. But was it indeed only Me, or chiefly My eye, that slept? Was it not your faith? *You* say, 'Where is the Lord?' but *I* say, 'Where is your faith?'" It is a mistake, brethren, we are all making every day. We say,—"The Lord sleeps—the Lord sleeps." But what is it,—"Your faith" sleeps. I begin by asking every one I am now addressing, "Where is your faith?" "Where is *your* faith?" Now tell me, is it in the First Great Source? or, is it in second causes? 1. It is astonishing how many men are putting their faith upon second causes! I can imagine the fisherman in the storm, looking at the wind and the gathering clouds, partly because they come with less trouble; partly from long habit; partly from the aversion which there is in the mind of men to everything spiritual; but chiefly because men imagine they have no right to go up straight to God. Hence almost all men are found trying means as if they were ends; and God's instruments as if they were gods. For instance, one man has a friend, and he hangs upon that friend, and you may see him behaving to that friend as if he considered that friend the arbiter of his life. Another is a man in business, and his study is about nothing every day but "his connection," and it is plain that he looks to nothing but "his connection" to determine his rise or his ruin in the enterprise in which he is embarked. A third man is a farmer, and you will hear him talking about "the weather," as if the crops had no other father but the sun and the rain. A fourth is a politician, and he makes the world turn—as upon a pivot—on the consideration whether this administration shall be in, or that. All are making their system of cause and effect; and they do not calculate upon the shadow of a doubt that if there is a prescribed cause, there must be the predicted event. Their whole hearts—their whole faith is in second cause. Now, brethren, we do not hesitate to arraign this trusting in second cause as sheer idolatry. It is the essential of God that He is final, and what is final is made God. 2. But I will turn to another class of life's voyagers, and say, again, "Where is your faith?" Is it not in yourselves? Perhaps the fishermen on the Galilean lake thought it very little for them to cross those oft-traversed waters, and would have laughed at the idea of there being any danger in their barque landing in safety on the other side. Yet how little booted their skill and their confidence! There are two distinct ways in which persons put faith in themselves. One is, in trusting there is a sufficient measure of goodness in their own hearts: the other, is by admitting their hearts are very bad, but still, taking a compensation in something that they are doing. 3. But I turn to the third class, and I ask again, "Where is your faith?" and a thousand voices will answer me almost in this church, "Why, in God"; but I reply, "In what God?" But you say, "Oh, Him that is all mercy and all goodness." Ah! and "all just!" Is not God all just? would He be just if He forfeited His own word? And has not He said it, "The soul that sinneth it shall die"? Has not He said, "Except ye repent, ye shall all likewise perish"? Has He not said, "He that believeth not shall be damned"? Has not He made a particular requirement of you, that you must keep His whole law; and has He not made it as sure, as necessary a thing, that every sin shall lead on to misery, as every seed leads on to its own harvest? O, tell me, is it possible—in any view you may take of good government—that any breach of its laws should pass unpunished? Is not the suffering of the offender part of the mercy—the centre of the mercy—of a grand administrator? Else, would not license, aye, and premium, too, be given to crime? and must not the whole empire pass into recklessness and misery? (*J. Vaughan, M.A.*)   *Where is your faith?*—1. "I believe in God." How lightly, how carelessly, we repeat those solemn words, and yet what a universe of meaning lies in them! 2. Do we believe? Do we at all know what belief means? Do we suppose it to mean, "I am familiar with these formulæ, I see no special reason for rejecting them." Thou believest that there is one God. Thou doest well. The devils also believe; nay more, they tremble. 3. "I believe," but, while with orthodox self-satisfaction we repeat our creeds, on which soul has dawned the tremendous responsibility of our belief, the transcendent obligation of all that it entails? 4. What, then, is wanting? Faith is wanting—that faith which is a possessing principle, an irresistible enthusiasm. Real faith—not the ineffectual pretence; not the faith which makes idols of formulæ; not the faith which delights in rigid systems and fantastic self-delusions, groping in mediæval traditions for a dead and material and exclusive Christ. Had we but faith as a grain of mustard-seed we should remove the mountains which overshadow and threaten to fall on us. (*Archdeacon Farrar.*)   *Fear rebuked:*—One day when Stonewall Jackson, with his sister-in-law, was crossing the boiling torrent, just below the American falls at Niagara, in a slight boat manned by two oarsmen, the current so swirled the boat that the lady became terrified, believing they were going to the bottom. Jackson seized her by the arms, and turned to one of the men and said, "How often have you crossed here?" "I have been rowing people across, sir, for twelve years." "Did you ever meet with an accident?" "Never, sir." "Never were capsized? never lost a life?" "Nothing of the kind, sir!" Then turning in a somewhat peremptory tone, he said to the lady, "You hear what the boatman says, and unless you think you can take the oars and row better than he does, sit still and trust him as I do." (*Mackay.*)

Vers. 27–40. A certain man who had devils long time.—*The demoniac in the tombs as he resembles the unconverted sinner:*—Observe the parallel that exists between this poor demoniac and the unconverted sinner. I. PREVIOUS TO CONVERSION. 1. Possessed by an unclean spirit. 2. Living among the dead. 3. Disordered in intellect. 4. His own tormentor. 5. In a state of utter destitution and wretchedness. 6. Beyond the power of human assistance or restraint. II. AT CONVERSION. 1. The means employed: the Word of Christ. 2. The influence exerted: the almighty power of Christ. 3. The effect produced: (1) The unclean spirit expelled. (2) The naked one clothed. (3) The wanderer sitting at the feet of Jesus. (4) The maniac in his right mind. III. AFTER CONVERSION. 1. Desiring to remain with Jesus. How natural—wishing to forsake all, in order to be near the Great Physician. 2. Christ's command, whatever it may be, is immediately obeyed. (*J. J. Rew, M.A.*)   *Plain words with the careless:*—1. A man may know a great deal about true religion, and yet be a total stranger to it. There are no sounder theoretical believers than devils, and yet their conduct is not affected by what they believe, and consequently they still remain at enmity to the Most High God. 2. There are a great many bad prayers prayed in the world. The man said, "I beseech Thee, torment me not." A sinner's prayer for his own misery is often a grim and awful thing to look upon, from its horrible earnestness. I. A VERY MISCHIEVOUS MISAPPREHENSION. It is currently thought among mankind, that to receive the gospel of Christ would be to cease to be happy, to give up all joyfulness and cheerfulness, and to doom one's self to a life of melancholy. 1. Now, I will admit that if men will go on in their sins, the gospel will, if it gets at their consciences, make them miserable.   It will act as salt to raw wounds, or as a whip to rebellious backs.   2. Again, I must make another admission, namely, that a great many people, at the time when they become serious for the first, and give themselves to Christ, are rendered, for a time, very miserable.   The terrors of the Lord are upon them, and they are feeling the burden of sin—it is no wonder that a cloud hangs over their brows.   3. But, now that I have admitted this, I want to ask those who say that Jesus Christ would make them miserable, a question or two.   I have admitted a great deal—now, be fair and open with me in return.   You are afraid of being made miserable.   Are you so mightily happy, then, at the present moment?   Excuse me if I say that I rather question whether those Elysian fields of yours are so very delightful.   A man cannot sin without bringing upon himself some sorrow even in this life.   4. There is another question I would like to ask you, and that is: If you reply that you are happy now, I should be glad to know whether the present happiness which you enjoy, or say you enjoy, will last you very long?   The leaves are now falling very rapidly from the trees, and they remind us that we, too, must die.   Will your mirth and your jollity support you in the dying hour?   5. But now, we will go farther in dealing with this mischievous misapprehension.   You have a notion that if Jesus Christ should come into your heart, you would have to give up your pleasures.   Now, what pleasures?   The pleasures of the hearth and family fireside?   The pleasures of seeing your children growing up around you to call you blessed?   The pleasures of doing good?   The pleasures of discharging your duties as in the sight of God?   The pleasures of a quiet conscience?   None of these pleasures will Christ take away from you.   Still you say, " If I were a Christian it would make me melancholy! "   Make you melancholy to believe that you are on the way to heaven, and that when the trials of this poor life are over, you shall be with Jesus for ever?   I cannot imagine it.   Let not Satan's lie deceive you.   6. One thing I will also say, and then have done with this point.   You believe that religion is a happy thing, though you pretend you do not.   You must confess, and you do confess, that you desire to die like a Christian.   II. A QUERULOUS QUESTION.   " What have I to do with Thee? "   This is a question which we have heard many times.   Poor people often ask it.   I heard a workman say, " Well, I have nothing to do with religion ; I know it is all very well for my master, for parsons, and fine ladies, and aristocrats, and old women, but it is of no use to me ; I have to work hard, and I have a family to bring up, and it has nothing to do with me."   Now, give me your hand, my good fellow, and, believe me, you are quite mistaken.   Why, there is nobody in the world whom it has more to do with than it has with you, for "the poor have the gospel preached to them."   But very often the wealthy say, "What have we to do with Thee? "   Lavender kid gloves and the gospel are not always well agreed : the upper circles are none the nearer heaven because of their imaginary elevation.   There are also certain learned gentlemen who are instructed in metaphysics and philosophy who patronizingly inform us that the restraint of religion is a very proper thing to keep the working classes in some kind of order, but really they themselves are several degrees above it.   Thus they say, as plainly as they can, " What have I to do with-Thee? "   Oh, my brethren, educated, refined, wealthy, as you may be, the gospel of Jesus has everything to do with you.   The giant minds of Milton and of Newton found ample room in the gospel ; they delighted to bathe, like leviathan, in the ocean of Divine truth.   There are two or three matters in which all of you have to do with Christ, whether you will or not.   1. It is because of His intercession that you are alive to-night.   2. It is entirely owing to Him that you are now in a place where the gospel can be proclaimed to you.   3. At the last great day, if you have nothing to do with Him as a Saviour, you will have to appear before Him as a Judge.   We *must* have to do with Christ.   (*C. H. Spurgeon.*)   *A Chinese demoniac :*—A short time ago our Christian servant had a great trial ; but it resulted, as trials have done to some of the rest of us, in the strengthening of his faith in God.   His brother became insane, was very outrageous, and getting worse every day.   Our servant always said he was sure his case was similar to that of the man who lived among the tombs in Gadara.   At length his mother grew quite tired of him, and, thinking his case hopeless, sent him to the Ya-men to be killed.   He was to be beheaded in two days.   We joined in asking God to heal him.   Next morning he was much better, and in a few days he was quite well.   The underlings then refused to let him out, except they received a good deal of silver.   We thought this unfair, as he had had no food from them, and we declined to assist.   Again we unitedly brought him before God, asking

Him to bring him out.   Next morning we sent his brother to ask the mandarin to let him out, which he did.   He stayed four days with us, heard the gospel, and went home quite happy to his wife and family, 120 *li* from the city.   (*J. Smith.*) *The Gadarene demoniac :*—On landing, after a night of storm, our Lord was met by one who was scarcely human.   The contrast between the rugged shore and the calm sea was not so striking as that between the wild demoniac and the calm and peaceful Son of God.   This was a meeting of the representatives of two different kingdoms, the kingdom of darkness and that of light—of hate and of love ; of misery and of peace.   The Gadarene knew who Jesus was, yet, full of terror, he cried, " What have I to do with Thee ? " and implored Him to depart.   But the Lord had to do with him, and would not therefore depart, but commanded the demons to depart, and they did so ; and then the wild man came to his right mind, and sat clothed at the feet of his Deliverer, meek and calm as a wearied child.   1. We have in this man's history a most instructive evidence of the capacity of an immortal being to sink into the depths of sin and misery.   What was essentially wrong in this man?   It was his wrong mind.   He was delivered from that by being brought to his right mind.   2. Look at the meeting of the demoniac with the Saviour.   It was verily a crisis in the sad life of this miserable man.   The inner conflict in this man's spirit on meeting Jesus represents the struggle in many a heart, during a similar crisis in its history.   3. Observe the effects of this great act of love on the hitherto miserable demoniac.   What outward force failed to accomplish, inward principle effected.   His outward physical condition was the effect and sign of his inward reformation.   Such will be the results, more or less, in every case where a soul is truly brought to the knowledge and love of God in Jesus Christ.   Terror will give place to love.   4. Notice, further, that when Jesus cast out the demon, the Gadarene prayed that he might be allowed to follow Him.   This prayer offered up by a true disciple was the only one, connected with the incident, which Jesus did not answer in the way requested.   The demons prayed that they might be permitted to enter the herd of swine, and their prayer was granted.   The Gadarenes prayed that Jesus would depart out of their coasts, and their prayer was also granted.   Some prayers may be answered in judgment, and some refused in mercy. 5. But why did this man ask to be allowed to follow Jesus?   (1) It may have been personal love ; or (2) it may have arisen from a trembling fear lest the dreadful demons of the olden time should return with the departure of Jesus ; or (3) his prayer may have been offered from shame for his countrymen, who had asked the Lord of life and of peace to leave their coasts.   But the worse the people were, the more they needed a missionary.   And what a missionary this man would be ! (*Norman Macleod, D.D.*)   *Destructive power :*—On one occasion Christ's power operated in a direction that was merely destructive.   A legion of devils besought Him to let them enter a herd of swine (a terrible illustration of the intolerableness of life in hell), and on obtaining permission the whole herd, to the number of 2000, ran into the sea, and was destroyed.   Much has been said against the people who besought Christ to leave their coasts on finding their swine destroyed ; they have been charged with sordidness, selfishness, and low ideas of the value of human amelioration.   Though we may steal a cheap reputation for magnanimity at the expense of these unfortunate people, yet they were right after all in desiring such a man as they took Christ to be to depart from their midst.   Their request was the expression of a great principle in the human constitution, implanted there by the Creator.   Men cannot be benefited by mere power, but they are necessarily reduced to a meaner manhood by the presence of a power that is destructive.   The history of despotism proves this.   People never beg thunder and lightning to continue amongst them, but they often wish that summer would never go away.   (*J. Parker, D.D.*)   *Insanity is much nearer the kingdom of God than worldly-mindedness :*— Men with shattered reason felt the spell, while the wise and strong-minded too often used their intellect, under the bias of passion or prejudice, to resist the force of truth.   In this way we may account for the recognition of Jesus by the Gadarene demoniac.   (*A. B. Bruce, D.D.*)   *A Saviour and not a tormentor :*—We may be sure of this, that just as the Saviour did not land on the coast of the Gadarenes to torment them, but to save them from the demons and sins that were their real tormentors ; so He did not come into the world to torment us, but to save us from evil passions and desires, than which there are no worse tormentors.   This, however, is what some people do not believe.   They think that the religion of Christ is a tormenting religion, and that it torments in two ways : (1) By putting restraint upon our conduct; and (2) by taking up all our time.   As to the first—in comparison with slavery to self the service of Christ is perfect freedom. As to the second—it takes no more time to do everything to the glory of God, than to do everything to God's dishonour. (*E. J. Hardy.*)   *Hell on earth:*—1. We may learn from this account that evil spirits are real persons. There is a notion got abroad that it is only a figure of speech to talk of evil spirits, that all the Bible means by them is certain bad habits, or bad qualities or diseases. When I hear such language —and it is very common—I cannot help thinking how pleased the devil must be to hear people talk in such a way. How can people help him better than by saying that there is no devil? 2. We have no right to believe—we have every right not to believe—that these evil spirits can make us sin in the smallest matter against our own wills. (*Charles Kingsley.*)   *Legion :*—If we yield to temptations whenever they come in our way, we shall find ourselves less and less able to resist them, for we shall learn to hate the evil spirits less and less. We shall give place to the devil, as the Scripture tells us we shall ; for instance, by indulging in habitual passionate tempers, or rooted spite and malice. And so a man may become more and more the slave of his own nature, of his own lusts and passions, and therefore of the devils who are continually pampering and maddening those lusts and passions, till a man may end in complete possession. Few men in England, of course, would be fools enough to indulge the gross and fierce part of their nature till they became mere savages, like the demoniac whom Christ cured ; so it is to respectable vices that the devil mostly tempts us—to covetousness, to party spirit, to a hard heart, and a narrow mind ; to cruelty, that shall clothe itself under the name of law ; to filthiness, which excuses itself by saying, " It is a man's nature, he cannot help it " ; to idleness, which excuses itself on the score of wealth ; to meanness and unfairness in trade, and in political and religious disputes—these are the devils which haunt us Englishmen—sleek, prim, respectable fiends enough, and truly, their name is Legion. (*Ibid.*)   *Spirits in possession of a man :*—I. The CONDITION OF THE DEMONIAC. 1. The extent to which he was possessed. 2. The effects of the possession. II. THE DEMONIAC CURED AND CLOTHED. 1. He is brought to his right mind. 2. He appears in his right place. 3. He displays a right demeanour. (*A. A. Ramsey.*)   *A genuine case :*—The area which an unclean spirit is permitted, in taking possession of a man, is probably, in the present day, more limited than it was during our Lord's personal ministry on earth. But the effects are not less disastrous, if less extraordinary, than they were then. Let me supply an example from within the range of my own observation. He was a choice young man, son of a wealthy citizen in the metropolis. Favoured by birth, distinguished by amiability of disposition and superior natural talents, clever in business, skilled in the sciences, he was the acknowledged centre of a wide and admiring circle of relatives and friends. One day an evil spirit, which for weeks previously had been hovering about his path, whispering in his ear, and injecting thoughts of envy, evil, and unbelief into his mind, took possession of him. It was while, at an evening party, he sat before the piano, discoursing exquisite music to an eager, enthusiastic group of friends. Suddenly there came upon him what he afterwards described to me as an irresistible impulse. It instantly detached him from the most agreeable associations. He glided out of the glittering room, rushed from beneath his father's roof into the dark street, and almost before his absence from home was noticed, he was " among the tombs," gnashing his teeth in a frenzy of lustful passion, rending those beautiful garments of virtue which cannot easily be repaired, and wounding himself with weapons which inflict a deeper scar in the conscience than " stones " do in the flesh. There, in the sepulchral regions of vice, in the charnel-house of the morally dead, he " dwelt night and day for years." Neither could any man tame him. Again and again the task was tried and failed. Faithful reproofs, cogent reasonings, urgent entreaties, tender persuasions oft-repeated, were utterly fruitless in regard to his reformation. " Fetters " most strong and sacred were used to bind him. Fetters forged in the white heat of a mother's burning devotion. Fetters skilfully woven out of the deep treasures of a pious sister's heart. But they proved as ineffectual as did the seven green withes on the limbs of Samson. It was in an hour of direful wretchedness, when, in a paroxysm of mingled rage and remorse, he was rushing to the riverside, defiant of all that is holy and true, and seeking self-forgetfulness in the suicide's grave, that Jesus met him, arrested his steps, cast out the demon that so long had led him captive, and constrained him to turn his face homeward, penitently and tearfully saying, " I will arise and go to my father." (*Ibid.*)

Ver. 35. **Sitting at the feet of Jesus, clothed, and in his right mind.**—*Sitting at the feet of Jesus :*—Sitting at the feet of one is an expression which seems fitted not merely to describe local position, but to image forth the state of the mind of him who occupies it. And among these we may notice—1. Reverential affection for his Deliverer. Thus he sought to be near Him; yet would take the lowest place in His presence, from which he might look up to Him with admiring and loving regards. 2. Confidence in His power to save. "Sitting at the feet of Jesus: " the man out of whom the devils were departed, may have considered this as the place of safety. 3. Docility under His instructions. This was the position of an avowed disciple, according to the custom of the times, which assigned to the teacher a more elevated seat, while the scholars placed themselves at his feet. His place showed that he had been made willing to submit his own understanding to the wisdom of God, speaking by Him whom He had sent. And may we not conclude that there was not only acquiescence in the truth of what Jesus taught, but a deep and engrossing interest in the subjects of His discourse ? 4. Submission to His authority, and devotedness to His service. By sitting at the feet of Jesus, would not the man whom He had delivered from the power of the demons express his sense of the obligations under which he was laid now to obey and serve Him who had done so great things for him, and had had compassion on him? What might he say by the place he occupied and his mien there ? "O Lord, I am Thy servant, truly I am Thy servant, Thou hast loosed my bonds." I would only add two observations farther. 1. That, in cherishing such sentiments and affections toward Jesus, we will show that we have come to ourselves, that we are now in our right minds. 2. By cherishing such sentiments and affections towards Jesus we consult our true happiness. (*J. Henderson, D.D.*)　　*A three-fold blessing:*—Three ideas are suggested by the brief but expressive description in the text: I. REST—"Sitting." Repose one of our prime needs. Is there rest anywhere? Yes, at the feet of Jesus. II. RAIMENT—"Clothed." Character the soul's raiment. III. REASON—"In his right mind." There is such a thing as moral insanity, spiritual lunacy. Remember what is said of prodigal son—"And when he came to himself." How suggestive ! Sin deranges our being. To live without God is to be out of our true, proper, right mind. (*T. R. Stevenson.*)　　*Casting out devils:*—I. THE PICTURE AS A HISTORICAL FACT. The man sitting, sane, clothed, restful, decent, master of his own being, and all because of his closeness to the Lord. Explanation of all is in the clause—"At the feet of Jesus." II. THE INCIDENT, AS A SPECIMEN OF THE TRANSFORMING POWER OF CHRISTIANITY ON A WIDE SCALE IN THE WORLD'S HISTORY. 1. It conduces to the material well-being. It is well to note that the man was "clothed." 2. Its influence upon the mind. 3. Its power to deal with the sores and sins of single souls. The individual first, and the mass afterwards. Lessons : 1. There are no outcasts beyond the sweep of Christ's large mercy, beyond the leverage of Christ's great love. 2. Here is what God sends me to offer to every man and woman here—rest, for distraction ; peace, tranquility ; quiet of heart, of conscience, of memory, of soul, of hope. Self-command. Emancipation from the madness of sin. (*Expository Sermons on New Testament.*)　　*The demoniac recovered:*—I. In the first place, you observe, THAT IN THIS CASE A MALIGNANT DISORDER HAD BEEN ENDURED. 1. As to the nature of the disorder, the person before us is described as " a certain man which had devils long time." Foul spirits, or demons, had mysteriously, though really, been permitted to enter into his frame, and to render his corporeal and mental existence subservient to the will and power of Satan. That so long as you remain untouched by another, by a higher, and by a far more commanding agency, so long you are "led captive by the devil at his will." 2. Thus is illustrated the nature of the disorder ; and we find the statement also presented as to its effects. The recorded effects of the disorder upon the victim here alluded to, are most pitiable and touching. My brethren, the subjection of man to the moral dominion of Satan exposes him to effects, of which those we have now described furnish a solemn and a striking analogy. There is the perversion of reason. Again : there is the exclusion of the'soul from all associations which can constitute its comfort and its dignity. Then, again, there is the endurance of positive pain and agony. Indulgences are fraught with pangs ; and the passions which prompt them only infuriate and convulse. II. We have thus considered, that a malignant disorder had been endured ; and you will now observe, secondly, THAT A SIGNAL RECOVERY WAS EFFECTED. 1. As to the Being by whom the recovering agency was exerted, it was, we need scarcely remind you, the Lord Jesus Christ. The Lord Jesus Christ is the one Deliverer appointed for men, from their subjugation to the slavery of

Satan. Further: it will be observed, that the Saviour accomplishes the deliverance of man by the manifestation of Himself to them, in His person and in His work. The demoniac, you observe, saw the Redeemer; and it was in connection with His personal appearance that the cure was effected and achieved; and in this manner the Saviour also spiritually manifests Himself to the understandings of men. He presents Himself to man by His Word. He also presents Himself to men by His Spirit. 2. This, my brethren, is the Being by whom the recovering agency is exerted; and you are now to observe the extent to which that agency operated. We are informed in this beautiful narrative, that by some mystic charm the sufferer was attracted to the Saviour. What a change!—from the frenzied maniac, in his wild convulsions and his angry mien, to one quiet and clothed, rejoicing in privilege, and exulting in the hope of happiness! It was, indeed, the accomplishment of a new creation. III. Then, brethren, from this signal recovery effected, we are also to observe, THAT IMPORTANT RESULTS WERE SECURED. 1. Observe the effects as they were produced upon the minds of others. It is recorded, that the men who had been guilty of the unholy traffic, and who by the loss of their foul property had been abundantly reproved and judged, "were afraid." My brethren, what we desire to impress upon you here, is a fact which no genuine Christian will for a moment dream of disputing, that any real and well-ascertained conversion, by the energy of the Divine Spirit, through the work of the great Redeemer, must produce powerful influences upon the minds of those who can personally and truly observe it. Although, perhaps, you but imperfectly calculated and estimated them, it was an event which vibrated to the most distant regions of the universe. Anger was excited. Satan was angry, and his ministers of darkness were angry, when they saw you snatched from the burning, and taken from their thraldom and from their doom, into "the glorious liberty" and the glorious prospects "of the children of God." Ungodly men, perhaps, were angry. But not only anger: astonishment was produced. You were a wonder unto others; they saw that which amazed them. There was the drunkard sober. And then, not merely was there anger and astonishment—there was joy. Your parents, your partners, your children, your friends, they rejoiced over you, when you told them of what God had done for your souls. 2. Again, brethren, we have also to observe the effect on the mind of the individual himself. And love to his deliverer was produced. And love, brethren, to Him by whom we have been emancipated from the thraldom of sin and Satan is the inevitable, and ought to be legitimately the master-impulse of our existence. Then again: zeal for his deliverer was produced; for we are informed, in a subsequent part of the narrative, that "Jesus sent him away, saying, Return to thine own house, and show how great things God hath done unto thee." Christ, brethren, will have no indolent enjoyers of privilege with Him. We must look onward, brethren, to the grand and glorious consummation, when liberty shall reign over our apostate globe. (*J. Parsons.*)   *Conversion of a sorceress:*—A remarkable case is reported by Mr. Owen Watkins, one of the most devoted and honoured missionaries in the Transvaal. He describes the baptism of a woman who had for years been famous among her people as a witch doctor, and was supposed to have the power of discovering secrets of every kind. Two years ago Mr. Watkins saw her at a great festival, engaged in her fantastic rites, leading a wild dance of women, with weapons in her hands and strange charms hung round her. She jumped and leaped, and shouted, he says, "like one possessed of devils." All this has passed away now; she has broken with her old life, burnt her charms, renounced her fame and her power. The very difficulty of her conversion goes far to prove its reality. "Often when trying to pray she would rush away to the solitudes of the mountain, and there wander about like an unquiet spirit." This is not the experience of one to whom the spiritual life is not a reality; and the fact that one who had so strong a hold upon their fears and superstitions should have thus accepted the gospel of Christ's love is certain to impress the hearts of those who used to dread and worship her.   *God's power in changing the heart:*—If God should speak to Niagara, and bid its floods in their tremendous leap suddenly stand still, that were a trifling demonstration of power compared with the staying of a desperate human will. If He should suddenly speak to the broad Atlantic, and bid it be wrapped in flames, we should not even then see such a manifestation of His greatness as when He commands the human heart, and makes it submissive to His love. (*C. H. Spurgeon.*)   *Changed by the power of God:*—A believer was giving in a prayer-meeting his testimony as to God's grace and goodness, and said:—"On my way here to-night I met a ma who asked me where I was going. I said, 'I am going to prayer-meeting.' He said, 'There are a good many religions, and I think the most of them are delusions; as to the Christian religion, that is only a notion—that is a mere notion, the Christian religion.' I said to him, 'Stranger, you see that tavern over there?' 'Yes,' said he, 'I see it.' 'Do you see me?' 'Yes; of course I see you.' 'Now the time was, as everybody in this town knows, that if I had a quarter of a dollar in my pocket I could not pass that tavern without going in and getting a drink; all the people of Jefferson could not keep me out of that place. But God has changed my heart, and the Lord Jesus Christ has destroyed my thirst for strong drink; and there is my whole week's wages, and I have no temptation to go there. And, stranger, if this is a notion, I want to tell you it is a mighty powerful notion; it is a notion that has put clothes on my children's backs, and it is a notion that has put good food on our table, and it is a notion that has filled my mouth with thanksgiving to God. And, stranger, you had better go along with me—you might get religion too; lots of people are getting religion now.'" (*Dr. Talmage.*)   *The demoniac at the feet of Jesus :*—In the first instance he was demon-possessed, and in the next he was Christ-possessed.   I. We shall direct our attention TO CERTAIN VIEWS SUGGESTED BY HIS INSANE CONDITION, AS CHARACTERISTIC OF MEN WHO HAVE NOT BEEN REDUCED TO A STATE OF SPIRITUAL SOUNDNESS BY THE HEALING POWER OF CHRIST. Among the various wrecks of humanity our eyes can scarcely rest on a spectacle more melancholy and humiliating than that of a poor helpless object, dragging out a seemingly profitless existence in a state of soulless idiocy. Deprived of that reason by which our race is mainly distinguished from the inferior animals, he appears but as the shadow or mockery of a man, because seemingly in possession of no more than his external form. Easily then can we conceive how much more friends would have preferred death for him to all this; and all the more earnestly they might long for it from concluding that his living could serve no good end, or be anything more than an oppression to himself and others. But, withal, how mistaken in their calculations! He had, notwithstanding all their misgivings, been created for the glory of God. Miserable, feared, and pitied, as he was, fleeing from human habitations and tearing his own flesh; yet the wretched man, wretched whilst in this state, was living for the glory of God, for, as proved in the event, he was destined to become the subject of a miraculous cure by the great Physician; and in this way was to help in attesting the Divine commission of that Physician. Thus in the first instance, although the devil was allowed to show what power he had gained over him by his state of lunacy: he was next to be an instrument in Christ's hands, whereby the great Deliverer was to show in turn what supreme power He had over the devil himself, and what He was able to do in the reduction of moral as well as mental insanity; and thus clothe the spiritually naked, and put them in their right mind. In directing our attention to these views, we are able at once to perceive that this poor lunatic was of far more use in the scheme of God's grace than multitudes who have thought themselves far wiser men. Assuredly they who sit down contented anywhere else than at the feet of Jesus, are still in a state of infatuation, so that in application to those who live and die in such a condition, we may employ the language of Solomon and say, "Madness is in their heart while they live, and after that they go to the dead." Nothing save madness, and that which in the end proves the worst kind of it, could lead men to embrace the world as a portion, when they might have instead the kingdom of heaven for an inheritance. What but madness could lead them to encounter at any moment, the risk of hastening into everlasting companionship with the devil and his angels, when otherwise they might be in the blissful condition of securing for eternity the society of the ministering hosts of heaven, and the spirits of just men made perfect. One of the tokens of insanity affecting the helpless maniac mentioned in the text, consisted, as stated by Mark, in "cutting himself with stones." But would he have been any wiser if, like multitudes of our race, he had cut himself instead with gold or silver, or with some of the other glittering things for which worldly minded and ambitious men spend their lives? Would he have been less a madman if his cutting instrument of torture had been the drunkard's glass, wherewith to have administered deadly poison till he perished in ruin? Would he have been less a madman to have climbed the ladder of ambition, till losing self-command in the giddy height, he had fallen to perish in misery, as hath happened, in the judgments of God, to many of the proud and insatiable tyrants of the earth. Would he have been less a madman to have frequented scenes of licentious and degrading sensuality, till wasting, loathsome disease, more cutting than all the stones of torture he employed, had severed the slender thread of life, and sent him an early victim to the all-devouring tomb? They may not, like the maniac before us, have their habitation among the tombs, but they live and breathe in as death-like places, inhaling the noxious vapours of mammon's treasure-house, or the noxious fumes of the temple of Bacchus, or the pestilential atmosphere of the slaughter-houses of licentious indulgence. They may not appear actually bound in fetters and chains like the demoniac of the text; but they are more than iron-bound to their own lusts, and seemingly without such power as the demoniac had to snap them asunder. There are no chains so galling as those which are forged by enslaving passions or degrading appetites. "O that they were wise, that they understood this, that they would consider their latter end." II. We shall show WHAT WE HOLD TO BE INVOLVED IN THE SPIRITUAL CONDITION OF MEN, WHEN IT MAY BE SAID OF THEM THAT THEY ARE IN THEIR "RIGHT MIND," AND HAVE THUS BECOME TRULY WISE. The main thing to which we have to attend in the management of this is to weigh Scripturally what is implied in the situation here spoken of, as "sitting at the feet of Jesus." It was there that the demoniac was found after he was brought to his right mind, and it is there that any one will be who is truly wise. No one can be said to have "come to himself" till in that situation. Wherefore consider that to sit in the church is not to sit at the feet of Jesus. To sit in the reading even of His own Holy Book is not to sit at the feet of Jesus. To sit as ministers, elders, or deacons, in discharging any of the offices which belong to His house, is not to sit at His feet. To sit at His own holy table on sacramental occasions, to eat and drink in His name, and, as called for, in remembrance of Him, is not that which constitutes sitting at His feet. Men may do all these things in their season, and with much regularity during the currency of a long life, and yet be found in the end to have been nearer the feet of Satan than the feet of the Saviour. All these are important duties in their place; but if done in mere formality, or hypocrisy, tend not to salvation, but to ruin. 1. It implies laying down at His feet the whole burden of one's sin that He may pardon and purify—that He may forgive and cleanse from all pollution. It is only when men are in this state of consciousness as to the burden of sin, they will take any active part in placing themselves at the feet of Jesus; and when they come to this, it is because of the conviction there is no other place of safety for them. He is then seen as affording the only propitiation for sin, so that verily there is no other name under heaven whereby men can be saved. 2. Sitting at the feet of Jesus may be regarded as implying the willing reception for directions in faith and life of the heavenly lessons taught in His Word. No one, therefore, can be said to sit at His feet, and clothed in his right mind, who does not venerate the Scriptures, and apply to them for spiritual instruction. And it is just because there is so little ambition of this sort, if we may so speak, to be taught the legislation of heaven, by sitting at the feet of Jesus in learning, or becoming "mighty in the Scriptures," that there are so many blunders in civil legislation—so many blunders in education—and, we may say, so many blunders in preaching. They who have never been at the feet of Jesus learning His will, have not, like the demoniac, come to their right mind, and what are we to expect from the still infatuated, or from madmen, whether they be princes, or statesmen, or parents, or teachers? Mere science, worshipped as it may be, is of no use to man at the brink of the grave. He needs no geometry to enable him to measure its length and depth. He needs no chemistry to enable him to analyze the soil into which he is about to be laid. These and other branches of learning are of use in their proper place to living men, but are of no use to the dying. They are fit subjects for discussion in the halls of science, but serve no purpose in the chambers of sickness and dissolution. When the end is thus drawing nigh, nothing is of any value to the immortal spirit, except what is learnt by "sitting at the feet of Jesus." The Bible, which contains the learning thus to be acquired, may have been despised before, but it can scarcely be despised now. (*J. Allan.*) *Testifying to the power of God's grace:*—I have told you of African cruelty. Here is a story of what Jesus does when He gets into the hearts of such dreadful men. Some years ago there was a man called Africaner, a Kaffir, who was the terror of the whole neighbourhood. The mere mention of his name made the people tremble. Sweeping down upon towns and villages with his wild followers, he would murder all the men and even the children, would take the women as slaves, and having burnt the place, would drive the cattle back to his own territory. The bold missionary thought that the gospel of Jesus was able to save even this man, and he set out to preach to him.

When the people found where he was going, they begged him to remain. His friends implored him not to go. Nobody expected to see him again. On he went, and speedily came tidings that he had been murdered, one man declaring that he himself had seen his bones bleaching in the wilderness. But some years after, two men came back amongst the white people. They knocked at the door of the farmer's house; the farmer started and turned pale, "Why, this is the missionary's ghost," he cried. "No, no," laughed Mr. Moffat, "it is the missionary himself, in the flesh still." "Why, but you were murdered long ago," gasped the farmer. But Mr. Moffat soon let him know that he was no ghost, and joy came in place of fright as the wife and children gathered around him with glad welcome. "But however did you escape from that dreadful Africaner?" asked the farmer, as if he could not quite believe it yet. "Africaner is now a truly good man"; and Mr. Moffat told of his conversion. The farmer listened in amazement. "If that is really so," he said, "I have only one wish before I die, I should like to see this eighth wonder of the world, and I will go with you to see him." The missionary coolly turned to the man at his side. "See," he said, taking his hand, "here is Africaner." The farmer started in terror; looking at him he saw the face, but with such a new spirit shining in it that he cried, "O God, what a miracle of Thy power; what cannot Thy grace accomplish!" (*M. G. Pearse.*) *Friends of the devil :*—Whole villages (of the Kohls in India) were found in ruins ; for "an evil spirit has settled in them." "Get up! be off!" shouted the excited people to the missionaries as they camped on a little green knoll near the hamlet. "Why?" "That is our devil's place; you must not inconvenience our devil." (*Dr. Stephenson.*)

Vers. 38, 39. **Return to thine own house.**—*The blessedness of active service :*— The words of this refusal seem to suggest to us its cause ; for instead of staying with Him, our Lord bade the lately possessed man go home to his friends, and tell them the great things which God had done for him. And in giving him this charge He did two things. 1. He thus in mercy provided that they who in their blindness had besought Him to leave them, and who would not, like the dwellers in Judea, have other opportunities of hearing Him, should still be reached by His blessed gospel : and so this instance stands alone. For whereas in other cases He ordered those He healed to tell no man, here, on the contrary, He sent away the healed man, charged by Himself to deliver this message of mercy. 2. He hereby calmed the fears of the restored demoniac. He bade him believe that in labouring thus for Him, in declaring His name, in blessing others, he should find that presence, and so that safeguard from evil, for which his soul craved. He answered the fears of his heart, and told him that whilst he laboured for his brethren, he should himself be safe from the assault of those mysterious powers he dreaded. The very charge was a promise. He was a monument of mercy—he should be kept as one : he longed to be in his Deliverer's presence—he should be so : after another manner, indeed, from that for which he asked, but yet most truly, most closely, yea, perpetually ; wherever there was another to whom he could testify, wherever there was a tormented body, or a vexed spirit, there he might find anew his own Deliverer in bearing witness to His power. And these are our lessons. With every heart which the Saviour hath set free He has left this charge : "Go home to thy friends, and tell them how great things the Lord hath done for thee." Into all social life this light penetrates. Every man is to be to those around him a living preacher of the power of the Redeemer ; he is to walk amongst his fellows as a witness for Christ. From him, too, the powers of evil have been banished ; for him life wears another countenance ; he is no longer, if he lives, as he may, under the renewing influences of the Holy Ghost, the slave of dark, or sensual, or furious, or earthly spirits. Silently it may be—meekly and unobtrusively it must be, but yet most truly—he is to bear witness to that mighty Deliverer, who found him out in his extremity, and broke the fetters which had bound his spirit. True Christian men in their own station do raise the tone of life round them : in a thousand little instances which are occurring daily, they are bearing a witness for truth, for sincerity, for reality, for purity, for meekness, for self-denial, for a spiritual life—which is not lost. For so it is that, most secretly, society is leavened for good or for evil. II. And if this is our first lesson, our second lies close beside it. It is, that our own safety must consist in thus working for Christ. Even as from the recovered demoniac, so from us also, the powers of evil are to be kept off in our active fulfilment of our own charge. If these, then, are our lessons from our Saviour's charge to this delivered man, let us gather them up into two strictly practical conclusions. And, first, let us see what a serious thing life is, even in its smallest parts. But it is a serious thing to live; serious both to ourselves and to others. To others, because all our life has its influence on them; because if we live unchristian lives, we throw away a ministry of mercy which might have saved some of them; because the very lowest of us cannot waste his own life and not injure other men; because we cannot be untrue to ourselves without being untrue to them. Let this, then, be our first conclusion, that it is a serious thing to live; and then we shall find encouragement as well as true instruction in this, as our second, that the sense of our redemption is to be the great foundation truth of all our life. We must have faith in this if we would know our charge, or in the least fulfil it. We must believe that we have been redeemed: we must have felt that He has indeed redeemed us from sin and its powers, from guilt and misery, or we cannot love Him as our Deliverer; cannot thankfully receive His easy yoke; and cannot witness of this truth to others. This is the great foundation of a true and earnest life: our hearts must yearn after Him; must pray that we may be with Him; must fear to be parted from Him; must long to live in His presence, finding it shelter, and safety, and peace; and then He will manifest Himself unto us. (*Bp. Samuel Wilberforce.*)   *Exemplifying religion in domestic relations :*—I design to use the text to set forth the duty of exemplifying religion in the family and immediate domestic relations. I. THIS IS THE PROPER PLACE TO COMMENCE ALL OUR EFFORTS TO DO GOOD. 1. The dearest relations of the world are there. 2. The family is the place of our most powerful and constant influence. II. PEOPLE ARE GENERALLY BACKWARD TO PERFORM THIS DUTY. Is not this the very point of defect in the family training of many professing Christians? Do we not here come at the main reason, so far as human agency is concerned, why, in the domestic circles of some eminent Christians, there occur instances of sad indifference to Divine things, and of open profanity and irreligion? III. The direction of the text demands our special attention, because it contemplates a sphere where SOME PECULIAR DIFFICULTIES EXIST, which are apt to interfere with the exemplification of high religious consistency. The very intimacy of the domestic intercourse is often a snare and a hindrance to one who does not religiously govern himself and watch against temptation. The freedom of family intercourse, also, is apt to take off restraints to the indulgence of our passions, and to the display of our real dispositions, which are felt in more public scenes. Let us be mindful, that the greater the impunity with which we may transgress, the greater the danger. (*T. E. Vermilye, D.D.*)   *Vital principles of the kingdom :*—What are the principles that are to guide and rule our life when we become His subjects? This is our theme. I. The first principle that our text gives us is this, that CHRIST'S WILL AND NOT OUR WISH IS TO REGULATE OUR CONDUCT. We are to use our reason; but we are not to set ourselves up in judgment against Christ. Get a good start, by laying hold of this principle in the first instance—that Christ's will and not your wish is to regulate and rule your conduct. Remember that we have a right, whatever our wishes may be, to bring them before Christ. If you have strong desires concerning any matters in your hearts, you will find, if you lay them before Christ, He will not reproach you for doing so. He did not reproach this man for his prayer. The tender and wise Saviour knew what He was about. Instead of lacking in love to the man, He was overflowing with it, and He gave the best answer possible to his prayer, "Go home to thy friends, My good man; thou needest care, thou needest nursing. Do not think of becoming one of My followers; why thou wouldest soon have to give up that; go home to thy friends, and say what great things God has done unto thee." My dear friends, believe me, God will hear and answer your prayer if it be sincere, and if He does not answer it in your way, He will do so in a better way. Never swerve from this principle for an instant, that prayer is a reality. The little eaglet as it sees its mother spread her pinions to the breeze, cries, "Oh that I could fly!" and the mother answers the prayer by overturning the nest: her offspring thinks it cruel, but it is the only way its prayer can be answered. II. The second principle is, that USEFULNESS AND NOT ENJOYMENT IS TO BE OUR SUPREME CONCERN. Now a man that lives merely for his own personal enjoyment, although that enjoyment be of a spiritual kind, will find that he will very soon frustrate his own purposes and intentions, and instead of securing that for which he has so earnestly, but selfishly sought, it will evade his grasp and leave him altogether a stranger to it. Christianity is not the last spar of a wreck on which a man may float himself into the still waters of an eternal calm; but it is a life-boat, and every man must "man the life-boat," and try to rescue others from the wreck which sin and Satan had made. Dear friends, you shall have enjoyment, but your enjoyment must come by way of usefulness. This principle of the kingdom of Christ is the principle of all kingdoms over which Christ rules and governs. All life is constituted according to this principle—that it shall only exist in a healthy condition as it gives out of that which it receives. The Dead Sea is a dead sea because it receives all and gives nothing. The brook is beautiful and lovely because it is constantly flowing, and all in nature that is healthy, is healthy because it observes this rule. The clouds take the water from the sea, only that they may give it back again in fertilizing showers to gladden and refresh the earth. In return the earth gives us fruit, flowers and herbs, indeed, everything good for man and beast. III. Another principle closely associated with the foregoing is this, that OUR POWER FOR USEFULNESS DEPENDS UPON WHAT CHRIST HAS DONE FOR US. Christ said to this man, " Go and show what great things God hath done unto thee." Your power for usefulness will not depend upon what you say, so much as upon what you are; and your great concern, if you want to be useful, is to live lives which are not inconsistent with your profession. Seek first of all to have an experimental acquaintance with Christ's power upon your own heart. IV. The fourth principle according to the text is that—OUR FIRST PLACE OF USEFULNESS IS TO BE THE HOME. "Return to thine own house, and show what great things God hath done unto thee." We are to begin in the family circle first of all. (*W. Williams.*)   *The religious use of excited feelings :*—Natural in this man to wish to continue with our Lord. Doubtless his mind transported with joy and gratitude. Christ impressed this very attendance upon others. In the case before us He suffered not what at other times He had bidden. A lesson may be drawn from this for the use of those who, having neglected religion in early youth, at length begin to have serious thoughts, try to repent, and wish to serve God better than hitherto, though they do not know how to set about it. Even for those who have neglected Him He has found (if they will avail themselves of it) some sort of remedy of the difficulties in the way of obedience which they have brought upon themselves by sinning. I. WHAT IS THIS REMEDY? It is the excited feeling with which repentance is at first attended. II. How IS IT TO BE USED? The restored sufferer in the text wished to be with Christ. Eagerness and zeal may lead to a false devotion which makes men desirous of keeping themselves in Christ's immediate sight, rather than of returning to their own home, as He would have them, that is, to the common duties of life. Learn to live by faith which sees Christ and rejoices in Him, though sent away from His presence to labour in the world. (*J. H. Newman, D.D.*)   *An unanswered prayer :*—I. WHAT INDUCED THE MAN TO OFFER THIS PRAYER? 1. Possibly fear. 2. Doubtless also gratitude. Not now possessed but possessing. II. WHAT INDUCED OUR LORD TO REFUSE THIS PRAYER? 1. It was better for the man. Lest he should infer that the power of Christ was merely local, and not universal. 2. It was better for the man's friends. The home-circle should be the great missionary-field. There are occasions when it is right for a man to narrate his personal experience. Showing is usually safer than telling. 3. It was better for the land in which he lived. If Christ had permitted him to follow Him, the whole land of Decapolis would have remained in darkness. (*H. A. Nash.*)   *The home-mission work of Christians :*—1. Every man who is entitled to the name of Christian, knows in some degree what great things the Lord has done for him. 2. To every man, therefore, who knows this, however imperfectly or inadequately the blessing may be realized, the Lord says, " Go to thine own house," &c. 3. Look at their sphere of missionary labour, in which every Christian is to be the missionary agent. The circle made up of our relations, friends, companions, and those with whom we come most into contact. (1) Our own house has the first claim upon us. (2) To show to our own house what great things the Lord hath done for us, is the very duty which every kind of religious fervour demands, in order to prevent it from dying out like a fire that leaves nothing but ashes behind, or from being spent like a fresh flowing stream in mere noise and foam, without doing any practical good. (3) Our religion as seen in our own house is the best test of the reality of our Christian character. (4) Our home is the field which we can cultivate better than any other. 4. We are further taught, by the history of this Gadarene, the way in which this home mission work is to be carried on. It is chiefly by our life : by what we are. This influence of a good life, however, does not exclude a more direct showing by spoken word, of what the Lord has done for ourselves, and what He is willing and able to do for all. (*Norman Macleod, D.D.*) *Christian influence :*—And regarding Christ's treatment of this restored man, as in

entire analogy with His treatment of true Christians, let us learn—I. A LESSON IN
REGARD TO GOD'S ANSWERING OF PRAYER. If our prayers are proper and right, both
in their spirit and their objects, may we not come to the throne of grace assured
that they will be answered ? To which I answer—1. That according to the principle
just insisted on, that God's thoughts are not our thoughts, no man is competent
to decide positively whether the prayer he offers is in the right spirit. The petition
of this Gadarene may have originated in a selfish desire to be happy in Christ's
presence, rather than useful in His service. And if so, it was self-considered, an
improper prayer, and not to be answered. And so of other prayers. 2. But we
remark that, even were we certain that the prayer is such as God promises to
answer, there remains still a more important point to be considered—viz., the best
way of answering it. If the Gadarene prayed properly, desiring only his own
greatest good and God's greatest glory, then Christ may have seen that he would
grow more rapidly in grace, and bring more honour to his Saviour, by remaining
among his own countrymen ; and thus really answered his petition by sending him
away. And so it is always. God will assuredly answer all prayers that are proper
and good ; but then He answers them in His own way, and according to His own
higher wisdom. The Christian prays to be sanctified ; and this is a good prayer,
and if offered in a right spirit is sure to be answered. But how ! Ah, not according to the man's thoughts ! God lays His strong hand upon the man's idols. He
takes away his property ; He takes away his health ; He takes away his comforts ;
He lays the beloved of his home and heart into the unpitying grave—thus weakening his affections for the earthly and the carnal. "Ah," but says the Christian,
"this is not what I meant ! " Be it so ; yet if you prayed sincerely to be sanctified,
this is precisely what you asked for—for this is sanctification ! But passing now
from this great lesson of prayer, and considering the text as containing important
parabolic instruction, we learn here several lessons as to practical Christian
influence. I. We learn THE IMPORTANCE OF SUCH CHRISTIAN INFLUENCE. The text
most impressively teaches us that the law of Christian life is not spiritual enjoyment, but usefulness. And so it is with the Christian. If the end of his conversion
were his own spiritual enjoyment, then, as soon as he is converted, he would be
translated to Christ's presence in glory. There is nothing falser and fouler than
that low, narrow, selfish idea of conversion, which regards it only as the condition
whereby the man escapes from hell and gets into heaven. If such conversion
makes a man good, it is a goodness out of harmony with all other good things.
God's great law of goodness is not absorption, but diffusion. All God's glorious
things, from a flower of the field to a star in the firmament, are not receptacles,
but fountains. No man ever thought of one of God's angels as sitting selfishly on
a heavenly throne, contemplating in indolent rapture the sceptre he is wielding
and the diadem he wears. And if one of those professing Christians, who think
that all God requires of them is just to get themselves to glory, is a true child of
God, then he lacks at least one evidence of sonship—he does not resemble
his great Father. Of one thing we are certain, that every converted soul is
designed by Jehovah to be "the light of the world." And if Jesus Christ should
descend again to the earth, dwelling as of old time with mortals, and one of these
very happy and indolent Christians should come to Him, saying, " O Lord Jesus,
precious Saviour, let me ever sit at Thy feet in love, and rapture, and worship ! "
then, sure I am Christ would frown on him as a slumbering and selfish disciple,
and, like the restored man of Gadara, "would send him away." II. Passing this,
we learn from the text, THE SECRET, OR ELEMENT, OF ALL TRUE CHRISTIAN INFLUENCE.
Our Lord sent this restored man away, that he might bear witness for God unto
his kinsfolk and countrymen. But how was he to bear witness ? Why, simply by
making it manifest that the devil had gone out of him. But the power of his
witness was not in his lips, but his life. They *saw* that he was a changed man. A
hundred men might have come from Galilee, telling these Gadarenes of Christ, the
worker of miracles, and yet all their arguments and eloquence would have been as
nothing to one hour's converse with this restored man—yesterday known to all as
a raging demoniac, to-day a gentle and loving companion, in his right mind. His
power of testimony for Jesus was the power of his life. And in this lies the secret
of all true Christian influence. It is the easiest thing in the world to talk about
religion. But mere talk about religion is the poorest thing in the world. Every
true Christian will indeed talk about his Saviour. Out of the abundance of the
heart the mouth speaketh. Nevertheless, here as elsewhere, the utterance of the
lips is as nothing to the influence of the life. In the Divine economy, all grand

forces are comparatively gentle and silent. The shallow rill, that is dry on the mountain-side half the year, brawls more noisily at times than yon mighty river. The boy's sparkling rocket makes a louder demonstration in the night air than all God's starry constellations. And yet, in the silence of their sublime manifestations, how eloquently do these great forces of the universe bear witness for God ! And so it is of moral forces. The gentle movement of this restored man, amid his wondering countrymen, did more to convince them of Christ's saving power than a thousand noisy utterances. And so is it with the convincing power of a Christian life. The converted man is left in this world a witness for Jesus—a living illustration of the power and blessedness of a religious life. He is to the theologic truth of the Bible what practical experiments are to scientific truths in nature. As the chemist talks technically of elements in analysis and synthesis, and exhibits, in illustration, free gases and ponderous compounds ; and as the botanist discourses scientifically of the structure of plants, and the functions of their parts, and shows you his meaning by producing the petals of a lily, or a spike of lavender—so is it with spiritual science, in the hands of the Great Teacher. The Bible explains, and Christian life illustrates ; e.g., Faith, by definition, is " the substance of things hoped for." But, in order to make men understand it, I must be able to point to some man who, under its power, lives, as did Abraham, ever looking for a city whose maker is God. Trust in God is, by definition, an unswerving resting of the mind on Divine veracity and benevolence. But, to make a man comprehend it, it must be in my power to point to men who, under its influence, sit calmly, like Daniel in the lion's den ; or go resolutely, like the young Hebrews, into a fiery furnace. And so of all graces. In the Bible they are described, as in a written epistle—in Christian life they are illustrated, as in a "living epistle." And in this sense are we, mainly, witnesses for Christ. As the Gadarenes saw that the demoniac was restored, so must the world see that the sinner is converted. He must speak for Christ, as the flower and the star speak for God, in the beauty and glory of their physical manifestations. Without this abiding savour of a holy life, all else will prove but a mockery. III. Meanwhile, the text teaches us THE TRUE SPHERE OF THIS CHRISTIAN INFLUENCE. "Return to thine own house, and show how great things God hath done unto thee." We may not be able to understand all the reasons of this command. It is, however, quite evident, first, that his home would be the field of his most powerful influence—since those who had best known him in his demoniacal state would be the most thoroughly convinced of Christ's power of miraculous restoration. And, secondly, that his home would be the most appropriate field of his influence, since his kinsfolk had the first claim upon his sympathy and labours. And, were there no reasons but these, this direction of Christ teaches us this important lesson in regard of Christian influence—that its truest field, and its mightiest power, are alike always at home. Its mightiest power is at home, because the members of a man's own household, and the familiar friends of his own social circle, are the best judges of the genuineness of his conversion. It is very easy to put on seemings of godliness that shall deceive strangers ; but that must be a true piety, which, amid the daily vexations of life, and the unrestrained intercourse of the home circle, bears the image of Jesus. Meanwhile, a man's home is the fittest field for the exercise of his Christian influence. Religion, like charity, should begin at home. See that your own field is well tilled, ere you go abroad to other fields. Your own heart first ; then your own family ; then your own Church ; then your own country ; and then the whole world. This is God's great law of influence. The heart must be in strong health, if the circulation be vigorous and healthful in the extremities. The roots and trunk of a tree must thrive, if it would fling forth new branches. No matter, indeed, how largely a man expands—the larger his benevolence the better—if he expand harmoniously, from a healthy and permanent centre. Let him not mistake diffusion for expansion, nor a change of scene for an enlargement of influence. Would that all Christians, and all Christian Churches, would learn this simple lesson, which Christ taught to the restored man of Gadara. One fixed and steadfast sun, standing earnestly in its appointed place, and diffusing constant light and life over the small circle of worlds God has committed to its keeping, is worth more than a hundred erratic comets, flaming out in the heavens, and casting a fiery and locomotive glare on a thousand constellations. "Let me walk through broad Galilee, and stand up as a living witness for God before Greek and Jew ; before ruler and Pharisee." And though this request falls in with the dictate of human reason, yet, oh, deeper wisdom of the blessed Saviour ; Christ sent him unto his own kinsfolk, saying, "Go home! Go home!" IV. Moreover, the text teaches us THE MOTIVES OF THIS CHRISTIAN INFLUENCE. "Return to thine own house," said the Saviour. The text tells us he had "a home"; and faithful hearts, long agonized in his behalf, were to be comforted and blessed by his presence. And though, for his own sake, he preferred to be with Jesus, yet, for the sake of beloved kindred, he was willing to depart. Here was one motive, and a strong one. But the text gives us a stronger. 1. The Divine commandment—"Christ sent him away." He may not have had the intellect to understand why Christ thus ordered it; but he surely had the heart that, in its supreme love to his great Deliverer, rejoiced above all things to do His bidding. And here are the types of Christian motives, in labour for the Saviour. Here is, first, philanthropy, the love of our human kindred; a desire to save the sons and daughters of our one great Father. But yet, strong as this motive is, it is as nothing to that second and mightier one—the command of his Master. Christ, his great and gracious Saviour, hath commanded him, as the grand end of his earthly being, to labour to bring impenitent men under the power of the gospel. And this motive is omnipotent. "The love of Christ constraineth him." The love of my kindred might fail—but "the love of Christ constraineth me!" (C. Wadsworth.)

Ver. 40. **The people gladly received Him: for they were all waiting for Him.**— A welcome for Jesus:—When Jesus is waited for and welcomed, He delights to come. He is not waited for by all in our congregations; so that we may ask the question of our present hearers—Do you welcome Christ? Let it be answered by each one this day. I. A BEAUTIFUL SIGHT. "They were all waiting for Him." This waiting may be seen in several different forms. 1. A gathered congregation, waiting in the place where prayer is wont to be made. Want of punctuality, and irregular attendance, often show that Jesus is not waited for. 2. A praying company, an earnest Church, looking for revival, and prepared to co-operate in labour for it. Some Churches do not wait for the Lord's presence, and would not be ready for Him if He were to come. 3. A seeking sinner, sighing for mercy, searching the Scriptures, hearing the Word, inquiring of Christians, constantly praying, and thus "waiting for Him." 4. A departing saint, longing for home: saying, like Jacob, "I have waited for Thy salvation, O Lord" (Gen. xlix. 18). 5. An instructed Church, looking for the Second Advent (Rev. xxii. 17). It is good for the eyes to behold such sights. II. A SURE ARRIVAL. "Jesus was returned." We are quite sure that our Lord will graciously appear to those who are "all waiting for Him," since—1. His Spirit is there already, making them wait (Rom. viii. 23). 2. His heart is there, in sympathy with them, longing to bless them. 3. His work is there. He has brought them into that waiting condition, and now He has found a sphere wherein to display his grace to saints and sinners. 4. His promise is there, "Lo, I am with you alway" (Matt. xxviii. 20). 5. His custom is to be there. His delights are still with the sons of men (Prov. viii. 31). What countless blessings His coming will bring! III. A HEARTY WELCOME. "The people gladly received Him." 1. Their fears made Him welcome. They feared lest He might have gone for ever from them (Psa. lxxvii. 7). 2. Their hopes made Him welcome. They trusted that now their sick would be cured, and their dead would be raised. 3. Their prayers made Him welcome. Those who pray that Jesus may come are glad when He comes. 4. Their faith made Him welcome. Jairus now looked to have his child healed (see verse 41). 5. Their love made Him welcome. When our heart is with Him, we rejoice in His appearing. 6. Their care for others made Him welcome. Jesus never disappoints those who wait for Him. Jesus never refuses those who welcome Him. Jesus is near us now: will you not open the doors of your hearts to receive Him? (Rev. iii. 20.) (C. H. Spurgeon.) Hearty welcome:—A congregation cannot be said to welcome the Lord Jesus unless they are all there, which requires punctuality; unless they have come with design to meet Him, which implies prayerful expectancy; unless they are ready to hear from Him, which involves attention; and unless they are resolved to accept His teaching, which demands obedience. (Ibid.) Waiting for Jesus:—But do we, like the people of Capernaum, gladly receive Him, and are we all waiting for Him? The true child of God regards Christ as the "chiefest among ten thousand," and the "one altogether lovely." Rich are the promises made to those who thus faithfully wait upon Him. "They that wait upon the Lord shall renew their strength." "The Lord is good to them that wait for Him." "Wait on the Lord, be of good courage, and He shall strengthen thy heart." "Those that wait upon the Lord, shall inherit the earth." "Keep mercy, and wait upon thy God continually." "And mind this other thing, prescribe nothing to God. If thou hast begun to wait, faint not, give not up, wait on still. It were good reason, were it but upon little hope at length to find Him ; but since it is upon the unfailing assurance that in the end thou shalt obtain, what folly were it to lose all for want of waiting a little longer ? " Thus it is that God waits for us, and we wait for Him. He waits for the fit times and seasons of His own appointment, that He may be gracious ; and we wait patiently upon Him in the means and ordinances of grace, tarrying the Lord's leisure, until He bring it to pass. We must wait for Jesus at such times as He may appoint, and one of these special times is the Lord's Day. But we must wait for Jesus in the spirit which He requires. In order to a full enjoyment of Christ, there must be not only a waiting for Him, but also a glad receiving of Him. The coming in of Christ into the heart always begets gladness in that heart. This spiritual gladness is an important element of Christian character because, like sunshine, it brightens all within and reflects its glow on all without. But there are those who are conscious to themselves that they are not waiting for Christ, and have not gladly received Him. It is a blessed state to be in, to be waiting for Jesus—to have the soul in that position of expectancy that looks and longs for His appearing. (*Bp. Stevens.*)

Vers. 41, 42. **And, behold, there came a man named Jairus.**—*Christ and the ruler :*—"And behold there came one of the rulers unto Him." This shows us the helplessness of the greatest men. The word ruler indicates position, influence, power, personal supremacy of one kind or another. And yet here is a ruler coming to Jesus Christ for help. There is a point at which all human might becomes utter weakness. We should have said if any man can do without Christ it will be the man who bears the position and sustains the name of ruler. What is our rulership but a mockery in all the great crises and trying passions and terrible combinations of life? A very pretty thing for convenience sake, useful in a social point of view ; but when life is driven to extremity, our rulership is nothing better to us than a nominal honour, and sometimes nothing more than a taunting mockery. Know this, then, that there is no title, no position, no supremacy that can cut you off from the fountain of life and make you independent of Emanuel, Son of God. And said unto Him, My daughter lieth at the point of death—showing us the helplessness of the kindest men. The man before us was not only a ruler, but a father ; yet ruler and father were found at the feet of Christ. Kindness will do more than mere power. A father will always do more than a ruler. The ruler will work by law, by stipulations, by technical covenants, he will consult the letter of the regulations, and he will abide by the bond. But the father will interpret by his heart ; he will avail himself of all the suggestions of love ; he cannot be bound by the narrowness and limitations of the letter ; he does not work by the clock, he works by his heart. Yet the father, the kindest man, came, as well as the ruler, the greatest man. Office and nature, position and life, status and love, will one day have to come to Jesus Christ to make out their petitions and to urge their cases— for even the deepest, grandest, royalest heart feels that it wants something beyond itself, and that something it can only find in Emanuel, Son of God. And it is often not until the ruler and the father have exhausted themselves that they will come to Christ. This ruler was never so truly a ruler as when he fell on his knees and besought Christ to help him. There is an abasement that is exaltation. There is a humility that is the guarantee of the surest independence: (*J. Parker, D.D.*) *The faith of Jairus :*—If Jairus had not been quite sure that Jesus could save her, could he have left his daughter in the very article of death to seek Him out ? We may be sure that nothing short of an absolute conviction of Christ's power to heal and save would have drawn Jairus from his daughter's room. His faith had its reward. No sooner had he uttered his prayer than Jesus set out with him. But as they went, Jesus paused. Favoured by the darkness and by the throng which opened and closed about Him, "a woman having an issue of blood," &c. (ver. 43), came behind Him, and laid her wasted hand on the hem of His garment with a touch that drew healing virtue out of Him. To Jairus, at least at first, this pause must have seemed an almost intolerable vexation. Every moment was precious. Even the apostles, long after this, thought there was hope for Lazarus so long as he was only sick, but none when once he was gone. We cannot suppose that the faith of Jairus was keener than that of Peter and James and John. To him, therefore, this check must have appeared well - nigh fatal to his hopes

The calmness of Jesus, His determination to probe the case to the bottom, to discover who it was that had touched Him, to compel the abashed culprit to tell the whole story of her disease and cure, to teach and comfort and assure her—all this must have been a sore trial to the father's faith. Yet he is too generous, or too self-restrained, to utter a reproach, to urge haste. The delay had teaching for him and benediction. However he may have fretted at it, it brought him the very lesson and help he most needed. The healing of Veronica taught him that, though many throng and press on Jesus, the only touch that reaches Him is the touch of faith. When, too, he saw a woman healed who had been sick " twelve years," that is, just as many years as his daughter had lived, must not that have enlarged his conception of the healing virtue of Jesus? must it not, by teaching him how great things faith can do, have strengthened and confirmed his faith. But as faith is the measure of the gift, as we receive just as much as we can take, this delay, by confirming and enlarging the ruler's faith, made him capable of a larger blessing. As he passed on with Christ, after witnessing so great a miracle, he must, we think, have walked with a firmer step, and have lifted up his head with a more cheerful hope. It was necessary that he should be prepared for a great trial as well as for a great benediction. For his fears were verified. His daughter *had* died while they stopped to talk with the woman who had laid a furtive hand on the Healer's robe. And if by this time Jairus had not had a stronger faith than when he left home, he must have altogether lost faith. One other trial had still to be encountered. To hear of a death affects and awes the mind; but to stand in the presence of death, encompassed by all the signs of mourning and woe, bites more deeply, and rouses the emotions to greater vehemence. " The child is not dead," said Jesus, " but sleepeth." How could He say that the maiden was not dead? Simply because it was true. We are no more without life when we die than when we sleep. Whether Jairus understood our Lord's saying or not, it is obvious that the mourners did not understand it. " They laughed Him to scorn." Their scepticism assures us of the reality of the miracle. If *they* knew the maiden to be dead, *we* know that Jesus must be able to quicken the dead to life. (*S. Cox, D.D.*) We are apt to look upon the healing of the woman with the issue of blood as an interruption of the history of the raising of the daughter of Jairus; as a separate and distinct incident altogether. But there is in reality the closest connection between the two events. They are brought together by all the evangelists, not only because they occurred at the same time and in the same association, but because they help to explain one another. The two miracles fit in a striking way into each other. **1.** The beginning of the woman's plague was coeval with the maiden's birth. **2.** Is not the character of Jairus brought out clearly into contrast with that of the woman? We see the stronger faith of the woman, content with the minimum of means, and the weaker and more irresolute faith of Jairus which needed personal recognition and the support of sympathizing words, which demanded that Jesus should visit his daughter, and could not compass the thought that He could heal at a distance, and restore when the vital spark had fled. **3.** Jairus needed the discipline of the woman's cure. It prepared him for the miracle that was to be wrought for himself. (*H. Macmillan, D.D.*)

Vers. 43-48. Came behind Him, and touched the border of His garment.—*Life behind and life before Christ :*—We believe in the progressive character of the Christian life. It is like the increasing light, which comes to us first as the dim dawn, then as the grey morning, and afterwards as the noon-day brightness. This progress is connected with, indeed is essential to, our highest well-being. It is a progress from good to better, and from better to best. Let us devoutly think of our life in its relation to Christ. I. THE FIRST STAGE IS LIFE BEHIND CHRIST. And what a picture this woman presents, as she quietly presses her way through the thronging crowd, as if by stealth, to take away the needed boon. She had tried life away from Christ; and that had proved a failure. Now she tries life in contact with Christ; this proves an immediate success. When it is asked, What brought her to Christ at all? we can only answer, She was driven by her sense of need, and drawn by her faith in Christ. Driven and drawn. This, more or less, is the experience of all who come to Christ. A sense of their need drives them; a knowledge of His character draws them. II. THE SECOND STAGE IS LIFE BEFORE CHRIST. Had this woman gone away as stealthily as she came, she would have gone away but half-blessed; she would have touched His garment and been healed; she would **not** have tasted His love and been made happy. 1. Life before Christ is **life revealing**

itself to Him. And what a wonderful saying that is: "She told Him all the truth!" "All the truth" about what she had suffered; and that was a mournful tale. And we have not risen to the glory of life before Christ if we are not accustomed to go and tell Him every phase of our experience, all the truth about our sins and our sorrows, our hopes and our fears. There may be phases of experience which we have never breathed into any human ear; but we can whisper all in His ear, confident that He will neither betray our trust nor withhold His sympathy. It takes a great many keys to unlock all the rooms of a great house; but the owner carries a master-key that unlocks them every one. There are rooms in the house of the heart into which few, if any, of our friends are admitted; but the master-key is in the hands of Christ, and He can come and bring all heaven in His train. 2. Life before Christ is life working beneath His eye. The saintly Payson speaks of three classes of Christian workers, and represents them as occupying three circles around Christ. In the outer circle there are those who take rare side-glances at Christ; in the inner circle there are those who occasionally look up to catch His smile; and in the inner-most circle there are those who bring all their work and do it beneath His eye. These last, in the truest, fullest, gladdest sense, stand in the presence of Christ, and have life before Christ. 3. Life before Christ is life blessed with His friendship. He is my physician, and I am grateful to Him; but He is my friend, and I am happy in Him. Oh! what a glory comes into the experience of him whose life is blessed with the friendship of Christ! Others may doubt; he has the witness in himself. Tell him that Christ is only a mythical character. You might as well tell him that the flowers that are breathing their sweetness in his presence are only painted flowers, that the sun which is pouring brightness into his chamber is only an imaginary sun. He perceives the sweetness, he enjoys the brightness that come from Christ into his very soul; and with a confidence that no sophistry can shake, with a love that no power can quench, he tells every assailant, You may as soon reason me out of the consciousness that I am alive, as out of the better and more blessed consciousness that I have the very life of God in my soul. (*R. P. Macmaster.*)   *Christ's particular sympathy and friendship :*—When a lone woman came up in a crowd to steal something, as it were, some healing power out of His person, or out of the hem of His garment, He would not let her off in that im-personal way. He compelled her to show herself, and to confess her name, and sent her away with His personal blessing. He pours out everywhere a particular sympathy on every particular child of sorrow. We have seen that He can love as a man loves another, and that such is the way of His love. He has tasted death, we say, not for all men only, but for every man. We even dare to say for *me ;* who "loved me, and gave Himself for me." Nay, He goes even further than this Himself, calling us friends, and claiming that dear relationship with us. "The servant knoweth not what his lord doeth; but I have called you friends." He even goes beyond this, promising a friendship so particular and personal that it shall be a kind of secret or cipher of mutual understanding open to no other—a new white stone given by his King, " and in the stone a new name written, which no man knoweth saving he that receiveth it." (*H. Bushnell, D.D.*)   *The earnest touch :*—How many feel the reality of a personal relation to Jesus? How many consciously recognize that their lives are implicated with His life? 1. Of some, of many, it may be said that they touch Jesus with their respect. No doubt the religion of Christ is respected. Christianity is at least a respectable institution. Nevertheless, all this respect is not like that touch which was given in the earnest purpose of faith and need. II. There are those who touch Jesus with their opinions. But, held as mere opinions, their intellectual validity gives us no real contact with the Saviour. We may actually be what we claim to be, exclusive possessors and vigilant guardians of orthodoxy, and yet be far from Him. The essential thing is not what we think about Him, but what He Himself, in His per-sonal relations, in His healing, life-giving power, is to us. III. Again, there are those who seek to touch Jesus through sacraments and ceremonies. The idea of the woman appears to have been of this kind. She thought, " If I may but touch His garment, I shall be whole"; whereas we know that the virtue went out of Him. IV. There are those who touch Jesus timidly and fitfully. Their communion with Him is felt only in impulses of intermittent enthusiasm or seasons of excitement, or it is held as a secret of which they are ashamed. We must, indeed, respect the modesty of sincere faith, the sacred reticence that guards the deepest and truest feelings of the heart. We know that religious emotion may evaporate in words, and that sterling principle may be less demonstrative than the noisy ring of cant.

But, notwithstanding all imperfections, he who has really touched Jesus will in some way make the secret manifest, not in the mere profession of the lips, but in the confession of the life. (*E. H. Chapin, D.D.*)   *Who touched Me?*—I. THERE IS GREAT DIFFERENCE BETWEEN THRONGING AND PRESSING CHRIST, AND TOUCHING HIM, WITH FAITH.   II. SIMPLE FAITH IN CHRIST IS ALL WHICH IS NECESSARY TO SALVATION. III. THERE ARE PREPARATIVES FOR FAITH.   It may be said, "If believing in Christ be such a simple and easy thing, why can I not believe at once, and be saved?   I have tried to believe in Christ, but hitherto without success."   There are preparatives for faith.   Yes, as there are preparatives for cure, and healing, and rescue, so there are preparatives for faith.   Preparatives for cure and healing are being sick, or wounded, and feeling the need of remedies.   So the woman in the text had preparatives for faith in Christ by twelve years' experience of fruitless help from physicians.   Hope deferred had made her heart sick; she saw her property melt away; one new physician had encouraged her to expect from Him a cure; and she was sinking into the grave.   These were the preparatives with her for saving faith. So that we may say, in general, that the preparatives for faith are, a deep conviction that Christ alone can help us, and a persuasion that He must save us or we perish.   IV. THIS WOMAN AFFORDS US A STRIKING ILLUSTRATION OF OUR DUTY TO COME TO CHRIST, WITHOUT WAITING FOR HIM TO COME TO US.   V. SALVATION FOLLOWS INSTANTANEOUSLY UPON BELIEVING IN CHRIST.   VI. THERE IS NOTHING WHICH CHRIST SEEMS TO LOVE SO MUCH AS FAITH IN HIM.   (*N. Adams, D.D.*)   *The throng and the touch:*—The woman reached out her hand and touched the Saviour's garment.   What was it that moved her hand?   She believed.   But in what did she believe?   Not in herself, not in the motion of her arm, not that she was doing anything that was an equivalent for the cure, or would purchase it; nor yet did she believe that by standing aloof and waiting awhile till she was partly restored, made stronger or more presentable, by some skill of her own, she should be more likely to get the benefit desired; nor had she any theory whatever about the method in which the curative power was to take effect.   You do not find in her clear and urgent sense of need that strange inverting of all reason that we so often see in men when they hesitate about coming to seek heavenly grace in Christ's Church, pleading that they are "not good enough," not strong enough, healthful enough, to be blessed by it.   The soldier, after the battle, wounded and sick, bloodstained and feverish, creeps along the hot and dusty road, longing only to die under the old home-tree, and under the breath of a mother's lips.   He comes to a hospital, and sees it written over the door, "Whosoever will, let him come."   Does he creep back, pleading that he is not well enough to go in and be healed?   What, then, *did* the woman believe?   She believed that she was to receive something, a real blessing, from Christ.   This was what distinguished her, in her humility and obscurity, from the sentimental crowd around her.   This was that in her which was not in them.   Most graphic history of how many hearts!   She believed that she could have that new life by a touch.   The reaching out of her hand was an expression of that faith.   Another signal might probably have done just as well.   In other cases a prayer was as effectual.   But there must have been two things: the faith that she should receive the benefit, and some act to embody that faith and bring the benefit home.   With faith, action.   (*Bp. F. D. Huntington.*)   *Various touches:*—1. There is the unbeliever's "touch," like the impious touch of the unhallowed hands of the soldiers who nailed the Saviour to the cross of Calvary.   How many are there that rudely and profanely handle the Person of the Lord Jesus Christ: they cannot leave Him alone: yet even while they "touch" Him, they only so "touch" Him as to bring judgment and condemnation upon their own souls, because the "touch" is the sacrilegious touch of unbelief.   The Philistines were bold enough to touch the ark, but they found there was death in the touch.   2. Then again, there is the cold "touch" of the critic.   He is not profane: he is not irreverent: he is simply critical.   The character of Christ is the object in which they are performing their experiments.   3. Then again, there is the fashionable "touch," which is much more common.   Those who give this "touch" to our Lord are to be found in all our churches and places of worship, not unfrequently, probably once in a week; they have got their tribute to pay, and they pay it.   Society expects it of them.   4. Then there is the formalists' "touch," where the "touch" is everything, but the Touched nothing!   What is the most proper way of saluting Him whom you recognize as your Saviour?   How are you best to arrest His attention?   Form, form, form, from beginning to end.   5. There is one way in which a larger number of persons seem to "touch" Him without receiving any help than in

any other. It is the "touch" of indifference. There are many people who are
no critics: they won't give themselves the trouble for that. They will not be
unbelievers: they will not be at the pains to be infidels. These, then, my dear
friends, are some of the different ways in which we may "touch" Christ, and yet
get no healing benefit. We should ask ourselves, How are we to "touch" with
good effect? Again, there may be difficulties in our way: but few of us have
such difficulties as that poor woman. The very nature of her disease was one
which made her shrink back from anything like publicity. She might have waited
until He was not surrounded by a crowd—waited for a more favourable opportunity.
She says to herself, "I am going to be healed;" she does not say, "I am going to
try." How often do we hear that word "try." There are two little words beginning
with "TR:" the one is "TRUST," and the other is "TRY." I wish we were a little
tender of the first, and less of the second. So, through the crowd she makes her
way, draws near, stretches out her hand, and "she touched Him." And now we
have a blessed opening up of the inner life of Christ, which seems to bring Him
wondrously near to us. It is this: amidst all the subjects that occupied His mind,
there cannot proceed from Him the very slenderest favour to any of the creatures
whom He has made, but He is sensible of it. The reception of grace shall be a
mutual thing—a thing involving reciprocal consciousness, consciousness on our
part of our approach; consciousness on His part that we are approaching: consciousness on our part of our stretching out the hand of faith; consciousness on
His part of the flowing of the current of His own Divine healing. There shall be
no blessing stolen from an unconscious God. We shall not get it from Him when
He is asleep. We will not get it from Him when His attention is fixed upon anything else. It is when His own blessed God-consciousness comes into contact with
our human sense of need that the miracle of grace shall be performed. Is it not a
wonderful thing He can think of us!—that, while He is giving us blessings every
moment, He nevertheless gives every blessing consciously? How near this brings
God to us! (*W. H. Aitken, M.A.*) *The touch:*—I. Look at THE PATIENT. 1.
Her courage. She was a woman who had suffered from a very grievous malady,
which had drained away her life. Her constitution had been sapped and undermined, and her very existence had become one of constant suffering and weakness;
and yet what courage and spirit she displayed. She was ready to go through fire
and through water to obtain health. 2. Note also her resolute determination. She
would die hard, if die she must. She would not resign herself to the inevitable till
she had used every effort to preserve life and to regain health. It is a hopeful sign,
a gracious token, when there is a determination wrought in men that, if saved they
can be, saved they will be. 3. I admire also this woman's marvellous hopefulness.
She still believes that she can be cured. She ought to have given up the idea long
ago according to the ordinary processes of reasoning; for generally we put several
instances together, and from these several instances we deduce a certain inference.
Now, she might have put the many physicians together, and their many failures,
and have rationally inferred that her case was past hope. II. THE DIFFICULTIES
OF THIS WOMAN'S FAITH. They must be weighed in order to show its strength.
The difficulties of her faith must have been as follows: 1. She could hardly forget
that the disease was in itself incurable, and that she had long suffered from it. 2.
And then again she had endured frequent disappointments; and all these must
have supplied her with terrible reasons for doubting. Yet she was not dismayed:
her faith rose superior to her bitter experience, and she believed in the Lord. 3.
There was also another difficulty in her way, and that was, her vivid sense of her
own unworthiness. 4. I do not know whether the other difficulty did occur to her
at all, but it would to me, namely, that she had now no money. 5. Perhaps the
worst difficulty of all was her extreme sickness at that time. We read that she
was nothing better, but rather grew the worse. III. THE VANISHING POINT OF ALL
HER DIFFICULTIES. We read of her first that she had heard of Jesus. It is
Mark who tells us that, "When she had heard of Jesus." "Faith cometh
by hearing." The point to notice most distinctly is this. The poor woman
believed that the faintest contact with Christ would heal her. Notice the
words of my text: "If I may touch but His clothes." It is not, "If I may
but touch His clothes"—no, the point does not lie in the touch; it lies in what
was touched. Splendid faith! It was not more than Christ deserved, but yet it
was remarkable. It was a kind of faith which I desire to possess abundantly.
The slenderest contact with Christ healed the body, and will heal the soul; ay, the
faintest communication. Do but become united to Jesus, and the blessed work

is done. IV. HER GRAND SUCCESS. Let me remind you again, however, of how she gained her end. She gave to the Lord Jesus an intentional and voluntary touch. Yet note that she was not healed by a contact with the Lord or with His garment against her will : she was not pushed against Him accidentally, but the touch was active and not merely passive. And now see her grand success; she no sooner touched than she was healed; in a moment, swift as electricity, the touch was given, the contact was made, the fountain of her blood was dried up, and health beamed in her face immediately. Immediate salvation! I heard a person say the other day that he had heard of immediate conversion, but he did not know what to make of it. Now, herein is a marvellous thing, for such cases are common enough among us. In every case spiritual quickening must be instantaneous. However long the preparatory process may be, there must be a time in which the dead soul begins to live. There may be cases in which a blessing comes to a man and he is scarcely aware of it, but this woman knew that she was saved; she felt in herself that she was whole of her plague. She had next the assurance from Christ Himself that it was so, but she did not obtain that assurance till she had made an open confession. (*C. H. Spurgeon.*) *Faith rewarded:*—I. CONSIDER WHAT THIS SUFFERER SAID WITHIN HERSELF (Matt. ix. 21). 1. As displaying ignorance of the true nature of Christ. Impossible then to have the clear and distinct ideas that we may now. 2. As displaying not only ignorance, but error, along with truth. 3. Was her faith, then, a foolish credulity? Not at all. She knew the wonders He had wrought on others, and responded to the goodness and truth His language and demeanour expressed; and on this convincing evidence she trusted Jesus, and was healed. II. CONSIDER THIS FEELING TOWARDS CHRIST AS FINDING RECOGNITION WIDER THAN THE CHRISTIAN CHURCH. The world finds healing in the slightest contact with Christ. How vast the number, outside avowed followers of Christ, who crowd Christian sanctuaries Sunday after Sunday, with a more or less explicit conviction that it is good to be there. III. REMEMBER THAT CHRIST CALLS US, BEYOND SLIGHT CONTACT, TO THE CLOSEST UNION WITH HIMSELF. This turning of humanity to Christ is like the turning of flowers towards the sun, their life-giver. It exhibits a true and healthy impulse; but how many forget that it is but the first step of what should be a close and continual approach to Him! There is healing in His slightest touch, but what in a living union with Him who died that we might live for ever! (*T. M. Herbert, M.A.*) *The woman healed by a touch:*—1. A disorder which was endured. (1) The disorder was unavoidably marked by much and painful privation. (2) The disorder was long-continued and inveterate. (3) The disorder had been aggravated by bitter disappointment. 2. The remedy which was resorted to. (1) Observe the Being to whom the application was made. (2) The spirit by which the application was distinguished. (*a*) There was a display of confidence. (*b*) There was the spirit of humility. 3. The blessing which was obtained. (1) The communication of the blessing of healing was immediate. (2) The communication of the blessing was free. (3) The communication of the blessing was kind. (*Preachers' Treasury.*) *Cured at last:*—I. Consider, therefore, concerning this woman, WHAT SHE HAD DONE. She had been literally dying for twelve years. 1. She had resolved not to die if a cure could be had. She was evidently a woman of great determination and hopefulness. Insensibility has seized upon many, and a proud conceit : they are full of sin, and yet they talk of self-righteousness. No doubt some are held back from such action by the freezing power of despair. They have reached the conclusion that there is no hope for them. Alas! many have never come to this gracious resolution, because they cherish a vain hope, and are misled by an idle dream. They fancy that salvation will come to them without their seeking it. 2. Let us next note, that this woman, having made her resolve, adopted the likeliest means she could think of. Physicians are men set apart on purpose to deal with human maladies; therefore she went to the physicians. No doubt she met with some who boasted that they could heal her complaint at once. They began by saying, "You have tried So-and-so, but he is a mere quack; mine is a scientific remedy." Many pretenders to new revelations are abroad, but they are physicians of no value. 3. This woman, in the next place, having resolved not to die if cure could be had, and having adopted the likeliest means, persevered in the use of those means. Have you been to Doctor Ceremony? He is, at this time, the fashionable doctor. 4. But this woman not only thus tried the most likely means, and persevered in the use of them, but she also spent all her substance over it. Thus do men waste their thought, their care, their prayer, their agony, over that which is as nothing: they spend their money for that which is not bread. The price of wisdom is above rubies. If we had mines of gold, we might profitably barter them for the salvation of our souls. II. We have seen what the woman had done; now let us think of WHAT HAD COME OF IT. We are told that she had suffered many things of many physicians. 1. That was her sole reward for trusting and spending: she had not been relieved, much less healed; but she had suffered. She had endured much additional suffering through seeking a cure. Efforts after salvation made in your own strength act like the struggles of a drowning man, which sink the more surely. 2. There has been this peculiarly poignant pang about it all, that you are nothing bettered. 3. We read of this woman, that though she suffered much, she was nothing better, but rather grew worse. You are becoming more careless, more dubious than you once were. You have lost much of your former sensitiveness. You are doing certain things now that would have startled you years ago, and you are leaving certain matters undone which once you would have thought essential. 4. This is a sad, sad case! As a climax of it all, the heroine of our story had now spent all that she had. Welcome, brother! Now you are ready for Jesus. When all your own virtue has gone out of you, then shall you seek and find that virtue which goeth out of Him. III. This brings to our notice, in the third place, WHAT THIS WOMAN DID AT LAST. 1. Note well she resolved to trust in Jesus in sheer despair of doing anything else. 2. After all, this was the simplest and easiest thing that she could do. Touch Jesus. 3. Not only was this the simplest and easiest thing for the poor afflicted one, but certainly it was the freest and most gracious. There was not a penny to pay. 4. This was the quietest thing for her to do. She said nothing. She did not cry aloud like the blind men. 5. This is the only effectual thing. Touch Jesus, and salvation is yours at once. Simple as faith is, it is never-failing. IV. And now, poor convicted sinner! here comes the driving home of the nail. Do THOU AS THIS WOMAN DID. (*C. H. Spurgeon.*)   *The woman who touched:*—I. MEN'S FAILURES. Human physicians could not heal. Sin incurable by self. II. A SUPERSTITIOUS FAITH. Faith may grow in strange places. III. AN ACTUAL TOUCH. We want the same living connection with Christ, and it is possible still. IV. IMMEDIATE HELP. No need to wait long; prayer answered often sooner than we expect. V. A TREMBLER IN HIDING. Glad to have blessing from Christ, but fearing to reveal how obtained. VI. PUBLIC ACKNOWLEDGMENT. Christ requires this. We must bear witness, &c. Free men. VII. INDIVIDUAL RECOGNITION. Christ will not pass us in a crowd. VIII. GENEROUS ENCOURAGEMENT. He might have called her "rude" or "foolish." Not so. He calls her "daughter." IX. SPIRITUAL ENLIGHTENMENT. It was not any power lying in the touching of My garment; it was thy faith that saved thee. Conclusion: The only one in the crowd blessed. Why? Lack of faith, not lack of need. How near we may be to Christ, and yet not find true spiritual healing or renewal. (*T. Sherlock, B.A.*)   *The healing of Veronica:*—Who is this wan, feeble woman that struggles through the swaying crowd, and watches her opportunity to stoop and lay her hand on the Healer's garment? This, say the Evangelists, is a poor woman afflicted for twelve years with a disorder, a hæmorrhage, which was then held to warrant divorce—a disorder which rendered her "unclean" in the eyes of the law, so that she could neither enter temple nor synagogue. This, says Eusebius, was Veronica, a woman of wealth and repute, who dwelt in Cæsarea Philippi, at the northernmost extremity of the Holy Land, hard by the main source of the river Jordan, in a lonely valley at the foot of Hermon. "I, Eusebius, have seen her house in that city. And to this day [some three centuries after the miracle], before the gate of her house, on a lofty block of stone, there stands a brazen sculpture; on the one side, a woman drops on her bended knees, with hands outstretched as in supplication; and, opposite to her, stands a man, erect and tall, becomingly clad in a mantle, who extends His hand to the suppliant. At her feet there springs a certain strange plant, which rises as high as the hem of her garment; it is held to be an antidote to all forms of disease. This they say, is a statue of Jesus Christ." Eusebius goes on to argue the probability that Veronica caused it to be erected, since it was a custom of the Gentiles to erect statues to those who had healed them; and Cæsarea Philippi being, not a Jewish, but a Phœnician city, mainly inhabited by Greeks, we have every reason to believe that Veronica herself was a Gentile. But whoever she was, and whencesoever she came, she had heard of Jesus, and conceived a hope that He would heal her. A woman who had spent all that she had, only to suffer more from her doctors than from her disease, in her despair would be very apt to betake herself to One who at least demanded no fee, and who was reported to have wrought many marvellous cures. . . . But why does she select the hem, or border, of His garment? Perhaps because in her diffidence she thought herself unworthy to do more. Perhaps because in her faith she thought even this would be enough. Perhaps simply because she thought the border of His garment might be most easily touched without attracting attention. . . . Beyond a doubt, her faith, though genuine, was darkened by superstition. In His grace the Lord Jesus corrects and enlarges her conception; He disentangles the truth in it from the error. But mark how He does it, how patiently, how gradually. At first it is her superstition, rather than her faith, which is confirmed. . . . But why did He not let the poor woman creep quietly away with her boon? Why compel her to tell her sad story of womanly pain and suffering in so many ears? Simply because He loves her too well to let her go away with half a blessing. Simply that He may teach her that it is her faith, and not, as she thought, her mere touch, which has saved her. It is a pathetic story, a story—1. Full of hope and gracious incentive for all who believe, however weak their faith may be. 2. Conveying also a lesson of warning. Many thronged and pressed upon Christ; many touched His clothes; yet only one touched Him. 3. Teaching also a lesson of invitation. According to the Hebrew law she was impure, and made all she touched impure; but she ventured to touch Jesus, and, instead of making Him unclean, He makes her clean and whole. Now, whatever our sins may have been, we can hardly be farther from hope than she. And however faintly we may turn to Christ, however ignorantly, we can hardly do less than she who hid herself in the darkness and the crowd, and laid trembling fingers on the edge of His garment, to see what would come of that. Jesus did not know her or her story—did not know even that it was she who had touched Him. Yet she was healed. Why? Because His will is always for the health and salvation of men. Virtue is stored up in Him, and flows forth from Him at every touch of faith. (*S. Cox, D.D.*)

THE WOMAN WHO CAME BEHIND HIM IN THE CROWD.

Near Him she stole, rank after rank;
    She feared approach too loud;
She touched His garments' hem, and shrank
    Back in the sheltering crowd.

A shame-faced gladness thrills her frame:
    Her twelve years' fainting prayer
Is heard at last; she is the same
    As other women there.

She hears His voice; He looks about;
    Ah! is it kind or good
To drag her secret sorrow out
    Before that multitude?

The eyes of men she dares not meet—
    On her they straight must fall:
Forward she sped, and at His feet
    Fell down, and told Him all.

His presence makes a holy place;
    No alien eyes are there;
Her shrinking shame finds god-like grace,
    The covert of its care.

"Daughter," He said, "be of good cheer;
    Thy faith hath made thee whole";
With plenteous love, not healing mere,
    He would content her soul. (*G. MacDonald.*)

Glimpses of Jesus:—I. The sensitiveness of Christ. "Who touched Me?" Ruskin has said truly, "We are only human in so far as we are sensitive." II. The yearning of Christ for nearer personal fellowship with men. The question must be interpreted by the result. Evidently what He desired was to bring the woman nearer, and to establish more direct and abiding relationship between her and Himself. III. THE JOY OF CHRIST IN CONFERRING BENEFITS UPON HUMAN SOULS. Mark—1. The loving address—" daughter." 2. The comfortable words—" Thy faith hath made thee whole." 3. The gracious dismissal—" Go in peace." Learn—1. That we should come to Christ in our need. 2. That we should commune with Him with the greatest freedom and openness. 3. That we should confess gladly and gratefully before men all the good we have received at His hands. 4. That we should comply with all His solicitings, and ever seek nearer and dearer fellowship with Him as our Saviour and our God. (*W. Forsyth, M.A.*) *The Healer:*—We have to trace the history of a touch. Let us inquire—I. WHY THIS TOUCH ATTRACTED THE PARTICULAR ATTENTION OF THE SAVIOUR? 1. It was the touch of a sufferer whose case before that touch had been desperate. 2. It was the touch of faith. 3. It was a touch that wrought an instant and perfect cure. II. WHY DID THE SAVIOUR ASK THE QUESTION, " Who touched Me ? " This excited the wonder of the disciples. 1. Not from ignorance. 2. Not from exhaustion. 3. Not from displeasure. But (1) To show that He marks the difference between thronging and touching Him. (" Many," says Ambrose, " press upon Christ, in outward ordinances, but believers touch Him ; it is by faith that He is touched, so as to have virtue from Him.") (2) To enlighten and invigorate the faith of her who touched Him. (3) To assert His right to be glorified for what He has done. 4. That the interview might issue in the bestowment of His benediction. (*C. Stanford, D.D.*)

> Oh, dost Thou ask who touched Thy garment? Oh,
> Sweet Master, hast Thou not turned back and viewed
> How round Thee throng and press the multitude?
> " Not all who throng and press for Mine I know ;
> But trembling, falling, one now Mine draws near,
> To tell of garment touched and ended woe,
> The things she sought not, nor has heard, to hear ;
> Things present, things to come, her deeds revealing,
> The fount of sin whose flowing none may stay,
> Till breaks on Calvary the Fount of Healing,
> All wounds to staunch, all tears to wipe away.
> This Flesh, My garment, feels but faith's right hand ;
> Ah : many near Its hem, unhealed will stand ! " (*A. M. Morgan.*)

Virtue is gone out of Me :—Virtue at one time meant strength. Now it is used to denote purity. Jesus meant that power had gone out from Him. It is worth while to note that virtue cannot leave one and pass to another without a loss to the giver. There can be little doubt that the sacred body of Jesus had to suffer for being the medium of healing, and that very costly was the honour of being the shrine of Divinity. I. Virtue is gone out of Me to ONE WHO FAILED TO GET HELP ELSEWHERE. As a last resource, she came and tried Jesus. Is she not a picture of many among us, who try everything but the right thing, and also go anywhere rather than to the Saviour ? There is Dr. Merryman. He has a very large practice. He is the most popular of all the soul doctors, and has an amazingly large connection among young people. If some one goes to him complaining of a sad heart, he will prescribe a change, lively society, the theatre, dancing, &c. There is another of these impudent quacks. I mean Dr. Devotee, who, like the famous Dr. Merryman, has a large number of patients, but they are generally rather older ; indeed, many of them have been under Merryman till they were tired out; then they have gone over to the other side of the way to try if Devotee could help them. If you go into his waiting room, you will see some who have had disappointments, blighted affections, &c. When you are shown into his room, you notice how very grave he is—none of the flippancy of the other. He does not approve of Merryman's prescriptions. Fasting and prayer and seclusion are his remedies. There is yet another of these medical gentlemen you must look in upon. This is where Dr. Apathy lives. He is the favourite doctor among men of business and commerce. They will tell you, " Merryman is all very well for the youngsters, and Devotee suits the women, but for a sensible practical man, commend me to Apathy. Bless you, what I suffered before I went to him ! I could not sleep at nights for thinking I might lose my soul. Really business began to suffer ; so I went to him, and he soon put me to rights. When I told him my symptoms, he said, ' I understand you, my dear fellow, you need a sedative. Stick to your newspaper, and give up all that nonsense about family prayer.'" II. Virtue has gone out of Me to ONE WHO HAS OVERCOME GREAT DIFFICULTIES. This poor woman must have found it very difficult to come to Christ, for at least two reasons. 1. She was ceremoniously unclean. And so are we. Yet we should not let this deter us. 2. There was the difficulty of the crowd. The people thronged Him; and no wonder, for He was on His way to heal the ruler's daughter. The crowd was between her and the Lord. III. Virtue has gone out of Me to ONE WHO HAS FAITH. Do not wait till you have altered this, or improved that; all that can be done afterwards. IV. Virtue is gone out of Me to one WHO MUST CONFESS THE TRUTH. (*J. Champness.*) *The cost of service:*—I. IN NATURE, WE HAVE WHAT HAS LATELY BEEN TERMED THE PERSISTENCE, OR CONSERVATION OF FORCE. II. THIS LAW OF COST IS ALSO ECONOMIC LAW. In agriculture, what we call the bounty of nature, the gift outright, comes a long way short of what is needed even for merest comfort. The spontaneous products of nature are scanty. So of all industry and useful art. To begin with, there is the cost of raw material, come whence it may, from earth, or sea, or air. Houses, and their furnishing, tax the quarries, the clay-yards and the forests. Our wardrobes suggest cotton-fields, flax-fields, silkworms, flocks of sheep, herds of cattle, birds of the air, wild animals of sea and land, from pole to pole. Even wigwams and bearskins are no gratuities. Every coarsest want supplied, every adornment, every luxury, means work. Good things, fine things, cost. III. THIS LAW OF COST IS ALSO MENTAL LAW. Mind is very much more than mere passive capacity; it is vital, organizing force. Learning, rightly apprehended, is not mere passive reception, as of water into a cistern, bringing with it all the accidents and impurities of roof or aqueduct. It is water in oak, or elm, making its way up through living tissue, filtered as it ascends, shaking out its leafy banner, hardening into toughest fibre. IV. BUT THIS LAW OF COST IS PRE-EMINENTLY SPIRITUAL LAW. The so-called passive virtues either are not virtues, or are not passive. Humility, patience, self-denial, and the forgiveness of injuries, are battles and victories. So it has been, and so it shall be, in essence, to the end. Redemption cost infinitely in eternity, and must cost in time. Human history almost began with martyrdom. The blood of righteous Abel inaugurated the stern economy. Scarcely a people have ever been evangelized without the baptism of blood. Scarcely a man has ever been signally useful without the baptism of some great sorrow. We learn in suffering what we teach in song. (*R. D. Hitchcock, D.D.*) *Real contact with Jesus: a sacramental meditation:*—I. First, then, IN THE USE OF ALL MEANS AND ORDINANCES LET IT BE OUR CHIEF AIM AND OBJECT TO COME INTO PERSONAL CONTACT WITH THE LORD JESUS CHRIST. 1. Note, first, she felt that it was of no use being in the crowd, of no use to be in the same street with Christ, or near to the place where Christ was, but she must get at Him; she must touch Him. She touched Him, you will notice, under many difficulties. There was a great crowd. It is very easy to kneel down to pray, but not so easy to reach Christ in prayer. 2. Observe, again, that this woman touched Jesus very secretly. Beloved, that is not always the nearest fellowship with Christ of which we talk the most. Deep waters are still. Nathaniel retired to the shade that no one might see him, but Jesus saw him and marked his prayer, and He will see thee in the crowd and in the dark, and not withhold His blessing. 3. This woman also came into contact with Christ under a very deep sense of unworthiness. 4. Notice, once again, that this woman touched the Master very tremblingly, and it was only a hurried touch, but still it was the touch of faith. II. THE WOMAN IN THE CROWD DID TOUCH JESUS, AND, HAVING DONE SO, SHE RECEIVED VIRTUE FROM HIM. In Christ there is healing for all spiritual diseases. There is a speedy healing. There is in Christ a sufficient healing, though your diseases should be multiplied beyond all bounds. III. And now the last point is—and I will not detain you longer upon it—IF SOMEBODY SHALL TOUCH JESUS, THE LORD WILL KNOW IT. Now, as Jesus knows of your salvation, He wishes other people to know it. (*C. H. Spurgeon.*) *She was not hid:*—I. First, then, we say concerning this woman, that HER HIDING SEEMED VERY EXCUSABLE. I have already said that if, in any instance, a cure might have been concealed, this was one; and it was so for many reasons. 1. Because of this woman's natural timidity, and because of the nature of her malady. 2. In addition to this, remember that the Saviour did not court publicity. He laid no injunction upon those whom He healed that they should tell every one of the marvel. 3. There was another reason why she might have thought she need not make a public confession, and that was, that the Saviour was at that time exceedingly occupied. 4.

Excuse might also have been found for the healed woman in the fact, that her cure would make itself known by its results. When she reached home everybody would see that she was quite another person ; and when they asked how it came to pass, she could tell them all about it. 5. Another pretext might have served this woman, if she desired an excuse. She might truthfully have said, " It is evident that an open confession is not essential to my cure, for I am cured." II. Secondly, HER HIDING WAS NOT PERMITTED BY THE SAVIOUR. Her being brought out had the best of consequences. 1. For, first, an open confession on her part was needful in reference to the Lord's glory. Beloved, the miracles of Christ were the seals which God gave to His mission. If the wonders which He wrought were not made known, the seals of His mission would have been concealed, and so would have lost much of their effect. If this woman concealed her cure others might do the same ; and if they all did it, then Christ's commission would have no visible endorsement from the Lord God. 2. Further, remember that our Lord's miracles were illustrative of His teaching. 3. But the confession had to be made for the sake of others. Do any of you wish to live unto yourselves? If you do, you need saving from selfishness. 4. Do you not think that her public declaration was required for the good of our Lord's disciples? When they heard her story, did they not treasure it up, and speak of it to one another in after days, and thereby strengthen each other's faith? 5. But especially she had to do this for her own good. The Saviour had designs of love in bringing this poor trembler forward before all the people. By this He saved her from a host of fears which would have haunted her. She had been a very timid and trembling woman, but now she would shake off all improper timidity. I have known many persons cured of timidity by coming forward to confess Christ. Our Lord also gave her an increased blessing after her confession. He gave her clearly to know her relationship to Him. He said, " Daughter! " Next notice that He gave a commendation to her faith—" Thy faith hath made thee whole." Then the Lord gave her a word of precious quieting. He said, " Go in peace." As much as to say : Do not stop in this crowd, to be pushed about or stared at, but go home in quiet. III. Thus I have already reached my last point : YOUR HIDING OUGHT TO BE ENDED. 1. Do you not think you owe something to the Church of God, which kept the gospel alive in the world for you to hear? 2. May I be permitted also to say, I think you owe something to the minister who led you to Jesus? 3. Besides, you owe it to yourselves. Are you going to be mere bats, fluttering out when none will observe you, and hiding from the light? Are you going to be like mice, which only come out at night to nibble in the pantry? Quit yourselves like men ! 4. You owe it to your family. You should tell your household what grace has done for you. 5. Do you not think you owe it to your neighbours to show your colours? 6. Now let me hear some of your objections, and answer them. I hope I have been answering them all through my sermon. Here is one. " Well, you know, I am such an insignificant person. It cannot make any difference what I do." Yes, and this woman was a very insignificant person—only a woman ! God thinks much of the lowly : you must not talk so. Do not excuse yourselves through pretended humility. " But coming out and joining a Church, and all that, is such an ordeal." So it may be. In this woman's case, it was a far greater ordeal than it can be to you. Jesus does not excuse one of his healed ones from owning the work of His grace. A dear lady, who has long since gone to glory, was once an honoured member of this Church : it was Lady Burgoyne, and when she wished to unite with us she said to me, " Dear sir, I cannot go before the Church. It is more than I can manage to make a confession of Christ before the members." I told her that we could make no exception for anybody, and especially not for her, who was so well established in the faith that she could surely answer a few questions before those who were brethren and sisters in the Lord. She came bravely, and spoke most sweetly for her Lord. Some of you may remember her, with her sweet countenance, and venerable bearing. When she had owned her Lord, she put both her hands on mine, and said emphatically, " With all my heart I thank you for this ; I shall never be ashamed of Christ now. When aristocratic friends call upon me I will speak to them of my Lord." She did so constantly. You never found her slow to introduce the gospel, whoever might be with her. She frequently said to me, " Oh, what a training that was for me ! I might have been a timid one all my days if I had not made that confession before the Church." Now I say to you, if it be an ordeal, undergo it for Christ's sake. " Alas ! " says one, " I could not tell of what the Lord has done for me, because mine is such a sorrowful story." Was it not so with this woman? " I have so little to tell," says one. That is a good reason why you should tell it, for it will be all the easier for you to do so. He that has little to tell should tell it straight away. "But perhaps people may not believe me." Did I tell you that you were to make them believe you? Is that your business? "Ah!" says one, "but suppose after I had confessed Christ I should become as bad as ever." Suppose that this woman had supposed such a sad thing, and had said, "O Lord, I cannot confess that Thou hast healed me, for I do not know how I may be in six months' time." She was not so mistrustful. (*Ibid.*)   *Grasping the* "*hem*":—Dr. Simpson on his death-bed told a friend that he awaited his great change with the contented confidence of a little child. As another friend said to him that he might, as John at the last supper, lean his head on the breast of Christ, the doctor made answer, "I fear I cannot do that, but I think I have grasped hold of the hem of His garment." (*Dr. Koenig's Life of Dr. Simpson.*)   *The touch of faith*:—A lady was being shown through a corn mill, worked by a river which ran close by the walls. But all the wheels were in silent inaction. "Where is the power?" she asked. She was shown a handle, and told to press upon it. She did, and the mighty force was instantly turned on, the wheels moved, and the place was alive with activity. The power of God moves in upon us at the touch of faith. (*Methodist Times.*)

Vers. 49–56. **Thy daughter is dead.**—*Christian consolation under bereavement by death*:—Now the great grounds of Christian comfort in times of bereavement are two. One relates to those you have lost; the other relates to yourselves. The first is, that those who have died in Christ have made a blessed and happy change in leaving this world for that where they are now. And the second is, that if you and they be both united to Christ, you have the confident assurance that you shall meet again. And, indeed, brethren, when we think of the first of these, we are constrained to feel and lament our want of faith. No truth can be plainer than that heaven is better than earth—a hundred things go to prove that; but it is only now and then that we are lifted up to a height of spiritual insight and fervour in which we truly feel that it is so. Strong convictions, large but vague, are often indicated by little things; just as floating straws show the direction of a great wind. And there is one little peculiarity in our common way of speaking which shows our natural unbelief in the grand Christian doctrine, that to the believer "to die is gain." Speaking even of friends who, we most firmly believe, have fallen asleep in Jesus, you know we habitually speak of them as though they were objects of pity; we speak of our *poor* friend, our *poor* sister, our *poor* little child, that died. This is, doubtless, a manifestation of that curious inconsistency with which, I have already said, we think of the departed. Surely we should rather say "blessed", "happy"; for have they not gone from this world of sin and sorrow and anxiety into the land of holiness, peace, and rest? But there is another reason why we should not mourn unduly for the dead who die in the Lord, one that touches us who remain more nearly. It is this, that we hope to meet them again; we know that if our own death be that of the righteous, we shall certainly meet them again. They have left you in this world, and you will miss their kind advice, and their warm affection, and their earnest prayers; but death can neither drown remembrance nor quench love: and they are remembering you and waiting for you, and theirs will be the first voices to welcome you entering the golden city. Now, let me remind you, in concluding, that all this strong consolation belongs only to such as have believed in Christ, and as mourn the loss of Christian friends. And the two practical lessons from this thought are, that if we would not have death part us eternally from those dear to us, we ought first to make our own calling sure by God's grace, that we may not on the judgment day see them on the right hand of the throne, and ourselves cast out to perdition; and next, that we should care for the souls of those dear to us as well as for our own, lest upon that great day any such should accuse us of that neglect which ended in everlasting separation, saying that if we had warned them as we ought, they had not come to this end of woe! Do you sometimes think, as you sit by the warm winter-evening fireside, and hear the keen blast shake the windows, and howl mournfully through the leafless boughs, and as you look round on the cheerful scene within, with its warm light and its blazing fire, do you sometimes think then how, out in the dark of the winter night, the snow lies white or the rain plashes heavy above some dear one's grave; how the sharp blasts roar round the headstone that marks where such a one sleeps—sleeps cold, and motionless, and alone; and does it seem to you a hard thing and a sad thing that in that dreary melancholy of the grave the departed one of the family must lie and slumber, while the fire is blazing bright on the hearth of the old home, till it seems to you a natural thing to weep for the dead, condemned to that cold negation of all that is bright and cheering? And do you sometimes think, in the long beautiful twilights of summer—summer, with its green grass and its bright flowers —that surely it is a loss to those that are gone that *they* cannot see the softened evening light, nor breath the gentle air? but that in their cold and narrow bed they still must rest and moulder, knowing nothing of the sweet scenes that surround them; not seeing the daisies in the sunshine over them, nor feeling the soft breeze sighing through the grass that lies upon their breast? If you do these things, then remember that it is not the dead you loved that moulder in that grave; it is but the cast-off robe, the shattered cottage of clay, that is turning there to the dust; it is the weak fancy of erring humanity to dream that what in our friends we loved has part or portion there. Remember that dwelling above, in light and glory, they never miss the warmth of the winter evening fireside, or the calm of the evening in June. (*A. H. K. Boyd.*)   *Death and life:*—I. DEATH AND LIFE ARE TERMS WHICH HAVE A SPIRITUAL AS WELL AS A PHYSICAL MEANING. A dead man physically is not always truly dead, and a live man physically is not always truly alive. The first occasion on which the ominous words—life and death—were used ought to teach us the mystery hidden in these terms. In the Garden of Eden there was the tree of life, which could not be merely physical life, since Adam was alive before and after he had access to that tree. And there again was another tree, with which the sentence was coupled, " The day thou eatest thereof, thou shalt surely *die.*" Of that tree Adam ate, and so died—although physically he continued to live for nine hundred and thirty years. No one can have failed to notice how decidedly our Lord corrects the earthly, carnal, and limited ideas of the Jews in reference to the great mysteries of life and death. How often He used words which were beyond, aside from, and even against the common mode of speaking; not, surely, for the sake of singularity, but in order that he might recall and affirm the whole truth. When, *e.g.*, people were indulging in loud and formal lamentation over the death of the ruler's daughter—as if she were literally lost for ever—as if her death were death in the fullest sense—as if the separation of her soul and body were the saddest event which could befall her or her family; when our Master saw through, not only the obtrusive formality of this loud grief, but penetrated the false notions on which rested the deep grief of her parents and those who sincerely lamented with them, He bade them know that their lamentations were out of place, for that she was not dead, but asleep. And when they who were wailing for her laughed Him to scorn; and when they, too, who wept for real sorrow, were incredulous—He demonstrated the truth of His assertion, for " He took her by the hand, and the maid arose." II. DEATH, IN ITS POPULAR MEANING, IS BEST EXPRESSED BY THE TERM SLEEP. In giving to the separation of soul and body the title " sleep," Christ has disclosed to us the true doctrine of the resurrection of the body, together with a warning, and comfort, which must not pass without distinct notice. 1. The doctrine. The exact phraseology of the Creed teaches us with authority the evangelical truth that we shall rise again; but the lesson can be also learned in the fact that the body of the Jewish maiden— when deprived of the soul—slept. They who sleep, awake again; if the dead body be not dead, but asleep, that is to say, if the term " sleep" be the most accurate one which He who gave us speech could single out, to describe the fact of physical death, then no dogmatic statement, no decree of council, could more clearly affirm the fact of the resurrection of the body. 2. The warning. There is no power in sleep to change one's moral character; as we lie down, we rise up again when awake. Again, in sleep, though the body be motionless, the spirit is active. There are dreams that trouble, as well as those that please. 3. The comfort. Is it no comfort to be told that the friend you thought to be dead only sleeps? Is it not a perfect protection against over-much sorrow to receive the great mystery set forth here? There was a time when Christians took great consolation from this very truth, when it made them ready to die, and resigned to see those near them die at the call of God. Go look at the catacombs of Rome, and see in the records which those faithful caverns have preserved of the creed and life of our Christian forefathers—how the early Christians thought of death. The inscriptions are full of faith. Here a mother " sleeps in Jesus "—there a child " sleeps in Jesus '— husband, wife, and friend—they all " sleep "—there is no sign of death in the catacombs. Our martyred forefathers of the early Church may teach us how to live, to die, to bury, and to mourn for our dead. Our Master teaches us in the text that we are not to sorrow for the sainted dead as those who have no hope. They "sleep." They shall rise. (*Bishop W. H. Odenheimer.*) *The ruler's daughter raised to life :*—I. That sometimes while dealing with the Saviour the storm becomes darker than before. We cry for pardon, and feel a growing sense of guilt. We pray for sanctification, and the power of corruption seems to revive. We hope for deliverance, and our difficulties multiply. II. Let us never deem importunity in prayer troublesome. III. It is never too late to apply to the Lord. IV. The way to obtain present ease, and certain relief, is to exercise faith under every discouragement. How well are "Fear not" and "Believe only" coupled together! Our Saviour could have healed the child at a distance, and with a word; but He chooses to go "to the house of mourning"—to teach us to go there. A family in such a condition is a very affecting and improving object. We melt into pity as we see the emblems of death. The world loses its hold of our minds. "Weep not: she is not dead, but sleepeth." 1. He spake modestly. Another would have said, "Come; examine this patient; see, there are no remains of life in her—you will witness, before I begin, that there is nothing to aid my operations." But He would not magnify the action He was going to perform. He sought not His own glory. 2. He spake figuratively. Sleep is the term commonly, in the Scripture, applied to the death of all believers; and it is peculiarly just. Sleep is the pause of care—the parenthesis of human woe. 3. He spake in reference to His present intention. Instead of a burial she was going to be raised to life. 4. He said this also to try His hearers. Accordingly, it showed their disposition. Here we are led to note two things. First: How much more are men governed by their natural views and feelings than by the word of truth; and how easily are they befooled in Divine things by their sense and reason! Secondly: We observe that a serious state of mind is the best preparation for Divine truth. "A scorner," says Solomon, "seeketh knowledge, and findeth it not." After they had made a declaration, which they could not retract, concerning the certainty of her death, "He put them all out"; and, as the Resurrection and the Life, He "took her by the hand, and called, saying, Maid, arise," when, lo! the fountain of life is warmed, the blood begins to liquefy and flow, the pulse beats again; she breathes; she looks—"her spirit came again, and she arose straightway: and He commanded to give her meat." This order was to show—1. The reality of the miracle, by the use of her faculties. 2. It evinced the perfection of the miracle: she was not restored to the state in which she died—that was a state of sickness, in which food was rejected; but to the state she was in before her disease—a state of health and appetite. 3. It was also to mark the limitation of the miracle: nothing further was to be done preternaturally; but her life, which had been restored by extraordinary agency, was to be preserved, as before, by ordinary means. It also distinguished this miracle from that of the final resurrection. The resurrection will produce a spiritual body, requiring neither sleep nor food; but this damsel was raised only to a natural life, subject to the same infirmities as that of other people, and liable to die again. Let us conclude. 1. If our Saviour so amazed the spectators, and honoured Himself, by the revival of one body newly dead, what will it be when He shall come to be glorified in His saints, and to be admired in all them that believe; when He shall speak, and "all that are in the graves shall hear His voice, and shall come forth—they that have done good unto the resurrection of life; and they that have done evil unto the resurrection of damnation"! Again: It is worthy of remark that of the three persons whom our Lord raised from the dead, Lazarus was the loved and *only* brother of Martha and Mary; the young man was the *only* son of his mother; and the damsel the *only* daughter of Jairus: so touched is He with the feeling of our infirmities; so much regard does He show to relative affection. (*W. Jay.*) *Consolation for mourners :*—I. In the text we perceive A DEEP SORROW EXPRESSED— "They all wept and bewailed her." But, as we have said, where a bereaving providence is felt, the genuine expressions of sorrow will not be wanting, nor are they out of place. 1. This is natural. 2. To weep and bewail the loss of beloved relatives and friends is also consistent and affectionate. II. To THE CONSOLATORY IDEA OUR TEXT COMMUNICATES—"Weep not; she is not dead, but sleepeth." Many believers, through fear of death, are all their lives subject to bondage; but the consoling representation of our text strips it of all its terrors, for, surely, if we sleep, we do well. 1. Now the spirit is unconfined. 2. This is a consoling idea.

because in sleep bodily labour is suspended. 3. The idea in the text is consoling, because our sleeping friends will awake again. III. We now consider, thirdly, THE VALUABLE INSTRUCTION WHICH THIS SUBJECT SUPPLIES. 1. We may learn the necessity of faith in the Redeemer. Every spiritual blessing is promised alone to those who believe in the Saviour. 2. Our subject to-day teaches us the folly of an inordinate fear of death. 3. Once more, our subject reminds us of the duty of daily preparation for our approaching change. (*T. Gibson, M.A.*) *The Christian's death a sleep:*—First, character; secondly, comparison; and, thirdly, conclusion. I. We shall speak upon CHARACTER. It is entirely through the death and the resurrection of the Lord Jesus Christ that the death of the believer receives and presents so mild, so peaceful, so softened a character as sleep. II. We shall now consider the COMPARISON in the text, or the several striking resemblances between death and sleep, and how they beautifully describe the condition of departed saints; and—1. Sleep is exclusively applicable to the body, it does not appertain to the spirit; often while the body sleeps, the soul is conscious, and busily active in dreams of the most astonishing character. 2. Death and sleep have a marked resemblance. Sleep is certainly a type of death. Ovid, the Roman poet, said, " O fool, what is sleep but the image of cold death? " 3. Death, under the figure of sleep, represents a state of rest, a state of sweet repose. 4. Sleep is useful, is most profitable to the body. By sleep the powers of the body are strengthened, and refreshed, and fitted for the labours of the future day. 5. Sleep is absolutely essential. Who could live for any protracted period without sleep? 6. Sleep delightfully illustrates the prospect of restoration. We expect at lying down to rest to-night, to awake and to arise to-morrow morning. III. We proceed to the CONCLUSION, or the inferences which the living should draw from the state of the dead, and especially the happy dead. 1. Are you yet unrenewed, uuchanged by the Spirit of God? 2. Are you the children of a spiritual resurrection, passed from death to life, translated out of darkness into amazing light?—while we live here, let us live. 3. Let us act as believers in parting with believing friends. (*T. Sharp, M.A.*) *The daughter of Jairus:*—Subject: the delay of Christ in going to the house of Jairus, and allowing the child to die before He reached there. I. CHRIST'S MASTERLY INACTIVITY. II. HOW IT CAME TO PASS. III. WHAT GOOD IT DID. IV. PRACTICAL SUGGESTIONS. 1. If we really feel our need of Christ we shall not mind how, when, or where, we seek Him. 2. Christ could not take a walk without doing good and being sympathetically ready to do it. 3. Christ never felt any call amiss to Him. 4. This miracle teaches that Christ can love the youngest. 5. We cannot do better than closely imitate the manner, spirit, and method of Christ's working. (*R. H. Lovell.*) *The Master of Life:*—When the title which is here translated " Master " was in common use, it meant the master of a school. Using the word in its English sense, every man is more or less, in relation to one thing or another, a master; but in Christ alone does the term find its full and perfect realization. I. VIEW THESE WORDS AS ILLUSTRATED BY THE NARRATIVE TO WHICH THEY BELONG. Was it of no use to trouble the Master? II. VIEW THESE WORDS AS ILLUSTRATED IN THE HISTORY OF OUR OWN EXPERIENCE. " Trouble not the Master," cries the specious philosopher, the mocking secularist, the trivial worldling. Unbelief, Pride, Despondency, Indolence, all say, "Trouble not the Master." Test some of these objections. 1. " Trouble not the Master," for there is no real power in prayer. 2. For the help you ask is too great for Him to render. 3. For the help you ask for relates to matters too insignificant for His dignity to notice. 4. For you have no assurance of His love. 5. For this is not the right time for your supplication. Be deaf to every voice that bids you " trouble not the Master," and listen to the voice from heaven that is for ever saying, " Ye that make mention of the Lord, keep not silence, give Him no rest, till He establish, and till He make Jerusalem a praise in all the earth." (*C. Stanford, D.D.*) **Fear not, only believe.**—*Manly faith:*—This encouraging direction was spoken by Christ to a man in the very crisis of his acutest agony, and was so efficacious in its influence that it lifted its recipient at once to the highest rank among the heroes of a victorious and manly faith, the faith that (1) is persistent and triumphant in its contest with difficulties in the gravest perils of human experience; (2) Opens, and keeps open, the nature for evermore to the highest, holiest, and helpfullest; and (3) Eagerly avails itself of all contemporary life-interpreting facts. I. " Only believe." Yes, " only," but what an only! Put yourself in this man's position. " Only believe," meant for Jairus attempting the hardest task mortal man ever engaged in. II. Short as this sentence is, it is an ellipsis, and on the way in which it is completed depend the chances of our gaining a true conception of what a manly faith is, not less than a clear notion of this ruler's act. Only believe—what? whom? Oh! if "only" some of our teachers would take the trouble to think this clause out to its fullest significance, the passage would cease to be a miserable fetish, and become a spiritual power. What was this ruler's faith? A correct idea? Yea, verily, for faith without knowledge is superstition. A feeling? Most surely. A tender regard for the Saviour glows in the scene, and faith works by love, and inspires courage never to submit or yield. Obedience? Yes! every step he took alongside of Christ revealed it. But was this all? Knowledge, love, obedience? No! The act is complex. Go to its roots, and you cannot set it out in a short phrase, or dispatch it in a definition. It is vital, like life; and like life, indefinable. It is an opening of the entire nature, in all its powers and faculties, to Christ, to receive of His energies, so that Christ is flowing into him, healing and strengthening him, and sustaining him as he journeys along, and finally giving him a complete victory over himself and his painful and distressing lot. III. But it must not be forgotten that this quickening and stimulating counsel was enforced by an actual and positive fact, illustrative of that very heroism—of faith to which this perplexed and agitated man was encouraged. The direction is set in a background that brilliantly illumines and enforces it; for I cannot avoid thinking that the dangerous delay in reaching the poor man's home, and the obvious determination of Christ to bring the tired and trembling woman to the front, and to compel the confession of her sad and lengthened illness, and of her speedy cure, was meant to encourage this believer in his difficult task. There is always close to us the human fact interpreting and enforcing the Divine direction, if only we have eyes to see and ears to hear the message of our Lord. God never gives us words alone. IV. Let me ask you to take this direction and apply it to yourselves as this man took it. Cling to Christ, the truth, hold fast the gentle and healing hand of Christ. (*J. Clifford, D.D.*) *On the death of little children :*—Let me speak of the spirit and work of Christ in the home of a sick child. 1. By the death of little children the unity of home life is broken up. 2. There is something which we call unnatural in this manner of death. 3. The bereavement of children is a bereavement that so often never seems to be fully repaired till the bereavement shall be over, and the separated have met again face to face. 4. There is for us, however, over their tiny graves, a glorious "nevertheless." We can enter into the joy of the word of the Lord that assures us that our loved children, numbered among the dead, are yet not dead, but only sleeping. (1) It is a great blessing which God confers on a home when its inmates can say : "Part of our family is in heaven." (2) Those who form this part so perfectly blessed are for ever safe from all moral dangers and ills. (3) And this because they are ever pure, without fault before the throne of God. (*T. Gasquoine, B.A.*) *Our lost children :*—"She is not dead." This He said of all our children we have seen lying thus. Christ here reveals to us, as truth, what the poets of all ages have been telling the world. Our children are not lost. They sleep. The burden has been too much, the road too broken, the light too dim for their eyes. (*E. Aston*). *Not death but sleep :*—I. The words of the messenger (ver. 49) may serve to REMIND US OF THE LIMITS WHICH ORDINARILY OUR UNBELIEF SETS TO OUR FAITH. "While there's life there is hope," we are accustomed to say. But "if in this life only we have hope in Christ, we are of all men most miserable." Christ has the same power over death now as He had when on earth. The difference between His treatment of death now, and His treatment of it then, is not in kind—it is only in circumstance and scene. Cling to the belief that Christ has abolished death, and brought life and immortality to light, and that one day your loved ones shall be restored to you and you to them, and, when set over against the consolation which that belief has power to yield, the question of the *time when* will come to matter less and less to you. II. Looking at the text itself we find in it—1. That when Christ reached the house of Jairus the relatives and neighbours who had assembled in the death-chamber, were, according to Eastern custom, bitterly weeping and loudly bewailing the loss which had just befallen the family ;and—2. That He bade them cease their mourning. WHY, THEN, DID CHRIST SAY TO THEM "WEEP NOT"? Surely their grief was pardonable and even fitting. Surely it would have argued the possession of a callous heart and an unsympathetic nature if they had been unmoved in that house of mourning that day. It seems to me that we must invest these words in the mouth of Christ with the tenderest look and the most sympathetic tone, and that we must regard them not as condemnatory of a grief that was natural, but as a gentle chiding of sorrow that was hopeless, and therefore unbelieving.

> " Weep not for them ! it is no cause of sorrow
> That theirs was no long pathway to the tomb;
> They had one bright to-day, no sad to-morrow
> Rising in hope, and darkening into gloom.
>
> Weep not for them ! give tears unto the living;
> O waste no vain regret on lot like theirs !
> But rather make it reason for thanksgiving
> That ye have cherished angels unawares."

III. THE REASON WHICH CHRIST GAVE WHY THEY WERE NOT TO WEEP. " She is not
dead." And yet the very next verse tells us that they all knew very well that she
was dead. How came Christ then to deny a fact so patent to all ? It was because
He set His face and " the whole weight of His thought and speech " against the
merely natural and temporal views of men as to what death is—" The illuminating
significance of the fact of Christ's indisposition to use the word death." IV. We
have seen that Jesus said, and why He said, that the daughter of Jairus was not
dead. How, then, does He explain the wondrous and awful change which has come
over her visible form? HE SAYS THAT SHE IS SLEEPING. Perhaps never was a
time, since men began to seek out the analogies in things, when they did not see
and speak of the striking similarity between Death and his twin-brother Sleep.
But is this fact enough to account for Christ's use of the similitude ? I think not.
" If Christ had done nothing more for humanity," says Munger, " than give to it
this word "sleep" in place of " death," He would have been the greatest of benefactors.
To that which seems the worst thing, He has given the best name, and the name is true.
It is a great thing that we are able to take that almost sweetest and most soothing word
in our tongue—sleep—and give it unto death : sleep that ends our cares and relieves
us of our toils, that begins in weariness and ends in strength." Out of sleep there is
awakening, and the light of the eternal morning gladdens the vision of all who fall
asleep in Christ. (*J. R. Bailey.*)   *Talitha cumi :*—Very tender is the word
in which Jesus addresses the dead child, as if she were still living. St. Mark alone
records the original Aramaic expression, " Talitha cumi," which had doubtless been
indelibly impressed upon the memory of St. Peter, from whom St. Mark, who was
his special friend and companion, must have obtained it. And the original expression is recorded, because it cannot be translated without losing much of its
charm and significance. It contains a term of endearment derived from a Syrian
word signifying "lamb," often applied by fond parents to their children. It is as
if the Good Shepherd had said, in bringing back in His bosom to the fold of the
living this lost lamb that had wandered into the land of forgetfulness, " My little
lamb, I say unto thee, arise." By the word of love and the touch of power, the
spirit is re-called from the everlasting spring, and the hills of myrrh, to the forsaken tabernacle. The wave of life rushes back to the quiet heart, the pulse is set
beating anew ; a warm glow diffuses itself through the frame and mantles on
the cheeks and lips. She rises from the couch as from a profound dreamless sleep,
in mute astonishment at the strange scene around her, all the feebleness of her
illness gone. The sun of her life — as happens in the natural world on the
borders of the Arctic regions in summer—just dipped below the horizon for a
little, and then rose again ; and dawn and sunset shone in the same sky. (*H.
Macmillan, LL.D.*)

> The Saviour raised
> Her hand from off her bosom, and spread out
> The snowy fingers in His palm, and said,
> " Maiden ! Arise ! "—and suddenly a flush
> Shot o'er her forehead, and along her lips
> And through her cheek the rallied colour ran;
> And the still outline of her graceful form
> Stirr'd in the linen vesture ; and she clasp'd
> The Saviour's hand, and fixing her dark eyes
> Full on His beaming countenance—arose.   (*N. P. Willis.*)

He commanded to give her meat :—The command of Jesus to give the restored
child meat was intended, we may suppose, to serve several purposes : to supply (1)
a physical want, and in so doing to give clear, unmistakable proof of the reality of
the life restored to perfect health ; (2) to calm the apprehensions and the great

astonishment of the parents; and (3) to show that the course of nature, though violently interrupted for once, must be resumed according to the usual order. Jesus descended from the region of the supernatural to the region of ordinary life, from the working of a miracle to the satisfying of a commonplace want. And by that circumstance He teaches us the important lesson, that the spiritual life which He has imparted by Divine power must be sustained by human means. (*H. Macmillan, LL.D.*) *Death pleasingly described:*—It would seem that the Romans had even an aversion to mention death in express terms, for they disguised its very name by some periphrasis such as, *Discessit e vita*—" He has departed from life "; and they did not say their friend had died, but that he had lived—*vixit!* Even among a people less refined the obtrusive idea of death has been studiously avoided. We are told that when the Emperor of Morocco inquires after any one who has recently died, it is against etiquette to mention the word " death "; the answer is, " His destiny is closed." (*I. D'Israeli.*) *What withers on earth blooms in heaven:*—A delicate child, pale and prematurely wise, was complaining on a hot morning that the poor dew-drops had been too hastily snatched away, and had not been allowed to glitter on the flowers like other happier dew-drops, that live the whole night through and sparkle through the moonlight, and through the morning onwards to noon-day. "The sun," said the child, "has chased them away with his heat, or has swallowed them up in his wrath." Soon after came rain, and a rainbow; whereupon his father pointed upwards. "See," said he, "there stand the dew-drops gloriously re-set—a glittering jewelry—in the heavens; and the clownish foot tramples on them no more. By this, my child, thou art taught that what withers on earth blooms again in heaven." Thus the father spoke, and knew not that he spake prophetic words; for soon after the delicate child, with the morning brightness of his early wisdom, was exhaled, like a dew-drop, into heaven. (*Jean Paul Richter.*) *A glorified memory :*—Christian parents have a rich inheritance in the memories of their sainted children, and in the living treasures laid up in heaven. "Years ago," says Dr. W. M. Taylor, "when I was leaving my Liverpool home to fulfil an engagement in the city of Glasgow, the last sight on which my eyes rested was that of my little daughter at the window in her grandmother's arms. As the carriage drove me away, she waved her hand in fond and laughing glee, and many a time during my railway ride the pleasant vision came up before my memory, and filled my heart with joy. I never saw her again! The next morning a telegram stunned me with the tidings of her death; and now that earthly glimpse of her has been idealized and glorified, and it seems to me as if God had set her in the window of heaven to beckon me upward to my eternal home. I would not give that memory for all the gold on earth. I would not part with the inspiration that it stirs within me for all that the world could bestow."

CHAPTER IX.

Vers. **1, 2. Then He called His twelve disciples together.**—*The apostolic authority :*—1. Its extent. 2. Its grounds. 3. Its puɪpose. 4. Its limits. (*Van Oosterzee.*) *Charge of our Saviour to the twelve :*—I. To whom they were to go. 1. Not to the heathen. It was more favourable to the progress of Christianity, even among the Gentiles, that the Jews should be first instructed, because, as they already believed in the unity and attributes of God, and possessed the prophecies, they were much better fitted than any other nation, at the commencement of Christianity, to be the instructors of the world. 2. Nor to the Samaritans, although, in travelling from Judæa to Galilee, it was necessary to pass through their country. Our Saviour foresaw that when the Jews should adopt the Christian religion the new benevolent spirit which that religion would diffuse among them would banish all national animosities, and dispose them to contribute with delight to spread the knowledge of Christianity among the Samaritans, and henceforth to acknowledge them as brethren. II. The preparation they were to make. It is, rather, the preparation they were not to make (ver. 3). What could be the reason of this singular prohibition? We answer, that it was evidently the intention of Jesus, in their first mission, to teach them to rely with confidence on the providence of God, who would show them that they were special objects of His care, would cause all their wants to be supplied, and thus to convince them that they were engaged in the business of heaven. III. WHAT THEY WERE TO DO. 1. Proclaim (1) the coming of the kingdom ; (2) the need of reformation. 2. While uttering this proclamation, they proved that they had received Divine authority to make it ; for they were empowered, during this journey, to perform miracles by curing all sorts of diseases. At the same time, to distinguish them from those impostors who pretended to cure all distempers, the apostles were prohibited from receiving money in the form of rewards or presents: "Freely ye have received, freely give " ; acting in this disinterested manner like servants of the God of bene- volence, they were not to be confounded with selfish and designing men. 3. As they had been prohibited from carrying with them the usual accommodations for a journey, they were to depend on the hospitality of those whom they visited. 4. They were enjoined to behave with courtesy to every person they visited. They had come to communicate most important information, and it was necessary to secure the most favourable attention. Besides, civility is an essential part of that benevolence which we owe to our neighbours ; and he that is destitute of it neglects to use the means of cultivating the kindly feelings in himself, and in those with whom he associates. 5. When repulsed, they were to shake off the dust from their feet—a significant action which was evidently intended to leave a salutary impression. (*J. Thomson, D.D.*)   *A host of heralds :*—When we are told that Jesus Christ sent His disciples forth to "preach the kingdom of God," the word Luke uses means to herald. All Christians are heralds when they speak of the coming of their King. And the characteristics of heralds, before any other persons, are just these : they cannot be inconspicuous, and they must not be timid. Hence, ancient sovereigns used to dress their heralds in unusual and showy garments, so as to attract attention wherever they went; and they furnished them with horns and trumpets, so as to enable them to make a noise which should compel people to hear them. 1. The chief reproach levelled at the Church by the wild race of wicked men around us is that we are not sincere in our professions of longing for the coming of Christ's kingdom. They laugh at a host of heralds so tame and bashful. Why do Christian people never speak up honestly, and do their avowed errands like men ? 2. Of course, the proper reply to all this violence is not found in any waste of furious declamation or any massing of forcible logic. Our remedy under such hateful attacks is found in undertaking at once the work which is urged. We shall never hear any more about our derelictions in duty if we are patiently doing duty. 3. Now, it ought to be remembered that this plan of pro- mulgation of the gospel was the choice of an infinitely wise God. There can be no doubt that it would have been an easy thing for Him just to convert the world at a stroke by an irresistible impulse of the Holy Spirit's influence; no doubt He could have turned men's hearts into obedient holiness by some suddenness of Divine disclosure ministered possibly through a song of hosts of angels. But He chose to take time for it, and he chose to put the ultimate accomplishing of such a work into the hands of Christian men and women. 4. It might be well to dwell a moment upon the great grace of God towards us in granting such a favour. Next to being rich and imperial ourselves, it certainly would be very fine to be the almoner of an emperor distributing his wealth to the poor. There was wonderful benediction to us in that God fashioned a form of practical evangelization, which would allow play for all kinds of characteristic human endowments. By putting these into rapid and repetitious service, all of those who love Him would share in the grand result. 5. Moreover, the wisdom of such an arrangement can never be questioned. Making men heralds to other men would economize force in exercise, for it would build up intelligence and grace as it exhausted it. Personal activity in doing good promotes growth in all Christian excellence. Love increases by just loving. Hope enlivens itself by just hoping. Zeal gets on fire, and keeps on fire, by just arousing the heat. Knowledge is augmented in all cases more by the effort of teaching others than by simply studying for one's self alone. To the man who rightly uses the five or ten talents extra talents are given from the Lord's money. 6. Right here, therefore, let us find an explanation of that low state of hypochondriac feeling which oppresses some Christians. They need spiritual exercise. Wilberforce was asked, once when he was labouring hardest, if he had in these times no anxiety, as he used to have, concerning his soul's interests; and he replied, "I do not think about my soul; I have no time for solicitude concerning self; I have really for- gotten all about my personal salvation, and so I have no distress." 7. It is possible, therefore, that sometimes it may become actually necessary for the Church itself to be taught by alarm. The heralds may have grown listless. A real sense of peril is of value. "Oh, do that on our souls," prayed Richard Baxter once, "which Thou wouldst have us do on the souls of others !" Once when Napoleon was crossing the Alps, his army grew laggard, and held back. He ordered the music to play, as if on parade. This was enough for most veterans in the ranks ; but he observed that the trumpeters were tame, and their feeble strains of ordinary encouragement were not sufficiently seductive to draw away the minds of the rank and file from the awful weariness of the ascent of the mountain. One regiment especially just toiled along in a spiritless and forlorn array ; these he gathered together, and then he ordered the bands to play the home-songs of the peasant people in order that thoughts of sunny scenes behind them might kindle the men's enthusiasm. Even that failed among some of the sad platoons ; and there were some conscripts who only wept beneath an inveterate gloom. Finally, that shrewd commander marshalled the worst of all into one battalion, and put them in the lead. Then suddenly he ordered the trumpets to sound the charge of battle. That was a solitary challenge that no soldier of a French army ever refused. No one could know how they came to be attacked by a foe in the icicles of the high Alps ; but is mattered nothing. Wild indeed was the excitement which ran through that hitherto dispirited host, for they supposed the enemy was upon them, and the quick instinct of war instantly flashed along the lines. The very bands played with splendid clangour of brass and shrill screaming of reeds on the frosty air. What that call meant pealing among the ravines was victory ! Most men need some sort of inspiration in religious life just to keep them up to duty. Woe to the heralds with trumpets in their hands if they lapse away into a feeble silence ! (*C. S. Robinson, D.D.*)   *Preaching the kingdom :*—We have here the commission of the twelve apostles. I. THEIR AUTHORITY. This they received from the great Head of the Church. II. THEIR QUALIFICATIONS. 1. Notice the two words used. (1) Power ; the ability to do a thing. (2) Authority ; the lawful right to do it. 2. Two realms referred to. (1) The spiritual realm of darkness ; (2) the physical realm of human nature. III. THEIR GREAT MISSION. 1. To give spiritual light and comfort. 2. To relieve those who were physically disabled and tortured. (1) Christ is Physician for both soul and body. (2) All His ministers should do what they can for the bodies as well as for the souls of men. IV. THEIR MARCHING ORDERS. They were to be encumbered with nothing superfluous. V. THEIR OBEDIENCE. Instructive to us—(1) in its promptness ; (2) in its exactness ; (3) in its thoroughness. Lessons : 1. Every disciple should be a witnesser for Christ. 2. Though some of the particular things laid down here are not obligatory on us, the prominent features in their equipment are still needed. (1) The power and authority; (2) the willingness to give up everything superfluous ; (3) prompt, exact, and thorough obedience. 3. Every one whom Christ sends forth may confidently expect every needed equipment if he ask. 4. Surely the fields are now ripe for the harvest. 5. Let us not only pray that God will send labourers, but be willing to be labourers ourselves. (*D. C. Hughes, M.A.*)   *Missionary work is God's work :*—Who would not be a missionary? His noble enterprise is in exact accordance with the spirit of the age, and what is called the spirit of the age is simply the movement of multitudes of minds in the same direction. They move according to the eternal and all-embracing decrees of God. The spirit of the age is one of benevolence, and it manifests itself in numberless ways—ragged-schools, baths and washhouses, sanitary reform, &c. Hence missionaries do not live before their time. Their great idea of converting the world to Christ is no chimera ; it is Divine. Christianity will triumph. It is equal to all it has to perform. It is not mere enthusiasm to imagine a handful of missionaries capable of converting the millions of India. How often they are cut off just after they have acquired the language ! How often they retire with broken-down constitutions before effecting anything ! How often they drop burning tears over their own feebleness amid the defections of those they believed to be converts ! Yes ! but the small band has the decree of God on its side. Who has not admired the band of Leonidas at the pass of Thermopylæ? Three hundred against three million. Japhet, with the decree of God on his side, only three hundred strong, contending with Shem and his three millions. Consider what has been effected during the last fifty years. There is no vaunting of scouts now, no Indian gentlemen making themselves merry about the folly of thinking to convert the natives of India, magnifying the difficulties of caste, and setting our ministers into brown studies and speech-making in defence of missions. No mission has yet been an entire failure. The old world was a failure under Noah's preaching. Elijah thought it was all up with Israel. Isaiah said, "Who hath believed our report, and to whom is the arm of the Lord revealed?" And Jeremiah wished his head were waters, his eyes a fountain of tears, to weep over one of God's plans for diffusing knowledge among the heathen. If we could see a larger arc of the great providential cycle, we might sometimes rejoice when we weep. But God giveth not account of any one of His matters. We must just trust to His wisdom. Let us do our duty. He will work out a glorious consummation. Fifty years ago missions could not lift up their heads. But missions now are admitted by all to be one of the great facts of the age, and the sneers about "Exeter Hall" are seen by every one to embody a *risus sardonicus*. The present posture of affairs is, that benevolence is popular. God is working out in the human heart His great idea, and all nations shall see His glory. . . . Let us think highly of the weapons we have received for the accomplishment of our work. "The weapons of our warfare are not carnal, but spiritual, and mighty through God to the casting down of strongholds." They are—Faith in our Leader, and in the presence of His Holy Spirit; a full, free, unfettered gospel; the doctrine of the Cross of Christ—an old story, but containing the mightiest truths ever uttered—mighty for pulling down the strongholds of sin, and giving liberty to the captives. This work requires zeal for God and love for souls. It needs prayer from the senders and the sent, and firm reliance on Him who alone is the author of conversion. Souls cannot be converted or manufactured to order. Great deeds are wrought in unconsciousness, from constraining love to Christ; in humbly asking, "Lord, what wilt Thou have me to do?" in the simple feeling we have done that which it was our duty to do. The effect works, the greatness of which it will remain for posterity to discern. The greatest works of God in the kingdom of grace, like His majestic works in nature, are marked by stillness in the doing of them, and reveal themselves by their effects. They come up like the sun, and show themselves by their own light. The kingdom of God cometh not with observation. Luther simply followed the leadings of the Holy Spirit in the struggles of His own soul. He wrought out what the inward impulses of his own breast prompted him to work, and behold, before He was aware, he was in the midst of the Reformation. So, too, it was with the Plymouth pilgrims, with their sermons three times a day on board the *Mayflower*. Without thinking of founding an empire, they obeyed the sublime teachings of the Spirit, the promptings of duty and the spiritual life. God working mightily in the human heart is the spring of all abiding spiritual power; and it is only as men follow out the sublime promptings of the inward spiritual life that they do great things for God. The movement of not one mind only, but the consentaneous movement of a multitude of minds in the same direction, constitutes what is called the spirit of the age. This spirit is neither the law of progress nor blind development, but God's all-eternal, all-embracing purpose, the doctrine which recognizes the hand of God in all events, yet leaves all human action free. When God has prepared an age for a new thought, the thought is thrust into the age as an instrument into a chemical solution—the crystals cluster around it immediately. If God prepares not, the man has lived before his time. Huss and Wiclif were like voices crying in the wilderness, preparing the way for a brighter future; the time had not yet come. Who would not be a missionary? "They that be wise shall shine as the brightness of the firmament, and they that turn many to righteousness as the stars for ever and ever." Is God not preparing the world for missions which will embrace the whole of Adam's family? The gallant steamships circumnavigate the globe. Emigration is going on at a rate to which the most renowned crusades of antiquity bear no proportion. Many men go to and fro, and knowledge is increased. No great emigration ever took place in the world without accomplishing one of God's great designs. The tide of modern emigration flows towards the West. The wonderful amalgamation of races will result in something grand. We believe this, because the world is becoming better, and because God is working mightily in the human mind. We believe it, because God has been preparing the world for something glorious. And that something will be a fuller development of the missionary idea and work. There will yet be a glorious consummation of Christianity. The last fifty years have accomplished wonders. On the American continent, what a wonderful amalgamation of races we have witnessed, how wonderfully they have been fused into that one American people—type and earnest of a larger fusion which Christianity will yet accomplish, when, by its blessed power, all tribes and tongues and races shall become one holy family. The present popularity of beneficence promises well for the missionary cause in the future. Men's hearts are undergoing a process of enlargement. Their sympathies are taking a wider scope. The world is getting closer, smaller—quite a compact affair. "The world for Christ" will yet be realized. (*David Livingstone, LL.D.*) *Authority for missions :*—When a Roman magistrate was appointed to conduct a campaign he could not even assume the command of an army until he had been invested with the special powers comprehended in the *imperium* or right of military command. And to this day when governments are called upon to undertake extraordinary enterprises they are in the habit of endowing their officers with extraordinary powers. So Jesus, when sending His disciples to combat with the powers of evil, gave them special authority and miraculous power. (*Sunday School Times.*) *Insignificant beginnings :*—Not many years ago the Queen of Great Britain was proclaimed Empress of India. That event was announced throughout India with all the pomp of empire. Contrast with this earthly splendour the manner in which the new kingdom of Christ was proclaimed on earth. Twelve poor disciples preached it in an insignificant province of the Roman Empire. (*Ibid.*)   *A missionary's healing work :*—In the first verse of this lesson is a strong reminder of the most efficient style of missionaries to-day. Saying nothing about the power and authority over all devils, to cure diseases is no small part of the modern missionary's task. It is plain enough to most Christian people who keep up with the general run of accounts from the mission field, that medical training greatly adds to a missionary's influence. Indeed, it seems almost superfluous to say a word more on the subject. But when one thinks how much physicians are needed among a people where regularly trained physicians do not otherwise exist than through the efforts of the missionaries; how many diseases have been scourges which are quite within the power of medical science; to how many people a physician can gain the access denied to every one else; what opportunities a physician has for making many his grateful friends for life; it will not be wondered that medical training and a physician's work are wonderful aids in advancing the kingdom. It is no wonder either that Luke, the physician, was particular to notice this branch of the apostolic commission; or that it was actually given by our Lord. Even a quack, or a skilful physician who insists on extortionate fees, is a man of power; though such a one may do the missionary work great harm. He would be feared. Unless he both preaches the kingdom of God—preaches in the old sense, not sermonizes by the hour-glass— and heals the sick, he is worse than useless. (*Ibid.*)   *The call to Christian work :*—I. THE CALL TO CHRISTIAN WORK. These twelve apostles were men specially called by Christ, some from their fishing, one from the receipt of custom. We must not think that they were elected to the exceeding privilege of personal relations with Christ. It would be true to say that, through all the ages, God does not elect to privilege, He selects for duty. II. THE FORM OF CHRISTIAN WORK. 1. Every one who is "sent" has a message to deliver. It is a message of sovereign grace. It is a message that has to be set in precise adaptation to men's needs. It is a message that makes practical demands on all to whom it is addressed. 2. Every one sent is expected to scatter temporal blessings as he goes about doing his higher spiritual work. "Heal the sick" only represents the work of the unusually endowed. III. THE SPHERE OF CHRISTIAN WORK. These apostles were bidden go to "the lost sheep of the House of Israel." Lost sheep! They can be found by us all close at hand. IV. THE SPIRIT OF CHRISTIAN WORK. "Freely ye have received, freely give." True workers for Christ must be heedless of "self"; they must gain full hold and mastery of "self." (*The Weekly Pulpit.*)   *A love of preaching :*—The late Rev. Rowland Hill remarks—"Old as I am, I am just returned from a long missionary ramble; but I feel I am getting old. Oh that I may work well to the last!" In all his journeys, even when he had reached a period beyond that usually allotted to man, he was disconcerted if he did not find a pulpit ready for him every evening. In one of his letters, fixing his days for preaching on his road to some place, he says, "Ever since my Master has put me into office I have ever esteemed it my duty to remember His admonition, 'As ye go, preach.'" His general answer to invitations to houses on his route was, "I shall be happy to come to you, if you can find me a place to preach in."   *Simplicity in preaching :*—Arthur Helps tells a story of an illiterate soldier at the chapel of Lord Morpeth's castle in Ireland. Whenever Archbishop Whately came to preach it was observed that this rough private was always in his place, mouth open, as if in sympathy with his ears. Some of the gentlemen playfully took him to task for it, supposing it was due to the usual vulgar admiration of a celebrity. But the man had a better reason, and was able to give it. He said, "That isn't it at all. The Archbishop is easy to understand. There are no fine words in him. A fellow like me, now, can follow along and take every bit of it in." *The mission of the twelve :*—1. It was one which had for its especial object the welfare of men, both as to soul and body. 2. In His instructions to these first ministers of the gospel, the Master seemed especially to warn them against any needless regard to their own appearance, or any undue considerations for their own comfort or ease. Simplicity, frugality, and paramount regard to their work, were the principles which they were to illustrate, and these have always been considered becoming to true ministers of the gospel in the purest days of the Church. These first apostles were to cultivate warm fraternal fellowship with the people among whom they were to labour, mixing with them and their families in the ordinary intercourse of life, and kindly receiving that hospitality which was freely offered, though never demanded. 3. We are not to consider that these directions of our Lord establish any fixed rules in respect to the support or costume or social relations of His ministers. They were rather adapted to a special and peculiar service; they were conformable to the customs and usages of the times and the country. 4. The injunction to shake off the dust from their feet in leaving a place where they were not welcomed and their teaching was not received, does not inculcate anything like a spirit of denunciation and bitterness, but simply a protest against the unbelief which manifested itself in this manner, and was like the custom, well known to the Jews, of shaking their garments when they came from a heathen city into their own country. The scribes taught that the dust of heathenism defiled those on whom it rested. (*E. P. Rogers, D.D.*) *Practical suggestions :*—1. An apostle is a sent one, but not self-sent. 2. A true shepherd must not mistake the love of the fleece for the love for the flock. 3. The Church is to remember that her " angels " are still in the flesh, and require at least an average provision for the needs of the flesh. It is a poor way to advance the spirituality of a minister, to begrudge him his bread. 4. Spirituality is not a thing belonging necessarily to riches or to poverty. All the worldliness is not with the rich. All the spirituality is not with the poor. 5. All true and faithful ministers may justly claim to be in the best sense in an apostolic succession. 6. Ostentation and luxury are a reproach to the ministers of Christ. 7. The Christian missionary emulates his Master, who came as the " sent One " from heaven, " to seek and to save that which was lost." 8. That is a true and practical Christianity which is not forgetful of the wants of the body while ministering to the necessities of the soul. 9. Every Christian is bound to be a missionary, even though he be not ordained as a preacher. The spirit of missions is the spirit of Christ, and when the whole Church is imbued with that the Lord's prayer will be answered, " Thy kingdom come." (*Ibid.*) *The kingdom of God :*—The whole circle of doctrines taught by Christ revolves about this central point—that He represented to men the kingdom of God. What is this kingdom of God which Jesus preached in His gospel? and how does the knowledge of this kingdom bring us under obligation to repent, and give us encouragement to believe? The answer to these questions must be sought in the meaning of this phrase, as it required to be understood by the Jews of Christ's own time. To the men whom Christ addressed, the kingdom of God was no new idea; or rather it was no new phrase—but it can hardly be said to have represented any definite idea to a generation that had so far lost the meaning of their own law and history. If we study closely the religion of the Old Testament, we shall find that all its doctrines, laws, and institutions grow out of this fundamental thought, that God, who Himself is pure and spiritual, is the true and only Redeemer of all those who desire to be no more estranged from Him. This truth was formally embodied in the doctrine of a kingdom of God in this world, the nucleus of which was His redeemed people of Israel. The political constitution of Israel as a nation was but a frame for this spiritual kingdom. The true conception of the kingdom stands out in the predictions of Jeremiah concerning the days of the Messiah. When this prophet wrote, the political kingdom had run itself down into disgrace and bankruptcy, through the vices of the kings and the general wickedness of the people; but although the monarchy should be overthrown, and king and people be carried away captive, the kingdom of God in the true Israel—as represented by the prophet and by all believing souls—could not be destroyed. This view of the kingdom of God may be interpreted to us by our familiar conceptions of the national and historical spirit in a people, as distinguished from the form of government and the practical administration of affairs. If, for instance, one loses confidence in a ministry, he does not abandon constitutional government as a failure. It was the spiritual conception of a kingdom *within* Israel itself—that did not embrace all Israel, and yet was greater than Israel, because it did possess, and should hereafter more and more possess, souls outside the pale of the Jewish commonwealth—that Jeremiah seized so vividly at the very moment when the national monarchy was sinking into nothingness. With this spiritual conception of the kingdom—the presence of God as a Saviour realized to the soul—it is easy to understand how Jesus preached the gospel of the kingdom of God. Coming at a time when the Jews were vassals of the Roman power; when deprived of every symbol of their nationality save their temple and its worship, they were yearning for a deliverer; to the nominal people of God thus subjugated by military rule, yet clinging to the ancient promise of a Messiah who should restore the glory of the theocracy, He said, "I bring to you the good news of the kingdom of God; in Me Jehovah once more comes to you as a Deliverer; the time predicted by Daniel is fulfilled; the new covenant promised by Jeremiah is brought to you in My gospel; repent of the sins that have humiliated and well-nigh destroyed you; renounce your vain hopes of deliverance and trust in Me as your Saviour; repent and believe the gospel, for the kingdom of God is at hand." (*J. P. Thomson.*) *The kingdom:*—1. Is within. One becomes a subject of it in his own consciousness. 2. Has laws for the regulation of the life, though purifying and ennobling the heart. 3. Has its privileges. Every subject is treated as a son. 4. Has its rewards, both present and prospective. (*Ibid.*) *The twofold mission: preaching and healing.*—It is in obedience to this mandate that our missionaries, before they go abroad, not only spend a number of years at some theological college where they may prepare themselves for the work of proclaiming the gospel, but generally spend a year or so in the hospitals, gaining some knowledge of medicine that they may alleviate the physical woes of the people among whom their lives are to be spent, and so, it may be, reach the soul through the body. At home the two functions are discharged by different persons, and yet it seems to me that minister and doctor should be in completest sympathy, and recognize each other as severally working towards the same end. Some doctors have I known, who while attending to the physical wants of their patients could find time not only to speak the kindly and reassuring words which come so well from the lips of men who belong to the healing profession, but also to say some word which might point the afflicted one to that great Healer and most beneficent Physician, who is the Redeemer of our whole nature. It is a proof of the close alliance which ought to subsist between preaching and healing, that hospitals are a direct fruit of Christianity. "Neither the religion nor the philosophy of Greece and Rome tended to comfort the poor. The divinities were cruel; the Stoic affected to despise the sufferings of the indigent; the Epicurean took no thought of them. Throughout the vast regions of Mogol, India, and China, the use of hospitals is unknown to this day. In no country did Christianity find such institutions existing. The history of their rise and progress can be traced in few words. In the year 380 the first hospital in the West was founded by Fabiola, a devout Roman lady, without the walls of Rome. St. Jerome says, expressly, that this was the first of all. And he adds that it was a country-house, destined to receive the sick and infirm, who before used to lie stretched on the public ways. The pilgrim's hospital at Rome, built by Pammachius, became also celebrated. In 330, the priest Zotichus, who had followed Constantine to Byzantium, established in that city, under his protection, a hospital for strangers and pilgrims. St. Basil, who founded the first hospitals of Asia, mentions a house for the reception of the sick and of travellers, near the city of Cæsarea, which became afterwards the ornament of the country, and like a second city. St. Chrysostom built several hospitals at Constantinople." Coming down to modern days, it is significant that the three oldest London hospitals, St. Thomas's, St. Bartholomew's, and Bethlehem, were founded about the middle of the sixteenth century, immediately after the Reformation, and that the reign of George II., in which Wesley and Whitefield preached from end to end of the land, was the period at which "a considerable accession was made to the number of English hospitals, and at which society became alive to the value of such institutions." (*J. R. Bailey.*) There is certainly no other feature of the old civilization so repulsive as the indifference to suffering that it displayed. The constant association of human suffering with popular entertainments rendered the popular mind continually more callous. Very different was the aspect presented by the early Church. Charity was one of the earliest, as it was one of the noblest creations of Christianity; and independently of the incalculable mass of suffering it has assuaged, the influence it has exercised in softening and purifying the character, in restraining the passions, and enlarging the sympathies of mankind, has made it one of the most important elements of our civilization. (*W. E. H. Lecky, M.A.*)   *Bodily healing a preparation for spiritual instruction:*—Although China has reached what some are pleased to call the highest degree of civilization of which a nation is capable without the gospel, it presents, I believe, more physical suffering, for want of medical knowledge, than any other nation on the face of the the earth. The multitudes of sick, and lame, and blind which crowd the streets of this and other cities, are ample evidence of her deplorable condition in this respect. In an institution like this, a good surgeon may almost every day of his life make the blind receive their sight, the lame walk, the deaf hear, and the paralytic whole; besides bringing hundreds together under the most favourable circumstances, to have the gospel preached to them. I might be allowed to give one example of the influence which even one successful case exerts, not only upon an individual or a family, but upon a locality or neighbourhood. Last spring I operated on a man's eyes for artificial pupil. For several years previously he had only just been able to distinguish day from night, light from darkness. Three days after the operation he was able to read the ordinary character, and on the fifth day he left the hospital. He was a boatman, and lives about half-way to Nankin, on the Northern bank of Yang-tsze river. Two months afterwards he arrived again in Shanghai with his boat, and brought six blind people to the hospital, five men and one woman, from his own neighbourhood, and they not only wanted to have their sight restored, but made enquiries about the Christian religion, which they said their friend who brought them had told them about. . . . One man," continues the doctor in another report, " a shopkeeper, who had been blind for three years, readily submitted to the operation for cataract. I need not say that he was much delighted when, on the twelfth day after it, he was able to read the New Testament character with facility. This man left the hospital in very high spirits, declaring that he would make known the gospel doctrine to all his friends and neighbours." (*Dr. Henderson.*)   *Delight in preaching:*—What cross do you suppose *I* take up in preaching? Just the same kind of a cross a mountain rill takes up that gushes forth all summer long. Why does it gush forth? Because it is its duty? No; because it cannot help it. It is its nature; and it goes ringing down the dell to please itself, not to please the heavens, or the clouds, or anything else—though it may please them all. And it is because it is to me pleasanter than anything else that I preach. I might preach if it was not so pleasant; but I am entitled to no thanks because I preach. The whole professional life of a minister who has health, and a healthy theology, ought to be pleasant. (*H. W. Beecher.*)

Ver. 3. **Take nothing for your journey.**—*Travelling without any burden:*—It is easy travelling if you have no burden. They were on His business, sent by Him, and He assumed their care, and forbade them to trust themselves, or any other but Him. What a load of care goes off with this, what a burden of responsibility is removed; but what faith and humility is needed! Some of them had been called away from full nets (Luke v. 11), and it takes faith to follow under such circumstances. Many would start if they were permitted to carry the fish, but they are afraid. Afraid—of what, or whom? How strange to their eyes would some of us appear, as we go forth to our work, clothed in rags of self-righteousness and wrappers of pride, loaded with burdens of care and sin? Too much like the Israelites, leaving Egypt with flocks and herds, clothes and kettles, bread and kneading troughs; delivered from bondage, but knowing nothing of the manna, or the water from the rock. Others are afraid to go, fearing to swing off from their earthly base of supplies, and trust the promises of God. But it is all explained in the word, " Lo, I am with you alway." And what for? 1. Surely to provide. Is He not the Creator? And what would come of all their care if He did not provide? How long would it take them to create a barley-corn, or make a fish? 2. Surely to direct. What would their ignorance have accomplished without Him? And, with such a captain, what need of vexatious study over plans and methods? 3. Surely to lead. In the march through an unknown wilderness, or through a trackless desert, or over an unknown sea, to an unknown port, what progress without a guide and a pilot? 4. Surely to carry all their burdens (Psa. lv. 22; 1 Pet. v. 7). And, if he wishes to carry them *all*, why need we refuse or complain? Is it not because, He knows our weakness, and because of His strength? And is this all? Oh on !

Surely it is because He will be our companion. What are the power and wisdom and riches without the love ? " If Thy presence go not with me, carry us not up hence " (Exod. xxxiii. 15). (*Sunday School Times.*)   *Apostolic simplicity :*—The Rev. H. Davies, sometimes called " the Welsh Apostle," was walking early one Sabbath morning to a place where he was to preach. He was overtaken by a clergyman on horseback, who complained that he could not get above half a guinea for a discourse. " Oh sir," said Mr. Davies, " I preach for a crown !" " Do you ? " replied the stranger; " then you are a disgrace to the cloth." To this rude observation he returned this meek answer, " Perhaps I shall be held in still greater disgrace, in your estimation, when I inform you that I am now going nine miles to preach, and have but sevenpence in my pocket to bear my expenses out and in ; but I look forward to that crown of glory which my Lord and Saviour will freely bestow upon me when He makes His appearance before an assembled world."

Ver. 4. **And whatsoever house ye enter into.**—*Fireside preaching :*—They went from town to town, receiving hospitality, or rather taking it for themselves, according to custom. The guest in the East has many privileges; he is superior to the master of the house, who has the greatest confidence in him. This fireside preaching is admirably adapted to the propagation of new doctrines. The hidden treasure is communicated, and payment is thus made for what is received ; politeness and good feeling lend their aid ; the household is touched and converted. Remove Oriental hospitality, and it would be impossible to explain the propagation of Christianity. Jesus, who adhered strongly to good old customs, encouraged His disciples to make no scruple of profiting by this ancient public right, probably already abolished in the great towns where there were hostelries. Once installed in any house, they were to remain there, eating and drinking what was offered them, as long as their mission lasted. (*Renan.*)   *Willing hospitality :*—When travelling in the East no one need ever scruple to go into the best house of any Arab village to which he comes, and he will always be received with profuse and gratuitous hospitality. From the moment we entered any house it was regarded as our own. There is not an Arab you meet who will not empty for you the last drop in his water-skin, or share with you his last piece of black bread. The Rabbis said that paradise was the reward of willing hospitality. (*Schöttgen.*)

Vers. 5, 6. **Shake off the very dust.** — *No connivance with those who reject the gospel :*—The Jews were accustomed, on their return from heathen countries to the Holy Land, to shake off the dust from their feet at the frontier. This act signified a breaking away from all joint participation in the life of the idolatrous world. The Apostles were to act in the same way with reference to any Jewish cities which might reject in their person the Kingdom of God. The rejection of the gospel is not the rejection of a mere theory on which men may innocently entertain different opinions. It is the rejection of a message which, if faithfully received, reveals God, and subdues us to Him, and transforms us into His likeness. It is the refusal of the only remedy for moral evil which God has given to man. And notice that this remedy, being offered to us by men sent by God, may be rejected in rejecting their message or their preaching. The faults or idiosyncrasies of the preached are taken no account of by the Lord. It is one with what He says elsewhere, " He that heareth you, heareth Me, and he that despiseth you, despiseth Me, and he that despiseth Me, despiseth Him that sent Me." (*M. F. Sadler, M.A.*)   *Dust :*—What can seem of less consequence, or more worthless, than a pinch of dust ? You have but to open your fingers and the wind blows it away in a moment and you see it no more. Yet if but one small grain of dust is blown into your eye it will give you a great deal of trouble. One of the terrible plagues of Egypt sprang from a handful of dust, which God commanded Moses to fling into the air. Every little grain scattered into millions and millions of invisible poison-atoms floating through the air ; and wherever they settled, on man or beast, dreadful boils and ulcers broke out. In the great deserts of Arabia and Africa the stormy wind sometimes brings such clouds of sand-dust, hot and stifling, that they hide the sun, and make the day as dark as night. The travellers have to lie flat on their faces, and the horses and camels to bend their noses down close to the ground, or they would be suffocated. Sometimes whole caravans have thus perished ; and even a great army was once destroyed and buried in these terrible clouds of hot dust. In Egypt, temples and cities have been buried under hills of sand, made up of tiny grains, which the wind has kept sweeping up from the desert for hundreds of years. Very great things,

you see, may come from very small things—even from dust. (*E. R. Conder, D.D.*)
Dust witnessing to the actions of people :—Once, in a certain part of Germany, a
box of treasure that was being sent by railway was found at the end of the journey
to have been opened and emptied of the treasure, and filled with stones and
rubbish. The question was who was the robber ? Some sand was found sticking to
the box, and a clever mineralogist having looked at the grains of sand through his
microscope, said that there was only one station on the railway where there was
that kind of sand. Then they knew that the box must have been taken out at that
station; and so they found out who was the robber. The dust under his feet,
where he had set down the box to open it, was a witness against him. Suppose
when people take off their shoes or boots when they come home, every grain of dust
could have a tiny tongue and tell where it came from ! What different stories they
would have to tell ! " We," say one little pair of shoes, " are all covered with sand
from the sea-shore, where we have been running about all day," " We," say a strong,
clumsy pair of boots, "have been all day following the plough." "And we have
brought sand from the floor of country cottages"; " and we, dust from the unswept floors of poor garrets "; " and we, mud from many a lane and court and
alley." Well-used shoes these; that are busy day after day, carrying comfort to
the poor, and the sick, and the sorrowful. And here are a pair of elegant high-
heeled boots with hardly a speck on them, for they have done nothing but step
from the carpet to the carriage, and from the carriage to the carpet : I am afraid
they have no story worth telling. And here are the village postman's shoes, stained
with mud of all colours, and thick with dust from twenty miles of road and footpath, park sward and farmyard, as he trudged his daily round. Here is a solitary
shoe, for its poor old owner has but one leg, and a wooden stump for the other; and
it is laden with the dust of the crossing he has been sweeping, for a few pence, all
day long. Some people, I am afraid, would rub and wipe their shoes for a long
time, as hard as they could, if they thought the dust under their feet would tell
tales of where they have been. At every step you take, you bring something away
with you and leave something behind. (*Ibid.*)   *Heralds of Joy :*—If a herald were
sent to a besieged city with the tidings that no terms of capitulation would be offered,
but that every rebel without exception should be put to death, methinks he would
go with lingering footsteps, halting by the way to let out his heavy heart in sobs and
groans ; but if instead thereof, he were commissioned to go to the gates with the
white flag to proclaim a free pardon, a general act of amnesty and oblivion, surely
he would run as though he had wings to his heels, with a joyful alacrity, to tell to
his fellow-citizens the good pleasure of their merciful king. Heralds of salvation,
ye carry the most joyful of all messages to the sons of men ! When the angels
were commissioned for once to become preachers of the gospel, and it was but for
once, they made the welkin ring at midnight with their choral songs, " Glory to God
in the highest, and on earth peace, good-will toward men." They did not moan out
a dolorous dirge as of those proclaiming death, but the glad tidings of great joy
were set to music, and announced with holy mirth and celestial song. " Peace on
earth; glory to God in the highest" is the joy-note of the gospel—and in such a
key should it ever be proclaimed. We find the most eminent of God's servants
frequently magnifying their office as preachers of the gospel. Whitfield was wont
to call his pulpit his throne ; and when he stood upon some rising knoll to preach
to the thousands gathered in the open air, he was more happy than if he had assumed the imperial purple, for he ruled the hearts of men more gloriously than
doth a king. (*C. H. Spurgeon.*)

Ver. 7. Herod the tetrarch heard.—*Herod in perplexity :*—" Perplexed." This
is a singular word. When we have a pictorial dictionary we shall see a very
graphic illustration of the meaning of this term. This word διηπόρει imports
that the man who was in this condition was perplexed, really stuck in the
mud. That is the literal import of the word. He could not move easily, and in all
his movement he was trying to escape—now he was moving to the right, then he
was moving to the left; now forward, now backward, now sideward ; he was making
all kinds of motion with a view to self-extrication, and he could not deliver himself
from this mood of hesitancy and incertitude. Herod was perplexed about Christ,
and curiously perplexed ; for his instinct put down his dogma, his conscience blew
away as with a scornful wind his theological view of life and destiny. Why was
Herod perplexed ?—" Because that it was said of some, that John was risen from
the dead ; and of some, that Elias had appeared ; and of others, that one of the

old prophets was risen again" (vers. 7, 8). Why did Herod trouble himself about these dead men? As a Sadducee he did not believe in spirit or in resurrection. If he had been quite faithful and stedfast to his creed, he would have said in answer to all these rumours—Whoever this man may be, he has nothing whatever to do with another world, for other world there is none; as to resurrection, dismiss the super-stition and forget it. But Herod had never been in this situation before. Circum-stances play havoc with some creeds. They are admirable creeds whilst the wind is in the south-west, and the way lies up a green slope, and birds are singing around us, and all heaven seems inclined to reveal its glories in one blaze: then we can have our theories and inventions and conjectures, and can play the little tricky con-troversialist with many words: but when the wolf bites us, how is it then? When all the money is lost, when the little child lies at the last gasp, when the doctor himself has gone away, saying it will be needless for him to return—how then? Men should have a creed that will abide with them every day in the week without consulting thermometer or barometer; a creed that will sing the most sweetly when the heart most needs heaven's music; a great faith, an intelligent, noble, free-minded faith, that says to the heart in its moods of dejection, All will come well; hold on, never despair, never give up; one more prayer, one more day, in a little while. A faith of this kind saves men from perplexity; it gives the life of man solidity, centralization, outlook, hope. It is an awkward thing to have a creed that will not bear this stress. Herod's Sadduceeism went down when a tap came to the door by invisible fingers. We can do what we will with matter; if the fingers are of bone and flesh they can be smitten and broken; but who can touch invisible fingers? Then what have we to take down by way of comfort? We have declared that we know nothing, and have taken quite lofty pride in our boundless ignorance, but here is a hand at the door, and the door must be answered, and you must answer it. Herod was perplexed, hesitant, now on this side, now on that side; he could not tell what to do. So are men perplexed about Christ to-day who do not believe in Him. It is one of two things in regard to this Son of Man: cordial, loving, positive trust, the whole heart-love poured out like wine into a living flagon; or it is now unbelief, now uncertainty, now a prayer breathed to the very devil that he would come and take possession of the mind so as to drive out all per-plexity and bewilderment. The latter course ends in deepening confusion and darkness. The only thing that will bear the stress of every weight, the collision of every conflict, is faith—simple, loving, grateful faith: Lord, increase our faith. (*J. Parker, D.D.*)   *The might and impotence of the conscience:*—I. ITS MIGHT. 1. It faithfully reminds of the evil committed. 2. Judges it rightly. 3. Chastises it rigorously. II. ITS IMPOTENCE. It is not able—1. To undo the past. 2. To make the present endurable. 3. To make the future hopeful. (*Van Oosterzee.*)   *Insincere unbelief:*—That practical unbelief distrusts itself, disavows itself, and punishes itself. I. ALL SUCH UNBELIEF, LIKE HEROD'S, DISTRUSTS ITSELF. Scepticism is never wholly satisfied with its own creed; never rests confidently on its own reasonings. So it was with Herod. As a Sadducee, he rejected the doctrine of the Resurrection, whether of angel or spirit. And yet, suddenly startled from his self-possession by an alarm of conscience, he is seen in the text to affirm strongly the truth whose denial was fundamental to his system! Sincere faith is serene, self-possessed, reliant. The traveller on the king's highway walks calmly and confidently, because he feels that his feet are on adamant; while he, in a marsh or a quicksand, is all restless and excited, through his distrust of the road. This very vapouring of un-belief in behalf of its tenets is significant of insincerity. II. That all unbelief, like Herod's, not only distrusts itself, BUT OFTEN, AND IN THE END, ALMOST ALWAYS DIS-AVOWS ITSELF! It may clamour against the hard things of revelation, as opposed to its instincts and its reason; yet will ever and anon make practical confession that they seem not unreasonable. This is strikingly exhibited in this history of Herod. Yea, and the text's illustration on this point goes much further. It shows, not only that the Resurrection is a reasonable doctrine, but that all the Bible teaches as to the effects of that Resurrection upon its subjects is as well reasonable and philosophic. These teachings may be embraced in two particulars—the positive identity, and the greatly enlarged powers and faculties of the Risen Immortal. 1. The Bible affirms this identity. The creature raised from the grave is to be the same creature who goes down into it. Death has no power to destroy or alter human nature. He says, "It is John. It is John the Baptist. He is risen from the dead!" 2. The Bible teaches that, along with this identity, the raised body shall possess powers and faculties very greatly enlarged. Indeed, there is in human nature something instantly responding to the voices of revelation. And it is by reason of this that unlearned and weak-minded Christians do maintain their faith so grandly against all the assaults of philosophic infidelity. They cannot argue for the truth, but they can apprehend it. And this natural moral sense exists originally in all men. The Bible never came to a human spirit that did not at some time respond to its felt truthfulness. III. Passing this, observe, That all such unbelief, like Herod's, POSITIVELY PUNISHES ITSELF. Conscience! Conscience! It was itself a resurrection-power within him! And look at the Tetrarch now! His cheek pale, his lip quivering, his wild eye glaring upon vacancy! He starts from his couch! The wine-cup drops from his hand as he whispers with white lips, "It is John the Baptist—he is risen from the dead!" Ah me! What aileth the Tetrarch there amid princes and nobles? John the Baptist sleeps still in his distant grave. But a simple thought long buried within his murderer's soul hath been unsepulchred! He thought to silence the living voice of God's prophet, but that voice in the dark chambers of his soul will wake echoes for ever! Here then we say is a striking illustration of the power of a roused conscience as God's avenger of sin. I have no room nor necessity here for an argument for retribution. I have only to do with this natural illustration. I am not prophesying what God will do, but only showing what man himself does! It is a favourite postulate, even of the infidel philosophy, that no impression once made on the thinking principle is ever obliterated. And it has doubtless happened unto you all to observe, how some trifling thing—a remark in conversation, the view of a familiar landscape, a strain of some long-forgotten harmony, yea, a thing so slight as the rustle of a falling leaf, or the breath of a flower's perfume—has awakened in the mind a long train of recollections. Thoughts long forgotten move again powerfully within us; we are borne away suddenly to other scenes; we live virtually in other times and other conditions. The magic of memory has summoned from the past shadowy forms, faces, voices, it may be of the dead. They rise upon us, they move before us, as life's great realities, and for the time we are under their mysterious power as our angels or avengers! Now, whether or not conscience be but a modification of memory, certain we are it follows the same great law. Conscience, too, may be beguiled for a season of its avenging power. But this you cannot do—you cannot destroy it. Sin, sin it is, as an operative principle within you, that, by arming conscience with an eye of fire and whip of scorpions, gives to the "worm" its fang, and to the "fires" their fierceness. Believe, if you will, that God is too merciful to make a hell. Yet you know, for you have seen, that every sinful man is making it. This is the law of man's moral nature, and under it you are all working out your own retribution. You are doing it always, each one for himself. (*C. Wadsworth.*) *Herod desiring to see Jesus :*—It is a striking sentence with which Luke concludes his narrative—" He desired to see Jesus." We are indeed told that many prophets and kings desired to see the things which the disciples of Jesus saw. Was this Prince of Galilee among those prophets and righteous men, earnestly longing for one glimpse of that mystery, which even angels desire to look into? Was his the desire of a longing holy heart? The evangelist leaves us in no doubt, for his desire was fulfilled; he did see Jesus. And I cannot but think that there is much significancy in the fact that the same writer who records the desire, is the only one who gives us the account of its accomplishment. The aged Simeon, too, desired to see Jesus, and when he saw Him, he said, "Lord, now lettest Thou Thy servant depart in peace, for mine eyes have seen Thy salvation." Certain Greeks, too, came to Philip and said, "Sir, we desire to see Jesus, and when Jesus heard it, He said, The hour is come that the Son of Man should be glorified." Thomas desired to see his risen Lord, and when he saw Him, he exclaimed, "My Lord and my God." Herod desired to see Jesus, and when he saw Him, "he and his men of war set Him at nought and mocked Him!" Herod will once more see Jesus, and it will not be then Herod "mocking Jesus," but, saith the Lord, "Because I have called, and ye refused; I have stretched out My hand, and no man regarded; but ye have set at naught all My counsel, I also will laugh at your calamity, I will mock when your fear cometh." (*B. Bouchier, M.A.*) *An accusing conscience :*—When Professor Webster was waiting his trial for murder, he is said to have complained of his fellow prisoners for insulting him through the walls of his cell, and screaming to him, "You are a bloody man." On examination, the charge was found wholly groundless. The accusing voices were imaginary—merely the echoes of a guilty conscience. *Conscience awakened :*— The long-forgotten sin is now remembered. Like the ground-swell after a storm, which, mariners tell us, appears long after the tempest has ceased, and far off from its *locus*, they come up in awful vividness before us. . . . As when a flash of lightning reveals but for a moment the dangers of the shipwrecked crew, so now there is an awful recollection of all our past transgressions. They have long been covered up, but only covered like the beautiful carvings of some old minster, or the frescoes on its walls were covered, before the hand of the restorer was brought to bear upon them. They were always clear and open before the eyes of Him with whom we have to do. Now we see them for a little with something of the insight that pertains to Him. (*J. G. Pilkington.*)　　*Emblem of a troubled conscience :—* There is a species of poplar whose leaves are often rustled by a breeze too faint to stir the foliage of other trees. Noticing the fact one day when there was scarcely a breath of air, Gotthold thought with himself, "This tree is the emblem of a man with a wounded and uneasy conscience, which takes alarm at the most trifling cause, and agitates him to such a pitch, that he knows not whither to fly." *A guilty conscience :—*It gives a terrible form and a horrible voice to everything beautiful and musical without. It is said of Bessus, a native of Pelonia, in Greece :—Being one day seen by his neighbours pulling down some birds' nests, and passionately destroying the young, they severely reproved him for his ill-nature and cruelty to those little innocent creatures that seemed to court his protection. He replied that their notes were to him insufferable, as they never ceased twitting of the murder of his father. The music of the sweet songsters of the grove are as the shrieks of hell to a guilty conscience startled from its grave. Let Byron describe its anguish, for who felt it more than he ?—

> "The mind that broods o'er guilty woes,
> Is like the scorpion girt by fire ;
> In circle narrowing as it glows.
> The flames around their captive close,
> Till inly searched by thousand throes,
> And maddening in her ire,
> One sad and sole relief she knows,
> The sting she nourished for her foes
> Whose venom never yet was vain,
> Gives but one pang and cures all pain,
> And darts into her desperate brain :
> So do the dark in soul expire,
> Or live like scorpion girt by fire.
> So writhes the mind remorse has riven,
> Unfit for earth, undoomed for heaven,
> Darkness above, despair beneath,
> Around it flame, within it death."　　(*D. Thomas, D.D.*)

*Torments of conscience :—*It is said of Charles IX., that he could never bear to lie awake at night unless his thoughts were diverted by the strains of music in an adjoining apartment; and of Tiberius, it is asserted that he declared to his senators that he suffered death daily.　　*Bad actions personified :—*Not in the sky, not in the midst of the sea, not if we enter into the clefts of the mountain, is there known a spot in the whole world where a man might be freed from an evil deed. Each action brings with it its inevitable consequences, which even God cannot change. "In a region of black cold," says an Eastern sage, "wandered a soul which had departed from the earth, and there stood before him a hideous woman, profligate and deformed. 'Who art thou?' he cried. To him she answered, 'I am thine own actions.'"

Ver. 10. **Aside privately.**—*The profit of restful retirement :—*I had a friend once (he is now in heaven) who was one of those men that give their whole heart to business, and believe in nothing else on week days, while even on Sundays their worship is, never to be still if they are religious men, but to be doing something from daylight to bed-time. One summer day the feeling came over him that he would wander away, just for once, into the silence, and take one whole day of perfect rest. It was toward an upland he took his way, wandering by some small lakes of an exquisite beauty, and enjoying every moment of his holiday ; until away on in the afternoon, when he had drunk deep of the quietness, and was lying on his face in the grass, happening lazily to lift his head all at once, as by a flash, he saw that one of these lakes could be tapped for his mill-dam, and so give him water enough to tide him over the summer dryness and prevent his wheel from stopping, when it ought to go right on. He went home at sunset, blessing himself for his good fortune as well as for the leisure, which was likely to turn out a better day's work than he had done for a long time, took a survey of the land next day, and when he told me the story he had made his connection with the new reservoir, and it answered entirely his expectation. I have often thought of my friend's adventure since then as an illustration of a lesson we are rather loth to learn in this busy land of ours—how springs and reservoirs of blessing may sometimes be opened to us through a perfect quietness we can never find through incessant toil. We do not believe in rest as devoutly as we believe in work. It does not seem possible we can ever do as good service either for God or man to be still as to be stirring. In this intense life we easily believe that to do nothing one whole day is for that day to be nothing. It is as if we should do nothing in a boat alone among the rapids of the St. Lawrence. The majestic motion and contention of the life about us overcomes us so that the gracious word contemplation in the old, sweet sense, is about as strange to the most of us as Sanscrit. We contemplate the very heavens to remember how many millions of miles the sun travels in an hour. Work while it is day is the watchword of our age, and it is always day. Time means the time to do things. " Let us then be up and doing" is indeed our psalm of life. We fight the idea of the philosopher that God cannot have rested on the seventh day and hallowed it, and then often illustrate our own belief by filling the seventh day as full of care as the rest. (R. Collyer.)

Ver. 11. He received them.—*Christ welcoming seekers :*—In the Revised Version we read, " He welcomed them," in place of, " He received them." An instructive improvement, of which we may make evangelical use. I. First, may the Holy Spirit help us while we dwell upon THE FACT that Jesus welcomed those who sought Him. 1. We observe, first, that our Lord received all comers at all times. The time mentioned in our text was the most inconvenient possible. He was seeking rest for His disciples, who were weary after their labours. A great sorrow was on them also, for John had been beheaded, and it was meet that they should solace their grief by a short retirement. At this time, too, our blessed Lord desired obscurity ; for Herod was inquiring for Him. It was most inconvenient, therefore, to be followed by so great a crowd. Is it not wonderful that under such circumstances our blessed Lord should welcome the insatiable throng ? I think, too, that the Master desired just then to hold a conference with His apostles as to the work they had done, and the future which was opening up before them. 2. Our Lord received all sort of comers. They were a motley throng, and I fear that few, if any, of them were actuated by any high or exalted motive. He never rejected any because they were (1) poor; (2) diseased; (3) too young ; (4) too old. 3. Once more : our Lord receives all with a hearty welcome. He did not merely allow the people to come near, tolerating their presence ; but " He welcomed them." II. Now I come to use this as AN ENCOURAGEMENT. If Jesus Christ when He was here on earth welcomed all that came at all hours, then He will welcome you, my friend, if you come to Him now ; for the circumstances are just the same. 1. You are the same sort of person as those whom Jesus used to welcome. They were good-for-nothing bodies ; they were persons that were full of need, and could not possibly bring a price with which to purchase His favour. Are you not just like them ? 2. And then there is the same Saviour. Jesus Christ is the same gracious Pardoner as He was in the days of His flesh. III. Thirdly, we use our text as A LESSON. If Jesus Christ welcomes all that come to Him, let all of us who are His followers imitate His example, and give a warm welcome to those who seek the Lord. Men are brought to Jesus by cheerfulness far sooner than by gloom. Jesus welcomed men. His looks said, " I am glad to see you." In winning souls use an abundance of smiles. Have you not seen in one of our magazines an account of seven people saved by a smile ? It is a pretty story. A clergyman passes by a window on his way to church. A baby was being dandled there, and he smiled at the baby, and the baby at him. Another time he passed ; the baby was there again, and once more he smiled. Soon baby was taken to the window at the hour when he usually passed. They did not know who the gentleman was ; but one day two of the older children followed to see where he went on a Sunday. They followed him to church, and as he preached in a winning way, they told their father and mother, who felt interest enough in their baby's friend to wish to go. Thus in a short time a godless family that had previously neglected the worship of God was brought to the Saviour because the minister smiled at the baby. I never heard of anybody getting to heaven through frowning at the baby, or at any one else. Certain wonderfully good persons go through the world as if they were commissioned to impress everybody with the awful solemnity of religion: they resemble a winter's night without a moon; nobody seems attracted, nor even impressed, by them except in the direction of dislike. I saw a life-buoy the other day covered with luminous paint. How bright it seemed, how suitable to be cast upon the dark sea to help a drowning man! An ordinary life-buoy he would never see, but this is so bright and luminous that a man must see it. Give me a soul-winner bright with holy joy, for he will be seen by the sorrowing soul, and his help will be accepted. (*C. H. Spurgeon.*)   **Healed them that had need.**—*Real grace for real need :—*I. THOSE WHOM CHRIST HAS SAVED WILL ALL CONFESS THAT THEY HAD NEED OF SAVING. 1. All the saved saints confess that they had need of healing through their natural depravity.   2. Many have been led to feel that in addition to ordinary original sin, evil tendencies had in the case of some of us assumed peculiar shapes and dreadful forms of besetting and constitutional sin—quick temper; pride; animal passions, &c.   Apart from grace, we had been sinners before the Lord exceedingly.   A Scotch gentleman was observed to look very intently upon the face of Rowland Hill : the good old man asked him, "And what are you looking in my face at?"   The observer replied, " I have been studying the lines of your face."   "And what do you make out of them?" said Rowland.   "Why, I make out," said he, "that if the grace of God had not changed your heart you would have been a great rascal." "Ah!" said Rowland, "you have made out the truth indeed."   Many of us have to confess humbly that in us there was pressing need of healing, for if healing had not come, we should not only have been sinful as others, but should probably have taken the lead in iniquity, and been carried away by the wild sweep of inward passion to the utmost excess of riot.   3. Brethren, this need of healing will be confessed by the saints in this further respect, that there was not only in us a tendency to sin, but we had grievously sinned in act and deed before conversion. 4. There was need of healing because, in addition to having sinned, we wilfully continued in it.   II. UNSAVED HEARERS HAVE NEED OF SAVING.   1. Because you are inclined to evil.   2. Because of your actual sins.   3. You do not feel this as you ought.   4. You are unable to pray.   5. Your feelings, your desires after good things, are very often damped.   Perhaps this morning you are sincerely in earnest, but to-morrow you may be just as careless as ever.   III. Our third point is to thee, O needy sinner.   JESUS CAN SAVE THEE.   Christ can save you, for there is not a record in the world, nor has there ever been handed down to us by tradition a single case in which Jesus has failed.   (*Ibid.*) *Power to heal :*—A great writer of fiction has remarked that "a man might be a great healer, if he would, without being a great doctor."   We may add, without being a worker of miracles.   " A man may be a great healer without being a great doctor."   The doctor, so far as his profession is concerned, has to do chiefly, if not entirely, with diseases of the body.   He is as an agent and instrument, the saviour and the healer of the body.   As a friend to the patient, he often ministers to the mind and heart; but these services are distinct from his profession.   Without being a doctor a man may be a great healer.

" Canst thou not minister to a mind diseased,
Pluck from the memory a rooted sorrow?"

Around us all there are sick minds, wounded spirits, broken hearts and diseased souls, to be cured, and healed, and relieved by means which God has given us. Around us all there are wounds in families, wounds in friendships, and wounds in communities, to which we may apply a healing power.   "Whole," "sound," "healthy," are words descriptive of but few persons, and of but few households, and of but few communities.   In this world of ours there is evidently a great work of healing to be wrought.   There is a great need of healing, and there are great healing powers.   There is a spiritual disease very like that malady of body known as atrophy.   It is a condition of weakness in the direction of evil.   The Apostle Paul refers to it when he observes, "When we were yet without strength, in due time, Christ died for the ungodly."   For this disease there is but one physician, and there is but one remedy.   The woman of Samaria was a great healer, when she brought the men of her city to the Messiah.   All are " healers " who guide men to

Jesus. I desire to awaken your ambition to be in this world of sorrow and sin—great healers. 1. You may heal by the tongue. "How forcible are right words." "A wholesome tongue is a tree of life." "The tongue of the just is as choice silver." "Pleasant words are as a honeycomb." 2. You may heal by the light of the countenance. Honest laughter has a stirring power. Genuine and kindly smiles have a healing power. A countenance alive with sympathy and bright with love heals. 3. You may heal by the hand, by what the hand may find to do in the sphere of ministration and of service. All help has healing power, if delicately and wisely and kindly administered. 4. You may heal by your purse. Solomon saith, "Money is a defence." "Money answereth all things." In the broad work of healing, money is a mighty agent. Without doubt, in some cases almsgiving spreads and confirms moral disease and spiritual sickness. But as buying bread for the hungry and clothes for the naked and medicine for the sick, as procuring dwellings for the homeless, and as relieving the fatherless and the widow, as redeeming from debt those who are under pecuniary obligations to others, money does much in the service of healing. 5. You may heal by your presence. Presence, even though the tongue be silent; presence, even though the hands be tied and bound by inability; presence, even though there be no silver nor gold, has oftentimes a healing power. Presence speaks, for it tells of sympathy; presence cheers, it diverts the thoughts and lessens the burden; presence will sometimes have in it a wealth of consolation. 6. You may heal by your social influence. The respect and esteem which men cherish toward you may be used to serve and to comfort others. Thus did Esther use her influence with the King Ahasuerus, to heal the wound inflicted on the safety and honour of the Jews (Esther iv. 13, 14). Influence with those who can serve others is as truly a talent as our individual ability. 7. You may heal by making intercession for others. This is a power which all possess. Its effectiveness is not as manifest as that of other agencies, but without doubt it is as real. There is more of mystery adhering to this agency than to other means, but our faith in it is not less strong. The achievements of prayer, as recorded in holy Scripture, are wonderful, as redeeming life from destruction, as securing the forgiveness of iniquities, and as healing diseases alike of body and of spirit. 8. You may heal by teaching Jesus Christ. To the truth of this saying multitudes in heaven and upon earth bear constant and willing witness. (*S. Martin, D.D.*)

Vers. 13–17. **Five loaves and two fishes.**—*Feeding the five thousand :*—I. All the people of God are stewards of the household of faith, and to God must they render an account. II. We are to adopt all lawful means by which to escape impending danger. When our Lord was exposed to danger from Herod, though possessed of all power, he adopted human means to escape that danger. We must not allow any fear of encountering perils to deter us from duty. III. We ought to esteem no sacrifice too great to be made for Christ and His gospel. The people referred to in the text did not think it too much to leave their comfortable homes; but, forsaking all, went into the desert to listen to Him who spake as never man spake. If called to hazard all, and even our life, for the gospel, let us commit ourselves to God. IV. Our Lord welcomes all who come to Him by faith. When the people came to Him from the villages round about, He refused none, but healed all who had need. V. Wherever true Christianity exists in the heart, it will manifest its presence by a spirit of benevolence. The disciples saw the night coming on, and wished the multitude to be dismissed, that they might retire to the comforts they needed. Christianity rejoices not only in our own salvation, but also in that of others. VI. When human aid fails, Divine power is made manifest. VII. We should so receive and enjoy the blessings of heaven as to glorify God. When our Lord received the food, He returned thanks for it, and pronounced a blessing upon it. VIII. When the mind reposes by faith on the Saviour, there will be ample supplies of grace and favour. Christ never said to the seed of Jacob, "Seek ye My face in vain." Conclusion : In all situations of danger let the people put their trust in Jehovah, remembering that He who is for them is much greater than all who can be against them. (*J. Henderson.*)　　*Lessons from the miracle of multiplying the loaves :*—1. We learn from this miracle that it is our duty to do what we can to supply the bodily wants of others. 2. We here learn that those who follow Christ may trust to Him for the necessaries of life. 3. We are here reminded of the duty of what is commonly called "saying grace" at meals. This was our Lord's practice; and it is a duty often enjoined in Scripture. 4. From the particular direction our Lord here gave as to the fragments, we draw the general rule that nothing should be lost, or wasted. To waste our substance is a sinful abuse of God's gifts. It is one thing to be generous and hospitable; it is quite another to be thoughtless, extravagant, and wasteful. Such wasting is not only offensive to God, but unjust and unkind to our fellow creatures. (*J. Foote, M.A.*) *Ability developed by responsibility :*—The vast hunger of the world is a vast responsibility upon the Church and a vast blessing. Christians must supply bread, or the people will perish. The necessity drives them to Christ, compels the bringing forth of their talents and resources, and works enlargement in volume and value. I. Christ deals with us on principles of a wise economy, builds his supernatural work on our natural resources, and makes a little do the work of abundance. II. Christ always makes that which we have and bring to Him for His blessing adequate for the needs of the hour. He takes us into partnership with Himself both in His work and its rewards. III; Weakness made strong in effort for Him. (*Anon.*) *Food for hungry souls :*—The Lord helps our souls as He helps our bodies, through the aid of ordained means. and sometimes He may cause these means to fall short, and then may supply them as suddenly and abundantly as He multiplied these loaves and fishes. A person may have but little learning—he may be quite unable to read, and may seem to himself as if he did not well understand what he hears—and yet, if he have the fear of God in his heart, and try to live accordingly, he shall eat and be filled with spiritual meat and drink. One good lesson, one verse, one prayer may be a treasure to him which he shall never lose. He may be a good way from Church, he may have few helps at home; but if he really try to make the most of what little he has, God can and will make a good deal of it—*to him*. Half a prayer remembered as having been learnt in childhood; an old loose Bible or Testament on a shelf; the remembrance of some good Christian formerly known, his sayings, his tone of voice, his manner of coming in and going out—all these and other such things are as the scanty fare of that multitude, which became abundant under His creative hand. (*John Keble, M.A.*) *Enough for all when Christ distributes :*—I. THE PEOPLE'S BODY NEED, AND SOUL NEED. II. GOD'S PROVISION FOR BODY AND FOR SOUL. III. GOD'S METHOD OF SUPPLY TO BODY AND TO SOUL. Ordinary. Miraculous. Moral. (*The Weekly Pulpit.*) *Christ in a fourfold aspect :*—I. Christ in MIRACULOUS BENEFICENCE. Omnipotence is ever instinct with love. II. Christ in SOCIAL ORDER. Not a God of confusion. III. Christ in FRUGAL ARRANGEMENT. Nothing in nature runs to waste. IV. Christ in the PATRONAGE OF HOSPITALITY. "Give ye them to eat." Help each other. Conclusion: Follow Christ in all this. (*D. Thomas, D.D.*) *The miraculous feeding of five thousand :*—The disciples had just returned from the mission in which they had been engaged, and "told Him all that they had done." The considerate Master saw that they were exhausted by the fatigue and excitement of their labours. He accordingly seeks to secure them quiet. This they could not have in Capernaum (see Mark vi. 31). They take passage privately in a vessel to a desert place near to Bethsaida. In vain did they look here for solitude. They had been observed by the eager multitude, who followed on foot, and were at the landing-place before them. The Lord has compassion on them, and is solicitous for their physical as well as their spiritual well-being. On finding that there are five loaves and two small fishes, He gives the disciples directions for the orderly arrangement of the multitude into companies; and when all were in perfect order He took the loaves and the fishes, and blessed and brake and gave the disciples to set before the multitude. As they passed from hand to hand, the loaves and fishes multiplied so as to become more than sufficient for the great multitude. Every year in the harvest we see this miracle repeated. 1. Learn that order is Christlike, is Divine. 2. That economy is Divine. All the evangelists are careful to record that they gathered up the fragments left. Liberal profusion and true economy always go hand in hand. 3. Learn to relieve the wants of others even when we have but little. It is ours also to feed the hungry. Especially with the bread of life. (*D. Longwill.*) *Jesus and His bounty :*—I. THE PROBLEM OF THE DISCIPLES. The desert place, the night, the multitude without food, presented a problem that might well constitute a reason for anxiety to any who were of a sympathetic nature. The circumstances were new and surprising, and were such as to test the weakness, or bring out the strength, of their confidence in the Master's wisdom and power. We all need to be surprised in life. It is the unexpected that shows us what we are. The disciples were perplexed, and very human they were in their perplexity. For the time they seem to have forgotten several things. 1. That the people had followed their Master and not them, and that *they* were connected with the people through Him. Had the people followed them there would be nothing to do but to send them away. If the case to-day were between the disciples and the multitude, it would be hopeless. 2. That the Master knew as much, and more, of the multitude than they did. 3. That the Master was moved with compassion towards the people. They had forgotten the most important elements of the problem. They had been looking at the multitude and the night; had been realizing the difficulties very vividly. We, too, look at our multitude, and see the darkness in which they are involved, and tremble as we think of the possible, if not the inevitable issue of what we see. But we do not see the whole when we tremble. God is above the night, and pities all who are in it. God knows, and God pities, and that ought to be enough for our faith, if not for our reason. At length the disciples made their petition, saying, "Send the multitude away." The very fact that He was there to receive their requests ought to have reminded them of some of the many things which they had forgotten. For if *they* had thought, had not He much more than they? II. THE SOLUTION OF THE MASTER. "Give ye them to eat." 1. The command seemed extravagant, but they knew that it had not been His habit to gather in where He had not scattered abroad. It made them feel how inadequate they were, with the little they had, to obey it. They had only five loaves and two fishes, do as they would, with a multitude to feed. The loaves were, however, just what the people needed. We have all some little which, if wisely used, may be of benefit to our fellows. We have mind, heart, and opportunity. 2. The Master took the five loaves and the two fishes from the disciples, and manifested His great power through that which they gave Him. He brought them into the fellowship of His mystery. He blessed the loaves which they brought. Our first condition of usefulness is to take the little we have to Christ, if we have only the little. That which is blessed by Him is equal to all that life's occasion demands. 3. After the blessing came the breaking, but it does not seem that the loaves appeared to be more than five after they were blessed. 4. Although there is enough and to spare, there is nothing to be wasted. (*J. O. Davies.*) **Give ye them to eat.**—*Duty not measured by our own ability :*—The narrative suggests and illustrates the following important principle :—THAT MEN ARE OFTEN, AND PROPERLY, PUT UNDER OBLIGATION TO DO THAT FOR WHICH THEY HAVE, IN THEMSELVES, NO PRESENT ABILITY. God requires no man to do, without ability to do ; but He does not limit His requirements by the measures of previous or inherently contained ability. He has made provision in many ways for the enlargement of our means and powers so as to meet our emergencies. And He does this on a large scale, and by system—does it in the natural life, and also in the works and experiences of the life of faith. 1. To begin at the very lowest point, it is the nature of human strength and fortitude bodily to have an elastic measure, and to be so let forth or extended as to meet the exigencies that arise. Muscular strength and endurance are often suddenly created or supplied by some great emergency for which they are wanted. 2. So, also, it is in the nature of courage to increase in the midst of perils and because of them, and courage is the strength of the heart. 3. Intellectual force, too, has the same elastic quality, and measures itself, in the same way, by the exigencies we are called to meet. Task it, and for that very reason it grows efficient. It discovers its own force by the exertion of force. All great commanders, statesmen, lawgivers, scholars, preachers, have found the powers unfolded in their calling, and by their calling, which were necessary for it. 4. The same thing is true, and quite as remarkably, of what we call moral power. Not seldom is it a fact that the very difficulty and grandeur of a design, which some heroic soul has undertaken to execute, exalts him at once to such a pre-eminence of moral power that mankind are exalted with him, and inspired with energy and confidence by the contemplation of his magnificent spirit. The great and successful men of history are commonly made by the great occasions they fill. As with David, so with Nehemiah, Paul, Luther. A Socrates, a Tully, a Cromwell, a Washington, all the great master-spirits, the founders and law-givers of empires and defenders of the rights of man, are made by the same law. 5. How childish, then, is it in religion, to imagine that we are called to do nothing save what we have ability to do beforehand ; ability in ourselves to do. We have, in fact, no such ability at all, no ability that is inherent, as respects anything laid upon us to do. Our ability is what we can have, and then our duty is graduated by what we can have. This is the Christian doctrine everywhere. 6. This doctrine opposed to two opposite errors : (1) That of those who think the demand of the religious life so limited and trivial as to require but little care and small sacrifice ; and (2) that of those who look upon them as being so many and so great, that they are discouraged under them. (*H. Bushnell, D.D.*)　　*Between the Lord of life and the famishing multitudes :*—1. The multitude in a desert place was representative to the Saviour's mind of vaster multitudes all over the earth. 2. The bread He supplied for men's bodies was suggestive of the bread He was to supply for their souls. 3. The position of the disciples, then, is the position of the disciples still—we stand between the Lord of life and the famishing multitudes. We may still hear the words ringing in our ears, " Give ye them to eat." I. IT IS A COMMAND ON BEHALF OF THE FAMISHING MULTITUDES. 1. They have not the knowledge of God. 2. They have not the knowledge of the meaning of life. 3. They have not the knowledge of the gospel. II. IT IS A COMMAND FROM THE LORD OF LIFE. 1. He has compassion on the multitudes. 2. He has provided bread for the multitudes. 3. It is His prerogative to command to give to the multitudes. III. IT IS A COMMAND TO DISCIPLES AS STANDING BETWEEN THE LORD OF LIFE AND THE FAMISHING MULTITUDES. 1. We are to sympathize with the multitudes. 2. We are to be the medium of communication between Christ and the multitudes in the distribution of bread. 3. We are to distribute to the multitudes in hope. The day is coming when the Church, turning to its Lord, shall say, " All the famishing multitudes are now fed." And after its task has been accomplished it will feel so strong in the means of extension, that there will be, as it were, twelve baskets over, out of which many more might have been fed. (*R. Finlayson, B.A.*)　　*Confidence in Christ's power to supply necessity :*—During the retreat of Alfred the Great, at Athelney, in Somersetshire, after the defeat of his forces by the Danes, the following circumstance happened, which, while it convinces us of the extremities to which that great man was reduced, will give us a striking proof of his pious, benevolent disposition. A beggar came to his little castle there and requested alms, when his queen informed him "that they had only one small loaf remaining, which was insufficient for themselves and their friends, who were gone in quest of food, though with little hopes of success." The king replied, "Give the poor Christian one half of the loaf. He that could feed five thousand men with five loaves and two fishes can certainly make that half loaf suffice for more than our necessity." Accordingly, the poor man was relieved, and this noble act of charity was soon recompensed by a providential store of fresh provisions, with which his people returned. (*W. Buck.*) *Valuable fragments :*—A carpet from the San Francisco Mint was burned the other day, and yielded £505 worth of gold dust, which had fallen in imperceptible particles during five years' use. In life take care of the minute things. These particles of gold seemed little indeed as they floated away, but they made a grand total. So it will be in life if we improve every moment of time, every scrap of knowledge, every degree of influence, every opportunity of being good, getting good, doing good. A wise economy of the grains of gold brings out massive talents some day. Take care and value apparently mean things. The carpet on which men walked in the Mint was sown with gold, although they knew it not. All our common things, tasks, duties, are full of the dust of gold. That on which men trample would yield crowns for their head if they only knew it and walked wisely. Make the best of a life of trifles, and we shall one day be astonished at the splendid result. God will not let our good doings perish, small as they may be. He will gather up the fragments to our eternal enrichment. The body will dissolve in the crucible of the grave, the earth be burned up as the carpet was, but the fine gold of true human life shall be gathered up in an eternal weight of glory. (*Christian Journal.*)　　*Saying grace at meals :*—Without meaning to say that any precise form, or length, or numeration of particulars, is necessary, the following hints may be given as of general application. A grace is a prayer before, or after meat, which circumstances require to be short, but which ought always to be solemn and earnest, never formal and careless. It most expressly requires an acknowledgment of God as the Author of our mercies, and a petition for His blessing along with them : and, as presented by Christians, it ought, in some way, to refer to the gospel, and spiritual things, and be concluded in the name of Christ. At a solitary meal, the duty must by no means be neglected ; and then one's own private feelings may be more particularly consulted as to the matter. At a social meal, time and circumstances, in what is indifferent, may be, and ought to be, considered; but all present ought to hear what is said, and join heartily in it, else it is no grace, no act of blessing and thanksgiving of theirs. Children ought to be early instructed in the nature of this duty, and taught and accustomed reverentially to discharge it. Nor ought it ever afterwards to be discontinued. The due observance of this pious custom adorns the best furnished table, and ennobles and sweetens the plainest fare. Let no man, who should be expected to discharge this honourable service before others, whether he be minister, or landlord, or other person residing, or taking a lead for the time, be afraid or ashamed so to do. (*J. Foote, M.A.*) *Ancient graces before meals :*—From the earliest time our Lord's act has been taken as a model, and the Jewish custom, being reconfirmed by our Lord's example, has passed into the practice of Christian people. Examples remain of the early graces, as used both in the Eastern and Western Churches. The "Apostolical Constitutions" furnish the following as a prayer at a mid-day meal: "Blessed art Thou, O Lord, who feedest me from my youth up, who givest food to all flesh. Fill our hearts with joy and gladness; that, always having a sufficiency, we may abound unto every good work, in Christ Jesus our Lord, through whom be glory and honour and power unto Thee, world without end, Amen." This prayer, slightly varied, is also given to be said after meals in a treatise improbably ascribed to St. Athanasius. (*Biblical things not generally known.*) *Divine provision, human distribution :*—1. Rationalizing tendency to explain away miracles on natural grounds wrong, but like many wrong things, a perversion of that which is right. It is a right and a reverent thing not to suppose a miracle where natural explanation sufficient. Peculiarity of New Testament miracles, which distinguishes them from absurd stories of apocryphal Gospels, that they all have a worthy purpose, and a purpose which could only be attained by the putting forth a supernatural power. But not everything, even in a miracle, is miraculous, for—2. Christ multiplied the loaves miraculously, but He distributed the provision thus made by natural means, human instrumentality. Necessity for miracle ceased with rendering supply sufficient. 3. We have in this an illustration of the method of God's working. God does not need human co-operation to enable Him to carry out His purposes. But He chooses that, while the power which makes the provision is of necessity Divine, the instruments of its distribution shall be human. Reason to be found in constitution of human nature and in blessedness of results. Good for recipient that he shall receive from brother-man. More blessed still for distributor. 4. Each disciple would feel it an unspeakable privilege to be made a dispenser of Christ's beneficence. Can you imagine one holding back? How is it now, with us? 5. The personal responsibility involved in this law of human instrumentality. Suppose one of the disciples had begun to argue with himself that it was folly to give away what they might need for themselves, and had hidden away a loaf in the folds of his robe, may we not imagine that in that case the reverse of the miracle would have been enacted? "What I gave I kept," &c. (*J. R. Bailey.*) Gave—"kept giving"; the tense shows the manner in which the increase of bread took place. (*A. Carr, M.A.*)

Vers. 18-20. **Whom say the people that I am ?**—*One of Christ's conferences with His disciples :*— I. OUR LORD'S PRAYER. Brethren, "He ever liveth to make intercession for us," and if "the effectual fervent prayer of a righteous man availeth much," what are we to think of that Intercessor whom the Father heareth always? It was the privilege of Jacob's family to have a friend at court, and that friend was their own brother. It was the privilege of David to have a friend at court, and that friend was the king's own son. Ah, Christians, both these are combined in your privilege; you have both in Him who now appears in the presence of God for us. II. OUR LORD'S INQUIRY. "He asked them, Whom say the people that I am?" This is a frequent question, arising not only from curiosity, but vanity. It would be indeed well if we were anxious to know what God says of us, for "it is a light thing to be judged of men: He that judges us is the Lord," and upon His decision depends our happiness or misery. But how frequent is the inquiry, "What do people say of me?" As to some, the answer would be, "Why, nothing at all; they do not even think of you; they do not know enough of you to make you the theme of their discourse." "But what do people say of me?" asks another. Why, they say, "Your tongue walketh through the earth; some call you 'the Morning Herald,' and others, 'the Daily Advertiser.'" "But what do people say of me?" asks another. They say that you are very hard-hearted and close-fisted; that you are a "busy-body in other men's matters"; they say that you are such a Nabal that a man cannot speak to you; they say that you are wiser in your own conceit than seven men that can render a reason. It would be well in certain respects if we knew what people say of us—what friends say of us; yes, and what enemies say of us, too. I remember Archbishop Usher says in an address to God, "Lord, bless me with a faithful friend; or, if not, with a faithful enemy, that I may know my faults, for I desire to know them." But Jesus was meek and lowly of heart; He, therefore, did not ask this question from pride or vanity. Nor did He ask it from ignorance. He knew all the numerous opinions afloat concerning Him. But this question seems designed to affect them, to bind them to Himself, and to furnish them with further instruction upon it. III. Observe THE CHARGE here given. "And He straitly charged them, and commanded them to tell no man that thing." We should rather have supposed that He would have ordered His disciples to go and publish it, but His thoughts are not as ours; "There is a time for every purpose under the heaven." It seems to be a general law of heaven, that knowledge of every kind should gradually spread. There are some things which must precede others, and make way for them. It is thus you deal with your children, keeping back for a time things from their knowledge. Thus a wise instructor will do with his pupils, he will teach them as they are able to bear it. And this was the method of our Saviour Himself in dealing with His disciples. Had our Lord then immediately proclaimed Himself as the Messiah, it is easy to suppose what insurrections might have taken place by those who would have endeavoured to make Him a king, and to keep Him from suffering. Besides this, the prohibition was only for a limited period. After His resurrection from the dead He appeared to His disciples, and said, "Go ye into all the world, and preach the gospel, beginning at Jerusalem"; and Peter, to whom He here spake, filled Jerusalem with His doctrine, and said to the murderers of the Savour, "God hath made this same Jesus whom ye crucified both Lord and Christ." IV. Observe HIS SUFFERINGS. "The Son of Man must suffer many things, and be rejected of the elders and the chief priests and the scribes, and be slain." You see, first, that He foreknew them. Secondly, He foretold them, to prepare His disciples for their approach. Thirdly, He describes them. V. Observe HIS GLORY. "And be raised the third day." We have demonstrations in proof of this. See the witnesses as they come before their adversaries. Believers have other kinds of evidences. They have the witness in themselves; they know the power of His resurrection; they have felt it raising them from a death of sin to a life of righteousness; that "like as He was raised up from the dead by the glory of the Father, even so should they also walk in newness of life." (*W. Jay*.) *The Lord's question :*—Who say ye that I am? 1. A question of conscience. 2. A question of controversy. 3. A question of life. 4. A question of the times. ((*Van Oosterzee*.) Jesus will have His disciples—1. Independently recognize Him as the Christ; 2. Voluntarily confess Him as the Christ. (*Ibid*.) *Jesus the Christ :*—I. THE WORLD'S JUDGMENT "Whom do men say that I, the Son of Man, am?" So, too, in our own time is there infinite divergence among the builders who reject the chief stone of the corner. To some He is the object of a hatred which, in its malignity, would construe His good as evil—others simply pass Him by as though His claims were unworthy of serious thought—others regard Him with respect and veneration, exhaust the resources of language in their attempts to picture His moral beauty, will do anything but trust in Him as a Saviour. To some He is a man full of imperfections, "in consistency of goodness far below vast numbers of His unhonoured disciples," to others He is the perfect man, the noblest of all creatures, everything but God. These diversities may be considered under two aspects. 1. The disbelief of the intellect, including all those phases of opinion held by men who distinctly reject the claim of the Lord Jesus to the honours of the Godhead, who do not regard His life and death as the ground of the sinner's acceptance with God, and who deny that faith in Him is the condition of salvation. There is a certain amount of respect which this theorist is willing to pay to our Lord. He tells us that Jesus has done for religion what Socrates did for philosophy, and Aristotle for science, that He fixed the idea of pure worship, and that He has thus exerted a wondrous power over the heart of humanity. Yet he would have us believe that He was Himself a self-deluded enthusiast, who yielded His mind up to the idea of His own Messiahship, until He was driven, though almost unconsciously, to act a part in order to sustain His own pretensions, and whose miracles, where they are not the pure inventions of His evangelists, were deceptions practised either by Himself or by some too-zealous followers to impose on popular credulity. The power which Christianity exerts cannot be ignored, and it is necessary to give some explanation of the way in which it has arisen. It is simply impossible to persuade the world that it owes some of its mightiest impulses, and has consecrated some of its noblest affections, to a being who, after all, was nothing more than the creation of the too luxuriant fancy and the too fond affection of a few Jewish disciples, who had contrived to throw around the humble life of an unlettered peasant of Galilee the unreal glory of legends and traditions. Rationalists, therefore, set before us a Jesus from whom they would have us believe this marvellous power has proceeded. Jesus of Nazareth would thus be removed from the page of history, but this other Jesus would not take His place. 2. We note a more frequent and formidable antagonism in the unbelief of the heart. Disbelief involves a certain exercise of mind as to the claims of Christianity. Unbelief may be nothing more than simple passive indifference. Disbelief says there is no Christ, no atonement, no redemption. Unbelief says if there be a Christ I will not worship Him ; though there be an atonement I care not to seek its blessings; though there be a Redeemer, of His salvation I care not to partake. Disbelief take up an attitude of positive opposition, and would fain disprove the claims of the gospel. Unbelief may often use friendly words, and do some kindly deeds on behalf of the truth— may treat it with seeming reverence, and even make generous contributions for its support—will, in truth, do everything but receive its message and submit to its power. The practical issue is the same. How many different causes serve to create this secret distaste of the heart to the religion of Christ. In some it is the all-absorbing passion of worldliness which holds the spirit back from faith. In others the pride of self-reliance revolts against a scheme of salvation which ascribes nothing to human merit, and therefore leaves no place for human boasting. II. THE CHRISTIAN'S CONFESSION. "And Simon Peter answered and said, Thou art the Christ, the Son of the living God." And in relation to it we observe— 1. That it is entirely independent of the world's judgment. The unanimity of the entire world in an adverse opinion ought not to shake, could not shake the un-doubting confidence of a Christian heart in Jesus. What to Peter were the sneers of Sadducees, the scorn of priests and Pharisees, the various opinions that divided the multitude? Even were the intellect confounded, and the arguments of its logic all silenced, and did the reasoning against the authority of the gospel appear unanswerable, the heart, out of the depths of its own consciousness, would cry out, " Still there is a gospel, still there is a Christ, and He is my Saviour, my Lord and my God." 2. It is the expression of a personal faith. The trust which Christ acknowledges, and over which He rejoices, is that which the soul itself reposes in Him, and which is infinitely more than the acceptance of any creed or the associ-ation with any Christian Church. It is nothing less than the man's own sense of dependence on Christ as a Redeemer. What can be the value of any so-called belief which stops short of this? Orthodoxy, as fair as the marble statue and as cold, as symmetrical in its proportions and as lifeless in its nature, is a wretched substitute for the living trust of a true soul, which may fall into some errors, but has, at least, this one cardinal excellence, that it cleaves to the Lord with full pur-pose of heart. Such was the spirit that prompted the words of Peter. He was far from being a perfect man. 3. This faith is the fruit of Divine teaching. "Flesh and blood hath not revealed it unto thee, but My Father which is in heaven." Peter had not reached the conviction thus boldly uttered by means of greater intellectual vigour, or in virtue of any special opportunities of observation, but solely through the grace of God. There were others who knew the great facts in connection with the life and ministry of Christ, on whom they had made no such impression as they had produced on him. It was God alone who made him, as He makes all believers, to differ. The prejudices and passions of the heart, which opposed the acceptance of the gospel, will never yield except to a power Divine. 4. The confession is the necessary outward expression of the heart's inward trust. "With the heart man believeth unto righteousness ; and with the mouth confession is made unto salvation." There are various modes by which a man may confess Christ. But there is one act for which no other can be a substitute—unmeaning, nay, rather, self-condemning if it stand alone—but itself the proper supplement to every other deed of holy service. To confess Christ, we must seek to be like Him, but we must also obey Him by bearing His name, and uniting with His people to show forth His death until He come. My brother, are you one of those who shrink from this special confession of Christ? (J. G. Rogers, B.A.)   Alone praying :—The bloom of the hawthorn or White May looks like snow in Richmond Park, but nearer London, or by the road side, its virgin whiteness is sadly stained. Too often contact with the world has just such an effect upon our piety; we must away to the far-off garden of paradise to see holiness in its unsullied purity, and meanwhile we must be much alone with God if we would maintain a gracious life below. (*C. H. Spurgeon.*) *Alone with God :—* One Sabbath night (says a Scotch clergyman), after discoursing on a very solemn subject which had stirred my own soul, I took a walk before going home. It was clear starlight, without any moon, and the heavens looked down upon me with all their sublime impressiveness. I found myself unconsciously walking in the direction of the mill. I had not gone far when I met a friend pacing slowly up and down by the side of a stream near his house. As soon as I came up, he said : "Mon, I couldna gang hame direct frae the chapel the nicht. After hearing your sermon, I wanted to be alane wi' God ; and I never feel His presence so much as when I am, too, in a nicht like this." *Praying alone :—*A minister, visiting the cottages of the poor, met a little boy who had been taught at school the duty, as well as the privilege of prayer. He said, " Do you love to pray, my little fellow ? " " Oh yes, sir ! " " But in so small a house, with so large a family, when and where do you pray ? " The boy answered, " I go to bed with the others ; and when they are asleep, I rise." " But then you, yourself, must be sleepy ; how do you keep awake ? " asked the minister. " I wash my hands and face in the pitcher where the cold water is kept ; then I do not feel sleepy." *What men say of Christ :—* 1. Christ did not ask this question for information. 2. He did not ask it because He desired the applause of men. 3. He did not ask it because He intended to form His course according to the reply. 4. But what He did ask it for was that He might ground His disciples in the deepest faith. The answer to His question suggests—I. THAT PEOPLE HAVE DIFFERENT OPINIONS CONCERNING CHRIST. II. THE OPINIONS HELD OF HIM WERE HIGH AND HONOURABLE. III. FOR ALL THAT THEY FELL FAR SHORT OF THE REALITY. IV. IT IS IMPORTANT THAT WE SHOULD HAVE THE TRUE ESTIMATE OF HIM : that of Peter—"The Christ of God." There is a great difference between believing Him to be the Son of God, and believing Him to be Jesus of Nazareth only. 1. You can never trust Him for your spiritual safety if you believe in Him merely as a man. 2. If you believe in Him only as a man, He can never satisfy the yearnings of your spirit. Who is He then? He is not only the greatest of men, but the Son of the Living God, the Saviour of the world. (*Thomas Jones.*) *Jesus—the Christ :—*Peter's confession remains the central article of the creed of Christendom. I. IT IS A FACT THAT JESUS OF NAZARETH ACTUALLY LIVED. II. IT IS A FACT THAT JESUS OF NAZARETH LIVED SUBSTANTIALLY AS REPORTED IN THE FIRST THREE EVANGELISTS. I specify these three Evangelists because their testimony is sufficient for the traditional picture of Jesus, and because their testimony is admitted by those who regard the fourth Gospel as a book of later date, and of less strictly historic character. Any one who is suspicious of the substantial accuracy of our Gospels cannot better treat his haunting fear of legend and myth than by a study of the apocryphal Gospels. (*R. H. Newton*). *The Christ of God: Tokens of the true Saviour:—*I. WHAT DID PETER MEAN BY THIS PHRASE-OLOGY ? Undoubtedly he intended to express his belief that Jesus was the true Messiah. II. HOW DID PETER AND THE OTHER APOSTLES DISCERN IN SO SATISFACTORY A MANNER THAT JESUS WAS NO IMPOSTOR, AS SOME PRETENDED, BUT WAS INDEED THE CHRIST OF GOD? 1. It may be answered that their common sense was sufficient to discover this. 2. Though common sense might convince them of the excellence of the Saviour's character, they had more—there was a Divine impression on their minds giving clearer sight and more satisfactory conviction (See Matt. xvi. 17). 3. To this may be added, the discernment arising from their own faith, giving them experience of His faithfulness and goodness. 4. *We* may add, having more to judge upon than Peter had, we know this is the Christ of God by the effects of His death, the wondrous influence it has had, and still has. III. LET US, THEN, TRY OUR PERSONAL HOPES BY THIS DESIGNATION OF THE ONLY SAVIOUR ABLE TO REALIZE THEM. It is only the real Christ of God that saves with a real pardon, a real sanctification, a real crown of glory. 1. Is the Christ of the Socinians the Christ of God ? 2. Let us look at the Christ of the Antinomians. 3. There is another sort of Christ spoken of by the self-righteous, who regard the Saviour only as a help, in case they cannot sufficiently help themselves. 4. Are not even believers apt to form notions such as injure the character of the Christ of God ? (*Isaac Taylor of Ongar.*) *Making known the obscured Christ :—*Not long ago there was a researcher of art in Italy, who, reading in some book that there was a por-trait of Dante painted by Giotto, was led to suspect that he had found where it had been placed. There was an apartment used as an outhouse for the storage of wood, hay, and the like. He sought and obtained permission to examine it. Clearing out the rubbish, and experimenting upon the whitewashed wall, he soon detected the signs of the long-hidden portrait. Little by little, with loving skill, he opened up the sad, thoughtful, stern face of the old Tuscan poet. Sometimes it seems to me that thus the very sanctuary of God has been filled with wood, hay, and stubble, and the Divine lineaments of Christ have been swept over and covered by human plastering, and I am seized with an invincible desire to draw forth from its hiding-place, and reveal to men the glory of God as it shines in the face of Christ Jesus! It matters little to me what school of theology rises or what falls, so only that Christ may rise and appear in all His Father's glory, full-orbed, upon the darkness of this world! (*H. W. Beecher.*)　*Christ the true Messiah:*—At a solemn disputation which was held at Venice, in the last century, between a Jew and a Christian, the Christian strongly argued from Daniel's prophecy of the seventy weeks, that Jesus was the Messiah whom the Jews had long expected, from the predictions of their prophets. The learned rabbi who presided at this disputation was so forcibly struck by the argument that he put an end to the business by saying, " Let us shut up our Bibles, for if we proceed in the examination of this prophecy it will make us all become Christians." (*Bishop Watson.*)

Ver. 22. **The Son of Man must suffer many things.**—*Christ foreseeing the Cross:*— I. We have here set forth in the first place OUR LORD'S ANTICIPATION OF THE CROSS. Mark the tone of the language, the minuteness of the detail, the absolute certainty of the prevision. That is not the language of a man who simply is calculating that the course which he is pursuing is likely to end in his martyrdom; but the thing lies there before Him, a definite, fixed certainty; every detail known, the scene, the instruments, the non-participation of these in the final act of His death, His resurrection, and its date—all manifested and mapped out in His sight, and all absolutely certain. II. OUR LORD'S RECOGNITION OF THE NECESSITY OF HIS SUFFERING. He does not say "shall," but "must." His suffering was necessary on the ground of filial obedience. The Father's will is the Son's law. But yet that necessity grounded on filial obedience, was no mere external necessity determined solely by the Divine will. God so willed it, because it must be so, and not it must be because God so willed it. That is to say, the work to which Christ had set His hand was a work that demanded the Cross, nor could it be accomplished without it. For it was the work of redeeming the world, and required more than a beautiful life, more than a Divine gentleness of heart, more than the homely and yet deep wisdom of His teachings, it required the sacrifice that He offered on the Cross. III. Now, note further, HOW WE HAVE HERE ALSO, OUR LORD'S WILLING ACCEPTANCE OF THE NECESSITY. It is one thing to recognize, and another thing to accept, a needs-be. This "must" was no unwelcome obligation laid upon Him against His will, but one to which His whole nature responded, and which He accepted. No doubt there was in Him the innocent instinctive physical shrinking from death. No doubt the Cross, in so far, was pain and suffering. But that shrinking might be a shrinking of nature, but it was not a recoil of will. The ship may toss in dreadful billows, but the needle points to the pole. The train may rock upon the line, but it never leaves the rails. Christ felt that the Cross was an evil, but that never made Him falter in His determination to bear it, His willing acceptance of the necessity was owing to His full resolve to save the world. He must die because He would redeem, and He would redeem because He could not but love. So the "must" was not an iron chain that fastened Him to His Cross. Like some of the heroic martyrs of old, who refused to be bound to the funeral pile, He stood there chained to it by nothing but His own will and loving purpose to save the world. And oh! brethren; in that loving purpose, each of us may be sure that we had an individual and a personal share. He must die, because "He loved me, and gave Himself for me." IV. Lastly, notice here OUR LORD'S TEACHING THE NECESSITY OF HIS DEATH. This announcement was preceded by that conversation which led to the crystalizing of the half-formed convictions of the apostles in a definite creed—" Thou art the Christ, the Son of the living God." But that was not all that they needed to know, and believe and trust to. That was the first volume of their lesson-book. The second volume was this, that "Christ must suffer." And so let us learn the central place which the Cross holds in Christ's teaching. (*A. Maclaren, D.D.*)　*On the humiliation and sufferings of Christ:*—Why does the Saviour say He "*must* suffer"? I. It was at that time, and in the sense our Saviour then spake it, necessary for this reason, because otherwise the prophecies that went before concerning Him could not have been fulfilled. This reason our Saviour Himself gives (Matt. xxvi. 53; Mark xiv. 48; Luke xxiv. 26, 44). The same reason is alleged also by the apostles in their preaching (Acts xvii. 2; 1 Pet. i. 10). II. The death of Christ was necessary to make the pardon of sin. But the death of Christ was necessary, at least in this respect, to make the pardon of sin consistent with the wisdom of God in His good government of the world, and to be a proper attestation of His irreconcilable hatred against all unrighteousness. III. The practical inferences from what has been said are as follows. 1. This doctrine concerning Christ's dying for our sins is a strong argument for the indispensable necessity of our own repentance and reformation of life. 2. The consideration of Christ's giving Himself a sacrifice for our sins is, to them who truly repent, an encouragement to approach with confidence to the throne of grace in our prayers to God through Him (Rom. viii. 32). 3. The death of Christ is a great example to us of patient suffering at any time in well-doing, when the providence of God shall call us to bear testimony in that manner to His truth (1 Pet. iii. 17). (*S. Clarke, D.D.*)

Ver. 23. **If any man will come after Me, let him deny himself.**—*Self-denial:*—What is self-denial? A very interesting and very important inquiry to us who are already the subjects of Divine grace. Perhaps we have not got too much of it in modern Christianity. I cannot help thinking that our Christianity in these days would be considerably improved if we had a little more of it infused into our daily lives. What is it? It is just when we begin to yearn for the likeness of Christ, and long to be conformed to His image—when we begin to see clearly that the path which the Master trod was one of humiliation and reproach, and that there are plenty of sorrows to be borne, and plenty of difficulties to be battled with—it is just then that Satan will, if he can, prevent even this new-born light arising within our soul, and endeavour to turn that very light into darkness. And he has succeeded only too well in former ages in diverting these religious instincts into a wrong and a mischievous channel. There are two false theories about self-denial which I want to guard you against. First, there have been some who have fallen into the error of thinking that, in some way or another, self-denial has to do with the expiation of our guilt; that the offering of a life of self-denial is a kind of satisfaction to be made to God for all the sins and all the imperfections of human nature. You cannot accept a theory of this kind without its producing at once its natural effect upon your own experience, which will become then and there intensely legal. For your very self-denial will be submitted to in the spirit of bondage; it will be the sufferings of a slave, and of a felon, and not the willing undergoing of hardship on the part of a reconciled and rejoicing child. Yet again; there is another false form of self-denial which is based upon a misconception of our relation to the pleasurable. It is assumed that we are not intended to enjoy pleasure here. Now observe, this is simply a new edition of the ancient lie which was suggested by the great tempter to our first parents in Paradise. "Hath God indeed said that ye shall not eat of the trees of the garden? He has placed you in Eden, surrounded you with delights, amid all these varied trees, and all these delicious and charming fruits: and does that God whom you call "your Father" exhibit any fatherly tenderness towards you in precluding you from the natural gratification of an appetite He has Himself created. How hard must that Father be! How little sympathy there can be in His nature! Can you serve, love, confide in such a God?" This was the venom which was first of all infused into the soul of our first parents. And when such a conception is received, even though it may seem to produce the effect of an austere or self-denying life, it will necessarily have the effect of interfering with our relationships with God. When our views of the character of God are in any way interfered with, and we begin to entertain a false ideal of Him, our whole religious life must suffer from it, because the knowledge of God is the great source both of power and of enjoyment throughout the whole course of our spiritual experience. There is nothing wrong in pleasure in itself; on the contrary. God has "given us all things richly to enjoy"; and yet there may be a great deal of harm in the indulgence of pleasure; and unquestionably a large proportion—perhaps far the largest proportion—of the sins that are committed in human history are committed because men deliberately make up their minds to pursue the pleasurable. Having indicated to you these two false forms of self-denial, let us endeavour to consider, if we really can, what it is that our blessed Lord does teach. First of all, let us take hold of the word, and see if we can learn a lesson from it. The meaning would be more accurately conveyed to our minds, as English people, if we use the word "ignore" instead of "deny." The word used in the original indicates such a process as would take place where a man would refuse to admit his own identity. Supposing one of us had a property left to us, and we were brought before the magistrate in order that our personal identity might be ascertained; and supposing that we swore before competent authority that we were not the persons we were supposed to be, and that we actually were; such a process would be a denying of ourselves, and in the act of denial we should be ignoring our own natural right, and thus precluding ourselves from the enjoyment of it. The first step, then, in a really Christian life, or rather, shall I say, in the life of a disciple—for I am not speaking now of first principles—of what takes place, for the most part, at conversion: I am speaking of what takes places in point of time subsequently to conversion: at any rate it comes second in order—if we are really willing to be disciples, Jesus says to every one of us, "If any man will come *after Me.*" Before we go any further, let us ask ourselves, "Is that what we wish to do?" How many a believer, if he were just to speak the honest truth, would say, "Well, my wish is to go to heaven." Well, that is a right wish; but it is not the highest wish. "My wish is to escape condemnation." Well, it is a right wish; but it is not the highest wish. Is your heart set upon going after Christ? If our minds are really made up to follow Him, then He points out to us the condition of such a relation: and the first is, "Let him deny himself." You cannot follow Jesus unless you deny yourself. Why? Because He took the way of self-denial. How did He do it? Was He an ascetic? No. "John the Baptist came neither eating nor drinking: the Son of Man came eating and drinking." Did He ever fast? Yes. And when, and why? When He had a very definite object in doing so: when He did so in pursuance of the Divine direction. Did He ever exclude Himself from society. Yes: but why? Sometimes to spend a short season in prayer: sometimes a whole night, so that He might prepare for some serious conflict with the forces of hell, or that He might fit Himself for doing some special work, as when He named His twelve disciples. There was an object in these outward acts of self-denial. He presented to the view of all a body that was under the control of the mind, and a mind that was under the control of God. Had He no sufferings? A great many. Had He no pain? Greater than ever was borne. How was this? He bore pain with an object. He suffered because He had a purpose in view. How was it inflicted? Did He bring it upon Himself? Nay, verily: as I have already said, He never courted pain. How did it come? It came in the fulfilment of the Father's will. It came because He would cleave to the path which the Father had laid down for Him. The cross lay in His way, and He took it up: He didn't go to look for one: He did not manufacture one for Himself: but there it lay in His way, and He raised it. It was a heavier cross than ever you or I will be called upon to bear—a cross so heavy, that His frail, human nature sank beneath its load: even the tender-hearted women who saw Him toiling up to Golgotha with that terrible burden, burst into tears as they saw the Man of Sorrows pass by, as they watched His tottering steps, and beheld Him sinking under the fearful burden. But although the load may not be so heavy, there is a cross for every one of us. We shall not escape it if we follow Him. Have you made up your minds to escape the cross, dear friends? If that is the determination with which you set out on your spiritual pilgrimage, then you must also make up your mind to lose the society of Jesus. He does not say, "If any man will go to heaven, let him take up his cross": but He says, "If any man will come after Me. I am going forth on My journey: before Me lie the shadows of Gethsemane, and My vision finds its horizon crowned with the Cross of Calvary. There it stands before Me in all its grim horror. I am going on step by step towards it. Every pulsation of My blood brings Me nearer to it; and I have made up My mind; My will is fixed, My face is set like a flint; the will which reigns within My bosom is the will of the Everlasting God Himself. I am content, My God, to do Thy will. And now this is the course I take: and if any of you want to follow Me, you must go the same road. You can only maintain fellowship with Me by placing your steps where Mine have fallen. 'If any man,'—whether he be the highest saint, or whether he be only a **new-born babe** in Christ—'if any man will come after Me, let him deny himself, and take up his cross, and follow Me.'" (*W. H. Hay Aitken, M.A.*)   *The Christian law of self-sacrifice:*—I. THE GROUND OF THIS REQUIREMENT. Why is it necessary? 1. The Christian law of self-sacrifice is involved in the supreme and universal moral law. Love is, in its essential character, sacrificial. The law of self-sacrifice is only the law of love seen on the reverse. So holy love ascends, from sin and weakness, to Christ the Deliverer, complete in perfection and mighty to save. Thus manifested, it is faith receiving redeeming grace from His willing hand. But this ascending love is, in its very nature, an act of self-abandonment and self-devotement. In it the soul accepts its Master, yielding its whole being to the plastic hand of the Perfect One, to receive the impress of His thought and will. It is trust in Him as Saviour: it is complacency in His character, adoration of His perfections, aspiration to be with Him and like Him, submission to His authority, loyalty to His person; but, in every manifestation, it is an act of self-surrender to the mighty and gracious One who is drawing the heart to Himself. The same is the characteristic of love descending and imparting—love active in works of beneficence and justice. This needs no argument. I proceed to consider the condition of man under this law. 2. The second ground of the requirement of self-renunciation is the fact that sin is essentially egoism or self-ism. As love is essentially self-abnegation, sin is essentially self-assertion: a practical affirmation of the absurdity that a created being is sufficient for himself; therefore a repudiation, by the sinner, of his condition as a creature, and an arrogating to self of the Creator's place. It has four principal manifestations, in each of which this essential character appears. It is *self-sufficiency*, the opposite of Christian faith. It is *self-will*, the opposite of Christian submission. It is *self-seeking*, the opposite of Christian benevolence. It is *self-righteousness*, the opposite of Christian humility and reverence, the reflex act of sin; putting self in God's place as the object of praise and homage. 3. The third ground of the law of self-sacrifice is the fact that redemption—the Divine method of delivering man from sin and realizing the law of love—is sacrificial. The substance of Christianity is redemption. Its central fact is the historical sacrifice of the Incarnation and the Cross. Christianity, therefore, as a fact, as a doctrine, and as a life, is a sacrificial religion. Thus the law of self-renunciation is grounded in the essential character of Christianity. 4. We may find a fourth ground of the law of self-renunciation in the constitution of the created universe; for this is an expression of the same eternal love which manifests its sacrificial character in Christ. Here our ignorance does not permit us to construct a complete argument; but glimpses of the law we can trace. It appears in the natural laws of society: a child is brought into the world by its mother's anguish, and nurtured by parents' toil and suffering. In turn the child grown up, wears out life, perhaps, in nursing a parent through a long sickness, or in the infirmities of age. It is shadowed even in physical arrangements: the dew-drop, which sparkles on a summer's morning, exhales its whole being while refreshing the leaf on which it hangs. When, in the early spring, the crocus lifts its pure whiteness from beneath the reeking mould, when the iris puts on its sapphire crown, when the rose unfolds its queenly splendour, it is as if each graceful form said: "This is all I have, and all I am; this fragile grace and sweetness—I unfold it all for you." The wild berries nestle in the grass, or droop, inviting, from the vine, as if saying: "This lusciousness is all my wealth; it is for you." The apples, golden and red, glowing amid the green leaves, seem to be thoughtfully whispering God's own words: "A good tree bringeth forth good fruit." The field submits, without complaint, to be sheared of its yearly harvest mutely waiting the return of blessing at the good pleasure of Him that dresseth it; symbolizing the patient faith of him who does good, hoping for nothing again, except from the good pleasure of God, who is not forgetful to reward the patience of faith and the labour of love; on the contrary, the land which bears thorns and thistles, though it is allowed to keep its own harvest to enrich itself, yet (emblem of all covetousness) is rejected and nigh unto cursing. The sun walks regally through the heavens, pouring abroad day; and the stars shining all night, seemingly say: "We are suns; yet even our opulence of glory we give to others; our very nature is to shine." Do not say that this is all fanciful. The creation was cast in the mould of God's love; and each thing bears some impress of the same. II. THE PRINCIPLE OR SPRING OF SELF-SACRIFICE IN THE CHRISTIAN LIFE. This is love itself; a new affection, controlling the life and making the acts of self-denial easy. Happiness is not bottled up in outward objects—the same definite quantity to be secured by every man who obtains the object. A man's affections determine the sources of his happiness: he finds his joy in what he loves; and is incapable of enjoying its opposite. Whether, then, any course of action is to be a source of happiness or the contrary, depends on what the man loves. The upspringing of a new affection, as the love of a first-born child, opens on the soul a new world of joy. But religion is an affection. It is not a sense of duty, under whose lash the soul creeps through its daily stint of service. While sinful affection rules the heart, religion comes to the sinner an outward law, bristling all over with prohibitions, and every touch draws blood; it goes against the grain of every desire and purpose;

every object which it presents, and every duty which it requires, is repulsive ; it is self-denial from beginning to end.   Then the sinner is incapable of finding enjoyment in religion ; and to bid him enjoy it, is, to use an illustration from South, as if Moses had bidden the Israelites to quench their thirst at the dry rock, before he had brought any water out of it. But when the new affection wells up in the heart, all this is changed. A new world of action and joy opens to the man. Religion is no longer an outward law, commanding him against his will ; but an inward affection, drawing him in the way of his own inclination. This new affection, which is the principle of Christian self-renunciation, is specifically love to Christ, whether existing as faith in Him or devotedness to Him. It is evident, therefore, that Christian self-denial is primarily that first great act of renouncing self in self-devoting love to Christ. It is the surrender of self to Christ in the act of faith. You are liable to think Christian self-denial less than it is : for you think it is giving some of your property, relinquishing some pleasures, drudging through some duties ; whereas, it is immeasurably more than this ; it is giving your heart ; it is giving yourself. It also appears, as to the method of self-denial, that sin is not torn off by force, but drops off through the growth of the new affection ; as a man drops his childish plays, not by a self-denying struggle, but because he has outgrown his interest in them. So always self-denial is accomplished, not by a dead lift, but by the spontaneous energy of love. It further appears that self-denial, in the very act of exercising it, is strangely transfigured into self-indulgence ; the Cross, in the very act of taking it up, is transfigured into a crown. It is a false charge that Christianity, by the severity of its self-denial, crushes human joy. Had you emancipated a slave, who had touched the deepest abasement incident to that system of iniquity, and had become contented with his slavery ; had you educated him and opened to him opportunity of remunerative industry, so that he is now incapable of being happy in slavery, and shudders at his former contentment, would you feel guilty of crushing his happiness, or pity him for the sacrifice which he has made ? But he did sacrifice the joys of slavery ; yes, and gained the joys of freedom. An emblem this of the sacrifice which Christianity requires. The joys of sin are sacrificed, the joys of holiness are gained : the snow-birds are gone, but the summer songsters are tuneful on every spray within the soul as it bursts into leaf and blossom beneath the returning sun.   All religious services once repulsive, prayer and praise formerly frozen words rattling like hail around the wintry heart, all works of beneficence once chafing to the selfish soul, all are now transfigured into joy. Under the power of the new affection, what was once self-denial accords with the inclination ; the soul has become incapable of enjoying its former sins, and regards it as self-denial to return to them, shuddering at them as an emancipated slave at his contentment in slavery, as a reformed drunkard, in the enjoyment of virtue, of home, and plenty, at his former hilarious carousals. Only so far as sin yet " dwelleth in us " is the service of Christ felt to be a self-denial or recognized as a conflict. But it will be objected that the innocent, natural desires must be denied in Christ's service. Here, in justice, it should be said, that self-denial of this kind is incidental to all worldly business, not less than to the service of Christ. Can you attain any great object without sacrifices ? Is the enterprising merchant, the successful lawyer, or physician, a man of luxurious ease ? It follows, from the foregoing views, that they who enter deepest into the spirit of Christian self-renunciation, are least aware of sacrificing anything for Christ. The more intense the love, the less account of service rendered to the beloved ; as Jacob heeded not the years of toil for Rachel through his love for her. Be so full of love that you will take no note of the sacrifices to which love inspires you. Love to Christ, then, is the spring of all acts of self-denial. Love much, serve much. When the tide is out, no human power can lift the great ships that lie bedded in the mud. But when you see the leathery bladders of the sea-weed swinging round, and bubbles and chips float past you upwards, then you know that the tide is turned, and the great ocean is coming to pour its floods into the harbour, to make the ships rise " like a thing of life," to fill every bay and creek and rocky fissure with its inexhaustible fulness. So you may see toils and sacrifices of Christian service seeming too great for your strength ; yet if your affections are beginning to flow to Christ, and your thoughts and aspirations are turning to Him, these are indications that love is rising in your hearts, with the fulness of God's grace behind it, to fill every susceptibility of your being within its Divine fulness, and lift every burden buoyant on its breast. Here we see the fundamental difference between asceticism and Christian self-renunciation. Asceticism is a suppression and denial of the soul's affections; Christian self-renunciation is the introduction of a new affection displacing the old. The former is a negation of the soul's life; the latter a development of a new and higher life. The former produces a constrained performance of duty, a restraint of desires which do not cease to burn, a sad resignation to necessary evils; the latter produces a new affection which makes duty coincide with inclination, quenches contrary desires, and quickens to positive joy in the accomplishment of God's will. III. THE PRACTICAL IMPORTANCE OF THE CHRISTIAN LAW OF SELF-RENUNCIATION IN INDIVIDUAL DEVELOPMENT AND SOCIAL PROGRESS. I affirm that individual development and social progress depend on the Christian law of self-renunciation. Recurring again to the two phases of a right character, the receptive and the imparting, or faith and works, compare, as to their practical efficacy in developing each of these, the Christian scheme of self-abnegation and redemption, and the infidel scheme of self-assertion and self-sufficiency. 1. As to the receptive phase of character, or faith. Here the aim must be to realize a character marked by reverence for superior power, wisdom, and goodness, and trust in the same; humility, in the consciousness of sin and need; aspirations for the true, the beautiful, and the good; loyalty to superior authority; and that peculiar courage in the vindication of truth and right which springs from loyal confidence in a leader powerful in their defence. This side of a holy character necessarily receives immediate and large development in the Christian scheme of redemption by Christ's sacrifice and salvation by faith in Him. It presents the objects of trust, reverence, aspiration, and loyalty, not as abstractions, but concrete in the personal Christ; and thus introduces the peculiar and overpowering motive of Christianity, affectionate trust in Christ as a personal Saviour. The philosophy of self-assertion has no legitimate place for this class of virtues. Consequently, carried out it cannot recognize them as virtues, but must leave them to be despised as weaknesses or defects; like those ancient languages which give no name to humility and its family of virtues, and name virtue itself not godliness but manliness. It has given us the pregnant maxim that work is worship, in which it expresses its inherent destitution of the element of faith, and declares that the only availing prayer is our own endeavour. But the impossibility of realizing a perfect character, without this class of virtues, is too apparent to admit of their total exclusion. 2. I proceed to consider the practical efficacy of these contrasted schemes in the sphere of works; in the development of active and imparting love, of the energies of a wise philanthropy. Here it is unnecessary to add to what has already been adduced to show that Christianity is effective in this direction. But leaving these considerations I confine myself to this single suggestion: the self-abnegation involved in the sacrificial character of Christianity is the only effectual preservative of the personal rights of the individual in his devotement to the service of the race. How grandly, in contrast, Christianity develops universal love, in its Divine activity, and yet upholds the individual in his Divine dignity. The Christian surrenders himself, without reserve, to God his Creator and Redeemer; and, in love to Him, freely devotes himself to the service of his fellow-men, a worker, together with God, in the sublime work of renovating the world; a worker, with God, in designs so vast, that the very conception of them ennobles; in enterprises so godlike that labouring in them lifts to a participation in the Divine. He is no longer the tool of society, but its Christ-like benefactor. The very fact that he kneels in entire self-surrender to God, forbids abjectness to man. He will not kneel to man, but he will die for him. 3. Besides the efficiency of these schemes in developing the different phases of character, I must consider their efficacy in developing the natural powers of thought, action, and enjoyment. Here we meet the objection that man cannot be developed by negation and suppression; and that self-denial, being a suppression of the soul's life, cannot develop it. But this objection is already sufficiently answered; for it has been shown that self-denial is not a negation, but the reverse side of a positive affection. Its power to develop is continually exemplified. The Church and the world are, as the Scriptures represent, antagonistic, not co-ordinate. Each develops the natural powers; but the development which Christianity effects in self-abnegation, is the normal, harmonious, and complete development of man. Here, then, I must contrast the two types, of progress and of civilization, which the two are fitted, respectively, to produce. 1. In the sphere of intellect, the one gives us rationalism and scepticism; the other, faith and stability. 2. In the sphere of social life, the one develops the outward activity, the other the inward resources. The one stimulates grasping and self-aggrandizement; the other, the spiritual life. The one is concerned with what a man gets ; the other, with what he is. The one is adequate to make man develop a continent ; the other, to develop himself and the continent. 3. In the sphere of political life, the one insists on freedom, the other on justice, mercy, and reverence for God. (*S. Harris, D.D.*) *Of self-denial :*—I. First, I am to show you the NATURE of this duty. Soul and body make up ourselves, and consequently, the powers, inclinations, and appetites, of both are to be restrained ; and because the mind and outward man are influenced upon by external objects, these also must in their due measure be denied and renounced. The operations of the soul are to be looked after in the first place ; and amongst them the understanding is the leading and principal faculty ; and, therefore, if this be taken care of, the rest will be more easily governed. But what is it to deny or renounce our understandings? 1. Such things as are unprofitable and useless to us. Those nice and fond speculations, trifling and impertinent, wanton and curious disquisitions, in ranging after which, the mind is diverted from the more solemn employment of religion, are no ways worthy of a Christian. 2. Much more doth it become us to check ourselves in our inquiring after things that are unlawful for us to pry into ; and those are either diabolical arts or Divine secrets. But sanctified minds decline the studying of these impious and diabolical mysteries, following the example of the Ephesian converts, who condemned the volumes of their black art to the flames. No excuse can legitimate our inquisitive search into these hellish intrigues, and our familiar conversing with them. And the latter (I mean Divine secrets) are to be admired and adored, not wantonly pried into. These abstruse and profound intricacies are not arrogantly to be ransacked, lest they confound us with their mighty depth, and quite overwhelm us with their glory. We must not think to bring down these lofty things to the level of our shallow capacities ; we must not criticize here, but believe. It is true, reason is the first-born, the eldest and noblest of the faculties ; and yet you must not refuse to offer up this darling, to sacrifice this Isaac. Let not reason persuade you to search with boldness into those mysteries which are inscrutable, and which ought to be entertained with silence and veneration. We renounce all modesty and humility when we attempt to fathom this abyss. This being rectified, the will (which is the next considerable operation of the mind) will follow its conduct, and become regular and orderly. This self-denial, as it respects the will, is comprehended in these two things, namely, our submitting to what God doth, and to what He commands. In the next place then, the affections are to be denied, for these are part of a man's self. But indeed, all of them ought to be tutored and kept in order ; their extravagancies must be allayed and charmed, for it is not fit the superior faculties should truckle to these inferior ones ; it is absurd and ridiculous that the beast should ride the man, and the slave domineer over the master, and the brutish part have dominion over the rational and Divine. Which leads me to the second main ingredient of the duty of self-denial, viz., the restraining and moderating the bodily and sensual desires. And this discipline consists in setting a strict guard and watch over the bodily senses ; for these are so many doors that open to life or death, as the Jewish masters say well. The sight is generally the inlet to all vice. If the motions of intemperance be urgent and solicitous with us, the wise man hath furnished us with an antidote, "Look not upon the wine," &c. (Prov. xxiii. 31). The sense of hearing also must be mortified and restrained, for this is another door at which sin and death do enter. We read that Polycarp used to stop his ears at the wicked speeches of heretics. Stop up all the passages and avenues of vice, especially block up these cinque ports by which the adversary uses to make his entrance. Third thing I proposed, in order to the explaining of the nature of self-denial, viz., that we must give a repulse to all external invitations whatsoever, whereby we are wont to be drawn off from our duty. And of this sort are— 1. Those which our Saviour takes particular notice of and warns us against (Luke xiv. 26). The bonds of nature oblige us to love our relations, but the injunctions of the gospel engage us to love our souls, and Christ much more (Matt. x. 37). Who sees not that persons are apt to be perverted by their near relatives? The first and early deceit was by this means. Adam, through the enticement of his wife, violated the Divine command. Solomon was corrupted by his wives (1 Kings xi. 4), and Jehoram was misled by his (2 Kings viii. 18). So it is particularly recorded of Ahab, who sold himself to work wickedness, that "his wife stirred him up " (1 Kings xxi. 25). Constantine the Great, in his latter days, by the instigation of his sister Constantia, who favoured the Arians, banished good Athanasius, and sent for Arius out of exile, and favoured his party. The Emperor Valentinian, by the impulse and artifice of his mother, Justinia, was harsh to the orthodox Christians, and countenanced the Arians. Valens was corrupted by his lady, who was an Arian, and made him such a one as herself. Justinian the emperor was wrought upon by his Queen Theodora, who had a kindness for the Eutychian heresy. Irene, who was empress with her son, another Constantine, caused him to favour the worship of images, she being for it herself; and then the second Nicene council was held, which decreed the adoration of images. And there are almost innumerable other instances to prove that persons are apt to be biassed and led away from their duty by the powerful enchantments of their beloved relations. But he that hath attained to that part of self-denial which I am now treating of will not listen to these charmers, though they charm never so cunningly. 2. Self-denial must show itself in renouncing of vainglory, and all inordinate desires of honours and preferments. Ambrose was preparing for flying, when he was like to be chosen Bishop of Milan. Basil the Great hid himself; Chrysostom declined it as much as he could. Gregory Nazianzen, when he was preferred to the bishopric of Constantinople, soon resigned it and retired to a solitary life at Nazianzum. Eusebius refused to be Bishop of Antioch. Ammonius Perota (mentioned by Socrates) cut off one of his ears, that by that means he might avoid the being preferred to a bishopric; for voluntary maiming themselves in those days made them incapable of that office. Nay, we are told, that a good father died with fear as they were bearing him to his episcopal throne. He died for dread of that which others so long for, and are like to die because they miss of it. 3. The sinful pleasures and delights of the flesh are to be abstained from by all the true practisers of self-denial. An eminent instance of this was Joseph, the modest, the chaste Joseph, who repulsed the solicitations of his mistress. 4. Wealth and riches: when you begin to desire and covet them inordinately; when your hearts are set upon them, when by plain experience you perceive that they damp your zeal for religion, and when the ways you make use of for acquiring them are prejudicial unto, and inconsistent with the keeping of a good conscience, you have no more to do in this case than to quit them with a resolved mind, to part with the unrighteous Mammon for durable and heavenly riches. 5. and lastly, To mention several things together, your self-denial ought to discover itself, in renouncing whatever it is that administers to pride, or lust, or revenge. Thus you see your task in all the several parts and divisions of it. Every Christian for Christ's sake is to deny his personal self (*i.e.*, his soul, the undue exertments of the understanding, will, and affections; his body, *i.e.*, all its carnal and sensual appetites, so far as they are hindrances to virtue); his relative self, his father, mother, wife, friends, and acquaintance, when they tempt him to vice; his worldly self (if I may so call it), houses, lands, goods, possessions, honours, pleasures, and whatever we are wont to set a high value upon; about all these this grace is commendably exercised. II. Secondly, it remains now that I convince you of the REASONABLENESS of this doctrine, which will appear from these ensuing particulars. 1. It might be said that there is restraint and hardship in all religions that ever were on foot in the world, and so it ought not to be thought strange in the Christian religion. Concerning the Jews it is notoriously known that their lives commenced with an uneasy and bloody circumcision; and by their Mosaic Law they were tied up to an unspeakable strictness all their lives long. They were forbid some meats which were wholesome enough, and very palatable. And afterwards they stinted themselves as to some drinks, and would by no means taste of the wine of idolatrous nations. They were religiously confined as to their garb and apparel, and to their converse and behaviour, their rites and ceremonies, which rendered their condition very uneasy, and almost insupportable. Should we look into the religion of the Gentiles, that will be found to be clogged with very great severities; and though one would think they should have made it as pleasant and enticing as possibly they could, yet he that takes a survey of some of its rites and laws shall discover inhumane and bloody usages, austere and cruel practices prescribed by them. And even among their wisest and soberest philosophers, restraint and self-denial were ever reputed laudable and virtuous. Some of them refused the richest offers of princes, and others of them voluntarily quitted their estates and revenues, and embraced poverty, and reckoned their greatest wealth to be the contempt of it (of which I shall give you some instances afterwards). At this day the people of Africa, on the coasts of Guinea, do all of them abstain from one thing or other, in honour of their fetishes, their little portable gods. Need I take notice of the deluded sect of Mahomet, to whom is granted a shameful indul gence in most things, yet their prophet would not give them their freedom as to all things, but peremptorily denied them the pleasure of the grapes and of swine's flesh. I will not insist here on the superstitious austerities and unreasonable restraints which another sort of men enjoin in their Church, and which are so readily submitted to by great numbers among them. 2. I offer this to your consideration, that there is not any man, *sui juris*, at his own disposal. If we acknowledge God for our Creator we have upon that very score all the reason in the world to own His right of commanding us. If we received our being from Him, it is but just that all our actions should be governed by Him. Seneca excellently speaks: God is our King and Governor, and it is our freedom to obey Him. On this account it is reasonable that we should not follow our own fancies and humours, and do what we will. But if we consider likewise that we are bought with a price, we may infer thence that we are not our own, but are for ever at the pleasure of Him that ransomed us. A Christian must not do what he would, that is, what his sinful inclinations prompt him to. He must be confined within bounds; he is a person pre-engaged, and must not, cannot be at the beck of every foolish lust. Third consideration, which will evince both the necessity and equity of this Christian duty. To be kept in and confined, to be limited and curbed by holy and just laws, to be commanded to walk by rules, and not to be suffered to be licentious, and to do what we please; this is the most safe, and therefore the most happy condition that can be imagined. It is undoubtedly the greatest kindness that God could confer upon us, to fence us in with laws, and to deny us many things which we eagerly desire; for He sees that what we so exorbitantly crave would be our ruin. How dangerous and mischievous to the world would an unrestrained liberty prove? For as 'tis a true aphorism of Hippocrates: The more you nourish morbid bodies, the more hurt you do them; so the more you fasten this inordinate desire in your souls, the more you harm and mischief yourselves. You think it may be to stint and satisfy your desires by giving them what they crave; but that is the way rather to increase them. One pleasure doth but make way for another. And besides, the pleasures which some luxurious persons entertain themselves with now will not be pleasures afterwards. The present delights will in time grow out of date, and some others must be sought for. 4. Still by way of reason consider, that to deny ourselves is the fairest and most convincing evidence of the sincerity of our hearts. By this we give an undeniable experiment of the free and plenary consent of our wills. We give a demonstration of the uprightness of our souls by refraining from whatever is forbidden us by the Divine laws. But Abraham was an instance of the contrary temper; very hard things were commanded him, and he obeyed them without disputing; whence there was a full trial made of his sincerity, and that he loved and feared God in the truth of his heart. 5. Natural reason, common prudence, and every day's practice commend unto us this Divine grace of self-denial. Wise men in a tempest are persuaded to throw their richest lading overboard, and commit it to the devouring element; that is, they are willing to part with their goods to save their lives. It is reckoned by us as wisdom, to deprive ourselves of some good and ease for a while; to make sure of a greater and more lasting one afterwards. We expose ourselves to danger that we may be safe. To recover health we submit to unpleasant potions; though the physic proves as hateful as the disease, yet we are reconciled to it, by considering that it will be profitable to our bodies afterwards; by the loss of a limb we are content to secure the whole. Prudence and reason justify all this, and shall they not much more reconcile us to the painful remedies which our great and good Physician prescribes? 6. Let me set before you some great and eminent examples to justify the reasonableness of this duty of self-denial. First, let me propound to you the example of Christ Jesus, our blessed Lord and Master. " He pleased not Himself," saith the apostle (Rom. xv. 3). And then, what a signal demonstration of self-denial was His Passion and Death. But, besides this, there are other examples, viz., of patriarchs, prophets, apostles, and divers holy men, who have been noted for their self-denial. Let me now provoke you to a godly emulation by some instances even of heathen men. If some pagans could arrive to some measure of self-denial by their natural light and reason, surely you, who profess higher principles, will be ashamed to come short of them. Plato tells us of his master, Socrates, that when his friends and relatives, and those who bore a great affection to him, came to him in prison, and wished him by all means to submit to the Senate of Athens, and thereby to save his life; his answer was: " Oh, my Athenians, I must needs profess to you, that I greatly respect and love you; but I tell you plainly, I am resolved to obey God rather than you." Most divinely spoken, and like a true denier of himself. That was a gallant action which is recorded of Cato the younger, a notable Roman captain, who, marching through the hot sands of Lybia, grew extremely thirsty ; and when one of his soldiers brought him some water in his helmet, which he had got with great difficulty and pains, he poured it out upon the ground, as a testimony that he could bear thirst as well as his soldiers. Xenophon relates of Cyrus, the King of Persia, that he would not so much as see the fair Panthea, the wife of King Abradaras, who was taken in battle, and reserved on purpose for him by one of his captains. And when one told Cyrus that her beauty was worth the beholding, he answered, that therefore it was much more necessary to abstain from seeing it. And truly this Cyrus is propounded by Xenophon as one of the greatest instances of self-denial and moderation in all particulars, many of which you'll find distinctly set down by that excellent historian, who also acquaints us that his soldiers and followers were trained up to severity and abstinence, and the exactest self-denial. 7. and lastly : If we would seriously consider that heaven shall be the reward of self-denial, this would make the performance of this duty easy. III. Now, in the third and last place, I will offer those MEANS AND HELPS whereby we may attain to this grace and duty which I have been treating of. If, then, thou wouldest effectually practise this evangelical duty of self-denial which is so excellent and yet so difficult, thou mayest be assisted by such proper helps as these : 1. By daily flying unto God for succour, by praying to be rescued and delivered from thyself, according to that good Father's devout Litany, "O Lord, deliver me from myself; shield me from my own depraved nature; defend me from my own wild desires and affections ; teach me to moderate my passions." 2. Prayer must be backed with endeavours, and your endeavours must begin within. You must strike at the root, the original cause of all the disorders in your life, viz., your inward lusts and desires. Democritus, who, it is said, put out his eyes as a remedy against lust, did, perhaps, doubly enhance their inveiglement by imagination. Your first business therefore is to correct it within, to regulate your desires and inclinations, and then you may safely look abroad, and not fear any actual or outward exorbitances in your lives. 3. Consider seriously the high calling whereunto God hath called you, and wherein you ought so to behave yourselves, that you do nothing which may disgrace and dishonour your profession. 4. Let us weigh our condition well, and often urge it upon our thoughts, that we are but strangers and pilgrims, and being upon our journey, it would be unreasonable to expect that we should have everything according to our mind. 5. It is requisite that you entertain right notions concerning the things of this world. Lastly, act by a principle of evangelical faith, and you will find that that doth wonderfully facilitate the exercise of self-denial. With a steadfast eye look beyond this present life ; pierce through this horizon to another world, and you will easily restrain your sinful appetites and desires, you will overcome all the blandishments, suavities, and allurements of this life. Besides, this is that which promotes and facilitates all our duties, and reconciles us to all difficulties, and renders all estates and conditions welcome, and makes Christians yoke easy and pleasant. It is the most excellent, and it is the most useful grace, and that which renders us masters of ourselves. (*J. Edwards, D.D.*) *Christians must expect afflictions :*—Be prepared for afflictions. To this end would Christ have us reckon upon the cross, that we may be forewarned. He that builds a house does not take care that the rain should not descend upon it, or the storm should not beat upon it, or the wind blow upon it ; there is no fencing against these things, they cannot be prevented by any care of ours ; but that the house may be able to endure all this without prejudice. And he that builds a ship, does not make this his work, that it should never meet with waves and billows, that is impossible ; but that it may be light and staunch, and able to endure all weathers. A man that takes care for his body does not care for this, that he meet with no change of weather, hot and cold, but how his body may bear all this. Thus should Christians do ; not so much to take care how to shift and avoid afflictions, but how to bear them with an even quiet mind. As we cannot hinder the rain from falling upon the house, nor the waves from beating upon the ship, nor change of weather and seasons from affecting the body, so it is not in our power to hinder the falling out of afflictions and tribulations ; all that lies upon us, is to make provision for such an hour, that we be not overwhelmed by it. (*T. Manton, D.D.*) *Self-denial :*—It is not what a man takes up, but what he gives up, that makes him "rich towards God." Now what ought a follower of Jesus to give up for his

Master's sake? 1. Of course every man who would become a Christ's man must renounce everything that God's Word and a healthy conscience set down as wrong. All sins are "contraband" at the gateway of entrance to the Christian life. The sentinel at the gate challenges us with the command—"Lay down that sin!" 2. We must give up whatever, by its direct influence, tends to injure ourselves or others. Here comes in the law of brotherly love. The safe side of all questionable amusements is the outside. 3. Give up whatever tends to pamper the passions, or to kindle unholy desires. Paul's noble determination to "keep his body under," implies that there was something or other in Paul's fleshly nature which ought to be kept under. It is also true of almost every Christian that somewhere in his nature lies a weak point, a besetting tendency to sin; and just there must be applied the check-rein of self-denial. Even eminent Christians have had to wage constant battle with fleshly lusts. Others have had sore conflict with irritable, violent tempers. When a servant of Christ is willing to take a back seat, or to yield the pre-eminence to others, he is making a surrender which is well-pleasing to his meek and lowly Master. One of the hardest things to many a Christian is to serve his Saviour as a "private," when his pride tells him that he ought to wear a "shoulder-strap" in Christ's army. 4. Another very hard thing for most persons to give up, is to give up having their own way. But the very essence of true spiritual obedience lies just here. It is just here that self-sufficiency, and vanity, and waywardness, and obstinacy are to be met. Here they must be sacrificed to that demand of the Master's, that He shall rule, and not we. 5. The last rule of giving up which we have room for in this brief article is, that time, ease, and money must all be held tributary to Christ. In these days of stylish equipage and social extravagance, how few Christians are willing to give up to Jesus the key to their purses and bank-safes! Too many go through the solemn farce of writing "Holiness to the Lord" on their property, and then using it for their own gratification. (*T. L. Cuyler, D.D.*) The necessity of self-denial:—I. ONE'S COMING AFTER CHRIST. This is the thing which some do aim at, and all should. 1. Christ in the world was in the way to His kingdom, the kingdom of heaven (Luke xix. 12). 2. Accordingly He was in the world, not as a native thereof, but as a stranger travelling through it, with His face always away-ward from it, home to His Father's house. 3. Our Lord Jesus made His way to His kingdom through many bitter storms blowing on His face in the world, and is now entered into it (Heb. xii. 2). 4. There is no coming into that kingdom, for a sinner, but at His back, in fellowship with Him (John xiv. 6). 5. There is no coming in at His back into the kingdom, without following Him in the way (Psa. cxxv. 5; John xv. 6). II. ONE'S DENYING HIMSELF TO COME AFTER CHRIST. 1. Implies two things. (1) That Christ and self are contraries, leading contrary ways. (2) That the self to be denied is our corrupt self, the old man, the unrenewed part. 2. Wherein it consists. In a holy refusal to please ourselves, that we may please God in Christ. Hence, in self-denial there is (1) Faith and hope, as the necessary springs thereof. (2) A practical setting up of God as our chief end, and a bringing down ourselves to lie at His feet. (3) An unlimited resignation of ourselves unto God in Christ—"first gave their ownselves to the Lord" (2 Cor. viii. 5). Faith taking hold of God as our God, according to the measure of faith, the whole man is swallowed up in Him; God is all, and we become nothing in our own eyes: the whole soul, the whole man, the whole lot, is resigned to Him. (4) A refusing to please ourselves in anything in competition with God; but denying the cravings of self, as they are contrary to what God craves of us (Tit. ii. 12). III. ONE'S TAKING UP HIS CROSS, AND THAT DAILY, AND FOLLOWING CHRIST. 1. God will lay down the cross for every one who seeks heaven, that they shall have nothing ado but to take it up. "In the world ye shall have tribulation" (John xvi. 33). They shall not need to make crosses to themselves, nor to go out of their way to seek a cross: God will lay it down at every one's door. He had one Son without sin, but no son without the cross (Heb. xii. 8). 2. He will lay it down daily to the followers of Christ, that they may have a daily exercise in taking it up, and bearing the cross of the day. "Sufficient unto the day is the evil thereof" (Matt. vi. 34). A change of crosses may be got, but there will be no end of them as long as we are here. 3. We must not be choosers of crosses. Every one must take up his own, allotted to him by sovereign wisdom. 4. We must not trample on the cross, and step over it, but take it up (Heb. xii. 5). The sullen manliness and Roman courage wherewith some bear their crosses is the produce of self-will, not of self-denial: and speaks contempt of God, not submission to Him. When heaven is our party, it becomes us to stoop, and not to make our faces like flint, lest God be provoked to dash us in pieces. 5. Yet neither must we faint at the sight of the cross ; for at that rate we will not be able to take it up (Heb. xii. 5). 6. As we must not go off the road of duty to shift the cross, so we must not stand still till it be rolled out of our way, but take it up, and go forward. It is easy going off the way, but not easy coming on again. There are quagmires of sin and sorrow on every side of the cross, where the shifters of it may come to stick (1 Tim. vi. 9). 7. We must take up no more for our cross than what God lays down ; not what Satan and our own corruptions lay to it : it will be our wisdom to shovel that off in the first place, and we will take up the cross the easier. 8. But however heavy the cross be, we are not to refuse it. Our very life, which of all worldly things is dearest to us, must be laid at the Lord's feet, and we ready to part with it for Christ. 9. We must yoke with the cross willingly and submissively : God can lay it on us, whether we will or not ; but He will have us to stoop, and take it up on us (James i. 2). 10. We must bear it, going evenly under it, till the Lord take it down. It is what belongs to the Lord to take it off ; it is our part to take it up. There must be an exercise of patience in our coming after Christ (Luke xxi. 19). 11. We must follow Christ with the cross on our back. (*T. Boston, D.D.*) *Erroneous ideas respecting self-denial :*—There is a current idea that it is a fine thing to go through self-imposed trials—to do what is disagreeable just because it is disagreeable : it is noble to climb Alpine heights—not because the slightest good is to come of your doing so—not because you have the faintest idea of what you are to do when you reach their summit ;—but just because it is difficult and dangerous to climb them, and most men would rather not. Some people now-a-days appear to think that when our blessed Lord uttered the sublime words which form the text, He meant that we are to be always seeking out a tribe of petty disagreeables—constantly finding out something we don't like to do, and then doing it : some people, I do believe, have a vague impression in their minds which they have never put into shape, but which really comes to this, that God would be angry if He saw His creatures cheerful and happy. Oh, the wicked delusion ! God is love ! When will men believe that grand foundation-truth ! You may see something like God's feeling in the kindly smile with which the kind parent looks on at the merry sports of his children, delighted to see them innocently happy. But believe it, brethren, there is nothing the least like God, in the sour, morose look of the gloomy fanatic, as he turns with sulky indignation from the sight of people who venture to be harmlessly cheerful. (*A. H. K. Boyd, D.D.*) *Various particulars in which self-denial must be practised :*— Let us consider, then, for a little, what is implied in the self-denial to which we are here called. It does not imply a disregard to our own true interest and happiness, for these are always found, at last, to be inseparably connected with the path of duty. But it implies that we are to be denied to ourselves, as depraved and sinful creatures—that we are to be denied to that spirit which would set up ourselves, our own wills, as the rivals of God—that we are to be denied to everything which would, in any way, interfere with our submission and fidelity to Jesus Christ. 1. More particularly, if we are to be the disciples of Christ, we must be denied to our own wisdom. While we are to use the natural wisdom, the reason, which God hath given us, we are not to trust in it as sufficient to show us the way of life. There is more hope of a fool, than of those who are wise in their own conceit. The wisest must not glory in their wisdom. 2. We must be denied to our own righteousness. We must renounce all trust in ourselves, plead guilty before God, and cast ourselves on His free mercy, by faith in His Son's righteousness. 3. We must be denied to all obviously sinful propensities and habits. Christ is willing to save us *from* our sins, but He will not save us *in* our sins. 4. We must be denied, not only to what is obviously sinful, but also to every earthly enjoyment, when it comes into competition with our regard to Christ. We must, for example, be denied to those bodily indulgences which, though in themselves innocent, when under due restraint, become incompatible with spirituality of mind, when felt to be essential, or very important, to our happiness. We must " keep under our bodies, and bring them into subjection." 5. We must be denied to our reputation. Though we are to value a good name in the world, if it can be had consistently with faithfulness to our Lord ; we are cheerfully to forego it, if it cannot be retained but at the expense of our conscience. 6. We must be denied to our friends. Should they attempt so to influence us, we must be denied to their solicitations, allurements, and upbraidings. It sometimes happens that the greatest foes to a man's salvation, are those of his own household. 7. We must be denied to our property, so as to be ready to undergo any sacrifice of our substance—to our ease, so as to be ready to undergo any torture—to our liberty, so as to be ready to go to prison—and to our very life, so as to be ready cheerfully to lay it down, rather than prove unfaithful to our Redeemer. (*J. Foote, M.A.*) *Increasing need of self-denial :*—They who climb lofty mountains find it safest, the higher they ascend, the more to bow and stoop with their bodies; and so does the Spirit of Christ teach the saints, as they get higher in their victories over self-corruption, to bow lowest in self-denial. (*W. Gurnall.*) *Self-repression :*—It is reported of Agrippina, the mother of Nero, who being told "that if ever her son came to be an emperor he would be her murderer," she made this reply : "I am content to perish, if he may be emperor." What she expressed vaingloriously, we should do religiously. "Let us perish, so our neighbours, our relations, and our country, be bettered." (*Archbishop Secker.*) *Joy from self-denial :*—A man takes a musical instrument, and undertakes to bring up one part of it so that it shall sound louder than any other part. The moment he brings it up so that it sounds a little louder than the others, people say, "Yes, I think I do hear that upper note," but it is so faint that a person has to put his hand to his ear to hear it. But by and by the man works the instrument so that out rolls this upper note so clearly that, although the under notes are there, everybody says, "Ah, now it has come out, now I hear it; it is all right now." And a man that denies himself in the truest Christian way does it so that the joy of the upper feelings rolls clear over the pain and suffering of the lower feelings. Where this does not take place, the self-denial is very imperfect. (*H. W. Beecher.*) *Various forms of self-discipline :*—Now, it is evident that the selfishness of one man is not the same as the selfishness of another. There is a man whose self lies in his intellect. He makes much of his own intellect. He is always leaning upon it. Now, that man has much to do, to become a very little child—to become a fool—to submit his own intellect absolutely to the teaching of the Holy Spirit and the Word of God—to receive the deep, mind-confounding mysteries of the gospel with a perfect simplicity, and to let Christ be all his wisdom. Another man's self is pleasure. That pleasure may take different forms. It may be in the form of the mere indulgence of his bodily appetites ; or it may be in worldly amusements ; or it may be in the pride of life ; or it may be in money ; or it may be in business ; or it may be in ambition. Now, if that man think that he can take those things, and the spirit of those things along with him ; if he think he can enjoy them and religion, he will find the gate too strait for him to pass, and the road too narrow for him to go. That is the man who must be continually learning to say "No" to himself. He must put the strongest rein upon the neck of his own desires. And even supposing that the pleasures which make that man's selfishness are of a very quiet, and, you may say, innocent, character, still that man must remember that self-renunciation in this life must not be confined to those things which are sinful, but much more he must practise it in innocent things—for it is a true thing, that most men perish through the unlawful use of lawful things. Therefore that man must deny himself, even, for instance, in his legitimate business—or in his best domestic affection—or in his holiest or purest of all engagements. But there is another form of self, and the more dangerous, because it takes the aspect of religion. When a man has laid down for himself a certain way of salvation, and begins in his own strength, goes on in his own wisdom, and ends in his own glory, turning his self-complacent virtues into saviours. Oh! how that self must be unloved! He denies self at the foundation, because he will have no other foundation but grace: he denies self in the work, because he will know no other but the finished work of his Saviour: he denies self in the end, because he will have no other end but the glory of God. (*J. Vaughan, M.A.*) *Shirking the cross :*—Rev. E. Paxton Hood in a sermon, "Crucifixion and Coronation," said, life means discipline to all of us in some way or other, and if we attempt to shirk our cross, we shall find that God fits one presently somehow or other to our shoulders, the meaning of which we shall find by and by. I am tempted sometimes to throw down the cross; I have said, "No, I won't have it;" but lo! I have found that although I have thrown it behind me and thought I had eluded and escaped it, there was one which still had to be fitted to the shoulders further on, whether I would or would not. (*E. Paxton Hood.*) *Self-denial is the first law of grace :*—A number of ministers were once dining together after an ordination, and when one of them seemed unduly attentive to the good things before him, he met with the approval of the host, who said, "That's right! To take care of self is the first law of nature." "Yes, sir," said an old minister sitting near, in reply ; "but to deny self is the first law of grace!" *Self-denial is the sign of a Christian:* The

devil once met a Christian man, and said, " Thou sayest, ' I am a servant of God.'
What doest thou more than I do? You say that you fast ; so do I. I neither eat
nor drink." He went through a whole list of sins, of which he said he was clear ;
but at last the Christian said, " I do one thing thou never didst, I deny myself."
There was the point in which the Christian came out. (*C. H. Spurgeon.*)   *Self-
sacrifice :*— The mortar with which the swallow builds is the mud from cart-wheels,
sides of wells, and such-like places. This it makes more adhesive by moistening
it with its own saliva. As the bird parts with a portion of its own substance to
cement its nest, so should we be prepared to give up, not that which costs us
nothing, but which may involve much self-denial and self-sacrifice on our part,
that which we love and cherish most, as Abraham was prepared to offer up Isaac
at the bidding of God. (*H. Macmillan, D.D.*)   *Cross-bearing :*—That the faith
of Christ does in sober truth involve a daily cross-bearing ; and that it is agreeable
to reason and the Divine nature that thus it should be—this is the proposition
which we have to establish. I. The words of Christ are of a nature which, it is
probable, the disciples by no means appreciated to the full at the time when they
were uttered. Since the crucifixion of the Son of God, the Cross has to us associations of the most affecting kind. We cannot hear of taking up a cross without
having our thoughts drawn back to the scenes of the last Passover—the street of
grief—the fainting Redeemer—Simon the Cyrenian—the hill of Calvary. To take
up a cross is to fulfil the spirit of His sacred life in the lowest depth of His humiliation. Let us consider how it fares with man's intellect when he adopts the religion
of the Crucified. It is sometimes the custom to assert that everything is easy and
plain in the gospel system ; that the heart and the conscience respond at once to its
revelations and commandments ; that the words of Christ do so awake an echo in
the human soul that he who has heard can no more doubt than he can doubt his
own existence. We believe all this to be quite wrong. Rather do we believe that
there are vast difficulties in the way of a thorough and complete adoption of the
truth in Jesus. The Bible represents that such would be the case. This is the
meaning of all those passages which speak of the Cross of Christ as " being to the
Jews a stumbling-block, and to the Greeks foolishness." This is the explanation
of the fact, again and again dwelt on by St. Paul, that " not many wise men after
the flesh are called." This is the ground of that mysterious confession of the
Saviour himself—" I thank Thee, O Father, Lord of heaven and earth, that Thou
hast hid these things from the wise and prudent, and revealed them unto babes."
The fact is, the deeper we reflect upon the revelation of God, the more shall we
find to baffle and confound. Be ye well assured, that if in your system of religion
there is nothing out of your grasp ; if everything is according to reason, and
nothing beyond it ; if you are never called upon to accept upon trust, to believe
without sight, then is your system not that of God. It is against reason that this
should be. Reason herself cries out that she ought to be baffled in measuring God,
that she ought to be shipwrecked on the ocean of His perfection, lost in the pro-
fundity of His counsels. It is against revelation, for revelation ever speaks of
mortification and self-denial, as requisite in those who accept her. Let Christ be
God, acknowledge Him, with St. Peter, to be the Son of the Blessed, and reason
echoes His answer, and sets to her seal that it is true. " If any man will come
after Me, let him deny himself, and take up his cross daily and follow Me. II.
But we turn for a brief moment to other illustrations of the text. We consider it
indeed, as a verse calculated in an especial degree for the age in which we live :
viewed not only with reference to matters of faith, but of practice. This is not
peculiarly an age of cruelty, or rapine, or licentiousness ; but it is, we think, pre-
eminently an age when men dream only of pleasing themselves. To be prosperous
is to win applause. " So long as thou doest well unto thyself, men will speak good
unto thee," was the proverb of the Psalmist, and it has met with a complete fulfilment in our generation. And very expedient therefore do we reckon it, that we
should occasionally turn aside to contemplate a severer model ; and remember that
it is not the highest law of our being to please ourselves ; that even when it
involves no positive crime, self-pleasing is not the noblest or safest rule of man.
Who are they who stand forth in the dimness of vanished years—landmarks in the
wilderness of time, giant rocks by which we cross the ocean of the past? They
are not the men who looked to themselves alone, and followed the impulse of the
moment, alike in their serious pursuits and in their sports. These selfish ones
have no record among posterity ; there is none that remembereth, nor any that
regardeth. The living men ; they who being dead yet speak, are the men who

thought first of others and last of themselves; who were ready to abandon country, and kinsfolk, and friends, to help the poor out of the dust and the feeble out of the mire. But why, amongst Christian people, linger here upon the threshold?—deeper and holier thoughts lie beyond. If we are not falsely called, if our whole profession is not a lie, we are followers of Christ. And what of Him our Master and Example, says the apostle? "Even Christ also pleased not Himself." And if in other things, then in this let us walk according as He walked. We cannot be like Him if we are always in pleasure and never in pain : not like Him if we indulge ourselves in every wish that rises within, in every taste and fancy. Moreover, to leave undone that which we cannot do, this is not self-denial; not to buy what we cannot pay for, this is not self-denial; not to labour when otherwise we must starve, is not self-denial. These are crosses laid upon us by God's providence, not crosses which we ourselves take up. Of our own free will we must forego pleasant things, and perform disagreeable tasks, leaving undone for His sake what we might have done, and doing in His name what none could make us do, if we would be like Him who bowed the heavens and came down. So act, young and old, and we tell you not that thus acting ye become shadows in the world of the Son of God Himself; that ye perpetuate His life upon earth; nay, more, we tell you that without so acting, without this self-restraint and self-discipline, it is but a false confidence of peace here and hereafter on which ye build. (*Bishop Woodford.*)   *Christ's terms of discipleship :*—I. THE TERMS OF DISCIPLE-SHIP are—1. Self-denial. 2. Endurance—"Take up his cross daily." 3. Perseverance—"And follow Me." II. THE REASONS GIVEN. 1. Because selfishness brings ultimate loss. 2. Because sacrifice brings ultimate salvation. III. THE MOTIVE INCULCATED—"For My sake." (*A. F. Barfield.*)   *Bearing the cross :*—What is this cross, and how are we to bear it? I. THE CROSS OF JESUS CHRIST IS THE INSTRUMENT AND THE SIGN OF SALVATION. Are we, then, to understand this literally? No. We must follow the spirit and not the letter. Everywhere the cross is before us, beside us, in us. II. THERE ARE THREE WAYS OF BEARING THE CROSS, OR THE CONTRADICTIONS AND SORROWS WHICH AFFLICT US. I do not here speak of those frivolous spirits which shake off the cross when it presents itself, and seek to escape it by diversions. 1. There are those who carry their cross with anger, with indignation, in revolt against providence or destiny. 2. Others, more reasonable, carry their cross with stoicism, in bearing up against it by a violent reaction of pride or of false dignity. 3. The only way to make suffering profitable is to accept it Christianly, that is, with patience and resignation. (*Abbé Bautain.*) *The law of daily Christian life :*—If we mean to be disciples of Christ indeed, we shall have every day—1. Something to put away for Christ's sake—"Let him deny himself." 2. Something to take up and bear for Christ—"Take up his cross." 3. Something actively to do for Christ's sake—"And follow Me." (*R. Tuck, B.A.*) *Self-denial the test of religious earnestness :*—Jesus told His disciples that they were not worthy of being His disciples unless they bore the cross for His sake. 1. To us Christians the cross is the symbol of salvation, self-devotion, obedience to our Father, loyalty to our Saviour. But to those who heard Jesus it was a symbol (1) of terrible pain; (2) of shame unspeakable; (3) of the burden of guilt. It is, then, in this light that we must look at what our Lord says of the cross. 2. All this is summed up in the one word self-denial. It is self that makes us shrink from the cross. 3. To guard against mistake let us remember that while we deny ourselves we must follow Jesus. There is a self-denial which is not a following of Jesus. (1) Men often deny themselves in one respect in order to indulge themselves in another. (2) Self-denial for its own sake is not a following of Jesus. The way of the cross is the way to heaven, and the crown of thorns prepares for the crown of glory. (*Canon Liddell.*)   *The conditions of service :*—Penalties accompany prizes. The more holy, resolute, defined the life, the greater the antagonism. A religion that lays hold of the deepest depths of thought, that is real, boundless, and inexhaustible, is only to be had on three conditions. 1. "Let him deny himself"—not cripple or degrade self, but govern it. 2. "Take up the cross." Not your neighbour's, but your own cross. Take it up; do not walk round it and admit it only, but take it up, every muscle strained; honestly on your shoulders carry it. 3. "Follow Me." Take the consequences of open avowal. The path is plain. It leads not to the monastery. No more social, loving man ever lived than the Master. Keep in touch with Him; grasp His hand; listen to His voice. (*New Outlines on New Testament.*)   *Following Christ :*—Those who companied with Jesus while He lived were scarcely in danger of losing their lives.

After His death persecution threatened the lives of Christians, and, while the
Christian life became more dangerous, the real and Christian living grew more
rigid, and the denying of self, which was required by the circumstances of our
Lord's day, grew and expanded until it was made to mean that all bodily delights
and joys of the senses and affections were either positively wrong or infirmities
which should be discouraged. The ascetic life, not because for the passing moment
it might be more prudent or more useful—as, for instance, when the soldier in
campaign patiently undergoes privation, eats mouldy bread, and drinks polluted
water, not because it is a fine thing to eat such bread and drink such water, but
because the circumstances of the campaign demand it—the ascetic life for its own
sake was enforced in the Early Church. There is an asceticism for the sake of a
higher good which at times may be necessary and most laudable, but the difference
is between the mother who goes without food that she may still the hunger of her
little ones, and the monk or hermit who reduces himself to an unlovely skeleton
because self-denial is intrinsically good. Yes, the spirit of Christianity in this
respect became pagan; it was but a new Stoicism without its philosophy.
(*W. Page Roberts, M.A.*)   *Self-denial:*—What is self-denial in its Christian
sense ? For clearly when we deny ourselves *we* are the deniers ; it is one
self denying another self, the real self, clothed with Divine authority, denying
the lower and usurping self. It is our soul's denial of the selfish part of
us. It is the supremacy of our sense of right among the multitude of our
prompters, or against the resistance of our inclinations. It is the starving
and binding up of ungenerous desires, that nobler desires may have free course
and be glorified. It is a command over the sensual passions of anger, fear,
envy, jealousy, and irritable impatience, that other powers, which bring only
strength and joy and love, may be the masters of our being. If it mortifies a lower
self-love, it is that a nobler self-knowledge may lift a meek and strong heart to
God. If there were no higher demands of our nature, there would be no reason
that the lower ones should be restrained. For self-denial is no monkish
virtue; no recluse's safety; no ascetic's way of recommending himself to God;
no pale, timid shadow shrinking from the light, and denying itself the
natural joys of man ; no self-inflicted pain, the price paid here for escape
from pain hereafter ; no abject creeping on the earth that a Power to
whom abjectness is pleasing may deign to cast His eye upon us—it is the
upward life of a child of God, loving what God loves, refusing to be in bondage to
anything that would remove him from the light of his Father's face. (*J.
H. Thom.*)   And take up his cross daily. — *Of taking up the cross ; or,
patience under all kinds of sufferings :*—There are two great hindrances and
impediments of Christianity, the one inward, the other outward. I. Ourselves, the second is the afflictions and crosses of the world. The former
must be denied, the latter taken up. First, I shall consider the words more
generally, and show that it is our duty and concern to entertain with patience
and submission the afflictions and crosses of what kind soever which are our allotment in this world. As to the first, namely, the nature of that patience which is
required of us under our crosses and afflictions, it contains in it these following
things :—First : Christian patience imports a quiet and sedate temper of mind, and
shuts out all inward repining and murmuring. Secondly : There is not only a
silence of the soul, but of the tongue, which is another ingredient of this duty.
This excludes all repining words, all desponding language. Thirdly : In a humble
confession and acknowledgment, which is the next exertment of the duty in the
text. Fourthly : This duty speaks not only a religious confession and humiliation,
but likewise faith and hope, and waiting upon God ; a depending on Him for
strength to be enabled to bear the cross, and for a happy issue out of it. Fifthly :
This virtue is accompanied with cheerfulness and rejoicing, with praising and
blessing of God for His fatherly love in afflicting. II. I undertook to offer
such reasons and arguments as I apprehend may be of force to excite
you to the practice of this important duty. 1. Consider, that impatience and
fretting are no ease at all to us in our calamities, but, on the contrary, they render
our grievances heavier and more intolerable. They do but nail us faster to the
cross, and put us to greater and more exquisite pain. The silly bird entangles and
hampers itself by its struggling to free itself from the snare wherein 'tis catched.
We never find ourselves bettered by our reluctancy : all that we purchase by it is a
more grievous durance. It is observable that the Israelites never found any mitigation of their punishments and judgments by their murmuring against God, but

they rather lay the longer under the lash for it. 2. We are to consider on the other side that submission and holy silence are the best way to put a happy period to our afflictions. It is so certainly in the nature of the thing itself, for patience lightens our burden; but it is much more so by the order and appointment of Providence. God is pleased to think thoughts of mercy and deliverance when He beholds our spirits wrought into a humble frame. 3. The serious consideration and persuasion that God is the author and disposer of all our afflictions is another prevalent argument to excite us to a humble submission and resignation. 4. Another is this, that we have provoked God, by our ill behaviour, to inflict these temporal evils upon us. 5. It should be a great support and stay to our minds to consider the vast advantages which accrue to us by the bodily and temporal crosses which are our allotment in this life. Every good man is a gainer by his crosses and distresses. The refiner casts the gold into the fire, not to make it worse, but better, namely, by purifying it. 6. A steady view of future happiness will effectually promote this. Some objections which may be raised in defence, or at least in excuse, of impatience. I begin with the first plea, and that is this: Nobody's case is so bad as mine; so great are my troubles, so heavy is my burden. I see that many have no afflictions, but I can't see that any one is visited in that degree that I am. To which I answer—1. All persons are generally inclined to think that their own troubles are the greatest, and that none have the like. It is, as it were, natural to men in distress to imagine that none are so miserable as themselves; but they do not know what pressures others lie under and are tormented with. But—2. Suppose that thy distresses and grievances far exceed those of some others, yet there is no room for impatience if thou considerest these following particulars: (1) It may be thou hast great and strong lusts, and these must be extirpated by afflictions of that quality. The remedy must be proportioned to the disease. Lesser afflictions would not awaken and rouse thee out of thy security, would not stir thee up to fly to God, and to beg mercy and pardon; even as men do not repair to a physician for a small indisposition, or to a surgeon for a scratch. (2) Perhaps thou art one on whom God hath bestowed great and vigorous graces, and 'tis His pleasure that these should be exercised, and the degrees of them manifested. Strong faith and love will endure strong trials. The greater ability and strength thou hast, the greater is the burthen which thou mayest expect to be laid upon thee. (3) Great afflictions make way for great temporal blessings. When men intend to build high, they lay the foundation very low. (4) Great afflictions make way for great spiritual blessings; that is, the increase of grace and holiness, and the manifesting them to the world. Abraham's faith was enhanced by the greatness of his trial, and he became the pattern of belief to all succeeding ages. (5) It is to be considered that no affliction is so great but God can deliver thee out of it; and 'tis His usual method to magnify His power and wisdom by delivering His servants out of the greatest. Another complaint is this: My afflictions are many and various, and heaped upon me in great numbers, and this is it that shocks my patience, and even destroys it. I shall answer—1. Are not thy sins many, and often repeated? And then 'tis no wonder that thy crosses are so too. Thou canst not justly complain of the variety of thy grievances, when thou reflectest on the multitude of thy offences. 2. There is sometimes a necessity of the multiplicity of afflictions, because what one doth not effect another must. 3. If we were used to one sort of affliction only, it would become familiar to us, so that we should not mind it, and consequently it would not be serviceable to us; as sometimes physic of one sort, if often taken, loses its virtue. 4. Let us not immoderately lament and bemoan our condition, as if we were the only persons that had many afflictions heaped upon us. If we look into the sacred records, we shall find that the best and holiest men have been treated after this manner. Their calamities and distresses have been many, and of divers kinds. 5. Are the afflictions of good men many and various? So are their comforts: as the fore-mentioned apostle testifies, " As our sufferings abound, so our consolation also aboundeth " (2 Cor. i. 5). 6. God is able to rescue us out of many evils and distresses as well as out of a single one. "He delivereth in six troubles, yea, in seven "; that is, in sundry and various troubles (Job v. 5). But the complaint rises yet higher: My afflictions are not only great and many, but long and tedious; insomuch that my patience will be tired out before they leave me. But consider—1. Whether they are not short in comparison of the many days and years of ease, health, and plenty that thou hast had. 2. It may be thy sins have been a long time indulged by thee, and then thou hast no reason to repine at the length of thy afflictions. 3. Think of this, that thy afflictions are long, that they may accomplish the work for which they were sent. Thy lusts and evil habits have been long growing, and are now rooted and fastened in thee : wherefore there is need of some lasting cross to root them out. 4. Art not thou conscious to thyself that God hath a long time called thee to repentance, and yet thou hast not been obsequious to that merciful call ? 5. Complain not of the length of thy afflictions, seeing they may be serviceable to prevent the eternal and never-failing torments of hell. 6. Thy afflictions are of more than ordinary duration, that they may sufficiently exercise thy faith and all other graces, and make them conspicuous and renowned. 7. Our longest pressures and troubles are but short in comparison of future glory. This being so hard a work, I will offer to you those means and helps in the use of which, by the Divine assistance, you may be effectually enabled to discharge this difficult duty, if ever the providence of God shall exact it of you. 1. That you may take up the cross, see that you deny yourselves. This makes way for that, and that can never be done without this. Most rationally, therefore, is self-denial enjoined here by Christ in the first place. 2. That you may suffer death for Christ, prepare yourselves beforehand by your other lesser sufferings. 3. That you may not shrink and fall back in that day when you are called to lay down your lives for Christ, consider the absolute necessity of professing His name and owning His cause. Weigh our Saviour's peremptory words, namely, that if you confess Him before men, He will confess you before His Father; but if you deny Him before men, He will deny you before His Father (Matt. x. 32, 33). (*J. Edwards, D.D.*) *The duty of taking up the cross :*—It may appear difficult, at first sight, to comprehend the goodness of God in afflicting us, or commanding us to afflict ourselves. Could not He render us holy, without rendering us miserable, by way of preparative? Doubtless He could have done it; and He could have produced all men as He created the first man, at their full growth; but His wisdom has seen it fit that we should pass through the pains and hazards of infancy and youth, in the latter instance; and, in the former, that through tribulation and affliction we should enter into His heavenly kingdom. It is His will; and therefore, though no reason could be assigned, silence and submission would best become us. But there are many. 1. It is obvious to remark that Christianity did not bring afflictions into the world with it; it found them already there. The world is full of them. Men are disquieted, either by the tempers of others, or their own; by their sins, or by their follies; by sickness of body, or sorrow of heart. 2. Let us reflect how it came to be so, and we shall find still less cause of complaint. The misery of man proceeded not originally from God; he brought it upon himself. 3. From what we feel in ourselves, and what we see and hear of others, every person who has thought at all upon the subject must have been convinced that, circumstanced as we are, "it is good for us to be afflicted." Naturally, man is inclined to pride and wrath, to intemperance and impurity, to selfishness and worldly-mindedness; desirous to acquire more, and unwilling to part with anything. Before he can enter into the kingdom of heaven he must become humble and meek, temperate and pure, disinterested and charitable, resigned, and prepared to part with all. The great instrument employed by heaven to bring about this change in him is the cross. (*Bishop Horne.*) *The daily cross :*—I. It is an INSTRUCTIVE command. Divine commands teach as well as prescribe; and this command teaches—1. That the Christian's path in this life is one of continued trial. 2. This command teaches that continued trial arises from the opposition of self to the will of God. The Saviour's words evidently imply this; showing that the daily bearing of the cross chiefly consists in the daily denying of self. 3. We are taught by this command that the daily trial must not be passively endured merely, but readily borne. Heathen philosophers of old could declaim on the folly of repining under troubles which could neither be prevented nor escaped. 4. This command teaches us that the taking up the daily cross is one eminent and distinguishing mark of true discipleship. "Follow Me," He saith; "not in speaking with the tongues of men and of angels, not in the gift of prophecy, not in the understanding of all mysteries and all knowledge, not in the faith that could remove mountains; but in the denying thyself in the daily bearing of the cross." This likens to Christ; this gives a just title to the name of "Christian," and is a distinguishing mark of true discipleship. II. It is a PLAIN command. Surely if any man refuses to follow Christ in the path of self-denial it cannot be because the meaning of the command to do so is hard to be understood; but because he abhors the sacrifice that is required. III. It is a WISE command. True wisdom is evidenced by selecting the most suitable means for effecting important ends. 1. One great end of this com-

mand is the spiritual and everlasting good of individual men. 2. Another important end of this command is the purity of the universal Church. IV. It is a
GRACIOUS command. 1. It was dictated by faithful kindness. 2. It prescribes the
way to real happiness. 3. It calls disciples to tread the same glorious path which
Himself had trodden before. Concluding observations : 1. No man belongs to
Christ who is destitute of the spirit required by this command. 2. The meekly
bearing of daily crosses is the best preparation for heavier trials. 3. Daily grace is
necessary for bearing the daily cross. (*Essex Congregational Remembrancer.*)
Personal cross-bearing :—I. EACH MAN HAS HIS OWN CROSS. Are there, then, any
principles which will guide us in answering the question, " What is my cross ? " 1.
Anything that hinders your highest life in God must be given up, and to give it up
may be your cross. 2. Anything than hinders your largest and fullest service for
Christ. One of the most distinguished oculists living in London to-day was a great
cricketer in his early years, and after he commenced practice he used to seek in
that noble game a relief from the anxiety and pressure of his professional work.
He found out, however, very soon, that the game interfered with the steadiness of
hand so imperative in a man touching one of the most delicate organs of the human
body ; he found out, in a word, that he could not be a great oculist and a great
cricketer at the same time, and he at once resolved to give up the cricket—it interfered with the serious business of his life. In a higher sense this may be true of
us. II. EVERY MAN MUST TAKE UP HIS CROSS. Our Lord is not speaking in the
text of those crosses which come to us whether we like or not ; but of voluntary
crosses—self-denials which the soul inflicts on itself. Such crosses we may either
take up, or may shut our eyes to them and not see them, or may see them and pass
them by. Christ does not compel us to take up our cross. We are free to refuse
it. But remember, no man can go to heaven unless he feels the cross somewhere.
There must be the cross in us as well as the cross for us. And it is a daily cross, a
daily surrender of self. It is easy to make a great sacrifice once ; but it is hard to
make a little sacrifice every day—and that is what is required. It is the test of our
discipleship. If we fail here we fail everywhere. I remember reading—I think
it was in the Indian Mutiny—of a siege which the British army conducted ; how
they captured, after long fighting, the walls of the city they had besieged ; but the
native garrison within only slowly and stubbornly retreated, fighting their way step
by step, until at last they entrenched themselves in the citadel, and there defied
the British troops. So it is with us. Who has not known this experience ? Self
may be beaten by Christ in the outworks of life ; it may retreat from Christ ; it
may yield one point after another ; or, to vary the metaphor, you may throw open
room after room in the soul to Christ until all the soul is open save one little room :
into it self has retreated ; there it has entrenched itself. Until Christ is master of
that room, He is not master of you. Hold one thing back, you hold all ; yield one
thing, you yield all. Yes, a man's cross is just that which he finds it most
difficult to yield. (*G. S. Barrett, B.A.*) *Taking up one's cross :*—This has
become a phrase, because it just hits the facts of life. One would like to
trace the history of that phrase. But here are samples of crosses which some
of you have to take up. A feeble and ailing body which ties you to one
place and robs you of many joys—that is a cross. The peevishness or perversity or jealousy of a dweller in your house you cannot escape—that is a
cross. To be denied the rank, preferment, or place to which you are entitled,
by the mischance of fortune or the arrogance of powerful caprice—that is a
cross. The unfaithfulness of friends and the infidelity of those you have done
your best to serve—that is a cross. To be childless for some is a cross. Unrequited affection is a cross. The ill deeds of those who are dear to you is a cross.
To be misunderstood, maligned, or hindered is a cross. To have your home made
so desolate by death that each day stares cold and lonely upon you—that is a cross ;
and if I were to go on for an hour I should not complete the long sum of the world's
crosses. What are we to do with them all ? " Take them up," says Christ ; that is,
recognize them as your portion, and bear them uncomplainingly. " Take them up
daily," mark the word ! just as you put on your dress. They may chafe you at
first, but as you think of Him whose servant you are, and whose eye is your
guiding-star, and who Himself set you an example in bearing His cross, the burden
will grow lighter until you scarcely feel its pressure. (*W. Page Roberts, M.A.*)
The cross is near at hand :—An old mystic once said a true word : " Never run
after a cross, and never run away from one." No, you need not run after it.
The cross is near you, with you, in you, if you will only see it. (*G. S. Barrett, B.A.*)

The crucial test:—Lord Bacon, in his great work, speaks of the supreme value of testing our hypotheses in natural science by what he calls the *experimentum crucis*—the experiment of the cross, or, as we should say, a crucial test. There is a crucial test in the kingdom of Christ. *The dignity of cross-bearing:*—Till Christ spoke of bearing the cross, the phrase had no special meaning. Under His use it has become proverbial. Cross-bearing is now understood to mean self-denial. A remarkable change of feeling has come about regarding the symbol itself. The cross in those days was a mark of shame. To the apostles it was as abhorrent as are the gallows to-day. But now the cross is honourable. The Crusaders wore the emblem on their clothing; orders of knighthood distinguished themselves by it; churches lift up the symbol as their conspicuous designation; it is even regarded as one of the choicest ornaments of jewellery. This change of sentiment is due to the fact that Christ "endured the cross, despising the shame." The symbol is honourable; so ought to be that which is symbolized. In fact, self-denial has come to be considered an essential quality of nobility in character. Recently, a company of unbelievers followed one of their number to the grave, bearing over his body the emblem of the cross. The fact was noticed as inconsistent, but they stoutly defended their action, saying that the cross, with that which it symbolized, was worthy to be the distinguishing characteristic of manhood. Christ, the first and great cross-bearer, taught them, no less than all the world beside, this fact. It is heroic. We are thrilled with interest at the effort made to rescue six men imprisoned in a coal-mine. Twelve thousand feet of earth are pierced to reach them; a great body of men are busy, at a great expenditure of money and at risk of life, toiling for five days and nights. At last they are saved, and the land rejoices. Just what was then done to save earthly life the Church must do to save spiritual life. And yet the temptation remains to avoid self-denial. Cross-bearing we love to commend in speech, but shrink from in action. (*A. P. Foster.*)

Ver. 24. **For whosoever will save his life shall lose it.**—*The gain of loss :*—I. WHAT IT IS TO LOSE THE LIFE. The term "lose," as here employed, is to be understood in the sense of parting with, giving up, surrendering; and when the act is done it is to be treated as something entirely gone, completely lost. You observe another thing here, also, that this is not loss in the ordinary way. Usually when anything is lost, it is either by carelessness, indifference, or bad management, but always against the will of the loser. And even in cases where none of these conditions apply—where the utmost care, attention, and good management are exercised, and losses occur, they would be prevented if possible. But this is not so in the case before us. Jesus says, "Whosoever *will* lose his life," or "Whosoever *will* save his life," showing that in either case the act is deliberate and willingly done. No man is forced into a sinful life, nor is any man compelled to become a Christian; in both cases the will of the actor is left free and unfettered, hence his responsibility. And it is just here where the test becomes so keen and crucial—the life—the entire life. Men would more readily accept discipleship if the conditions were easier, if they could be met half-way with some compromise. But we are met by men who raise objections to this doctrine of complete and unconditional surrender to Christ. They say it is too hard a thing for human nature to do, that men must be more than human to comply with such conditions. That it is more than human nature in itself can accomplish we freely admit. II. WHEN AND IN WHAT WAY DOES A MAN WHO LOSES HIS LIFE FIND IT? 1. The gain is present. Self-love, love of the world, or the things of the world, as a primary and all-absorbing principle of the soul, is ruinous to the entire life—the soul. But the man who sets his affections on Christ and things above—such a man saves his soul and secures his interests for eternity. This consecration to Christ brings present gain. A man gives himself up to the service of God, and what follows? He keeps his life. A Christian man only can be said to be a living man. He has Divine life in the soul, born of God, re-created after the similitude of the heavenly. Has he not gained then richly, abundantly, yea, transcendently, in giving up his life for Christ's sake? 2. The gain is eternal. The advantages and pleasures of a Christian life, as they relate to the present only, more than compensate for any sacrifice which that life involves. But see! how rich to repletion is the Divine method of repayment—"he shall keep it to eternal life." "Ye are dead,"—referring to the old nature where death unto sin has been produced—"and your life"—the new creation, or life Divine in the soul—"is hid with Christ in God"—safe, inviolable, doubly secure, kept by Divine power and grace unto the time of eternal redemption. This is the now—the present, the here, of probation and pilgrimage. And are not these honours and immunities the loss of which worlds could not compensate? Oh then! who would not lose the life for Christ's sake? Loss by Christian service is a misapplied term; there is no real loss, for even in those times when we are apt to think the loss or sacrifice the greatest and most severe—when we have to suffer for conscience' sake, then the compensating principle is working most vigorously in our lives, giving back to us an increase of riches that gold cannot purchase; advancing, refining, and fitting us for nobler company, and writing for us some fresh record that shall give increased emphasis and sweetness to the Master's "Well done" at the last. This subject suggests three thoughts. 1. The present makes the future. The NOW is everything to us. 2. This is the time of preparation. That of retribution. 3. For what, then, are you living—Self or Christ? "Whatsoever a man soweth, that shall he also reap." (*J. T. Higgins.*) *Gaining life by losing it :*—The highest life, by thinking of something else than your life at all, of something else than yourself, than either of your own body or your own soul. Quit thinking about yourself and your own life; that is how man shall attain the true life, by losing himself in something else! Now, this is apt to seem a contradiction and a paradox. Is not the first principle in doing anything this—to keep the thing steadily before you and aim right at it? It seems a sort of getting at the true life round a corner; going in one direction in order to get into another. And yet it is not so. See! It is true that with respect to the work man has to do outside himself, the way to do it is to keep it directly in view, aim consciously at it. But what I want you to notice is, that the moment you come to the operations of mind or life in man himself, not merely in this higher life Christ speaks of, but in almost any part of his nature, in man himself, the opposite principle comes in—this very principle which seems so paradoxical, the principle that losing the life, letting it go, not thinking of it, is the surest way of saving it. This is not only true with regard to coming to the best for one's soul, it is true of coming to the best even in the commonest faculties and qualities of life. Why, you see the truth of it every day even in such a common thing as the operations of mind and memory. You want the name of a person or of a place. It is something you know perfectly well—you know it, you say, as well as your own name. Yet you cannot recall it; no! and the serious thing is that the harder you try to recall it, the more it won't come. Dr. W. B. Carpenter tells how some years ago an English bank cashier lost the key of the vault. In the morning it was not on hand. The whole business was at a stand. What must be done? He certainly had it the night before and put it somewhere—but where he could not remember. A sharp detective was sent for, and when he had inquired into every circumstance connected with the affair, he said, "The only way is for you to go home and think of something else." And the man did go home; probably found it very hard work to get interested in anything else but at last something attracted his attention, set him thinking in quite a different direction, and then, almost directly, it flashed into his mind where he had put it—and all was right. Take a higher operation of mind than mere memory. Did you ever try to cross a stream by some rather awkward stepping-stones, or by a rather narrow plank? Or have you tried to walk at some dangerous height? or, in fact, anything requiring a particularly clear, steady head? If you have, you know that it is to be done exactly by not thinking about it. If you begin looking down at the stepping-stones, or at the water, or at the depth beneath you, and thinking about it, and about how you shall go through with it, you are lost. Whereas, if you are so occupied, thinking about something else, that you hardly notice the stepping-stones; if you are on some errand in which you are so eager that you are not thinking of yourself—that losing yourself is your safety—you may go perfectly safely over places and heights that afterwards, when you do come to think about them, will make you dizzy to look at. There, too, life is safest by not thinking about saving it. Take another matter—the preservation of health. One condition of keeping in good health is not to think about your health, but to be wholesomely occupied with quite other thoughts. Think about your health, begin feeling your pulse, watching your symptoms, considering all the things which might possibly be the matter with you, and you may think yourself into an illness. Why do physicians so often order " change of scene " and " something to distract the mind," but that the patient may be led to lose himself, and so find the health which he could not gain while anxiously thinking of himself? And so, when there is some epidemic about, how true you constantly see it that " he that will save his life shall lose it." The most dangerous thing of all is to be constantly thinking and scheming how to escape infection. And so it is even in life's most tremendous crisis and trials and perils. In those terrible days of persecution, when the Christian might any hour be taken before some magistrate, and have it put to him to say a word or two cursing and denying Christ, or else to be thrown to the wild beasts in the amphitheatre, or put to any cruel torture that happened to have come in fashion— they believed their Master's words. They didn't worry themselves about saving life, and they did "find it." They found it even here—here, as Christ had said, a hundred-fold, even with their persecutions. The life they had was a nobler, happier life, because it was not occupied in thinking of its own safety, and when they lost it, why, they found it elsewhere. Yes; for these are the things which make us feel man's immortality. It is not when I see men in a mad rush for safety; it is not when I see men setting such store on the mere life that they will sacrifice everything for it, that I am most impressed with life's deathless quality, but just the opposite. When I read—and every week there is some instance of the kind—of those who in the wrecked ship or the burning building are content to let life go in order to help others; when I read of such brave men as that lifeboat crew who, a while ago, pushed off into the raging sea out to the stranded ship, and the storm was so awful that their own boat swamped, and eight of them were drowned; or when I hear such a story as that of the colliers in a mine only five miles from my old Lancashire home, where there was one of those awful explosions, and the men from some lower levels came rushing up right into the danger of the deathly afterblast, when the only chance of escape was by another shaft; and one man knew this, and stood his ground there in that dangerous passage warning the men, as they came rushing along, that their only safety was the other way, and when they urged him to go that other way, saying, "No; some one must stay there to guide the others"—ah! these are the things which make you feel that immortality is real. For the moment you touch this—not self-preservation, but self-renunciation —you feel that there is something in such life of quite other sort than that gross matter by which it can be crushed or burned or drowned; something against which those brute substances and forces are as powerless as a sledge-hammer against steam. I know it seems a hard doctrine. The whole spirit of the common world rises up against it. "We must look to ourselves," men say. Yes, I know how natural this is, and I know that it has its place. I do not want to speak intolerantly or condemnatorily about self-interest. Self-interest, if it is not the highest thing, is one of the useful forces of the world. Self-interest has set man grappling with nature, has taught him the arts of self-protection, has trained him to dig and plant, and spin and weave, has sent him sailing and discovering over the world, has raised the human race from savagism to civilization. Yes, and it has all this, and this kind of thing, to do perpetually. Self-interest is one of the great, strong, permanent forces at the base of life! It is part of nature; but it is not the whole of nature, and it is not the highest nature. Through these self-motives, more and more disciplined and restrained, man should be ever rising higher. The world's best life and work are always leading on to this higher quality in life and work, of losing self, forgetting self. The very things which begin with self do not come to their best till self is lost, forgotten. If you only want to be a public speaker, well, you may begin your practising for it—perhaps you have to do—by thinking about yourself; but you will never come to any real eloquence till you have got away past that, till in some hour of passionate feeling you have forgotten yourself in your subject. The physician may study medicine in order to earn his own living; but he will be a poor doctor who does not by and by become so interested in his work, and in trying to do good to his sick patients, that he constantly forgets himself. So with all the real excelling power in life. The real power to do any worthy thing in the world depends upon our loving that thing more than ourselves. The moment you rise to that—forget yourself, think of something else, some one else—that moment your work takes on a higher quality. The merest hand-worker goes to work for his own need, but he will find his work happier, and do it better, whenever he forgets his own interest in thinking of his employer's interest. And just so the employer carries on his business primarily for his own self-interest. (*B. Herford, D.D.*) *Life through death :*—Men are saved only as they get the better of themselves; the higher self treading down and treading out the lower self. What is virtue but sharp conflict all the way along, and in death alone the victory? If ever we enter heaven, we go in on our shields. To escape with our lives is to lose our lives. To be slain is to live for evermore. I. IT IS COMMONLY REQUIRED OF US TC

SACRIFICE A LOWER GOOD IN ORDER TO GAIN A HIGHER. Not always, but almost always. The rule is, with regard to the good things of this world, that every man shall take his choice, and then abide by it; selecting some one thing that he wants, and consenting to forego all the rest. The world is thus turned into a vast bazaar, where everything is ticketed and has its price, but where no man makes more than one purchase at a time. Especially true is it that a lower sort of good has to be given up for a higher. If we may not have God and Mammon for our friends, still less may we reverse the order, and have Mammon and God. All that a man may win of earthly good he must be ready to sacrifice, if need be, in order to save his soul. You may call the demand a hard one; but all the analogies of our ordinary life endorse and favour it. As pleasures are trampled on in the chase after gain, and gold has no glitter for a proudly aspiring eye, so is it no more than just and fair that he who would shine as a star in heaven, should be willing to have his light eclipsed and quenched on earth. Pleasure, money, fame—each has its price; and nobody complains of it. The soul, too, has its price. Its redemption is precious. It may cost us all we are worth, and all we covet, to save it. The life temporal may have to be flung utterly away in order to make sure of the life eternal. The men who burnt Polycarp thought they were taking his life. They would have taken it, had they persuaded him to deny his Lord. II. By FIRST SECURING THE HIGHER GOOD, WE ARE PREPARED PROPERLY TO ENJOY THE LOWER, AND ARE MORE LIKELY TO SECURE IT. The principle I wish to emphasize is, that no worldly good of any sort can be well secured, or properly enjoyed, if pursued by itself and for its own sake. This may be seen in our most ordinary life. The man whose aim is pleasure may, indeed, secure it for a while; but only for a while. It soon palls upon his senses, disgusts and wearies him. So of gold. So also of fame. The best way to win renown is not to work for it, not to think of it, but to work for something higher; to work for God and work for man, forgetting self, and, by and by, it will be found that both God and man are helping us. He that most utterly forgets himself is the one most surely and most warmly remembered by the world. General Zachary Taylor, the twelfth President of the United States, spent forty years of his life in comparatively obscure, but very faithful, service at our Western outposts; receiving no applause from the country at large, and asking for none; intent only upon doing promptly and efficiently the duties laid upon him. By and by events, over which he had exercised no control, called him into notice upon a broader theatre. And then it was discovered how faithful and how true a man he was. The Republic, grateful for such a series of self-denying and important services, snatched him from the camp, and bore him, with loud acclaim, to her proudest place of honour. And this was done at the cost of bitterest disappointment to more than one, whose high claims to this distinction were not denied, but who had been known to be aspiring to the exalted seat. And so through our whole earthly life—in all its spheres and in all its struggles. To lose is to find; to die is to live. It is so also in our religion. We begin by abjuring all; we end by enjoying all. He that loves God with all his heart, and serves Him with all his powers, working here, with a self-forgetting devotion, in the world where God has planted him; willing to forego pleasure, gain, renown, and everything for Christ, shall find that everything comes back to him— if not in its material fulness, yet in its essential strength and spirit. Am I charged with preaching that "gain is godliness"? Not so, my friend. But godliness is gain. It begins by denouncing and denying all; it ends by restoring all. First it desolates, and then it rebuilds. In conclusion—1. We may learn the great mistake committed by men of the world in their chase after worldly good. They make it an end. They must reverse the present order of their lives. They must learn to seek first the kingdom of God. They must abandon themselves to the service of Christ. 2. We may learn why it is the happiness of Christians is so imperfect. They have only partially denied themselves; are only partially resigned to the love and service of their Maker. Hence they are still in part devoted to the world and fettered by it. Not till the last link is sundered, and their souls entirely absorbed in Christ, can they attain to a perfect joy. Not till they are wholly dead can they wholly live. (*R. D. Hitchcock, D.D.*) *Self-seeking involves a cross equally with self-abnegation:*—Does the cross terrify you by its dark shadow? Do those nails seem so sharp—that thorny crown so terrible—that spear so pointed—that darkness so heavy? Stay for a moment, while you listen to these solemn words: "What is a man profited if he should gain the whole world, and lose his own soul?" You are running away from the cross; but there is a cross being prepared for you. Remember that the cross was the instrument of a felon's execution; and while you are flying away from the unfriendly shadow, behind the veil there is a ghastlier cross being erected for you. You are asserting your own will, you are loving your own life. You shall "lose it"; and lose it by your own irrational self-love. You have elected to live for yourself; you are running after what you conceive, in your own blindness and deception, to be your own self-interest. Do you not find, even now, O child of the world! that your self-interest is deluding you? The bubbles you grasp burst in your hand; the flowers you gather fade at your touch; as you go along life's journey you are conscious of the approach—ever becoming more and more terrible—of a cloud of darker sorrow, while the present sense of blank disappointment becomes more and more appalling! Years creep on upon you; the effect of age is felt: the body is shattered as you near the end of your journey; the human strength decays; the joys of life are withered, and, one by one, as your earthly possessions slip from your grasp—then, what then? " Say ye to the wicked, It shall be ill with him, for the rewards of his hands shall be given unto him." You have fled from suffering into the arms of suffering; you have endeavoured to escape from the cross, you find your portion in the cross for all eternity. Thus it is that the man prepares his own doom, and is himself the creator of his own misery. (*W. H. H. Aitken, M.A.*) *Individuality :*—This is one of those sayings of Christ which have aroused in men opinions of the most opposite character. It has been received on one side with scorn, on the other by reverence. It has been considered as a piece of unpractical sentiment; it has been hailed as the very inmost law of all life. Any spiritual theory of life which tends to destroy, and not to assert, the individuality of man is an inhuman theory, and, as such, false. Any explanation of this text must account for the fact of the desire of individuality. We must keep our individuality, but we ought to take care that it is true and not false individuality. The key to distinguish them from each other is given in the text. It speaks of a double nature in man; one which asserts itself, the other which denies it. The first has a seeming life which is actual death; the second has a seeming death which is actual life; and, therefore, if life is inseparably connected with individuality, the development of the selfish nature is false individuality; the development of the unselfish nature is true individuality. Individuality is not isolation. (*Stopford A. Brooke, M.A.*) *Losing the life to find it :*—It was my fortune last year, in going from Torcello to Venice, to be overtaken by one of the whirlwinds which sometimes visit the south. It was a dead calm, but the whole sky high overhead was covered with a pall of purple, sombre and smooth, but full of scarlet threads. Across this, from side to side, as if directed by two invisible armies, flew at every instant flashes of forked lightning; but so lofty was the storm—and this gave a hushed terror to the scene—that no thunder was heard. Beneath this sky the lagoon water was dead purple, and the weedy shoals left naked by the tide dead scarlet. The only motion in the sky was far away to the south, where a palm-tree of pale mist seemed to rise from the water, and to join itself above to a self-enfolding mass of seething cloud. We reached a small island and landed. An instant after, as I stood on the parapet of the fortification, amid the breathless silence, this pillar of cloud, ghastly white, and relieved against the violet darkness of the sky, its edge as clear as if cut out with a knife, came rushing forward over the lagoon, driven by the spirit of the wind, which, hidden within it, whirled and coiled its column into an endless spiral. The wind was only there, at its very edge there was not a ripple; but, as it drew near our island, it seemed to be pressed down upon the sea, and, unable to resist the pressure, opened out like a fan in a foam of vapour. Then, with a shriek which made every nerve thrill with excitement, the imprisoned wind leapt forth; the water of the lagoon, beaten flat, was torn away to the depth of half an inch; and, as the cloud of spray and wind smote the island, it trembled over it like a ship struck by a great wave. We seemed to be in the very heart of the universe at a moment when the thought of the universe was most sublime. The long preparation, and then the close, so unexpected and magnificent, swept every one completely out of self-consciousness; the Italian soldiers at my side danced upon the parapet and shouted with excitement. For an instant we were living in Nature's being, not in our own isolation. It taught me a lesson; it made me feel the meaning of this text, "Whosoever will lose his life shall find it"; for it is in such scanty minutes that a man becomes possessor of that rare intensity of life which is, when it is pure, so wonderful a thing that it is like a new birth into a new world, in which, though self is lost, the highest individuality is found. (*Ibid.*) *Saved by willing to lose :*—Two men were sinking a shaft. It was a dangerous business, for it was necessary to blast the rock. It was their custom to cut the fuse with a sharp knife. One man then entered the bucket, and made a signal to be hauled up. When the bucket again descended, the other man entered it, and, with one hand on the signal-rope and the other holding the fire, he touched the fuse, made the signal, and was rapidly drawn up before the explosion took place. One day they left the knife above, and, rather than ascend to procure it, they cut the fuse with a sharp stone. It took fire. " The fuse is on fire ! " Both men leaped into the bucket, and made the signal, but the windlass would haul up but one man at a time; only one could escape. One of the men instantly leaped out, and said to the other, " Up wi' ye; I'll be in heaven in a minute." With lightning speed the bucket was drawn up, and the one man was saved. The explosion took place. Men descended, expecting to find the mangled body of the other miner; but the blast had loosed a mass of rock, and it lay diagonally across him ; and, with the exception of a few bruises and a little scorching, he was unhurt. When asked why he urged his comrade to escape, he gave an answer that sceptics would laugh at. Well, they may call it superstition or fanaticism, or whatever they choose. But what did this hero say when asked, " Why did you insist on this other man's ascending ? " In his quaint dialect he replied, " Because I knowed my soul was safe: for I've gie it in the hands of Him of whom it is said that ' faithfulness is the girdle of his reins,' and I knowed that what I gied Him He'd never gie up. But t'other chap was an awful wicked lad, and I wanted to gie him another chance." All the infidelity in the world cannot produce such a signal act of heroism as that. Carlyle refers to this story in one of the chapters of his "Life of Sterling."

Ver. 25. What is a man advantaged.—*A wreck :*—Did you ever see a wreck ? I remember being one winter's night in a little town on the coast of Wales. We were sitting by the fire, cheerful, and we heard, while there, a sudden noise: we looked out into the night ; there was a deep fog over the sea ; we could scarcely see the cliffs ; the wind was very high ; there was a drizzling rain ; and suddenly we heard the scream of voices ; then the boom of the guns over the water; then stillness ; then the clatter of feet along the street; the life boat and the life buoy. Human life in danger. We thought we discried the dark mass heaving over the black billows, lit up by the ray of the guns and the blue lights ; but the sound of the surf and the roar of the breakers carried all away ; they carried *her* away. That night she struck on the rocks. I walked down in the morning to look at her lying on the beach. I could not help saying, " How human this is; how life-like ! " There she lay—the pride and hope of her owners—stripped ; masts, sails, shrouds, broken, ragged, torn, gone ; and yet much had depended on her. She had been launched with many hopes and expectations. All gone—a melancholy wreck ! The winds howled through as they lifted her ragged shrouds. She could not, as once she might have done, repel them and make them her ministers. The sun shone on her, through her cabin windows and port-hole, but awakened no answering glory on her deck. She was a lost ship—melancholy type of a lost soul. (*E. Paxton Hood.*) *The loss of the soul :*—I. Man has a soul. The soul touches the highest part of the universe. Nature ministers to nature ; but nature cannot feed the soul. The fruits, and grapes, and animals cannot contribute to the being of the soul. God, who is its Parent, can alone minister to it. This is that difference between the spirit of the beast which goeth downward, and the spirit of man which goeth upward. " We are dust and Deity," says a great poet : most true. This is our original. Turn into reality the great fact that you have a soul. Did you ever hear how Fichte awoke the consciousness of his hearers ? He pointed to the wall, the white wall. " Gentlemen," said he, " I want you to think the wall. Have you thought the wall ? Now, think the man that thought the wall." Ah ! to do that is to realize to ourselves our soul. II. It is of infinite value. 1. Think of its power. (1) It can sin. It is capable of moral wrong. The soul has had power to disturb the universe. (2) It can suffer. Oh, how it can suffer, remorse, conscience, despair ! Nay, we estimate the greatness of the soul by its power to suffer. (3) It can think. How it can think ! can be even wild with thought, and rend the poor body as the strong wind rends oaks and rocks ! 2. Its duration. For ever : no cessation. III. A soul may be lost. Nay, every soul in the world is, in fact, lost. Do you know it? do you feel it? Lost ! ! For there are but two ways in the universe—God's and man's. To be lost, is to wander into the far country, and to attempt to feed an angel nature with the husks that the swine eat. Picture to yourselves the man on the dark moor at night among the

mountains—amidst the mists—lost. I may mention four causes of the loss
of the soul. 1. Ignorance. 2. Error. 3. Passion. 4. A perverted will: underlying the whole. These are the marks of human nature in its present state.
And to be lost, is to love our natural state, and to persist in it. You may
remember an incident in the united lives of two men, with whose labours and
lives, it may be, you have on the whole little sympathy. When Francis
Xavier, the youthful, the eloquent, the noble, was engaged in the pursuits of
his varied and wonderful mind, in Paris, in the university, and its more
romantic neighbourhood, as he yielded himself to the fascinations mingling
around him, there stepped forth and spoke to him a plainly dressed and
powerful preacher of lofty bearing and stern deportment, mighty in the assumption of a voluntary poverty—Ignatius Loyola. "Francis," said he, "'What shall
it profit a man, if he gain the whole world, and lose his own soul?'" He would
not let the youth go. He attended the hall where Xavier delivered his eloquent
prelections; he stood and listened before the orator's chair; but when the applause
had subsided, and the crowd had retired, then he was by the side of the eloquent
scholar. He touched him on the shoulder; "Francis," said he, "'What shall it
profit a man, if he gain the whole world, and lose his own soul?'" Noble as he
was, Xavier was not rich; his affairs became embarrassed; he needed help. The
stern apostle of voluntary poverty did not forsake; he came to him with assistance;
he produced mysterious aid; but, as he put the bag into the hands of his friend,
he was ready with his old question, "Francis, 'What shall it profit a man, if he
gain the whole world, and lose his own soul?'" They wandered together by the
banks of the Seine; they trod together through its groves of trees, and wound their
way into its lovely recesses; but even as the enthusiastic and imaginative Xavier
paused, enraptured before the spectacle of some astonishing beauty, some enchanting
or spell-compelling spot, the voice thrilled through him: "Francis, 'What shall
it profit a man, if he gain the whole world, and lose his own soul?'" And the
reader knows that earnestness subdued the eloquent scholar, and he became the
comrade and the disciple of Ignatius Loyola. You have heard of the Mammoth
Cave in America—a world under the ground—how many miles no one can tell,
rivers, lakes, chambers, immense territories all in darkness, where the light of the
sun never penetrated. But nineteen miles within the cave, 450 feet beneath the
soil, there was yet a descent called the Bottomless Pit. Down into that no man
would go; they had sounded 150 feet, and yet had not reached the depth; no man
would go; the guide refused 500 dollars offered him to go. At length a poor man
came, a young man, and he determined he would descend. Ropes were procured,
and he descended 150 feet. He walked among those galleries of darkness, alone,
through those depths and corridors of gloom; he began to ascend, but as he
ascended he stayed to throw himself into an interminable cave on the side of the
pit; there as he roamed through its fissures, his light went out—no light—and
alone in that gloom—lost! And the light was kindled again; but he found, as he
began to ascend, the rope was on fire. Ah! what shall he do now? What think
you, ascending—looking up to that faint ray, and the fire burning—burning. But
it *was* extinguished, he *was* saved. But is it not the very picture of a poor soul?
In the deep night, the light extinguished. And sometimes those very powers by
which he might ascend,—his passions, his intellect, his will, only kindling to ruin
him—affections which might unite to God, turning to fire to separate him for ever.
IV. And why? FOR THE SOUL MAY BE SAVED. Surely no person will say, "What
shall I do to be saved?" But if so, I have only to say, "Believe in the Lord Jesus
Christ, and thou shalt be saved." And if you say, I cannot believe, in a word, I
have only to say—say thou to God, "I will not let Thee go except Thou bless me."
Pray, and you shall not fail to obtain the knowledge of Christ and Him crucified.
(*Ibid.*)   Save your soul :—If temporal affairs impose upon a man a large measure
of labour and solicitude, how much more should he exercise the utmost diligence
in behalf of his eternal welfare? I. NOTHING IS MORE NECESSARY THAN TO SAVE
OUR SOULS. 1. The chief solicitude of God is for our salvation. 2. The question
is of everlasting weal or woe. 3. Therefore Jesus warns us with the most tender
anxiety—(1) To work our salvation *before* all things. (2) To work our salvation *in*
all things. (3) To take care of our salvation *at all times*, and give it our own
personal attention. II. NOTHING IS MORE RARE THAN THIS SOLICITUDE. 1. Everywhere we may observe an all-absorbing care for temporal affairs and earthly
possessions. (1) The heart of man is attached to them; restless his desire to
acquire them; great his sorrow at their loss. (2) All activity of man is centred

upon them. Men are grovelling in the dust. 2. Negligence in regard to heavenly things. (1) No earnest examination of the condition of the soul. (2) Carelessness in regard to the means of salvation. 3. Men appear to be without conscience in regard to the salvation of others. (1) Careless parents, educating their children for everything except the one thing necessary. (2) Cruel seducers, showing heartless indifference to their own and others' salvation. 4. Let us look back at our past life. (1) How many opportunities has God granted us to save our souls! Time, the Word of God, misfortunes, &c. (2) How little is it that we have given to God! What use have we made of our time? For whom have we laboured? Have we laid up treasures for the world to come? (3) What folly! All our trouble for nothing! We run after the mists and clouds, and neglect that which is everlasting. We frustrate the merciful designs and endeavours of God. (*Tourbe.*) *Money given as the punishment of avarice:*—We read of a Spanish general who was so fond of money that the enemies into whose hands he had fallen, tortured and killed him by pouring melted gold down his throat in mockery of his covetousness. So Satan now often makes money unlawfully acquired, the very means of tormenting the miserable beings who have sold their consciences to obtain it. (*Family Treasury.*) *Bad bargains:*—A Sunday-school teacher, when speaking about the passage, "Buy the truth, and sell it not," said that the man who buys the truth, at whatever cost, makes a good bargain. He then asked his boys if any of them remembered an instance in the Scriptures of a bad bargain. These answers were given—1. "Esau made a bad bargain when he sold his birthright for a mess of pottage." 2. "Judas made a bad bargain when he sold Jesus for thirty pieces of silver." 3. "He makes a bad bargain, who, to gain the whole world, loses his own soul." *The world cannot give peace:*—There was one living who, scarcely in a figure, might be said to have the whole world. The Roman Emperor Tiberius was at that moment infinitely the most powerful of living men, the absolute, undisputed, deified ruler of all that was fairest and richest in the kingdoms of the earth. There was no control to his power, no limit to his wealth, no restraint upon his pleasures. And, to yield himself still more unreservedly to the boundless self-gratification of a voluptuous luxury, not long after this time he chose for himself a home on one of the loveliest spots on the earth's surface, under the shadow of the slumbering volcano, upon an enchanting islet in one of the most softly delicious climates of the world. What came of it all? He was, as Pliny calls him, "*Tristissimus ut constat hominum,*" confessedly the most gloomy of mankind. And there, from this home of his hidden infamies, from this island where, on a scale so splendid, he had tried the experiment of what happiness can be achieved by pressing the world's most absolute authority and the world's guiltiest indulgencies into the service of an exclusively selfish life, he wrote to his servile and corrupted senate, "What to write to you, conscript fathers, or how to write, or what not to write, may all the gods and goddesses destroy me, worse than I feel that they are daily destroying me, if I know." Rarely has there been vouchsafed to the world a more overwhelming proof that its richest gifts are but "fairy gold that turns to dust and dross." (*Archdeacon Farrar.*) *A crime against the life of the soul:*—When, a half-century ago, the famous Kaspar Hauser appeared in the streets of Nuremberg, having been released from a dungeon in which he had been confined from infancy, having never seen the face or heard the voice of man, nor gone without the walls of his prison, nor seen the full light of day, a distinguished lawyer in Germany wrote a legal history of the case, which he entitled, "A Crime against the Life of the Soul." It was well named. . . . But it is no worse than the treatment some men bestow upon their own souls. . . . As the poor German youth was at length thrust out into the world for which he was unfitted, with untrained senses in a world of sense, without speech in a world of language, with a dormant mind in a world of thought, so many go out of this world with no preparation in that part of their nature that will most be called into use. (*Theodore T. Munger.*) *Secure the soul:*—What wise man would fetch gold out of a fiery crucible, hazard himself to endless woes, for a few waterish pleasures, and give his soul to the devil, as some Popes did for the short enjoyment of the Papal dignity? What was this but to win Venice, and then to be hanged at the gates thereof, as the proverb is. In great fires men look first to their jewels, then to their lumber; so should these see first to their souls to secure them, and then take care of the outward man. The soldier cares not how his buckler speeds, so his body be kept thereby from deadly thrusts. (*J. Trapp.*)

Ver. 26. **Whosoever shall be ashamed of Me.**—*Shame of Christ, and its con-sequences :*—I. A COURSE OF CONDUCT SPECIFIED. " Ashamed " of Christ—1. In a sceptical rejection of Him as the true Messiah. Jews. Infidels. 2. In an unbelieving disregard to His demands and authority. 3. In a compromising spirit of conformity to the world. 4. In a neglect of His ordinances, and in avoiding a public profession of Him before men. 5. In an unwillingness to consecrate all we are and have to His service. II. THE INEVITABLE RESULTS DECLARED. " Of Him shall the Son of man be ashamed," &c. The result shall be—1. That such shall receive a similar return. 2. Christ shall be ashamed of them. 3. He will be ashamed of them in the day of His glory. 4. He will be ashamed of them when the dispensation of grace will have ceased for ever. (*J. Burns, D.D.*) *False shame :*—I. WHAT THERE IS IN CHRIST AND HIS WORDS OF WHICH MEN ARE ASHAMED. 1. Their reason is perplexed by the mystery of His person. Indeed, it may be said that Christ was a mystery in His day both to His disciples and to His enemies. If He had not been a mystery, He would not have been a Saviour. No man who is merely on the level of man both in his intellectual and moral nature can be the Saviour of man. It was because the men of His age did not see this truth that they so stumbled at His words. And men may be offended at Him, and ashamed of Him, still, because of the mystery which attaches to His person. They cannot com-prehend it. It combines in one the earthly and the heavenly, the finite and the infinite, the human and the Divine ; and reason cannot compass and explain a union of such contrasted properties and attributes. It cannot understand even man himself. Still less can it understand God. And yet it would fain understand the God manifest in the flesh. 2. But this is not all. Some men are ashamed because their pride is humbled by the nature of His work. For what is that work ? It is a work which assumes, at the very beginning, the helplessness of man. Christ would never have been known by man as a Saviour but for this helplessness. He did not come to vilify our nature, and make it seem worse than it really is. But He did come to convince the world of sin ; and this could not be done without humbling the pride of man. II. But let us now consider IN WHAT MANNER MEN MAY SHOW THAT THEY ARE ASHAMED OF CHRIST. There are several ways. The shame of some is seen in their shrinking from the profession of His name. Everywhere you see men shrinking from responsi-bility, fearing responsibility, declining responsibility. They like to be un-attached. They want to feel free. Do not be ensnared in the too common mistake that it is only the becoming a Christian that creates the obligation to live a holy life. That is a duty whether you are or profess to be a Christian or not. Then as to the other aspect of shame, namely, that of shrinking from the responsi-bility of giving yourself openly to the Church of Christ ; you may shrink from it, but the duty remains. We can show our shame of Christ by silence and by com-pliance. We can show it by silence ; by the cowardice with which we hear religion ridiculed, and not rebuke the mocker ; by the cowardice which will hear the oath, or the impure and immoral sentiment, and not remind the swearer or the unclean person that neither profanity nor uncleanness will ever enter into the Kingdom of Heaven. There is too much silence among Christian men when the honour of Christ is at stake. And this is all the sadder when you see how courageous men will be in defence of their friends. But men may show their shame of Christ by compliance, as well as by silence. By compliance I mean doing as the world does, not because it is right, but because the world does it. (*E. Mellor, D.D.*) *The monstrous shame :*—1. In the first place, there are people ashamed of Christ's name. They recoil at the idea of being called Christians. If you should call them world-lings, they would stand that. If you should call them half a dozen other names, they would stand that. But the idea of their being Christians ! They are embar-rassed. They say : " You are mistaken. Have I ever given any signs of being pious ? Did you ever see me weak ? Did you ever see me pray ? No, sir ! I want you to understand that I am not a Christian." Ashamed of the sweetest name that ever thrilled the lips of men, or woke up the harps of heaven ! Ashamed of that name which now costs so little to avow ! Ashamed of that name which was the last word on the dying lip of your father, and in the song with which your mother sang you to sleep in those times before the evil days came, when you forgot her counsel and broke her dear old heart ! 2. Again : I find that there are people ashamed of Christ in the person of His friends. " John, who was that you were seen going through the street with yesterday ? " He, a worldly young man, flushes up and says : " I wasn't with that Christian man, I just happened to meet him. I wasn't walking with him." Ashamed of being associated with those who are living for eternity, but not ashamed of being with those who live for time ! 3. Still, further, there are people ashamed of Christ in His book. If you found them reading a novel, or a poem, or an essay, or any worldly book, they would not be embarrassed; but if you come suddenly upon them and find them reading the Bible, how flustered they would be ! how excited ! how they would try to have you think they were not reading at all. My text intimates that the tide is going to turn after awhile. The same feeling which some men now have toward God, God will have toward them. " Whosoever is ashamed of Me and of My Word, of him will the Son of Man be ashamed when He cometh in His own glory, and of the Father, and of the holy angels." He comes ! He will cry through all the earth and the sea : " Gather together those people who are ashamed of Me. Fetch up their bodies from the graves. Fetch up their souls from the dungeons. Gather them together." And, as He looks at the long array of blanched faces, He will be ashamed of them. He will remember their cowardice. He will say : " These are the people who were ashamed of Me. These are the people who, by their comrades and friends, were kept away from heaven, and these are the people who lost their souls. I am ashamed of them, of their sin and cowardice. They cannot sit with My people. They cannot share My royalty. Out with them ! Executioners, bind them hand and foot, and cast them into outer darkness. They despised Me. Now, I despise them. Away with them for ever ! " (*Dr. Talmage.*) *On dishonouring Christ* :— I. THE CONDUCT WHICH IS HERE CONDEMNED. 1. An evasion or rejection of those truths which are peculiar to the gospel, because they are hostile to carnal reason. 2. The refusal to make those sacrifices which an attachment to the gospel of Christ must induce, on account of their apparent harshness and severity. 3. An abandonment of the public profession of religion, because of the hatred or hostility which it would excite. II. THE CONSEQUENCES WHICH THIS CONDUCT INVOLVES. Those who have treated the Saviour with evil, shall, at His glorious coming, receive evil in return. As they have rendered to Him, it shall be rendered to them again. 1. As to the grounds on which this doom proceeds, they are such as will fully justify the sentence given. (1) It is an opposition to the essential principles on which the Divine Governor proceeds in the management of His intelligent creatures. A rejection of the rewards of eternity for those of time. (2) It is base ingratitude against the arrangements of infinite love. It is taking the sceptre of God's benevolence ₄nd dashing it in pieces against His justice. 2. The results which the view of condemnation thus stated should produce. (1) Engage at once in the service of Christ. (2) Be not ashamed of the testimony of the Lord. (*J. Parsons.*) *Am I ashamed of Christ ?*—I. WHAT IT IS TO BE ASHAMED OF CHRIST AND OF HIS WORDS; AND WHAT IS REQUISITE TO EVIDENCE THAT WE ARE NOT IN SUCH A CASE. Every one who is unwilling to sacrifice his temporal ease and pleasures, or to lay down his life for the sake of Christ, and who neglects to persevere in a steady and uniform course of obedience to His commands, in spite of all opposition and of every indignity that may be cast upon him, is considered—Jesus being His own interpreter—as ashamed of Christ. But some meek and lowly person, with much humility of mind, and great fear and trembling, may perhaps anxiously and eagerly inquire—not being without hope that he is ready to own his Lord—How must I act in order to prove the sincerity of my desires, and to evidence that such is the language and feeling of my heart? To this it is replied, It is undoubtedly requisite that there should be—1. A confession of the Lord Jesus. 2. A readiness to defend the Saviour's cause. II. WHENCE DANGER ARISES OF BEING ASHAMED OF CHRIST. 1. The simplicity of the gospel itself. Against this point the men of the world have frequently directed the weapons of their wit and jesting. Thus of old, by the polite and learned Greeks, the doctrines of the gospel were considered as foolishness. And in modern times, the wise of this world affect to sneer at the doctrines of the Cross, and mock at those who espouse truths so humiliating. 2. The character of the age in which the profession of Christ is to be maintained. In the days of our Lord it laboured under this peculiar disadvantage—it was to be professed in an adulterous and sinful generation. Awful as this language may appear, yet it conveys but too striking and faithful a picture of the manners and character of the present age. 3. The sense of fear, under apprehended danger. The cry, as directed against Jesus, that oft falls upon the ear, is, " Away with this fellow from the earth "; and the question that follows upon it is, " Art not thou one of this man's disciples ? " Immediately we begin to fear, and perhaps reply, " We know not the man." Alas ! this shameful fear too often gains the victory, and leads the disciples of Christ to base desertion in the hour of danger. III. WHAT WILL BE THE FINAL AND AWFUL CONSEQUENCES OF YIELDING TO THE THREATENING DANGER. "Of him also shall the Son of man be ashamed, when He cometh in the glory of His Father, with the holy angels." It is justly remarked that the day is coming when the cause of Christ will appear as bright and illustrious as it now seems mean and contemptible; for, as Christ had, so His cause shall have a state of humiliation and exaltation. (*Essex Remembrancer.*) *The folly and guilt of being ashamed of Christ :*—I. WHAT IS IMPLIED IN BEING ASHAMED OF CHRIST. 1. The sentiment of shame. Fear of the world's laughter and companions' sneers. 2. The principal causes. (1) The pain of singularity. (2) The power of ridicule. (3) The want of sincerity. 3. The consideration of the effects, as well as the causes of this principle, will assist in explaining its nature. One of the most certain consequences of being ashamed of duty, is to lead to boldness and audacity in vice. Shame is, perhaps, the evidence of a middle character, neither virtuous nor abandoned. It is always accompanied with some remaining reverence for God. But, judging from the licentious face of the world, that other sinners are not subject to the same constraints, it blushes for this sentiment as for a weakness. Endeavouring to cover its belief, or its fears, it assumes a greater show of infidelity and license than perhaps is real. It soon affects to talk in the style of the world, to divert itself with serious persons, and at length with serious things. But conscious insincerity urges them to extremes to cover its own deceptions. And men being prone to form their opinions, no less than to derive their feelings from sympathy, these mutual appearances contribute to create at length, that vice and infidelity to which all, in the beginning, only pretend. It is, besides, a principle of human nature, that pretence itself will ultimately form those dispositions and habits which it continues to affect. II. THE FOLLY AND GUILT OF BEING ASHAMED OF CHRIST. 1. Its folly. (1) In being ashamed of our true glory. (2) In hoping to avoid, by renouncing religion, an evil which cannot be shunned among men, I mean detraction and ridicule. (3) In fearing an imaginary evil, that is, reproach for real virtue and piety. (4) And finally, in exposing ourselves to infinite danger, for the sake of covering a fruitless deception. 2. Its guilt. (1) In exalting the authority of man above the glory of God. (2) In ingratitude to Him who was not ashamed of us. (3) In promoting vice by the pernicious influence of our example. (*S. S. Smith, D.D.*) *Confessing Christ :*—St. Augustine relates, in his "Confessions," that one Victorinus, a great man at Rome, who had many rich heathen friends and relations, was converted to the Christian religion. He repaired to a friend of his, also a convert, and told him secretly that he too was a Christian. "I will not believe thee to be a Christian," said the other, "until I see thee openly profess it in the church." "What," said Victorinus, "do the church walls make a Christian?" But directly the answer came to his own heart—"Whosoever shall be ashamed of Me and of My words, of him, also, shall the Son of man be ashamed when He cometh in the glory of His Father, with the holy angels." He was ready to bear the scorn and persecution of his heathen friends, that he might honour his Master in a public confession of His name. It cost something to acknowledge Christ in those early days of His church. When Symphorianus, a young Roman, acknowledged himself a believer in Jesus, he was seized and scourged nearly to death, and then dragged away to a place of execution. His heroic Christian mother walked by his side, not shrieking and bewailing his terrible fate, as her mother's heart prompted, but encouraging and cheering him with such words as these—"Son, my son, remember life eternal! Look up to heaven! Lift up thine eye to Him that reigneth there! Life is not taken from thee, but exchanged for a better." At these words, the young man's heart was wondrously cheered, as if God had sent an angel to strengthen him. He went to the block with a face all glowing with holy joy. What power but that of a "living God" could sustain a mother and son in such an hour? What a glorious exchange was such a belief for the dead system of heathen worship in which they had been born! (*Biblical Treasury.*) *Necessity of confessing Christ before men :*—Lieutenant Watson, once a gay young aristocrat, was awakened and converted by means of a few earnest words spoken by a brother officer (Captain Hawtry), when he was actually preparing for a ball. Growing rapidly in grace, and confessing Christ from the first and constantly, he was soon led, while serving in the Peninsula, under Wellington, to hold meetings in his own quarters for the soldiers, who were spiritually in a very destitute condition. Many of these were converted, but the officers generally mocked, calling Lieut. Watson "Coachie," saying he drove the mail-coach to heaven, and crying after him, "Any room for passengers inside or outside to-night?" One officer, however, Lieut. Whitley, a man of refined and scientific mind, behaved differently, and although he reasoned with Watson, he always behaved as a gentleman. The result of quiet conversations was that he became seriously interested in the gospel. " One day," says Mr. Watson, " on his repeating the question, 'How am I to get the Spirit?' I replied, 'The Lord said, "Ask and ye shall receive."' He said, 'I hope I have asked, though feebly.' I remarked, 'Jesus said again, "If a man will be My disciple, he must deny himself, and take up his cross and follow Me."' 'What did He mean by that?' he said. I told him, 'You can now have a practical proof. You know we have a public meeting, will you take up your cross and come to-night?' 'Anything but that,' he said. 'But you must remember the words of Jesus,' I told him: ' " Whosoever shall be ashamed of Me and of My doctrine in this sinful generation, of him will I be ashamed when I come in My glory."' 'Oh,' he exclaimed, 'I will go.' And he went under great exercise of mind." Of course, the going was greatly blessed to him, and soon after " the Lord filled him with joy and peace in believing. He now became most valiant for the truth, and ceased not, wherever he was, to speak of Jesus." *Tom Baird, the carter:*—Dr. Norman Macleod says: " Tom Baird, the carter, the beadle of my working man's church, was as noble a fellow as ever lived—God-fearing, true, unselfish. I shall never forget what he said when I asked him to stand at the door of the working man's congregation, and when I thought he was unwilling to do so in his working clothes. 'If,' said I, ' you don't like to do it, if you are ashamed——' ' Ashamed!' he exclaimed, as he turned round upon me. ' I'm mair ashamed o' yoursel', sir. Div ye think that I believe, as ye ken I do, that Jesus Christ, who died for me, was stripped o' his raiment on the cross, and that I—Na, na, I'm proud to stand at the door.' Dear, good fellow! There he stood for seven winters, without a sixpence of pay; all from love, though at my request the working congregation gave him a silver watch. When he was dying from small-pox, the same unselfish nature appeared. When asked if they should let me know, he replied, 'There's nae man leevin' I like as I do him. I know he would come. But he shouldna' come on account of his wife and bairns, and so ye munna tell him!' I never saw him in his illness, never hearing of his danger till it was too late." *Christ's threefold glory:*—Not without a purpose, we may reasonably believe, did our Lord take this opportunity of asserting the threefold glory in which He should appear as the anointed Judge of human kind. It becomes us to pause for a few moments, that we may, if possible, distinguish the separate rays of His final manifestation, and then turn them, in their united effulgence, on the cowardly who have been ashamed of their Redeemer. Christ shall come, this is the first assertion, " in His own glory "; and this is especially His glory as Mediator, that glory which accrued to Him as the recompense of His sufferings, when He was " exalted on the right hand of God "; when He " received a name which is above every name," and was appointed to administer the affairs of this creation, as " head over all things to His Church." Though the mediatorial kingdom be subordinate to the Divine, and though there is yet to come a day, when all rule, and all authority, and all power having been put down, this kingdom shall be delivered up to the Father—very glorious is it through its appointed duration. There is a glory in it which should especially commend itself to creatures like ourselves ; not the glory of the fact, that on a throne of ineffable majesty sitteth one, who, though " found in fashion as a man," guides every spring and regulates every movement throughout a crowded universe—but the glory of another fact, that this Man won to Himself this unlimited sovereignty, through humbling Himself for our sakes to the death upon the cross ; that He exercises it upon our behalf, that He may shield us from the second death which is due to our sins. Christ " shall come in His own glory," forasmuch as it will be in virtue of His office as Mediator, that He shall ascend the great white throne. And wondrously resplendent may we believe that glory shall be, forasmuch as it is to be proportioned to the depth of His humiliation, and to the intenseness of His agony in the garden and on the cross. But nevertheless, this is only the glory which appertains to Him as man; and stupendously brilliant as a creature may be when God puts upon him as much honour as a finite nature can admit, we still imagine something immeasurably more dazzling when we think of the glory of a being who is uncreated and infinite. Oh! Christ shall not come in His own glory alone—the glory appertaining to Him as Mediator and as man; He shall come also in " the glory of His Father "—the glory of essential Deity, which appertains to Himself as well as to the Father, seeing that He and the Father are one. I know not—tongue cannot express, thought cannot reach—what this glory shall be. It is utterly beyond us even to imagine a manifestation of Divine glory, as distinct from that glory which has been put upon the Son in His creative capacity; but we are distinctly taught the fact, and we know, therefore, that when "the sign of the Son of man" shall be seen in the heavens, and every eye of the earth's mighty population shall be fastened on the descending Judge, there shall be more discernible than a mere human form, however "clothed with light as with a garment." It shall be made evident, through some, at present, incomprehensible means, that there is actual Divinity, as well as actual humanity, in the person of Christ; and they who have here striven to prove Him nothing more than a creature, degrading Him to a man, and denying Him to be God, shall read at once their false-hood and their condemnation in that "glory of the Father" which shall be super-added to His own glory as Mediator. Neither is this all. There is yet a third glory in which Jesus Christ shall appear—"the glory of the holy angels." What does this mean? Is it only that the Mediator shall be attended with ten thousand times ten thousand ministering spirits? that the firmament shall be lined with the heavenly host, who shall swell His triumphs, and assist at His coronation as universal Lord? More than this is probably intended, seeing that Christ is to be actually invested with the glory of the holy angels; and this He could hardly be if merely accompanied by their processions. But you are to remember that "all things were made by Christ, and that without Him was not anything made that was made"; and the angels are the loftiest beings in creation, and may justly be taken as its representatives. So that, to come in "the glory of the holy angels" may be to come in the glory of the Creator; there may be some immediate and incontro-vertible demonstration of the fact that Christ reared the universe, and replenished with animation the infinite void. Or, again, let it be remembered, that "holy angels" owe it to Christ that they were confirmed in their allegiance, and are still preserved from apostasy. Then are holy angels a crown upon the brow of the Redeemer, just as the saints who have been ransomed by His blood. Or, once more, the law was given by the ministration of angels. To come, therefore, in the "glory of the holy angels," may be to come in the glory of the legal administration; Christ's "own glory" being the glory of the gospel, and His Father's the glory of creation. So that to come in the triple glory is to come to judge men according to those several degrees of light under which they lived—that of nature, that of the law, and, the most glorious, that of the gospel. But, whichever be the more correct interpretation, enough is revealed to set in overwhelming contrast the base presence before which men are ashamed of Christ, and the inconceivable magnificence before which Christ shall be ashamed of men. (*H. Melvill, B.D.*) *Witnessing for Christ* :—There are three main failures, so to call them, for which Christians will be condemned at the day of account. I. DISOBEDIENCE—CONSCIOUS AND WILFUL—TO THE GOSPEL LAW. II. FALSE AND MERELY OUTWARD PROFESSION. III. THE FAILURE TO PROFESS THE TRUTH OF WHICH THEY ARE SECRETLY CONVINCED. (*Canon Liddon.*) *Ashamed for being ashamed of Christ* :—A soldier in hospital three times picked up the hymn, "Will you go?" which was scattered as a tract, and twice threw it down again. The last time he read it, he thought of it, and, taking his pencil, wrote deliberately on the margin these words : "By the grace of God, I will try to go. John Waugh, Company G, Tenth Regiment, P. R. V. C." That night he went to a prayer-meeting, read his resolution, requested prayers for his salvation, and said : "I am not ashamed of Christ now; but I am ashamed of my-self for having been so long ashamed of Him." He was killed a few months after. How timely was his resolution! *Not ashamed of Christ* :—I remember hearing of a young convert who got up to say something for Christ in the open air. Not being accustomed to speak, he stammered a good deal at first, when an infidel came right along and shouted out, "Young man, you ought to be ashamed of yourself, standing and talking like that." "Well," the young man replied, "I'm ashamed of myself, but *I'm not ashamed of Christ.*" That was a good answer. (*D. L. Moody.*)

Vers. 28-36. **He took Peter, and John, and James.**—*The Transfiguration* :—
I. THE SCENE OF THE TRANSFIGURATION. II. THE PURPOSE OF THE TRANSFIGURATION. 1. Its intent touching Jesus. To strengthen and brace His spirit for the solemn and awful work before Him. 2. Its interest touching Moses and Elias. For them it must have been a new revelation of the wisdom and glory of God in the con-summation of His eternal purpose to redeem a ruined world. 3. Its intent touching

the three apostles. To rectify their conceptions of the Messiah. III. THE
SIGNIFICANCE OF THE TRANSFIGURATION. 1. It marks the topmost step in the progressive glorification of the manhood of Jesus Christ. His incarnation and His
whole life upon earth was a humiliation; but side by side with that humiliation
there was going on a process of glorification. From infancy His person had been
the centre of a widening circle of epiphanies, manifesting forth the glory which
was progressively unfolded within the Tabernacle of His humanity. 2. It may be
looked upon as the inauguration of the New Covenant. The law and the prophets,
having prepared the way for the new dispensation of grace, mercy, and peace, in
Christ Jesus our Lord, now appear as His attendant ministers, at once to bear
witness to Him, and to learn from Him the mystery of redemption. Then, having
borne their testimony, they give way to Him, and the voice of God proclaims Him
the Head and Lord of all. 3. It represents to us the investiture of Jesus Christ as
High Priest. The Father was now robing His Son in the sacred garments of His
holy priesthood in which he was to offer the great sacrifice for the sins of the
whole world, and, bearing upon His heart the names of His people, to pass through
the veil—that is to say, His flesh—into the Holy of holies in the heavens, now to
appear in the presence of God for us. 4. It is, above all, designed to exhibit to us
the transcendent value of the sufferings and death of Christ. In the Basilica at
Ravenna there is a mosaic of the sixth century, representing in emblematical form
the Transfiguration of Christ—a jewelled cross set in a circle of blue studded with
golden stars, in the midst of which appears the face of Christ, the Saviour of the
world; while from the cloud close by is thrust forth a Divine hand that points to
the cross. Those early artists were right in their reading of this sublime event.
The Transfiguration sets the cross of Christ in the centre, surrounds it with a
radiant firmament of God's promises and of the prophecies of the Old Testament,
and shows us the hand of God Himself, emerging from the cloud of glory, and
pointing to the cross, as though God the Father would say to man what John the
Baptist said, "Behold the Lamb of God," &c. 5. It has a prophetic significance.
Standing on Hermon with these three apostles, a long vista stretches out before us
into the distant future, including in its scope that great day when the Son of God
shall take to Himself His power, His mighty power, in order to reign. His kingdom
has come at last; and what is the manner of it? It is a kingdom of redeemed men—
of men who stand, like Moses and Elias, with Christ in glory, not only redeemed,
not only delivered from sin and suffering and sorrow and trial and pain, but transformed and transfigured with that same glory by which the person of Jesus is
inwrapped. 6. It has a symbolic import. It symbolizes the transformation and
transfiguration of our spirits, our whole reasonable, moral, and spiritual nature
into the image of Jesus Christ our Lord. CONCLUDING LESSONS: 1. If we desire
to behold the glory of the transfigured Redeemer, we must climb with Him the
mount of prayer. 2. Learn from this great scene the metamorphic power of prayer.
There are holy men and women, even in this our practical age, and amid the
practical duties of life, whose spirits are manifestly transformed, who, already in
this mortal life, are seen walking with Christ in the white robes of self-renouncing,
self-forgetting love. If we ask the secret of this new transfiguration, the answer
can only be, "They are men and women who breathe the atmosphere of fervent
prayer. 3. Consecration to the path of suffering is the preparation for transfiguration. Oh, the mystery of suffering, the mystery of sorrow, the mystery of
bereavement! Oh, the mystery of loneliness and of affliction in this world! But
see, it vanishes like the morning mist, as we discover that they who tread the path
of suffering are preparing for the Mount of Transfiguration. 4. Learn from this
scene the true relation of the contemplative to the active life. We cannot spend
our lives on the mountain-top of vision, or of ecstasy, or of contemplation. "It is
good to be here," says the mystic, "beholding the vision of the glory of God."
"It is good to be here," says the ascetic, "apart from the world, disciplining the
soul, striving to obtain purity of heart." "It is good to be here," says the student,
"revelling in the contemplation of the Divine, beholding the glory of God in
history, in philosophy, in revelation." But we may not thus spend our lives. The
voice of God calls us down to grapple with the problems and the duties which wait
on every side. Sin is here! sorrow is here; darkness is here; unbelief is here.
If God has revealed to us the glory of His Son, it is not that we should give our
lives up to its contemplation, but that we should gain thereby inspiration and
strength to tread the path of duty or of suffering, that we should consecrate ourselves to the work of lightening the darkness, and lessening the suffering, and

cleansing the defilement, of the world in which we live. (*R. H. McKim, D.D.*)
Our Lord's Transfiguration:—I. TRANSFIGURATION DOES NOT SEEM TO HAVE BEEN AN
UNUSUAL EXPERIENCE WITH OUR LORD. He was accustomed to go apart to pray—to
ascend mountains and spend whole nights in devotion. He was accustomed to
meet heavenly beings there. He was accustomed to shine among them as the light.
All this we know. But once He took three earthly witnesses, and permitted them
to see those angels, who "strengthened Him," "comforted Him," "ministered to
Him." Some, at least, of these celestial visitors were seen to be pious men who
had lived and tried to do God's will on earth. One of them certainly had died,
and been buried as we must be. Look upon this lantern. Its sides are unflecked
crystal. No stain dims their transparency. Each ray of the Drummond light that
blazes within them is perfectly transmitted. Such a light in such a body was Jesus
Christ when His soul had been kindled by converse with Moses and Elias upon the
theme which at His birth made heaven sing. II. WHAT LESSONS DID CHRIST MEAN
TO TEACH HIS DISCIPLES BY GOING THUS ONCE INTO HIS CLOSET WITHOUT HAVING
SHUT TO THE DOOR? 1. He showed them the source of His strength. Such seasons
of communion with heaven are needed by His disciples. We need experiences
which remind us that we are citizens of eternity—experiences which will make the
events of the markets, of the graveyard, and even wars and rumours of wars, seem
insignificant, except so far as they move us to consider the "sign of the Son of
Man." 2. Christ strengthened His disciples to meet the trouble that was coming,
by showing them what that trouble meant. The thing of which blind mortals had
been ashamed is the thing in which heaven glories! Is it not plain that the three
who most needed this lesson were Peter, who had protested most vehemently
against the cross, and James and John the throne-seekers? Peter, who will take
the sword to assault the High Priest's servant, and the sons of Zebedee, who would
call down fire from heaven after the manner of Elijah before he learned to understand the power of Christ revealed in the still, small voice? Did not these most
need to be taught that the throne of God was the cross? 3. But why did the
Master forbid the three to mention the heavenly interview until after He should
arise from the dead? Plainly a prominent purpose of the peculiar experience
granted them was, to impress their minds with a consciousness of the sympathy of
the two worlds. The scene must have made them feel that heaven and earth were
adjacent mansions in their Father's house; that the door was always swinging.
As their Master retired at will into celestial companionships, so might they. But
this was a lesson they did not need to use while He, their Guide, their Friend,
their Saviour, was with them in the world. "Hear ye Him!" was the sole
direction they required then. But the time was drawing near when they would
need to use the lesson learned upon the mount. That time was not when Jesus
hung upon the cross, not even when His body lay in the sepulchre, but when He
had risen, and they would be tempted to believe that their continued communion
with Him was an illusion, an "idle tale." And most of all after the ascension
would they need to realize the meanness of heaven and earth. (*W. B. Wright.*)
The redeeming majesty of the Son of God:—I. LOOK AT THE CIRCUMSTANCES WHICH
THE EVANGELISTS RECORD. 1. The scene was a mountain. It is not fanciful to say
that mountains seem to have a power of attracting to themselves the great things
of men. Natural advantages may account for it in part; symbolism may account
for it still more. Physical qualities present a strong claim, spiritual significance a
stronger. However some may disesteem the more ethical relations of the material
to the mental, we believe that men have been wise in seeking for types as well as
space in the outward world, and that their religions, whether of human origin or of
Divine origin, as among the Jews, have embodied a deep truth in connecting their
sacred scenes and sacred services with "the ancient mountains" and everlasting
"hills." When the Son of God appeared in glory, the earth assisted in his
temporary enthronement, and the local accident harmonized with the spiritual
import of that august event. 2. The company who witnessed it. These witnesses
were enough to attest the reality of the occurrence. But why select them? Why
not permit all the apostles to be thus privileged? The answer to this may not be
within our knowledge. It is, however, probable that they were more intimately
related to the Saviour than the rest. They had a closer fellowship; they could
follow Him further; they required a higher preparation. They perhaps loved
more, could bear more, and needed more. And thus, as He showed Himself to
all of them more than to the world, so He showed Himself to some of them more
than to the rest, admitted them to the deeper things of His spirit, and the stranger

facts of His history, now permitting them to behold His "sorrowfulness unto death," and now permitting them to be "eye-witnesses of His Majesty." 3. The time it took place. A week after the conversation which Christ had with His apostles at Cæsarea Philippi, when Peter declared his belief in His Messiahship, and Christ predicted His sufferings. The immediate season was night, for what took place on their descent from the mount, Luke says, was "on the next day." Hence the disciples fell asleep. The darkness of the night would add to the solemnity of the scene. And may we not say that the seasons of our greatest glory are commonly connected with gloom, and that the evil of sorrow and shame help the display of the moral lustre of the soul? But the circumstance to which I would especially call attention is that Christ was "praying." The obvious lesson to be drawn from our Lord's conduct on this and other occasions is, that not only should we always indulge the spirit of prayer, but that we should enter into the greatest events and experiences with peculiar devotion; that special temptations, special duties, special sufferings, and special good, all call for special wrestling with God; that instruction and strength, fortitude and honour, are to be sought from heaven; that only in prayer can we meet our enemy, only in prayer can we fulfil our vocation, only in prayer can we drink the cup of love, and only in prayer can we gain "the Spirit of glory and of God." II. THE MEANING AND DESIGN OF THIS GLORIOUS SCENE. 1. It had immediate reference to the circumstances of Christ and His disciples. Jesus was now entering upon the last and most sorrowful portion of His career. He was probably within a fortnight of His death. It was not the dying, but the attendant circumstances that made the future so distressing to the mind of Jesus. In another sense than that of the disciples, "He feared as He entered the cloud." He was chastened and oppressed by the anticipation of His peculiar woe. And, doubtless, "He received from God the Father honour and glory," on the occasion before us to strengthen Him for the coming conflict. But if the Transfiguration was meant for Christ, it was also meant for the disciples. It was intended to reward and establish the conviction of His Messiahship, which they had lately expressed. It was intended to extend and exalt their conceptions of His character and work. 2. The Transfiguration has a meaning to ourselves, as a type of the redeeming majesty of the Lord Jesus Christ. (1) Christ is glorified. He is personally transfigured in heaven. He is "changed," and His body is a "glorious" one, the beauteous type of the restored bodies of all who "die in" Him. This body exists in light. Ineffable brightness invests it. Far different is it from what is below—the seat of infirmities, and pains, and death. Far different is its state from its state below—one of want, exposure, injury, and shame. (2) The glory of Christ is the glory of One who is appointed the Lord and Lawgiver of man. He is to be "heard." (3) It is the glory of One who passed to honour through suffering and death. Most notable is it that the theme of conversation with the glorified messengers was His decease. (4) It is the glory of One whom both worlds obey and honour. (5) It is the glory of One in whom all history finds its meaning and its honour. (*A. J. Morris.*)　　*Christ's Transfiguration:*—I. INTRODUCTION. 1. The time. Luke says, "about an eight days," Matthew and Mark, "after six days." The reconciliation is easy. Matthew and Mark spoke of the space of time between the day of prediction and the day of Transfiguration exclusively; Luke includes them both. 2. The persons chosen to attend Him in this action. (1) Why three? (Deut. xvii. 6.) And as John speaks (1 Ep. v. 7, 8) of three witnesses in heaven and three on earth, so here are three and three, three from heaven—God the Father, Moses, and Elias; and three from earth—Peter, James, and John. (2) Why those three? Many give divers reasons. Peter had led the way to the rest in that notable confession of Christ (Matt. xvi. 16), and is conceived to have some primacy for the orderly beginning of actions in the college of the apostles. James was the first apostle who shed his blood for Christ (Acts xii. 2), and John was the most long-lived of them all, and so could the longer give testimony of those things which he heard and saw, till the Church was well gathered and settled. 3. The place. A high mountain. (1) For elevation. (2) For secrecy. 4. The preparative action. Prayer. II. THE TRANSFIGURATION ITSELF. 1. Its nature. It was a glorious alteration in the appearance and qualities of His body; not a substantial alteration in the substance of it. It was not a change wrought in the essential form and substance of Christ's body, but only the outward form was changed, being more full of glory and majesty than it used to be or appeared to be. (1) How His body, now transfigured, differed from His body at other times during His conversing with men. Though the fulness of the Godhead dwelt in Him always, yet the state of His body was disposed so as might best serve for the decency of human conversation; as the sun in a rainy, cloudy day is not seen, but now as it might cover His Divine nature, it would break out in vigour and strength. (a) It was not a change or alteration of the substance of the body, as if it were turned into a spiritual substance; no, it remained still a true human mortal body with the same nature and properties it had before, only it became bright and glorious. (b) As the substance of the body was not changed, so the natural shape and features were not changed, otherwise how could it be known to be Christ, the shape and features were the same, only a new and wonderful splendour put upon them. (c) This new and wonderful splendour was not in imagination and appearance only, but real and sensible. (2) How His body transfigured differed from His glorified body. (a) Partly in the degree and measure, the clarity and majesty of Christ's glorified body is greater and more perfect. Here is a representation, some delineation, but not a full exhibition of His heavenly glory. (b) Partly in continuance and permanency this change was not perpetual, but to endure for a short time only, for it ceased before they came down from the Mount. (c) The subject or seat of this glory differed, the body of Christ being then corruptible and mortal, but now incorruptible and immortal. If Christ's body had been immortal and impassible, then Christ could not die. (d) Here are garments, and a glorified body shall have no other garments than the robes of immortality and glory in heaven. Christ shall be clothed with light as with a garment. 2. Its objects. (1) To show what Christ was. The dignity of His Person and office. (2) To show what Christ should be; for this was a pledge with what glory He should come in His Kingdom (Matt. xvi. 27); it prefigured the glory of His second coming. (3) To show what we shall be; for Christ is the pattern. Uses: 1. Be transformed, that you may be transfigured (Rom. xii. 2). The change must begin in the soul. 2. Be contented to be like Christ in reproaches, disgraces, and neglect in the world, that you may be like Him in glory. Your Lord is a glorious Lord, and He can put glory upon you. 3. To wean our hearts from all human and earthly glory; what is a glorious house to the palace of heaven; glorious garments to the robes of immortality? The glory of Christ should put out the glory of these petty stars that shine in the world, as the sun puts out the fire. We have higher things to mind; it is not for eagles to catch flies, or princes to embrace the dunghill. 4. Since this glory is for the body, do not debase the body, to make it an instrument of sin (1 Thess. iv. 4). "Possess your vessels in sanctification and honour," do not offend God to gratify the body, as they do (Rom. xiv. 13) who make provision for the flesh to fulfil the lusts thereof. Do not spare the body to do God service (Acts xxvi. 7). (*T. Manton, D.D.*) And it would be good for us also to be on the mount, for we, too, need to see Jesus transfigured. Some would say, if they were honest, that while they have a certain admiration for Christ, they see nothing transcendent in Him. To them, He is only one among the great—one among great peaks, not the greatest peak of all. They are not on the height where He is to be seen. They must ascend the mount of knowledge and faith, where alone His glory is to be seen. Have *we* seen this glory of Christ? Some say, "These 'visions' are a questionable good; they lead people into saying foolish things." But notice, it was only Peter who spoke, John and James were silent; Peter would not have spoken so if he had taken time to think, but Peter was always impetuous. What, then, was the good to the disciples? It struck down their prejudices. It silenced all objections to the death of Christ. The Church has come during the last fifty years to enjoy a vision of the Transfiguration of Christ—that is, to see more than in previous centuries the glory of His character and of His death. Christ is more prominent, more precious to the Church than ever before. It has consequently been delivered from many prejudices, and has been prepared for the great trial of anti-christian criticism. It is good for us to be here in this generation. But if this be true of the Church at large, let it be true also of our own individual lives; you have difficulties about His death. Could you but see His glory these difficulties would vanish away. Or you have trials of various kinds—they will seem insignificant on the Mount of Transfiguration. But how shall we get on to the mount? how obtain these glorious views of Christ? Be guided by the circumstances before us. It comes (1) by abiding with Christ; (2) by free communion with Christ; (3) by increasing devotion to Christ. The excellence of a great picture or book or character does not always appear at first. So we must have some good knowledge of Christ, some acquaintance with Him. Let there be an earnest study of these Gospels. Be not impatient. See how freely these three talked with Christ. There must not only be thought about Christ, but free talk with Him. (*T. Goodrich.*) *Christ's Transfiguration:*—I. THE FINAL CAUSE : why Christ was transfigured. 1. The Redeemer of souls lived in great humility upon earth, nay, like an abject worm, to attract the love of the Church ; now He changed Himself into this admired excellency, to increase their faith. 2. By this apparition the three disciples saw in what form He would come to judgment. 3. He did represent Himself as the argument and idea of that beautiful reward which the bodies of the just shall have in the general resurrection. 4. For this once Christ looked like a person of Divine authority, that the minds of His disciples might not be cast down with despair at the cross. 5. The fifth and last reason hath a moral use. There is an old man with his corruptions to be metamorphosed in us all, *sicut Pelias recoctus,* as the fable goes, that Medæa bathed the body of Pelias with certain magical drugs, and from a decrepit old man transmuted him into a vigorous youth. This is a figment ; for no man spent his young years so well, to deserve at God's hands in this world to be young again : but there is a renovation in the spirit of our mind. God will not know us in our own form and filthiness, unless we put on the image of Christ. As Jacob obtained his father's blessing, not in his own shape, but in the garments of Esau ; so we must sue our blessing, having put on the righteousness of Christ ; then the Lord will receive His servant, and say unto thee, as Jacob did unto Esau, " I have seen thy face, as though I had seen the face of God." II. THE EFFICIENT CAUSE: from whence this splendour was derived. Many obscure points will come to light by asking this question : Whether this lightsome beauty like the sun did appear in our Saviour's face from the beatification of His human soul, or from the union of His Divine nature? First, you must understand, that the great school-man, Aquinas, took the best end of the cause into his hand, when he answered to neither of those two members, but rather to the purpose of the question in this wise, *fuit hæc qualitas gloriæ, sed non corporis gloriosi, quia nondum erat immortalis.* " This Transfiguration was a quality of glory, but not of a glorified body, because He was not yet passed death, and raised up to be immortal and impassible." In this distinction is covertly included, that it was not such a brightness as the soul shall communicate to the body, when it is reunited in a joyful resurrection, but was created at this time by the Divine power, to foretell and shadow what would come to pass with much increase in the kingdom of God. *Prælibatio regni Dei fuit hæc transfiguratio,* says Cajetan : this was but the landskip or pattern of the true happiness which shall be in the kingdom of heaven. III. THE EFFECT ITSELF. Alteration in His countenance : whiteness and glistering in His raiment. It is a good thing to be safe under His mercy, the cheerful aspect of His face doth promise that at the least. And doth not this glistering transmutation assure us likewise, that His grace shall shine in our hearts to produce the fruits of life : " The life is the light of men," says St. John ; and by inversion it is true to say, that this light is the life of the soul. Though this which I have said already be much, yet this prospective of admirable light leads us further ; for in this transformation the Master did show what liveries of glory the servants should wear when they should dwell with Him in His kingdom for ever. All the light which is in this world is but like a glowworm to the day, in respect of that mirror of marvellous light in the heavenly Jerusalem, where millions of millions of saints shall be gathered together, and every saint shall shine more sweetly and majestically than the whole globe of the sun ; what a ravishing object will this be ? What an unutterable concurrence of illumination, especially when the sense of the eye shall be perfecter than the eagle's a thousandfold, and no whit dazzled to behold it ? " O Lord, what good things hast Thou laid up for them that fear Thee ? " And thus you see what the Transfiguration in our Saviour's countenance did portend—light of grace in this world ; light of glory in the next ; and light of mercy and comfort in respect unto them both. I conceive that in the resurrection of the just every countenance which had disfigurement in it, or any monstrous disproportion, shall be new shaped and fashioned. Because that great workmanship of God which abideth for ever shall be conspicuous to all eyes with most exact decency and comeliness. One thing more may yet be expected from me to be spoken of for the finishing of this point. St. Luke says, that " His countenance was altered, and His raiment glistered." Was that all ? Was His face only glorified with light, and not the rest of His body ? There are some that hold how His whole body was transfigured and bedecked with light, and that the radiancy of the body did shine through the garments and make them brightsome ; and they think that St. Matthew's text doth favour this opinion, for he speaks of a total transfiguration first, and then of the shining of the face—" He was transfigured before them, and His face did shine as the sun." The matter is not great which way the truth stands. But I assent to that which is the more probable *tenent*, that the rays of splendour did issue out from no part of His body, but from His face only. As the face of Christ did bear the greatest share of ignominy at His passion—being buffeted, being spit on, being pricked with thorns—so the honour of His Transfiguration did light upon his face rather than upon any other part of the body, because God's reward shall make amends in every kind for the despite of Satan. The Jews did strip Him of His garment, and arrayed Him with a robe of scorn, and then led Him to be crucified: so God, to show that His Son deserved no such ignominy, made His garments to shine with unspeakable purity. As lapidaries say of a true diamond, that whereas other precious stones have some colour in their superficies well known by name, as the ruby and sapphire, but the colour of the diamond cannot be well called by any name, there is a white gloss and a sparkling flame mixed together, which shine fairly, but render no constant colour: so we cannot say what manner of show the raiment of our Saviour did make. These two did concur to the composition of the beauty, candour, and *lux*; a whiteness mixed with no shadow, a light bedimmed with no darkness. (*Bishop Hacket.*) *Thoughts [on the Transfiguration:*—1. An illustration of the personal character of Jesus, and the connection which exists between eminent devotion and Divine manifestation. 2. The Divine dignity of the Son of God. 3. The susceptibility and the need of Jesus as Son of Man. 4. The importance of Christ's redemptive work. Of all subjects that they might have chosen, the heavenly visitants talk with Him about His coming death. 5. Christ's supremacy and authority. "Hear Him." 6. From the whole incident we may learn—(1) The weakness and poverty of humanity. (2) What a grand and glorious thing it may become. (*T. Binney.*) *Lessons:*—1. This event gives us an insight into the unseen world. 2. An assurance of Christ's Divine personality. 3. The subject of converse was the Atonement. 4. It is quite in accordance with man's imperfect condition at present, that Peter's rapture so soon came to a close. 5. The Transfiguration suggests to us the nature of our own condition hereafter. (*F. Jacox.*) *The mountain where the Transfiguration took place:*—Where did the Transfiguration take place? An old tradition tells us on Mount Tabor; but though I am always reluctant to refuse assent to these traditions if I can find reason to believe them, yet no traditions are of apostolic authority, and I cannot believe that which assigns the Transfiguration to Mount Tabor. We know that the preceding conversation took place at Cæsarea Philippi. Now this is far off from Mount Tabor, but near to that city is a mount which may be called *the* mount of the Holy Land, the snow-clad mount of Hermon. And what place so fitting for a retreat as that? We have no hint in the Bible of any long journey taken from Cæsarea Philippi to Mount Tabor of the tradition, while the solitude which our Lord would naturally seek would not be found there, for Mount Tabor was fortified by stations and garrisons of Roman soldiery. Then, again, the whole setting of the story, according to the imagery of St. Luke, seems to imply that the incident took place on some snow-clad height. Tabor is not snow-clad, but all the year through the heights of Hermon are clad with snow. There is no doubt, then, to me, that one of the lower slopes of Hermon was the scene of the Transfiguration of our Lord. (*Canon Body.*) *Arguments in favour of Hermon as the scene of the Transfiguration:*—There can be little doubt that Mount Hermon (*Jebel es Sheikh*) is intended, in spite of the persistent, but perfectly baseless tradition which points to Tabor. For (1) Mount Hermon is easily within six days' reach of Cæsarea Philippi, and (2) could alone be called a "lofty mountain" (being 10,000 feet high), or "the mountain," when the last scene had been at Cæsarea. Further (3), Tabor, at that time, in all probability was (Jos. *B. J.* i. 8, § 7, *Vit.* 37), as from time immemorial it had been (Josh. xix. 12), an inhabited and fortified place, wholly unsuited for a scene so solemn; and (4) was moreover in Galilee, which is excluded by Mark ix. 30. "The mountain" is indeed the meaning of the name "Hermon," which being already consecrated by Hebrew poetry (Psa. cxxxiii. 3), and under its old names of Sion and Sirion, or "breastplate" (Deut. iv. 48, iii. 9; Cant. iv. 8), was well suited for the Transfiguration by its height, seclusion, and snowy splendour. (*Archdeacon Farrar.*) *Arguments in favour of Tabor as the scene of the Transfiguration:*—The tradition which has pointed to Tabor has been often contradicted, yet the objections raised against this are, according to our opinion, not well founded. That this tradition existed even in the time of Jerome, and that the Empress Helena for this reason erected a church on Tabor, proves of itself not much, it is true. Yet it may still be called remarkable, that tradition designates a place so far distant from Cæsarea Philippi, where our Saviour had just before been found (Matt. xvi. 13). Without sufficient ground in the apostolic tradition, it appears probable that they would not have assumed the theatre of the one event to be so far removed from that of the other. For the other mountains which have been thought of instead of Tabor, viz., Hermon, or Paneas, there is almost less yet to be said. Yet it must not be forgotten that about a week intervened between the Transfiguration and the first prediction of the Passion, in which time the Saviour may very well have traversed the distance from Cæsarea to Tabor, which, it is true, is considerable. If the Saviour, moreover, after He left the mountain, returned to Capernaum (Matt. xvii. 24–27), this town was scarcely a day's journey from Tabor. The single important difficulty is that raised by De Wette, following Robinson, that at this time there was a fortification on the summit of Tabor. But although Antiochus the Great fortified the mountain, 219 B.C., it is not by any means proved that in the time of Jesus this fortification was yet standing, and though, according to Josephus, this mountain, in the Jewish war, was fortified against the Romans, this, at all events, took place forty years later. Traces of these fortifications are found apparently in the ruins which have since been discovered, especially on the south-western declivity; but in no case is it proved that the whole mountain was built over in the time of Jesus. (*Van Oosterzee.*)   *Why a mountain was chosen for the Transfiguration :*—A valley is as capable of God's glory as a mountain, for " God is God of the valleys as well as of the hills," whatsoever Benhadad, the king of Syria, said to the contrary; but Christ chose this high hill as well for the exercise of prayer, as for the mystery of His Transformation. There may seem to be two intentions that He desired such a place for prayer, *quia cœli conspectus liberior, quia solitudo major :* First, upon the higher ground there is the more free contemplation of heaven, the place to which we lift up our eyes and our hearts in prayer; for though our Lord is everywhere, both in heaven and earth, and under the earth, yet thither we advance our devotions as to the chief throne of His Majesty. Next, our Saviour left a concourse of people beneath, and went to the mountain to pour out His devotions there as in a solitary sequestration, where he should not be troubled. Into such unfrequented hills He did often retire alone, as if He would teach us to bid all the world adieu, and all earthly thoughts, when we utter our supplications before our Heavenly Father: neither doth it seem expedient to act the miracle of the Transfiguration upon a meaner theatre than an exceeding high mountain, to show what ascensions must be in their soul who have a desire to be exalted to God's glory. (*Bishop Hacket.*) *We must climb if we would see Christ :*—Our heart, according to its own evil inclination, cleaves unto the dust like a serpent, our thoughts are of low stature, like Zachæus; if they will climb up, let it be for no other end, or errand, but, as he did, to see Christ. There are two mountains, says Bernard, which we must ascend, but not both at once. First, there is the mountain where the Son of God did preach (Matt. v.), and after that go up to the mountain where He was Transfigured (Matt. xvii.). *Non solum meditemur inpræmiis, sed etiam in mandatis Domini :* I beseech you first meditate upon the sayings and commandments of God, and afterward upon His Transfiguration, upon the reward of glory : and not, as it is the vain custom of the world, run on presumptuously upon assurance of glorification, and to forget the true order, first to ascend upon the mountain of obedience. (*Ibid.*) *The transfiguring look :*—As Jesus prayed there on the mount, " the fashion of his countenance was altered." And so we may say that, as man prays—or, in other words, as in any posture man comes in contact with the great realities of religion and of the soul, and expresses his relation to these—the fashion of *his* countenance alters, the look of humanity is transfigured. I affirm that there is no mode of action, no posture of being, so grand, so hopeful, so pregnant with suggestion, as that of man praying—one in whom culminates the fullest expression of Christian belief and service. It is a transfiguring look, which lifts him above all sin and frailty and dust and shadow, and exhibits him as a child of God and an heir of immortality. Higher than any mere intellectual achievement is this uplifting and surrender of the soul. Newton grasping the firmament in his thought is not so sublime a spectacle as Newton when he kneels and adores. And as with individual instances, so with the collective humanity. Its supreme expression is in the act of faith and worship. Wherever to-day humanity heaves with the great ground-swell of religion, and all outward distinctions dissolve in the light of spiritual relations— I say that there this humanity is transfigured; it is lifted above its sins and miseries and frailty, and all that gives occasion for sceptical distrust. For as man prays—as his nature assumes its highest expression—the shadows of his mortality disappear, and the fashion of his countenance is altered. Even at the risk of some repetition, let me specify that which has now been generally suggested. I. I observe, then, in the first place, that the very attitude of religious faith contradicts sceptical theories of human nature. In trying to estimate the worth and the purpose of any being, it seems reasonable that we should adopt for our standard the highest manifestations of that being. As an illustration of my meaning, I remark that we estimate any individual man, not by what he may be doing at any specified time, not by the weakness or failure of some particular occasion, but by what he has done in his highest moods, what he is capable of doing at his best. We do not expect that Demosthenes will always give us an "Oration for the Crown," that Shakespeare will always write a "Hamlet," or Tennyson an "In Memoriam." But surely it is by these productions, and not their poorest, that we rate such men. We measure their calibre by their broadest circle of achievement, and stamp the recognition of genius upon that which they have done, and can do, in the full swell of their powers. Now apply this illustration to classes of being. There are fools and knaves and tyrants and sensualists; there are such as Caligula and Benedict Arnold and George IV.: but here, also, are Pauls and Fénélons and Florence Nightingales; here are men and women writing a Christian martyrology in letters of blood and fire on the walls of amphitheatres; here are Latimers and Ridleys holding unblenching hands in the flame; here are Pilgrims clasping Bibles to their breasts as they sail over stormy seas. Nay, let us get away from these scenic instances of history, here, right around you, are poor widows in bare garrets, kneeling, with God-seeing eyes; here are oppressed and suffering men clinging to their simple belief in an infinite Helper, and feeling the consolation of Jesus breathing upon their sorrow; here are poor brethren of ours, pressed by grievous temptations, lifting up their souls to Him who can make them strong in their moral conflict, and with swift strokes of supplication cleaving down help from the Almighty. Here is a man called to lie down and die, leaving a sick wife, leaving little helpless children; feeling the mortal terror creeping inward to his heart, as the mortal agony creeps over his flesh; but still looking up to the Father, laying hold of immortality, and in that one touch of faith making the coarse sheet that soon is to be his shroud more glorious with heaven's light than the hearse of Napoleon, rumbling through the streets of Paris and blossoming with a hundred victories. In such, in a thousand ways, here is the spectacle of man praying—man summoning faith and devotion, and taking hold of unconquerable strength, lifted into unfading light; and, I ask, what do you make of this? I maintain that thus estimating humanity by its highest, not by its lowest attitudes, this weak, sinning, dying creature refutes all sceptical conclusions, and the fashion of its countenance is altered. II. I proceed to observe, in the next place, that in this expression of our nature we find a refutation of any extreme claim of action as opposed to worship, and also of science as setting itself in the place of religion. Action cannot occupy the place of prayer. As the very motive power of our action, we need the inspiration and the vision which are revealed to faith. Nor can science be substituted for religion. The soul of man requires a light that we cannot find through the telescope, or at the end of the galvanic wire. It cannot rest or be satisfied with the mere discernment of natural laws. It cannot steer through the mystery of life with no other chart than the physical constitution of man. It needs a heavenly Father and a redeeming Christ. Christ the revealer, Christ the glorified, Christ the transfigured, represents something without ourselves and above ourselves. He presents a point of reconciliation between the human and the Divine, that no one else—no Plato, no Socrates, no oracle of scientific truth, no modern type of philanthropy—can give. In the light which streams upon us from the personality of Jesus the fashion of man's countenance is altered. III. In closing, let me say that the fact which we have been considering, not only refutes false theoretical, but unworthy practical conclusions. Construct, in theory, a universe that will justify profaneness or licentiousness, meanness and fraud, lack of principle and lack of love. How awful the system of things in which such lives would be logical conclusions! A universe in which there are no foundations of "eternal and immutable morality," no source for Divine light like that which shone upon Jesus and from Jesus on the Mount of Transfiguration! But if we are children of God and heirs of immortality, what then should be the scope and standard of our lives? Oh, my brethren! if there *is* a world from which a supernatural splendour fell upon the face of the praying Jesus— if there *was* such a Jesus, revealing such things to men—if these things are real— it is not merely the fashion of man's countenance that alters, but the entire fashion of human life! Then, not those things concerning which men think and act as though they really made up the substance of our being, but those we seek for and cling to in solemn moments, in our best hours and in our last—these are the supreme, the eternal fashion, all else being uncertain and perishable. (*E. H. Chapin, D.D.*) *Lessons from the Transfiguration :*—1. One use of this scene was to give to the favoured disciples a clearer idea of the nature of Christ's kingdom. 2. Another use of this scene was to disclose more than had yet been seen of Christ's personal majesty and true glory. 3. We may note a third use of the Transfiguration in the confirmation it afforded to the harmony of Christ's teaching with that of Moses and the prophets. 4. The Transfiguration scene was of use in helping to show the place, in heavenly as well as earthly interest, of the death of Christ. 5. A fifth and very important use of the Transfiguration was in the glimpse it afforded of the heavenly world. 6. The one other use of this wonderful scene to be noticed, is the lesson of patience it teaches, with respect to our earthly temptations, conflicts, and work. (*H. M. Grout, D.D.*) *Transfiguration during prayer :*—O the wise God, that would have the glory of transfiguration fall upon Himself at no other time but in the fervour of prayer. Miserable men are those that desire not to be transfigured and to cast off the old man ; but more miserable that think to be transfigured without continual prayer. An hypocrite would seem to be a transformed man ; Satan would appear to have transformed himself into an angel of light ; hypocrites and devils all love to make a show of transfiguration, but they did never pray to God to change their inside, which is nothing but filthiness, and to be renewed in the spirit of their mind ; hold on, and cease not to pray, till you be changed into new men. As a distiller keeps his extractions at the furnace till he see them flower and colour as he could wish ; so, as long as we feel the relics of the old Adam remaining, especially while we feel them reign and get the dominion over us, we must ply our Saviour day and night with a restless devotion and a flagrant importunity ; and I am sure while we pray, not the fashion of our countenance, but the fashion of our heart shall be altered. Well, I pray you remember, that when our Saviour went up into the mountain, as well to be transfigured as to pray, yet the text names this only, that "He went up into the mountain to pray"; that name stands in chief, and drowns the mention of the other business, as if prayer were a greater work than that resplendent Transfiguration. And what needed He to pray, but to bring us upon our knees humbly and frequently before His Father, and our Father. (*Bishop Hacket.*) *The beauty of Jesus Christ :*— And what was that glory ? What made His face shine ? What was the light which enveloped His form ? We know that it was the glory of God, a glory not from without but from within, a light shining from the essential beauty of the Godhead within, not flashed from without. The Transfiguration, then, was not a miracle, but a witness of the abiding presence of Christ's Divinity : His whole Being shone, and like Moses, when gazing day and night upon the image of God till it became, in a measure, stamped upon him, and the "skin of his face shone," what did He do? Moses, we are told, put a veil over his face to hide it from the people of Israel, and so it was with Christ : He veiled His glory. If He had been outwardly true to what He bore within Him He would have been seen always with His glory unveiled ; it would have been about Him in the manger at Bethlehem—transfigured Babe ! in His home at Nazareth—transfigured Boy ! it would have shone about Him during His ministry in Galilee—transfigured Man ! and, at the last, on Calvary's Cross—transfigured Sufferer ! But under the very conditions of coming as man among men, the Godhead within was veiled, and the outcoming of those rays held back which would have made for ever beautiful the Sun of Righteousness. For a moment there is no restraint, for a moment He knows the beauty of repose as in His solitude He holds communion with His Father, and all the beauty from within shines forth, and He is transfigured. The beauty of Jesus Christ ! not an outward beauty, such as appeals to the physical part of man. "When we see Him there is no beauty that we should desire Him." He does not stand out as an Apollo of the Greeks or as a Samson of the Bible stories. "As the apple-tree among the trees of the wood, so is my Beloved." As the apple-tree, you notice, not as the cedar ; yet if there is no physical beauty, there is a beauty of His own in every feature, every action, every part, for the transfiguration beauty was the beauty of God. God had communicated His beauty to His Son, for "in Him dwelleth all the fulness of the Godhead bodily "—the perfect beauty of an intellect which is permeated with light, of a heart which is filled with love, of a will lifted up wholly to the will of God, of a conscience at perfect peace, of an imagination sanctified by the most perfect imagery. For the fact remains, which is so true of Him, and, in a great measure, of our fellow-creatures, that the spirit moulds the countenance. There is such a thing as a saint-like countenance, wherefore where there is the indwelling of the Divine there is a beauty of face and figure, movement, speech, and tone, which nothing else can give. (*Canon Body.*) *The irradiation of our Lord's raiment :*—The evangelists, in their record of the Transfiguration scene, seem to concentrate the attention of Christian people on the irradiated garments in which our Lord's sacred form was enveloped. Indeed, the description of the irradiation of the garments of Christ is certainly fuller than the description of His transfigured humanity. St. Matthew tells us that "His raiment was white as light " ; St. Mark, that "His raiment became shining, exceeding white as snow, so as no fuller on earth can white them"; and St. Luke, as our text reminds us, that "His raiment was white and glistering." Therefore, in studying the history of the mystery of the Transfiguration our duty is carefully to notice this feature, and to seek to learn the lesson that the glorified beauty of the raiment of Christ teaches us. The scene of the Transfiguration is one which each of us can easily paint for ourselves by an effort of the imagination. Jesus Christ was, no doubt, poorly clad, probably in the garb that a mechanic was wont to wear in those days. His clothing was not the clothing of "soft raiment," for "they that wear soft raiment are in kings' houses " ; not in the palace of a king among a favoured few dwelt the Incarnate Son of God, but in a cottage where His lot was cast among the toiling many ; and there He dwelt for thirty years, clothed surely in raiment of the most homely nature, probably made by His mother's own hands, and woven from the wool of the flocks. And if the raiment of our Lord had no beauty of form or material to make it lovely, so, too, it must have borne signs of wear, the stains and marks of daily toil. Thus clothed, then, our Lord passed to the Mount of Transfiguration ; and, whilst He prayed "He was trans-figured before them." The light of the essential Godhead within broke forth, and, lo ! as its rays shone through the veil of His humanity, it pierced the poor garments in which He was clothed, which, though worn and stained, now became white with a supernatural whiteness, and, though lacking beauty, now became beautiful with a supernatural beauty. Sweet vision of irradiated garments ! what an abiding spiritual meaning it shows forth ! St. Augustine, in a notice which occurs in his "Commentary on the Psalms," says "The raiment wherewith Christ was clad is His Church." Sweet, sacred vision of a transfigured Lord associated with an irradiated Church; showing forth the abiding relationship of Christ with His Church through endless ages of glorified eternity, and His closest union with this Church, which He has put on as a mystic garment shining with the glory of His own mystic beauty. In this glorified raiment of Christ we see shadowed forth His Church under all conditions of time and of eternity. The Church exists, and is eternally predestinated in the fulness of time to be the glorified vesture of her Lord ; the Church, which is God's elect, admitted by baptism and by the cleansing waters of the holy font brought into this election, this *ecclesia* of God. Is not the Church in her making like the garments of our Lord? Mary takes of the wool of the flock, and therewith weaves the raiment which He puts on in all its meanness and poorness, and then glorifies. Just so with the Church. In what is she poor, do you say? Surely her poverty is in the men and women within her who are lacking in purity and in beauty ; but our Lord stretches out His hand and brings them into union with Himself; not a hypostatical union, such as the union of the Divine and human natures in Himself, but a sacramental union, which can be severed, like the putting on of the garments with which He was clad. Then, having as it were put them on to lie on His Sacred Heart, He works in them the work of justification, taking from them the soil of guilt, and by the work of renewal ever removing from them all spots and wrinkles, till passing from glory to glory, and going from beauty to beauty, the just become more and more pure in the sight of God. He gives them not only purity but beauty ; Christ acts on the pure and makes them lovely ; He communicates to them His own Divine beauty, till in time the Church on earth becomes " white and glistering " with the glory He imparts. And what is the glorification of the Church? What is the consummation of sanctification ? What is the end of justification? Is not the goal to be absolutely beautiful ? is it not that when we awake we may find that we are beautiful even in the sight of God ? Yes, in the glorified raiment of Christ we see a pledge of His work in His Church, a pledge which in her perfect day shall be accomplished, yet for its accom-plishment it is necessary that her members co-operate with Him in a three-fold way. The members of Christ's Church must be channels of Divine grace. Men and women touching the garments of Christ were made whole ; as, for instance, that poor woman who had suffered for many years from a sad disease, and who stretched forth her hand in the crowd, saying within herself, "If I may but touch His garment I shall be whole "; but Christ said not, "Who touched my raiment? " but "Who touched Me? " (as St. Luke tells us), for His raiment had been but the means of conveying His own healing power: and in the same way Christ has made His Church the instrument through which He distributes truth, and grace, and peace ; and if her members would reach forth to her essential glory in eternity they must reach forward to her Divine mission in time, and become, like His garments, channels of His grace to those around. Is it not so? Have you thought that those same garments were probably on the hill of Calvary ? But where do we see them then? No longer clothing that sacred form, but thrown at the foot of the cross, given over to the Roman soldiery, His very vesture the prize of a gambling game which they were playing just beneath Him. As with the raiment of Christ so must it be with His Church. The Church can only pass to her Divine glory under the same conditions by which Christ passed to His ; the Church must not only imitate Him in His active ministry, but share His sufferings: she, too, must go to her Gethsemane, and pass along her way of sorrow, and hang down upon her cross of shame, and pain, and humiliation ; and only as she patiently perseveres in walking on the road of the Cross can she hope to reach to the glory awaiting her above. There is only one ladder from earth to heaven, that is the ladder of our Saviour's Cross. And it is necessary for us always to keep this vision of the transfigured raiment of Christ before our minds ; for this reason, that we never look at any creation of God aright unless we keep in sight the ideal of that creation as it is in the mind of God, otherwise we form a wrong conception of it. God's ideal cannot be realized here and now. If we look at the world in its present conditions only, should we not find it hard to justify the dealings of God with men ? But these conditions are only accidental ; sin came into the world, and with it poverty, crime, pain, death. God has mysteriously permitted a temporary marring of His creation, but that which mars it does not come from God, therefore it cannot last. We Christians are saved from being pessimists because we know that the present conditions are not final. There is a time, at the coming of our Lord, when error will be banished by truth, iniquity by righteousness; when universal knowledge will cover the face of society; when peace shall be the only condition of mind among God's people. Look with eyes brightened by faith, then, even though we see antichrist developed, yet our hope shall be bright, aye, brighter than before, for the development of antichrist is the very pledge of the coming of Christ. And so, too, with the Ideal of man ; none have ever realized, even if they have grasped, their own ideal ; and certainly no one can ever have grasped their ideal as it is in the mind of the Creator, far less have carried that out. What is this ideal ? is it not conformity to the perfection of God Himself? "Be ye therefore perfect, even as your Father which is in heaven is perfect." Yet we know by experience that, here and now, we cannot conform to this perfection ; and so the Church, here and now, fails to realize her ideal: to-day she is of the earth earthy, as poor, and stained, and marred as the garments of Jesus before they were transfigured by His imparted glory. Often perplexities meet us when we try to reconcile the actual condition of the Church with the ideal. But on the Mount of Transfiguration we see this—that in His own time and way Christ will realize the ideal of His Church. Till then let us live in faith and hope, refusing to let our faith be staggered by the Church's troubles in time, but giving ourselves up to His service, lying, as His sacred garments did, at the foot of His cross, in sure and confident expectation that He will realize His own ideal, and that in eternity we shall see Jerusalem the Golden, shining with the glory of God and of the Lamb, and the Church, as His vesture, lying on His bosom in closest union with her Lord! (*Ibid.*) *Luminous hours :*—To every one of us, first or last, come these luminous hours. But they are transient. As the Transfiguration on the Mount was designed to teach the disciples how to conduct themselves when the exigencies which were to come upon them should be developed, so these luminous hours which come to all men ought to be used by them to determine their duties and courses. It is when you are on the mountain-top that you should take your land-marks and steer toward them, and when you go down and lose sight of them, keep straight across the valley until you rise so that they greet your vision again. Not when you are in the valley can you tell which way to travel, unless you have learned it on the top of the hill.

Another thing. After all the beauty and sublimity of this wonderful miracle wrought upon the person of Jesus Christ, and after all the instruction connected with it, it still comes back to me, in the light of the apostle's joyful yet sad utterance, "Now we see through a glass, darkly; but then face to face." We are all of us ignorant; we know in part; but the time is drawing near when neither upon this mountain, nor at Jerusalem, nor upon Mount Hermon, nor upon any earth summit, shall we need to receive instruction, or have any luminous hours, or pass through this or that experience; but when we shall stand in Zion, and before God, and shall see Him as He is, and shall be like Him, and shall rejoice with Him for ever and for ever. (*H. W. Beecher.*) *The Transfiguration:*—This remarkable story divides into two parts the ministerial life of Christ. It is the central point of His public career. It is connected, in thought, with His baptism by the voice from heaven. It is connected with His death by the conversation with Moses and Elias. We must not forget the appropriateness of the comparison of the whiteness of Christ's garments to snow, for above the apostles' heads was the dazzling snow which illuminates the peak of Hermon. Observe—I. CHRIST'S LOVE FOR MOUNTAIN-SOLITUDES. This is only one instance out of many, and it brings before us the sensitive humanity of Christ. Christ loved nature. All the world to Him was sacramental. It should be so with us. Celestial messages and grace should flow to us through every sight and sound which touches and exalts the heart. II. THE TRANSFIGURING GLORY. It supplies us with a principle. The outward form takes its glory or its baseness from the inner spirit. III. THE VISION. Moses and Elias represent the law and the prophets, and Christ is the end of them both. All the revelation given in the past culminated in the revelation which He gave. The glory of the law and of the prophets was fulfilled and expanded in His perfect glory. The whole of the Old Testament, so far as it was spiritual, was taken up into the New. The unity of the Old Testament with the New was declared, and the superiority of the New Testament over the Old. IV. The apostles not only saw a vision, but they heard A CONVERSATION. Strangely in the midst of radiant glory, of ecstatic joy, intervened the thought of death and sorrow. Learn that eternal life is giving, that eternal joy is the sacrifice of self; that the human is only then transfigured into the Divine life when the pain of sacrifice is felt as the most passionate ecstasy. That is the transfiguration power. That thought transfigures the world of humanity. It is the life of heaven with God. (*Stopford A. Brooke, M.A.*) I. THE LEADING FEATURES OF THE TRANSFIGURATION ITSELF. 1. The prayers of Christ. 2. The witnesses of the Transfiguration. 3. The manner of the Transfiguration. 4. The appearance of Moses and Elias. 5. The subject of their conversation with Jesus. II. THE DESIGN OF THE TRANSFIGURATION. 1. To accredit the Divine mission of our Lord. 2. To connect the different dispensations of revealed truth together, to give an authorised sanction to Old Testament announcements, to affix the signet of heaven to all the ancient types and prophecies, and to show that Christ was the glory, the substance, the terminating object of them all. 3. To afford a practical demonstration of man's immortality. 4. To asssure us that in the life of the world to come we shall know each other. (*D. Moore, M.A.*) *The prayers of Christ:*—Communion with God is a condition of spiritual elevation. I. NOTICE TWO OR THREE THINGS WITH REGARD TO SUCH ELEVATIONS. 1. They presuppose a somewhat advanced condition of the spiritual life. 2. They are fraught with the richest, keenest bliss. 3. They are given not merely for their own sake, but as means to important and practical ends. II. WHAT IS THE RELATION WHICH PRAYER SUSTAINS TO THESE ELEVATIONS? The evangelist evidently wishes us to understand that there was a connection between the Saviour's praying and His being transfigured, that in some way the one was the consequence and the outcome of the other. 1. Prayer draws us away from the presence of distracting objects. 2. Prayer relieves us from the pressure of worldly toil. 3. Prayer calls out the finer, better feelings of our nature. 4. Prayer opens to us all the treasures of God's own being. III. REFLECTIONS. 1. It is not necessary for our prayers to be consciously and intentionally directed towards this particular end. 2. Let us be thankful that such elevations are possible to us. 3. Let us show our thankfulness by putting ourselves constantly in that prayerful attitude which is the one chief condition of spiritual exaltation. (*B. Wilkinson, F.G.S.*) *The Transfiguration:*— Christ ever seemed to live in view of the two worlds, even as He belonged to both. The Transfiguration, viewed as an example of intercourse between the seen and the unseen, appears not like a magician's marvel, based on optical illusions; but an example of what it seems natural should always be—heaven opened, its glory visible, its great inhabitants present to converse, and Peter's proposition, what we should all feel, natural. I. JESUS TRANSFIGURED. Tendency in the inner nature of everything to clothe itself with an appropriate external shape. Hereby was given to the world, for once, a fit investment for His exalted soul, a supreme exposition of the old poet's lines—

> " There shone through all His fleshly dress
> Bright shoots of everlastingness."

II. JESUS TRANSFIGURED AS HE PRAYED. These words, which mean so much, given only by Luke. III. THE TRANSFIGURATIONS OF PRAYER. Such scenes are not repeated. This was given, as the poet says of sunsets—

> " that frail mortality may see,—
> What is? Ah no, but what can be."

But though the law of conformity between the material and the spiritual be not so closely observed, it tends to fulfil itself everywhere. It is deeply true to-day, that the nature which habitually prays, which habitually seeks heaven, becomes heaven-like; precisely as it is true that the nature which habitually stoops to debasement becomes debased, and its debasement can be read in the countenance. (*T. M. Herbert, M.A.*)   *The Transfiguration of Christ :—*This singular and beautiful incident in the life of our blessed Redeemer I propose to set before you in detail, as befitting the occasion of this sermon, and because it is an incident not only most interesting in itself, but also one which presents to us an idea of that transfiguration into glory which we shall ourselves sometime experience, if by perseverance in the faith we attain to the resurrection of the just. It was into a high mountain, St. Mark informs us, that Jesus led the chosen three, Peter and James and John, by themselves apart from the rest. This is the true sense of the passage in St. Matthew : not that the *mountain* stood apart from other mountains, but that our Lord took with Him three of His disciples apart from the rest. Nevertheless tradition has long asserted this high mountain to be Tabor, a solitary hill indeed, and apart from others—a hill studded with trees, rising like a rounded mass of verdure out of the plain of Galilee to the height only of 1,700 feet. But there stands another hill in Palestine that rises high above all the hills of Palestine, with snow-clad summits towering to an altitude of 10,000 feet above the level of the Mediterranean. It is the hill of Hermon : nay, rather it is a mountain, the only mountain that deserves the name in the Holy Land. The northern barrier it is of the Holy Land ; that lofty barrier which " set the last limit to *His* wanderings who was sent only to the lost sheep of the house of Israel." To some one or other of the southern peaks of Hermon modern research has assigned the scene of the Transfiguration. But leaving the question of place undetermined, we may briefly remark in passing that hills and mountains and high places were often the exalted platforms of exalted events. On Mount Sinai was the law delivered. Up the slopes of Moriah was Isaac led to the sacrifice. On the hill of Rephidim Moses built an altar, and stood with the rod of God in his outstretched hand. From the summits of Ebal and Gerizim sounded the blessings and the curses. Elijah sacrificed on Carmel. On the hill of Zion stood the Temple. " I have looked up to the hills," we read in the Psalms ; and from the Mount of Olives our blessed Lord was wont to look up to heaven, which is God's hill—from those hallowed heights prayers ascended from Christ, and Christ Himself ascended bodily. But to return to the text—into this high mountain—whether it was Tabor or Hermon, or neither, but some hill country on the shores of lake Tiberias, our Saviour went up. For what purpose? For the purpose of devotion and prayer. St. Luke expressly asserts that " He went up to pray," and moreover, that " as He prayed, the fashion of His countenance was altered, and His raiment became white and glistering." " The fashion of His countenance was altered." For this was a transfiguration, not a transformation : there was no change of form ; the shape of the head and the outline of the features, and the symmetry of the body all remained the same ; only the *figure* or *fashion* of His countenance was altered : and His face did *shine*, did shine " as the *sun* " : and His *raiment* became dazzling *white*, as the *light*, white as *snow*, white as no fuller on earth can whiten. His *form*, I say, was unaltered, but the fashion of that form underwent a change. His whole sacred person seemed to be *living* with light, living with the light of the glory which is above the brightness of the sun; this intense unearthly light struggling through the veil of the flesh, streaming through the threads of His raiment, flashing from the inner man to the outer—why so? Why from the inner man to the outer? Because the spirit of Jesus was then rapt in prayer to His Father when His body began to be transfigured. For prayer—fervent prayer—is a great power; it is the silent engine that bends heaven to earth; it is the power which moves the hand which moves the world. The countenance of a holy man rapt in prayer seems to be illumined from within, and is, as it were, a transfiguration begun. It was this surpassing splendour of the heavenly glory which long afterwards again riveted the gaze and dazzled the eye of one of the spectators of this wonderful scene. What St. John afterwards saw, in a trance, in a vision on the Lord's day, that he was commanded to write. And he wrote, " I saw one, like unto the Son of Man " (the beloved disciple recognized his risen and ascended Master)—" I saw one, like unto the Son of Man, clothed with a shining garment down to the foot and girt about the breasts with a golden girdle. His *head* and His *hairs* were *white* like wool, as white as *snow*, and His eyes were as a flame of fire, and His feet like unto fine brass, as if they *burned* in a furnace, and His voice as the voice of many waters, and His countenance was as the sun shineth in his strength." But, brethren, this vision of glory on the heights of the mystic mountain, this brief heaven upon earth in the life of our Lord, this beautiful insertion of a golden link in the iron chain that bound His career, this brilliant intrusion of the Transfiguration into the dreary uniformity of His humiliation, was not without human witnesses. Peter and James and John—the legal number of three—were witnesses of the Transfiguration on the mount, even as they were afterwards witnesses of the Agony in the garden. On *both occasions* they slumbered and slept. On the present occasion something there was in the majesty of heaven descending to earth which seems to have overpowered the senses of the chosen three. And yet, while their Master was standing and praying near them in the mount, to watch the light of love looking out of His earnest eyes, to see His soul outpoured in those palms outspread, was enough, one would think, to bring His followers, the chosen three, to their senses and to their knees. Yet it was not so, for they saw but heard not; or if they heard they heeded not; or if they heard and heeded, it was but for a little while. Soon somehow their ears became dull, their spirits drowsy, their eyes heavy; they felt a film of stupor rising and spreading between themselves reclining and their Saviour standing. He in the attitude of one praying, they in the posture of men drooping, listless, lethargic, unconcerned, indifferent, with dreamy eyes and heads nodding in a bewilderment. So the disciples slumbered and slept, but their Master watched and prayed. And as they slept and as He prayed, as they slept the sleep that is cousin to death, and He prayed the prayer that is akin to life, then in the dull stupor of their prostration, and in the holy rapture of His supplication, was ushered in the first act in the Divine drama of the Transfiguration. How it was ushered in, what it was, is not recorded. For when the chosen three awoke out of their sleep, the glory had already set in; and they, lifting up their eyes, " beheld the glory, the glory as of the Only Begotten of the Father." And they saw also standing in that glory together with Jesus two *human forms*. The three attendants, Peter and James and John, themselves outside the glory, beheld the two companions of Jesus standing with Him inside the glory. These two human forms, " whether in the body or out of the body," I know not, were Moses and Elias: Moses the publisher of the law, Elias the chief of the prophets, both of them seen shining in the same light with Christ Himself, who gave the law and sent the prophets. Moses and Elias, admirable to the Jews for their miracles, beautiful to God for their holiness. Moses and Elias, each admitted to conference with God in Horeb; both of them types of Christ; both of them fasters of forty days; both of them dividers of the waters, messengers of God to kings; both of them marvellous in their life, mysterious in their end. A chariot of angels came and took away Elias; he was sought by the prophets and not found. Michael, the archangel, strove with the devil for the body of Moses; and he was sought by his people and not found. But strange to say, both Moses and Elias were destined to be found at last without seeking. Many centuries after their disappearance three fishermen of Galilee found the two prophets of God both together, standing with the Messiah, shining in fellowship with the brightness of His glory on some mountain or other in Galilee. Doubtless, other than human spectators were gazing upon this marvellous scene of the transitory glory. We may well believe that myriads of angels, ever moving on the wings of ministration, on this occasion also clustering around the peaks of Tabor, did in amazement behold Him between two saints transfigured, whom afterwards they beheld in horror between two thieves disfigured. Meanwhile Peter and James and John, from the outer twilight of the sunshine of this world, were looking with an astonished curiosity into that heavenly circle of sevenfold brightness, which ensphered in one glory the shining three, Jesus and with Him Moses and Elias. And as they gazed they heard Moses and Elias speaking—speaking still as of old prophetically and of Christ, for they spake of His decease, or, as St. Luke writes, they "foretold His departure." This they did, not to inform Him that He was to die, for this He knew long before ; nay, He Himself communicated it to them, for He was the Word of the Father, and they were but two voices or echoes of that Word—the two prophets inside thus spake in order that the three disciples outside might hear, and that, hearing from two heavenly witnesses what they had before heard from their Divine Master, they might by the threefold testimony be settled, strengthened, established in the belief of the coming passion. And now behold a bright cloud overshadowed them! The outer skirts of the central glory began to advance—to enlarge their borders and to encompass the chosen three. Peter and James and John stand for a while in the golden suburbs of the heavenly Jerusalem. "A bright cloud overshadowed them." He who "tempers the wind to the shorn lamb" softened the dazzling brightness with a luminous curtain. Nevertheless, even in the haze of the cloud that relieved the blaze, they were affrighted. The majesty was veiled to them, yet they were afraid. The glory was tempered to them, yet they trembled. But if the subdued flashing of the clouded splendour alarmed them, the thunder of the voice that came out of the cloud appalled them. It was the voice of God! "This is My Son, My Beloved, in whom I am well pleased : hear ye Him." At the sound of that Divine voice the three disciples fell upon their face and were exceedingly afraid. And Jesus approaching them, as was His wont, did not rebuke them either for their past drowsiness or for their present terror, but gently said, "Arise, and be not afraid." And lifting up their eyes they saw no one save Jesus only. This was the last scene of this Divine drama. All had now vanished—Moses, Elias, the cloud, the voice, the glory. The *mountain* remained standing, as it stood before, but not more solid and real than the glimpse of heaven of which it had been the brief stage. Peter and James and John, who had drooped and slumbered, who had gazed upon the scene and wondered, who had heard the voice and had fallen and been raised and comforted, they also remained near the spot. And last, but not least, *Jesus*, too, remained on the scene; *but* the beauty of comeliness, the brightness of majesty, the glory of His countenance had departed from Him. This was the second time that He relinquished His glory for us and for our salvation. He was now to outward view just what He was before the change, a man to common eyes of no mark, of no desire. Now, as before, He was in the form of a servant, a man of sorrows and acquainted with grief. He knew what was in store for Him : that from the summits of the glory He must descend into the garden of the agony ; from the garden of the agony bearing the cross of shame He must be lifted up on the tree of the curse. That Divine face which had so lately shone with the light of God must be smitten and buffeted and spit upon ; that sacred brow and those stainless hands that had just now glistened with a heavenly brightness must be bruised with thorns and pierced with nails ; that raiment which had been woven anew with threads of light must be stript from His body and divided as a spoil. As He came down from the mount of the Transfiguration He knew that He must *die*. He knew as He descended from that happiness that He must descend still further, that henceforth His path lay terribly downward. He knew that He, bearing the nature of all men, must step by step pass down the steep stair of the humiliation, from the glory to the agony, from the bitter sharp agony to the awful tragedy. He knew that He, the Messiah, the Redeemer of men, the Creator and the Restorer of the world, the Holy One of Israel, the Son of God, must for some hours hang upon the tree, in the daylight a mark of mocking men, in the darkness a butt of scoffing fiends. In this storm of hate, in this wild rage of popular fury, the sea and the waves roaring, cries of blasphemy, shouts of derision shocking His pure ears, from all sides looks of malignant glee, glances of triumphant scorn meeting His meek eyes—He knew that thus and thus He must depart, alone in His passion, abandoned of His fellow-men, deserted by the chosen three, forsaken of the twelve elect, forsaken even in His inmost consciousness of His God. He knew, I say, as He descended from the mount of the Transfiguration that He must *die*—must die the

death of a common malefactor, in order that He might become the common Benefactor of mankind and the *propitiation*, not only for the sins of His Church, but for
the sins also of the whole world. (*T. S. Evans, D.D.*)   *Above the cloud :*—An alpine
traveller has told us how, one day, he set out from Geneva, in a dense and dripping
fog, to climb one of the hills in the range of the Grand Salève; and how, after ascending for some hours, he came out above the mist, and saw the cloudless sky above him,
and around him on every hand the snowy battlement of the glorious mountains.   In
the valley lay the fog, like a waveless ocean of white vapour ; and as he stood on the
overhanging crags, he could hear the chime of bells, the lowing of cattle, and the
sound of labour coming up from the villages that lay invisible beneath ; while now
and then, darting up out of the cloudy sea, there came a bird, which after delighting
itself awhile in the joyous sunshine, and singing a glad song to greet the unexpected
brightness, dived down again and disappeared.   Now, what that brief time of
unclouded radiance was to the bird which had left the drizzling dulness of the
lower world beneath it, that was the experience of the Transfiguration to our Lord
Jesus.   His earthly life, as a whole, was spent in the valley, beneath the clouds of
suffering and sorrow ; and it was only at rare intervals that He emerged above it,
and stood on the mountain-top in the glorious majesty of His native Godhead.   Of
such occasions, that of the Transfiguration was, by far, the grandest.   It stands
alone, even among the marvels of His history, rising above them with as much
magnificence as does the mountain on which it took place above the surrounding
plain.   (*W. M. Taylor, D.D.*)   *The countenance as an index :*—The human face is
a "book where men can read strange matters."   Said Dr. Bellows in a recent
sermon : "There is an œcumenical council in the soul of man," a conflict of
opinions good and evil, a debate on the great truths of duty and destiny ; and we
might carry out the figure and say that the doings of this great council in the soul
cannot be kept secret by closed lips, for the face is a bulletin-board that constantly
indicates the working of the heart.   We have all seen how anguish of heart
"disasters the cheeks" and furrows the face, and writes upon it the epitaphs of
buried hopes ; we have seen "faces tramped as hard as a highway by the hoofs of
pain and oppression," and every one is thus familiar with the fact that sorrow
engraves its story in the countenance.   But look, also, into the faces that glare at
you from the dens of infamy ; faces that seem to contain the ruins of the ten commandments ; faces that hurt you more than a blow ; faces where "from the eyes
the spirit wildly peeps" ; faces like petrified vices, not a finger-touch of God left
whole upon them, and you will realize that vice as well as misery makes its trade-
mark on the visage while it ravages the heart.   Great soul-artists always recognize
the fact that we are to see the mind in the visage.   Dickens makes even the dogs
to lead their blind masters up side alleys to escape the cruel face of Scrooge, while
on the other hand, the little boy in the churchyard looks with tears into the face of
"little Nell," as her countenance is being transfigured by approaching death to see
if she is already an angel, as the neighbours have said she will be soon.   (*W. F.
Crafts.*)   *Modern transfigurations :*—But these transfigurations are not out of date.
In the sweet hour of prayer, and around the mercy-seat, it is is still true of many
a believer, "as he prayed the fashion of his countenance was changed."   I have
seen faces that shone with the light of a new experience ; faces that caused me to
look steadfastly, for they were as the faces of angels by this transfiguration from
within.   Often I meet a face which is a transfiguration of trust and joy ; often I
feel the outshining of a mystic glory and peace as I gaze within a face that is itself
a gospel, a living epistle known and read of all.   Recently there knelt at the altar
of mercy a man whose face was horrible with agony and remorse.   At length he
cried, " My sins are washed away in the blood of the Lamb ! " and he looked up
beautiful, as it were, with the face of an angel.   "The beauty of the Lord our God
was upon him."   "Beholding, as in a glass, the glory of the Lord, he was changed
into the same image."   *The transforming power of communion with God :*—
Whether that communion take the form of prayer, or a childlike confidence, or a
searching after truth and life, it has this power.   Contrast the portraits of Luther
and Loyola ; George Canning and George IV. ; John Milton and Charles I. ; or
more pertinently still, the portrait of Bunyan, the wild, godless tinker of 1650, with
the same Bunyan of twenty years later, the thinking, praying, dreaming maker of
laces in Bedford jail for conscience' sake.   Or picture to yourself the appearance
of John when the fisherman on the Galilean sea—what his face was when with
indignant anger he said, " Shall we call down fire from heaven and consume them ? "
—and what he was and his face was, when after intimate communion with the

Father through Christ Jesus, he stood by the Cross—and what later still, when old and sainted, he repeated his one text and sermon, " Little children, keep yourselves from idols." *(John Christian, D.D.)*

Vers. 30, 32. Moses and Elias : who appeared in glory, and spake of His decease. —*The decease at Jerusalem :*—I. IN THE DECEASE AT JERUSALEM, THERE IS THE DEATH OF THE SINLESS CHRIST. II. THIS DECEASE AT JERUSALEM WAS A DEATH PURELY AND PERFECTLY VOLUNTARY. III. IN THE DECEASE AT JERUSALEM, WE HAVE A DEATH WHICH APPEARS TO BE MORE IMPORTANT AND PRECIOUS THAN EVEN LIFE. IV. IN THIS DECEASE AT JERUSALEM, WE HAVE THE ONLY INSTANCE OF A MAN BEING A SACRIFICE FOR SIN. V. IN THIS DECEASE AT JERUSALEM, WE HAVE A DEATH THAT IS TO BE REMEMBERED AND COMMEMORATED FOR EVER. *(H. J. Bevis.)* *The conference on the Mount :*—1. What they spake of none could Divine, unless it had been told us, and the Evangelist Luke telleth us, that it was of His death. This argument was chosen—(1) Because it was at hand. The next solemn mediatory action after this was His death and bloody sufferings; after He was transfigured in the Mount, He went down to suffer at Jerusalem. (2) This was an offence to the apostles that their Master should die (Matt. xvi. 22, 23). (3) This was the Jews' stumbling-block (1 Cor. i. 23). (4) This was prefigured in the rites of the Law, foretold in the writings of the Prophets. (5) It was necessary that by death He should come to His glory, of which now some glimpse and foretaste was given to Him. (6) The redemption of the Church by Christ is the talk and discourse we shall have in heaven. The angels and glorified saints are blessing and praising Him for this (Rev. v. 9, 12). (7) It is an instructive pattern to us, that Christ in the midst of His Transfiguration, and the glory which was then put upon Him, forgat not His death. In the greatest advancement we should think of our dissolution. If Christ, in all His glory, discoursed of His death, surely it more becometh us, as necessary for us to prevent the surfeit of worldly pleasures ; we should think of the change that is coming, for " Surely every man at his best estate is vanity" (Psa. xxxix. 5). In some places they were wont to present a death's head at their solemn feasts ; merry days will not always last, death will soon put an end to the vain pleasures we enjoy here, and the most shining glory will be burnt out to a snuff. 2. The notion by which His death is expressed, His decease ἔξοδον, which signifies the going out of this life into another, which is to be noted. (1) In respect unto Christ His death was an "exodus," for He went out of this mortal life into glory, and so it implieth both His suffering death, and also His resurrection (Acts. ii. 24). (2) With respect to us ; Peter (2 Eph. i. 15) calls His death an "exodus." The death of the godly is a " going out," but from sin and sorrow, to glory and immortality. The soul dwelleth in the body as a man in a house, and death is but a departure out of one house into another; not an extinction, but a going from house to house. 3. The necessity of undergoing it. "Accomplish." (1) His mediatorial duty, with a respect to God's ordination and decree declared in the prophecies of the Old Testament, which, when they are fulfilled, are said to be accomplished. Whatsoever Christ did in the work of redemption was with respect to God's will and eternal decree (Acts iv. 28). (2) His voluntary submission which He should accomplish, noteth His active and voluntary concurrence ; it is an active word not passive, not to be fulfilled upon Him, but by Him. (3) That it was the eminent act of His humiliation ; for this cause He assumed human nature. His humiliation began at His birth, continued in His life, and was accomplished in dying ; all was nothing without this, therefore there is a consummation or perfection attributed to the death of Christ (Heb. x. 14). *(T. Manton, D.D.)* *A revelation of the heavenly life :*—Moses and Elias are standing humbly in the presence of Jesus Christ (as He had once sat at the feet of the Rabbi in the Temple), holding converse with Him, acknowledging all their ignorance, telling Him all their perplexities, responding to Him with the response of perfect assent to His every utterance. Of what did they speak ? They spoke of " His decease, which He should accomplish at Jerusalem." This word "decease" should, in my opinion, have a larger application ; it is the same word as St. Peter used when he spoke of the death which he was about to die, which is also translated as "decease"; it should be rather "exodus." We may be certain of this ; it was not merely of the historic fact of Christ's death of which they spoke, they wanted to know the deep meaning underlying that fact, and this could only be understood when His death was studied in connection with the many mysteries before and after. Of this, of all those mysteries which found their centre in the Cross of Calvary, did they speak on the

Mount of Transfiguration, and thus revealed to the apostles and to us what is the heavenly life of which our life here is the prelude, what is that eternal state to which we are all rapidly journeying. First, then, it is of primary importance to consider that heaven is a state rather than a locality. Don't misunderstand me. I do not say there is no space which we call heaven to-day, no space where that sacred humanity still exists which the Incarnate Saviour took upon Himself, and which has since been in some sense subject to laws of creaturely existence, and therefore subject to space. Wherever Jesus Christ is there is heaven, and yet if you ask where this heavenly life will be lived, in what locality the heavenly life will be lived, then I shall answer that probably, though of this no one can be certain, probably the sphere of that life will be mainly this earth. The last vision in the Apocalypse is not the vision of the Church ascending, but her advent on the "new earth." "I saw the holy city, new Jerusalem, coming down from heaven, prepared as a bride adorned for her husband." Insignificant as this planet is in the wonderful cosmos, yet it has been chosen among God's creations as the scene in which the great mystery of love should be carried out, in which the incarnate life of the Son of God should be lived ; out of the dust of this earth His sacred body was formed, on this earth He lived His life, on this earth He died His death, and from this earth He ascended into heaven, and carried into the presence of the Father, to be for ever there, the body formed of the dust of this earth. This earth is the scene of the humiliation of Jesus Christ, of the humiliation of His Church, of the whole family of mankind ; is it not likely to be the centre of that plan in which the glory of Jesus Christ, the glory of His Church and of mankind, shall be consummated ? I state, then, as a pious opinion, that this earth will be the centre of that life of bliss which the glorified Church will live. And where more fitting ? We have no reason to believe that the great work of Redemption has been carried out in any of the other worlds in God's great plan of creation, nor do we even know that those worlds are inhabited by living souls. And yet the great question is, not where shall that heavenly life be spent, but what is that life? And the answer is plainly and distinctly given in the Revelation which we are studying, that the heavenly life is a state of conformity to God. Church life is revealed to us as lived under three conditions, of which two are present conditions and one future: the first is the militant life on earth ; the second is the waiting life in paradise—the life of souls waiting in that dear place of rest for the coming of their Lord in glory—and the third is the life of perfect conformity to Jesus Christ. Here we are ever reaching forward to that conformity, and yet none of us can ever be perfect ; in paradise I venture to believe that there will be growth for those waiting souls, an ever-increasing conformity with Jesus ; for "the path of the just is as the shining light, that shineth more and more unto the perfect day." That "perfect day" is the coming of our Lord, when we shall see Him as He is, when we shall be wholly conformed to God, when, waking up after His likeness, "we shall be satisfied." By the heavenly life we understand that state of glory which is entered on by the resurrection—for as baptism is our birth into the Church militant, so death is our birth into the Church expectant, and the resurrection our birth into the Church glorified. The state of expectation is only over when He, whom we look for, shall appear, and we shall enter into the state of conformity. What is this conformity ? I answer, that my perfect conformity is my attainment of my perfect individuality ; no one can be perfectly conformed to God in the sense that they can express in themselves every beauty that is in Him ; for is it not true that He is the Sun and we are only the stars, and we know that " one star differeth from another star in glory " ? Conformity to Christ is this, my perfect realization of the Divine thought for me ; God is not mirrored in each member of the Church, but in the whole Church ; one ray of His beauty is mirrored in one, and one in another ; I was created to reflect one ray ; He who created me " telleth the number of the stars, and calleth them all by their names," and, as "one star differeth from another," so one man from another man. If I may say it, the great Creator never uses the same mould twice ; having used it once He throws it away, and so the characteristics of one are not the same as another. God has placed me in this world with an individual purpose of life to develop, and any system which takes God's creations, on whom is stamped individuality, and forces them into the same pattern, is immoral, is a marring of God's plan. There must be space in His Church : "Thou has set my feet in a large room." So, when I am truly myself when I can fulfil my highest aspirations, when I can live out my fullest resolves, when I can perfectly express the idea of my individual being which God has

revealed to me, then at last I have gained conformity to Christ, then I know what it is to rest in the heaven of God. Oh! joy to be my ideal self! joy when conduct shall square with conviction, when conviction shall square with aspiration, and aspiration shall square with resolve! Oh! the utter rest to lie at the feet of Jesus, true to Him because utterly true to myself! Moses will be Moses there, Elias will be Elias there, each before Jesus Christ in His own individuality and personality. But what is the life which awaits me there? The answer comes clearly and distinctly—a life lived in the power of Jesus Christ. The first great hunger of each human creature is heart-hunger, the first great thirst is heart-thirst; if love, then, is our greatest need, be sure of this, God created us to be loved, and, therefore, He created us to possess and to be possessed by Himself, who is absolute Beauty and perfect Love; and so, whether our love flows out first to those dear ones whom He has given us to love, whether our first love is given to Him or only indirectly to Him, of this be sure, we cannot know heart-rest until we rest wholly in His love. The time will come when we shall have not only an intellectual but an actual apprehension of His love, when we shall live by sight and not by faith, and as we gaze on the Word Incarnate, the sight of God's beauty mirrored there will draw up to us His embrace, and the joy of God's love will attract us to Him eternally. This, then, is heaven, to rest in the love of God. Then if our first great longing is for love, our second is for knowledge. The heart longs for love, the mind for knowledge: and here, in time, we cannot satisfy this longing. The more we know, the more we become conscious of our ignorance; the more we feed the mind, the more it hungers for that which it has not. Here we know "in part." But there, in the heavenly life, the partial knowledge shall be made complete; and I shall study the truth, not only as it has been revealed, but with the aid of the great First Cause, of God Himself; and as I see God I shall know the rest that comes with the perfect knowledge of the truth as it is in Him. And how shall we study to know God? As we can see the Father only as He is mirrored in the Son, so we can only hear His voice as revealed to us through the Incarnate Word. And our study will surely be the study of those mysteries which gather round His sacred form—the mystery of His Incarnation, the mystery of His Death, the infinite mystery of His Resurrection and of His Ascension (for in each is a manifestation of the Infinite). And so, through all the ages of eternity, there will be an eternal festival—an eternal Christmas, an eternal Lady Day, an eternal Easter, and an eternal Ascension—that I may receive into my mind the meaning of these mysteries, and give back to God my mental satisfaction by uttering heaven's eternal creed and offering heaven's ceaseless worship. Then, thirdly, if in heaven the cravings of our heart for love and of our intellects for knowledge will be satisfied, so, too, will our desire for unity. To some the thought of individuality is not attractive; it is not personal isolation they long for, but corporate union. The two ideas are not antagonistic. True, "the King's daughter is all glorious within, her clothing is of wrought gold." But why? Because each separate thread is of wrought gold. We see in the Revelation how every precious stone was used in the completion of the heavenly city, which could not be perfect without the perfection of each stone; and so here a life of perfected individuality may be the same as a life of perfected unity. Moses and Elias stood side by side, they knew one another, they shared a common study, they asked common questions, they received the common truth, though Peter and James and John, with their own individual characteristics of zeal and love and patience, as they stood there with them, and heard the Voice out of the cloud, "This is My beloved Son," knew Moses to be Moses, and Elias Elias; so in heaven ours will be no mere life of individual isolation, in which the enjoyment of personal love, the tasting of personal truth, the offering of personal worship, will be our one thought. No; the perfection of the lives of the saints blends in one perfect communion: there saint with saint holds converse, lives a common life, offers a common worship. (*Canon Body.*)
Christ crucified:—Such words never were, never could with truth and fitness, be applied to any but the one death. I. The first point to be noted here is, THE VOLUNTARY CHARACTER OF THIS DEATH. There was no power, no law of nature that made death a necessity to the Lord Jesus. That pilgrimage into the regions of the tomb He could undertake or decline, according to His own pleasure. He died simply because He willed to die. He might have left the world in a very different way. Like His own servant Elias, with whom He conversed of this decease, He might have returned to heaven in a chariot of fire; or, if He must taste death in order that He might be perfectly like unto His brethren, His departure might have

been calm and tranquil, in the stillness of home, amid the sympathies and tears of loving friends. Such a death would surely have been sufficient, if the end of His ministry had been simply the manifestation of God in the flesh. Instead of a close so fitting to a life of purity, He chose to accomplish a decease, in which He should be "numbered with the transgressors." Surely for this there must have been wise and sufficient reason. The fact that He died thus, is the proof that the great design of His advent could be fulfilled only by such a death. With Him it was the centre-fact of His whole history. II. THE IMPORTANCE ATTACHED TO THIS DEATH. He had work to do in the world beside, a bright example to give; the true ideal of a human life to set before man; a perfect righteousness to win; a thousand blessings to scatter; His own deep love and sympathy with human sorrows to discover: but His great work was this—to die. III. THE TRUE MEANING OF THIS DEATH. The New Testament speaks in various ways—sometimes it employs the language of type and symbol—sometimes it gives us distinct and explicit statements—but all its representations of this death converge to one point, and enforce one grand idea. "Christ our Passover is sacrificed for us." Here is an expressive metaphor—one whose signification it cannot be hard to discover. What is the meaning of the apostle? The Paschal Lamb died for the deliverance of the nation —through his death the nation escaped the sword of the destroying angel—the animal was slain, the blood was sprinkled, and the people were saved. So was Christ our Passover sacrificed, that we might be delivered—His death is our life—in virtue of His blood of sprinkling we are purified and accepted. "The decease which He should accomplish at Jerusalem." Thus, then, did the man Christ Jesus ever keep before Him that goal of suffering and humiliation to which His steps were tending. Not ignorantly did He rush on perils and death, entering on a path whose end He did not discern until retreat had become impossible. Knowing what the work was, He had deliberately undertaken it, and throughout all its stages, the issue was ever present to His eye. Very early in His ministry did He indicate that He was set apart to this service—was anointed unto sacrifice. (*J. G. Rogers, B.A.*) *Two divisions in the glorified Church:*—Why were these two men with Jesus in the vision? Is it not because when at length the Church shall reach her state of glory there will be within her two distinct classes? We are told, that when our Lord comes, the "dead in Christ shall rise first," and at the sound of the trump, and at the call of His voice, the "fields of Paradise" shall be deserted, and they shall all be caught up to meet their Lord in the air, henceforth to seek Him in His beauty and to be His daily delight. But what of those who are not in the "fields of Paradise" at the time of the coming of our Lord? Shall they die? Shall they know that mysterious experience which we call death, the separation of the soul from the body? No, for then it would be a purposeless experience. "They shall not die, but shall be caught up together with them in the clouds, and shall be ever with the Lord." Therefore the glorified Church shall be the assembly of those who, some from life and some from Paradise, are gathered into the presence of Christ. And do we not see these two classes represented in the ancient saints who talked with our Lord on the Mount of Transfiguration? Moses, we know, died; and we remember the cause of his death there in the wilderness, and the mysterious conflict over his body between Michael the archangel and Satan. Elijah died not; he never experienced this crisis of existence, but, we are told, "went up by a whirlwind into heaven." So the two great divisions of the glorified Church are fittingly represented by these two Old Testament characters, one of whom died the most arresting death there recorded, and the other died not. (*Canon Body.*) *Death an exodus:*—1. It is strange how much we can find in that great scene on the Holy Mount, to illustrate this conception, and to impress it on our minds. Look at the speakers—Moses, Elijah, Christ. Was not the death of Moses an exodus? A sacred mystery hangs over the decease of the "Man of God." "He who died by the kiss of the Eternal" is a not infrequent synonym for Moses in the Rabbinical schools. Elijah, again, was rapt, we are told, and carried up into heaven, as by a whirling cloud of fiery chariots. If, therefore, any of the sons of men should be permitted to pass from the spiritual world to hold converse with Christ in the moment of His glory, these were the two men. They had already and fully achieved the exodus or journey of death, and had passed into the large fair land beyond. "They talked with Him of the exodus He should accomplish at Jerusalem." If we love and follow Him, we need not doubt that we shall be made partakers of His death in this high sense—that for us, as for Him, death will be an exodus, a journey home. 2. The more we study this conception of death the more instructive and suggestive we shall find it to be. The illustration which the figure suggests, and was intended to suggest, is the exodus of Israel from Egypt. If we consider what that exodus was and implies, if we then proceed to infer that death will be to us very much what their exodus was to the captive Hebrew race, we shall reach some thoughts of death, and of the life that follows death, which can hardly fail to be new and helpful to us. The exodus was a transition from bondage to freedom, from grinding and unrequited toil to comparative rest, from ignorance to knowledge, from shame to honour, from a life distracted by care and pain and fear to a life in which men were fed by the immediate bounty of God, guided by His wisdom, guarded by His omnipotence, consecrated to His service. And if death be an exodus, we may say that, by the gate and avenue of death, we shall pass from bondage to freedom, &c. (*S. Cox, D.D.*) *The central truth of the Transfiguration:*—I. CHRIST GLORIFIED IN CONNECTION WITH HIS DEATH. There are two transfigurations—that of the Mount and that of the Cross; and it is impossible to understand either, save in the light of the other. He who was on the Mount was still the Man of Sorrows, and He who was on the Cross was still the Divine Son. The death on the Cross gave its glory to the mountain-scene; the declaration on the Mount makes the death all-radiant with triumph. II. CHRIST GLORIFIED THROUGH HIS DEATH, REFLECTS BACK A RADIANCE ON MOSES AND ELIJAH. III. AS MOSES AND ELIJAH ARE THUS GLORIFIED BY CHRIST, THEY RETIRE FROM VIEW AND GIVE PLACE TO HIM. (*W. M. Taylor, D.D.*) *Celestial visitors:*—When we read of the reappearance of Moses and Elias after their long absence, our first feeling is that of wonder; it is to us a miracle, a strange thing, for the dead do not return. But why view it thus? The wonder is, not that Moses and Elias were seen in the holy Mount, but that the separation between us and the blessed dead should be so complete. Their long unbroken silence is the strange thing when you think of it. We long to know more of them and of the world in which they dwell. We know from this narrative—1. That human spirits are not annihilated when they disappear from this world. 2. That human spirits have a personal existence after death. 3. We see in Moses and Elias what all faithful souls shall be, when the great redemption is completed—as like unto God as possible. (*Thomas Jones.*) *The thought of death amid the raptures of the Transfiguration:*—Jesus was lifted by His rapture above the fear of death. He spoke calmly of His decease with the messengers from the unseen world, whose very presence testified of death conquered and the grave despoiled. His acutest pain was transformed into His highest joy, as the body of His humiliation was transfigured by the glory of heaven; and at that supreme moment, when His life was at the brightest, He could have willingly lain it down, and passed into the dark shadow feared of man. This true to human experience. Jacob on seeing Joseph again—"Now let me die"; Simeon, with the infant Saviour in his aged arms—"Now lettest Thou Thy servant depart in peace." And outside the domain of Scripture we find numerous examples of the same strange intermingling of the highest glory of life with the thought of sorrow and death. It is indeed on mounts of transfiguration, when our nature is irradiated by some great joy, that we love to speak of our decease. We fear not to enter into the cloud of death when we are transfigured by the passionate intensity of our feelings. Our joy transforms the pain of dying into its own splendour, as the sun changes the very cloud into sunshine. All thoughtful writers have described this remarkable human experience. Æschylus, in his "Agamemnon", pictures the herald returning from the Trojan War as so overjoyed at revisiting his native land that he was willing to die. Goethe represents one of his most beautiful creations—the loved and loving Clara—as wishing to die in the hour of her purest joy; for earth had nothing beyond the rapture of that experience. Shakespeare puts into the lips of Othello, at his joyful meeting with Desdemona, after the perils of his voyage to Cyprus were over, the passionate exclamation:—

> " If it were now to die
> 'Twere now to be most happy: for I fear
> My soul hath her content so absolute,
> That not another comfort like to this
> Succeeds in unknown fate."

It is said of Benjamin Franklin that his exultation was so great when he succeeded in attracting the lightning from the clouds by means of his kite, and thus proving its identity with the electricity of the earth, that he could willingly have died that very moment. Miss Martineau, in her "Retrospect of Western Travel," describes the grandeur of a storm which she encountered on the Atlantic, as producing a similar triumph over the fear of death. "In the excitement of such an hour," she says, " one feels as if one would as soon go down in those magnificent waters as die any other death." I remember, on one occasion, having something of the same feeling. I was travelling at night in a mountain region, when a terrible storm came on. The rain poured in torrents; the thunder pealed among the rocks; flash after flash of lightning linked the hills together, as with chains of fire. A pall of blackness covered the sky from end to end. Hundreds of torrents poured down the heights into a lake, as if direct from the clouds; the sheen of their foam looked weird and ghastly in the illumination of the lightning, and their roar drowning the crash of the thunder ; the sound of many waters, here, there, and everywhere, filling earth and sky. Amid all this appalling elemental war, 1 felt a strange excitement and uplifting of soul, which made me indifferent to danger, careless what became of me. Such moments reveal to us the greatness of our nature, and fill us with the intoxication of immortality. Death in such glorious circumstances seems an apotheosis. He comes to us as it were with the whirlwind and the chariot of fire, to lift us above the slow pain of dying, in the rapture of translation. (*H. Macmillan, LL.D.*) *The conference during the transfiguration :*—In this discourse I shall first direct your attention to the account given of the persons who conversed with our Lord, and then to the subject of their conference. I. THE PERSONS WHO CONVERSED WITH OUR LORD WERE TWO MEN. 1. It may be thought that two angels would have rendered the scene more splendid, but there was a peculiar propriety in employing men. 2. They were men of high eminence under the former dispensation. 3. We are told that these visitants appeared in glory. They came from heaven, and though their honour and felicity there were very high, they felt no reluctance to descend to this mountain. They were not called to relinquish their splendour or to cover it with a veil, as our Lord is said to have " emptied Himself," when he appeared in our world. The glory which invested them must have been very great, since it was visible amidst the brightness spread around our Lord. 4. They talked with Jesus. It is not said that they talked with one another. They descended, not to hold intercourse with the disciples, but with their Master. II. Let us now attend to THE SUBJECT OF THEIR CONFERENCE. It was the decease which He should accomplish at Jerusalem. 1. They spake of the moral glory which Jesus should exhibit in His departure. Great was the glory of Moses in the going forth from Egypt. 2. They spoke of the important ends to be gained by His death. It reconciles the mind to labours and sufferings, when we are assured that valuable ends will be gained by them. Let me specify some of these ends. They talked of the glory which would result from His death to all the Divine perfections. The expiation to be made for sin was another end. I must mention further, the salvation to be gained by His death for millions of human beings. 3. We may consider them as speaking of the influence of His death. 4. They spoke of the rewards which would be conferred on Him for His obedience to the death. Let me now state shortly, some of the reasons why this theme was chosen for conference on the Mount. 1. It was done to animate and invigorate the Son of Man for the scene before Him. 2. We may find another reason for the choice of the topic in its peculiar importance. 3. They talked of this subject for the sake of the disciples. 4. They did it for the benefit of the Church in all ages. 1. Let Christians live more under the influence of this death than ever. 2. Let good men prepare for their departure. 3. Let me call on the disciples of Jesus, with kindred feelings to those of Moses and Elias, to commemorate their Saviour's decease. And let those who never approach the Lord's table consider that, were their conduct general, the death of Christ might sink into oblivion on earth. (*H. Belfrage.*)

Ver. 33. **It is good for us to be here.**—*Raise up your eyes heavenward :*—I. If you frequently remember heaven, it will be A GREAT CONSOLATION IN YOUR MANY TRIBULATIONS HERE. 1. Affliction shall be no more. (1) No separation. (2) No grief. (3) No pains. 2. In heaven we shall find an everlasting reward for our tribulations. II. If you frequently remember heaven, you will be ENCOURAGED IN THE VARIOUS STRUGGLES OF LIFE. 1. Heaven is your peaceful home. (1) No enemy. (2) No struggle. 2. Heaven is the abode of infinite glory. (*Joseph Schuen.*) *On the top of Tabor :*—I. THEY HAD A VISION OF CHRIST'S DIVINITY. Not His distinct, unveiled Godhead—*that* would have been an insufferable blaze ; *that* Jehovah Himself hath told us can no man look upon and live. On the form of a servant He wears His coronation robes, and is at one and the same time a mystery and a revelation—God manifest in the flesh! What an honour and a privilege was this! II. THEY HAD A VISION OF GLORIFIED SAINTS. Thou too, my friend, for good or ill, will live on through all the ages. Not only men, but retaining their individuality, in form and feature as in the days of their flesh. III. THEY HAD A VISION OF THE FATHER'S PRESENCE. There came a cloud and overshadowed them; not an ordinary cloud, but the bright Shekinah-cloud, in which Jehovah did ever manifest His presence—the medium through which He ever made His communications to a favoured few. IV. THEY SAW A VISION OF JESUS ONLY. This, I think, was the chief end and aim of this great event. (*J. J. Wray.*) *Our wishes are not always wise:*—Peter's instance showeth us two things. 1. That we are apt to consult with our own profit, rather than public good. It is our nature, if it be well with ourselves, to forget others. 2. How much we are out when we judge by present sense, and the judgment of flesh. Well then, let us learn by what measure to determine good or evil. 1. Good is not to be determined by our fancies and conceits, but by the wisdom of God: for He knoweth what is better for us than we do for ourselves. 2. That good is to be determined with respect to the chief good, and true happiness. 3. That good is not always the good of the flesh, or the good of outward prosperity; and therefore certainly the good of our condition is not to be determined by the interest of the flesh, but the welfare of our souls. 4. A particular good must give way to a general good, and our personal benefit to the advancement of Christ's kingdom, and the glory of God. 5. This good is not to be determined by the judgment of sense, but by the judgment of faith; not by present feeling, but future profit. That which is not good may be a means to good. If we come to a person under the Cross, and ask him, What! Is it good to feel the lashes of God's correcting hand? to be kept poor, sickly, exercised with losses and reproaches, to part with friends and relations, to lose a beloved child? he would be apt to answer, No. But this poor creature after he hath been exercised, and mortified, and gotten some renewed evidences of God's favour; ask Him then, Is it good to be afflicted? Oh yes, I had been vain, neglectful of God, wanted such an experience of the Lord's grace. Faith should determine the case when we feel it not. Well then, let us learn to distinguish between what is really best for us, and what we judge to be best. Other diet is more wholesome for our souls than that which our sickly appetite craveth. It is best many times when we are weakest, worst when strongest, all things are good as they help on a blessed eternity, so sharp afflictions are good. (*T. Manton, D.D.*) *Peter's rash judgment:*—I propound six questions on this. 1. Could it be good for them that Christ should entrench Himself in Mount Tabor, and never go to Jerusalem to be crucified? Lord, grant us not our own wishes when we desire evil unto ourselves; for this apostle unwittingly desired as much mischief to fall upon his own head as the devil could wish. 2. And might not Peter counsel Him without offence against this ignominious death? No, my beloved; for it is not to be excused how he knew not the Scriptures, that this was the course appointed for the redemption of the world. The hungry could not eat their bread until it was broken; we could not quench our thirst with the water of life till it was poured out of His wounds. 3. I ask, if that condition of life be well chosen in this world which appears, as this did to Peter, to be exempted from all affliction? Danger is the best sentinel in the world to make us watch our enemies. Fear is the best warning-bell to call us often to prayer. Tribulation is the best orator to persuade us to humility. 4. Where shall the dove rest his foot? If we would be contented with the present state we enjoy, yet all things will change, and though all things should remain as they are, and never change, yet we would never be contented. The sea is a new sea every tide, the earth is a new earth every month, or every quarter at the longest distance, the same mutability whirls us about, and the things that we possess. What content then could Peter take in one hill, though it were furnished with a most desirable vision? How quickly would it have cloyed him to have been long there, like a lark, hopping upon one turf of grass? Though God prepare for us a new heaven, and a new earth, yet He must give us a new heart likewise to delight in them for ever. For it is not the object alone, but the disposition of the soul which receives it, that must make us say, "When I awake up after Thy likeness I shall be satisfied with it." 5. Should we call that good which is appropriated to ourselves, and not communicated to many? When every man is his own end, all things will come to a bad end. Blessed were those days, when every man thought himself rich and fortunate by the good success of the public wealth and glory.

Every man thinks that he is a whole commonwealth in his private family. Can the public be neglected and any man's private be secure? It is all one whether the mischief light upon him or his posterity. There are some, says Tully, that think their own gardens and fishponds shall be safe when the Commonwealth is lost. 6. To the last question briefly in a word: Could it be the supreme good of man to behold the human nature of Christ only beatified? Surely, the human nature shining as light as the sun was a rare object, that Peter could have been contented with that, and no more, for his part for ever, yet the resolution of the school holds certain, that blessedness consists essentially in beholding the Divine nature which is the fountain of all goodness, and power; and in the fruition thereof, accidentally it consists in beholding Christ's human nature glorified, and in the consequent delectation. These things must not be enlarged now, because I am prevented by the time. (*Bishop Hacket.*) *Balloon religion:*—Peter is in ecstasy amid these surroundings. He desires to remain on the Mount. He says in rapture, "It is good for us to be here." He would rather remain there for ever, than go down from the mountain and engage in the practical duties of life. But his request is denied him. Sometimes, in revival meetings, you have felt in the same way. There are duties outside of the revival. Longfellow, in one of his poems, pictures a youth, who, in winter, seizes a banner and begins the ascent of a mountain. He gradually leaves behind him the fields, the stores, the workshops, the dwellings, and the neighbours. As he rises higher and higher he shouts, "Excelsior." His voice grows fainter and fainter, until heard no more. He has gone so high, that the atmosphere in which he moves has become too thin to sustain life, and he dies. So it is no uncommon thing to see professed Christians taking the banner of the Cross and crying, "Hallelujah," "Amen," rise higher and higher, emotionally, until they leave behind them this practical world. They lose sight of the duties of every-day life. They are too high up to give much attention to such matters as speaking the truth, keeping their temper, restraining their tongue from slander, and paying their debts. They have become too religious to give much concern to these things. But these persons soon reach an altitude where the atmosphere is too thin for them to live, and they die. It is one thing to be religious on the Mount of Transfiguration, and another thing not to deny our Lord in the world below. Instead of this gushing religion, let us have one that touches the ground. (*Irving A. Searles.*) *A three-tent heaven:*—Peter forgot the other disciples, the great world beneath, and the generations yet to come. How narrow and insignificant this proposed heaven, compared with the one seen by the Patmos exile, who beheld "a great multitude which no man could number." But Peter is not the only follower of Christ who would be satisfied with a little three-tent heaven. This spirit is the death-warrant of missionary enterprise. What shall be said of a Christian who is satisfied if he can only gain heaven for himself, even if the rest of the world is lost? Away with the idea of a three-tent heaven! (*Ibid.*) *Holiness in religious assemblies and in every-day life;*—1. The wish Peter here expresses is exceedingly natural. 2. It is seemingly pious. 3. It expresses a desire not altogether free from selfishness. 4. Like other selfish wishes, Peter's was mistaken. "Not knowing what he said" indicates the blind manner in which it was cherished and expressed. 5. We have said enough already to indicate why Peter's wish was not gratified. But why, if in form it had to be denied, might it not have been granted in substance? Supposing that Peter's main object in wishing to remain there was the better and holier mood which he would have been able to maintain, why might not the spiritual condition have been granted to him, even though the surrounding circumstances could not be perpetuated? The same questions in effect are sometimes asked now. Say some, "The Lord is able at once to sanctify you wholly." But to ask why, if God is able to sanctify us, we are not sanctified instantaneously by His power, is very much the same as to ask, why does not God make us other than men? Why does He not change us into things into which He can put whatsoever He pleases, while, for the possession of it, as we have no will in the matter, we shall be entitled to no praise, as for the lack of it we are subject to no blame? The answer is, because He has destined us for something nobler; that, while free to choose the wrong, ours might be the merit of making the right the object of our desires and aspirations, and prayers and strivings, until having, through diligent and untiring effort, gained the victory over evil, and attained to the possession of all that is well-pleasing in His sight, we hear from His lips the eulogy which can never be pronounced on those who are *made*, only on those who do, and labour, and fight, "Well done, good and faithful servant," &c.

(*W. Landels, D.D.*) *The overshadowing cloud :*—Like the clouds that overhang and surround us, so the sorrows of life come and go, and alternate our days with changeful light and shade. Let us gaze at this cloud overshadowing these apostles, that we may learn something of the clouds that may now and hereafter overshadow our hearts. I. THE CLOUD OVERSHADOWING THE DISCIPLES. 1. When did it overshadow them? At the moment at which they were witnessing a new and unexpected revelation of the majesty and glory of Jesus. How unlikely that a cloud should then arise! 2. What cloud was it that overshadowed them? It was a cloud of salvation. It came in mercy. II. THE FEAR OF THE DISCIPLES AS THEY ENTERED THE CLOUD. Why did they fear? 1. Perhaps because it was a cloud. 2. Because there was mystery in the cloud. Their fear implied their deficiency of love. III. THE VOICE IN THE CLOUD. The voice of God, testifying to them of Jesus. It was the very testimony they needed, and it was vouchsafed to them in answer to the prayer of Jesus. In all the clouds that overshadow us, in all the sorrows that assail us, there is a Divine voice addressing us; and the design of the testimony is to exalt Jesus in our hearts. (*W. T. Bull, B.A.*) *The cloud :*—Our whole happiness and power of energetic action depend upon our being able to breathe and live in the cloud; content to see it opening here and closing there; rejoicing to catch through the thinnest films of it, glimpses of stable and substantial things; but yet perceiving a nobleness even in the concealment, and rejoicing that the kindly veil is spread where the untempered light might have scorched us, or the infinite clearness wearied. (*J. Ruskin.*) *The fear of the disciples :*—What is meant by the expression "as they entered the cloud," will be understood by all of you who have ever climbed to the summit of some high mountain, and may be imagined by those who have seen the lofty peak of some towering hill enveloped in a robe of mist. When, as you stand in the cool air of the mountain-top, the cloud descends upon you, you seem rather to be rising up into it, and as it hides from your view the way you have come, and the wide reach of the surrounding country, you are seized and oppressed with a sense of loneliness and mystery which may well explain what is said of the disciples in the text. And the kind of fear which is here spoken of is just that which is most trying and hardest to bear, that namely of some unknown evil that may befall you in the gloom. We create for ourselves more evils than we are called to endure. We climb the shadows before we reach the hills. To be the slave of presentiments is to deprive life of the pleasure which it was intended to have in store for us, and so to weaken ourselves that when the expected trouble befalls us it crushes and overwhelms us. (*J. R. Bailey.*) *The voice from the cloud :*—Is there not rich and consoling meaning to be got out of the fact that the voice spake to the disciples *out of* the fearful cloud? Does it not show that the cloud itself was the token of the Divine presence? Does it not teach us that the very events and experiences we fear the most may be those which shall most surely bring God nigh to us? The cloud and the voice are inseparably connected in the narrative—the cloud which conceals, and the voice which reveals. It is not that there was a cloud here, and a voice there. It was from the midst of the cloud that the voice came. And, did we but know it, there is a Divine presence in, and a Divine voice issuing from every cloud. Let us learn to be thankful for the cloud, instead of fearful of it, if, without it, we should not hear the reassuring voice. (*Ibid.*) *The overshadowing cloud :*—Think of the cloud as a symbol—I. OF THE MYSTERIES OF REVELATION AND OF HUMAN LIFE. II. OF THE SORROW THAT OFTEN VEILS THE PURPOSES OF GOD'S LOVE, AND YET IS THE KEY TO THE SECRET RICHES OF THAT LOVE. III. OF DEATH—THE VEIL THAT HANGS BETWEEN US AND THE GREAT HEREAFTER. (*J. Waite, B.A.*)

Vers. 34–36. **They feared as they entered into the cloud.**—*Entering the cloud :*— I. THE GLOOM OF THE CLOUD OFTEN SUCCEEDS THE GLADNESS OF THE LIGHT. Delight even in our divinest experiences is not to be all. These disciples had a hard work to do yet. God has reasons for the darkness as well as for the light. II. THE ENTERING INTO THE CLOUD WAS A MATTER OF FEAR. Fear on entering! It is often the first experience that we dread. The awful solitude of Glencoe strikes you most on entering; by degrees, you see colour among the rocks, beauty in the vale. Overcome first fear, and then, as you merge into some dread experience, the mind will become accustomed to the change. No sorrow is so great as it seems. III. THERE IS A VOICE IN THE CLOUD, AND IT IS THE VOICE OF GOD. A cloud and a voice! Yes, the conjunction is beautiful even in a human sense. It is under the cloud of misconception that a friend's voice is all-sustaining; it is under the cloud of some dark trial that the tender tones of love make sweetest music. This was the voice of God. That in itself is deepest solace and truest inspiration. Speak, Lord! Enoch heard that voice when he walked with God. It is a Father's voice. In the cloud, if we are the children of the world, there will be heard only our own voice—the voice of repining—the voice of distrust—the voice of mourning—or, worst of all, the voice of despair! IV. THERE IS A SOLITARY VISION AFTER THE CLOUD. They saw "Jesus only." Beautiful in one sense, though they were disappointed that other visions were gone. V. THERE IS A TRANSFIGURATION LAND, WHERE THERE ARE NO CLOUDS. Then the voice will come from the throne, not from the cloud. There are no clouds there; faith needs no more trial; character no more test. Christian transfiguration is not completed here; we are renewed, but not glorified yet. But in ourselves we have a prophecy of perfected life, even the earnest of the inheritance. (*W. M. Statham, B.A.*) *The overshadowing cloud, and the voice that comes from it:*—The first thing that claims attention is—THE OVERSHADOWING CLOUD. It is not necessary for us to go on far in life before we find clouds coming to cast their shadows over us. We know that the elements are there out of which overshadowing clouds are in constant process of formation. And we know too that there are active agents all the time in operation on those elements. There are the rivers and lakes and seas about us, spreading out their broad water surfaces. And there is the sun with his genial beams, turning that water into vapour, and sending it off on its floating voyage through the air, to form into clouds which shall cast their shadows over our pathway. And just so it is in our experience of life in its moral or spiritual aspect. We carry in us, and find around us, the elements and agents that are occupied continually in forming the clouds that come and overshadow us. In the sickness and death of those we love, or in the visitation of personal sickness, in the loss of property, in the disappointment of our reasonable expectations, what clouds arise continually from all these varied sources! How darkly their shadows fall upon us! The apostles were on the Mount of Transfiguration. Jesus in all the glory of His coming kingdom stood in the midst of them. They stood at the very vestibule of heaven, with all the radiance of its glory beaming around them; and yet, even on that towering summit—a point of elevation in brightness and bliss, such as dwellers on this globe had never reached before—"there came a cloud and overshadowed them." And so it must be with us. We must expect the clouds to come and cast their shadows over us. This side of heaven we cannot get beyond their reach. "There came a cloud and overshadowed them," has been descriptive of the experience of God's people from the beginning. If we look at the lives of Abraham, Job, Jacob, David, or any of God's servants, as written in the Bible, we see how broad and deep these shadows have lain upon their pathway. II. THE FEELING WITH WHICH THIS EXPERIENCE IS GENERALLY MET. "And they feared as they entered into the cloud." Nothing is more natural to fallen men than fear in reference to God and eternity. And it is not difficult to point out the causes of it. 1. One of these is our consciousness of sin. Fear cannot find room where sin has not gone before it. 2. There may be a failure to understand the views which the Scriptures give us of God's providence; or an unwillingness to believe those views. Either of these things will give rise to the fear of which we are speaking. This is the Bible view of God's providences towards His people. Could anything be brighter, or more cheerful? Then why should Christians fear when the cloud comes? There would be no room for fear if we only had simple faith in these Bible views of providence. Fear springs from the want of faith. In the darkest hour of Luther's trying life the Elector of Saxony was the only earthly defender who stood by him. For a time it was doubtful whether the Emperor Charles V. might not send an army against the elector and crush him. "Where will you be," said some one to Luther, "if the emperor should send his forces against the elector?" It was under the sustaining influence of the principle we are now considering that that heroic man sublimely said, "I shall be either *in* heaven or *under* heaven." He could enter the darkest cloud without fear. III. THE VOICE FROM THE CLOUD. "There came a voice out of the cloud. saying, This is My beloved Son; hear Him." And this is the design of all God's afflictive dealings with His people. The cloud comes upon us, with its overshadowing gloom, to check us in the too eager pursuit of other things, and to enable us to see Jesus, and understand His character and work. A soldier had lost his right arm from the shoulder during the last war. To an agent of the Christian Commission, who visited him, he said, "It seems to me I cannot be grateful enough for losing my arm. It was dreadful to me at first." Thus he

" feared as he entered into the cloud."　"But," he continued, "it has ended in bringing me to Jesus. And now, I can say with truth, ' It is better to enter into life halt or maimed, rather than having two hands or two feet to be cast into outer darkness." Thus God lets the clouds of trial come and overshadow us, that we may be prepared to see the light, and glory, and infinite sufficiency, and preciousness, that are to be found in Christ.

> " Sorrow touch'd by love grows bright,
> 　With more than rapture's ray;
> And darkness shows us worlds of light
> 　We never saw by day."

And then this voice from the cloud quickens to duty, as well as points to Jesus. " This is My beloved Son; hear Him." Such was David's experience when he said, " Before I was afflicted I went astray; but now have I kept Thy word." The voice from the overshadowing cloud had quickened him in duty. There are two trees. One is growing on a fertile plain, the other is perched high up on the mountain-side. The lowland tree will lean to this side or that, though it be but a summer breeze that bends it, or a bank of cowslips from which its trunk leans aslope. But let the storm and the avalanche do their worst to the hardy pine-tree of the Alps, it will cling to its little ledge on the side of the precipice and grow straight. Its roots point down to the centre of the earth; and the more the storms rock it, the hardier, and the stronger, and the straighter it will grow. And the same law holds in spiritual growth as in that which is natural. The voice from the overshadowing cloud quickens to duty and strengthens for service. And there is no nobler sight to contemplate than that of a child of God, whose confidence in Him cannot be shaken —not fearing when the clouds gather, nor faltering when the tempests burst. And thus we have attempted to speak of the overshadowing cloud; of the fear with which it is entered; and of the voice that comes from it. The cloud, the fear, the voice. There is just one lesson we may carry away with us from the consideration of this subject. It is this: If we are true Christians we never need fear the developments of God's providences. However darkly the clouds may gather, or however fiercely the storms may burst, they cannot harm us. We need not fear. (*R. Newton.*)　*The cloud and the voice :*—With a natural cloud the facts we associate are obscurity, dimness, a degree of mystery, a hiding of the light—sometimes very mercifully softening and tempering what would be more dazzling than the delicate organ of sight could bear—yet a body so attenuated, transparent, and movable, that we feel the darkness is transient. It may pass away from the face of the sun; it may be touched by his beams, transfigured to the eye, and made almost like another sun in splendour. Such, under the laws of light and air and water and attraction, are the properties of the cloud in nature. Now, in that succession of special disclosures of the Divine Presence and care for man, of which the Bible is the completest record and Christ the perfect incarnation, it is striking to see how each principal act of revelation is covered with a cloud—a palpable veil of mystery. From the beginning to the end you see the persistent and remarkable reappearance of this symbol. Considering how these different books of the Bible were produced, and what a variety of authors, periods, countries, stages of literary culture, they proceed from, this is more than a coincidence—it is design. It discloses a general truth. As men are brought near to the very sight and feeling of their Lord, an obscurity overshadows them; there is a shrinking; reverence hides the face; the angels even, admitted to the brightest day, veil their eyes with their wings; no sight is clear enough, no faith is bold enough, not to need the screen. "They feared as they entered into the cloud." 1. Most of our deepest acquaintance with religious truth comes by a discipline of some severity. To pass out of a life of indifference and self-indulgence into one of purity and prayer requires a painful effort. If you can look back to any time when your life took a new starting-point, or rose to a higher aim, you will remember there was some hard conflict connected with it. Suffering is not only the consequence of sin, but the instrument of recovery. It is a means of penitence, and so a minister to the only real peace. 2. The second point on this practical side of the doctrine is that it is when we are entering into this cloud—having only the dark side of it before us, and its damp and chilly folds closing around us—that we are afraid. The purpose of the cloud is to shut out all that we are not meant to see. It is also a kind of background for the heavenly vision. This is only one way of expressing the exact and eternal contradiction of right and wrong. The true life is born by a painful travail. 3. For, thirdly, there comes, as the Evangelist writes, " a voice out of the cloud," which is sufficient, if we will hearken to it, to guide us through the dark, into the light, where the sun is never dim. 4. " Hear Him." Hear Him, and He will scatter the cloud from about you with the breath of His mouth. (*Bishop Huntington.*) *The cloud :*—I. The Lord did show that He could frame a better piece of architecture of a sudden than Peter could imagine to build : he spake of three tabernacles, which would be long in piecing together ; God in a moment creates one cloud to receive them all better than a hundred tabernacles. Such a one as Moses and the Israelites had in the wilderness to shadow them against all offence. Such things the heathen did drive at in their poetical fictions : but I am sure the Lord is able to pitch a cloud between His chosen and their enemies, that the hand of violence shall not touch them, neither shall any evil come nigh their dwelling. II. A cloud did interpose itself to qualify the object of the Transfiguration, and to make it fit for the disciples to behold it : the cloud indeed was very bright, yet it was dark and opacous in respect of Christ's body, which did exceed the very light of the sun. In this life we must look through a cloud, we must expect to see Him as in a glass darkly, hereafter we shall see Him face to face. Mark the infirmity of man's nature in this sinful corruptible condition, and let us learn humility ; it was not enough that Peter, John, and James were not transformed in the Mount, as Christ was—no, nor as Moses and Elias were, our vile flesh is not receptive of such celestial excellency—but to abase them and us further, a shady cloud opposed itself before their eyes, because we are not fit nor worthy to behold such pure happiness in these days of vanity. " Such knowledge is too excellent for me," says David," I cannot attain unto it." III. This cloud was set up for a land-mark to limit curiosity, and to drive men off from approaching too near to pry into the Divine secrets. Where God sets up a cloud it is a manifest sign that those are our bounds, and we must not break them. IV. And I am sure this reason searcheth the true cause of the cloud as near as any. God the Father in the Old Testament was wont to utter His voice out of the thick clouds of the air, and so He continues His holy will in the gospel, and therefore prepared this cloud to preach from thence the words which follow, " This is My beloved Son," &c. (*Bishop Hacket.*) *A cloud of protection :*—Where God covers anything with a miraculous shadow, it promiseth that the Divine protection is round about it. Leonidas the Grecian was told that his enemies came marching in such full troops against him, that their darts when they threw them up would cover the light of the sun : Leonidas puts it off with this stout courage, *Tum in umbrâ pugnabimus ;* " Then we will fight in the shade." A courageous word, and made very fit for a Christian's mouth. Believe in the Lord, and we are all under His custody and defence ; beseech Him to stretch His wings upon us, and the Holy Ghost will overshadow us, *In umbrâ pugnabimus,* to that shadow we betake ourselves to shun the fire of anger, and the heat of concupiscence ; under that shadow will we fight against our ghostly enemies. Why did not the disciples know their own strength and assurance when this cloud did overshadow them ? Did not the Lord declare that He took them into His protection ? (*Ibid.*) *Man and mystery :*—I. MAN IN CONTACT WITH MYSTERY. The disciples now stood face to face with " The Cloud." 1. Every science is an attempt to solve Nature's mysteries, to discover Nature's secrets. 2. Nor in the realm of Religion does man have less frequently to do with mystery. In the fact that man has thus to do with mystery, we have a sign of the finiteness of our nature. II. MAN ALARMED AT MYSTERY. There are many mysteries, such for instance as some in the physical world, contact with which does not awaken fear. Some in the natural world. As when stupendous nature seems to be the enemy of man, so that it arrays itself in plague, storm, earthquake, against the feeble, the unoffending, the good. Some in intellectual speculation. Those who climb the mountain of inquiry often " fear as they enter the cloud." Some in personal experience. And there will be death. In the fact that man is thus alarmed at mystery, we have one proof of the sinfulness of our nature. To a pure being mystery would have no dread. III. MAN ENLIGHTENED IN MYSTERY. But the cloud became a sanctuary ; the mystery a revelation. For out of it there came a voice, saying, " This is My beloved Son : hear Him." So hearing the Divine teaching about the ever-living, ever-present Christ, we connect Him and mystery together thus : Christ is the moral of all mysteries. The cloud settled on the mountain, and enwrapped the three disciples, solely to perfect the revelation of Christ to them. Thus every mystery in human life is meant, and adapted, to train us for Christ. Does mystery discover to us our ignorance, so that we feel as those that grope in darkness, and stretch forth imploring hands, and strain eager eyes for light? That yearning, thus intensified under the pressure of mystery, is a yearning for Christ, "the Light of the World." Does mystery make us realize our feebleness, so that we feel as a leaf driven before the winds of circumstances, a waif tossed on the waves of the unresting ocean of the material universe, and cry for strength? That cry is for Christ, "the arm of the Lord revealed." Christ is the interpreter of mystery. There are mysteries that He solves for us now by the record of His wonderful words. Christ is the controller of all mystery. Not alone hath He "the keys of death and hell," though verily these two are among the deepest of all mysteries; but He is the Sovereign of the future, for to Him "is subject the world to come." (*U. R. Thomas*). *The Lord Jesus as Mediator:*—1. From the occasions upon which this voice came from heaven; at His Baptism, which was Christ's dedication of Himself to the work of a Redeemer and Saviour, and now at His Transfiguration, to distinguish Him from Moses and the other prophets, and publicly to instal Him in the mediatory office. 2. The matter of the words show His fitness for this office, for here you have—(1) His dignity; not a servant, but a Son (Heb. iii. 5, 6). (2) The dearness between God and Him. 3. His acceptableness to God, who is well-pleased with the design, the terms, the management of it. II. This work of Mediator Christ executeth by three offices of King, Priest, Prophet. III. That though all the three offices be employed, yet the prophetical office is more explicitly mentioned, partly as suiting with the present occasion, which is to demonstrate that Christ hath sufficient authority to repeal the Law of Moses which the prophets were to explain, confirm, and maintain till His coming. (*T. Manton, D.D.*) *Christ, the great Prophet, must be Head:*—I. That Christ is the great Prophet and Teacher of the Church appeareth.—1. By the titles given to Him. (1) He is compared with Moses, the great Lawgiver among the Jews (Deut. xviii. 15). (2) He is called the Angel or Messenger of the Covenant (Mal. iii. 1). 2. By the properties of His office. He has three things to qualify Him for this high office. (1) Absolute supreme authority; and therefore we must hear Him and hearken to Him. (2) All manner of sufficiency and power of God to execute this office (John iii. 34). (3) There is in Him a powerful efficacy. As He hath absolute authority to teach in His own name, and fulness of sufficiency to make known the mind of God to us; so He hath power to make His doctrine effectual. And when He dealt with His disciples, after He had opened the Scriptures, He opened their understandings (Luke xxiv. 25). So He opened the heart of Lydia (Acts xvi. 14). He can teach so as to draw (John vi. 44, 45). He can excite the drowsy mind, change and turn the rebellious will, cure the distempered affections, make us to be what He persuadeth us to be. There is no such teacher as Christ, who doth not only give us our lesson, but a heart to learn; therefore to Him must we submit, hear nothing against Him, but all from Him. II. About hearing Him; that must be explained also. First, What it is to hear. It being our great duty, and the respect bespoken for Him. In the hearing of words there are three things considerable; the sound that cometh to the ear, the understanding of the sense and meaning, and the assent or consent of the mind. Of the first, the beasts are capable, for they have ears to hear the sound of words uttered. The second is common to all men, for they can sense such intelligible words as they hear. The third belongeth to disciples, who are swayed by their Master's authority. Secondly, How can we now hear Christ, since He is removed into the heaven of heavens, and doth not speak to us in person. The revelation is settled, and not delivered by parcels, as it was to the ordinary prophets. Now we hear Christ in the Scriptures (Heb. ii. 3, 4). Thirdly, The properties of this hearing or submission to our Great Prophet. 1. There must be a resolute consent or resignation of ourselves to His teaching and instruction. All particular duties are included in the general. 2. This resignation of our souls to Christ as a Teacher, as it must be resolute, so it must be unbounded and without reserves. We must submit absolutely to all that He propoundeth, though some mysteries be above our reason, some precepts against the interest and inclination of the flesh, some promises seem to be against hope, or contrary to natural probabilities. 3. It must be speedy. No delay (Heb. iii. 7). 4. Your consent to hear Him must be real, practical, obediential, verified in the whole tenor and course of your lives and actions; for Christ will not be flattered with empty titles: "Why call ye Me Lord, and Master, and do not the things which I say?" (Luke vi. 46). Many study Christianity to form their opinions, rather than reform their hearts and practice. The great use of knowledge and faith is to behold the love of God in the face of Jesus Christ, that our own love may be quickened and increased to Him again. If it serve only to regulate opinions, it is but dead speculation, not a living faith. III. The reasons why this Prophet must be heard. 1. Because He is the only beloved Son of God. 2. Because the doctrine of the gospel which He speaks is the most sweet, excellent, and comfortable doctrine that can be heard or understood by the heart of man. Uses: I. Of conviction, to the carnal Christian for not submitting to Christ's authority. 1. Do you seriously come to Him that you may have pardon and life? 2. Do you respect the word of the gospel, entertain it with reverence and delight, as the voice of the great Prophet? Do you meditate on it, digest it as the seed of the new life, as the rule of your actions, as the charter of your hopes? 3. Do you mingle it with faith in the hearing, that it may profit you? 4. Do you receive it as the Word of God? 5. Doth it come to you as the Mediator's word, not in word only, but in power? 6. Do you hear Him universally? 7. Do you hear Him so as to prefer God, and Christ, and the life to come, above all the sensual pleasures and vain delights, and worldly happiness, which you enjoy here? II. ADVICE TO WEAK CHRISTIANS. 1. To excite themselves to obedience by this "hear Him" when dead and lifeless. 2. When you do renounce some beloved lust, or pleasing sin, urge your hearts with Christ's authority. Remember who telleth you of cutting off your right hand, and plucking out your right eye. How can I look the Mediator in the face, if I should wilfully break any of His laws, prefer the satisfaction of a base lust, before the mercies and hopes offered me by Jesus Christ. 3. In deep distresses, when you are apt to question the comfort of the promises, it is hard to keep the rejoicing of hope, without regarding whose word and promise is it (Heb. iii. 6). (*Ibid.*) *The cloud a blessing :*—Man is harrassed by groundless fears. Who has ever looked for blessings in a cloud? Were we appointed to collect the riches of the universe, how many would pass by the clouds, as though in their dark and troubled breasts no treasure could be found! How often have we trembled as we have entered into the cloud of bereavement, or sorrowful apprehension; and yet in such a cloud have we heard a voice, as did the trembling disciples! In the cloud which they dreaded they heard the Divine voice; henceforward, then, let us gratefully remember that even a cloud can contain a blessing, and that sometimes fear is but the quaking harbinger of joy. (*J. Parker, D.D.*) *Keeping a secret :*—It is a privilege to be trusted. Sometimes the trust is a burden. Few can keep secrets. The disciples were able to do so. We are told concerning one thing that they had seen that they kept it close. I. THE SECRET HELD. A vision of Christ's glory among beings of another world. That vision had been—1. Instructive. 2. Assuring. 3. Elevating. II. THE REASONS FOR THE MAINTAINED SECRESY. 1. The spiritual attainments of the disciples were not sufficiently advanced for them to speak freely of what they had seen without some damage to themselves. A sneer of some doubter might have weakened their belief at that time. 2. Christ had enjoined silence. He was in no haste to astonish the world. 3. The outside world was not in a fit state to receive the knowledge of that vision. A time was sure to come when the disciples could speak openly and effectively. Peter doubtless made frequent references to it (2 Peter i. 16). We may remember that—(1) We have no need to refrain from speaking of what Christ has done in giving us peace. (2) Whatever witness we bear should be the outcome of a real experience. Anyhow, we should endeavour to let the praise of Christ be on our lips and reflected in our lives. (*Homiletic Magazine.*)

Vers. 37–43. **Master, I beseech Thee, look upon my son.**—*The devil's last throw :*—I. OUR HOPES ARE ALL AWAKENED. Here is a poor youth, but bad as he is, terribly possessed as he is, he is coming to Christ. Prayer has been offered for him by his father, and Jesus is near. All looks well! For a hungry man to be coming to a dinner is not enough: he must actually reach the table and eat. For a sick man to be coming to an eminent physician is hopeful, but it is not enough; he must get to that physician, take his medicine, and be restored. That is the point. To be coming to Christ is not enough: you must actually come to Him, and really receive Him; for to such only does He give power to become the sons of God. II. OUR FEARS ARE AROUSED. "As he was a-coming, the devil threw him down, and tare him." How does the devil do this? Well, we have seen it done in this way: When the man had almost believed in Christ, but not quite, Satan seemed to multiply his temptations around him, and to bring his whole force to bear upon him. I have known in addition to all this that Satan has stirred up the anxious one's bad passions. Passions that lay asleep have suddenly been aroused. Moreover, the man has become thoughtful, and from that very fact doubts which he never knew before have come upon him.   III. OUR WONDER IS EXCITED.   This cure was perfected at once, and it remained with the youth.   The Saviour's cures endure the test of years.   " Enter no more into him " preserved the young man by a life-long word of power.   I never dare to preach to anybody a temporary salvation.   (*C. H. Spurgeon.*)   *The comer's conflict with Satan :*—I. THE DEVIL'S DOINGS. When this child came to Christ to be healed, the devil threw him down and tare him.   1. First of all he does this by perverting the truth of God for the destruction of the soul's hope and comfort.   2. But Satan is not very scrupulous, and he sometimes throws the coming sinner down and tears him by telling horrible falsehoods. Many a time when the soul is coming to Christ, Satan violently injects infidel thoughts.   3. Then if the devil cannot overcome you there, he tries another method ; he takes all the threatening passages out of God's Word, and says they all apply to you.   II. THE DEVIL'S DESIGN.   Why does he throw the coming soul down, and tear it ?   1. Because he does not like to lose it.   2. Sometimes, I believe, he has the vile design of inducing poor souls to make away with themselves, before they have faith in Christ.   3. When the soul is coming to Christ he tries, out of spite, to worry that soul.   III. THE DEVIL'S DISCOVERY.   I will give the poor sinner a means of detecting Satan, so that he may know whether his convictions are from the Holy Spirit, or merely the bellowing of hell in his ears.   1. In the first place, you may be always sure that that which comes from the devil will make you look at yourselves and not at Christ.   2. You may discern the devil's insinuations in another way ; they generally reflect upon some attribute of God.   IV. Now, in the last place, we have to consider THE DEVIL'S DEFEAT.   How was he defeated ? Jesus rebuked him.   Beloved, there is no other way for us to be saved from the castings down of Satan but the rebuke of Jesus.   (*Ibid.*)   *Spiritual power, impaired and restored :*—I. SPIRITUAL POWER IS NEEDED FOR THE CASTING OUT OF DEVILS. We, weak men, in our own strength cannot successfully grapple with evil in ourselves or others.   You may charm the serpent for a little time.   You may tame the wild beast.   You may put him into a cage and restrain him in many ways.   The sweet music of David did charm to rest the evil spirit of Saul.   But the grim fact remains that the foul fiend is not cast out.   Every generation has witnessed the failure of man in this unequal struggle with evil.   All the forces of civilization are called into eager requisition in the conflict—art, and education, and refinement, and philanthropy, and social reform, and the administration of law.   The failure is confessed by the deepest and purest spirits of the Grecian culture.   In Rome an iron will entered into conflict with evil, but the failure was more conspicuous still than in Athens.   In the East the religious instinct, often under the guidance of gloriously gifted men, has laboured to cast out the spirit of evil.   But all the centuries and all the generations have sunk in hopeless failure.   We are forced to return to the plain, simple teaching of God's Book, that we need a power not our own, the power of God to overcome.   1. We need this spiritual power to cast evil out of ourselves.   You have often tried self-denial.   You have tried occupation and work.   You have tried religious duties.   You have tried the practice of moral precept.   2. But in like manner we need spiritual power to cast the spirit of evil out of others.   The early disciples found it so.   II. THERE IS NO TRUE SPIRITUAL POWER WITHOUT FAITH.   Let us observe, that in order to lose spiritual power it is not necessary to commit a flagrant sin.   Samson committed a flagrant sin and lost his strength.   The disciples were guilty only of this, that their faith was not vigorous and growing, yet they stand before the world shorn of their strength as completely as Samson when he shook himself as at other times.   Observe, again, that the disciples themselves do not appear to have been conscious beforehand of this departure of power.   They come down to the scene of work, and like Samson they wist not that their strength had departed from them.   Doubtless in their failure it did not occur to them to suspect themselves.   What, then, is the first condition of true spiritual power ?   It is the possession of a living and growing faith.   Who are the men who have wielded great spiritual power in all ages ?   They are the men of faith.   The men of unbelief die and are forgotten, even their gifts and accomplishments only serve to build their tomb or write their cold epitaph. But the men of faith are the heroes of the race and the kings of the Church of God. It is given to them like Israel to be princes, having power with God and with men. It is the men of faith who subdue kingdoms, and work righteousness, and stop the mouths of lions.   Faith imparts power because it lays hold of the truth, and it is the truth which purifies.   It imparts power because it quickens and inspires all the faculties of the soul. It imparts power because it establishes an alliance between God and man, by which Divine help is given in moments of need. It imparts power by means of its innate courage and invincibility. III. THERE IS NO LIVING FAITH WITHOUT EARNEST PRAYER. The sequence of spiritual ideas is simple and beautiful. The evil spirit could not be cast out without special spiritual power. Power could not co-exist with unbelief. And now unbelief can be extinguished only by prayer. This kind goeth not out but by prayer and fasting. In these practical and bustling days there is abundant recognition of the value of what is called a working Christianity. Why could not we cast him out ? The weeping mother feels the bitterness of this question as she witnesses her wayward boy disregarding her counsels and rejecting her reproof. Why could not I tame the evil passion and guide the wandering feet ? Or the sabbath-school teacher wails out the despairing confession of failure at the end of years of busy work with his class. O think, what conquests lie before us if in Christ's name we be endued with new power from on high. (*S. Prenter, M.A.*) *Fasting :*—Here was a demon of extraordinary strength, and he could be vanquished only by extraordinary prayer and fasting. Fasting is connected with extraordinary spiritual attainments and achievements. These disciples lacked the higher form of prayer, and its profounder spirit. There is a faith which removes mountains ; a prayer that unlocks heaven, and vanquishes the powers of hell. But Christ here shows that they are connected with fasting. I would, then, observe that—I. WE FIND THIS PRINCIPLE CONFIRMED BY THE WHOLE HISTORY OF FASTING, IN THE SCRIPTURES, AND IN THE CHURCH, FROM THE CHRISTIAN ERA DOWNWARD. 1. We turn, first, to the Jewish Church. It is not affirmed whether the patriarchs knew anything of fasting as a religious service ; but Moses, in entering into the Mount, to commune with God concerning the foundation of the Old Testament Church, for forty days abstained from food—of course by Divine direction, and by miraculous aid. It is quite remarkable that the three persons who appeared on the Mount of Transfiguration had all performed this extraordinary fast of forty days—Moses, Elijah, and Christ. If, now, we look at the several occasions on which it was employed by the devout members and eminent leaders of the Jewish Church, we shall receive a strong impression that it has some connection with the higher exercises, attainments, and achievements, of piety, or with cases of especial appeal to the Most High. When Saul was buried, having been the first King of Israel, and having been slain ingloriously, the people assembled to recover his insulted corpse, and decently inter it. Then they fasted seven days. When David's child was dangerously ill, he lay on his face, and mourned, with fasting and prayer. The psalmist, speaking of the afflictions brought on him by his enemies, says, " I humbled my soul with fasting." The great day of atonement, when the people brought their sins particularly to mind, was a day of fasting. Another use of it was to prepare the mind for specially intimate communion with God, or for very important service to the Church. Ezra's fasts had reference, too, to great reformations ; and, in 1 Sam. vii. 6, we find a fast to have been the first stage in one of those glorious revivals which refreshed and preserved the ancient Church. Another occasion was the looking to God for especial help. When the eleven tribes were driven to the necessity of punishing Benjamin, almost to extermination, they " went up, and came unto the house of God, and wept, and sat there before the Lord, and fasted that day until even." So, when Haman had procured the terrible decree that was to annihilate the Jewish people, Esther, with her maids of honour, gave themselves to fasting and prayer for the deliverance of their people ; and with what success, you remember. 2. If we now follow the history of fasting into the times of Christ, the apostles, and the early Christian Church, we see it having the same solemn import and connections. We begin with the Great Exemplar. Jesus did many things as a Jew, or a worshipper under the old theocracy, because that system was not yet abolished. In such matters He is not an example, only so far as the spirit of obedience and order is concerned. But this fasting was not Jewish. It obeyed no law of Moses. It was human. It was spiritual in the highest degree, and a most fitting opening to His glorious ministry, and His wondrous life as the Saviour of men. After the apostolic times, the Church preserved fasting ; and, at length, when aiming to fix a uniform observance of sacred seasons, she set apart the time supposed to be the same as that of our Saviour's fast and temptation in the wilderness, to be solemnized with the anniversary exercise of abstinence. And I believe all her eminent men, of every communion, have been distinguished for this exercise. I do not remember any of any age who considered it as obsolete or useless. Down to the time of the Reformation, no true Christian any more thought of neglecting fasting than prayer. After the Reformation we find two classes: those who chose to confound the Romish abuse with the institution itself, and so despised it; and those who practised it in primitive simplicity. And I repeat my impression that the men most eminent for piety, in every branch of the Protestant Church, used this means of grace. What, then, is—II. THE NATURE OF FASTING AS A RELIGIOUS EXERCISE? 1. It is a spiritual service. "Is this the fasting or day for soul-humbling that I have chosen; the mere bowing down of the head like a bulrush, and spreading sackcloth and ashes under him?" No. He says: I require you to fast in spirit; to cease from your injustice and cruelty. So that the abstinence from food, more or less rigid, is but a means to a spiritual end. It may often, indeed, be bodily beneficial to omit a meal, even in good health; but that is not a religious service, it is a medical regimen. 2. Fasting is in no way a meritorious service, nor a magical instrument. 3. It is the expression of an earnest religious purpose. The heart of him who fasts aright is, at the time, peculiarly concentrated. The heart is fixed on one great object, with peculiar earnestness of desire. Moses did not fast for the sake of laying up a store of merit for himself, or for some other person. The founding of God's Church; the promulgation of Jehovah's law; the opening of a new stage in the work of redemption; these were the mighty charges lying on his soul. And he fasted, as a natural means of aiding his self-abasement and his spirituality of mind. This earnestness of purpose is seen not only in being fixed on a definite object; but also in the consecration of time and person to that specific object. That is an eminent advantage. Our life is wasted with vague intentions and scattered labours; our consciences are cheated with good resolutions that we never find time to execute. By making the object definite, the mind is concentrated, clear, calm, and strong. By fixing the purpose, the character is rendered firm. By executing it, the conscience assumes its proper ascendency, and something definite is attained and accomplished. There is gain in another direction by this setting apart time to accomplish a definite object. Hindrances are removed. 4. It is consonant with peculiar degrees of repentance. Repentance includes a distinct contemplation of our personal sins. To that, such a season is very favourable. It includes sorrow for sin. Indeed, the natural effect of sorrow is to diminish the appetite for food. There is also in repentance a congeniality with fasting, because both express a kind of holy revenge against sin. 5. Fasting accords with a season set apart for peculiar efforts to attain to personal holiness. 6. Fasting agrees, too, with the peculiar exercise of love to Christ. He peculiarly desires that we remember His sufferings. "Do this in remembrance of Me." His fasting was a part of His suffering, and a part in which we can imitate and share with Him. 7. A peculiar fitness in making a fast to accompany our peculiar onsets on Satan's kingdom. The first thing we need, in waging the battles of the Lord, is to believe that there are any battles to fight; that Satan and his demons are realities. Then we need to know that they are too formidable for us; and yet that they are not invincible. This kind can be driven forth, but it must be "by fasting and prayer." We can become the organs of the Spirit of God by fasting and prayer. We must look to God in our attacks on Satan. And religious fasting is an acceptable service. He accepted it of Moses and Nehemiah, of Jesus and of the apostles. We see how the Church is to become efficient. (*E. N. Kirk.*)   *The devil throwing down :*—1. Satan endeavours thus to throw down by suggesting perplexing considerations regarding the supposed magnitude of the worldly sacrifices that must be made by the returning sinner. 2. The devil endeavours to throw down the sinner that is awakened and a-coming to Christ, by false representations of the life of godliness, as if, through imaginary moroseness and austerity, it were adverse to happiness. 3. The devil also endeavours at times to throw down the awakening sinner, by raising doubts in his mind, whether his sins are not too many and aggravated to leave him in hope of their being forgiven. (*J. Allan.*)   *Satan's rage :*—Satan hates the slightest approach to Jesus. An old writer says, that Satan, whenever he knows his time is short, exercises his power all the more fiercely; "like an outgoing tenant that cares not what mischief he does" before leaving the house. So with Satan here. Rather than give up the soul, he will tear it, throw it down, make it wallow and foam, insomuch that it is "rent sore," and "he was as one dead; insomuch that many said, He *is* dead." (*F. Whitfield, M.A.*)   *Inability through not believing :*—It is said that Admiral Dupont was explaining to Admiral Farragut the reasons why he failed to enter Charleston harbour with his fleet of ironclads. He gave this and that and the other reason. Farragut remained silent till he had ended, and then said, "Ah, Dupont! there is one reason more." "What is that?" "You did not believe you could do it." A Church not believing the world's conversion possible will fail to accomplish it. To win victories for Christ the heart must be hopeful. That which kept Livingstone undaunted, and bore him on through numberless perils, until he died kneeling, with his hands clasped in prayer, was the thought "Africa for Christ!" *Bring thy son hither :*—I. JESUS INVITES MEN TO BRING ALL THEIR TROUBLES AND BURDENS TO HIM. II. HE ENCOURAGES US TO BRING TO HIM NOT ONLY OUR OWN INFIRMITIES, BUT THOSE ALSO OF OUR DEAR ONES. III. HE SYMPATHIZES WITH US IN, AND IS ABLE TO SAVE US FROM, NOT SPIRITUAL TROUBLES ONLY, BUT THOSE ALSO WHICH ARE PHYSICAL AND TEMPORAL. (*Anon.*)

Ver. 44. **The Son of Man shall be delivered.**—*Repeated predictions :*—As the time of our Saviour's death was approaching, He thought proper to repeat the prophecy of it again and again. For this various reasons may be assigned. 1. It was necessary to show that the death of Christ was an appointed as well as an important event in the plan of Divine providence. 2. It tended to prove that it was voluntary on the part of Jesus, and not the debt of nature, as it is on the part of those who are merely human. 3. It was necessary for the fulfilment of ancient prophecy, and consequently to prove that Jesus was the predicted Messiah. 4. It was requisite to show that He was a prophet in the highest sense of the word, and that not a part, but the whole future dispensation was thoroughly known to Him. 5. The frequent repetition of the prophecy of His death tended also to prepare the minds of the disciples for what might otherwise have overwhelmed them. (*J. Thomson, D.D.*)

Vers. 46–48. **Which of them should be greatest.**—*The greatest in the kingdom of heaven :*—I. Who ARE NOT the greatest in the kingdom of heaven ? 1. The lofty in birth and the rich in possession have no claim, on such grounds, for this distinction. 2. Nor the loftiest in intellect. 3. Nor yet the man who—(1) works the most ; (2) suffers the most ; (3) gives the most—in the service of God. II. Who IS the greatest in the kingdom of heaven ? 1. The humble man. 2. He who is the most docile. 3. He who is most unworldly. 4. He who is most loving in spirit. 5. He who cherishes a forgiving spirit. (*T. W. Aveling.*) *Unhappiness of striving to be great :*— "Some time since," says Dr. Payson, in a letter to a young clergyman, "I took up a little work purporting to be the lives of sundry characters as related by themselves. Two of those characters agreed in remarking that they were never happy until they ceased striving to be great men." **A child.**—*How children are emblematic of conversion :*—Let us consider how little children furnish an apt emblem of conversion, or rather, of those who are being converted. 1. More particularly, and in reference to those qualifications in which the disciples now showed that they were very deficient, and yet of which we must all be possessed, if we are to be saved—little children are comparatively humble. Whatever seeds of evil may lurk in their minds, it is almost impossible that they should imagine themselves equal to those who are grown up. They are almost unavoidably sensible of their inferiority and dependence. And this is the state of mind towards God, to which we, as sinners, must be brought. Let us not think more highly of ourselves than we ought to think ; but let us think soberly. Let us not imagine that we are rich and increased in goods, and have need of nothing ; but let us feel and confess that we are wretched, and miserable, and poor, and blind, and naked. 2. Intimately connected with this disposition of humility is a disposition of teachableness ; and of this, too, children are, in a considerable degree, possessed. Aware that their parents and teachers surpass them in knowledge, they look to them that they may learn of them ; and they are at first very much disposed to believe and receive, without gainsaying and without doubt, whatever they tell them. In this, too, we mark an essential feature in the character of true converts in relation to God. 3. Once more, here, children are comparatively free from worldliness and ambition. This world does not yet obviously appear to be their idol. They do not form plans or labour for the riches and the honours of public life. They readily associate with their inferiors, and do not aim at surpassing competitors for exalted stations. (*J. Foote.*) *True greatness :*—Apparently this was the first occasion on which the spirit of rivalry manifested itself among the disciples of our Lord. Followed close upon a scene which might well raise their hopes of personal distinction. Three of their number had just been witnesses of the Transfiguration ; they had seen their

Divine Master in that dazzling vesture of glory which betokened His coming accession. And it is conceivable that the special favour conferred upon the three who were admitted to that wonderful vision set all thinking. Then, too, it has been suggested that our Lord's own promises to His disciples may have served to stir ambitious longings in their hearts. 1. Our Lord rebuked the first exhibition of the competitive spirit among His followers by taking a child and pointing to him as the true pattern of the essential grace of the gospel. The greatest is the humblest. 2. This ideal appeals to the best instincts of the human heart. (*Canon Duckworth.*) *Children and childhood :*—It is very good to me, in reading the Bible, to notice how much of the interest and hope of the world is made to depend upon the children that are unborn when the hope springs up. The hope of humanity rests in the children. When the Spartans replied to the king who demanded fifty of their children as hostages, "We would prefer to give you a hundred of our most distinguished men," it was only an expression of the ever-lasting value of the child to any commonwealth and to every age. The great hope is always in the new birth. This the deepest reason for the unspeakable loyalty and reverence for children that so constantly filled the heart and life of Christ. 1. If it be true, then, that the hope of the world lies in the cradle, in what relation do we, who are now responsible for this new life, stand to it? 2. If we are wise and faithful to our trust there is in each child the making of a man or a woman who shall be a blessing and be blessed. 3. What is it, then, to receive a child in the name of Christ? This question would need no answer had there not been so many mistakes made about this simple, natural, and beautiful truth. (1) Have faith in the Son of Man in the child. Guide and govern with best wisdom and love the life that is of the earth, earthy. (2) Guard and reverence the Son of God in the child— the life that is from above. (*R. Collyer.*)   *Christianity and childhood :*— Greek art gives us no children. Nay, it is equally true, though perhaps not so surprising, that up to the thirteenth century there were no Gothic children either. It was only when art was touched by Christianity, and when the Madonna and Child became the light of every honest heart and the joy of every pure soul, that pictures of children were possible. The tradition of the Beautiful Child lasted long. Then came a dark period in which children were ground to death by our millwheels, and the wealthy patrons of art could not conceive of the children of the poor except in vice and misery; and it is only now that you are beginning to restore the quiet earth to the steps of children. (*Ruskin.*)   *Unobtrusiveness of the truly great :*—Travellers tell us that the forests of South America are full of the gem-like humming-bird, yet you may sometimes ride for hours without seeing one. They are most difficult to see when perched among the branches, and almost indis-tinguishable flying among the flowering trees ; it is only every now and then that some accidental circumstance reveals the swarm of bejewelled creatures, and they flash upon the vision in white, red, green, blue, and purple. It is somewhat thus with society—the noblest, the most beautiful characters are not the obtrusive ones. Going through life carelessly, one might think all the people common enough; reading the newspapers, one might suppose the world to contain only bad men; but it may comfort us to remember the truly great and good shun observation and walk humbly with God. (*W. L. Watkinson.*)

Vers. 49, 50. **Forbid him not.**—*Casting out devils :*—This, one of the shortest of the recorded conversations of Jesus, contains but a single remark made in response to a single statement of the disciples. I. JESUS WAS HERE DEALING WITH THAT HARDEST CONDITION IN WHICH WRONG AND RIGHT ARE MIXED TOGETHER. There was good in the jealousy of the disciples for Jesus, even though it misled them. There was evil in the narrowness into which it led them. There were four people involved : 1. The man out of whom the devil was being cast. To him the interference of the disciples must have seemed a cruel thing. 2. The man who was casting out the evil spirit. We can understand his bewilderment. Shall I refrain from doing this thing which it is so evident that I have power to do? 3. The disciples. No doubt they were men who rejoiced to see any good work done in the world, and yet they bade this man to cease the work he was doing. 4. Behind all, Jesus Himself, looking upon the whole transaction, and declaring at once, without any hesitation, "Forbid him not." II. IS THIS A STORY OF THE CEN-TURIES AGO, OR IS IT NOT THE STORY OF WHAT IS ALWAYS TAKING PLACE? Wherever Christian men, in very virtue of their loyalty to Christ, incline to limit the opera-tions of His power in the world, there are these four. III. EVERYTHING THAT IS

GOING ON IN THE WORLD MUST BE PLACED EITHER UPON ONE SIDE OR THE OTHER SIDE. Everything that is making the world better is on the side of Christ. Everything that is degrading humanity is against Christ. How clear this principle is! How Jesus is always pointing us to the great test of results. IV. THIS TEST APPLIED— 1. To our personal lives. 2. To our fellowship with Churches around us. There is only one way in which we shall enter into such sympathy with Jesus that we can have His large spirit, and that is by catching that which was in His mind, His soul, the intense value He set upon the end. He rejoices so in the driving out of the devil that any one who would drive out the devil should have His commendation and His praise, His permission to do it, and His thanksgiving that it had been done. (*Phillips Brooks, D.D.*) *Need for toleration :*—" Seeing a tree grow somewhat irregular in a very neat orchard," says Mr. Flavel, " I told the owner it was a pity that that tree should stand there, and that if it were mine I would root it up, and thereby reduce the orchard to an exact uniformity. He replied, that he rather regarded the fruit than the form, and that this slight inconvenience was abundantly preponderated by a more considerable advantage. ' This tree, which you would root up, hath yielded me more fruit than many of those trees which have nothing else to recommend them but their regular situation.' I could not," adds Mr. Flavel, " but yield to the reason of this answer, and could wish it had been spoken so loud that all our conformity men had heard it, who would not stick to root up many hundreds of the best learners in the Lord's orchard because they stand not in exact order with other more conformable but less beneficial trees, who destroy the fruit to preserve the form." Such, alas, is the prejudice of our minds, that we are too prone to condemn those who do not view things exactly as we do. We lay down plans and rules for ourselves, and then blame others if they do not follow them. Too often also are we mistaken in our opinions of others, and imagine that they are only cumberers of the ground, when probably they bring forth the fruits of righteousness in greater abundance than ourselves. (*W. Buck.*)

Vers. 51–56. **He steadfastly set His face to go to Jerusalem.**—*Christ hastening to the cross :*—I. THE PERFECT CLEARNESS WITH WHICH ALL THROUGH CHRIST'S LIFE HE SAW THE INEVITABLE END. II. OUR LORD'S PERFECT WILLINGNESS FOR THE SACRIFICE WHICH HE SAW BEFORE HIM. III. THERE WAS IN CHRIST A NATURAL HUMAN SHRINKING FROM THE CROSS. That steadfast and resolved will held its own, overcoming the natural human reluctance. " He *set* His face." All along that consecrated road He walked, and each step represents a separate act of will, and each separate act of will represents a triumph over the reluctance of flesh and blood. We are far too much accustomed to think of our Saviour as presenting only the gentler graces of human nature. He presents those that belong to the stony side just as much. In Him is all power, manly energy, resolved consecration; everything that men call heroism. (*A. Maclaren, D.D.*) *Why did Christ go up to Jerusalem ?*—He went there to precipitate the collision and to make His crucifixion certain. He was under the ban of the Sanhedrim, but perfectly safe as long as He stopped down among the hills of Galilee. He was as unsafe when He went up to Jerusalem as John Huss when he went to the Council of Constance with the Emperor's safe-conduct in his belt ; or as a condemned heretic would have been in the old days if he had gone and stood in that little dingy square outside the palace of the Inquisition at Rome, and there, below the obelisk, preached his heresies. Christ had been condemned in the council of the nation; but there were plenty of hiding-places among the Galilean hills, and the frontier was close at hand, and it needed a long arm to reach from Jerusalem all the way across Samaria to the far north. Knowing that, He steadfastly set His face to go to Jerusalem, and, if I might use the expression, went straight into the lion's mouth. Why? Because He chose to die. (*Ibid.*) *The face toward Jerusalem :*—Every step of the Lord Jesus Christ left a footprint for His followers to study. This incident, too often overlooked as unimportant, has some suggestive lessons for the Christian. 1. It teaches that we should never shrink from a path of duty, however many may be the obstacles we encounter. 2. Such an uncompromising religion must not expect any help or hospitality from the world. Jesus found Himself on hostile soil as soon as He set foot in Samaria. 3. It was probably about the time of His repulse by the Samaritans that Jesus delivered those solemn injunctions to His followers about taking up their cross daily if they would be His disciples. He drew a sharp line, and made a clean issue. It is a religion of this fibre that the times demand. Such living brings happy dying. Dean Alford asked that it might be inscribed on his tombstone:

" This is the inn of a traveller on his way to Jerusalem." Let us determine so to live that, when Death calls our names on his roll, we may be found with our faces steadfastly set toward "Jerusalem the Golden." (*T. L. Cuyler, D.D.*) *Steadfastness in the path of duty* :—The Master's example teaches us to march unflinchingly forward in the path of duty, with our faces steadfastly set toward God. This is not an age of heroic Christianity. There is more pulp than pluck in the average Christian professor when self-denial is required. The men and women who not only rejoice in doing their duty for Christ, but even rejoice in overcoming uncomfortable obstacles in doing it, are quite too scarce. The piety that is most needed is a piety that will stand a pinch ; a piety that would rather eat an honest crust than fare sumptuously on fraud ; a piety that can work up stream against currents ; a piety that sets its face like a flint in the straight, narrow road of righteousness. (*Ibid.*) *Boldness of the decided man* :—The decisive man walks by the light of his own judgment : he has made up his mind ; and, having done so, henceforth action is before him. He cannot bear to sit amidst unrealized speculations : to him speculation is only valuable that it may be resolved into living and doing. There is no indifference, no delay. The spirit is in arms : all is in earnest. Thus Pompey, when hazarding his life on a tempestuous sea in order to be at Rome on an important occasion, said, " It is necessary for me to go : it is not necessary for me to live." Thus Cæsar, when he crossed the Rubicon, burned the ships upon the shore which brought his soldiers to land, that there might be no return. (*Paxton Hood.*) *The battle-face* :—Oliver Cromwell's men just before the battle used to look at their general, and whisper to each other, " See, he has on his battle-face." When they saw that set, iron face they felt that defeat was impossible. Determined striving towards one point is the best way of gaining that point. Try to walk in a straight line over a field of snow, keeping your eyes fixed on the ground as you walk. When you look back on the track, you find it far from straight. Walk over the field again, this time keeping your eye fixed on some definite point ahead. That will keep you in the straight line, and will save you from fruitless wandering on this side or that. Jesus, keeping the end of His work in view, set His face towards it. So should we do with our work. (*Sunday School Times.*) **Wilt Thou that we command fire ?**—*Our Lord and the Samaritans* :—The conduct of these Samaritans in refusing to receive Christ and His disciples, was, indeed, very sinful ; but the transport of rage into which that conduct threw His disciples, or at least some of His disciples, and the proposal which it provoked them to make, were most lamentable and most unchristian. That John, especially, whose usual temper was so gentle and so affectionate, should have been so forward in this affair, is very strange, and ought to be considered as an instructive warning of the necessity for the most charitable and meek to be constantly on their guard against the first risings of prejudice, passion, and false zeal, lest the fierce spirit obtain the mastery over them. They imagined that they were influenced by a purely religious spirit—by a hatred of sin, and a regard to the honour of Christ : whereas, they were really led to make such a proposal by the original prejudice which, as Jews, they indulged against the Samaritans, and, still more, by their now irritated pride, party feeling, blind zeal, personal resentment, violence, and passion. I. LET US ADMIRE, AND IN OUR SPHERE AND MEASURE IMITATE, THE NOBLE FIRMNESS DISPLAYED BY OUR LORD AND MASTER ON THIS OCCASION. II. LET US BEWARE OF RESEMBLING THESE SAMARITANS IN NOT RECEIVING THE LORD JESUS CHRIST. Though they were not immediately destroyed, yet their sin was great ; nay, the very circumstance of the merciful forbearance shown towards them, manifests, with peculiar clearness, the heaviness of the guilt they incurred by rejecting such goodness. III. Let us observe how plainly EVERY KIND AND EVERY DEGREE OF PERSECUTION ARE HERE FORBIDDEN. Fire from heaven might prove a doctrine to be true ; but fire kindled under any such pretence, by men, or any other species of persecution, could prove nothing but their own bigotry and cruelty. Indeed, such is the constitution of the human mind, that it is ready to call in question, or to suspect, even the truth itself, when any attempt is made to support it by such means. IV. In all we do, and especially in what we do under the name of religion, LET US CAREFULLY CONSIDER WHAT MANNER OF SPIRIT WE ARE OF. " The servant of the Lord must not strive, but be gentle unto all men." V. LET US BE VERY THANKFUL WHEN WE THINK OF THE GRACIOUS PURPOSE FOR WHICH THE SON OF GOD IS HERE SAID TO HAVE COME INTO THE WORLD. (*J. Foote, M.A.*) *A visit from Christ* :—We are not told the name of the village, and it is well the Scriptures are silent on the matter, for the name deserves to be buried in oblivion ; and all those who perpetrate such inhumanity should have an opportunity of blotting out such disgrace. Nor do we know who were the messengers whom Christ sent to make ready for Him. Perhaps they were disciples, or followers, or adherents—anyhow, they were doubtless in sympathy with Him. The Saviour, then, desires to become the Guest of men in this world. He is ever sending messengers before His face to prepare His way. Here, then, we have—I. PIONEERS—"He sent messengers before His face." Pioneers in every sphere are those who go in advance and prepare the way, or act as heralds and announce the coming of those who are to follow. His coming is anticipated by the many and varied mercies and blessings of life, even as the glory of day is heralded by the early dawn. The loving Saviour we may be sure is close to the bounties of Providence and the privileges of the gospel. Education, too, is always in advance of Him. He sends it forth on its beneficent mission to give men right ideas, and to awaken in them a sense of need and longing. Education, too, like the sappers and miners, goes forward to remove obstructions, to cut down wild, luxuriant growth, to make a way through the wilderness, and to bridge over the ugly, dangerous chasms. The mercy of grace, religious instruction, the service of the sanctuary, the preaching of the Word—these are like the predictions which went before the Saviour, like the stars of the morning, true harbingers of the coming day. Yes, Jesus Christ is near the Temple and the teaching there—near the institutions and ordinances of worship. He is not far from pain and sorrow, from affliction, bereavement, and death. Now all these pioneers have come to you, my friends ; have come to you with a mission in the interests of Christ, and for your eternal good. The question, therefore, arises: How have they been received? What has been the result of their visits? II. PREPARATION—"To make ready for Him." The pioneers in all time have gone before Christ to prepare His way, and the things of which I have spoken, and which come into our every life, are sent not only to herald the approach of the Saviour, but to help men to realize His nearness with their deep and present need of Him. When the light of the morning comes peeping in at the window, it tells the world that the sun has arisen and will soon flood the earth with brightness and glory. The dawn ever predicts the day, and prepares for it, and it ever seems to say to men, " Give it welcome ; up with the blinds ; open the windows, and let the light of the day come in." When the blade, the leaf, the blossom appear, they speak of the coming summer and harvest, and suggest that every barn and granary be got ready. And so when Christ sends His messengers in advance of Him, He desires that they should prepare for Him. There are three things which the pioneers of Christ seek to do—inform, awaken, and command, and all are intended to prepare for a full and hearty reception of Christ. They inform—tell men that Christ, that infinite goodness and love are in the events, in the experiences of life, and that Christ is coming near through them—is thus visiting to bless. They say, "He is coming," and the soul asks, "Who is He?" Zaccheus, hearing that Christ was to pass that way, had his curiosity aroused, and was thus moved towards the sycamore tree, that He might see Jesus, who He was. They command—coming from Christ and for Him, they declare His will, His requirements; they tell men to make ready for Him, and to give Him welcome and entertainment, to put away prejudice and indifference, to turn out all intruders, and to let the rightful owner of their spirits in; and that they would rightly regard these visitations, and the voices which speak —for they are in truth the voice of Christ—and their message may be summed up in one verse, " Behold I stand at the door and knock." III. PREJUDICE—"They did not receive Him." The Samaritans did not because of their antipathy to the Jews; they allowed prejudice to overcome discretion, and even reason itself; but they did not know Christ, or they would not have acted thus, nor were they conscious of what they lost by rejecting Him. IV. PASSING—"They went to another village." Jesus went from those who were unwilling, to others who were disposed to entertain Him, and this He is doing to-day. Anxious to enter every heart, He passes by the indifferent and obstinate. He does not force Himself upon man. (*John James.*) **Ye know not what manner of spirit ye are of.**—*Intolerance rebuked :—* 1. We may notice here, in the first place, the power and evil of prejudice. The Samaritans seem in general to have been very favourably disposed towards our Lord, as was seen on various occasions. Why, then, did they now refuse to receive Him ? It was because He was going up to Jerusalem to the Passover. They claimed that Mount Gerizim was the place where men ought to worship ; but our Lord was on His way to worship at the Temple, on Mount Zion, and thus showed that He favoured their old enemies the Jews, and declared His preference for their religion.

When Christ came from Judæa to Jacob's well they kindly received Him. If He would renounce the Jews, become a Samaritan prophet, and teach in their synagogues, they would have welcomed Him most cordially; but forasmuch as "He steadfastly set His face to go to Jerusalem," they would have nothing to do with Him. Thus they lost their last opportunity of hearing Jesus, for He was now on His way to be crucified. Nor were the disciples much better in the spirit they displayed than the Samaritans. 2. We may notice, secondly, the mischiefs of a wrong interpretation of Scripture. "Wilt Thou that we command fire to come down from heaven and consume them, as Elias did?" Now Elias' conduct was very different from theirs, and his example gave no sanction to their proposed vengeance. Upon a perversion of Scripture, the supreme divinity of Jesus has been denied, the atonement rejected, good works pronounced unnecessary, a future punishment discarded; yea, all the thousand forms of error, and all the monstrous sects of Christendom have been based upon just such a mistake as these disciples made, in pleading the seeming sanction of Elijah's example, for that which it did not warrant. 3. We have, in the third place, in our Lord's conduct on this occasion, a beautiful lesson of tolerance towards those who are in error. 4. We may also learn from our Lord's treatment of these Samaritans, how to estimate the comparative evil of error. 5. We have in the conclusion of this history, the glorious end of the Saviour's mission. "He came not to destroy men's lives, but to save them." His whole work was one of salvation. His miracles were those of healing. His teaching was for the saving of the soul. (*W. H. Lewis, D.D.*)

Our Lord's treatment of erroneous zeal:—I. NOTICE WHAT IS IMPLIED IN THE PROPOSAL OF THE TWO DISCIPLES. 1. This proposal discovers at least some acquaintance with the writings of the Old Testament, for it refers to an event which happened many centuries before, and which is remarkable in the history of Elijah. 2. It appears that the disciples had some distrust of their own judgment, and were willing to submit to Christ's direction. Their language is, Lord, wilt Thou that we should do this? They would do nothing rashly, nothing but what He approved; and in this they furnish an example worthy of imitation. 3. The language implies strong faith: "Wilt Thou that we command fire from heaven?" The disciples felt persuaded that if the Lord gave authority, the miracle would be performed. They had commanded unclean spirits out of persons, and were obeyed; and why might they not expect the same, if they called for fire from heaven? 4. They had a zeal for God, though not according to knowledge; it was sufficiently fervid, but not well directed. It was promised to the disciples that they should be baptized with the Holy Ghost and with fire; that they should be endowed with extraordinary gifts and extraordinary zeal, yet not for the purpose of destroying men's lives, but to save them. 5. Their zeal expressed great indignation against sin, and in this it was commendable. 6. It was a zeal which expressed great affection for their Lord and Master. To see Him slighted and insulted, shut out of doors, and denied the common necessities and civilities of life, was more than they could bear; they therefore wished to resent such churlish behaviour. 7. There was, however, too much asperity in their zeal, and a want of Christian meekness and charity. II. OBSERVE THE TREATMENT THEY MET WITH FROM THEIR LORD : "He turned and rebuked them, and said, Ye know not what manner of spirit ye are of." There is a mixture of mildness and severity in this reproof. He upbraids them with ignorance, and especially ignorance of themselves, and of the motives by which they were influenced. 1. They were unacquainted with the infirmities of their own spirit, the temper they derived from constitutional causes, and which had been insensibly confirmed by habit. 2. They were not aware of the principles and motives by which their present conduct was influenced. The springs of action ought at all times to be severely inspected, because if an action be materially good, it is not morally and intrinsically so, unless its principle be good also. A corrupt motive depraves and renders unacceptable to God the most laudable actions. Conclusion: 1. From the instance before us we see what a mixture of good and evil there may be in the same persons. 2. If Christ's immediate disciples, who had the advantage of such instructions and such an example, did not know what manner of spirit they were of, no wonder that so many misapprehensions and mistakes are found amongst us. Who can understand his errors? 3. We see that particular actings of the mind may be wrong, even where the general frame and temper of it is right. 4. Though the disciples did not well know the motives by which they were influenced, yet Christ did, for He searcheth the reins and the heart. He knoweth what is in man, and needeth not that any one should testify. All the Churches shall know this, and He will give to every man according to his works (Matt. **ix. 4**; Mark ii. 8; Rev. ii. 23). (*B. Beddome, M.A.*)   *The vindictive spirit rebuked:* — You can't make Eliases. You may do just the very thing Elias did, and so make the greater fools of yourselves. Elias is sent when the world needs him—son of thunder, son of consolation, each will be sent from heaven at the right time, and be furnished with the right credentials. But how delightful it is to set fire to somebody else! The dynamitard is a character in ancient history. Would it not be convenient for the Church always to have in its pocket just one little torpedo that it could throw in the way of somebody who differed in opinion from somebody else! The Lord Jesus will not have this; He said, "Ye know not what manner of spirit ye are of." The spirit of Christianity is a spirit of love, a spirit of sympathy, a spirit of felicity, a spirit that can weep over cities that have rejected the Son of Man. Then said He, or said the historian—the words might be His, for they are part of His very soul—"For the Son of Man is not come to destroy men's lives, but to save them" (ver. 56). Tell this everywhere. Go ye into all the world and say to every creature, "The Son of Man is not come to destroy men's lives, but to save them." The strongest man amongst us might devote his life to that sweet, high task. The brightest genius that ever revelled in poem or picture might devote all its energies to the revelation of that sacred truth. There are destroyers enough. Nature itself is often a vehement and unsparing destroyer. We are our own destroyers. There needs to be somewhere a saviour, a loving heart, a redeeming spirit, a yearning soul, a mother-father that will not let us die. (*J. Parker, D.D.*) *Ungodly nature of revenge:*—A young man who had great cause of complaint against another, told an old hermit that he was resolved to be avenged. The good old hermit did all that he could to dissuade him; but, seeing that it was impossible, and the young man persisted in seeking vengeance, he said to him, "At least, my young friend, let us pray together before you execute your design." Then he began to pray in this way: "It is no longer necessary, O God! that Thou shouldst defend this young man, and declare Thyself his protector, since he has taken upon himself the right of seeking his own revenge." The young man fell on his knees before the old hermit, and prayed for pardon for his wicked thought, and declared that he would no longer seek revenge of those who had injured him. *False zeal:*— "Ye know not what manner of spirit ye are of"; that is, ye own yourselves to be My disciples, but do you consider what spirit now acts and governs you? I. The OPPOSITION OF THIS SPIRIT TO THE TRUE SPIRIT AND DESIGN OF THE CHRISTIAN RELIGION. 1. This spirit which our Saviour here reproves in His disciples, is directly opposite to the main and fundamental precepts of the gospel, which command us to "love one another," and "to love all men," even our very enemies; and are so far from permitting us to persecute those who hate us, that they forbid us to hate those who persecute us. They require us to be "merciful, as our Father which is in heaven is merciful"; and to "follow peace with all men," and to "show all meekness to all men." 2. This spirit is likewise directly opposite to the great patterns and examples of our religion, our blessed Saviour and the primitive Christians. II. The UNJUSTIFIABLENESS OF THIS SPIRIT UPON ANY PRETENCE WHATSOEVER OF ZEAL FOR GOD AND RELIGION. (*Archbishop Tillotson.*)   *Religious repulsions:*—This little exquisite bit of human nature and Divine nature stands recorded in the Bible among a hundred other dramas, brief but significant. The Samaritans and the Jews were two very religious, very conscientious peoples. That they were religious was evident from the fact that they hated each other so thoroughly that they would have no dealings one with another. Of all hatred there is none like religious hatred. The Samaritan was a bastard Jew. When you come to look at the conduct of the Samaritans you naturally feel a good deal of surprise; for it is other people's inhospitality that surprises us, not our own. But when you turn round and look at the disciples what do you think of them? You have genuine Jewish orthodoxy against the orthodoxy of the Samaritans, and both of them were hatred. I do not wonder that the old Oriental nations sacrificed men to their gods, and that human offerings were burned on their altars. The whole religious world has been burning victims to their gods, their creeds, and their consciences ever since. Of the two here the Jews show to the least advantage. The Samaritans only wanted not to have anything to do with Jesus. The disciples on the other hand, wanted to burn up the Samaritans, to pulverise them to ashes. On the whole, I think the Samaritans were a little more religious than the Jews. What did the Saviour do? He quietly went to another village, but not until He had rebuked these disciples. And see how the rebuke was administered. Not as most

of us would have done it. "Ye know not what manner of spirit ye are of," &c.
(*H. W. Beecher.*)   *Misdirected enthusiasm :*—The next worst thing to being destitute of enthusiasm altogether is to expend it on the wrong objects. As the poet
says—

> " What is enthusiasm ?   What can it be
> But thought enkindled to a high degree,
> That may, whatever be its ruling turn,
> Right or not right, with equal ardour burn ?
> That which concerns us, therefore, is to see
> What species of enthusiasts we be."

Here was enthusiasm, and enthusiasm for Christ; but it was expending itself in
unchristian, and even anti-Christian channels. We are constantly meeting,
in our every-day experience, with instances of misdirected enthusiasm. The
important thing to do is to discover Christ's idea of Christianity, and to let
our enthusiasm go forth into the same channels in which His was wont to
flow. If this be our earnest and constant endeavour, then, although we may
sometimes make mistakes, although we may, like the Boanerges, incur the
rebuke, "Ye know not what spirit ye are of," it will be a gentle rebuke—one
of pity rather than of condemnation. (*Prof. Momerie, M.A., D.Sc.*)   *The story
of the Sons of Thunder :*—The Samaritans believed that their copy of the Law was
the only authentic one; that God had forsaken Zion and chosen Gerizim, and
placed His Name there; that it was in their country that the Messiah was destined
to appear, and not in Judæa. It was in connection with this latter article of their
belief that the conversation arose which is related in the text. It is the common
assumption that what the Samaritan villagers were guilty of was merely a breach
of hospitality. I believe there was something far worse. Jesus had been there
before, and they had treated Him hospitably then. It is said that before setting
out on this journey Jesus sent messengers before His face. It cannot be that these
were only couriers, to provide food and shelter. They were heralds, specially sent
to tell the Samaritans that the Messiah was coming. It was this that urged them
to refuse Him food and shelter. John and James, fresh from the Transfiguration
scene, and knowing that He was certainly the Son of God, were indignant at the
rejection of His claims, and wanted to call down fire upon the Samaritans. They
recalled a passage from Elijah's history, which seemed to them to furnish a precedent for their conduct. Christ in effect says to them : " Elijah acted according
to his lights; you must act up to yours." Christ did not censure the conduct of
Elijah, but He told them that they were forgetting the influence of the spirit of
Christianity: "I came not to destroy men's lives, but to save them." (*Canon
Luckock.*)   *The Spirit of Christ and of Elijah :*—Rénan tells us that in the
pictures of the Greek Church Elijah is usually represented as surrounded by the
decapitated heads of the Church's enemies. And Prescott tells us that in the
sixteenth century the brutal inquisitors of Spain tried to justify their fiendish
deeds by appealing to Elijah's act of calling down fire from heaven. They did not
understand, or would not, that that act of Elijah's was for ever condemned by One
who was at once Elijah's Master and Elijah's God. Elijah, and the old heroes,
doubtless, had not learnt to distinguish between the sinner and the sin. It was
reserved for after times—it required the teaching of the Son of God Himself to
teach men that. The spirit of Elijah was a spirit of justice, of righteous retribution, of terrible vengeance; the spirit of Christ was a spirit of tenderness, of
compassion, of love. But, because the religion of Christ is a religion of love, do
not fancy that it is therefore a religion of sentimentalism, fit only for weak women
and effeminate men. The spirit of Elijah is passed away, replaced by the spirit
of Christ, which is a spirit of meekness, but of justice too, and a spirit of hatred
against intolerable wrong. (*J. Vaughan, B.A.*)   *Peace and war—from a Christian
standpoint :*—I. THE SPIRIT OF WAR IS CONDEMNED BY THE GENIUS OF CHRISTIANITY.
1. It very often springs from vainglory. 2. Or revenge. 3. Or sordid ambition.
II. THE SPIRIT OF PEACE IS INCULCATED BY OUR RELIGION, AND IN PROPORTION AS
CHRISTIANITY PREVAILS WILL THAT SPIRIT OF PEACE BE DIFFUSED AMONG MANKIND.
1. It tends to the preservation of human life, and happiness, and property, and
social order. 2. It allows of the development of all good and great principles,
and the progress of mankind in virtue, morality, and piety. 3. Christianity must
be on the side of peace, because of its Divine Author and Exemplar. III. PRAC-
TICAL CONCLUSIONS. 1. Let us cherish the spirit of peace. The great thing is to

have the right temper. 2. Let us pray that our national councils may at all times be controlled and permeated by the spirit of peace. 3. We should labour for Christianity for this amongst other reasons, that it is only through Christianity, and the spread of it, that we shall ever attain to an era of universal peace. (*Dawson Burns, M.A.*) On persecution :—I. Persecution for conscience' sake— that is, inflicting penalties on men merely for their religious principles or worship— is plainly founded on an absurd supposition, that one man has a right to judge for another, in matters of religion. II. Persecution is also evidently inconsistent with that obvious and fundamental principle of morality, that we should do to others as we might reasonably desire they should do to us. III. Persecution is likewise in its own nature absurd, as it is by no means calculated to answer the ends which its patrons profess to intend by it. IV. Persecution evidently tends to produce a great deal of mischief and confusion in the world. V. The Christian religion, which we here suppose to be the cause of truth, must, humanly speaking, be not only obstructed but destroyed, should persecuting principles universally prevail. VI. Persecution is so far from being required or encouraged by the gospel, that it is directly contrary to many of its precepts and indeed to the whole genius of it. (*P. Doddridge, D.D.*) To save.—*Christ, the Saviour of human life :*—We may regard the text in the light of a prophecy. Whatever Christ announced as the purpose of His coming, was to be accomplished upon earth throughout successive ages. The Saviour of human life—this is the character which Christ here assumes to Himself, or of which He predicts, that it will be proved to belong to Him, as the religion He was about to establish makes way among men. Now there is nothing more interesting than the tracing the temporal effects which have followed the introduction of Christianity. We shall not now enter upon this wide field of inquiry ; but our text requires us to consider Christianity as beneficial under one special point of view—as making provision for the saving of human life. 1. It has done this by overthrowing the tenets and destructive rites of heathenism. 2. By contributing to the civilization of society, it has, in many ways, spread a shield over human life. 3. Add to this the mighty advances which have been made under the fostering sway of Christianity, in every department of science. 4. There is, however, a far higher sense, in which our Lord might affirm that He had come to save human life. You are to bear in mind that death, bodily death, had entered the world, as the direct and immediate consequence of Adam's transgression, and that the counteracting this consequence, was one chief object of the mission of our Redeemer. 5. Now we have treated our text as though the word "life" were to be literally taken, or interpreted with reference exclusively to the body ; but it is often very difficult to say whether the original word denotes what we mean by the immortal principle and spiritual part of man, which never dies, or merely the vital principle—that, through the suspension of which the body becomes lifeless. And if the words before us may be applied to the destruction and the salvation of the soul, as well as of life in the more ordinary sense, it is indispensable that we say something of them in this their less obvious meaning. "I live," said the great apostle, "yet not I, but Christ liveth in me" ; and life indeed it is, when a man is made "wise unto salvation"—when, having been brought to a consciousness of his state, as a rebel against God, he has committed his cause unto Christ, who "was delivered for our offences, and raised again for our justification." It is not "life"—it deserves not the name, merely to have power of moving to and fro on this earth, beholding the light and drinking in the air. It may be life to the brute, but not to man—man who is deathless, man who belongs to two worlds—the citizen of immensity, the heir of eternity. But it is "life," to spend the few years of earthly pilgrimage in the full hope and certain expectation of everlasting blessedness—to be able to regard sin as a forgiven thing, and death as an abolished—to anticipate the future with its glories, and the judgment with its terrors, and to know assuredly, that He who shall sit upon the throne, and "gather all nations before Him," reserves for us a place in those "many mansions" which He reared and opened through His great work of mediation. It is life to live for eternity ; it is life to live for God ; it is life to have fellowship with what the eye hath not seen, and the ear hath not heard. And this life Christ came to impart ; He came to give life to the soul. (*H. Melvill, B.D.*) Christ's mission :—I. The nature of Christ's mission. 1. To open up a new era under a dispensation of unbounded mercy. 2. This mission of our Lord's did not interfere with the course of nature, or natural law. It refers to our spiritual life. II. The duties which these words lead us to infer. 1. The first is that of not being satisfied with any other life than that which Christ came to give or to save. 2. Another duty is that of encouraging feelings of charity towards others. 3. That the object of our Saviour's mission has been fulfilled, is being fulfilled, and will be so hereafter, is indisputable. (*W. D. Horwood.*)   *The Son of Man the Saviour of life :*—Christ came into the world both as Destroyer and Saviour. He came to " destroy the works of the devil."   He came not to destroy the law, but to fulfil it. He came not to destroy men's lives, but to save them. The preservation of human life was characteristic of our Lord's public ministry. And Christianity in its very nature is a life-saving religion. Consider three or four of the great destructive agencies at work in the world, and the way in which Christianity opposes itself to them in principle, and practically proves itself victorious over them. I. WAR. The late Dr. Dick calculated, in 1847, that from the earliest period down to that year 14,000,000,000 of human beings had fallen in battle. Christianity condemns war and inculcates peace. II. SLAVERY. Here we have another great scourge of human life. Christianity sets its face against this monstrous iniquity. True that Christ and His apostles did not in a direct manner attempt to abolish it. Nevertheless, I affirm that Christianity is opposed to slavery, and will prove its death. Jesus Christ came to liberate the captive. III. HEATHEN IDOLATRY and its human sacrifices. IV. INTEMPERANCE. Sixty thousand deaths annually result from the use of intoxicating liquors. Christianity condemns intemperance. Sobriety is enjoined as a Christian virtue. (*W. Walters.*)   *Christ a Saviour :*—The design of Christ's coming into our world is here expressed—I. NEGATIVELY. Life is exposed to destruction. By sin it was forfeited. By law it is condemned. By justice it is demanded. By death it is claimed. II. POSITIVELY. The Son of Man is a Saviour. He came to reveal salvation. He came to procure salvation. He came to bestow salvation. He is coming to perfect salvation. III. THE ASSURANCE THE SINNER HAS OF CHRIST'S INTEREST IN HIS SALVATION. Of God's readiness to give salvation. Of the Spirit's power to apply salvation. Of the joy a personal salvation secures. " Now is the accepted time; now is the day of salvation." (*A. Macfarlane.*)

Vers. 57-62. **Lord, I will follow Thee.**—*Faring wholly with Christ :*—We have here, in connection, the story of three inquirers who came in turn to Christ. I. THE PROVIDENTIAL CONDITIONS OF THE NEW LIFE ARE ABSOLUTELY EXCLUSIVE (vers. 57, 58). The bold proffers of this scribe were met by the pathetic announcement of what their acceptance involved afterwards. 1. Our Lord's earthly career was hard and lonely. 2. Christ's followers were forewarned that they must fare entirely with Him (Matt. x. 24; John v. 18, 19). 3. Henceforth, therefore, believers were to consider themselves shut up to the lot they had accepted. We have a right to expect all solaces, defences, and sustenances in Christ; but we must rely upon Him for them. Honours and human praises, emoluments and ease, are excluded. II. THE SPIRITUAL RELATIONSHIPS OF THE NEW LIFE ARE ABSOLUTELY EXCLUSIVE (vers. 59, 60). We are told in Matthew's Gospel that this man was already instructed to some extent; he was one of Jesus' " disciples." The duty was accepted; only a mere human wish was interposed. 1. The Bible employs the tenderest names for its illustrations of relationship between believers and God. " Thy Maker is thy husband." 2. The purpose of this use of terms seems to be to show that all lower relationships are overridden by the higher. 3. Our Saviour Himself set the fine example of this surrender. More affectionate or devoted child there never lived; but He began to draw aside from all home entanglements as He reached the conscious nearness of His public work. III. THE PERSONAL EXPERIENCES OF THE NEW LIFE ARE ABSOLUTELY EXCLUSIVE (vers. 61, 62). We cannot help imagining there must have been some deft allusion here to Elisha's history in this reply of our Lord (1 Kings xix. 20). Elisha desired the same privilege, not as an excuse for delay, but only as a tender duty of respect to those who loved him at home. He was actually at the plough when he was called by the casting of Elijah's mantle upon his shoulders. 1. Gospel experience is generous. It supplies room for all; but those who reject the offer must be left behind. 2. Gospel experience is indivisible. Philosophically speaking, it is impossible for any man to love two things supremely: " No man can serve two masters; ye cannot serve God and Mammon." That old familiar call, My son, give Me thine heart," means the whole heart. " A double-minded man is unstable in all his ways" (1 Chron. xii. 33; Psa. xii. 2).   3. Gospel experience is uncompromising. All attempts to combine religion with worldliness are injurious (2 Kings v. 18). Naaman asks the privilege of going into the house of Rimmon with a show of devotion so as to keep his place at court,

4. Gospel experience is immortal. "The world passeth away, and the lust thereof; but he that doeth the will of God abideth for ever." This part of our nature is what projects itself forward beyond the confines of time. (*C. S. Robinson, D.D.*) *Following Jesus :*—I. FOLLOWING JESUS AS SEEN IN HIS CHARACTER FOR OBEDIENCE. 1. His obedience was prompt. 2. His obedience was characterized by inflexibility of purpose. 3. His obedience was characterized by perfect self-abnegation. II. FOLLOWING JESUS AS ILLUSTRATED IN THE SPIRIT HE MANIFESTED (vers. 52–56). III. FOLLOWING JESUS AS ILLUSTRATED IN WHAT HE REQUIRES OF HIS DISCIPLES. 1. He requires that spirit of holy heroism which will cheerfully endure all hardship and opposition for His sake. 2. He requires implicit and prompt obedience. 3. He insists upon the absolute supremacy of His will. (*D. C. Hughes, M.A.*) *He who looks back is unfit :*—Self-examination is wise and well when we try ourselves by tests divinely appointed, and not by ideals of moods and feelings which we conjure up ourselves. Scripture is fertile in tests for self-examination of the right sort. Three kinds of spurious disciples. See whether you are like either of them. I. THE DISCIPLE UNREADY FOR SELF-DENIAL. The merely impulsive follower must learn that to be ranged in the company of real disciples means glad share in the Lord's woe as well as weal. Do we follow our Lord out of such definite and principled yielding of ourselves to Him that we will go where He leads? II. THE DISCIPLE ENTANGLED. Christ can accept no second place. He must reign. His kingdom involves our entire and self-consecrating submission. Have we made obedience to Jesus the structural principle of our lives? III. THE DISCIPLE IRRESOLUTE. Not ready definitely and at once to set out on the Christian march : there are other things, farewells, &c., which must be first attended to. The emphasis is on that word "first." Perhaps, when these things which ought to be second have been first done, the man may follow. Plainly, he is doubtfully balancing. He is at cross-purposes, has not organized his life under one masterful principle. (*W. Hoyt, D.D.*) *Three applicants :*—We may dismiss the old conceit that sought to identify these three persons with three apostles, Judas, Thomas, Matthew. It is hardly credible that these apostles, already named as apostles in this Gospel, would be now introduced here as "a certain man," "another," "another." They would have been mentioned by name, surely, if they had been meant in person. "A certain scribe," "another of His disciples," "another"; this is all recorded of them in the Gospels—not enough to identify the individuals, but sufficient to accentuate the cases. One of them, the last of the three, seems to have been shaping for discipleship for some time, and was now making full proffer of it. These men differed apparently in their dispositions. The first seems bold and impulsive, as his loud avowal would show—"I will follow Thee whithersoever Thou goest." The second looks modest and thoughtful, as the piety he expresses toward his father would indicate—"Lord, I will follow Thee, but suffer me first to go and bury my father." The third appears cautious and calculating ; so we infer from his desire to smooth things first with his relations—"Lord, I will follow Thee ; but suffer me first to go bid them farewell that are at home at my house." Again: These persons differed, very evidently, in their gospel ideas. They all recognized the Messianic mission of Jesus, but diverged in their thought of its character and aim. The first regarded Him as the Christ certainly, but, like many more, imagined that it was a temporal kingdom, with temporal attendings, that He was aiming at, and that it would be well to be with Him in this aim of His, the direct way to the things of this life ; hence his gushing proffer, "I will follow Thee whithersoever Thou goest." The second also regarded Him as the Christ, but perceived His aim to be rather a reign of "spirit and truth" than of might, and, spiritualized as he was, and waiting with the few for "the consolation of Israel," he would assuredly follow this Son of David when his dying father should be buried and the way all clear ; hence also his sincere but delaying request, "Lord, I will follow Thee ; but suffer me first to go and bury my father." The third, like the others, regarded Jesus as the Messiah, and with the second perceived the spirituality of His aim, and felt drawn into sympathy with Him in His spiritual gospel, a follower in heart of His blessed Person. But the flesh shrank where the spirit was willing in him ; he would rather not break with his family if he could but go and settle matters with them so as to stand well in their eyes while yet he followed Jesus ; hence also his true but somewhat trimming proffer, "Lord, I will follow Thee ; but let me first go bid them farewell that are at home at my house." Farther : These men differed, as may be gathered from their sentiments, in the risks they ran of coming short in discipleship—the chief point in the narrative. The first was, without

doubt, on his way to serious disappointment; the second was, without perceiving it, asking for a dangerous delay ; and the third was, though not very conscious of it, attempting a compromise that would surely prove disastrous. (*J. Chalmers, M.A.*) *A would-be disciple repulsed :*—We are further informed by Matthew (viii. 19), that this man was a scribe, consequently a man of education, and of considerable respectability and social importance. 1. His avowal of attachment was unsolicited. To most men this would probably have increased the value of his decision. This spontaneous offer must be the dictate of a sincere and honest heart. But He who knows what is in man penetrated all the disguises and subtle reserves within, and discerned the real bias, the ulterior motives, and mean and mercenary views of this adventurer. There was no conscious need of the Saviour in him ; no previous work of the word of Christ upon his heart. The true disciples of Christ are attached to Him by obligations of everlasting gratitude: they have been recipients from Him of the greatest blessings God can bestow and man receive. But this man makes no profession of love. 2. Yet his profession was extensive—"Lord, I will follow Thee whithersoever Thou goest." He seems to anticipate some inconvenience, to be prepared for some self-denial, to look at the probability of danger, and to form some estimate of the cost involved. But then it was his own estimate, and altogether erroneous. It was well for him that he was not exposed to the fury of that boisterous night. That very first lesson would have shown that the scribe was ignorant of the principles of the doctrine of Christ. 3. Yet his plans were all laid ; he did not solicit any delay. He was ready to step into the boat, to go anywhere—as he thought, and to do anything, when the Saviour put before him the picture of His own abject condition—"Foxes have holes," &c. Disappointed and vexed that his overtures of service should not be immediately and respectfully accepted, chagrined that he should have stooped to one whose circumstances were so indigent, all the bright prospects that he had cherished in the mind's eye are dispelled, and he retires, teaching us that those who indulge carnal views of a Christian life have " neither part nor lot in the matter." What an opportunity he for ever lost of entertaining the King of kings ! " Not where to lay Thy head ! My house is Thine ; eat at my table ; sleep on my bed." And if the gracious Saviour had declined the invitation, He would have accepted the heart from which it came. In some direction or other this miserable scribe was related to the large family of By-ends, who think "to make a gain of godliness "; for it is certain that the Friend of Sinners never did, and never will, reject the approaches of one humble, genuine candidate for His favour. (*W. G. Lewis.*) *The faithful followers of Christ must expect troubles in this world :*—1. The time. In Matt. viii. 19, it is when Christ had a mind to retire, and had declared His purpose to go into the desert ; in Luke, when He steadfastly set His face to go to Jerusalem. Both may agree; the one more immediately, the other more remotely; first to the desert, then to Jerusalem. 2. Here is a resolution professed : " Lord, I will follow Thee whithersoever Thou goest." Where take notice—(1) Of the ready forwardness of the scribe. He was not called by Christ, but offered himself of his own accord. (2) Observe the largeness of the offer, and unboundedness of it, " whithersoever " ; as indeed it is our duty to follow Christ through thick and thin. 3. Christ's answer and reply : " And Jesus said unto him, Foxes have holes, and the birds of the air have nests ; but the Son of Man hath not where to lay His head." By the tenor of Christ's answer, you may know what ails him, and on what foot he limped ; for this is spoken either by way of preparation to enable him to keep his resolution, or rather by way of probation, to try the truth and strength of it ; whether it were sincere and sound ; yea or nay: as the young man was tried (Mark x. 21). So here, we hear no more of this scribe; our Lord knew how to discover hypocrites. Two things were defective in this resolution. (1) It was sudden and rash, not weighing the difficulties. They that rashly leap into a profession, usually fall back at the first trial. Therefore we must sit down and count the charges (Luke xiv. 28). (2) There was a carnal aim in it. He minded his own profit and honour ; therefore Christ in effect telleth him, " You had best consider what you do, for following of Me will be far from advancing any temporal interest of yours." " He did not discourage a willing follower, but discover a worldly hypocrite," saith Chrysologus. The doctrine we learn from hence is this :—They that will sincerely follow Christ, must not look for any great matters in the world, but rather prepare themselves to run all hazards with Him. This is evident—1. From Christ's own example ; and the same mind should be in all His followers : " They are not of the world, even as I am not of the world " (John xvii. 16). Our estranging of our hearts from the world is an evidence of our conformity to Christ. Christ passed through the world to sanctify it as a place of service; but His constant residence was not here, to fix it as a place of rest; and all that are Christ's are alike affected. We pass through as strangers, but are not at home as inhabitants or dwellers; and if we have little of the world's favour, it is enough if any degree of service for God. 2. From the nature of His kingdom. His kingdom is not of this world (John xviii. 3, 6). It is not a kingdom of pomp, but a kingdom of patience. Here we suffer with Christ, hereafter we reign with Him. The comforts are not earthly, or the good things of this world, but heavenly—the good things of the world to come. This was the scribe's mistake. 3. From the spirit of Christ. His spirit is given us to draw us off from this world to that which is to come (1 Cor. ii. 12). Use 1. Is information. (1) With what thoughts we should take up the stricter profession of Christianity—namely, with expectations of the cross. Christ will try us, and the world will hate us; therefore let us not flatter ourselves with an easy passage to heaven. (2) It informeth us what fools they are that take up religion upon a carnal design of ease and plenty, and will follow Christ to grow rich in the world. (3) It informs us what an unlikely design they have in hand who would bring the world and Christ fairly to agree, or reconcile their worldly advantages and the profession of the gospel. And when they cannot frame the world and their conveniences to the gospel, do fashion the gospel to the world, and the carnal courses of it. Use 2. Is instruction. When you come to enter into covenant with Christ, consider—(1) Christ knoweth what motives do induce you: " He needeth not that any should testify of man, for He knoweth what is in man " (John ii. 25). (2) If the heart be false in making the covenant, it will never hold good. An error in the first concoction will never be mended in the second (Deut. v. 29). (3) That Christ cannot but take it ill that we are so delicate and tender of our interests, and so impatient under the cross, when He endured so willingly such great things for our sakes. (4) If you be not dead to the things of the world, you are not acquainted with the virtue and power of Christ's cross, and have not a true sense of Christianity, cannot glory in it as the most excellent profession in the world (Gal. vi. 14). (5) We are gainers by Christ if we part with all the world for His sake (Mark x. 29, 30); therefore no loss should seem too great in obeying His will. Certainly a man cannot be a loser by God. (6) All worldly things were confiscated by the Fall, and we can have no spiritual right to them till we receive a new grant by Jesus Christ, who is the heir of all things (1 Cor. iii. 23). (*T. Manton, D.D.*) *The warning to an ill-calculating professor :*—This man was in his proffer animated by the hope of temporal good with Jesus. Far back in his mind was the thought of the restored kingdom of David under this his Messianic Son, and of a name and a place and no small honour therein by His side; and the glowing thought produces the loud but ill-calculating profession, "I will follow Thee whithersoever Thou goest." Could the Lord Jesus receive such mistaken profession as this? Would He allow this man to become His disciple from so spurious a motive, and under so erroneous an expectation? Did not the man need a word of warning to save him from the disappointment he was positively courting, and to set him right as to what he might reckon on in the kingdom he was seeking to enter? Yes, the man needed such a word, and gets it, plain and direct and strong: " Foxes have holes, and birds of the air have nests; but the Son of Man hath not where to lay His head." As if He would say, " You would follow because you expect worldly good with Me. You are mistaken; for worldly good I reject for Myself, and promise not to My followers. Poor and despised and rejected I am among men; and so will My followers be for long time to come. If you receive My Word and abide in it, then shall you be My disciple indeed; and you shall know the Truth and the Truth shall make you free. But, as to other things, count the cost; reproach will be your lot with Me rather than honour; poverty will be your burden with Me instead of wealth; you must suffer with Me if you would reign with Me." In this way did the Lord Jesus strip this man of his worldly notion in seeking to follow Him and throw him back from all worldly consideration on to spiritual conviction if he would be His disciple. And in similar way does He ever seek to check in seekers all worldly motive for following Him—and many there are in every age who need such checking as to their profession of the name of Christ. One man thinks it will advance his worldly prospect if he become a Christian; another thinks it will gain him reputation and a character in life; another thinks it will open to him a wider sphere of acquaintances and friends; and so, without any particular conviction as to their need of Christ as their Saviour, they join themselves to His people and call themselves by His name. But it is unworthy motive this in every form of it. It is the desire of the multitude of whom He said, "Ye seek Me because ye did eat of the loaves," and He declines now as He declined then to be followed on any such terms. He will have you follow Him for Himself, because of His grace, and not for any worldly advantage, if you are to be with Him in the gospel; and He sends you back into your hearts with the summary check, "The Son of Man hath not where to lay His head," to see if you will take your lot with Him without reserve. He leaves you no choice, friend, but unreserved surrender if you would be His. (*J. Chalmers, M.A.*) *The election of Christ:*—There are words here that seem harsh. Stern they may be; harsh they cannot be. I. THEY ARE DISCRIMINATING, which harsh words never are. No one was more regardful of individual differences than Christ. II. THEY ARE DISCRIMINATING, SO FAR AS WE CAN SEE, IN THIS WAY: The second case stands on a different footing from the first and third. In two respects. 1. The reply in the second case is more stern and uncompromising; because—2. There was in this case a distinct call. The first and third were volunteers. III. IT IS NOT TO BE SUPPOSED THAT THOSE REJECTED THUS, IF REJECTED, WERE EXCLUDED. All are not chosen for such lonely work. He only gave some to be apostles. There are diversities of gifts. The many are called; the few are chosen. Man is called; men are chosen. Thank God, we all find our level sooner or later. (*P. T. Forsyth, M.A.*) *The true interpretation of religion:*—I. From this passage we may naturally consider THE GREAT NUMBER WHO REGARD RELIGION AS SIMPLY A POETIC EMBELLISHMENT, AN ÆSTHETIC SPECIES OF ETHICS, AN ACCOMPLISHMENT. The New Testament idea of religion is no such thing as this. That idea is that religion is life itself. No man ever got religion; if he ever had any, he lived it. To follow Christ is not a mere polish of things that are substantial, valuable, and needful in this life: it is the reconstruction of the whole man upon a higher pattern. II. THE IDEA IS CURRENT THAT RELIGION IS A LIMITATION AND RESTRICTION INSTEAD OF AN ENJOYMENT AND AN EXALTATION, that it is, therefore, to be put off as long as it is safe to put it off. You can begin to be a Christian instantly. But you cannot accomplish it instantly. The work is progressive; it is life-long; but when once entered upon heartily it is the sweetest, the noblest, and the best work with which life can concern itself. III. From the passages read we may LEARN THE WAY IN WHICH MEN ARE ACCUSTOMED, WHEN FROM VARIOUS CONSIDERATIONS THEY ARE MOVED TO A CONSIDERATION OF HIGHER THINGS, TO TREAT THEIR ASPIRATIONS AND THEIR LUMINOUS HOURS. The two or three instances which are grouped together here, represent men that either are moved to follow, or are called to follow, the Christ-life; and the invitation is, in the second case, the same as if it had been an impulse proceeding from the party himself. You will observe, then, from the whole attitude of Christ, and from what we know of His nature, that He saw through the hollow pretences of these men. One wanted to follow Him with the expectation of loaves and fishes, and honours, and prerogatives. Another wanted to follow Him; but he wanted first to go home and bury his father. The inspiration was not strong enough to constitute a spring of action and of life. The guise of filial piety. Christ's reply—spiritualizing it—was, "Let men that do not care for the kingdom of God perform the rites of sepulture; as for you, follow Me." And then, in the other case in which the man was willing to follow Christ, he wanted to go back and say "good-bye" to his father and mother, and brothers and sisters, before he went. This was almost frivolous; for the following of Christ could not be a separation from all that was dearest to him in this life. As it was then, so it is now. Mostly these alleged reasons of doubt, of occupation, of pleasure, and of bias are simple excuses. Men do not wish to enlarge their lives. They are content with smallness. Sin has beggared them. They not only are living upon penurious doles on the lower plane of life, but they are content to live so. I say to every one that has been wandering, and is wandering, and yet at times is haunted with longings, "Seek first the kingdom of God and His righteousness, and all other things shall be added unto you": but seek that first; seek it in earnest; seek it at once; seek it with all your heart; make it your life; and then life will be a thousandfold greater, fuller, and richer to you. (*H. W. Beecher.*) *Testing sincerity:*—After the siege of Rome, in 1849, Garibaldi issued to his followers this appeal: "Soldiers, your efforts against overwhelming odds have been unavailing; I have nothing to offer you but hunger, thirst, hardship, and death; let all who love their country follow me." And hundreds of Italian youths did follow him, because they loved him and because they loved their country; and, therefore, they could endure trial with greater joy than any selfish pleasures could bestow. (*Archdeacon Farrar.*)   The poverty of Christ :—Richard Fitzralph, Archbishop of Armagh, became celebrated as an opponent of the shameless mendicant orders in the fourteenth century. During one of his visits to London he found the ecclesiastics warmly discussing the subject of the poverty of Jesus; and being asked to preach on the subject, he taught as follows:—"Jesus Christ, during His sojourn upon earth, was always a poor man; but He never practised begging as His own spontaneous choice. He never taught any one to beg. On the contrary, Jesus taught that no man should practise voluntary begging." (*Reformation Anecdotes.*)   Enduring hardship :—When Felix Neff undertook the pastorate of the High Alps, a neat cottage was built for him at La Chalpe, one of the few pleasant spots in his vast parish. But his anxiety to reach all his scattered people was such, that two or three days in each month was all that he spent there. With a staff in his hand and a wallet on his back, he travelled from this starting-point twelve miles westward, sixty eastward, twenty southward, and thirty northward. While strength lasted, he did not allow himself a single day of repose, and never slept three successive nights in the same bed.

Vers. 59, 60. **Let the dead bury their dead.**—*Christ's invitation put off :*—We have now before us one of those who excuse themselves from immediate compliance with the Saviour's demands—"Lord, suffer me first to go and bury my father." Perhaps you have been sometimes disposed to pity this man, and to think it rather a hard case that such an act of charity and necessity should be denied. Never fear, my brethren, for the character of Christ. It was an Eastern proverb, "When I have buried my father I will do so-and-so." Mark that the man does not say his father was already dead. Had that been the case, he must, at this very time, have been engaged in the funeral preparations instead of joining the crowd in the Saviour's presence. The interment of the dead was required to take place before the sunset of the day on which they expired. He had an aged sire who could not live long, and when he was gone, and the property divided —in other words, at his own leisure—he would be a Christian. He is a type of the large class who want heaven in their own time and on their own terms. (*W. G. Lewis.*)   *Following Christ the great business of life :*—I. THAT THE ATTAINMENT AND PRACTICE OF TRUE RELIGION IS THE MOST IMPORTANT BUSINESS IN WHICH WE CAN BE ENGAGED. It is so, because it is the necessary preparation for a happy immortality. We have commenced a course of being that shall never end. Our faculties, now in their infancy, and but just budding, shall exist and expand for ever and ever. If so, then man's great concern should be to secure a blissful immortality. II. THAT TO THIS GREAT BUSINESS OF RELIGION ALL OTHER CONSIDERATIONS SHOULD BE MADE TO GIVE WAY. This second proposition is the necessary sequence of the first. If religion is the most important business, then everything else should yield to it. You conduct your temporal business on this principle. You endeavour to ascertain the relative importance of each department, and you make the lesser bend to the greater. (*J. H. Beech.*)   *No excuse against a speedy obeying Christ's call :*—The reasons of Christ's refusal. Christ would show hereby—1. That all human offices and duties must give place to the duty we owe to God. Duty to parents must be observed, but duty to God must be preferred before that or anything whatsoever. 2. He would teach us hereby that the ministry requires the whole man, even sometimes the omission of necessary works, much more superfluous : "Give thyself wholly to these things" (1 Tim. iv. 15). The words are now explained; the practical notes are these two—First, that nothing in the world is a matter of such great weight as to be a sufficient excuse for not following of Christ. Secondly, that those who are called to follow Christ should follow Him speedily, without interposing any delays. For the first point, that nothing in the world is a matter of such great weight as to be a sufficient excuse for not following of Christ, I will illustrate it by these considerations. 1. There are two sorts of men. Some understand not their Lord's will, others have no mind to do it (Luke xii. 47, 48). Some understand not the terms of the gospel; they think to have Christ and the pleasures of the flesh and the world too. 2. They that have no mind to follow Christ put off the matter with dilatory shifts and excuses. To refuse altogether is more heinous, and therefore they shift it off for a time. *Non vacat* is the pretence—I am not at leisure. *Non placet*, I like it not; is the real interpretation, disposition, and inclination of their hearts, for excuses are always a sign of an unwilling and backward heart. When they should serve God there is still something in the way, some danger, or some difficulty which they are loth to encounter with. Secondly, that those who are called to follow Christ should follow Him speedily, without interposing any delays. Consider—1. Ready obedience is a good evidence of a sound impression of grace left upon our hearts. When our call is clear, there needeth no debate or demurring upon the matter. 2. The work goeth on the more kindly when we speedily obey the sanctifying motions of the Spirit, and the present influence and impulsion of His grace. To adjourn and put it off, as Felix did (Acts xxiv. 25), doth damp and cool the work—you quench this holy fire; or to stand hucking with God, as Pharaoh did, the work dieth on your hand. 3. There is hazard in delaying and putting off such a business of concernment as conversion to God. We know not the day of our death, therefore we should get God to bless us ere we die. A new call is uncertain (2 Cor. vi. 1, 2). It may be He will treat with us no more in such a warm and affectionate manner. It is a hazard or uncertain if the Spirit of God will put another thought of turning into your hearts, when former grace is despised (Isa. lv. 6). 4. Consider the mischiefs of delaying. Every day we contract a greater indisposition of embracing God's call. We complain now it is hard; if it be hard to-day, it will be harder to-morrow, when God is more provoked, and sin more strengthened (Jer. xiii. 23). (*T. Manton, D.D.*) *Christ stimulating sluggish discipleship :*—This man is one of the people that always see something else to be done first when any plain duty comes before them. Sluggish, hesitating, keenly conscious of other possibilities and demands, he needs precisely the opposite treatment from his light-hearted and light-purposed brother. Some plants want putting into a cold house to be checked; some into a greenhouse to be forwarded. The diversity of treatment, even when it amounts to opposition of treatment, comes from the same single purpose. And so here the spur is applied, whilst in the former incident it was the rein that was needed. I. Note, then, first of all, THIS APPARENTLY MOST LAUDABLE AND REASONABLE REQUEST. "Lord, suffer me first to go and bury my father." Nature says "Yes," and religion enjoins it, and everything seems to say that it is the right thing for a man to do. The man was perfectly sincere in his petition, and perfectly sincere in the implied promise that, as soon as the funeral was over, he would come back. He meant it, out and out. If he had not, he would have got different treatment, and if he had not, he would have ceased to be the valuable example and lesson that he is to us. So we have here a disciple quite sincere, who believes himself to have already obeyed in spirit, and only to be hindered from obeying in outward act by an imperative duty that even a barbarian would know to be imperative. And yet Jesus Christ read him better than he read himself; and by His answer lets us see that that tone of mind into which we are all tempted to drop, and which is the characteristic natural tendency of some of us, of being hindered from doing the plain thing that lies before us, because something else crops up, which we also think is imperative upon us, is full of danger, and may be the cover of a great deal of self-deception; and, at any rate, is not in consonance with Christ's supreme and pressing and immediate claims. The tempter which says "Suffer me first to go and bury my father" is full of danger, never knows but that, after he has got his father buried, there will be something else turning up equally important. There was the will to be read afterwards, you know, and if he was, as probably he was, the eldest son, he would be executor most likely, and there would be all sorts of things to settle up before he might feel that it was his duty to leave everything and follow the Master. And so it always is: "Suffer me *first*," and when we get to the top of that hill, there is another one beyond. And so we go on from step to step, getting ready to do the duties that we know are most imperative upon us, and sweeping preliminaries out of the way; and so we go on until our dying day, when somebody else buries *us*. Like some backwoodsman in the American forests who should say to himself, "Now I will not sow a grain of wheat until I have cleared all the land that belongs to me. I will do that first, and then begin to reap." He would be a great deal wiser if he cleared and sowed a little bit first and lived upon it, and then cleared a little bit more. Mark the plain lesson that comes out of this incident, that the habit, for it is a habit with some of us, of putting other pressing duties forward, before we attend to the highest claims of Christ, is full of danger, because there will be no end to them if we once admit the principle. And this is true not only in regard of Christianity, but in regard of everything that is worth doing in this world. II. Now LOOK AT THE APPARENTLY HARSH AND UNREASONABLE REFUSAL OF THIS REASONABLE REQUEST. It is extremely unlike Jesus Christ in substance and in tone. It is unlike Him to put any barrier in the way of a son's yielding to the impulses of his heart and attending to the last duties to his father. It is extremely unlike Him to couch His refusal in words that sound, at first hearing, so harsh and contemptuous, and that seem to say, "Let the dead world go as it will; never you mind it, do you not go after it at all or care about it." But if we remember that it is Jesus Christ who came to bring life into the dead world that says this, then, I think, we shall understand better what He means. I do not need to explain, I suppose, that the one "dead" here is the physical and natural "dead," and that the other is the morally and religiously "dead"; and that what Christ says, in the picturesque way that He so often affected in order to bring great truths home in concrete form to sluggish understandings, is in effect: "Ay! For the men in the world that are separated from God, and so are dead, in their self-hood and their sin, burying other dead people is appropriate work for them. But your business, as living by Me, is to carry life, and let the burying alone, to be done by the dead people that can do nothing else." Now, the spirit of our Lord's answer may be put thus: It must always be Christ first, and everybody else second; and it must therefore sometimes be Christ *only*, and nobody else. "Let me bury my father, and then I will come." "No," says Christ, "first your duty to Me"; first in order of time, because first in order of importance. And this is His habitual tone, "He that loveth father or mother more than Me is not worthy of Me." Did you ever think of what a strange claim that is for a *man* to make upon others? This Jesus Christ comes to you and me, and to the whole race, and says, "I demand, and I have a right to demand, thy supreme affection and thy first obedience. All other relations are subordinate to thy relation to Me. All other persons ought to be less dear to thee than I am. No other duty can be so imperative as the duty of following Me." What business has He to say that to us? On what does such a tremendous claim rest? Who is it that fronts humanity, and says: "He that loveth father or mother more than Me is not worthy of Me?" He has a right to say it, because He is more than they, and has done more than they all, because He is the Son of God manifest in the flesh, and because on the cross He has died for all men. Therefore all other claims dwindle and sink into nothingness before Him. Therefore, His will is supreme, and my relation to Him is the dominant fact in my whole moral and religious character. And He must be first, whoever comes second, and between the first and the second there is a great gulf fixed. Remember that this postponing of all other duties, relationships, and claims to Christ's claims and relationships, and to our duties to Him, lifts them up, and does not lower them, ennobles and does not degrade, the earthly affections. (*A. Maclaren, D.D.*) *Let the dead bury their dead:*—The meaning of this passage may perhaps be this: "If necessary, leave the dead unburied, but at all events obey My call to go and proclaim the kingdom of God." The Christian should be willing and prepared to leave his dearest dead unburied, or to slight any other tender natural affection, the indulgence of which would be in conflict with a plain command or call of God; not that such a conflict commonly exists, or may be brought about at pleasure, which, so far from being pleasing in the sight of God, is really the sin committed by the hypocrites who said "Corban," when they ought to have supplied the wants of their dependent parents. 1. There is still a special call of Christ to individuals, not only to believe in Him, but to preach His kingdom. Without attempting to define this call at present, I may observe that it is neither miraculous on one hand, nor a matter of business calculation on the other, but a complete judgment or conclusion to which various elements contribute, such as intellectual and physical capacity, without which a call is inconceivable—providential facilities and opportunities, opening the way to this employment more than to all others—the judgment and desire of others, and especially of those best qualified by character and situation to sit in judgment on the case. I might add a desire for the work, which, in a certain sense, is certainly included in a call, but which is apt to be confounded with a mere liking for the outward part of the profession—for example, with that mania for preaching which is sometimes found in grossly wicked men, and has been known to follow them, not only to their haunts of vice, but to the prison and the madhouse. There is also a desire which results from early habit and association, the known wish of parents, pastors, and other friends, or the fixed inveterate habit of regarding this as a man's chosen calling, even when every evidence of piety is wanting. The desire which can be referred to any of these causes is entirely distinct from that which God produces in the heart of His true servants, as a part of their vocation to the ministry. 2. This vocation, where it really exists, is paramount to every personal and selfish plan, to every natural affection, even the most tender, which conflicts with it. 3. This conflict is not usually unavoidable, though often so regarded by fanatics. The first duty of the Christian is not to desire or create, but to avoid it ; but if unavoidable, his next is to obey God rather than man. 4. Our Saviour did not deal indiscriminately with all cases of desire to enter His immediate service. The remark is at least as old as Calvin, that in this case He repelled the man who wanted to go with Him everywhere, and urged the man to follow Him at once who wanted to go home for what appeared to be most necessary purposes. So far as His example is a guide to us in these things, we are bound, not only to persuade, but to discourage, as the case may be. 5. There is no more danger of excluding those whom God has called by faithful presentation of the whole truth, than t ere is of preventing the conversion of His chosen ones by showing them the true tests of faith and repentance. The man who can be finally driven back in this way ought to be so driven. He whom God has called will only be confirmed in his desire and resolution by such warnings against self-deception, though he may pass through the discipline of painful doubt and hesitation for a season. (*J. A. Alexander, D.D.*) *Religious impressions not to be checked :*—I. The importance of a prompt and resolute devotedness of mind to the great concern of religion. This is, in other words, to follow Christ ; and it includes three things. 1. The candid reception of His revelation. 2. To follow Christ involves a surrender of ourselves to Him as our Saviour and Governor. There must be transactions of a personal nature between every such individual and Christ. First, he must seek to Him, and to God by Him, for reconciliation. Next, he must pay attention to the institutions of Christ. They must have his punctual and cordial regard. Moreover, every such person must be careful to comply with the moral precepts of the New Testament, as well as its more spiritual injunctions. 3. To follow Christ imports also ardent solicitude for the prevalence of His religion. II. The egregious folly of stifling impressions in favour of such devotedness, by worldly considerations. Our Lord's language implies this : "Follow Me; and let the dead bury their dead." Leave the cares of the world to those who have no such call of God upon their hearts, but by no means postpone compliance with it for their sake. It is peculiarly sinful, then, to stifle religious impressions by the influence of worldly considerations. Yet—1. Some are prevented from an immediate compliance with their convictions by the notion that there is a happiness to be found in the world, which they, in that case, would be required to abandon. An entire mistake. Religion imposes no gloomy austerities, no unnecessary self-inflictions. 2. Some are prevented from going the full length of their religious convictions by the remonstrances of worldly relatives and friends. 3. The prompt devotedness of other minds is prevented by some particular worldly object of pursuit upon which they are at that moment intent, and which promises, by its attainment, soon to leave them at liberty. But this is the artifice of Satan. It quiets the present alarm ; it hinders the heart, at this time, from closing with the call of God. (*J. Leifchild.*) *Action and grief : a meditation for a church-yard :*—And are not these strange words for one so loving as our Lord? How mighty was the attractive force of our Lord's character ! When He spake, they were compelled to leave all, and to follow Him. I. "Lord, suffer me *first.*" Ah ; that is the cry of nature. "I will come to Thee, but suffer me *first.*" "*First* suffer me to be disappointed, and *then* I will follow *Thee ;* first, build my house upon the sand, and *then* I will come, O Rock, to *Thee.* First, worship and waste my affections on the clay, and *then* I will come to *Thee.*" "Suffer me *first* "; but Jesus answered, "Follow *thou* Me." 1. Follow Me. I am Life, and you seek life, but then you have only death ; as long as you linger there, you do but seek the living among the dead. 2. Follow Me. You seek love, and here nothing loves you ; that which loved you has gone, and, if you would regain what loved you, you must follow Me. 3. Follow Me. I am not only Life—I am the only Master of the kingdom of life. I am the Way to the life. In following Me, you do not leave behind you merely dead affections ; you rise to the true kingdom of the affections. Action, action, action. Life is in action, in following more than in musing. The music of the harp is beautiful, but that has not served the world so well as the music of the hammer ; and even all poetry is action—all true poetry is. (*E. Paxton Hood.*) *Meaning of the prohibition :*—We are not to suppose, by this prohibition, that Christ disallows or disapproves of any civil office from one person to another, much less of a child to a parent, either living or dying; but He lets us know—1. That no office of love and service to man must be preferred before our duty to God, to whom we owe our first and chief obedience. 2. That lawful and decent offices become sinful when they hinder greater duties. 3. That such as are called by Christ to preach the gospel, must mind that alone, and leave inferior duties to inferior persons. (*W. Burkitt.*) *Preach thou the kingdom:*—There are many of you who are busily engaged in legitimate occupations, and devoting yourselves in various degrees to various forms of good, touching the secular condition of the people around us. May I hint to you, "Let the dead bury their dead; preach thou the gospel"? A Christian man's first business is to witness for Jesus Christ. And no amount of diligence in legitimate occupations or for the good of others will absolve him from the charge of having turned duties upside down if he says, "I cannot witness for Jesus Christ. I am so busy about these other things." This command has a special application to us ministers. There are hosts of admirable things that we are tempted to engage in now-a-days, with the enlarged opportunities that we have of influencing men, socially, politically, intellectually, and it wants rigid concentration for us to keep out of the paths which might hinder our usefulness, or, at all events, dissipate our strength. Let *us* hear that voice ringing always in *our* ears : "preach thou the gospel of the kingdom." (*A. Maclaren, D.D.*) *Our just obligation :*—These words seem at first harsh and severe. Our Lord's teaching gives no sanction, however, to the monstrous error that the new life releases men from obligations which they may have found irksome. The common relations of life are a discipline whereby we are trained to spiritual perfection. What did our Lord say, and under what circumstances? 1. The man probably heard of his father's death when he was with Christ, and wanted to return to the funeral. But the father was dead, and the son could do nothing for him now. If he had neglected him in life, he could not now repair the neglect. 2. Still you say natural affection impels a man to discharge the last offices of love. Yes ; but there are reasons which justify a man in being absent from his father's funeral. This was a very solemn and critical time. The man appears to have been selected as one of the seventy ; and if he had gone home, he would have been detained some days by the ceremonial law ; his purpose might have been weakened ; so even in the hour of his grief he is commanded to do this great service. 3. "Let the dead bury their dead." Does this show contempt for the unspiritual? No ; our Lord never spoke with contemptuous indifference of such; it was his very eagerness that they should rise to a new and better life that led Him to call this man away. 4. The whole narrative suggests that critical moments in a man's life bring critical duties. If God is near us now in a very special and solemn manner, then that principle enters our life and regulates our duty. (*R. W. Dale, LL.D.*) *Following Christ:*—I. WHAT IS INCLUDED IN FOLLOWING CHRIST? 1. By following Christ the disciple is brought into a new relation. 2. At all times the religious relation is more important than the natural one. (1) It is formed by the will and choice of the individual himself. (2) It is wider in its sympathies. (3) It is a relation which will never fail. II. THE DISCIPLE OF CHRIST HAS NEW RESPONSIBILITIES. 1. He has to learn of Him. 2. He has to suffer with Him. 3. He has to move on towards Him. III. THE DISCIPLE IS BROUGHT TO POSSESS NEW PRIVILEGES. 1. He has the most powerful incentive to work in this world. He has the most glorious hope with regard to the world to come. (*H. C. Williams.*) *Living preaching :*—When the Master gave the command, "Go thou and preach," He meant "Go thou and shine ; go thou and bear much fruit; go thou and do good ; go thou and teach the poor ; go thou and save the drunkard; go thou and heal the sick ; go thou and witness for Me ; go thou and live out this beautiful and sublime religion of the Cross." 1. A life of obedience to Christ is the most effective way of glorifying our Saviour. It has been well styled "the strongest manifestation of God to the world." 2. There is no other preaching of the Word that makes so many converts to the truth. 3. Every man is a preacher, and every life a sermon. What sort of a discourse are you making, you, and you, and you? (*T. L. Cuyler, D.D.*) *Ways of preaching Jesus:*—There are a great many ways of preaching Jesus without standing in a pulpit. Wilberforce proclaimed the gospel of love on the floor of the British Parliament, though he never wore a surplice, and never had the ordained hand of a bishop on his honoured head. George Stewart was an apostle of the Cross when he organized a Christian mission for our soldiers' camps during the civil war in America. John Macgregor was another when he gathered the shoeblack brigade in the streets of London. Hannah More preached Jesus in English drawing-rooms, and Elizabeth Fry in Newgate prison walls, and Sarah Filey amongst the negro freedmen of our Southern plantations. Sometimes God gives a single precept to a man to carry out, as when the Roman Catholic Father Matthew wrought grandly and gloriously for the reformation of Irish drunkards, and William Lothian for the recovery of poor lost women from the streets of Glasgow. Our Lord scatters His commissions with a munificent liberality. The "Dairyman's Daughter" murmuring the voice of Jesus, till we heard it across the Atlantic; Hannah Burton testifying to the power of Christ to sustain her—all these were most effective preachers of the unsearchable riches of Christ. (*Ibid.*)　　*Supremacy of duty :*—An officer who served under Stonewall Jackson, having gone to visit some relatives without applying for leave, was detained late at night by a severe rain-storm. About two o'clock in the morning, hearing a loud shouting at the gate of the house, he rose, and found his brother there with a message that he must report himself at daybreak. He returned immediately, through the drenching rain and mud, to find all quiet at the camp, and the captain not yet risen. Inquiring of the adjutant the meaning of the message, he received for reply : "That is to teach you that a soldier in the face of an enemy has no business away from his post." (*Mackay.*)

Vers. 61, 62. **Looking back.**—*Danger of religious indecision :*—1. This man wished to follow Christ, but there was something of more urgent necessity that must first be attended to. What folly, to put off attention to concerns of soul. Life is uncertain. Every delay is a step towards final impenitence. 2. The person who made this resolution, evidently made it in his own strength. Vain promise. Without grace we cannot follow Christ. 3. The resolution, when formed, seems to depend on the consent of his friends; for, though he speaks only of taking his leave, he probably wished to know whether they approved of the step he was about to take. Had he been influenced by proper motives, instead of leaving them behind, he would rather have endeavoured to bring them with him, to follow Jesus in the way. 4. Instead of following Christ cheerfully and with all his heart, he appeared somewhat dejected at the thought, and must go and take leave of his friends, as if he were about to die, and should see them no more. Such are the melancholy apprehensions which some persons entertain of true religion; they imagine it would be injurious to their worldly interest, and unfit them for the common duties and enjoyments of life, and that therefore they must take a final leave of the concerns of the present world. 5. By going home to his friends, he would expose himself to great temptation, and be in danger of breaking the resolution already formed. (1) This subject may serve as a warning to those who trifle with the calls of the gospel. Here was a looking back, a lingering after the world, and Christ pronounces such to be unfit for the kingdom of God (ver. 62). (2) Nothing but a decided attachment to Christ, and a determination to sacrifice all for His sake, can constitute us His disciples. (3) Let us beware of the ensnaring influence of worldly connections, and of every inordinate affection; for these, rather than grosser evils, are the ordinary impediments to our salvation (Matt. xvi. 26). (*Theological Sketch-book.*)　　"*Lord, I will follow Thee : but——*" :—"Lord, I will follow Thee : but——." I. First, here comes a man who says, "Lord, I will follow Thee; but I WANT A LITTLE MORE ENJOYMENT OUT OF LIFE BEFORE I BECOME A CHRISTIAN." His notion is that religion is decidedly a melancholy affair, and that from the moment that he becomes a follower of Christ, he must bid adieu to all merriment and pleasure. Secretary Walsingham, an eminent statesman in the time of Queen Elizabeth, in the latter period of his life, retired to a quiet spot in the country. Some of his former gay associates came to him, and made the remark that he was now growing melancholy. "Not melancholy," replied he, "but serious." The mistake of those frivolous courtiers is precisely the mistake made by thousands, that of confounding seriousness with melancholy. The deepest joy is serious, and being serious is stable. Away with the notion that the pleasures of the world are denied to a believer! II. The next objector comes forward and says, "Lord, I would follow Thee; but THE NATURE OF MY BUSINESS PREVENTS ME." When Adam Clarke was a young man, his employer once bid him stretch short measure to make it enough; but his reply was, "Sir, I can't do it; my conscience won't allow me." He lost his situation, but God found him another. It never pays in the long run to have God against you. It all depends on how your money comes to you, whether it is better to have it or to want it. Be sure of this, that character and a good conscience are the best capital. III. Number three starts up, and, in loud and self-asserting tones, proclaims that he has a mind to be religious, but DOES NOT FIND THAT CHRISTIANS ARE ANY BETTER THAN OTHER PEOPLE. This is a polite way of hinting that they are possibly a little worse. I met with a case in point only the other day. I was visiting in the same house with a man who had been under deep religious impressions, and was "almost persuaded," but he had been repelled by the conduct of certain persons who bore the Christian name. "They were the most unprincipled fellows I ever knew, and their religion disgraced everything they touched." Stop, my friend; say, "their hypocrisy disgraced everything they touched." To speak the truth, it was not their religion, but their want of religion, that made them the rogues and scamps they were. IV. "I would be a Christian," says another, "but YOU KNOW ALL THESE THINGS ARE MATTERS OF MERE SPECULATION. WE CANNOT ARRIVE AT CERTAINTY ON THE SUBJECT OF RELIGION." The objection is plausible, but it is shallow and insufficient. 1. The evidence in favour of Christianity is far stronger than that demanded in respect to other matters which you daily accept, and in which great interests are involved. 2. That evidence furnishes the fullest demonstration of which the nature of the subject admits. V. I am only to name another objection, and it is perhaps the most insidious and fatal of all. "Lord, I will follow Thee; but—THERE IS NO HURRY; THERE IS TIME ENOUGH." Remember, a resolution like that, though it quiets conscience, is worth nothing. (*J. T. Davidson, D.D.*)   *The broken column:*—When you have walked through a cemetery, you have frequently seen over a grave a broken column intended to memorialize the death of some one who was taken away in the prime of manhood, before as yet his life had come to its climax. I shall take that picture of the broken column to represent my text. It is a broken text. You expected me to go on and to conclude the sentence: I have broken it off abruptly. That broken column shall also represent the broken resolutions of full many who were once in a hopeful state. As if prepared to witness a good profession, they said, "Lord, I will follow Thee," when there came a heavy blow from the withering hand of sin; and the column was broken short with a "but." So let my text stand. I will not finish it. But so let not your determination stand. The Lord grant by His effectual grace that while you mourn with sincere grief the grave of many a fair resolve which never attained the maturity of true discipleship—cut off with the fatal "*but*" of indecision; you may now be quickened to newness of life. Thus you shall come to the fulness of the stature of a man in Christ. Thus, as a building fitly framed together and growing to completeness, you shall be made meet for a habitation of God through the Spirit. "Lord, I will follow Thee: but—." How remarkably does Scripture prove to us that the mental characteristics of mankind are the same now as in the Saviour's day! We occasionally hear stories of old skeletons being dug up which are greater in stature than men of these times. Some credit the story, some do not, for there be many who maintain that the physical conformation of man is at this day just what it always was. Certainly, however, there can be no dispute whatever among observant men as to the identity of the inner nature of man. The gospel of Christ may well be an unchanging gospel, for it is a remedy which has to deal with an unaltering disease. The very same objections which were made to Christ in the days of His flesh are made to His gospel now. The same effects are produced under the ministry of Christ's servants in these modern times as were produced by His own ministry. Still are the promised hopes which make glad the preacher's heart, blasted and withered by the same blights and the same mildews which of old withered and blasted the prospects of the ministry during our Lord's own personal sojourn in the world. I. First, then, TO EXPOSE YOUR OBJECTIONS. I cannot tell man by man, what may be the precise let that causes you to draw back, but perhaps, by giving a list, I may be directed to describe full many a case exactly, and with precision. Some there be who say, and seem very sincere in the utterance, "Lord, I would be a Christian, I would believe in Thee, and take up the cross and follow Thee, but my calling prevents it. Such is my state of life that piety would be to me an impossibility. I must live, and I cannot live by godliness, therefore I am to be excused for the present from following Christ." "Yes, but," saith another, "if it be not in our calling, yet in my case it is my peculiar position in providence. It is all very well for the minister, who has not to mingle with daily life, but can come up into his pulpit and pray and preach, to make little excuse for men; but I tell you, sir, if you knew how I was situated, you would say that I am quite excusable in postponing the thoughts of God and of eternity. You do not know what it is to have an ungodly husband, or to live in a family where you cannot carry out your convictions without meeting with persecution so ferocious and so incessant, that flesh and blood cannot endure it." "Besides," says another, "I am just now in such a peculiar crisis; it may be I have got into it by my sin, but I feel I cannot get out of it without sin. If I were once out of it, and could start again, and stand upon a new footing, then I might follow Christ." "Yes," says another, "I would follow Christ; I have often felt inclinations to do so; and I have had some longings after better things: but the way of Christ is too rough for me. It demands that I should give up pleasures which I really love." "But," saith another, "that is not my case. I can say I will follow Christ, but I am of such a volatile, changeable disposition, that I do not think I ever shall fulfil my purpose." II. Soul, thou who sayest, "I will follow Christ, but—," I now come to EXPOSE THINE IGNORANCE AND THE ILL STATE OF THY HEART. Soul! thou hast as yet no true idea of what sin is. God the Holy Spirit has never opened thine eyes to see what an evil and bitter thing it is to sin against God, or else there would be no "buts." Picture a man who has lost his way, who has sunk into a slough; the waters and the mire are come up to his very throat. He is about to sink in it, when some bright spirit comes, stepping over the treacherous bog, and puts forth to him his hand. That man, if he knows where he is, if he knows his uncomfortable and desperate state, will put out his hand at once. Again: soul, it seems plain to me that thou hast never yet been taught by the Holy Spirit what is thy state of condemnation. Thou hast never yet learnt that the wrath of God abideth on thee. What shall I say more? Yet this once again I will admonish thee. O thou procrastinating, objecting sinner, thou hast never known what heaven is, or else thou wouldst never have a "but." III. LET ME SHOW THEE THY SIN. When thou saidst, "But," thou didst contradict thyself. The meaning of that rightly read is this, "Lord, I will *not* follow Thee." That "but" of thine puts the negative on all the profession that went before it. I wish, my hearers, that this morning you would either be led by grace to say, "I will believe," or else were permitted honestly to see the depravity and desperate hardness of your own hearts so as to say, "I will not believe in Christ." It is because so many of you are neither this nor that, but halting between two opinions, that you are the hardest characters to deal with. I know a gentleman of considerable position in the world, who, after having been with me some little time, said, "Now that man is going away, and I shall be just what I was before"; for he had wept under the Word. He compared himself, he said, to a gutta-percha doll; he had got out of his old shape for a little while, but he would go back to what he was before. And how many there are of you of this kind. You will not say, "I will not have Christ"; you will not say, "I will not think of these things." You dare not say, "I disbelieve the Bible," or, "I think there is no God, and no hereafter"; but you say, "No doubt it is true, I'll think of it by and by." You never will, sinner, you never will, you will go on from day to day, harping that till your last day shall come, and you will be found then where you are now, unless sovereign grace prevent. (*C. H. Spurgeon.*) *Conditional discipleship:*—This third character, like the first, volunteers his declaration of attachment to the Saviour, appending to it a condition—"Lord, I will follow Thee, BUT let me first go bid them farewell, which are at my house." BUT—ominous word, treacherous poison, undermining the best resolves, and spoiling the fairest speeches. It is said of Augustine that he used to say, "Lord, convert me, but not yet." "Lord, I will follow Thee, BUT I am not yet good enough." If this be the utterance of real humility, know thou that it is not unworthiness, but unwillingness that alone disqualifies us from following Jesus. It is unconditional determination that He demands. D'Aubigné, the great church historian, says that when he was a student at college, he was much beset by doubts and difficulties in relation to questions connected with Divine truth; and it was his wont to repair to an old Christian, in very humble life, whose rich experience had often served to help the young student. But at length, upon preferring some grave difficulty, D'Aubigné received an unexpected rebuff, for his aged friend replied, "Young man, I shall not answer any more of these questions of yours. If I settle them one day, new perplexities arise the next day. The great question for you is—'Do you mean to belong altogether to Christ?'" That is the shortest way of setting at rest these misgivings. Give yourselves to the Saviour, and He will smooth your path, and show the way. (*W. G. Lewis.*) *The danger of backward looks:*—This man was in the spirit of true discipleship, resolved to follow Jesus, and actually beginning it. But he felt a desire first to return to his relatives and give his last commission to them, and bid them farewell: "Lord, I will follow Thee; but suffer me first go bid them farewell that are at home at my house." This request had something of a backward look in it; it indicated somewhat of a desire to trim between Christ and His kindred;

at least there was a positive danger in it to the discipleship he had just avowed; for, once away from the Master's side and among his own unbelieving kindred, he would be beset by them as to the step he was taking; he would be expostulated with and warned against it, and threateningly dissuaded from it; tears, entreaties, influences of all sorts would be brought to bear on him to turn him from his intent and keep him at home as he was wont to be. And then, perchance, his mind would waver, and his resolution become shaken, and his faith fail, or be much unfitted for the high calling of the gospel. This danger the Lord Jesus keenly perceived, and clearly points out: and, while not forbidding him from doing as he desired, yet warns him to beware: "No man," &c., as if He said, "No man who follows Me can at the same time turn towards the world; if he do so he will fail in his following, perhaps in the way of it, certainly in the work of it. Such trimming is treason to Me, and shows those pursuing it unfit for My kingdom and work." (*J. Chalmers, M.A.*) *Fatal delay:*—Some time since, in a little watering-place in the west of Scotland, I was pointed to a spot where, a few years ago, a sad and strange incident had occurred. Several workmen were engaged in calking the bottom of a vessel that had been drawn up on the sandy beach. On a sudden the cry was raised that the ship was listing over, and all the men started to their feet, and hastened to escape—all but one poor fellow, who was late in stirring, and the huge hulk fell upon him, imprisoning his lower extremities and loins, but leaving head and chest uninjured. At first it was thought there was little danger, for the ship rested gently on him, and the sand was soft. So they tried to shore up the vessel, and willing hands brought ropes, and blocks, and wedges, and earnest strength. But they soon discovered that the thing was impossible, from the nature of the bottom. The man was jammed there, and they could not extricate him. There was just one awful hour before the advancing tide would cover him. Oh! with what agonizing entreaty did he appeal to them to rescue him. It was too late. He saw the tide of death approaching, but he had not the power to rise and escape; and none could deliver him. Another hour; and as the vessel calmly rose and glided on the waters, the pale corpse floating in to shore seemed to preach the solemn lesson, that even a few moments' delay may be fatal. And so has it happened with many a soul, that, trifling with his season of grace, has resolved to get up and follow Christ at some future day; but that day came, and he could not stir; all capacity for resolve had passed away; his heart was dead and motionless as a stone. If you have but half a desire then to follow Christ, let no "buts" block the way, those flimsy objections which drown so many in perdition, and make *you* the *butt* of Satan's ridicule; but instantly arise, and say with Peter (though in a Divine strength that will not fail you), "Lord, why cannot I follow Thee *now?* I will lay down my life for Thy sake." (*J. T. Davidson, D.D.*) *Danger of procrastination:*—A recent discovery at Pompeii has brought to light the fact of a priest fleeing from the temple when the warning came of the city's approaching doom. But the treasures of the temple—why should he leave them? He is supposed to have returned to obtain them. Again he sets out, but had not proceeded far before the destruction came and he was lost. Had it not been for the treasures, his life had been spared. *Danger in delay:*—Cæsar had a letter given him by Artimedorus the morning he went to the senate, wherein notice was given him of all the conspiracy of his murderers; so that with ease he might have prevented his death: but neglecting the reading of it, he was slain. What can be done to-day, therefore, delay not till to-morrow. (*W. Buck.*) *The virtue of perseverance:*—1. MOTIVES. 1. The unchangeableness of God. 2. The unchangeableness of Divine charity. 3. The nature of virtue. II. MEANS. 1. Prayer. 2. Energy. 3. Frequent reception of the Holy Communion. 4. The remembrance of heaven. (*Bishop Ehrler.*) *The evil of looking back:*—This man offered himself, but his heart was not sufficiently loosened from the world. 1. His request. He offers himself to be a disciple of Christ, but with an exception—that he might take his farewell at home, and dispose of his estate there, and so secure his worldly interests. You will say, what harm in this request? Elijah granted it to Elisha (1 Kings xix. 21). I answer—(1) The evangelical ministry exceedeth the prophetical, both as to excellency and necessity, and must be gone about speedily without any delay. The harvest was great, and such an extraordinary work was not to be delayed nor interrupted. (2) If two men do the same thing, it followeth not that they do it with the same mind. Things may be the same as to the substance or matter of the action, yet circumstances may be different. Christ knew this man's heart, and could interpret the meaning of his desire to go home first. (3) Those that followed Christ on these extraordinary calls were to leave all things they had, without any further care about them (Matt. xix. 21 ; iv. 19, 20 ; ix. 9). Therefore it was preposterous for this man to desire to go home to order and dispose of his estate and family, before he complied with his call. (4) In resolution, estimation, and vow, the same is required of all Christians, when Christ's work calleth for it—" So likewise, whosoever he be of you that forsaketh not all that he hath, he cannot be my disciple " (Luke xiv. 33). 2. Christ's answer, which consists of a similitude, and its interpretation joined together. (1) The metaphor or similitude. Taken from ploughmen, who cannot make straight furrows if they look back. So, to look back, after we have undertaken Christ's yoke and service, rendereth us unfit for the kingdom of God. Putting our hands to the plough is to undertake Christ's work, or to resolve to be His disciples. Looking back denotes a hankering of mind after the world, and also a return to the worldly life. For, first we look back, and then we go back. 1. Upon what occasions we may be said to look back. A double pair I shall mention. The first sort of those : (1) That pretend to follow Christ, and yet their hearts hanker after the world, the cares, pleasures, and vain pomp thereof. (2) When men are discouraged in His service by troubles and difficulties, and so, after a forward profession, all cometh to nothing—" If any man draw back, My soul shall have no pleasure in him " (Heb. x. 38). The former is looking back, and this is drawing back. The one arises out of the other ; all their former zeal and courage is lost, they are affrighted and driven out of their profession, and relapse into the errors they have escaped. There is a looking back with respect to mortification, and a looking back with respect to vivification. (*a*) With respect to mortification, which is the first part of conversion. So we must not look back, or mind anything behind us, which may turn us back, and stop us in our course. (*b*) With respect to vivification, or progress in the duties of the holy and heavenly life. So the apostle telleth us—" But this one thing I do, forgetting those things which are behind, and reaching forth unto those things which are before " (Phil. iii. 13), &c. Farther progress in holiness is the one thing that we should mind, and that above all other things. 2. How ill it becometh those that have put their hands to the spiritual plough. (1) In respect of the covenant into which they enter, or the manner of entrance into it, which is by a fixed unbounded resignation of themselves unto God. Till this be done, we are but half Christians. (2) With respect to the duties of Christianity, or that part of the kingdom of God which concerneth your obedience to Him, you are never fit for these while the heart cleaveth to earthly things, and you are still hankering after the world. A threefold defect there will be in our duties. (*a*) They will be unpleasant. (*b*) They will be inconstant. (*c*) Imperfect in such a degree as to want sincerity. (3) In respect of the hurt that cometh from their looking back, both to themselves and to religion. (4) With respect to the disproportion that is between the things that tempt us to look back, and those things that are set before us. (*a*) The things that tempt us to look back are the pleasures of sin and the profits of the world. Both are but a temporary enjoyment (Heb. xi. 25). (*b*) The things that are before you are God and heaven ; reconciliation with God, and the everlasting fruition of Him in glory. (*T. Manton, D.D.*) *The danger of looking back :*—I. Many seem disposed to follow Christ, and yet are kept back by their domestic and worldly affairs. II. The concerns of religion are so very important, that they admit no excuse nor delay. 1. Religion is the most important concern, infinitely more so than any domestic and worldly concern. 2. Worldly business is no excuse for neglecting religion, because both may go on together, if a man will "guide his affairs with discretion." 3. To this I add —that business and domestic affairs will flourish the better, if religion be minded as the principal thing. III. Those who have engaged in the service of Christ, must be resolute and persevere to the end. Application : 1. How lamentable is the conduct of mankind in general ; so widely different from the maxims of our Lord and Master. 2. What great need have we to watch over ourselves, lest domestic affairs hinder us in religion. 3. Let us be solicitous to persevere to the end. (*J. Orton.*) *Christ demands decision in religion :*—I. THERE IS A GREAT WORK, WHICH IT BEHOVES US ALL TO LABOUR IN. 1. All are interested in reaping the advantages of it. 2. All must alike feel the sad consequences of neglecting it. 3. It is a work that requires immediate attention. II. WHEN WE TAKE UP RELIGION WE MUST GO ON WITH IT, and never allow ourselves to be diverted from our object by any worldly considerations. We must be determined to serve Christ faithfully, to serve Him above all, and to serve Him for ever. No reservation ; no division of affection or interest between Christ and other things. III. IF, AFTER BEGINNING GOD'S WORK, WE LOOK AWAY FROM IT, AND TURN OUR THOUGHTS AND HEARTS AGAIN UPON THE WORLD, WE UNFIT OURSELVES

FOR THE KINGDOM OF GOD. (*W. Curling, M.A.*)　　　*Fatal significance of a hind look :*—The professed Christian, to demonstrate his sincerity, to do his work effectually, and to prove his adaptedness for a higher sphere, must keep his face Zionward. Because, if he looks back, he shows—1. That he is not deeply interested and fully occupied by the employment in which he is professedly engaged. 2. That the ties of his earthly relationships are stronger than those which bind him to heavenly things. 3. That he has surrendered himself to temptation. Conclusion : As the first look to Christ and the first step towards the Cross are encouraging and hopeful, so the first look away from the Saviour and the first step aside from the path of duty are discouraging, dangerous, appalling. Apostasy is thus reached by an accelerating motion. (*Anon.*)　　*Spiritual ploughing :*—Life is here figured as a field which God has set us to plough. I. Upon it THREE CLASSES OF MEN appear. 1. There are those who move without regard to their orders or their duty. Their purpose is to live as easily and pleasantly as possible. They mean to enjoy the present ; to enjoy virtuously, if that may be, but to enjoy. What questions may be asked them by and by, they refuse to consider. Of such the text says nothing. 2. There are others trying to plough with their eyes behind them. They have seized the plough in order to be drawn by it to heaven. But they have found life no summer sea over which they can be carried smoothly gliding. They have found it an unbroken prairie that must be ploughed as it is passed. They are continually tripped and thrown by unexpected obstacles. They do not find the joy they crave. When demands upon their energies increase, they are disturbed. When tribulation or persecution ariseth because of the Word, " by and by they are offended." Thus they learn by sad experience that religion which is not wings is always chains. 3. But there are men who begin and continue the Christian life as the instructed ploughman runs his furrow. II. Let us mark THREE POINTS IN THE MASTER'S ILLUSTRATION which give reply to certain questions often asked of Christians by the world, by their own hearts, by the Holy Spirit. 1. Why does God's kingdom come so slowly ? Why is the Church not stronger ? One could scarcely glance upon the ploughman at his work, remembering Christ's words the while, and ask these questions twice. The marvel would rather seem to be that the kingdom does increase. Survey the field of Christian ploughmen. Some are absorbed in watching and in criticising other people's furrows. Some are gazing back upon their own, recalling past experiences, at times anxiously, which is bad ; at times proudly, which is worse. How few are eagerly alert to the work they themselves are set to do ! How few are even sure that they have furrows to plough ! 2. The Lord's words bring an answer to another question of serious practical import. It is said the Church is losing, if she has not already lost, her hold upon young men. Yet in our Lord's lifetime it was the young and the strong whom He attracted to Him and gathered round Him. Why is it not so now ? Is not an answer found in this, that we no longer preach Him with the old heroic ring ? All are not mourners. All are not heavy-laden. There are many who carry life as a hunter bears his gun through an unflushed preserve. Has Christ no words for them ? Ay, verily ! But how rarely are those words repeated ? In the New Testament the Christian is painted, not as one flying from a doomed city, but as a stalwart farmer ploughing the old growths of the old world, until visions of a new earth no less than of a new heaven fill his horizon. 3. One other question presses upon many who read the text. " Let me first go bid them farewell which are at home, at my house." Was the Master's reply intended to rebuke the disciple for loving his family—to teach him not to care for wife and child ? Altogether the reverse, I think. The man assumed that to follow Christ was to forsake his family. It was the fatal blunder made by most Christians some centuries later, when they conceived that to run away from their duties, and try to save their souls by hiding in caverns or monasteries, without a thought of the world their Master came to deliver, was the proper way to obey Him. To grant the man's request would have confirmed him in his error. It was needful to teach him that he could effectually care for wife and child only by following with unswerving gaze and unfaltering foot the Lord who gave them to him. No man ever obeyed Christ in singleness of heart without discovering that fact. This disciple, if he obeyed, learned it in due time, and learned it effectually, though when or how he learned it we are not told. (*W. B. Wright.*)　　*No looking back :*—The Saviour's reply to this man embodies a great principle which regulates the Christian life. As though He said, The meanest occupation in life demands of men fixedness of attention and devotedness of purpose. The ploughman, the oarsman, the helmsman, the engineman, must each have the fixed eye, and so must the Christian man.

Without perseverance there is no success in worldly undertakings, and without this not the most resplendent grace can bring a man to heaven. Some turn back at the very commencement of the pilgrimage. The figure of the plough points out the fact to us that labour for Christ is the law of the kingdom. (*W. G. Lewis.*) *Danger of trifling with religous impressions :*—While the Holy Spirit pleads with us, when conscience wakes and talks with us, let none of us trifle with the impressions that are made. There is no process so perilous as that by which men come into familiarity with Gospel truth, and go away partially enlightened and imperfectly convinced. How many there are who, like the three men we have been considering, come near to Christ, but are only *almost* saved. The northern steel is hardened by alternate exposure to heat and cold, and thus often are men's hearts indurated. They come into the warm atmosphere of the public means of grace, and go out into the world to become less and less approachable by Divine truth. There are not a few who have outlived all power of susceptibility to God's Word. They could not shed a tear over sin if they would. (*Ibid.*) *Putting the hand to the plough :*—To put the hand to the plough, is to enter ostensibly upon some undertaking, to embark in some pursuit with an apparent purpose of securing its object ; and to look back, implies that divided state of mind, and that irresoluteness of purpose which are a virtual abandonment of the end proposed, and are, therefore, fatal to success. We are thus taught that a wavering and undetermined state of mind in religion is as fatal as it is in any other pursuit, that it can never form that character which qualifies for the kingdom of God. I. Among those who, in the language of the text, put the hand to the plough and look back, may be mentioned the following classes. 1. Those who would become religious were it not that they wish first to secure some worldly good. 2. The same thing is true of those who are prevented from coming to a decided purpose in religion by certain embarrassments and difficulties. 3. The same thing is true of those who, in times of deep affliction, sudden danger, or alarming sickness, have formed resolutions to become religious, and who abandon them on a change of circumstances. 4. The same charge lies against those who have been the subjects of special religious awakening, and who afterward return to stupidity in sin. II. Its utter insufficiency to form the Christian character. 1. An undecided purpose in religion is sure, sooner or later, to abandon its object. 2. An undecided, fluctuating purpose in religion greatly impairs the energies of the mind, and thus defeats its object. 3. That an undecided purpose in religion cannot form the Christian character, is evident from the fact that it still leaves the soul as completely under the dominion of sin as if it had no existence. 4. An undecided purpose in religion grieves the Holy Ghost and fearfully exposes to judicial abandonment of God. (*N. W. Taylor, D.D.*) *Crooked ploughing :*—It seems a very easy process to a man who has never tried, as he stands looking over the fence and sees the plough glide smoothly through the field. One would think all you have to do, would be to take hold of the handles and put the point of the coulter in the sod, and then tell the horses to start ; but to send the plough through at equal depth of earth, and, without being stopped by stone or stump, make a clear, straight furrow from one end to the other, requires a good deal of care. Many a one has lost his patience in the process, and when he first began to plough, has been knocked flat by the plough handles. Here is a boy that attempts to plough, but instead of keeping his eye on the beam of the plough or on the horses that are dragging the plough, he is looking this way and that, sometimes looking back to the end of the field from which he started. The husbandman comes down in the field and says : " My boy, you will never make a ploughman in that way. You must keep your eye on your work, or I shall discharge you, and put some one else in your place. See here, what a crooked furrow you have been making." Now it is this illustration that Christ presents in order to show up the folly of that man who, once having started toward heaven, is averted this way and that, often looking back to the place from which he started. (*Dr. Talmage.*) *Concentration :*—If you can dismiss from your minds the figure of the modern farmer, with his polished ploughshare leaving the deep, clean furrow in its wake, and put in its place the figure out of which Jesus made this little picture —the Eastern ploughman doubled over the pointed stick which serves as a plough —you will see at once how vividly the absurdity of a man's ploughing and looking behind him at the same time would have impressed Christ's hearers. Even a modern ploughman, with the best modern plough, will make sad work if he do not keep his eyes straight before him. Anyway, that is true of ploughing which is true of any other kind of work. One whose interest is half in front and half behind him will be only a half-way man in anything to which he may set his hand. All good work requires concentration. No good work is done into which a man does not throw himself wholly. A man cannot plough, and be looking behind him half the time. Such a man is not fit for a ploughman. You say, Of course not. That is a law of all good work, that a man cannot do it well with half his attention ; but why not, then, a law of work and life in the kingdom of God ? We have a great deal yet to learn about the words of Christ ; and one of the most important things is, that these apparently commonplace truths and familiar laws which He so often cites are merely sides, or ends if you please, of truths and laws which hold in the whole spiritual world. It is not, that, in this little picture of an incompetent farm-hand Christ gives us something like a law of the kingdom of God. He states the law itself. Good work requires the entire committal of the worker. It is the law of Christian service and of ploughing alike. It is this fact which lifts utterances like our text out of the region of commonplace. They seem commonplace where they touch us, but their line runs out to truths which are not commonplace. The law of the plough followed up appears as the law of the kingdom of God. (*M. R. Vincent, D.D.*) *Reasons why men look back from the plough:*—1. I remark, that many surrender their religious impressions because, like this man in the text, they do not want to give up their friends and connections. The probability is that the majority of your friends are not true Christians. 2. Again, I remark, that sometimes people surrender their religious impressions because they want to take one more look at sin. They resolved that they would give up sinful indulgences, but they have been hankering for them ever since, thirsty for them, and finally they conclude to go into them. So there is a man who, under the influence of the Spirit, resolved he would become a Christian, and as a preliminary step he ceases profanity. That was the temptation and the sin of his life. After awhile be says : "I don't know as it's worth while for me to be curbing my temper at all times—to be so particular about my speech. Some of the most distinguished men in the world have been profane. Benjamin Wade swears, Stephen A. Douglass used to swear, General Jackson swore at the battle of New Orleans, and if men like that swear, I can ; and I am not responsible anyhow for what I do when I get provoked." And so the man who, resolving on heaven, quits his profanity, goes back to it. In other words, as the Bible describes it, " the dog returns to its vomit again, and the sow that is washed to her wallowing in the mire." Oh, my friends, there are ten thousand witcheries which, after a man has started for heaven, compel him to look back. 3. I remark, again, there are many who surrender their religious impressions because they want ease from spiritual anxiety. They have been talking about their immortal soul, they have been wondering about the day of judgment, they have been troubling themselves about a great many questions in regard to religion, and they do not find peace immediately, and they say, " Here, I'll give it all up. I will not be bothered any more " ; and so they get rest ; but it is the rest of the drowning man who, after half an hour battling with the waves, says, " There's no use ; I can't swim ashore ; I'll drown " ; and he goes down. Oh, we do not hide the fact that to become a Christian demands the gathering up of all the energies of the soul. (*Dr. Talmage.*) *No retreat :*—When Garibaldi sailed from Genoa in 1860, to deliver Sicily from its oppressors, he took with him a thousand volunteers. They landed at Marsala almost in the face of the Neapolitan fleet. When the commander of Marsala, returning to the port, saw two steamers, he gave immediate orders to destroy them. Garibaldi, having landed his men, looked with indifference, almost with pleasure, upon their destruction. " Our retreat is cut off," he said exultingly to his soldiers ; " we have no hope but in going forward ; it is to death or victory." Which it proved to be we know full well, the brave hero soon returning as complete conqueror. *No retreat possible to the Christian soldier :*—Among the prisoners taken captive at Waterloo there was a Highland piper. Napoleon, struck with his mountain dress and sinewy limbs, asked him to play on his instrument, which is said to sound so delightfully in the mountains and glens in Scotland. " Play a pibroch," said Napoleon ; and the Highlander played. " Play a march " ; it was done. " Play a retreat." " Na, na," said the Highlander, " I never learned to play a retreat." *Never look back :*—In the East, when men or women leave their house, they never look back, as " it would be very unfortunate." Should a husband have left anything which his wife knows he will require, she will not call on him to turn or look back ; but will either take the article herself or send it by another. Should a man have to look back on some great emergency, he will not then proceed on the business he was about to transact. When a person goes along the road (especially in the evening) he will take care not to look back, "because the evil spirits will assuredly seize him." When they go on a journey, they will not look behind, though the palan-keen, or bandy, should be close upon them; they step a little on one side, and then look at you. Should a person have to leave the house of a friend after sunset, he will be advised in going home not to look back: "as much as possible keep your eyes closed; fear not." Has a person made an offering to the evil spirits? he must take particular care when he leaves the place not to look back. A female known to me is believed to have got her crooked neck by looking back. Such observations as the following may be heard in private conversation:—"Have you heard that the Camàran is very ill?" "No; what is the matter with him?" "Matter! why, he has looked back, and the evil spirit has caught him." *Sermon to young men:*—A noble resolution frustrated by a "but"! A life full of promise and of hope broken off by a "but"! A crown lost, a kingdom forfeited, an eternity marred by a "but"! A "but" was this man's ruin, and it may be also yours. I take it in this way, that each one present who is not following Christ may write in his or her own objection. 1. It is possible that with some of you the worldly life seems preferable on the score of pleasure. 2. Or you perhaps say: "At present I am so absorbed in business that I have no time to follow Christ." 3. Or perhaps that which has kept you back is fear of the reproach or the scorn of others. 4. Or you have formed an intention to follow Christ, but not now. "Let me first go," &c. Any excuse that will save you from immediate decision! What, think you, is peopling the regions of the lost? Is it crime? No. It is simple neglect of the gospel. Satan asks no more than that you should neglect it. He seeks not that you shall blaspheme it, or that you shall disbelieve it, or that you shall neglect and despise it. He only asks that you will neglect it. If you will only say, "Lord, I will follow Thee, but——" that is all he wants. (*H. Wonnacott.*)   *Irresolution:*—I will follow Thee, but—1. Not yet. 2. I will let no one know it (Mark viii. 38). 3. I will see how others go (Psa. xlii. 4). 4. There are so many ways (John xiv. 6). 5. I have not sufficient convic-tion (Acts xxiv. 25). 6. I must make myself better (Matt. ix. 13). 7. I do not know how (Acts xvi. 31). 8. It will affect my worldly position (Matt. xvi. 26). 9. I shall lose my situation (Matt. vi. 24). 10. The doctrine of election stands in my way (Heb. vii. 25). 11. I am not certain that Thou wilt forgive and receive me (Jer. xxxi. 34). 12. I cannot do certain things which a profession of religion requires of me (Mark x. 21, 22). 13. I will wait God's time (2 Cor. vi. 2). 14. I have not the heart to do it (Psa. xxxiv. 18). Application: 1. The propensity of an awakened sinner is to put off conviction day after day. 2. The excuses and pro-mises of the sinner are to ease his conscience. 3. Excuses are enough to prevent submission. 4. Are you ready to cast yourselves into the arms of Jesus Christ? (*E. Schnadhorst.*)   *The power of a "but":*—I. MANY ARE CONTINUALLY SAYING, "LORD, I WILL FOLLOW THEE," WHO YET DO NOT FOLLOW CHRIST. They have a reverence for sacred things; their head-belief is scriptural and unhesitating; they know both that their lives are wrong and their hearts sinful, and the remedy for the evil; but there is always something in the way of their present decision. II. Inquire into SOME OF THE CAUSES WHICH OPERATE TO KEEP BACK SUCH AS I HAVE BEEN DESCRIBING FROM DECISION FOR CHRIST. 1. With some, as with the man of the text, natural ties. "Let me first go and bid them farewell which are at home at my house." "A very natural wish!" you say. And so in some circumstances it would be. When Elijah summoned Elisha to follow him, the son of Shaphat said: "Let me, I pray thee, kiss my father and my mother, and then I will follow thee." And the prophet, stern man though he was, assented (1 Kings xix. 19, 20). Why then does Christ act so differently on a similar occasion? We may conjecture that Elisha's parents would be rather gratified than otherwise that their son should become the servant of the great prophet. The parents of this man who came to Christ, on the other hand, would not, it may be, feel that it was any advance or promotion for their son to give up his occupation and follow the fortunes of the poor carpenter's son. Christ may then have apprehended that if the man returned home he would never come back, deterred from doing so by the persuasions of his relatives. Elisha was called from the plough to follow the prophets; this man was called from his occupation to put his hand to the plough. "Oh, but it was the gospel-plough," you say. Yes, but gospel-ploughing was not popular in those days. But whatever it was that rendered this man's temporary return home a probably permanent one, whatever it was that made it perilous to his spiritual interests to go and bid farewell to his parents, I gather from Christ's rebuke that it was some-thing which the man knew, and knowing, did not consider as he ought. We may be sure that for him to do as he proposed would have been actually to prefer his relatives to Christ, the lesser duty to the larger, his affection to Christ's claim. Do natural ties ever keep us from following Christ? I am afraid that, in some cases, they do. Unbelieving wife or husband; worldly parent, scoffing brother or sister. 2. Plea of being too young yet. 3. Worldly preoccupations. Must "get on" in business, provide for family and old age. As if it was not possible to be both diligent in business and fervent in spirit. No man has a right to barter his soul for worldly gain. III. "Choose you this day whom you will serve." Let there be no hindering "but." Christ suffered no "but" to come between Him and the fulfilment of His loving purposes for our redemption. Shall we hesitate to follow Him when He bids us? (*J. R. Bailey.*) *Perseverance:*—A man's work is what his will is. If he throws his will into his work, it will be done. If his heart and will are not in his work, it will be but half done. "He that endureth to the end, the same shall be saved." I. What is perseverance? It is holding out steadily to the end. The question is of two kinds: 1. Active perseverance. The availing ourselves of the lights of truth when we see them. 2. Passive perseverance. When there is perseverance on our part there is also perseverance on God's part. Perseverance on God's part a sovereign gift which we cannot merit. 3. This gift of perseverance consists of three things: (*a*) The special guidance of God to guard us from running into temptation; (*b*) God will guard those whom He guides; (*c*) the continual renewal of God's grace. II. How is perseverance lost? One mortal sin will destroy it. There are sins which are not considered deadly which are in reality more deadly because they contain more subtle poison, *e.g.*, pride, jealousy, anger, sloth. III. How is perseverance to be sustained? By fidelity to the voice of conscience; by maintaining a delicacy of conscience. 1. Dwell much upon God's love to you. 2. Meditate upon those who have fallen. 3. Learn that there must be a strong, fervent will throwing itself into perseverance. (*Cardinal Manning.*) *The plough and the kingdom:*—The picture of a slouching plough-man is the form into which our Lord throws the lesson of the closing section of this chapter. 1. The first man, an enthusiastic volunteer, had conceived of no difficulty in the case. Nevertheless, our Lord will not let a man enter His service without a full knowledge of its conditions. The man shall never have it to say that he was entrapped into sacrifices and labours upon which he did not count. 2. The next man is a ready man, like the first, but a more cautious man. No one would be more ready than Christ to acknowledge such a claim as he urged. But this case was peculiar. When a community, in the old colonial days, was suddenly attacked by the Indians, every man must drop everything else, and go out to repel the savages. He must leave his team unyoked in the field, his plough in the furrow, his sick wife in the house, his dead child or father unburied, and seize his gun, and take his place in the ranks. You are to remember further that this was the man's only chance to attach himself to Jesus. The Lord was going forth from Galilee to return no more. According to the Jewish law, the pollution from the presence of a dead body lasted seven days. By that time the man's first enthusiasm would have become chilled, and Jesus would be out of reach. The man evidently thought that it was only a question of a little delay in following Christ; Jesus knew that it was a question of following Him now or never. 3. Then comes a third. He offers himself also; but he, too, is not ready to go at once. He wants to go home and take leave of his family and friends. And in this case, as in the last, Christ assumes that there is a moral crisis. He must decide promptly; and if he decides to follow Christ, he must promptly forsake all, once for all, and follow Him. Christ says to Him, in effect, "If you go after me, the course is straightforward. If part of your heart is left behind with friends and home and old associations, it is of no use for you to go. You are not fit for the kingdom of God, any more than a man is fit to plough a field who is constantly turning from his plough and his team to look backward." 1. The lesson of the text is that of committal—the truth, that to follow Christ is to commit one's self wholly and irrevocably to Christ. This law of entire committal is familiar enough to us in its worldly applications. When you choose a calling in life, it is said of you, "He is going to devote his life to business, or to law, or to medicine." 2. As a consequence, when you enter your plough in this spirit of entire committal, you agree to take whatever comes in the line of your ploughing, and to plough through it, or round it, and in no case to turn back because of it. The kingdom of God is full of surprises, and you will come upon a good many unexpected things, and hard as they are unexpected. There are curved as well as straight lines in God's plans, ends reached by indirection as well as directly. A farmer likes to cut straight furrows, but God is more concerned about our making a fruitful field than a handsome one. Any way, straight or crooked, you commit yourself to what comes. God selects the field for us with its conditions—rocks in one man's field, stumps in another's. Last week there came into my study a pastor of many years' standing—a faithful, able, useful servant of God. He told me of sickness and prostration, of burdens lifted in struggling churches, of divisions and dissensions among his people, of final success; and he brought down his hand with emphasis as he said, "I have learned this one thing through it all, that God's work is bound to go on any way; and that the only thing for us to do is to stand in our place and do our work whatever comes." My brethren, you all know something about this in your own lives. You have all felt the jar when the plough struck a stone. Not one of you has been able to make straight furrows always. But there is no such thing as failure of faithful work in God's kingdom. And the simple reason of that is because it is in God's kingdom, and not man's. 3. The text presents us with a question of the present, a present responsibility. It is not a question whether you will be fit for heaven by and by, but whether, by absolute and entire committal to Christ, you are fit for the service of the kingdom here and now. (*M. R. Vincent, D.D.*) Christ required implicit consecration, with no mental reservation, no hankering after the old manner of life. (*J. P. Thompson.*) *Prompt decision:*—Father Taylor, the sailor preacher, was brought up in a place near the city of Richmond (United States) by a lady to whom he had been given in charge. One day, when he was about seven years old, he was picking up chips for his foster-mother, when a sea captain passed by and asked him if he did not wish to be a sailor. He jumped at the offer, never finished picking up his chips nor returned into the house to bid his friends good-bye, but gave himself to the stranger without fear or thought. As a sailor he underwent many hardships, being at one time a prisoner of war in England; and he finally became, and was for over forty years, pastor of the Seamen's Bethel, Boston, and an eminent and useful preacher. (*Biblical Treasury.*) *Duty permits no deliberation:*—Nero once tried to disgrace some of the great Roman nobles to as low a level as his own by making them appear as actors in the arena or on the stage. To the Roman noble such an appearance was regarded as the extremest shame and disgrace. Yet to disobey the order was death. The noble Florus was bidden thus to appear in the arena; and doubtful whether to obey or not, consulted the virtuous and religious Agrippinus. "Go, by all means," replied Agrippinus. "Well, but," replied Florus, "you yourself faced death rather than obey." "Yes," answered Agrippinus; "because I did not deliberate about it." The categorical, imperative "you must," the negative prohibition of duty, must be implicitly, unquestioningly, and deliberately obeyed. To deliberate about it is to be a secret traitor, and the line which separates the secret traitor from the open rebel is thin as the spider's web. (*Archdeacon Farrar.*) *Making a way to return:*—About the time of the reformation a certain bishop who had embraced the new doctrines, and to whom it was therefore of no use, presented a relic (a dead man's toe) to the Church at St. Nicholas, Switzerland. He made the present conditionally with the power of resuming it if he should return to his old ways. (*Sir John Forbes.*) *Looking back:*—The son of Carey, the Indian missionary, went to Burmah as a missionary, but there he became an ambassador for the Burmese king. He then lived in great worldly pomp and state, but his father mourned that he had so demeaned himself as to stoop from being God's ambassador to be the ambassador of an Eastern king. All worldly things are only like the shadows of a dream; there is nothing substantial about them. But the honour and blessings which come from God are satisfying and abiding. (*H. R. Burton.*)

CHAPTER X.

Ver. 1. **The Lord appointed other seventy.**—*Our Lord's instructions to the seventy :*—I. Christ sent out the seventy by pairs. II. Our blessed Lord fairly and faithfully warned the seventy of the difficulty and danger of the charge which they were undertaking. III. Our Lord cautions His missionaries against an over curious and minute regard to accommodation preparatory to

THEIR ENTERING ON THEIR MISSION, AND WHILE EMPLOYED IN EXECUTING THE BUSINESS OF IT. IV. OUR LORD RECOMMENDS TO THE DISCIPLES UNDIVIDED, UNDEVIATING ATTENTION TO WHAT WAS SPECIALLY COMMITTED TO THEM. V. OUR LORD'S INSTRUCTIONS TO THE SEVENTY RESPECTING THEIR WORK AND THE MANNER IN WHICH THEY WERE TO PERFORM IT. VI. CHRIST ENCOURAGES HIS DISCIPLES WITH THE ASSURANCE THAT HE SHOULD CONSIDER THE RECEPTION WHICH THEY MET WITH, AS GIVEN TO HIMSELF. (*H. Hunter, D.D.*) **Two and two.**—*Two and two before His face :*—Yet questions of high interest immediately arise. Why should there be any forerunners? What were they sent to do? In order to the full, personal influence and reign of Christ anywhere, there is a law of necessary preparation. Very impressive it is to see that God, when He has any great gift to communicate, proceeds by pre-arrangement. He never bursts into His family with thunders of revelation too sudden or loud for them to bear. Take the one signal event which stands in the centre of all history, —the personal coming of the Son of God on the earth. The prophetic spirit of His nation had been looking out for Him, as nightly watchers on Mount Moriah looked out for the dawn toward Hebron, two thousand years. In fact, to eyes that see the divinity in the Saviour's face at all, it is not difficult to discern, all along those earlier ages, heralds like "the other seventy also," going before that Face into the places whither He Himself was afterward to come. Now on that great scale of time and space we have a picture, in colossal proportions, of what goes on in every one of our own breasts. Conscious of it or not, agencies are at work in us to make ready, if we only will, for the entrance of the Lord of the heart into His home and dwelling-place there. Having created us for Christian service, as the true end and real glory of our being, our Father takes pains to fit and to fashion us for that destiny, with all its honour and all its joy. By secret influences, untraceable as the wind that bloweth where it listeth, silently pressing on the springs of feeling and principle within us; by strange sorrows and misgivings there. That we may become wise and strong and pure in our grief, this process of personal preparation is in continual operation. The heralds are out, sent by Him who is coming after them. The "other seventy" are proceeding on their errand. We ourselves are the cities and places whither He would come. Again, it appears from the Lord's sending of the seventy that all personal efforts and public movements for extending truth and increasing righteousness in the world are really parts of His work, and are dependent on His spiritual power. Christendom everywhere is full of beneficent activities. The benefactions of this late age, half-blind though they may be, or forgetful of their Author, were born at Bethlehem, and grew in stature at Nazareth, and conquered their enemies—selfishness and pride and wrath—at Calvary, and went out among the nations with the apostles. If we had seen one of the seventy walking in some by-way of Jericho or Bethany, we might have seen no badge of Christ upon him, and wondered at his eager gait or absorbed expression. But he was going where the Master sent him, and the Master's mantle was on him, and the Master's secret in his soul. Thither, after him, the Master Himself would come, to reaffirm and fulfil his words, to deepen, sanction, complete his work. (*Bishop F. D. Huntington.*)

Ver. 2. **The harvest truly is great.**—*The gospel harvest :*—I. THE STATE OF THINGS WHICH OUR LORD DESCRIBES. 1. A plenteous harvest. (1) A great number of souls. (2) Great diversity in souls. 2. This vast and varied crop is ready for the sickle. This is proved—(1) By the moral and spiritual necessities of the world. A genuine philanthropist wants no other demand upon his efforts than the misery of His fellow men ; and a genuine Christian requires no other proof that men are ready for the gospel than the fact that they need it. Here lay one of the great mistakes of the Church of a former age. She did not think of sending the gospel, because men did not clamour for it. (2) But if our duty be plain in the presence of silent and uncomplaining woe, how much more when misery is suppliant and clamorous at our feet! The world is now conscious of its maladies; and knows full well what can heal them. 3. The labourers are few. They toil on, willing rather to die than to abandon their work. One and another drops and dies, exclaiming, as did the immortal Waterhouse, "more missionaries! more missionaries!" and the very heathen repeat and prolong the cry! II. THE INJUNCTION FOUNDED ON THE ABOVE DESCRIPTION. 1. To whom are our prayers to be addressed? To "the Lord of the harvest." (1) He is the owner and proprietor of the harvest. They are bought with a price. The enemy had usurped possession of the great Creator's claim. (2) And must He not, therefore, take a deep, an unspeakable interest in them ? Think you that He can be indifferent whether this harvest is reaped or not? (3) And it is God's absolute and inalienable right to choose and employ His labourers. 2. We are called, then, to pray that God would graciously exert His prerogative in the appointment of His own labourers to reap His own fields. What does this prayer imply? (1) He exerts this prerogative, in part, by the inward operation of His Holy Spirit. (2) We are to pray, not only that God would call and qualify, but also send out labourers into His harvest. And here we must have regard to His mode of administration. He does for man what man cannot do for himself, but requires him to do all that is in his power. We cannot give the piety, and the intellectual and spiritual gifts ; but it is our duty and privilege to furnish the means for sending the men whom God has raised up. 3. Does any one ask, Why, if God is the Lord of the harvest, having such exclusive prerogatives, and so deeply interested in the matter, He should be entreated to do that which it so nearly concerns His honour not to leave undone ? We answer, Such sceptical inquiries become not the position of finite and mortal creatures. The objection would apply to all prayer for any blessing ; and call in question the whole adminis-tration of heaven. (*J. H. James.*)   *The abundance of the harvest, and the scarcity of the labourers :*—I. Let us first look at THE HARVEST. It is too vast to be taken within the verge of one short sermon. China, India, Burmah, and Japan, Africa, the West Indies, South America, Russian Tartary, Persia, and the islands of the South Sea—all this is too vast for our consideration at the present oppor-tunity. II. THE LABOURERS. "The labourers are few." Let us consider—III. THE SAVIOUR'S PLAN FOR INCREASING THE NUMBER OF THE LABOURERS. 1. We observe in the first place, that where persons offer this prayer in sincerity, they make a solemn acknowledgment that God must do all the work. 2. In the second place, when a minister and a congregation offer up this prayer and solemnly enter into its spirit, they mean that, when God raises up such men, they will furnish the means to convey them to the heathen, and support them when they get there. 3. In the third place, when young men utter this prayer, they mean that, if it is the will of God, they are ready to become labourers. 4. Observe, in the last place, that when Christian parents offer up this prayer, they express their willingness that their children should go. (*R. Knill.*)   *Harvest ripeness :*—It is just to go and gather in Christ's sheep that are scattered abroad all over the world. In the notion of a harvest we cannot rid ourselves of the idea of ripeness—and I shall take a twofold view of this. There are some of the Lord's family, and it falls to my lot not unfrequently to meet with such in whom we cannot fail to discern the presence of life; their knowledge of themselves as sinners is manifest, their view of Christ as a Saviour is encouraging, and even their reliance upon Him—but there is a want of ripeness, there is a rawness, a greenness, a defectiveness, a youthfulness. The harvest is coming on, beloved ; let us look to our ripeness, the ripeness of all our faculties, as exercised in the things of God, the ripeness of all the graces called into full exercise, so that faith shall no longer be like a grain of mustard seed, but like the ripe ear, waving and bending with its weight—so that love shall no longer be faint and glimmering, as if it were but a spark, but fanned to a flame, rising high, and soaring to its native source ; so that humility shall no longer be a piece of mockery, something openly expressed but never felt, but that which debases the soul in its own esteem, and keeps it in the dust at the feet of Jesus ; so that hope shall not be merely the hope of the hypocrite, but a sure and steadfast thing as the ripeness we speak of—"Entering into that within the veil." Moreover, there is a ripeness in grace, and there is a ripeness in sin. The sickle is coming, beloved, and therefore examine which state of ripeness you are in. When God was about to destroy the seven nations of Canaan, and told Moses of His deferring it for a time, while the children of Israel travelled forty years in the wilderness, He gave this as the reason, that the iniquity of the Amorites was not quite full—their sin was not yet completely ripe. Moreover, I saw in some fields some fine heavy corn, which was sadly "laid," as they call it, bent down to the ground, and not exposed to the sun, so that it will be a long time before it gets ripe. What a picture of a great number of real Christians ! They are so earth-bound, so fond of this world, so laid low in their grovelling desires after it, that they cannot be expected to get ripe very fast. That corn gets ripe the fastest that lifts its head the highest, and gets away from the ground and the weeds. Beloved, if you would be ripe Christians, I tell you that you must get it by being lifted above the world and its vanities, enjoying intimacy with God, fellowship with the Most High, aspiring to heaven, and enjoying communications from above. (*J.*

Irons.) *The labourers and the field :*—Note here—1. That God's Church is a harvest field. 2. That the ministers of God are labourers in His harvest, under God, the Lord of the harvest. 3. That to God alone doth it belong to send forth labourers into His harvest, and none must thrust themselves in till God sends them forth. 4. That the number of faithful labourers is comparatively small and few. 5. That it is the Church's duty to pray, and that earnestly and incessantly, to God the Lord of the harvest, to increase the number of faithful labourers, and to send forth more labourers into His harvest. (*W. Burkitt.*) *The husbandry of God :—* 1. Great is the harvest. 2. Few are the labourers. 3. God alone can restore the just relation between harvest and labourers. (*Van Oosterzee.*) *God the Lord of the harvest :*—1. God determines the time of the harvest. 2. God appoints the labourers for the harvest. 3. God guards the success of the harvest. 4. God deserves the thank-offering of the harvest. (*Ibid.*) *The need of immediate workers :*—Captain Allen Gardiner, on the inhospitable coast of South America, where he slowly perished with hunger, in the hope of attracting the notice of some passing vessel, wrote on the cliff in large letters "DELAY NOT, WE ARE STARVING." Years after, the words were seen; but it was too late, the bleached bones of the brave hero of the cross strewed the beach. Help had been delayed, and he had perished. The like cry of a dying world for the Bread of Life, ringing in the ears of the people of God who have enough and to spare, will surely not be much longer unheeded. A few have responded already, but what are these among so many? Oh that we would each one arise and do our utmost daily, expecting to see mighty results now! (*J. C. Fullerton.*) *A prayer for more labourers :*— Leonard Keyser, a friend and disciple of Luther, having been condemned by the bishop, had his head shaved, and being dressed in a smock-frock, was placed on horseback. As the executioners were cursing and swearing because they could not disentangle the ropes with which his limbs were to be tied, he said to them mildly, "Dear friends, your bonds are not necessary; my Lord Christ has already bound me." When he drew near the stake, Keyser looked at the crowd and exclaimed, "Behold the harvest! O Master, send forth Thy labourers!" And then ascending the scaffold, he cried, "O Jesus, save me!" These were his last words. "What am I, a wordy preacher," said Luther, when he received the news of his death, "in comparison with this great doer of the Word?" (*J. H. M. D'Aubigne.*) *Christ's harvest and Christ's reapers :*—I. CHRIST MEANT HIS SEVENTY DISCIPLES TO GO FORTH AND GATHER THAT WHICH HAD ALREADY GROWN AND RIPENED. 1. He saw a harvest of piety, for instance, waiting for Himself, and the proofs of His Messiahship. 2. I think He saw also another sort of harvest, or another element in that harvest—the moral element. There were many highly moral people living in the world who had become disgusted with religion and its priests. II. THE CHARACTER OF THE HARVEST-MEN HE EMPLOYED. It is at once painful and disheartening to perceive that He did not select, either as individuals or as a class, the professed teachers of religion. He employed no class of men as such. He dealt only with persons and their individual consciences, and so acting, it is easy to discover the sort of people He could call and use as His harvest-men. III. AS THESE WERE PEOPLE MORALLY AND SPIRITUALLY LIKE HIMSELF (TO SOME REAL EXTENT AT LEAST), HE WAS RESTRICTED GREATLY IN THE NUMBER OF GATHERERS, AS HE WAS RESTRICTED IN THE METHOD OF INGATHERING TO BE EMPLOYED. IV. I REMARK UPON THE MODE IN WHICH THE HARVEST WAS TO BE GATHERED. How were the pious and the moral to be brought in? I might properly answer, on a principle of natural selection. They were to preach the gospel of Christ, and illustrate, enforce, and commend that gospel by the beauty and perfectness of their own holy lives. They would thus become witnesses for God, as He was a witness for God. V. TAKE NOW THE PRACTICAL LESSON. Piety in you and me, who profess to be Christ's real friends, is to attract whatever piety we come in contact with. There is plenty of unattached piety waiting to be attracted by you and me. The Lord sent out twelve, then seventy. That great world-clasping system we call Christianity had once so few supporters and missionaries. Do you ask how many it wants now? I will tell you. It wants every man, woman, and child, into whose soul the grace of God has come, that every other life found in the vast field of human activity may be brought with a throb of love and a song of joy, a gathered ear all ripe and golden to the great Lord of the harvest of souls. (*J. McDougall.*)

Ver. 3. **As lambs among wolves.**—*Counsels of prudence :*—I. THE NATURE OF PRUDENCE. In general, it is a discerning and employing the most proper means of obtaining those ends, which we propose to ourselves. It is an important branch of prudence to avoid faults. One false step sometimes ruins, or, however, greatly embarrasses and retards a good design. Prudence likewise supposeth the maintaining of innocence and integrity. We may not neglect our duty to avoid danger. II. THE NECESSITY, GROUNDS, AND REASONS OF PRUDENCE. These are chiefly the wickedness and the weakness of men. Good men, therefore, are obliged to be upon their guard, and make use of some methods of defence and security. Nay, if there were no bad men, yet there would be need of prudent behaviour, because some who have not much reflection or experience are apt to put wrong constructions upon harmless actions. A great part of prudence lies in denying ourselves, so as to keep some way within the limits of virtue. III. SOME RULES AND DIRECTIONS concerning a prudent conduct, with regard to our words and actions. 1. The first rule of prudence I lay down is this, that we should endeavour to know ourselves. He that knows not himself may undertake designs he is not fit for, and can never accomplish, in which he must, therefore, necessarily meet with disappointment. 2. Endeavour to know other men. It is a point of charity to hope the best of every man, and of prudence to fear the worst. 3. Watch, and embrace opportunities. 4. Advise with those who are able to give you good counsel. 5. Restrain and govern your affections. (*T. Lardner.*) *A lamb among wolves :*—One of the most conspicuous instances of moral courage which history affords is the following : The veteran Stilicho had conquered Alaric and his Goths. The Romans invite the hero and his ward—a stupid, cowardly boy, the Emperor Honorius—to gladiatorial games in honour of the victory. The empire has been Christian for a hundred years, yet these infamous and brutalizing shows still continue. They are defended with all sorts of devil's sophistry. The games begin ; the tall, strong men enter the arena ; the tragic cry echoes through the amphitheatre, " Ave Cæsar, morituri te salutamus ! " the swords are drawn, and in an instant's signal will be bathed in blood. At that very moment down leaps into the arena a rude, ignorant monk. " The gladiators shall *not* fight," he exclaims. " Are you going to thank God by shedding innocent blood ? " A yell of execration rises from these 80,000 spectators. " Who is this wretch that dares to set himself up as knowing better than we do ? Pelt him ! Cut him down ! " Stones are hurled at him ; the gladiators run him through with their swords ; he falls dead, and his body is kicked aside, and the games go on, and the people—Christians and all—shout applause. Aye, they go on, and the people shout, for the last time. Their eyes are opened ; their sophistry is at an end ; the blood of a martyr is on their souls. Shame stops for ever the massacre of gladiators ; and because one poor, ignorant hermit has moral courage, " one more habitual crime was wiped away from the annals of the world." (*Archdeacon Farrar.*)

Ver. 4. Salute no man by the way.—*No time to be lost :*—" Salute no man by the way." It is remarkable that such an injunction should be given by our Divine Master, so distinguished as He was for amiable feelings and condescension, while at the same time He immediately added an exhortation to pay the usual courtesy, by desiring them, when they entered a house, to " salute the family." The reason of this apparent inconsistency is easily discovered. In eastern countries, we are told, that salutations between travellers meeting on a journey are attended by so many questions, by so many expressions of welcome often repeated, and so many tedious forms, as seriously to retard their journey. Now, if such interruptions often occurred, as might be the case on a much-frequented road, the object of their journey might be in a great measure frustrated. When such despatch was required as our Saviour deemed necessary on this occasion, those tedious forms of customary civilities were to be omitted. It is true, that in the charge which our Saviour gave to the twelve, He uttered no prohibition to salute the travellers which they might meet with on the way. But it was properly given to the seventy disciples, because haste, which was not required at the mission of the twelve, was then become necessary. (*J. Thomson, D.D.*) *Salutation :*—They were to waste no time on such ceremonies which were clearly excessive. We, however, are in no great danger of carrying the ceremony of salutation to excess. It befits us, therefore, to take heed how we minify even the few salutations which we have. " Good-bye " is all we have left of " God be with you " ; for men are ashamed any longer to use that. Instead of the grand salutation, " God be with you," you shall hear men who are parting say, " Well, old fellow, take care of yourself ! " Men are substituting a coarse way of greeting and saluting each other, instead of giving those reverent, dignified, pleasure-giving, respect-inspiring salutations which belong to antiquity, and which should belong to every refined society—and to none so much as that which calls itself Christian. (*H. W. Beecher.*)

Vers. 5-7. **Peace be to this house.**—*The work and success of the ministry :*— I. THE WORK AND OFFICE OF MINISTERS. They are appointed by the Prince of Peace to be the messengers of peace. 1. The ministers whom Christ here sends forth are supposed to enter into private houses ; and that under the character of Christ's ambassadors, and in the execution of their office. (1) Sometimes they were forced into such corners. Though the message they brought had everything in it to recommend them to an universal acceptance, yet it is probable in many places they were not permitted to preach in the synagogues ; the rulers there who had a jealous eye upon them would take care to keep them thence ; and they then retired into private houses, and preached to as many as would come to hear them there. Those who cannot do what they would for God and the souls of men, must do what they can, and God will accept of them. (2) They always embraced such opportunities of spreading the gospel, and doing good to the souls of men, as visiting people at their houses gave them. Our Lord Jesus preached wherever He visited. 2. They are instructed to say, "Peace be to this house ; " that is, to the inhabitants of it ; to all under this roof ; to the master of the family, for be he ever so great he needs this blessing ; and to all the members of the family, for be they ever so mean they are not excluded from this blessing. Ignatius's bishop was to take cognizance even of the servants of the families that belonged to his charge. (1) We are to preach peace to all. (*a*) Reconciliation, and no war. (*b*) Riches and no want. (2) We are to pray for peace to all. (*a*) We must earnestly desire the welfare and salvation of precious souls ; and not be cold and indifferent about it. (*b*) These desires of the salvation of souls must be offered up to God in prayer. (*c*) It is good to let those we preach to know that we pray for them. We must not only say to God, "Peace be to this house," but we must say it in the hearing of those that dwell in it. II. THE SUCCESS OF MINISTERS. As to those to whom we minister—the success is varied ; not the same with all. On some, the peace comes which we preach and pray for ; on others, it does not. 1. The text gives us encouragement to hope that some shall be the better for our praying and preaching ; we shall meet with those who are sons of peace, who are disposed to submit to the commands, and qualified to partake of the privileges, of the gospel peace. Who are the sons of peace, on whose heads, and hearts, and houses, the blessings of peace shall come ? I answer—(1) Those who are so by the designation of the Divine counsel ; the chosen of God, whom He hath set apart for Himself to be vessels of mercy. (2) Those who are so by the operations of the Divine grace. 2. Wherein shall those who are thus the sons of peace be the better for our ministry ? We are here told that our peace shall rest upon them, that is—(1) Our " prayers " for them shall be heard. (2) Our "preaching " to them shall answer the end, and be effectual. (3) The fruit of both shall remain. 3. The text also shows us that we ought not to be overmuch discouraged in our work, though there be many who are never the better for our praying and preaching. Let us now make some application of all briefly. 1. Let this awaken us who are ministers to be faithful, and serious, and diligent *in* delivering our message ; as those who are in some measure sensible of the vast importance of the work we are employed in, and the dispensation that is committed to us. 2. Let us, when we have done what we can, look up to God for the success. 3. Let us be very careful that we do not, by any irregularity in our conversation, hinder the success of our praying and preaching, and defeat the ends of them. 4. What success of our labours we have the comfort of, let God have all the glory of. (*Matthew Henry.*) *Christian courtesy :*— I. THE BREADTH OF CHRISTIAN COURTESY. The kindly greeting, " Peace be to this house," was to be addressed to every family into which the seventy might enter. II. THE DEPTH OF CHRISTIAN COURTESY, the reality and meaning of their greeting, are brought before us in verse 6. Christ is telling them that their words are not to be a mere formal salutation ; He suggests that an influence of peace shall actually go out from them, to " rest upon " the house that receives them ; returning to them if rejected. The soul of Christian courtesy is faith ; our greetings are prayers. Trust in God is the animating principle of social kindness ; graciousness of disposition rests upon the grace of God. III. THESE ARE THE TWO FOUNDATIONS OF GENUINE CHRISTIAN COURTESY: 1. The sense of our Christian mission. 2. The certainty that we shall find many prepared for the Lord. 1. Christ sent His disciples to "heal the sick," to "cast out devils," and to say to all, "the kingdom of God is come nigh unto you." Could they doubt whether they would be received? Would not the sick man hail them from his couch? and the demoniac come trusting them to heal him? Their confidence that they were come on a blessed errand, that it was given to them to comfort the sorrowful, to sustain the sinking, to still the restless, and to proclaim the blessed name of Christ, would fill them with a confidence, a frankness, and a tenderness, that would secure them a welcome. With what words could they enter any house but those which Christ bade them first to speak? they were full of peace, they were charged and laden with peace; peace was the light of their eye, it was the spring of their footstep, it must breathe in their every tone. It would come forth from them because it was so fully in them; the messengers of peace could say no other words, no words before these, in whatsoever house they entered, "Peace be to this house." It is just this sense of a mission which Christ has entrusted to us, a holy, blessed message He has given us to utter, which is needed to make us frank and courteous to all men. Selfishness is the root of all moroseness and ungeniality. 2. The assurance that we shall find a people prepared for the Lord. Some households would reject the disciples, but not all; the son of peace would be beforehand with them in many a house, their prayer should be answered, and their peace should rest upon it. IV. I have already anticipated somewhat I had designed to say under our fourth head—THE BLESSED-NESS OF CHRISTIAN COURTESY. "If the son of peace be there, your peace shall rest upon it"; rest upon the household, and on you too while you are in it. The unforeseen welcome given you by many who return your cordial greeting; the humility, the heartiness, the joy with which they listen to your words; God's answer to the prayer of your greeting; in all this, you and they will share together. But look for a moment at the last clause of the verse, "If not, your peace shall turn to you again." Christ tells His disciples that some will reject them; not all our hope will be fulfilled. "If," you ask, "if my frank intercourse with the ungodly does not bless them, will it not injure me? But I fear lest I shall be depraved by too great frankness with worldly men, some of whom will continue worldly. Shall I not be charged with inconsistency?" To all these questions we have Christ's answer, "your peace shall turn to you again." No man is ever degraded by his love for the ungodly. Christ's name is not dishonoured by the tender, gracious association of His people with the lost souls to whom He sends them. You know of whom it was said, "this Man receiveth sinners, and eateth with them." You may be misjudged by your fellow-Christians, but you will not be misjudged by your Lord. (*A. Mackennal, D.D.*) *Christ's first message is peace:*— Here we may observe the method of our Saviour. He, coming to fight against the pomp, the covetousness, the luxury of the world, first offers terms of peace, and instructs His disciples as God did Moses: "When thou comest nigh unto a city to fight against it, then proclaim peace unto it" (Deut. xx. 10). As we read of Tamerlane, He first hangs out His white flag of peace, not His black nor His bloody colours. He fights not against us to destroy us, till we have wearied His mercy, and stood out too long. First He tenders peace: but it is the wickedness of the wicked, the obstinacy of the enemy, that draws His sword. For God doth not, as Nimrod, destroy men for pleasure: He doth not set them up as a mark, and then shoot deadly arrows at them. He seems rather to carry peace and war *in sinu*, "in His bosom," as Fabius did in the skirt of his gown; and leaves it to our choice, which we will have. First peace shows itself, in His love, in His precepts; nay, in His threatenings and fearful menaces. He opened the mouth of His servant Noah, a "preacher of righteousness," before He "opened the windows of heaven, and broke up the fountains of the great deep" (Gen. vii. 11). He opened the mouth of His servant Moses, before the earth opened her mouth to swallow up Dathan and Abiram and their complices (Numb. xvi.). He doth not undermine us with double voices and double counsels and a holy dissimulation, as some call it, crying, "Peace," when He girds Himself with strength, and prepares Himself to battle; saying, "Peace," to that house which He meaneth to level with the ground. But He sends His ambassadors, and "Peace" is the first clause in their commission: "first" they must salute us, before He will strike us; "first" wish "peace," before He will furbish His sword. (*A. Farindon, D.D.*) *Proclaim peace:*—A writer in a Scottish magazine told of an earnest minister, who, thinking all his labours among his people fruitless, was so disheartened that he made up his mind to leave them. When meditating about a farewell sermon, he was struck with the words of this verse, and felt as if Christ were saying to him, "Ungrateful servant, are you not satisfied with this promise of Mine? Hold on, then, proclaiming peace." This accordingly he did, with renewed vigour. *Fireside ministry :*—These missioners were pioneers going in advance to waken thought, create expectation, inspire confidence, and announce the nearness of the revealing Christ. They took their orders from His lips and their methods from His life. The Master's charge to them is still vital; it has sterling and perennial value for us men in the midst of our accumulated social evils, our hoary and deep-seated social vices. Stripped of Oriental accident and incident, and expressed in the English of the hour, it supplies an invaluable recipe for the healing of our sick and diseased human life, and for the guidance of our Churches in their home missionary activities. Go to the people, get close to them, enter their houses and their hearts, make your mission domestic, be social and sociable, friendly and human, go not from house to house in a hurry, as though figures were redeemed souls, but stay long enough to win love; invite trust, and do nothing to thwart expectation; make men feel your tenderness is instinctive, and your desires real; prove that you work and speak on the common ground of manhood, and then you will have a right to say, "The kingdom of God is come nigh unto you," and the heart will feel the presence of that unseen rule, and the conscience confess its august authority. 1. According to the mind of our Teacher all really helpful human work must be rooted and grounded in loving friendship, and energized by an unhesitating trust in the men it seeks to cleanse and ennoble. Renan has said that the fireside preaching of the seventy missioners was one of the capital causes of the success of early Christianity. And surely, not even in our Lord's day, was this policy of making friends first, converts afterwards, more needed than in our own time. 2. The next stage in the work of the seventy, beyond the ministry of friendship, is that of compassionate healing. Christianity, like its Author, is essentially healing. 3. But the crowning service of man to man is the interpretation of life in the light of Divine ministration. The priests of friendship and healing have free course and are glorified only when they acknowledge God's sovereignty over the heart and soul. The supreme good is not a perfectly healthy body. The missioners did not reach the climax of their work until they said, "The kingdom of God is come nigh unto you." This is fireside preaching at its best. (1) This saying is a pertinent and necessary sermon on a physical text. "Do not stop at the healing of the body. Trace out the Divine handwriting on the renovated body, and say, 'See here, the kingdom of God is come nigh unto you.'" That is a blessed if difficult task. But (2) this unique declaration has this additional significance, that Christ Himself was on His way to these healed folks, and that their physical salvation was only an earnest bestowed by His advanced couriers of what He was also to give if only they would welcome Him. (*J. Clifford, D.D.*) *Only souls can save souls :*—Carry no purse, no wallet, no shoes. Go to your work with such perceptible signs of trust in men as shall at once disarm suspicion and inspire confidence. (*Ibid.*) *Deferred remuneration :*—Christmas Evans' parishioners seem to have been marked by an insatiable appetite for sermons, and by a singular disregard for the temporal comfort of the preacher. Once, when he had preached away from home, and had received less than his expenses, an old woman remarked to the great pulpit orator, "Well, Christmas, you have given us a wonderful sermon, and I hope you will be paid at the resurrection." "Yes, yes, no doubt of that," answered the preacher humorously, "but what am I to do till I get there? And there's the old white mare that carries me, what will she do? There will be no resurrection for her." *Ministers badly paid :*—I wonder whether some of the people who come to hear Christ's servants ever ask themselves the question, "How do these ministers live and pay their way?" "I thought they preached for souls," said one of these spiritual mendicants to Mr. Spurgeon, who required an able and intelligent preacher for the munificent sum of £60 a year. "So they do," replied the famous preacher; "but they would need some thousands of souls of your size to keep them from starving." (*Henry Varley.*)

Ver. 9. **The kingdom of God is come nigh unto you.**—*Nearness to the kingdom :*— This is a part of the discourse which Christ gave to His disciples when they were going forth to preach under His ministration. Their message was, "The kingdom of God is come nigh unto you." They were Jews in Jewry. They were preaching to their own countrymen—especially in Galilee; and this was a part of their message : the approach of the kingdom of God to all those that heard. Nothing more striking than the spiritual insight of our Lord. What is spiritual insight?

As it existed in our Master, it was a perception of developed and perfect forms of morality and religion as constituent elements of human life in the broadest statement. It included—1. A far more exalted idea of right and wrong than has been developed by human society. 2. A perception of character and conduct far more exalted than any that ordinary life develops. 3. A perception of the whole sphere of man. To Him life was a unit, and the life beyond was a part of it. Beyond all darkness He saw life and man in their higher relations, and in their possibilities. This higher spiritual condition, this perfectness of human nature in its aggregate emotions, now and hereafter, He called " The kingdom"; " The new kingdom"; " The kingdom of heaven"; " The kingdom of God"; and it was this that He told His disciples to preach when they went abroad.   Whenever outward circumstances brought men to a place where the influences that acted upon them tended to develop their higher nature, and carry them forward along the path of perfectibility, or where their state of mind tended to make them perceptive of truths which at other times had little power with them, or where they were by outward things made sensible to things insensible, lifting them to the relation of the heavenly life, then He spoke of them as being near the kingdom of God.   They were in a condition out of which should easily and naturally come spiritual development.   What were some of those times?   What may we gather in regard to them from a general inspection of Christ's ministry, and of His teachings to the people, and from our own experiences?   1. Times of general religious interest in communities bring the kingdom of God very near to men.   2. Any revelation to a man's consciousness of his exceeding need of change, of development, of exaltation; any influence which shall strike through a man, giving him a discriminating power by which he can separate between right and wrong, between better and worse, between good and better—any such revelation or influence brings him near to the kingdom of heaven. 3. Anything that brings to the personal consciousness and experience of a man a sense of his degraded condition may be said to bring the kingdom of God near to him.   4. Anything that reveals to a man the reality of his whole estate, and shows him a higher and supernal life, and gives him a consciousness of the stern, terrific danger that threatens him, is bringing him to the border of God's kingdom.   5. All the perceptions of concrete goodness which men gain, and which strike into their mind, bring them near to the kingdom of heaven.   6. All experiences of the unsatisfying condition of earthly life, are, or may be, instruments of bringing men to the very border of the kingdom of God.   7. Any cause of thought in ourselves, or any cause of thought in others brought to bear upon us, which opens clearly the nature of manhood, or the possibilities of the future endless development of human life, brings men not far from the kingdom of God. (*H. W. Beecher.*)

Vers. 10–12. **They receive you not.**—*Opportunity wasted:*—I. THE OBJECT TO WHICH THIS ALLEGATION RELATES—" The kingdom of God." 1. The gospel is designated " the kingdom of God," because it is constituted by God.   There is claimed on its behalf, strictly and truly, a Divine origin. 2. The gospel is designated " the kingdom of God," because it is the ordained instrument of God to restore His authority over the minds of men. II. THE FACT WHICH THE ALLEGATION AFFIRMS.   " The kingdom of God is come nigh unto you"—1. In the sacred and inspired writings. 2. In the proclamations and appeals of the ministry. 3. In the conversion of other men. 4. In the partial impressions of your own mind. III. THE DEPORTMENT WHICH THE ALLEGATION DEPRECATES. 1. Continued carelessness of the truth. 2. Continued rejection of the truth. (*J. Parsons.*) *The grace of salvation coming near us:*—I. WHEN MAY THE KINGDOM OF GOD (OR THE GOSPEL) BE SAID TO COME NIGH TO AN INDIVIDUAL OR A PEOPLE? 1. When it comes within the hearing of the ear. 2. When it reaches the understanding. 3. When it gains access to the conscience. II. WHY THE GOSPEL SALVATION IS BROUGHT NIGH TO SOME WHO ARE FINALLY LOST.   (*D. A. Clark.*)   *Symbolical action:*—To " shake off the dust of their feet " as a witness against any city which had wholly rejected their message, signified that they had no more part or lot with the inhabitants—that they would retain nothing of theirs, no, not so much as what accidentally cleaved to their sandals.   This was one of the many outward significant symbolical acts of which the special messengers of God made constant use.   Thus Jeremiah put on a yoke, and hid a girdle by the side of the Euphrates; thus Agabus bound St. Paul's girdle round his own hands and feet; and Paul himself and Barnabas on one occasion used this very sign of shaking off the dust of their feet against the Jews of Antioch in Pisidia, who had rejected God's word spoken by their mouth. We have given up altogether the use of such signs, and I believe have lost much by our rejection of them. (*M. F. Sadler.*)   *No room for excuse :*—The Rev. William Grimshaw, an early Methodist of eccentric manner, frequently would preach before the doors of such as neglected the parish worship. "If you will not come to hear me at the church," he would say on these occasions, "you shall hear me at home ; if you perish, you shall perish with the sound of the gospel in your ears." (*G. Stevens.*)

Vers. 13–15. Woe unto thee.—*The sentence of Chorazin :*—We may conceive some inhabitant of these Jewish towns demanding with astonishment, How can these things be? Shall we who are the children of Abraham be rejected, and the heathen be preferred in our stead? The Almighty Judge, we may hence collect, in the apportioning of rewards and punishments, regards not the actual amount of profligacy or virtue, but takes into consideration also the means of improvement enjoyed, the kind of information and light vouchsafed. He could estimate, in Tyre and Sidon, debased as they were by ignorance and idolatry, a disposition not indifferent to those proofs of Divine revelation, which to Bethsaida and Chorazin were exhibited in vain. He judges according to that hidden temper, according to that inward disposition; not by the acts committed, but by the circumstances also under which they are done. Nay, He judges of a degree of faith never actually called into existence. I. The first conclusion to be drawn from the text thus explained relates to the future condition of those millions of mankind who depart this life in ignorance of a Saviour's name. The sacrifice of Christ made atonement for the whole race of mankind. And though so many millions are ignorant of His name, yet in some of them is discerned a spirit which would enable them to have repented at His preaching. By that spirit it may be hereafter determined whether or no the merits of Jesus Christ are imparted for the salvation of their souls. II. Secondly, we may learn, from this view of the text, the probability of our being greatly mistaken in our views of the future judgment. III. And here, thirdly, it may be observed, that mankind are too ready to draw hasty conclusions, from anything which they can interpret as a manifest interference of Divine Providence for the punishment of sin. IV. Such, too, let us in the last place remember, is the sentence recorded against every one of us ourselves, if we know these things and do them not ; if we acknowledge these mighty works and yet repent not. Let us not then be deceived by the blessings of outward prosperity. They form part of our trial. (*C. Girdlestone, M.A.*)   *The danger of impenitence where the gospel is preached :*—I. I observe from this discourse of our Saviour that miracles are of great force and efficacy to bring men to repentance. II. I observe, likewise, from our Saviour's discourse, that God is not always obliged to work miracles for the conversion of sinners. III. I observe farther, from our Saviour's discourse, that the external means of repentance which God affords to men, do suppose an inward grace of God accompanying them, sufficiently enabling men to repent, if it be not their own fault ; I say, a sufficient grace of God accompanying the outward means of repentance, till, by our wilful and obstinate neglect and resistance, and opposition of this grace, we provoke God to withdraw it from the means, or else to withdraw both the grace and the means from us : otherwise impenitence, after such external means afforded, would be no new and special fault. IV. I observe from this discourse of our Saviour's, that an irresistible degree of grace is not necessary to repentance, nor commonly afforded to those who do repent. V. I observe from the main scope of our Saviour's discourse, that the sins and impenitence of men receive their aggravation, and consequently shall have their punishment proportionable, to the opportunities and means of repentance which those persons have enjoyed and neglected. For what is here said of miracles, is by equality of reason likewise true of all other advantages and means of repentance and salvation. VI. Sixth and last observation, and which naturally follows from the former, is this : that the case of those who are impenitent under the gospel is of all others the most dangerous, and their damnation shall be heaviest and most severe. (*Archbishop Tillotson.*)   *Chorazin :*—It stands in the midst of such desolation as must be seen to be believed. Millions of boulders cover the ground everywhere as far as the eye can reach. The terrible volcanic energy in this district ceased long before the historic period—how long no one can tell—and hence the aspect of the landscape must have been the same in Christ's day as at present. One very interesting feature of the ruins is that many of the dwelling-houses are still tolerably perfect, though in the days of St. Jerome (A.D. 331–420), Chorazin had long been deserted. They have stood tenantless for at least 1,500 years, and may well have been standing in the days when our Lord from time to time wandered among them, doing those mighty works which were yet, as at Bethsaida and Capernaum, ineffectual to bring the population to thoughtfulness and repentance. It helps one to realize better the daily life of our Saviour, to see in what poor barren spots He laboured; following the lost sheep of the house of Israel to such a forbidding wilderness. (*C. Geikie, D.D.*) *The guilt of a privileged people :*—Max Müller in the preface to his essays tells us of a Hindu who, having been converted in Benares, greatly wished to visit England. He had heard that it was a land of Bibles, a land of preaching, a land of churches and chapels, and he longed to see it. He expected to find the Christian land Christ-like. At length he arrived there. Max Müller adds that never shall he forget the deep dejection of the man when he discovered the Christianity of Europe to be so unlike that of the New Testament. In fact, nothing but keeping to the teachings of the Bible kept him from an utter relapse into idolatry.

Ver. 16. **He that heareth you heareth Me.**—*A Christian minister the voice of Christ :*—We send an ambassador to England ; there is a difference of opinion between our Government and that of England. The ambassador is in a circle in society, but he does not take his opinions from the English people ; he cares nothing what they think on national subjects ; the crowd around him may be indignant against this country, but the ambassador listens not to the voice of the populace around him. He bends a listening ear for the telegraphic communication from Washington, and whatever words he hears those he utters, no matter how they may be received, no matter what the people or the crown may think. He stands an American in the midst of English society ; he thinks the thoughts and has the feelings of the Government at Washington ; he dares to say words however unpleasant to the English crown because the power that sustains him, though it is invisible, he knows to be real. Well, now, so is it with a man, principally the true minister of Christ. For instance, he goes into a community where all are infidel or all are heathen. What the sentiment of the populace is he asks not ; what the people will think of him for uttering his words he cares not, but he bends his ear and listens for words from the throne, and when God says : " Speak in the hearing of the people," he speaks the words that are given to him and stands unmoved. He may behold the rack, the stake, the torch, and the fagots kindling about it, and the wild beasts, but his thoughts and conversation are in heaven ; he stands unmoved, and he is looking at the unseen. (*M. Simpson, D.D.*)

Vers. 17–20. **The seventy returned.**—*The seventy :*—I. COMMISSION OF THE SEVENTY. 1. They were commissioned of Christ. 2. They were commissioned of Christ to prepare the way before Him. 3. They received special directions when commissioned. (1) Every one deeming himself commissioned of Christ should carefully study his Lord's " marching orders." (2) To ignore these instructions is to prove unfitness for the Lord's service. II. ENDOWMENT OF THE SEVENTY. Miraculous and spiritual power. III. IDENTIFICATION OF THE SEVENTY WITH CHRIST. 1. His gospel they were to preach. 2. Himself they were to represent. (1) Such identification is the mark of every minister of Christ. (2) Such identification devolves on hearers of the gospel a responsibility simply unspeakable. IV. RETURN OF THE SEVENTY. 1. The spirit in which they returned. Rejoicing. 2. The ground of their rejoicing. (1) The power with which they were invested. (2) This ground not sufficient. (3) Why? (*a*) Because of its temporariness. (*b*) Because of its dangerous tendency. 3. The true ground for Christian joy. Names written in heaven. (1) More permanent. (2) More glorious. (3) More satisfactory. V. CHRIST'S JOY IN THE SEVENTY. Because of the honour the Father conferred on them. Lessons : 1. Whom Christ commissions He sufficiently endows. 2. Not great power, position, or genius the true ground of the minister's joy, but a " name written in heaven." (*D. C. Hughes, M.A.*) *Reporting to Christ :*—This mission and re-assembly representative for all time. This is the order of all real Christian movements and missions—from Christ to Christ. I. THE DISCIPLES' REPORT. We see them—1. Acting under a sense of responsibility. 2. Conscious of Christ's continued presence and power with them. The only universal guarantee of success. 3. Taking note only of secondary and superficial circumstances of success. A false guage. How careful we should be in our estimates of Christian work! II. THE MASTER'S RECEPTION OF IT. He awaits them with—1. An interpretation : " I was beholding." Whilst they laboured He was watching and praying. He saw Satan's downthrow. He encouraged them, and all who should follow them, to take deeper and higher views of their work. 2. A promise. 3. A caution. The true source of satisfaction is acceptance with God, and conscious communion with Him. (*St. John A. Frere, M.A.*) *Return of the seventy :*—I. GOSPEL WORKERS IN LARGE NUMBERS MAY BE SPEEDILY EQUIPPED AND PROFITABLY EMPLOYED. Let the Church multiply " seventies " who shall go forth two by two, and will not the Lord be sure to follow? II. FAITHFUL SERVICE FOR CHRIST BRINGS GLAD SURPRISES. Often these victories are over self. Plans for life, before worldly and selfishly ambitious, are revolutionized. Fame's siren song is without power to charm, its spell broken. Wealth for its own sake ceases its fascinations. Sad memories, disappointments, defeats, that once brought shadows and heart-ache, though not forgotten, lose their power to hurt. Habits, appetites, once dominant with more than despot's thrall and merciless cruelty, are exorcised ; and the utter hopelessness of despair gives away to the buoyancy of glad faith. In Christian work, faculties take a wider range and greater efficiency than would otherwise have been possible. Slow lips become eloquent, intellects sluggish and unfruitful are cleared and competent, hands idle and inapt are active and dexterous. III. A COMPLETE TRIUMPH OF HIS GOSPEL IS A VISION EVER PRESENT WITH OUR LORD. IV. SOLDIERS IN THE LORD'S ARMY ARE PROMISED A COMPLETE SAFETY FROM THE POWER OF THE ENEMY. We know that the promised power over serpents and scorpions was literally bestowed. Paul, at Melita, unharmed shook the deadly viper from his hand ; but the twentieth verse means more than immunity from natural evil. To-day, the words of Paul to Timothy are true : " Yea, and all that will live godly in Christ Jesus shall suffer persecution." How explain the apparent contradiction? 1. We may understand that physical protection and preservation will be given to all who are about the Lord's business. Paul might be shipwrecked, but his life was safe until he had preached the gospel " at Rome also." 2. The Christian has fewer points of attack open to the enemy. The pure in heart are repelled by that which allures the impure. The lowly mind does not see the high things which dazzle and intoxicate. 3. The enemy is permitted power over the children of God, only thereby to bring to himself more utter defeat. 4. To all who suffer for Christ, pain is not hurt nor loss. It brings a divine ministry, the forerunner of promotion and sure joy. Christ in the soul brings a kingdom invulnerable to the enemy. Poverty, stripes, and imprisonment, all earthly ill, are powerless to invade that domain. V. THE DISCIPLE OF CHRIST SHOULD REJOICE MOST, NOT IN VIEW OF VICTORIES HERE, BUT BECAUSE OF COMING REWARDS IN HEAVEN. (*S. L. B. Speare.*) *Mission of the seventy disciples :*—I. THE MISSION OF THE SEVENTY DISCIPLES IS HERE IMPLIED. 1. The purpose for which they were sent. 2. The way in which they were sent. (1) They were sent out in pairs. (2) They were to prosecute their work without loss of time. (3) The manner in which they were to conduct themselves in their visits, and that in reference to those who received and those who rejected them. II. THE SUCCESS THEY MET WITH IS HERE DECLARED. 1. Exceedingly novel. 2. Pre-eminently strange. 3. Not by any skill or energy of their own. " Through Thy name." III. THE FEELING WITH WHICH THEY REGARDED THEIR SUCCESS IS HERE SHOWN. 1. They rejoiced in the fact that success had attended their efforts. 2. That beings so hateful and dangerous were overcome. 3. The happiness which they had been instrumental in diffusing. 4. In the success of the great cause with which they were identified. IV. A CONSIDERATION IS URGED WITH THE VIEW OF MODERATING THEIR JOY, AND DIRECTING IT INTO ANOTHER AND HIGHER CHANNEL. We see here the comparative estimate in which miraculous gifts and saving grace should be held. What is the former without the latter? It is possible to possess the one without the other (Matt. vii. 21–23). To have cast out devils, and to be ourselves at last cast out among devils, will be horrible indeed ! 1. What is meant by having our names written in heaven. It signifies that we are citizens of the celestial city, that we are freemen of the New Jerusalem, and that all its honours and privileges are ours by a rightful title. 2. How the fact may be ascertained. If we are citizens of heaven our conversation is there; we are strangers and pilgrims on earth ; like the patriarchs of old, we are looking for a city which hath foundations, whose builder and maker is God. 3. Those may well rejoice who have satisfactory grounds for concluding that this privilege is theirs. (*Expository Outlines.*) **I beheld Satan as lightning-fall from heaven.**—*Looking back upon our earthly life:*— These words refer to a definite moment in Jesus' life. That same hour in which He sent forth the seventy, He beheld Satan fall from Heaven. Yet that was a prophetic vision of the Lord. When He saw Satan falling, Jesus was in spirit above time, beholding as one finished whole, from the beginning to the end, the history of God's conquest of evil. While the seventy were going forth to win their first unexpected success in His name, the Lord in prophetic anticipation was looking back upon His work and theirs as a work already accomplished ; as even the devils, to their surprise, began to be subject unto them, His Spirit went forward to the final triumph of redemption, and, as one looking back from its completion, Jesus beheld Satan fallen. Throwing ourselves forward in the pure imaginations of faith into the world to come, let us seek to look back and down upon this world as though we already were beyond it. Surrendering ourselves to our faith, and with our powers of spiritual imagination lent to the aid of our faith, let us seek humbly to imitate our Master, and look upon our world as He looked upon this earth, when, as from a position in eternity, He saw Satan fall from heaven. I. In the first place, if we look upon our own lives as one looks back upon a way already trodden, and a work already accomplished, we shall gain a truer sense of the proportions of things. If we can succeed in transporting ourselves beyond the present, and regarding its occupations as already past; if we can draw back, as it were, in our own souls from the events of now and here, and regard our whole life, past, present, and future, as one undivided and completed whole ; then we cannot fail to gain a more just estimate of the real proportions of events in our lives, and to correct, as in a large view from beyond, our present sense of the relative importance of things. And just this true sense of proportion in life is hard for us to keep in the nearness of present things ; yet it is essential to large, happy living that we should gain and keep it. II. In the second place, in so far as we can put ourselves in the exercise of our own faiths beyond this life, we shall gain in many respects a different, and in all a more just estimate of our own real attainments. We shall see more clearly what we may expect to win for ourselves from life. Look down now upon what you have made, or are making, for yourselves in this world from this higher position after your own death. Measure what you are seeking to attain by its worth as judged by that estimate from beyond. From this point of view let us seek to determine what are the real attainments which a human being may reach in this world. That artizan, for example, has stood up faithfully for years to his work. He dies. The arm loses its strength, and the hand its cunning. What can he have gained by years of faithful work in making square-joints, honest insides, or lines true to an infinitesimal ? What can the workman be conceived as keeping hereafter as the reward of all his labour under the sun ? Not the eye, not the arm of flesh ; yet the doctrine of the resurrection stands in the Scriptures as the pledge that our life here and hereafter is to be in all its powers one continuous life ; and though this body shall return to dust, the discipline and capacity of the man, which is to be gained through the right exercise even of these bodily powers, is something which may count in the life of man for ever. Even in the honest and best exercise of his bodily senses a man may be training himself for the quick and skilled use of those powers of spiritual embodiment which shall succeed these mortal powers. That artist, for instance, who one evening as we gained the crest of a hill, with an exclamation of delight, counted instantly five different hues upon the horizon where my duller eye had only seen at first glance one resplendence of the setting sun, may have gained in that quick sense of colour a power which shall be carried on as a possession of the soul into the spiritual body, enabling that trained artist's spirit hereafter to see with instantaneous and enhanced delight the hues and harmonies of colour of the new heavens and the new earth. Hence I venture to say that the training and discipline of any power in the honest work of a lifetime may be so much real attainment for immortality—so much gain carried in the man himself through death into the world of larger opportunity. A man, therefore, should perform all his labour on this earth not as though what he does now is all of it, but as an heir of immortality. Jesus lived for two worlds at one and the same time. He was the Son of Man who was in heaven, as the Scripture says. All true, deep life must have something of the sense of heaven in it as a present fact. III. We are led, thus, to the third remark that only as we strive to throw ourselves forward into the life beyond, and to consider our whole existence here as it is in its relation to the man and his life then and there, can we form a safe estimate of the *worths* of things. Such and such opportunities are brought now within reach of a young man or woman. What are they worth ? Success is a safe happiness to the Christian man who can look down upon it as from out the kingdom of heaven. Success is a danger and snare of soul to that man who is not himself already in his heart above it. This position, finally, as of one looking back upon this world, which we all need sometimes to take in the Christian imaginations of faith, is the position from which in a little while we must be judging all things both in life and death. Our whole life erelong shall be one finished picture in the retrospect. And may it lie then behind us in the softening, hallowing light of God's grace! By the grace of God, the penitent, converted man, even now judging himself from out the hereafter, as Christ did the world, may say: From my life I saw sin falling; from the heaven of my desires I beheld Satan fallen; —Behold God alone is reigning. (*Newman Smyth, D.D.*) *Satan lamed by his fall from heaven:*—There is a strangely widespread belief that Satan is lame, and that this was caused by his fall. In classical mythology we find limping Vulcan ; and Hephaistes was lamed by his fall when hurled by Zeus from Olympus. Our idea of the devil always includes the clubbed or cloven foot. (*Biblical Things not Generally Known.*) **Power to tread on serpents and scorpions.**—*Scorpions:*—Of these Tristram says: "They swarm in every part of Palestine, and are found in houses, in chinks of walls, among ruins, and under stones, whether in dry or moist situations. It is always necessary before pitching tents to turn up every stone, however small, lest a scorpion should be secreted ; as, when disturbed or roused by the warmth of the camp, these troublesome pests will strike at and sting any person or object within reach. So numerous are they that in the warmer parts of the country every third stone is sure to conceal one. . . . I have known an instance of a man dying from the effects of a scorpion's sting, which he had received in the throat when leaning against a wall in which the creature was secreted." The scorpion is described as having much the appearance of a small lobster; it has two claws, extending from near the head, eight feet, and a long, jointed tail, terminating in the sting, which inflicts a painful and sometimes fatal wound. The largest and most dangerous species is black, and about six inches long. *Suicide of the scorpion:*—Mr. Allen Thomson, in a letter published in *Nature*, says : "While residing many years ago during the summer months at the baths of Lucca, in Italy, in a somewhat damp locality, my informant, together with the rest of the family, was much annoyed by the intrusion of small black scorpions into the house, and their being secreted among the bed-clothes, in shoes, and in other articles of dress. It thus became necessary to be constantly on the watch for these troublesome creatures, and to take means for their removal and destruction. Having been informed by the natives of the place that the scorpion would destroy itself if exposed to a sudden light, my informant and her friends soon became adepts in catching the scorpions and disposing of them in the manner suggested. This consisted in confining the animal under an inverted drinking-glass or tumbler, below which a card was inserted when the capture was made, and then, waiting till dark, suddenly bringing the light of a candle near to the glass in which the animal was confined. No sooner was this done than the scorpion invariably showed signs of great excitement, running round and round the interior of the tumbler with reckless velocity for a number of times. This state having lasted for a minute or more, the animal suddenly became quiet, and turning its tail or the hinder part of its body over its back, brought its recurved sting down upon the middle of the head, and, piercing it forcibly, in a few seconds became quite motionless, and, in fact, quite dead. This observation was repeated very frequently; in truth it was adopted as the best plan of getting rid of the animals, and the young people were in the habit of handling the scorpions with impunity immediately after they were so killed, and of preserving many of them as curiosities." *Power of spiritual life:*—Brainerd, in his narrative of his work among the American Indians, confesses his great embarrassment. "When I have instructed them respecting the miracles wrought by Christ, they have quickly referred to the wonders of that kind performed by their diviner; . . . a fatal obstruction to some of them in the way of receiving the gospel." Yet, though Brainerd could do none of these mighty works, he was the means of the conversion of that very diviner by the influence of his own life and the spiritual truths which he taught. (*J. M. Buckley.*) *Divine protection:*—Mr. Gobat, the late Bishop of Jerusalem, when engaged as a missionary in Abyssinia, retired on one occasion, in a season of deep spiritual depression and gloom, into a cavern, and there poured out his heart in earnest supplication, beseeching that God would not desert him, but encourage him in his trials. He remained in the cavern for some time. When he rose from his knees, his eyes had become accustomed to the darkness, and he saw that he had been there with a hyena and her cubs, which yet had, marvellously, not been permitted to attack him. At the very time when he deemed himself forgotten, he received this striking manifestation that the God of providence was nigh to shield and protect him. (*Memoirs of Bishop Gobat.*)   *Immunity from snake-bites :*—The Psylli, according to Pliny, were so characteristically endowed with this immunity (from snake-bites), that they made it a test of the legitimacy of their children ; for they were accustomed to expose their new-born babes to the most venomous serpents they could find, assured that if their paternity was pure Psyllic they would be quite unharmed. Of this tribe was the ambassador Hexagon, who, boasting of his powers before the Roman consuls, submitted to the crucial test which they suggested, of being enclosed in a vessel swarming with poisonous reptiles, which, says the legendary story, hurt him not. (*Philip H. Gosse, F.R.S.*) **Rejoice, because your names are written in heaven.**—*The supreme joy :*—I. Christian citizenship is man's highest blessedness. This is the first thing I have to endeavour to illustrate and impress. 1. And in the forefront of all I set this consideration, namely, that the having the name written in heaven implies the Divine acceptance of us, as attested to our consciousness. Indeed, brethren, this is a blessed thing ; blessed in itself, and blessed, moreover, in all its bearings and influences upon all our life. For, to know that we are at peace with God and are now the objects of the Divine complacency, O how it bathes everything with its own sunshine ! Look out upon the world with eyes purged by the euphrasy of God's acceptance of you through Christ, and you will see it flushed with a thousand beauties never seen till now, and brightened with glancing lights and splendours where before it was all darkness and gloominess to you. 2. Emancipation from the thraldom of sin, and introduction into the glorious liberty of the children of God. " Free." " Free indeed." Yes, it is a glorious freedom that is conferred upon the heavenly citizen. " He is the freedman whom the truth makes free; and all are slaves besides." It is not liberty merely to have no gyves upon your wrist and no clanking fetters about your feet. That is a poor thing in comparison of that inward deliverance from the tyranny of evil which enables a man to stand up in the blessed consciousness that he is now master even of himself. Besides, the freedom of the children of God has another side. It is not only a freedom from sin, it is also a freedom unto God and unto holiness. 3. Then, further, in this citizenship there is also an immunity from care. Now, I say, when a man becomes a citizen of heaven he is set free from this care, as well as from sin. The charter of the New Jerusalem assures him that having secured the highest good all lesser good shall be added unto him. 4. Then, too, in illustrating the blessedness of the Christian citizen I ought to speak of the " strong consolation " which is ministered to him in all times of his adversity and sorrow. An immunity from trial is not indeed among his privileges. That would not be for his real good. No ; as steel acquires its fine temper in the fire, as the sweetest music issues from the darkened cage, as spices must be bruised if we would breathe their odours, so " blessed are they that mourn " ; " blessed are they that weep now." A blessedness is theirs which the always prosperous and the ever merry cannot know. 5. Last of all, and best of all, beyond all this wealth of earthly advantage and benefit there is laid up for the Christian citizen the blessedness of the life to come. To have the name written in heaven is to be able " to read our titles clear to mansions in the skies." II. And now it will not need, I think, that I should argue the point of the text, viz., that enrolment in heaven should constitute our master-joy. For all rational beings their chief good should and must form their chief joy. III. And so, in conclusion, and as the practical outcome of the subject for ourselves, let me say— 1. First, to those of you who can rejoice in the assurance that your names are written in heaven. Take care that this joy maintain its supremacy within you. Be sure that you allow no other joy to displace it or to overtop it. Observe it—I do not say—even as our Lord does not say in the text, rightly understood—that you are not to rejoice at all in anything save and besides your Christian felicity. That were ingratitude to God. That were an irrational asceticism. Nay, but if you have health of body and soundness of mind, rejoice in this physical blessedness, as being of priceless advantage to you. 2. And, to those of you whose names are not yet written in heaven, let me say that this supreme joy of religion, so far from extinguishing such of your earthly pleasures as are innocent and legitimate, would inconceivably brighten and increase them. (*T. Akroyd.*)   *Why may I rejoice ?*—I. The joy which needs moderating. The joy of triumph over evil spirits, the joy of having preached the gospel and wrought wonders—in a word, the joy of gifts, power, and success. This needs moderating—1. Because it is so apt to degenerate into pride. 2. Again, this joy which needs to be moderated should be restrained by the reflection that it is no evidence of grace in the heart that we possess gifts, or that we are successful. Talents are possessed even by wicked and slothful servants. Grace without talent will save, but talent without grace will only increase our condemnation. 3. Moreover, it is very unsafe to rejoice unduly in the work which we have done, because the work after all may not turn out to be all that it appears. It is too early to begin to rejoice until the fire has passed over our life-work. 4. This joy, again, however good our work may be, is to be moderated, because it does not prove that we are any more gracious than others of far less gift and usefulness. 5. Again, this joy in success needs to be kept under tight rein because it is not an abiding joy. If thou, O man, rejoice to-day because of subject devils, what wilt thou do to-morrow, when the devils break loose again? What if He should send thee among Samaritans, who will not even hear thee, and thou shalt have to go from city to city and wipe off the dust of thy feet against them? 6. Once again, this joy, if we were to be filled with it to overflowing, would be found unable to bear the strain of trial, trouble, temptation, and especially of death. II. THE JOY WHICH NEEDS EXCITING. "Because your names are written in heaven." 1. The joy which our Lord commends is one which springs from faith, while the other joy arises alone from sight. 2. This joy consists in knowing our election—"knowing, dearly beloved, your election of God," knowing that your names were written in heaven. To be God's choice is the choicest of delights. 3. Brethren, this is a joy which can be cultivated. How are we to cultivate it? If we desire to have much of this joy we must make the fact sure. We must be certain that our names are written in heaven, or else we cannot rejoice in it. III. Now, lastly, into this joy the Saviour enters, and we have to look, in the third place, to THE JOY OF THE LORD IN SYMPATHY with it, and so we add to our text the first sentence of the 21st verse—"In that hour Jesus rejoiced in spirit." Why did He rejoice? 1. Because grace was given. 2. Jesus was also glad at the Father's choice. He said, "I thank Thee, O Father." He looks at these seventy babes out of whose mouth He has ordained strength, and He says, "I thank thee, O Father, for having chosen these." 3. Notice the spirit in which Jesus puts His thanksgiving—He is satisfied with the choice because it is God's choice. "Even so, Father," said He, "for so it seemed good in Thy sight." 4. Then our Saviour went on to rejoice because the grace of God given to us has revealed to us Christ, and revealed to us the Father, for He says, "no man knoweth who the Son is, but the Father; and who the Father is, but the Son, and he to whom the Son will reveal Him." 5. Jesus exulted because there was a fellowship about all this, for He speaks of His knowing the Father and the Father knowing Him, and then of our knowing the Father because the Son has revealed Him unto us—all of which implies a wondrous communication and communion with the Father and with the Son. Now, this, I take it, is the cream of joy, a joy in which Christ partakes as He has fellowship with the Father and with us, and of which we partake as we have fellowship with Him and with the Father. (*C. H. Spurgeon.*) *The successful minister's safeguard:*—I. THE JUSTIFICATION OF THE REJOICING SPIRIT WHICH THE SEVENTY NOW EXHIBIT. 1. It was in spiritual matter. 2. It was with a self-renouncing disposition that they expressed it. 3. Their report is brought direct to the feet of their Master. 4. There is evidently no mistake in their report, no delusion on their part. II. THE JUSTIFICATION OF THE CAUTION OR SUGGESTION WHICH CHRIST HERE UTTERS. 1. To rejoice genuinely, in even the very highest work done for the soul of another, must have its dangerous side. It does not guide a humbling look into oneself. 2. It may have a directly disastrous effect, feeding spiritual pride, contributing to self-confidence, and absolutely calling off the attention of the soul from itself. 4. On the other hand, rejoicing in the conviction or in the certainty that one's own "name is written in heaven," leads one to review all that is most desirable to review. (*Philip C. Barker, M.A.*) *The highest eulogy:*—"Your names are written in heaven." 1. How it is to be understood. 2. How desirable it is. 3. How alone it is to be obtained. (*Van Oosterzee.*) *The certainty of salvation:*—1. Its only ground. 2. Its all-surpassing worth. (*Ibid.*) *The noblest source of joy:*—Heaven is here compared to a city or corporation, in which a list or record is kept of all the citizens or freemen who are entitled to its privileges and immunities. "How may I know whether my unworthy name be written in heaven? who can open and read the records of heaven, and show me whether my name is registered there?" I answer, This is a secret that may be discovered; for all that have their names written in heaven, may be distinguished by their characters, their temper, and practice, while upon earth. And their characters are such as these : 1. They are deeply sensible of the vanity of all earthly things, and that heaven alone is a sufficient portion and happiness. All that are registered as citizens of the heavenly Jerusalem, have a superlative esteem of that privilege, and count all things but loss in comparison of it (Matt. xii. 24–26; xiii. 45, 46). 2. All that have their names written in heaven have a heavenly nature ; a nature very different from that of the men of this world, and like that of the citizens of heaven. And is this your temper ? or is it earthly and sensual ? 3. All that have their names written in heaven have a peculiar love for all their fellow-citizens, who are heirs of heaven. They love them as members of the same corporation with themselves (1 John iii. 14). 4. If your names are written in heaven it is the chief business and concern of your life to obtain an interest in heaven. And do you thus seek the kingdom of heaven ? (Matt. x. 12 ; Luke xvi. 16). I. If your names are written in heaven, this is the greatest cause of joy you can possibly have; a joy that may swallow up every other joy. II. If your names are not written in heaven, you can have no cause of solid, rational, and lasting joy in any thing. (*President Davies.*) *The true doctrine of election :*—This opinion is not believed by thee, but is only pretended, as a cloak for thy wickedness and idleness ; for if thou dost believe that, if God hath elected, He will save thee however thou livest, why are not thy practices answerable to such principles ? Why dost thou not leave thy ground unsowed, and thy calling unfollowed, and say, If God hath decreed me a crop of corn, I shall have it, whether I sow my ground or no ; and if God hath decreed me an estate, I shall have it, though I never mind my calling? Why dost thou not neglect and refuse eating, and drinking, and sleeping, and say, If God hath decreed that I shall live longer, I shall do it, though I never eat, or drink, or sleep ? For God hath decreed these things concerning thy ground, estate, and natural life, as well as concerning thine eternal condition in the other world. (*G. Swinnock.*) *Insured election :*—A senator related to his son the account of the book containing the names of illustrious members of the commonwealth. The son desired to see the outside. It was glorious to look upon. " Oh, let me open it," said the son. " Nay," said the father : " it's known only to the council." Then said the son, " Tell me if my name is there ? " " And that," said the father, " is a secret known only to the council, and it cannot be divulged." Then he desired to know for what achievements the names were inscribed in that book. So the father told him ; and related to him the achievements and noble deeds by which they had eternized their names. " Such," said he, " are written, and none but such are written in the book." " And will my name be there?" said the son." " I cannot tell thee," said the father; "if thy deeds are like theirs, thou shalt be written in the book; if not, thou shalt not be written." And then the son consulted with himself ; and he found that his whole deeds were playing, and singing, and drinking, and amusing himself, and he found this was not noble nor temperate nor valiant. And as he could not read, as yet, his name, he determined to "make his calling and election sure." And thus, by patient continuance in well-doing, the end is crowned with glory, honour, immortality, and eternal life.

Vers. 21, 22. **Jesus rejoiced in Spirit.**—*Christ glorifies His Father and magnifies Himself :*—Learn hence—1. That till God reveals Himself, His nature and will, no man can know either what He is, or what He requires—" Thou hast revealed." 2. That the wise and knowing men in the world have in all ages despised the mysteries of the gospel, and have therefore been judicially blinded by God—" Thou hast hid these things from the wise and prudent." When men shut their eyes against the clearest light, and say they will not see, God closes their eyes and says they shall not see. 3. That the most ignorant, if humble, and desirous of spiritual illumination, are in the readiest disposition to embrace the gospel revelation—" Thou hast revealed them unto babes." 4. That this is not more pleasing to Christ than it is the pleasure of His Father—" Even so, Father, for so it seemed good in Thy sight." Observe—Our Saviour magnifies Himself : 1. His authority and commission—" All things are delivered unto Me " ; that is, all power is committed unto Me, as Mediator, from God the Father. 2. His office to reveal His Father's will to a lost world—" No man knoweth the Father but the Son, or the Son but the Father " ; that is, no man knoweth their essence and nature, their will and pleasure, their counsel and consent, their mutual compact and agreement betwixt themselves, for saving a lost world, but only themselves, " and those to whom they have revealed it." Learn thence, That all saving knowledge of God is in, by, and through Christ ; He, as the Great Prophet of His Church, reveals unto us the mind and will of God for our salvation.

(*W. Burkitt.*) *Lessons :*—1. Let me ask you if you resemble Christ in rejoicing at the success of true religion ? He greatly rejoiced in spirit, and gave thanks to His Father, that Satan was dethroned, and that, though some were obstinate, others were blessed with a saving discovery of Divine things. 2. Beware of being proud of your own wisdom and prudence, and cherish the humility and teachableness of babes. 3. We should learn, from the twenty-second verse, never to separate the truths of what is called natural religion from the gospel. The idea that there is, or can be, any true and acceptable religion whatever, apart from the revelation of Christ, is here shown to be quite preposterous. The true Witness declares that no man can know the Father except he to whom He shall reveal Him. 4. Let us be thankful for the precious religious privileges which we enjoy, and careful to improve them. " Blessed are the eyes which see the things that ye see." 5. Lastly : Are we blessed, because our eyes see, and our ears hear these things?—then, Christian benevolence should lead us to feel for those who enjoy no such privileges, and to do everything we can to extend them to the utmost corners of the earth. (*Jas. Foote, M.A.*) *The Saviour's joy :*—The sublimity of this joy we feel the more, when we compare with it that of the seventy. They rejoice in the great things, He in the good brought to pass; they have their joy directed to the outer, Jesus His to the moral world ; they rejoice alone in the present, Jesus also in the past and the future ; they are disposed to self-praise, Jesus to thankful adoration. (*Van Oosterzee.*) *Christ's joy :*—1. An example of the joy which the Lord sometimes experienced upon earth. 2. An image of the joy which He now experiences in heaven. 3. A presage of the blessedness which He shall hereafter taste when the kingdom of God shall be fully perfected. (*Ibid.*) *The joy of Jesus :*—It is remarkable that this is the only instance on record in the Gospels in which our Lord is said to have rejoiced. Yet I do not think it would be fair to infer from the fact of a solitary mention of His rejoicing that He did not rejoice at other times ; on the contrary, our Lord must, despite His sorrow, have possessed a peaceful, happy spirit. He was infinitely benevolent, and went about doing good ; and benevolence always finds a quiet delight in blessing others. Moreover, our Lord was so pure that He had a well of joy within which could not fail Him. Besides, Christ Jesus was a man of faith ; faith's highest exposition and example. He it was, who " for the joy that was set before Him endured the cross, despising the shame." His faith must, therefore, have anticipated the reward of His passion, and have brought the joy thereof home to Him even while He sorrowed here. It is clear that joy was not a distinguishing feature in our Lord's life, so as to strike the beholder. Peace may have sat serenely on His brow, but nothing of the exuberant spirits which are seen in some men, for His countenance was marred with lines of care and grief. The words here used are very emphatic. " He rejoiced." The Greek word is much stronger than the English rendering ; it signifies " to leap for joy." It is the word of the blessed Virgin's song, " My spirit hath rejoiced in God my Saviour." Strong emotions of delight were visible upon our Lord's face, and were expressed by the tones of His voice as well as by His words. It is clear that He was greatly glad. The text also says, He " rejoiced in spirit " : that is, deep down in the very centre of His nature, in that largest and most capacious part of His human being, the Redeemer rejoiced. I. Our Lord's joy was JOY IN THE FATHER'S REVELATION OF THE GOSPEL. 1. I call your attention to the fact that He ascribed all that was done to the Father, and joyed that the Father was working with Him. 2. The Saviour's joy was that through the Father's grace men were being enlightened. 3. Further, our Saviour's joy lay very much in this, that this revelation to men was being made through such humble instruments. 4. And yet, further, His great joy was that the converts were of such a character as they were. 5. Our Lord's joy sprang from one other source, namely, His view of the manner in which God was pleased to save His people. It was by revealing these things to them. There is, then, to every man who is saved a revelation, not of anything over and above what is given us in the Word of God ; but of that same truth to Himself personally and with power. In the word is the light ; but what is needed is that each man's eye should be opened by the finger of God to see it. II. OUR LORD'S MODE OF EXPRESSING HIS JOY. 1. His joy finds tongue in thanksgiving. 2. He found expression for His joy in declaring the Father's sovereignty. 3. He delighted in the special act of sovereignty which was before Him, that the Lord had "hid these things from the wise and prudent, and had revealed them unto babes." His voice, as it were, went with the Father's voice ; He agreed with the Father's choice, He rejoiced in it, He triumphed in it. III. Thirdly, and briefly, I want you to see

OUR LORD'S EXPLANATION OF THE FATHER'S ACT. The Father had been pleased to hide these things from the wise and prudent and to reveal them unto babes, and Jesus Christ is perfectly satisfied with that order of things, quite content with the kind of converts He has and the kind of preachers that God has given Him. The Lord Jesus does not need prestige. 2. See how the Lord explains it yet further, by showing that human wisdom cannot find out God. Next, learn that the sovereignty of God is always exercised in such a way that the pure in heart may always rejoice in it. God never did a sovereign act yet that the loving Christ Himself could not rejoice in. The ultimate honour of the gospel is secured unto God alone, let that be our last lesson. (*C. H. Spurgeon.*) **Revealed them unto babes.** *Why God reveals to babes :*—The babe is the representative of the receptive spirit. Its characteristic is trust, openness to impression, and freedom from prejudice. The disciples were babes who lay open to the Divine message, and did not interpose theories and traditions. They were poor and knew it, and were willing to become rich. To them God revealed. But the revealing to a certain disposition is of necessity the hiding from its opposite. I. To REVEAL TO BABES HARMONIZES WITH GOD'S CHARACTER AS A FATHER AND ILLUSTRATES IT. "Babe" is the counterpart to "Father"—"wise and understanding" has no such relation. The wise and understanding might have a special relation to an almighty Taskmaster, an infinite Schoolmaster and Prizegiver; but certainly not to an infinite Father. A father's heart is not attracted to the brilliance or power in his family, but to the want. The gospel is salvation by the free gift of God. Any true conception of the evil of sin, and its effects on the soul, renders other ideas of salvation incredible. We call God Father, and ask His forgiveness. Salvation by grace is bound up with the Divine arrangement, which reveals to babes. The distinction of the babe is just here—he is adapted to salvation by grace. II. IT GLORIFIES GOD AS LORD OF HEAVEN AND EARTH TO REVEAL TO BABES. That God is Lord of heaven and earth makes His lowliness not less, but more needful and credible. The more you extend the empire of God, the more necessary it is for the heart to feel that God is lowly, and to have abundant proof of it. The higher and mightier you conceive God to be, the less it will appear credible to you that He should show preference to force of any kind. III. BY REVEALING TO BABES THE FATHER AND LORD OF HEAVEN AND EARTH MANIFESTS THE SUPREMACY OF THE MORAL ELEMENT. What a calamity it would have been if the highest blessing had been in any way specially associated with intellectual qualities. This would have been to confirm and glorify the false estimate already so prevalent and so disastrous. But when God passes by the soaring imagination, the lofty intellect, the keen understanding, and puts His main blessing into the lowly heart and open spirit, when He comes down to the very lowest form of the moral and spiritual, the mere sense of want, the mere hunger for better things, and gives infinite eternal wealth to that—what a rebuke He conveys to pride of intellect; what honour He confers upon plain heart and conscience. Now is the false judgment of the world reversed. Now substance is put in place of show. Now spirit is exalted over form. Now right is put on the royal seat. IV. IT GLORIFIES GOD AS FATHER AND LORD OF HEAVEN AND EARTH TO REVEAL TO BABES ; FOR IT SHOWS HIS DESIRE TO REVEAL AS MUCH AS POSSIBLE, AND TO AS MANY AS POSSIBLE. Had God then revealed to the wise and understanding, He would have hidden from the world as a whole. By revealing to babes He gives hope to universal humanity. The babe slumbers in every soul however artificial or proud, and may be wakened up by some simple touch of pathos, or glimpse of memory, as well as by disaster. God who reveals to babes shows that it is man himself that He wants, not man's accomplishments, not man's energies, and distinctions and elevations, but man. V. THE APPOINTMENT OF A PERSONAL SAVIOUR GLORIFIES GOD AS FATHER AND LORD OF HEAVEN AND EARTH, AND IS PECULIARLY ADAPTED TO BABES. Jesus is the typical original Babe, the perfect, infinite example of the receptive spirit; therefore He reveals the Father, and is the refuge of men and the rest for the weary. On account of the very vastness of the lordship of heaven and earth a person is needed to bring God near, to show that it is a lordship, and not a mere system ; and that there is a heart at the centre. The gospel is salvation by a person. Trust in Christ saves us. This suits the babes, and, therefore, at bottom, all men. (*J. Leckie, D.D.*) *The child-heart :*—I. THE INTELLECTUAL CONTRAST. The world, Christ would tell us, is divisible into the simple and the wise. Our Lord rejoices that the larger section is not excluded from participation in the things of the kingdom of God ; that men do not need worldly wisdom and the prudence of experience in order to knowing the truths of salvation. No exclusive sentence is written over the portals of Christianity. It is adjusted to the lowest and meanest capacity. Christ's mission was to all humanity, and He rejoiced in that fact. II. THE MORAL CONTRAST. He wishes to tell us what is essential—that it is only to the child-heart that revelation will be made. We know the contrast between the child-heart and a heart sophisticated by life. Worldly and hardened hearts cannot receive the revelation of the things of heaven. 1. It is even so in regard to the world of beauty around us. We fill our hearts with cares, and immerse ourselves in business, so that we cannot see the beauty of a landscape which entrances the child-heart. 2. It is true also of noble actions or ideas : only the care-free child-heart feels their beauty and sublimity. 3. When a great evil is to be dealt with, we notice how slowly the consciences of worldly-wise, practical men rise to a great public duty, and how swiftly the child-heart perceives the line between right and wrong. III. THE PRACTICAL RESULT. Christ rejoices that none are excluded from His kingdom. But no gigantic effort of intellect will enable us to climb over the battlements of heaven. Wisdom is nearer to us when we stoop. (*Bishop Boyd Carpenter.*)   *Revelation to the lowly :*—I. THE FACT. 1. A childlike mind is required in those who would receive Christ and His kingdom. 2. The first disciples were children and men of childlike mind. 3. In the present day, the gospel is for the childlike. II. THE SECRET. 1. The nature of the truth revealed requires a childlike mind for the reception of it. (1) Its novelty. It is not contrary to true reason ; but it is aside from and different from the old results of human reason. (2) Its unworldliness. The eyes that are wearied with poring over earthly lore are often too worn to bear the light of heavenly truth. This requires a healthy, fresh vision. (3) Its lowliness. A gospel for the simple is not necessarily a simple gospel. 2. The method of the revelation requires a childlike mind for the reception of it. It is not given by logical demonstration, but through act and life. We must see it with the soul's eyes. For the clearness of this spiritual vision we need (1) simplicity and self-forgetfulness, (2) trustfulness, (3) purity—children's graces. III. THE THANKSGIVING. Why? 1. It is according to God's will. 2. It redounds to the glory of God. (1) As an evidence that the revelation comes from heaven and is not got by man's wisdom. It is not stolen Promethean fire. (2) As a proof of the power of God. He can teach highest truth to lowliest scholars. (3) As a sign of the goodness and condescension of God. 3. It proves the breadth of revelation. 4. It brings to us the best discipline in revelation. (*W. F. Adeney, M.A.*)   *The kingdom of God, now as ever, hidden from the wise and prudent, and revealed unto babes :*—1. This *is not* different : (1) In the days of the Saviour ; (2) In later ages ; (3) In our time. 2. This *cannot* be different. (1) Objective cause in the nature of the gospel. (2) Subjective cause in the human heart. (3) Supernatural cause in the counsel of God. 3. This *may not* be different ; for, even in this way—(1) The divinity of the gospel is confirmed ; (2) The requirements of the gospel are satisfied ; (3) The trial of the gospel is assured. (*Van Oosterzee.*)   *Divine truths hidden and revealed :*—Whilst Jesus deemed it needful to warn His disciples against self-exaltation because of what they had been the means of doing, He Himself found in the successes which had accompanied their labours a ground for grateful rejoicing.   In these successes He saw the first-fruits of a rich and glorious harvest ; and He broke out into the exclamation—" I thank Thee, O Father ! " &c.   By the expression, " these things," our Saviour meant the great Divine truths which He had come into the world expressly to reveal, which He had commissioned these seventy disciples to announce in the towns they visited, and for the rejection of which He had a little while before upbraided the cities of Galilee.   With respect to these Divine truths, Christ here makes a two-fold statement.   I. HE SPEAKS OF THEM AS HAVING BEEN HIDDEN FROM SOME. 1. Divine truths were not hidden from these people through any want of outward revelation.   2. Nor through any lack of intellectual ability to understand them. They were " the wise and prudent."   3. Nor through any influence exerted by God for the purpose.   " Thou hast hid," &c., must be interpreted in the broad light of our Saviour's teaching as a whole.   4. In what sense, then, are we to understand that Divine truths were hidden from these people?   To answer this question we must first answer another, namely, Who were the wise and prudent from whom these truths were concealed ?   (1) They were not really the wise and prudent.   (2) They supposed themselves to be so, and gloried in the supposition.   There is in such a case an element of retribution of which we must not lose sight.   The retribution consists in this—that these people, having wilfully shut their minds against the revelations of God's truth, are left by God to the consequences of their self-inflicted

blindness. II. HE SPEAKS OF THEM AS HAVING BEEN REVEALED TO OTHERS. The
word "babes" is clearly intended to be antithetic to the words "wise and prudent."
As by the wise and prudent, the Saviour meant those who were proud, ostentatious,
self-sufficient, thinking of themselves more highly than they ought to think, and
looking down on others with a cold indifference or a supercilious contempt; so by
babes He meant those who were humble, teachable, self-distrustful, feeling themselves to be destitute of all real good, and being willing to receive help and blessing
from whatever quarter or in whatsoever way it might come.   To such as these
Divine truths were revealed, and only to such.   1. It was not because they had
been favoured with a greater amount of light respecting these truths. 2. It was not
because they had been supplied with better means of preparation for the reception
of these truths.   3. It was not because they had been made the exclusive objects
of a selecting love.   4. It was because they were in a fit and proper mood for the
reception of spiritual truths.   With respect to this revelation of Divine truths to
the humble we have to notice two things, each of which suggests a practical lesson
well worth learning: (1) It was a source of grateful joy to the Saviour's heart. (2)
It had His cordial and unqualified acquiescence.   In conclusion, let us remember
that if we would be as babes to whom Divine truths are revealed, we must not only
bow before God in self-abasement and contrition, but we must look for the revelation
of those truths through Jesus Christ. This point comes out in ver. 22, "All things
are delivered," &c. (*B. Wilkinson, F.G.S.*)   *The simplicity of mystery :*—In that
hour Jesus rejoiced in Spirit. How few such occasions occurred in His life! What
hour was it?   When He saw, humanly speaking, a glimpse of God's method of
unfolding His governmental purposes, and His beneficent plans and designs. "I
thank Thee that Thou hast hid these things from the wise and prudent," from
intellectual giants, from merely clever people, from so-called genius, and sagacity
and intellectual power. "Who is greatest in the kingdom of heaven?" Jesus did
not summon the proudest king, or the mightiest thinker, but He set a child in the
midst of them, and said, "The child is always the greatest." So you will find it
all throughout life, that when you have been most happy, when you have been most
childlike, you have seen things most clearly; not when you have put on the cap of
your genius, and have taken the sceptre of your power, and robed yourself in the
official dignity of a passing moment or a transient situation; but when you have
stripped yourself of your own greatness, and have sat down, and said, "Lord, teach
me."   Religion, as propounded to us by Jesus Christ, is not a riddle to be solved
by the intellectually great.   It is a revelation to the heart; it is a word spoken to
sin; it is a gospel breathed upon sorrow; it is a word of liberty delivered to those
that are bound; a subtle sympathy—something not to be named in high-sounding
phrases, or to be wrought out in pomp of words.   If you have been in the habit of
going to church for the purpose of settling some critical argument, for the purpose
of hearing the minister through the medium of your scholastic accumulations and
of your native power of intellect, I do not wonder you are numbered with the lean
kine who, having devoured much, are none the better for their gluttony; but if you
go hungering and thirsting after righteousness, if you have left your big self outside, and have come in, just enough of you to breathe and confess sin, just enough
to be a mere spot on the floor of the sanctuary—a mere cripple, with only breath
enough to say, "God be merciful to me a sinner," you were never disappointed.
If in hymn, or psalm, or high anthem, or exposition, or reading of the Word Divine,
you have received satisfaction, great answers, infinite gospels, you have secretly
blessed God for His revelations. The disciples were compared to babes, and the
babes received the great revelation.   It will be found that simplicity itself is the
chief mystery of God.   Some things are so simple that we won't believe them. I
know sceptical minds who, if they were asking me which is the way to the Thames,
and I were to say "This," would doubt the answer because of its brevity and
simplicity.   If I could have conveyed the indication of the route by a roundabout
process, they might, perhaps, have been led to believe that I meant what I said,
though they did not know what I meant.   Do not look so far from home for your
blessings; do not make mysteries where God intends you to find simplicity.   (*J.
Parker, D.D.*)   *The babe-spirit :*—Observe, I am speaking about the beginning, in
developing this doctrine of the babe-spirit, and not about the end. And even at the end
thou shalt find out the great mystery of the unity between the man and the child that
He, the child Jesus, and the man Christ Jesus are one and the same. The greater
the man, the greater the simplicity; the greater his acquisitions, the more beautiful
his modesty; the more wonderful his power and influence, the greater his readiness

to consider, and oblige, and do good. From the greatest expect the best; from the master more than from the servant; from the disciple rudeness and rejection, from the Master, " Forbid them not, let them come." (*Ibid.*)   *God revealed unto babes*:—That the sage should miss what the infant can see seems at first but little possible, and still less a subject for thankfulness. It would appear to discourage the highest attributes of our nature, to throw contempt on the patience of thought, and cruelly to visit the prayer for light with the deeper darkness. Can it be that the more pains we take to know, the less will the truth be found; that the rich and practised mind is at a disadvantage compared with the inexperienced and empty? And if so, why exult in the frustration of the noblest of human aims, and the confiscation of the prize to those who have no aim at all? Tertullian dwells with a savage satisfaction on the supposed exclusion from the kingdom of God of whatever we hold fair and great in the old heathen world, and richest for the adornment of all time; and exults in peopling it with hordes of triumphant barbarians like himself. Is this the spirit of Christ's thanksgiving? Are we required, out of sympathy with it, to believe Socrates an outcast and clap our hands as he vanishes from hope? to stifle our reverence for Æschylus and Plato, for the Scipios and Antonines—and declare God's preference for mendicant monks and illiterate missionaries? Must we condemn as secular and carnal our own natural admiration for the gifts of wisdom—the disciplined powers, the large and supple thought, the accurate expression, of a well-cultured nature—and force ourselves into harmony of taste with the raw religion of unmellowed sectaries, their loud voice, their rude speech, their narrow zeal, their tumultuous aspirations? Far from it. It is not intellect from which God hides Himself, but selfishness and pride; which may belong alike to taught and untaught, and darken the soul of sophist or of clown. There is light both in the " base " and in the " wise ": but in the former it is wholly spontaneous; in the latter it is chiefly derivative. In its infancy the soul simply apprehends what is given it to perceive, lies confidingly in the bosom of nature, and lets the morning beams come into the full and wondering eyes. It is the loss of the habit of natural trust, the tendency to anxious quest of something distant instead of pure repose on what is here, that according to Christ's prayer, hides God from the wise and prudent. And, conversely, it is the surrender to spontaneous light and love, the simple passing out upon it into life, without doubt of its guidance or scrutiny of its claims, that reveals Him unto " babes." How profoundly true this is—that in Divine things the little child may know what the great philosopher may miss—will appear if you only think what God is, and whether He is likely to be discovered on any explorer's track or by any artifice of calculation. Two things science enables us to do, from which all its triumphs spring. It shows us how to put the parts and products of nature into true classes; and it qualifies us to foresee phenomena else unsuspected. But God is neither a being to be classified, nor a phenomenon to be foreseen. (*Dr. Martineau.*)   *It is the great marvel of the Christian character* that the completest self-sacrifice gives the completest self-possession; that only the captive soul, which has flung her rights away, has all her powers free; and that simply to *serve* under the instant orders of the living God, is the highest qualification for command. This is the meaning of that great saying of Cromwell's: " One never mounts so high as when one knows not whither one is going ": a saying which the wise and prudent scorned as a confession of blindness, but which reveals to simpler minds the deepest truth. (*Ibid.*)   *Two types of human greatness are there*—the Pagan and the Christian—the moral and the religious—the secular and the Divine. The former has its root and essence in trying hard; the latter, in trusting gently: the one depends on voluntary energy, the other on relinquishment of personal will to cast every burden upon God. (*Ibid.*)   *To commune with God* there is need of no subtle thought, no foreign tongue, no newest philosophy: " the pure in heart shall see " Him; and Fox and Bunyan can more truly make Him known, than " Masters of Sentences " and "Angelic Doctors." (*Ibid.*)   *Learning the alphabet of religion*:— A man came to his pastor one night to learn the way of salvation. He was a very learned man, but he said: " I know nothing of Divine truth. I come to you to learn—as a child. I come to learn the very alphabet of religion." His pastor replied: " My friend, when you return home, open your Bible and read prayerfully the third chapter of John. Think of it. Study it. That will be A. Then turn to Isaiah, fifty-fifth chapter. Study it. Believe it. That is B. A B, *ab*, almost *Abba Father*." (*Handbook to Scripture Doctrines.*)   *Humility of Pascal*:—The curate who attended Pascal on his dying bed, struck with the triumph of religion over the pride of an intellect which continued to burn after it had ceased to blaze, would frequently exclaim, "He is an infant—humble and submissive as an infant!" (*Life of Pascal.*) *The receptive spirit:*—The Rev. John Foster, whose sceptical tendencies were the source of much distress of mind, was finally led to say: "I have felt the necessity of dismissing subtle speculations, and of yielding a humble, cordial assent to mysterious truth, just *as* and *because* the Scriptures declare it, without asking 'How can these things be?' The gospel is to me a matter of urgent necessity. I come to Jesus because I need pardon." **The Son will reveal Him.**—*Deity revealed:*—I. THE MYSTERY OF DEITY IN SELF-EXISTENCE. He is an unknown God where there is no supernatural revelation of Him. Reason is baffled, because it is under the fall. Eternal self-existence. How wonderful! It exceeds all power of calculation. II. THE INCARNATE SON OF GOD REVEALING. Now mark, I beseech you, that all this glory of the Father, made to shine in the face of Jesus Christ, is unknown to the sinner as long as he is blinded. III. THE SALVATION SECURED THEREBY. Contrived and bestowed by God the Father. Carried out by God the Son. It is, therefore, infallible, and it secures the glory of Jehovah. (*J. Irons.*) *The power bestowed on Christ by the Father:*—1. Unlimited. 2. Legitimate. 3. Beneficent. 4. Ever-enduring. (*Van Oosterzee.*) *The unique relation between the Son and the Father:*—1. How far it is the object of our faith. 2. How far it can be the object of our knowledge. (*Ibid.*) *The relation between Father and Son:*—1. The highest mystery. 2. A revealed mystery. 3. Even after the revelation yet continually a partially concealed mystery. (*Ibid.*) *Christ the Revealer of God:*—Christ, as you see here, speaks of Himself. What does He say of Himself? 1. Does He not claim to be Divinely constituted as a Revealer of God? "All things are delivered to Me of My Father." 2. Our Lord speaks here also of the glorious mystery of His own person and character. No man, nor angel, nor archangel, nor any intelligence in this or in the heavenly world, knoweth who the Son is but the Father. It takes an Infinite Being to comprehend an Infinite Being. 3. Christ alone knows God in perfection—"No man knoweth who the Father is but the Son." What an awful sense of loneliness—a loneliness which is unutterable—would be involved in our idea of God, unless we had some light given to us by Jesus Christ, concerning His relation to the Father. 4. Jesus Christ is and can alone be the Revealer of God to us—"And he to whom the Son will reveal Him." (1) He can be known to whom the Son will reveal Him. (2) The way to the knowledge of God is by meekness, humility, submission, trustfulness, love. (*W. Dorling.*)

Vers. 23, 24. **Blessed are the eyes which see the things that ye see.**—*The gospel privileges:*—I. THE THINGS HERE SPOKEN OF. The blessings of Christ's revelation. II. TO WHOM THEY WERE DEVISED. Not only to the great, but to the good. Not merely to the mighty kings of Nineveh, Assyria, Babylon, Egypt, Greece, and Rome, but to the holy and righteous—to Moses, to David, to Elijah. III. TO WHOM THEY WERE REVEALED. To the poor, despised, illiterate; to fishermen on the Galilean sea; to the sisters at Bethany; and, following in their train, to us at the present, whatever our character or position. IV. THE OVERWHELMING PRIVILEGE WE ENJOY. More favoured than kings; more honoured than prophets; higher in the scale than all who have gone before. V. THE HEIGHT OF OUR RESPONSIBILITY. If the prophets scarcely were saved, how shall it be with the present generation, if they neglect the privileges they enjoy? (*The Preacher's Analyst.*) *Difference between the patriarchal, Jewish, and Christian dispensations:*—It is a common, but very just observation, that we are seldom duly sensible of the value of our blessings till we are deprived of them. This remark is applicable to our case, under the Christian dispensation. How few persons bless God that they dwell in the "days of the Son of Man"! The way to know how much we are distinguished, is, carefully to compare our situation with that of our fellow-creatures. I. Let us survey the state of the HEATHEN WORLD. Place yourself, for a moment, amongst them, and consider what would then be your situation with respect to knowledge and virtue. 1. As to knowledge—everything among the heathens was obscure and uncertain. 2. In the heathen world also vice dreadfully prevailed. And what authority was there to check its prevalence? What principles strong enough to enable men to resist it? Their worship was base and degrading, offered in general to idols representing beings who were described as the patrons of corruption. II. But let us turn our eyes from the state of the heathens, to the fairer view of those who were in some measure enlightened by Divine knowledge. To speak first of the PATRIARCHAL DISPENSATION—One great instance of its inferiority was its want of clear and sufficient authority. Probably the laws and observances enjoined by it were first communicated by God to Adam, and transmitted by him to his children. Now it is easy to see that such a religion would become more and more obscure, imperfect, and corrupt in every succeeding generation. Many things would be forgotten, many misunderstood, many improperly added. On the MOSAIC DISPENSATION we now proceed to offer a few remarks. It may be considered as having been inferior to the Christian in the following particulars. 1. It was chiefly composed of types and shadows, of forms and ceremonies. 2. The Jewish dispensation abounded with severe and burdensome impositions. 3. The Mosaic dispensation is inferior to the Christian, inasmuch as the latter is founded upon better promises—better, as being of a more sublime and excellent nature, as being promises of spiritual and eternal things; such as grace, pardon, peace, and eternal life. 4. Another remarkable circumstance, in which the superiority of our dispensation consists, is, the larger and more abundant communication of the Holy Spirit. 5. Further: The Christian dispensation excels the Mosaic in the manner of its establishment. 6. The Christian dispensation is superior to the Jewish, in respect to the spirit of its institution. The spirit of the gospel is a spirit of liberty. (*John Venn, M.A.*) *National privileges:*—This is a noble text, and yet an awful one, for if it does not increase our godliness, it will certainly increase our condemnation. It tells us that we, even the meanest amongst us, are more favoured by God than the kings, and judges, and conquerors of the old world; that we have more light and knowledge of God than even the prophets David, Isaiah, Jeremiah, and Ezekiel, to whom God's glory appeared in visible shape. It tells us that we see things which they longed to see and could not; that words are spoken to us for which their ears longed in vain; that they, though they died in hope, yet received not the promises, God having provided some better things for us, that they without us should not be made perfect. 1. Now, what was this which they longed for, and had not, and yet we have ? It is this— a Saviour and a Saviour's kingdom. All wise and holy hearts for ages—as well heathen as Jews—had had this longing. They wanted a Saviour—one who should free them from sin and conquer evil. They longed for a heavenly kingdom also. They saw that men got worse and worse as time rolled on, and that all the laws in the world could never make them good. They longed for a kingdom of God, a golden age, a regeneration of the world, as they called it, and rightly. 2. And now this kingdom is come, and the King of it, the Saviour of men, is Jesus Christ, the Son of God. Long men prayed, and long men waited, and at last, in the fulness of God's good time, just when the night seemed darkest, and, under the abominations of the Roman Empire, religion, honesty, and common decency seemed to have died out, the Sun of Righteousness rose on the dead and rotten world, to bring life and immortality to light. 3. And that we might not doubt that we too belonged to this kingdom, God has placed in this land His ministers and teachers, Christ's Sacraments, Christ's Churches, Christ's Bible; that from our cradle to our grave we might see that we belonged, as sworn servants and faithful children, to the great Father in heaven and Jesus Christ, the King of the earth. 4. Thus, all that all men have longed for we possess; we want no more, and we shall have no more. If, under the present state of things, we cannot be holy, we shall never be holy. Blessed indeed are the eyes which see what you see, and hear what you hear; prophets and kings have desired to see and hear them, and have not seen or heard ! But if you, cradled among all these despised honours and means of grace, bring forth no fruit in your lives— shut out from yourselves the thought of your high calling in Christ Jesus, what shall be your end but ruin? He that despises Christ, Christ will despise him. And say not to yourselves as many do, " We are church-goers—we are all safe." I say to you, God is able, from among the negro and the savage—aye, God is able of these stones to raise up children, while those of you, the children of the kingdom, who lived in the Church of your fathers, and never used or loved her or Christ her King, shall be cast into outer darkness, where shall be weeping and gnashing of teeth. (*Charles Kingsley.*)

> Vainly they tried the deeps to sound
> Even of their own prophetic thought,
> When of Christ crucified and crowned
> His Spirit in them taught:
>
> But He their aching gaze repressed
> Which sought behind the veil to see,

For not without us fully blessed
  Or perfect might they be.

The rays of the Almighty's face
  No sinner's eye might then receive;
Only the meekest man found grace
  To see His skirts and live.

But we as in a glass espy
  The glory of His countenance,
Not in a whirlwind hurrying by
  The two presumptuous glance.

But with mild radiance every hour
  From our dear Saviour's face benign
Bent on us with transforming power,
  Till we, too, faintly shine.

Sprinkled with His atoning blood
  Safely before our God we stand,
As on the rock the prophet stood,
  Beneath His shadowing hand.

Blessed eyes which see the things we see!
  And yet this tree of life hath proved
To many a soul a poison-tree,
  Beheld, and not beloved.   *(John Keble.)*

Our privileges :—The privileges here referred to.   What are the things we see and
hear ?   Many answers might be given.   We might tell of the progress of science,
commerce, civilization—progress that is stupendous, amazing; and there is nothing
of all this but has its value.   But these are not the things that make us "blessed."
What are they ?   An Infant, cradled in a manger, shepherds and wise men bowing
near—a meek and lowly Man, standing in the midst of a crowd, teaching and
healing, while mockery and hatred look on—a Sufferer stretched upon a cross,
"His visage marred more than any man, and His form more than the sons of
men "—an opening sepulchre, and a figure rising, ascending, received up into glory
—these are the things we see.   Meanwhile, we hear the song of angels, proclaiming
the birth of Messiah, and foretelling His glory—we hear the sweeter voice of
Messiah's self, when " gracious words proceed out of His mouth."   Such are the
things we see and hear : all of them, you perceive, referring to Christ—His Incarnation, Teaching, Life, Death, and Resurrection.   And this is the gospel !   In
this God reveals His purposes of mercy.   Such is the gospel as we receive it—
more complete than when our Lord spake the words of the text to His disciples.
The position of ancient saints with regard to these privileges.   " Many prophets
and righteous men have desired," &c.   The fact here stated is two-fold : they had
the desire—but it remained ungratified.   Take some passages by way of illustration.
Christ says of Abraham : " He rejoiced to see My day : and he saw it "—that is,
he exulted with the desire to see, and, by lively faith, clearly pictured it forth.   Here
then is a specimen of the position of the patriarchs—Just as Moses climbed Mount
Pisgah, and looked on Canaan, though he never crossed the Jordan : so Abraham
climbed the mount of faith, and descried the distant scenes of our Lord's life.
How natural was the desire !   The man who has taken an earnest part in some
great undertaking naturally longs to see it accomplished.   " They desired to see
the things that we see, and to hear the things that we hear."   And yet—their
desire remained ungratified.   In this there is much that is instructive.   **1.** See the
calm steady procession of the purposes of God !   He has appointed a time for
everything and nothing can derange His plan.   **2.** See the trial He gives His
people's faith !   It is so still, is it not ?   How many of our heart's desires He denies
us now.   The faith of the ancient saints was tried—and strengthened by trial ; and
thus they became " strong in faith, giving glory to God."   **3.** Brethren, let us
prize our privileges.   Here they are, in rich abundance ; yet how often are we dull
and cold in the midst of them all !   **4.** Impenitent man—beware !   You, too, are
surrounded by privileges.   Isaiah, David, Daniel never saw what *you* see.   **5.** Some
are coming after us, who will know more than we do.   When we pass away, others

will arise; and in regard to position, we are to them as the prophets were to us. 6. But those who have gone before—have not they, too, outstripped us? Think—what do they see and hear? We cannot tell! 7. O happy time when the whole Church shall be complete in glory! (*F. Tucker.*)

Ver. 25. **Master, what shall I do to inherit eternal life?**—*The lawyer's question:*—The question of the lawyer is the question of the human heart everywhere. You will find it asked and answered in all the world's religions. The answers fall into two classes. 1. One set of replies thinks of the better life as a thing external to a man's own being, procurable by something that a man can do, by bodily self-denial or suffering, or by religious rites or ceremonies. 2. The other class of answers amounts to this—that nothing that is merely outside a man or comes to him from without can ever meet his wants. The true ideal life of humanity is in its very essence a life; it is not doing, it is being. The orthodox doctrine in Christ's time taught very definitely what was the pathway to eternal life. The religious teachers laid it down that the life God wants men to live was a life of obedience to the law of Moses. The preaching of Jesus Christ did not quite tally with the orthodox teaching of the time. The Pharisee and the penitent, the harlots and publicans, were distinctly conscious that Christ was preaching a new gospel. The gospel of the Pharisees was orthodox; therefore the gospel of Christ was heresy. They were bent upon getting a case against Him, and yet it was not easy. He Himself fulfilled the law, conformed to all its requirements and statutes, and never spoke disrespectfully of it. How were they to catch Him? One day a crafty lawyer had a very happy thought. He determined to cross-question Christ, to force Him to declare His inner hostility to the creed of the Pharisees, His inner antagonism to the law of God: "What shall I do to inherit eternal life?" A fair, honest question, and yet in the very wording of it the note of discord comes out. Jesus is confronted with a man whose notion of eternal life is utterly different from His. It is impossible to answer that man. Instead of answering, Jesus turns questioner. He must bring out the man's own notions, and then, when He has got them, it may be possible to show him how threadbare, how poverty-stricken, how wrong they are. "What do you find in the law? How readest thou?" The lawyer, taken aback, gives the regulation reply. He could not repeat the whole law, but there was a summary of it, a standing condensed statement of it, and this he repeats to Jesus: "Thou shalt love . . ." Now, what have we to say to that answer? Is this the pathway to eternal life? What more could a man do to make the music of his life majestic, heavenly, splendid? Loving God utterly, and loving all men as you love yourself—no doubt that is life eternal. The scribe's answer is the true answer; yet in the scribe's mouth it was an utter lie, and a damning heresy, that was sending men's souls to ruin. Christ could accept the definition of the lawyer. "Thou hast answered right." But then the meaning that He felt in those words was a meaning utterly different from that of the Pharisee; and there you have the explanation of His preaching. He took the very same text that the scribes took, but what a different sermon He preached from it, and what a different application against theirs! He did not say "Obey"; He said the word that must come before obey: He said "Love." The least bit of love will do more to make you keep the commandments than any amount of studying them, or any amount of selfish resolve to make a good thing out of the commandments for yourself. The essence of the Pharisee's gospel was selfishness. Save yourself by keeping on the right side, and not giving God a chance against you. What a God, and what a soul! I think that Jesus, as soon as the scribe had given his reply, looked him straight in the face. The look meant, "Dare you pretend that you do that?" and the man felt it, and therefore, we read, was eager to justify himself. The man's conscience was uneasy. He instantly said, "Yes, but who is my neighbour?" It is where the heart is cold that definitions come in. "Who is my neighbour? How many men can claim love from me?" said the scribe. Christ did not answer that, but He made a picture in order to ask the scribe this question, "Who is the man who plays the neighbour's part?" He told of a man who started from Jerusalem to go to Jericho, and was attacked on the way by thieves, who certainly did not play the part of neighbour by him. There came on the road a priest and a Levite. Christ had not that foolish idea that the clergy should never be held up to rebuke or scorn when they deserve it. Do not misjudge the priest and the Levite. You say they did a heartless thing. They did not; they had not heart to do it. Their sin was not in not doing something, but in being heartless. That is the very point of the story. And if you had met these men after hearing of it, and had asked them how they could do such a thing, they would have assured you that they did not see any man like that. They would have told you that they saw a man who had been fighting, or who had got drunk, or who was an impostor. Or they would have told you they were going to a religious service at Jericho, and had not the time for it. All we can say of them is that they had not heart. And Christ paints the other side of it. There came along a Samaritan, a man of a different religion, a man who had been taught of the Jews that he owed them no kindness. He appeared to be a business man, and probably it would be more to him to lose his market than to the clergy to be late for the religious service. He saw the man, and he saw the first passer-by that had seen him; he saw the wretchedness of it—and he had a heart, and that is all. He did not say, "Is there anything in the Decalogue bearing on this?" And he certainly did not say, "Is that man a neighbour? He is a Jew. Where does he come from?" If he had begun going to the law, he would never have done it. And now, mark how the story has answered the question. As soon as it is finished Christ turns to the scribe, and asks, "Who played the neighbour's part?" Not the priest, not the scribe, not his own fellow-countrymen. It was that Samaritan. Nobody could deny it. Even the lawyer acknowledges it. That was a beautiful thing to do, and Christ drove it home with the rejoinder, "Go thou and do likewise"; and He sent that man away saying to himself, "No amount of reading the law would ever make me able to do that; more than that, my reading of the law must be all wrong." Christ had made that man understand that what he wanted was the real love of the real, living, loving God, and the real, common human love to his fellow-men. Where have you and I to learn that love for God and love for man? I will tell you. At the feet of Christ, and by His side, in fellowship with Him, we shall learn to love God with all our heart, and soul, and mind, and strength, and our neighbour as ourself; and that is eternal life. (*Professor Elmslie, M.A.*)   *Inheriting eternal life:*—1. You will observe that the man who asked this question was a lawyer, a man of education and of good standing; a man, therefore, from whom good behaviour and reverence of spirit might reasonably have been expected. You would think that when such a man spoke he would speak soberly, he would mean, under such circumstances, exactly what he said. You find, however, that the inquiry—the very greatest that can possibly engage human attention—was put in a spirit of temptation. The lawyer was not an earnest man. He asked a right question, but he asked it in a wrong spirit. See, then, the possibility of asking religious questions irreligiously. Learn the possibility of asking great questions in a merely controversial spirit, without any profoundly anxious desire to know the answer that God will return to such inquiries. God understands the irony of our attitude. The Living One knows whether we are hungering and thirsting for Him; He can see through our hypocrisies and concealments, and only into the broken heart and the contrite spirit will He come with redemption and life and helpfulness and grace. So that at the very beginning there is to be no mistake about this. We know the conditions upon which alone we receive the revelations of God—that we be quiet, self-renouncing, reverent, sober, anxious about the business; and wherever these conditions are forthcoming, some light will be flashed upon the life, and some healing word will be dropped into the sorrow of the heart. 2. Jesus Himself answered one question by asking another; and so He not unfrequently disappointed men who had undertaken to ensnare Him in His speech. They thought that if they did but put a case to Him He would instantly commit Himself, and they would entrap Him and take Him captive, and make a fool of Him. Here is a man probably accustomed to put questions, and to put questions again upon the answers that are given, and so to cross-examine those with whom he came in contact. Jesus undertakes to deal with him according to the spirit which he presents; and before He lets him go He will show what the man's meaning is and his nature, and He will expose him as he never was exposed before. Thus quietly He begins: "What is written in the law? Thou art a lawyer, a man of reading, a man of many letters, and of much understanding probably—how readest thou?" God has never left the greatest questions of the human heart unanswered. The great answer to this question about eternal life was not given first of all by Jesus Christ as He appeared in the flesh. Jesus Himself referred to the oldest record; inferentially He said—That question has been answered from the beginning; go back to the very first revelation and testimony of God, and you will find the answer there. Yet the question is put very significantly: "How readest thou?" There are two ways of reading. There is a way of reading the letter which never gets at the meaning of the spirit. There is a way of reading which merely looks at the letter for a partial purpose, or that a prejudice may be sustained or defended. And there is a way of reading which means, I want to know the truth; I want to see really how this case stands; I am determined to see it. He who reads so will find no end to his lesson, for truth expands and brightens as we study her revelations and her purposes. He who comes merely to the letter will get but a superficial answer in all probability. It was, therefore, of the highest importance that the lawyer should tell how he had been reading the law. 3. The lawyer, please to remember, knew the answer when he asked the question. He said, " What shall I do to inherit eternal life ? " and all the time the answer was in his own recollection had he but known it. Alas ! we do not always turn our knowledge into wisdom. We know the fact, and we hardly ever sublimate the fact into truth. We know the law, and we fail to see that under the law there is the beauty and there is the grace of the gospel. 4. " This do," said Jesus, " and thou shalt live." What had the lawyer to do ? To love the Lord his God with all his heart and with all his soul and with all his strength and with all his mind. Love is life. Only he who loves lives. Only love can get out of a man the deepest secrets of his being and develop the latent energies of his nature and call him up to the highest possibility of his manhood. Criticism never can do it ; theology never can do it; power of controversy never can do it. We are ourselves, in all the volume of our capacity, and in all the relations of our original creation, only when life becomes love and our whole nature burns with affection towards the God and Father of our Lord Jesus Christ. Let us look less at our knowledge and our intellectual capability and our training and our circumstances, and more at the degree of our religious love. The end of the commandment is charity ; the summing up of all true law is love. Do we, then, know this mystery of religious love ? or is ours a religion that hangs itself upon the outward letter and the ceremonial form ? Then observe that the law goes still further than love to God, it includes love to one's neighbour. Hear the exact expression of the text—" And thy neighbour as thyself." Love of God means love of man. Religion is the Divine side of philanthropy ; philanthropy is the practical side of religion. We must first be right with God or we never can be right with man. 5. Was the lawyer satisfied ? Read : "But he, willing to justify himself, said unto Jesus, And who is my neighbour ? " It was the question of a sharp man, but not the inquiry of an honest one. Such a question as this does not need to be answered in words. Every man knows in his own heart who his neighbour is ; and only he who wishes to play a trick in words, to show how clever he is in verbal legerdemain, will stoop to ask such a question as this. Why did he ask the question ? Because he was willing to justify himself. It is precisely there that every man has a great battle to fight, namely—at the point of self-justification. So long as there is any disposition in us to justify ourselves are we unprepared to receive the gospel. One of the first conditions required of us at the Cross is self-renunciation. Am I to suppose that any one is asking now, What shall I do to inherit eternal life ? Do not misunderstand that word *do*. It may be so employed as to convey a wrong sense. The obtaining of eternal life does not come through any action or merit of our own. There is not a certain journey that is to taken, a labour which is to be performed, a specific duty that is to be discharged. What, then, is there to be ? Consciousness of sin, conviction of guilt in the sight of God, self-despair, self-torment, such a knowledge of the nature and reality of sin as will pain the heart to agony ; and then a turning of the eyes of faith to the bleeding Lamb of God, the one sacrifice, the complete atonement; a casting of the heart, the life, the hope, upon the broken body of Jesus, Son of God ! Dost thou so believe ? Thou hast eternal life ! This eternal life is not a possession into which we come by and by. We have hold of it now ; for to love the Son of God is to begin eternity, is to enter upon immortality ! How is this life to be exhibited ? In other words, how is it to prove its own existence and defend its own claim ? By love. God is love. And if we be in God we shall be filled with love. Let us then retire, knowing that there is in our hearts and minds information enough upon these great questions, if so be we are minded to turn that information to account. Let no man say he will begin a better life when he knows more. Begin with the amount of your present knowledge. Let no man delude himself by saying that if he had a good opportunity of showing charity to a stranger he would show it. Show charity, show piety at home. Let no man say that if he was going down a thief-haunted road, and saw a poor man bleeding and dying there, he would certainly bind up his wounds. Do the thing that is next thee; bear the Cross that is lying at thy feet; start even upon the very smallest scale to love, and thou shalt grow in grace. (*J. Parker, D.D.*)

Ver. 26. **How readest thou ?**—*Profitable reading of the Bible :*—As there are always among violets some that are very much sweeter to us than others, so among texts there are some that are ,more precious to us than others. When I go to the Bible, it is not once in a hundred times that I read a whole chapter for my own devotions. As one that goes out into the field to rest does not take the first spot that presents itself, but waits till he finds a nook where the mosses and the flowers and the shrubs are right, and then sits down and feasts his eyes on the beauties around, so I wander along till I come to a passage which, though I cannot tell why, I read over and over and over again. One or two verses or sentences, perhaps, will linger in my head all day, like some sweet passage in a letter, or like some felicitous word spoken by a friend, coming and going all the time. I find often that one single text, taking possession of the mind in the morning, and ringing through it during the whole day, does one more good than the reading of a whole chapter. Frequently some one thing that Christ said fixes itself in my mind, and remains there from morning till night. (*H. W. Beecher.*) *The law of God, the guide of youth :*—I. In following out this question to a satisfactory reply, we may, in the first place, inquire, WHAT IS WRITTEN IN THE LAW, AND HOW WE SHOULD READ, ON THE SUBJECT OF FAITH, IN THE GOSPEL ? Does not the law of God tell you what the faith of the gospel is, especially all that God has revealed respecting His Son ? II. But, in the second place, we must not only TAKE WHAT IS WRITTEN IN THE LAW, IN ORDER TO OUR BELIEF, BUT IN ORDER TO OUR PRACTICE. The "law" holds out, not only testimony to be believed, but precepts to be obeyed. III. But, in the third place, let us inquire, WHAT IS WRITTEN IN THE LAW CONCERNING THOSE FEELINGS WHICH WE OUGHT TO CULTIVATE ? IV. But again, there is another important subject, on which it is our duty to be informed. WHAT IS WRITTEN OF THOSE ENJOYMENTS HELD OUT IN THE GOSPEL ? V. Then, WHAT IS WRITTEN IN THE LAW ON THE SUBJECT OF TRUST IN THE LORD ? VI. For again, WHAT IS WRITTEN IN THE WORD OF GOD CONCERNING DANGER ? It states, the only danger to be apprehended is, the danger arising from sin. VII. Let us inquire, however, further, WHAT IS WRITTEN IN THE LAW CONCERNING HOPE ? VIII. But next, WHAT IS WRITTEN IN THE LAW CONCERNING THE TIME WHEN THE MIND SHOULD THUS GIVE ITSELF WHOLLY TO GOD ? (*J. Burnet.*)

Ver. 27. **Thou shalt love.**—*Love to God and our neighbours :*—I. THE LAWYER'S QUESTION. No evidence of his having put it in a malicious spirit. Quite a fair question. Also a most intelligent question. He wished to try Christ's pretensions and knowledge—a perfectly blameless, indeed praiseworthy wish. Yet, although the lawyer's intellect was not at fault, his heart, in some measure at least, was. He did not feel, as he ought, the seriousness of the question he proposed, and his own personal interest in it. He put it too much to try Christ, too little to get instruction for himself. II. CHRIST'S MANNER OF DEALING WITH HIM. He did not answer him, but made him answer himself –obviously, in order to turn his attention in upon himself. III. THE LAWYER'S ANSWER. A marvellously good answer. He joins to a precept in Deuteronomy another in Leviticus, and so replies to Christ's question in words altogether appropriate and divine. Our Lord Himself had used the same words in the same way. He had found none better in which to sum all duty and the whole consequence of religion. IV. CHRIST'S APPLICATION. Have we here Christ Himself teaching salvation through works, not through faith ; through doing, not by belief ? Yes, there is no doubt about it ; His words are perfectly plain and decided—" Do, and thou shalt live." But, do what? "Love," &c. A safe kind of teaching salvation through works ! If by doing this, but only by doing this, man is to be saved through doing, then that only makes it clear as the sun that not by doing will any man be saved. Such a law condemns us all utterly. It is one thing to be a hearer of the law, even an intelligent and studious hearer of it, and quite another to be a doer of it. What it demands is obedience—strict, perfect, absolute obedience. V. THE LAWYER'S DIFFICULTY. He secretly feels that salvation on such terms is not to be had, but he does not like to acknowledge this even to himself, and still less to Him whose words have found him out. He fights against the conviction. He wishes to justify himself, for he cannot bear the thought that Moses and his law—all that he had hitherto been accustomed to depend upon for eternal life—will fail him, and even turn against him. To justify himself, he puts to our Lord the question, "Who is my neighbour?" No question about God, or love to God. Why? Feeling that with respect to that his case was hopeless, he tries to get off on the second commandment, flattering himself there was at least some chance of acquittal on that count. The mere fact of his putting such a question showed him at fault. How could he have fulfilled the law of neighbourly love if he didn't even know who his neighbour was? VI. CHRIST'S DEFINITION OF A NEIGHBOUR. Again our Lord seeks to get the lawyer to answer himself, so as to condemn himself; He seeks to help him not only to the right answer to his question, but to convince him that the very question itself showed that he had not the love he spoke of, and not the love which he rightly said was demanded by the law. He seeks to do so by vividly setting before him, in a singularly beautiful parable, the nature of genuine and practical love, as exhibited by the Samaritan, in contrast with a merely formal respect for the law, as illustrated by the priest and the Levite. Then, when He has thus got his conscience to bear witness to the depth and breadth and exceeding comprehensiveness of the law, He again tells him to go and do it, to go and obey it as the Samaritan had done. This our Lord again tells him to do, not supposing that he really could do it, but indirectly to convince him that he has not done it, and to lead him to find out that it is not in his power to do it. Christ wishes through the law to draw him to Himself. (*Professor R. Flint.*) *The two great commandments:*—I. THE MANNER AND OCCASION OF THEIR DELIVERY (see Matt. xxii. 36, where our Lord Himself gave them). In the text He draws them from the lips of His questioner. Notice, also, that even these two great commandments were not on these occasions invented for the first time by our Divine Lawgiver (Deut. vi. 5; Lev. xix. 18). Words that had been lying dormant He brought to life. II. THEIR CONTENTS. 1. One supreme affection is to rule over our whole being—the love of God. The intellect must seek truth with undistracted, fearless zeal; else we do not serve God with our whole mind and understanding. The bodily powers must be guarded and saved for the healthy discharge of all that Providence requires of us in our passage through life; else we do not serve Him with our whole strength. The affections must be kept fresh and pure; else we do not serve Him with our whole heart. The conscience must not have stained itself with secret sins, unworthy transactions, and false pretences; else we do not serve Him with our whole soul. There was an old barbarian chief who, when he was baptized, kept his right arm out of the water that he might still work his deeds of blood. That is the likeness of the imperfect religion of so many Christians. This is what they did who of old, in their zeal for religion, broke their plighted faith, did despite to their natural affections, disregarded the laws of kinship and country, of honour and of mercy. 2. The second of these commandments is like the first. It is the chief mode of fulfilling the first. (1) The measure of the love we owe to others is just what we think owing to ourselves. Observe the equity of this Divine rule. It makes us the judge of what we ought to do. It imposes upon us no duty that we have not already acknowledged for ourselves. Every one of us knows how painful it is to be called by malicious names, to have his character undermined by false insinuations, to be overreached in a bargain, to be neglected by those who rise in life, to be thrust on one side by those who have stronger wills and stouter hearts. Every one knows also the pleasure of receiving a kind look, a warm greeting, a hand held out to help in distress, a difficulty solved, a higher hope revealed for this world or the next. By that pain and by that pleasure judge what you should do to others. (2) The object towards which this love is to extend—"Thy neighbour." Every one with whom we are brought into contact. First of all, he is literally our neighbour who is next to us in our own family and household—husband to wife, wife to husband, parent to child, brother to sister, master to servant, servant to master; and then in our own town, in our own parish, in our own street. With these all true charity begins. But, besides these, our neighbour is every one who is thrown across our path by the changes and chances of life—he or she, whomsoever it be, whom we have any means of helping—the unfortunate sufferers whom we may perhaps meet in travelling—the deserted friend whom no one else cares to look after. III. THEIR RELATIVE POSITION TO THE OTHER PARTS OF THE CHRISTIAN DISPENSATION. These two commandments are the greatest of all. On them the rest of God's revelation depends. By keeping them we inherit the greatest of all gifts: "This do, and thou shalt live." (*Dean Stanley.*) *The sufficiency of these two commandments:*—It has been observed that sometimes when a man is told that religion and morality are summed up in the two great commandments, he is ready to say, like one who first beholds the sea,

> "Is this the mighty ocean?
> Is this all?"

Yes, it is all; but what an all! We know well here what is the view of the ocean. We look out from these shores on that vacant expanse, with its boundless horizon, with its everlasting succession of ebb and tide, and we might perhaps ask, What is this barren sea to us? How vague, how indefinite, how broad, how monotonous; yet, when we look closer at it, it is the scene on which sunlight and moonlight, shade and shadow, are for ever playing. It has been the chosen field for the enterprise, for the faith, for the charity of mankind. It is the highway for the union of nations and the enlargement of churches. It is the bulwark of freedom, and the home of mighty fleets, and the nurse of swarming cities. And so these two commandments. They seem at first sight vacant, vague, and indefinite; but let us trust ourselves to them, let us launch out upon them, let us explore their innermost recesses, let us sound their depths, and we shall find that we shall call forth all the arts and appliances of Christian love. We shall find that they will carry us round the world and beyond it. To love the Lord our God with all our heart, with all our mind, with all our soul, with all our strength—what new fields of thought and activity ought this to open to us when thoroughly studied! It is in proportion as the Bible teaches us the true perfections of God that it becomes to us the Book of God; it is in proportion as the gospel discloses to us those perfections in the most endearing and the most intelligible forms that it becomes to us the revelation of God in Christ; it is in proportion as our hearts and consciences are filled from the fountain of all goodness, that we are able to enter into the true spirit of God, who is worshipped in spirit and in truth. It is, or it ought to be, for the sake of these great commandments that we value and strive to improve the sanctifying and elevating influences of Christian worship, Christian civilization, Christian friendship, Christian homes, and Christian education. It is for the sake of better understanding what God is, and how He wishes us to serve Him, that we value these indications of His will which He has left us in the sure footsteps of science, in the manifold workings of history, of art, of poetry, and of all the various gifts and graces which He has bestowed on earth and on man. "Let no man," says Lord Bacon, "let no man out of weak conceit of sobriety or ill-applied moderation think or maintain that a man can search too far, or be too well supplied, in the Book of God's Word or the Book of God's works." That is at least one result of the endeavour to love God with all our understanding and with all our soul. And again, "to love our neighbour as ourselves"—what a world of Christian duty is here disclosed! How eagerly, for the sake of better serving our neighbours, should we welcome any one who will tell us what is the best and safest mode of administering charity, what is the best mode of education, what is the best means of suppressing intemperance and vice. How eagerly should we all cultivate the opportunities which God has given us, not for keeping men apart, but for bringing them together; how anxiously we should desire to understand the character of neighbouring nations, neighbouring Churches, neighbouring friends, so as to avoid giving them needless offence—so as to bring out their best points and repress their worst, making our own knowledge of our own imperfections and faults the measure of the forbearance which we should exercise to them. How eagerly should we rejoice in everything which increases the countless means that Christianity and civilization employ for the advancement and progress of mankind. These are some of the means of loving our neighbour as ourselves. (*Ibid.*) *The two great commandments* :—1. Let us now consider the first great commandment, "Thou shalt love the Lord thy God." The great principle which animated the Jews was not love but fear; "Fear God and keep His commandments" with them comprehended the whole duty of man. Accustomed to see their enemies punished by the immediate interference of the Deity; and sensible of the sufferings inflicted on themselves for their idolatry and their incessant hankering after the imaginary gods of the heathens, they contemplated the true God rather as an object of fear than of love. Accordingly, in the Old Testament it is the power, the greatness, the holiness, the terrible justice of the Almighty, that is chiefly exhibited, because the Jews were not fitted for the guidance of higher motives. But, in the New Testament, the goodness, the mercy, the loving-kindness of God are displayed in the most affectionate and attractive form. Every page beams with the benevolence of the Deity. What a beautiful picture of the goodness and mercy of God is exhibited in the parable of the prodigal son! As fear arises from contemplating the power and justice of God, so love is produced by meditating on His wisdom and goodness. But as it is a matter of the highest importance that we should be enabled to determine with certainty whether we really love God, it may be justly asked, What is the plainest and most undoubted proof of love to God? We answer, That which the Scripture declares it to be. He who hath ears to hear, let him hear. "This," says the Apostle John, " is the love of God, that ye keep His commandments." There is another question still which requires our serious consideration, What are we to understand by loving God with all our heart, with all our soul, and with all our mind? The meaning is, that our desire to please God should be the highest and most vigorous principle, disposing us at all times to prefer our duty to God to every other consideration, and especially to the gratification of all our selfish passions. II. We come now to the second great commandment, "Thou shalt love thy neighbour as thyself." It is scarcely necessary to observe that there is no inconsistency between loving God and loving our neighbour. It is perhaps of more importance to remark that we cannot sincerely and correctly observe the one without attending to the other, for they are parts of one whole. Accordingly, the Apostle John says, " If a man love not his brother, whom he hath seen, how can he love God, whom he hath not seen? " 1. To love our neighbour is never to do him any injury ; for, says the Apostle Paul, " love worketh no ill to our neighbour." Consequently, we ought not to cherish any evil passion against him. 2. We ought also to be always anxious to do our neighbour all the good in our power. 3. But we are required to love our neighbour as ourselves. Then self-love must be a principle which God has implanted, and which He approves, otherwise He would never have recommended it as the standard of our benevolence. Self-love is a desire of happiness; and, if we have just views of happiness, it will never lead us astray. Self-love, too, is to be distinguished from selfishness. The selfish man is wrapped up in himself, and is terrified to do any good to his neighbour, lest he should diminish his own happiness. But the man who is guided by rational self-love knows that the more he goes beyond himself, the more good actions he does to others, the more he will increase and extend his own happiness. III. Consider the observation which our Saviour made on the value of these two grand divisions of the moral law : " On these two commandments hang all the law and the prophets." By the law and the prophets we are sure are meant the books which contain the law of Moses and the books written by the prophets. These books are here represented by our Saviour as being fixed and suspended to the two commandments and supported by them, so that if the two commandments were withdrawn, the law and the prophets being thus deprived of their necessary support, would fall to the ground, and lose their value and intended effect. (*J. Thomson, D.D.*) *Love to God and our neighbour :*—I. Love to God. 1. A principle Divinely implanted in the renewed hearts of believers. 2. It implies a high esteem of God. 3. It implies an earnest desire for communion with God and the enjoyment of Him. 4. Love to God is a judicious principle. 5. An active principle. 6. A supreme love. He must have our whole heart. II. Love to neighbour. 1. This grace, too, like the former, is a divinely implanted principle. 2. Loving our neighbour implies that we entertain benevolent dispositions towards him. 3. It implies that we speak well of him. Love tries to conceal reports prejudicial to our neighbour. It imputes his faults, if it can, rather to inadvertence than to habitual premeditated wickedness. In a word, true love deals faithfully and closely with a man's faults when it gets him by himself ; but as tenderly as possible with them in the presence of others. To this let it be added, that love to our neighbour implies that we do him all the good offices in our power. What avail professions without performance, when it is in our power to perform kind actions? (*Jas. Foote, M.A.*) *Condensed commandments :*—When the late Rev. Dr. Staughton, of America, resided at Bordentown, he was one day sitting at his door, when the infidel Thomas Paine, who also resided there, addressing him, said, " Mr. Staughton, what a pity it is that a man has not some comprehensive and perfect rule for the government of his life." Mr. Staughton replied, " There is such a rule." "What is that? " asked Paine. Mr. Staughton repeated the passage, " Thou shalt love the Lord thy God with all thy heart, with all thy mind, with all thy soul, and with all thy strength ; and thy neighbour as thyself." " Oh," said Paine, " that's in your Bible," and immediately walked away. *The law of love :*— I. The law of love is not inferior to that of the ten commandments ; in other words, love of God and man includes all which these teach at greater length. What saith the first commandment? "Thou shalt have no other gods before Me." Is not there even more than this contained in our text? Let love, to any object whatever, reign in a man's heart, and his whole being revolts from the idea of doing any injury to the object of his affection. The law of love binds us to keep the first commandment. So with the second. It is obvious that they who have true love to the Lord God as the one spiritual King, eternal, immortal, and invisible, will loathe the attempt of the heathen idolaters to represent the attributes of Deity in the lineaments of a creeping thing, or of a beast, or of a bird, or of the physical nature of man. Or take the third. Does this tell any more than the simple direction, Love God? Could yonder wild blasphemer dare to call for God's damnation on his own soul or on that of his fellow-man, to swear by the name of the Holy One, to thread his sentences with oaths, if he had ever learnt to love the great Jehovah whose name he thus dishonours? Take the fourth. If any Jew had spoken of this as a burdensome enactment, it would only have shown that he had not learned to love his God. Then, mark the fifth commandment—"Honour thy father and thy mother." We need not say that this is love. What makes a happy home, with kindly trusting parents, and fond, clambering children, with a gleam of heaven shooting across the scene, and a warm glow resting on it all?—what but love? And is not the fifth commandment fulfilled in this? Then take the sixth, and say if it is possible that love can kill. See the skulking figure, with the deadly knife in his hand, with the restless glance of his suspicious eyes, as though he felt that he is watched: see him draw near the victim, who slumbers, all unconscious of danger and death, and say what would stop that murderous hand but love for his fellow-man? So with the seventh. Lust breaks through this rule, which love would keep; for lust is selfishness, while love forgets all self. So, briefly, with the eighth. Love would prevent a man from "whatsoever doth, or may, unjustly hinder his own or his neighbour's wealth or outward estate." Again, take the ninth. What would stop the voice of slander, and hush the tale of shame, and seal the lips of the liar whose malignant tongue knows no restraint, and stop the story of slander, which circulates so easily over a parish or a nation—what, but this self-same love? And, once more, look at the tenth commandment. What would check the growth of coveting, and withdraw one man's eye from another's scant possessions—what but love? Ahab could not have done the deed of Jezreel if his soul had contained the slightest love for Naboth. Thus we see that all the commandments are embraced in love; and, in the same way, it would be easy to show that on its twofold rule hang all the law and the prophets. II. But, further, the law of love is superior, because—1. It is positive. 2. It is exhaustive. 3. It begins at the heart. 4. It leads us directly and at once to feel our need of the Spirit of God. (*A. H. Charteris, D.D.*) *The love of God:*—I. THE LOVE OF GOD RECOMMENDS ITSELF BY ITS NATURE. 1. It is the most sublime virtue. (1) The most sublime of the Divine and moral virtues (1 Cor. xiii. 13). (2) The fertile mother of all other virtues and their brightest ornaments. (3) All-powerful in its effects, keeping the heart, so prone to sin, from the depths of spiritual ruin; moving and exciting to, and furnishing the necessary strength for, apparently impossible undertakings. (4) The virtue of the inhabitants of heaven, its exercise being the constant work of angels and saints. 2. It confers on us the highest dignity. (1) By this virtue we are elevated above all creatures of this visible world. They serve God by absolute necessity, but they cannot love Him. (2) By this virtue we are elevated above ourselves. All other virtues remind man of his misery and lowness—faith reminds him of his spiritual blindness; humility, of his foolish pride; chastity, of the disgrace of sensuality. Charity alone elevates without reminding you of your weakness, rendering the soul, as it were, infinite. (3) This virtue confers on us a true nobility. (*a*) We obtain the freedom of the children of God. (*b*) We reach by it our perfection, it being "the bond of perfectness" (Col. iii. 14). (*c*) We enter into the most intimate relation with God, being in a manner deified. 3. The greatest beauty of our holy religion. 4. In the love of God we find true happiness. (1) In this world. Divine love—(*a*) renders man infinitely rich by the possession of God; (*b*) fills the heart with the sweetest delights; (*c*) causes heavenly peace, which cannot be disturbed either by tribulations or by the sting of the passions; (*d*) sweetens what is most bitter—all sufferings, and especially death. (2) For eternity. Divine charity is the pledge of life everlasting (1 John iv. 16; 1 Cor. ii. 9). II. HOW MUCH GOD DESERVES OUR LOVE. 1. He is the most perfect Being. 2. He is our greatest benefactor. 3. He is infinitely merciful. (*Eberhard.*) *How we may be convinced that we love God :*—I. Do you love God as you ought to love Him? 1. He requires a love of faithfulness and obedience. (1) Do you obey all that He commands? (2) Do you obey in such a manner as He requires of you? (3) Do you obey because God commands? 2. He requires a love of subjection and dependence. Do you possess this love? God is your sovereign Lord, you are His servant, and, as such, you should submit to His dispositions. (1) God deals with- you and your possessions as He wills, that you may lift up your eyes heavenward. Do you say with Job, "The Lord gave," &c. (Job i. 21). (2) God humbles you that you may honour Him by your humility. Do you complain, as though God was unjust? (3) God sends you diseases and afflictions. Do you embrace the cross? (4) God scourges with the rod of His wrath the degenerated human race. Do you honour and love Him in this also? 3. A love of preference. Do you love God more than all else? 4. A love of equality. Do you love whatever God loves, and hate whatever He hates? 5. A love of attention and complacency. Does it afford you delight to reflect on God, to converse with Him by prayer, &c.? 6. A love of zeal. 7. A love of desire. Do you long for the possession of God? II. What we have to do in order to inflame our hearts with the love of God. 1. We should often call to mind certain eternal truths, and ponder over them. Such truths are the following. (1) All visible things say to us that God is infinitely lovable. (2) God has infinitely loved us. (3) God wills that we should love Him. 2. We should banish from our heart all impure flames of sensual passion. 3. We should endeavour to have a great devotion. (*Segaud.*) *Of the love of God :*—I. The nature of this love. We may describe love in general to be an affection or inclination of the soul toward an object, proceeding from an apprehension and esteem of some excellency or some conveniency therein (its beauty, worth, or usefulness), producing thereon, if the object be absent or wanting, a proportionable desire, and consequently an endeavour to obtain such a propriety therein, such a possession thereof, such an approximation or union thereto, as the thing is capable of; also a regret and displeasure in the failing so to obtain it, or in the want, absence, and loss thereof; likewise begetting a complacence, satisfaction, and delight in its presence, possession, or enjoyment; which is moreover attended with a good-will thereto, suitable to its nature; that is, with a desire that it should arrive unto and continue in its best state; with a delight to perceive it so to thrive and flourish; with a displeasure to see it suffer or decay in any wise; with a consequent endeavour to advance it in all good, and preserve it from all evil. The chief properties of the love we owe to God are these: 1. A right apprehension and firm persuasion concerning God, and consequently a high esteem of Him as most excellent in Himself and most beneficial to us. 2. Another property of this love is an earnest desire of obtaining a propriety in God; of possessing Him, in a manner, and enjoying Him; of approaching Him, and being, so far as may be, united to Him. 3. Coherent with this is a third property of this love, that is, a great complacence, satisfaction, and delight in the enjoyment of God in the sense of having such a propriety in Him; in the partaking those emanations of favour and beneficence from Him; and, consequently, in the instruments conveying, in the means conducing to such enjoyment, for joy and content are the natural fruits of obtaining what we love, what we much value, what we earnestly desire. 4. The feeling much displeasure and regret in being deprived of such enjoyment in the absence or distance, as it were, of God from us; the loss or lessening of His favour; the subtraction of His gracious influences from us: for surely answerable to the love we bear unto anything will be our grief for the want or loss thereof. 5. Another property of this love is, to bear the highest goodwill toward God; so as to wish heartily and effectually, according to our power, to procure all good to Him, and to delight in it ; so as to endeavour to prevent and to remove all evil, if I may so speak, that may befal Him, and to be heartily displeased therewith. II. To the effecting of which purposes I shall next propound some means conducible; some in way of removing obstacles, others by immediately promoting the duty. Of the first kind are these ensuing : 1. The destroying of all loves opposite to the love of God ; extinguishing all affection to things odious and offensive to God; mortifying all corrupt and perverse, all unrighteous and unholy desires. 2. If we would obtain this excellent grace, we must restrain our affections toward all other things, however in their nature innocent and indifferent. 3. The freeing of our hearts also from immoderate affection to ourselves; for this is a very strong bar against the entrance, as of all other charity, so especially of this ; for as the love of an external object doth thrust, as it were, our soul outwards towards it ; so the love of ourselves detains it within, or draws it inwards; and consequently these inclinations crossing each other cannot both have effect, but one will subdue and destroy the other. These are the chief obstacles, the removing of which conduces to the begetting and increasing the love of God in us.   A soul so cleansed from love to bad and filthy things, so emptied of affection to vain and unprofitable things, so opened and dilated by excluding all conceit of, all confidence in itself, is a vessel proper for the Divine love to be infused into: into so large and pure a vacuity (as finer substances are apt to flow of themselves into spaces void of grosser matter) that free and move-able spirit of Divine grace will be ready to succeed, and therein to disperse itself.   As all other things in nature, the clogs being removed which hinder them, do presently tend with all their force to the place of their rest and well-being; so would, it seems, our souls, being loosed from baser affections obstructing them, willingly incline toward God, the natural centre, as it were, and bosom of their affection; would resume, as Origen speaks, that natural filter (that intrinsic spring, or incentive of love) which all creatures have toward their Creator; especially, if to these we add those positive instruments, which are more immediately and directly subservient to the production of this love. They are these: 1. Attentive considera-tion of the Divine perfections, with endeavour to obtain a right and clear appre-hension of them.   2. The consideration of God's works and actions; His works and actions of nature, of Providence, of grace.   3. Serious regard and reflection on the peculiar benefits by the Divine goodness vouchsafed to ourselves.   4. An earnest resolution and endeavour to perform God's commandments, although on inferior considerations of reason; on hope, fear, desire to obtain the benefits of obedience, to shun the mischiefs from sin.   5. Assiduous prayer to Almighty God that He in mercy would please to bestow His love on us, and by His grace to work it in us.   These are the means which my meditation did suggest as conducing to the production and growth of this most excellent grace in our souls. III. I should lastly propound some inducements apt to stir us up to the endeavour of procuring it, and to the exercise thereof, by representing to your consideration the blessed fruits and benefits (both by way of natural causality and of reward) accruing from it; as also the woful consequences and mischiefs springing from the want thereof. (*I. Barrow, D.D.*)   *Love renders all our services acceptable:*—It is not so much the thing done, as the spirit in which it is done, which is of such great moment. For love is an affection of the heart and will, and we know that very small tokens, the merest trifles, will evince it; and that, when it is evinced, it has a peculiar power of winning its way both with God and man.   Suppose a great fortune laid out in building churches, or relieving the poor, under the pressure of servile fear, and with the design of expiating sin, or a great philanthropic enterprise inaugurated and maintained from ambitious motives; can it be supposed that such acts, however it may please Him to bless the effects of them, go for anything with God as regards the doer of them.   And, on the other hand, suppose some very simple, commonplace action, something not going at all beyond the circle of routine and daily duty, done with a grateful, affectionate feeling towards God, and from a simple desire to please Him, and to win His approval—can it be supposed that such an action, however trifling in itself, does not go for something, nay, for much, with God? The love of Him with all the heart, and mind, and soul, and strength, is "the first and great commandment."   One movement of that love gives to the commonest action the fragrance of a sacrifice; while, without one movement of it, the costliest offering must of necessity be rejected. "If a man should give all the substance of his house for love, it would utterly be contemned." (*Dean Goulburn.*)   *Love may be cultivated:*—How shall we cultivate this charity?   Now I observe, first, love cannot be produced by a direct action of the soul upon itself. You cannot love by a resolve to love.   That is as impossible as it is to move a boat by pressing it from within.   The force with which you press on is exactly equal to that with which you press back.   The reaction is exactly equal to the action. You force backwards exactly as much as you force on.   There are religious persons who, when they feel their affections cooled, strive to warm them by self-reproach, or by unnatural efforts, or by the excitement of what they call revivals—trying to work themselves into a state of warm affection.   There are others who hope to make feeble love strong by using strong words. Now, for all this they pay a price. Effort of heart is followed by collapse.   Excitement is followed by exhaustion.   They will find that they have cooled exactly in that proportion in which they warmed, and at least as fast. It is as impossible for a man to work himself into a state of genuine fervent love as it is for a man to inspire himself.   Inspiration is a breath and a life coming from without. Love is a feeling roused not from ourselves, but from something outside ourselves. There are, however, two methods by which we may cultivate this charity. 1. By doing acts which love demands. It is God's merciful law that feelings are increased by acts done on principle. If a man has not the feeling in its warmth, let him not wait till the feeling comes. Let him act with such feelings as he has; with a cold heart if he has not got a warm one; it will grow warmer while he acts. You may love a man merely because you have done him benefits, and so become interested in him, till interest passes into anxiety, and anxiety into affection. You may acquire courtesy of feeling at last, by cultivating courteous manner. The dignified politeness of the last century forced man into a kind of unselfishness in small things, which the abrupter manners of to-day will never teach. And say what men will of rude sincerity, these old men of urbane manners were kinder at heart with real good-will, than we are with that rude bluffness which counts it a loss of independence to be courteous to any one. Gentleness of manner had some influence on gentleness of heart. So in the same way, it is in things spiritual. If our hearts are cold, and we find it hard to love God and be affectionate to man, we must begin with duty. Duty is not Christian liberty, but it is the first step towards liberty. We are free only when we love what we are to do, and those to whom we do it. Let a man begin in earnest with—I ought; he will end, by God's grace, if he persevere, with the free blessedness of—I will. Let him force himself to abound in small offices of kindliness, attention, affectionateness, and all those for God's sake. By and by he will feel them become the habit of his soul. By and by, walking in the conscientiousness of refusing to retaliate when he feels tempted, he will cease to wish it; doing good and heaping kindness on those who injure him, he will learn to love them. For he has spent a treasure there, "And where the treasure is, there will be the heart also." 2. The second way of cultivating Christian love is by contemplating the love of God. You cannot move the boat from within; but you may obtain a purchase from without. You cannot create love in the soul by force from within itself; but you may move it from a point outside itself. God's love is the point from which to move the soul. Love begets love. Love believed in, produces a return of love; we cannot love because we must. "Must" kills love; but the law of our nature is that we love in reply to love. No one ever yet hated one whom he believed to love him truly. We may be provoked by the pertinacity of an affection which asks what we cannot give; but we cannot hate the true love which does not ask but gives. Now, this is the eternal truth of Christ's gospel, "We love Him because He first loved us." "Beloved, if God so loved us, we ought also to love one another." "God is love." (*F. W. Robertson, M.A.*) *Is it necessary to understand God in order to love Him?*—It is said that it is impossible to love God; and the reason alleged is, He is beyond our understanding. The very description of His being Omnipotent, Omniscient, Omnipresent, are terms that daunt us. "I cannot form any conception of such vastness as this. I can measure the mountains, but these even make me falter as I give out the lengths and heights of their measurement. How much more so, when the measurement is simply immeasurable? When it is vast, infinite, is it not also vague? I cannot understand, and therefore I will not love." But is that true? Men and women, is it true that I cannot love where I cannot understand? Go into the midst of your own homes, and watch the face that looks up from her work to glance at you. The toil of your business, the anxiety of your duties, or, if you are scientific, the vastness of those lucubrations which are occupying your time, the splendid calculations, the measureless periods and vast issues which you are considering, occupy your mind; but is the very smallest tittle of these in any degree comprehensible by her who sits beside you? Is it not rather true, in the words of our own laureate, that "Though she cannot understand, yet she loves." She loves, and though she knows that your mind is expatiating in vaster fields than her intellect can follow, yet still that very vastness of your knowledge and comprehension, in comparison with hers, gives her no uneasy sense of a vague might which she cannot love, but rather gives her a sweet sense of confidence in might which she cannot fathom. Or, the child that leaps to greet you on the threshold of your home —are you going to discredit the reality of its little love, because it cannot penetrate the mysteries of the Stock Exchange, or understand the fluctuations of shares and of bills? You know perfectly well that it is very possible, nay, daily life proves it certain, that there are hundreds among us who give out a full unalloyed love, even where their comprehension is staggered by the vastness of that which they cannot understand. So is it surely with God. This great world, this limitless heaven above us, those stars, whose distances we have not calculated, these worlds hung in dizzy space, do they give us such an overwhelming sense of His vastness as to make it impossible for us to love Him? Do they not rather, if we understand that not a little flower blows, nor little stream trickles to its valley below, but does so under His guidance, and is directed by His hand, give us the vastest confidence in Him, whose boundless nature is so great, that, fall where we will, we cannot fall out of the embrace of His love? No, it is false to say you cannot love where you cannot comprehend. (*Bishop Boyd Carpenter.*) *Love the law of life:*—What a strange and startling command, to be ordered to love! If self-dictation over the heart is impossible, as we suppose, who is the master that can pretend to command us to love him? What tyrant, in his most imperious moment ever dreamed of such a demand? Yet God assumes the entry even of this last refuge. It is a rule of His dominion that He shall be loved. Love of God—love of our neighbour: these constitute the sole titles of admission to the kingdom, the sole claims on life. We may plead a hundred other obediences, but no other is of any avail whatever. One command, and one only, has been given, " Thou shalt love." One thing then certainly Christ, our King, presumes to do; He presumes to have the entire command of our affections. What can justify such a claim? I. Who is it who demands love of us? It is our Maker, who made us not by any binding necessity, nor yet for any play or pastime of His own, but solely because the very core of His innermost Being is Fatherhood: He is God because He is the Eternal Father; the Fatherhood is His Godhead. Fatherhood is the love which passionately delights in seeing its own life's joy reproduced in another. Sonship is that love which passionately delights in recognizing that its life is owing to another, belongs to another, is dedicated to another. Love, then, is a natural necessity between human parent and child; and love, therefore, belongs by the same necessity to our Divine relationships. God has undeniable right to this demand; but—II. Who are we that we should love God? We go our own way; we follow our own tastes; we have joys and sorrows, friends and foes of our own. All this fills up our days and occupies our minds; and where is there any room for the love of a far-away invisible God? We are here on earth to find out what love means: and all true love begins in the love of God who loved us. At whatever risk, at whatever cost, we must attain to this love. How, then, to put some meaning into it? We must secure and foster the condition of our sonship; and what does this signify? It signifies this: that the entire movements of our lives must set outward, away from ourselves. (*Canon Scott Holland, M.A.*) *Love to God:*—These words never came from men. Earth never could have heard them if they had not come down from heaven. I. Here we see the very heart of God. He is Love who speaketh thus. II. This is the first and great commandment; because all else flows from it. III. As love only seeks, so only love wins love. IV. Love satisfies love. V. As God's love is the source of our love, so it is the pattern of our love. (*Mark Guy Pearse.*) *Loving God with the heart:*—I. To love God with the heart is to delight in pleasing Him. II. To love God with the heart is to delight most of all in His presence. III. To love God with the heart is to hold ourselves and all we are as belonging to God. (*Ibid.*) *Morality and religion:*—You will observe there are several " ands " in the passage, and that all the earlier ones, though very useful, are merely additions; but here ["and thy neighbour"] is an equalising copulative, a word which brings two sentences together as the two sides of an equation, and which will not permit you to take the first part of the sentence as the declaration of the Saviour, but which requires you to take it in its wholeness. It is not enough to " love the Lord thy God," nor is it enough to " love thy neighbour as thyself," you must do both; and therefore that "and" stands as none of the others do, and as almost no other such single common word does in the great realm of literature. The love of God is put first in order, probably from the dignity of the personage spoken of; it is in the order of importance, but not of time. We do not first love the Lord our God with all our heart, and then learn to love our neighbour as ourselves. We learn to love our neighbour, and from that point, through practice, we come to a condition in which we love our God. So then, these two members or sides of this wonderful sentence, this charter of human life, may be said to represent religion and morality. " Thou shalt love the Lord thy God "—that is, thou shalt worship Him, reverence Him, acknowledge Him, and look up to Him, in every inflection of experience—this stands appropriately for religion; and the other—"Thou shalt love thy neighbour as thyself "—stands appropriately and properly for morality. I. WHAT, THEN, IS THE SPHERE AND FUNCTION OF MORALITY; its educating force; its final intent? Morality includes—1. Duties to oneself, personal duties, sustenance, defence. 2. Social duties—the duties of the family and the neighbourhood. 3. The relations in which we stand to the larger community represented by the Government in all its forms. Here, then, I pause in the discussion, having shown in the first place what moralities are—namely, that they are in their highest and best sense, those duties which men owe to themselves, to their households, to civil society, to their social relations in this world and in time; and also, that morality, in one form and at each stage, prepares for the next higher development of it and the next advance in growth; and likewise, interiorly, that every true morality tends to develope itself in a higher class of faculties. So that, finally—II. EVERY MORALITY THAT DOES NOT GO ON TO A SPIRITUAL FORM IS STOPPED AND DWARFED. Men say, "I am not a religious man, but still I do about as well as I know how." Is that rational? What would you say of men who should voyage to a distant country, and make only those provisions which were necessary for them while they stayed at home? Death cuts men in two, and leaves the bottom here, and there is no top to go there. Do not understand me as saying that morality is of no use. It is very useful; it is the seed-ground of immortality; and I go further and say, it is better that you should have that, even if you have no religion, than that you should have no religion and not that either. Therefore when I preach that you must be born again, when I preach that the new life in Christ Jesus, wrought by the power of God, must be in you, do not think that I undervalue the lower forms by which you come to the possibility of these things. They are of transcendant importance, but do not believe that they are enough. Straw that never ripens its grain is straw, plants that throw out leaves and do not blossom are mere grass and herbs and not flowers. Trees and vines that bring forth no fruit are not fruit vines, nor fruit trees. (*H. W. Beecher.*) *Loving God with the mind:*—Christ claims that God is to be loved with all our nature. They who love God, then, with the heart only, do sin. You are to love God with all your mind, with your brain, and thought, and power; with reason and with argument; with learning and knowledge. No pretence that you love God with your heart absolves you from loving Him with your mind. Did it ever strike you that being ignorant is disservice to God; so much withdrawn from the Almighty? To the degree that you refuse to study the sublime in nature: to that degree I have no pity for your ignorance. It is a failure in your service; a coldness in your love to God. If you love God with all your mind you will do what you do when you love a great author. You may say, "Of all authors I think Shakespeare the greatest; but I have never read one of his plays, never studied one of his sonnets." Indeed! what do you do, then, to show your love to Shakespeare? "Oh, I talk about him." He who loves an author well, turns his pages again and again; weighs his words and marks their construction. If he reads the "Merchant of Venice," he studies it attentively, and proposes to himself to go back to his labour of love again and again. I don't know who is your darling; but I know it is the author with whom you are most familiar. And that is what loving God with all your mind is. The three great volumes of God which you should study are before every one of you: Nature, History, and the Bible. (*George Dawson.*) *The second great commandment:*—Practically a new chapter was opened in the history of morals when Jesus announced that within this solitary principle of duty, "Thou shalt love thy neighbour as thyself," room could be found for every commandment in the Second Table of the Decalogue. 1. The affection which fulfils the whole law is an ethical principle, and not simply an instinctive or generous affection. 2. The neighbour-love which fulfils God's law possesses a compass as wide as the species, and is thereby raised above every rule of moral obligation which obtained popular currency before Christ. 3. This neighbour-love which fulfils the law forms an express counteractive and equivalent to selfishness as a motive of conduct. 4. This golden rule will carry us a great deal further than the merely negative virtue of working no harm, which, in its terms, is all that the Decalogue calls for. (*J. O. Dykes, D.D.*) *The Saviour's great rule:*—There are fundamental truths which lie at the bottom, the basis upon which a great many others rest, and in which they have their consistency. There are teeming truths, rich in store, with which they furnish the mind; and like the lights of heaven, are not only beautiful and entertaining in themselves, but give light and evidence to other things, that without them could not be seen or known. Our Saviour's great rule, that we should love our neighbours as ourselves, is such a fundamental truth for the regulating human society, that I think that by that alone one might without difficulty determine all the cases and doubts in social morality. Truths such as this we should endeavour to find out and store our minds with. (*W. Locke.*) *The sum of duty like the ocean:*—When a man is told that the whole of religion and morality is summed up in the two commandments, to love God and to love our neighbour, he is ready to cry, like Charoba in Gebir at the first sight of the sea, "Is this the mighty ocean? is this all?" Yes! all; but how small a part of it do your eyes survey! Only trust yourself to it; launch out upon it: sail abroad over it; you will find it has no end; it will carry you round the world. (*British Weekly.*) *Loving God with the mind:*—I have known people love God with the heart, and yet talk as if the works of God were not worth studying. What is the use, they say, of studying God in his works? Ah! he who loves a woman well, loves the very trinkets she wears. Whoso loves a man well, loves every hair of his head. All, everything, even the smallest thing, is glowing with preciousness, and is made glorious by the deep love of the heart. For a man, therefore, on the plea of loving God with his heart, not to love Him with his mind, is to offer but a part. Who are you, that you should look upon Nature in her beauty, and behold the green fields and the trees, every leaf of which is full of the life of God, every blade of grass a passing mystery, a consummate divineness—who are you that you should turn from that volume and say, "I love God with my heart and not with my mind." There is no excuse for you if you know nothing about Nature. Do you say you have no time for these things? One flower from your table, if you will study it, will be more than a garden; one rose is worth more attention than all your furniture. No time? You can find plenty of time to study your own foolish garments; and have you no time to study the garments of God? Whoso shall watch the sun, and ask a few questions about his rising, shall find that one hour of study shall make him more instructed than before in regard to the great works of God. Therefore, a part of loving God with the mind is to study God's works. It is not "necessary to salvation," as it is called, but it is necessary to large love, for God is not loved with the mind by stupid people. (*George Dawson.*) **Thy neighbour as thysel'.**—*Fraternal charity:*—I. Works of Christian charity are acceptable to God. We infer this—1. From the urgency with which this commandment is enjoined upon us by Jesus Christ. (1) He places it on a par with the love of God (Matt. xxii. 37–39). (2) He urges it as being emphatically His own (John xv. 12). (3) He states most anxiously the true meaning of this commandment—a precaution usually observed with matters of the greatest importance (John xiii. 34). 2. From man's relation to God: he being his Maker's image and likeness. The essence of Christian brotherly love consists in loving our neighbour for God's sake; not only from reverence for the Divine commandment, but from sacred reverence and love for God's own nature which is reflected in man. 3. From God's view of charitable works. He considers them as done to Himself. II. The value of charitable works for our own temporal and eternal welfare. The rewards or effects of fraternal charity are as follows—1. An abundance of Divine blessings, by which God restores a hundredfold what, from love towards Him, we give to His poor children. 2. Divine mercy, which opens its treasures principally to the merciful. 3. An exceedingly great reward in eternity. (*P. Beckx.*) *Of the love of our neighbour:*—I. The object of this duty. Our neighbour, *i.e.*, every man with whom we have to do, especially every Christian. II. The qualification. 1. Loving our neighbour "as ourselves" doth import a rule directing what kind of love we should bear and exercise toward him; or informing us that our charity doth consist in having the same affections of soul, and in performing the same acts of benefi-cence toward him as we are ready by inclination, as we are wont in practice to have or to perform toward ourselves, with full approbation of our judgment and con-science, apprehending it just and reasonable so to do. 2. Loving our neighbour as ourselves imports also the measure of our love towards him; that it should be commensurate with, and equal in degree to that love which we bear and exercise towards ourselves. This is that perfection of charity to which our Lord bids us aspire, in the injunction, "Be ye perfect, even as your Father in heaven is perfect." That this sense of the words is included, yea, chiefly intended, divers reasons will evince; for—1. The most natural signification and common use of the phrase doth import thus much; and any one at first hearing would so understand the words. 2. It appeareth by comparing this precept with that to which it is annexed, "of loving God with all our heart and all our soul"; which manifestly designeth the quantity and degree of that love; consequently the like determination is intended in this precept, which is expressed to resemble that, or designed in like manner to qualify and bound our duty toward our neighbour. 3. If the law doth not signify thus much, it doth hardly signify anything; not at least anything of direction or use to us; for no man is ignorant that he is obliged to love his neighbour, but how far that love must extend is the point wherein most of us do need to be resolved, and without satisfaction in which we shall hardly do anything; for as he that oweth money will not pay except he can tell how much it is; so to know the duty will not avail toward effectual observance of it, if its measure be not fixed. 4. Indeed, the law otherwise understood will rather be apt to misguide than to direct us; inducing us to apprehend that we shall satisfy its intent, and sufficiently discharge our duty, by practising charity in any low degree or mean instance. Also— 5. The former sense, which is unquestionable, doth infer and establish this: because similitude of love, morally speaking, cannot consist with inequality thereof; for if in considerable degrees we love ourselves more than others, assuredly we shall fail both in exerting such internal acts of affection, and in performing such external offices of kindness toward them, as we do exert and perform in regard to ourselves; whence this law, taken merely as a rule, demanding a confused and imperfect similitude of practice, will have no clear obligation or certain efficacy. But, farther, the duty thus interpreted is agreeable to reason, and may be justly required of us. 1. It is reasonable that we should love our neighbour as ourselves because he is as ourselves, or really in all considerable respects the same with us. This explained. 2. It is just that we should do so, because he really no less deserves our love. Justice is impartial, and regards things as they are in themselves; whence, if our neighbour seem worthy of affection no less than we, it demands accordingly that we love him no less. 3. It is fit that we should be obliged to this love, because all charity beneath self-love is defective, and all self-love above charity is excessive. 4. Equity requires it, because we are apt to claim the same measure of love from others. 5. It is needful that so great charity be prescribed, because none inferior to it will reach divers weighty ends designed in this law; viz., the general convenience and comfort of our lives in mutual intercourse and society. 6. That entire love which we owe to God our Creator, and to Christ our Redeemer, exacts from us no less a measure of charity than this. 7. Indeed the whole tenour and genius of our religion imply an obligation to this pitch of love on various accounts. 8. Lastly, many conspicuous examples, proposed for our direction in this kind of practice, do imply this degree of charity to be required of us. III. An objection answered. If, it may be said, the precept be thus understood, as to oblige us to love our neighbours equally with ourselves, it will prove unpracticable, such a charity being merely romantic and imaginary; for who doth, who can, love his neighbour in this degree? Nature powerfully doth resist, common sense plainly doth forbid that we should do so: a natural instinct doth prompt us to love ourselves, and we are forcibly driven thereto by an unavoidable sense of pleasure and pain, resulting from the constitution of our body and soul, so that our own least good or evil are very sensible to us: whereas we have no such potent inclination to love others; we have no sense, or a very faint one, of what another doth enjoy or endure; doth not, therefore, nature plainly suggest that our neighbour's good cannot be so considerable to us as our own? especially when charity doth clash with self-love, or when there is a competition between our neighbour's interest and our own, is it possible that we should not be partial to our own side? Is not, therefore, this precept such as if we should be commanded to fly, or to do that which natural propension will certainly hinder? In answer to this exception I say, Be it so, that we can never attain to love our neighbour altogether so much as ourselves, yet may it be reasonable that we should be enjoined to do so; for laws must not be depressed to our imperfection, nor rules bent to our obliquity; but we must ascend toward the perfection of them, and strive to conform our practice to their exactness. But neither is the performance of this task so impossible, or so desperately hard (if we take the right course, and use proper means toward it) as is supposed; as may somewhat appear if we will weigh the following considerations. 1. Be it considered that we may be mistaken in our account, when we do look on the impossibility or difficulty of such a practice, as it appeareth at present, before we have seriously attempted, and in a good method, by due means, earnestly laboured to achieve it; for many things cannot be done at first, or with a small practice, which by degrees and a continued endeavour may be effected; divers things are placed at a distance, so that without passing through the interjacent way we cannot arrive at them; divers things seem hard before trial, which afterward prove very easy. It is impossible to fly up to the top of a steeple, but we may ascend thither by steps; we cannot get to Rome without crossing the seas, and travelling through France or Germany; it is hard to comprehend a subtle theorem in geometry, if we pitch on it first; but if we begin at the simple principles, and go forward through the intermediate propositions, we may easily obtain a demonstration of it. If we would set ourselves to exercise charity in those instances whereof we are at first capable without much reluctancy, and thence proceed toward others of a higher nature, we may find such improvement, and taste such content therein that we may soon arise to incredible degrees thereof; and at length, perhaps, we may attain to such a pitch, that it will seem to us base and vain to consider our own good before that of others in any sensible measure; and that nature which now so mightily doth contest in favour of ourselves, may in time give way to a better nature, born of custom, affecting the good of others. 2. Let us consider that in some respects and in divers instances it is very feasible to love our neighbour no less than ourselves. 3. We see men inclined by other principles to act as much or more for the sake of others, than they would for themselves—instances of patriots and friends. 4. Those dispositions of soul which usually with so much violence thwart the observance of this precept, are not ingredients of true self-love, by the which we are directed to regulate our charity, but a spurious brood of our folly and pravity, which imply not a sober love of ourselves. 5. Indeed, we may farther consider that our nature is not so absolutely averse to the practice of such charity, as those may think who view it slightly, either in some particular instances, or in ordinary practice. Man having received his soul from the breath of God, and being framed after His image, there do yet abide in him some features resembling the Divine original. This shown by our natural sympathy with distress and misery, by our admiration of pure benevolence, and contempt of sordid selfishness, &c. 6. But supposing the inclinations of a depraved nature do so mightily obstruct the performance of this duty in the degree specified, yet we must remember that a subsidiary power is by the Divine mercy dispensed to us, able to control and subdue nature, and raise our faculties far above their natural force. 7. There are divers means conducive to the abatement of this difficulty, the issue of which may be safely referred to the due trial of them. 1. Let us carefully weigh the value of those things which immoderate self-love affects in prejudice to charity, together with the worth of those which charity sets in balance to them. 2. Let us also consider our real state in the world, in dependence on the pleasure and providence of Almighty God; the thought that we are members of one commonwealth, and of the Church, under the government and patronage of God, may disengage us from immoderate respect of private good, and incline us to promote the common welfare. 3. There is one plain way of rendering this duty possible, or of perfectly reconciling charity to self-love; which is, a making the welfare of our neighbour to be our own; which if we can do, then easily may we desire it more seriously, then may we promote it with the greatest zeal and vigour; for then it will be an instance of self-love to exercise charity; then both these inclinations conspiring will march evenly together, one will not extrude nor depress the other. 4. It will greatly conduce to the perfect observance of this rule if we studiously contemplate ourselves, strictly examining our conscience, and seriously reflecting on our unworthiness and vileness. If we do so, what place can there be for that vanity, arrogance, partiality, and injustice, which are the sources of immoderate self-love? 5. Lastly, we may from conspicuous examples and experiments be assured that such a practice of this duty is not impossible. (*I. Barrow, D.D.*) *Love to man the offspring of love to God :*—I hold that the power to love man always grows in proportion to the love that you have to give. That is the New Testament thought upon the subject. That is what our Lord meant when He added—and remember He added it scrupulously, because He wished, as it were, to link it with the former—" The second is like unto it—Thou shalt love thy neighbour as thyself." Not like it in being a repetition of words cast in the same form, but like it in this, that, as child is like parent, so the duty of loving the neighbour resembles the duty of loving God, and springs from it, is caused by it, is necessitated by it. Look at it, and say, is it not true? Whenever a great man dies, there is immediately an anxiety possessing the public mind to be possessed of little tokens of his life. What do those anxieties mean? Do they not mean that our love for the one that has gone makes us love everything that his hand has touched? All that bears the impress of his hand we love. The fabulous sums given for autographs are the proof of this, that the love for any single being passes on to all that he has made. Surely that is true. Not one man stands before the world who has learned to love God but has loved that which is made by God. You look now into the face of human-kind—they are not an accidental brotherhood, the outgrowths of creation, the evolutions of a law merely. They may be that, but they are far more—they are the offspring of God—they are made in His image. You see His likeness everywhere. Man is the autograph of God, and loved by those who love God. Nay, more—go to your homes and learn that you always loved that which was loved by those whom you loved. Why is it that you treasure that little drawer with all those sweet tokens in it—a little knot of ribbon, a small bunch of hair, a faded leaf, a pair of little shoes; what is it that makes you draw them forth and weep silent tears alone? Because these are expressions of a love which has gone. There were hands that handled those little shoes and placed them upon the tiny feet, and hands and feet have grown cold now. There in the little rough work where the small sketch is seen, the hand that traced it will trace no more—it is tracing fairer scenes in the presence of God. All that has caused anxiety, all that has caused care and toil, commends itself as a thing to be loved, because it was loved by one who has gone. So also is it when you regard humanity as the work of God. You must regard humanity, from the Christian point of view, as the redeemed work of God. Upon every son of man there is the mark of blood, and it is the blood of Christ that redeemed him. That blood is the pledge of the love which suffered, and although humanity be utterly contemptible at times, though you despise its meanness, though you turn away with disgust and loathing from its equivocations and falsehoods, yet at the moment you ɔ̣ad, like the Israelites of old, the mark of blood there on their foreheads, you know that, not for their own sakes merely, but for the sake of Him who hung upon the cross to consecrate humanity in redemption to Himself, they must be loved by you. (*Bishop Boyd Carpenter.*) *Love is the secret of obedience :*—There was once a catechist preaching in China, and as he was teaching, a Chinese coolie came in and said, " What is that in your hand ? " The missionary said, " It is a measure, and it is like your measures, it has got ten divisions " (the Chinese do not divide into twelve inches, but ten). " What do you measure ? " said the coolie. " I measure longs and shorts—long hearts and short hearts. Sit down and I will measure you." The coolie sat down, and the catechist began to measure. He took the first commandment, "Thou shalt have none other gods but Me." "Is your heart shorter than that commandment, or longer ? " The Chinese man said, "Oh, I am afraid it is very short." As the catechist went through all the Ten Commandments the poor man found his heart was too short, and did not come up to any of them. The catechist said, " You see your heart is too short. How shall we make up the deficiency ? who will supply what is wanting? " Then he talked to him about Jesus Christ; how He would make up his shortcomings; how Christ's obedience was as if he had kept the whole law himself. So, perhaps, some child will say, " I cannot do God's commandments." Do not say " I cannot "; it is not a good thing to say " I cannot." There was a poor man, and his hand was all withered and powerless ; and Christ said to him, " Stretch out your hand." Could he ? Not before Christ told him; but when God told him to " stretch out his hand," He gave him power. When God tells you to do those things you cannot do of yourselves, He gives you power. " God's biddings are God's enablings." Supposing you got a piece of cold iron, and I said, " Make me a pretty thing out of that." You would say, " I cannot bend that cold iron; melt it, and something might be done." Your heart is like a piece of cold iron, and what will melt it? *Love*, that will make your heart soft, and then you can keep " God's commandments." God says at the beginning of the Ten Commandments, " I am the Lord *Thy* God." Which is the important word there? " *Thy* God." If you cannot say " My God," you cannot keep His commandments. If you keep these commandments, you will become happy, holy, and useful. (*British Weekly Pulpit.*)

Ver. 28. **This do, and thou shalt live.**—*Eternal life promised the obedient :*—I. WHAT IS IMPLIED IN OBEYING GOD'S COMMANDS. It is easy to see in what obedience to the Divine commands consists. It must consist in doing what the commands of God require. The two great commands of the law require love to God and love to man. And to exercise this love is to obey these commands. II. GOD PROMISES ETERNAL LIFE TO ALL WHO OBEY HIS COMMANDS, or exercise those holy and benevolent affections which His commands require. III. WHY GOD PROMISES

ETERNAL LIFE TO ALL WHO SINCERELY AND CORDIALLY OBEY HIS COMMANDS. **1.** God does not promise eternal life to all who obey His commands, because their sincere and cordial obedience atones for their sin, and lays a foundation for pardon, for forgiveness, or justification in His sight. After men have once sinned, their future obedience can make no atonement for past transgression. Perfect obedience is their constant and indispensable duty. **2.** Nor does God promise eternal life to those who obey Him, because their obedience merits eternal life. Though obedience to the Divine commands is really virtuous and intrinsically excellent, yet it is not meritorious. The obedience of a creature can lay no obligation upon his Creator. **3.** He does promise eternal life to them because their obedience is a proper ground, reason, or condition, for bestowing upon them such a gracious and unmerited reward. (*N. Emmons, D.D.*) *The necessity of moral obedience :*—I. THE INCULCATION OF MORAL OBEDIENCE AS A SCRIPTURE REQUISITE TO SALVATION. Why was the gospel given? What did Christ come into the world for? Doubtless to relieve wretchedness, to dissipate error, to revive hope, to take away condemnation, to make death and the grave unfeared, to light up with brightness the whole face of the world. But was this all? Was it not also to destroy sin, to promote holiness, to cast out Satan from His dominion, to repair the broken and effaced image of paradise, to magnify the victories of the cross, to illustrate the agency of a new principle in man's heart, to form a character which angels might consort with, and God might look upon? We must insist upon such moral obedience as man has power to render, as being vital to his salvation; must close the doors of the kingdom of heaven against everything that defiles; must propound as an eternal axiom of the heavenly moralities, that in every nation he that feareth God, and worketh righteousness, and he only, is accepted of Him. "This do, and thou shalt live." II. THE PERFECT COMPATIBILITY OF SUCH A SUPPOSITION WITH OUR RECEIVED VIEWS OF THE DOCTRINE OF JUSTIFICATION BY FAITH. If I am asked to show a man the way of salvation, I am as little at liberty to omit saying to him, "Believe on the Lord Jesus Christ," as I am, in reference to the unchanging demands of the moral law, to omit saying, "This do and thou shalt live." But it will be said, if you thus insist upon moral obedience, or works of godliness as vital to salvation, do you not in effect make these works an element of justification? I answer, We do; but not a meritorious element, any more than we make faith a meritorious element. Faith itself is a work; is put down in Scripture among our commanded endeavours after obedience. "Then said they unto Him, What shall we do that we may work the works of God? Jesus answered and said unto them, This is the work of God, that ye believe on Him whom He hath sent." Let us not put asunder what God hath joined together; let us not weaken the everlasting bond which unites the faith of justification with the sanctities of life. (*D. Moore, M.A.*)

Vers. 29–37. **And who is my neighbour ?**—*Self-justification :*—"The lawyer said—" Then comes his own particular plea or excuse, to which I intend to pay little or no attention now, it was so completely and triumphantly answered by Jesus Christ. Read His parable in reply. Next to the parable of the prodigal son, it is the sweetest word ever spoken even by the lips of Jesus Christ. I. I intend each man to fill up the sentence for himself, only having from the lawyer the preface: "He, willing to justify himself, said—" What words do you insert after the word "said"? How is it with your self-justifying and self-excusing heart? Do I hear correctly when I say you are now reasoning thus—"If I am sincere in my spirit and convictions, no matter whether I believe what is in the Bible or not, all will be well with me here and hereafter"? Is that a correct statement of what you are now thinking? It sounds well. I admit, with all candour, that it seems to sound conclusively and to admit of no refutation. Yet it surely will admit of a question or two being put, in order that we may fully understand the position. You speak of sincerity. I ask, What are you sincere in? Does anything turn upon the object of your sincerity? If you are sincerely giving to a customer over your counter what you believe to be the thing he has asked for, will you be fully justified in the day that you find you have poisoned the man? You sincerely believed that you were giving him precisely the very ingredient that he asked for, and that he had paid for, but you do not give him that ingredient, but something else, and ere the sun go down the man will be dead. What does sincerity go for there? If you indicate to a traveller, sincerely, to the best of your knowledge, the road along which he ought to go to reach a certain destination; if it be the wrong road, and if in some sudden darkness the man should fall over a precipice, will your sincerity obliterate everything like self-reproach ? Were you sure it was the road ? " No, but I was sincere in thinking it was." Did you explain to the man that you were speaking upon an assumption? " No, I thought there was no occasion to do so, I felt so sure." But you see that the mere element of sincerity goes a very short way in cases of that kind. We love sincerity. Without sincerity life is but a mockery, the worst of irony! But what are we sincere in ? Have we ascertained that the object of our sincerity is real, true, and deserving of our confidence? We are responsible not only for the light we have, but for the light we *may* have. There is a sincerity of fanaticism, as well as a sincerity of philosophy. There is a sincerity of ignorance, as well as a sincerity of knowledge. Merely, therefore, to say, " I am sincere," is to say nothing. We must inquire, what is the object upon which your sincerity fixes itself? what is the degree of its intelligence, and what is the degree of its conscience? When any man has returned clear earnest answers to these inquiries, my belief is that he will find himself short of something, and that that something which is absent will be found to be the truth as it is in Jesus—the Cross, the one Cross, out of which every other cross that is true and useful must be made ! II. But he, willing to justify himself, said, " I have been looking round, and it strikes me that I am every whit as good as other people that are about me." Would it be rude to contradict you? Will it be polite to admit the truthfulness, generally, of what you say? Either on the one hand or the other it does not touch the point at all. If the question lay between you and me, it would be right for each to compare himself with the other, and to exalt his superiority at the expense of his brother's infirmities. The case is not as between one man and another. We err in circumscribing the question so. The question is between the soul and God ; between the heart and the absolutely right ; between man and Jesus Christ ; between right and wrong. When you compare yourself with another man, especially to your own advantage, you are not in the spirit which is likely to elicit the truth and lead you to sound and useful conclusions. Your disposition is wrong ; your temper is wrong. You must cease such a method of comparing advantages and honours, and must go to the absolute and final standard of righteousness. III. But he, willing to justify himself, said, " Though I do not believe and act as they do who call themselves Christians, yet I trust to the mercy of God." The man who makes this plea talks in some such fashion as this: " I do not care for doctrines ; I do not care for churches ; theologies trouble me very little indeed ; if I live as wisely as I can, and do what is tolerably fair between one man and another, I shall trust to the mercy of God, and I believe all will be right at last." Do you know what you are talking about in talking so ? Do you understand the value and the force of your own words ? Are you aware that the word mercy is one of the words in our language which it is very difficult to understand? What is mercy? In your estimation, perhaps, it is mere physical sensibility, simple emotion—a gush of feeling. Is that mercy? No. What is mercy? The highest point of justice—justice returning and completing itself by the return. Mercy is justice in tears! Mercy is righteousness with a sword just transforming itself into a sceptre ! Is mercy a mere freak of sentimentality ? Do you think God will say at last, " Well, well, come in, come in, and say nothing more about it " ? I would not go into His heaven if the conditions were such ! It would be no heaven. Where there is not righteousness at the centre, there is no security at the circumference. Where the throne is not founded upon justice, mercy is but a momentary impulse, to be followed by a terrible recoil. What do you mean, then, when you talk about trusting to His mercy at last? Trust to His mercy at first. Where is His mercy ? It is in the life, the ministry, the death, the resurrection, and the whole mediation of Jesus Christ! IV. But he, willing to justify himself, said, "There is so much mystery about religion that I cannot really attempt to understand it." I answer, There is mystery about religion, but there is ten thousand times more mystery without it. There is mystery with the Bible, but there is nothing but mystery without it. There is a mystery of grace ; yes, and there is a mystery of sin. Life is a mystery. All that is great touches the mysterious. Would I part with the mystery! Nay, verily. Are not the clouds God's as well as the blue sky ? Are not the mists around the mountain tops His, as well as the bases of the mountains and the foundations of the earth? Is He Himself the living God, not the culmination of all mysteries, the sum of all wonder— the Alpha and the Omega—not to be understood, but loved and served ? There is a point in my religious inquiries where I must close my eyes, look no more, but rest myself in the grand transaction which is known as faith in the Son of God. V. But he, willing to justify himself, came at last to this : " There are so many denominations of Christians, that it is impossible to tell which is right and which is wrong." Think of a man going off on that line ! Think of a man saying that he has been looking round and sees that there are so many denominations, that really he has made up his mind to give up the whole thing ! Does he know what he is talking about ? Is he really serious when he speaks so ? Shall I follow his example? If I do it will be to show how great is his folly. " I have been looking round, and see so many different regiments in the country that really it is impossible to tell which is right and which is wrong, and I do not think I shall have anything to do with the country." Yes, there are many regiments, but one army ; many denominations, but one Church ; many creeds, but one faith ; many aspects, but one life ; many ways up the hill, but one cross on the top of it. Don't lose yourself among the diversities, when you might save yourself by looking at the unities. " There are so many mountains about, that I really do not know that there can be any truth in geography." Many mountains—one globe ! Conclusion : If, then, there is not to be self-justification, what is there to be ? Self-renunciation. A man must empty himself of himself before he is in the right condition to understand lovingly and gratefully the offer which Jesus Christ makes men. God guests with the contrite and companies with the self-renouncing soul. I will go to my Father, then, and will say unto Him, not, " Father, I was tempted ; somebody lured me away ; I did not intend to leave Thee, but I was beguiled " ; but I will say unto Him, " Father, I have sinned ! " This, then, is the ground of coming to God ; the ground of self-denial, self-renunciation, self-distrust, self-hatred, on account of sin. " Oh ! Israel, thou hast destroyed thyself, but in Me is thy help." " Come unto Me all ye that labour and are heavy laden and I will give you rest." " Jesus cried and said, If any man thirst let him come unto Me and drink." " I am come that they might have life, and that they might have it more abundantly." Who accepts the invitation to-night ? Some have accepted it. Pray that this word may not be spoken in vain ! Some require just one more appeal, and they will decide. Take this, my friend, as the appeal you want. " Now is the accepted time ; now is the day of salvation." (*J. Parker, D.D.*) *Parable of the man who fell among thieves :*—1. By the man that went from Jerusalem to Jericho, I understand is meant fallen man, who originally in the first Adam went from God. 2. By " falling among thieves," may be meant that mischief and misery which hath befallen man by sin, Satan, and other enemies of the soul. 3. By " stripping him of his raiment," may be meant all our first or original righteousness. Righteousness being often compared to raiment, or to a garment. 4. By " wounding him," may be intended that sad and fearful privation of the soul in every faculty thereof by sin. 5. By " leaving him half dead," may be meant the spiritual death of the soul, which is half, nay the better half of the man. 6. By " the priest passing that way and going on one side," may be meant, the law or priesthood of Aaron ; by the Levite may be meant legal sacrifices, and by their both passing by, and not pitying or helping this poor distressed man, may signify that there is no help, no cure, no salvation by the law, nor sacrifices of the law, for undone sinners. 7. By " the Samaritan," I understand is meant our Lord Jesus Christ, who is said to pass by and see us in our blood—" Now as I passed by, I looked upon thee, and saw thee polluted in thy own blood " (Ezek. xvi. 6, 8). This was a blessed look indeed, a look of pity and compassion—" When he saw him, he had compassion on him." " And he went to him," which may refer to two things. (1) To Christ's coming into the world to assume our nature. (2) It may refer also to His gracious coming to a wounded sinner by His Word and Spirit, in helping him to apply the virtue of His own precious blood to his wounded soul. 8. Binding up his wounds, and pouring in oil and wine, may be meant, Christ infusing of His Spirit and precious grace into his soul ; grace, as well as the Holy Spirit, being compared to oil. (*B. Keach.*) *Mankind wounded and robbed by sin and Satan :*—I. In what respects sin and Satan may be compared to thieves. 1. Thieves are enemies to honest men, and of which they are in danger continually. 2. Thieves often in a secret and felonious manner have taken away all that men had in their possession, leaving them in a very poor and distressed condition who were very rich before. 3. Thieves many times lead poor travellers out of the king's highway, into some blind or secret place, and there bind them hand and foot, as well as take away all they have. So sin and Satan—(1) With the bond of ignorance. (2) Hard heart. (3) Unbelief. 4. Thieves are a great terror to honest men, and they strive to avoid them as much as they can, and also to defend themselves against them with their utmost power and skill. So the Lord Jesus arms us with spiritual armour, wisdom, and courage, to resist the flesh, world, and devil. 5. Thieves wait a fit opportunity to come upon a person or family, even when they are most secure, or asleep in their beds. So Satan and other spiritual enemies watch a fit time when a child of God is most secure, or in a sleepy or slothful condition. II. Sin and the evil are the worst of thieves. 1. Because they are soul-thieves, and seek to rob us of our choice and chiefest treasure. 2. Because they are cruel and bloody thieves, murdering thieves. 3. Because none have escaped them. 4. Nay, and they have not only murdered the whole world of ungodly sinners, but they have also wickedly slain and murdered the Lord Jesus Christ. 5. Sin and the devil, &c., are the worst of thieves, because they are old thieves and murderers. "The devil was a murderer from the beginning" (John viii. 44). 6. They are the worst of thieves, considering their great subtilty, policy, and craftiness. 7. Because of their great power and strength. Who is a match for them? (*Ibid.*) *Parable of the Good Samaritan:*—I. The Saviour here reminds us that IN THE WORLD THERE IS SORE DISTRESS. Upon this man a band of ruffians rushed out : and, seizing, they stripped him of his raiment, beat him, and left him half dead ; and all, so far as appears, with no fault of his own. There is poverty and pain and sorrow, for which the sufferer is not, at least directly, responsible. It must, however, be owned that the chief woes of the world come of sin. There are no thieves and robbers so cruel as worldliness and wrong-doing, irreligion and vice. II. THERE ARE THOSE WHO TO ALL THIS PAY LITTLE HEED. "The priest and the Levite were both in a hurry. They had been a month at Jerusalem, and were expected and wanted at home. Their wives and children were anxiously waiting for them. The sun would soon be down, and this was a lonely road even by daylight. Neither of them understood surgery, they could not bind up a wound to save their lives. Moreover, the poor man, already half dead, would be quite dead in an hour or two, and it was a pity to waste time on a hopeless case. The robbers, too, might be back again. Then, the man might die, and the person found near the body be charged with murder." Good excuses, every one! And so it comes to pass that the world's miseries go unrelieved; the world's sins unrebuked; the world's perishing ones unsaved. III. But, now, in contrast with all this, our Saviour shows us that, IN THE PRESENCE OF DISTRESS, TRUE LOVE, FORGETTING SELF, HASTENS TO ITS RELIEF. (*H. M. Grout, D.D.*) *Parable of the good Samaritan:*—I. THE DISTRESSED CONDITION OF A FELLOW-CREATURE. Of what vileness men are capable—in some respects more to be dreaded than the savage beast of prey that roams abroad in the forest. II. THE EMBODIMENT OF SELFISHNESS IN TWO TRAVELLERS WHO ARE PASSING BY. III. AN EXHIBITION OF LOVE AND MERCY WHERE WE SHOULD NOT HAVE EXPECTED TO FIND IT. 1. The Samaritan's eye affected his heart. 2. His feet hastened to the sufferer. 3. His hands ministered to him. IV. THE INEVITABLE CONCLUSION to which the querulous lawyer was forced. 1. Think of the Samaritan, and admire his spirit. 2. Have equally generous feelings toward all thy suffering fellow-creatures. 3. Imitate him when such circumstances shall be presented before thine eyes. Learn—1. The fallacy of that religion which is devoid of mercy and compassion. 2. See under what an awful delusion professors of religion may live. As in the case of the priest and Levite. 3. Cherish the spirit, and imitate the conduct of the Lord Jesus—"Who went about doing good." (*J. Burns, D.D.*) *The good Samaritan:*—1. It is not always convenient to be good. A free-and-easy manner of life is not goodness, and no more is good-nature. There is no goodness without a self-denial which runs right against self-convenience. 2. Again, it is not always agreeable to be good. Thorns lacerate the hand which gathers roses. In the Divine service the question is not what we would prefer. No one can enjoy the scene of suffering or be gladdened by its moans—this is not natural ; yet we must always relieve such wants. 3. Once again, goodness implies a heavy cost. One who is truly good never locks up his pocket-book so that he cannot be benevolent. The Samaritan was good long before he bound up the bruises of the sufferer and provided for him. The event simply evoked what he already was. We do not become good by doing such acts as these, but such acts as these declare our nature. We observe yet further, this goodness wins the respect of the world. (*David O. Mears.*) *Lessons from this parable:*—I. THAT MAN IN ALL HIS VARIETIES AND CONDITIONS IS TO BE RECOGNIZED AS OUR NEIGHBOUR AND BROTHER. II. THAT NATIONAL PREJUDICE AND RELIGIOUS DISTINCTION SHOULD ALL GIVE PLACE TO THE EXERCISE OF CHARITY. III. THAT IT IS OUR DUTY TO OVERCOME EVIL WITH GOOD. In conclusion: consider some motives which call for the exercise of charity. 1. The relation in which we stand to God and to one another in the present world. 2. The genius of our holy religion demands it. (*J. Pulling.*) *The good Samaritan:*—Two things must strike every attentive reader. The first is, that the parable was not so much an answer to the question formally put by the lawyer, as an exposure of the state of heart which the putting of that question revealed. The inquirer wanted a definition of the word "neighbour." The Lord answers by showing him true neighbourliness in contrast with selfish indifference. Thus the parable does not tell us in form who our neighbour is, but it shows us how true love works. But the second peculiarity of this parable is, that it is not an allegory, each figure in which represents a spiritual analogue; but simply an illustrative example of the working of benevolence, as contrasted with that of selfishness. It is designed to show us what we must avoid, as well as what we must cultivate, if we would truly and fully love our neighbour as ourselves. I. THE KINDNESS OF THE SAMARITAN WAS OF THE SPIRIT, AND NOT MERELY OF THE LETTER. With him love meant the doing of everything within his power, for all who required his help; and, therefore, without asking any questions or making any excuses, he gave the poor man all the assistance he could. If we do that only which is formally prescribed, and if, where the law leaves a blank to be filled up by circumstances, we act as if there was no law at all, then we have yet to learn what true benevolence is; nay, more, we have yet to learn what kind of a book the New Testament is : for it is not a list of distinct precepts, each of which is applicable to only one case; but it is a book of living principles of universal application, and he who really understands them, and has a heart to feel their obligation, will be at no loss to find occasion for their manifestation. II. THE SAMARITAN'S BENEVOLENCE WAS NOT HINDERED BY ANY PREJUDICES OF NATIONALITY OR RELIGION. III. THE SAMARITAN'S BENEVOLENCE WAS NOT HINDERED BY ANY CONSIDERATIONS OF PERSONAL CONVENIENCE. What genuine neighbour-love does, it will do thoroughly. Love is ready to sacrifice up to the extent of the necessity which it seeks to meet. IV. THIS MAN'S BENEVOLENCE TOOK ITS FORM FROM THE NATURE OF THE MISERY WHICH HE SOUGHT TO RELIEVE. He did the very things which the sufferer needed to have done for him, and he did these at once. He might, indeed, have put himself about in many other ways, under the idea that he was helping the unfortunate traveller; but nothing could have met the case save the method which he adopted. He had no stereotyped mode of showing mercy, which he sought invariably to follow; but he did in each case just what each required. Now, this is very important, because, for lack of attention to it, many people's benevolence, though it may be very well meant, is a total failure. V. IF OUR BENEVOLENCE WOULD BE OF THE HIGHEST ORDER, WE MUST EXERCISE IT OUT OF REGARD TO HIM WHO DIED TO SHOW MERCY TO OURSELVES. Thus our humanity will rise into Christianity, and our benevolence will be baptized into the name of the Lord Jesus. I conclude with the story of an incident in the life of my grandfather, which I have often heard from my father's lips. It was more than a hundred years ago, when wheeled conveyances were rarely used in the rural districts of Scotland, and the custom was to convey grain to the mill in a sack laid over a horse's back. The good man was making such a journey once, over a rough bridle-path; and the horse stumbled, so that the sack fell off. As he was perplexed, and wondering what to do, he saw a man on horseback in the distance, and had just made up his mind to ask him for assistance, when he recognized in him the nobleman who lived in an adjoining castle; and then his heart sank again within him, for how could he request *him* to help him? But he did not need to ask him, for he was noble by a higher patent than any monarch could confer; and, when he came up, he dismounted of his own accord, saying, "Let me help you, John." So between them they put the load again upon the horse; and then John, who was a gentleman too, though he did wear "hodden grey," taking off his broad Kilmarnock bonnet, made obeisance, and said, "Please your worship, how shall I ever thank you for your kindness?" "Very easily, John," was the reply. "Whenever you see another man as sorely needing assistance as you were just now, help him; and that will be thanking me." So, as we contemplate the sacrifice of Christ on our behalf, we cry, "What shall I render unto Thee, O Lord, for all Thy benefits toward me?"—and there comes this answer : "Whensoever thou seest a fellow-man needing thy succour as much as thou wast needing Mine when I gave My life for thee, help him, and that will be thanking Me." "Inasmuch as ye do it," &c. (*W. M. Taylor, D.D.*) *The good Samaritan:*—Take the scene of this parable as the wayside of life. The road through this world is a dangerous way, leading through the wilderness, stained by many crimes, haunted by many robbers. Travelling along this highway of life, I see crowds of persons, of all sorts and conditions of men. And I see, moreover, that all of them bear scars upon them, as though they had been wounded, and many I see are lying by the wayside in sore distress. All have at some time or other fallen among thieves. There is a famous picture by the great French painter which illustrates this. It represents a number of different people journeying through the valley of this world. The way is rough and gloomy, and all bear signs of having known weariness and sorrow. The king is there in his royal robes, and wearing his crown ; but his brow is furrowed with care, and he seems to ask, like our own King Henry—

> " Gives not the hawthorn bush a sweeter shade
> To shepherds, looking on their silly sheep,
> Than doth a rich embroider'd canopy
> To kings, that fear their subjects' treachery ? "

The poet is there crowned with laurel, but his eyes are sad, as though he felt how poor a thing is fame ; how valueless the garland which to-day is, and to-morrow is cast into the oven. He looks with a yearning glance, as though searching for something not yet found. There, too, is the minister of state, who directed the fortunes of empires. " Whom he would he slew, and whom he would he kept alive." But his head is bowed with trouble, and he seems to look wistfully to the time when " the wicked cease from troubling, and the weary are at rest." Among the crowd there are women ; the widow with veiled head, and tearful eyes ; the mother clasping her dead child ; the poor slave, cowering beneath the lash of the taskmaster, and stretching out her chained hands for pity. There, too, are many sick folk. Blind men sit in darkness by the wayside ; cripples drag their maimed bodies wearily along ; beggars grovel in their sores and raggedness. And all these different people seem to turn their faces longingly to one place, where a bright light breaks over the dark valley, and where there stands One with outstretched arms, and loving smile. It is Jesus, the Good Samaritan, who is ready to help these travellers on the road of life ; it is the Good Physician, who has medicine to heal their sickness ; and who says to every suffering heart, king and beggar, desolate widow, weary warrior, childless mother, " Come unto Me, all ye that are weary and heavy laden, and I will give you rest." (*H. J. Wilmot-Buxton, M.A.*)   *The lawyer and the Samaritan:*—I. THE LAWYER. 1. He had thus much to recommend him, that he was an orthodox Israelite. 2. He seems to have been a sincere inquirer after truth. 3. Another thing we notice in this lawyer is the accuracy and truthfulness of his knowledge and views of the law. 4. But there was one great deficiency in his case. Theoretical orthodoxy is not always accompanied with practical righteousness. A man may confess a good creed, and yet lead a very unworthy and sinful life. People may know and approve the law, and yet not keep it. He had " answered right." But he was not righteous. II. THE SAMARITAN. 1. A heretic as to his faith. He was an errorist, and in this respect compares very unfavourably with the Jewish lawyer. It was not his Samaritanism that the Saviour wishes to recommend to us. His churchliness was thoroughly defective and reprehensible. 2. But there is one thing in him that is good, and this it is that the Saviour wishes to recommend to us. He had human sympathy. His mercy was not restrained by sectional antipathy and religious animosities. Conclusion : It was the Samaritan's mercy that needed to be added to the lawyer's orthodoxy, in order to a full and acceptable piety. Orthodoxy without humanity is worthless ; humanity with heterodoxy is better as regards the comfort of this world ; but orthodoxy with humanity—a pure worship with universal charity—fills out the complete picture of what the law requires, and what practical Christianity really is. (*J. A. Seiss, D.D.*)   *Christian compassion :* — I. ITS SPHERE OF ACTION. 1. On whom it is exercised. On those who stand in need of it. 2. How far it reaches. To all. II. ITS NATURE. It is—1. A feeling. 2. Manifests itself in deeds. III. ITS WORKING. 1. It gives help instantly and without delay. 2. Voluntarily. 3. Does what is required, and as well as it can. 4. Is full of self-denial, for (1) It fears no dangers ; (2) no troubles ; (3) no cost ; (4) no labour. 5. It is indefatigable, and completes the work. (*F. G. Lisco.*)   *Service of love :*— 1. Willingly begun. 2. Unweariedly continued. 3. Never completed. (*Van Oosterzee.*)   *Debt of love :*—1. Measureless. 2. Undeniable. 3. Blessed. (*Ibid.*) *Good Samaritan love :*—1. Whom it profits. 2. How it manifests itself. 3.

Whence it come. (*Harless.*) *The glory of true love :*—1. It inquires not. 2. It hesitates not. 3. It is not afraid. 4. It tarries not. 5. It willingly sacrifices, and leaves nothing unfinished. (*Florey.*) *Love makes neighbours :*—It is love that makes man neighbour to man. The true neighbour is the man who has a compassionate heart and a friendly spirit. Where this is wanting, it avails not that a man lives next door, or belongs to the same congregation, or is a member of the same club or union or profession ; it ought to be so, that these external associations quicken our friendliness, and so they often do, and where love exists they find expression for it in many suitable ways ; but these external bonds can never supply the place of love. No doubt the people who saw how careful the Samaritan was of his *protégé* would say, He must be his brother, or his neighbour, or an old friend ; for the truth is that genuine compassion and affection make a man brother, neighbour, a friend, of all. It is not, then, by any marks in others that you can test who is your neighbour ; but only by what is in yourself, viz., humanity of disposition, friendliness, compassion, or whatever name you choose to give it. Love alone can determine who is your neighbour. (*Marcus Dods, D.D.*) *Humanitarianism :—* I. Earliest of all, there is indicated here that THE RECOGNIZED AIM OF THE ENTIRE GOSPEL IS SIMPLY TO SAVE HUMAN SOULS (see verse 25). II. From the reply our Lord gave to him we learn, next, that THE GRAND SOURCE OF ALL INFORMATION ON THIS SUBJECT IS GOD'S WORD, REVEALED IN THE INSPIRED SCRIPTURES (see verses 26–28). III. Hence, we reach another lesson : THE MAIN OFFICE OF THE LAW OF GOD THUS REVEALED IS TO CONVINCE MEN OF SIN (see verse 29). Evidently this man was not at all satisfied. There was just one subtle implication in this courteous commendation of Jesus that stung his conscience. He knew he had never obeyed the command he had quoted. IV. Our Lord follows his extraordinary lead, and so we have another lesson : THE LAW OF GOD ACCEPTS EVEN HUMANITARIANISM AS ONE OF THE TRUTHFUL TESTS OF A REAL RELIGIOUS CHARACTER. 1. In the beginning of the parable, Jesus shows what constitutes a neighbour, meeting the lawyer's interrogatory in its exact terms : "And who is my neighbour ? " (see verse 30). 2. A neighbour, so the story went calmly on to say, is one who is close to us in circumstances of common exposure. All these people were in the perilous and infested road between Jerusalem and Jericho. 3. A neighbour is one who has received misfortune which might happen to any one of us in the same circumstances. Robbers are never specially particular concerning what respectable people they plunder. 4. A neighbour is one who is left near us helpless, and must suffer more unless succoured at once. The force of the figure turns on that. Thus, having explained what it was to be a neighbour, Jesus proceeded to show further by the parable what it must mean to love one's neighbour as one's self (see verses 31–35). (1) A priest (see verse 31). Perhaps he was one of these refined, fastidious men, full of soft sensibility, and could not force his delicate feelings to bear the sight of abject suffering, especially when no one was near to sustain and praise him. Possibly he could pity the wounded neighbour, but could not afford just then either the time or the twopence. It may be, housed in his comfortable quarters that night in Jericho, he took it out in blaming the Government for the tolerance. (2) A Levite (see verse 32). No better than the other : no reason to suppose he would be : a Levite was just a little priest : "like master, like man." Still, it is fair to say he went across to see what was the matter. Perhaps he found there was too much the matter. Perhaps prudence suggested the robbers might return. Now please remember these were the friends this lawyer would have stood up for ; a sacred calling certainly involves sacred duties. (3) A Samaritan (see verses 33–35). He had love in his heart and succour in his hands. V. So ends the parable ; and now, as we return to the story for our final lesson, we learn that MERE FORMAL DEVOTION CANNOT EVEN ABIDE ITS OWN TEST, WHEN FORCED TO IT (see verses 36, 37). (*C. S. Robinson, D.D.*) *The good Samaritan :*—I. THE WORLD IS VERY FULL OF AFFLICTION. 1. Frequently the greater afflictions are not occasioned by the fault of the sufferer. 2. Very much distress is caused by the wickedness of others. 3. Certain paths in life are peculiarly subject to affliction. Our mines, railways, and seas show a terrible roll of suffering and death. Many a needlewoman's life is truly a path of blood. II. THERE ARE MANY WHO NEVER RELIEVE AFFLICTION. 1. The two men here mentioned were brought to the spot by God's providence on purpose to render aid to the sufferer. 2. They were both of them persons who ought to have relieved him, because they were very familiar with things which should have softened their hearts. 3. They were, moreover, bound by their profession to have helped this man. 4.

They were very well aware of the man's condition. 5. Yet they had capital excuses. III. THE SAMARITAN IS A MODEL FOR THOSE WHO DO HELP THE AFFLICTED. 1. He is a model if we notice who the person was that he helped. (1) One who could not repay him. (2) A total stranger. (3) One rejected by his own people. (4) One of a different faith from himself. 2. He is a model to us in the spirit in which he did his work. (1) Without asking questions. (2) Without attempting to shift the labour from himself on to others. (3) Without any selfish fear. (4) With self-denial. (5) With great tenderness and care. IV. WE HAVE A HIGHER MODEL than even the Samaritan—our Lord Jesus Christ. 1. Our Lord Jesus Christ has done better than the good Samaritan, because our case was worse. We were not only half but altogether dead in trespasses and sins. 2. What the Samaritan gave to the poor man was generous, but it is not comparable to what the Lord Jesus has given to us. He gave him wine and oil ; but Jesus has given His heart's-blood to heal our wounds : he *lent* himself with all his care and thoughtfulness ; but Christ *gave* Himself even to the death for us. (*C. H. Spurgeon.*) *The good Samaritan :—* I. THE OCCASION OF THE PARABLE. 1. The general circumstances (vers. 25-28). 2. The specific question (ver. 29). II. THE APTNESS OF THE PARABLE. 1. This parable shows the Divine idea of true neighbourliness. 2. This parable shows the grand principle and obligation of Christian endeavour at home and abroad. 3. This parable shows the secret of true happiness. (1) The robbers who stripped and wounded their victim did not become happy in their deed. (2) Neither priest nor Levite was happy in his cowardly selfishness. (3) It was the good, benevolent, tender-hearted Samaritan whose soul was filled with a happifying satisfaction. Practical lessons: 1. Selfishness is not 'the Divine ideal of a true and noble life. 2. Happiness is not an emotion, but the fruit of love. 3. The true good Samaritan is Jesus Christ Himself. (*D. C. Hughes, M.A.*) *The good Samaritan :—* I. THE CIRCUMSTANCES WHICH LED TO THE UTTERANCE OF THIS PARABLE. 1. A sinister question put to our Lord by a lawyer. 2. Our Lord's method of meeting cavillers (see ver. 26). 3. The lawyer's remarkable answer to our Lord's question. 4. Our Lord's candour. 5. The caviller unimpressed by his own profound answer, and still under the dominant power of self. II. THE PARABLE. 1. The topography of the scene is noticeable. 2. The touching story of the parable. (1) The pitiable victim of the thieves. (2) The pitiless passers-by. (3) The pitiful Samaritan. III. THE APPLICATION. 1. Jesus enabled the lawyer to answer his own perplexing question. This is a great gift. 2. Jesus brought home the truth to the lawyer's conscience, so that he could not shake it off. Lessons : 1. Let us learn not to despise the questionings of men, but seek to turn them to practical account. 2. Let us learn that the crown of all human excellencies, the unquestionable evidence of true piety, and the golden girdle which is yet to bind in one holy Christly brotherhood the human race, is to love God with all our heart, mind, and strength, and our neighbours as ourselves. 3. Let us learn the utter hollowness of formal religion. 4. Let us learn that an immortality of honour is only for those whose heart throbs with Christly sympathy. 5. Let us learn that our Lord has here drawn for us His own portrait in the delineation He has given us of the "good Samaritan." (*Ibid.*) *The good Samaritan :—* I. A GRAPHIC PICTURE OF HUMAN NEED AND MISERY. 1. Much of man's suffering is inflicted by his fellow-man. 2. His condition, apart from aid, human and Divine, appears helpless and hopeless. II. A SAD ILLUSTRATION OF MAN'S TOO COMMON INDIFFERENCE TO HIS FELLOW-MAN. III. AN INSTRUCTIVE EXAMPLE OF TRUE CHARITY. Note the several movements of benevolence, as exemplified in the story. 1. An observant eye. 2. A sensitive heart, that will not steel itself against a neighbour's misfortunes, saying, "All is owing to the operation of general laws, and it is unreasonable to allow one's self to be affected by the inevitable afflictions of mankind." 3. An absence of bigotry. 4. A ready hand, to carry out the benevolent desires of the heart. 5. Self-forget-fulness and self-denial, leading to a disregard of personal comfort and even of personal safety. 6. A combination of tenderness and wisdom. 7. An endeavour to interest others in the work in which we are engaged ourselves. As this Samaritan procured the services of the host, so many good people multiply their own bene-ficence by calling forth that of others. 8. Liberality. There are occasions for gifts as well as for services ; it is well to be found responsive to such claims. 9. Foresight. A wise man will look forward, and consider how that which is begun may best be carried on. IV. A SUGGESTION OF THE DIVINE MOTIVE TO BENEVOLENCE. It is vain to disconnect morality from religion. Our relation to God governs our relation to our fellow-creatures. V. AN ILLUSTRATION OF REDEMPTION. (*J. R.*

Thomson, M.A.)   The bloody way :—The road connecting Jerusalem with Jericho ran through a wild, dreary, and mountainous solitude, suited by the gloomy and inaccessible fastnesses on either side of it, to harbour thieves, robbers, and other outlaws from society, and so particularly infamous in the time of our Lord for the horrid depredations and murders perpetrated by the ruffians that infested it, that it went under the name of "The Bloody Way." Herod the Great had dismissed about 40,000 men who had been engaged in building the Temple, many of whom, through want of employment, as Josephus informs us, became robbers and haunted the road to which this parable refers. *Fallen among thieves* :—" Among thieves ! " Come with me to the dead-house. There lies a lifeless form just brought in by rough yet kind-hearted men from the river. It is the body of a woman. Push back the masses of dishevelled hair, and you look into a young and beautiful face, and wonder whose child she is. Last night when the the city was quiet, and those who had homes had sought them, and the poor street arab had coiled himself into an empty cask, this child of sorrow noiselessly stole on to the bridge, climbed the parapet, gave one long, low wail of despair, then madly leaped into the river. There was a splash, a struggle, and then the dark waters rolled on as before, and as they have done over hundreds of such frail children of men as this one who lies before us in the dead-house. What does it mean ? It means that she has fallen among thieves, who have robbed her and left her to die. "Among thieves ! " Yonder stands a gloomy building, with high walls and gates, as heavy and massive as those of the old castles of the Middle Ages. Get inside. See that youth. Who is he ? Where does he come from ? His father is a godly man, his mother is a holy woman. Once he was the joy of the home. Now see his convict's dress, look at his sad, worn face, and you shudder as the lock clicks upon the door of his cell. What does it mean ? It means that he "fell among thieves." (*C. Leach.*) *The good Samaritan* :—This parable reveals in the brightest light—I. THE CHRISTIAN'S HEART. It is like the Samaritan's as he stands over yon panting, bleeding man: it is full of compassion. This word "compassion," as used by Christ, has the greatest force and feeling in it. It means that His whole body tingled, and thrilled, and was warmed with loving pity, as your body was when you stood over against your dying brother or sister, and felt as you had never felt before. Very great must have been the Samaritan's compassion when, without a moment's delay, he stooped to the bleeding man. We are weak and slow in Christ's work because we are weak in compassion. A boy was showing me his model steam-engine, in which the steam was made by a spirit-lamp. He lighted his lamp, but the engine moved not till a certain temperature was reached. Compassion is the moving force in us, but it does not move us till it grows hot within the heart. The Samaritan also reveals—II. THE CHRISTIAN'S HAND. It is the ready agent of a compassionate heart. First the heart, then the hand ; that is the order in the kingdom. Watch the Samaritan's hand. It is not the hand of a sluggard. How quickly it moves ! The story gives us the idea of hearty haste. He did not linger till compassion was chilled by worldly prudence. He knew that his first thoughts were best. I dare say he did not think about it at all: he just did it at once. A new book tells that a Glasgow merchant died lately without a will, leaving a widow, one son, and two daughters. The son in London received a telegram, came down the same evening, and settled his father's fortune on his mother and sisters. He was asked why he had been in such a hurry. "I dared not wait," was his noble reply. "Had I waited, my resolution might have cooled, and I might have claimed all the law allowed me. I felt that it was right to do what I have done, and I wished to commit myself before selfishness could come in." Many a noble purpose dies of cold and delay in its infancy. 2. It is not the hand of a weakling. See it binding up wounds, pouring in oil and wine, setting the traveller on his beast, bringing him to the inn, tending him all through the night, taking out the purse and giving to the host. The hand moved by love is not easily tired, is not flighty but steady, and carries through what it begins. 3. It is not the hand of a hireling, who works only for pay. The Samaritan was not rich: he travelled with one ass and without a servant. Besides the wine, and oil, and bandages, and two pence to the host, he lost a whole day's work, and probably a whole night's rest. He had reward enough in an approving conscience reflecting the smile of God, in the home-bred sweets of a benevolent mind, and in the thought that he was imitating his Father in heaven. 4. It is not the hand of earthly ambition. The Pharisees gave alms to be seen of men. Had the Samaritan been like them, he also would have passed by on the other side. III. THE CHRISTIAN'S

SPHERE. The lawyer made it very narrow. He loved his friends and hated his enemies, and was sure that these Samaritans were no neighbours of his. But Christ teaches that there are no limits or exceptions to the love of man. (*J. Wells, M.A.*) *The parable of the good Samaritan:*—I. THAT God has established a principle of universal dependence through every part of His intelligent creation. As creatures we have a twofold dependence—a dependence upon God, and upon our fellows. II. THAT among men, and especially among fallen and guilty men, the principle of benevolence, which expresses itself in a readiness to administer to the necessities of others, is not only a mere arrangement of wisdom and goodness, but has in it the force of duty and obligation. III. The benevolence enjoined in the parable before us derives great force from the terms in which it is expressed. " Thou shalt love thy neighbour as thyself " is the language of the law. " Who is my neighbour ? " asks the lawyer. The answer is, " Every man in distress is thy neighbour." IV. THAT they are unhappily often counteracted in practice. The introduction of sin has subjected us to misery, and rendered us more dependent upon each other; but it has also introduced principles into the heart which are subversive of those charities to which our very necessities and common dangers ought to give birth. Like mariners in a storm, like soldiers in a battle, we ought to be at hand to each other ; but there are principles which too frequently separate man from man, and harden the heart against every emotion of pity. We might specify many of these, but we will confine our attention to one, suggested by the parable; I mean religious bigotry. V. LASTLY, let me observe, that the universal and undistinguishing philanthrophy, so affectingly urged in the parable of our Lord before us, must be fostered and matured by every consideration we can pay to the nature of our religion. (*R. Watson.*) *Chance :* — There are some who utterly proscribe the name of *chance* as a word of impious and profane signification ; and indeed, if it be taken by us in that sense in which it was used by the heathen, so as to make anything casual, in respect of God Himself, their exception ought justly to be admitted. But to say a thing is a *chance*, or casualty, as it relates to second causes, is not profaneness, but a great truth, as signifying no more than that there are some events, besides the knowledge, purpose, expectation, and power of second agents. And for this very reason, because they are so, it is the royal prerogative of God Himself, to have all these loose, uneven, fickle uncertainties under His disposal. (*Dr. South.*) *Unrelieved misery :*—Which of us has not been guilty of passing by on the other side, of leaving misery unrelieved because it was not clamorous? This unfortunate, lying half dead by the roadside, could make no importunate supplications for relief, could not sit up and prove to the priest that it was his duty to help him, could not even ask help, so as to lay on the priest the responsibility of positive refusal ; and so he got past with less discomfort, but not with less guilt. The need is often greatest where least is asked. And how many forms of misery are there lying within our knowledge as we journey along the bloodstained road of life, but which we pass by because they do not bar our progress till we give our help, or because it is possible for us to put them out of our mind and live as though these things were not. A lost child is crying on the streets, but it is awkward to be seen leading a dirty, crying child home, so we refuse to notice that the child is lost ; a man is lying as if he were ill, but he may only be intoxicated, and it looks foolish to meddle, and may be troublesome, so we leave him to others, though another minute in that position may, for all we know, make the difference between life and death. You read a paragraph of a paper giving a thrilling account of a famine in China, or some other great calamity ; but when you come to a clause intimating that subscriptions will be received at such and such a place, you pass to another column, and refuse to allow that to make the impression on your mind which you feel it is beginning to make. In short, you will, in these and many like circumstances, wait till you are asked to help; you know you could not in decency refuse if you were asked, if the matter were fully laid before you and all the circumstances detailed, but you will put yourself out of reach before this can be done, you will not expose your-self to the risk of having your charitable feelings stirred, or at any rate of having your help drawn upon; you will, if possible, wipe the thing from your mind, you will carefully avoid following up any clue, or considering steadily any hint or suggestion of suffering. (*Marcus Dods, D.D.*) *Backwardness to good works :*— I. The first and chief plea, under which men generally take shelter, is that of inability, because of straitened circumstances, heavy taxes, &c. Before this plea can be accepted, we must ask ourselves whether there be no unnecessary expenses that we support, such as are unsuitable to our circumstances.   II. There are those that plead unsettled times, and an ill prospect of affairs (whether wrongly or rightly, is not the case; but there are those that plead these things) as impediments to the exercise of charity.   For in such an uncertain world, who knows but that he may want to-morrow what he gives to-day?   III. There are men sensible enough of their obligations to charity, and resolved, some time or other, to discharge them; but they desire to be excused from that duty for the present, and put it off, perhaps, to a will and a deathbed, and think it sufficient if they begin to do good in the world any time before they leave it.   Seldom do either of these proceed from a principle of goodness; nor are they owing to a love of virtue, but to a fear of punishment.   IV. It is alleged that the increase of charity tends often to the increasing and multiplying the poor; and by that means proves a mischief to the commonwealth, instead of a support and benefit.   V. And last thing (I shall mention) by which we are apt to excuse our backwardness to good works, is, the ill success that hath been observed to attend well-designed charities; with relation both to the objects on which they are placed, and the hands through which they are conveyed.   Our part is, to choose out the most deserving objects, and the most likely to answer the ends of our charity; and when that is done, all is done that lies in our power; the rest must be left to Providence.   (*Bishop Horne.*)   **A certain Samaritan.**—*Good news for you:*—The good Samaritan is a masterly picture of true benevolence.   I. The sinner is WITHOUT MORAL QUALIFICATION FOR SALVATION, but Christ comes where he is.   1. Remember first, that when the gospel was first sent into the world, those to whom it was sent were manifestly without any moral qualification.   2. Recollect again, the Biblical descriptions of those whom Christ came into the world to save, which prove to a demonstration that He comes to the sinner where he is.   3. But, thirdly, it is quite certain from the work of grace itself, that the Lord does not expect the sinner to do anything or to be anything in order to meet Him, but that He comes to him where he is.   4. The godlike character of the grace of God proves that He meets the sinner where he is.   If God forgive little sinners only, then He is little in His mercy.   5. The spirit and genius of the gospel utterly forbid the supposition that God requires anything in any man in order to save him.   II. In the second place, there are very many of the lost race of Adam, who say that they are WITHOUT ANY MENTAL QUALIFICATION.   III. But yet again, I think I hear another say, "I am in despair, for I CANNOT FIND ANY REASON IN MYSELF, OR OUT OF MYSELF, WHY GOD SHOULD FORGIVE SUCH A PERSON AS I AM."   So then, you are in a hopeless state, at least you see no hope.   The Lord meets you where you are by putting the reason of your salvation altogether in Himself.   IV. We proceed to our fourth point.   "Oh," says one, "but I am WITHOUT COURAGE; I dare not believe on Christ, I am such a timid, trembling soul, that when I hear that others trust to Christ I think it must be presumption; I wish I could do the same, but I cannot; I am kept under by such a sense of sin, that I dare not."   V. I hear one more complaint.   "I am WITHOUT STRENGTH," saith one; "will Jesus come just where I am?"   Yes, sinner, just where you are. You say you cannot believe; that is your difficulty.   God meets you, then, in your inability.   First, He meets you with His promises.   "Him that cometh to Me I will in no wise cast out."   Cannot you believe now?   (*C. H. Spurgeon.*)   **The good Samaritan:**—The first object that arrests our attention is a man lying by the wayside robbed, stripped, wounded, half dead.   Now, all that we know about this man was that he had been taking a journey from Jerusalem to Jericho; and even this is full of suggestion.   He had his back turned upon the "city of the vision of peace" and his face turned towards the city of the curse.   Cursed was Jericho—cursed in the moment of its first destruction, and cursed in the moment of its restoration.   He was turning his back upon the place which had been built for God's glory, for the especial abode, so to speak, of the Divine presence, and his face towards the place which had been built in distinct defiance of the Divine will, the very existence of which was a monument of human rebellion.   Such is the ill-omened character of the journey which the traveller has undertaken.   Is it not just such a journey that man has undertaken?   If we look at human history, what is it but a continuous going down from Jerusalem to Jericho?   Dear friends, as it has been with human history in the abstract, so has it been with each of us individually.   As we look upon our own history, what has it been?   One continual going away farther and farther from God, wandering from "the city of peace," and voluntarily exiling ourselves into the region which is blighted with God's curse.   First, there is "the robbing."   Satan is the great master robber.   How much has he robbed us of? First, he has robbed us of all the blessedness of Paradise. Further, this man was not only robbed, he was also "stripped." They were not content with taking his money, they must needs take his garments. That is just what Satan has done with us. He has stripped us of all with which we cover our shame. There are some of us who have endeavoured to put on a garb of respectability, and to cover ourselves with that, just as our first parents sewed fig-leaves together to cover themselves. And that is not all. He is not content with robbing and stripping you; he goes even further; with ruthless hands he "wounds" those whom he has already robbed. How many of us are there here who do not know what it is to be wounded, inwardly wounded? Ah! he knows how to wound. Wounded! How are you "wounded?" Not only by the malice of Satan, but by the accusations of conscience. How are you "wounded?" Not only wounded by Satan, not only wounded by conscience, but also wounded by your truest and best Friend. For there is One who wounds that He may heal. "Faithful are the wounds of a friend!" But that was not all. The man was not only wounded, but he was "left half dead." In what sense is the sinner half dead? So far as his spiritual condition is concerned he is quite dead, but so far as his moral nature is concerned he is half dead; that is to say, he is rapidly losing all his moral powers, but he is not altogether lost. The man is not only half dead; he is fast dying; his life is ebbing out in that flowing blood. Every moment that he lies there he grows weaker. Now let us look at it again. The first that passes that way is the priest. The priest cannot do anything for him, or does not do anything for him. And, dear friends, all the ordinances in the world, however precious and however valuable they are in themselves, will not restore lost vitality. The Levite passes by—he can do nothing. "If there had been a law given which could have given life, verily righteousness should have been by the law." This is just where the law fails. But the next to come along that road is one of a different race. He was the very last man that this poor dying Jew had a claim upon. "He was a Samaritan." And Jesus passes by, not on the wings of His sovereign power, not in the majesty of His eternal sway, but He passes by in human form, a traveller amongst the sons of men. He passes by along life's dreary, dusty journey; He threads the mazes of life's wilderness, and on His way He "hears the groanings of such as are in captivity, and the sorrowful sighing of those who are appointed to die." (*W. H. M. H. Aitken, M.A.*) *Compassion :*—"He had compassion on him." Premising that, we can rest assured there is more to follow. He began with pity, and all the rest is a mere matter of detail. In the light of this one luminous word "compassion," the poor man is seen already right away home, the idol of his happy family, surrounded with bright-eyed, curly-headed, pretty little prattlers, bounding with joy, and his fond wife heaping blessings on the nameless benefactor. "He had compassion on him"—an expression this, big with salvation. He drew out his sympathetic soul first of all, and wrapped that warm around him, and made him understand that smaller gifts and minor mercies would soon be forthcoming. The oil, the wine, the bandages, the beast, the inn, the pence, the care, are all only so many forms of the large-hearted "compassion" with which he started. And the unfortunate individual, who had been callously "passed by" with indifference by cold and formal ecclesiasticism, is now at length happily rescued by the religion of humanity. (*D. Thomas.*) *Sympathy more than pity :*—"He set him on his own beast"—the one act in which the Samaritan's Samaritanism was most deeply lodged, and most gently and suggestively evinced. The Samaritan had nothing left him but to walk. So we conclude. The weariness of it denoted less to him than his co-traveller's comfort denoted. His own comfort was in having his companion comfortable. His consciousness was of the other man. He *became* practically the other man for the time; felt his bruises as his own bruises; forgot that he was not working for himself in working for him. He felt not *for* him, which is nothing but pity; but he felt *with* him, he felt *in* him, which is sympathy and gospel. Becoming the other man—that is Samaritanism : seeing with his eyes, feeling with his sensibilities, subject to his limitations, obnoxious to his exposures. Sympathy is two hearts tugging at one load, bent beneath one sorrow. (*C. H. Parkhurst, D.D.*) *True help :*—We can help a man only by identifying ourselves with him, getting into his circumstances, getting into him, becoming he. . . . If you have a temptation that you want to get the mastery over, the man for you to go to for counsel and relief is the man who has been in your place and gained the victory that you want to gain. The best man to convert a drunkard is a converted drunkard. The power to appreciate temptation is the prime condition to being able to help others out of temptation. In a certain way it holds that the more bad and awkward situations a good man has been in, the richer may prove his ministry and the more various his apostleship. Almost all the men in the Scripture story that ever proved a great advantage to anybody had at some time been themselves in sad need of succour. The first step God took towards making us become like Him was for Him to become as far as He could like us. If you have any doctrinal perplexity, your resort for assistance will always be to some one whose doctrinal experience has been complicated in the same way. And it is not by any means enough to be able to understand another man's difficulty, burden, temptation; we need to go a little farther and feel it as our own difficulty, burden, temptation, just as the Samaritan not only appreciated his fellow-traveller's distresses, but felt them as his own distresses, and therefore set him on his own beast; and as Christ not only understood our sins, but Himself put Himself behind our sins, underneath them, carried them, and in such a whole-hearted way, as really to suffer the pain and penalty of them. There is always more or less of the vicarious when there is any good done, any release wrought, any redemption effected. (*Ibid.*) *A good Samaritan among the Maoris :*—In our journeyings, says the *Waikato Times*, a newspaper published in New Zealand, we have to record the various traits of man, be he European or Maori—all have to be faithfully noticed by our pen. Whether his characteristics are of the animal or intellectual kind, whether his sympathies are with the refined or debased. In this instance it is our great pleasure to have to record one of the most Christian and good Samaritanlike acts that we remember to have read or published. A few nights ago—a bitter cold night it was—Amopui, a native, was returning to Cambridge, and when some distance from the township saw the prostrate form of a man—a European—on the road. It appears that the poor fellow, with one leg only, had travelled overland all the way from Napier, had crossed creeks, surmounted hills, and threaded his way through the bush. But nature gave way at last, and he fell, when Amopui found him, utterly worn out, helpless and exhausted. But for this timely assistance, Charles Parmeters (for this was the European's name) would in all probability never have seen the light of another day. The Maori lifted him up, and carried him into Cambridge, and those who know the heavy, sandy road on the other side of the bridge can judge what the labour must have been. Amopui took him to his tent, and attended to him the night through; but the noble fellow's good deeds did not end here. In the morning he got a subscription list, and by dint of perseverence collected nearly £9, which he handed over to the police authorities to be expended in sending the poor cripple on to Auckland. Amopui is well known in Cambridge as being a straight-forward and honest native, and will now more than ever be universally respected. If there be no other recognition in this sphere of this good action, the story should find a corner in every paper and magazine in the world, and should be printed in gold. *Humane assistance :*—The day after the action near Alexandria, where the brave Abercrombie fell, the General was riding over the field of battle, attended by two orderly dragoons, to see if there were any wounded, French or English, who had escaped notice the evening before, when, on turning round a wall by the sea-side, he was struck with the appalling sight of more than a hundred French soldiers, who, with their officers, huddled together, desperately wounded by grape and cannon shot from an English brig of war. From being collected in the recess of the wall they had escaped notice on the previous day of search, and were exposed to the night air, and with undressed wounds. Here the General saw a man, evidently English, in the garb of a Quaker, actively employed in the heavenly task of giving his humane assistance to those poor, brave sufferers; giving water to some, dressing the wounds of others, and affording consolation to all. Upon inquiry, he found the benevolent individual to be Dr. John Walker, who was himself almost exhausted, having been thus nobly employed from daybreak without any assistance. *Rescue the perishing :*—A venerable servant of Christ said to me just at the time that I was accepting my first living, "If you would really wish to be useful to those with whom you are brought into contact, remember there is only one way of doing it: like the blessed Master of old, you must yourself be moved with compassion, or else you never can help them." The man who has been himself much in the society of the good Samaritan will partake of his feelings, and, like his Master, will be "moved with compassion." "But a certain Samaritan, as he journeyed, came where he was: and when he saw him, he had compassion on him." He might naturally have turned aside and said, "Oh, it is only one of those miserable Jews; the fewer we have of them the better; let him be." The first thing he had to overcome was natural prejudice, and it is rather a strong one with some people. But he did not stop to inquire whether he was a Jew or a Samaritan; he was a man—a brother; and the Samaritan acted accordingly. I remember hearing the story of a little incident that occurred in the streets of Edinburgh some years ago. A coach was driving rapidly down the narrow streets of the town. A poor little child of some two years of age crept into the middle of the road, and there it was in utter helplessness standing by itself, while the galloping horses were drawing nearer and nearer every moment. Just as they approached the spot where the poor little helpless infant was standing, a woman, who had just happened to come to the door of her house, darted forth like a flash of lightning, grasped the child in her arms, and, at the peril of her own life, saved it from imminent destruction. A passer-by remarked to the poor terrified woman when she reached the other side, "Well, woman, is that your child?" "Na, na," she said, "it's nae my bairn." "Well, woman," he said, "what for did you risk your life for a child when it was not yours?" With a beaming eye and a flushed face, the noble woman replied, "Aye, but it's some-body's bairn." That was real humanity! The true spirit of a woman asserted itself within her nature. And if that be humanity, dear friends, what ought to be Christian humanity? What would have become of us if the Lord Jesus Christ had asked the question, "Who is My neighbour?" He might have pointed to where Gabriel, Michael, and the other ministering spirits stand before the throne, and say, "Behold My neighbour." What daring intelligence of heaven or hell would ever have suggested that the Lord Jesus Christ could find His "neigh-bour" in a fallen world, amid the children of sorrow and the slaves of hell? Who would have ever thought that God would have chosen us to be His "neigh-bours?" that He should have come where we are, that He should bend over us with a heart glowing with love, and pour into our wounds the sweet solace of His own anointing oil, or breathe into our lifeless being the supernatural energy of His own eternal life—who would so much as have suggested this? Not less than this Divine love has actually effected. Here is a call for each of us, children of God. Go to your own home as "a saviour." Go to the crowded streets, and courts, and lanes of this town as "a saviour." (*W. H. M. H. Aitken, M.A.*) *Who is my neighbour?*—I. That religious profession and service have no necessary connection with real goodness. II. We see that neighbourship is not cancelled by a difference of religion. But surely no differences of religion can cancel the duties which are anterior to all revealed religion whatsoever. If men do not see as we see, they are still men. And yet who does not know that a diversity of religious faith frequently operates as a check on all natural sympathy, and that poverty has often to starve on because it does not happen to lie within the enclosure of some theological shibboleth? III. We see from this parable that true neighbourliness involves the spirit of sacrifice. (*E. Mellor, D.D.*) *The obligation of the strong to the weak:—* The phrase "by chance" used in the parable describing the coming of the three men upon the wounded traveller is the same in structure with our word "con-current." The priest, the Levite, and Samaritan were not travelling that road and did not meet the half-dead stranger by hazard, but by the concurrence of events which Providence controlled the three were brought to one who needed help. Such is the claim of Christian charity, the combination of events which brings us into proximity to suffering involves the obligation of ministering to it. This claim has its binding force from two principles—I. Power or advantage of any kind is not a personal possession, but a trust. "I am a debtor both to the Greeks and to the barbarians; both to the wise and to the unwise," wrote Paul. He owed the Greeks nothing. They had persecuted him. The barbarians he had never seen. But Paul was conscious that God had conferred upon him great gifts and experiences. Because he had them he was bound to make others partake of them. Every such man had a claim upon Paul. His ignorance and wickedness gave the claim. That is the claim that the heathen and the newly-settled portions of our land have upon us. "Communism," as one has said, "is only the refracted image of a supreme truth, the truth of the indebtedness of the strong to the weak, as that however is dimly discerned by intoxicated brains, through bloodshot eyes." The half-dead man had a claim upon priest and Levite and Samaritan. Priest and Levite were faithless to the trust God's providence brought them opportunity to administer. II. Love to men also makes the claim of the weak upon the stronger of binding force. This love comes into our hearts when we are awakened to the truth of the brotherhood of man, and realize God's love toward us. In antiquity there was nothing beyond national ties to bind man to man. (*G. E. Horr.*) *The humanity of Christianity and other religions :*—A Chinese Christian thus described the relative merits of Confucianism, Buddhism, and Christianity :—" A man had fallen into a deep, dark pit, and lay in its miry bottom groaning and utterly unable to move. Confucius walked by, approached the edge of the pit, and said, ' Poor fellow, I am sorry for you; why were you such a fool as to get in there? Let me give you a piece of advice: if you ever get out, don't get in again.' ' I can't get out,' groaned the man. That is Confucianism. A Buddhist priest next came by, and said, ' Poor fellow, I am very much pained to see you there. I think if you could scramble up two-thirds of the way, or even half, I could reach you and lift you up the rest.' But the man in the pit was entirely helpless and unable to rise. That is Buddhism. Next the Saviour came by, and, hearing his cries, went to the very brink of the pit, stretched down and laid hold of the poor man, brought him up, and said, ' Go, sin no more.' That is Christianity." *A good Samaritan :*— Oberlin was travelling on one occasion from Strasbourg. It was in winter. The ground was deeply covered with snow, and the roads were almost impassable. He had reached the middle of his journey, and was so exhausted that he could stand up no longer. He commended himself to God, and yielded to what he felt to be the sleep of death. He knew not how long he slept, but suddenly became conscious of some one rousing him up. Before him stood a waggon-driver, the waggon not far away. He gave him a little wine and food, and the spirit of life returned. He then helped him on the waggon, and brought him to the next village. The rescued man was profuse in his thanks, and offered money, which his benefactor refused. " It is only a duty to help one another," said the waggoner; "and it is the next thing to an insult to offer a reward for such a service." " Then," replied Oberlin, " at least tell me your name, that I may have you in thankful remembrance before God." " I see," said the waggoner, " that you are a minister of the gospel. Please tell me the name of the good Samaritan." " That," said Oberlin, " I cannot do, for it was not put on record." " Then," replied the waggoner, " until you can tell me his name, permit me to withhold mine." *Neighbourly kindness :*—A fire having broken out in a village of Denmark, one of the inhabitants, a poor man, was very active in affording assistance; but every endeavour to extinguish the flames was in vain. At length he was told that his own house was in danger, and that if he wished to save his furniture, not a moment was to be lost. " There is something more precious," replied he, " that I must first save. My poor sick neighbour is not able to help himself : he will be lost if I do not assist him. I am sure he relies upon me." He flew to his neighbour's house, rushed, at the hazard of his life, through the flames, and conveyed the sick man in his arms to a place of safety. A society at Copenhagen showed their approbation of his conduct by presenting him with a silver cup filled with Danish crowns. *Generosity and liberality :*—This parable is very strong as a dramatic representation. It touches the common sense of all races. It is just as plain to the ignorant as it is to the learned. The good Samaritan stands admired by all sects and races, and occasionally is imitated. There is to be drawn, however, something further from this narrative. A fine philosophical distinction lies hidden here, quite aside from its general drift. The breaking down of all limitations to kindly feelings is the main drift; and in executing that something else was accomplished. When the Samaritan rescued the sufferer, that was GENEROSITY. He acted upon the impulse of his heart. Generosity springs out of the heart; it is the child of emotion. It acts in an inferior sphere. It acts quickly. But how easily might one, after relieving this man who had suffered from the thieves, have left him for other folks' kindness, saying, "I have done my part." When, having rescued him, he began to think for the unseen wants of the days to come, and provided for them, that was LIBERALITY. It was not generous. It was not acting from the senses and sight. It was acting from reflection, from a higher moral quality of equity. (*H. W. Beecher.*) *The good Samaritan:*—From this story there are many lessons to be learnt. 1. It shows how easy it is for us men of the sanctuary to be far less tender-hearted than the laymen who pass their lives amid matters which have nothing absolutely to do with God. 2. It shows how easily the religious conscience can reason itself out of the responsibilities resting upon it for the discharge of the everyday duties of life. 3. It has also a lesson in the practical character of general philanthropy, for behind the persons of the narrative it shadows out the character of the Divine Person taking compassion on suffering humanity, and placing the wounded man in the true home of souls to the end of time. (*Canon Liddon.*) *The good Samaritan:*—No words, perhaps, ever spoken on earth have had more effect than those of this parable. What was the power and the spirit of this parable? What gave it its strength in the hearts of men? This—that it told them that they were to help their fellow-men simply because they were their fellow-men. Not because they were of the same race, the same religion, the same sect or party, but simply because they were men. In a word, it commanded men to be humane, to exercise humanity, which signifies kindness to human beings simply because they are human beings. One can understand our Lord preaching that; it was part and parcel of His doctrine. He called Himself the Son of Man. He showed what He meant by calling Himself so by the widest and most tender humanity. But His was quite a new doctrine, and a new practice likewise. The Jews had no notion of humanity. All but themselves were common and unclean. The Greek, again, despised all nations but his own as barbarians. The Romans, again, were a thoroughly inhuman people. Their calling, they held, was to conquer all the nations of the earth, to plunder them, to enslave them. They were the great slave-holding, man-stealing people. Mercy was a virtue which they had utterly forgotten. Their public shows and games were mere butcheries of blood and torture. To see them fight to death in their theatres, pairs after pairs, sometimes thousands in one day, was the usual and regular amusement. And in that great city of Rome, which held something more than a million human beings, there was not, as far as I am aware, one single hospital or other charitable institution of any kind. There was, in a word, no humanity in them. But the gospel changed all that miraculously and suddenly, both in Jew, in Greek, and in Roman. While men had been heathens, their pattern had been that of the priest, who saw the wounded man lying, and looked on him, and passed by. Their pattern now was that of the good Samaritan, who helped and saved the wounded stranger simply because he was a man. In one word, the new thing which the gospel brought into the world was humanity. The thing which the gospel keeps in the world still is humanity. (*Charles Kingsley.*) *Between Jerusalem and Jericho:*—I. A certain man fell among thieves. HERE IS THE BLACK MARGIN WHICH SURROUNDS CIVILIZED SOCIETY. II. There came a priest that way, as also a Levite and a Samaritan. So, THE ESCAPE OF SOME IS NOT TO BE TAKEN AS A CONDEMNATION OF OTHERS. All the four went down the same road, yet only one of them was unfortunate! What a temptation for the three who escaped to say, It must have been his own blame; we passed down the very same road, and did not hear so much as the fluttering of a leaf. III. The priest passed by on the other side; so did the Levite—THE THING WHICH IS ALWAYS BEING DONE BY A NEGATIVE AND DO-NOTHING RESPECTABILITY. There are two sides in life. 1. The side on which men are dying; and—2. "The other side." We can choose our side. On the first side we shall find—1. Something to shock our sensibilities. 2. Something to interrupt our speed. 3. Something to tax our resources. On the opposite side we shall find a clear path to infamy and the hell of eternal remorse. IV. The priest passed by, and so did the Levite—SO SACRED NAMES ARE NO GUARANTEE FOR SACRED SERVICES. It is a terrible thing for the nature to fall below the name. A name is a promise. A profession is a responsibility. V. But a certain Samaritan had compassion on him. THERE ARE UNEXPECTED SOURCES OF HELP IN LIFE. You have found it so in business; others have found it so in sympathy; others in periods of great perplexity. This reflection of great value as showing—1. That we all need help. 2. As protecting men from despair. 3. As showing that we ourselves may become the unexpected helpers of others. In the distribution of help we are not to be limited (*a*) by theological creeds; (*b*) by natural prejudices; (*c*) by personal dislikes. We are to help humanity as such. The Christian application of this study is obvious. 1. Life is a perilous journey. 2. Lost men will never be saved by formal piety. 3. The true Helper is the very Being whom we have offended. The Teacher of this parable is the Exemplar of its beneficent doctrine. The teacher should always be the explanation of his own lesson. (*J. Parker, D.D.*) *The spirit of love:*—The priest and the Levite knew the law, which was written in a book, perfectly. They had nothing to learn about that. The words of it rose at once to their lips; they could confound any one who disputed it. And yet when they were called to fulfil this law—when their neighbour lay on the ground needing their help, they did not remember it at all. It was a long way from them. They were to love their neighbour as themselves, no doubt. But who was their neighbour? Not this poor creature, though he was a Jew, a son of Abraham, an heir of the covenant. They owed him nothing; they were going on their own errands; what was he to them? That is to say, they had the law of love upon tables, but they had it not written on their hearts. They were serving God for hire; they could do things which they thought would profit them, and avoid things which they thought would injure them, but they did nothing because they had God's mind; they did nothing because they felt to men as He feels towards them. But this Samaritan, although he had never studied the words of the law as they had; though he had not a hundredth part of the blessings which belonged to them; though he had probably a great many mistakes and confusions in his head from which they were free, had this law of love in his heart, and showed that he had. God had written it there. And therefore he did not ask whether this poor half-dead traveller by the roadside belonged to his village, or his town, or his country, or his religion. He had nothing to do with any of those questions, supposing there was any one able to answer them. This was his neighbour, for he was a man. That was quite enough, and therefore he at once did what his neighbour wanted, what he would have had another do to him. Here was a lesson for the lawyer; one which he might be learning day by day, which would last him as long as he remained on earth, and long after that. If he would keep God's commandments, he must give up his pride as a lawyer, his pride as a Jew; he must become simply a man, just like this poor despised Samaritan. He must understand that God cared for men, and therefore he must care for them. (*F. D. Maurice, M.A.*)　　*Christian socialism:*—The attention drawn to the condition of the poor is one of the most encouraging signs of the times. Is that a desirable state of civilization in which such multitudes are doomed to so degraded and wretched a condition? Can it be that this is a necessity, or that it can be consistent with the will of that loving Father of whom we are told that it is not His will that one of His little ones should perish? What has Christianity to say to such questions as these? It will not do for it to stand 'dumb and helpless in the presence of these perplexities, which are troubling numbers of thoughtful minds, and that dense mass of wretchedness which lies as a heavy burden upon loving hearts. There is special need for the exercise of Christian influence because of the perils by which our social system is at present menaced. It is the imperative duty of the Christian teacher to discount the extravagant expectations which too many indulge as to what others—Parliament, or the Church, or rich people—can do for them, and to make them understand that it is but little real and enduring help which all combined can give to those who have not learned how to help themselves. This is one part of the message of Christianity to the poor; but those who speak it can only hope to succeed if they are able also to teach some lessons, equally necessary to be learned, and perhaps equally impalatable, to those on the opposite side. 1. One of the first of these certainly is that the well-being of men is of infinitely higher importance than the success of trade. A nation can afford to lose some of its wealth; but it cannot afford to have in its midst a number of men whose condition is a scandal to its religion, a reproach to its civilization, a standing menace to its institutions. 2. The principle which must govern a Christian's conduct in the transaction of his business must also regulate the distribution of his wealth. He cannot indulge in the arrogant spirit which says, "This is all my own, and I can do with it as I will." It is not his own, for the reason that he himself is not his own. 3. But behind all this must be the spirit of true sympathy—a love without hypocrisy—gracious, generous, spontaneous, free. The change wanted is in human hearts, rather than in the arrangements of society. The true sympathy will quietly produce these, and when that sympathy is not active, even they would fail of the desired result. (*J. G. Rogers, B.A.*)　　*The good Samaritan:*—Here is my neighbour, here is one for whom I am bound to care. It matters not what the need or distress may be, love will be ready to supply the need or relieve the distress to the utmost of its power. 1. It may be bodily suffering. It was bodily suffering that the good Samaritan was represented as displaying his compassion for. Christ's miracles were mostly miracles of mercy. If we had enough of true love, I believe we should send out medical missionaries to the heathen, even though we had no hope of securing converts to the gospel. The crowding together of human beings into wretched dwellings under conditions obnoxious to both physical and moral life are evils which might engage the most anxious thoughts, and elicit the deepest sympathies of every Christian man and woman in our large towns. 2. It may be the subtle mischief of unbelief, which is, no doubt, slaying its thousands in the present age, and sapping the strength and endangering the future of society. 3. It may be the burdens of a spirit labouring under a sense of sin, burdens only to be removed by the soul's directly closing with Christ's invitation to come unto Him for rest. It may, in a word, be any sorrow and any sin. All around us there are multitudes of wounded men and women whom we ought not to pass by without helping them. Have we, then, been striving, as in duty bound, to fulfil the old, old law of love, the royal law which sums up all law? Have we been faithfully endeavouring to meet the demands made upon us by a world around us with its multitudinous mass of wounded and dying men? Surely we need to humble ourselves, because we have so greatly failed in this respect. (*Professor Flint, D.D., LL.D.*) *Theory and practice of humanity :*—The Rev. Mr. Kelly, of Ayr, once preached an excellent sermon from the parable of the man who fell among thieves. He was particularly severe on the conduct of the priest who saw him, and ministered not unto him, but passed by on the other side; and in an animated and pathetic flow of eloquence, he exclaimed, "What! not even the servant of the Almighty! he whose tongue was engaged in the work of charity, whose bosom was appointed the seat of brotherly love, whose heart the emblem of pity; did he refuse to stretch forth his hand, and to take the mantle from his shoulders to cover the nakedness of woe? If he refused, if the shepherd himself went astray, was it to be wondered at that the flock followed?" The next day, when the river was much increased in height, a boy was swept overboard, from a small boat, by the force of the current. A great concourse of people were assembled, but none of them attempted to save the boy; when Mr. Kelly, who was dressed in his canonicals, threw himself from his chamber window into the current, and at the hazard of his own life saved that of the boy. (*W. Baxendale.*) *Unfeeling conduct :*—Cold comfort can some ministers render to afflicted consciences: their advice will be equally valuable with that of the Highlander who is reported to have seen an Englishman sinking in a bog on Ben Nevis. "I am sinking!" cried the traveller. "Can you tell me how to get out?" The Highlander calmly replied, "I think it is likely you never will," and walked away. (*C. H. Spurgeon.*) *Christlike compassion :*—A good many years ago there laid in the streets of Richmond, Va., a man dead drunk, his face exposed to the blistering noonday sun. A Christian woman passed along, looked at him, and said, "Poor fellow." She took her handkerchief and spread it over his face, and passed on. The man roused himself up from his debauch, and began to look at the handkerchief, and, lo! on it was the name of a highly respectable Christian woman of the city of Richmond. He went to her, he thanked her for her kindness; and that one little deed saved him for this life, and saved him for the life that is to come. He was afterward Attorney-General of the United States; but, higher than all, he became the consecrated disciple of Jesus Christ. (*Dr. Talmage.*) *The blessedness of helping others :*—Edward Irving, when a young minister, got himself much laughed at and plagued by carrying a poor Irishman's pack for some distance on his back. But Irving nobly replied, "The poor fellow was very tired, and his countrymen had been very kind to me." The gentle and good George Herbert also once helped a poor countryman to raise his fallen and heavy-laden horse. Mr. Herbert dirtied himself, and his friends said he demeaned himself; but he really thus ennobled himself, and got such gratitude and such a blessing from the poor man and from God, as made him exceedingly happy. A medical man once said to a very rich lady who was very miserable, and thought she had all sorts of ailments, "Do something for somebody." She followed this advice, and by adopting a course of active benevolence, this prescription so completely cured her of her misery and fancied ailments, that she could soon dispense with her doctor. By every means let us try to lessen the evil and misery there is in the world, and to increase good and happiness everywhere. We shall never lessen the light of our own candle by lighting another. (*H. R. Burton.*) *Heart-compassion :*—And no marvel, for this you know the heart is the first mover and master-wheel in spiritual works, that regulateth all and keeps all right and constant. (*N. Rogers.*) *Willing philanthropy :*—These liquors that pour out themselves, and drop of their own accord, are esteemed better than those which are squeezed and pressed out by violence. These give, but it is grudgingly; their gift sticks long in their hands before they part with it. It is long before the purse can be found, then before the hand can get in, then before they can get change. And when they give they do it in such a manner, as if the hand had stole from the heart unawares, and that the eye were displeased with the discovery of the theft. But *qui moratur, neganti proximus est* (saith one), yea many times a quick denial is to be preferred before a slow grant. (*Ibid.*) *The priest and Levite :*—1. Spiritual persons in a special manner should be pitiful (see Tit. i. 7, 8; 1 Tim. iii. 2). You may read 2 Kings iv. 1. The distressed widow comes to a prophet to bemoan her condition; every one would not be sensible of her affliction; if they did pity her, yet little hopes there was that they would relieve her. A prophet she hopes will do both. Into Elisha's ear she unloads her griefs. The like course takes David, and flies unto Abiather the high-priest when he was an hungry and in distress (1 Sam. xxii). And no wonder, for they are God's chaplains-in-ordinary; they serve that Master who is merciful; Him they should imitate, and learn to " be merciful as He is merciful" (Luke vi. 36). What scholar but will imitate his master's exercise ? 2. They have received more mercy, and drunk deeper in that cup than others have (2 Cor. iv. 1, 2). Whoever they are, it is expected they should not be wanting in this duty. 3. In every good duty ministers should be examples unto others, in word, in conversation, in charity, &c. (1 Tim. iv. 12). Charity becomes all men, but above all men the men of God. If we want bowels in us where shall men find them ? If mercy be a lamp in others, it must be a bright star in our breasts. A jewel more precious than all the stones in Aaron's breastplate. For—1. We are men of God, and therefore should fly all covetous and earthly practices. Fishes love the salt waters, yet birds of the air fly upwards towards heaven, and whilst the ant (a creature housed in the earth) makes abundant provision for herself, "the fowls of heaven neither sow, nor reap, nor carry into barns." Oh! how unnatural is it that they, next heaven by vocation, should yet in respect of conversation be furthest off! Nothing further from heaven nor more unlike God than uncharitableness. 2. We preach charity and mercy, that is the sum and main scope of all our sermons, it being the abridgment of the law and the tenor of the gospel. Faith is the centre, love the circle. All our doctrines and conclusions are but lines drawn from the centre to the circumference. Nay, as we preach charity, profess charity, and pray for charity, so we must open our doors to charity and give it entertainment. (*Ibid.*) *Entertaining the Satanic thief :*—This being so, how comes it to pass that we take such delight in the company of these ? What traveller lighting into the company of a suspected person doth not soon shake him off ? Better is a blank than an ill filling. Or what wise man would invite a thief to come unto his house, and being come would make him the best cheer, show him the best room, lay him in the best bed, &c., when he is told for certain that he means to spoil him? And yet this entertain-ment hath Satan from us, when no thief so mischievous as he. What thief but leaves something behind him ? " Some gleaning grapes shall remain " (as the prophet shows, Jer. xlix. 9). They " steal but till they have enough," but this thief carries all away that good is. Not a member of the body, not a power of the soul, not a good instruction in the head, not a good motion in the heart, but he steals away (Matt. xiii. 4.) (*Ibid.*) *Personal contact with suffering .*—We need to be brought out of our luxurious houses and into personal contact with needy ones. God has linked the poor and rich together. Sir Robert Peel's daughter wore a beautiful ermine coat, that was purchased from a fashionable store in the West End of London, but which had been worked upon in one of the lofty tenement houses of East London. The sewing-woman who made the cloak was ill with fever, the con-tagion of which was carried in the beautiful cloak that soon enwrapped the peer's daughter, from which she died. So God says, " Neglect no portion of your city, or it will send back its pestilential airs into your homes and your children's hearts." There is no possibility of redemption until we go out and find those that are in need, clasp hands over the chasm that divides us from the unfortunate, look into their faces and tell them that we are akin to them in need. I may not be incorrect in thinking that the priest and Levite went back to Jerusalem, and reported to the secretaries of various societies, saying that they had better send down at once and relieve this wounded man on the highway. If they did, those two men did what a majority of people are doing to-day. They report their cases to somebody else to relieve, instead of, as largely as possible, going and doing it themselves. There is nothing that so relieves and cheers as the presence of the donor with his donation. If it comes through agencies, it never blesses to the extent that the touch of your hand does the poor woman who needs your encouragement and cheer. In conver-sation with Octavia Hill, last May in London, she said, in regard to the tenements of London : " We have more model tenements than we can take care of. My present work is to train women that will go down and oversee them." If you get families out of poor tenements into the model ones, ten chances to one they will sink to the level in which they are accustomed to live; and the great thing to do in London is to get a corps of workers who will oversee those tenements, and give inmates constant counsel. Remember that the happy man makes the happy world, and not the happy world the happy man. (*G. M. G. Dana.*) *The need of sym-*

pathy :—The great undertakings that we have entered upon in the name of charity have been those that have had their beginnings in this feeling of sympathy. I do not suppose John Howard would have undertaken his mission to the prisons of the world if he had not been first moved by a fellow-feeling for those who were confined in dungeons that had never been exposed to publicity, and whose cruelties and sufferings had never been made known to the public. He never could have aroused all British Christendom unless he had borne himself the strait-jacket, and subjected himself to some of the tortures that prisoners were compelled to endure. He spoke from a personal experience concerning their sufferings, and respecting brutal punishments from which hitherto there had been no escape. Dr. Guthrie, with others, did a great work in Edinburgh in behalf of the street boys, awakened thereto by his sympathy with them in their life of hardship and peril. Artist-like, he detected the possibilities of these otherwise wasted and blighted lives. He saw what could be made of them, and therefore appealed with impassioned eloquence to the dull and uninformed public of Scotland's metropolis, urging the importance of training these street Arabs till they might develop into merchants and useful citizens—ay, even through patient instruction unfold those latent powers which would enable them to become benefactors and men of genius. You may hold in your hand a diamond glittering in the ring you prize or sparkling in the pin which is a cherished keepsake, and observing its beauty, its pureness, try to estimate the value of the gem. So, too, you may hold in the other hand a piece of charcoal, which smuts the fingers touching it, and you will see nothing to admire in the latter. The brilliance of the one but makes the dullness of the other more apparent. Yet these two are substantially the same : they are differentiated by the processes to which each has been subjected, and because of which they are so wide apart in work and appearance. In like manner do those we meet differ. A fortunate environment, great privileges, fill some with noble hopes, and make possible a glorious life. The little *gamin* of the street, devoid of all this, eking out his career in the dark tenement and noisome alley, has little at first to attract you. But there may be locked up in him capacities now unsuspected. Under certain conditions, and with the guiding hand of some gifted teacher, he may become the artist of whom the community will be proud, or the architect able to build the cathedral famed for its lines of beauty, or the philanthropist whose good works will bless generations and embalm his name in the fragrant odours of loving hearts. When we learn to sympathize with such young life, then will we understand the significance of all schemes of child-saving and all efforts to reclaim erring youth. The true artist always has this sympathy. Hence, he is quickly interested in the rude etchings shown him, the work of some tyro in art. He inquires about the subject who has thus revealed the signs of slumbering genius, waiting for the helping word and needed culture which some master is able to afford. He knows what can be made of one already revealing talents that else must go to waste. "I can teach him," he says, "till he shall become an artist able with his own brush to immortalize his name, or the sculptor carving out of the shapeless marble the speaking statue, or the architect constructing the dome for some noted fane, which shall seem to be hung in the air, full of grace, a marvel of human skill." (*Ibid.*) *Every natural man is a wounded man* :—Cast your eye upon what part you please, you can see nothing but wounds and bruises (Isa. i. 5). His mind that is blind (Jer. x. 14, li. 17 ; Eph. v. 8). Vain (Prov. xiv. 12 ; Eph. iv. 17 ; 1 Cor. i. 21). Foolish (Tit. iii. 3 ; Isa. xxix. 13 ; Job xi. 12). His will rebellious and adverse (Rev. viii. 7, vii. 14, vi. 19 ; Matt. xxiii. 37 ; Jer. xviii. 12, xliv. 16, 17). His memory marvellous weak and feeble (Luke xxiv. 6, 7, 8 ; Heb. xiii. 2 ; 2 Pet. iii. 5). His conscience that is benumbed (Eph. iv. 19 ; Heb. ix. 14 ; Gen. x. 15). Turmoiled (John viii. 9 ; 1 John iii. 20 ; Acts ii. 37, xxiv. 26). Impure (Tit. i. 15 ; Heb. x. 22). Superstitious and erroneous (Mark x. 19, 20 ; Luke xviii. 12 ; Matt. xv. 2, 3 ; John xvi. 2). His affections are unruly and disordered ; they stand quite cross and contrary unto God (Gal. xv. 24 ; Rom. x. 2 ; 1 Kings xxii. 8, xxi. 4 ; Jas. iv. 12). His outward members are all instruments of sin (Rom. vi. 13, 19, iii. 13 ; Psa. lii. 4 ; 2 Pet. ii. 24). (*N. Rogers.*) *The needy and helpful placed side by side in this world* :—We are accustomed to admire the wisdom and foresight that spread layers of iron ore and layers of coal near each other in the crust of the earth that the one might give the melting heat which the other needed ; but the Divine government is a much more minute and pervading thing. The same Omniscient Provider has appointed each meeting between those who are in want and those who have abundance ; and for the same reason, that the one may give what the other needs, and that both may be blessed in the deed. But He who lays the plan watches its progress, and is displeased when men do not take the opportunity that has been given. When He has brought the strong to the spot where the weak are lying He is displeased to see them pass by on the other side. (*W. Arnot.*)   *Love not selective :*—The point on which attention is fixed is not, Who of all mankind have a right to receive kindness? but, Are you willing to show kindness, as far as you have opportunity, to every human being who is in need? The scribe desired to select a few who might rank as his neighbours, hoping that by limiting their number he might show kindness to each, without any substantial sacrifice of his own ease. The Lord shows him that love is like light : wherever it truly burns it shines forth in all directions, and falls on every object that lies in its way. Love that desires to limit its own exercise is not love. Love that is happier if it meet only one who needs help than if it met ten, and happiest if it meet none at all, is not love. One of love's essential laws is expressed in those words of the Lord, that the apostles fondly remembered after He had ascended, "It is more blessed to give than to receive." (*Ibid.*)   *Brotherhood of men :*—A man was standing by a hole which had been excavated, in which work- men were engaged in tossing out the dirt that it might be enlarged, when suddenly it caved in, burying those at the bottom. He stood idly looking on, as those sum- moned to rescue the buried shovelled the dirt as rapidly as possible to reach the bodies below, until a woman started out of a shanty near by, and called out, "Jim, your own brother is down yonder!" He instantly stripped off coat and vest, and dug for dear life ; and why? Because his brother was among those entombed. Our brothers are in danger, our brothers are deaf and dumb, our brothers have defective minds, our brothers have lost their reason ; and we need the inspiration that will send us to work as vigorously as the man just described. Then we will say that no expenditure is too great for redemption of the erring, and no personal effort should be spared to reform the fallen. Those who are now under the power of sin, who are swelling the ranks of our criminals that become the burdens of society, need to be sought out and saved. (*G. M. G. Dana.*)

Vers. 38–42. **Martha received Him into her house.**—*Christ's visit to Martha and Mary :*—I. The conduct of Christ is to be considered. 1. It is observable that as soon as He entered the house, He attended to the great work for which He came into the world. 2. It is further observable that Christ noticed the manner in which the two sisters were employed, and that the rule of his judgment was the claim of His doctrine upon their attention. II. Consider the most prominent particulars of the conduct of the two sisters, by way of illustrating the grounds of our Lord's remarks. 1. In Martha there was an error of judgment : not of that kind which proves the entire want of real piety, but which implies great oversight, and a disregard to existing circumstances. 2. She neglected a religious opportunity. Christ was travelling with His disciples, and hence His stay would be short. It was a privilege of rare occurrence to have Him as a guest. But by Martha it was neglected, and the reason was not one of necessity but of choice. It was not because affliction, or acts of mercy to others prevented her, but because she deprived herself by gratifying a useless inclination. 3. There was evil passion in her conduct. It was the warmth of her temper which prompted her to make the appeal, "Lord, dost Thou not care that my sister hath left me to serve alone?" She felt irritated because her sister did not think and act like herself. She measured her sister's conduct by her own line, and hence her rash reflection on Mary's composure. III. Make a few observations in order personally to improve the subject. 1. The narrative evidently gives the highest importance to the concerns of the soul. 2. Let the examples set before us in the text be regarded as very instructive in this respect. One is an example by which we are warned against the evil of earthly-mindedness. Influenced in such a way the heart is in danger of being entangled so as not only to be kept from attending to what is better, but to think it strange that others should differ from ourselves. We sustain a serious loss without being sensible of it. The other is an example which we ought to imitate. In Mary we witness that readiness to hear Divine instruction, that improvement of a present opportunity, that subordination of temporal things to spiritual, which show the seriousness and correct preference of the mind—the purity and fervour of the affections. Hers was thinking and acting for eternity. 3. The narrative teaches us in what way we are to expect the notice and approba- tion of our Divine Redeemer. Not when pursuing our own plans, not when devoting ourselves to worldly concerns ; but when honouring His word, when learning His will and seeking His grace. (*Essex Congregational Remembrancer.*) *Lessons from the incident at Bethany :*—I. CONSIDER THE DILIGENCE OF THE SAVIOUR IN THE IMPROVEMENT OF TIME. He goes about doing good. He always pays for His entertainment. In the parlour as well as the temple, He furnishes admonition and counsel. No sooner does He enter this house than we find Him teaching. II. OBSERVE, HOW IMPROPER IT IS FOR A FOLLOWER OF THE LORD JESUS TO BE SENSUAL AND SELFISH. Mary who hears His word pleases Him better than Martha who prepares His meal : yea, Martha even grieves Him by her assiduity to entertain Him. He would rather feed than be fed. III. SEE WHAT DIVERSITIES THERE ARE IN THE FOLLOWERS OF OUR LORD. Many things diversify the degree and the exercises of religion. Thus the stations in which Providence places good men differ ; one shall be favourable to devotion, another shall afford less leisure and create more distraction. Constitutional complexion also has its influence. Thus some Christians are more inclined to contemplation and the shades ; other are formed for the active virtues. The difficulties which chill the timid serve only to rouse and animate the bold and courageous. Religion, like water, partakes a little of the nature of the soil over which it runs. IV. WE MAY MEET WITH HINDRANCES IN RELIGION FROM THOSE WHO SHOULD BE OUR ASSISTANTS. Such are friends and relations. Michal ridicules the holy joy of David. A brother may discourage a brother. A sister may reproach and repel a sister. Our foes may be those of our own household. Yea, even by religious friends and relations we may sometimes be injured. They may be wanting in sympathy. They may censure and condemn our actions from ignorance of our circumstances and motives. V. HOW ANXIOUS SOEVER WE MAY BE ABOUT MANY THINGS, ONE THING ALONE REALLY DESERVES OUR ATTENTION : " one thing is needful." It is, hearing the Saviour's words ; it is, an attention to the soul ; it is—religion. What ! is nothing else necessary ? Yes ; many things. But, compared with this, they are less than nothing and vanity. Other things are accidentally needful—this is essentially so. Other things are occasionally needful— this is invariably so. Other things are partially needful—this is universally so— needful for prosperity and adversity ; needful for the body and the soul ; needful for time and eternity. Some things are needful for some individuals, but not for others ; but this is needful for all. (*W. Jay.*) *Lessons :*—1. This passage suggests important cautions as to domestic, and all worldly affairs. The difficulty here is to pursue the proper medium—to pay sufficient attention to these matters, and yet not to carry that attention to an excessive and hurtful length. On the one hand, let all needful attention be paid by the pious mistresses of families to have everything in their house in a judicious, orderly, and comfortable state, according to the station of life in which they are placed ; and let them conscientiously avoid all indolent, careless, and slovenly habits, as they would avoid bringing a scandal on their profession, and prejudicing the worldly against it. In describing the virtuous woman, Solomon says, " She looketh well to the ways of her household, and eateth not the bread of idleness." On the other hand, this care must not be carried to excess ; it must not be the chief business ; it ought to be managed so as not to interfere with, but to promote, the one thing needful. One breach of duty, in consequence of excessive domestic care, occurs when it is the means of preventing secret and family worship altogether, or of impeding their regular and calm exercise ; and this is very similar to the situation to which Martha now reduced herself. Another sinful error, in this respect, is that of giving or requiring from servants more time and attention to the preparation of food, and to other family concerns, on the Lord's-day, than is necessary. 2. Improve this passage as a test of your state and character. Ask yourselves, What has had the chief place in your thoughts—the world and its cares, or Christ and His salvation ? 3. Consider the folly, guilt, and danger of neglecting the one thing needful, and the good portion. 4. Let me earnestly urge you all to make Mary's choice. (*Jas. Foote, M.A.*) *Mary and Martha :*—I. Let us clear the way, by a brief statement as to WHAT THESE SISTERS WERE NOT. It is clearly wrong to take them as representatives severally, of the worldly and heavenly sides of life. It was not for diligence in housewife's tasks that our Lord took Martha to task, if He did take her to task ; and it was not contemplative piety that He commended in Mary, if He really did commend her. Nothing is more striking, in the life we are called to follow, than the way in which we are taught to serve God. We are called to serve God, actively if possible, passively at any rate, but in any case to serve Him. Mere gazing, mere reading, mere listening, mere dreaming, have never prospered as forms of Christian life ; and we can be certain that it was not for anything that could be so named that Mary was commended by the Lord. The law for our spiritual life is, "Diligent in business, fervent in spirit, serving the Lord." Martha served; Mary sat at His feet; and the Lord, by what He said, did not put any mark of disapproval on Martha's serving. II. Let us try to gather up THE TRUE LESSONS OF THE INCIDENT. 1. Observe the word "also" in ver. 39. It refers to something that had gone before. She was Martha's sister. It can hardly refer to that. Must not this be the meaning—she had joined with Martha in receiving their Guest, had taken part with Martha in the household tasks; and *also*, in addition to that, when all she considered needful was done, she sat at the Master's feet. 2. Observe next, that what brought Martha with her complaint to Jesus, was not her sister's freedom from service and neglect to fulfil her household duties, but just this—she was "cumbered with much service." A temporary entanglement with many things; a confession that she was unable to undertake her tasks. What we have to deal with is not her whole life, but a special and exceptional moment of it—that moment when Patience was not allowed to have its perfect work in her, when Care sat on the hearth. Caught in this moment of weakness, and weighed down by the very burden which her love had taken up, she stumbled at what seemed, but was not, the indifference of her sister, and came to the Lord and said, "Dost Thou not care that I am left to do all the work alone?" 3. Now let us turn to the words and meaning of the Lord. They are not to be taken as words in a sermon, but as words spoken in the quiet atmosphere of the house, with holy emphasis attached to them. "Dear Martha! Art thou troubled so? My coming has proved indeed a burden to thee. Do not suffer My coming to be a burden; do not trouble about many things for the table; one thing is enough for Me." Then consider the words about Mary. Martha wanted our Lord to tell Mary to rise from sitting at His feet, and come and help in the preparation of the meal; she was grudging her the place she had taken. The Lord replies: "Oh Martha! only look. It is not the seat of honour; it is the lowliest place. It is at My feet. She has not taken thy place as head of the house, but simply the retired place, the place of a disciple, at My feet—the humblest place there was at the table. She has chosen that good place which shall not be taken from her." III. WHAT DO WE GAIN BY SURRENDERING THE OLD FAMILIAR INTERPRETATION? 1. We gain, first of all, an escape from the mere conventional reading of the story. We gain what painting does when taken from the monastic attitudes and golden halos which surround the heads of mediæval martyrs, and get back to natural forms, to nature and to humanity. 2. And next, we gain an immense freshness in the reading and application of this story, instead of having to descend to lower levels of Christian truth. Mary and Martha are brought nearer and more akin to us, seem to be more certainly our own flesh and blood. (*Alex. Macleod, D.D.*) "*Now it came to pass, as they went, that they entered,*" &c. In this we have two things observable—1. The nature of the place, which Christ at this time turned into—"He entered into a certain village." 2. The party that entertained Him, and took Him in upon His entering into the town—"A certain woman named Martha, received Him into her house." To speak a word of the first, THE NATURE OF THE PLACE—"He entered into a certain village." We see here that Christ did not only take care of cities and great towns. This was the temper and disposition of Christ, to condescend so far to such places as these are, for the scattering of His heavenly Word and doctrine amongst them. And thus there is a very good reason for other ministers likewise to do, upon occasion, in divers regards. 1. Because here's an opportunity of doing good, as well as elsewhere. There are souls to be saved in the villages, as well as in the great cities. 2. There's encouragement of a man's ministry in these, as well as in other places, and sometimes more. All religion is not compassed and comprehended within the walls of a city. 3. For a difference of gifts, and various improvements of those abilities which God pleases to dispense. The second is THE PARTY THAT ENTERTAINED HIM. "And a certain woman named Martha received Him into her house." 1. The protection and blessing which she was likely to receive from His person and presence with her. The presence of holy men casts a blessing upon the places where they are; which are in so much the greater safety and security for their sakes. As Jacob tells Laban, "God has blest thee since my coming to thee"; *te-ragli*, alms-foot; "since I set my foot within thy doors." Such a Guest was Christ to Martha, a blessing and protection to her. 2. The benefit she should have from His instruction, and doctrine, and conversation, and communion with Him. "This day is salvation come to this house," *i.e.*, in the means (Luke xix. 9). **3.**

The special love and affection which she bare unto Him by way of thankfulness, and requital to Him. It is said, "Jesus loved her" (John xi. 5). And now she shows her love to Him again. She had taken Christ at first into her affections, and now she takes Him into her house. It follows in the text: "And she had a sister called Mary, which also sat at Jesus' feet, and heard his words." 1. I say, Christ was here to good purpose, as indeed He was everywhere else. From whence we learn the like duty, and disposition, and practice, both ministers and others; where we see any coming forward in religion, to promote them, and bring them on further all we can. Thus did Christ here to these two sisters, Martha and Mary; He took occasion, from his presence with them, to establish them further in religion. Here there are divers rules which, by the way, are to be observed by us; as, namely these: 1. That we always carry about us a full heart. We should be full of heavenly meditations, that so we may the better be fitted for heavenly discourse. 2. We must also have respect to the company we converse withal. There's a casting of pearls before swine; which our Saviour has given us warning of. 3. To time and season: "Everything is beautiful in its season," and a word spoken then, "is like apples of gold in pictures of silver." The second is that which is expressed. The different entertainment of Him by these two sisters: Mary, she sat at His feet, and heard His word; but Martha, "she was cumbered about much serving." We'll speak to the carriage of them both, &c. 1. Of the carriage of Mary: "She sat at His feet, and heard His word." Wherein we have divers things observable of us. 1. Here was her wise improvement of the opportunity for the good of her soul. She was not sure to have Christ always, therefore she would make use of Him while she had Him. 2. "She sat at His feet." Here's another expression of her carriage; which has also its several intimations contained in it; as especially these two: 1. Her reverence and composedness of carriage and quietness of mind. A roving and unsettled hearer can never be a good hearer (Psa. xlvi. 10). For this purpose we should come with preparation and premeditation aforehand; labouring to disburden our minds of those cumbrances which are apt to molest us. 2. Here was her humility: "She sat at His feet." We have many hearers sometimes which do not sit at the feet, but rather at the head of their teachers; which will be teaching those which should teach them (Col. ii. 18). 3. She heard His word. She attended to the things which were spoken; as is said of Lydia. 2. Delight. She had a sweet savour and relish of them, and complacency in them. 3. Reposition. She retained them, and laid them up in her heart. And thus much for the carriage of Mary. The second is, Martha's carriage herself, which was very different from it. 1. I say, Here is her own behaviour for for her own particular: "She was cumbered about much serving:" that is, in the friendly entertainment of Christ's person. But, accordingly as it is here qualified in her; so it had somewhat which was vicious in it. 1. Luxury and excess. She was too large in her entertainments. It may be she provided more than was fitting for such a time. 2. Curiosity for the manner. "She was cumbered" about it. She was too punctual, and curious, and exact in her preparations, that she thought nothing good enough. 3. There was a turbulency and unquietness of spirit. Sometimes it proceeds from unskilfulness; as those things which people have no skill in, they are troublesome to them to go about them. Sometimes it proceeds from unaccustomedness; as those things which they are not used to, they are disquieting when they undertake them. But more especially, it does arise from a weakness and impotency of mind. And so much for her own behaviour. The second thing here considerable, is the censure of her sister's carriage; yea, upon the point of Christ Himself: wherein also there were many weaknesses and infirmities involved at once. As—1. There was a spice of pride and vain-gloriousness in her obsequiousness: "Lord, dost Thou not care that my sister hath left me to serve alone?" As who should say, Dost Thou not take notice of how much pains I take to entertain Thee? While she finds fault with her sister, she does implicitly commend herself; which is oftentimes the end of such speeches. She saw she outstripped her sister in this service, and now she would needs be commended for it. The remedies of this distemper are these: (1) A reflection upon our weaknesses and failings other ways. (2) A consideration that all we do, is a due debt. (3) That others may be better in other respects, &c. That's the first. 2. Here was a spice of envy and censoriousness of her sister's forwardness in religion: "Lord, dost Thou not take care that my sister," &c. Here was a quarrelling and contending with her sister; as one weakness brings in another. From pride comes contention (Prov. xiii. 10). And this is joined with envy, and censure, and emulation.

She would needs be thought the best of the two, and she pleased herself in her own good performances; and hence falls upon her sister. And where there's one neglects the world for the looking after their souls, there are hundreds which lose their souls for attending too much upon the world. And that's a second infirmity here observable. 3. Here was a spice also of impiety, in interrupting the good discourse of Christ. Those which have no mind to listen themselves, when they come at any time to the hearing of the Word; they are the forwardest to distract others: and those |which care not themselves to discourse, will not suffer others to do it neither. 4. Here was a great deal of incivility in her carriage to her Guest Himself; a great deal of fondness, and trespassing upon the rules of hospitality; and that in sundry particulars, that we may see the unseasonableness of this passion in this pious woman. 1. She does here commend her own diligence and care of entertainment—" I am left alone to serve." What a sad thing is this! As she desired to be commended by Christ, which we spake of before; so, for want of it, she commends herself for her own attendance: this was absolutely contrary to the rules of hospitality and entertainment. 2. Which was as bad on the other side; she finds fault with her Guest, and picks a quarrel with Him, which now was a stranger to her. This was another trespass upon entertainment. 3. She puts Christ, which was a stranger, upon finding fault with His own entertainment, which was another ridiculous business. For though Christ, as He was in His proper person, might justly find fault with anything; yet, take him now under t he notion of a Guest, here it was not so proper for Him. 4. There was this incivility and disrespect to Christ her Guest, and so a trespass upon hospitality; that she wrangles with her sister in His presence, which was very unseemly. (*J Horton.*) 1. Here is the reprehension itself; He checks and reproves Martha : and thus it may be amplified to us according to a various and different apprehension and notion, in which we may here look upon her: and that especially threefold. (1) As she was a good and godly woman. (2) As she was a kind and friendly woman. (3) As a woman beloved. 1. She was good, and yet Christ reproves her, and checks her, where she was now amiss. Whence we note; that even those which are good, are to be reproved when they do that which is evil. And good reason for it : For—(1) The goodness of the person does not change the nature of the action. Sin is no better than sin, whosoever they be that commit it. 2. The goodness of the person sometimes makes the action worse. 3. Those which are good may be better ; and this is a means so to make them ; therefore the rather to be reproved in this regard. Indeed, in the reproof of good persons, there are some cautions which are fit to be observed. (1) That we be sure to reprove them for that which is evil, and no other (1 Sam. i. 14). (2) We must do it with another kind of spirit, than those which are commonly profane persons; looking upon them as brethren and sisters in Christ. 3. So order the business as near as we can, that our reproof of good persons may not reflect upon goodness itself. 2. We may look upon her as a friendly woman. She was one that entertained Christ ; took Him into her house. Whence we note, that the receiving of courtesies from any persons, does not discharge us from our duty towards them; where, by our place and occasions, we are called to the reproving of them. This, then, it serves, for the use of it, to meet briefly with two sorts of persons. 1. With people, who think by their courtesies sometimes to stop the ministers mouths where they show any testimony of respect and kindness. 2. It meets also with some ministers : their pusillanimity and lowness of spirit in this regard, which are silent, and meal-mouthed, where at any time they receive courtesies, and will not reprove where things are amiss. The second is the matter of reproof, or the thing which He reproves her for : "Thou art careful, and troubled about many things." In which passage of Christ's to her, there are divers particulars couched, as reprovable in this good woman. 1. Here was a mistake in her, and misapprehension of Christ Himself. She did not judge aright of Him in this particular. That we are all apt, by nature, to think we please Christ most, when we abound in outward services and performances to Him. Martha, because she stirred herself in the entertainment of Christ in her house, therefore she thinks she has now quitted herself, though she neglect, and let pass His doctrine. 2. Another thing reprovable here in Martha, was, as a misapprehension of Christ, so a misplacing of her own affections. She looked after that which was but trivial, and nothing to speak of, the providing of her feast, &c., and neglected the main chance of all, which was the word of Christ. "Thou art careful, and troubled about many things" ; where that which expresses "many things" is in the

Greek τὰ πολλά ; that is, ordinary, and common, and vulgar things, τὰ τυχόντα. And here we learn thus much; that it is a great fault in Christians, and those who are professors of religion, to have their minds and thoughts taken up about slight and trivial matters (Col. iii. 2). This minding of such things is very unfitting in these respects. 1. In regard of the unsuitableness of these things to their minds ; they are things below a Christian spirit. Take an heart which is sanctified by grace, sprinkled with the blood of Jesus Christ, has the Spirit of God dwelling in it ; and how far are these outward things inferior to it ? as much, and a great deal more, than the sports and pastimes of children are to the thoughts of grown and grave men. 2. Because they have better, and other things to take their minds up. 3. Because they little conduce to that end to which themselves are appointed. Our main end is a better life, and to be fitted and prepared for that. The third and last thing which Christ seems here to tax in Martha, is her solicitude and distraction of spirit and excess in this business. 1. Here was her excess and superfluity, in the word "many things," as a note of variety. Christ did not find fault with her hospitality, but she was too curious, and superfluous in it. We are very ready and subject to over-shoot ourselves in things lawful and necessary, and to go beyond our bounds in them. And this now leads us to the second thing, which is the last observable in this verse ; and that is, Martha's solicitude and distraction. First, she was cumbered. Secondly, she was careful. Thirdly, she was troubled. 1. Distraction, it does no way further or promote. " Which of you, by taking care, can add one cubit to his stature ? " (Matt. vi. 27). 2. Distraction, it does very much hinder, and put back ; both formally, and demeritoriously ; forasmuch as it weakens the mind, and makes it unfit for service. 3. Distraction, it does contract a great deal of guilt with it. It is a very vicious and inordinate affection, as that which casts a disparagement upon His promises and care over His people. For this purpose, it may be very pertinent to consider both the causes and remedies of this distemper ; and the one will very fitly and pertinently follow upon the other. The causes of it are partly these : 1. Sometimes a dependence too much upon outward means. He which trusts to outward means, will be distracted ; because these, they oftentimes fail, and give a man the slip. 2. A limiting of God's providence to such a particular way. This is another thing which causes distraction. 3. An over-prizing and over-valuing such a project and design. Our distractions are oftentimes according to our estimations ; where we make too much of anything, it will be sure to trouble us, when it falls contrary to us. Lastly. A special cause of distraction is a special sickness which is upon the soul in this regard : weak things are apt to be unquiet ; and frowardness, it causes trouble. Now, the remedies against distraction are likewise these : 1. A commending of ourselves and our ways to God by prayer (Phil. iv. 6). 2. A consideration of our call to such and such businesses and ways which we fall into. 3. A meditation on the promises which God has made in such and such conditions. (*J. Horton.*) *But one thing is necessary, or needful :*—This is the one thing which is necessary. And here there are two things further to be explained. First, how this is said to be " one thing." And, secondly, how this, alone, is said to be necessary, as if none were so but this. 1. How it is said to be but one. For if we speak of spiritual matters, we know that there are divers and sundry things of this nature, and they have their varieties in them. There is the Spirit of God, and there is the Kingdom of God. These, they are not one, but many, in the kinds and in the operations of them. To this we answer : That these all, they come to one, and tend to one purpose in conclusion. 1. This is that which is most noble and excellent in its own nature, that is mainly and principally to be regarded, and looked after by us ; which, of all other things, is most noble and excellent, considered in itself. It is that which does indeed excel all the comforts and contentments of this world ; they are nothing in comparison with it. There is an emptiness and a defectiveness in them, and such as will be unable to satisfy at another day : whereas this, it makes a man fully and completely happy. Now, this is this "one thing" in the text. It can be least spared of all other things besides. 2. It is of the greatest influence, and extent, and usefulness to us ; it is that which we have occasion for in the whole course and compass of our lives, and we cannot properly do anything without it. It manages all callings, and all providences, and all affairs whatsoever they be. And a man cannot carry himself in them so decently, and as becomes him, that wants it. That man that neglects his soul, there is nothing else which can be well minded by him. 3. It is of the greatest continuance and duration. 4. This is also the main purpose for which every man was sent into the world ; therefore it is mainly to be regarded and looked after by him. For this end was I born, and for this cause came I into the world, that I should live according to the truth. The consideration of this point may be thus far useful to us. 1. To teach us where especially to spend our chiefest thoughts and endeavours. And that is, upon this one thing, which is so needful and necessary for us, as we have heard it is. We see here where to begin, and fasten our studies: 1. To take care of necessaries, before we take care of superfluities. We count him to be a madman, in reference to the world, who looks after flowers, and pictures, and music, and such things as these; and, in the meantime, suffers himself to starve, and want bread. Well, there is a time coming when things will appear in another kind of view than now they do; when this "one thing needful" will appear to be needful indeed. Now, therefore, this is that which in the first place we should work ourselves into; an apprehension of the necessity of religion. The way hereunto is first of all to get a spiritual favour and relish and appetite in us; what makes men to think meat to be needful, but because their stomachs call for it from them, and their mouths crave it at their hands? And so, what is that which makes men to think grace to be necessary? It is because they have gracious dispositions in them, which accordingly we must labour for. This will make us, with the prophet David, to think the word of God to be to us as our necessary and appointed food. 2. Labour to be convinced of the vanity and insufficiency of the creature. This will make us to think one thing necessary; that is religion, and nothing else. For, it may be, we think it necessary; but other things as necessary as that; and this divides our cares about it. 3. Get our hearts freed from those lusts and corruptions which are in them, and are apt to prevail over them; that's another way to make us to mind this one thing necessary. A covetous heart will never prize this "one thing," nor care for attaining unto it. Secondly. Seeing "one thing is needful," we should therefore not only mind this "one thing" itself, but also mind everything else in reference to that one. We should make all our projects, and actions, and undertakings, subordinate and subservient hereunto; whatever we do, we should examine what connection it hath with this; how it furthers our salvation? how it advances the glory of God? 1. In matters of doctrine, and opinion, look at the "one thing needful" here. There are many frivolous and unnecessary disputes which the world sometimes is troubled withal; which take up men's heads, and minds, and divert them from better things. They never consider the influence or extent of those things which they hold, as to the making of a man better or worse; but indifferently rush upon them without any heed or regard at all. 2. In the duties and exercises of religion, look still at the one thing which is needful; and that according to the particular nature and quality of them. There are many religious performances, which have that which is merely accessory to them. In prayer, to pray in the Holy Ghost; in hearing, to receive the word with meekness; in fasting, to afflict the soul; in communicating, to feed upon Christ; and so of the rest. 3. In our employments and the works of our ordinary callings let us have an eye also still to this; consider what that is which is principally required of us. Lastly. In all the several passages and contrivances and occasions in the whole course of our lives, let us still have a regard to that which is of greatest concernment. Again, further, take it in men's dwellings, and the contrivances of their habitations; they should still look at that which is most needful, not only as to corporal or secular accommodations, but as to spiritual. Men commonly look at the goodness of the air, at the convenience of the soil, at the pleasantness of the situation; what it is for trade, what it is for health, what it is for pleasure; and it may not be amiss in them to do so. But is there nothing else to be regarded by them, but only these? or, are these the chief, and the principal? What are the means for Heaven? and salvation? and spiritual improvements? So again likewise for marriage, and the altering of men's conditions in the world, what is the one thing needful? The third is this: that feeling but one thing is needful, we should therefore take heed of all needless and frivolous distractions in ourselves. 4. We learn from hence how to judge both of others, and likewise of ourselves. If there be but "one thing" which is needful, let us see what we are, according to the abiding, and the abounding of this "one thing" in us. We commonly reckon of ourselves from other qualifications and endowments. No, but let us do it rather by this. No, but we count him a rich man, that has a great deal of gold, and silver, and jewels, and plate, and the like. And so it is here in this particular, as to the whole compass of happiness; he is not so happy a man that does abound with outward accommodations as he that doth abound with the excellencies of grace, and the adorning of the inward man. **All perfections besides, without these, are very imperfect ; and such as being** truly considered, are of no account at all. Lastly. Seeing "one thing is needful," we have here also a very good account of God's dealings and proceedings with His people here in the world, as a special ground and argument of satisfaction, and contentation unto them. Seeing He provides this one thing for them, they have no cause to murmur against Him, as to some outward and worldly deprecations. Again, further, this may also satisfy us in all the hard and severe courses which God seems sometimes to take with His children, when He lays His corrections upon them here in this life, as a means to work out their corruptions, and to prepare them for an heavenly condition: all this is needful and necessary, and such as cannot be well omitted. Physic, it is as needful as health, which is procured by it. That the way to be freed from superfluous cares, is to divert, and so turn to necessary. The looking after salvation will take men off from distraction about the world and the things that belong thereunto. This we gather from the course which was taken by our Saviour with Martha in her present condition, who suggests this unto her as that which was most seasonable for her. This it does upon a twofold account. 1. As it is another thing; and so it does it by way of interruption. 2. As it is a greater thing; and so it does it by way of absorption. 1. I say, as it is another thing; and so it does it by way of interruption. Diversions, they break the force of anything, and check it in its full pursuit. As inordinate bleeding in one part is cured by opening of a vein in another, and the violence of it is stopped by revulsion; even so it is here. 2. As it is a greater thing, and so it does it by way of absorption, and swallowing up; the greater devours the less. As when a man is in care about his life, he forgets some small and petty matter that troubled him; even so it is here. When men are made sensible of the concernments of their souls and their future salvation, other matters do not so closely stick by them as otherwise they would. This, it serves to give us account of so much inordinacy as there is in the world. Therefore we are commonly troubled about many things because this one thing is so neglected by us. We should still have this sentence in our remembrance—that "one thing is needful" and we should accordingly be affected with it. 1. By way of specification: Seeing there is "one thing needful," therefore be sure to mind that; and, at the least, not to neglect it. 2. By way of order: Seeing it is the "one thing needful" therefore take care of that first; mind religion afore anything else. 3. By way of measure and degree: Seeing it is the "one thing needful,' therefore give it the greatest care and endeavour. And to make it full and complete, let us take it also in its full latitude and extent. Religion, it is the "one thing needful," and it is needful for all persons, and all ages, and all conditions. It is needful for people in their youth to look after their souls then, and to begin with God. And it is needful for people in their old age, that so they may end their days in peace, and exchange this life for a better. (*J. Horton.*) *And Mary hath chosen that good part, which shall not be taken away from her :*—1. Here is His judgment itself, which is in a way of praise and commendation; "Mary hath chosen that good part." Christ commends Mary for her choice. Where there are divers things observable of us. We will take them as they offer themselves to us to be handled by us. 1. We learn from hence thus much: That it is the commendation of a Christian to make choice of such ways as are best and most approvable to Christ. If there be any way better than other in the course and tenour of his life, to be sure to pitch and fasten upon that. This is also commendable in every one else besides, and that upon these following grounds. 1. It is an argument of a good and sound judgment; it is an argument of persons well grounded and principled in religion, and that know what belongs unto it. 2. It is an argument also of a gracious and savoury spirit. Men choose commonly according to their affections, and there is much of their spirit in those things which they fasten upon. We may see what is within them, and what principles they are acted by, according to that which they make choice of. A spiritual heart is most affected with spiritual objects, and places its greatest delight and contentment in such things as these. 3. It is an argument of some courage and self-denial and resolution of mind. For the better part, it is not commonly without opposition and resistance in the world. Lastly. It is also an argument of an elect and chosen vessel. It is a sign that God has chosen us, when we choose Him, and such ways as these, which are good and pleasing to Him. We see in other matters for the world, how careful men are (what they are able) to make the best choice that may be, and there is nothing good enough for them, so exact and curious are they. And how much rather should they then choose the best in spiritual matters. The way hereunto is first of all to beg direction of God Himself for the guiding of us. Alas! we are but fools of ourselves without His Spirit to teach us, and therefore we must have recourse to Him. 2. We must also seriously weigh and compare one thing with another. Good election, it proceeds from good deliberation. 3. Take in the advice and experience of well-grounded and experienced Christians to help us. Lastly. To labour to be acquainted with the power of religion ourselves. Religion, it is a matter of election; it is not a business of chance, but a business of choice. We are not to be carried only by others principles, but by principles of our own, not only to take the better part, but to choose the better part; that is, to take it out of a liking of it, and out of an affection to it; at least, to do so at last, and before we have done. And, further, they have also more delight and contentment in it. That which is forced, it is commonly burdensome, and men undertake it with a great deal of reluctancy, and are not themselves in it. But that which comes from them upon their own choosing, it is so much a great deal more pleasing and acceptable to them. We do not hereby advance the power of nature, as if we could do it of ourselves, without the grace of God assisting us; for that we cannot do. In the last place, we may here take notice of the object itself here propounded—"that good part." For the better opening of this point unto you I shall briefly do two things. 1. Show you what, in religion, may be lost and taken away from us. And—2. What may not. For somewhat is considerable in both. 1. For what may be lost. And we may take it in these particulars. (1) The outward means of salvation, that may be sometimes lost, and taken away. (2) Liberty of outward profession, and expression of the several graces of the Spirit, that may be restrained also. (3) The sense and feeling of grace in us, that may also be taken away, and removed from us—we may lose that. Now, further — 2. (which is more proper to the text) We may here consider what it is which cannot. Now, sure it holds good of religion that it cannot be taken away, as is here expressed in this particular case of Mary. (1) In regard of its root and principle—This " shall not be taken away." Thus Job intimates of himself, when he was deprived almost of everything else; yet, that the "root of the matter was found in him" (Job xix. 28). And (Isa. vi. 10) a godly man is compared to an oak, " whole substance is in him, when he casts his leaves." The second is in regard of its operations and effects which it works in the heart. The better part shall not be taken away thus; it still leaves somewhat behind it, which is sure to stick fast. (3) In regard of its reward and recompense both here in this life, and in another world; it shall not be taken away so neither. (*J. Horton.*) *Martha and Mary :*—Some are full of fever and excitement; some live in the shade. 1. The essence of the Christian religion is, that it is a religion of receiving. Martha was studious of giving; Mary, of receiving. Both had reference to Christ; nevertheless, Martha was reproved, while Mary was praised. Now, brethren, be persuaded of this—those please God most who take in most, and dwell in the calm contemplation of His glory till we reflect something of His likeness. 2. But the difference between Martha and Mary did not, after all, lie so much in what they did, as in the spirit in which they did it. Martha worked anxiously. Mary's mind rested. Had Martha gone about all her business with a heart quiet and at ease, I do not suppose that she would ever have been reproved. Now what is the great end for which Jesus lived and died—the end of ends, next to the glory of God? That you may have peace—that the soul of the sinner may be quiet, and rested, and happy. Christ had more pleasure in Mary's peace than He had in Martha's work. 3. But once more. Mary had learnt to do what Martha could not do—to concentrate her mind. She could gather all to one single point, and that point was Christ. It is impossible to suppose that Martha had not several motives as she bustled about that day in the house. Was not she thinking about who was looking at her? Had not she some desire for admiration? Were not there some grovelling feelings, and some unnecessary cares? " Martha, Martha, thou art careful and troubled about many things." (*J. Vaughan, M.A.*) *Martha and Mary :*—I. THE MARTHA SPIRIT IS VERY PREVALENT IN THE CHURCH at this period—prevalent in some quarters to a mischievous degree, and among us all to a perilous extent. 1. There is a considerable tendency among Christian people, in serving Christ, to aim at making a fair show in the flesh. Jesus would be better pleased with a grain of love than a heap of ostentatious service. 2. The Martha spirit shows itself in the censuring of those persons who are careful about Christ's word, who stand up for the doctrines of the gospel, who desire to maintain the ordinances as they were delivered unto them and who are scrupulous and thoughtful, and careful concerning the truth as it is in Jesus. Mary, treasuring up every word of Christ, Mary, counting each syllable a pearl, is reckoned to be unpractical, if not altogether idle. Contemplation, worship, and growth in grace are not unimportant. I trust we shall not give way to the spirit which despises our Lord's teaching, for if we do, in prizing the fruit and despising the root we shall lose the fruit and the root too. In forgetting the great well-spring of holy activity, namely, personal piety, we shall miss the streams also. 3. The Martha spirit crops up in our reckoning so many things necessary. To bring us back to first principles, "one thing is needful," and if by sitting at Jesus' feet we can find that one thing, it will stand us in better stead than all the thousand things which custom now demands. To catch the Spirit of Christ, to be filled with Himself, this will equip us for godly labour as nothing else ever can. 4. The censurable quality in the Martha spirit appears in the satisfaction which many feel with mere activity. To have done so much preaching, or so much Sunday-school teaching, to have distributed so many tracts, to have made so many calls by our missionaries, all this seems to be looked at as end rather than means. If there be so much effort put forth, so much work done, is it not enough? Our reply is, It is not enough, it is nothing without the Divine blessing. 5. Once more, Martha's spirit is predominant in the Church of God to a considerable extent now, in the evident respect which is paid to the manifest, and the small regard which is given to the secret. II. THE MARTHA SPIRIT INJURES TRUE SERVICE. 1. It brings the least welcome offering to Christ. 2. It brings self too much to remembrance. III. THE MARY SPIRIT. I have to show you that it is capable of producing the noblest form of consecration to Christ. Its noblest results will not come just yet. Martha's fruits ripen very quickly, Mary's take time. While she was sitting at Christ's feet, she was forming and filling the springs of action. You are not losing time while you are feeding the soul. While by contemplation you are getting purpose strengthened and motive purified, you are rightly using time. When the man becomes intense, when he gets within him principles vital, fervent, energetic, then when the season for work comes he will work with a power and a result which empty people can never attain, however busy they may be. If the stream flows at once, as soon as ever there is a shower, it must be little better than a trickling rivulet; but if the current stream is dammed up, so that for awhile nothing pours down the river bed, you will in due time, when the waters have gathered strength, witness a torrent before which nothing can stand. Mary was filling up the fountain head, she was listening and learning, feeding, edifying, loving, and growing strong. The engine of her soul was getting its steam ready, and when all was right her action was prompt and forcible. 1. The manner of her action was being refined. Her estimate of Christ was truer than Martha's. Those who think not, who meditate not, who commune not with Christ, will do commonplace things very well, but they will never rise to the majesty of a spiritual conception, or carry out a heart-suggested work for Christ. 2. That sitting of Mary was also creating originality of act. Martha is in a hurry to be doing something—she does what any other admirer of Jesus would do, she prepares meat and a festival ; but Mary does what but one or two besides herself would think of—she anoints Him, and is honoured in the deed. She struck out a spark of light from herself as her own thought, and she cherished that spark till it became a flaming act. (*C. H. Spurgeon.*) *Martha; or, thoughts on the active life:*—The name of Martha suggests to the minds of most of us, I fancy, the thought of an anxious, troubled, and perhaps a somewhat fussy woman, with a short temper and a hasty tongue. That I think is the picture that many of us have drawn of Martha in our own minds. But you must remember that there is something to be said on the other side, something to be said on Martha's behalf; and while we do not shut our eyes to Martha's faults, we may learn something from that which is recorded to her credit. Martha, herself, the managing spirit of the household, is the person who invites the Lord Jesus Christ to come and take His abode for a season in her house. And here let me say that it is a happy thing when a strong mind and a vigorous will are turned in the right direction, and employed for the right purpose. It is something to be thankful for if we have such qualities as a strong mind and a vigorous will to present to the Lord for His service; and although these are not unfrequently coupled with an ungentleness and hastiness which are not altogether lovely, nay, may sometimes be repulsive and painful, yet let us acknowledge the fact that God can utilize that element in our temperament which Satan seeks to abuse, and that where a strong will and a vigorous determination may be employed by the devil with the worst possible results, such natural characteristics, dedicated to the service and glory of God, may prove of priceless value. Now we must remember that Martha had to face a good deal in inviting Jesus Christ into her household. The test was a severe one to her, because it was to try her in her weakest point. There were thirteen hungry men to be provided for, and then no doubt some of the neighbours would also be expecting an invitation to meet this Jesus, who had come among them, and about whom there was so much talk. Perhaps, too, there may have been other unpleasant consequences that she may have had to think about. Jesus Christ not unfrequently may have seemed a troublesome guest, in other ways besides those that I have referred to. His presence may sometimes have exposed people to an amount of hostile criticism and censure which they would fain have avoided. One thing is clear, she was a brave woman, whatever faults she may have had. It required a good deal of moral courage to invite this much-maligned and much-abused Man into her house, and to treat Him as a loved and honoured guest. But Martha's courage was equal to the occasion. And, my dear friends, we too shall find it no light matter to receive Jesus into our hearts and into our homes. And it is as well that we should clearly understand what the consequences may be if we take so important a step. The question will have to be asked over and over again, " Is this and that in accordance with the mind of Him whom we have received and welcomed as our guest?" for we must bear in mind that wherever Christ goes He declines to occupy a subordinate position. It is possible for some of you to do what Martha did. You may be the means of introducing Jesus Christ into your household; and although His presence may cause a disturbance, just think what an honour it is to be the means of introducing the King of kings and Lord of lords into the household which belongs to Him, but which has not previously recognized His claims. Think of the beneficent results that may flow from your action—how the purifying and elevating influences of the Divine Presence may reach one person after another, until at last you can look around with holy joy, and exclaim, " As for me and my house we now serve the Lord." Not long since, at the close of a mission that I had conducted in the North of England, a gentleman, a man of property, returned to his country house, from the large town where I was working, a changed man. On his arrival he summoned into his dining-room all his household, servants and all; and standing up before them all, he addressed them to this effect: " My dear friends, I have to confess with shame and sorrow that this has not been hitherto a Christian household. It has not been regulated upon Christian principles. I, as your master, have not been setting you a Christian example; but, on the contrary, all my influence has been thrown into the wrong scale. I cannot express the amount of sorrow I feel as I look back over the past. But I have called you all together to tell you that, through God's mercy, a great change has taken place in me, and now my supreme desire is that this household should be a Christian household, and that all that is done in it should be done just as the Lord would have it done." Turning to the butler, he said, " We have never hitherto had family prayers; but now understand that at such an hour in the morning, and such an hour in the evening, you ring the bell, and we will all gather together and acknowledge God in our family." And he added, " Be sure you make no difference; whoever may be in the house, whether they be worldly or whether they be religious people, make no distinction. From this time forth Jesus Christ must be Master in this household; we have ignored and dishonoured Him too long." It must have needed some courage, no doubt, to make such a declaration as that. But oh! do you not think he had his reward in the joy and satisfaction he must have felt as he knelt for the first time, surrounded by his family, at the feet of a reconciled God, and thus publicly received Jesus into his house? And remember you may be the means of introducing Christ into your household, even if you be not at its head. The humblest member of the family, or even one of the servants, may be the means of bringing Christ in, and by and by the influence and effect of His presence may be recognized and felt by all. Dear friends, do you think Martha ever regretted receiving Jesus Christ into her house? Martha received Jesus, but little did she know, when she did so, how soon she was to stand in terrible need of His sympathy and comfort and help! Ah, dear friends, sweet are such uses of such adversity as this! blessed are the sorrows that bring out such new and fresh revelations of our wealth in Christ! It is only this that can make our sorrows fruitful of good. But it is time that we should look at the other side. So far we have been saying all we could in

Martha's favour, but we must not shut our eyes upon her faults; for there is much to be learned from considering the faults and failings even of those whose hearts are in the right place, if we approach the consideration of these in the spirit of charity and humility. It is evident that Martha got some harm as well as some good out of Jesus' visit; for she seems here to be sadly flustered and flurried, and even somewhat peevish and irritable. She seems indeed to have been out of temper with the Master as well as with her sister, and to have implied some little reproach on Him as well as on Mary. But why all this disturbance and irritation? Surely it all came of this, that she was thinking more of serving Christ than of pleasing Him. If she had paused to reflect, she must have seen that a sharp, half-reproachful word, and the obvious loss of composure and temper, would cause the Master a good deal more pain than the best-served meal in the world could give Him pleasure. She was busy about Christ, but she failed to enter into sympathy with Christ. Here we have a very important lesson taught us, and one that we need to have impressed upon our minds as Christians and as Christian workers. Our object in life should not be so much to get through a great deal of work, as to give perfect satisfaction to Him for whom we are doing the work. If Martha had looked at things from His point of view she would have felt differently about Mary, differently about those household cares that were troubling her. But Martha in her attempts to serve Christ, though scarcely conscious of it, was really serving herself. Her great desire was, that everything should pass off well. Everything was to be clean and tidy, and well served and well managed, so that nobody should make any unfavourable criticism upon the whole entertainment. We are bound to offer Christ our very best, and nothing done for Him should be done in a slovenly, slip-shod, negligent way, as if anything were good enough for God. She was right in her principle, and yet she failed in carrying it out, and in that failure denied her Guest the very thing that pleased Him best. Martha is quite indignant, and doesn't care to conceal it. And you know people of her class, while they are very useful in a Church, and do a great deal of work, are very frequently indeed, like Martha, somewhat short-tempered. They have a great deal of energy, and a great deal of enthusiasm; but when things do not go exactly as they wish, the hasty word soon slips out, and the unpleasant thought is harboured, and that soon takes all the joy and all the blessing out of Christian work. How often is the work of the Church marred by this hasty spirit, and the Master is grieved in our very attempts to honour Him! And the same spirit, still, I fear, not unfrequently mars a useful life, and desecrates our sanctities. Yes, there is something better than service; there is something grander than doing. It is well to serve; but better still to offer acceptable service. It is well to do; but it is better still to do things in the right way. Martha had her own idea of what the right way was, and it was a worldly idea. What Martha needed was sympathy with Jesus Christ's spirit, to come within the charmed circle of His inner life—to understand His object and aims, to appreciate His longing desire, not to feed Himself with outward food, but to feed a famishing world with the revelation of God in His human form; to reciprocate His spiritual desires for those He sought to lift to a high and heavenly level of experience. This was where Martha went wrong, and this where Mary went right. As it was, Mary chose the good part which could not be taken from her, and Martha missed it, and by her very conduct showed that the Master was right in describing that good part as the one thing needful. Christian workers, let us learn our lesson. It is not enough to receive Jesus into our homes and into our lives—this we must do before anything else—but we need to sit at His feet, to gaze on His spiritual beauty, to hear His words, to yield ourselves wholly to His spiritual influence. Thus, and only thus, shall we find ourselves possessed of the one thing needful; and while hands or feet or brain are busy—or while all are busy together—there shall be a great calm within; there will be speed without feverish haste, and activity without bustle, and our work shall become sabbatic, and our lives an unbroken sanctity. Whatever happens let us not be too busy to sit at Jesus' feet. (*W. H. Aitken, M.A.*) *Mary ; or, the contemplative life :*—These two sisters have been regarded, and rightly regarded, it seems to me, as illustrating to us, in their character, two contrasted elements of spiritual experience. Martha represents the active life, and Mary represents the contemplative life. For we know, and do let us bear in mind, that Christian work in itself is intensely interesting; indeed, there is nothing more likely to become **engrossing.** We all know how absorbed men may become in their own special pursuits. For instance, we have read about Sir Isaac Newton, and how absorbed he used to be in his mathematical and astronomical researches, until he was scarcely able to give a thought to the common duties and circumstances of life, but used frequently to make the most ridiculous blunders about commonplace things, because he took so profound an interest in, and was so fully occupied with, his own great discoveries. And so it is with other branches of knowledge. When men devote their attention to a particular branch of knowledge or science, it becomes a sort of passion, and they no longer find it necessary to stimulate themselves to exertion in that particular; rather they have to check or curb themselves, in order to prevent their minds from becoming too deeply absorbed in their favourite studies. And it sometimes happens that when the mind is given over to some special pursuit, interest in their work becomes so keen that men seem to lose all power of checking themselves, and their brains go on working, as it were, automatically, when they don't intend them to be working at all. I well remember some years ago hearing a touching story of a late Cambridge professor, who was one of the greatest Greek scholars of our time. For some few months before he died he was advised by his friends to shut up his books, give up his studies, and go as much as possible into social life, in order that he might be drawn away from those subjects in which his mind had become so absorbed that his constitution was impaired; indeed, he was threatened with softening of the brain. On one occasion he was in a drawing-room, surrounded by cheerful company, when a half-sad smile passed over his countenance as he observed to a friend, " What is the use of you shutting up my books and not allowing me to work? While I have been here I have traced the derivations of three distinct Greek words, and detected their connection with certain Sanscrit roots." Such was the force of his ruling passion. Now if we can become so absorbed in intellectual researches, is it a wonder that we should become even more absorbed in those higher pursuits in which it is the privilege of Christian people to engage? To be doing God's work; to be endeavouring to make people happy; to be the means of regenerating human hearts and lives, and of reforming the homes of the vicious and degraded; to be restoring those that are fallen, and rescuing those that are tempted—is not this necessarily a most engrossing work, and one that should employ all our energies? It is well, my friends, indeed it is necessary, that we should be interested; for no man ever yet did anything well until he threw his whole heart into it and felt an interest in it. Yet in this very interest lies the danger; for may not the work become everything to us, and He for whom we work be allowed to fall into the background, and eventually be almost forgotten? Nor is it only our work that suffers. We suffer ourselves; for our very work has practically slipped in between us and the Lord for whom we are working, and thus becomes to us, instead of a means of grace, drawing us nearer to God, on the contrary, rather a barrier between ourselves and God. How shall we guard against this error? Yon mediæval monastic would reply, " Give up your work, tear yourself away from the activity of life, seclude yourself in the desert; and then you will be able to enjoy the fellowship of Christ and to enter upon the life of vision, the mystical blessedness of apprehension of the Divine." That is one answer; but it is not such as is given here, and we know what it has brought about in bygone ages. Let us look for an answer to all such misapprehensions to the scene that lies before us. On the one side, there is busy Martha; on the other, quiet, contemplative Mary. We are not told to be imitators of either Martha or Mary, but we are told to be imitators of the Lord Jesus Christ. Was there ever such a busy life as Christ's? Was there ever such a contemplative life as Christ's? He moved forward in the quietness of assured power. He was a true Quietist; for His life was very still, and yet its very stillness told. We may learn a good deal in this respect from observing outward objects. The mightiest things are not always the noisiest things. You go down to one of your own quays, and there you will see the little donkey-engine, on the deck of one of your ships, that is being employed in loading or unloading its freight. What a fuss it makes! Your ear is at once painfully arrested by its clatter and noise; but when you come to examine it, you find it is only a small and insignificant thing, in spite of the noise it makes. It is very useful, no doubt, and does its own work; but it does it very fussily, and that work is not a very great one. You descend into the vessel, and there you see the colossal engine which is to take the ship, donkey-engine and all, across the ocean; and it does all that work without making half as much noise as the little insignificant piece of mechanism that you have been listening to.

Or take a picture from Nature. Look at yonder little bubbling rill flowing down the mountain side, dashing in and out between the rocks, and making a noise which can be heard a considerable distance away. You follow the stream until eventually it is absorbed in a great river, which flows smoothly, calmly, and quietly along in all the majesty of its strength. Perhaps it is strong enough to bear up the navy of a great nation, and yet it does not make the noise that the little stream did. Do let us endeavour, dear friends, in this somewhat noisy age, to distinguish between noise and power. We sometimes think that noise is power, and that if we can create a certain amount of bustle we are doing a large amount of work. I think our work is done well just in proportion to the absence of bustle from it. Now to correct this noisy fussiness we need to learn to imitate Mary and to sit at Jesus' feet, and in silence and stillness of soul to hear His words. No amount of service will make up for the loss of this inward and secret fellowship of the soul with Christ—this hidden life of love, in which Christ and the consecrated heart are bound together in a certain holy intimacy and familiarity. This it is that sanctifies even the most commonplace toil, and the loss of this robs even the holiest things of their sanctity. Notice then, first, Mary sat at Jesus' feet as a learner; and if we desire to learn, here it is that we must receive our lessons. Several thoughts suggest themselves to our minds as we see her sitting there. Let us dwell upon them for a few moments. First, sitting at His feet, she is taking the place of the lowly; and only those who wish to be such can learn of Jesus. The proud and self-confident, whether they be intellectually proud, or morally proud, or spiritually proud, will ever have to go empty away; but " such as are gentle, them shall He learn His way." Next, observe, it is the place of *true* honour and dignity; for it is better to be a junior scholar in the school of Christ than to be a distinguished philosopher untaught by Him. Next, let me point out to you that while she was sitting here she was in a position, not only to learn by Him, but to learn of Him. It was not merely that she heard the truth from Him; it was rather that she found the truth in Him. He was Himself to her the Truth. And we, too, dear brethren, need to discern the difference between learning about Christ or learning by Christ and *learning* Christ. We may be good theologians and yet bad Christians. We cannot sit with Mary now before a visible Christ, but we can contemplate His moral features even as she gazed upon His outward countenance, and we can hear His spiritual teaching even as she heard His outward voice. And there is a sense in which we may be said to know more of Christ than at this time Mary did or could know; for she had never gazed upon the cross, and read the more perfect revelation of the Divine character as it is written there. Come, let us look at Mary, that we may learn to be a learner. How impressed she is with His superior wisdom; how little confidence has she in her own. Nay, the more she learns, I doubt not, the more she feels her ignorance. Oh, blessed is the ignorance that brings us so near to infinite wisdom, and blessed the child-like simplicity that enables us to understand what to the world may seem inexplicable! Then see how absorbed she is. I can never believe that Mary was selfish and inconsiderate. If she had been, I feel sure Jesus would have gently reproved and not commended her. When Mary is next introduced to our notice she is again at Jesus' feet, and this time she is at His feet as a mourner. Blessed are those mourners whom sorrow drives to Jesus' feet; for they shall indeed be comforted! Refer for a moment to the passage (John xi. 32): " Then when Mary was come where Jesus was, and saw Him, she fell down at His feet, saying, Lord, if Thou hadst been here, my brother had not died." Oh, blessed are the trials that bring us to Jesus' feet! The sorrows of this world harden and embitter some people. They grow sour and selfish. I dare say she felt as if she had never loved Him so much before, as she loved Him then when she saw those tears of His. When we feel crushed with sorrow, do let us try to remember that Jesus Christ Himself was the Man of sorrows. Now, dear friends, let us look at Mary once again. We have seen her at the Lord's feet as a learner, and we have seen her there as a mourner: and now, in John xii., we shall see her at the Lord's feet as a worshipper. Turn for a moment to the beginning of that chapter: " Then Jesus, six days before the Passover, came to Bethany, where Lazarus was which had been dead, whom He raised from the dead. There they made Him a supper; and Martha served." Dear Martha! how I love her for it! Always true to her character; never weary of waiting on such a Guest, and this time not even in her own house. Even in the house of Simon Martha must wait upon her Lord; no mere hireling or slave shall be allowed to minister to Him while Martha's willing hands and heart are near. The truest form of worship is, first of all, the presentation to God of all that is most precious, all that is most costly, that we have or that we are.   (*W. H. Aitken, M.A.*)   *The good part chosen :*—I. First of all, I would speak of THE DECISION. "Mary," saith our Lord, "hath chosen." She had made up her mind; she had taken her choice. She had discerned what she loved; she had seen what was for her good; she had great courage, and, caring not for the praise or the blame of others, she determined to hold fast what she had chosen. How valuable is this decision of character! How valuable it is, even in the children of this world! How many statesmen, generals, leaders of men, have been distinguished by it! Look over the lists of the men who have moved the world, or who have led vast armies to battle; take such men as Julius Cæsar, such men as the Emperor Napoleon; and mark how decision of character—bold, unflinching, unhesitating decision of character—is their leading feature. And mark how, in all the Word of God, we find this a leading characteristic of God's servants. We find Noah boldly and decidedly making the ark in the face of an ungodly and unbelieving world; we find Abraham leaving his father's house, to go to a land he had never seen; we find Moses forsaking the pleasures of Egypt, looking for recompense in the unseen reward; we find Joshua saying to the people, "As for me and my house," whatever ye do, "we will serve the Lord"; we find Daniel going down to the lion's den, choosing to meet with what was to all appearance a dreadful death, rather than deny his principles; we find Paul the apostle opposing a world in arms against him, and withstanding even his brethren, when there seemed to be an article of the faith impugned. And coming later, we find men like Athanasius, ready to meet the world and the Church too, when they seemed to be against them—men like Martin Luther, opposing all the professing Church of their day, when they saw the professing Church opposing the Bible. In all these men we find the same bold, firm, uncompromising decision of character. But when we turn to the world at large, how uncommon is this very decision of character which has such power and possesses such influence! Doubting they live, doubting they hear our sermons, doubting they come to our means of grace, doubting they pass through the course of this world, and doubting, hesitating, lingering, undecided, too often they lay down their lives, and leave this world for another! Dear brethren, for your own comfort's sake, for your own happiness' sake, for your own usefulness' sake in this world, if ever you would know the joy and peace of the gospel, if ever you would be useful in your day and generation, and have influence on the minds of men, cultivate this decision of character. Very beautiful is that allegory in which John Bunyan describes what happened to his pilgrim, when the interpreter took him up to the door of an elegant and well-furnished palace, within which were men and women taking their ease and in the enjoyment of all happiness; and at the door of the palace, and all round the entrance of it, there stood a body of armed men to withstand every one who would enter. Many come up to the palace; they dare not go forward; they fear the conflict; they shrink from the attempt. At last one bold man is described as coming up to the gate, saying to the person who had charge of the palace, "Set down my name, Sir," and, putting a helmet on his head, and a sword in his hand, forcing his way through the armed men, when he hears a pleasant voice saying—

"Come in, come in ;
Eternal glory thou shalt win."

There was Christian decision. That man is a model, a pattern, an example, to every one who would be a faithful soldier of Christ, laying hold on eternal life, fighting a good fight, warring a good warfare—to choose boldly and act decidedly —to go straight forward, not fearing any opposition that he may have to meet with. II. Turn we next to THE CHOICE that Mary made. She chose "the good part." Now, what is it that our Lord Jesus Christ here calls the "good part"? Mary had not chosen the riches of this world; she had not chosen the honour, or the rank, or the learning of this world: she had chosen none of those things that the world commonly thinks good. She sat at Jesus' feet; she heard the words of Jesus ; she drank in the instruction that the Lord Jesus Christ is ever ready to give to those who listen. Because she did this—because she so gave evidence of the state of her heart—the Lord says of her here, "She hath chosen the good part." That "good part" was the good of her everlasting soul; a knowledge of God, as revealed in the face of Jesus Christ. How many things, my brethren, are called "good" that do not deserve the name! How many things are said to be for man's good, and yet how little do they avail! How little comfort they can give him! and how short a time he is able to enjoy them! How many things are called "good" that will not last! They will not wear. Who that has eyes to see, who that has mind to observe, can fail to know, that what the world calls good does not give perfect happiness? Do those that have the most of them really enjoy what they possess? Like the two boys, Passion and Patience, spoken of in "The Pilgrim's Progress," so are the children of this world and the children of God. Passion must needs have his best things now; he has them, and lavishes them away. Patience waits for his best things, and when he has them keeps them. So the children of God may "endure hardness" for a season; they may seem to fail to prosper for a time; but they look forward, they wait, they know that their good things are yet to come, and that when their good things come, they shall not be taken away from them. III. Pass on, finally, to THE CHARACTER OUR LORD GIVES TO THE PORTION THAT MARY CHOSE. He says it is "that good part which shall not be taken away from her." That favour of God which Mary sought, that peace of God which Mary longed for, that indwelling of the Holy Ghost which Mary craved, that spiritual wisdom after which Mary hungered and thirsted—all these abide for ever; he that has them shall never lose them; they are riches and treasures that shall never fade. In the time of health they are a man's best companions; in the time of sickness they "make all his bed." And now, in concluding, I would ask you all to take heed to make a right choice. And put not off that choice to a future day. Shall I not call on all the young persons that I see here in such numbers, to follow the example of her whose conduct we have this day been considering—to choose that good part which shall not be taken from them? I call upon you, as knowing that I may not meet you all face to face in this church again, to seek that peace with God that she sought after—that favour of God for which she longed. (*Bishop Ryle.*) *One thing is needful:*—What we want to bring about in ourselves is the due balance and equipoise between the principle of faith and the principle of action, so to pass through things temporal that we finally lose not the things eternal; to be in such a way convinced that but *one* thing is needful as not to destroy all stimulus and interest for the *many* things in which we find ourselves of necessity involved. First, then, it must be observed that the inward harmony of soul which is proposed must not be sought by the means of partitioning off the one province from the other, and fixing limits between them, by concluding a peace between the world and God, and giving part of our day to one, and part to the other. What we want, then, is a piety that shall be energetic and efficacious through our whole life, through every act we do, every word we speak, every breath we draw. We should not distinguish our day into one part given to God, and the rest to ourselves, but it should be all of one colour and texture. The one thing needful which we want to secure is a penetrating and all-powerful motive, universal in its extent to apply to our every act, minute, special, practical, to ensure its being brought out into our conduct, not lodged as a dormant creed in our understanding. We should not have *any* worldly employments, for our whole life should be a religious act. This is the inward and outward harmony which constitutes a sound being, when all our movements flow naturally from one central governing thought. Such a character is not a compound of two tendencies ill at ease in one another's neighbourhood, and subsisting by a forced compromise, but a uniform whole in which one pure aim informs each separate impulse. Life is then not a state of rest or equilibrium produced by opposite forces, but a sustained motion towards a fixed point. This habitual reference of everything we do to a single ruling motive is absolutely necessary for anything like consistency of action and of character. See the strength of will and steady power which a man derives from consistent adhesion to any, even the lowest purpose. Even obstinacy, which is mere perseverance without a purpose, and is more often mischievous than useful, has something about it respectable. Much more does the steady persevering pursuit of an object of importance, whatever it be, command the esteem of men at large. When the "various talents" are united with the "single mind," they give their possessors a moral weight and mastery which is instantly recognized, and to which all around pay a willing homage. (*M. Pattison.*) *On unity of effort in the service of God:*—We will, therefore, in this chapter offer some remarks on the principle of spiritual policy which we should adopt, if we desire successfully to meet that discouragement which results from distraction of mind. The principle is thus given us by our blessed Lord—"One thing is needful." Let there be one idea at the foundation of your spiritual character, round which that character forms itself: let one single principle be the foundation of all your obedience to God's commandments. You will never succeed while you are paying equal attention at one and the same time to every department of the Divine law. Again, it is the law of the natural characters of all of us that one particular feature or class of features stands out prominently, and gives its complexion to the whole character. We may be quite sure that our spiritual characters will form themselves in the same way. They will have a pervading colour, they will manifest a particular leaning, whether we wish it or not. Our minds are so constituted that each feature of them cannot be equally developed. Nor, indeed, is it consistent with God's design in regard to His Church that it should be so. But again, and this has a most important bearing on the question at issue—all growth proceeds upon the principle which we are recommending. Natural growth means the gathering together of particles of matter round a single nucleus, which nucleus appropriates and assimilates those particles. If we take a small fragment of the blossom of a flower, and examine it with a powerful microscope, we shall see that it consists of a series of colour-cells, ranged in perfect order (like the cells in a honeycomb, or the stones in a tessellated pavement), which contain the pigment of the flower. Originally there was but one single cell, containing the vital principle of the whole flower ; but as the germ was fed by the dews and rains of heaven, and by the moisture of the earth, it gathered to itself particles from the elements which surrounded it, and gradually formed a neighbour cell, and then another, and another, until the whole resulted at length in this magnificent mosaic of cells, so far superior to any pavement which King Solomon had in his palace, or even in his temple. Well, spiritual growth proceeds by the same rule as natural ; it is for the most part a development out of one sentiment, an accretion round the nucleus of one idea. It is our part to watch this law of our minds, and to endeavour by prayer and forethought, and wise effort, to turn it to account. Now, practically, how is this to be? 1. There can be no doubt that the besetting sin, or fault, if any one is prominent, should be the first quarter in which the Christian should turn his thoughts, and prayers, and efforts. His particular shortcoming is an indication by God in what part of the field his work lies. At all events it is certain that " the one thing needful" for those beset with any moral and spiritual infirmity, is to rid themselves of it, rooting it, as far as possible, out of their hearts, with loathing and abhorrence. Until this is achieved, there is no business for them of equal importance. 2. But supposing that, on a survey of our character, it should not appear that any one fault or sin has a greater prominence than another (though this will rarely be the case), we may then set ourselves to choose, according to our own inclinations, some broad Scriptural principle which may be made the foundation of our own spiritual character. Or we might attempt to make poverty of spirit—the subject of the first Beatitude—the leading thought of our religious character. We might set ourselves to cultivate this grace as the " one thing needful." Having chosen our principle, whatever it be, it will be part of the business of every morning to anticipate the occasions on which it may be brought into exercise. It will be well to say, in conclusion, one word of advice as to the sort of principle which it is desirable to choose for the purpose of building upon it a holy life. Choose not, then, too narrow a principle—by which I mean one which gives no scope for exercise or trial, except on rare occasions. Suppose, for example, that submission to the will of God under the loss of friends were chosen as the principle. There is not here room enough for every-day practice. Bereavement, much as it behoves us to conduct ourselves well when it does come, is of rare occurrence. On the other hand, too broad a principle will destroy the unity of aim and endeavour, which is recommended. Too broad a principle is in fact more principles than one, and so defeats the end. Finally, choose a principle to which your mind is naturally drawn when in a right frame. We are all attracted by different lines of thought in religion, and no man has a right to impose upon his neighbour his own line. (*Dean Goulburn.*)   *Love at home:*—I. LOVE AT LEISURE.   When the evening comes on, and all the members of the family are around the fireside, then love rests and communes, forgetting all care, happily at home, oblivious of the outside world, and of time itself. Like Mary—1. We would feel ourselves quite at home with Jesus our Lord. 2. We would be free from worldly care—leaving all with Jesus. 3. We would even be free from the care of His service, the battle for His kingdom, and the burden of the souls committed to our charge. 4. We would sweetly enjoy the happy leisure which He provides for us, as we muse upon the rest-giving themes which He reveals so clearly, and makes so true to us. (1) His work for us, finished, accepted, abidingly effectual, and perpetually overflowing with priceless blessings. (2) His great gifts received, which are greater than those to come. (3) All other needful and promised benedictions of grace, sure to come in due season (Rom. viii. 32). (4) All our future, for time and for eternity, safe in His dear hands. Let us, without fear, enjoy leisure with Jesus—leisure, but not laziness—leisure to love, to learn, te commune, to copy. Leisure in a home where others are cumbered (see verses 40–42). Leisure to sit, and to sit in the most delightful of all places. II. LOVE IN LOWLINESS. "At Jesus' feet." In this let each one copy Mary. Let me be, not a busy housewife and manager, which any one may be, and yet be graceless; but—1. A penitent, which is an acknowledgment of my unworthiness. 2. A disciple, which is a confession of my ignorance. 3. A receiver, which is an admission of my emptiness. III. LOVE LISTENING—"And heard His word." She could not have heard if she had not been at leisure to sit, nor if she had not been lowly, and chosen to sit at His feet. Be it ours to hear that love-word which says, "Hearken, O daughter, and consider" (Psa. xlv. 10). Listening to what Jesus says in His Word, in His creation, in His providence, and by His Spirit in our soul. Listening to Himself. Studying Him, reading His very heart. Listening, and not obtruding our own self-formed thoughts, notions, reasonings, questionings, desires, and prejudices. Listening, and forgetting the observations and unbeliefs of others. Listening, and bidding all cares lie still, that they may no more disturb the reverent silence of the heart. How sweet! How instructive! How truly "the good part"! IV. LOVE IN POSSESSION. 1. In full enjoyment. 2. In perfect satisfaction. 3. In full assurance. (*C. H. Spurgeon.*) *Reflection and action*:—This was a scene at Bethany. It precedes the other accounts. If I mistake not, it is the earliest notice of this remarkable household. 1. Let us look at the scene itself. Martha, full of gladness and alacrity, and such affection as she had, was serving Him. It was household service. I do not suppose that she was without any sensibility of His loftiness and nobility; but her way was not in the interchange of soul qualities with soul qualities. She was practical. She was entirely domestic. She took a worldly view of this adorable personage, and felt as though the best thing she could do was to minister to His comfort. As she was thus, with anxious household cares, ministering, Mary was sitting still, at the feet of Jesus. Martha, seeing her sitting there, had not the least idea that anything was going on. Mary's feet were still, her hands were quiet. She neither sewed nor knit. She wove no flowers into wreaths or bouquets. She said nothing. She was not doing anything. There are a great many persons who do not suppose that there is anything going on unless there is some buzz and bustle, unless there is some outward show and development. Of the method of the soul they have no insight. Their whole brain-life expends itself in a rushing forth of intense activity. They have no idea of the lake that is hid far up in the mountain recesses, on which the day shines and the night sends down its starry beauty, and which does nothing except reflect the heavens. Ask the mill-brook that comes tearing down the gorge, and wipes the sweat off at every mill-wheel, what it is doing, and what it is, and it says, "I am working, working, working; I am an enterprising brook; but that lazy old lake up there in the mountain-top never did anything in the world for its living." And yet that lake in the midst of the mountain has some beauty and some merits to the poet. Now, Martha, in her soul, loved her sister, but she did not know much of that higher experience of the soul to which her sister had attained; and, instead of saying, "Mary, why do not you come and help me?" she said, "Master, see, she doesn't help me; tell her to come and help me." Christ's reply is significant. 2. Look for a moment at these two women as types of human society. Martha ticked and kept time; she talked all the while; she was a very useful person. Hers was a valuable character. There is room in all the world for such persons. On the other side, Mary was reflective. She was full of thought, and of various thought. Above all things she was hungry for the food of thought. Doubtless, in her own quiet way, she fulfilled the daily duties of practical life: as a sleep-walker, or as one sunk in a reverie, with all the absent-minded mysteries that fall to the lot of such persons. And when Christ came her thought was, "Now I shall receive; and her heart lay open in His presence as a flower to the dew, or as the grass to the rain, that she might live and grow by the feeding of her soul. 3. The perfect person is one who combines, in suitable degrees, both of these elements. There is the workshop of life below, and there are the serene hills, the crystal domes above. They have their hours for meditation; they also have their hours for labour and for communion with men. 4. But there are very few perfect people in the world; and the lineage of those who are born with a high moral endowment joined to an active temperament seems almost at times to have run out. Those, then, that are all activity, and those that are recluse, silent and meditative, ought to have enough in themselves to form an easy intercommunication, so that they shall accept one another. 5. The Church should also have precisely the same thing. No Church has any perfect members in it, and too often Church people associate themselves together, the intensely zealous with the intensely zealous, and the extremely intelligent with the extremely intelligent; but we are all of us so imperfect that we need somebody else here and there, for it takes about ten or fifteen persons to make one, and fill up all his deficiencies. "Receive ye one another." The imaginative are to take the practical, the practical are to take the imaginative, and both are to rejoice in the rich-souled silence of others; and let those who are given to a life of meditation look with toleration upon persons who have the art of developing and giving out into life. God receives them all and uses them all. 6. Let those who mourn because they have been set apart to be thinkers, and to dwell in the solitude of their own genius, remember that perhaps they are more active than they know. The largest and best work that ever is done in this world is done in silence. Go into the meadows over which birds sing, and out of which grass and all flowers spring. The silent attraction of all those roots is a greater power than all the steam engines on the face of the earth. Or go into the forests. There is no measure of gigantic power which is comparable with the strength which is developed in their internal tubes. It is not measurable by all the machinery on earth. And yet it is silent. Activity? Yes. There is the buzzing factory. It has turned out its thousands of yards of cotton every day, and is a very noble thing, doing a great deal of good. But yonder, off against the rocky shore, on the dangerous reef, stands the lighthouse. It neither spins nor turns a single wheel. All day long the lazy thing suns itself; and all night long it simply stands shining. But far off, beyond its own vision, are ships that come toward the shore; and they see its light; and they know where the rock, the shoal, and the danger are; and they pass on and make their port in safety. It has no trumpet, it does not speak, it sends out nothing but simply a light; and 10,000 ships are blessed by it. (*H. W. Beecher.*)　　*Thought and activity :*—We read in the biography of old Dr. Lyman Beecher that the young lady he married, Roxana Foote, had thought herself converted at five or six years of age, though far from satisfying the exactions of an apostle of absolute election ; but at least she was the Mary among the three granddaughters of General Andrew Ward, who used to say that when the girls first came down of a morning, Roxana would put some thoughtful question, suggestive of study and meditation, while Harriet's voice could be heard briskly calling out, "Here! take the broom; sweep up; make a fire, make haste." Harriet's namesake, Dr Beecher's celebrated daughter (Mrs. Stowe) is fond, like other American lady-novelists, of referring to the Bethany sisters, as often as not in a vein of humour; where, for instance, Mrs. Twitchel characterises her indispensable "help," Cerinthy Ann, as "one of the most master-hands to turn off work. Deacon was a-saying, if ever she was called she'd be a Martha, and not a Mary." (*F. Jacox.*)

MARY TO JESUS IN THE HOUSE.

"O Master! when Thou comest, it is always
A Sabbath in the house. I cannot work :
I must sit at Thy feet, must see Thee, hear Thee!
I have a feeble, wayward, doubting heart,
Incapable of endurance or great thoughts,
Striving for something that it cannot reach,
Baffled and disappointed, wounded, hungry;
And only when I hear Thee am I happy,
And only when I see Thee am at peace.
Stronger than I, and wiser, and far better
In every manner is my sister Martha.
Thou seest how well she orders everything
To make Thee welcome; how she comes and goes,
Careful and cumber'd ever with much serving,

While I but welcome Thee with foolish words !
When'er Thou speakest to me I am happy;
When Thou art silent I am satisfied.
Thy presence is enough, I ask no more.
Only to be with Thee, only to see Thee
Sufficeth me.   My heart is then at rest."   (*Longfellow.*)

CUMBERED ABOUT MUCH SERVING.

Christ never asks of us such busy labour
    As leaves no time for resting at His feet;
The waiting attitude of expectation
    He ofttimes counts a service most complete.

He sometimes wants our ear—our rapt attention,
    That He some sweetest secret may impart;
'Tis always in the time of deepest silence
    That heart finds deepest fellowship with heart.

And yet He does love service, where 'tis given
    By grateful love that clothes itself in deed ;
But work that's done beneath the scourge of duty,
    Be sure to such He gives but little heed.

Then seek to please Him, whatsoe'er He bids thee,
    Whether to do—to suffer—to lie still ;
'Twill matter little by what path He leads thee,
    If in it all thou seek'st to do His will.   (*Anon.*)

Activity and rest :—I noticed once that in the ocean there was a beauty and power
quite peculiar to its rest, as well as its motion.   Once in a while there would come
a day when the waters would leap into white foam in their strife with the great
calm cliffs; and then a day when the blue waters would melt into the sky full of
innocent dimples, which made you feel as if the tides were laughing with content.
But this was what I noticed besides : that in the clear waters rested the full sun,
while in the unresting waters you saw only broken lights.   There was shining on
the edges, but not in the deeps ; a stormful grandeur, but no mirror of the quiet
heavens.   It was in a summer vacation, when I was glad enough to find reasons
for lounging all day long on the sweetest bit of land I ever found west of the
heathery Ramald's Moor, where I wandered a quarter of a century ago.   And so I
said to myself, Beautiful is the activity that works for good, and beautiful the
stillness that waits for good.   Blessed the self-sacrifice of the one and the self-
abnegation of the other.   Martha gives up everything that she may be hospitable,
and is cumbered with much serving; and Mary sits still.   But still the voice of the
Lord tells her, and tells us through her, that she hath chosen the good part.   I
would like, then, if I could do it, to include both in their turn in the sum of my
life.   We cannot help believing in work ; but there are days when we should be
glad because we are quiet.   When both the strong motion and the strong
emotion of existence should be done with for a while, and all things be as naught
to us except the pure stillness, which, like the still sea I saw, only drank in the
sun and glassed his clear shining through its whole heart. (*R. Collyer.*)   *Variety
in God's works :*—There is astonishing variety in God's works.   What different
creatures, plants, and other objects there are in the world ; and probably not two
of them precisely alike.   " One star differed from another star in glory."   How
the forms and faces of human beings and various animals vary in appearance and
expression.   And, it is said, no two blades of grass, nor leaves of any tree, are
exactly similar.   Then, as to dispositions, some creatures are bold and fierce,
others are fearful and timid ; and even in any single family we find diverse tempers
and inclinations.   In a well-appointed army and navy there are many regiments,
ranks, services, ships, &c., and probably all are necessary in order to greatest
efficiency.   In a large house, or place of business, or manufactory, there are
individuals filling different posts, who have separate duties.   In a flower garden,
or nosegay of any pretensions, we find flowers of various forms, colours, and perfumes.   In the grand and gorgeous sunrise or sunset, the most lovely tints,

wonderfully blended, produce pictures, in comparison with which man's most admired paintings appear mean and paltry. Thus in God's Church and family, for beauty, utility, and perfection, we find the greatest conceivable variety. Take the characters referred to in our lesson. Martha was a good woman, diligent in business, a careful housewife, an excellent manager, and we suppose a model mistress of a family, only she was probably too anxious, and perhaps rather bad tempered; Mary was quiet, devout, thoughtful, one who might be in danger of spending too much time in her closet, or about good things, as her sister would spend too little. Could they have been blended, Romans vii. 11 would have been perfectly observed. Lazarus was probably an amiable, easy man, who would lovingly and simply believe in Jesus. But Thomas was a doubter. He was thoughtful, cautious; one who would "count the cost" before he would commit himself to any enterprise, and who would not take anything for granted, but would require irrefragable evidence for his faith. (*H. R. Burton.*) **Cumbered about much serving.**—*Domestic cares:*—I. THE TRIAL OF NON-APPRECIATION. This is what made Martha so mad with Mary. The younger sister had no estimate of her older sister's fatigues. As now, men bothered with the anxieties of the store, and office, and shop, or coming from the stock exchange, they say when they get home: "Oh, you ought to be over in Wall-street in these days; you ought to be in our factory a little while; you ought to have to manage eight, or ten, or twenty subordinates, and then you would know what trouble and anxiety are." Oh, sir! the wife and the mother has to conduct at the same time a university, a clothing establishment, a restaurant, a laundry, a library, while she is health officer, police, and president of her realm! She must do a thousand things, and do them well, in order to keep things going smoothly; and so her brain and her nerves are taxed to the utmost. If, under all this wear and tear of life, Martha makes an impatient rush upon the library or drawing-room, be patient, be lenient. O! women, though I may fail to stir up an appreciation in the souls of others in regard to your household toils, let me assure you, from the kindliness with which Jesus Christ met Martha, that He appreciates all your work from garret to cellar; and that the God of Deborah, and Hannah, and Abigail, and grandmother Lois, and Elizabeth Fry, and Hannah More, is the God of the housekeeper. II. THE TRIAL OF SEVERE ECONOMY. This is what kills tens of thousands of women—attempting to make five dollars do the work of seven. How the bills come in! The woman is the banker of the household; she is the president, the cashier, the teller, the discount clerk; and there is a panic every few weeks! This thirty years' war against high prices, this perpetual study of economies, this life-long attempt to keep the out-goes less than the income, exhausts millions of housekeepers. O! my sister, this is a part of the Divine discipline. If it were best for you, all you would have to do would be to open the front windows and the ravens would fly in with food; and after you had baked fifty times from the barrel in the pantry, the barrel, like the one of Zarepath, would be full; and the shoes of the children would last as long as the shoes of the Israelites in the wilderness—forty years. Beside that, this is going to make heaven the more attractive in the contrast. III. SICKNESS AND TROUBLE. IV. OVER-RESPONSIBILITY. (*Dr. Talmage.*) *Over-carefulness:*—Did you never see persons that are kind-hearted and good-natured but that are continually anxious? Not that they are peevish; not that they are cross; but they are filled with anxiety. Did you never see a boiler that carried just enough steam, so that there was no sound in the machinery? And have you never seen a boiler that carried a little too much steam, so that it hissed at every rivet, making a disagreeable sound day and night? There are persons that carry a little more steam than they can work, and that sing and hiss all the time; and Martha was one of those. Where this anxiety is brought suddenly in collision with those that are associated with us, and expresses itself with sharpness, it is called chiding if you are charitable, and fretfulness or peevishness if you are a little cross yourself. And so it seemed to be in Martha's case. When Christ came, nothing must be left undone that could be done for Him. Every room must be set aright. (*H. W. Beecher.*) *Martha's interference:*—Is Martha a little offended, and a little jealous? Has she often tried to reclaim her musing sister from what she thinks vagrancy of mind, and now considers that she has an opportunity to get her effectively reproved? How tyrannous may we become by the excess of our temperament, even towards those whom we best love! If Martha has her special opportunity of serving, and wisely employs all her active shrewdness, may not Mary have her special opportunity of listening, and wisely employ her meditative intelligence? Why should Mary be Martha any more than Martha Mary? "Lord, bid her that she come and sit at Thy feet with me, and hear Thy word." Would not such an invocation have been as proper a one as Martha's? They who are careful about many things must take care of this too: that, encumbering themselves, they be not burdensome to others also. Our excellency may become the occasion of our fault. We may be fussy because kindly busy, when only by being busy, but not fussy, can we provide a comfortable meal, as well as a sufficient one. (*T. T. Lynch.*) *Worry:*—When the English lost the town of Calais in the reign of Queen Mary, she is said to have declared that at her death the name Calais would be found engraved upon her heart. The loss of the French town was the sorrow of her life. Most of us, my friends, have some name or another which sorrow has graven on our hearts, and printed in deep lines upon our faces. It may be a disappointment which will last all our lives; it may be the remorseful memory of a fault which cannot be atoned for here, or the name of one long dead and gone. It is not of these great sorrows of which I would speak now. Do you know what makes the stones on the sea beach so smooth and polished? They were rough fragments of rock once, and they have been smoothed and shaped into what they are, not by a furious tempest, when the waves rose mountains high, but by the constant action of the tide day after day, year after year. The deep furrows and channels in the face of the cliff were not formed by a flood, but by the continuous falling of a tiny stream of water. So, my brother, those grey hairs of yours, and those lines and furrows in your face, were not caused by some terrible, crushing calamity, but by the daily action of little troubles and anxieties which we call worry. These worries are some of God's teachers in the great school of this world. Properly met, they help on our education; if misused, they simply lead us into sin. How then shall we meet worry? First, I would say, don't meet it half-way. Don't torture yourselves with the thought of what may happen; don't neglect the sunshine of to-day, because it may rain to-morrow. It is simply want of faith in God to be always fearing what has not, and never may, come to pass. Excellent was the advice of the wise American President, "Never to cross the great and big muddy creek till you come to it." When the worry does come, try to look beyond it, try to see the land over the troubled waves, and to find the dawn after the dark night. There is a bright side to every trouble, if we would but look for it. There are some who love to shut themselves up in a dark room, as it were, with their troubles, and they will tell you that there is no sunshine outside. My advice to you is, keep out in the sunshine as much as you can, and the troubles will not seem half so dark or threatening. 2. Next, think less of self, and more of others. When things come to vex and annoy you, turn your thoughts to the troubles of others. Go and look at the real sorrows of your neighbour, and in helping them you will find your own burden easier to carry. 3. Lastly, yet above all, pray about your worry. Take it to Jesus Christ, tell Him all about it in plain language, ask Him to help you, so that your trouble may not drive you into sin, but lead you to your Saviour. Take up your cross, my brothers, you who are careful and troubled about many things. Bear with the crooked tempers, and the sharp tongues, and the ill-kept homes, and the narrow means, and the thousand worries of life, and these crosses shall one day bud and blossom for you into palms of victory. (*H. J. Wilmot Buxton, M.A.*) **One thing is needful.**—*The essential thing :*—While the "one thing needful" may have had reference to the immediate matter of Martha's anxiety, it is also applicable to her own spiritual need, she being deficient in that element of inward life out of which all orderly methods and untroubled activities proceed. Thus, both fact and symbol lead us from those "many things" about which Martha was too careful, to the contrast of that "good part" which was Mary's choice. I. ONE THING IS NEEDFUL AS A MOTIVE POWER. Love for God, for Christ, for all that is good. Only this can keep the appetites in their place. II. ONE THING IS NEEDFUL AS A PRINCIPLE OF ACTION. The love of goodness for its own sake. III. ONE THING IS NEEDFUL AS AN ELEMENT OF LIFE. The soul's communion with God. (*E. H. Chapin, D.D.*) *Mary's better choice :*—I. THE CHARACTERISTIC OF THIS CHOICE— "Shall not be taken away." Earthly goods are all transitory; but this is abiding. II. THE COMMENDATION OF THE CHOICE. 1. Good in itself—its effect. 2. Good in its substance—Jesus. 3. Best in its association. Christ is more than the property; He is the joint possessor. "Partakers with Christ. III. THE CHANNEL FOR ALL THIS COMFORT. "Chosen." 1. No violence done to our freedom. 2. Sweet consciousness that we *gave* ourselves to Christ. (*S. H. Tyng, D.D.*) *The one* *thing needful:*—However far apart the streams may appear to flow, there is in the life one great ocean where they all meet, and in which they are all absorbed. Now, the Saviour, who was so entirely consecrated to one great object, would teach us an important truth in these words, and it is this—That it is a mistake to divide one-self among many cares and troubles. The great secret of life is to seize upon *one* thing, which will determine all else, and in the light of the context this one thing seems to be—a personal interest in Jesus Christ." I. THIS IS THE ONE THING NEEDFUL TO GIVE LIFE A WORTHY AIM. If we would start aright, we must start at the feet of the Great Master. Here alone can we find reliable direction how to live. This is the way: walk ye in it. But who will set our feet upon that path? Jesus will. It is Jesus alone that teaches us to live so as to attain the object which God Himself had in creating. II. THIS IS THE ONE THING NEEDFUL TO GIVE LIFE ANY REAL VALUE. The alchemists of old, who paved the way for the modern science of chemistry, were, it is said, searching for a substance which contained the original principle of all matter, and had the power of dissolving all things into their primitive elements. Here was the one thing needful to give value to all material objects brought into contact with it. We do not suppose this was ever discovered by them, or that it ever existed save in their wild imagination; but there are many present, I trust, who have found in effect a spiritual equivalent—that one thing needful which gives value to all brought into contact with it, that philosopher's stone which turns everything into glittering gold in the eye of Heaven itself. Even all the life becomes consecrated—the ruling of nations, the regulating of households, obeying monarchs, obeying parents, obeying masters, even what often seems trivial, eating and drinking. This one thing needful can set value to all. III. THIS IS THE ONE THING NEEDFUL TO SUPPORT US UNDER THE TRIALS OF LIFE. We may glide easily, in virtue of a slight external impulse, along the levels of our life, we may go down the slopes ourselves, but if we mean to climb triumphantly over the rugged hills, we must link ourselves to a mighty Saviour. IV. THE ONE THING NEEDFUL TO FACE THE GREAT HEREAFTER. (*T. Nicholson.*) *True religion exemplified in Mary:*—There can be no doubt as to what our Lord means by the " one thing " and the " good part " He here commends. They are both of them true religion. It does more, observe, than praise this blessed thing; it partially describes it. I. We will begin with the latter of these two questions, and look at this Scripture as DISTINGUISHING BETWEEN CHRISTIAN AND CHRISTIAN. Both these sisters were undoubtedly sincere followers of our Lord; they were both converted, holy women. But yet we see here a great difference between them, and such a difference as natural disposition will not of itself account for. The main source of it lay elsewhere—one was high in spiritual attainments, the other was a learner in the same school, but as yet had learnt much less in it. We may discover in Mary two marks of a highly spiritual mind. 1. Notice, first, her composure; her composure, I mean, as to worldly things. 2. Observe in Mary another thing—an earnest desire of spiritual instruction. " She sat," we read, " at Jesus' feet." But love for Him, we say, might have placed her there. She wished, perhaps, to be near her holy Guest and enjoy His society. " No," says the evangelist, " she sat at His feet, and heard His word." Warm-hearted as she was, she forgets or half forgets the friend in the teacher. Martha, on the contrary, had no such feelings. She appears to have turned aside altogether from our Lord's instructions at this time, and to have done so almost without regret. She let the stream of heavenly wisdom flow by her untasted and unheeded. And indifference like hers is by no means uncommon now. There are some really Christian persons, who manifest a frame of mind exactly similar to it. They know very little of Divine things, and seem almost indifferent whether or not they ever know more. It is mournful that a dying sinner should be a thoughtful, inquiring man among his goods and merchandise, his sheep and cattle, shrewd and penetrating, taking nothing on trust, and sifting to the bottom everything that concerns him; and yet the same man put his mind to sleep as he opens his Bible or enters a church. Worldliness of heart only can account for this. " Much serving " leads us away from our great Teacher. Our low degree of knowledge is the result of a low degree of piety. We are not growing in grace, therefore we are not growing, nor desiring to grow, " in the knowledge of our Lord and Saviour Jesus Christ." Knowledge and grace are as closely connected as the day and the light. If any of you should think I have laid too much stress on the two things I have noticed in Mary, and made too much of them, mark this—they are the exact points in which at this moment she most visibly resembled our Lord. He was quiet in a house of bustle; so was Mary.

He made much of heavenly wisdom, for He began to teach it as soon as He entered that house; she made much of it also, for she sat down at His feet to learn it. You know what follows—the more we resemble Christ, the holier we are; the more like Him, the nearer we are to Him. II. We are now to view this Scripture as DISTINGUISHING BETWEEN THE REAL CHRISTIAN AND ALL OTHER MEN. 1. It tells us that, with the real Christian, religion is a needful thing; it is known and felt to be such. The question is, be it what it may, has it this feature of sound piety—do you feel it to be absolutely necessary for you? Do you find that you need it at all times and in all things? Is it in your estimation of supreme importance? 2. But further—our Lord tells us here that true religion is something that is chosen; it is a matter of deliberate and serious choice. The religion that saves the soul, lays hold of the soul before it saves it, and the whole soul. It commends itself to the judgment, it wins the affections, it captivates the heart. It is first seen to be a necessary thing, then felt to be a blessed thing, then determined on as a thing which above all others shall be chosen, and followed, and held fast. (*C. Bradley, M.A.*) *The choice of Mary :*—I. Our Saviour in the text speaks of true religion as ONE THING; and He appears thus to represent it in contradistinction to those many things which harassed and distracted the mind of Martha. True religion is something more than bearing the name of Christ, making an outward profession of religion, using with diligence the means of grace, supporting an external decency of conduct, or being kind and charitable to the poor. What is it? It is a conformity of heart and life to the will of God as made known to us in holy Scripture; or it is a compliance with it both outwardly in our bodies, and inwardly in our souls. And in this view it is fitly represented as one thing. This one thing, however, consists of many parts—repentance, faith, holiness, &c. II. Our Saviour in the text represents true religion as a NEEDFUL THING. 1. What He means is, that it is so much more needful than other things, that our chief care and attention should be directed to it; and that nothing else ought to be allowed for a moment to come in competition with it. Other things pertain to the body, and to the life that now is; whereas religion regards the soul, and the life which is to come. And as the soul is more precious than the body, and eternity more important than time, so is true religion infinitely more needful for us than every earthly blessing whatsoever. 2. Nor is true religion a blessing we need only occasionally. We want it at all times and in all circumstances, whether we are in prosperity or adversity, in sickness or in health, in trouble or in joy. 3. Nor will the time ever come when true religion will not be needful for us. It will be as needful for us in death as it is in life, as necessary in eternity as it is in time. It will then indeed, if possible, be unspeakably more needful for us than ever. Death and eternity will stamp on it a value and an importance of which we can now form but a faint conception. III. It is still more. Our Saviour here represents it as a GOOD PART OR PORTION. 1. It insures a supply of our temporal wants. St. Paul tells us that it "is profitable unto all things, having promise of the life that now is," no less than "of that which is to come." 2. True religion enriches us. It puts us in possession, not indeed of the unrighteous mammon, but of the true riches. While those who have no religion are represented in Scripture as "poor, and blind, and naked, and ready to perish," those who have it are described as "possessing all things." It is expressly said to them, "All things are yours, and ye are Christ's." 3. True religion contributes in a most essential manner to our contentment and happiness. IV. True religion is A LASTING PORTION. It is a "good part, which shall not be taken away from us." This cannot be said of any worldly portion. Our earthly possessions are only for a time, and that often a very short time. (*D. Rees.*) *The one thing needful :*—The mere posture of sitting down and listening to the Saviour's word was nothing in itself: it was that which it indicated. It indicated, in Mary's case, a readiness to believe what the Saviour taught, to accept and to obey—nay, to delight in, the precepts which fell from His lips. And this is the one thing needful. He that hath it hath the spirit of grace and life. To sit at Jesus' feet implies submission, faith, discipleship, service, love. We must not learn of Christ like unwilling truant boys, who go to school and must needs have learning flogged into them; we must be eager to learn; we must open our mouth wide that He may fill it, like the thirsty earth when it needs the shower, our soul must break for the longing it hath towards His commandments at all times. We must rejoice in His statutes more than gold, yea, than much fine gold. When we are moved by this spirit, we have found the one thing needful. I. To begin, then, here is a word of CONSIDERATION, which, as I have already said, is interjected into the middle of our

Lord's brief word to Martha. Shall I say a word that should discourage your industry? I will not ; but, but is there nothing else ?—is this life all? Is making money everything ? II. Our text speaks of NECESSITY—one thing is a necessity. If this be proven, it overrides all other considerations. We are nearly right when we say proverbially, " Necessity has no law." If a man steal, and it be found that he was dying of hunger, he is always half forgiven, and charity has been known to excuse him altogether. Necessity has been frequently accepted as a good excuse for what else might not have been tolerated ; and when a thing is right, and necessity backs it, then indeed the right becomes imperative, and pushes to the front to force its way. Necessity, like hunger, breaks through stone walls. The text claims for sitting at Jesus' feet that it is the first and only necessity. Now, I see all around me a crowd of things alluring and fascinating. Pleasure calls to me ; I hear her syren song—but I reply, " I cannot regard thee, for necessity presses upon me to hearken to another voice." Philosophy and learning charm me : fain would I yield my heart to them ; but, while I am yet unsaved, the one thing needful demands my first care, and wisdom bids me give it. Not that we love human learning less, but eternal wisdom more. Pearls? Yes. Emeralds ? Yes ; but bread in God's name —bread at once, when I am starving in the desert ! What is the use of ingots of gold, or bars of silver, or caskets of jewels, when food is wanting ? If one thing be needful, it devours, like Aaron's rod, all the matters which are merely pleasurable. All the fascinating things on earth may go, but needful things we must have. If you are wise, you will evermore prefer the necessary to the dazzling. About us are a thousand things entangling. This world is very much like the pools we have heard of in India, in which grows a long grass of so clinging a character that, if a man once falls into the water, it is almost certain to be his death, for only with the utmost difficulty could he be rescued from the meshes of the deadly, weedy net, which immediately wraps itself around him. This world is even thus entangling. All the efforts of grace are needed to preserve men from being ensnared with the deceitfulness of riches and the cares of this life. The ledger demands you, the day-book wants you, the shop requires you, the warehouse bell rings for you ; the theatre invites, the ball-room calls : you must live, you say, and you must have a little enjoyment, and, consequently, you give your heart to the world. These things, I say, are very entangling ; but we must be disentangled from them, for we cannot afford to lose our souls. In order to enter heaven, it is necessary that our nature should become like the nature of Christ. By sitting at His feet, and beholding Him, we become changed into the same image from glory to glory even as by the Spirit of the Lord. Some things in this world are necessary, after a measure, but this is necessary without measure ; infinitely needful is it that you sit at Jesus' feet, needful now, needful in life ; needful in life for peace, in death for rest, and in eternity for bliss. This is needful always. Many things have their uses for youth, others come not into value till old age ; but one thing, the one thing, is needful for childhood, and needful for palsied age ; it is needful for the ruddy cheek, and the active limb, and needful upon the sick bed ; needful in the world, and in the Church, needful everywhere, and always. In the highest and most emphatic sense, " one thing is needful." III. Thus much about the necessity, the next word is CONCENTRATION ; " One thing is needful." I am glad it says " one thing," because a division of ends and objects is always weakening. A man cannot follow two things well. Our life-blood suffices not to fill two streams or three ; there is only enough water, as it were, in our life's brooklet, to turn one wheel. It is a great pity when a man fritters away his energies by being " everything by turns, and nothing long " ; trying all things, and mastering nothing. Oh, soul, it is well for thee that there is only one thing in this world that is absolutely necessary, give thy whole soul to that. If other things are necessary in a secondary place, " Seek first the kingdom of God and His righteousness, and all these shall be added unto you." One thing is needful, and this is well arranged, for we cannot follow two things. If Christ be one of them, we cannot follow another. It is an unspeakable mercy that the one thing needful is a very simple one. Little child, thou couldst not climb the mountain, but thou canst sit down at Jesus' feet ; thou canst not understand hard doctrine, but thou canst love Him. IV. The last word is IMMEDIATENESS, and there is no need that we say much upon it. One thing is a necessity, a necessity not of the future only, but of to-day. It is not written, " it shall be needful," on certain coming days, to sit at Jesus' feet ; but it is so now. Young man, one thing is necessary to you while yet young ; do not postpone it till advanced years. (C. H. Spurgeon.)　　　The one thing needful :—I. THAT THERE

MUST BE ONE PREDOMINATING INTEREST IN THE LIFE—not a multiplicity of interests, swaying the mind by turns—" Thou art careful and troubled about many things: but one thing is needful." Variety seems to you to be an essential element of happiness; and the systematizing of life, by reducing its component actions to one and the same principle, appears to exclude variety, and to involve such a repetition and recurrence of the same idea as cannot fail to be dull. Is this your view? Then let me address myself to answer it; for it admits of an answer most satisfactory and conclusive. We fully admit that, as human nature is constituted, variety is an essential element of happiness. In our present state of existence, a continual recurrence of one action, however exciting, or of one strain of thought and feeling, however interesting, could not fail of becoming tedious and wearisome. Our nature, moral and intellectual, needs change. But in what has been said we have not been advocating uniformity of occupations, whether mental or bodily, but only the pervading of all occupations, diversified as they may be, by an unity of principle. Occupations the most various may be engaged in with one leading design. Business the most trivial and commonplace may be executed with a ruling aim and in a lofty spirit. Is it not evidently feasible to reduce our life from an unconnected series of movements, flowing from whatever impulse is at the time uppermost, to a system, composed, indeed, of divers parts, and exhibiting divers operations, but actuated by a common principle, and working towards a common end? And what we assert is that, without such organization, life is destitute of happiness, and destitute of dignity. Busy and bustling it may be—chequered with many incidents it may be; but it will always be agitated by an instinctive restlessness. II. THAT THIS PREDOMINATING INTEREST MUST NOT BE OF A TRANSIENT NATURE—must have reference not to time, but to eternity. " Mary hath chosen that good part, which shall not be taken away from her." Every worldly interest must one day recede. If it have no reference to eternity, it must one day be taken away. If it be an interest which we are unable to carry with us beyond the barriers of the grave, the consistent prosecution of it may indeed impart a fugitive dignity to our few brief years of existence, but will never adequately develop the energies of our moral nature, and will never confer happiness—a boon unattainable, wherever the insecurity and precarious tenure of the object of pursuit is continually recurring to the mind. What remains then, brethren, but that we should set before you the ruling principle which governs, and pervades, and communicates unity to, the various actions of the Christian's life—the one good part which, when all objects of earthly interest are to our apprehensions dwindling into their native insignificance, shall not even then be taken away from him? This ruling principle, defined according to its motive, is the constraining love of a crucified Redeemer: defined according to its aim, it is the glory of God. (*Dean Goulburn.*) *The single need:*—Christ's words imply no disapproval of active service as against a contemplative or meditative life. It is not Martha's activity that He is rebuking, but her anxiety and distraction. He who went about doing good, and who said, " My meat is to do the will of Him that sent me," was not the one to rebuke active ministry. The point of His rebuke lies in enforcing the pursuit of one thing as against many things. It may have been that the peculiar form of the expression grew out of the feast itself. Martha has provided, with much worry and care, many things to eat. To sustain life, only one thing is absolutely needful; or, as some read it, "There is need of few things, or of one." Be this as it may, the lesson is plain: the life of the soul depends on one thing; the whole energy of the soul should be concentrated upon that. Suppose a man who had never seen a great machine-shop, and who knew nothing of the power of steam or water, were set down in a great hall full of lathes and looms and circular saws, and required to set the machinery in motion: how many men he would call in! how many separate contrivances he would apply to each machine! how he would bustle about from wheel to wheel, from lathe to lathe, now heaving away at a great trip-hammer, now cutting his fingers on a circular saw, now turning round the driving-wheel of a lathe! And at this point the experienced engineer comes in, and laughs as he sees the poor man's perplexity, and says to him, "My friend, all this trouble is unnecessary; only one thing is needful"; and he slips a belt over a drum, and pulls a lever, and behold! the whole hall is in a whirl—lathes, saws, trip-hammers, all in motion, without a hand on any of them. Or, here is a schoolboy with his arithmetic before him, and a whole page of "examples" to work out: and he takes each example by itself, and tries to think his way through it; trying all sorts of experiments, applying one method to one, and another to another, and getting more confused every minute. Presently the teacher looks over his shoulder at his slate covered with a chaotic mass of figures, and glances at the boy's hot and troubled face, and says to him, " You are taking a good deal of unnecessary trouble. This is not as hard as it looks : only one thing is needful ; all these examples are illustrations of one law." And he sits down, and explains a simple principle to the lad ; and then the work becomes a delight. The boy has a clue in his hand which leads him straight through the whole labyrinth of figures. He turns from the multitude of details to the principle, and finds that the details arrange themselves, and the answer comes right every time. So that there is nothing arbitrary or unnatural, or even unfamiliar, in the gospel's summing itself in one thing, and concentrating men's attention on that. When a man buys an estate of so many acres, he does not ask for separate titles for the woodland and the pasture and the streams and the mines. He wants one title to the estate. He pays so much ; and then, if there is gold or coal or an oil-well on the estate, that is his. The purchase of the estate gives him command of all its possibilities, whether apparent or latent. And so, when God would lead a man to spiritual power and riches by the most direct road, He leads him to Christ. He says : " Receive Him implicitly. Only that one thing is needful ; the rest follows, the rest is contained in Him, all things are in Him—all power, all grace, all wisdom, all spiritual possibilities of every kind ; and, therefore, when you receive Him, you receive all these things with Him." The first thing with us all, the *one* thing, is to get home to Christ—not merely to read about Him or to speculate about His character, but to get face to face with Him. We contemplate too many things : we range all along the vast circumference of duty, instead of striking direct for the centre ; we live by law, which takes up duty in detail, instead of by love, which masses and carries all details. We too often act as if God had merely recognized us as His children, and given us the freedom of His house, and then left us to ourselves to work out our life as best we could. That is not God's way. When He makes us His children through faith in Christ Jesus, He assumes the care of our life in all its details. He not only turns us loose in His house : He goes with us into every corner, and shows us its treasures. He not only gives us the freedom of His domain : He assigns each of us His plot of ground, and stands by us while we try to sow the seed and water the growths, and teaches us how to be workers for and with Him ; and as for our care, all that tends to distract and cumber and confuse us He bids us cast it all on Him. Christian life, I say, is simple. It may seem to us that there is a little support on which to cast such a burden and problem as life is to most of us, but we shall do well to try it. Day before yesterday I had occasion to go to the lower part of the city by the elevated railroad ; and, as I got out at Hanover Square, I looked down upon the street far below, and a thought something like this went through my mind : Supposing that, without any knowledge of the existence and mode of working of an elevated railway, I had been placed on this train while asleep or unconscious, and had awakened at this station, and been told that I must get down to that street. I get out of the train, and find myself on a narrow platform. I look down on either side, and say, " No way down there, except by being dashed to pieces." Instinctively I follow those in front of me. Steps, but the door is shut : no getting down there. I follow still. A door, but it opens into an enclosure. I follow still. Another door, and there are steps which lead me safely and easily down to the street. I might have stood still, and distracted myself with a dozen devices for getting down. I might have gone bustling about, looking for a rope or a ladder. There was only one thing needful, and that was, to follow those who knew the way. So in our Christian experience, one thing is needful—the part which Mary chose, to hear Jesus' words and to follow Him. (*M. R. Vincent, D.D.*)　　*The one thing needful :*—We learn from the text that true religion is needful, and is a good thing, and will never be taken away from those who possess it. We shall endeavour to show the excellence and necessity of Divine knowledge with its accompaniments, by several considerations. I. This knowledge is necessary to our reconciliation with God. This is to him the good part which he has chosen fo r his heritage, and equally needful for all. Of this knowledge, Christ is the sum and substance. II. The second consideration which serves to show the necessity and excellence of the knowledge of Divine truth, is, that in this knowledge, and the holy affections which flow from it, consists the highest dignity and supreme excellence and felicity of human nature. In proportion to our knowledge will be our love ; and from this perennial fountain will flow uninterrupted happiness. III. A third consideration which goes fully to justify the choice of Mary is, that the good part on which she had fixed her affections, should never be taken away from her. (*A. Alexander, D.D.*) *The one thing needful:*—1. The text reminds us that we are endowed with the power of choice, and are responsible for its exercise. "Mary *hath chosen* the good part." It was her own act, and she was commended for it. This truth is perfectly consistent with the assurance that we are saved, "not of ourselves, it is the gift of God." Universally it is true that "without Him we can do nothing." Yet it is also true that, as He does help us, we are able to do very much and are bound to do it. 2. Let me urge the importance of youth as a season for exercising this choice. A train of carriages once set in motion on the rails, easily goes forward on the same track. Most persons go through life as they first set out. If you, in youth, deliberately neglect the "one thing needful," your wrong choice now may be your evil genius in old age, and your ruin eternally. 3. Let me then urge on you the great motive to a right decision which the text suggests. "Many things" on the one hand, the "one thing needful" on the other, solicit your preference. The world sets before you its various objects of desire—wealth, ease, learning, pleasure, fame, power, admiration. Let me remind you that, however desirable, they are not *necessary*. Moreover, all these "many things" are fleeting, as well as non-essential. They can only be for a little while. Beauty, riches, rank, admiration, health, life, will be taken away. (*Newman Hall, LL.B.*) *Scriptural religion the one thing needful:*—It is the one thing needful for—1. The safety of man. 2. The usefulness of man. 3. The support and comfort of man. 4. The present and eternal well-being of man. (*J. Smyth, D.D.*) *The care of our souls, the one thing needful:*—I. WHEREIN THIS CARE OF OUR SOULS CONSISTS. 1. The due care of religion and our souls doth consist in the distinct knowledge, and in the firm belief and persuasion of those things which are necessary to be known and believed by us in order to our eternal salvation. 2. The due care of our souls consists in the frequent examination of our lives and actions, and in a sincere repentance for all the errors and miscarriages of them: in a more particular and deep humiliation and repentance for deliberate and wilful sins, so far as we can call them to our remembrance; and in a general repentance for sins of ignorance, and infirmity, and surprise. 3. The due care of our souls consists in the constant and daily exercise of piety and devotion, both in private and in public, if there be opportunity for it, especially at proper times, and upon more solemn occasions; by fervent prayer to God, and by hearing and reading the Word of God with reverence and godly fear; by frequenting His public worship, and demeaning ourselves in it with that solemnity and seriousness which becomes the presence and service of God. 4. The due care of our souls consists also in avoiding those things which are pernicious to our salvation, and whereby men do often hazard their souls. 5. The due care of our souls consists in the even and constant practice of the several graces and virtues of a good life; or, as the apostle expresseth it, in "exercising ourselves always to have a conscience void of offence towards God and men." For herein is religion best seen, in an equal and uniform practice of every part of our duty; not only in serving God devoutly, but in demeaning ourselves peaceably and justly, kindly and charitably towards all men; not only in restraining ourselves from the outward act of sin, but in mortifying the inward inclination to it, in subduing our lusts, and governing our passions, and bridling our tongues. II. I proceed now, in the second place, TO CONVINCE US ALL, IF IT MAY BE, OF THE NECESSITY OF MINDING RELIGION AND OUR SOULS. When we call anything necessary, we mean that it is so in order to some end, which cannot be attained without it. We call those things the necessaries of life, without which men cannot subsist and live in a tolerable condition in this world; and that is necessary to our eternal happiness, without which it cannot be attained. Now happiness being our chief end, whatever is necessary to that, is more necessary than anything else; and in comparison of that, all other things not only may, but ought to be neglected by us. 1. That religion is a certain way to happiness. And for this we have God's express declaration and promise—the best assurance that can be. He that cannot lie, hath promised "eternal life to them who, by patient continuance in well-doing, seek for glory and honour and immortality." 2. It is certain also that there is no other way to happiness but this. We must be like to God in the temper of our minds, before we can find any felicity in the enjoyment of Him. 3. If we neglect religion, we shall certainly be extremely and for ever miserable. (*Archbishop Tillotson.*) *The one thing needful:*—But why is this concern which is so complex called one thing? I answer: Though salvation and holiness include various ingredients, and though the means of grace are various, yet they may be all taken collectively and called one thing ; *i.e.*, one great business, one important object of pursuit, in which all our endeavours and aims should centre and terminate. 1. It is also said to be one, in opposition to the many things that are the objects of a worldly mind. 2. It may also be called the one thing needful, to intimate that this is needful above all other things. 3. This is so necessary, that nothing else deserves to be called necessary in comparison of it. This shows you also, not only why this is called one thing, but why or in what sense it is said to be necessary. It is of absolute and incomparable necessity. 1. However well you have improved your time for other purposes, you have lost it all, unless you have improved it in securing the one thing needful. The proper notion of time is, that it is a space for repentance. Time is given us to prepare for eternity. 2. Whatever else you have been doing, you have lost your labour with your time, if you have not laboured above all things for this one thing needful. A child or an idiot riding upon a staff, building their mimic houses, or playing with a feather, are not so foolish as you in your conduct, while you are so seriously pursuing the affairs of time, and neglecting those of eternity. 3. This is not all: all your labour and pains have not only been lost while you have neglected this one thing, but you have taken pains to ruin yourselves, and laboured hard all your lives for your own destruction. We were far from having any such design. But the question is not, what was your design? but, what is the unavoidable consequence of your conduct, according to the nature of things, and the unchangeable constitution of heaven? Whatever you design in going on in sin, the wages of sin is death, eternal death. 4. If you have hitherto neglected the one thing needful, you have unmanned yourselves, acted beneath and contrary to your own reason, and in plain terms behaved as if you had been out of your senses. If you have the use of your reason, it must certainly tell you for what it was given to you. And I beseech you tell me what it was given to you for but to serve the God that made you, to secure His favour, to prepare for your eternal state, and to enjoy the supreme good as your portion? (*President Davies.*)   *One thing is needful:*—1. In order rightly to employ the time of life. 2. In order rightly to enjoy the joy of life. 3. In order rightly to endure the burdens of life. 4. In order rightly to await the end of life. (*Van Oosterzee.*)   *One thing only is necessary :*—Run to and fro in the world, and in that great emporium and mart of toys and vanities find out one thing that is necessary if you can, though you search it, as the prophet speaks, with candles. Is it necessary to be rich? Behold Dives in hell, and Lazarus in Abraham's bosom. Is it necessary to be noble? "Not many noble are called." Is it necessary to be learned? "Where is the scribe? where is the disputer of this world?" Everything hath its necessity from us, not from itself; for of itself it cannot show anything that should make it so: it is we that file these chains, and fashion these nails of necessity, and make her hand of brass. Riches are necessary because we are covetous; honour is necessary because we are proud and love to have the pre-eminence. Pleasure is necessary because we love it more than God. Revenge is necessary because we delight in blood. Lord, how many necessaries do we make when there is but one? one, *sine quo non debimus*, without which we ought not, and *sine quo non possumus*, without which we cannot be happy; and that is our assimilation and being made like unto Christ, in whom alone all the treasures of wisdom, and riches, and honour, all that is necessary for us are to be found (xiv. 18–20 ; Col. ii. 10). (*A. Farindon.*)   *One thing is needful :*—The other day I stood outside of a church in my native county, in Scotland. I never was inside that church but once, and that was, I am afraid to say forty years ago, certainly thirty-five, at least, and I heard there a minister whom I had never heard before or since, and he preached from this text, "One thing is needful," and although years passed before I was converted to God, I can say here to-night, as before Him, that word went home to my soul in power, and never left me. That one short sentence taught me that I was wrong, and that I should never be right until I came to Christ. It followed me for years, until God in His infinite mercy led me to put my trust in that blessed Saviour whom I hope I still love and seek to serve. (*W. P. Lockhart.*) *Need of both Martha and Mary :*—We need to combine the theoretical and the practical, the doctrinal with the experimental. Either extreme, exclusively, is to be avoided. Do not be ascetic when the world is full of work—good, honest, remunerative work, that requires the best wisdom for its performance. Three doctors of divinity were dining together. The character of the model wife was discussed. The first thought that Martha, of Bethany, filled the bill. The second, somewhat at a loss, thought he should prefer Mary. The third, when appealed to, immediately replied, " Oh, I think I should choose Martha *before* dinner, and Mary *after* it." May we all sit at the feet of Jesus as learners, that we may become all the more useful and helpful as workers. (*L. O. Thompson.*) *The only thing of importance :*—In Whitefield's Tabernacle, Tottenham Court Road, is an inscription to a once celebrated sculptor, designed with the tomb by himself. It runs as follows: " What I was as an artist, seemed of some importance while I lived; but what I really was, as a believer in Christ Jesus, is the only thing of importance to me now." *The good part best :*—St. Bernard, the son of a Knight of Burgundy, having devoted himself to a monastic life, persuaded four brothers, of whom the two elder were, like their father, stout fighting men, to follow his example. Only the youngest remained for a secular life, and he was but a child. As they were finally leaving the paternal castle, one of them said to the boy: " Nivard, you are now owner of all our property." " What?" replied the boy, "you have heaven, and I the earth; that is no fair division !" *Realizing the love of God as the one thing needful :*—A little girl in Paris, seven years old, was observed to read the New Testament continually. Being asked what pleasure she found in doing so, she said, " It makes us wise, and teaches us how to love God." She had been reading the history of Martha and Mary. " What is the one thing needful?" asked her friend. " It is the love of God," she replied, very earnestly. *The better part :*—The preference which Jesus manifested for the character of Mary, has, I believe, been often esteemed more poetical than just. It has been accused as a romantic judgment, giving countenance to the mischievous belief that the qualities best adapted for this world are uncongenial with the spirit of the other. The passage has been read not without a secret pity for the good Martha; and many a worthy housewife has thought within herself, " It seems rather hard that this is what we get for our pains." From the outside it looks so easy to sit still and gaze upon the face of heavenly goodness,—so pleasant to take in the lessons of holy truth, that those who see the attitude from amid the toil and heat of the common day, regard it only as a mental luxury, a coolness from the tree of life upon the grass of thought; more fit to be envied of men than applauded of the Son of God. And yet there is the deepest truth discoverable in this verdict of Christ; and the whole history of individual character, and of collective society, leads us to the same result. Those to whom life is a succession of particular businesses, however intelligent, energetic, and conscientious, must rank in the scale of human excellence below those to whom life is rather the flow of one spirit. (*J. Martineau, D.D.*) *The one thing needful :*—It is an unspeakable mercy that the one thing needful is a very simple one. To sit at Jesus' feet in humble submission and quiet rest—He the Master and I the little child; I the vessel waiting to be filled and He my fulness; I the mown grass and He the falling dew; I the raindrop and He the sun that makes me glisten in life with diamond brilliance, and then exhales me in death to be absorbed in Him—this is all in all to me. Let love permeate everything and other virtues will grow out of it, as flowers spring from the soil. So when we say that sitting at Jesus' feet is the one thing needful, we have not uttered a mere truism; it comprehends a world of blessing. (*C. H. Spurgeon.*) I. I WISH TO SPEAK OF SOME THINGS WHICH ARE NEEDFUL IN A SECONDARY OR SUBORDINATE SENSE. Cultivation of the mind; care for the body; diligence in business; faithfulness as a citizen. II. THE ONE THING WHICH OUR LORD HERE REFERS TO AS BEING NEEDFUL. She sat. She sat at Jesus' feet. She heard His word. III. SOME OF THE OBJECTIONS WHICH ARE MADE WITH REGARD TO DECISION FOR CHRIST. 1. It is a humbling thing. 2. Christianity is unmanly. 3. There are some very limp Christians. 4. There will have to be a very great deal of self-denial if I become a Christian. 5. It is such a difficult thing to live a Christian life. These objections will not bear examination. (*W. P. Lockhart.*) *One thing is needful :*— Write down a line of ciphers ! You may add thousands, multiplying them till the sheets they fill cover the face of heaven and earth—they express nothing. Now take the lowest number of the ten, the smallest digit, and place that at their head ; magic never wrought such a change ! What before amounted to nothing, rises instantly by the addition of one figure, one stroke of the pen, into thousands, or millions, as the case may be ; and whether they represent pounds or pearls, how great is the sum of them ! (*T. Guthrie, D.D.*) **Mary hath chosen that good part.**—*The good part of Mary :*—I. It would appear, on our Lord's own authority, that there are TWO WAYS OF SERVING HIM—by active business, and by quiet adoration. And further, these two classes of His disciples do not choose for themselves their course of service, but are allotted it by Him,

Martha might be the elder, Mary the younger. I do not say that it is never left to a Christian to choose his own path, whether he will minister with the angels or adore with the seraphim; often it is: and well may he bless God if he has it in his power freely to choose that good portion which our Saviour especially praises. But, for the most part, each has his own place marked out for him, if he will take it, in the course of His providence; at least there can be no doubt *who* are intended for worldly cares. The necessity of getting a living, the calls of a family, the duties of station and office, these are God's tokens, tracing out Martha's path for the many. Let me, then, dismiss the consideration of the many, and rather mention who they are who may be considered as called to the more favoured portion of Mary; and in doing so I shall more clearly show what that portion is. First, I instance the old, as is natural, whose season of business is past, and who seem to be thereby reminded to serve God by prayer and contemplation. Next those, who minister at the altar, are included in Mary's portion. "Blessed is the man whom Thou choosest and causest to approach unto Thee," says the psalmist, "that he may dwell in Thy courts." And next, I may mention children as in some respects partakers of Mary's portion. Till they go out into the world, whether into its trades or its professions, their school-time should be, in some sort, a contemplation of their Lord and Saviour. Further, we are told, on St. Paul's authority (if that be necessary on so obvious a point), that Mary's portion is allotted, more or less, to the unmarried. I say more or less, for Martha herself, though unmarried, yet as mistress of a household, was in a measure an exception; and because servants of God, as St. Paul, may remain unmarried, not to labour less, but to labour more directly for the Lord. "The unmarried careth for the things of the Lord, so as to be holy both in body and in spirit. And this I speak for your own profit, that ye may sit at the Lord's feet without being cumbered." And, further still, there are vast numbers of Christians, in Mary's case, who are placed in vaaious circumstances, and of whom no description can well be given; rich men having leisure, or active men during seasons of leisure, as when they leave their ordinary work for recreation's sake. Certainly our Lord meant that some or other of His servants should be ever worshipping Him in every place, and that not in their hearts merely, but with the ceremonial of devotion. And, last of all, in Mary's portion, doubtless, are included the souls of those who have lived and died in the faith and fear of Christ. Scripture tells us that "they rest from their labours"; and in the same sacred books that their employment is prayer and praise. II. MARY'S PORTION IS THE BETTER OF THE TWO. Our Lord's words imply, not that Martha's heart was not right with Him, but that her portion was full of snares, as being one of worldly labour, but that Mary could not easily go wrong in hers; that we may be busy in a wrong way, we cannot well adore Him except in a right one; that to serve God by prayer and praise continually, when we can do so consistently with other duties, is the pursuit of the "one thing needful," and emphatically "that good part which shall not be taken away from us." (*J. H. Newman, D.D.*) *The worthy portion:*—I. THE ONE THING. This one thing is not one dish, as Theophylact; nor unity, as Augustine; nor one grace, whether faith, hope, or charity, as others. But this one thing is the Christian care that every one ought to have of his own salvation, because—1. The cares of Mary and Martha are opposed. 2. This was the good part chosen by Mary, namely, a care how to be saved. 3. To this is perseverence promised, for as salvation is the good part of the elect, which shall never be taken away, so neither shall this care to attain that end by the means, for God preserves it by means. II. How IS IT NECESSARY? 1. In order above and before all things. "First seek the kingdom of God" (Matt. vi. 33), that is, to get into the estate of grace, as Israel must seek manna the first thing they do in the morning. 2. This one thing is simply necessary for itself, all other things for this. 3. It is transcendently necessary far beyond all things in the world, for this is alone sufficient for happiness and salvation, all they insufficient. 4. It is perpetually necessary while we live, lest beginning in the spirit we end in the flesh. The crown is set on the head of the conqueror. III. BUT WHY IS IT SO NECESSARY? 1. Because this one thing neglected, all other things are unprofitable, yea, all other things are vile without it; what would the gain of the whole world profit him that loseth his soul? How doth the apostle esteem all things loss and dung in comparison of Christ in the means? All without one's self, authority, wealth, favour, honour; yea, and all within one's self, knowledge, wisdom, memory, discourse, and the most excellent gifts which the apostle had in abundance, all dung and loss. 2. All actions, words, thoughts, profession, and the whole course not accompanied with this care, do swerve and err, and being not of faith are sinful, idle, hurtful; everything is lossful that helps not toward heaven, or that hinders heaven from being still held in our eye. 3. God delighteth only in such as in whom He espieth this care. 4. This one thing and care affordeth a man the surest comfort in the world, yea, in the agony of death it cheers the heart to have had a care of the best things. The point is this. In the most earnest affairs of this life a Christian must never forget the one thing necessary; as here we see, the care of salvation must take place of the care of entertaining Christ's own person. And why? 1. The excellency of grace and glory, of Christ and His gospel, is such as should draw all eyes from off these shadows and vanishing contentments to the surpassing brightness of it. What is earth to heaven, earthly goods to heavenly grace? What is gold and silver but dust of the earth, and base things to enter comparison with the blessings of the gospel? What a sin and shame is it to set the moon above the sun, to prefer pottage before the blessing, swine before Christ, and husks before the bread in our Father's house? 2. The dignity of the soul requires the chief care to keep and save it. It is a particle of Divine breath, called the precious soul of man (Prov. vi. 26), not made for the body, but the body to be the tabernacle of the soul, and the soul's instrument to work by, so precious, as that the ransom of it must be beyond all corruptible things; not gold and silver can deliver it, but only the precious blood of Christ (1 Pet. i. 18, 19). And the soul being lost, what recompense can be given? 3. The presence of grace makes a man serious in this care for the one thing necessary. It lets a man see the danger of the soul without it. It shows the means of recovery out of this woeful estate. It enables him to behold the worth of grace. Labour, then, to discern and conclude, that this is the one thing necessary. To do which, we must do three things. 1. Inform our judgments aright, which are the best things. They are such as serve to the main end, to uphold and maintain Christian life. 2. Resolve to do that which rightly-informed judgment suggests. 3. Avoid the lets and hindrances by which this care of the one thing necessary is usually put off; two specially. First, carnal and proud conceits. Martha must be counted a good housewife, and may not disgrace herself now at such a time, and Christ may be heard another time, or if not, she is well enough; she hath given Christ entertainment. Oh, but he is the best husband and she the best housewife who provide best for their souls, who have care that everything lie handsome and cleanly within, who hear Christ upon all occasions, and give Him not a meal's-meat in their houses, or entertain His disciples and ministers at their tables, but give Him entertainment in their hearts; without which care the best entertainment is not worth a rush, no, not if Christ's own person were at thy table; for many will say at that day, "We have eaten and drunk with Thee," to whom He shall profess, "Depart from Me, I know you not." Secondly, evil example. It was so common for women to bestir themselves at such a time, as Martha makes a complaint of Mary to Christ, because she did not help her, saying, "Bid her come help me." But happy was Mary that attended Christ, though alone. If many run in byeways and see not the one thing necessary, yea, and account it the most unnecessary of all, we must not go in their way, but sit down (though alone) at the feet of Christ. (*T. Taylor, D.D.*) *Mary's choice:*—Nay, this whole life is a life of necessities, how then is there but one thing necessary? I answer, it is true these things are necessary in their compass and sphere for this present life, but this life itself is nothing without a better being, and we had better not be than be and not be translated hereafter to a better life, and therefore Christ applies Himself to these means, as to that which conducteth us to that better life, which is only absolutely necessary. But, it may be urged, is not Christ's righteousness, faith, God's Spirit, more than one; and yet are they not all necessary? I answer, though they be diverse, yet they run all to one end. Even as many links make one chain, so all these tend to make a man one, that is a Christian; and therefore a wise soul considers them as one thing, and runs over them all at one view. And first, consider in everything what reference it hath to this one thing, what reference it hath to grace and glory. So long as we neglect this, the devil cares not what we have, whither we go, in what company we are; all is one to him. Secondly, carry ourselves respectively according to the necessity of the things that we are to be busied about, whereof some are more, some less necessary, according as they have more or less good in them. Those that cannot stand with this main one thing, cut them off, for other things that are necessarily required for our well-being in this life, as our daily bread, our callings in these, and the like. Thirdly, take heed of faithless cares, and beg wisdom to despatch business so as they prejudice not the main, and look still how they aim at the main end. As travellers and warriors do unburden themselves of things less necessary, so let us take heed of entangling ourselves in the cares of this life (2 Tim. ii. 4). Fourthly, in all business we should observe what the main end is, and labour to direct them to that main end. All other things are temporal, and death buries them, but grace and glory are in extent equal to our souls, extending to all eternity. Grace and the fruits thereof is our own ; all other things are not ours. Grace brings us to the greatest good, and advanceth us to the true nobility of sons and heirs of God, and grace makes us truly wise. It makes us wise to salvation ; it makes us truly rich with such riches as we cannot lose. Grace is so good, it makes ill things good, so as afflictions with the word and grace are better than all the pleasures in Pharaoh's court in Moses's esteem (Heb. xi. 25). Seeing it is thus, let us be animated by this example of Mary ; and to that end, first, beg the Spirit of revelation to open our eyes to see the high prize of our calling, the happiness thereof ; and to get a sense and taste of the pleasures thereof, that we may judge by our own experience. For the meanest Christian out of experience knows this to be the good part ; and this it is which the apostle prays for (Phil. i. 10), that the Philippians may approve the things that are excellent. The word signifies in all sense and feeling, to approve the things that are excellent, or do differ. Secondly, let us endeavour to balance things, by laying and comparing them together. For comparison gives lustre ; and thus shall we see the difference and the excellency of some things above others, and the sooner be able to choose. Thus did David ; and the effect thereof was this, "I have seen an end of all created perfection, but thy commandments are exceeding broad or large " (Psa. cxix. 96). Thirdly, labour for spiritual discretion to discern of particulars. This is, as it were, the steward to all actions, teaching what to cut off, what to add. In all particular affairs of this life, what time and what place fitteth best, tells what company, what life, what way is the best. And when we have done this—fourthly, proceed on and make this choice. If we do not choose it only, but stumble upon it, as it were, it is no thank to us. Though it be the fashion nowadays ; men read the Word, and go to church ; why? Not that they have, by balancing and the spirit of discretion, made choice of this as the best part, but they were bred up in it ; and they went with company, and custom hath drawn them to it ; they happen on good duties it may be against their wills ; and this is the reason of those many apostates that fall off to embrace this present world, as Demas did (2 Tim. iv. 10) ; for they not being grounded, must needs waver in temptation. Fifthly, in the next place, when we have made this choice, we must resolve with a deliberate resolution to stand by this choice. It is not enough to make an offer, or to cheapen, as we say, but come with resolution to buy, to choose. So David, " I have chosen the way of truth, and have stuck to Thy statutes   (Psa. cxix. 30, 31) ; and (ver. 57), " I have said," that is, set down with myself, "that I would keep Thy words": for the will rules in our souls. If we be good, our will is good. There are many wicked men that understand and are persuaded what is best ; but for want of this resolution and will they never make this determinate choice ; and many rail at good men and persecute them. Let such know that God will not take men by chance. If they choose the worst part, they must look for to reap the fruit of their choice. Sixthly, in the next place, come we often, and sit at Christ's feet, as Mary here came to the ministry. "He that heareth you heareth Me," saith Christ. Live under a powerful plain ministry. Lastly, labour to draw on others to this choice. By so much the more earnest endeavour, by how much the more we have been a means to draw them to ill heretofore, and this will seal up all the rest, it being a sure sign of our perfect and sincere choice.   (*R. Sibbes, D.D.*) *Mary's choice :*—As the head and the foot are both needful in the body, so Mary and Martha are both needful in a commonwealth ; man hath two vocations, the one earthly by his labour, the other heavenly by his prayer. There is the active life, which consisteth in practising the affairs of this life, wherein man showeth himself to be like himself ; and there is the contemplative life, which consisteth in the meditation of Divine and heavenly things, wherein man showeth himself to be like the angels ; for they which labour in their temporal vocations, do live like men ; but they which labour in spiritual matters, live like angels. A nurse which hath her breast full of milk doth love the child that sucks it from her ; and Christ which hath His breast full of heavenly milk is glad when He hath children to suck the same ; let us therefore, as the apostle willeth us (1 Pet. ii. 12), " laying aside all maliciousness, and all guile, and dissimulation, and envy, and all evil speaking, as new-born babes, desire the sincere milk of the word, that we may grow thereby," to be perfect men in Christ Jesus. Let us breathe after the fountain of the living water, which springeth up into eternal life; and as the fainty hart desireth the water-brook to quench his thirst (Psa. xlii. 1). (*H. Smith.*)   *The service of rest* :—— Here were two services, both earnest, both from loving hearts, both for Christ, both greatly to be emulated——the one active, the other passive——one doing for Christ, the other receiving from Christ, one toiling, the other sitting at the feet. But Christ had no hesitation which He preferred, and has left it beyond a question, that, in that instance at least, the service of work was inferior to the service of rest. But now, we must be careful before we proceed that we understand very accurately what rest is. Idleness and rest are two of the most diametrically opposite things in the whole world. Idleness is a selfish thing, done on no principle, to please nature. Rest is a holy thing, done measuredly, and with a purpose, to please God, and to fit to work. An idle man never rests. Who has not found the restlessness of inactivity, and that the hardest thing we ever do is when we do nothing? But what is rest? Rest, being a relative term, is essentially retrospective and pro-spective. It pre-supposes that there has been labour; for where there is no fatigue, there is no rest. And it is not rest worthy of a man unless it be preparatory to work which is to follow, and which is to be the better for the temporary inter-mission. But what is the present character of rest, and how are resting-times to be spent? I say generally, as Mary spent her opportunity in the house at Bethany, as David the solitude of his chamber, as Paul the desert, as Christ the mountain. Perhaps we should be right to say, rest is not so much a cessation from work as a change of employment. Whereas the work was outward, in rest it is inward; still, more rest than work. Never, brethren, are we better practising for heaven than when we are learning the service of rest. Do not be afraid, in your hours of sickness and weakness, to take the comfort of the thought. (*J. Vaughan, M.A.*)   *The best dish* :——There is a touch of playfulness in our Lord's reply to Martha. He takes an image from the very table about which Martha was so unnecessarily and unduly anxious: for the words rendered "Mary hath chosen the good part," mean "Mary hath chosen the good portion, the best dish, the Benjamin's mess." It is as though He had said to the careful and fretted housekeeper: "You are very kind, Martha; you are doing your best to please Me, and to give Me as good a dinner as you can: and yet it is Mary who has brought Me the best dish, the food I like most. She is nourishing and refreshing My spirit with her love and sympathy. She is giving Me an opportunity of feeding her with the bread of life and the wine of the kingdom. Our fellowship with each other is the true feast. And you, O you poor Martha, are so taken up with your dainties that you are losing the feast!" Obviously, our Lord stoops to Martha's level, to the busy housekeeper's point of view, and play-fully rebukes her for her mistake. Her mind is full of dishes and dainties, so full, and so bewildered, that she is forgetting the best dish of all. She wants to serve Him and do Him honour; but she is pre-occupied with thoughts of how she may do her best for Him. And so He teaches her that she will best serve both herself and Him by casting aside her cares, and giving herself up to the joy of communion with Him. Now if you ask me to name this best dish, to tell you exactly what the one thing needful is, I am a little puzzled how to reply; not, however, because I do not know what it is. First, I will tell you what I think the one thing needful is. I believe it is that love for God and man which quickens and sustains the true life within us, and redeems us from all anxieties for the many things of our outward life. But if you rise into this pure, deep, and trustful love, you will be saved from all these base and vexing cares and fears. You will do your best in your several stations. You will be as diligent, as prudent, as skilful, as you can; and then you will leave the results of your faithful discharge of duty with God; fearing no evil, because you know there is no want to them that fear Him. And is not that the very best thing you can do, the best dish of which you can eat? What else has life to offer that is half so good? This is the dish of which Mary ate with Christ, and of which the young ruler refused to eat, at least for a time. And, last of all, it is the best dish, the best portion, because it can never be taken away from us. We lose much as life goes on, more than you can yet imagine. We lose health and energy both of body and of mind; the fineness of our intellectual perceptions is dulled, and the firmness of our intellectual grasp relaxed. We lose our very senses ——not going out of our minds, I do not mean that, but——our eyes grow dim, and our ears hard of hearing, and our tongues trip, and our natural force is abated.

We lose, or partly lose, our very memories, so that our own past grows hazy to us, or even dark. We lose the power to do much that we once loved to do, and to enjoy much that was once pleasant to us. We lose our friends, or at least the presence and use and enjoyment of our friends, losing at the same time the faculty of forming new friendships. And, at last, we lose life itself, and with it all that we have gained. But there is one thing we never lose, if once we have had it—the love of God. We never lose the one thing needful, the one only thing which enables us to bear all other losses, and even turns them into gain. (*S. Cox, D.D.*) *The one thing needful:*—Philip Henry left in his will the following important passage: " I have now disposed of all my property to my family; there is one thing more I wish I could give them, and that is, the Christian religion. If they had that, and I had not given them one shilling, they would be rich; and if they had not that, and I had given them all the world, they would be poor." *The one thing needful:*—An Asiatic traveller tells us that one day as he was crossing a desert, he and his party found the bodies of two men laid upon the sand beside the carcass of a camel. By their side lay a small bag of dried dates, two leathern bottles, quite empty, and on further examination he noticed that the stomach of the dead camel had been cut open, as if to get at the water, which, as is well known, that animal can carry on its desert journeys for a considerable time. A further glance at the swollen lips and blackened tongues of the two men made it evident that they had died during the most agonizing pains of thirst. " I was much stirred," says the traveller, " when I found that both men had in the belt around their waist a large store of jewels of different kinds, which they had doubtless been crossing the desert to sell in the markets of Persia. I warrant the poor wretches would have bartered many a jewel for a few delicious draughts of water." (*J. Jackson Wray.*) *The good part:*—You have chosen the better part, and it shall never be taken from you (Luke x. 42); and therefore behave as bravely when you have little as when you have much. You shall be sure to enjoy all in God and God in all; and what would you have more? Seneca once told a courtier who had lost his son, that he had no cause to mourn, either for that or ought else, because Cæsar was his friend. Oh, then, what little cause have the saints to mourn for this or that loss, considering that God is their portion! I have read of a company of poor Christians, who were banished into remote parts, and one standing by seeing them pass along, said, that it was very sad for those poor people to be thus hurried from the society of men, and made companions with the beasts of the field. " True," said another, " it were sad indeed if they were carried to a place where they could not find their God; but let them be of good cheer, for God goes along with them, and will enrich them with the comforts of His grace wheresoever they go." Would you not laugh to see a man lament bitterly for the loss of his shoe-strings when his purse is safe? or for the burning of a pig-sty when his dwelling-house is safe? and why then should a Christian lament for the loss of this or that, so long as God is with him? (*Thomas Brooks.*) *What cannot be taken away:*—There is a story in Foxe's " Book of Martyrs " of a woman who, when she came to be tried for her religion before the Bishop, was threatened by him that he would take away her husband from her. " Christ," was her reply, " is my husband." " I will take away thy child," said he. " Christ," said she, " is better to me than ten sons." " I will strip thee," said he, " of all outward comforts." And again came the answer, " Yes, but Christ is mine, and you cannot strip me of Him." (*W. Baxendale.*)

CHAPTER XI.

Ver. 1. Lord, teach us to pray.—*The Christian taught to pray:*—I. What the request implies. 1. A conviction of the importance of prayer. This, in this case, seems to have had its origin in the habits and example of Christ. He prayed often and much; in sorrow, and in joy; alone, and with His disciples. 2. This request implies also some knowledge of the real nature of prayer. The disciples had heard their Master pray. They had witnessed His fervour, the seriousness, the abasement, and perhaps something of the elevation, of His spirit in His supplications, and their understandings were opened. Prayer appeared to them in a new light. Before, it was a ceremony; it was now an inward, spiritual service. They regarded it for the first time as the work of the heart, and conscious that their own hearts had hitherto been but little engaged in it, their request was, "Lord, teach us to pray." They wished their prayers to be in future of a higher and more spiritual character, and, beyond this, they scarcely knew, perhaps, their own meaning or object. 3. An impression, too, of the difficulty of prayer is plainly to be traced in the disciples' words. And this undoubtedly sprung out of their conviction of its importance, and their newly-acquired knowledge of its real nature. That which is so important must, they concluded, be done aright; and that which is so spiritual, they were conscious they could not do at all; and thus they were constrained to seek help and instruction. 4. Besides intimating a conviction of the importance, the real nature, and the difficulty of prayer, it plainly indicates also a desire for an increased ability to pray. II. How MAY WE EXPECT SUCH A PETITION AS THIS TO BE ANSWERED? In the instance before us, it was answered at once. We owe to it the well-known prayer we call the Lord's prayer—a model of supplication, which claims at once our admiration and gratitude. But with all its excellencies it is in itself powerless. It could not teach these disciples to pray. It showed them indeed what their prayers ought to be, but it did not communicate to them the power of making their prayers like it. Our Lord well knew this. Accordingly, as soon as He had given His disciples a pattern for their supplications, we find Him immediately directing them where to go for the ability to follow it. He sends them to the Holy Spirit for the inward principle of prayer, urging them to importunity in their petitions for His grace, and assuring them at the same time that their importunity shall not be lost. How then does this Holy Spirit teach us to pray? In many ways. Among others, in these four: 1. By discovering to us our spiritual poverty; showing us our wants and help-lessness, or giving us a more lively sense of them. 2. Affliction, too, is often made to answer the same gracious end. 3. At other times Christ stirs up the soul to prayer, by giving it an enlarged view of the Divine promises and goodness. 4. Sometimes the Holy Spirit carries us yet farther. He teaches us to pray by giving us clearer views of Christ as a Mediator and Intercessor. You are aware, brethren, that I might still go on. I might say, Christ teaches us to pray by much that is passing around us, by what we call accidents—events that make, perhaps, a whole parish or nation start; crushing, and crushing in an hour, the hopes and prospects and happiness that seemed almost out of the reach of decay or change. And He teaches us by deliverances, by bringing us to the edge of some precipice, and then, as our foot goes over it, snatching us away from it; showing us in the same moment our danger and our deliverance. (*C. Bradley, M.A.*) *Christ the Teacher of prayer:*—I. THE DISCIPLES' REQUEST:—1. This was a pertinent request, con-sidering them as dependent, needy, sinful, and dying creatures. 2. A seasonable request, as Christ had been just now praying before them, and was shortly to be taken from them. 3. A short and comprehensive request, much being contained in a few words. 4. It would also appear to have been an acceptable request, for it was immediately answered, and that in a very gracious manner. II. WHAT WAS IMPLIED IN THE REQUEST. 1. A consciousness of the importance and necessity of prayer. The breath of the newborn soul. Prayer softens our affections, sweetens our enjoyments, and is the principal means of keeping up an intercourse with heaven. God approves of it, and the soul is every way benefited by it. 2. A sense of weakness and inability, and that this duty cannot be performed aright without Divine assistance. 3. It also implies that those who are appointed of God to instruct others, will, among other things, teach them to pray. III. THE PROPRIETY OF THIS APPLICATION, AS MADE TO CHRIST:—1. None ever prayed like Christ—so pertinently, fervently, and effectually. 2. As none ever prayed, so none ever taught like Christ. 3. It was Christ who taught John to pray, else He could not have taught His disciples. He teaches those who are teachers of others. (*B. Beddome, M.A.*) *The disciples' request:*—I. WHAT IS IMPLIED IN THIS REQUEST? Clearly it implies—1. A conviction of the propriety of prayer. 2. It implies a sense of their need of being taught. 3. It implies a sincere desire to learn. 4. It implies something of the true spirit or disposition of prayer already possessed. 5. The request implies a high opinion of the ability and grace of Christ. II. THE MANNER IN WHICH THE REQUEST WAS REGARDED. We may observe, in the general, it was answered. The disciples said, "Lord, teach us to pray." **The Lord Jesus did teach** them. 1. By convincing us more clearly of the necessity of prayer. **2.** By giving us more impressive views of our wants. **3.** By strengthening our faith in Divine promises. **4.** By instructing us in the great utility of His own mediation. **5.** By increasing our pleasure and delight in the duty. (*T. Kidd.*)   *Lord, teach us to pray :—*After listening to a fervent prayer we sometimes say, " We wish we could pray like the person who has offered it "; how much more should we have thus wished, if we had heard Jesus Christ pray! No doubt His manner was very impressive, sincere, fervent, reverent. **1.** "Lord, teach us to pray," because we are ignorant in asking. St. Paul says, " We know not what we should pray for as we ought." A consciousness of inability to pray aright grows with a Christian's growth. **2.** Again, a sense of our sinfulness, as well as of our ignorance, should cause us to offer the petition in our text. Who does not feel at times as if it was a wonder of mercy that God does not cut us down in anger, even while in the act of praying, so miserable and defective are our purest offerings! What a gift of prayer would it be if our God would enable us always to delight in the duty, restrain every wandering thought, and fix our whole soul in sweet and full communion with Him! Can you think of many things more desirable in this world, Christians, than the perfect spirit of prayer? If we could enjoy always as much as we do in our happiest devotional seasons, that would be a blessed privilege; but, alas! our happy seasons are few and far between, and even in them there was much imperfection. "Lord, teach us to pray." **3.** To make us prevalent in prayer, we have need also to offer the petition in our text. We might have unnumbered mercies more than we do enjoy if we prayed for them aright. There are favours in God's right hand for ourselves, our children, our friends, and fellow-creatures, the bestowal of which is suspended on our faithfulness in asking. Here is more than life, here is eternal welfare resting on our prayers to God. **4.** And who can so well teach us how to pray as that blessed Saviour to whom the request of our text was addressed! Prayer was His frequent work on earth, intercession is His employ in heaven. He knows what pleas will prevail with God, and He can put them into our hearts and order them aright upon our tongues. (*W. H. Lewis, D.D.*)   *Teach us to pray :—***1.** It would be difficult, I think impossible, to prove that our Lord ever commanded His disciples to pray. He always assumes that they pray; teaches them plainly that unless they pray they cannot do what they must do. He moved His disciples to pray, not by telling them to do so, but by exciting in them desires which compelled them to supplication. You cannot pray by direct force of resolution. You must put yourself under conditions which will inspire desire for communion with God. **(1)** Because for most men it is hard to pray, and easy to pretend, we are warned against that easily besetting sin. The hypocrites wanted of the king only to be seen in his company. They stood at his door that they might be mistaken for his friends. The same temptation assails us at all times, and is acutely dangerous now. It is insidious as malaria. **(2)** Most of us say grace before our meals. If we realize who feeds us, we cannot help doing so, unless we are brutes. Most of us have family worship. If we are alert to spiritual facts, it will be more natural to omit our meals than our devotions. But what are the motives we often hear unblushingly advanced for continuing these spiritual exercises? The children will be surprised if they do not hear grace at table! For the sake of the example upon them, daily prayers must be inexorably maintained! But is it permitted to pray that we may be seen of children, and forbidden to pray that we may be seen of men? The " closet " is the cure for hypocrisy in prayer. **2.** When we pray, we are forbidden to use vain repetitions as the heathen do. There are men, good men, men meaning to be honest, who think their prayers must be right if couched in Scriptural phrases. Many say prayers every night and morning, who never pray except when they are scared. Repeating David's or Isaiah's petitions, or even our Lord's Prayer, is not necessarily praying because we do it on our knees. Saying over even the Lord's Prayer is for us a vain repetition until we so understand its meaning and so sympathize with its spirit that the words express our real desires. For " vain repetitions " are simply " empty phrases," sayings which do not express what we really mean. The cure for this habit of making vain repetition lies in creating right desires. We must learn to know what we need, and to desire that. Therefore we are told—**3.** When we pray, to pray after this manner. The prayer tells us what we need, but rarely crave. If we were sure that one wish, and one only, would be granted us this day for the asking, would that wish be the petition which stands first in the Lord's Prayer? **(1)** We shall not pray effectively until we pray according to the mind of God. **(2)** Few of us do greatly desire the things God desires for us. (3) We need such a change of heart as shall make us crave what God declares we need. And this is only another way of saying—(a) That we cannot pray effectually until we can sincerely pray in the manner of our Lord's Prayer. (b) That few of us can yet do that. (c) That we need to learn to do so. (*W. B. Wright.*)　　*Barrenness in prayer :*—There are, no doubt, many who have experienced at times an intense dissatisfaction with their prayers. They seem so lame, so cold, so profitless, till you are inclined to exclaim, "What a weariness, what a mockery it is!" You are constantly disappointed with yourselves. The heart that seemed so full has run empty ere you reached your knees. You have nothing to say; all your thoughts have fled from you; and the intense longing comes across your heart that some one would teach you how to pray. I do not pretend to supply the want here indicated; but I wish to touch upon some of the causes of this trying sense of barrenness in prayer. I. SELF-CONCEIT. We are very slow to learn the lesson of our own inability. We feel at some time, perhaps, that our hearts are prompted by an earnest desire to pray. We grow keenly alive for the moment to our own wants; but when we attempt to pray, we find the edge of that sense of need is gone. The heart appeared full, but when we knelt we found it empty. Vexed and disappointed, we murmur at our privation, but are too blind to see its cause. We cannot see that our own self-conceit lies at the root of our failure. We thought we could do it of ourselves—we anticipated rich heart-communion; but we were miserably mistaken, because we did not realize that we are not sufficient of ourselves to think anything as of ourselves, but that our whole sufficiency is of God. We need, then, to pray for the gift of the Holy Spirit. This is the very dawn of spiritual light, the very threshold of prayer. II. SELF-IGNORANCE. They tell God that they have sinned, that they have grievously broken His commandments; they ask God to give them true repentance, and to forgive them for Jesus Christ's sake. Such a prayer might be from a certain heart a true and noble expression of spiritual longing; but with the persons alluded to this prayer is the stereotyped plate from which all their prayers for themselves, morning and evening, are struck off. With very little variation, and in the most conventional way—though, perhaps, with very real desire—they confess that they are sinners, unworthy and polluted, but there is not the confession of a single definite sin, or if there is, it is perhaps the result of some very rare circumstance which has impressed some special transgression more vividly upon their minds. To realize our sinfulness, we must adopt a more particular mode of dealing with our own hearts, taking them to task; recalling each special sin, and confessing it before God. III. SELFISHNESS IN PRAYER. By this I mean that spirit in prayer which confines all our supplications to our own individual needs. Often God visits us with barrenness because we fail to grow in heart-sympathy and Christian longing for the welfare of others. It is the very law of Christ that His love should spread, as it is the law of hydrostatics that pressure should circulate in all directions through a volume of water; and when we in a niggardly forgetfulness of others violate that law, we are met with the punishment of a straitening in ourselves. (*Bishop Boyd Carpenter.*)　*Acceptable prayer, the gift of Christ :*—I. I shall begin by mentioning TWO QUALIFICATIONS THAT ARE INDISPENSABLY NECESSARY, AS PREPARATORY TO ACCEPTABLE PRAYER. 1. The first of them is a due sense of our wants. Christ alone by His Spirit, teacheth this first preparatory lesson. "Lord, teach us to pray," by revealing to us our guilt and misery, our vileness and our helplessness. 2. The second qualification which is indispensable, as preparatory to acceptable prayer, is an acquaintance with the true way of access to God. Alas! the tendency of our corrupt hearts is, to resist this Divine appointment. O, then, what need is there to ask of the Lord a right understanding, a cordial approbation, of that way which He hath appointed. II. Supposing you, then, to have made some proficiency in these two preparatory lessons, I proceed, in the second place, to mention SOME PARTICULARS, WITH RESPECT TO WHICH EVEN THE WELL-INSTRUCTED CHRISTIAN WILL HAVE PERPETUAL OCCASION TO USE THE LANGUAGE OF MY TEXT, "Lord, teach me to pray." 1. The power of devout attention while praying is one of those gifts which we must obtain by prayer. 2. Spirituality in our devotional exercises is another gift, for which we must often pray. 3. Furthermore, the Christian has need to pray for simplicity and godly sincerity in his prayers. 4. We must request of the Saviour that a patient confidence in God may accompany all our prayers. (*J. Jowett, M.A.*)　　*The rule of direction in prayer :*—I. WE NEED DIRECTION IN PRAYER. This is evident from—1. God's greatness. 2. Our own guiltiness. 3. The importance of the subject. 4. Our weakness and aptness to go wrong. 5. The danger of mistaking and miscarrying in prayer. II. WHAT RULE GOD HAS GIVEN for our direction in prayer. 1. A general rule in the whole of the Bible, where His will is revealed. (1) It furnishes us abundantly with matter of prayer, in all the parts of it—petition, confession, &c. (Psa. li. 4, 5 ; Phil. iv. 6). And whoso has the Word of God dwelling richly in him, will not want matter for prayer, for himself or for others. There is a storehouse of it there, of great variety ; and we are welcome to the use of it, agreeable to our own case. (2) It fully directs us as to the manner of prayer : as, for instance, that we must pray with sincerity (Heb. x. 22) ; with humility (Psa. x. 17); in faith (James i. 6); and with fervency (James v. 16). And there is no qualification necessary in prayer, but what we may learn from the Holy Word. (3) It furnishes us with the most fit words to be used in prayer. Do ye want words to express your desires before the Lord ? He has given us His own words in the Bible, that we may use them according to our needs (Hos. xiv. 2). 2. There is a special rule given us by Jesus Christ for that end, namely, that form of words which Christ taught His disciples, commonly called " the Lord's Prayer." (1) The Lord's Prayer is given us as a directory for prayer, a pattern and an example, by which we are to regulate our petitions, and make other prayers. (2) It may also be used as a prayer, so that it be done with understanding, faith, reverence, and other praying graces. Inferences : 1. How gracious and ready to hear prayer is our God, who has been pleased Himself to direct us how to pray to Him ! 2. Let us acquaint ourselves with the blessed Word, that contains such a full rule of practice as well as faith ; and study the Holy Scriptures, that we may be the better instructed to pray. 3. See the absolute necessity for prayer in a Christian life.   (*T. Boston, D.D.*)   *Prayer :*—What is prayer? I. IT IS AN OFFERING UP OF OUR DESIRES TO GOD. These are, as it were, the soul of prayer, without which the most elegant and warm expressions that can possibly be invented and used would not be acceptable to God.   II. Our request must be FOR SUCH THINGS AS ARE AGREEABLE TO THE WILL OF GOD. Things which are not so it is not fit we should receive; and for that reason we should not be rash and hasty to utter anything before God.   III. Our prayers are to be offered up to God IN THE NAME OF CHRIST ; for His sake ; in dependence upon the merit and intercession of the beloved Son of God, in whom the Father is well pleased.   IV. CONFESSION OF SIN IS A BRANCH OF THAT WORSHIP WE CALL PRAYER. V. A THANKFUL ACKNOWLEDGMENT OF GOD'S MERCIES justly claims a place in this part of Divine worship. (*John Whitty.*)   *Prayer :*—I. WHAT IS PRAYER ? The presenting of our requests to God, and breathing out our desires before Him. In prayer—1. The heart must be the agent. 2. God is the object. 3. Jesus Christ the medium. 4. Prayer must be our constant exercise.   II. WHY SHOULD WE DESIRE TO BE TAUGHT HOW TO PRAY ? 1. Because of the importance of prayer. 2. Because of our natural ignorance of this duty. 3. Because God desires us to be proficient in this duty. III. WHY SHOULD WE DESIRE THE LORD TO TEACH US HOW TO PRAY ? 1. Because He was distinguished for this holy exercise. 2. Because He is our Master, and in all things we are to hear Him. 3. Because with Him is the spirit of prayer. 4. Because He is our great High Priest. Application : 1. Let us cultivate the gift of prayer. 2. Covet the true spirit of prayer (1 Cor. vii. 5). 3. Commence and conduct all our affairs in connection with prayer (Philip. iv. 6.) 4. Continue instant in prayer (Luke xviii. 1). 5. In the exercise of faith look for the returns of prayer. (*J. Burns, D.D.*)   *Forms of private prayer :*—In the case of *public* prayer the need of forms is evident; but it is not at first sight so obvious that in *private* prayer also we need use written forms, instead of praying extempore (as it is called) ; so I proceed to show the use of them. 1. Let us bear in mind the precept of the wise man, " Be not rash with thy mouth, and let not thine heart be hasty to utter anything before God ; for God is in heaven, and thou upon earth ; therefore let thy words be few."   Prayers framed at the moment are likely to become irreverent.   What need have we of humble, sober, and subdued thoughts ! as becomes creatures, sustained hourly by His bounty ; as becomes lost sinners who have no right to speak at all ; and still more, as grateful servants of Him who bought us from ruin at the price of His own blood. Therefore, to avoid the irreverence of many or unfit words and rude half-religious thoughts, it is necessary to pray from book or memory, and not at random. 2. In the next place, forms of prayer are necessary to guard us against the irreverence of wandering thoughts. A chief use of them is that of fixing the attention. 3. Next, they are useful in securing us from the irreverence of excited thoughts. They are accused of impeding the current of devotion, when, in fact, that (so called) current is in itself faulty, and ought to be checked. To be excited is not the ordinary state of the mind, but the extraordinary, the now-and then state. Nay, more than this, it ought not to be the common state of the mind; and if we are encouraging within us this excitement, this unceasing rush and alternation of feelings, and think that this, and this only, is being in earnest in religion, we are harming our minds, and (in one sense) I may even say grieving the peaceful Spirit of God, who would silently and tranquilly work His Divine work in our hearts. 4. Further, forms are useful to help our memory, and to set before us at once, completely, and in order, what we have to pray for. It does not follow that when the heart is really full of the thought of God, and alive to the reality of things unseen, then it is easiest to pray. Rather the deeper insight we have into His majesty and our innumerable wants, the less we shall be able to draw out our thoughts into words. 5. And further, the use of a form as a help to the memory is still more obvious, when we take into account the engagements of this world with which most men are surrounded. The cares and businesses of life press upon us with a reality which we cannot overlook. Shall we trust the matters of the next world to the chance thoughts of our own minds, which come this moment, and go the next, and may not be at hand when the time of employing them arrives, like unreal visions, having no substance and no permanence? 6. And this use of forms in prayer becomes great, beyond power of estimating, in the case of those multitudes of men, who, after going on well for a while, fall into sin. Chance words and phrases of the Church's services adhere to their memories, rising up in moments of temptation or of trouble, to check or to recover them. And hence it happens, that in the most irreligious companies a distinction is said to be observable between those who have had the opportunity of using our public forms in their youth, and those whose religious impressions have not been thus happily fortified; so that, amid their most reckless mirth, and most daring pretence of profligacy, a sort of secret reverence has attended the wanderers, restraining them from that impiety and profaneness in which the others have tried to conceal from themselves the guilt and peril of their doings. 7. Such is the force of association in undoing the evil of past years, and recalling us to the innocence of children. Nor is this all we may gain from the prayers we use, nor are penitent sinners the only persons who can profit by it. Let us recollect for how long a period our prayers have been the standard forms of devotion in the Church of Christ, and we shall gain a fresh reason for loving them, and a fresh source of comfort in using them. I know different persons will feel differently here, according to their different turn of mind; yet surely there are few of us, if we dwelt on the thought, but would feel it a privilege to use, as we do (for instance, in the Lord's Prayer), the very petitions which Christ spoke. He gave the prayer and used it. His apostles used it; all the saints ever since have used it. When we use it we seem to join company with them. Who does not think himself brought nearer to any celebrated man in history, by seeing his house, or his furniture, or his handwriting, or the very books that were his? Thus does the Lord's Prayer bring us near to Christ, and to His disciples in every age. No wonder, then, that in past times good men thought this form of prayer so sacred, that it seemed to them impossible to say it too often, as if some especial grace went with the use of it. Nor *can* we use it too often; it contains in itself a sort of plea for Christ's listening to us; we cannot, so that we keep our thoughts fixed on its petitions, and use our minds as well as our lips when we repeat it. And what is true of the Lord's Prayer, is in its measure true of most of those prayers which our Church teaches us to use. It is true of the Psalms also, and of the Creeds; all of which have become sacred, from the memory of saints departed who have used them, and whom we hope one day to meet in heaven. (*J. H. Newman, D.D.*) *Forms of prayer:*—Common sense tells us, that when people unite together in public worship, if their thoughts are to run in the same channel, they must agree beforehand what is to be the subject of their petitions, and the very words in which they are to be offered, if there is to be any certainty, satisfaction, and regularity in devotion. To sing out of a book is the same in principle as praying out of a book, and if the one is spiritual and right, so is the other also. Public worship should embrace confession, penitence, implorations, ascription, and thanksgiving. The prayer offered to God in His holy place should be sober, solemn, reverential, filial, scriptural, offered in faith, through the merits of the Divine Redeemer. Such, most emphatically, are the devotions of the Prayer Book. A Presbyterian minister, no less distinguished for his abilities than for his

Christian charity, has lately given this little sketch from his pastoral experience. In looking up scholars for a mission-school, he was led to visit a poor woman, on her sick-bed, in the upper room of a crowded, comfortless tenement-house. The room was entirely dark, the only inlet of illumination being the swinging, two-paned ventilator overhead. Waiting until his eyes became accustomed to the dimness, he discovered that the apartment was merely a small closet, about six feet square. A shapeless mass of humanity was buried under a heap of coarse, tumbled coverlets, the victim of rheumatism; having occupied the same comfortless room for fourteen years. Although a member of the Church, no minister of the city knew of her existence, she having come from another place, and bringing no certificate of membership to commend her to pastoral care and oversight. When asked by the visitor whether she had ever given up her faith and hope, her pale, shrivelled face lighted up, as she answered, very decidedly, " Never ! " She declined his kind offers of pecuniary aid, but thankfully accepted his proposal to pray with her. He was struck with the fact that, in his repeated visits, she avoided speaking much of herself, and seemed to prefer to spend all the time in talking of God's love, and the Saviour's abundant grace. Remembering the strong attachment of Churchmen for the Prayer Book, the Presbyterian minister learned several of the beautiful collects by heart, and one day, while praying, suffered his voice quietly to run into the form. The sick woman recognized the first sentence of the dear old words with a start of surprise ; then she began to repeat the petitions aloud with him ; and when he finished she sobbed aloud, with humble, grateful tears. It was a repetition of good George Herbert's dying expression of childlike affection for his spiritual mother : " Give me the prayers of my mother the Church, no other prayers are equal to them ! "   (*J. N. Norton, D.D.*)   *How to pray :*—Would you pray to God in a proper way—1. Read a few verses of the Bible before you pray. Much of the language of Scripture is in the form of prayer, and by using it we find help in our approches to God. 2. Always go to God with faith in Jesus Christ. In His name you may ask for every blessing ; and through His merits, and for His sake, you may find all that can make you happy in this world, with a pardon of your sins, and a good hope of heaven. 3. Seek for the aid of the Holy Spirit, for He will show us what we need, help our weakness, put right desires into our hearts, and teach us how to pray aright. 4. Have something to say to God. Do not say words in an unmeaning way. Spend a few minutes in thought before you begin to pray, that you may not " mock God with a solemn sound." 5. Leave the answer to the love and wisdom of God. He will give to us those things which it is best for us to receive. *The praying Christ :*—We owe our knowledge of the prayers of Jesus principally to the Evangelist Luke. This fact tallies with the many other characteristics of the third Gospel which mark it as eminently the story of the Son of Man. Consider, then—I. How PRECIOUS THE PRAYERS OF JESUS ARE, AS BRINGING HIM VERY NEAR TO US IN HIS TRUE MANHOOD. II. THE HIGHEST, HOLIEST LIFE NEEDS SPECIFIC ACTS AND TIMES OF PRAYER. III. CHRIST'S OWN PRAYERS DO, IN A VERY REAL SENSE, TEACH US TO PRAY. 1. The praying Christ teaches us to pray as a rest after service. 2. The praying Christ teaches us to pray as a preparation for important steps (Luke vi. 12, &c.). 3. The praying Christ teaches us to pray as the condition of receiving the Spirit and the brightness of God. There were two occasions in the life of Christ when visible signs showed His full possession of the Divine Spirit and the lustre of His glorious nature—Baptism, and Transfiguration. Now on both these occasions, our Gospel, and our Gospel alone, tells us that it was whilst Christ was in the act of prayer that the sign was given (see iii. 21–22 ; ix. 29). 4. The praying Christ teaches us to pray as the preparation for sorrow. Gethsemane. (*A. Maclaren, D.D.*)   *Desire and prayer :*—Prayer is an attestance of desire, and desire is so natural to man that no man who lives is quite without it. Our human life is created in great part by desire. When men, who have been created to desire, turn themselves towards a Being who is supposed to have power over their destinies, desire naturally renders itself into prayer. The Son of God imparting to His disciples the true knowledge of the Father, did not fail to teach them concerning prayer. In His own practice He sets an example of earnest and sustained prayer. He deliberately taught His disciples to pray ; He bade them pray out of the fulness of their hearts, and not only so, but He gave His sanction to the use of forms by prescribing to them a form of words which would show them the desires they ought to entertain, and be a perpetual encouragement to such desires. We may derive a double benefit from our Lord's lofty teaching; we may be delivered from the covetous, self-regarding prayers which dishonour Him to whom they are offered, and have no healing or exalting influence on the worshipper who offers them ; and at the same time the true spirit of prayer, which is effectual with God, and on the wings of which we may rise upwards towards Him, may through His teaching be breathed into our hearts. The most Christian kind of prayer will be the utterance of a desire in our souls which is in harmony with God's purposes, and which we may believe to be breathed into us by God's Spirit. And though the essence of prayer is inward and spiritual, we rightly put it into words, and even use fixed words of prayer, because it belongs to our nature to translate our thoughts into words, and because forms are necessary modes of our life, and especially indispensable for whatever we are to do jointly or in common. (*Ll. Davies, D.D.*) *Jesus the Teacher of prayer :*—I. WHY JESUS IS TO BE REGARDED AS THE TEACHER OF PRAYER. It should be taken for granted that knowing how to pray is the first of all essentials. If we want information we may have it. There was once a man in Palestine who said that He was the Son of God, and what He did proved that what He said was true. When we would know how to pray, we, like the first disciples, think that if any one can tell us He can. He is the Teacher of prayer. That is His business. Now He is ascended, His disciples are always learning to pray, and He is always teaching. In all our approaches to the Infinite Unseen, we have first to do with Jesus; every prayer must reach His ear before we have the answer to it. II. HOW HE TEACHES. 1. Sometimes by means of an overheard prayer. It was so in the chapter of events to which the text belongs. 2. Jesus teaches us to pray by our troubles. " Nature in an agony is no atheist." 3. Jesus teaches prayer by revealing Himself as the one medium of prayer. 4. Jesus teaches us to pray by making His own Spirit the spirit of our lives. 5. Jesus teaches to pray by quickening the sense of difficulty. (1) One difficulty is realizing God. (2) Another is the frequent coldness of desire Godward. (3) Another, the effect on our souls of the atmosphere in which we have to live. (4) Another, vain thoughts. If, said Philip Henry, " our prayers were written down and our vain thoughts interlined, what nonsense there would be ! " (5) A kindred difficulty is the restlessness we often feel in the act of prayer. Every one of us can understand the entry made by homely William Smith of Coalville, in the diary of his soul : " While at prayer my mind was rather shifting. I had to bring it back and ask it to sit down." We are baffled and weighted by ignorance, by infirmity, and by countless things, which together make such a total that we feel inclined to think with Coleridge that " the act of praying, in its most perfect form, is the very highest energy of which the human mind is capable." The difficulty does not begin when we begin to pray under the teaching of Christ, but the *sense* of it does; and this He uses for carrying on His purpose. When you have made acquaintance with a thing through difficulties you are more sure of your ground. By quickening the sense of difficulty the Angel wrestles us into strength, and teaches the suppliant to say, " I will not let Thee go except Thou bless me." (*Dr. Stanford.*) It is remarkable that Jesus only teaches *prayer*, never the *philosophy* of prayer. The sentiment of not a few appears to be, that this philosophy is the very thing that we have first to learn. The first questions, even of Christians, are too often simply speculative; and in almost every one of the many treatises on prayer they have given to the world in recent years, a large space is taken up with the discussion of such questions. More than they are aware, they are influenced in this direction by the spirit of the times. Each young believer is now likely to be brought more or less in contact with some theorist who owns no higher teacher of religion than science, who smiles down upon him, assures him that the discoveries of science prove the alleged power of prayer to be impossible; and says, " It is useless for you to expect that the laws of nature will be set aside because you pray ! " " Who wants the laws of nature to be set aside ? " might be the reply. " Assuredly I do not. I know very little about the laws of nature, and even you know very little more. For aught your science can show, it may be quite possible for God to answer prayers, without in the least degree touching the settled constitution of the universe." Our conviction is that we find wrought into our very nature, as one of its primary principles, the instinct that prompts to prayer. (*Ibid.*) *A prayer about prayer :*—In this verse there are certain arguments for and encouragements to prayer, worthy of careful attention. I. PRAYER IS INSTINCTIVE. Four classes of persons here mentioned. In some respects very different from each other. One thing, however, they had in common, namely, prayer. Christ prayed. His disciples prayed. John prayed. His followers were like him. The world here in miniature. Man a praying being.

II. PRAYER IS CHRISTLIKE. Prayer was His habit. "I give myself unto prayer," was the experience of both David and David's greater Son. To some this is perplexing. They cannot understand why our Lord should pray. There would, however, have been far more mystery had He never prayed at all. The holier we become, the more frequent and fervent is our communion with our Heavenly Father. III. PRAYER IS CONTAGIOUS. The word is used for want of a better. What led His disciples to say, "Teach us to pray"? Had the Master been speaking of prayer? Not a word. It was on quite another occasion that He said, "Men ought always to pray." How was it, then, that the desire for increased power in devotion was awakened? It was through hearing and seeing our Lord pray. Prayer begets prayer. One live coal kindles another. There is an Eastern proverb, as true as it is poetic, "I am not the rose; but I have been with the rose, and therefore I am sweet." IV. PRAYER IS EFFECTUAL. "Teach us to pray." That petition was granted. And real prayer is always answered. It cannot fail. As Bishop Hall says: "I am sure that I shall receive either what I ask, or what I should ask." V. THE EXPRESSION, "AS JOHN ALSO TAUGHT HIS DISCIPLES," HAS MORE IN IT THAN AT FIRST SIGHT APPEARS. It is not the cry of false conservatism. We shall err if we suppose that he who uttered it simply wanted our Lord to follow in the track of another. Surely there was an argument, and a fine one, in the words. What did it mean? Something like this: "John was Thy servant, and he helped the devotion of his followers; wilt Thou, great Master, do less? John was only a herald and a forerunner, but he watched over his disciples; wilt not Thou, the promised and predicted One, do the same to us?" It was good reasoning. Better logic cannot be imagined. Let us take the benefit of it. Inspired by the faith which it teaches, be our prayers both frequent and fervent. (*T. R. Stevenson.*)   *Influence:* —We have here a simple illustration of the silent involuntary influence of our Lord. One of His disciples had observed Him praying, and struck with the grandeur and sweetness of the act, he asks to be taught how to pray. Without a commandment but by the power of His example, He influenced His disciple. I. IT IS A REAL INFLUENCE THAT OF EXAMPLE. He who is most a child of God in faith, hope, and love, is most of a king for God over himself and over others, wielding an irresistible power, and gaining widest triumphs. II. EXAMPLE OF THE INFLUENCE OF EXAMPLE. You see it in Christ in this incident. Teach me to pray, said the disciple; but he had more than half learned the lesson when he had looked on Christ praying. The evangelists never pause to extol the life of the Master. To tell the life was best to praise it. On the way to the cross, Jesus does not recommend patience—He *is* patience. On the cross, He does not speak of love—He *is* love as He never was before. III. THE APPLICATION OF THIS TRUTH. 1. To those who need encouragement. Some feel much the uselessness of their lives—no money, little knowledge, or eloquence. But you are not useless if you are true to what is pure and gentle and brave—true to Christ. Influence is not the less powerful because it is silent. 2. This truth speaks to those who need warning. Remember that no one lives to himself. The influence of selfish aims, unregulated tempers, illiberal gifts, goes forth where you little think, and does evil you would dread to acknowledge. What a minister for evil the very presence of an unrevered man is wherever he goes. But if you come to Jesus, though with souls most feeble and most sinful, you may become through Him most magnetic and mighty for the highest issues and the widest influences. (*Dr. W. Graham.*)   *Prayer necessary to maintain the spiritual life:*—The first true sign of spiritual life, prayer, is also the means of maintaining it. Man can as well live physically without breathing, as spiritually without praying. There is a class of animals—the cetaceous, neither fish nor sea-fowl, that inhabit the deep. It is their home; they never leave it for the shore; yet, though swimming beneath its waves, and sounding its darkest depths, they have ever and anon to rise to the surface that they may breathe the air. Without that these monarchs of the deep could not exist in the dense element in which they live, and move, and have their being. And something like what is imposed on them by physical necessity, the Christian has to do by a spiritual one. It is by ever and anon ascending up to God, by rising through prayer into a loftier, purer region for supplies of Divine grace, that he maintains his spiritual life. Prevent these animals from rising to the surface, and they die for want of breath; prevent him from rising to God, and he dies for want of prayer. "Give me children," cried Rachel, "or else I die." "Let me breathe," says a man, gasping, "or else I die." "Let me pray," says the Christian, "or else I die." (*T. Guthrie, D.D.*) *The difficulty of true prayer:*—"I have no difficulty," said he (Coleridge). "in forgiveness; indeed, I know not how to say with sincerity the clause in the Lord's Prayer which asks forgiveness *as we forgive.* I feel nothing answering to it in my heart. Neither do I find, or reckon, the most solemn faith in God as a real object, the most arduous act of the reason and will. Oh no, my dear, it is *to pray, to pray* as God would have us ; this is what at times makes me turn cold to my soul. Believe me, to pray with all your heart and strength, with the reason and the will, to believe vividly that God will listen to your voice through Christ, and verily do the thing He pleaseth thereupon—this is the last, the greatest achievement of the Christian's warfare upon earth. *Teach* us to pray, O Lord !" And then he burst into a flood of tears, and begged me to pray for him. (*Ed. Coleridge's Table Talk.*) *Thought in prayer :—*A prayer must have thought in it. The thought may over-burden it so that its wings of devotion are fastened down to its sides, and cannot ascend. Then it is no prayer, only a meditation or a contemplation. But to take the thought out of a prayer does not insure its going up to God. It may be too light as well as too heavy to ascend. I saw once, in a shop window in London, a placard which simply announced, " Limp Prayers." It described, I believe, a kind of a prayer-book in a certain sort of binding, which was for sale within; but it brought to mind many a prayer to which one had listened, in which he could not join, out of which had been left the whole backbone of thought, and to which he could attach none of his own heart's desire. (*P. Brookes.*) *Forms of prayer :—*I. And, first, on the use of prepared forms of prayer for public worship, or liturgies as we call them. That these were of Divine appointment under the Jewish dispensation there can be no question. The songs of Moses and Miriam, and the titles prefixed to a large number in the Book of Psalms, bear evidence of being composed for congregational use. Besides, through the writings of Josephus and other Hebrew historians, no inconsiderable part of the ancient Jewish liturgies have been preserved to us, and a remarkable coincidence has been discovered between the order and method of these early compositions with our own Book of Common Prayer. The forms of which we know the most are two—one for the service of the Temple, and the other for that of the Synagogue. In the synagogue form the order of public worship was prayer, reading of the Scriptures, and preaching. Their prayers, though not always the same, were always pre-composed, the most commonly used being eighteen, said to have been composed by Ezra at the time of the Captivity, all containing many sentences out of his Book. These forms were in use among the Jews in our Lord's time, and both Jesus and His apostles joined in them. Unsafe, therefore, as it might be, as a rule, to base an argument on the silence of Scripture, yet we can hardly suppose, that if our Lord had intended that in such an important particular the Christian worship was to differ from the Jewish, He would not have told His disciples so plainly, rather than first join in such pre-composed devotions Himself, and then institute a form, which from being expressed throughout in the plural number, must have been supposed to have been intended for public and social use. Here, then, is good reason to believe that the only recited congregational prayer preserved in the New Testament —I mean that contained in the 4th chapter of the Acts—was a form commonly used by the early Christians as suited to a time of persecution, for the whole assembly recited it together—" Then lifted up they their voice to God with one accord." The scriptural evidence, therefore, as far as it goes, is clearly in favour of set and prepared forms of public prayer. If we join to this the testimony of ecclesiastical history, there is no more doubt about the apostolic usage as a question of fact, than there is as a question of fact about the persecution of Domitian or the siege of Jerusalem. Even Pliny's letter to Trajan, at the beginning of the second century, alludes (contemptuously, of course) to these Christians meeting for daily worship, and reciting, as he says, a composed form ; whilst the liturgies attri-buted to St. Mark, St. Peter, and St. James, respectively, from which a good deal of our own liturgy is taken, whether really composed by those apostles or not, can be traced to a period sufficiently early to make the alleged authorship by no means impossible. Other testimonies might be cited, more convincing, because merely incidental, all assuming the usage itself to be one of common notoriety. II. Let me advert to a point which we shall all feel to be of great importance, namely, the use of prepared forms in our private devotions. Let me proceed, then, to point out some objections to prepared forms of private prayer, however spiritual and excellent they may be, if they be used exclusively. Thus it is obvious we are thereby confined in regard to the matter of our prayers, we restrict our conversation with heaven to a fixed routine of subjects, and preclude the mention of those hourly spiritual experiences, which though unseen, and unknown to the world, make up the great incidents of the soul's life, and may give, day by day, a new complexion to its prayers. We live in a world of change, and in the countless vicissitudes to which mind, body, and estate are alike exposed; the soul is subject to infinite varieties of emotion, for which no prepared form can provide corresponding expression. Again, there is a danger lest the exclusive use of forms should have a tendency to deaden the spirit of prayer. Let me conclude with a few practical directions which, whether with or without forms, cannot be neglected by those who would be taught how to pray. 1. As first, when you enter your closet, be composed, and reverent, and thoughtful. 2. Again, be honest and faithful with yourselves; let there be a great searching both of heart and life. 3. I say, aim to be comprehensive and yet specific. 4. Lastly, we must be earnest and persevering. The confession is humiliating, but it must be made. (*D. Moore, M.A.*) *The instructions of the Bible as to the matter and manner of prayer :*—The best of men need direction in prayer. Who may not adopt the language, " Teach us what we shall say unto Him : for we cannot order our speech by reason of darkness "? The Bible is a sufficient rule of conduct in all things pertaining to life and godliness. The subject-matter for prayer is to be found in the Word of God. There is not one of its doctrines, in all their richness and variety, that does not contain truths which the lips of prayer may make use of, and turn to good account at the throne of grace. The point is too plain to require either illustration or proof, that the mind must be furnished with the truth of God in order to be furnished with matter for prayer. The precepts of the Bible also teach us how to pray. They describe the spirit of prayer ; while they teach us what graces to ask for, and for what duties we need strength. The promises of the Bible are revealed for our instruction and encouragement in prayer. They teach us what blessings God is willing to bestow, and how willing He is to bestow them. The threatenings of the Bible teach us what we have reason to fear and deprecate ; while the very sins that are there recorded teach what we should pray against and deplore. God has also recorded a multitude of facts in His Word, that are comments upon its truths, its promises, and its threatenings, of which He condescends to permit His people to remind Him, and which furnish them with powerful considerations in pleading at His mercy-seat. There are instances of prayer, too, there recorded, which show us its spirit, its comprehensiveness, its appropriateness to times, and places, and circumstances, and men, as well as its fruit and power ; and which show us for what it is to be offered, and God's readiness to hear and answer. More than this ; the Bible teaches us where to go for assistance in prayer. " For through Him we have access by one Spirit unto the Father." In every act of true devotion, there is a concurrence of the Spirit's influence. Let your mind be richly furnished with all God's truth, and let your bosom be filled with devotional emotions, and then freely utter your requests before God. There is thought in prayer ; strong thought, and often close, compact, and connected thought. There is emotion, too, heavenly emotion. There is memory, too, in prayer ; and there is conscience and even imagination. This formula, commonly called the Lord's Prayer, contains the substance of prayer for His disciples. A question arises here, if we may not use this form in our supplications at the throne of grace ? The Christian ought not to be so much the enemy of forms, as to depreciate this most beautiful form of prayer ; nor so much of a formalist, as not to pray without it. Jesus Christ has nowhere authorized a restriction to any set form of prayer. The prayers of Abraham were not written prayers. Nor was the prayer of Eleazar at Haran ; nor the prayer of Jacob at Peniel ; nor the prayers of Moses and Aaron for Egypt and Israel. The prayer of Joshua at the defeat of Ai, the prayer of Manoah, of Samson, of Hannah, of Samuel at Mizpeh, of Elijah at Mount Carmel, of Hezekiah against Sennacherib, of Jabez, of Ezra, of Nehemiah, of Job, of Daniel, of Jonah, and of Habakkuk, were none of them dictated by the pen. Nor was the prayer of Zacharias, nor that of the publican, nor that of the disciples in any one exigence of their history. In the next place, forms of prayer invert the order of prayer ; they make the words lead the heart, and not the heart the words. True prayer flows from the heart ; the heart is the seat of supplication. Another objection to forms is, that they check the teachings of the Holy Spirit. Still another objection to forms of prayer is, that no set of prayers is, or ever can be, adequate to the necessities of the Church. It has been said that the example of the Primitive Christians is in favour of forms. Much has been written to prove the antiquity of liturgies, and Bishop Bull has strongly urged the probability of their being of Apostolic origin. The posture of the primitive Christians in prayer was such as to render it impossible to read prayers. They stood with their arms crossed on their breasts, their heads back, and their eyes often closed. It is confidently asserted by those who have made close search, that there is not such an expression as "reading prayers," to be found in the history of the first four centuries. In favour of forms, it is also said, that it is important to have matter to ponder upon, to pray with intelligence. We have only to reply, most certainly it is so ; but then there is more matter in the Bible than in a Book of Common Prayer. It is further urged, and we confess the objection has some weight that in extempore prayers, too much latitude is given to the speaker, that, on the one hand, his prayers may often be barren and dry ; and on the other, they may be redundant, and sometimes filled even with wild and extravagant notions. This is true ; it is an evil to be guarded against : and we have only to say, that we expect too much, when we expect perfect prayers from imperfect men. Once more, it is objected to prayers that are not thus formed, that the people cannot join in them. (*G. Spring, D.D.*) *The abridgment of the whole Gospel :*—Such plentiful rivers stream from this seven-headed fountain. So that as the seven arms of Nilus watered and made fertile all Egypt ; so doth this prayer, springing from seven petitions, which are deprecative or optative, water the whole Christain world, preventing and deprecating all mishaps, and supplying our wants. So that in this short prayer, as in a little orb, the Sun of Righteousness moves ; from hence doth every star, every faithful servant and counsellor of Christ (for they are incarnate stars) borrow a ray of light to illuminate and sanctify the body of his meditations. The Church in her liturgy and the preacher both enjoined to use it. A small quantity of this leaven seasons a great lump of devotion, and a few spirits give taste and quickness to much liquor. This prayer is a quintessence extracted by the greatest chemist that ever was, from Him that brought nature out of chaos, separated light from darkness, and extracted the four elements out of nothing. All parts of it are spirits. *Quæ enim spiritualior oratio ?* And the mixture of a few grains thereof with our prayers proves the strongest and best Christian antidote. (*Archdeacon King.*) *Giving God His own in prayer :*—It is a familiar and friendly tribute to present God with His own ; a petition clothed in Christ's words, will find the ready way to heaven, and a speedy access into the ears of God. (*Ibid.*) *The parts of the Lord's Prayer :*—So consider this prayer as it now lies all together, the plates and joints and several matters make but one Christian buckler to ward and avert all necessities that may befall us ; yet resolved into parcels, every limb and member, and gradation, is a perfect buckler to bear off our particular wants. It is like that famous target of Ajax that was Clypeus Septemplex, consisted of seven folds ; this is Oratio Septemplex, a prayer consisting of seven requests. That buckler was dart-proof, impenetrable, and this prayer an impenetrable shield to resist the fiery darts of Satan. If I would insist upon the allusion to the number of these petitions, I might compare this whole prayer to the constellation of the Pleiades, or seven stars in heaven ; or to the seven stars in the right hand of the Son of Man, being fit lights and tapers for the seven golden candlesticks there mentioned, to be set up in those seven Churches, and not in them alone, but in all the Churches of the world, where Christ's name is known and adored. Or I may liken the parts of this prayer to the seven planets, eminent above all other stars of the firmament. For as some of those planets move nearer to the earth, others higher and farther off, so is the motion of these seven petitions ; some of them move and solicit God for earthly things, as the four last of them ; others for heavenly and eternal, as the three first, "Hallowed be Thy name, and Thy kingdom come," &c. Saint Augustine hath taken their just height and motion, *Tres petitiones superiores æternæ sunt, quatuor sequentes ad hanc vitam pertinent.* (*Ibid.*) *Praying from a copy :*—I do not deny him a good artizan that works by the strength of his own phantasy : yet all will grant he works truest that works from a copy. And though a voluntary expressed upon an instrument show the sufficiency of the musician, yet I should think that musician who undervalues all set lessons in comparison of his voluntaries hath more of arrogance than skill. Just so is it in prayer. I prejudice no man's gift, and let me advise no man so much to prejudice this excellent gift of Christ's Prayer as to exalt his own meditations above it. (*Ibid.*) *The Lord's Prayer perfect :*—The matter is every way found complete and perfect. Every word in it hath its weight. There is not a superfluous word in it that could be spared. Nor is it any way defective. Whatsoever is lawful, needful, and meet to be asked in prayer is therein contained : yea, whatsoever is to be believed or practised by a Christian is therein implied. (*William Gouge.*)

The Lord's Prayer little, yet great :—The sense of it is as large as the body is little. (*Archdeacon King.*)

Ver. 2. **When ye pray, say.**—*Sermonic hints on the Lord's Prayer:*—1. Not a prescription of words. A great merit in prayer is that it most naturally expresses the feeling of him who offers it. A child's prattle is more acceptable to a parent than stately utterances put into his mouth. In Raphael's cartoon the adoring disciples surround the risen Lord in various attitudes, one kneeling, one with clasped hands, one with open palms, one with bowed head, and one shows excited reverence by the fact that he is allowing his robe to trail in the dirt; the great artist having seen that the highest expression of religious emotion must be the natural outcome of the soul, and bear the mark of the worshipper's individuality. Horace Bushnell used to go to sleep, as he said, "talking with God." Liturgies are useful to stimulate spirituality; but should be used to suggest, never to limit, religious thought. 2. The manner of the prayer is in general—(1) Of utmost simplicity. No elaboration. (2) Calmness. No oh's! only quiet confidence and consecration. 3. Analyzing more particularly the sentiments of the prayer, we observe that the model prayer gives a portraiture of a model man. (1) Filial faith. "Our Father." (2) Reverence. "Hallowed," &c. (3) Loyalty. "Thy kingdom come." (4) A conformed spirit. "Thy will be done." (5) Recognition of Providence. "Give us . . . daily bread." (6) Dependence upon grace. "Forgive us our debts." (7) Sincere charity. "For we forgive." (8) Dependence upon the Holy Spirit. "Lead us not," &c. (*J. M. Ludlow, D.D.*) *The Lord's Prayer like the Decalogue:*—The Lord's Prayer, like the Decalogue, falls in two: two tables of law, two leaves of petition. The first table of the law concerns our duties to God; the first leaf of the prayer concerns the glory of God. The second table respects our duties to man; the second leaf respects the needs of man. The first table contains the laws that are the hardest to obey sincerely; the first leaf, the petitions that are the hardest to pray sincerely. Obeying the laws of the first table is what qualifies us to obey those of the second. Praying the petitions of the first leaf is what qualifies us to pray those of the second. Yet we never suppose that the prayer was composed with any reference to the Decalogue. All resemblance ceases to be interesting as soon as it is felt to be imitation. Resemblance by imitation betrays the mechanic; resemblance without imitation argues the artist, the creator. The earth did not become spherical to imitate the sun, nor do the leaves on one branch become serrate to imitate each other. Those leaves unfold up into an outward likeness because they unfolded out of an inward likeness. The Decalogue was not made, it unfolded. The prayer was not made, it unfolded; it was not built, it grew. And because Decalogue and prayer both are unfolded from out the one mind of God, leaves upon one branch, blossoms upon one stem, they show the same hues and take the same orderly arrangement. (*C. H. Parkhurst, D.D.*) *The Lord's Prayer indicates the right way of looking at things:*—There is a fearful tendency in us all, which has infused itself most mischievously into our theology, to look first at our necessity or misery, only afterwards at our relation to God, and at His nature. The last are made dependent upon the former. We are conscious of a derangement in our condition; simply in reference to this derangement do we contemplate Him who we hope may reform it. We have just been tracing this process in heathenism. A mischief is felt; if there is a mischief there must be a deliverer. Undoubtedly the conscience bears this witness, and it is a right one. But the qualities of the deliverer are determined by the character or locality of that which is to be redressed, or by the habits of those who are suffering from it. From this heathenish habit of mind the Lord's Prayer is the great preserver. Say first, "Our Father." This relation is fixed, established, certain. It existed in Christ before all worlds, it was manifested when He came in the flesh. He is ascended on high, that we may claim it. Let us be certain that we ground all our thoughts upon these opening words; till we know them well by heart, do not let us listen to the rest. Let us go on carefully, step by step, to the Name, the Kingdom, the Will, assuring ourselves of our footing, confident that we are in a region of clear unmixed goodness; of goodness which is to be hallowed by us; which has come and shall come to us, and in us; which is to be done on earth, not merely in heaven. Then we are in a condition to make these petitions, which we are ordinarily in such haste to utter, and which He, in whom all wisdom dwells, commands us to defer. Last of all comes this "Deliver us from evil." When we are able to look upon evil, not as the regular normal state of the universe, but as absolutely at variance with the character of its

Author, with His constitution of it, with the Spirit which He has given to us, then we can pray, attaching some real significance to the language, deliver us from it. Then we shall understand why men looked with faith to the aid of their fellow-men; to princes, and chieftains, and lawgivers, and sages. They were sent into the world for this end, upon this mission. They were meant to act as deliverers. They were to be witnesses of a real righteous order, and to resist all transgressors of it. We can understand why strong men felt that they had better act for themselves, than depend upon foreign help. For the Father of all put their strength into them, that they might wield it as His servants in His work; it was His Spirit who made them conscious of their strength, and of that purpose for which they were to use it. We can see why these hopes were so continually disappointed though they had so right a foundation; why they were driven to think of higher aid, of invisible champions, because those upon the earth proved feeble, or deserted the cause, and served themselves. It is true that the hosts of heaven are obeying that power which the hosts of earth are commanded to obey; that they are doing His service by succouring those who are toiling below; it is true, because He who rules all is not a destiny, but a loving will; not an abstraction, but a person; not a mere sovereign, but a Father. All creation is ordered upon this law of mutual dependence and charity; but it is only in the knowledge and worship of the Highest, that we can apprehend the places and tasks of the lower; when He is hidden, these are forgotten; society becomes incoherent; nothing understands itself; everything is inverted; the deliverer is one with the tyrant; evil and good run into each other; we invoke Satan to cast out Satan. See, then, what a restorative, regenerative power lies in this prayer! (*F. D. Maurice, M.A.*) *Introductory remarks :*—1. The first thing to be noted is the brevity of this prayer. In most religions the efficacy of prayer has been supposed to depend on its length. The notion is that the gods will do nothing for men unless they are teased. This prayer rebukes and corrects that idea. 2. How was this prayer to be used? (1) Was it to be used exclusively? Clearly not, since in the Acts we have the record of several prayers which did not follow this form, and yet were answered abundantly. (2) Ought we always, when we pray, to use these words—to include this prayer in all our supplications? No; I do not think our Lord means to require that. We shall often wish to pray in these words; but He means that our desires shall be free to utter themselves in their own way. The prayer is a model, in its simplicity, brevity, directness, but not a prescribed form; a staff, not a fetter, for the praying soul. (*Washington Gladden, D.D.*) *The peculiar worth of the Lord's Prayer :*—Not so much in particular expressions, as rather in the tenor and spirit, in the arrangement and climax of the whole, lies its peculiar worth, and those who can assert of the "Pater Noster" that it is only a joining together of Rabbinic expressions, might assure us with the same right that from a suitable number of single arms, legs, and members, one could compose an animated human body. We honour much more the wisdom of the Saviour in this, that He would teach His disciples no chords which would have been entirely strange to their unpractised lips, and in vain do we seek here for the traces of a limited Judaistic spirit. So brief is it, that it does not even weary the simplest spirit, and yet so perfect that nothing is therein wholly forgotten : so simple in words that even a child comprehends it, and yet so rich in matter that the principal truths and promises and duties are here presupposed, confirmed, or impressed, so that Tertullian rightly named it "breviarium totius evangelii." How often soever it may have been misused, especially where it has been turned into a spiritless formula of prayer, while men have forgotten that it only expresses the lofty fundamental ideas which must prevail in the exercise of prayer, it remains yet continually a gold-mine for Christian faith, a standard for Christian prayer, a prop for Christian hope. (*Van Oosterzee.*) *The Lord's Prayer :*—Edwin Booth, the celebrated tragedian, was a man who threw into his impersonations an amount of heart and soul which his originals could scarcely have equalled. He did Richard III. to the life, and more. He had made human passions, emotions, and experiences his life's study. He could not only act, but feel rage, love, despair, hate, ambition, fury, hope, and revenge with a depth and force that amazed his auditors. He transmuted himself into the hero of his impersonation, and he could breathe a power into other men's words which perhaps never was surpassed. And what is rather remarkable, when he was inclined to give illustrations of this faculty to private circles of friends, he nearly always selected some passages from Job, David, or Isaiah, or other holy men of old. When an inquiring young professor of Harvard University went to him by night to ask a little advice or instruction in qualifying himself for an orator, the veteran tragedian opened the Bible and read a few verses from Isaiah in a way that made the Cambridge scholar tremble with awe, as if the prophet had risen from the dead and was uttering his sublime visions in his ears. He was then residing in Baltimore, and a pious, urbane old gentleman of the city, hearing of his wonderful power of elocution, one day invited him to dinner, although strongly deprecating the stage. A large company sat down to the table, and on returning to the drawing-room, they requested Booth, as a special favour to them all, to repeat the Lord's Prayer. He signified his willingness to gratify them, and all eyes were fixed upon him. He slowly and reverentially arose from his chair, trembling with the burden of two great conceptions. He had to realize the character, attributes, and presence of the Almighty Being he was to address. He was to transform himself into a poor, sinning, stumbling, benighted, needy suppliant, offering homage, asking bread, pardon, light and guidance. Says one of the company present: It was wonderful to watch the play of emotions that convulsed his countenance. He became deathly pale, and his eyes, turned tremblingly upwards, were wet with tears. As yet he had not spoken. The silence could be felt; it had become absolutely painful, until at last the spell was broken as if by an electric shock, as his rich-toned voice, from white lips, syllabled forth, "Our Father, which art in heaven," &c., with a pathos and fervid solemnity that thrilled all hearts. He finished; the silence continued; not a voice was heard, nor a muscle moved, in his rapt audience, until, from a remote corner of the room, a subdued sob was heard, and the old gentleman (the host) stepped forward, with streaming eyes and tottering frame, and seized Booth by the hand. "Sir," said he, in broken accents, "you have afforded me a pleasure for which my whole future life will feel grateful. I am an old man, and every day, from boyhood to the present time, I thought I had repeated the Lord's Prayer; but I never heard it before—never!" "You are right," replied Booth; "to read that prayer as it should be read caused me the severest study and labour for thirty years, and I am far from being satisfied with my success." *The fulness of the Lord's Prayer:*—I used to think the Lord's Prayer was a short prayer; but as I live longer, and see more of life, I begin to believe there is no such thing as getting through it. If a man, in praying that prayer, were to be stopped by every word until he had thoroughly prayed it, it would take him a lifetime. "Our Father"—there would be a wall a hundred feet high in just those two words to most men. If they might say "Our Tyrant," or "Our Monarch," or even "Our Creator," they could get along with it; but "Our *Father*"—why, a man is almost a saint who can pray that. You read, "Thy will be done"; and say to yourself, "Oh! I can pray that;" and all the time your mind goes round and round in immense circuits and far-off distances: but God is continually bringing the circuits nearer to you, till He says, "How is it about your temper and your pride? how is it about your business and your daily life?" This is a revolutionary petition. It would make many a man's shop and store tumble to the ground to utter it. Who can stand at the end of the avenue along which all his pleasant thoughts and wishes are blossoming like flowers, and send these terrible words, "Thy will be done," crashing down through it? I think it is the most fearful prayer to pray in the world. (*H. W. Beecher.*) *The Lord's Prayer contains the essence of the Old Testament:*—When at Jerusalem I read this prayer to one of the rabbis, he said, "There is not one single prayer, not one single demand, which is not already contained in the Old Testament." I said, "Very well, let us see." "Now," I said, "can you give me a parallel passage to 'Hallowed be Thy name?'" He quoted in an instant the forty-third verse of the eighth chapter of First Kings. "Hear Thou in heaven Thy dwelling place . . . that all people of the earth may know Thy name to fear Thee." And farther, he said, "'Blessed be the name of the Lord'; what means this but 'Hallowed be Thy name'?" "Let us go on—'Thy kingdom come!'" He immediately gave me the passage from the seventy-second Psalm. "He shall come down like rain upon the mown grass: as showers that water the earth. In His days shall the righteous flourish; and abundance of peace so long as the moon endureth. He shall have dominion also from sea to sea, and from the river unto the ends of the earth." "Let us go on—'Thy will be done in earth, as it is in heaven!'" "Does not the psalmist tell us—'Teach us to do Thy will, O Lord?'" "Let us proceed—'Give us this day our daily bread?'" "You find this prayer in the Proverbs—'Give me neither poverty nor riches, feed me with food convenient for me.'" "Forgive us our debts, as we forgive our debtors!" "This you find in the one hundred and thirty-second Psalm—'Lord, remember David, and all his afflictions,' and in the seventh Psalm, and the fourth verse—'If I have rewarded evil unto him that was at peace with me.'" "Lead us not into temptation." He said at once—"O Lord, correct me with judgment; not in Thine anger, lest Thou bring me to nothing." And then he quoted the Apocrypha, with which he was well acquainted. "Take away the desire of sensuality; to the spirit of licentiousness do not deliver me." "What is this but 'Lead us not into temptation'?" "Deliver us from evil." He quoted—"Deliver me from the workers of iniquity." I said, "Have you done?" He said, "Yes." "Then," I said, "you have just shown that our blessed Lord was in the right, when He told the Jews, that He 'came not to abolish the Law, but to fulfil it.' And have you in the whole of the Old Testament a prayer which is not contained in the Lord's Prayer?" He admitted that there was not one. So you see how this prayer, the Lord's Prayer, according to the testimony of a Jew opposed to Christianity, is an abridgment, a wonderful abridgment, of the whole of the gospel, and of the whole of what Moses and the prophets have told us. So that the great and holy Stolberg says—"the child prays in it in simplicity, and the learned in vain tries to fathom its depths." (*J. Wolff, D.D.*) *The Lord's prayer:*—In the prayer our Lord taught His disciples, all the relationships in which we stand to God are taken up. The believer prays as—I. A CHILD FROM HOME. "Our Father," &c. II. A WORSHIPPER. "Hallowed," &c. III. A SUBJECT. "Thy kingdom come." IV. A SERVANT. "Thy will be done." V. A BEGGAR. "Give us," &c. VI. A DEBTOR. "And forgive us," &c. VII. A SINNER AMID TEMPTATION AND EVIL. "And lead us not," &c. (*Classified Gems of Thought.*) *The Lord's prayer given as a pattern:*—We have here a ground-plan to fill in, and on whose lines we may build the structure of our petitions every time we pray. 1. Observe, IT IS NOT ONE OF OUR LORD'S OWN PRAYERS THAT IS GIVEN FOR A PATTERN. It is out of the question that we should offer for our daily prayer the very words once used to express the prayers of Christ for Himself. When, therefore, the disciples asked for a pattern of prayer that they might pray just like Christ, the spirit of this the opening sentence in His reply was—"No, your prayers are not to be just like Mine. I pray after that manner. After this manner, pray ye. I pray as the *Lord ;* but when *ye* pray, say "—and then He gave them these words. II. You will take notice that this pattern was granted after the petition—Teach us to pray AS JOHN ALSO TAUGHT HIS DISCIPLES. The speaker, and those for whom he was the spokesman, had no doubt, been in the school of John before they had come into that of Jesus. Yet you are ready to wonder how they could have thought of Him just then. They had just overheard that sacred secret, a secret prayer of Jesus. You say each one ought to have felt his whole being tenfold alive and awake in that moment of glory and exaltation, and you think there ought then to have been no room for the memory of anything mortal. Yet that prayer at once reminded them of their old Master, and their first wish was that Jesus would use John's method of teaching them to pray. He must have been a tremendous man to leave an impression on the minds of his scholars that was keen even in the sharpness of such an excitement. There was much imperfection in this petition. The disciples had no right to speak to their Lord in anything like the tone of dictation. While they asked Him to teach them, they told Him how to do it, and indicated the kind of teaching they preferred. But Jesus passed by the fault, recognized the necessity, and was pleased to formulate a prayer for the help of their weakness, and also of our own; for on us also His eye rested as He gave it, and all who are trying after closer fellowship with God, may now feel their way, think their way, and pray their way, through these great words. III. Take note of the fact that THIS PATTERN WAS GIVEN TWICE. Christ had already given it in the Sermon on the Mount. These suppliants, as if they had never heard of it, asked Him to give what He had already given. How was this? We suppose that besides the disciples who came from John to Jesus at the commencement of his ministry, and the story of whose call is told in the opening of the Fourth Gospel, there were others whose enrolment came later, and that some of these having been with John during the first delivery of the Lord's prayer, made the appeal which led to this, the second delivery. Strange that they should have been content to miss so much! Why did they stay with John after he had pointed out Jesus to be the Saviour? and how could they stop looking at the finger-posts instead of travelling in the road? Perhaps they considered themselves, so to speak, to be all the time, scholars in Christ's school, though in John's class, and as spiritual infants still needing his elementary lessons. They had come late to school. They had more to learn than their classmates. They had missed the Sermon on the Mount. Their new companions, spiritually dull and slow, had not told them that the Lord had already given a pattern of prayer; they therefore asked for one, and the compassionate Saviour gave them the substance of His former words. This was only like Himself, the Teacher who has infinite patience with our dulness, stoops to us, repeats His lesson, and is for ever saying, "Learn of Me, for I am meek and lowly in heart." IV. THIS PATTERN OF PRAYER MUST ALWAYS BE TAKEN IN CONNECTION WITH, AND BE EXPLAINED BY, THE WHOLE OF THE CHRISTIAN REVELATION. It is a mistake to take this, or any other sectional part of revelation, as if it were the whole—a mistake to treat this as Christ's final disclosure of grace. V. THE PATTERN IS MEANT FOR THE USE OF ALL THE CHILDREN OF GOD, WHATEVER THEIR DIFFERENCES IN AGE, CAPACITY, OR ATTAINMENT. It fits the child, it fits the man, it fits the father and mother, it fits the youngest saint, and the saint with reverend head. VI. THIS PATTERN IS INTENDED TO FURNISH CERTAIN RULES AND METHODS OF PRAYER. 1. Petitioners are here taught brevity. 2. They are taught to shun vain repetition. (See Matt. vi. 7.) 3. They are taught to pray using these very words. The second announcement of the pattern was prefaced by the phrase, "When ye pray, say," &c. But mark the proviso. The point is that we may only say it when we *do* pray. Prayer is a distinct thing from the vehicle of prayer. Beautiful as this frame is, it is only a vehicle of praying life, not a substitute for it. 4. It is a social prayer. 5. They are taught to pray after this manner. VII. IT IS RIGHT TO CALL THIS PATTERN PRAYER THE LORD'S PRAYER. Some would prefer to call it the Rabbi's prayer. Others the Disciples' prayer. We might as well say of the Remembrance Feast, that it is not the Lord's Supper but the Disciples' Supper, for only the disciples are to keep it. As the Lord's Supper is a remembrance feast, this is a remembrance prayer, always to be in our ears, always before our eyes, to show what we should pray for, and how we should pray; until, "at our Father's loved abode our souls arrive in peace." (*Dr. Stanford.*) **Our Father, which art in heaven.**—*The preface of the Lord's Prayer:* — I. WHAT OUR BEING DIRECTED TO CALL GOD "FATHER" IN PRAYER TEACHES US. 1. That the children of God alone can pray acceptably. 2. That it is through Jesus Christ we have access to God in prayer (Eph. ii. 18), because it is through Him alone that God becomes our Father; by Him, for His sake, we are adopted into the family of heaven (John i. 12). 3. That coming to God in prayer, we must come in the name of His Son, as the alone foundation of all our confidence in and expectation from God (John xiv. 13). 4. That the Spirit of adoption, the Spirit of Christ in His people, is the principle of all acceptable praying to God; for by Him it is that we are enabled to call God Father (Gal. iv. 6), and therefore it is called "inwrought prayer" (James v. 16). 5. That we should draw near to God in prayer with child-like dispositions and affections towards Him. (1) Though He be very kind and admit us into familiarity with Him, yet we must come with a holy reverence (Mal. i. 6). (2) Though we have offended God, and be under the marks of His displeasure, we must come with confidence, whatever we want, whatever we need (Eph. iii. 12). (3) That God is ready and willing to help us, and we should come to Him in that confidence (Matt. vii. 11). II. WHAT OUR BEING DIRECTED TO CALL GOD "OUR FATHER" TEACHES US. Negatively: not that we may not pray, saying "My Father," or that we are always to speak plurally, saying, "We pray." For we have Scripture examples for praying in the singular number (Ezra ix. 6; Luke xv. 18, 19). But—1. That we are not only to pray secretly by ourselves alone, but with others, joining with them in public and private. 2. That we are to pray, not only for ourselves, but for others also, according to Scripture example and precept (Acts xii. 5; 1 Tim. ii. 1, 2). Praying with and for others is a piece of the communion of saints. And it is one of the privileges of God's family on earth, that they have the prayers of all the family there. III. WHAT WE ARE TAUGHT BY OUR BEING DIRECTED TO ADDRESS OURSELVES TO GOD AS "OUR FATHER IN HEAVEN." 1. That we are to eye His sovereign power and dominion over all, in our addresses to Him, believing that He is able to help us in our greatest straits, that nothing is too hard for Him, but He can do whatsoever He will (Psa. cxv. 3). This is a noble ground for faith. 2. That we should be filled with heavenly affections in prayer (Psa. cxxiii. 1). And that God's glorious greatness above us should strike an awe upon us in our approaches to Him (Eccl. v. 2). 3. God's glorious and wonderful condescension, who vouchsafes to look from His throne in heaven unto us poor worms on earth (Isa. lxvi. 1, 2). 4. That we go to God as those who are strangers on this earth, and to whom heaven is home, because it is our Father's house (1 Peter i. 17), looking on this world as the place of our pilgrimage, and the men and manners of it as those we desire to leave, that we may be admitted into the society of angels, and consort with the spirits of just men made perfect. Inferences : 1. Let us see here the miserable condition of those who have no ground to call God Father. 2. There is no right praying without faith. (*T. Boston, D.D.*) *The preface of the Lord's prayer :*—I. To WHOM WE ARE TO DIRECT OUR PRAYERS; to God, the omnipresent God, who fills heaven and earth. He can hear a thousand, or ten thousand million petitioners at the same time, if there were so many, and know distinctly what every one asks. And further, we pray to an infinitely wise God, who knows what is fit should be granted us, and what not. II. UNDER WHAT CHARACTER OR DENOMINATION God (according to our Saviour's direction here) is to be addressed; as our Father in heaven. 1. God sustains the character of a Father in the Scripture style in a threefold respect; that is, with reference— (1) To creation. (2) To external separation. (3) To adoption and regeneration. 2. We are to call upon Him as our Father in heaven. Lord, art not Thou God in heaven? O Lord God of heaven. But Christ would direct us to make our supplications to God with the deepest humility, in consideration of the infinite distance between God and us, and with admiration of His amazing condescension in permitting us to speak to the great possessor of heaven, and to implore His presence and blessing who is exalted infinitely above us. III. THE MATTER, AND THE MANNER, of prayer. The Lord's Prayer may be considered—1. As a directory. 2. We may take the Lord's Prayer as a method. 3. We may consider the Lord's Prayer as a form. (*John Whitty.*) *Pater, Father :*—I can conceive of two ways or methods of reaching the notion of a fatherhood in the Deity, or of arriving at the use of this form of address to the Supreme Being, and calling Him Father. The first may be characterized as an ascending, the second as a descending, process; the first having its rise in an earthly and human relation, the second in a relation that is heavenly and Divine. I. The earthly and human relation of a child to a parent— a son to a father—is very close and tender. II. Here we touch the other and higher view which, as I think, Scripture suggests and warrants of the relation now in question; the relation in respect of which we call God Father, and invoke Him as Our Father. It is essential to the very being of the Supreme that He should be a Father, and that of Him there should be a Son. From all eternity, accordingly —in the terms of the Creed of the Council of Nice—the Son is of the Father, "begotten of His Father before all worlds; God of God, Light of Light, very God of very God." He is "the everlasting Son of the Father," "begotten, not made." The relation therefore of paternity or fatherhood in God precedes creation, as well as redemption; and is indeed from everlasting. For before all worlds the Son is in the bosom of the Father. And the infinite, ineffable complacency subsisting between the Father and the Son, realized in the unity of the Holy Spirit with them both, is the true prototype and original model or pattern of the fatherly relation and the fatherly affection of which all who are in the Son are partakers, and in virtue of which they call God Father, and invoke Him as their Father. (*R. S. Candlish, D.D.*) *Pater noster, Our Father :* — The use of the plural form in this invocation is surely significant. We are taught, not only to call upon God as Father, but to call upon Him as our Father. We are to say, Our Father; and that too even in secret prayer. Plainly, therefore, thou dost not apprehend thyself, even in such secrecy, to be quite alone with thy God as thy Father. Others are associated by thee with thyself in this filial utterance, and in the fellowship of filial relationship which it expresses. One at least, or more than one, must be felt by thee to be embraced along with thyself in the invocation. Otherwise thou couldst not well say, with a full and deep sense of reality and truth, Our Father. I. One at all events there surely is—the Master Himself who gives thee this gracious form of address. The Lord Jesus joins Himself to thee, and invites thee to join thyself to Him, so that the invocation may be common to both;—a joint invocation; jointly His and thine—" Our Father." 1. Let us consider here, in the first place, the gracious condescension of the blessed Son of God in His joining Himself to us at the first. Let us behold Him drawing near to us as a brother, in order that we and He together may say, Our Father. For it is as a brother that He draws near to us and stands by us; it is in the character of a brother, "a brother born for adversity." He takes our nature. He takes our place. He takes as His own the very relation in which we stand to God as apostate rebels, disobedient subjects, guilty and condemned, outcast and estranged. He sounds the lowest depths of its degradation, and tastes the bitterest agony of its curse. He makes common cause with us. 2. And now— thou art at home. The gracious interview is over. The reconciliation is complete. The Father hath met thee, and embraced thee, and welcomed thee as His child.

Thou canst scarcely believe for very joy. But thou shalt see greater things than this. For now, secondly, in that Father's dwelling thou hast constant fellowship with Him as a Father. And in that fellowship thou art permitted and enabled to join thyself still always to Him who in thy distress joins Himself to thee. II. But when we say, Our Father, we associate with ourselves others in this fellowship of prayer besides the blessed Lord. He indeed is pre-eminently our fellow, in this act of filial devotion ; and others are so, and can be so, only in Him. But there is room in this fellowship for a wide enough brotherhood. 1. All who are within the reach of saving mercy and redeeming love may be comprehended in its embrace. Men—all men—become dear and precious to me now. To every man—to any man —I can now go, and with all tenderness of fraternal pity and brotherly affection, plead—Brother, Brother—weary and wasted in that far country! To thee, as to me, Christ Jesus, the elder brother, cries, Come! Let us go, thou and I together— let us go home with Him, the elder Brother, saying—all three of us together —Our Father. 2. But a narrower line, at least as regards this earth, must here be drawn. I am called to sympathize with the blessed Jesus, not merely in His going forth among the lost and guilty children of men, that He may win them back to His Father's dwelling, and get them to unite with Himself in saying to Him, Our Father. But I am to sympathize with the blessed Jesus also in His going in and out among those whom He has actually brought again to that dwelling, and whom He is ever presenting there as His brethren to His Father and theirs. Let them all have a place in our heart when we say with Christ, Our Father. And that we may make room in our hearts for them all, let us see that by the help of that very Spirit of adoption—that Spirit of His Son—which the Father sends forth into our hearts—the Spirit "not of bondage and of fear, but of power and of love and of a sound mind"—we banish whatever tends to harden, or deaden, or straiten our affections. 3. Is this all the family? Is this the whole brotherhood? Is it merely the comparatively small company of believers among men that we have to associate with us, when in Christ, and with Christ, we say, Our Father? Nay; if there be a narrow limit to the household of faith on earth, there is ample room and verge enough elsewhere. For, not to speak of the multitude of the redeemed already around the throne, have we not the holy angels for our fellows in this filial address to God? For they also, as well as we, have an interest in the Son ; " the first-begotten," whom the Father bringeth into the world, saying, "Let all the angels of God worship Him." Reverently—believingly—they worship Him— though, alas! too many of the bright host, through pride and unbelief, refuse. The chosen ones kiss the Son, and in the Son receive themselves the adoption of sons. (*Ibid.*) What sacred associations cluster round the word Father! The very mention of it carries us back to the dawning of our consciousness, when we learned our earliest lessons at a parent's lips. But to the thoughtful and religious soul the earthly significance does not exhaust the meaning of this holy name; for God at first designed that the human fatherhood should be the miniature of that relationship in which He stood to men, and He wished them to understand that the love of parents to their children on earth is but as a drop to the ocean of fatherly love which is in Himself. I. When we can truly and intelligently call God " our Father," NEW LIFE IS GIVEN TO OUR DEVOTIONS. I am persuaded that much of our lack of enjoyment in prayer, and much of the lifelessness and artificialness in our devotions generally, must be traced to the fact that we have not thoroughly received the spirit of adoption, and have lost the idea of God's Fatherhood. Why should we be in terror of a father? What liberty is that which our own son enjoys! See how he comes bounding into our room, calculating that we will be thoroughly interested in all he has to say, and knowing that when he lays hold of our heart he has taken hold of our strength! But is it different with God? II. When we can truly and intelligently call God our Father, NEW JOY IS GIVEN TO THE DISCHARGE OF DUTY. Heaven's own sunshine would illuminate our pathway, if every morning we went forth to do our Father's business ; and the driest and most uninteresting things of daily life would acquire a new importance in our eyes, and would be done by us with gladsomeness, if we but felt we were doing them for a Father. Let us try this heavenly specific and we shall soon find that the glory of love will halo for us all common things with its own celestial radiance, and duty will merge into delight. III. When we can truly and intelligently call God Father, a NEW SIGNIFI-CANCE IS GIVEN TO OUR EARTHLY TRIALS. The Lord Himself hath said by the mouth of Solomon, " He that spareth the rod hateth the child," and He is too wise a Father to think of training His children without discipline. By trials He keeps them from falling away; He leads them to bethink themselves and return when they have been backsliding, and He prepares them for the discharge of arduous and important duties. Some time ago, while sojourning in the Housatonic valley, I was greatly interested in passing through a paper manufactory and observing how the filthy rags were put through process after process, until at length the pulp pressed between heavy rollers came out upon the other side a seamless web of fairest white, having the mark of the maker woven into it. Let this illustrate God's purpose with His children. When He subjects them to one species of trial after another, it is only that at the last they may come forth purified and refined, having enstamped upon them His name and character, to be " known and read of all men." IV. When we can truly and intelligently call God our Father, a NEW GLORY IS GIVEN TO OUR CONCEPTION OF THE HEAVENLY WORLD. Jesus teaches us to say, " Our Father which art in heaven," and so leads us to look upon that land as our home. Home is the centre of the heart, and so, by enabling us to call God our Father and heaven our home, Jesus centres our hearts there, and gives us such an idea of its blessedness that we scarcely think of the outward accessories of its splendour, because of the delightful anticipation that we cherish of being there " at home with the Lord." O that God, through faith in Jesus Christ, would give to each of us this noble conception of heaven! Then, on true and rational principles we shall desire the better country, and at length have fulfilled to us the beautiful German beatitude, " Blessed are the home-sick, for they shall reach home." (*W. M. Taylor, D.D.*) *Christ's revelation of the Fatherhood of God :*—I believe that the word "Father" is applied to God seven times in the Old Testament; among the innumerable references to the Supreme Being which crowd almost every chapter of all the books of the Old Testament but one, He is mentioned just seven times as a Father—five times as the Father of the Hebrew people, twice as sustaining that relation to individuals. Of these two intimations that God is the Father of individual men, one is a promise to David that God will be a Father to his son Solomon; the other is a prediction that by and by men will pray to God calling Him Father—a prediction fulfilled in this prayer. For there is not any record of any *prayer* in the Old Testament in which God is addressed as Father. " In the vocative case, as an address to God in prayer," says Dean Mansel, the name of Father " does not occur in the Old Testament." It was, then, practically a new thought about God which our Saviour gave His disciples when He taught them about God. They had always known Him as the Eternal, the Creator, the Self-Existent One, the Supreme Ruler, the Judge, the Lord of Hosts and of Battles, the Captain of the armies of heaven; but this thought of Him as the Father in heaven was one that was very far from all their common thoughts of Him. This word took them into a new world. It was to them as if they had been standing for a long time before the grim outer wall of some old castle which they had been summoned to enter—standing there and looking doubtfully at the forbidding granite battlements, with cannon and sentries on the ramparts with suggestions of gloomy passages and dungeons and chains within—when all at once a little door opened, and they saw within the wall a pleasant garden, with flowers and fountains and cool retreats, and caught a breath of the sweetest odours, and heard a burst of melody from singing birds and happy children playing in the sun. Such an opening into the very heart of God did this word " Father " make for all who had stood for long in the cold shadow of the old monarchical conception of His character. (*Washington Gladden, D.D.*) *Inferences :*—1. The truth contained in this new name of God is the true constructive idea in all theological science. Build all your theologies on this foundation. Hold fast to the idea of uniform law, of a nature of things which God has established, under which sin is punished; but when you speak of the personal character and government of God, of His direct interference in the affairs of men, of what He does supernaturally, in the order of history, remember that He is our Father. 2. The word suggests to us also the dignity of human nature. Man is made in the image and likeness of God. He who was before all worlds, He whose will is the source of all laws, He who is the life of all that live, the Omnipotent, the All-Wise, the Eternal God, is our Father. 3. The word not only lifts up and glorifies every humblest human creature, it binds together in one brotherhood, in one family, all that dwell upon the face of the earth. It is the grand leveller of ranks and hierarchies; the charter of fraternity; the prophecy of peace and goodwill among men. 4. Again, what help and inspiration there is for us in the thought of the relationship here pointed out. Take it home to yourself. Try to make out something of what it means when you say that God is your Father. 5. Our Father *in heaven !* Where it is I know not ; what it is no man fully knows. But it is where our Father is. And whoever is with Him is not far from heaven. Something of the melody of its music, something of the fragrance and the beauty of its sweet fields, steal into his heart even while he walks along the dusty ways of this lower world. (*Ibid.*)   *Our Father :*—I. The expression implies that God has communicated to us His own QUALITY OF LIFE (see Gen. i. 27 ; Col. iii. 10). Traces of the Divine in man, though marred by the fall. 1. Our intellectual faculties. 2. Our aesthetic nature. 3. Our power of loving. 4. Our moral sense. 5. Our native impulses to goodness. 6. Our disposition for Divine communion. 7. Our hopefulness. 8. Our free agency. II. The expression implies also that God holds us in INTIMATE RELATION TO HIMSELF. 1. He holds us in the intimacy of affection (John xvii. 23). 2. He holds us in the intimacy of communion. A parent desires the society of his children. (1) Therefore God gives us the command and the spirit of prayer. (2) He communicates to us His thoughts in the Bible, and His own impressions of truth and virtue through the influence of His Holy Spirit. (3) He dwells within us, making even our bodies His temples. 3. He visits us with an intimacy of service. (1) His Providence secures our temporal well-being. (2) His Grace provides our atonement. (3) His Spirit serves our spirits in sanctifying them. (*J. M. Ludlow, D.D.*)   *Our Father, in heaven :*—I. THE RELATION OF GOD TO US AS A FATHER. 1. God is a Father three ways. (1) God is a Father by eternal generation ; having, by an inconceivable and ineffable way, begotten His Son, God co-equal, co-eternal with Himself ; and therefore called the " only begotten Son of God " (John iii. 16). (2) God is a Father by temporal creation ; as He gives a being and existence to His creatures. (3) God is said to be a Father by spiritual regeneration and adoption. And so all true believers are said to be the sons of God, and to be born of God (John i. 12, 13). Now that God should be pleased to take this into His glorious style, even to be called Our Father, it may teach us—First. To admire His infinite condescension, and our own unspeakable privilege and dignity (1 John iii. 1). Secondly. It should teach us to walk worthy of this high and honourable relation into which we are taken ; and to demean ourselves as children ought to do, in all holy obedience to His commands ; with fear and reverence to His authority, and an humble submission to His will. Thirdly. Is God thy Father ? This, then, may give us abundance of assurance, that we shall receive at His hands what we ask, if it be good for us ; and, if it be not, we have no reason to complain that we are not heard, unless He should turn our prayers into curses. Fourthly. Is God thy Father ? This, then, may encourage us against despair, under the sense of our manifold sins against God, and departures from Him ; for He will certainly receive us upon our repentance and returning to Him. 2. The next thing observable, is the particle *Our*, Our Father : which notes to us, that God is not only the Father of our Lord Jesus Christ, but He is the Father of all men, by creation and providence, and especially the Father of the faithful, by regeneration and adoption. (1) Let us esteem one another as brethren. (2) If thou art mean and low in the world, this should teach thee to be well content with thy present state and condition ; for God is thy Father, and a Father to thee equally with the greatest. (3) Since when we pray we must say, Our Father, this teacheth us, to interest one another in our prayers. II. The next expression SETS FORTH HIS GLORY AND GREATNESS—" which art in heaven." " But is not God everywhere present ? Doth He not fill heaven and earth, and all things ? " True. But this expression is used—1. Because heaven is the most glorious place of God's residence, where He hath more especially established His throne of grace, and there sits upon it. 2. Our prayers are directed to our Father in heaven, because, though He hears them wheresoever they are uttered, yet He nowhere hears them with acceptance but only in heaven. And the reason is, because our prayers are acceptable only as they are presented before God through the intercession of Christ. Now Christ performs His mediatory office only in heaven ; for He performs it in both natures, as He is God and Man ; and so He is only in heaven. And, therefore, we are still concerned to pray to our Father in heaven. (1) Since we are directed to pray to our Father in heaven, we may be sure that there is no circumstance of time or place, than can hinder us from praying. For heaven is over thee, and open to thee, wherever thou art. (2) Is thy Father in heaven ? Thy prayers then should be made so as to pierce the heavens where God is. (*Bishop Hopkins.*)   *The opening Invocation :*—This Invocation lifts upwards the child's brow, and claims in heaven and in the King of that country a filial interest. I. The FILIAL ; he sees in the Most High a Father. II. The FRATERNAL ; he comes not with his private needs and vows alone, but with those of his race and brotherhood, " Our Father." And—III. The CELESTIAL; though we are now of the earth, and attached to it by these mortal and terrene bodies, we are not originally from it, nor were we made to be eternally *upon* it. We are *of* heaven, and *for* heaven; for there and not here our Father is, and where He is our true home is. Conclusion: Let the Churches ponder these great truths. In the *filial* principle of our text they will find life and earth made glorious, by the thought that a Father made and rules them; and, above all worldly distinctions, they will prize and exult in their bonds through Christ to Him—rejoicing, mainly as Christ commanded His apostles to rejoice, in this that their names are written in heaven. In the *fraternal* principle we shall aright learn to love the Church and to compassionate the world; and in the principle *celestial*, we shall be taught to cultivate that heavenly-mindedness which shall make the Christian, though feeble, suffering, and forlorn in his worldly relations, already lustrous and blest, as Burke described in her worldly pomp, and in the bloom of her youth, the hapless Queen of France: " A *brilliant orb*, that seemed scarce to touch the horizon." More justly might the saint of God be thus described; having already, as the apostle enjoins, his conversation in heaven, and shedding around the earth the splendours of that world with which he holds close and blest communion, and towards which he seems habitually ready to mount, longing to depart that he may be with Christ, which is far better. (*W. R. Williams, D.D.*) *The Divine Father:*—Rev. Dr. Jonas King once went to visit the children in an orphan asylum. The children were seated in a schoolroom and Dr. King stood on a platform before them. " So this is an orphan asylum," said he. "I suppose that many of you children would tell me that you have no father or mother, were I to ask you." " Yes, sir; yes, sir," said some little voices. " How many of you say you have no father? Hold up your hands." A forest of hands were put up. " So you say, you have no father? " " Yes, sir; yes, sir." " Now," said Dr. King, " do you ever say the Lord's prayer? Let me hear you." The children began: " Our Father who art in heaven——" " Stop, children," said Dr. King; " did you begin right? " The children began again: " Our Father who art in heaven——" " Stop again, children," said Dr. King. " What did you say? Our Father? Then you have a Father; a good, rich Father. I want to tell you about Him. He owns all the gold in California; He owns all the world; He can give you as much of anything as He sees is best for you. Now, children, never forget that you have a Father. Go to Him for all you want, as if you could see Him. He is able and willing to do all that is for your good." *God's head-quarters:*—" Why do we say in the Lord's prayer, ' Who art in heaven,' since God is everywhere? " asked a clergyman of some children. For a while no one answered; at last, seeing a little drummer-boy who looked as if he could give an answer, the clergyman said: " Well, little soldier, what say you? " " Because it's head-quarters," replied the drummer. *The address :*— The first part of the Lord's prayer I have called the address, or the invocation because in it we invoke or call upon God by name, and tell Him, as it were, that we are going to speak to Him, and beg Him to listen to what we are about to say. 1. The name of " Father," by which we are commanded to call upon God, is one of the most remarkable things in the whole prayer. To us, indeed, who have been accustomed to it from infancy, it may seem almost a matter of course to call God, Father. But to do it, and that too with a certainty that He approves of it, is so far from being a matter of course that, if God had not expressly authorized and commanded us, we should never have dared to address Him by that name; we should have felt it too great a presumption to claim relation with the Lord of the universe. Any one may see what a step Christ gave us toward heaven by commanding us to address our Maker, not as our God and King, but as our Father. Any one may see and feel what a pledge the name contains that God will listen to our prayers. 2. Every privilege has its corresponding duty. Let us consider what duties the privilege, which Christ has bought for us, of calling God our Father, brings with it. (1) The first and chief duty is the behaving to Him as children should behave to their father. (2) The knowledge that God is our Father, and can do whatsoever He pleases, should fill us with faith and a courageous trust in Him. (*A. W. Hare.*) *Our Father :*—We are commanded to say " Our Father," and not my Father, to teach us not to pray for ourselves alone, but for the whole family of God and Christ on earth. When we say " Our Father," we ought to bear in mind that God has other children beside us, children who have equal claims on His mercy and love, children whom He loves as well as us. We should remember, too, that, if we are all the sons of one common Father, we must all be brothers and sisters. Here is a fruitful subject for self-examination. Do we love as brothers? Do we live together as brothers ought to live, in peace and concord? Do we help each other to the utmost of our power? Do we rejoice in our brother's prosperity, though the like may not befall ourselves? Do we feel that concern for their welfare, not in body only, but in soul, which ought to live in the hearts of all such as declare themselves before God to be members of one great family, but in the same breath for our brethren also? (*Ibid.*)   *Which art in heaven:*— Remember where that Father dwells. It is a Father which is in heaven that you are to pray to. Therefore He must be—1. most gracious; or He would never have allowed you to call Him by such a name. 2. He must be most powerful; for He is high above all things. 3. He must be most wise; for He made the world. 4. He is everlasting, and will endure without a change, when the heavens and the earth have passed away. Having then a Father, who is so powerful and so wise, and who is also unchangeable and everlasting, what an anchor of hope must this thought be to us! (*Ibid.*)   *Our Father:*—Does this familiar conception of the Fatherhood of God impair our reverence for Him? Let the children of the most loving parents answer the question. 1. This view of the Divine nature has its momentous bearings on the type of piety which we should cherish in ourselves and promote in others. The child of kind human parents shows his piety to them, not by despising their gifts and spurning the tokens of their love, but by enjoying all of them to the full, with his loving parents constantly in his thoughts, using their gifts as they would have them used, and deeming himself most happy when he can pursue his pleasure in their presence, and with their participation. By parity of reason, the true child of God manifests his piety, not by dashing from him the cup of joy put full to his lips, but by making his joy gratitude, his gladness thanksgiving, by using the world as not abusing it, by close adherence to the laws which always accompany the gifts and make them immeasurably the more precious, and by never losing thought of the benignant presence of Him who has all a Father's gladness in seeing His children happy. 2. Were these views made prominent in religious teaching, and especially in the religious culture of the young, religion would not be the unwelcome theme it now is to so many, nor would the offices of Christian worship be regarded with the indifference now so sadly prevalent. 3. Fatherhood implies distinctive love for the individual child, and thus, of necessity, a personal interest in the child's well or ill-doing, right or wrong conduct, good or bad character. 4. Whether the child finds privilege and happiness, or restraint and irksomeness, in the human father's well-ordered household, depends on his own choice, his own character. God's child, too, can be happy in His universal house, only through love of the father, and conformity to the ways of the house. The child of God who has not a child's heart must go to his own place, and that cannot be a place of privilege or joy. But he is self-banished, self-punished. He has forsaken his own mercies. It is not God's love that is withdrawn from him; but he has taken himself from the shelter and joy of that love. (*Prof. Peabody, D.D., LL.D.*)   *Carlyle and the Lord's prayer:*—"'Our Father which art in heaven, hallowed be Thy name, Thy will be done'—what else can we say? The other night, in my sleepless tossings about, which were growing more and more miserable, these words, that brief and grand prayer, came strangely into my mind, with an altogether new emphasis, as if *written* and shining for me in mild pure splendour on the black bosom of the night there; then I, as it were, *read* them word by word, with a sudden check to my imperfect wanderings, with a sudden softness of composure which was much unexpected. Not for perhaps thirty or forty years had I once formally repeated that prayer; nay, I never felt before how intensely the voice of man's soul it is—the inmost aspiration of all that is high and pious in poor human nature, right worthy to be recommended with an 'After this manner pray ye.'" (*Thomas Carlyle.*)   *God realized as a Father:*—I have been told of a good man, among whose experiences, which he kept a record of, this, among other things, was found after his death, that at such a time in secret prayer, his heart at the beginning of the duty was much enlarged, in giving to God those titles which are awful and tremendous, in calling Him the great, the mighty, and the terrible God; but going on thus, he checked himself with this thought, "*And why not my Father?*" (*Matthew Henry.*)   *The Fatherhood of God:*—A Jew entered a Persian temple, and saw there the sacred fire. He said to the priest, "How do you worship fire?"   "Not the fire: it is to us an emblem of the sun and of his animating light," said the priest. Then asked the Jew, "Do you adore the sun as a deity? Do you know that he also is a creature of the Almighty?" The priest answered that the sun was to them only an emblem of the invisible light which preserves all things. The Israelite continued, " Does your nation distinguish the image from the original? They call the sun their god, and kneel before the earthly flame. You dazzle the eye of the body, but darken that of the mind; in presenting to them the terrestrial light, you take from them the celestial." The Persian asked, " How do you name the Supreme Being?" "We call Him Jehovah Adonai; that is, the Lord who was, who is, and shall be." " Your word is great and glorious, but it is terrible," said the Persian. A Christian approaching said, " We call Him Abba, Father." Then the Gentile and the Jew regarded each other with surprise. Said one, " Your word is the nearest and the highest; but who gives you courage to call the Eternal thus?" " The Father Himself," said the Christian, who then expounded to them the plan of redemption. Then they believed and lifted up their eyes to heaven, saying, " Father, dear Father," and joined hands and called each other brethren. (*Krummacher.*) · *Of the preface to the Lord's prayer :*—I. The INTRODUCTION to the Lord's prayer—" After this manner, therefore, pray ye." Our Lord Jesus, in these words prescribed to His disciples and us a directory for prayer. The ten commandments are the rule of our life; the creed is the sum of our faith; and the Lord's prayer is the pattern of our prayer. As God did prescribe Moses a pattern of the tabernacle, so Christ hath here prescribed us a pattern of prayer—"After this manner, therefore, pray ye," &c. Not that we are tied to the words of the Lord's prayer; Christ saith not, " after these words, pray ye"; but " after this manner"; that is, let all your petitions agree and symbolize with the things contained in the Lord's prayer; and indeed, well may we make all our prayers consonant and agreeable to this prayer, it being a most exact prayer. Tertullian calls it, a breviary and compendium of the gospel; it is like a heap of massy gold. The exactness of this prayer appears—1. In the dignity of the Author; a piece of work hath commendation from the artificer, and this prayer hath commendation from the Author; it is the Lord's prayer. As the moral law was written with the finger of God, so this prayer was dropt from the lips of the Son of God. 2. The exactness of this prayer appears in the excellency of the matter. I may say of this prayer, it " is as silver tried in the furnace, purified seven times." Never was there prayer so admirably and curiously composed as this. As Solomon's Song, for its excellency, is called " the song of songs," so may this well be called " the prayer of prayers." The matter of it is admirable. 1. For its succinctness; it is short and pithy, *multum in parvo*, a great deal said in a few words. It requires most art to draw the two globes curiously in a little map. This short prayer is a system or body of divinity. 2. Its clearness. This prayer is plain and intelligible to every capacity. Clearness is the grace of speech. 3. Its completeness. This prayer contains in it the chief things that we have to ask, or God hath to bestow. There is a double benefit ariseth from framing our petitions suitably to the Lord's prayer. 1. Hereby error in prayer is prevented. It is not easy to write wrong after this copy; we cannot easily err, having our pattern before us. 2. Hereby mercies requested are obtained, for the apostle assures us God will hear us when we pray " according to His will." And sure we pray according to His will, when we pray according to the pattern He hath set us. II. THE PRAYER ITSELF, which consists of three parts : (1) A preface; (2) petitions; (3) the conclusion. First. The preface to the prayer. 1. " Our Father." 2. " Which art in heaven." To begin with the first words of the preface. " Our Father." Father is sometimes taken personally—" My Father is greater than I": but Father in the text is taken essentially for the whole Deity. This title, Father, teacheth us to whom we must address ourselves in prayer; to God alone. Here is no such thing in the Lord's prayer as, " O ye saints or angels that are in heaven, hear us!" but " Our Father which art in heaven." In what order must we direct our prayers to God? Here is only the Father named; may not we direct our prayers to the Son, and Holy Ghost? Though the Father only be named in the Lord's prayer, yet the other two Persons are not hereby excluded; the Father is mentioned because He is first in order; but the Son and Holy Ghost are included, because they are the same in essence. Princes on earth give themselves titles expressing their greatness, as " high and mighty "; God might have done so, and expressed Himself thus, " Our King of glory, our Judge"; but He gives Himself another title, " our Father," an expression of love and condescension. God, that He might encourage us to pray to Him, represents Himself under this sweet notion of a father, " our Father." The name Jehovah carries majesty in it, the name of Father carries mercy in it. In what sense is God a Father? 1. By creation; it is He that hath made us—"We are also His offspring"; "Have we not all one Father?" But there is little comfort in this; for so God is Father to the devils by creation; but He that made them will not save them. 2. God is a Father by election. 3. God is a Father by special grace. Such only as are sanctified can say, "Our Father which art in heaven." What is the difference between God being the Father of Christ, and the Father of the elect? God is the Father of Christ in a more glorious transcendent manner. Christ hath the primogeniture. What is that which makes God our Father? Faith—"Ye are all the children of God by faith in Christ Jesus." An unbeliever may call God his Creator, and his Judge, but not his Father. Faith doth legitimate us and make us of the blood-royal of heaven—"Ye are the children of God by faith." Wherein doth it appear that God is the best Father? 1. In that He is most ancient—"The Ancient of days did sit." A figurative representation of God who was before all time, this may cause veneration. 2. God is the best Father, because He is perfect—"Your Father which is in heaven is perfect"; He is perfectly good. Earthly fathers are subject to infirmities. 3. God is the best Father in respect of wisdom—"The only wise God." He hath a perfect idea of wisdom in Himself; He knows the fittest means to bring about His own designs; the angels light at His lamp. In particular this is one branch of His wisdom, that He knows what is best for us. An earthly parent knows not, in some intricate cases, how to advise his child. He is the only wise God; He knows how to make evil things work for good to His children. He can make a sovereign treacle of poison; thus He is the best Father for wisdom. 4. He is the best Father, because the most loving—"God is love." The affections in parents are but marble and adamant in comparison of God's love to His children; He gives them the cream of His love, electing love, saving love. No father like God for love! If thou art His child, thou canst not love thy own soul so entirely as He loves thee. 5. God is the best Father, for riches; God hath land enough to give to all His children, He hath unsearchable riches. He gives the hidden manna, the tree of life, rivers of joy. God is ever giving to His children, yet hath not the less; His riches are imparted, not impaired; like the sun that still shines, yet hath not the less light. He cannot be poor who is infinite. 6. God is the best Father, because He can reform His children. 7. God is the best Father, because He never dies—"Who only hath immortality." Earthly fathers die, and their children are exposed to many injuries, but God lives for ever. Wherein lies the dignity of such as have God for their Father? 1. They have greater honour than is conferred on the princes of the earth; they are precious in God's esteem. 2. God confers honourable titles upon His children; He calls them the excellent of the earth, or the magnificent, as Junius renders it. 3. This is their honour who have God for their Father—they are all heirs; the youngest son is an heir. (1) God's children are heirs to the things of this life; God being their Father, they have the best title to earthly things, they have a sanctified right to them. Others may have more of the venison, but God's children have more of the blessing; thus they are heirs to the things of this life. (2) They are heirs to the other world; "heirs of salvation," "joint heirs with Christ." 4. God makes His children equal in honour to the angels. How may we know that God is our Father? All cannot say, "our Father": the Jews boasted that God was their Father—"We have one Father, even God." Christ tells them their pedigree: "Ye are of your father the devil." They who are of satanical spirits, and make use of their power to beat down the power of godliness, cannot say, God is their Father; they may say, "our father which art in hell." Well, then, how may we know that God is our Father? 1. By having a filial disposition. This is seen in four things. First. To melt in tears for sin. A child weeps for offending his father. He grieves for sin (1) as it is an act of pollution. Sin deflowers the virgin-soul; it defaceth God's image; it turns beauty into deformity. (2) He who hath a childlike heart, grieves for sin, as it is an act of enmity. Sin is diametrically opposite to God. (3) A childlike heart weeps for sin, as it is an act of ingratitude; sin is an abuse of God's love; it is taking the jewels of God's mercies, and making use of them to sin. God hath done more for His children than others. Second. A filial, or childlike, disposition is to be full of sympathy; we lay to heart the dishonours reflected upon our heavenly Father; when we see God's worship adulterated, His truth mingled with the poison of error, it is as a sword in our bones, to see God's glory suffer. Third. A filial disposition, is to love our heavenly Father; he is unnatural that doth not love his father. A childlike love to God is known, as by the effects, so by the degree; it is a superior love. We love our Father in heaven above all other things; above estate, or relations, as oil runs above the water. A child of God seeing a supereminency of goodness, and a constellation of all beauties in God, he is carried out in love to Him in the highest measure. Fourth. A childlike disposition is seen in honouring our Heavenly Father—"A son honoureth his father. How do we show our honour to our Father in heaven? 1. By having a reverential awe of God upon us—"Thou shalt fear thy God." 2. We may know God is our Father, by our resembling of Him; the child is his father's picture. Wicked men desire to be like God hereafter in glory, but do not affect to be like Him here in grace; they give it out to the world that God is their Father, yet have nothing of God to be seen in them; they are unclean; they not only want His image, but hate it. 3. We may know God is our Father, by having His spirit in us. 4. If God be our Father, we are of peaceable spirits—"Blessed be the peace-makers, they shall be called the children of God." Grace infuseth a sweet, amicable disposition; it files off the ruggedness of men's spirits; it turns the lion-like fierceness into a lamb-like gentleness. They who have God to be their Father, follow peace as well as holiness. 5. If God be our Father; then we love to be near God, and have converse with Him. An ingenuous child delights to approach near to his father, and go into his presence. David envied the birds that they built their nests so near God's altars, when he was debarred his Father's house. See the amazing goodness of God, that is pleased to enter into this sweet relation of a Father. God needed not to adopt us; he did not want a Son, but we wanted a Father. God showed power in being our Maker, but mercy in being our Father. If God be a Father, then hence I infer, whatever He doth to His children, is love. But will God be a Father to me, who have profaned His name, and been a great sinner? Wherein lies the happiness of having God for our Father? 1. If God be our Father, then He will teach us. What father will refuse to counsel his son? A man may see the figures upon a dial, but he cannot tell how the day goes, unless the sun shine; we may read many truths in the Bible, but we cannot know them savingly, till God by His Spirit shine upon our soul. God teacheth not only our ear, but our heart; he not only informs our mind, but inclines our will; we never learn till God teach us. 2. If God be our Father, then He hath bowels of affection towards us. If it be so unnatural for a father but to love His child, can we think God can be defective in His love? That you may see God's fatherly love to His children: (1) Consider God makes a precious valuation of them—"Since thou wast precious in My sight." A father prizeth his child above his jewels. (2) God loves the places they were born in the better for their sakes—"Of Zion it shall be said, This man was born in her." (3) He chargeth the great ones of the world not to prejudice His children; their persons are sacred—"He suffered no man to do them wrong; yea, He reproved kings for their sakes, saying, Touch not Mine anointed." (4) God delights in their company; He loves to see their countenance, and hear their voice. (5) God bears His children in His bosom, as a nursing father doth the suck-ing child. (6) God is full of solicitous care for them—"He careth for you." A father cannot always take care for his child, he sometimes is asleep; but God is a Father that never sleeps. (7) He thinks nothing too good to part with to His children; He gives them the kidneys of the wheat, and honey out of the rock, and "wine on the lees well refined." He gives them three jewels more worth than heaven; the blood of His Son, the grace of His Spirit, the light of His counten-ance. (8) If God hath one love better than another, He bestows it upon them; they have the cream and quintessence of His love. God loves His children with such a love as He loves Christ. 3. If God be our Father, He will be full of sympathy—"as a father pitieth his children, so the Lord pitieth them that fear Him"—(1) in case of infirmities; (2) injuries. 4. If God be our Father, He will take notice of the least good He sees in us; if there be but a sigh for sin, God hears it. God spies the least good in His children; He can see a grain of corn hid under chaff, grace hid under corruption. 5. If God be our Father, He will take all we do in good part. A father takes a letter from his son kindly, though there are blots or bad English in it. What blottings are there in our holy things? 6. If God be our Father, then He will correct us in measure. "I will correct thee in measure"; and that two ways: First, It shall be in measure, for the kind; God will not lay upon us more than we are able to bear. He knows our frame. He knows we are not steel or marble, therefore will deal gently. Second, He will correct in measure for the duration; He will not let the affliction lie on too long. A sting a-wing. 7. If God be our Father, He will intermix mercy with all our afflictions; if He gives us wormwood to drink, He will mix it with honey. In every cloud a child of God may see a rainbow of mercy shining.

As the limner mixeth dark shadows and bright colours together, so our heavenly Father mingles the dark and bright together, crosses and blessings ; and is not this a great happiness, for God thus to chequer His providences, and mingle goodness with severity ?　8. If God be our Father, the evil one shall not prevail against us. God will make all Satan's temptations promote the good of His children.　(1) As they set them more a-praying.　(2) As they are a means to humble them.　(3) As they establish them more in grace ; a tree shaken by the wind is more settled and rooted ; the blowing of a temptation doth but settle a child of God more in grace. Thus the evil one, Satan, shall not prevail against the children of God.　9. If God be our Father, no real evil shall befall us—"There shall no evil befall thee."　It is not said, no trouble ; but no evil.　What hurt doth the furnace to the gold ? it only makes it purer.　What hurt doth afflictions to grace ? only refine and purify it. What a great privilege is this, to be freed, though not from the stroke of affliction, yet from the sting !　Again, no evil befalls a child of God, because no condemnation— "no condemnation to them that are in Christ Jesus."　10. If God be our Father, this may make us go with cheerfulness to the throne of grace.　Were a man to petition his enemy, there were little hope ; but when a child petitions his father, he may hope with confidence to speed.　11. If God be our Father, He will stand between us and danger ; a father will keep off danger from his child.　God calls Himself a shield.　God is a hiding-place.　God appoints His holy angels to be a lifeguard about His children.　Never was any prince so well guarded as a believer. 12. If God be our Father, we shall not want anything that He sees is good for us ; "They that seek the Lord shall not want any good thing."　God is pleased some- times to keep His children to hard commons, but it is good for them.　13. If God be our Father, all the promises of the Bible belong to us ; God's children are called "heirs of promise."　14. God makes all His children conquerors.　First, They conquer themselves.　Though the children of God may sometimes be foiled, and lose a single battle, yet not the victory.　Second, They conquer the world.　Third, They conquer their enemies ; how can that be, when they oft take away their lives ? God's children conquer their enemies by heroic patience.　A patient Christian, like the anvil, bears all strokes invincibly ; thus the martyrs overcame their enemies by patience.　15. If God be our Father, He will now and then send us some tokens of His love.　God's children live far from home, and meet sometimes with coarse usage from the unkind world ; therefore God, to encourage His children, sends them sometimes tokens and pledges of His love.　What are these ?　He gives them a return of prayer, there is a token of love ; He quickens and enlargeth their hearts in duty, there is a token of love ; He gives them the firstfruits of His Spirit, which are love-tokens.　16. If God be our Father, He will indulge and spare us—"I will spare them, as a man spareth his own son that serveth him." 17. If God be our Father, He will put honour and renown upon us at the last day. (1) He will clear the innocency of His children.　God's children in this life are strangely misrepresented to the world.　(2) God will make an open and honourable recital of all their good deeds.　18. If God be our Father, He will settle a good land of inheritance upon us—"Blessed be the God and Father of our Lord Jesus, who hath begotten us again to a lively hope, to an inheritance incorruptible and undefiled." God's children shall not wait long for their inheritance ; it is but winking, and they shall see God.　19. If God be our Father, it is a comfort, first, in case of loss of relations.　Hast thou lost a father ?　Yet, if thou art a believer, thou art no orphan, thou hast an heavenly Father, a Father that never dies, "who only hath immortality."　Second. It is a comfort in case of death ; God is thy Father, and at death thou art going to thy Father.　If God be our Father, we may with comfort, at the day of death, resign our souls into His hand : so did Christ—"Father, into Thy hands I commend My Spirit."　If a child hath any jewel, he will, in time of danger, put it into his father's hands, where he thinks it will be kept most safe. Our soul is our richest jewel, we may at death resign our souls into God's hands, where they will be safer than in our own keeping.　What a comfort is this, death carries a believer to his Father's house, "where are delights unspeakable and full of glory !"　Let us behave and carry ourselves as the children of such a Father, in several particulars.　1. Let us depend upon our Heavenly Father, in all our straits and exigencies ; let us believe that He will provide for us.　2. If God be our Father, let us imitate Him.　3. If God be our Father, let us submit patiently to His will. What gets the child by struggling, but more blows ?　What got Israel by their murmuring and rebelling, but a longer and more tedious march, and at last their carcases fell in the wilderness ?　4. If God be our Father, let this cause in us a childlike reverence—" If I be a Father, where is My honour?" If you have not always a childlike confidence, yet always preserve a childlike reverence. 5. If God be our Father, let us walk obediently—" As obedient children." 6. If God be your Father, show it by your cheerful looks that you are the children of such a Father. Too much drooping and despondency disparageth the relation you stand in to God. 7. If God be our Father, let us honour Him by walking very holily—" Be ye holy, for I am holy." A young prince asking a philosopher how he should behave himself, the philosopher said, "Remember thou art a king's son." Causinus, in his hieroglyphics, speaks of a dove, whose wings being perfumed with sweet ointments, did draw the other doves after her. The holy lives of God's children is a sweet perfume to draw others to religion, and make them to be of the family of God. Justin Martyr saith, that which converted him to Christianity, was the beholding the blameless lives of the Christians. 8. If God be our Father, let us love all that are His children—" How pleasant it is for brethren to dwell together in unity!" 9. If God be our Father, let us show heavenly-mindedness; they who are born of God do set their "affections on things that are above." What, a son of God, and a slave to the world! What, sprung from heaven, and buried in the earth! 10. If God be our Father, let us own our Heavenly Father in the worst times; stand up in His cause, defend His truths. What may we learn from this, that God is in heaven? 1. Hence we learn that we are to raise our minds in prayer above the earth. God never denied that soul his suit who went as far as heaven to ask it. 2. We learn from God's being in heaven, His sovereign power. "By this word is meant, that all things are subject to His governing power." "Our God is in the heavens, He hath done whatever He pleased." God being in heaven governs the universe, and orders all occurrences here below for the good of His children. 3. We learn God's glory and majesty; He is in heaven, therefore He is covered with light; "clothed with honour," and is far above all worldly princes as heaven is above earth. 4. We learn, from God's being in heaven, His omnisciency. "All things are naked, and opened to His eye." 5. We learn from God's being in heaven, comfort for the children of God; when they pray to their Father, the way to heaven cannot be blocked up. One may have a father living in foreign parts, but the way, both by sea and by land, may be so blocked up, that there is no coming to Him; but thou, saint of God, when thou prayest to thy Father, He is in heaven; and though thou art ever so confined, thou mayest have access to Him. A prison cannot keep thee from thy God; the way to heaven can never be blocked up. "Father," denotes reverence; "Our Father," denotes faith. In all our prayers to God we should exercise faith—" Our Father." Faith is that which baptizeth prayer, and gives it a name; it is called "the prayer of faith"; without faith, it is speaking, not praying. Faith is the breath of prayer; prayer is dead unless faith breathe in it. Faith is a necessary requisite in prayer. The oil of the sanctuary was made up of several sweet spices, pure myrrh, cassia, cinnamon: faith is the chief spice, or ingredient in prayer, which makes it go up to the Lord, as sweet incense—" Let him ask in faith"; "Whatsoever ye shall ask in prayer, believing, ye shall receive." Faith must take prayer by the hand, or there is no coming nigh to God; prayer without faith is unsuccessful. As Joseph said, "You shall not see my face, unless you bring your brother Benjamin with you," so prayer cannot see God's face, unless it bring its brother faith with it. This makes prayer often suffer shipwreck, because it dasheth upon the rock of unbelief. O sprinkle faith in prayer! We must say, "our Father." 1. What doth praying in faith imply? Praying in faith implies the having of faith; the act implies the habit. To walk implies a principle of life; so to pray in faith implies a habit of grace. None can pray in faith but believers. 2. What is it to pray in faith? (1) To pray in faith, is to pray for that which God hath promised; where there is no promise, we cannot pray in faith. (2) To pray in faith, is to pray in Christ's meritorious name—" Whatsoever ye shall ask in My name, that will I do." (3) To pray in faith, is; in prayer to fix our faith on God's faithfulness, believing that He doth hear, and will help; this is a taking hold of God. 3. How may we know that we do truly pray in faith? We may say, "our Father," and think we pray in faith, when it is in presumption: how, therefore, may we know that we do indeed pray in faith? (1) When our faith in prayer is humble. A presumptuous person hopes to be heard in prayer for some inherent worthiness in himself; he is so qualified, and hath done God good service, therefore he is confident God will hear his prayer. (2) We may know we pray in faith, when, though we have not the present thing we pray for, yet we believe God will grant it, therefore we will stay His leisure. A believer, at Christ's word, lets down the net of prayer, and though he catch nothing, he will cast the net of prayer again, believing that mercy will come. Patience in prayer is nothing but faith spun out. 1. It reproves them that pray in formality, not in faith; they question whether God hears or will grant—" Ye ask and receive not, because ye ask amiss." Unbelief clips the wings of prayer, that it will not fly to the throne of grace; the rubbish of unbelief stops the current of prayer. 2. Let us set faith awork in prayer, " our Father." O pray in faith! Say, " our Father." And that we may act faith in prayer, consider (1) God's readiness to hear prayer. Did God forbid all addresses to Him, it would put a damp upon the trade of prayer; but God's ear is open to prayer. The Ediles among the Romans had their doors always standing open, that all who had petitions might have free access to them. God is both ready to hear and grant prayer; this may encourage faith in prayer. And whereas some may say, they have prayed, but have had no answer: First. God may hear prayer, though He do not presently answer. We write a letter to a friend; he may have received it, though we have yet had no answer of it. Second. God may give an answer to prayer, when we do not perceive it. (2) That we may act faith in prayer, consider we do not pray alone. Christ prays over our prayers again; Christ's prayer is the ground why our prayer is heard. Christ takes the dross out of our prayer, and presents nothing to His Father but pure gold. Christ mingles His sweet odours with the prayers of the saints. (3) We pray to God for nothing but what is pleasing to Him, and He hath a mind to grant; if a son ask nothing but what his father is willing to bestow, this may make him go to him with confidence. (4) To encourage faith in prayer, consider the many sweet promises that God hath made to prayer. The cork keeps the net from sinking: the promises are the cork to keep faith from sinking in prayer. God hath bound Himself to us by His promises. The Bible is bespangled with promises made to prayer. (5) That we may act faith in prayer, consider, Jesus Christ hath purchased that which we pray for; we may think the things we ask for in prayer too great for us to obtain, but they are not too great for Christ to purchase. (*T. Watson.*)

Our Father which art in Heaven :—I. From these words we learn, first, that GOD IS A FATHER—" When ye pray, say 'Father!' " At the very outset, let us beware of taking this blessed word, Father, figuratively, or, to use the language of the theologians, as an accommodation. Rather is it precisely the opposite. It is the human fatherho od which is an accommodation to the Divine, not the Divine which is an accommodation to the human. For the spiritual exists before the material, as the substance exists before the shadow it casts. The meaning, the final cause, of the earthly fatherhood itself, what is it but to testify to and interpret the heavenly? Hence the deep solemnity of the Parental Institution. The parent is to the infant the image and representation of the Parent in Heaven. And the first lesson the infant learns is Fatherhood. Happy if in learning it he learns the Divine Fatherhood as well as the human! Thus, the parental institution is the Heavenly Father's means of lifting His earthly children to His own Divine Fatherhood. And now let us ponder the Divine Fatherhood in light of the human, and note some of the meanings it has for us. And, first, Fatherhood means sirehood, or communication of nature. Animals are God's creatures; men are God's children. This is the very point which the Lord urges when He exhorts His disciples to trust the Heavenly Father. " Behold the birds of the air; they are not God's children; yet your Heavenly Father feedeth them; will He not much more feed you, who are His sons?" This Divine inspiration or inbreathing it is which makes man God's image, God's offspring, God's son. How august the Divine record of man's genealogy: "Who was the son of Enoch, who was the son of Seth, who was the son of Adam, who was the son of God." Sirehood, then, is entailment of nature, and sonhood is inheritance of nature. As the difference between parent and babe is a difference in degree rather than in kind, so is the difference between God and man. Man shares finitely in God's infinite nature. And this is true for all men. God is not only a Father; God is the Father. True, Holy Scripture speaks of adoption, or a special sonship. As an earthly father discriminates between his children, admitting the dutiful ones to special intimacies, partnerships, bequests, and the like, so it is with the Heavenly Father. There is a sonship of nature in the sphere of manhead; and there is a sonship of grace in the sphere of Christhead. Again: Fatherhood means authority. The government by the Father is natural, direct, personal, supreme, inextinguishable. And this is God's government. It is based on Fatherhood. Just as an earthly father has the natural right to rule his offspring, so it is with the heavenly. Parentage, in simple virtue of its being parentage, is imperative. God is Father-King. And authority means the right—and, when needful, the duty—to punish. Alas, how often in this fallen world is punishment needed, *e.g.*, to vindicate authority or to amend character! And observe precisely the basis of the right to chasten: it is not age, or strength, or stature; it is Fatherhood. No man has the right to punish his neighbour's child, however vicious he may be: none but the child's own father has that right; and he has that right because he is father. Let us beware then of sentimental views of God's Fatherhood. But let us beware of the opposite extreme. There may be slavish views of God as well as sentimental. Particularly is this the case among the heathen; their God is force. Witness Jupiter Tonans, Thor, Siva, and the like And so, once more, Fatherhood means Love. The Heavenly Father's love is shown in the realm of Providence. Just as an earthly father reveals his fatherhood by arranging the conditions and providing for the welfare of his children, so does the Heavenly Father reveal in the same way His Fatherhood. And as the earthly father does not leave the wants and affairs of his children—their market and clothing and school and health and holiday expenses—to be regulated by machinery, but exercises over them his personal vigilance and guardianship, being, in short, a sort of Providence; so the Heavenly Father does not leave the wants and affairs of His children to the blind operations of Nature's laws and the inexorable sequences of fate, but He exercises over them a personal vigilance, protection, and guidance. What man, accustomed to take broad and observant views of human history, does not see that the wisest and strongest of men are often but as little infants in the Heavenly Father's hands, sheltered by Him, guarded by Him, led by Him, arranged by Him? God's Providence grows out of God's Fatherhood. But the crowning proof that the Heavenly Father loves us is seen in the Incarnation of His Son, II. But our text teaches a second lesson. It is this: ALL MEN ARE BROTHERS—"When ye pray, say: 'Our Father!'" Each is to carry the race with him, making his closet the world's oratory. As long as He who is no respecter of persons, and with whom is no variableness or shadow of turning, invites Jew and Gentile, Mongolian and Caucasian, Nubian and Anglo-Saxon, to call Him Father, so long are Jew and Gentile, Mongolian and Caucasian, Nubian and Anglo-Saxon, brothers. These two words—Our Father—for ever settle the question of the moral unity of the race. Mankind is more than an aggregate of individuals; it is a family group; we are members of one another. Moreover, these words for ever settle the missionary question. In these words—Our Father—is born and fostered and will triumph the missionary enterprise, the true "Enthusiasm of Humanity." III. But our text teaches a third lesson; it is this: GOD IS OUR HEAVENLY FATHER—"When ye pray, say: 'Our Father who art in Heaven.'" And first, negatively: the term Heaven, as occurring in our text, must not be taken in the local sense. Containing in Himself all things, God cannot be contained in anything. "Lo, heaven and the heaven of heavens cannot contain Thee." Affirmatively: the heaven of our text is the moral heaven rather than the local. To express moral excellence by terms of altitude is an instinct. How naturally we use such phrases as these: "Exalted worth, high resolve, lofty purpose, elevated views, sublime character, eminent purity!" How naturally, too, we use opposite phrases: "Low instincts, base passions, degraded character, grovelling habits, stooping to do it!" In like manner, pagans instinctively localize their gods on mountain-crests: *e.g.*, the Persians on Caucasus, the Hindoos on Meru, the Greeks on Olympus. So the Jews themselves, when fallen into idolatry, consecrated high places and hill-tops. Doubtless here, too, is the secret of the arch, and especially the spire, as the symbol of Christian architecture—the Church is an aspiration. Loftiness being the symbol of whatever is morally excellent, to say that our Father is in heaven is to ascribe to our Father every moral excellence. And, first, heaven suggests our Father's immensity. Nothing seems so remote from us or gives such an idea of vastness as the dome of heaven. Again: heaven suggests our Father's sovereignty. Be not rash, then, with thy mouth, and let not thy heart be hasty to utter a word before God: for God is in heaven and thou upon earth; therefore let thy words be few. Again: heaven suggests our Father's spirituality. Nothing seems so like that rarity of texture which we so instinctively ascribe to pure, incorporeal spirit, as that subtle, tenuous ether which it is believed pervades the clear, impalpable sky, and, indeed, all immensity. Again: heaven suggests our Father's purity. Nothing is so exquisite an emblem of absolute spotlessness and eternal chastity as the unsullied expanse of heaven, untrodden by mortal foot, unswept by aught but angel wings.

Again: heaven suggests our Father's beatitude. We cannot conceive a more perfect emblem of felicity and moral splendour than light. Once more: heaven suggests our Father's obscurity. For though God Himself is light, yet there are times when even the very heavens themselves obscure His brightness. "Why has Christ commanded us to add to the address, Our Father, the words, Who art in heaven?" asks the Heidelberg Catechism. And the answer is: "That we may have no earthly thought of the heavenly majesty of God." A true and noble answer. The term—Father—expresses God's relation to us—it is fatherly. The term—heaven—expresses that Father's character—it is heavenly. Thus our text give us God for Father, man for brother, heaven for character. (*G. D. Boardman, D.D.*)　　*Our Father in heaven:*—I. A TENDER RELATIONSHIP. 1. A tender relationship between us and God: "Our Father in heaven." Well, when you pray, what do you do? to whom do you speak? I fancy some speak to themselves, some to those to whom they say their prayers, many to no one at all. The heathen sees his idol, and speaks to it, and you cannot understand that. But you see nothing, hear nothing, feel nothing, and so when you close your eyes and pray, it is as if you had no one to speak to. But you know how it is when you write to your absent father. You see or hear or feel nothing, and yet you know that you are speaking to him, and that the words you are writing will one day come under his eye, and serve the purpose in view. And so with your "Father in heaven." He is a real personal God, not who was once, but who is now, "which art in heaven." When you think of God, you often think of Him with fear, with terror. He is such a holy God, He so hates sin, and is so just in punishing it, and so mighty. And when you pray, if you think at all about the matter, your thoughts of God are such as these, and you only fear Him. But what says the text? "Our Father in heaven." You may be afraid of others, not of a father. You may stand in doubt of others, not of a father. If there is any one you can trust and love and feel at home with, it is a father. There is a little child crying as if his heart would break. I do all I can to pacify him, but can make nothing of it. My well-meant efforts seem only to make him worse. But when his father comes in sight, how the little one stretches out his hands, how his face is lighted up, and when once fairly in his father's arms, how his sorrow is hushed! Who is so kind and considerate and tender as a father? And such is God. I wish I could persuade you to believe in God's love and tenderness as a Father. There is nothing which you may not tell Him. There is nothing which you may not ask of Him. There is nothing too little—too trifling. I wish I could convince you of that heavenly Father's love. What it would do for you! I can suppose that, in the spring or summer time of the year, when the flowers are so beautiful, you have a little favourite flower. You planted it with your own hand, you water it daily, you watch it constantly, you are bent on seeing it come into bloom. The plant is somewhat sickly, and the long-watched bud seems as if it would drop off without ever opening, till you bring it out of the shade, and set it in the sun; and what you could not force in any other way, takes place quite naturally under the genial heat and sunshine of a summer's day. Such is the effect of coming under the sunshine of the heavenly Father's love. It would do for you what the shining sun does for the flowers—making them healthy and beautiful, a joy to all onlookers. The very word, how it should melt, and draw, and gladden you—"Our Father!" What a word this is to be applied to God! what a name for us to call Him by! There is no petition which we could address to Him at all equal to it. It is a prayer in itself, the most powerful that could be offered. Let me suppose that one of you boys or girls were drowning, that from the sea, or from some neighbouring lake or river, one of you were to send the shrill cry, "Father!" I need not tell you what would follow: I need not describe how your father would be up and off in a moment, how he would rush to the quarter from which the sound came. Not a word more would be needed, it would ask all you required, it would contain at once petition and argument—no prayer would be like it—"Father!" A mother once told me, that from the time her children began to call her "mother," the word had a power over her which she could not describe. She might be in the attic, busily at work, but if, three stories below, she heard her boys calling "Mother!" it went to her heart. The very name was so sweet—it had such a power over her—that she would at once throw down her work and hurry to them. And now that they are grown-up men, it is still the same. I have heard the call, and soon has followed the sound of hurrying footsteps, and the gentle, "Well, dear?" in reply. Now, if this be so, if the name father or mother has such a power with earthly parents, what power may we not suppose that word, "Our

Father," from the lips of His children, to have with the "Father in heaven"? 1 do not know any words sufficient to express the honour of standing in such a relationship to God. Nor would it be easy to tell what we should be to such a God, how we should love and serve and obey Him. Let me just make one remark here. Those who call God "Father," should be like Him. Have you not often been struck with the likeness of children to their parents? There are not a few children whom I could name, though I had never seen them before, just from their likeness to their parents. I have said to a child on the street, "Your name is so-and-so; isn't it?" "Yes." "I was sure of it: he is so like his father." Now, so should it be with those who call God "Father." The likeness should be such that everybody should see it. Ay, and the name should help us to be like Him. I cannot, for very shame, use that name and do as I have been doing. Just as an ill-doing son might well change his name, and try to be as unlike his father in appearance as possible, as feeling it a disgrace to be so unworthy of him; so, many of us would almost do well to give up this name, unless we are more worthy of it. Not long ago, the chaplain in one of our prisons told me, that among the prisoners to whom he ministered, he had met with a soldier whose name had been on the prison-books again and again, but who had always given a false name, assigning as the reason, that he could not bear the thought of his father's honoured name being on the prison-books in the person of his unworthy son. 2. A tender relationship between us and Christ. This remark explains the last. This is necessary in order to the last. But for this, the other could not be. We were not always sons. We were strangers. We were enemies. "Ye are all the children of God, by faith in Christ Jesus." "Predestinated unto the adoption of children, by Jesus Christ." The relationship between us and Christ is that of brotherhood. 3. A tender relationship between us and others. No believer needs to be, is, can be, alone. Whenever he comes to Christ, he comes into the family. II. THE CHARACTERISTICS OF TRUE PRAYER. 1. It should be trustful: "Our Father—our Father in heaven." Trustful as regards His ability to do what is asked. Little children have extraordinary notions as to what their fathers can do. To hear them speak, you would almost think they believed in a father's power to do anything. You must have noticed this in others, or in yourselves. If there is a heavy load to be lifted, which a child cannot move, more than likely he will tell you his father could lift it. If any one threatens to do him harm, though a far stronger man, he says he will tell his father, as if he could put all to rights. Prayer should be trustful, as regards God's willingness to do anything, His love: "Our Father." Once more, prayer should be trustful, as regards God's wisdom: "Our Father in heaven." How often do others give us what our fathers would deny! I find the thought on which I have been dwelling, of trust in "our Father," beautifully illustrated in a most interesting little book, entitled, "Nettie's Mission: Stories illustrative of the Lord's Prayer." Three little children were spending the evening together, when a violent thunderstorm came on, which obliged them to stay where they were, all night. "Just before prayer time, Mr. Thorn told them that they might each choose the Bible verse they liked best, and tell why they loved it. 'I know what my verse will be for this night,' said Margery. 'I don't know where to find it, but it says, 'The Lord of glory thundereth.' Why did you choose that verse, Margery?' asked Mrs. Thorn. 'Because I think it so nice, when you hear that awful noise, to know it is God. It makes me think of one day long ago. Aunt Annie was out, and I heard a great noise up in the loft, when I thought I was all alone in the house; and I was so frightened, I screamed, and father's voice called out, "Don't be afraid, little Margie; it's only father." And now, when it thunders very loud, it always seems as if I heard God say, "Don't be afraid, little Margie; it's only Father;" and I don't feel a bit frightened. Don't you think it's a real nice verse?'" In travelling lately in a railway carriage, a friend told me the following facts with which he was personally conversant. Some years ago, a vessel, crossing to this country from the Continent, was overtaken by a storm. One of the passengers, much alarmed, asked a young sailor-boy on board, if there was danger. He said there was, but added, "Like as a father pitieth his children, so the Lord pitieth them that fear Him." The ship reached the port in safety, and not long since the fact was called to mind in this interesting way: On board one of our steamers, a clergyman told the captain what I have told you, adding that he was the passenger, and that the boy's trustful word had had such effect on him, that it had led him to seek the Saviour, and ultimately to become a minister of the gospel. "And I," answered the captain, "am that sailor-boy!" I give you the story, in substance, as it was told to me; that Christian sailor and his friend being, I believe, still alive. 2. Prayer should be reverent: "Our Father in heaven." The word "Father" implies that, still more "in heaven." How particular you are when you speak to one higher in rank than yourself! What thought it gives you beforehand! How anxious you are to have all right, as regards your dress, your hair, &c., how in the porch outside, you might been seen, with your cap or your handkerchief, wiping the dust off your shoes ; and after you have rung the bell, how your heart beats before the door is opened, and you are ushered in! With what reverence people appear before and speak to the Queen! The highest men among us would be not a little anxious to-day, if they had to appear before her Majesty to-morrow. And what about appearing before God, and speaking to God? 3. Prayer should be in the name of Jesus. 4. Prayer should be unselfish. (*J. H. Wilson, M.A.*) *God a Father :*—A strong and practical belief of the Divine being and presence lies at the basis of all true devotion. An atheist cannot pray. "He that cometh to God, must believe that He is, and that He is the rewarder of them that digilently seek Him." Prayer is the language of nature, because it is the language of want; it is the language of a creature to his Creator, of a child, dependent, helpless, benighted, to his unearthly Parent. From whatever station in human life, or portion of the world, or degraded state of human society; from whatever throne or dungeon, from whatever liberty, or whatever servitude, any one of the vast family of man may affectionately and dutifully address his thoughts to heaven, he shall find a Father's ear, and the heart of a Father. His family is large and widely dispersed ; it is composed of millions upon millions, scattered over every continent and island, every sea and shore, every mountain and valley, every palace and every log-cabin; nor is any one of them denied the relation of children. One of the obligations of piety is founded on this natural relation which men sustain to God as the parent source of their being. When we adopt the language, "Our Father who art in heaven," we are also reminded of the still more endearing relation which exists between their Heavenly Father, and those who constitute His spiritual family. The Scriptures and facts instruct us that every son and daughter of Adam is by nature alienated from God, and a child of wrath. Even under the old dispensation, the people of God were not denied the hopes and consolations of this filial relation. The language of Moses to the people of Israel is, "Ye are the children of the Lord your God." "Doubtless Thou art our Father," is the language of the prophet. The beautiful language of his prayer is, "Our Father." There are two thoughts of interest in this emphatic phraseology. "Thou art my God," says the Psalmist, "and I will exalt Thee." Elsewhere he says, "God, our own God, shall bless us." There are the actings of an appropriating faith in words like these. But this is not all which these cheering words express. The social character of this prayer may not be passed over in silence. It is "Our Father." The social character of religion is too little known by the men of the world, and appreciated too little by Christians. True piety has indeed much to do with individual character and obligations. It cannot exist without secret meditation, and solitary communion with God. Yet is it designed to call into exercise and consecrate all the social principles of our nature. There are common interests, and there are individual interests, to be prosecuted in joint supplication. God is not only the hearer of prayer, but the hearer of social prayer. The social relations flourish only under the genial influence of Christianity. They have never been known in their purity in Pagan lands, however elevated by science, and refined by the courtesies of life. The gospel alone purifies and elevates them, and gives them principle. "Our Father who art in heaven!" how strong the bond! Here the worst affections are subdued, and the best called into exercise. The powers of earth and sin are here subdued, suspicion and jealousy, envy and hatred. Nor may the thought be lost sight of, that union is the soul and strength of prayer. If "united action is powerful action," so is united prayer powerful prayer. Why should the social principle be pressed into every other service, save the service of God ; and why, while men associate for the purposes of business, pleasure, literature, accomplishments, science, and the arts, are there so few associations for prayer? Shall every other society be sought, rather than the society of God's children? There is also in this brief address a sublime ascription. "Our Father, who art in heaven!" The Divine Being is not confined either to the heavens or the earth. He "filleth all in all." He is in heaven ; highly exalted as God over all; reigning there in invisible majesty, and dwelling in light that is inaccessible and full of glory. He is venerable for His greatness. He decks Himself with light as with a garment, and is arrayed in majesty and excellency. There is great imperfection in earthly parents compared with God. Earthly parents know not how to adapt their bounty at all times to the wants of their children. There is no such defect, and no such mistake with God. But nothing restricts God's power to give : giving does not impoverish, withholding does not enrich Him. The love of earthly parents is strong ; it survives separation, annihilates distance, forgives disobedience, rebellion, and neglect. It does not perish even with the infamy of its objects, nor will it yield its claims to the stern and inevitable demands of the grave. It outlives life ; feeds on recollected joys and hopes, and lavishes on the marble and on the turf that tenderness of which the dead are unconscious. It is a self-sacrificing and uncomplaining, coveting even weariness, and watchings, and pain for those it loves. But it is not indestructible. Let the spirit of this first sentence in the Lord's prayer counsel us to cherish more befitting impressions of the God we worship. He is no unbending tyrant, no hard master ; but the best and kindest of fathers. (*G. Spring, D.D.*) *Our Father :*—1. Christ here teacheth us to call God " Our Father " ; and by God's providence and fatherly goodness we are incorporated as it were and kneaded together, that by softness of disposition, by friendly communication, by mutual praying, we may transfuse ourselves one into another, and receive from others into ourselves. And in this we place the communion of saints. 2. In the participation of those privileges and characters which Christ hath granted and the Spirit sealed, calling us to the same faith, baptizing us in the same laver, leading us by the same rule, filling us with the same grace, sealing to us the same pardon, upholding us with the same hope. 3. In those offices and duties which Christ hath made common, which Christ requires of His Church: " Where my fear watcheth not only for myself, but stands sentinel for others ; my sorrow drops not down for my own sins alone, but for the sins of my brethren ; my joy is full with others' joy ; and my devotion is importunate and restless for the whole Church." I cry aloud for my brother, and his prayers are the echo of my cry. We are all joined together in this word *noster,* when we call God " our Father." (*A. Farindon.*) *Love abroad :*—Our love is so chained to ourselves that she cannot reach forth a hand to others. She is active and vocal at home, but hath the cramp and cannot breathe for the welfare of our brethren, *impetu cogitationis in nobis ipsis consumpto,* " having consumed and spent herself at home." (*Ibid.*) *Of applying God's Fatherhood to ourselves :*—A particular persuasion of God's fatherly affection to ourselves is then especially requisite when we pray unto Him. We cannot in truth say unto Him, " Our Father " without such a persuasion. The benefits of that particular persuasion are great and manifold. For—1. It distinguisheth the sound faith of true saints from the counterfeit faith of formal professors and trembling faith of devils. They may believe that God is a Father, but they cannot believe that God is their Father. 2. It maketh us more boldly to come to the throne of grace. " I will go to my Father." 3. It maketh us to rest upon God more confidently for provision for all things needful, and protection from all things hurtful. For this particular relation of God's fatherhood to us showeth that God taketh an especial care of us, to whom the promise of God's care especially belongeth. 4. It doth much uphold us in all distresses. 5. It strengtheneth our faith in all the properties and works of God. 6. It affordeth much comfort against our manifold infirmities. 7. All that can be said of God's fatherhood will bring no comfort to a man unless he can apply it to himself. Children do not go to a man for the things they want because he is a father of other children, but because he is their own father. (*William Gouge.*) *God hath abundance of blessing for all :*—Concerning the abundance of blessing which this our common Father hath, it appeareth to be sufficient for all, in that Christ directeth all to go to Him, and that for others as well as for themselves, and not to fear to put Him in mind that He is the Father of others as well as of ourselves, and that He hath others to bless as well as us. So as God is not like Isaac, who had but one blessing, and having therewith blessed one son, could not bless the other. He is as a springing fountain which ever remaineth full, and continueth to overflow, though never so much be taken out of it. Men that are very chary in keeping standing ponds private to themselves suffer springs to flow in common for others. Thus doth God's fatherly bounty flow out to all that in faith come to partake thereof. (*Ibid.*)   *Of God's being in heaven :*—How is God's greatness set forth? By His mansion place which is in heaven. A mansion place is an usual means of greatness or meanness. When we see a little thatched ruinous cottage we may imagine that he is a poor mean person that dwelleth there. Thus Eliphas setteth out the baseness of men who "dwell in houses of clay, whose foundation is in the dust." But if we see a fair and stately palace, we think that he is a great personage that inhabiteth there. Great Nebuchadnezzar did thus set out his own greatness: "Is not this great Babylon that I have built for the house of the kingdom and for the honour of my majesty?" Many do so pervert this description of God's greatness, as thereby they much impeach the excellency of His majesty. For—1. Some thence infer that God may be circumscribed and compassed in a place. 2. Others thence infer that He is so high as He cannot see the things below, which Eliphas noteth to be the mind of the profane in his time who say, "Is not God in the height of heaven? How doth God know?" 3. Others thence infer that though it be granted that God seeth the earth and all things done thereon, yet He ordereth them not, which was the conceit of many philosophers. Why is God thus set forth? 1. To make our souls ascend as high as possibly can be when we pray unto Him. Above heaven our thoughts cannot ascend. 2. To distinguish God from earthly parents, and to show that He is far more excellent than they, even as heaven is higher than the earth, and things in heaven more excellent than things on earth. 3. To show that He is free from all earthly infirmities, and from that changeableness whereunto things on earth are subject. 4. To set Him forth in the most glorious manner that can be. As kings are most glorious in their thrones, so is God in heaven, which is His throne. 5. Because His glory is most manifested as in heaven, so from heaven. What direction doth it give for the manner for prayer? 1. That in prayer we conceive no image of God. For whereunto can He, who is in heaven, be resembled? 2. That we conceive no earthly or carnal thing of God who is in heaven. 3. That we measure not God, His Word, nor works by the last of our reason. He is in heaven; we on earth. This, therefore, is to measure things heavenly with an earthly measure, which is too scanty. 4. That we apply all the goodness of earthly parents to God after a transcendent and supereminent manner. For as the heaven is higher than the earth, so great is His mercy, &c. 5. That with all reverence we prostrate ourselves before God our Father in heaven. 6. That we make no place a pretext to keep us from prayer. For as the heaven and the sun therein is everywhere over us so as we cannot withdraw ourselves out of the compass thereof, so much more is God in every place over us. Is our Father which is in heaven tied to one country, or to one place in a country more than to another? An heathenish conceit! For the heathen imagined their Apollo, from whom they received their oracles to be at Delphi, Cuma, Dodona, and such other places. 7. That we lift up pure hearts in prayer. For heaven, where God is on His throne of grace, and whither our souls in prayer ascend, is a pure and holy place. 8. That our prayers be made with a holy subjection to God's will. 9. That in faith we lift up eyes, hands, and hearts into heaven. 10. That our prayers be so sent forth as they may pierce the heavens where God is. This is to be done with extension not of voice, but of spirit. The shrillest sound of any trumpet cannot reach unto the highest heaven, nor the strongest report of any cannon. But ardency of spirit can pierce to the throne of grace. 11. That we pray with confidence in God's almighty power. 12. That we pray with courage, not fearing what any on earth can do to hinder the fruit and success of our prayers. (*Ibid.*) *Of the direction which God's being in heaven giveth us for the matter of prayer:*—What direction doth this placing of God in heaven give us for the matter of prayer? It teacheth us what things especially to ask. 1. Things of weight and worth meet for such a Majesty to give. When subjects prefer a petition to their sovereign sitting on his throne, or chair of estate, they do not use to make suit for pins or points. This were dishonourable to his majesty. Shall we then make suit to this highest Majesty being in heaven for toys and trifles? Shall a dice-player pray that he may win his fellow's money? Shall an angry man pray to God that he may be revenged on him with whom he is angry? Shall any one desire God to satisfy his lusts? 2. From this placing of God in heaven we are taught to crave things heavenly, which are (1) Such as tend to the glory of God that is in heaven. (2) Such as help us to heaven. If the things which we are here taught to pray for be heavenly, how is it that temporal blessings come in the rank and number of them? As appendices and appurtenances to heavenly and spiritual blessings, for so they are promised. "First seek the kingdom of God, and His righteousness; and all these things shall be added unto you." As when a man purchaseth manors and lands, the wood in hedgerows for fire-boot, plough-boot, and other like purposes is given in the gross. Or more plainly, when a man buyeth spice, fruit, comfits, or any such commodities, paper and packthread is given into the bargain. So if thou get heavenly blessings, temporal things, so far as they are needful for thee, shall be cast in. 3. From placing God in heaven we are taught to crave heaven itself, that we may be where our Father is, and where we may most fully enjoy His glorious presence. (*Ibid.*) *Our Father which art :*—From the greatness of His love to us when we call Him Father. From the liberal communication of His goodness to us in that we say "Our Father." From the immutability of His essence, intimated in these words, *Qui es*, "Which art." From the high domination and power He hath over us when we say *In Cœlis*, "Which art in heaven." (*Archdeacon King.*) "*Our*," *better than mine and thine :*—*Meum* and *Tuum*, these words, "Mine" and "Thine," have been the seeds of envy and contention ever since the world was habitable. From these little grains hath the law's large harvest grown up. These were they which at first invented, and ever since exercised our terms—the common barristers, causes of all rents and schisms in the commonwealth's body. These have blown the coals of strife, occasioned brothers to go to law with brothers, nay, brothers to destroy one another. If Abel should have asked Cain upon what quarrel he killed him, he could have stated his controversy in no other terms but *Meum* and *Tuum*— "Thy sacrifice is better accepted than mine." These have been the accursed removers of neighbours' bounds and landmarks, have entitled the vigilant oppressor to another's patrimony. These were the bloody depositions that cost Naboth his life; had he relinquished his right to the vineyard, and not called it mine—" I will not give thee my vineyard "—he had preserved a friend of Jezebel and a life too. These two little monosyllables, "mine" and "thine," they are the great monopolists that span the wide world, that, like Abraham and Lot, divide the land betwixt them, yet cannot agree, but are ever wrangling and quarrelling about their shares; like those two factious brethren, Eteocles and Polynices, who never could be reconciled, living nor dead, for when they had slain one the other, and were put on one hearse, one funeral pile, their ashes fought, and the flames that burnt the bodies, as sensible of the mortal feud which was betwixt them living, divided themselves. How many actions and suits begun upon these terms "mine" and "thine" have survived those that commenced them first, and descended from the great-grandfather to the heir in the fourth generation? Since then these two had occasioned so much strife, so much mischief in the politic body, Christ would not have them admitted to make any faction or rent in the mystical body of the Church. But as He was the Reconciler of God and man by His blood, so would He show Himself the Reconciler of man and man, shutting up all opposition of mine and thine in this one word, as the common peacemaker, *Noster*, Our Father. (*Ibid.*) *A lesson of humility :*—He would not have any to prize themselves so much as to scorn and disvalue all below them. God is a God of the valleys as well as the hills, nor is He a Father of the rich and noble, but of the poor too. Be their qualities and degrees never so different in the account of the world, summed up in the account of this prayer, they are all even. As but one sacrifice was appointed for the rich and poor, so Christ hath appointed but one prayer, but one appellation for them all, *Pater Noster*, Our Father. The king and the beggar, the lord and the slave, all concur and say, "Our Father." God is no partial Father, nor is His ear partial; He hears and accepts the one as soon as the other. For our prayers do not ascend in their ranks, nor doth the poor man's petition stay to let the great ones go before; but when we pray, God comprehends us all under one common notion of sons and suitors. (*Ibid.*) *God our Father :*—The spirit of adoption is shed abroad in our hearts, and its cry is "Abba, Father." Now I need not say, I am sure, that of all feelings in the world there is none which is so likely to exhibit itself by outward signs and proofs as this—none so impossible to conceal, and of the existence of which, in consequence, we need have so little doubt. In the first place, then, let us see what proofs there may be of this love of God within us! First, as a matter of course, like any other passion or strong feeling which takes possession of us, it will be constantly present to us. Let the urgent business be over, and the burthen, so to say, removed from the mind, it returns like an unstrung bow instantly to its own bent. It delights to recover its liberty, and those beloved thoughts which for the moment had been driven into the background, resume their natural place, and become the first without an effort. Thus it is, as we all know, that the man of pleasure finds thoughts of pleasure uppermost; he does not seek for them; they come. The man whose heart is set on gain finds worldly speculations occupying him whether he will or not, I believe without exception, and so on through all the varieties of human pursuit! The favourite

thought comes! Now this is what I mean in regard to God. **In all** the intervals
which our worldly occupations leave, which in those whose hearts are not given up
to them, are very many, it is the thought of our heavenly Father which presents
itself most naturally and unaffectedly to us. Secondly. There is another principle
which flows naturally out of this constant presence of the thought of God in our
secret souls, and it is one of the most delightful, if not the most so, which comes
out of those treasures of grace which enrich the converted soul, even the feeling of
trust, an entire confidence without reserve or drawback, in Him whom we love. It
is just that sort of reliance, without check or a doubt of suspicion, which you see
in an innocent child towards an affectionate parent. Thirdly. Another proof of
the love of God, as a real living principle within us, is the readiness with which
men encounter difficulties, or make what the world calls sacrifices of gain or
pleasure, in order to further the holy will of Him whom they serve. Fourthly.
Another evidence of the love of God or not, is the delight, or otherwise, with which
the soul traces out in all things the signs of God's presence, and the proof of His
manifold mercies towards us. Finally, there is another sign of this love of God,
which is, perhaps, the strongest and best of all. I mean love to other men's souls,
and a longing for their eternal happiness. (*J. Garbett, M.A.*) **Hallowed be Thy**
name.—*On hallowing God's name :*—1. A man does not hallow the name of God who
does not speak of Him most reverently. He helps to hallow it who endeavours to
prevent others from profaning it. 2. The man who would hallow the name of God
should be very diligent in publicly worshipping Him : he who is diligent in attending on the public worship of God thereby honours God Himself, and also protests
against the conduct of those who honour Him not; and may not he who wishes
to hallow the name of God do something by his influence towards persuading
others to hallow it? 3. Every man who wishes to do as he prays should be
careful to honour God in his household; the master of a house should hallow
God's name by daily gathering his family about him, and praising Him and
making supplication before Him; he should hallow God's name, too, by teaching his
children to fear it, by bringing them up in the fear of it; he should make it his
constant effort that God should be recognized as the Lord of that house that His
name should be hallowed in his family however it may be profaned in others.
(*Bishop Harvey Goodwin.*) *Hallowing God's name :*—This petition relates to what
is called " declarative glory "—a prayer that God's name may be made known, and
honoured by all His creatures. 1. The desire that God's name may be " hallowed"
implies that we have a just sense of His majesty and holiness. He who is really
anxious for the honour of God's name will respect His Holy Word, His house, His
day, His sacraments, and all the institutions of His Church. 2. The petition,
" Hallowed be Thy name," is a prayer that all people may learn to love and obey that
gracious Father in whose service we find such freedom and delight. 3. This petition
should also remind us of the various ways in which our Heavenly Father is treated
with disrespect and contempt. 4. Once more, the petition, " Hallowed be Thy name,"
may be regarded as a devout response of faith and hope to the prophet's vision of
coming glory (Mal. i. 2). Two classes of persons should consider the subject of
this sermon as applicable to them. 1. It speaks loudly to those who, while living
upon the daily bounty of a gracious providence, to all intents and purposes ignore
the very existence of God. The greatest miracle in the world is our heavenly
Father's patience toward the unthankful and the evil. 2. Must not even the
professed followers of Christ acknowledge, with deep mortification, their own neglect
to promote the honour of God? (*J. N. Norton, D.D.*) *The petition for the*
advancement of God's glory:—I. WHAT IS MEANT BY THE NAME OF GOD. The
" name " of God is any perfection ascribed to Him, whereby He has been pleased
to make Himself known to men. 1. God's titles are His name. 2. God's attributes are His name. And there are two ways whereby God has made known Himself
and His name to us: by His works and by His Word. II. WHAT IT IS TO HALLOW
THIS NAME OF GOD. We can add nothing to His infinite perfections, nor to the
lustre and brightness of His crown; yet then are we said to sanctify and glorify
God, when, in our most reverend thoughts, we observe and admire His holiness
and the bright coruscations of His attributes; and when we endeavour by all holy
ways to declare them unto others, that they may observe and admire them with us
and give unto God that holy veneration which is due unto Him. III. WHAT IS
CONTAINED IN THIS PETITION. 1. In that Christ hath taught us to make this the
first petition in our prayer to God, we may learn that the glory of God is to be
preferred by us before all other things whatsoever. 2. In that this petition is

placed in the beginning of the Lord's prayer, it intimates to us that in the very beginning and entrance of our prayers, we ought to beg assistance from God, so to perform holy duties that God may be glorified and His name sanctified by us in it. It is a good and needful request to beg of God the aid and help of His Spirit to enable us to hallow His name in the succeeding requests we are to make. 3. Observe that when we present this petition before God we beg three things of Him. (1) Such grace for ourselves as may enable us to sanctify and glorify Him. (2) Graces likewise for others to enable them thereunto. (3) That God would by His almighty providence direct and overrule all things, both good and evil, to the advancement of His own glory. (*Bishop Hopkins.*)   *Hallowing God's name :—* I. WHAT IS MEANT BY THE NAME OF GOD. 1. God Himself. Names are put for persons. 2. Everything whereby He makes Himself known to His creatures. II. IN WHAT SENSE GOD'S NAME IS TO BE HALLOWED OR SANCTIFIED. Not effectively. " Holy *is* His name " ; it cannot be made more so. 2. But manifestly and declaratively, viz., when the holiness of His name is manifested, declared, shown, and acknowledged, " They shall sanctify My name " (Isa. xxix. 23). The holy name in the dark parts of the earth and in the dark men of the earth is a candle under a bushel ; it has a glorious light, but it is not seen ; the bushel being removed, and the splendour breaking forth to open view, it is hallowed; men then show, declare, and acknowledge it. III. WHY GOD'S NAME IS SAID TO BE HALLOWED OR SANCTIFIED RATHER THAN GLORIFIED. 1. Because God's holiness is His glory in a peculiar manner. 2. Because it is the manifesting of His holiness, in the communicating of it to the creature, that brings in the greatest revenue of glory from the creature to God. The truth is, none are fit to glorify Him but those who are holy (1 Pet. ii. 9). IV. THE IMPORT OF THIS PETITION. God's name is hallowed—1. By Himself, manifesting the glory of His holy name. And this He doth in all the discoveries which He makes of Himself to His creatures. 2. By His creatures, they contributing to His glory, by showing forth His praise, and declaring the glory of His name. So we pray in this petition. (1) That God would by His overruling providence hallow His own name and glorify Himself (John xii. 28). (2) That God would by His powerful grace cause the sons of men, ourselves and others, to glorify Him and hallow His name. V. WHY IS THIS PETITION PUT BY OUR SAVIOUR FIRST INTO OUR MOUTHS ? The reason is, because the glory of God or honour of His name is the chief end of our being and of all others. And therefore it should lie nearest our hearts (Rom. xi. 36). Inferences—1. The dishonour done to God by one's own sin and the sins of others must needs go near the heart of a saint (Psa. li. 4). 2. Habitual profaners of that holy name are none of the children of God, whose main care is to get that name hallowed. 3. Holiness is the creature's glory, and its greatest glory, for it is God's glory, and therefore unholiness is its disgrace and dishonour. (*T. Boston, D.D.*) *What the first petition implies :—*I. We must pray that God will enable us to sanctify Him in our hearts, in our words, and in our actions. 1. In our hearts. We must pray that holiness to the Lord, the holy Lord God, may be engraven there. We must pray further: that we may always maintain in our hearts a reverent esteem of God, as a Being of infinite, unblemished purity, &c. 2. We must likewise pray, that we may sanctify the name of God with the tongue. 3. We are here directed to pray, that we may sanctify the name of God by practical obedience. II. We must likewise pray, that God by His providence will dispose of all things for His own glory, as the universal Lord and Ruler, of whom, and through whom, and to whom are all things, and whose throne is for ever and ever; who has the hearts of all in His hand, universal nature at His command, from the meanest worm or insect to the highest of all the angelic orders in heaven ; and who has wisdom and power sufficient to govern all in the best manner and to promote the best end. (*John Whitty.*) *The hallowing of God's name :—*I. THE TERMS OF THE PRAYER. To implore that God's name may be hallowed, is to ask that it may be treated with due reverence, as befits the holy. In heaven it is so treated (Isa. vi. 3). But what is God's " name " ? It stands for His character, and includes all those signs and deeds by which God makes known to us His moral essence ;—all the manifestations which He has given of His nature and purposes ;—as well as in the narrower sense of the titles and appellations which He has chosen to proclaim as His own. As His Scripture, or His Word, is a fuller and clearer manifestation of His character than is contained in this material structure—the handiwork of God, the visible Creation ; so, consequently, this volume of Divine Scripture and the revelation there made are an important part of His name. As the Son, in His incarnation, yet more clearly and yet more nearly manifested God, He, the embodying Messiah, is called the Word of God. For as the word or speech is the embodiment of human thought, so His humanity was the embodiment of the Divine thought, or rather, of the Divine Spirit. Moses had, when sheltered in the cleft of the rock, heard the name proclaimed. Elijah caught its " still, small voice." But Christ was the distinct, full, and loud utterance of the name—articulate, legible, and tangible—complete and enduring. And all the institutions which Christ Himself established, or which His apostles after Him ordained by His authority, since those institutions bear His name, or illustrate His character, are to be regarded as coming within the scope of the text. II. THE SINS CONDEMNED BY THIS PETITION. 1. The profanity which trifles with God's name and titles is evidently most irreligious ; and it is, though so rife a sin, most unnatural, however easily and however often it be committed. Other sins may plead the gratification of some strong inclination—the promise of enjoyment or of profit, which they bring with them, and the storm of emotion sweeping the tempted into them. But what of gain or of pleasure may be hoped from the thoughtless and irreverent—the trivial or the defiant use of that dread name, which angels utter with adoring awe ? That the sin is so unprovoked adds to its enormity. That it is so common, fearfully illustrates the wide removal which sin has made of man's sympathies from the God to whom he owes all good ;—rendering him forgetful alike of his obligations for past kindnesses, and of his exposure to the coming judgment. How murderously do men guard the honour of their own paltry names, and how keenly would they resent, on the part of a fellow-sinner, though their equal, the heartlessness that should continually, in his narratives, and jests, and falsehoods, call into use the honour of a buried father, and the purity of a revered and departed mother, and employ them as the expletive or emphatic portions of his speech—the tacks to bestud and emboss his frivolous talk. And is the memory of an earthly, and inferior, and erring parent deserving of more regard than that of the Father in heaven, the All-holy, and the Almighty, and the All-gracious ? And if profanity be evil, what is perjury, but a daring endeavour to make the God of truth and justice an accomplice in deception and robbery ? The vain repetitions , of superstitious and formal prayer ; the acted devotions of the theatre, when the dramatist sets up worship on the stage as a portion of the entertainment ; and the profane intermixture in some Christian poets of the gods of heathenism with the true Maker and Ruler of Heaven, re-installing, as poets both Protestant and Catholic have done, the Joves and Apollos, the Minervas and Venuses of a guilty mythology, in the existence and honour, of which Christianity had stript them—will not be passed over, as venial lapses, in the day when the Majesty of heaven shall make inquisition of guilt and requisition for vengeance. And so, as to those institutions upon which Jehovah has put His name, just as an earthly monarch sets his seal and broad arrow on edict and property, the putting to profane and common uses what God has claimed for sacred purposes, betrays an evident failure to hallow His name. 2. But from the sins in act, which this prayer denounces, let us pass to the sins more secret, but if possible yet more deadly, those of thought—the errors and idolatries of the heart. Jehovah's chosen and most august domain is that where human legislators cannot enter or even look—the hidden world of man's soul. And in the speculations, and in the mute and veiled affections of that inner sphere, how much may God be profaned and provoked. III. Consider the DUTIES to which this prayer, for a hallowing of our Father's name, pledges us. 1. As, in order to hallow God's name, we must ourselves become holy, repentance and regeneration are evidently required to acceptable service before the Lord our God. Are Christians called vessels of the house of God ? It is needful that they be purified " to become vessels meet for the Master's use." 2. And, as a consequence of this growing holiness, Christians must grow in lowliness and self-abasement. 3. Pledged thus to holiness, and to lowliness as a consequence of understanding the true nature and the wide compass of holiness, Christians are again, in crying to their Father for the sanctification of His name, pledged to solicitude for the conversion of the world. (*W. R. Williams, D.D.*) *The sacred name :* — What "name" is this that our Lord here teaches us to "hallow" in our prayers ? God has been known by many names. He was first revealed as Elohim, the God of nature, the Creator—a name to which in the early Scriptures no moral attributes are attached. He was known also to the early patriarchs as El-Schaddai—the God Almighty. He was known also as the Holy One of Israel, and as the Lord of Hosts. Above all, He declared Himself by that name which in our version is rendered Jehovah—or for which the word LORD in small capitals is substituted,—which seems to mean the Self-existent and Eternal

Being. And now Jesus teaches us to address Him as our Father. Which of these names are we here bidden to hallow? As soon as we ask this question, it at once becomes plain that "name" is not used here in the narrow verbal sense of which we have been speaking, but in a wider and larger sense. It is not merely the letters and syllables that spell the name by which God is known, that our Lord teaches us here to sanctify. The petition includes, I suppose, all the names by which God has revealed Himself. There is no word that is large enough to hold all the truth that God has told men about Himself. He must needs choose many different words under which to declare to men different attributes and phases of His character. And when all these words are uttered, the half is not told. And it is not only by words that He has made Himself known. In the order and the beauty of the universe He discloses Himself; in the movements of the race; in the person of His Son; and in the heart of the humble and contrite believer. Indeed the whole of creation, the whole of providence, the whole of history, is simply God's method of revealing Himself. Now, as I understand this first petition, it includes the thought that all these distinct but conspiring revelations of God are to be reverenced. Whatever helps us to a fuller knowledge of Him—His nature, His character, His purposes, His works—ought to be held sacred. But the name of God stands for God Himself, and I suppose that when we intelligently offer this prayer we express the desire not only that the various revelations which God has made to men may be reverently treated, but that God Himself may be honoured in our thoughts and in our conduct. (*Washington Gladden, D.D.*) *On hallowing God's name:*—To hallow is either to make holy or to consider and recognize as holy. We cannot by our words nor by our deeds add any essential holiness to the Holy One of Israel; but we can think holy thoughts about Him; we can sanctify Him in our hearts. And in this petition we are taught to ask that our thoughts of God may be freed from error and cleansed from corruption; that our conception of His character may be corrected and enlarged and hallowed, so that it shall come nearer to the ineffable Divine reality. Moreover, the name of the Lord is hallowed, by our adding, as we can, to the respect and honour in which His name is held among men. The true child of God desires that all men should love and revere his Father in heaven; that not only the goodly fellowship of the prophets, &c., should praise Him, but that all men everywhere should honour Him; that earth as well as heaven should be filled with the majesty of His glory. 1. We cause His name to be hallowed in the earth by telling the truth about Him. One reason why many men do not hallow His name is simply that they do not understand His character. They have been told many things about Him that are not true. You are not hallowing the name of God when you make statements about Him which give the impression that He is unjust, or tyrannical, or cruel. 2. We can cause His name to be hallowed, also, by showing men that we honour and love Him. Good as well as bad sentiments are contagious. The unconscious influence of reverent hearts and praising lives will help to lift the thoughts of others to the same sublime realities. 3. Of praising lives, I said. For it is not chiefly by the reverent demeanour and the devout speech of God's children that the glory of their Father is promoted, but by the fidelity and nobility and beauty of their conduct. If we proclaim that He is our Father, then those who do not acknowledge Him will look to see what manner of spirit we are of. And if in our lives men see the purity and truth, the manliness and honour, the fidelity and charity that belong to all who learn of Him and abide in His fellowship and are transformed into His image, they cannot help honouring Him in whom we live and move and have our being. (*Ibid.*) *Selfishness excluded:*—This first petition of the Lord's prayer, without saying anything about it, deals a most effective blow at the central evil of human nature—our selfishness. Men are apt to be nearly as selfish in their religion, nearly as egotistic in their prayers, as in any other part of their lives. But this petition turns their thoughts wholly away from themselves. "Our Father, who art in heaven," we say; and now that our thought is lifted up to the Infinite Giver, what shall we ask for first? For the easing of our pains, the supply of our wants, the pardon of our sins, the saving of our souls, the welfare of our friends? No; these are things to ask for, but not first. "Hallowed by Thy name"! Away from ourselves to God our thought is quickly turned. "Begin to pray," this petition says, "by ceasing to think of yourselves; by remembering that your small personality is not the centre round which this universe revolves." "Seek first the kingdom," &c., is the Master's great command, and here He frames it into the first petition of the prayer that is to be always on our lips. "After this manner, therefore, pray ye. Self must be the fulcrum on which your prayer will rest, but it is not the power that lifts you heavenward. It is by looking out and not in, up and not down, that a man escapes from the bondage of sin into the liberty of the sons of God. (*Ibid.*) *Some things upon which God has recorded His name :*—1. Outward nature is stamped with the Divine name. Our Lord set us the example of sending worshipful thoughts to the Heavenly Father at the hint of the grass, the lilies, the sparrows, our hair, fountains, clouds, &c. The man of science ought to be the most devout of all, for, as Max Müller says : " The eye of man catches the eye of God beaming out from the midst of all His works." 2. Our human nature bears the name of God. To revere God fully, I must revere His image in myself. To abuse my nature in any way is blasphemy. Especially are conscience, the impulse to pure love, faith, hope, &c., Divine characters impressed upon us, to ignore or debauch any of which is sacrilege. 3. Providences, especially those in connection with our own lives, are to us God's names. Every blessing is a souvenir inscribed with the name of the Giver ; and every affliction is the branding which the Great Shepherd of our souls has put upon us to mark us and assure us that we are His. 4. The Bible bears God's name. It is a series of His Fatherly letters to us. 5. Jesus Christ is, above all, the name of God, which could only be articulated in the pulsations of a grand life. (*J. M. Ludlow, D.D.*) *Hallowing God's name :*—God's name—that is, His nature or character. It is for the hallowing of this that Jesus teaches us to pray. Not that God's name can be more truly holy in itself at one time than another. The name of the Holy One of Israel is always equally holy in itself ; just as the sun is always equally hot and glorious. To us, however, the sun is sometimes hotter and sometimes colder, sometimes brighter, and sometimes less bright ; sometimes, too, we lose sight of it altogether, and are left in night and darkness. So it is with God's name. Though in itself it is always holy, all-holy, yet by us sinners it is more reverenced and more hallowed at one time than another. There is a summer of the soul, when we look in the sunshine of God's countenance ; and there is also a winter of the soul, when our souls are cold and wither for the want of His cheering, enlivening presence. There is a night, too, of the soul, when we lose all sense and feeling of His holiness, and are, as it were, left in the darkness of sin. Therefore, in praying that God's name may be hallowed, we pray that there may be no more spiritual winter, no more spiritual darkness, but that the souls of all men may at all times feel the same bright and gladdening sense of God's true nature and character ; we pray that all men may at all times think of God truly as He is. Now there is much need, believe me, of praying for this. I. There is much need of praying that we may all of us always cherish true and holy and reverent thoughts about God. 1. The hardened sinner dishonours God's name, by robbing Him of His justice and hatred against sin. 2. The despairing sinner dishonours God in another way, by forgetting His mercy and lovingkindness. When we pray that God's name may be hallowed among the sons of men, we pray, in other words, that they may have such a true and lively sense both of His justice and of His mercy, as may lead them at once to fear and to love Him. II. But since we are made up of soul and body, not only does it behove us to sanctify and hallow our Father and Saviour in our hearts and souls, we must also hallow Him with our bodies, and with outward actions— for instance, with our tongues and voices—by telling forth all His praise, especially by joining in the public service of the Church. III. Let us hallow God's name by reverencing everything belonging to Him, His Word, His day, His sacraments, His ministers, His people. (*A. W. Hare.*) *Religious reverence :*—Reasons for the decline of it. 1. Technical theology, in attempting to delineate the Divine attributes, has dwarfed them, by using about them terms that describe human necessities and limitations, even human infirmities and passions. 2. There are certain stages of scientific research that are unfavourable to religious awe and devotion. Reverence and science have, however, no essential antagonism, and cannot be permanently or long divorced. 3. Another reason for the decline of reverence among us has been the decline of parental authority and domestic discipline. 4. There is also a style of religious instruction for the young which generates irreverence. I refer to the mania for explanation, which belittles all that is great, and degrades all that is lofty in the endeavour to make truths vast as immensity and eternity comprehensible by the youngest and feeblest mind. (*Prof. Peabody, D.D., LL.D.*) *The primal obligation of reverence :*—If there is One, by and in whom alone I live, to whom my whole consciousness lies open, whose power and love throb alike in every pulse of light from the far-off stars, and in every beat of my own heart ; to whom there is no far nor near, no great nor small ; to whom my least needs are known,

and my least desires precious; who is to me more than I can comprehend in the dearest names of human love, and is no less the tender and compassionate Father of myriads upon myriads in every realm of His universe—to feel all this is to worship and adore, and to say, in profoundest reverence, " Hallowed be Thy name."
(*Ibid.*)　*Irreverence in speech :*—Trifling with a name is disrespect to the person to whom it belongs. In the filial relation irreverence of speech and the corresponding deficiency in conduct uniformly coincide, the two being reciprocally cause and effect. The former, however, would of itself produce the latter. Were a son who really honoured his father and mother tempted by bad example to talk flippantly about them, and to call them by names unworthy so sacred a relation, irreverence in feeling and conduct would be the swift and inevitable consequence. The Hebrews dared not pronounce, even on solemn occasions or in reading the Scriptures, Jehovah, the most sacred name of God—a reticence which must have made blasphemy the rarest of sins. Would that we might take a lesson from them as to the needless use of the Divine name, even at sacred times and on sacred themes, much more as to its utterance on ordinary occasions! The frivolous or profane use of that name cannot long co-exist with a reverent spirit. Early and of necessity it lapses into practical atheism. It is a social offence against which no stress of indignation can be excessive. As *lèse-majesté* against the Sovereign of the universe, it is the climax of human audacity. As a sin against one's soul, I will not say that it is irreparable; for I do not believe that recuperative power is denied to any being under the reign of infinite love; but of all forms of guilt and wrong it has this bad pre-eminence, that it fouls the only fountain for its own cleansing, desecrates the very shrine before which lowly, awe-stricken worship is its only token of repentance and condition of forgiveness. (*Ibid.*)　*Of the first petition in the Lord's prayer :*—This petition, " Hallowed be Thy name," is set in the forefront, to show that the hallowing of God's name is to be preferred to all things. I. It is to be preferred before life : .we pray, " Hallowed be Thy name," before we pray, " Give us this day our daily bread." When some of the other petitions shall be useless and out of date ; we shall not need to pray in heaven, " Give us our daily bread," because there shall be no hunger; nor, " Forgive us our trespasses," because there shall be no sin ; nor, " Lead us not into temptation," because the old serpent is not there to tempt : yet the hallowing of God's name shall be of great use and request in heaven ; we shall be ever singing hallelujahs, which is nothing else but the hallowing of God's name. Every Person in the blessed Trinity—God the Father, Son, and Holy Ghost— must have this honour, to be hallowed ; Their glory being equal, and Their majesty co-eternal—" Hallowed be Thy name." 1. What is meant by God's name? (1) By God's name is meant His essence—" The name of the God of Jacob defend thee "; that is, the God of Jacob defend thee. (2) By God's name is meant anything by which God may be known; as a man is known by his name. God's name is His attributes, wisdom, power, holiness, goodness; by these God is known as by His name. 2. What is meant by hallowing God's name? To hallow, is to set apart a thing from the common use to some sacred end. As the vessels of the sanctuary were said to be hallowed, so to hallow God's name, is to set it apart from all abuses, and to use it holily and reverently. In particular, hallowing of God's name is to give Him high honour and veneration, and render His name sacred. When a prince is crowned, there is something added really to his honour ; but when we go to crown God with our triumphs and hallelujahs, there is nothing added to His essential glory ; God cannot be greater than He is, only we may make Him appear greater in the eyes of others. 3. When may we be said to hallow and sanctify God's name? (1) When we profess His name. (2) We hallow and sanctify God's name when we have a high appreciation and esteem of God ; we set Him highest in our thoughts. (3) We hallow and sanctify God's name when we trust in His name. (4) We hallow and sanctify God's name when we never make mention of His name but with the highest reverence; God's name is sacred, and it must not be spoken of but with veneration. The Scripture, when it speaks of God, gives Him His titles of honour—" Blessed be the most high God "; " Blessed be Thy glorious name, which is exalted above all blessing and praise." (5) We hallow and sanctify God's name when we love His name. (6) We hallow and sanctify God's name when we give Him a holy and spiritual worship. Then we hallow God's name, and sanctify Him in an ordinance, when we give Him the vitals of religion, and a heart flaming with zeal. (7) We hallow and sanctify God's name when we hallow His day— " Hallow ye the Sabbath-day." (8) We hallow and sanctify God's name, when we ascribe the honour of all we do to Him—" Give unto the Lord the glory due unto

His name." This is a hallowing God's name when we translate all the honour from ourselves to God—"Not unto us, O Lord, not unto us, but unto Thy name give glory!" The king of Sweden wrote that motto on the battle of Leipsic: "*Ista a Domino facta sunt*"; "The Lord hath wrought this victory for us." (9) We hallow and sanctify God's name by obeying Him. How doth a son more honour his father than by obedience? (10) We hallow and sanctify God's name when we lift up God's name in our praises. God is said to sanctify, and man is said to sanctify. God sanctifies us by giving us grace, and we sanctify Him by giving Him praise. Especially, it is a high degree of hallowing God's name, when we can speak well of God, and bless Him in an afflicted state—"The Lord hath taken away, blessed be the name of the Lord!" Many will bless God when He gives, but to bless Him when He takes away is in an high degree to honour God and hallow His name. (11) We hallow and sanctify God's name when we sympathize with Him; we grieve when His name suffers. (a) We lay to heart His dishonour. How was Moses affected with God's dishonour! He broke the tables. (b) We grieve when God's Church is brought low, because now God's name suffers. (12) We hallow and sanctify God's name when we give such honour to God the Son as we give to God the Father. (13) We hallow God's name by standing up for His truths. Much of God's glory lies in His truths; God's truths are His oracles. God's truths set forth His glory; now when we are zealous advocates for God's truths, this is an honour done to God's name. (14) We hallow and sanctify God's name, by making as many proselytes as we can to Him; when, by all holy expedients, counsel, prayer, example, we endeavour the salvation of others. (15) We hallow God's name when we prefer the honour of God's name before the dearest things. (a) We prefer the honour of God's name before our own credit. This is a hallowing God's name, when we are content to have our name eclipsed, that God's name may shine the more. (b) We prefer the honour of God's name before our worldly profit and interest—"We have forsaken all and followed Thee." (c) We prefer the honour of God's name before our life—"For Thy sake are we killed all the day long." (16) We do hallow and sanctify God's name, by an holy conversation—"Ye are a royal priesthood, a peculiar people: that ye should show forth the praises of Him who hath called you." 1. See the true note and character of a godly person; he is a sanctifier of God's name—"Hallowed be Thy name." 2. I may here take up a sad lamentation, and speak, as the Apostle Paul, weeping, to consider how God's name, instead of being hallowed and sanctified, is dishonoured. Theodosius took it heinously when they threw dirt upon his statue; but now, which is far worse, disgrace is thrown upon the glorious name of Jehovah. Let us hallow and sanctify God's name. Did we but see a glimpse of God's glory, as Moses did in the rock, the sight of this would draw adoration and praise from us. That we may be stirred up to this great duty, the hallowing, adoring, and sanctifying God's name, consider—1. It is the very end of our being. Why did God give us our life, but that our living may be a hallowing of His name? Why did He give us souls but to admire Him; and tongues, but to praise Him? The excellency of a thing is, when it attains the end for which it was made; the excellency of a star is to give light, of a plant to be fruitful; the excellency of a Christian, is to answer the end of his creation, which is to hallow God's name, and live to that God by whom he lives. 2. God's name is so excellent that it deserves to be hallowed—"How excellent is Thy name in all the earth!" "Thou art clothed with honour and majesty." God is worthy of honour, love, adoration. We oft bestow titles of honour upon them that do not deserve them; but God is worthy to be praised; His name deserves hallowing. He is above all the honour and praise which the angels in heaven give Him. 3. We pray, "Hallowed be Thy name": that is, let Thy name be honoured and magnified by us. Now, if we do not magnify His name, we contradict our own prayers. 4. Such as do not hallow God's name, and bring revenues of honour to Him, God will get His honour upon them—"I will get Me honour upon Pharaoh." 5. It will be no small comfort to us when we come to die that we have hallowed and sanctified God's name: it was Christ's comfort a little before His death; "I have glorified Thee on the earth." (*T. Watson.*) "*Hallowed be Thy name*":—Now there are two reasons why this prayer, "Hallowed be Thy name," is especially needful. The first springs from our own limitations as finite creatures. Sons of God though we are, we are finite, and God is infinite; and, therefore, our conceptions of Him will be commensurate with ourselves: that is to say, will be finite; and, so far, imperfect, meagre, unworthy. But there is a second reason why we ought to offer this prayer—"Hallowed be Thy name!" We are not only finite, and therefore, must necessarily have stinted conceptions of God ; we are also fallen, and, therefore, must necessarily have sinful conceptions of Him. How we mistake God's character, purposes, providences, justice, love, authority—in one word, His Fatherhood ! To hallow our Heavenly Father's name, then, is to have His name hallowed in the sphere of our own thoughts, feelings, desires, purposes, in a word, our characters. It is to pray : "Enlarged be our conceptions of Thee, O infinite One ! Chastened be our feelings toward Thee, O Holy One ! Exalted be our purposes in reference to Thee, O Mighty One ! Celestialized be our characters before Thee, O All-seeing One !" Again : To hallow our Heavenly Father's name is to have it hallowed in the sphere of our own words. Once more : To hallow our Heavenly Father's name is to have it hallowed in the sphere of our own lives. For the life without answers to the life within. Our opinions concerning God control our practices. Remembering, then, that our lives represent our views of God, what constant need there is of praying: "Father, Hallowed be our lives !" In drawing our meditation to a conclusion, I ask you to observe. First—That the knowledge of God's name has been an unfolding purpose. Again : The hallowing the Heavenly Father's name is the purpose or final cause of creation itself. (*G. D. Boardman, D.D.*) "*Hallowed be Thy name*" :—Regarding this petition I have three remarks to make. I. The place which this petition occupies in the Lord's prayer. It occupies the very first place, as the most important thing in all the prayer. There is a young artist, who has spent many a weary day on a painting, which, as his masterpiece, will, he hopes, secure for him both fame and fortune. No one may enter the room but himself. He carries the key in his pocket. His first thought is his picture. If any harm were to befall it, he would be a ruined man. But one day you see the smoke issuing from his house, and then the flame darts out, and all is in a blaze. There can be no coming back. Whatever he most values, each must seize at once, and run for life, so that the choice tells the value he attaches to his burden. Not a look does he cast at his precious piece of workmanship, but through smoke and flame you see him bearing, not the picture, but his old bedridden father !— so important to him as to eclipse all else. Now, just as the youth regarded the interests of his father, as momentous above all else, so what concerns God should, with every man, come before what concerns himself ; and that, not as differing from, but as having pre-eminently to do with, himself. How often most of us have passed this great petition lightly by, with little thought of what it meant, and with little desire that our prayer should be granted, when we said, "Hallowed be Thy name." And yet it concerned ourselves and others, the Church and the world, unspeakably more than anything of a temporal kind we could have asked. II. The meaning of this petition. The name of God is that by which He makes Himself known. I remark, that the prayer asks—1. That God's name may be known. Unless it be known, it cannot be hallowed. You have seen a person's shadow : you could learn something about him even from that. You have seen one of those likenesses taken from the shadow which the head casts on the wall; you can gather something from that. But when you see a well-finished portrait, it makes all the difference. It is almost as good as seeing the person himself. Now God in His works gives us the shadow, the dim profile. But God in His Word, and, above all, God in His Son, Jesus Christ, gives us His likeness, His portrait, so that we find Jesus saying, "He that hath seen Me hath seen the Father." 2. That the name of God may be reverenced and honoured. He is the King; He is the Creator; He is God. He made all things. He upholds all things. The hosts of heaven praise Him night and day. 3. That the name of God may be loved. This is higher than the last. III. The bearing of this petition. See its bearing—1. On the literal name of God. Everything pertaining to God is holy, and should be reverenced and honoured. Especially, "holy and reverend is His name." We have here the third commandment, "Thou shalt not take the name of the Lord thy God in vain," turned into a prayer. 2. Its bearing on God's House. Long ago, the temple was called the holy place, as the place where God had His dwelling. 3. Its bearing on God's Word. The Bible is God's letter, and may well be honoured and prized. And yet how often is it otherwise, both with the book itself, and what it says ! Look at the back of it, and what have you there? "The Holy Bible." In all your dealings with your Bible, reading it or listening to it, or otherwise having to do with it, remember that word, "Hallowed be Thy name." 4. Its bearing on God's Day. It is called the Lord's Day. He calls it, "My holy day." 5. Its bearing on the Son of His love. This was the best of all God's gifts—His only-begotten and well-beloved Son. He was peculiarly

the name of God—the Revealer of the Father, regarding whom He says,
is in Him." (J. H. Wilson, M.A.) *The name of God hallowed:*—In expr
this first and greatest desire of every devout mind, it is of some importance to ins
tute the inquiry, How is so desirable an end to be brought about? We confess our
inability to honour God aright. We ask that He would make us fit to honour Him,
and to give Him the glory which is due. 1. This is done, in the first place, by our
becoming acquainted with God. Many a man fails of receiving due honour from
his fellow-men, because he is not known. It needs but to become acquainted with
his excellencies, in order to love and respect him. His excellencies may be unpre-
suming and retired, and need searching out; or they may be obscured by his humble
condition or covered by a veil of prejudice, and require to be inspected by an impartial eye, that they may be appreciated. No man honours God while he remains
ignorant of Him. We respect the Deity, from a consideration of His Divine excellence; nor can we fail, at least, to respect him, if we know Him. 2. The name of
God is also hallowed by a reverential treatment of Him in our thoughts, words, and
actions. "As a man thinketh in his heart, so is he." Low, unworthy thoughts of
God, will lead neither to complacency, gratitude, nor honour. 3. God's name is
hallowed by a suitable regard to all His institutions and ordinances. Just as "truth
is in order to goodness," institutions are for the sake of principles. And such are
all the institutions of a pure Christianity. The institutions which the Great
Founder of religion has appointed, coincide with the great end for which the entire
system of Christianity itself was revealed. They are the visible symbols of great
and important principles, and the means by which they are advanced and perpetuated. The gospel cannot live without them. Prostrate these, and you exter-
minate true religion from the earth. 4. The name of God is also hallowed by the
exhibitions which He Himself makes of His own excellence. When we pray that
God's name may be hallowed, we pray that He Himself would make it holy and
venerable, by more and more extended and refulgent exhibitions of His glory.
There is another general inquiry, the answer to which may serve still further to
illustrate the import of this petition: Why does this petition hold so high a place in
this summary of prayer; and why is it so desirable and important that God's name
should be hallowed? Great and eternal interests depend upon the honours of His
name. We shall dwell a few moments upon the reasons which justify these general
remarks. 1. Our Heavenly Father's name and honour are justly great and endeared.
It is the greatest, most endeared name in the universe. Angels cannot bear to see
it dishonoured, because He is God their Maker and Sovereign; His children cannot,
because He is their Father, and they have all the honourable, honoured sentiments
of children. 2. That God's name should be hallowed, is also demanded by the great
interests of holiness in our world. 3. Inseparable from these suggestions also is
the thought that the happiness of creatures requires that God's name should be
hallowed. Let God be brought into view, and a holy mind will be happy; let God
be withdrawn, and it is miserable. The happiest moment of the Christian's life, is
when he enjoys the most enlarged and most impressive views of God, and dwells
with adoring wonder on His boundless and unsearchable perfections. (G. Spring,
D.D.) *God's name our first regard in prayer:*—Could we raise our devotion to
this pitch, it were indeed in its proper zenith. But our prayers for the most part
are blemished with some partialities and by-respects, and ourselves are more respected in them than God. If they be petitory, we request some good for ourselves;
if eucharistical, we give thanks for some good we have received; if deprecatory, we
request to be preserved from some evil. Still ourselves have the chiefest part; and
our prayers are like the Parthian horsemen, who ride one way, but look another;
they seem to go towards God, but indeed reflect upon ourselves. And how many
of us would fall down before God if we did not stand in need of Him? And this
may be the reason why many times our prayers are sent forth like the raven out of
Noah's ark, and never return. But when we make the glory of God the chief end
of our devotion, they go forth like the dove, and return to us again with an olive-
branch. It is a nice observation of Quadrigarius in Gellius, that darts and arrows
which are shot upward do fly more level, and more surely hit the mark, than those
which are shot downwards. But it is most true in our prayers, which are called
"ejaculations," because they are darted from us as shafts out of a bow: those that
fly upward to God, and aim at His glory, do more fix upon and take Him than those
other which fly downward upon ourselves. (A. Farindon.) *Of the particulars to
be prayed for under the first petition:*—Unto how many heads may those particulars
which in the first petition we are taught to pray for, be referred? Unto three

especially. For we are taught there to desire—1. Such graces in ourselves as may enable us to hallow the name of God. 2. Such graces in others as may enable them thereto. 3. Such an overruling providence in God, as may direct everything thereto. What are the graces which we desire for ourselves to the foresaid end? Such as are requisite for every power of our soul, and part of our body to make them fit instruments of hallowing God's name, as—1. For our understanding, we desire knowledge of God; that (as the apostle prayeth) "God would give to us the Spirit of wisdom and revelation in the knowledge of Him." 2. For our will, we desire a thorough and full submission of it to God, as to our sovereign Lord. 3. For our mind and will jointly together, we desire faith, whereby we give all due credence to the truth of God's Word, and believe in Him. This is a great honour done to God; "for he that receiveth His testimony, hath set to his seal that God is true." 4. For our heart, we desire that it may be wholly set upon God; and that He may be made the object of all our liking affections. 5. For our speech, we desire to mention the name of God, as we have occasion, with all reverence; yea, and to take all occasions of speaking of the glory of His name. 6. For our life and outward actions, we desire that they be holy, just, and blameless. What graces do we desire for others to the hallowing of God's name? All those which we are to desire for ourselves. What things do we desire that God by His overruling providence would turn to the hallowing of His name? Everything whatsoever, as—1. The virtues of His saints, whereby else they may be puffed up. 2. The peace and prosperity of His saints, whereby else they may be drawn away from God. 3. The failings and folly of His saints, as He did turn the envy of Joseph's brethren to the accomplishment of His word. 4. The troubles and crosses of His saints, that they sink not under the burden of them. 5. The wicked plots and practices of His enemies, and of the enemies of His Church. 6. All that all creatures do; that thus in all places, at all times, in and by all things, the name of God may be hallowed. All things whereby we ourselves are enabled to hallow God's name; whether in our soul, as the gifts and graces thereof; or in our body, as health, strength, agility, and dexterity to anything that maketh to that end; or in our calling, whether it appertain to Church, commonwealth, or family; or in our outward estate. (*W. Gouge.*) To what heads may the duties, which by reason of the first petition we are bound unto, be referred? What are we bound unto in regard of ourselves? To make the best use that we can of all the means which God affordeth to enable us to hallow His name, by giving us knowledge of God. 1. So to behold the creatures, and meditate on them, as we may discern the stamp of God in them, and the evidences which they give of His wisdom, power, justice, mercy, providence, &c. David also by this means had his heart even ravished with an holy admiration of God (Psa. viii. 1, &c.). 2. To take more distinct notice of God in and by His Word. The Scriptures are they that testify of God. 3. To take all occasions of stirring up our glory (as David styleth our tongue) to speak of, and to spread abroad the glory of God's name. 4. To order the whole course of our life, so as it may be worthy of the Lord, and a means to bring honour to His name. What are we bound unto in regard of others? To do our uttermost endeavour to draw on others to hallow God's name; for this end we ought—1. To instruct such as are ignorant of God in the knowledge of God. 2. To draw them to set their whole heart on God, by commending to them the greatness and goodness of God, so as they may be enamoured therewith. 3. To encourage them to all good works whereby God is glorified. (*Ibid.*) What are we to bewail in regard of the first petition? 1. Atheism, which is an utter denying of God. 2. Ignorance of the true God. 3. Errors of God. 4. Light esteem of God. 5. Neglect of due worship. 6. Undue using of His name. 7. Profaneness, and all manner of impiety. 8. Contempt of His image in such as He hath set over us. (*Ibid.*) *The conquering name :*—This petition stands in the head of the troop, being brought up before the others to acknowledge the power of that name which could give success to all we sought for in the rest of them. Constantine wore that victorious motto in his banner, *In hoc vinces.* Well may I write upon the front of this petition, *Hoc nomine vinces ;* by this name shalt thou obtain the victory. (*Archdeacon King.*) *Thought better than speech :*—Thy understanding will be more sharp and clear to discern Him without a name. Better is it only to conceive than to name God, for our conceit is more ample than our language; and 'tis more glory to God, when in a silent contemplation we confess Him far greater than we can utter. Let us be religious to sanctify, not curious to search His name. For thy service and adoration thou needest know no other name but God. That title is enough to give aim to thy petitions; that object powerful to grant them. (*Ibid.*)

God's attributes :—Rather I should think it a good moral way of expressing God's infinity by an infinite number of attributes. What hurt or blemish is it to the diamond, though you put several rates upon it? the quantity and the lustre is still one and the same; so is God. Neither do those attributes of His which began in time, cause any alteration or change in His eternity. One and the same piece of money is successively called a price, a debt, a pawn, a tribute; yet those appellations change neither the metal, nor the weight, nor the impression. How much easier, then, may we apprehend the immutability of God's substance amidst these His attributes—"In whom there is no shadow of change." (*Ibid.*) **Thy kingdom come**:—*God's kingdom*:—I. The kingdom for which Christ has taught us to pray. A spiritual kingdom. The prayer has for its objects—1. The spread of the gospel among men. 2. The saving reception of the gospel by man. II. Why the coming of this kingdom is accounted desirable. This will appear when we consider the numerous and valuable blessings which it invariably brings: such as—1. The light which it spreads. 2. The liberty which it grants. 3. The peace which it promotes. 4. The laws which it enforces. 5. The purity which it establishes. III. The considerations which should induce us to pray for the coming of this kingdom. We have an inducement in the consideration—1. That the Sovereign of this kingdom has an indisputable right to universal rule. 2. This kingdom has not yet come to the full extent of the dominion promised. 3. The universal establishment of this kingdom is ultimately certain. IV. The duty of those who pray for the coming of this kingdom. It is their duty—1. Personally to receive the gospel. 2. Personally to promote the spread of the gospel. 3. Personally to persevere in prayer for the success of this gospel. (*W. Naylor.*) *Reasons for missionary exertions:*—I. We pray that the kingdom of God may come, because of the wretchedness which prevails where His kingdom is not established. The very religion of the heathen is their misery. II. The gospel is in itself a mighty blessing. III. We desire that the gospel may be carried into all lands, because it leads to unspeakable blessings hereafter. (*Archbp. Sumner.*) *The reign of heaven:*—The mere mention of a kingdom suggests the idea of power and glory. 1. The kingdom of God, although not a temporal one, is a real one. 2. The kingdom for whose advancement we so often pray is a peaceable kingdom, and one which is constituted in the very person of the King Himself. 3. The kingdom of our blessed Lord, for whose prosperity we are permitted to pray and labour and endure, admits of unlimited extension throughout the world. 4. We should offer this petition for ourselves, that the Spirit of God may so rule in our hearts that every thought and desire may be subdued to the obedience of Christ. It is heart work, much more than head work, which is to make us fit for this kingdom. Religion is an inward principle, calling for personal self-denial and effort; and as vegetation is more advanced by the gentle dews and showers than by violent torrents of rain, so is it with the growth of grace in the soul. 5. When we offer the petition, "Thy kingdom come," we not only pray for ourselves, but also for those who enjoy fewer religious privileges than we do. The philanthropist is not satisfied to enjoy his abundance, nor the patriot his liberty, alone. The true Christian, like his Divine Master, would have all to be saved, and he feels pity for those who know not the way of life. Zeal for the honour of God, and for the advancement of His kingdom, may be exercised without the slightest infringement on the rules of Christian charity. One of our American bishops, on entering a beautiful church in Spain, was accosted by a Romish priest, who inquired if he was a Catholic. "Yes," was the prompt reply, "Catholic, but not Roman." The good priest grasped his hand and said, "It is sad that those who love Jesus should differ. We will tell it to Him, and, some day, His prayer will be answered, and we shall all be one." As the two parted for ever this side the grave, the Spanish priest said, with evident sincerity and emotion, "Pray for me!" Whenever such a spirit shall prevail among the disciples of Christ, the dawn of the millennium will be close at hand. The acting upon St. Augustine's famous rule will be helping the good cause: "In things essential, unity; in things questionable, liberty; in all things, charity." (*J. N. Norton, D.D.*) *The coming of God's kingdom :*—1. We must distinguish of God's kingdom. Now the kingdom of God is twofold; either universal, or more particular and peculiar. The one is His kingdom of Power; the other is His kingdom of grace. It is this latter that is meant here. Now this kingdom of grace is His Church, and may be considered two ways. (1) In its growth and progress. (2) In its perfection and consummation. In the former respect, it is the Church militant here upon earth; and, in the latter, it is the Church triumphant in heaven: for both make up but one kingdom, under divers respects. 2. The next thing in order is, to show how this kingdom of God is said to come. This word, " come," implies that we pray for a kingdom that is yet in its progress; and hath not yet attained the highest pitch of that perfection which is expected and desired. Now this peculiar kingdom is said to come in three respects. (1) In respect of the means of grace and salvation : for where these are rightly dispensed (I mean the Holy Word and Sacraments) there is the kingdom of God begun and erected; and therefore we find it called " the word of the kingdom " (Matt. xiii. 19). (2) In respect of the efficacy of those means. When all ready and cordial obedience is yielded to the laws of God, then doth this kingdom come, and the glory of it is advanced and increased. (3) In respect of perfection. And so it comes when the graces of the saints are strengthened and increased; when the souls of the godly, departing this life, are received into heaven; and when the whole number of them shall have their perfect consummation and bliss, in the glorification both of soul and body, after the general resurrection. And thus we have seen how the kingdom of God may come. 3. In the next place, we must inquire what it is we pray for when we say, " Thy kingdom come." (1) I answer, there are various things lie couched under this petition, as— (*a*) We pray that God would be pleased to plant His Church where it is not. (*b*) This petition intimates our earnest desire that the Churches of Christ, where they are planted, may be increased in the numbers of the faithful : that those, who are as yet enemies to the name and profession of Christ may be brought into the visible Church; and that those in it who are yet strangers to a powerful work of grace, may, by the effectual operation of the Holy Ghost, be brought in to be members of the invisible Church. (*c*) We pray that all the Church of Christ, throughout the world, may be kept from ruin. That they may not be overrun with superstition or idolatry : that God would not, in His wrath, remove His candlestick from them; as He hath, in His righteous judgment, done from other Churches which were once glorious and splendid : we pray, likewise, that God would make up all breaches, and compose all differences, and silence all controversies. (*d*) It intimates our humble request to God that His ordinances may be purely and powerfully dispensed. (2) This petition likewise respects the Church triumphant in heaven. (*a*) We may well pray that the whole body mystical of Jesus Christ, and every member of it, may be brought to the full fruition of heaven and happiness; that daily more may be admitted into the heavenly fellowship, till their numbers as well as their joys be consummate. (*b*) We may also pray that the bodies of all the saints may be raised again, united to their souls, and made glorious in the kingdom of heaven. (*Bp. Hopkins.*) *Thy kingdom come* :—1. WHAT IS MEANT BY THE KINGDOM OF GOD. A fourfold kingdom. 1. The kingdom of His power. 2. The kingdom of His gospel. 3. The kingdom of His grace. 4. The kingdom of His glory. Use 1. Submit yourselves contentedly to the disposals of Providence. If God be King over all, is there any fault in the administration; nay, is not all well done, yea, best done ? 2. Submit yourselves to the good sceptre. Are ye subjects of the gospel-kingdom ? Then it becomes you to be subject to the laws, to observe the ordinances, and to be submissive to the officers of the kingdom. 3. Let our royal Master have your hearts for His throne, and set up His kingdom of grace there. 4. Labour and be restless till ye get your interest in the kingdom of glory secured. And this is done by closing with Christ for all the ends for which He is given of God. It is dangerous to delay this. II. THE IMPORT OF THIS PETITION. The four kingdoms are sweetly linked together, and stand in a line of subordination, the end of which is the kingdom of glory, the kingdom of grace being subordinate to it, the gospel-kingdom to that of grace, and the kingdom of power to the kingdom of the gospel. Therefore I must begin with the kingdom of glory. 1. What is the import of this petition with reference to the kingdom of glory ? It imports—(1) That the kingdom of glory is not come yet— " It doth not yet appear what we shall be " (1 John iii. 2). The King has not yet erected that kingdom. The King's coronation-day for that kingdom (2 Thess. i. 10) is not yet come. (2) That it will come. The King really designs it. From eternity He decreed it (John xvii. 24). (3) That it is the duty and disposition of the saints and children of God, to desire the coming of this kingdom, and that themselves and others may be brought into it (2 Tim. iv. 8). 2. What is the import of this petition with reference to the kingdom of grace? There is no getting into the kingdom of glory but by coming through that of grace. So that desiring the coming of the former is desiring the coming of the latter too. It imports—(1) That all men naturally are without this kingdom, under the dominion of Satan (Eph. ii. 2, 3).

(2) That we cannot bring ourselves or others into it (John vi. 44). (3) That we cannot, where it is set up, maintain and advance it against the enemies of it (2 Cor. iii. 5). (4) That it is the duty and disposition of the children of God to desire that the Lord Himself may bring forward His kingdom. 3. What is the import of this petition with reference to the kingdom of the gospel? By it one is brought into the kingdom of grace. So desiring the coming of the one, we desire also the coming of the other. It imports—(1) That there are many impediments in the way of the propagation and efficacy of the gospel which we cannot remove. (2) That the Lord Himself can remove all the impediments out of the way, and make the gospel triumph over them all, persons or things, sins or troubles, that are laid in the way to hinder it (Isa. lvii. 14). (3) That it is the duty and disposition of the children of God to desire the advancement of the kingdom of the gospel. (4) That God would exert His power for all this. 4. What is the import of this petition with reference to the coming of God's kingdom of power? It is by the power of God that all these great things must be brought about. So the desiring of the coming of the gospel, is the desiring of the coming of this kingdom too. It imports—(1) That these things will not be done unless Omnipotency interpose. The work is great, the hands employed in it are feeble, and there is great opposition. It will stick, if heaven put not to a helping hand. (2) That it is the duty and disposition of the children of God, to desire that God would exercise the kingdom of His power in the world, as may best conduce to these ends (Isa. lxiv. 1, 2). III. THE REASONS OF THE CONCERN OF THE CHILDREN OF GOD FOR THE COMING OF HIS KINGDOM. 1. The new nature in them moves that way (Isa. xliii. 21). 2. It is their Father's kingdom. How can they help being concerned for it? 3. Their own interest lies in it. Use 1. Of information. (1) The excellency, usefulness, and necessity of the glorious gospel. It is the kingdom of God. (2) That the cry for the ruin of the kingdom of God can be no other but the cry of the family of hell. (3) That the kingdom of our Lord will triumph over all its enemies, and drive over all opposition. 2. Of trial. Try by this whether ye be of the family of God or not. Have ye a kindly concern for the coming of His kingdom? Do your hearts say within you, "Thy kingdom come"? If it be not so, God is not your Father; but if so, He is. (*J. Boston, D.D.*) *The prayer for the coming of God's kingdom:*—I. What is meant by the KINGDOM? 1. Not that general kingdom of God which extends to all the world, and all ages of it. 2. Nor the kingdom of grace, whereby God rules in the hearts of His people; for God always has thus ruled in such as He was pleased to subdue to Himself. This cannot, therefore, be what Christ directly pointed at, though the increase of that kingdom, by the addition of real members to His Church, may be included in that petition. 3. Our Saviour did not direct His disciples to pray that a worldly kingdom may be set up under the Messiah. 4. Nor can we judge that Christ directed them to pray that the kingdom of glory might come immediately, or in a short time. For the gospel was to be preached to all nations, and a Church to be gathered to Christ through a succession of many ages before that end would come. However, that glorious everlasting kingdom seems to be included. 5. The gospel dispensation, which was to be put under Christ, God's anointed, as the Lord and head of it, to whom all judgment was committed, was plainly intended in this place. II. What we are to understand by the COMING of this kingdom. This includes, we may suppose, three things. 1. That the prophecies which related to the kingdom of the Messiah might be accomplished. That that kingdom might be actually set up, of which it was said, it should have no end; that throne of God erected, of which David wrote, "that it should be for ever and ever." In a word, that all that God had spoken by His prophets of that nature might be fulfilled; and that the commencement of that kingdom might soon take place, which John had preached as then at hand. 2. That it might appear that Christ was the Lord's anointed, though His kingdom would not come with observation, with such external pomp and splendour as would raise admiration. 3. The coming of the kingdom of God must be understood as meaning the increase and advancement of it, as well as its commencement. III. What were the DISCIPLES to pray for in this petition? Undoubtedly they were to pray for the completion of those things which had been promised and prophesied concerning the kingdom of Christ. IV. What are WE to pray for in this petition? Are we not to offer up this request in the very same sense, to ask the very same thing the disciples of Christ did, to whom He delivered these instructions about prayer, how to pray, and what to pray for? I answer, no; undoubtedly we are not to use these words in the same sense they did. It was proper for those who lived before Christ's coming, and

looked for redemption, to pray for the advent of the Messiah; that the desire of all nations might come : it would be absurd and impertinent for us to do so, since we know that in this sense the kingdom (*i.e.*, the gospel dispensation) began almost two thousand years ago. 1. We must pray, that the kingdom of Satan may be destroyed. 2. We must pray, that the borders of Christ's kingdom may be enlarged; that more of the kingdoms of the earth may be added to it; that His interest may grow and flourish; and the kings and princes of this world, who are not yet acquainted with Christ, the universal Lord, may bring their glory and honour into His Church. 3. We must pray, that the number of true believers may be increased: that Christ may have numerous faithful subjects subdued to Him, a willing people, to whom His yoke is easy, and His burden light; who do not only confess His name, and attend upon His ordinances and the like, but sincerely honour, esteem, and love Him, and desire grace to enable them to adorn their holy profession by strict obedience to His gospel. And we should pray that in all the Churches of Christ truth and holiness and peace may prevail; that the true gospel doctrine may be universally and faithfully preached, gainsayers convinced, and their mouths stopped, errors confuted, and all corruptions removed as to worship or Church-government. And that holy discipline, according to the gospel direction, may be kept up, where it is already used; and restored, where it is dwindled away into nothing, through lukewarmness and negligence, or by pride and ambition and covetousness turned into tyranny and oppression. 4. Under this head of prayer we may make mention of ourselves, and pray that our own souls may be subdued to Christ, and that His kingdom may come in us. 5. We should pray for that glorious state of the Church, which the Scripture gives us ground to believe there will be before the end of the world. A millennium, or thousand years' reign of Christ, is spoken of in the Revelations, when the devil is to be bound a thousand years, and Christ to reign in some eminent sense for that term. 6. We are directed by this petition to pray that the kingdom of glory may be hastened. Practical reflections: 1. We should heartily commiserate the unhappy parts of the world where the gospel of the kingdom is not preached, and from whom the mystery of redemption is altogether hidden. 2. We should be heartily thankful that unto us it is given to know the mysteries of the kingdom of heaven. 3. It is a shame and reproach to such a nation as this, that so little of the holy fruit of the gospel is to be seen among us; and so much vice and impiety, as (all things considered) can hardly be equalled among the heathen. Will they not rise up in judgment with us in the last day, and condemn us as more guilty than themselves? 4. We should fear the righteous judgment of God, and pray that God will pour out His Spirit upon us; upon magistrates, ministers, and all sorts of people; that the glory may not depart from us, but that the kingdom of God may be advanced and flourish among us, in righteousness, and peace, and joy in the Holy Ghost; and that that kingdom may come in our own hearts. 5. Those that pray that the kingdom of Satan may be destroyed, should take care that they do not anything to promote it by practising unlawful things themselves, or by conniving at such things, or encouraging them in others. Should we do this, our own prayers would condemn us. (*John Whitty.*) *The coming of God's kingdom of grace :*—The kingdom here intended is the dominion of His grace—that provision of His infinite mercy, by which He is to subdue our sinful race into cheerful allegiance, and exulting homage, and general service. This, as yet, has come but in part. Its full and final establishment has been long the theme of prophecy, and the burden of prayer. The movements of God in His kingdom of Providence had respect from the beginning to the development of this kingdom of grace. Let us now consider the several aspects of this kingdom. I. It is spiritual. As man's noblest nature is his inner, invisible, and spiritual one, it is to this mainly that God and the religion of God look. The power that is to change the face of earth, and the history of the race, is not an army, not a fleet, not a treasury; but a word of salvation—something of the mind, and for the mind—and it is a Spirit renewing and sanctifying—the creative Spirit come down, to rear again and restore our fallen, created spirits. Now, as the Holy Ghost is the great primal agency in advancing and upholding the spiritual dominion of God on earth, aught that grieves or repels Him—aught that assumes to replace Him in His prerogatives, or claims to mortgage Him to a certain ecclesiastical communion, or to imprison Him in certain ordinances, as dispensed by a certain order of men, and, above all, aught that forgets our dependence on Him, or affects independence of Him and His aids, is so far a hindrance in the way of the coming of this spiritual empire. To enter ourselves Christ's Church, or to aid others in advancing it, we must be born of the Spirit. II. It is social. Though religion begins with the individual, it, after having renovated the inner world of the heart, necessarily affects the outer world, or the man in all his relations to his fellow-creatures; both those of like feelings with himself, or men spiritually minded, and those also who are not yet in affinity and sympathy with him, or, as the Scripture calls this last class, the men who are carnally minded. If a man is a true disciple of Jesus, he is, or ought to be, the better man in all his relations to worldly society, as far as those relations do not assume to control and overtop his duties and relations to heaven. Education and commerce and art—so far as they keep themselves in a position of due deference to a pure Christianity—will elevate and bless society. So far as they shall rival or defy her, they cannot fail to disappoint the hopes which they excite, and to bloat the body politic into a diseased appearance of prosperity, the unsoundness of which any great reverse of affairs will soon betray. Pauperism, slavery, and the question of labour in our times can be reached most safely and effectively by Christian principles diffused throughout the community. III. But whilst this religion, beginning in the individual and spiritual man, works inevitably its way outward upon all social relations and interests and maladies, it is, unlike the government and institutions of earth, eternal. So Daniel described it, "a dominion that shall never end." The Churches of earth are but like the receiving-ships of a navy, from which death is daily drafting the instructed and adept recruit for his entrance upon service in the far and peaceful seas of the heavenly world. Christ asks the heart and the homage of the deathless spirit; and, as death moulders and disperses for a time the bodily tabernacle, He neither loses His rights in, nor His care over, the spirit which that bodily tabernacle for the time housed. Now the kingdom of heaven has already known, amid seeming and local reverses, its stages of regular extension and advancement. It has overspread a large portion of the globe. The most powerful nations of the world are its nominal adherents. Missions are diffusing it on this very Sabbath amongst tribes whose names even our fathers knew not, and in empires which those fathers deemed hopelessly barred against the access of our faith. Prophecy assures us that this shall go on with still augmented zeal, and still expanding conquests. The Jews shall be brought in. Mahommedanism shall fall, and is even now evidently withering. Antichrist shall be shattered. These are stages in the social development of Christ's blessed kingdom. But behind and above them come higher developments in the individual Christian. The righteous here have in their earthly homes but lodges in the wilderness. The most prosperous of earthly churches is but a green booth, reared by pilgrims beside the fountains of Elim, and which is soon to be forsaken in their onward march beyond the line of the present visible horizon. But in the heavenly Canaan there is a fixedness of tenure, and perpetual repose, and fulness of felicity—of knowledge—and of holiness. Towards this crowning and culminating state of the Redeemer's kingdom all the earlier and inferior stages tend. Zion's sorrows are disciplinary; her reverses but school her for a more successful onset on the powers and strongholds of darkness; and with the destinies of her Redeemer embarked in her, and with infallibility and Omnipotence united in her Helmsman, her course, like His, is "conquering and to conquer." Now, when the Word of God speaks of this kingdom, it sometimes alludes to its incipient, and sometimes to its advancing, and sometimes again to its final stages. In its spiritual and individual beginnings it is within us. In its social leaven reaching the tribe, the nation, and the race, it is around us. In its last and triumphant day it is no longer a matter of time and earth. It is beyond and above. It has come in splendour never to wane, in power never to be lessened; and the kings of the earth bring their glory into its gates never to be closed. To pray, then, for Christ's kingdom, is to pray for the conversion of sinners and the edification and sanctification of disciples. (*W. R. Williams, D.D.*) *Thy kingdom come:*—1. Consider the boldness of Christ in speaking these words. Here is a single thought of His, which is the sublimest ideal ever presented in human speech—something which, heretofore, was utterly unknown on earth, in its true scope and fulness. Christ here announces the fellowship of the human with the Divine nature, the sanctification of man's will and temper, and its union with God's purpose and plan. In the midst of all the rivalries of the race, Christ stands as the index of a spiritual kingdom, for the prevalence of which His disciples are to pray. He perfectly, they—timid and passionate—very imperfectly, represented the kingdom of God to be set up in the world. 2. Think what light is cast upon the gospel by this utterance of the Son of God. The Word of life was to regenerate the world. 3. The true standard by which we are to measure society. The test is, How far is the Divine idea realized? Is the kingdom of God set up? 4. Here, again, we find the criterion of judgment as to what constitutes individual renown in history. 5. We are reminded by these words of the great opportunity of life. We may co-operate with God in bringing, first our own souls into harmony with His will, and then leading other spirits under the sweet dominion of His royal law. (*R. S. Storrs, D.D.*) *The eternal kingdom :*—The kingdom of God is in its essence a spiritual kingdom; the seat of His dominion is in the thoughts and affections of men; the tokens of its sway are a deepening purity and a growing love among the children of men. Of course it takes hold on things outward also, and shapes them by its law; it changes the manners and the fashions and the laws and the social relations of men; it is not in its essence meat and drink, but it rules the lives of men who are its loyal subjects whether they eat or drink or whatever they do. Still it affects the forms and fashions of men only as it transforms the thoughts and the desires of men; it works from within outward; its forces are all spiritual, though its manifestations are visible in all the realms of life. And it includes everything that is true, everything that is pure, everything that is lovely, everything that is honest and brave and sound and sweet in the universe. Whatsoever is good is of God, and is a sign of the rule of His kingdom in the world. Whatsoever shows improvement— whether it is from good to better, or from worse to better—is a token of the progress of God's kingdom in the world. Wherever morality and purity are gaining, wherever the vile are becoming less vile, and the cruel less cruel, and the coveteous less coveteous, there the kingdom of God is advancing. "There is none good but one, that is, God," said our Lord Himself; and there is no good in any man, from the feeblest virtue in the worst man to the grandest integrity in the best man— there is no good in any beneficent institution, or in any kindly custom, or in any refinement of social life—that is not a Divine inspiration; that is not the result of obedience to the Divine law; that is not, therefore, a token of the presence and the prevalence in some degree of God's kingdom. When we intelligently offer this petition, then, we are asking for nothing less than this, that the light and love and power of God may increase and abound everywhere in the world. "But why, then," it may be asked, "should we say, 'Thy kingdom come'?" If God's kingdom is the sum of all beneficent forces, of all holy influences, of all truth and all love and all righteousness, why should we pray that it may come? It is here already. The world has never been wholly destitute of righteousness. God has never been without a witness on the earth. Why then do we pray, "Thy kingdom come"? Why do we wish or ask in March that summer may come? That would surely be a proper wish, and might be a fitting prayer. Yet all the elements of the summer are here to-day. The earth, from whose fruitful breast the summer springs, lies waiting here; in her veins a myriad lives are throbbing; the mighty prince of light is shining down on us every day; air and light, and moisture and warmth, all the forces that make the summer, are here; every day the sun is wheeling his chariot a little higher into the sky; every day the empire of the light enlarges, and the realm of night is narrowed; yet, though the elements and forces out of which the summer comes are here, we might wish to have them here in greater fulness and in greater power. And so this petition asks, not that righteousness and peace and joy in the Holy Ghost may begin on the earth, for they began to be long ago, but that they may continue, and that they may increase. Probably it is the increase of this kingdom that is more specifically intended. It is a fuller, a broader, a more glorious manifestation of these great principles and forces. It is a prayer that the lives which are not now under their sway may be brought into subjection to them; that the institutions that now are ruled by selfishness and strife may be pervaded by them; that the homes in which vice and greed and worldliness now reign may be cleansed and hallowed by the spirit of purity and love; that the societies in which frivolity and vanity now rule may be ruled by soberness and modesty and quietness; that many lands which are now habitations of cruelty may hear and obey the gospel of goodwill. It is not a prayer that the leaven may be brought and placed in the measures of meal, but that its subtle, transforming influence may extend until it shall pervade the whole lump. It is not a prayer that the mustard seed may be planted, but that its growth may be hastened by the gentle dews of God's grace and the sunlight of His truth until it shall become a great tree, whose branches shall be vocal with the songs of Paradise, and in whose shade all the weary of the world may rest. (*Washington Gladden, D.D.*)　　*The most comprehensive petition:*—This is the most comprehensive petition of the Lord's prayer.　Indeed, it is the most comprehensive petition that it is possible for man to utter; there is hardly anything that we ask for that is not summed up in this prayer.　It is a prayer that the whole world may grow better and brighter; that all the people in the world may grow gentler and stronger, and truer and kinder, and happier year by year.　And it is a recognition of the fact that this can come to pass only as the world is filled with the knowledge of God and ruled by His law; only as the people in the world come to know Him better and to obey Him more perfectly. (*Ibid.*)　　*Answers to this petition:*— People sometimes question whether prayer is ever answered; but here is a prayer that Christians have been offering now for eighteen hundred years, and if you want to know whether it has been answered, read the whole of history since Christ ascended.　"Thy kingdom come!" the disciples prayed, and presently a bloody persecution fell upon them in Jerusalem, and drove them forth from the holy city, and made them homeless wanderers.　That was a strange way of answering the prayer.　But "they that were scattered abroad went everywhere preaching the Word."　Up and down the rugged roads of Palestine they went proclaiming the glad tidings of great joy.　It was not long before the messengers found their way over the heights of Mount Taurus, and here and there a centre of light was kindled in the dark provinces of Asia Minor; then the voice came to Paul summoning him to Macedonia, and Europe was invaded by the intrepid apostle, who planted the standard of the gospel on the classic fields of Philippi and on the heights of the Areopagus.　From these small beginnings the leaven of Christianity has spread, until now nearly a third part of the human race acknowledge Jesus Christ as Lord. . . . "Thy kingdom come!" good Christians prayed.　And He who hears the cry of His children came down to earth and stretched forth His hand to woman, so long the slave of man's power, and the drudge of his indolence, and the victim of his passions, and lifted her up, and clothed her motherhood with dignity, and her womanhood with divinity, and gave us by her hand the blessings of home, the best of all earth's precious things.　"Thy kingdom come!" the strong of faith were crying; and a Presence unseen by men stood among the prisoners in the dungeons that were festering dens of disease and vileness, and laid its gentle hand upon these hapless children of the evil, and lifted the weight of hate and scorn that made their lot so desperate, and sought to lead them forth to ways of purity.　"Thy kingdom come!" God's children cried; and the victims of insanity saw a beam of hope through the mental darkness in which they were walking, and found themselves no longer chained and scourged like criminals, but gently led and kindly treated.　"Thy kingdom come!" was the voice of millions who groaned in slavery, and of millions more who remembered their brethren in bonds as bound with them; and one by one the fetters have snapped asunder — the strong shackles of the Roman law, the wounding cords of feudal villenage, the degrading toils of British slavery, the prescriptive manacles of Russian serfdom—until even in our own land, and in our own day, "our eyes have seen the glory of the coming of the Lord," as He comes proclaiming liberty throughout the land to all the inhabitants thereof.　"Thy kingdom come!" the children of the light were pleading; and the hierarchies that sought to confine the thought of men were baffled and paralyzed, and the Bible was unchained, and the ways that lead to the mercy-seat were opened to the feet of all penitent believers.　Thus it is by these mighty changes which have liberated and elevated and enlightened the children of God that God's kingdom has been coming through all the ages, with increasing glory and enlarging power. (*Ibid.*)　　*Ways in which we may hasten the coming of God's kingdom:*—Even the children can help to bring, in many places, this kingdom of God for which they daily pray.　I heard a mother telling the other day of her children who had quarrelled sometimes, as many children do, I fear, but who had both been made so thoroughly sorry and ashamed on account of one of their quarrels that they were careful for many days after that not to say a bitter word, or to do a hateful deed. So peace came to that home through the prayer and the watching of these two Christian children; and peace, you know, is one of the signs of the kingdom of God in the world.　And I hope that when the children offer this prayer, they will remember that this is one of the ways in which it is answered, and in which they may help in answering it.　And wherever we help one another to the living of better lives—to be more truthful or upright or honourable or kind, to be more faithful in our duties to God or to men—there we are helping to answer our prayer, and to hasten the coming of God's kingdom. (*Ibid.*) *Loyalty to God :*— Reverence recognizes the majesty of God; loyalty His authority. We might revere a foreign king; we are loyal only to our own. Many are able to feel the former sentiment who are apparently uninfluenced by this. They go in crowds to worship, confessing that it is good and seemly to do so, but never think of leaving their homes for the sake of obeying a Divine precept in doing an act of justice or charity in God's name. Lord Bacon was a very reverential man, but not loyal, for he was an unrighteous man. Robert Burns must have had some hallowing sense of Divine things to have written the "Cotter's Saturday Night"; but he was not an honest subject of God, for he did not keep the seventh commandment. "The kingdom" is that condition in which God's laws are perfectly kept, and His promises fulfilled. The kingdom of God, with its hallowing influences, presses against our generation, and against every man in it, as really as the upper ether presses against the earth's atmosphere. The righteousness of the kingdom presses upon our consciences; our moral natures are as sensitive to it as our nerves are to the slightest motional influence. We cannot keep out the sense of justice and judgment, awakening complacency or dread, according to our lives. We are all and always conscious of spiritual realities about us and within us. When we pray, "Thy kingdom come," we ask that the same righteousness which makes heaven perfect may come to reign in all men's lives, not dimly discerned through conscience and reflected in the Bible precepts, but as it is in the character of God our King. We pray that the love which makes heaven happy may fill every human soul, not as we feel it in our kindliest charity, but as it is in God who "is love": we pray that Christ may come, in whom Divine righteousness and love were embodied, and win all hearts to His sway. And if we are honest in the prayer we open our own hearts to receive the kingdom, that upon it may be put those laws of holiness and love. The petition sincerely uttered is thus a formula of consecration. An illustration of spiritual loyalty to our King may be taken from a historical scene. When William the Conqueror assumed dominion in England, each of his barons knelt before him bareheaded, and, placing his hands within those of his superior, swore—"Hear, my lord, I become liege-man of yours for life and limb and earthly regard, and I will keep faith and loyalty to you for life and death. God help me." Whereupon the kiss of the king invested him with his portion of the land. (*J. M. Ludlow, D.D.*) *Appreciation of God's kingdom:*—It is the state of a man's mind which qualifies him to enjoy any one of God's kingdoms. What is the celestial kingdom of suns and stars to him whose eye is downward looking? Tell him that in yonder space "there are 1,000 stars seen by the naked eye, and each of them is the centre of a planetary system; that it has been computed that 100,000,000 might be seen by the telescope were they explored"; but his soul is not awakened to these stupendous and distant realities, and that celestial kingdom rings no peal of harmonies, no everlasting chime in his ears. The world is what we make it. It is a market-place, or the portico of a temple, or a school where character is disciplined for eternity, or a sphere of government where the ground wears the stamp of God's footsteps to the observant eye; the world is either of these to us according to our culture, our knowledge, our life. So this kingdom of God is to you according to your point of observation. It is appreciated or neglected as you are wont to prize or to despise the spiritual world and spiritual influences. Do you think that the greatest thing in the world is a soul ruled by God? A soul receptive of influence to guide its convictions and to give conscience dominion over the passions? Are you wont to think that falsehood, excess, enmity, impurity, ignorance—the curses which turn the earth into a wilderness—shall be weeded up as sure as there is a God in heaven; weeded up out of the soil of men's affections by the mighty power and all-subduing love of the gospel of His Son? Is it a bent of your mind, a resolute habit of thought, that you will not dishonour your Maker's purpose or character by suspecting that He could make this earth for a horde of guilty and unbridled passions to riot in; for war and cupidity, for envy, lust, and avarice; that it is no part of your creed that disease and the cry of the lazar-house are the natural state of mankind? No; they were brought in by evil, by malignant influences; brought into a world which its Maker pronounced to be "very good"; brought in by sin. But as God did not bring them in, He will rid the earth of them. Their sentence is already pronounced. The throne is set. Judgment is passed. Let them revel their appointed time. To your eye they are doomed; creation has groaned under their weight too long already, but the hour of its redemption is come; to your ear it is already striking; and "Behold, I make all things new: new heavens, and a new earth." "Belief is something towards its own realization." Grotius, in describing the success of the Batavians in breaking the Spanish yoke, says beautifully, "*credendo fecerunt.*" By believing they could do it—they did it. So he who prays, "Thy kingdom come," from his heart, hastens its coming, and sees it come. (*B. Kent.*)   *A slave's definition of the words, "Thy kingdom come."*—A female slave in Travancore, at a public examination of candidates for baptism, in reply to the question, What is meant by the words, "Thy kingdom come"? (when the silence of others made it her turn to speak), modestly said, "We therein pray that grace may reign in every heart." The most learned divines could not have answered the question better.   *God's kingdom not of this world:*—No doubt many of us have heard the well-known story which is told of the early Dominican monk, St. Thomas of Aquinum. He was one day sitting in the Vatican with Pope Innocent the Fourth, and large masses of gold and silver were being carried into the treasury. "The day has passed, you see," said the Pope, in a self-satisfied manner, "when the Church could say, 'Silver and gold have I none.'" "Yes," replied St. Thomas, "and with it has also passed the day when she could say to the paralytic, 'Rise up and walk.'" No, it is not endowment but fidelity which God regards—the establishment of a connection between the Church of any country and the State must never, in any sense, be regarded as an establishment of the "kingdom of God." (*W. S. Carter, M.A.*)   *God's threefold kingdom:*—What is this kingdom, the coming of which our Lord thus commands us to ask and wish for? The kingdom of God, so far as we have any concern with it in this prayer—so far as it is still to come, and must therefore be something different from that rule and dominion which He is always exercising over every part of His creation—is a threefold kingdom. I. There is His kingdom and authority over the souls of all true believers, which we call HIS SPIRITUAL KINGDOM. II. There is His kingdom upon earth, or His Church, which we call HIS VISIBLE KINGDOM, because it is visible to all men, and all may see it. III. There is HIS HEAVENLY KINGDOM, which is to come after the resurrection, and to last for ever. (*A. W. Hare.*)   *Thy kingdom come:*—I never felt the power of this petition more impressively than when once standing in the midst of a leafless wood. It was a clear day in early spring. Every cloud had been withdrawn from the canopy. The trees were perfectly naked, and their great branches were like arms outstretched in prayer. To me they seemed to be saying: "O spring, come and clothe us with thy beauty; summer, come and enrich us with thine abundance; we are patiently waiting for thee; through the long winter storm we have tarried for thee; thy kingdom come." I, too, a poor, leafless human tree, lifted up my entreaty, saying, with a full heart, "O fairer Spring, O richer Summer, O purer Light, come, clothe me, adorn me, make me beautiful; O, Saviour, Thy kingdom come." (*Dr. J. Parker.*)   *Thy kingdom come:*—1. Human life is one great WANT. 2. This want should turn human life into one noble ASPIRATION. 3. This aspiration can only be noble as it is lifted up towards A FATHER. 4. This Father must be asked to come in all the power and splendour of A KINGDOM. (*Ibid.*) *The kingdom of God:*—I. WHAT IS THIS KINGDOM? 1. The term in its primary signification no doubt suggests a material territory, with a personal sovereign, laws, offices, institutions. But without any effort we transfer this organization to that which is ideal, and use the term in a figurative sense. We are accustomed to speak of a kingdom as representing some particular section of created things; as, for example, the animal kingdom, the vegetable kingdom, the kingdom of letters. The principle of life, and not any particular mode or form of its development, must be the same in the several members of the kingdom. In like manner, the phrase "kingdom of God" is intended to comprise all who are spiritually related to God—all who are partakers of the Divine nature, and are subservient to the Divine rule and government. The complete development of that kingdom is, I take it, the meaning of the term here; and towards that our prayer is directed, though in reality the kingdom itself has already come. 2. This thought suggests another. We have spoken of a common life, a Divine life which constitutes citizenship in the kingdom of God, of laws by which this life is governed, of principles by which it is animated. Let us amplify this idea, so as to see what are the moral forces at work within the kingdom. "The kingdom of God is within you." It is not a thing to be seen; it is a power to be felt. This view of the kingdom is purely a personal one. Its principles must be apprehended, so that he who is enrolled as its subject may possess the moral qualities pertaining to it. "The kingdom of God is not meat and drink; but righteousness and peace, and joy in the Holy Ghost." II. WHOSE IS THIS KINGDOM? It is the kingdom of God. But not of God only as God. It is the kingdom of the Father. Whose Father? My Father? Our Father. III. TO WHOM IS THE GOVERNMENT OF THIS KINGDOM COMMITTED? To Him who by the mysterious incarnation was at once Son of God and Son of Man. Both natures are needed in His capacity of Prince and Ruler. As God, He rules with Divine attributes; as man, He knows and feels for the governed. Let us take care to be in readiness to recognize this kingdom when it comes. (*T. Lessey.*) *Thy kingdom come :*—A soul truly devoted to God joins heartily in this petition, " Thy kingdom come!" 1. In these words this great truth is implied—that God is a King. He who hath a kingdom can be no less than a king—" God is the King of all the earth." And He is a King upon His throne—" God sitteth upon the throne of holiness." He hath His kingly prerogatives ; He hath power to make laws, to seal pardons, which are the flowers and jewels belonging to His crown. Thus the Lord is King. 2. He is a great King, " a King above all gods." He is great in and of Himself; and not like other kings, who are made great by their subjects. 3. God is a glorious King—" Who is this King of glory? He hath internal glory—" The Lord reigneth, He is clothed with majesty." Other kings have royal and sumptuous apparel to make them appear glorious to the beholders, but all their magnificence is borrowed; but God is clothed with majesty, His own glorious essence is instead of royal robes, and " He hath girded Himself with strength." He sets up His throne where no other king doth; He rules the will and affections ; His power binds the conscience. 1. (1) If God be so great a King, and sits King for ever, then it is no disparagement for us to serve Him. " To be a servant of God is to reign as a prince"; it is an honour to serve a king. If the angels fly swiftly upon the King of heaven's message, then well we may look upon it as a favour to be taken into His royal service. Theodosius thought it a greater honour to be God's servant than to be an emperor. Therefore as the queen of Sheba, having seen the glory of Solomon's kingdom, said, " Happy are these thy servants which stand continually before thee," so, happy are those saints who stand before the King of heaven, and wait on His throne. (2) If God be such a glorious King, crowned with wisdom, armed with power, bespangled with riches, then it shows us what prudence it is to have this King to be ours; to say, " My King and my God!" It is counted great policy to be on the strongest side. (1) If God be so glorious a King, full of power and majesty, let us trust in Him. (2) If God be so great a King, let us fear Him— " Fear ye not Me? saith the Lord: will ye not tremble at My presence?" (3) If God be so glorious a King, He hath the power of life and death in His hand. (4) Is God so great a King, having all power in heaven and earth in His hand? Let us learn subjection to Him. Obey the King of glory. 3. Comfort to those who are the subjects of the King of heaven; God will put forth all the royal power for their succour and comfort. (1) The King of heaven will plead their cause. (2) He will protect His people ; He sets an invisible guard about them. (3) When it may be for the good of His people, He will raise up deliverance to them. 4. Terror to the enemies of the Church. What kingdom doth Christ mean here? Neg. 1. He doth not mean a political or earthly kingdom. 2. It is not meant of God's providential kingdom ; " His kingdom ruleth over all "; that is, the kingdom of His providence. This kingdom of God's providence we do not pray should come, for it is already come. What kingdom then is meant here when we say, " Thy kingdom come "? Positively. 1. The kingdom of grace, which kingdom God exercises in the consciences of His people—this is God's lesser kingdom. When we pray, " Thy kingdom come "—(1) Here is something tacitly implied, that we are in the kingdom of darkness. (*a*) We pray that we may be brought out of the kingdom of darkness. (*b*) That the devil's kingdom in the world may be demolished. (2) Something positively intended. (*a*) We pray that the kingdom of grace may be set up in our hearts and increased. (*b*) We pray that the kingdom of glory may hasten, and that we may in God's good time be translated into it. These two kingdoms of grace and glory differ not specifically, but gradually; they differ not in nature, but only in degree. The kingdom of grace is nothing but the inchoation or beginning of the kingdom of glory ; the kingdom of grace is glory in the seed, and the kingdom of glory is grace in the flower; the kingdom of grace is glory in the daybreak, and the kingdom of glory is grace in the full meridian ; the kingdom of grace is glory militant, and the kingdom of glory is grace triumphant. There is such an inseparable connection between these two kingdoms, grace and glory, that there is no passing into the one kingdom but by the other. At Athens there were two temples, a temple of virtue and a temple of honour, and there was no going into the temple of honour but through the temple of virtue ; so the kingdoms of grace and glory are so close joined together, that we cannot go into the kingdom of glory but through the kingdom of grace. Many people aspire after the kingdom of glory, but never look after grace ; but these two, which God hath joined together, may not be put asunder ; the kingdom of grace leads to the kingdom of glory. How many ways is a natural man in the kingdom of darkness ? 1. He is under the darkness of ignorance—"having the understanding darkened." 2. Let us pray that God will bring us out of this kingdom of darkness. God's kingdom of grace cannot come into our hearts till first we are brought out of the kingdom of darkness. Why should not we strive to get out of this kingdom of darkness ? Who would desire to stay in a dark dungeon ? Go to Christ to enlighten thee—"Christ shall give thee light " ; He will not only bring thy light to thee, but open thine eyes to see it. That is the first thing implied in "Thy kingdom come "; we pray that we may be brought out of the kingdom of darkness. II. The second thing implied in " Thy kingdom come," we do implicitly pray against the devil's kingdom, we pray that Satan's kingdom may be demolished in the world. Satan hath a kingdom ; he got his kingdom by conquest ; he conquered mankind in paradise. Satan's kingdom hath two qualifications or characters. 1. It is a kingdom of impiety. 2. It is a kingdom of slavery. Let us pray that Satan's kingdom, set up in the world, may be thrown down. When we pray, "Thy kingdom come," here is something positively intended. 1. We pray that the kingdom of grace may be set up in our hearts and increased. 2. That the kingdom of glory may hasten, and that we may, in God's due time, be translated into it. I begin with the first, the kingdom of grace. When we pray, " Thy kingdom come," we pray that the kingdom of grace may come into our hearts. 1. Why is grace called a kingdom ? Because, when grace comes, there is a kingly government set up in the soul. Grace rules the will and affections, and brings the whole man in subjection to Christ ; grace doth king it in the soul ; it sways the sceptre, it subdues mutinous lusts. 2. Why is there such need that we should pray that this kingdom of grace may come into our hearts ? (1) Because, till the kingdom of grace come, we have no right to the covenant of grace. The covenant of grace is to an ungracious person a sealed fountain ; it is kept as a paradise with a flaming sword, that the sinner may not touch it ; without grace you have no more right to it than a farmer to the city-charter. (2) Unless the kingdom of grace be set up in our hearts, our purest offerings are defiled ; they may be good as to the matter, but not as to the manner ; they want that which should meliorate and sweeten them. (3) We had need pray that the kingdom of grace may come, because till this kingdom come into our hearts we are loathsome in God's eyes— " My soul loathed them." I have read of a woman who always used flattering glasses ; by chance seeing her face in a true glass, she ran mad. Such as now dress themselves by the flattering glass of presumption, when once God gives them a sight of their filthiness they will abhor themselves—" Ye shall loathe yourselves in your own sight for all your evils." (4) Till the kingdom of grace comes, a man lies exposed to the wrath of God—" and who knoweth the power of His anger ? " (5) Till the kingdom of grace come man cannot die with comfort ; only he who takes Christ in the arms of his faith can look death in the face with joy. But it is sad to have the king of terrors in the body, and not the kingdom of grace in the soul. 3. How may we know that the kingdom of grace is set up in our hearts ? (1) Men think they have the kingdom of grace in their hearts because they have the means of grace ; they live where the silver trumpet of the gospel sounds ; they are lift up to heaven with ordinances—" I have a Levite to my priest," sure I shall go to heaven. (2) Men think they have the kingdom of grace set up in their hearts, because they have some common works of the Spirit. How may we know the kingdom of grace is set up in us ? In general, by having a metamorphosis or change wrought in the soul ; this is called " the new creature." When the kingdom of grace is set up, there is light in the mind, order in the affections, pliableness of the will, tenderness in the conscience ; such as can find no change of heart, they are the same as they were, as vain, as earthly, as unclean as ever ; there is no sign of God's kingdom of grace in them. We may know the kingdom of grace is come into our hearts by having the princely grace of faith. We may know the kingdom of grace is come into our hearts by having the noble grace of love ; faith and love are the two poles on which all religion turns—" The upright love thee. " We may know the kingdom of grace is come into our hearts by spiritualizing the duties of religion—" Ye are an holy priesthood to offer up spiritual sacrifices." We may know the kingdom of grace is come into us by antipathy and opposition against every known sin—" I hate every false way." We may know the kingdom of grace is come into us, when we have given up ourselves to God by obedience; as a servant gives up himself to his master, as a wife gives up herself to her husband, so we give up ourselves to God by obedience. I fear the kingdom of grace is not yet come into my heart. 1. I cannot discern grace. A child of God may have the kingdom of grace in his heart, yet not know it. The cup was in Benjamin's sack, though he did not know it was there; thou mayest have faith in thy heart, the cup may be in thy sack, though thou knowest it not. The seed may be in the ground, when we do not see it spring up. 2. Before the kingdom of grace come into the heart there must be some preparation for it; the fallow ground of the heart must be broken up; I fear the plough of the law hath not gone deep enough; I have not been humbled enough, therefore I have no grace. God doth not prescribe a just proportion of sorrow and humiliation; the Scripture mentions the truth of sorrow, but not the measure. 3. If the kingdom of God were within me it would be a kingdom of power; it would enable me to serve God with vigour of soul; but I have a spirit of infirmity upon me, I am weak and impotent, and untuned to every holy action. There is a great difference between the weakness of grace and the want of grace: a man may have life, though he be sick and weak. 4. I fear the kingdom of grace is not yet come, because I find the kingdom of sin so strong in me. Had I faith, it would purify my heart; but I find much pride, worldliness, passion. Those sins which you did once wear as a crown on your head are now as fetters on the leg; is not all this from the Spirit of grace in you? Sin is in you as poison in the body, which you are sick of, and use all Scripture antidotes to expel. 5. Where the kingdom of grace comes it softens the heart; but I find my heart frozen and congealed into hardness; I can hardly squeeze out one tear. Do flowers grow on a rock? Can there be any grace in such a rocky heart? There may be grief where there are no tears, the best sorrow is rational. Labour to find that this kingdom of grace is set up in your hearts; while others aspire after earthly kingdoms, labour to have the kingdom of God within you. The kingdom of grace must come into us before we can go into the kingdom of glory. 1. This kingdom of God within us is our spiritual beauty; the kingdom of grace adorns a person, and sets him off in the eyes of God and angels. 2. The kingdom of grace set up in the heart is our spiritual defence. 3. The kingdom of grace set up in the heart brings peace with it—" The kingdom of God is not meat and drink, but righteousness and peace." There is a secret peace breeds out of holiness. 4. The kingdom of grace enriches the soul; a kingdom hath its riches. 5. When the kingdom of grace comes, it doth fix and establish the heart—" O God, my heart is fixed! " Before the kingdom of grace comes the heart is very unfixed and unsettled, like a ship without ballast. 6. This kingdom of grace is distinguishing; it is a sure pledge of God's love. How should we do to obtain this kingdom? 1. In general, take pains for it; we cannot have the world without labour, and do we think we can have grace? " If thou seekest her as silver." 2. Such as have this kingdom of God set up in them, it calls for gratulation and thanksgiving. What will you be thankful for, if not for a kingdom? If God hath crowned you with the kingdom of grace, do you crown Him with your praises. The second thing intended by our Saviour in this petition is, that the kingdom of grace may increase, that it may come more into us. And this may answer a question. Why do we pray, " Thy kingdom come," when the kingdom of grace is already come into the soul? Till we come to live among the angels we shall need to pray this prayer, " Thy kingdom come." Lord, let Thy kingdom of grace come in more power into my soul; let grace be more augmented and increased. When doth the kingdom of grace increase in the soul? When is it a flourishing kingdom? 1. When a Christian hath further degrees added to his graces; there is more oil in the lamp, his knowledge is clearer, his love is more inflamed; grace is capable of degrees, and may rise higher as the sun in the horizon. 2. Then the kingdom of grace increaseth when a Christian hath gotten more strength than he had. That grace which will carry us through prosperity will not carry us through sufferings; the ship needs stronger tackling to carry it through a storm than a calm. 3. Then the kingdom of grace increaseth when a Christian hath most conflict with spiritual corruptions. 4. Then the kingdom of grace flourisheth when a Christian hath learned to live by faith—" I live by the faith of the Son of God." 5. When a Christian is arrived at holy zeal. 6. Then the kingdom of grace increaseth when a Christian is as well diligent in his particular calling as devout in his general. 7.

Then the kingdom of grace increaseth when a Christian is established in the belief and love of the truth. 8. Then the kingdom of grace increaseth in a man's own heart when he labours to be instrumental to set up this kingdom in others. Wherein appears the needfulness of this, that the kingdom of grace should be increased. 1. This is God's design in keeping up a standing ministry in the Church, to increase the kingdom of grace in men's hearts. 2. We had need have the kingdom of grace increase, in respect we have a great deal of work to do, and a little grace will hardly carry us through. 3. If the kingdom of grace doth not increase, it will decay— "Thou hast left thy first love." If grace be not improved, it will soon be impaired. 4. To have grace increasing is suitable to Christianity. The saints are not only jewels for sparkling lustre, but trees for growth. They are called the lights of the world. Light is still increasing: first there is the daybreak, and so it shines brighter to the meridian. 5. As the kingdom of grace increaseth, so a Christian's comforts increase. How may they be comforted, who bewail their want of growth, and weep that they cannot find the kingdom of grace increase? 1. To see and bewail our decay in grace argues not only the life of grace, but growth. 2. If a Christian doth not increase in one grace, he may in another; if not in knowledge, he may in humility. If a tree doth not grow so much in the branches, it may in the root; to grow downwards in the root is a good growth. 3. A Christian may grow less in affection when he grows more in judgment. As a musician when he is old, his fingers are stiff and not so nimble at the lute as they were, but he plays with more art and judgment than before; so a Christian may not have so much affection in duty as at the first conversion, but he is more solid in religion, and more settled in his judgment than he was before. 4. A Christian may think he doth not increase in grace because he doth not increase in gifts; whereas there may be a decay of natural parts, the memory and other faculties, when there is not a decay of grace. Parts may be impaired, when grace is improved. 5. A Christian may increase in grace, yet not be sensible of it. I come to the second thing intended in this petition, "That the kingdom of glory may hasten, and that we may in due time be translated into it." When we pray, "Thy kingdom come," here is something positively intended. We pray, 1st, that the kingdom of grace may be set in our hearts; 2nd, that it may increase and flourish; 3rd, that the kingdom of glory may hasten, and that God would in His due time translate us into it. 1. What this kingdom of glory is. 2. What are the properties of it. 3. Wherein it exceeds all other kingdoms. 4. When this kingdom comes. 5. Wherein appears the certainty of it. 6. Why we should pray for its coming. First. What this kingdom of glory is. By this kingdom is meant that glorious estate which the saints shall enjoy when they shall reign with God and angels for ever. If a man stand upon the sea-shore he cannot see all the dimensions of the sea, the length, breadth, and depth of it, yet he may see it is of a vast extension; so, though the kingdom of heaven be of that incomparable excellency that neither tongue of man or angels can express, yet we may conceive of it to be an exceeding glorious thing, such as the eye hath not seen. 1st. What the kingdom of heaven implies. I. It implies a freedom from all evil. 1. A freedom from the necessities of nature. What need will there be of food when our bodies shall be made spiritual? Though not spiritual for substance, yet for qualities. What need will there be of clothing when our bodies shall be like Christ's glorious body? What need will there be of armour when there is no enemy? What need will there be of sleep when there is no night? 2. In the kingdom of heaven we shall be freed from the imperfections of nature. Since the fall our knowledge hath suffered an eclipse. (1) Our natural knowledge is imperfect, it is chequered with ignorance. Our ignorance is more than our knowledge. (2) Our Divine knowledge is imperfect—"We know but in part," saith Paul. 3. In the kingdom of heaven we shall be freed from the toilsome labours of this life. God enacted a law in paradise, "in the sweat of thy face shalt thou eat bread." Where should there be rest but in the heavenly centre? Not that this sweet rest in the kingdom of heaven excludes all motion, for spirits cannot be idle; but the saints glorified shall rest from all wearisome employment; it shall be a labour full of ease, a motion full of delight; the saints in heaven shall love God, and what labour is that? Is it any labour to love beauty? They shall praise God, and that sure is delightful; when the bird sings, it is not so much a labour as a pleasure. 4. In the kingdom of heaven we shall be freed from original corruption: this is the root of all actual sin. There would be no actual sin if there were no original; there would be no water in the stream if there were none in the fountain. What a blessed time will that be, never to grieve God's Spirit more! 5.

In the kingdom of heaven we shall be freed from all sorrows—"There shall be no more sorrow." Our life here is interlarded with trouble. Either losses grieve, or lawsuits vex, or unkindness breaks the heart. We may as well separate moisture from air, or weight from lead, as troubles from man's life. 6. We shall, in the kingdom of heaven, be freed from the immodesty of temptation. 7. In the kingdom of heaven we shall be freed from all vexing cares. 8. We shall, in the kingdom of heaven, be freed from all doubts and scruples. In this life the best saint hath his doubtings, as the brightest star hath his twinkling. 9. We shall, in the kingdom of heaven, be freed from all society with the wicked. 10. We shall, in the kingdom of heaven, be freed from all signs of God's displeasure. 11. We shall, in the kingdom of heaven, be freed from all divisions. 12. We shall, in the kingdom of heaven, be freed from vanity and dissatisfaction. II. In the kingdom of heaven there is a glorious fruition of all good. Concerning the fruitions and privileges of this heavenly kingdom—1. We shall have an immediate communion with God Himself, who is the inexhausted sea of all happiness; this divines call "the beatific vision." God hath all excellencies concentred in Him. If one flower should have the sweetness of all flowers, how sweet would that flower be! All the beauty and sweetness which lie scattered in the creature are infinitely to be found in God; therefore to see and enjoy Him will ravish the soul with delight. We shall so see God as to love Him, and be made sensible of His love. 2. We shall, in the kingdom of heaven, with these eyes see the glorified body of Jesus Christ. If the glory of His transfiguration was so great, what will the glory of His exaltation be? 3. We shall, in the kingdom of heaven, enjoy the society of "an innumerable company of angels." 4. We shall, in the kingdom of heaven, have sweet society with glorified saints; then the communion of saints will be illustrious. 5. In the kingdom of heaven there shall be incomprehensible joy. 6. In heaven there is honour and dignity put upon the saints. A kingdom imports honour. When all the titles and ensigns of worldly honour shall lie in the dust—the mace, the silver star, the garter—then shall the saints' honour remain. 7. We shall, in the kingdom of heaven, have a blessed rest. This rest is when the saints shall lie on Christ's bosom, that hive of sweetness, that bed of perfume. 8. The saints shall, in the kingdom of heaven, have their bodies richly bespangled with glory; they shall be full of clarity and brightness, as Moses' face shined that Israel were not able to behold the glory. The bodies of saints glorified shall need no jewels when they shall shine like Christ's body. 9. In the heavenly kingdom is eternity; it is an eternal fruition; they shall never be put out of the throne, "they shall reign for ever and ever." It is called "the everlasting kingdom," and "an eternal weight of glory." The flowers of paradise, of which the saints' garland is made, never wither. Well may we pray, "Thy kingdom come." What are the properties or qualifications of the kingdom of heaven? 1. The glory of this kingdom is solid and substantial; the Hebrew word for glory signifies a weight, to show how solid and weighty the glory of the celestial kingdom is. The glory of the worldly kingdom is airy and imaginary, like a blazing comet, or fancy. 2. The glory of this kingdom is satisfying—"With Thee is the fountain of life." How can they choose but be full who are at the fountain-head? "When I awake, I shall be satisfied with Thy likeness." The soul is never satisfied till it hath God for its portion and heaven for its haven. 3. The glory of heaven's kingdom is pure and unmixed; the streams of paradise are not muddied. There is ease without pain, honour without disgrace, life without death. 4. The glory of this kingdom is constantly exhilarating and refreshing; there is fulness, but no surfeit. Worldly comforts, though sweet, yet in time grow stale; a down-bed pleaseth a while, but within a while we are weary, and would rise. 5. The glory of this kingdom is distributed to every individual saint. In an earthly kingdom the crown goes but to one, a crown will fit but one head; but in the kingdom above the crown goes to all, all the elect are kings. God hath land enough to give to all His heirs. 6. Lucid and transparent. This kingdom of heaven is adorned and bespangled with light. 7. The glory of this kingdom is adequate and proportionable to the desire of the soul. The excellency of a feast is when the meat is suited to the palate; this is one ingredient in the glory of heaven—it exactly suits the desires of the glorified saints. 8. The glory of this kingdom will be seasonable. The seasonableness of a mercy adds to its beauty and sweetness; it is like apples of gold to pictures of silver. After a hard winter in this cold climate will it not be seasonable to have the spring-flowers of glory appear, and the singing of the birds of paradise come? Wherein the kingdom of heaven infinitely excels all the kingdoms of the earth. 1. It excels in the architect; other kingdoms have men to raise their structures, but God Himself laid the first stone in this kingdom. This kingdom is of the greatest antiquity; God was the first King and Founder of it; no angel was worthy to lay a stone in this building. 2. This heavenly kingdom excels in altitude; it is higher situated than any kingdom, the higher anything is the more excellent; the fire being the most sublime element is most noble. The kingdom of heaven is seated above all the visible orbs. If wicked men could build their nests among the stars, yet the least believer would shortly be above them. 3. The kingdom of heaven excels all others in splendour and riches; it is described by precious stones. Those who are poor in the world, yet, as soon as they come into this kingdom, grow rich, as rich as the angels; other kingdoms are enriched with gold, this is enriched with the Deity. 4. The kingdom of heaven excels all other kingdoms in holiness. Kingdoms on earth are for the most part unholy; there is a common sewer of luxury and uncleanness running in them. Holiness is the brightest jewel of the crown of heaven. 5. The kingdom of heaven excels all other kingdoms in its pacific nature; it is a kingdom of peace. Peace is the glory of a kingdom. A king's crown is more adorned with the white lily of peace than when it is beset with the red roses of a bloody war. There is no beating of drums or roaring of cannons; but the voice of harpers harping, in token of peace. 6. The kingdom of heaven excels in magnitude; it is of vast dimensions. As every star hath a large orb to move in, so it shall be with the saints when they shall shine as stars in the kingdom of heaven. 7. The kingdom of heaven excels in unity; all the inhabitants agree together in love; love will be the perfume and music of heaven; as love to God will be intense, so to the saints. Perfect love, as it casts out fear, so it casts out envy and discord. There Luther and Zuinglius are agreed; Satan cannot put in his cloven foot there to make divisions; there shall be perfect harmony and concord, and not one jarring string in the saints' music. It were worth dying to be in that kingdom. 8. This kingdom exceeds all earthly kingdoms in joy and pleasure; therefore it is called paradise. 9. This kingdom of heaven excels all earthly kingdoms in self-perfection. Other kingdoms are defective; they have not all provisions within themselves, but are fain to traffic abroad to supply their wants at home; King Solomon did send to Ophir for gold; but there is no defect in the kingdom of heaven; it hath all commodities of its own growth. 10. This kingdom of heaven excels all others in honour and nobility. 11. This kingdom of heaven excels all others in healthfulness. In the heavenly climate are no ill vapours to breed diseases, but a sweet aromatical smell coming from Christ; all His garments smell of myrrh, aloes, and cassia. 12. This kingdom of heaven excels in duration; it abides for ever. It is founded upon a strong basis, God's omnipotency; this kingdom the saints shall never be turned out of, or be deposed from their throne, as some kings have been, namely, Henry VI., &c., but shall reign for ever and ever. When shall this kingdom be bestowed? This glory in the kingdom of heaven shall be begun at death, but not perfected till the resurrection. Wherein appears the certainty and infallibility of this kingdom of glory? That this blessed kingdom shall be bestowed on the saints is beyond all dispute. 1. God hath promised it—"It is your Father's good pleasure to give you the kingdom"; "I appoint unto you a kingdom." The whole earth hangs upon the word of God's power; and cannot our faith hang upon the word of His promise? 2. There is a price laid down for this kingdom. Heaven is not only a kingdom which God hath promised, but which Christ hath purchased; it is called a "purchased possession." 3. Christ prays that the saints may have this kingdom settled upon them: "Father, I will that they also whom Thou hast given Me, be with Me where I am," that is, in heaven. 4. The saints must have this blessed kingdom by virtue of Christ's ascension: "I ascend unto My Father and your Father, to My God and your God." Where lies the comfort of this? Here it lies—Jesus Christ ascended to take possession of heaven for all believers. As a husband takes up land in another country in the behalf of his wife, so Christ went to take possession of heaven in the behalf of all believers—"I go to prepare a place for you." 5. The elect must have this blessed kingdom, in regard of the previous work of the Spirit in their hearts. 6. The elect must have this blessed kingdom by virtue of their coalition and union with Jesus Christ. They are members of Christ; therefore they must be where their Head is. Why should we so earnestly pray for this heavenly kingdom, "Thy kingdom come"? 1. Because it is a kingdom worth the praying for. 2. We must pray for this kingdom of glory, because God will not bestow this kingdom on any without prayer—"They seek for glory and immortality"; and how do we seek but by prayer? 3. We must pray that the kingdom of glory may come, that by going into it we may make an end of sinning. I think sometimes what a blessed time it will be never to have a sinful thought more! We must not pray, "Thy kingdom come," out of discontent, because we would be rid of the troubles and crosses of this life. 4. Because that all Christ's enemies shall be put under his feet. 5. We must pray earnestly that the kingdom of glory may come, that we may see God "face to face," and have an uninterrupted and eternal communion with Him in the empyrean heaven. 1. From all this you see then that there is nothing within the whole sphere of religion imposed upon unreasonable terms. When God bids us serve Him, it is no unreasonable request; He will out of free grace enthrone us in a kingdom. When we hear of repentance, steeping our souls in brinish tears for sin, or of mortification, beheading our king-sin, we are ready to grumble, and think this is hard and unreasonable—"But do we serve God for nought?" Is it not infinite bounty to reward us with a kingdom? This kingdom is as far above our thoughts as it is beyond our deserts. Our service cannot be so hard as a kingdom is sweet. 2. See hence the royal bounty of God to His children, that He hath prepared a kingdom for them, a kingdom bespangled with glory; it is infinitely above the model we can draw of it in our thoughts. 3. See hence that religion is no ignominious, disgraceful thing. Would a prince regard the slightings of a few frantics when he is going to be crowned? You who are beginners, bind their reproaches as a crown about your head, despise their censures as much as their praise; a kingdom is a-coming. 4. See what contrary ways the godly and the wicked go at death; the godly go to a kingdom, the wicked to a prison; the devil is the jailor, and they are bound with the "chains of darkness." 5. See then that which may make us in love with holy duties; every duty spiritually performed brings us a step nearer to the kingdom. As every flower hath its sweetness, so would every duty, if we would look upon it as giving us a lift nearer heaven. 6. It shows us what little cause the children of God have to envy the prosperity of the wicked. 7. Is there a kingdom of glory a-coming? then see how happy all the saints are at death; they go to a kingdom; they shall see God's face, which shines ten thousand times brighter than the sun in its meridian glory. The godly at death shall be installed into their honour, and have the crown royal set upon their head. In the kingdom of heaven the saints are crowned with all those perfections which the human nature is capable of. In the kingdom of heaven there is glory in its highest elevation; in that kingdom is knowledge without ignorance, holiness without sin, beauty without blemish, strength without weakness, light without darkness, riches without poverty, ease without pain, liberty without restraint, rest without labour, joy without sorrow, love without hatred, plenty without surfeit, honour without disgrace, health without sickness, peace without war, contentation without cessation. O the happiness of those who die in the Lord! they go into this blessed kingdom. And if they are so happy when they die, then let me make two inferences. (1) What little cause have the saints to fear death! Are any afraid of going to a kingdom? (2) If the godly are so happy when they die, they go to a kingdom; then what little cause have we to mourn immoderately for the death of godly friends. Shall we mourn for their preferment? 8. See the wisdom of the godly; they have the serpent's eye in the dove's head; wise virgins. Moses chose "rather to suffer affliction with the people of God." It was a wise, rational choice; he knew if he suffered he should reign. At the day of judgment those whom the world accounted foolish will appear to be wise; they made a prudent choice, they chose holiness; and what is happiness but the quintessence of holiness? 9. See the folly of those who, for vain pleasures and profits, will lose such a glorious kingdom. Lysimachus, for a draught of water, lost his empire; so for a draught of sinful pleasure these will lose heaven. We, too, much resemble our grandfather Adam, who for an apple lost paradise; many for trifles, to get a shilling more in the shop or bushel, will venture the loss of heaven. If Satan could make good his brag, in giving all the glory and kingdoms of the world, it could not countervail the loss of the celestial kingdom. Of reproof. 1. It reproves such as do not at all look after this kingdom of glory; as if all we say about heaven were but a romance, they do not mind it. That they mind it not, appears because they do not labour to have the kingdom of grace set up in their hearts. If they have some thoughts of this kingdom, yet it is in a dull, careless manner. Luther spent three hours a day in prayer. "Anna, the prophetess, departed not from the temple, but served God with fasting and prayers night and day." How zealous and industrious were the martyrs to get into this heavenly kingdom! They wore their fetters as ornaments, snatched up torments as crowns, and embraced the flames as cheerfully as Elijah did the fiery chariot which came to fetch him to heaven; and do we not think this kingdom worth our labour? 2. It reproves such as were once great zealots in religion, and did seem to be touched with a coal from God's altar, but since have cooled in their devotion, and have left off the pursuing the celestial kingdom. Whence is this? 1. For want of a supernatural principle of grace. That branch must needs die which hath no root to grow upon. 2. From unbelief—"An evil heart of unbelief, departing from the living God." 3. Men leave off pursuing the heavenly kingdom; it is from some secret lust nourished in the soul, perhaps a wanton or a covetous lust. Demas for love of the world forsook his religion. 4. Men leave off pursuing the kingdom of heaven out of timorousness; if they persist in religion they may lose their places of profit, perhaps their lives. How shall we know this kingdom is prepared for us? If we are prepared for the kingdom. How may that be known? Would we go to the kingdom of heaven? are we heavenly? 1. Are we heavenly in our contemplations? Do our thoughts run upon this kingdom? 2. Are we heavenly in our affections? Do we set our affections on the kingdom of heaven? This is the temper of a true saint; his affections are set on the kingdom of God, his anchor is cast in heaven, and he is carried thither with the sails of desire. 3. Are we heavenly in our speeches? Christ after His resurrection did speak of the things pertaining to the kingdom of God. Are your tongues tuned to the language of the heavenly Canaan? 4. Are we heavenly in our trading? Is our traffic and merchandise in heaven? Do we trade in the heavenly kingdom by faith? A man may live in one place and trade in another; he may live in Ireland, and trade in the West Indies; so, do we trade in the heavenly kingdom? They shall never go to heaven when they die who do not trade in heaven while they live. 5. Are our lives heavenly? Of exhortation to all in general. 1. If there be such a glorious kingdom to come, believe this great truth. 2. If there be such a blessed kingdom of glory to come, let us take heed lest we miss of this kingdom, let us fear lest we lose heaven by short shooting. Trembling in the body is a malady; in the soul a grace. How many steps may a man take in the way to the kingdom of God, yet miss of it! 1. He may be adorned with civility, he may be morally righteous, he may be prudent, just, temperate, he may be free from penal statutes; this is good, but not enough to bring a man to heaven. 2. He may hang out the flag of a glorious profession, yet fall short of the kingdom. 3. A man may be a frequenter of ordinances, and yet miss of the kingdom. 4. A man may have some trouble for sin, and weep for it, yet miss of the heavenly kingdom. 5. A man may have good desires, yet miss of the kingdom—"Let me die the death of the righteous!" 6. A man may forsake his sins, oaths, drunkenness, uncleanness, yet come short of the kingdom. Secondly, this fear is necessary, if we consider what a loss it is to lose the heavenly kingdom. 1. The eyes of the wicked shall be opened to see their loss; now they care not for the loss of God's favour, because they know not the worth of it. 2. A second aggravation of the loss of this kingdom will be, that sinners shall be upbraided by their own conscience. 3. A third aggravation of the loss of heaven will be to look upon others that have gained the kingdom. 4. A fourth aggravation is, this loss of the kingdom of heaven is accompanied with the punishment of sense. 5. A fifth aggravation of the loss of this kingdom will be to consider on what easy and reasonable terms men might have had this kingdom. 6. Aggravation of the loss of this kingdom, it will be an eternal, irreparable loss; heaven, once lost, can never be recovered. What shall we do that we may not miss of this kingdom of glory? 1st. Take heed of those things which will make you miss of heaven. 1. Take heed of spiritual sloth. 2. Take heed of unbelief. Unbelief kept Israel out of Canaan; so we see "they could not enter in because of unbelief." 3. If you would not miss of the heavenly kingdom, take heed of mistake, imagining the way to the kingdom of heaven to be easier than it is; it is but a sigh, or, "Lord have mercy!" 4. If you would not miss of the heavenly kingdom, take heed of delays and procrastinations. 5. If you would not come short of the kingdom of heaven, take heed of prejudice. Many take a prejudice at religion, and on this rock dash their souls. 6. If you would not miss of the kingdom of heaven, take heed of presumption. 7. If you would not miss of the heavenly kingdom, take heed of the delights and pleasures of the flesh. 8. If you would not fall short of the kingdom of heaven, take heed of worldly-mindedness; a covetous spirit is a dunghill spirit, it chokes good affections, as the earth puts out the fire. 9. If you would not come short of the kingdom of heaven, take heed of indulging any sin. 10. If you would not fall short of the kingdom of heaven, take heed of inordinate passion; many a ship hath been lost in a storm, and many a soul hath been lost in a storm of unruly passions. 11. If you would not fall short of the kingdom of heaven, take heed of injustice in your dealings; defrauding lies in two things. Mixing commodities—as if one mix bad wheat with good, and sell it for pure wheat, this is to defraud. 12. If you would not miss of the kingdom of heaven, take heed of evil company. 13. If you would not fall short of the kingdom of heaven, take heed of falling off; beware of apostasy; he misseth of the prize who doth not hold out in the race; he who makes shipwreck of the faith cannot came to the haven of glory. 2nd. The second means for the obtaining of the kingdom is serious consideration; most men fall short of heaven for want of consideration. 3rd. The third means for obtaining this kingdom is to keep up daily prayer. 4th. If you would obtain the heavenly kingdom get a love to heaven. Love puts a man upon the use of all means to enjoy the thing loved. 5th. If you would obtain the kingdom of heaven, make religion your business. 6th. If you would obtain the kingdom of heaven, bind your hearts to God by sacred vows. 7th. If you would obtain the kingdom, embrace all seasons and opportunities for your souls—"Redeeming the time." 8th. We obtain the kingdom of heaven by uniform and cheerful obedience. Obedience is the road through which we travel to heaven. 9th. If we would obtain this kingdom, be much in the communion of saints; one coal of juniper will warm and inflame another. 10th. If we would attain to this kingdom of heaven, let us be willing to come up to Christ's terms. Many will be cheapening, and bid something for the kingdom of heaven; they will avoid gross sin, and will come to church, and say their prayers; and yet all this while they are not willing to come up to God's price. How doth a Christian hold on till he comes to the kingdom? How doth he persevere? 1. By the aid of the Spirit. God carries on a Christian to perseverance by the energy and vigorous working of His Spirit. 2. Christ causeth perseverance and carries on a saint till he come to the heavenly kingdom by His intercession. The kingdom of heaven cannot be obtained without labour. A boat may as well get to land without oars, as we to heaven without labour. We cannot have the world without labour, and do we think to have heaven? What striving is there for earthly kingdoms, which are corruptible, and subject to change? With what vigour and alacrity did Hannibal's soldiers continue their march over the Alps and craggy rocks, and Cæsar's soldiers fight with hunger and cold! Men will break through laws and oaths, they will swim to the crown in blood; will they venture thus for earthly promotions, and shall not we strive more for an earthly kingdom? This is "a kingdom which cannot be moved," a kingdom where there is unparalleled beauty, unstained honour, unmixed joy; a kingdom where there shall be nothing present which we could wish were removed, nor nothing absent which we could wish were enjoyed. (*T. Watson.*) *Thy kingdom come:*—First: there is His natural kingdom, or His kingdom over the material creation. Secondly: there is God's supernatural kingdom, or His kingdom over the moral creation. For, let it be noted, our Father's kingdom, like all things of life, is a growth. And first, the kingdom of God, viewed as an inception, has its beginning with and in Jesus Christ. Not that the kingdom of God, as a spiritual sway, had not existed before the Incarnation. Prophets and patriarchs were members of it; but they were members of it anticipatively. The kingdom of God, then, surveyed as a beginning, had its root in Jesus Christ: and so it is called His kingdom, the kingdom of the Son, the kingdom of our Lord and Saviour Jesus Christ. And thus surveyed, the kingdom of God has already come. In those days came John the Baptist, preaching in the wilderness of Judea, and saying: Repent ye: for the kingdom of heaven is at hand. From that time, Jesus Himself began to preach and to say: "The time is fulfilled, and the kingdom of God is at hand: repent ye, and believe in the gospel." Again: the kingdom of God, viewed as a growth, has its unfolding in the Holy Ghost. For, being a spiritual kingdom— the building up of a spiritual character—it needs a spiritual architect, a spiritual workman, a spiritual ædile. God's kingdom is not food and drink, a matter of ceremonial distinction between clean and unclean; it is righteousness and peace and joy in the Holy Ghost. As such, the kingdom of God, since the Son departed and the Spirit came, has ever been and still is coming. The conversion of each separate sinner through all these centuries has been the setting up of a new and distinct duchy or principality in the empire of the Father. Once more: the kingdom of God, viewed as a consummation, has its end and completion in the Father. The kingdom for whose coming we are here taught to pray is, as we have seen, the kingdom of the consummation, when God shall be all in all. But as the coming of what is ultimate involves the coming of what is intermediate, and as the Christ must continue reigning till He hath made all His enemies His footstool, the prayer for the coming of our Father's kingdom involves prayer for the coming of His Son's. But it is not enough that we simply pray, "Thy kingdom come!" We must also work in the line of our prayer. (*G. D. Boardman, D.D.*) *Thy kingdom come :*—He who is "our Father" is also a King. This is a prayer which even children may offer. This is a matter with which even children have to do. In the war that not long since was raging on the continent of Europe, the interest and the work were not confined to those who were grown up. Not only in the universities and among the students, but in the schools, and among the young people generally, there was not only enthusiasm, but effort. They all felt that they could do, and should be doing, something. The war-spirit seemed to have made its way into the very infant schools. The very infants were quite becoming little soldiers. "What could such children know about these things?" you ask. Perhaps the best answer I can give, is to read to you an extract which I cut out of a newspaper at the time: "The energy, concord, and practical good sense shown by the Genoese ladies, in their labour of charity and patriotism, were marvellous. The first instalment of supplies for the wounded had been despatched on the 20th ult., under the superintendence of surgeons and their dressers. The chests contained bandages, compressers, lint, and shirts. They were forwarded to the central depot at Milan, and not a day too soon. Every class has vied in these offerings. Even the children of the infant schools had given up their money allowance for fruit, and for some weeks had eaten dry bread at their noonday meal, and, with the money thus saved, had bought materials for their contributions." Shall the names of Italy's king and captains be household words among the people? Shall the children of Italy be familiar with the names of Garibaldi, and Victor Immanuel, and La Marmora, and Cialdini, and rise into enthusiasm at the very mention of them? Shall they be interested in the movements of their armies, and talk among themselves of winning Venetia and Rome to the Italian crown, and shall *our* boys and girls take no interest in the coming of that kingdom of righteousness and peace, of which our text speaks? We do not want fighting of that kind, we want praying. Jesus said, "My kingdom is not of this world." I. THE PRAYER: "Thy kingdom come!" What is implied in it? 1. The destroying of the kingdom of Satan. Satan, too, is a king—a mighty king—the head of a kingdom, with wide-spread dominion, and many subjects. I have spoken of Italy. Not long since, that country was divided into a number of petty kingdoms and states. In some of these the people were groaning under the yoke of their oppressors. Their prisons were loathsome and filthy dungeons, filled with miserable prisoners, who were there for what, in this country, would not have been accounted crime at all. For having a Bible or tract in their possession, for getting it out of its hiding-place at dead of night, and gathering a few neighbours together to hear it read, for telling about Jesus and the way of salvation, they were imprisoned and banished. Don't you think, when they heard the tidings of Garibaldi's wonderful exploits, and of what he and his band of brave red jackets were bent upon doing for the whole country, as they listened to the distant bugle sound, and then to the crack of musketry closer at hand, as they heard it coming nearer and nearer—oh, don't you think *they* would devoutly pray, "Thy kingdom come," as they thought of the approach of one who would give them civil and religious liberty, who would break off the fetters from the prisoner and open the prison doors, and bring the reign of terror to an end? During the Indian Mutiny, when our countrymen were hemmed in on all sides by bloodthirsty rebels, who had been guilty of the most dreadful atrocities, and were waiting, like beasts of prey, ready to rush in whenever an opening was made, and subject their victims to what was worse than death—how they longed for the coming of the British soldiers, to break the power of the enemy, and bring to a speedy close his brief but dreadful supremacy! Had the mutineers got their will, we can hardly think what might have been—how women and little children would have been mercilessly tortured and slain, and brave men would have died a lingering and shameful death. Oh, how their hearts yearned for the quiet and safety of their far-off home; and as they went back, in thought, to the land of their birth, how earnestly they sighed, "Thy kingdom come!" And when at last there was the sound of distant bagpipes, telling that Sir Colin Campbell and his brave Highlanders were coming to the rescue, and their colours at length appeared flying in the wind, and the boom of cannon fell upon the ear, who shall ever tell how welcome it was, and how they wept for joy, as the restoration of British rule saved them from the hands of cruel foes? This petition asks the destroying of Satan's power (1) in ourselves. We have more to do with this than many of us fancy. (2) It asks the destroying of Satan's power in others. Drunkenness, profanity, carelessness, and crime, at home. It bears upon all these. (3) Slavery and oppression. This evil is not now what it was once. But in many parts of the world it still exists. (4) War. Is it not strange that men should take such delight in murdering each other? (5) Error and superstition. I have chiefly in view here, the gigantic systems of Popery and Mahometanism, which have cast their dark shadow over many beautiful lands—in Europe, Asia, South America, and other parts of the world. (6) Judaism —the religion of the Jew. There are thousands upon thousands of Jews, scattered all over the world, whose bitter hatred to the Lord Jesus is something wonderful, shared in, as it is, by the very children. (7) Heathenism. (8) Division among the professed friends of Christ. "By this," said Jesus, "shall all men know that ye are My disciples, if ye love one another." Now I have come to you to-day as a sort of recruiting-sergeant. Don't be alarmed. I have no wish to entrap you, and though I would fain have you to enlist under the banner of my King, I cannot, though I would, slip *His* shilling into your hand, and fasten the badge of the recruit to your bonnet, so that you should wake up as out of a sleep, and all of a sudden find yourselves soldiers. I only wish I had the power and the happiness to enlist you all. When settlers take possession of a new country, there are two things to be done. They must first clear the ground of what is on it, felling the great trees, as in the backwoods of America, or removing the brushwood and weeds that have got possession of the soil. But that is not enough. Stopping there, things would soon be again where they were. The old things have passed away, but the new things have not yet come in. They must cultivate the ground, sowing and planting, and prevent the springing up again of what is evil or useless by growing what is useful and good. When the ground is merely cleared, the work is but half done. If you were getting a property into your hands, with a house on it that was ugly to look at, and dangerous to live in, a ruin, it would not be enough that you took down the old house, and cleared away the rubbish. That would be necessary, indeed, but it would merely be a step in the right direction—a means towards an end. The old house once away, a new one would have to be set up in its place. You would have forthwith to begin to build, strongly and beautifully, and the perfection of the thing would be, to have, instead of the ruin, not a mere vacant site, but a comfortable and elegant dwelling. Now all this is just what must be in the other case. Satan's kingdom may be so far destroyed, but if the kingdom of God is not set up in its stead, Satan will come back again, and get firmer possession than ever. Just such a picture we have in Matthew (xii. 43–45), drawn by the hand of Jesus Himself. Let us see, then, what is meant by the advancing of the kingdom of grace. (1) The coming of Christ as King into our own hearts. Naturally we have rebel hearts, acknowledging Satan the usurper as king. Why not lay aside the prayer, as not needing it any longer? Because we need it still. Is not Ireland a part of Great Britain? Does it not belong to the British crown? Is not Victoria queen *there* as well as *here?* You say, "Yes; of course." Then why is regiment after regiment being sent across the Channel—cavalry, and infantry, and artillery, scattered all over the land? Because there are rebels in the country, who need to be overawed, conquered, and, if it may be, changed into loyal subjects. Now, Ireland at present, loyal as a whole, but with Fenians here and there, in town and country, not coming out openly and giving battle, but meeting in secret, having their drill at night, working in the dark, and every now and then being discovered and apprehended, is just like a Christian child or man. He is a subject of Christ, right at bottom, sound-hearted, loyal. But there are still traitors within—rebels—the remains of the old nature— evil tempers, evil habits, evil dispositions, evil tendencies, not indeed what once they were—unchecked, unresisted—but not rooted out, not dead yet. And so there is a constant fight kept up; and when you think they are fairly conquered, and you have seen the last of them, up they start, all of a sudden, and show their heads again—so that at times it is almost like a struggle for life. (2) The coming of Christ as King into the hearts of others. I can fancy one of you, with all the rest of your family, spending an hour on the ice, at some neigh- bouring loch. When you are in the middle of the loch, suddenly there is a creak, and in half a minute you are all in the water, struggling for life. The alarm is given. Ropes, and poles, and boats, and life-preservers, are all in requisition; but the ice is rotten, and, once it is broken, no one can get near. At length, with grea' difficulty, you are rescued, and words cannot tell how glad and thankful you are. But why don't you hurry home, and get off your wet clothes, and beside a blazing fire, or in a comfortable bed, get all right again? Why do you linger on the bank, the water dripping off you, half dead with cold? why look so wistfully, and seem as if you would rush back again—ay, *would*, if they did not prevent you by force? I think I hear you saying, "Don't you see my father, my mother, my sister, seizing the slippery surface only to lose hold of it again, or able only to stretch out the hands, or, benumbed and exhausted, giving in and going down?" I think I hear your piercing cry, "O my father, my father!—save him! What would my own life be to me without him? God save my beloved father!" Anything else than that, you would think strange indeed. The truth is, you cannot be rightly saved yourself, without having the desire, and sending up the prayer, and making the effort, that those you love may be saved as well. If you have no care about *their* salvation, you have reason to be in doubt about your own. In like manner, when you get anything good, if you are at all right-hearted, you have a desire that others should share it with you. If you are looking at a beautiful picture, the wish at once starts up that some friend were there to see it; and if you found him standing beside you, it would double your own enjoyment. If I were to find you ill-protected from the cold, on one of these winter days, going bare-footed, or with your hands all frost-bitten, or with no warm covering to wrap about you, and were to give you a pair of shoes and stockings or of warm gloves or a comfortable cloak or overcoat—if you were the only one that got this help, and the rest of your family were left starving as before—do you think you could take the things, or wear them, with any measure of comfort? When you saw your little brother's cold hands or feet or shivering body, could you help taking off what I had given you, and, at least, sharing the use of them with him? and would not your joy be increased a hundredfold, if I gave the same gift to all, and made all alike? 3. This petition implies the hastening of the kingdom of glory. We come now to consider—II. OUR DUTY in connection with it. 1. To pray. Many of us say this prayer who never pray it. Many repeat the words who have no desire for the thing. At the last great exhibition in London, there was one object that excited special interest. It was a speaking-machine, so contrived as to give utterance to certain sounds, like those of a human voice. Many of our prayers are as worthless as if they were uttered by such a machine, because they are not the prayers of the heart. Why, just suppose that the children of any town or district were to combine to get something they wanted very much from their parents or teachers, and were with one voice to ask it, would it not be a very difficult thing to refuse the request? Would they not be almost sure to carry their point? One great complaint just now, throughout the Churches, is the want of missionaries. Men cannot be got to go and tell the heathen the story of redeeming love, and preach among them the unsearchable riches of Christ. Would it not be a sad thing, if, on a harvest day, when the fields are covered with waving corn, all ready to be cut down, no one could be got to reap it, so that the grain began to fall out of the ear, or to rot upon its stalk? That is just a picture of the heathen world now. What would help to get them? One thing, I know, would help wonderfully—the prayers of our children. Another complaint in many quarters is, the want of blessing where the missionaries are. The hearts of some of them are failing, because there seems to be so little fruit of all their labours. They need—they ask your help. I saw lately, the picture of a party of children who had gone a bird-nesting. The nest was on the face of a cliff. One of the boys had a rope tied firmly round his waist, and was let gently down. In one sense he did the work; but did not everything depend on the others holding the rope? And when, having robbed the nest, he was attacked by the mother bird, I can fancy he was not so much afraid of that as of their letting him go; so that I think I hear his cries to those above, on whom all depended, "Hold the rope! Hold the rope!" One of the first missionaries who left this country to unfurl the gospel standard in India, said he would only consent to go down into the mine, on condition that his friends, whom he left behind, should thus "hold the rope." That is what they want and expect you to do now. They have gone instead of you; and from all lands, the missionaries' cry, to the children at home, amid all their dangers and discouragements, is, "Hold the rope! Hold the rope!" The holding of the rope is the offering of earnest believing prayer. 2. To work. It is not enough to pray. We must work as well as pray. The two should always go together—praying and working. Perhaps you say, "What can the like of us do? We cannot preach to people; we cannot go out as missionaries; we don't see that we can be of any use—that we can do anything at all in this matter." Well, you can do many things else. Many of you have a wonderful amount of energy. I have seen many of you at your games, and have watched you with not a little interest and pleasure as you made such tremendous efforts to come off first in the contest. Young people, who can master such difficult lessons at school, who can acquire a knowledge of Latin and Greek, and French and German; who are so well versed in geography, and arithmetic, and mathematics; who carry off prizes, and get no end of praise for your abilities and good qualities, you can surely do something for Christ. There is much of children's work that is lost. There is, perhaps, good got from it as regards the promoting of the general health of the body, but very little as regards the direct result. There are some things which a child cannot do so well as a man. There are some kinds of work which he cannot do at all—some burdens which he cannot carry. But there are things which he can do every whit as well—some better. A little body can get in at some openings where a big one cannot. A little hand can do some things which a big one cannot. In our large factories, children can go where old people cannot, and can do what others cannot. So in field labour. Work for Christ is often compared to the sowing of seed. Now, sometimes a young hand can drop a seed where an older one cannot. We are told of a Scotchman in another land, that missing the thistle of his native country, and longing to see it as at home, he procured a supply of seed, and when travelling to and fro, scattered it from his carriage window wherever he went. Dropping it here and there, it was not long ere the Scotch thistle bristled all over that region. Now, a child's hand can do that, and sow better seed than the Scotch thistle. It can sow the incorruptible seed of the Word in human hearts. Let me give you some illustrations. There is one who is described as "neither believing in heaven nor hell, God nor devil." There is no way of getting at him. Ministers and others have tried in vain to reach him. "He said if any parson dared to enter his room, he would smash his brains out with the poker." He is an infidel, and he is ill, how shall he be got at? A little girl repeats to him a hymn she has learned at the Sabbath-school, and as she goes on, he covers his face and weeps. The door is thus opened, and the man's heart reached, and when, a while after, he dies, among the last words he utters are three lines of that child's hymn, which he has learned to make his own :—

> " See smiling patience smooths my brow,
>   See the kind angels waiting now,
>   To waft my soul on high " ;

and his last wish is to have a sermon preached from the text, " This is a faithful saying, and worthy of all acceptation, that Christ Jesus came into the world to save sinners, of whom I am chief." 3. To give. It does not matter though it is little you have to give. Children should be early accustomed to give to the cause of Christ, and to give what is their own. Every family should be a little missionary society—praying, working, giving. " Sir," said a working man to Mr. Knill, of St. Petersburg, " I went last night to the missionary meeting, and I heard you speak of the love of Christ, and of the responsibility of Christ's people to seek the salvation of the heathen. I have professed many years to be a Christian, but I have never yet given anything to the Christian cause. I have come now to say that, by good health and constant work, I have saved up £10; and I have brought it, begging your acceptance of it, as my first contribution to the missionary society." Don't make a show of giving, any more than of working. Be like a youth in a small country town in Scotland, who afterwards became a good and useful man. His ambition was to give a piece of gold to the cause of Christ; and, when at last he had a half-sovereign, and the day had come when he was to put it into the plate at the church door, the attention of the two elders at the door was attracted by the careful way in which the lad put down his penny. On lifting it, there, between two pennies, lay the yellow coin ! (*J. H. Wilson, M.A.*) *The kingdom of God on the earth :*—We shall have still clearer views of this kingdom by specifying some of its great features. It possesses very remarkable characteristics, and is unlike every other kingdom. 1. It is emphatically distinguished by the character and authority of its Great Prince. At all times, under all circumstances, and in its whole procedure and administration, this kingdom is subjected to Him as its great and sole Monarch. Its common law and its positive statutes may be prescribed by no earthly and secular power. In no one particular may His decisions be departed from. 2. Another peculiarity of this kingdom will be found in the principles by which it is administered. "Justice and judgment are the habitation of God's throne"; these are the great principles on which it is built and stands firm. And in this pre-eminently consists the force and excellence of His claims upon the hearts of His subjects. His very law is clothed with new power by the grace that bringeth salvation. Principles which thus originate with the heart of the Deity, are fitted to address themselves to the hearts of men. Hence one peculiarity of the laws of this kingdom is the fact that they are spiritual, and go beyond the exterior man. They aim at the heart. 3. Another peculiarity of this kingdom is found in the character of its subjects. The subjects of this kingdom are they who are redeemed by the blood of its Prince, and sanctified by His Spirit. They possess a congeniality of mind with the spirit and tenor of God's Word; while their practical compliance with it is the effect of the love of God shed abroad in their hearts. 4. Another peculiarity of this kingdom, therefore, consists in its benevolent and hallowed influence. Depraved as the world is, its great security, under God, is in the practical influence of this Divine kingdom. 5. Another of the distinctions of this kingdom is, that it is a happy kingdom. The kingdom of God has come to them as suffering, perishing men, with the abundance of its light, the plenitude of its pardons, the redundancy of its grace. The malady and the misery which consisted in their departure from God, are healed by their being restored. 6. The only remaining characteristic of this kingdom on which I shall dwell is its perpetuity. It is a kingdom which "shall never be destroyed": it shall "not be left to other people": it shall "stand for ever." "Of this kingdom," said the angel Gabriel to Mary, "there shall be no end." The "gates of hell shall not prevail against it." *The means of extending God's kingdom:*—It is destined to advance; but the inquiry is one of interest, How and by what means is its advancement to be secured? Its conquests are not physical, nor political, nor military conquests; but spiritual victories, and are achieved by a spiritual armour. 1. There are preparatory measures by which the minds of men are rendered accessible to its influences. There is an intimate connection between the system of providence and the method of grace. One of the selected and ordained means of advancing the kingdom of God, ever has been the revolutions and conduct of His own mighty providence. His providence, in ways unseen, as well as seen, prepares the way for His gospel, and is the appointed precursor to herald its approach. The history of the past, as well as events that are taking place under our own observation, abundantly show how the many overturnings in the affairs of men, subserve the purpose of His mediatorial reign. Even the sword of the conqueror receives its commission from Him who purposes to follow it with the sword of His Spirit. 2. In addition to these preparatory arrangements, there are moral instrumentalities by which this kingdom is to be advanced. 3. Another of the means by which this kingdom is advanced, is the religious education of the young. I remark, then, once more, there is an appropriate place for another powerful agency in advancing the kingdom of God: I mean the power of prayer. (*G. Spring, D.D.*) *Thy kingdom come:* — In this petition we have three words, and all very observable. I. A noun—"Kingdom"; II. A pronoun—"Thy"; and—III. A verb—"Come." I. The kingdom which here we are commanded to pray for is not that which the Chiliasts or Millenaries fondly dream of, the enjoyment of pomp and pleasure and all temporal happiness upon earth for a thousand years together after the resurrection. This fancy they fetch from Rev. xx. and other places. II. I now proceed further, to unfold the nature of the kingdom of God. It is *Regnum Tuum,* "Thy kingdom." Which puts a difference betwixt this and other kingdoms. To speak something of these in their order. 1. First. In the kingdom of Christ and His laws neither people, nor senate, nor wise men, nor judges had any hand. The laws of Christ are unchangeable and eternal, but all human constitutions are temporary and mutable. 2. The second head wherein the difference of this kingdom from others is seen, is the power of it, which is extended not to the body alone, but to the soul also. Magistrates promulge laws, threaten, bind the tongue and hand; but have no influence nor operation on the hearts and wills of men. But in this our spiritual kingdom the King doth not only command, but gives us His helping hand that we may perform His command. But we must remember it is a kingdom we speak of; and Christ is a King, not a tyrant. 3. We pass now to the third head of difference, which consists in the compass and circuit of this kingdom, which is as large as all the world. In this respect all kingdoms come short of it, every one having its bounds which it cannot pass without violence. A foolish title it is which some give the Emperor of Rome, as if he had power over the most remote and unknown people of the world. Bartolus counts him no less than a heretic who denies it. But his arguments are no better than the emperor's title, which is but nominal. "The gospel must be preached to all nations," saith our Saviour (Mark xvi. 15). But as the sun hath its race through all the world, but yet doth not shine in every part at once, but beginneth in the east, and passeth to the south, and so to the west; and, as it passeth forward, it bringeth light to one place, and withdraweth it from another: so is it with the Sun of Righteousness; He spreads His beams on those who were in darkness and the shadow of death, and makes it night to them who had the clearest noon. Not that His race is confined, as is the sun's, but because of the interposition of men's sins, who exclude themselves from His beams. 4. And now to proceed to our fourth head of difference: As this is the largest of all kingdoms, so it is the most lasting. 5. We will conclude with the riches of this kingdom. If money were virtue, and earthly honour salvation; if the jasper were holiness, and the sapphire obedience; if those pearls in the Revelation were virtues; then that of our Saviour would be true in this sense also, "The kingdom of heaven would be taken by violence" (Matt. xi. 12). The covetous, the ambitious, the publicans and sinners, would all be *candidati angelorum*, "jointsuitors and competitors for an angel's place." Behold, then, in this kingdom are riches which never fail; not money, but virtue; not honour, but salvation; not the jasper and the sapphire, but that pearl which is better than all our estate. Having now made the comparison, the choice is easy. And a great folly it were to prefer the world to the Church. In the world the laws are mutable, here everlasting. In the world they have tongues many times to speak, but not hands to strike; here they both thunder and lighten. There power beats the ear, here it pierceth the very heart. The kingdoms of the world are bounded by place and time; this is unconfinable: more scope in the Church than in the world. The riches of the one are fading and transitory, of the other everlasting. And of this just and mighty and large and rich and everlasting kingdom we cannot but say, *Adveniat*, "Let it come." III. We pass now to the petition itself, to the verb *Adveniat*, "Let it come." Which breathes itself forth in an earnest desire to draw this kingdom nearer. Whether you take it for the gospel, which is the manifestation of God's will; or for the receiving of the gospel, which is the performing of His will; whether you take it for the kingdom of grace here, or for the kingdom of glory hereafter; *Adveniat*, "Let it come!" That is the language of every true Christian. "Where it is not yet come, 'let it come'; it cannot come soon enough. And when it is come, let it come nearer. When it is within us, let it be established there; and when it is established, let it be eternized there. Remove all obstacles, supply all helps, *ut adveniat*, 'that it may come'; that Thy kingdom of grace may entitle us to Thy kingdom of glory." I might name here many hindrances of the growth of the gospel; as heresy, which is a most poisonous viper biting not the heel but the very heart of it; infidelity, which robs Christ of His subjects, contracts His kingdom into a narrow room and into a small number; disorder, which rends it, which works confusion there. 1. Further: this *Adveniat* reacheth to the second advent of Christ, even to the end of all things. For of His kingdom of glory we say, "Let it come." And it is a word of desire, not of impatience. For though we cry out, "How long, Lord? how long?" (Rev. vi. 10) yet we are willing to stay His leisure. For it is also a word expressing our hope. And hope as it doth stir and quicken our desire, so doth it also temper it, that it be not irregular. 2. Secondly. *Adveniat* is a word expressing our faith. Though hope takes a long day, yet faith lays hold on the promises as if they were present, being "the substance, the evidence," the presence, "of things to come" (Heb. xi. 1). Faith is the life of hope, without which it cannot have existence. Hope doth suppose faith; but faith may be where there is no hope at all. 3. Lastly. This *Adveniat*, as it is the language of our hope and faith, so is it the dialect also of our charity and love both to God and our brethren. (*A. Farindon, D.D.*) *Of the difference betwixt the kingdoms of grace and glory*:—The kingdoms of grace and of glory are but one and the same kingdom, distinguished into two parts, which differ in six circumstances. 1. In time. The kingdom of grace is now present while here we live. The kingdom of glory is to come. 2. In place. This of grace is on earth; that of glory in heaven. 3. In condition. This is continually warfaring against many enemies, in which respect it is styled the Church militant; that triumpheth over all the enemies, in which respect it is called the Church triumphant. 4. In order of entering into them. This is to be entered into, and passed through before we can enter into that. The priest was to enter through the sanctuary into the *sanctum sanctorum*. 5. In the manner of government. This is governed and ordered by many subordinate means, as magistrates, ministers, and sundry ordinances. That immediately by God Himself. 6. In continuance. This hath a date, and is to come to an end. That is everlasting without end. (*W. Gouge.*) *How ought we to pray for particular Churches whose estate we know?* :—We ought to frame our prayers according to that we hear, see, or otherwise know of any. As—1. If any especial blessing be bestowed on any, to pray that it may be continued and increased. 2. If any mischievous plots be practised against any, to pray that they may be prevented. 3. If ministers or other members of any Churches be surprised, to pray that they may be delivered. 4. If persecution be raised against any Church, to pray that either that fire may be quenched, or else that sufficient courage and strength may be given to such as are persecuted to hold out, and endure the uttermost trial. 5. If any noisome weeds of idolatry, heresy, schism, or the like, sprout up in any Church, to pray that they may be rooted out. To sharpen our prayer herein, we ought oft to call to mind that which in this case is promised by Christ, "Every plant which My heavenly Father hath not planted shall be rooted up." This is that true use which we are to make of the knowledge that we have of the estate of any of God's Churches. (*Ibid.*) *Of the things to be bewailed under the second petition:*—All such things as any way make to the disadvantage or disparagement of the kingdom of Christ. As—1. That great sway which Satan hath in the world. 2. The small circuit of Christ's kingdom. 3. The mixture of Satan's subjects with Christ's in that small circuit. 4. The many clouds which obscure the light of the gospel. I mean the clouds of error, superstition, human traditions and such like. 5. The spoils of the Church made by open enemies. 6. Treacheries of false-hearted brethren. 7. Unfaithfulness in magistrates. 8. Unfaithfulness in ministers. 9. Desolation of seminaries. 10. Disorder of families. 11. Professors' unworthy walking. 12. Reproaches cast upon the saints. 13. Persecution raised against the Church. 14. Timorous backsliding of professors. 15. Schisms, sects, and dissensions in the Church. (*Ibid.*) *Prayer for the advancement of Christ's kingdom:*—1. The first motive, to which I request your attention, is the Divine command. We ought to pray for the advancement of this kingdom, because God, our rightful Sovereign, requires it of us. 2. A second motive, which should induce us to pray for the coming of God's kingdom is, that by this desirable event the Divine glory will be greatly promoted. 3. The benefits which will result to mankind from the coming of God's kingdom, furnish another powerful motive to induce us to pray for its advancement. The number and value of these benefits, as they respect the present life, may in some measure be inferred from a consideration of the nature and tendency of Christ's kingdom. It essentially consists, as has already been observed, in righteousness, peace, and holy joy. 4. We may therefore add, as another motive which should induce us to pray for the universal spread of Christ's kingdom, that He has promised, and even sworn by Himself, that this event shall infallibly take place. 5. As a farther inducement to do this, permit me to remind you that the time allotted for their fulfilment is rapidly advancing, and that the present appearance of the world and the dispensations of Providence plainly indicate that God is about to finish His work and cut it short in righteousness, and that the latter day of Christ's kingdom is beginning to dawn. 6. As a farther motive to induce you to this, consider the happy effects which it will have upon yourselves. Nothing can more directly or more powerfully tend to destroy every baleful, malignant passion in your breasts, or promote in them the growth of Divine benevolence, than frequently praying for the advancement of Christ's kingdom. That our prayers for this event may be acceptable to God, two things are indispensably necessary. (1) The first is, that they be accompanied by corresponding exertions. (2) The second thing necessary to render our prayers for the advancement of Christ's kingdom sincere and acceptable is, that we become willing subjects of His kingdom ourselves. (*E. Payson, D.D.*) **Thy will be done, as in heaven, so in earth.**—*Doing God's will:*—I. WHAT IS MEANT BY THE WILL OF GOD. 1. The will of God's commands (Heb. xiii. 24; Matt. vii. 21). God's will may be reduced to two heads: (1) Faith; (2) Holiness. 2. The will of God's providence (Psa. cxxxv. 6). It may be considered—(1) As directing to duty (Psa. xxxii. 8); (2) As ordering and disposing of events about ourselves and others (Matt. x. 29, 30). II. BY WHOM GOD'S WILL IS DONE IN HEAVEN. 1. By the heavenly bodies—sun, moon, and stars. 2. By the angels. III. THE IMPORT OF THIS PETITION. 1. With reference to the will of God's command. (1) A confession that—(*a*) The will of God is not done on earth as it is in heaven.

(*b*) There is in all men naturally an utter indisposition and unfitness for the will of God's commands. (2) A profession that—(*a*) It is the grief of their hearts, that God's will is not done by themselves or others, as it is done in heaven (Matt. xxi. 29). (*b*) That God by the power of His grace is able to reform this, and to frame the souls of men on earth to the doing His will, as in heaven. (3) A desire— (*a*) That He would by His grace remove from themselves and others all spiritual blindness and cause them to know His will (Eph. i. 17, 18). (*b*) That God by His grace would remove from themselves and others all weakness, indisposition, and perverseness, and cause them to obey and do His will, as it is done in heaven (Psa. cxix. 35). And here as in a glass we may see what sort of doing the will of God the saints aim at and desire. It is—(i) To do it evenly, without stumbling or changing their course. (ii) To do it unweariedly. (iii) To do it universally. (iv) To do it humbly. (v) To do it cheerfully. (vi) To do it readily, without delay. (vii) To do it constantly. 2. With reference to the will of God's providence. (1) A confession—(*a*) Of a natural aptness in all men to quarrel, repine, and murmur against the methods and disposals of Providence (Numb. xiv. 2). (*b*) Of a natural back-wardness to fall in with the designs of providence of one sort or other. (2) A profession—(*a*) of the saint's sorrow for this disposition of heart crossing the will of God; (*b*) of the faith of the power of grace to subdue the will to this conformity. (3) A desire for grace for a thorough compliance with the will of God's providence. (4) A consent to the will of God, a yielding of the heart that it may be done. IV. Why the saints have such a concern that the will of God may be done in earth, as it is in heaven. 1. Because it is most just, holy, reasonable, and equitable, in all things, and they see it so (Psa. cxix. 128). 2. Because the glory of God, which of all things is dearest to the saints, is deeply interested in this matter. 3. Because this would make a heaven on earth. If there were such a harmony betwixt earth and heaven, that God's will were done in the one as in the other, it would make on earth—(1) A heaven for beauty and order of all things. (2) A heaven for happiness. The happiness of men lies in their assimilation to God; and they are so far like Him as they conform to His will. (*T. Boston, D.D.*) *On doing God's will :*—This petition is often quoted as if it were merely a prayer for meek resignation ; or, as though it contained but an echo of the sobbings of Gethsemane. But whilst this is certainly included, the prayer seems to comprise much more ; and to ask for Christian energy as well as for Christian endurance ; and for diligence as much as patience. It is not only the motto of that blessed Redeemer, as He is beheld mutely suffering, but also as He is presented incessantly and effectually labouring. All Christ's obedience in life, as well as His obedience unto death, is embraced in the sentiment and spirit of the petition before us. There would be another incongruity in giving to the present sentence merely the narrow construction of resignation to suffering; it is that angels and saints in heaven could scarce be presented to us in the manner in which here they are, as our patterns. Patterns they could not well be of those who are enduring evils, since from all evil they are now and for evermore exempt. But give to the petition the wider scope of conformity to the Father's will—in action as well as in submission—let it be the Lord's will done, as well as the Lord's will borne—endeavoured as well as endured—and you may readily see how the glorified worshippers on high—those who continually and perfectly and cheerfully obey the Father's wishes—may well be made models for our imitation, and their zeal furnish a burning incentive to our flagging emulation. It is the language of adoring obedience. I. What is God's will? There are depths and heights in His will yet but very partially known. It is His will of control—that sovereign and all-governing purpose, which foresees and uses all occurrences and all influences, and all resistances even—providing for the eruptions and avalanches of our revolt, and of our sinful disregard of Him, and of our league with hell, and weaving even these into His wide plans. Much of this controlling and overruling Will is among those " secret things " which, as Moses declared, belong only to the Lord; whilst the " things revealed " belong more properly to us and to our children. The great outlines and last results of this controlling and sovereign purpose He has made known ; but its details and many of its relations are as yet inscrutable to our limited faculties. But there is another aspect of His will. It is His will of command ; what He requires of us, and what He disapproves in us. This He makes known by the voice of reason and conscience in part, but more perfectly in the book of His Scriptures, and by the influences of His Spirit. We see in human beings, even the just and the wise of the race, the same distinction between their will of control, and their will of command or counsel. Take, for instance, the illustrious Howard the missionary martyr, of benevolence to the imprisoned and forsaken. This good man had devised, from his experience and observation, certain rules for the better construction and governance of prisons. Now, if his will of counsel or command, so to speak (his precepts of wisdom and kindness), had been heeded by evil-doers, they would not be the inmates of prisons; and the other portion of Howard's studies, his law of control, would be no longer needed. But if men, in the abuse of their freedom, did wrong, then in his controlling will—his disposition to bring out of the case as it stood, not as he had wished it, but as they made it, the most good to society and to the transgressor himself—he had his prisons prepared and arranged for the detention and restraint of the evil-doer. So too, a civil government, upright and equitable, whose just laws are threatened with resistance by a portion or by an entire province of its subjects, may by its will of counsel or command, urge sincerely and kindly the men of the province to abide the civil law; but if they scorn the milder legislation, it may in its will of control, proclaim, and that justly and inevitably, martial law for the repression of the revolt, and for the avengement of its own dishonoured and imperilled authority. Now sin is an anomaly in God's dominions. He, allowing to His creatures in the angelic and human races the exercise of freedom, may have permitted sin to occur, whilst His will of command or legislation sincerely and strictly condemns it; but He so permits it only because in His will of control He will ultimately restrain its ravages, and make its wrath to praise Him. His precepts are one thing; His decrees, in the event of our rejecting His precepts, another. To leave room and range for the exhibition of man's real character, for the evolving of the blossom and the full-blown flower of his depraved heart—to allow verge and margin enough for the existence of a world of probation, and for the manifestation of Satan's nature and will, and for the true fruits of the tempter's infernal counsels—God gives but the will of His command to be fully known; and keeps as yet in reserve and comparative darkness the will of His control; just as a legislator, having given his subjects, ere their revolt, just and full statements as to his statutes, is not bound, if they spurn these, to add a full and minute plan of His campaigns, when, as the avenger, He comes forth to punish them for the infringement of those statutes. It is enough for justice, that the sinner should know that his transgression, persisted in and remaining unrepented of, will be assuredly and eternally visited. II. WHAT DOES THIS PETITION COMPRISE? Very comprehensive. 1. In offering this request, we by necessary implication ask that we may have grace earnestly and honestly to inquire, in all the channels through which it is to come to us, What His wishes are, and what He would have us His children do? So did Paul in the first agony of his conversion—"Lord, what wouldest Thou have me to do?" Conscience, then, will be cherished, and kept not as a tarnished but as a burnished mirror, that it may more clearly reflect the light and images cast upon it. Scripture will be pondered, habitually and prayerfully and practically. And as none of these petitions are isolated and selfish, but grasp our brother's needs as well as our own—to pray that God's will may be known is virtually to implore that the two Testaments of Revelation, the Old proclaimed by the prophets of the Saviour, and the New by the apostles of the Saviour, may be diffused abroad. It is to pledge ourselves at the mercy-seat that the prayers we offer shall be accompanied by plans and alms, and efforts for the translation and dispersion of these Scriptures among the whole brotherhood of our race. 2. It is, again, a prayer explicitly that the will, being once and in any way—by reading or hearing, by conscience or Scripture, or by the ministrations of the nursery, of the Sabbath-school or the pulpit—made known, it may be done by us. It is thus a prayer that God would give us the grace of obedience in action, that our lives and words and thoughts may practically carry out His law and exemplify His gospel. 3. But though obedience in action be required, it is not the sole meaning of the petition. Obedience must be shown in suffering as well as in toiling. And the obedience of suffering submits itself not only to the will of God's command, as requiring us to encounter all sacrifices of reputation and interest and ease that obedience to his precepts may occasion us; but it subjects itself also to the will of God's control, to His Sovereign and inscrutable Providence, which orders all events and overrules even the wickedness and wrath of man and of devils, for the accomplishment of its own wise purposes. (*W. R. Williams, D.D.*) *The reign of grace viewed in relation to the work of righteousness :*—I. IT IS HERE ASSUMED THAT THE WILL OF GOD IS DONE BY ALL THE INHABITANTS OF HEAVEN AS HE HIMSELF REQUIRES. The place, the parties, and the practice to which this statement refers, must, in succession, receive a distinct though brief consideration. 1. To determine the locality of heaven beyond the possibility of a reasonable doubt will, probably, for ever exceed the ability of man while on earth. 2. If, however, we cannot fix the locality of heaven, we can describe its inhabitants. 3. Having shown who the inhabitants of heaven are, we have to consider how they act. Every individual of this innumerable company serves God day and night in His temple. The obedience of each begins and ends in love. This sacred passion is fixed supremely on the Lord. II. THERE IS HERE A DOCTRINE TO BE ESTABLISHED. The phrase, "Thy will be done on earth, as it is done in heaven," certainly shows that in the opinion of its author God not only has, but will exercise the same authority over men on earth as over saints and angels in heaven. 1. Our first proof is to be obtained from the dictates of conscience. By conscience we mean that power of the human mind which approves the actions it considers right, and condemns those which it thinks wrong. By all its operations it recognizes a greater than human authority. 2. This momentous doctrine admits of further confirmation from the deductions of reason. The will of God is declared in His laws. These are framed with an especial reference to either matter or mind ; forming, in the one case, the basis of natural, and in the other, the foundation of a moral government. 3. To adduce direct evidence from Scripture in support of the doctrine the text implies. There are two individuals introduced to our notice on the sacred page, to whose history we need do little more than refer, for a confirmation of the truth that God will not suffer the wicked to prosper in their wickedness. These are Adam and Noah. III. A DUTY TO BE ENFORCED. 1. The objects for which the Christian is here taught to pray must be noticed in the order of their own importance. They are two—the one evidently supreme, and the other subordinate. As an ultimate object, we are to pray that the will of God may be done on earth as it is done in heaven ; and as though conscious that this end could be secured by no other means, we are to pray that His kingdom may come. 2. The importance of our prayers in regard to this matter will immediately appear, if we consider the manner in which they affect our own minds, and the numerous promises God has made both to hear and answer them. (1) It is impossible for any one to enter into the spirit of this petition without feeling the power of a true Christian philanthropy. All who can say, with the understanding and the heart, "Thy kingdom come," must be constrained to ask if they can in any way assist in its advancement. It would, perhaps, not be going too far to affirm, "that wherever these words have been properly employed in the worship of God, they have been expressive of a real concern for the welfare of man." (2) Prayer, when thus associated with exertion, is sure either more or less to prevail. God says to His Son, "Ask of Me and I will give Thee the heathen for Thine inheritance, and the uttermost part of the earth for Thy possession." For this He is doubtless asking personally in heaven and by His people on earth, for we are told that prayer shall be made for Him continually. And is it not answered as well as made? In reviewing our subject we naturally remark—1. That obedience to the will of the Creator is absolutely essential to the welfare of every intelligent creature. 2. Moreover, it is obvious that had there been no sin there would have been no suffering. 3. It is, therefore, certain that in order to be happy we must be in a state of acceptance with God. (*J. Jukes.*) *How is God's will done in heaven?*—A Sunday-school teacher was once questioning his class as to the meaning of the petition, "Thy will be done," when he said, "And how do you suppose that the angels, who are to be our patterns, do God's will?" Several very proper answers were given, and, at last, a little girl arose, and said, "Why, sir, they do it without asking any questions!" 1. It is certainly done zealously. No lagging nor loitering ; no lame excuses for neglecting God's will. Can we claim to be zealous, even in a moderate degree? Are we zealous enough to do things which really call for no special sacrifice nor endurance? II. The angels in heaven do God's will REVERENTLY. Contrast the four-and-twenty elders, whom St. John beheld in his vision, falling down before the Divine Redeemer, and casting their golden crowns in the dust (Rev. iv. 11), with the conduct of sinful mortals who treat God's Holy Temple with disrespect, and whose stubborn knees refuse to bend in prayer, and then say whether the lesson which the reverent behaviour of the angels shall teach has been very perfectly learned. III. God's will is also done in heaven WITH CHEERFUL ALACRITY. The grand passage from the vision of Isaiah (vi. 1–3) need hardly be quoted to prove this point. IV. Again: God's will is done in heaven PERSEVERINGLY. The angelic host "serve Him day and night in His Temple " (Rev. vii. 15); and "they rest not day and night" (iv. 8) in their exalted ascriptions of praise. While the weakness of our moral nature obliges us to rest, even from the offices of our religion, the blessed spirits in the better land move swiftly, without sense of weariness, and worship God with undistracted soul. What a change must come over us before those who fancy that they are patterns of propriety—because they attend public worship for a brief hour, morning and evening, on Sunday—will be prepared to serve God day and night, in the heavenly sanctuary. V. Angels, moreover, do God's will in heaven HARMONIOUSLY. Jealousy and envy find no admittance there. VI. Once more: God's will is done in heaven PERFECTLY. Imperfections and frailties mar our best services on earth. Angels no sooner learn the will of God, than it is promptly and perfectly obeyed. (*J. N. Norton, D.D.*) *The doing of God's will*:—I. THE PETITION ITSELF. 1. What this will of God is. (1) God's purpose is His will. (2) The precepts and commands are also the will of God. 2. What will it is we pray may be done. (1) It is clear that we especially and absolutely pray that the will of God's precept may be done, and that, not only by us, but by all men: for this will of God is the rule of our obedience, and according to it we ought to conform all our actions. And, because we are not sufficient of ourselves so much as to think anything of ourselves, much less to perform all those various and weighty duties of holiness which God hath enjoined us in His Word, therefore our Saviour hath taught us to beg of God grace and assistance to enable us to fulfil His will. And, indeed, there is a great deal of reason we should pray that His will of precept should be done on earth, if we consider—(*a*) The great reluctancy and opposition of corrupt nature against it. The Law is spiritual; but we are carnal, and sold under sin (Rom. vii. 14). (*b*) God's glory is deeply concerned in the doing of His will. For it is the glory of a king to have his laws obeyed. And so is it God's. (*c*) Our own interest is deeply concerned in it. (2) It is more doubtful, whether we are simply to pray that God's will of purpose should be done. (*a*) Because the will of God's purpose is secret and unknown, and therefore cannot so immediately concern us in point of duty; for secret things belong to God, but revealed things belong to us and to our children (Deut. xxix. 29). (*b*) Because this will of God shall, within the periods set by His eternal decrees, have its most perfect and full accomplishment. For, though His revealed will may be resisted and hindered, yet neither men nor devils can hinder His secret will and the purposes of His counsels: these shall take place, notwithstanding all their spite and oppositions; and therefore it seems not altogether so proper matter for our prayers. (*c*) Many things come to pass by the will of God's purpose which we ought not to pray for; yea, which we ought to pray against. As—not to instance in God's will of permitting the sins and wickednesses of men, which, beyond all exceptions, we ought to deprecate—let us but consider, common charity obligeth us not to pray for any evil of suffering to befall either ourselves or others; and yet we know that it is oftentimes the will of God's purpose to bring great and sore judgments upon kingdoms, and upon families and persons. And if we may indefinitely pray that this will should be done, this would be nothing else but to pray for the death and ruin of many thousands, whom yet the revealed will of God commands us to pray for, and to desire all good and prosperity to them. But yet, notwithstanding all this, we may doubtless pray that the will of God's purpose may be done, so far as it brings to pass those things which we are obliged to pray for by the will of His precept. (3) The next thing to be taken notice of is the particle "Thy "—"Thy will be done." And this carries in it both an emphasis and an exclusion. (4) The last thing to be inquired into, is, what is meant by God's will being "done on earth." And here, briefly to resolve this, that the will of God should be done on earth, signifies that it be done by men living on the earth; the place here being put for the persons in it. (*a*) That all men in the world, renouncing the will of Satan and their own corrupt wills, may readily subject themselves unto the will of God. (*b*) We pray that we may employ and improve the few and short days of this mortal life to the best advantage. II. THE MEASURE AND PROPORTION OF THE PETITION. That we may the more fully understand what it is we pray for, we shall inquire how the holy angels and blessed spirits do the will of God in heaven. 1. Their obedience is absolutely perfect. (1) They do all that God enjoins. (2) They do the whole will of God with all their might. 2. Their obedience is cheerful, not extorted by fear. (1) The will of God is done in heaven with zeal and ardency. (2) The will of God is done in heaven with celerity and ready dispatch. (3) The will of God is done in heaven with all possible prostration, reverence, and humility.

(4) The will of God is done in heaven with constancy and perseverance. (*Bishop Hopkins.*)　　*Practical reflections :*—I. We should not think it hard to be subject to the Divine government, obliged to do the will of God, and to submit to it. This is more reasonable, and more profitable for us, than to be left to our own liberty, to follow our own pleasure, and to choose our own circumstances. But we are not easily persuaded to think so. I suppose some will say, God, who is the Father of spirits, and the author of all the powers of the soul, has given us senses and appetites; and is it not lawful for us to gratify them? Doubtless it is; but within due bounds. God has given man reason too, by which his sensual inclinations and appetites are to be governed, as the superior faculty whereby we are distinguished from beasts; and He has given us His Word, containing His will, the law of nature, and positive ordinances, to which, as the subjects of God, we know we ought to endeavour to conform our heart and life. Now, if we will not use our understanding, if we follow not the dictates of reason, nor regard the voice of conscience, even natural conscience, and give up ourselves to sensual lusts and appetites, then we transform ourselves into brutes, and render ourselves contemptible to God, and to all wise men. II. Let us bless God that His will is revealed to us. III. Let us desire and endeavour to know the will of God as it is revealed to us. To have it in the Scripture is one thing, and to have it in the understanding, the memory, the heart, is another. IV. Let us do the will of God. " If ye know these things, happy are ye if ye do them. To him that knoweth to do good, and doeth it not, to him it is sin." The meaning is, that knowledge, without obedience, is so far from excusing men when they sin, or from extenuating the guilt, that it aggravates it. V. Let us go to the throne of grace, that we may obtain mercy to pardon our opposition to the will of God in thought, word, or deed; and for grace to help us proportioned to the work He has given us to do, and to our infirmities which disable us for it; that His grace may be sufficient for us, and His strength made perfect in our weakness. VI. Let us be exhorting one another to an obediential regard to the Divine law. So we are taught to do in many places of the Sacred Word. And let us take great care that we do not, on the contrary, lay a stumbling-block in the way of others, and tempt them to offend. We have guilt enough of our own, let us not be partakers of other men's sins; let us not enter into a confederacy against God. VII. Let us all labour to be prepared for that world wherein dwelleth righteousness. Where there will be no sin nor temptation to it, no inclination nor allurements to oppose the will of God; where we shall not tempt others, and where there will be none to tempt us. Happy place! where the holy God will rule without opposition. (*John Whitty.*)　　*The blessed will :*—This petition doubtless conveys to many of those who use it a lesson of simple submission. And undoubtedly it includes this. Sometimes the will of God conflicts with our plans, runs counter to our wishes, disturbs our repose, and then it is necessary that we should submit. In such times it is good for us to be able to say from the heart, " Thy will be done"; and therefore it is well for us to settle it in our thoughts beforehand that His will is a good will, and ought to be done; and that though for the present it may seem grievous, it is sure to bring forth the peaceable fruits of righteousness in all who trust Him and wait upon His Word. There is a mistake just here, however, against which we must be watching. It is possible to be too submissive. Submissiveness may degenerate into supineness. We ought to be measurably sure that the ills that threaten us are coming upon us by the will of God before we submit to them. A man is sitting upon a steep hill-side in the spring-time when he hears a noise, and, looking up, perceives a huge rock that has been loosened by the frost rolling down upon him. It is evident that the rock will pass directly over the place where he is sitting, and though there is time for him to escape, he sits still, saying, " It seems to be the will of the Lord that I should perish here, and His will be done." But this is not the will of God in the truest sense of the word. The will of God is that the man shall escape; the noise that warns him is the call that summons him to escape; his sitting still is not trusting God, nor submitting to God, but tempting God most wickedly. A man is suffering from dyspepsia, the result of his own imprudence in the use of food; or from nervous headache, the result of an intemperate indulgence in tobacco; and though he does not mend his habits, we hear him talk in the midst of his sufferings about being submissive to the trial God has put upon him. All suffering, he says, comes from the hand of God; it is His will that I should suffer; His will be done. But it is not God's will that this man should suffer; this is not the portion that God has chosen for him; it is the portion that he has chosen for himself. He is alto-

gether too submissive. It is only in a secondary sense that suffering can ever be said to be the will of God. His will is expressed in His laws; obedience to His laws brings health and happiness and peace; disobedience brings suffering. The suffering is a warning against disobedience, and a dissuasive from it. (*Washington Gladden, D.D.*)   *On doing God's will:*—To do God's will we must know what it is. How shall we find it out? The first and most obvious answer to this question is that His will has been revealed, and that we find it in His Word. It is especially to be found in the teaching of Christ and His apostles. Our Lord Himself has condensed the whole of God's law into two short commandments—"Thou shalt love," &c. He who perfectly obeys these two commandments perfectly does God's will. So then we find in this Holy Book such a declaration to us of the will of God as may serve to guide our feet into the ways of obedience. If we study the Word with a prayerful and teachable mind, we shall know more of His will than we shall ever find time and strength to do. And if, in all our study of the Bible, we sought this mainly—to find things to do—to get hints as to the kind of work God has for us, in the cleansing of our lives, and in the serving of Him and of our neighbours in the world; if we went to it as to an order-book in which we expected to find some definite direction for the doing of God's will to-day—I am sure that our study of the Bible would do us much more good than it now does. We are too apt to read the Bible and study the Bible as a mere perfunctory service. It is a thing to be gone through with, there is so much Bible-reading or Bible study to be done; it is a duty, and when it is done it is done, like any other duty. Or else we fall into the habit of thinking that there is a certain charm about it; that the study of the Bible in some mysterious way has a kind of alterative effect upon the character; so that to spend a certain time every week reading it will prove to be a means of grace. If we could get rid of all such formal and superstitious notions, and just remember that our main business with the Bible is to find out from it what God wants us to do, the book would speedily come to have new meaning and value. Mr. Matthew Arnold says that conduct is three-fourths of life, and that the Bible, far above all other books, is the book of conduct. We shall be safe, I am sure, in adopting his maxim, so that while we pray, "Thy will be done," we may search the Scriptures to find each day how to help in answering our prayer—what part of God's will we ought each day to be doing. (*Ibid.*) *God's will to be discovered in nature and providence:*—God's will is revealed not only in the Bible, but also in nature and in providence. We learn the will of God as we learn the will of a man, not only by attending to what He has said, but by observing what He is doing. His works, quite as distinctly as His words, indicate His will. So when I pluck in the meadow a violet or a crowfoot bloom, and look it in the face and see how deftly its petals are carved and how daintily they are painted, then I learn a little of what God's will is. Such a thing of beauty as this is an expression of His thought and of His love. He no more wills that I should be holy than that this flower should be beautiful. And although the flowers are not all perfect; although in an unkindly environment some of them have been maimed and scarred; yet of this we are always sure, that the flower which is most beautiful comes nearest to being the flower that God meant to make, and did make in the beginning. So when we see a human being of full stature and fair proportions, with a clear eye and a ruddy skin, and the wholesome beauty that springs from perfect health, we are able to say with equal assurance that God's will is revealed in the body which the soul inhabits, however poorly it may be done by the inhabitant. And though there are many decrepit and diseased bodies in which human beings make their homes, yet we are sure that those bodies which are soundest and most symmetrical and most beautiful are the nearest like what God means all the bodies of men to be. In like manner when we meet with a human life that is upright and modest and pure and beneficent, based on firm principles of justice and honour, working quietly but energetically for the building up of righteousness, we know that God's will is revealed in such a life as this more perfectly than any words can tell it, more clearly than any flower can show it, more fully than the shapeliest form and the comeliest face can reveal it. And when we go into a home in which love is the law, in which each member of the household seeks to live worthily, and in which all conspire together to seek one another's welfare and happiness, so that the law of the home seems to be, Each for all and all for each—then we are sure that God's will is made known to us in the life of this household; that something like this is what He would have every home to be. And if we should find ourselves in a community where peace, and order, and temperance, and thrift, and industry, and contentment abounded; where there was no squalid poverty, and no filth, breeding pestilence, and no enormous fortunes, and no profligate expenditures of wealth, and no extortionate capitalists who kept themselves wholly aloof from the workpeople by whose labour they were enriched, and cared not, so long as their dividends were undiminished, how fast the labourers were pauperized and brutalized; where there were no eye-servants, that worked only when they were watched, and no discontented, and surly, and suspicious employers; where the law of goodwill had prevailed over the law of supply and demand, making peace where there once was strife, and spreading plenty where there once was poverty—if we ever should find such a community as that we should know of a surety that God's will had found expression in its corporate life; we should say with confidence that every community on earth would be like this community when His will should be done on earth as it is done in heaven. (*Ibid.*)   *A conformed spirit: unquestioning submission:*—This exceeds mere loyalty. A man is loyal to an earthly kingdom if he keeps its laws, and pays the due tribute; but, at the same time, he may criticize the laws and wish they were different; may regard the Government's policy as unwise and an infringement of his personal liberty; and dislike the individuals having the administration. Gladstone is a loyal Englishman, though in the so-called Opposition. But the Christian who can use this petition would have no opposition party within God's kingdom. He loves the Sovereign, would delight in the administration, and desires that the details of the Divine will may become his will also. To fulfil the sentiments of the petition there must be— 1. Comformity of natural desire to His Providence. 2. Conformity of moral desire to His Law. 3. Conformity of spiritual desire to all His truth as taught either in His Word or by his Spirit. (*J. M. Ludlow, D.D.*)   *God's will must be the rule of our life:*—If a man lay a crooked stick upon an even level ground, the stick and ground ill suit together, but the fault is in the stick; and in such a case, a man must not strive to bring the even ground to the crooked stick, but bow the crooked stick even with the ground. So is it between God's will and ours; there is a discrepancy and jarring betwixt them; but where is the fault? or rather, where is it not? not in the will of God, but in our crooked and corrupt affections; in which case we must not like Balaam seek to bring God's will to ours, but be contented to rectify and order the crookedness of our wills by the rectitude and sanctity of the will of God, which must be the ruler and moderator of our wills; for which cause we are to cry out with David, " Teach me, O Lord, to do Thy will "; and with the whole Church of God, in that pattern of wholesome words, " Thy will be done in earth, as it is in heaven "; never forgetting that, too, of Christ Jesus Himself in the midst of His agony and bloody sweat, " Father, not My will, but Thine be done " (Luke xxii. 42). (*Augustine.*)   *God's will the best:*—A man must be untrue to his own moral convictions who can say to a God that violates his ideas of sanctity and Divine excellence, "Reign, rule." There must be presented to the human soul a deity that is better than man, in each and in every respect—so much better that it shall seem an infinite and unspeakable blessing that such a God should control all things, and should constrain men to become like Himself. Men have taught that God had a right to rule, simply because He was the strongest. It is true that the wisest, the best, and the strongest must take precedence. It is true, therefore, that God has a right to reign in heaven and on earth—everywhere—but not because He has power to reign. It is true that when you see the use that God makes of His power, you cannot help following with those that in the apocalyptic vision worshipped His power, and acclaimed praise to it; but when you look at the question narrowly and reduce it to its basis, no being in heaven or on earth has a right to reign, simply because he has power. Right goes with moral quality. If God's conscience is pure, and supreme over all consciences; if God's moral sentiments are themselves the very fountains from which our moral sentiments flow; if His wisdom is supreme and unerring; if His love is broader, deeper, higher, wider, and more full of bounty than any other love, these qualities raise him to supremacy. But the mere fact that God made men, is no more an argument that He owns them, than is the fact that I have children an argument that I own them. I have obligations to rear them; but when they come to man's estate, is the mere fact of paternity a reason why I may wring their necks off, or why I may make a slave of one, and put one in hateful preference over another? Paternity gives no one a right to set at naught the great moral distinctions which love and conscience have established in the world. It does not among men, and still less does it in God. Those doctrines, therefore, are inconsistent with a cheerful reliance upon the will of God, which have taught that God had a right to reign simply because He had power to do it; that we had no business to question that Divine power; and that, when men set up their images of ideas, their idols of teaching, saying "This is God," if men questioned them, they questioned the real God because they questioned these theoretic gods. And this idea that God had a right to reign simply because He was able to do it, would be despotism in heaven, as much more hateful than despotism is upon earth, as the sphere is broader, and the Being wiser and more comprehensive. God's wisdom, God's justice, God's truth, God's love, God's fidelity—these give Him —shall I say right?—*necessity*, to reign. These exalt Him, and on these stand the throne of the universe. (*H. W. Beecher*.)　　*Willingness that God should rule:*— Begin and say, "Our Father which art in heaven, Hallowed be Thy name. Thy kingdom come"—stop! if you say the next sentence, it is all gone—you are His— "Thy will be done." What! In you? In your reason? In your taste? In your affections? In God's providential counsels for you in the affairs of your family? Stand then, mother, over your little child that lies sick in the cradle, and say, if you can, "Our Father which art in heaven"—then God is your Father, and He loves your child better than you do—"Hallowed be Thy name. Thy kingdom come"—now do you dare look down into the face of your little child and say, "Thy will be done," if it is the will of God to take the child? Look upon your estate, that seems trembling, and about to totter and fall. Look upon your property that seems to take to itself wings and fly away. In my boyish days, in just such weather as this, in old Bethlehem, Connecticut, where I studied Latin by hunting pigeons, I have stood and seen among the young and tender leaves, thousands, myriads of pigeons. The trees seemed laden with them. And I see in the city here, rich men, all of whose branches are loaded down with money. At the report of a gun, or the flight of a stone, or a little shout, the pigeons, with a rip and a roar, all rose, and the air was clamorous, as they flew every whither; and in a minute the wood was still, with the exception, perhaps, of the bark of a squirrel. They had taken to themselves wings and flown away. And so the man that yester-day was branch-ful, to-day is branch-less. Everything is stripped from him, and gone. And can you stand in your barrenness and say, "Thy will be done"? Between two there has come the shadow and the darkness, and both hearts sorrow, and both yearn. Can you both say, in the sight of final, everlasting separation— in this world, everlasting—"Thy will be done"? Can you stand in the house of your pride, and say, "Thy will be done"? Is your God such a one that, for the sake of the sweetness in Him, for the sake of the beauty in Him, for the sake of the joy that you have in Him, for the sake of His glorious excellence, you can say of your pride, "God's will be done therein"? Can you say it of your vanity? Can you hush every passion to sleep with the name of God? (*Ibid.*) *God's will, not ours:*—This is the petition with which we have the closest concern. It shows us what ought to be the great aim and end of our lives—that we may be able to do the will of God. After praying to our Father that His name may be hallowed, and that His kingdom may come, we pray that His will may be done; for, unless His will be done, His kingdom cannot come, His name cannot be hallowed. Can a father be said to be honoured by his children while they are disobeying him? Can a king be said to reign over His subjects while they are rebelling against him? At the Fall man set up his own will against God's; and so his will became corrupt and tainted, as everything must become when God's purifying Spirit leaves it. Man set up his own will. This is the great disease and the main evil of our nature. It comes to us from our parents; it shows itself soon after our birth; and the seeds of it continue to lurk, even in the best of men, as long as they remain in the body. Having thus found out the cause of the disorder, we may more easily see how it is to be cured. We must get rid of that cause; we must root out that self-will which is the source of the whole evil. We must take God's will' for our rule and guide, and must endeavour by all the means in our power, by prayer, by meditation, by self-denial, to bring our own will first into complete obedience to God's, and then to make it one with God's. Then there is another portion of God's will which must also be taken into account. I mean that portion of it which is done towards us, and which exercises our patience and our faith, as that portion of it which is to be done by us exercises our obedience and activity. We must sacrifice our wills to the will of God, not merely by doing His will, but by suffering His will, with faith, submission, and contentment. (*A. W. Hare*.)　　*The measure and degree in which God's will ought to be done by us:*—"As it is done in heaven." The measure which Christ lays down for us is always an infinite measure, and the pattern is always a heavenly pattern. As Moses was commanded to make the tabernacle for the children of Israel according to the pattern showed to him in the mount, so we, too, are to frame the tabernacle of our Christian life, and all things belonging thereto, according to the perfect model of heaven. We are to pray and to strive that God's will may be done on earth as it is in heaven; that is, we are to do it as the angels do it. (1) Wholly; (2) readily; (3) cheerfully; (4) out of love to God, for His glory, and not for our own. (*Ibid.*) *The spirit of true resignation :*—As Richard Baxter lay dying, in the midst of exquisite pains which arose from the nature of his disease, he said, " I have a rational patience and a believing patience, though sense would recoil, Lord, when Thou wilt, what Thou wilt, how thou wilt." *Thy will be done on earth, as it is in heaven :*— This petition consists of two parts. I. The matter—" doing of God's will. II. The manner—" as it is in heaven." I. The matter of this petition is, " the doing of God's will " : " Thy will be done." 1. What is meant by the will of God? 2. What do we pray for in these words, " Thy will be done "? We must know God's will before we can do it; knowledge is the eye which must direct the foot of obedience. Knowing God's will may make a man admired, but it is doing God's will makes him blessed. (1) The bare knowledge of God's will is inefficacious; it doth not better the heart. Knowledge alone is like a winter-sun, which hath no heat or influence; it doth not warm the affections, or purify the conscience. (2) Knowing without doing God's will, will make one's case worse. Many a man's knowledge is a torch to light him to hell. Let us set upon this, the doing of God's will, " Thy will be done." 3. Why is the doing of God's will so requisite? (1) Out of equity. God may justly claim a right to our obedience; He is our founder. God is our benefactor; it is but just that, if God give us our allowance, we should give Him our allegiance. (2) The great design of God in the Word is to make us doers of His will. If you tell your children what is your mind, it is not only that they may know your will, but do it. All God's providences are to make us doers of His will. As God makes use of all the seasons of the year for harvest, so all His various providences are to bring on the harvest of obedience. Afflictions are to make us do God's will. (3) By doing the will of God, we evidence sincerity. (4) Doing God's will much propagates the gospel; this is the diamond that sparkles in religion. (5) By doing God's will, we show our love to Christ—" He that hath My commandments and keepeth them, He it is that loveth Me." What greater love to Christ, than to do His will, though it cross our own? " We do not revere the Prince if we hate His laws." It is a vain thing for a man to say he loves Christ's person, when he slights His commands. Not to do God's will on earth is a great evil. It is sinful, foolish, and dangerous. Either we must do God's will, or suffer it. (6) Whatever God wills us to do is for our benefit; behold here self-interest. As if a king commands his subject to dig in a mine of gold, and then gives him all the gold he had digged. God bids us do His will, and this is for our good. (7) To do God's will is our honour. (8) To do God's will on earth makes us like Christ, and akin to Christ. (9) Doing God's will on earth brings peace in life and death. (10) If we are not doers of God's will, we shall be looked upon as contemners of God's will; let God say what He will, yet men will go on in sin. This is to contemn God—" Wherefore do the wicked contemn God?" 4. In what manner are we to do God's will, that we may find acceptance? The manner of doing God's will is the chief thing. The schoolmen say well, " The manner of a thing is as well required as the thing itself." If a man build a house, if he doth it not according to the mind of the owner, he likes it not, but thinks all his charges lost; so if we do not God's will in the right manner, it is not accepted. We must not only do what God appoints, but as God appoints; here lies the very life-blood of religion. So I come to answer this great question, " In what manner are we to do God's will, that we may find acceptance?" (1) We do God's will acceptably when we do duties spiritually—" which worship God in the spirit." To serve God spiritually is to do duties from an inward principle. A crab-tree may bear as well as a pearmain, but it is not so good fruit as the other, because it doth not come from so sweet a root; an unregenerate person may do as much external obedience as a child of God; he may pray as much, hear as much, but his obedience is harsh and sour, because it doth not come from the sweet and pleasant root of grace. The inward principle of obedience is faith; therefore it is called " the obedience of faith." (2) We do God's will acceptably when we prefer His will before all other ; if God wills one thing, and man wills the contrary, we do not obey man's will, but rather God's. (3) We do God's will acceptably when we do God's will as it is done in heaven; that is, as the angels do it. To do God's will as the angels, denotes this much, that we are to resemble them, and make them our pattern. Though we cannot equal the angels in doing God's will, yet we must imitate them. A child cannot write so well as the scrivener, yet he imitates the copy. In particular—(*a*) we do God's will as the angels do it in heaven when we do God's will regularly; we go according to the Divine institutions, not decrees of councils, or traditions. This is to do God's will as the angels: they do it regularly; they do nothing but what is commanded. Angels are not for ceremonies; as there are statute laws in the land which bind, so the Scripture is God's statute law which we must exactly observe. The watch is set by the dial; then our obedience is right when it goes by the sun-dial of the Word. If obedience hath not the Word for its rule, it is not doing God's will, but our own; it is will-worship. There is in many a strange itch after superstition; they love a gaudy religion, and are more for the pomp of worship than the purity. This cannot be pleasing to God, for, as if God were not wise enough to appoint the manner how He will be served, man will be so bold as to prescribe for Him. To thrust human inventions into sacred things is a doing of our will, not God's; and He will say, "Who hath required this at your hand?" (*b*) We do God's will as it is done by the angels in heaven when we do it entirely, without mutilation; we do all God's will. He who is to play upon a lute must strike upon every string, or he spoils all the music. God's commandments may be compared to a ten-stringed lute—we must obey God's will in every command, strike upon every string, or we can make no good melody in religion. The badger hath one foot shorter than the other; hypocrites are shorter in some duties than others. Some will pray, not give alms; hear the Word, not forgive their enemies; receive the sacrament, not make restitution. How can they be holy who are not just? But who is able to do all God's will? Though we cannot do all God's will legally, yet we may evangelically, which is—First: When we mourn that we can do God's will no better; when we fail, we weep. Second: When it is the desire of our soul to do God's whole will. Third: When we endeavour to do the whole will of God. (*c*) We do God's will as it is done in heaven by the angels when we do it sincerely. First: To do God's will out of a pure respect to God's command. Thus the angels do God's will in heaven; God's command is the weight that sets the wheels of their obedience a-going. Second: To do God's will sincerely is to do it with a pure eye to God's glory. (*d*) We do God's will as it is done in heaven by the angels when we do it willingly, without murmuring. The angels love to be employed in God's service; it is the angels' heaven to serve God. "There is no virtue in that to which we are compelled." A pious soul goes to the Word as to a feast, or as one would go with delight to hear music. Not that a truly regenerate person is always in the same cheerful temper of obedience: he may sometimes find an indisposition and weariness of soul; but his weariness is his burden—he is weary of his weariness; he prays, weeps, useth all means to regain that alacrity and freedom in God's service that he was wont to have. Love is as musk among linen, that perfumes it; love perfumes obedience, and makes it go up to heaven as incense. (*e*) We do God's will as the angels in heaven when we do God's will fervently. The angels serve God with fervour and intenseness. Formality starves duty; when we serve God dully and coldly, is this like the angels? Duty without fervency is as a sacrifice without fire; we should ascend to heaven in a fiery chariot of devotion. (*f*) We do God's will as the angels in heaven when we give God the best in every service. The Jews might not offer to the Lord wine that was small or mixed, but the strong wine, to imply that we must offer to God the best, the strongest of our affections. Domitian would not have his image carved in wood or iron, but in gold: God will have the best we have; golden services. (*g*) We do God's will as the angels in heaven when we do it readily, and swiftly. The angels do not dispute or reason the case, but as soon as they have their charge and commission from God, they immediately obey. (*h*) We do God's will as the angels in heaven when we do it constantly. The angels are never weary of doing God's will; they serve God day and night. Constancy crowns obedience. Our obedience must be like the fire of the altar which was continually kept burning. Use 1. Branch 1: See hence our impotency; we have no innate power to do God's will. What need we pray, "Thy will be done," if we have power of ourselves to do it? Branch 2: If we are to do God's will on earth as it is done by the angels in heaven, see then the folly of those who go by a wrong pattern; they do as the most of their neighbours do. We must make the angels our patterns, and not our neighbours. If our neighbours do the devil's will, shall we do so too? If our neighbours go to hell, shall we go thither too for company? Branch 3: See here that which may make us long to be in heaven, then we shall do God's will perfectly as the angels do. Alas, how defective are we in our obedience here! Let us be doers of the will of God—"Thy will be done." First: It is our wisdom to do God's will. Keep and do these statutes, "for this is your wisdom." Second: It is our safety. Hath not misery always attended the doing of our own will, and happiness the doing of God's will? (a) Misery hath always attended the doing of our own will. Our first parents left God's will to fulfil their own, "in eating the forbidden fruit." And what came of it? (b) Happiness hath always attended the doing of God's will. Daniel did God's will contrary to the king's decree; he bowed his knee in prayer to God, and did not God make all Persia bow their knees to Daniel? (c) The way to have our will is to do God's will. You see you lose nothing by doing God's will. This is the way to have your will: let God have His will in being obeyed, and you shall have your will in being saved. 5. How shall we come to do God's will aright? (1) Get sound knowledge; we must know God's will before we can do it. (2) If we would do God's will aright, let us labour for self-denial; unless we deny our own will, we shall never do God's will. God's will and ours are contrary, like the wind and tide, and till we can cross our own will, we shall never fulfil God's. (3) Let us get humble hearts. Pride is the spring of disobedience. (4) Beg grace and strength of God to do His will. If the loadstone draw the iron, it is not hard for the iron to move; if God's Spirit enable, it will not be hard, but rather delightful, to do God's will. II. In this petition, "Thy will be done on earth, as it is in heaven," we pray that we may have grace to submit to God's will patiently in what He inflicts. The text is to be understood as well of suffering God's will as of doing it. 1. What this patient submission to God's will is not. There is something looks like patience which is not, namely, when a man bears a thing because he cannot help it; he takes affliction as his fate and destiny, therefore he endures that quietly which he cannot avoid. This is rather necessity than patience. 2. What is it may stand with patient submission to God's will? (1) A Christian may be sensible of affliction, yet patiently submit to God's will. We are bid to humble ourselves under God's hand, which we cannot do unless we are sensible of it. (2) A Christian may weep under an affliction, yet patiently submit to God's will. God allows tears. Grace makes the heart tender; grief shut up chokes us; weeping gives vent to sorrow. (3) A Christian may complain in his affliction, yet be submissive to God's will—"I cried to the Lord with my voice, I poured out my complaint before Him." 3. What is it that cannot stand with patient submission to God's will? (1) Discontentedness with Providence. Discontent hath a mixture of grief and anger in it, and both these must needs raise a storm of passion in the soul. (2) Murmuring cannot stand with submission to God's will. Murmuring is the height of impatience; it is a kind of mutiny in the soul against God. Murmuring is very evil; it springs—First: From pride: men think they have deserved better at God's hand. Second: Distrust; men believe not that God can make a treacle of poison, bring good out of all their troubles. Men murmur at God's providences, because they distrust His promises. (3) Discomposedness of spirit cannot stand with quiet submission to God's will. To be under a discomposure of mind is as when an army is routed, one runs this way, and another that, the army is put into disorder: so when a Christian is in a hurry of mind his thoughts run up and down distracted, as if he were undone. This cannot stand with patient submission to God's will. (4) Self-apology cannot stand with submission to God's will; instead of being humbled under God's hand, a person justifies himself. 4. What is this patient submission to God's will? (1) In acknowledging God's hand; seeing God in the affliction—"Affliction cometh not forth of the dust." (2) Patient submission to God's will lies in our justifying of God. Patient submission to God's will lies in the accepting of the punishment. This patient submission to God's will in affliction shows a great deal of wisdom and piety. The skill of a pilot is most discerned in a storm, and a Christian's grace in the storm of affliction; and indeed this submission to God's will is most requisite for us while we live here in this lower region. In heaven there will be no need of patience more than there is need of the starlight when the sun shines. In heaven there will be all joy, and what need of patience then? When do we not, as we ought, submit to God's will in our affliction? 1. When we have hard thoughts of God, and our hearts begin to swell against Him. 2. When we are so troubled at our present affliction that we are unfit for duty. 3. We do not submit as we ought to God's will when we labour to break loose from affliction by indirect means. The means for a quiet resignation to God's will in affliction are~~-~~ ~~de~~deration—"In the day of adversity consider." Consideration~~…~~ harp to charm down the evil spirit of frowardness and disco~~…~~ and unsubmissiveness of will to God is very sinful. (1) It is~~…~~ to murmur when God crosseth us in our will shows much~~…~~ quarrel with God's providence, and be unsubmissive to His will,~~…~~ and cause; it ariseth from pride. (3) Quarrelsomeness and~~…~~ God's will is sinful in the concomitants of it. It is joined wit~~…~~ heart. Evil thoughts arise; we think hardly of God, as if F~~…~~ or as if we had deserved better at His hands. Passions begi~~…~~ secretly frets against God. (4) Frowardness and unsubmissiveness to God's will ~~…~~ evil in the effects. It unfits for duty; it is bad sailing in a storm. Unsubmissiveness to God's will is very imprudent. We get nothing by it; it doth not ease us of our burden, but rather makes it heavier. The more the child struggles with the parent, the more it is beaten. The mischief of being unsubmissive to God's will in affliction, it lays a man open to many temptations. To bring our wills to God in affliction doth much honour the gospel; an unsubmissive Christian reproacheth religion, as if it were not able to subdue an unruly spirit. It is weak physic which cannot purge out ill humours; and surely it is a weak gospel if it cannot master our discontent and martyr our wills. We may the more cheerfully surrender our souls to God when we die, when we have surrendered our will to God while we live. The second means to bring our will to God in affliction is to study the will of God. 1. It is a sovereign will; He hath a supreme right and dominion over His creatures. A man may cut his own timber as he will. 2. God's will is a wise will; He knows what is conducive to the good of His people. 3. God's will is a just will—"shall not the Judge of all the earth do right?" 4. God's will is a good and gracious will; it promotes our interest. God's flail shall only thrash off our husks. 5. God's will is an irresistible will; we may oppose it, but we cannot hinder it. The rising of the wave cannot stop the ship when it is in full sail; so the rising up of our will against God cannot stop the execution of His will—"Who hath resisted His will?" Who can stay the chariot of the sun in its full career? The third means to submission to God in affliction is, get a gracious heart; all the rules and helps in the world will do but little good till grace be infused. The bowl must have a good bias, or it will not run according to our desire; so till God puts a new bias of grace into the soul, which inclines the will, it never submits to God. The fourth means to submission to God in affliction is, to get an humble spirit; a proud man will never stoop to God. Fifth means: Get your hearts loosened from things below; be crucified to the world. (*T. Watson.*)   "*Thy will be done in earth, as it is in heaven*":—Observe, then, that there are two ways of doing the Father's will: a right way, as, for instance, it is done in heaven, and a wrong way, as, for instance, it is done on earth. Not but that on earth our Father's will can be, and often is, done in a right way. But the cases, comparatively speaking, are so rare, that we must look elsewhere for our model, even as mariners in mid-ocean take their bearings, not from anything they can see around them, but from the heavenly bodies above them. What we are bidden, then, to pray is this: As Thy will is done in heaven, so, Father, may Thy will be done on earth! And now let us glance at some of the particulars of the way in which our Father's will is done in heaven. And first, our Father's will is done in heaven voluntarily. There are two kinds of loyalty. There is the loyalty of necessity. Such is the loyalty of the material creation. There is not an atom of matter throughout measureless immensity but that obeys God's will instantly, completely, everlastingly. The star nearest the outskirts of creation and the atom nearest earth's centre alike join in an obedience profound and unquestioning. But in all this profound obedience there is no liberty of choice. And this in large measure is the loyalty of earth. For even wicked men, as we have seen, are doing God's will; but they do it reluctantly, in spite of themselves. And this brings us to consider the other kind of loyalty, the loyalty of choice. This is the supreme prerogative of the moral creation as distinguished from the material. Again: Our Father's will is done in heaven consciously. Not always, not even generally, is it thus done on earth. Wicked men, as we have seen, are doing God's will; but they do it unconsciously. Not in way of personal absorption into Deity, as the Buddhist craves, but in way of conscious response, do the angels in heaven do their Father's will. It is their will to do His will. Again: Our Father's will is done in heaven totally, with the whole nature. Alas! it is not so done on earth. Take even the saintliest of His

; with what a partial, fractional heart do they serve Him! Though the is willing, the flesh is weak. In heaven reason, judgment, memory, imagi- n, language, motive, choice, resolve, tendency, activity, obedience, cheerful- ss, humility, gratitude, conscience, faith, hope, love, reverence, worship—every sensibility, every power, the nature as a whole and in each and every part, all, and without alloy, and in every one of the heavenly hosts, blend in a common incense of service and adoration. Again: Our Father's will is done in heaven joyously. Again: Our Father's will is done in heaven universally. Again: Our Father's will is done in heaven concurrently. And to each dweller in heaven is assigned his own part, be it voice or finger, in the ever-varying music of the skies; and each fulfils his own part in perfect time and chime, so that not a note is wanting or super- fluous, not a note dissonant, in the universal choir—archangel and saint, princi- pality and firstborn—all heaven itself, evermore moving in majestic concurrence and beatific melody. Again: Our Father's will is done in heaven uninterruptedly and everlastingly. How irregular and fitful is the obedience of many of God's children on earth! In way of conclusion, let it be observed: One there is who, in the sphere of manhood, has done the Father's will on earth even as the angels do it in heaven. "Then said I, Lo! I am come—in the volume of the book it is written of Me, to do Thy will, O God!" (*G. D. Boardman, D.D.*) "*Thy will be done in earth, as it is in heaven*":—You learn here what it is that makes heaven to be heaven. It is that God's will is done there—perfectly, always, in everything. That is what makes heaven. It makes heaven anywhere, everywhere. It brings heaven into a heart. It brings heaven into a home. It brings heaven into a street, or city, or land. If universal, it would make it to be heaven all the world over. When Garibaldi, the hero of Italy, entered on his career of conquest, or, rather I should say, of emancipation, many parts of Italy were groaning under oppression and tyranny; the prisons were crowded; justice was not to be had; liberty there was none. Ignorance and crime and misery was everywhere to be met with. As he advanced, throwing open the prison doors, giving the people freedom, leaving the way clear for all good influences being brought to bear on them, you might have asked, What makes the difference between one town or province and another lying close beside it, where no such changes had taken place? And you might have been told in answer, "The will of the Liberator, or of his royal Master, is done here!" And the same explains the difference between one heart and another, between the happy and good, and the evil and wretched among men; they are the one or the other, just according as the will of God is done among them, or not. I. A GREAT AUTHORITY—the will of God: "Thy will." If a master and a servant give opposite orders, I do not hesitate to obey the master; and if I am asked the reason, I say, *He* is my authority. At the mills, or any public works, if a foreman were giving certain orders, the workman or mill-girl might point to the printed regulations, signed by the manager, and having the seal of the company attached, and say, "That is my authority, which I may not disre- gard." If a railway servant were asked or bribed to do something that was a violation of rule, he would pull his instructions out of his pocket, and having first pointed to the paragraph that forbade him, he would put his finger on the signa- ture of the manager, and say, "That is my authority; I dare not." Now, I wish you were just as particular in the respect you pay to the authority of God as the mill-worker or railway-man is in his regard to the authority of his manager, deciding everything by the will of God. 1. The will of God is above that of magistrates and kings. 2. The will of God is above that of masters and mis- tresses. 3. The will of God is above that of parents. 4. The will of God is above our own will. II. A HARD LESSON—submission to the will of God: "Thy will be done." I have heard of a lady who, on being visited by a friend, said: "I was just trying to learn the Lord's prayer as you came in." "What," said her friend, "have you never learned the Lord's prayer?" "No," was the reply; "I have just got the length of the third petition, and I find it hard to learn: I cannot say yet, 'Thy will be done!'" It is called, "that good and acceptable and perfect will of God." The hardness lies in us—in our being so sinful and depraved, so ignorant and self-willed. If you were to take a straight rule, wouldn't you find it a hard thing to get a tree that had grown crooked and gnarled to lie alongside of it, so as just to answer to it? Luther got so far as to say, it was not, "*Thy* will be done," but "*My* will be done," so much had God's will become his. There is a godly woman sick unto death. She is asked whether she would live or die. "Which God pleaseth," is her reply. "But if God should refer it to you, which should you choose ?" "Truly if God should refer it to me, I should even refer it to Him again." See that deaf and dumb boy. As the school where he is is being examined, the question is written on a slate, "Why were you born deaf and dumb, while I can hear and speak?" "Never," says the narrator, "shall I forget the look of holy resignation and chastened sorrow which sat on his countenance as he took up the chalk and wrote, "Even so, Father, for so it hath seemed good in Thy sight." There is a Christian officer, well up in years, with an only and beloved son. During a siege, they are sitting together in their tent, when a shot carries off the son's head. What shall the father do? "He immediately arose, first looked down on his headless son, and then, lifting up his eyes to heaven, while the tears rolled down his cheeks, said, ' Thy will be done!'" Faith in God alone can bring us to this. Sight and sense will not suffice. There is a merchant travelling with a considerable amount of money, overtaken by a heavy rain and thoroughly drenched. He is inclined to murmur, and upbraid Him who sent it; but just as he comes to a wood, he gets other thoughts to occupy him, for a robber lies awaiting him, and the next moment the muzzle of a gun is pointed at him, the trigger is drawn, its click is heard, but the gun will not go off, for the rain has drenched the powder; and putting spurs to his horse, the traveller gets back in safety to his wife and family. The rain that he so grumbled at was the means of saving him. How this is to be got at—this submission—I cannot tell better than in the words of one who had his full share of trouble, but was never heard to repine: "I can teach you my secret with great facility; it consists in nothing more than making a right use of my eyes. In whatever state I am, I first of all look up to heaven, and remember that my principal business is to get there; I then look down upon the earth, and call to mind how small a place I shall occupy in it; I then look abroad into the world, and observe what multitudes there are who are in all respects more unhappy than myself. Then I learn where true happiness is placed, where all our cares must end, and what little reason I have to repine or complain." III. A HOLY PRAYER—that God's will may everywhere be supreme: "Thy will be done on earth," &c. Our last remark had reference more especially to the providence of God, this to the commands of God. The one spoke of submission, the other speaks of obedience. For, notice, the prayer is, that the will of the Lord may be done. He has a work and a will to be done, and we and others must be the doers. And then notice, it is "on earth." Many are willing that God's will should be done in heaven, not on earth. "We shall do His will when we get there." Nay, but in earth as in heaven. How can that be? Chiefly in the spirit of it. And how do they serve in heaven? The Word gives us glimpses, from which we may gather—1. That they do the will of God promptly. There is nothing of doubt or uncertainty—nothing of hesitation, or hanging back, or deferring. 2. They do it cheerfully. 3. They do it with all their might. Oh, what a waste of power there is on earth. 4. They do it always, constantly, unweariedly. "They serve Him day and night in His temple." 5. All do it. "Are they not all ministering spirits?" Like the different threads in a loom, all combine to make up the fair fabric with its leaves and flowers, so delicate in colour, and elegant in form, that delights the eye of the onlooker. (*J. H. Wilson, M.A.*) *The will of God performed on earth :*—God's right thus to give law is founded on His original and underived supremacy. The eternity of His existence, the supremacy of His wisdom, power, and goodness, so infinitely above those of all creatures, give Him the throne and make Him the monarch. That it is the perceptive will of God to which this prayer refers, cannot admit of a question. An object obtained cannot be the object of petition. This request cannot relate to God's purpose, because His purpose is accomplished as well on the earth as it is in heaven. "His counsel shall stand, and He will do all His pleasure." But it is not so with His law. His perceptive will is accounted as a strange thing; it is transgressed, abused, and vilified. How then is the will of God done in heaven? 1. The will of God is there done in all its parts. There is no form or modification of holy affection toward God, which does not there exist and is not acted out. Nor are there any violations there of the great law of love to fellow intelligences. There is no murderous hand, or malignant intention; no furious and revengeful passion; no harshness or cruelty; no unkindness, or even inattention and negligence. There are no revolting scenes of impurity, no haunts of licentiousness, and no lascivious eye. There is no lying tongue or covetous desire. 2. The will of God is there obeyed also by all its inhabitants. There is no jar in their society, and no discord in their song. 3. In heaven the will of God is also done with sincerity and cheerfulness. There is no hypocrisy there; no formal sacrifice is offered on that altar. In this low world, true religion is an exotic; an unnatural and unindigenous plant, confined and stinted in its growth, and sometimes a meagre, dwarfish, and ungainly thing. It partakes of the cold soil and cheerlessness of this low earth, never arrives at maturity, and sometimes blooms to fade. But what pencil can paint, or what poetry describe its beauty and fragrance, when transplanted to the skies? No longer some depressed and drooping floweret, it is like Sharon's rose, unfolding its leaves on its native bed. 4. In heaven the will of God is likewise done perfectly and for ever. The flow of holy affections is there constant and resistless, and " clear as crystal "; and their strength and vigour remain for ever unabated. There are no seasons of languor and declension, and no apostasy and backsliding. 5. It is not out of place to submit the remark, that the law of God is no less binding on the earth than it is in heaven. While every man should obey the law of God, merely because it is law, and an expression of His will, it is a right rule to which he is subject. It is as reasonable that the will of God be done on earth, as that it should be done in heaven. Is it reasonable for those immortal princes to obey their sovereign, and is it unreasonable for man? 6. Obedience to God's will would produce a high degree of happiness in the earth as well as in heaven. The foundation on which the happiness of thinking beings rests, is their obedience to the Divine will. 7. Still further: God would be as truly honoured and glorified by the obedience of earth, as He is by the obedience of heaven. He is eminently exalted by the sinless perfection of the heavenly world. 8. Nor is this all. In some respects, God is even more honoured by the obedience of earth, than by the obedience of heaven. The planet on which we dwell is a peculiar world. It has properties and relations altogether peculiar to itself. There are no such expressions of the Divine goodness made to any other world as are made to this. Nowhere does it assume the form of favour to the guilty, except to men. Others have gained the heavenly inheritance by their own righteousness; inhabitants of earth are the purchase of the Saviour's blood, and the reward of His obedience unto death. 9. Mournfully affecting to every Christian mind is the present condition of the Church and the world. 10. Yet, notwithstanding this, does this very prayer suggest a ground of hope. (*G. Spring, D.D.*) *Of the manner of following a perfect pattern :*—How can we do God's will as they do it, seeing they in all points do it most perfectly, and it is impossible for us to attain to such a perfection? 1. In such a manner as they do may we also do God's will, though not in so complete a measure. A candle giveth light in an house, even as the sun doth in the world: in such a manner, not in so great measure. There may be in quality and likeness a comparison betwixt things that are in quantity and measure very unequal. 2. All the saints even on earth have the beginning of that heavenly perfection wrought in them, which beginning the apostle styleth "the first fruits of the Spirit." Now we may be "confident of this very thing, that He who hath begun a good work in us, will perform it until the day of Jesus Christ: that we may be blameless in that day." 3. Our desire and endeavour may and must be beyond our ability, as shall be proved by and by. (*W. Gouge.*) *We are very prone to follow imperfections :*—As a stream where a breach is made will leave the channel to run in that breach, and by striving to run therein will make the breach greater and greater; so we, where we see any defect in the pattern, are ready not only to fail by that defect, but to be far worse. A proselyte made by a Pharisee proved twofold more a child of hell than the Pharisee. We are, by that corruption of nature which is in us, prone to swerve from the pattern which is set before us, even where the pattern itself is good and right. How much more shall we swerve when the pattern is defective? Yet by a perfect pattern we shall be kept the nearer, and held the closer to perfection. (*Ibid.*) *High shooting :*—A man that shooteth at a mark within his reach may shoot short for want of putting out his full strength. (*Ibid.*) What are the particulars for which by virtue of the third petition we ought to pray? 1. Such as concern the petition itself. 2. Such as concern the direction added thereto. To how many heads may the things which concern the petition itself be referred? To four especially. Which are these— 1. The rule itself, in this word "will." 2. The restraint of it, in this particle "Thy." 3. The extent of it, in this phrase "be done." 4. The place where it is to be done, "in earth." What desire we in regard of the rule? 1. Knowledge of God's Word; for in and by God's Word is His will revealed, and knowledge thereof is the ground of true obedience. "Give me understanding," saith the Psalmist, "and I shall keep Thy law: yea, I shall keep it with my whole heart." Desire of obedience without knowledge is very preposterous. An ignorant man's practise is like a blind man's wandering in by-ways. How can it otherwise be, but that such should fall into many dangers? 2. A conformity of our will to God's; or a readiness in our will and heart to yield to whatsoever we shall know to be God's will. 3. Strength of memory to hold fast God's Word, and that in the good directions and sweet consolations, in the precepts and promises thereof. 4. Life of conscience, both to cheer us up in doing the will of God, and also to check us when we swerve from the same, and not to suffer us to be quiet till we turn to it again. 5. Love of God's Word: that our hearts be so set upon it, as we make it our joy and delight. 6. Renovation of our outward parts, that they may be made instruments in their several functions, to execute God's will: that thus as there is a readiness to will, so there may be a performance also. What desire we in regard of the restraint of the fore-named rule in this word "Thy"? 1. A distinct understanding of the excellency and perfection of God's will. 2. A right discerning of the vanity and corruption of the creature's will, especially when it is not agreeable to God's. 3. A denial of our own will. 4. Mortification of the flesh. For "the flesh lusteth against the Spirit, so that we cannot do the things that we would." What desire we in regard of the extent of the fore-named rule? (be done). 1. An accomplishment of whatsoever God hath determined. 2. A contented submission to everything which God bringeth to pass. What desire we in regard of the place here specified for doing the will of God, "in earth"? 1. Grace well to use the time of this mortal life. For the time while we abide on earth is the day wherein we may work, and the time of doing good. 2. Universal subjection to God's will throughout this world. For this indefinite phrase, in earth, showeth that our desire ought to be extended to all that are on the face of the earth. To how many heads may their manner of obedience be reduced? To six especially: which are these that follow :—1. Sincerity. 2. Integrity. 3. Alacrity. 4. Sedulity. 5. Ardency and zeal. 6. Constancy. (*Ibid.*) *Of sins against the manner of doing good :*—What are failings against the direction which we ought to bewail? An evil manner of performing good things; as when they are performed. 1. Hypocritically, in show and appearance only, and not in truth. 2. Partially, or by halves; so far as seemeth good to ourselves, but no further. 3. Grudgingly, as if it were done more by compulsion then by any free disposition of will. 4. Negligently, and carelessly, without heed-taking, or such respect as beseemeth so weighty a matter. 5. Lukewarmly, without any fervour of affections. 6. Inconstantly, as if we repented of that good we had done, and thereupon refuse to hold on therein. (*Ibid.*) *Liberty is clogged with restraint :*—It is a negative freedom, like that which is indulged to prisoners who are allowed the liberty of the prison, to go freely about the house, but may not exceed that circuit (if you can call it a liberty not to wear shackles) or else have leave to walk abroad with their keepers, or be confined to one room, this is such : man is not left indifferent to himself, but still waited on by an abridgment. To speak more properly, man hath such a freedom over his will, as keepers have over lions in their grates, who permit them a kind of liberty : they do not tie them up, but let them walk about in their cells, and can choose, keeping them within those bounds, whether they shall do any hurt ; but it were a dangerous presumption to inlarge them further, as dangerous in their boldness, who dare impute to man the liberty of doing well, or give the latitude and scope to will, which, if it be not bridled and with a strait hand held in, is wilder than the wildest of creatures. Man may rudely cast and project good things, intend and mean towards well, yet all this is but purpose, but pretence, it is not action. He must wait on God for the finishing his good intents. For though he may cast the model, lay the platform of virtue, he cannot raise the work without higher assistance. "Except the Lord build the house," in vain is all other endeavour. (*Archdeacon King.*) *God's will seen in His Word :*—We will here call down our contemplation, and as they that look on the sun reflected in the water, see him more perfectly and more safely than if they should gaze on him in his own sphere wherein he moves; so will we behold the glorious Will of God by reflex in His Word. Thus looking on it, we shall be able to satisfy ourselves in so much as becomes Christians, not over-curious to understand. (*Ibid.*) *A bad copy :*—We must lead our lives in, but not by the world, *Sicut in Cœlis, non sicut in Terrâ*, earth is a bad copy, lame and imperfect. Let beasts make that their object, the level of their thoughts. Man's exalted strait form bids him look up, invites his contemplation to the things above, not the things below. That man degenerates from nature much, from grace more, that proposes unto himself low ignoble patterns. (*Ibid.*) *Knowing God's will not enough :*—It is not enough to know the Bible, or be able to repeat the several volumes of His will, unless a practice be joined to this speculative science of Christianity. Knowledge what to do, and forbearance to do what we know, hastens our condemnation, and adds weight to it. (*Ibid.*)

Ver. 3. **Give us day by day our daily bread.**—*The petition for daily bread :*— Human nature is made up of two parts, soul and body, and the Lord's prayer is so framed as to have direct reference to the wants of both. The petition for " daily bread," while, apparently, it is one of the smallest, is really one of the greatest of them all. It seems small, because—1. We ask for what so many already possess; 2. We ask it only for the small circle around our table; and 3. We ask it only for to-day. It is, nevertheless, a great petition, because—1. We ask that earthly bread may be changed into heavenly. 2. We ask God to feed all those who are in want. 3. We ask Him to supply the daily necessities of a waiting world. 4. We ask it to-day, and ever again to-day. All the blessings of this life, as well as those of the life to come, were forfeited by man's transgression in Eden, and the Almighty has a right to withhold, or to give, just as He sees fit. I. The fact that we thus apply to our Heavenly Father, teaches us our DEPENDENCE UPON HIM. II. A wholesome lesson of CONTENTMENT. III. FRUGALITY AND PATIENT LABOUR. IV. MODERATION. V. BENEVOLENCE. From whence do all good things come? Is not God the Author and Giver of them? Ought not those whom He has blessed with abundance be glad to share it with the children of want and suffering? Aye, can we, with a quiet conscience, offer the prayer, " Give us this day our daily bread," while our ears are deaf to the piteous appeals of the needy? VI. FAITH. The wants of the body are certainly important, but those of the soul are much more so. The petition which we are considering has reference to both. Not only do we implore our Heavenly Father to give us needful supplies of food for our bodily health, but nourishment for the soul. (*J. N. Norton, D.D.*) *Prayer for daily bread:*—I. The order. And that is remarkable upon two accounts. 1. Whereas this petition is placed in the midst, and encompassed about with others that relate unto spiritual blessings; so that, after we have prayed for the glory of God, our Saviour teacheth us to make mention of our temporal wants, and so to pass on again to beg spiritual mercies for our souls : this may instruct us, in the government of our lives, to use worldly comforts as here we pray for them. Spiritual and heavenly things are our greatest concernments, and should be our greatest care. With these we should begin, and with these we should end. 2. It is observable that though we are commanded to seek first the kingdom of God and its righteousness, with a promise that all other earthly things shall be added to us; yet here our Saviour places the petition for temporal blessings before the two petitions we present to God for spiritual blessings. (1) Our Saviour useth this method in His prayer in conformity to the method of Divine Providence towards us, which first gives us life and the necessities of it, and then orders us spiritual and heavenly blessings, as an accession and happy addition to those natural good things He bestows upon us. (2) Because we are usually more sensible of our temporal than of our spiritual wants, our Saviour therefore doth by degrees raise up our desires by the one to the other : for, seeing we are commanded to pray for the supply even of our temporal necessities, which are but trivial in regard to the necessities of our souls ; we cannot but be convinced that we ought to be much more earnest and importunate with God for spiritual mercies than for temporal, by how much our spiritual wants are more important and of vaster consequence than our temporal. II. The petition itself. 1. The matter of this petition, or that which we pray for, and that is bread : Give us our bread. By bread here is meant all temporal and earthly blessings, that contribute either to our being or to our well-being in this life. (1) Temporal mercies and blessings may lawfully be prayed for. (*a*) They are needful for us as the means that God hath appointed for the preservation of our temporal life and being ; in which we have so many opportunities to serve and glorify Him, and so many advantages to secure heaven and glory to our souls. (*b*) As temporal good things are needful for us, so God hath promised to give them to us. (2) They must be prayed for only conditionally ; for they are only conditionally promised. And these conditions are twofold : if they be consistent with God's pleasure, and if they be conducible to our good. Now God is said to give us our daily bread, and all the necessaries of life, especially two ways. (*a*) By producing them and bringing them to us. (*b*) God gives them by blessing them to us. 2. Let us consider the specification of this blessing, or the kind and quality of it, our daily bread. (1) We may pray for the supply of all our natural necessities. (2) Besides things that are naturally necessary, there are things that are civilly necessary; which are not so absolutely imperious as the other, yet these also oblige us to pray for supplies and relief. 3. In the words of this petition are designed our right and propriety to this daily bread : Give us our daily bread.   (1) Now right to a temporal enjoyment is threefold, either natural, or spiritual, or civil.   Natural by creation, spiritual by regeneration, and civil by human and legal constitution.   (2) Now when we pray for our daily bread, we pray—(a) That God would give us the good things of this life, to be obtained by us in a lawful regular manner.   (b) That He would bless and increase those good things that are rightfully our own.   (c) That He would bestow upon us a spiritual right in whatsoever we enjoy, through Jesus Christ, who is the Heir and Possessor of all things. (d) We pray that we may not desire nor covet that which is another's : for we are taught to pray only for that which we may justly call ours, to which we have as well a civil as a spiritual right and title.   4. We have in the words the limitation of the petition in respect of time. " Give us this day our daily bread." And, indeed, there is great reason why we should pray for it this day; for we every day stand in need of relief and supplies from God. Our wants and our troubles grow up thick about us, and unless God make daily provisions for us we shall be overrun by them. Food nourishes but a day, and that which we receive this day will not suffice us to-morrow.   There is a continual spring and fountain of necessities within us ; and, therefore, we must have continual recourse unto God by prayer, that He would daily satisfy and supply our wants as they daily rise up about us.   Again, by teaching us to pray for our temporal comforts this day, our Saviour tacitly intimates to us that we should be content with our daily allowance. It is enough, if we have our *dimensum*, our appointed food for the day.   (*Bishop Hopkins.*)   *Our daily bread :*—" Bread."   Life's commonest necessity, our physical care and craving ; and this most practical of gifts lies in the very middle of Christ's own model prayer for daily use !   And yet there are people who regard the Christian religion as visionary, contemplative, a matter that lies outside the circle of the actual ; a something above, beyond, and apart from the ordinary acts and experiences of life !   Yet here it is ! a thing of the pantry and the pocket, mingled and wrapped up with pardon and paradise.   It is a golden ladder, this religion of Jesus, bright with the vision of angels, and with its top among the stars, and resting hard by the throne of God.   And yet it is set up on earth amid tools and toil, business and bread.   " Give us this day our daily bread."   That cannot be the bread of idleness. It cannot properly be applied to the food which is received in charity, when there is no earthly reason why we should not go forth in manly independence, and earn our own loaf.   The prayer is not—" Give me this day somebody else's bread—give us this day bread anyhow, and from any quarter "; but, give us our bread : that which has fairly and honestly become ours, by the sweat of our own brow, by the honest toil of our own hands.   I remember reading the memoir of some good and successful man, who says, in reference to his first start in the world : " That was a sweet loaf, both crust and crumb, that I bought and paid for out of my first wages." You see, it was *his* daily bread.   Now, what-ever our station, our lot in life may be, let us seek, in this respect, to exhibit true self-respect and self-reliance ; and while we ask our God to give us daily bread, let us ask and strive, too, that it may be ours, not other people's; ours, not our creditors'; ours, not by fraud or wrong, but our own genuine property, which God hath enabled us to win.   But I must point your attention to one word more in this petition : " Give us *our* daily bread."   The model prayer has no exclusiveness. It is a stranger to selfishness.   It is not, " Give me *my* daily bread."   " Our Father " owns our brotherhood, and our brotherhood cares for the wants of others as well as our own ; and we cannot use this prayer aright, cannot hope to win the Father's gracious answer to it, unless we are open-hearted and open-handed to our brother's honest need.   Jesus would that we remember the poor.   The Jews have a capital proverb, " He that prays for another is heard for himself." Let us break our bread to the hungry, so shall our daily bread be sweeter to the palate and come more surely to the hand.   It is said of a certain lad who had listened long to his well-to-do father's prayers for the poor and needy, that after they rose from their knees, the boy appeared moody and silent.   " What are you thinking about, my son ?" said the father, who probably thought his prayers were bearing fruit in the boy. " I was thinking, father, that if I had your corn-bags, I would soon answer your prayers." I am afraid there is a good deal of similar devotion.   Brothers ! when ye pray, say, Give us this day our daily bread !   And do your best among God's poor ones to help to answer your own petitions.   " The bag is full," said a kindly farmer, "though enough has missed the mouth to give the birds a dinner." "Give us this day our daily bread." It breathes absolute dependence. You can't buy. God must give. Strength to gain it, skill to earn it, power to eat it—all are from Him. From Him the soil, the seed, the sun, the harvest. What hast thou that thou hast not received? How long the gifts have come to you! How bountiful they have been and still are! And, once again, before stern winter comes with shivering blast across the bare and empty fields—He hath sent bread enough and to spare. Our Father! May our hearts be filled with gratitude and our lives with praise. (*J. J. Wray.*) *The prayer for our daily bread :*—We are to regard this petition as a request for the supply of bodily needs, but we are not to stop there. It includes a prayer for the instruction of God's Word, which is often compared to food (Job xxiii. 12; Amos viii. 11; 1 Tim. iv. 6); and for the assistance and support of His grace, for strength to do His will, for that Bread which endureth unto everlasting life, which is contrasted by our Lord with the perishing support of the perishing life of earth. I. IT IS A PRAYER OF FAITH. 1. A cry of nature (Psa. civ. 21, 28). 2. By it man acknowledges his Benefactor. (1) While we recognize God as the Giver of all good things, and seek to Him for their supply, we must not ignore the means and channels which He has appointed for their conveyance to us. (2) Nor, again, while we ask God, our heavenly Father, to give us those things that He sees to be needful for us, must we dare to snatch in unlawful or forbidden ways what He does not offer, however imperious may seem to us the need (Deut. viii. 3; Matt. iv. 4). II. THE LESSON OF TRUST AND RESIGNATION follows naturally in thought from the spirit of faith which this prayer inculcates. First, "Thy will be done"; then, if it be in accordance with Thy will, "give us" what to us seems needful. III. CONTENTMENT WITH OUR LOT will naturally flow from this believing regard of God as the Giver of all good, and from resignation to His wise and loving will. 1. We ask for "bread," necessaries, not luxuries. 2. We ask not that our storehouses may be replenished and goods laid up for many years, but for the supply of the need of the coming day (Prov. xxx. 8, 9; 1 Tim. vi. 8; Matt. vi. 34). IV. OUR MUTUAL DEPENDENCE ONE UPON ANOTHER, as well as OUR COMMON DEPENDENCE UPON GOD. *Meum* and *tuum* do not belong to the Christian vocabulary; *Pater noster* is the Christian prayer and rule. We are stewards of God's bounty, which we must use for the common good (1 Cor. xii. 7; Gal. vi. 2; 1 Tim. vi. 17, 18; 1 Peter iv. 10). This rule applies not only to gifts of money, but also to the expenditure of time, of ability, and talent of any kind. (*A. C. A. Hall, M.A.*) *Enjoyment of God's daily mercies :*—I will say here, that if you would enjoy the blessing of daily bread which God gives you, you will do so best by receiving it and recognizing it as a gift from God. Two men go out to their labour until the evening; one reckless of God his Maker, and labouring because he knows he must work or starve; the other goes out, after raising the prayer, "Give us this day our daily bread," to obtain an answer to his prayers in the sweat of his brow, and he toils because that is the way in which it pleases God to give him his daily bread, and he bears in mind who is the giver of it, and he takes it as bread sent to him from heaven, and eats it with thankfulness. Which man will have most enjoyment of God's blessings? I think this last; for indeed, Christian brethren, we miss much of the happiness which may still be had in this world, because we are self-sufficient, and think we are indebted to ourselves for the supply of our wants, and not to God. Daily labour is hallowed, by being the means of supplying that for which we pray; and it is a great thing for us thus to connect our daily work with our prayers; the prayers which a man has offered up before commencing his task of toil in the morning, will shoot a ray of light through the occupations of the day, and tinge them with a glory which nothing else can give. And I would wish you thus to connect your daily life with your prayers; your prayers should be the life of your life, and your actions should be a comment upon your prayers. A man who would enjoy this life, in the way in which it was intended to be enjoyed, ought to look upon it in the spirit of the prayer, "Give us day by day our daily bread"; as a pensioner on God's mercy from day to day and from hour to hour, he will eat his bread with thankfulness, and will recognize in all mercies vouchsafed to him the hand of Him who gives him daily bread, and he will not live as a man separate from God, but as one bound to Him by very near ties. (*Bishop Harvey Goodwin.*) *Lessons on this petition :*—1. Reliance on God's Providence. You must not trust in your strength; you say you earn your bread for yourself, but who gives you strength to labour for it? in this, as in much higher things, "it is God that worketh in you";

a breath from Him and your strength may be laid low, and who will give you
your bread then ? 2. Christian simplicity. We pray for *bread*, and bread only
according to our wants ; what a protest is here against the spirit of the world,
the spirit of ever getting and never being contented ; the spirit which does not
belong to Christ and ought not to belong to His people. 3. The gratitude due
to God for all His manifold favours to us. For if we pray for daily bread for
the time to come, doubtless we must in our hearts give thanks for what we have
already received. 4. When you use the words, " Give us this day our daily bread,"
think how incapable the mere bread of this world is of feeding your souls to
immortality, and how lamentably poor, how poor beyond any beggary which words
can describe, you must be, if having bread to eat and raiment to put on, you have
no food for your souls and no covering to hide you from the wrath of God. (*Ibid.*)
The prayer for bread :—As we repeat this formula with its bread and private
interests deferred to the second leaf, I think it will occur to us sometimes how much
has still to be wrought within us before the order of desires in our heart will conform to the order of desires in this prayer, and before we can sincerely comply with
the requirement of our Lord, " After this manner, therefore, pray ye." So much
for the place which the petition of our text occupies in the prayer. Another of its
features of interest is that it authorizes us to carry our religion into the details and
every-day affairs of life—Give us bread. It singles out a common matter and puts
us in religious relation to it. It lets religion into the interior of life, instead of
putting it upon the margin as an appendix or after-thought. There is no danger
of giving to religion an exaggerated greatness, but there is of giving to it an
isolated greatness—holding it apart, pushing it into the firmament, and making an
inaccessible sun of it, instead of making of it the familiar sun*shine*, enswathing
every little thing with light, lying down among all the valleys, putting a finer life
into every blade of grass, and a beautiful tint on every bead of dew. There is truth
in what an Englishman has said : " We are not to look at religion itself, but at
surrounding things with the help of religion." Our text reminds us that we may
look at so common a thing as bread with the help of religion. Another fact of
which our text reminds us is, that God is the Author and Dispenser of our common
benefits ; that God is personally near us, and that His thought and interest run out
into all our little concerns. " O God, do *Thou* give to us bread ! " This petition
is composed in the spirit with which the whole of Scripture is animated, that
God is personally immanent in all which transpires, and personally sympathetic with
all which needs and suffers. " He watereth the hills from His chambers ; the earth
is satisfied with the fruit of Thy works. He causeth the grass to grow for the
cattle, and herb for the service of man." " Consider the grass, God arrayeth it ;
the lilies, God clotheth them ; the ravens, He feedeth them." Give us this day our
daily bread. All this is full of childlikeness and simple-mindedness. It makes
God's relation to us very immediate, and His goodness to us very direct and personal. It almost lifts us over on to the inner-side of God's mercy-seat, and sets us
almost at the exact spot where God keeps His bounties. It is, I say, a very childlike way of putting the case, " Give us bread to-day." It sounds a little foreign
and strange when uttered by persons of thoughtful and mature years. It sounds
like an echo from out different times and distant generations. Children pray in
that way to-day, but adults do not unless they are praying an inherited prayer
brought in from another age. And it is remarkable that although our Lord's prayer
is so short, room was made in it for the doctrine that in every event of nature God
is the personal agent. That is all involved in the petition of our text. The last
thing we shall notice about this petition is that it teaches us to ask God for one
day's benefits at a time : Give us this day (give us to-day) our daily bread. It looks
as though the petition contemplated quite another condition of things and state of
society from what now exists. Christ and His disciples could appreciate the exact
form of this request. We cannot. It is not easy to pray devoutly for sustenance
that we already have in store. We are not concerned for to-day. Our desires outrun the clock. We pray about to-day, but think about to-morrow and the day after.
We have all we need now, but are afraid we shall not have by and by. No man is
contented with enough ; and yet a man's life consisteth not in the *abundance* of the
things which he possesseth. To be discontented is to desire to find a week's manna
fallen on the morning of each day. " Give us this day our daily bread," then,
means that the Christian policy of life is to receive life's necessities, bear its burdens, meet its temptations, encounter its uncertainties, and endure its griefs one
day at a time, and to depend upon God to make us sufficient for each day's crosses

and emergencies. It is better to go to sleep to-night thanking God for what He has helped us to do to-day than asking Him to help us do as much, and more, to-morrow. " Give us to-day our daily bread,"—there is nothing in the Lord's prayer about to-morrow. It is Christian to feel as the night-traveller does, who knows that the road before his feet will become light just as fast as it is illuminated by the candle which he carries and which moves as he moves. (C. H. Parkhurst, D.D.) *Lessons from the fourth petition :*—1. Let us, as our Lord advises, " seek first the kingdom of God and His righteousness." This, if we will hearken to the Son of God, is our wisdom. Let us hear His counsel and obey His voice ; they that sin against Him wrong their own souls. We may be happy without abundance of the world, nay, without more than enough, more than a sufficiency for ourselves and our families ; and even without so much as that, as all those poor are, who are rich in faith and heirs of the kingdom which God has promised to them that love Him. But we can never be happy without an interest in that kingdom ; we should not if we were possessors of all the world, all the treasures and glory of it. Let us make our spiritual and eternal interest our first care, because it is, without doubt, the most important. Let us apply ourselves to our worldly business, only in subordination to our spiritual concerns. 2. Let none indulge themselves in idle-ness, and expect to be provided for by the labours or the charity of others, when they are able to take care of themselves. 3. On the other hand, let not our hearts be overcharged with the cares of this life. 4. Let us not indulge distrustful thoughts of God's providence ; no, not even when our affairs seem to be in the most discouraging situation. 5. Let such as have but little in the world be satis-fied, if they have enough ; nay, if they have not enough of their own which is the case of many who have a greater interest in God's fatherly love than those who have a larger share of the outward blessings of His providence. 6. Let not such as are in low circumstances envy such as are in possession of a larger share of the good things of the world. As the flower of the grass they pass away. A man that lives by his labour may be as happy as the wealthiest man in the nation. 7. Let such as have plenty of the world willingly contribute towards the support of such as are in want. God has given them a right to daily bread ; let us not withhold from them what God has given them. 8. Let us all labour after an interest in the true riches, a treasure in heaven that faileth not. The world, and all the enjoyments of it are passing away ; but there is an inheritance incorruptible, undefiled, and that never fades ; a world in which all will be rich, sit down with Christ in His throne, in glory, honour, and immortality. What great matter is it, if those who, (through God's peculiar grace) are heirs of that kingdom, if for the little while they are here they have no more than their daily bread? (*John Whitty.*) *The prayer for daily bread :*—I. WE HERE CONFESS OUR DEPENDENCE. A man may be proud of his industry, and economy, and skill ; a nation may exult over their enterprise and energy ; but are not these, or the qualities that win bread, and win it abundantly, themselves gifts of Heaven ? " Is it not He that giveth thee power to get wealth ? " The statesman or political economist who overlooks this palpable truth has little reason to boast of his discernment. All the praise of a man or of a measure—of a political leader, or of a party and its policy—that stops short of God, is like the stolidity of the heathen fisherman represented in Scripture as burning incense to his net and drag. Is it not He, that bestowed all the material constituents of wealth, the ores and gems hid in the recesses of the earth, as well as the harvests reaped from its fields ; and is it not His Providence that discovers to man, in the fitting age and hour, the treasures of Nature, and suggests all the inventions of Art? He who of old guided the flight of the quails over the tents of the chosen tribes in the wilderness, is not He, the same in skill, yet guiding the crowds of the fisher-men's finny spoil, beneath or far aside from their barks? Can the trapper of the Rocky Mountains, or the harpooner of the Pacific Ocean succeed, but as God maintains and guides their chosen prey? The Puritan fathers when they eked out the scanty supplies of their first years with the shell-fish of our coasts, and blessed God for showing them the "treasures," as they beautifully quoted the Scripture, " hid in the sand," were setting a lesson of pious acknowledgment, which their children in our days would do well to remember, when sifting other, and perhaps far more baleful treasures out of the golden sands of California. II. WE HERE PLEDGE OUR SYMPATHY. And how many need this ! Wherever population has become dense, and labour difficult to be obtained, pauperism has grown into a formidable evil. It is in many lands the great question of the times. The gaunt and hollow-eyed clan of the " Wants " are confronting the more sleek, but the less numerous, and the feebler house of the "Haves." Shall the sinewy grasp of Famine's bony hand be laid on the pampered throat of Luxury, and a violent social revolution assay to right for a time the dread inequality? We believe that to the lands which know not or scorn the gospel there are few enemies which they have more cause to fear than this famishing multitude—fierce, unrestrained, and illiterate—a Lazarus without a gospel and without a God, turning wolf-like in the blindness of its misery and its brute strength on a Dives without conscience and without mercy. The poor must be relieved, but not in indolence. The gospel must come in, and by its influence on personal conscience and on individual character, teach the poor self-respect, diligence, and economy and content; and require of the rich sympathy, and compassion, and bounty, for their more necessitous brethren. III. WE HERE PROMISE BY IMPLICATION, CONTENTMENT, AND MODERATION. We ask not from our God luxuries, but necessaries. One of the sins that called down from heaven the terrific bolt of the first French Revolution was that prodigal luxury of the nobility and court, which dared to run to all excesses of riot amid a famishing people, and with a bankrupt exchequer, with the selfish cry: "After us let there come the Deluge." It came for them. Fashion and pride rob charity. When the Egyptian queen, to make a draught of unparalleled costliness, melted a most precious pearl in her goblet; and when in the days of Charles V., a merchant-prince of Germany kindled a fire of cinnamon for his kingly guest; the gem and the wood might well perhaps be spared as far as referred to any immediate use which the poor could have made of them; but if the price of them were so much deducted from what might have fed needy thousands, this destruction of value, for purposes of mere ostentation, cannot certainly be regarded as being just. "Our superfluities," said Howard, "must give place to our brother's necessities." That maxim would replenish every poor fund and mission treasury under the cope of heaven. (*W. R. Williams, D.D.*) *The convenient food:*— This is the first petition that expresses a personal want of the petitioner. We have not thought as yet of our own necessities. Our minds have been led away over the universe of God; we have been made to take in the great purposes of the Divine love and the great attributes of the Divine character; and now with this preparation we come to think of our own personal needs. Plainly, we shall not be quite so selfish, quite so insistent, quite so querulous in our petitioning as we should have been if we had not been lifted up and led forth along these higher paths. 1. Our dependence on Him to whom we pray. For health to earn our daily bread, for wisdom to keep it and use it, we depend upon His Goodness. The habit of connecting our commonest gifts with the great Giver sanctifies and ennobles life. 2. For daily *bread* we are bidden to ask. Plain and simple food. A prayer the epicure would hardly think of offering. 3. *Daily* bread. Sufficient or necessary. Lesson of moderation in wants. We are not to pray for banks; or bins—or barns—or cellars-full, but only for our daily bread. 4. *Our* daily bread. Given to us; yet ours—ours when we have earned it, when by our own labour we have provided it for ourselves. Bread that we beg is not ours; bread that we take as lazy pensioners on some one else's bounty is not ours; bread that we steal is not ours; bread that we get from other people by fraud and extortion and overreaching is not ours; only the bread that we have earned by honest work and fair traffic is ours. 5. There are some who may seem to be absorbed by their circumstances from the duty of offering this prayer. Here is a man whose larders are full, whose cellars are crowded, whose barns are bursting with gathered grain, whose bank account shows a daily balance of many thousands. Is it not a little superfluous for him to say this prayer? No; for the prayer is not, "Give me my daily bread"; nor is it, "Give me and my household our daily bread"; it is "Give us this day our daily bread." It includes all mankind. He who thoughtfully takes these words upon his lips takes at the same time all human wants by sympathy upon his own soul, and craves the outpouring of the infinite bounty upon every needy human brother. (*Washington Gladden, D.D.*) *Prayer for daily bread:*—1. This is the first petition of the prayer in which we ask anything for ourselves, and we have reached the middle of it. The chief anxiety of the Christian should not be for his own good, not even for his spiritual good, but to exalt God. One will make most spiritual progress as he keeps self in the background. The essence of godliness is in becoming God's man. 2. Of the various petitions for our own good, this one alone relates to our secular interests; the others are moral or spiritual aspirations. Evidently our Lord thought it of comparatively little concern how these bodies brought us through the world, if they brought us through with moral safety. They are the rafts on which we cross the narrow time-river; and when the oldest man bends over the map of his eternity that time-river seems less than one of his own silvered hairs fallen upon it. 3. This petition for secular good is a very moderate one. Bread enough—that is all. Why did our Lord never teach us to ask for luxury, landed estates, bank stock, annuities, life insurance, &c. Perhaps He thought how little happiness depends upon these things; that they are more hurtful than helpful to average character; that they load a man with account-ability which he cannot meet unless he keeps growing nobler, more unselfish and spiritual as worldly goods increase—which is quite apt not to be the case. He saw that most people would have enough to do to discharge the ordinary duties of common life; to conquer temptations that spring out of every man's flesh, without adding to the lust of the flesh, the lust of the eye, and the pride of life. 4. Jesus here teaches us that we should have the habit of recognizing God in the commonest blessings of life. 5. Though Jesus chose a commonplace thing to remind us of our dependence upon God, it was not a commonplace thing in the sense of being little or trivial. Bread-Providence is one of the most astounding exercises of God's goodness and power. What marvels in the growth of grain and the chemistry of nutrition—that standing miracle of the connection of food and life! What wonders of local productiveness to meet the emergencies of crowded settlements. Observe the providence of God also in the trade-system of the globe, by which the products of one portion of the earth are enjoyed by the inhabitants of other portions. (*J. M. Ludlow, D.D.*) *Our bread not merely bodily sustenance:*—The prayer of Christian men must differ from the lion's roaring and the raven's crying. The end of their praying is that their bellies may be filled, but we must have as great a care for the food of our *souls*, wherefore we call it "panem nostrum," *our* bread. We do not call it "panem communem," such bread as is common to us with other creatures, but that special bread which is proper to man, who consists not only of body, but of soul and body, which must both be fed. (*Bishop Andrewes.*) *God's gift of bread:*—Does God give us our bread? Is it not a thing that we ought to work for, and not to pray for, unless we really desire to see manna come down out of the heavens again? Bread and earthly blessings generally represent to us human energy, wisdom, and prudence; and it will be a great loss to the world when they cease to do so. But so much the more reason is there that we should pray for bread, for then our prayer really approaches God as He is—a God working through secondary causes in His management of the earthly interests of men. Those first petitions of the Lord's prayer are prayers that a man's soul can appreciate, and to that soul God can and does speak directly. But leave those to stand alone, and we see God as of necessity one who does work at first hand; and that He is not and cannot be. It does not add to God's glory to think of Him as such a one. That throne of His, toward which we look up and pray with all our hearts, "Thy kingdom come," would not be more powerful or more kindly if it were where every commonest hand could touch it. That name of His, which lies close to our secret thoughts, would not be more hallowed if He walked among us, giving us our bread with His own hand. It is more wonderful to think of Him as bringing food to generation after generation through so many various and appro-priate channels. It is kinder to think of Him as one who stimulates His children respecting their powers; showing Himself in a thousand different ways, rather than by bringing supplies in one evident open way. Bread-fruit growing on the trees does not tend to the development of devotional or religious men. The countries in which you find the one do not show you the best specimens of the other. The inhabitants of those tropical lands look up just high enough to see the tree, and are satisfied. But bread brought from the earth by hard labour, eaten in the sweat of the brow, makes the man rise and praise God with all his developed faculties, and say, "Verily Thou art a God that hidest Thyself," and all the more wonderful because of that. (*Arthur Brooks.*) *The best answer to this prayer:*— A man comes and says to you, "Give me bread." It is the easiest way to give him the price of a loaf: it is harder, it is wiser, it is kinder, to find him work, to stimulate his energy, to encourage his flagging spirits, to procure friends for him. Sometimes he is passing through an intermediate wilderness, where he needs a little manna rained down for a time; and you are to imitate your God in doing it. But that is not the rule of working; nor is it God's. And yet, when you had thus set a man upon his feet, you would not for a moment think that you had not answered his cry for bread, or did not deserve his thanks. You would expect them all the more, and they would be more valuable as they came from the lips of an independent man, instead of from the parrot-like phrases of a pauperized human being. So we pray, and the best answer God can give is to make us men. We see its answer in every friend, in every strong thought, virtuous resolution, and energetic impulse. We learn to acknowledge Him everywhere. We trace Him from our table to the sunbeam that on some distant prairies ripened the wheat. He is diffused in all places. He is a God of wonderful resources. He is our God, meeting us at every point, speaking to us of the greatness and happiness of life. The prayer makes us respect ourselves, as we see God thus ready to mingle His power with ours, and to work with us everywhere. (*Ibid.*) *Our bread, not Thine :—* Give us *our* bread, not *Thine.* Let it be ours. It comes from God; our prayer shows that; and, therefore, when prayer has established that relation strongly, we need not be afraid to give that possessive pronoun all its force. Human possessorship is dangerous only when no such prayer is offered. Let the gifts come marked with your own name, speaking of personal responsibility, of personal duty, and God will become glorified more than ever. (*Ibid.*) *Our bread, not mine :—* You do not, you must not, want your neighbour's bread; you must want him to have that. Where is there a chance for dishonesty, where for oppression, when we pray such a prayer as that? No grinding the face of the poor, no withholding their wages, no reliance on their helplessness, when we have prayed that God would give them *their* bread. It is theirs, God gave it them; and we are to see that our hand never keeps back the blessing for which we pray. (*Ibid.*) *Prayer for each day's proper bread :—* There is another expression in the prayer which we must not overlook. In Matthew it reads, "Give us *this day* our daily bread"; in Luke, "Give us *day by day* our daily bread." In both, therefore, is that distributive idea of allotting to each day the proper character and quantity of its bread. For how the days do differ! At one time it is the diminution of supply that is wanted, to abate our pride, to increase our sense of dependence, to chasten and soften us; at another only a full table and prosperity can give us strength and encouragement. We labour on the same, day after day, trying to get all we can, the best and the most. We know not how to regulate our own lives; we are beyond ourselves. Our lives are too delicate for our hands to manage, and so we leave it to God. We can do nothing else, for we cannot see either the poverty or the fever of our blood. Unrequited labour is no contradiction, therefore; unexpected and apparently cruel disappointment is not to seem unaccountable. Neither of them is to make us say, "I will not labour, or I will not enjoy to be happy again." It is right for us to keep the stream of human life full of activity and work. Only He who presides over us, "our Father," knows when and where that flood shall be brought to bear on the machinery of life, so that it shall either produce the greatest results, or just let us have enough, perhaps scarcely enough to live on. In our earliest, simplest prayer, we embody this trust, which it is the work of all life to learn perfectly. We would not leave it out, as we see on every side men making shipwreck of themselves because they think that they know and understand all the wants of their own life. We can only determine to say and use it more constantly, to remember it under disappointment, to rejoice in it in prosperity, to feel sure that the Father alone can feed us with food convenient for us. (*Ibid.*) *Christ and daily bread :—* You cannot separate the external and the internal in life, and therefore you cannot separate Christ and our daily bread. The catechism phrase is, "I desire that God will send us all things that are needful both for our souls and bodies." God's gift to a world calling for bread is not a stone, no dead gift, but the presence of His Son. By that He strengthens us; we take up the old work stronger and better, and our prayer for daily bread is answered every day. (*Ibid.*) *The pilgrim fathers and the drought :—* It is well known that many of the good men who were driven from England to America by persecution, in the seventeenth century, had to endure great privations. A numerous party, who came out about 1620, were for a time supplied with food from England, and from the natives of the western wilderness. But as these resources were uncertain, they began to cultivate the ground. In the spring of 1623 they planted more corn than ever before, but by the time they had done planting their food was spent. They daily prayed, "Give us this day our daily bread"; and, in some way or other, the prayer was always answered. With a single boat and fishing-net they caught bass, and when these failed they dug for clams. In the month of June their hopes of a harvest were nearly blasted by a drought, which withered up the corn, and made the grass look like hay. All expected to perish with hunger. In their distress the pilgrims set apart a day for humiliation and prayer, and continued their worship for eight or nine hours. God heard their prayers, and answered them in a way which excited universal admiration. Although the morning of that day was clear, and the weather very hot and dry during the whole forenoon, yet before night it began to rain, and gentle showers continued to fall for many days, so that the ground became thoroughly soaked, and the drooping corn revived.　　*Daily bread :*—"God always hears when we scrape the bottom of the flour-barrel." So said the child of a poor widow to his mother, one morning, after she had prayed as only the needy can, "Give us this day our daily bread." Beautiful faith of childhood! Why may it not be ours? God always hears the prayers of His children, and He knows when to answer. Our spiritual as well as temporal wants are known to Him, and every sincere cry for help enters His compassionate ear. When we feel entirely our dependence on Him; when our stock of pride and self-confidence is exhausted; when earthly friends and earthly comforts fail us, the humble cry of "O my Father," the oftenest bring the speedy answer, "Here, My child." God always hears when we have reached the depths of need, and cry to Him for help.　　*Routine observance indispensable :*—This is a prayer for each morning—a daily prayer for daily bread, even for this day's bread. To offer this prayer, therefore, as many do, after the day or every repast of the day is finished, is to make it a thing of form, when it is nothing in the fact; which is about the worst dishonour that could any way be done it. Whether Jesus means this prayer to be used every morning or not, He does, at least, give honour and sanction to the daily observance of morning prayer. And it is under His sanction thus given, that I draw out now, for your consideration, this great law of practical Christian living : THAT WE NEED TO KEEP FIXED TIMES, OR APPOINTED ROUNDS OF OBSERVANCE, AS TRULY AS TO BE IN HOLY IMPULSE ; TO HAVE PRESCRIBED PERIODS IN DUTY AS TRULY AS TO HAVE A SPIRIT OF DUTY ; TO BE IN THE DRILL OF OBSERVANCE AS WELL AS IN THE LIBERTY OF FAITH. 1. The argument, commonly stated, as against the obligation of fixed times and ways of observance in religion, contains a fatal oversight. It is very true that mere rounds of observance, however faithfully kept, have in themselves no value; nothing of the substance of piety ; but they have an immense value when kept, and meant to be, as the means of piety. This, in fact, is the very particular blessing of prayer, that when we are averted from it, and slacked in all our inclination toward it, we may still get our fire kindled by it. When we go to it, therefore, by fixed times of observance, we do just what is necessary to beget fixed inclinations, and train the soul into a habit of abiding impulse. 2. Let me ask your attention now to the grand analogies of time and routine movement in the world you live in. What could we do in a world where there are no appointed times, no calculable recurrences, no grand punctualities? Such a world would be really valueless ; we could do nothing with it, and simply because it has no fixed times. And for just this reason God has consented to inaugurate the sublime routine necessary to its uses, determining the times before appointed, and the bounds of our habitation. And so very close does God come to us in this matter of times or of natural routine,· that our hearts beat punctually in it, our breath heaves in it like the panting tides of the ocean, and the body itself, and with it also the mind, is a creature of waking and sleeping, of alternating consciousness and unconsciousness, like the solar day and night of the world. And yet some cannot think it a matter sufficiently dignified to have any prescribed times in religion. Though God Himself is a Being of routine, though the everlasting worlds are bedded in routine, though their very bodies and minds are timed in it, like a watch, or the earth's revolution, still they are jealous of any such thing in religion, and refuse it, as an infringement on their liberty. 3. I refer you again to the analogy of your own courses in other things, and also to the general analogies of business. Which do we suppose to be in the best conditions of comfort, dignity, and good keeping, the savage tribes that have no set times for their meals, or we that feed in the exact routine of the civilized table? What figure of success will any man make in business who has no fixed hours? If, then, there is nothing men do with effect in the world of business, despising the law of times, how does it happen that they can expect, with any better reason, to succeed in the matter of their religion—their graces, charities, and prayers? Wherein does it appear to be absurd, to assume that the soul wants times of feeding as regular, and frequent, and punctual, as the body. 4. Consider the reason of the Sabbath, where it is assumed that men are creatures, religiously speaking, of routine, wanting it as much as they do principles, fixed times as much as liberty. A very considerable part of the value of the Sabbath consists in the drill of its times ; that it comes when we do not ask for it, commands us to stop when we desire to go on, calls us off to worship by a summons astronomically timed, and measured by the revolutions of the world. 5. The Scriptures recognize the value of prescribed times and a fixed routine of duty in other ways more numerous than can be well recounted. Thus in the old religion, the sacrifices, great feasts, &c. The holy men had all their times. If we have no times in religion but such as we take by mere impulse or inclination, we shall fall away at last from all times and all duties. Let any one take the ground, for example, that he will never pray except when he is drawn to it, and he will less and less frequently be drawn. (*H. Bushnell, D.D.*) *Our daily bread:*—The prayer for daily bread need not be a selfish one. It may be the expression of a pure and lofty desire. Our meat and drink and other most common necessities have a noble as well as a mean side. In this selfish world there may be found some men who do not live for self, and by whom the supports and comforts of life are sought and valued only as a means to the better doing of God's will. In their prayers the petition for bread follows naturally, " Thy will be done." The prayer for daily bread is a confession of our dependence upon God. All the prayer in the world, however, will not provide food for the man who is too lazy to work. We are creatures of manifold needs. The phrase, "necessaries of life," includes many other things than those which are required for our physical well-being. The higher part of our nature requires its daily bread. 1. To starve our finer faculties is no more allowable than to starve our bodies. The majority of men and women do not realize what it is to starve the mind. 2. But man is a social as well as an intellectual being. The social nature requires its appropriate food. We cannot be satisfied from ourselves. We require help and sympathy from others, and we require to give help and sympathy to others, as we require our daily bread. 3. But we have deeper wants still, which cannot be satisfied by the hardest work, the largest knowledge, or the dearest love. We have an inward spiritual life which can only be fed in communion with the Divine. We need God. Jesus spoke of Himself as " the Bread of Life." His mission was to feed the Divine life of the world. When we pray " Give us," &c., we pray for the love of God, the grace of Christ, and the fellowship of the Spirit, for faith in an eternal righteousness, for a sense of the unseen things, for earnest aims and holy affections, and immortal hopes, for everything that ministers to the growth and perfection of the spiritual life. (*J. Hunter.*) *Day by day:*—Not bread for to-morrow, but bread for to-day. We need not be anxious about the future. In this world and in all the worlds we are the children of a Father's tenderness and care. (*Ibid.*) *Us, not me:*—The Lord's prayer is the prayer of a family, world-wide, bound together by all the sympathies of a common Fatherhood. We are not separate beings with separate interests, but children at a common table, with common needs. The want of one is the want of all. If we pray the Lord's prayer in the Lord's spirit, we pray that the hungry may be fed, that the ignorant may be taught, that the idle may find work, that the lives of the lonely may be blessed with love, that men everywhere may be in communion with God, and partakers of the spirit of Jesus Christ, and we rise from our knees to live and work as we pray, to help God to give to His children and our brethren their daily bread. (*Ibid.*) *Bread:*—Observe what it is we are to pray for. Not for delicate food, or fine clothes, or a large house ; no, we are to ask for bread. Now what are we to understand by this word bread ? Surely not a crust of bread alone. For this plain reason, that there are other things as needful for our bodies as bread itself. What should we do without clothes to cover us, or a roof to put our heads under at night ? We may be sure that our Saviour did not mean us to disregard such things as these. Therefore, when He tells us to pray for bread, we may reasonably understand that petition as including all things which are really needful for our bodies. (*A. W. Hare.*) *Daily bread:*—A little girl in a wretched attic, whose sick mother had no bread, knelt down by the bedside, and said slowly, " Give us this day our daily bread." Then she went into the street and began to wonder where God kept His bread. She turned around the corner and saw a large well-filled baker's shop. So she entered confidently and said to the baker, " I've come for it." " Come for what ? " " My daily bread," she answered, pointing to the tempting loaves. " I'll take two, if you please—one for mother and one for me." " All right," said the baker, putting them into a bag and giving them to his little customer, who started at once into the street. " Stop, you little rogue ! " he said roughly ; " where's your money ? " " I haven't any," she said, simply. " Haven't any ! " he repeated. " You little thief, what brought you here, then ? " The hard words frightened the little girl, who, bursting into tears said, " Mother is sick, and I am so hungry. In my prayers I said, 'Give us this day our daily bread,' and then I thought God meant me to fetch it, and so I came." The rough but kind-hearted baker was softened by the child's simple tale, and instead of chiding her, said, "You poor dear child! Here, take this to your mother," and filled a large basket full for her. (*Henry T. Williams.*) *Bread the gift of God:*— I by chance let fall a piece of bread; the burgomaster and two peasants rushed forward, and, raising the fragment, placed it on the window-sill: "You have let fall the gift of God," said they. (*One Year in Sweden.*) *Of the fourth petition in the Lord's prayer:*—In this petition there are two things observable. I. The order. II. The matter. I. The order. First we pray "Hallowed be Thy name," before "Give us this day our daily bread." Hence we learn that the glory of God ought to be preferred before our personal concerns. 1. Do we prefer God's glory before our own credit? 2. Do we prefer God's glory before our relations? 3. We must prefer God's glory before estate; gold is but shining dust, God's glory must weigh heavier. 4. We must prefer God's glory before our life—"they loved not their own lives to the death." Who but a soul inflamed in love to God can set God highest on the throne, and prefer Him above all private concerns? II. The second thing in the petition is the matter of it—"Give us this day our daily bread." 1. See our own poverty and indigence; we live all upon alms, and upon free gifts—"Give us this day." 2. Is all a gift? then we are to seek every mercy from God by prayer—"Give us this day." The tree of mercy will not drop its fruit, unless shaken by the hand of prayer. Better starve, than go to the devil for provender. 3. If all be a gift, then it is not a debt. We cannot say to God, as that creditor said, "Pay me that thou owest." 4. If all be a gift, "Give us this day"; then take notice of God's goodness. There is nothing in us can deserve or requite God's kindness; yet such is the sweetness of His nature, He gives us rich provision, and feeds us with the finest of the wheat. Observe three things in God's giving. (1) He is not weary of giving; the springs of mercy are ever running. The honeycomb of God's bounty is still dropping. (2) God delights in giving—"He delighteth in mercy." (3) God gives to His very enemies. Who will send in his provisions to his enemy? The dew drops on the thistle as well as the rose; the dew of God's bounty drops upon the worst. 5. If all be a gift, see then the odious ingratitude of men, who sin against their Giver. How many make a dart of God's mercies, and shoot at Him? He gives them wit, and they serve the devil with it. 6. If God gives us all, let God's giving excite us to thanksgiving; He is the Founder and Donor of all our blessings, let Him have all our acknowledgments. "All the rivers come from the sea, and thither they return again"; all our gifts come from God, and to Him must all our praises return. We are apt to burn incense to our own drag; to attribute all we have to our own second causes. (1) Our own skill and industry. Or—(2) We oft ascribe the praise to second causes, and forget God. First, give. Hence I note—1. That the good things of this life are the gifts of God; He is the Founder and Donor. 2. From this word "give," I note, that it is not unlawful to pray for temporal things; we may pray for daily bread. (1) There is a great difference between our praying for temporal things and spiritual. In praying for spiritual things we must be absolute; but when we pray for temporal things, here our prayers must be limited, we must pray conditionally so far as God sees them good for us. (2) When we pray for things pertaining to this life, we must desire temporal things for spiritual ends; we must desire these things to be as helps in our journey to heaven. If we pray for health, it must be that we may improve this talent of health for God's glory, and may be fitter for His service. If we are to pray for temporal good things, then how much more for spiritual? Some may say, We have an estate already, and what need we pray, "Give us daily bread." Supposing we have a plentiful estate, yet we need make this petition, "Give us daily bread," and that upon a double account. (1) That we may have a blessing upon our food, and all that we enjoy—"I will abundantly bless her provision." "Man shall not live by bread alone." If God should withhold a blessing, what we eat would turn to bad humours, and hasten death. (2) Though we have estates, yet we had need pray, "give," that we may hereby engage God to continue these comforts to us. How many casualties may fall out! Secondly, "us"—"Give us." Why do we pray here in the plural? Why "Give us"? Why is it not said, "Give me"? Spiders work only for themselves but bees work for the good of others; the more excellent anything is, the more it operates for the good of others. The springs refresh others with their crystal streams, the sun enlightens others with its golden beams; the more a Christian is ennobled with grace, the more he besiegeth heaven with his prayers for others. It is matter of comfort to the godly, who are but low in the world, yet they have the prayers of God's people for them; they pray not only for the increase of their faith, but their food, that God will give them "daily bread." The fourth thing in the petition is, "our bread." Why is it called "our bread," when it is not ours, but God's? 1. We must understand it in a qualified sense; it is our bread, being gotten by honest industry. There are two sorts of bread that cannot properly be called our bread—the bread of idleness; the bread of violence. 2. It is called "our bread" by virtue of our title to it. There is a twofold title to bread. (1) A spiritual title; in and by Christ we have a right to the creature, and may call it "our bread." "All things are yours"; by what title? "Ye are Christ's." (2) A civil title, which the law confers on us; to deny men a civil right to their possessions, and make all common, opens the door to anarchy and confusion. See the privilege of believers; they have both a spiritual and a civil right to what they possess; they who can say, "our Father," can say, "our bread." Wicked men, though they have a legal right to what they possess, yet have not a covenant right; they have it by providence, not by promise; with God's leave, not with His love. Wicked men are in God's eye no better than usurpers; all they have, their money and land, is like cloth taken up at the draper's, which is not paid for; but this is the sweet privilege of believers, they can say "our bread "; Christ being theirs, all is theirs. O how sweet is every bit of bread dipped in Christ's blood! The fifth and last thing in this petition is, the thing we pray for, "daily bread." What is meant by bread? Bread here, by a synecdoche, is put for all the temporal blessings of this life, food, fuel, clothing: whatever may serve for necessity or sober delight. Learn to be contented with that allowance God gives us. If we have bread, a competency of these outward things, let us rest satisfied. 1. God can bless a little, "He will bless thy bread and thy water." A blessing puts sweetness into the least morsel of bread, it is like sugar in wine. 2. God, who gives us our allowance, knows what quantity of these outward things is fittest for us; a smaller provision may be fitter for some; bread may be better than dainties; every one cannot bear an high condition, no more than a weak brain can bear heavy wine. 3. In being content with daily bread, that which God carves for us, though it be a lesser piece; much grace is seen in this : all the graces act their part in a contented soul. As the holy ointment was made up of several spices—myrrh, cinnamon, cassia; so, contentment hath in it a mixture of several graces. There is faith, a Christian believes God doth all for the best; and love, which thinks no evil, but takes all God doth in good part; and patience, submitting cheerfully to what God orders wisely. God is much pleased to see so many graces at once sweetly exercised, like so many bright stars shining in a constellation. 4. To be content with daily bread, the allowance God gives, though but sparingly, doth keep us from many temptations, which discontented persons fall into. When the devil sees a person just of Israel's humour, not content with manna, but must have quails, saith Satan, Here is good fishing for me. Satan oft tempts discontented ones to murmuring, and to unlawful means, cozening and defrauding. 5. What a rare and admirable thing is it to be content with daily bread, though it be coarse, and though there be but little of it! What he hath not in the cupboard, he hath in the promise. 6. To make us content with daily bread, though God straitens us in our allowance, think seriously of the danger that is in an high prosperous condition. 7. If God keeps us to a spare diet, if He gives us less temporals, He hath made it up in spirituals; He hath given us the pearl of price and the holy anointing. 8. If you have but daily bread enough to suffice nature, be content. Consider it is not having abundance makes the life always comfortable; it is not a great cage will make the bird sing: a competency may breed contentment, when having more may make one less content; a staff may help the traveller, but a bundle of staves will be a burden to him. A great estate may be like a long trailing garment, more burdensome than useful. Many that have great incomes and revenues have not so much comfort in their lives as some that go to their hard labour. 9. If you have less daily bread, you will have less account to give. The greater revenues the greater reckonings; this may quiet and content us, if we have but little daily bread, our account will be less. 10. You that have but a small competency in these outward things, your provisions are short, yet you may be content to consider how much you look for hereafter. God keeps the best wine till last. (*T. Watson.*)   *Not long prayers :*—A dozen halfpennies look much more valuable than a single shilling. I saw a little girl lately, who began to cry when a sixpence, which she had got, was taken from her; but she thought she had made a wonderfully good exchange, and dried her tears, when, instead of the little sixpence, she got a big penny. And yet, you know how many large pieces of copper or bronze it would take, to equal in value a small piece of silver, and, still more, to be worth a piece of gold. So there are many long prayers which are not worth half so much as some very short ones. There are some, the repetition of which would take a quarter of an hour, of far less value than others that would not take you a quarter of a minute. A big crown piece, or a big copper penny, does not come so far short of the value of a gold guinea, as many long prayers do of the shortest petitions. It is the importance of the things asked, the need for them at the time, and the spirit of the prayers offered, that give them any real value, irrespective of the number of words made use of. *Give us this day our daily bread:*—You will also find the same prayer, in slightly different words, in Luke **x. 3**: "Give us day by day our daily bread." Let me, first of all, even at the risk of virtually repeating what I said at the beginning of a former address, call your attention to the place which this petition occupies in the Lord's prayer. I have seen a gentleman bringing his old mother into a room, leaning upon his arm. He got the best seat for her. He helped her before any one else. "Wouldn't I be unworthy of a son's name and place if I did not consult my mother's wishes before my own, and seek her pleasure above my own, and make what was mine ever second to what was hers?" Just so with God and His children. His will, His honour, His glory—these should ever be first; so that, even before getting the wants of the body supplied, before thinking of their daily bread, they must think of Him. I. This petition teaches the lesson of DEPENDENCE and THANKFULNESS: God the Giver of all good, and we the receivers. That is implied in the opening word, "Give." It acknowledges our dependence on God. II. This petition teaches the lesson of CHARITY—of caring for others as well as for ourselves. It does not say, "Give me *my* bread." I have seen two orphans. The elder, a girl, has her arm clasped round her brother, and as she looks at his pale cheeks, and bare feet, and tattered clothes, all heedless of herself, and only mindful of him, she says, "Have pity on *us*; help *us*; give *us*." That has a power that "give *me*" never would have had. This is a prayer for others. It is a prayer for the family, the father asking the blessing for all his household. III. This petition teaches the lesson of DAILY TRUST IN GOD. "Give us *this* day." When Israel was in the wilderness, we can fancy this prayer to have suited them well, "Give us this day our daily bread." They had no store, and yet they had no fear. How apt we all are to fear for the future, alike in youth and age. I might mention many instances of a more ordinary kind, occurring in common life, all pointing in the direction of trusting in God in any emergency. I prefer, however, to call your attention to one or two well-authenticated instances of a more remarkable, though without pretending at all to be of a miraculous, kind. I dare say many of you are familiar with the history of those Christians in the valleys of Italy, so well known as "the Waldenses," alike for their sufferings for the truth and their unflinching steadfastness. On one occasion they had been driven out from their homes, and when a large number, consisting of many hundreds, returned, what with the assaults of their enemies, and the want of food, their case seemed quite desperate. At this juncture, however, a thaw came on in these stormy regions, and, in the course of a night, the snow had so melted away, that next morning there stood a field of corn ready to be cut, almost as if it had come there by miracle, sustaining these Christian martyrs till other supplies came. During the persecution that raged in France at the time of the Massacre of St. Bartholomew, when so many Protestants perished, a minister, named M. Merlin, chaplain to the good Admiral de Coligny, hid himself in a hay-loft. Here, however, he was in danger of dying from starvation, and would have perished, but that every day a hen came and laid an egg near where he was, which preserved his life! We are told of another witness for the truth—a godly woman, who had great faith in God's providence, that, on being brought before a judge, and condemned for her religion, he tauntingly said to her, "I shall send you to prison, and then how will you be fed?" Her reply was, "If it be my Heavenly Father's will, I shall be fed from your table." And so it was. The wife of the judge, hearing this, was so struck with the woman's steadfastness and faith in God, that she supplied her with all she needed during her imprisonment, and herself found the same Saviour for whom the other suffered. Surely the Lord is worthy to be trusted. An old writer says of the child of God, "What he hath not in the cupboard, he hath in the promise!" IV. This petition teaches the duty of PRAYER FOR ALL COMMON MERCIES. We are told here to pray for "bread"; and bread includes all that is needed for the supply of our bodily wants. And then, "this day," implies that the prayer, as it is needful, so it should be offered every day. One day's food will not do for another, and so one day's prayer will not do for another. V. This petition teaches the lesson of DILIGENCE, HONESTY, and CONTENTMENT—"our bread." 1. It must be earned. 2. It must be honestly come by. Otherwise, you cannot say "our bread." 3. It must be "food convenient for you." You may not get all you would like. You may not get what other people regard as best for you. Look into that cottage, and see the aged saint, whose home it is, sitting at an uncovered table, with a crust of bread and a cup of water. The head is reverently bowed, the face is lighted up with a look of content, and thanks are given before partaking, for "All this, and Christ too!" Not long since, one whom I knew, a tradesman in humble life, was dying of consumption. Those who went about him remarked his contentment and his thankfulness. One day a bunch of grapes was handed in for the invalid, and when this, so much better than the "daily bread," was given, his heart was so full, that the only way in which he could get outlet to what he felt, was by asking his young wife to lock the door, that undisturbed, they might have family worship, in acknowledgment of this gift of God. When a friend of mine went in, a little after, they had just concluded their exercise, and the dying man, holding up the grapes, said, with a beaming face, "This is just like one of the clusters of Eschcol, telling what the promised land will be!" VI. This petition teaches the lesson of MODERATION IN OUR DESIRES—"Our *daily* bread." (*J. H. Wilson, M.A.*) Nor is it the penniless alone who must offer this prayer. The millionaire must offer it not less than the pauper. For, observe how many steps are involved in the obtaining a single loaf of bread. Trace the history of wheat from the day it is sown as grain in the poor man's field to the day it reappears as bread on the rich man's table. Look first at the grain itself. Tiny and simple as a kernel of wheat is, man, although skilful and strong enough to build empires, is not skilful and strong enough to build a solitary wheat-kernel. Each kernel is the product and gift of our Heavenly Father. This is the first step. Again : Wheat cannot grow without soil. And soil man cannot make. True, he can modify its character. But he and all the chemists in the world, sitting in conclave with Liebig at their head, cannot create one of those ingredients, which in their union constitute soil. Soil is the product and gift of our Heavenly Father. This is the second step. Again : The best quality of wheat may be put into the best quality of soil, and yet there be no harvest. Moisture, heat, light, electricity, chemical elements and agencies in most complicated and delicate forms, and these in due order and proportions—all these are indispensable to the sprouting, growing, and ripening of the wheat. And not one of them can man make. He may modify them, indeed; but not one of them can he create. They are the product and gift of our Heavenly Father. This is the third step. Again : The wheat may be cradled and gathered into granaries, and yet there be no bread. Skill is needed to take advantage of the laws of mechanics and of chemistry, to invent the machine that shall thresh and winnow it, and the mill that shall grind it, and the yeast that shall leaven it, and the oven that shall bake it. And skill, although man prides himself on it as though it were his own creation, is the gift of our Heavenly Father. This is the fourth step. Again : The wheat may already be in the form of bread, and yet not find its way to the table. Numerous and complicated laws of finance, laws of demand and supply, of labour and capital, of exchange and circulating medium, intervene between the producer and the consumer. And these laws are as much beyond the power of human alteration as the winds of heaven. True, man may modify their action, as the mariner does the action of the winds when he adjusts his canvas to the breeze. But he can no more create or alter or annihilate them than the mariner can turn an easterly wind into a westerly, or Euroclydon into a zephyr. (*G. D. Boardman, D.D.*) *Dependence for temporal blessings :*—Let us enforce the great principles contained in this request. I. One of these is, THAT FOR THE SUPPLY OF THEIR TEMPORAL WANTS, MEN ARE DEPENDENT ON GOD. When the Saviour puts the petition into our mouths, "Give us this day our daily bread," He not only teaches the abstract doctrine of our dependence, but that we should be in the habit of acknowledging it. Temporal enjoyments are no more the result of chance and contingency than the beautiful and wondrous world in which we dwell. Natural causes may be the means and instruments of their production, but they are not the authors of them. Nature herself teaches us that our insufficiency is absolute, while God's sufficiency is boundless. How many secondary causes, not one of which is under any human control, must be preserved in successful operation in order to secure his daily subsistence to a single individual of the human family! What a delicate and nice adjustment of all the laws of nature, in order to furnish him food to eat and raiment to put on! What a multitude of bodies in the planetary system must be constantly and wisely directed, in order to shelter him from the summer's heat and the winter's cold! To instructions like these we may also add the lessons of personal experience. You began the world poor; and God has not only taken care of you, but given you unexpected prosperity. II. Another principle contained in this request is, that WHAT IS THUS SUPPLIED TO THE CHILDREN OF MEN, IS TO THEM A MERE GRATUITY. It is all of His mercy, and not of our own deserving. Gabriel himself cannot say of the smallest and obscurest gem that adorns his crown that it is of his own procuring. And if man's dependence renders his daily bread God's gift, much more does his sinfulness render it so. As a sinner, he has no right to Divine blessings of any kind. It is not a thought to which the minds of Christian men are strangers, that their daily bread is conveyed to them in channels opened at the Cross. III. There is also another principle of great practical import contained in this request. It strongly inculcates AN IMPLICIT RELIANCE ON THE DIVINE GOODNESS AND BOUNTY FOR ALL THAT WE NEED. It is a great privilege to trust with undisturbed tranquillity on the bountiful providence of our Father who is in heaven. IV. There is yet another great principle involved in this request—it is THAT OUR DESIRES FOR TEMPORAL GOOD SHOULD BE MODERATE. "Give us this day our daily bread." This prayer regulates the amount of our wants, and the measure of our desires. (*G. Spring, D.D.*) *Prayer and pains:*—Although He is the great Giver of all temporal blessings, yet if it be by wisely appointed means and instruments that He gives, the application of these means and instruments is indispensable to the gift. It is so for every gift which God bestows. Men, in the common affairs of human life, never think of acting upon any other principle. 1. In the first place, there is nothing in man's dependence that dispenses with his own industry. The moral virtue of men depends, in no small degree, upon their industry and enterprise. 2. Another of the means, without which we may look in vain for temporal good to God as the Giver, is economy. He who wastes what God gives him, may not complain if He ceases to give. Nature and Providence are constantly reading us this lesson. One law is made to subserve a thousand purposes, and acts everywhere. Nothing is thrown away; nothing lost; nothing but accomplishes its appropriate end. If, then, such is the wise economy in the kingdom of nature; if the most worthless mineral, or the meanest vegetable, when decomposed, is resolved into elements which immediately enter into new combinations, and in other forms assist in carrying on the designs of Providence, surely nothing was given to men to destroy. 3. Nor do we hesitate, in the next place, to specify among the means of temporal prosperity, a sacred regard to the Lord's Day. 4. Another of the means of worldly good is a sacred regard to truth. Truth between man and man is the only solid basis of human intercourse. Without it there can be no confidence in the transactions of business; no order, no happiness in human society. 5. Another means of temporal prosperity is that genuine rectitude and integrity of character which secure honesty in our dealings with one another. 6. One more thought deserves consideration, as connected by the Divine appointment with temporal prosperity—it is a filial, respectful, and dutiful deportment towards parents. "Honour thy father and thy mother, that thy days may be long in the land which the Lord thy God giveth thee." Such are the ordinary means of procuring temporal blessings. Where these are faithfully adopted and pursued, men may consistently pray, "Give us this day our daily bread!" (*Ibid.*) *Foresight:*—Now consider how many movements not under human control are necessary in order to secure the simple bread of a single child in the household of God on earth. Think of the large plans of God's providence which the putting of the loaf on the table implies. The word "providence" means "foresight." To provide is *pro-video*, to "see before." What forethought the Father has had! what a long way He can see ahead! It is well that we have such a Father to think for us and to look ahead for us. I remember a striking passage in the Rev. William Arthur's "Fernley Lecture" which illustrates this truth with much philosophic precision and fulness. I cannot forbear quoting a sentence or two. "Our corn sprouts in direct dependence on a world distant from ours by millions and tens of millions of miles; and whether water or wind drives the mill that grinds the corn, the water runs and the wind blows immediately under the influence of sun and moon, which, so far as we know, have within their own bounds no miller waiting to grind, and no eater asking for bread. This order between sun and fields evidently is not ordained to terminate with the fields; but is aimed at a point farther on, where order must be kept up between them and beings of fragile mould, who can exist only by virtue of complex harmonies being sustained between themselves and the earth and the sun." " He that would if he could, crib and confine all human thought within the human sphere is forced by a question of bread to confess that the wheels which grind for the children of men their corn, are all turning in silence outside of the human sphere," . . . " rolling round in manifest relation with the daily renewed hunger of this needy family of ours." Science teaches that there are sources of supply higher than the clouds. The Saviour here teaches us that the sources of supply are to be referred back beyond the solar system, even to the Father in heaven, who keeps the windmills and water-mills of the universe going, to grind for the children the bread He gives. This is the forethought of the Father, the Father looking ahead. Other instances of this truth might be given. Physical science is showing us with bewildering wealth of illustration that the Father's foresight is infinite, and that the delicate movement and perfect adjustment of sun and earth, of solar system and our corn-sown fields, directly touches the question of our daily bread. The Father's providence carries us back to ages long before this earth-home was ready for the family. He was then laying in stores of coal and mineral for future use. Iron was laid up in the store-house of the earth incalculable ages before man was created; it was put there for man; and without it the vast system of our commerce and civilization could not have existed. There are also our coal-beds. The luxuriant tropical forests of pre-historic ages were engulfed and pressed, and changed by chemical action into coal for our use. You put a piece of coal on the fire; it ignites; combustion takes place; the gases and sunlight escape which were stored up there ages ago. It grew a tree which drank in the sunlight and gases of the atmosphere, and stored them to be released in the bright fire that warms you. Thus the same forethought of the Father gives us fuel that gives us food. Our Heavenly Father provides us with food and firing. The Father laid stores in the earth-home before the family came to live in it. (J. H. Batt.) Bread in answer to prayer :—The value of praying over these matters is seen in times of extremity. As God fed Elijah by means of ravens—birds of a ravenous disposition—so He sometimes in answer to prayer employs instrumentalities of a most unlikely kind to be almoners of His bounty. The following story is told in the Sword and Trowel for January, 1884 :—" Thomas Hownham, who lived in the North of England, a good many years ago, was once reduced to great straits. Having tried in vain to get work, he went out in the moonlight to a spot some way from his cottage, and there poured out his soul in prayer, his wife and children having gone to bed supperless, the little ones crying themselves to sleep. In an hour or two he returned. To his surprise he found inside the door a joint of meat and a half-peck loaf. He woke his wife and children, and they had a hearty meal together. How it came there he could not find out till twelve years after, when a rich but very miserly farmer died. Then a respectable servant who had lived long in his employ spoke of his master as having done one act of charity in the course of his life, though he afterwards regretted it. On the night in question he dreamed three times over that Hownham and his family were starving, and at last it had such an effect on him that he woke his two servants, and sent his man with bread and meat, which he left at the cottage. Next morning he was so vexed with himself at what he had done, that he charged both his servants never to say a word about it as long as he lived, or he would discharge them." (Ibid.) Of praying for temporal blessings :—What are we taught by the mention of bread in this prayer? Temporal things are to be prayed for. 1. These are good things in themselves. 2. They are very needful and useful. Needful (as means sanctified of God) for preserving our being in the world, which, like a lamp, would soon be extinguished if a continual supply of new oil were not added thereto. 3. The want of them is a great hindrance to the work of our calling, to works of charity and piety, and a temptation to injustice. (W. Gouge.) What instruction are we taught by this word " daily "? Our desire must be for no more than is needful for us. What may be accounted needful ? 1. That which very nature requireth, as meat and drink to feed the body, and clothing to keep it warm; without these the body cannot but pine away and perish. 2. That which is meet for the estate wherein God hath set us, as fit instruments for artificers, books for scholars, ammunition for captains and other soldiers. 3. That which is requisite for the charge committed to us. As, if a man have wife and children, that which is meet for them, as well as for himself, may justly be accounted needful. 4. That which is apparently needful for the time to come. Fathers ought to lay up for their children. (*Ibid.*) How doth God give bread, and the things here comprised under it? 1. By causing them to be brought forth. 2. By bringing them to us, so as we may partake of the use of them. Thus saith God to Israel, "I gave her corn, and wine, and oil," &c. (Hos. ii. 8). 3. By giving them a blessing. 4. By sanctifying them to us. (*Ibid.*) What are the particular good things for which, by reason of the fourth petition, thanksgiving is required? 1. Life itself. For every day that is renewed unto us affordeth matter of thanks even for that life which is lent us. 2. Health and strength in that life. 3. Sufficient means to preserve these. This Moses giveth in express charge to Israel, saying, "When thou hast eaten and filled thyself, thou shalt bless the Lord thy God." 4. Recovery of health and strength. For this did Hezekiah (as a perpetual testimony of his thankfulness) indite a psalm of praise, and cause it to be registered for all ages. 5. Good success in our pains. For this doth Abraham's servant give express thanks unto God (Gen. xxiv., 26, 27; xxxi. 5, &c.). 6. The extent of God's providence to our family, and to such as we ought to provide for. Jacob acknowledgeth thus much (Gen. xxxiii. 11, 20). 7. God's bounty extended to the places where we dwell. Sion was the city of David, and in Jerusalem was his habitation; he doth therefore praise the Lord for that peace, plenty, safety, and other like blessings which God had bestowed thereupon. 8. God's providence in keeping away, or removing any evils, as famine, plague, sword, plots and practices of enemies, with the like. 9. The common blessings which God bestoweth on the whole world. The consideration whereof much enlarged David's heart to praise the Lord. What are the duties after which we ought to endeavour by reason of the fourth petition? 1. Diligence in our calling. 2. Good conscience in getting the things that are needful for us. 3. Confidence in God for His blessing. 4. Faith in the Lord Jesus for a right to what we have. 5. Faithfulness in nourishing and cherishing our bodies with that which we have. 6. Temperance in using such things as are most usual and useful for us. 7. Contentment in that which God bestoweth on us. 8. Providence for such as belong to our charge. 9. Liberality to such as need. The extent of this particle "us" reacheth to all of all sorts. 10. Joy in the occasions of rejoicing which others have for God's blessing on their temporal estate. (*Ibid.*) Who may be accounted guilty of neglecting their own welfare? 1. They who care not what they do to their bodies. 2. They who over-rigorously punish their bodies. Many blinded with superstition and besotted with idolatry. 3. They who through too eager a pursuit of what they like, waste their natural vigour, as Esau, who followed his hunting till he was faint. 4. They who by immoderate passion shorten their days. It is taxed as a fault in Rachel, that she refused to be comforted. 5. They who through niggardliness afford not themselves things needful. 6. They who cast themselves into needless dangers. 7. Self-murderers. It is the main scope of this petition to desire preservation of life. (*Ibid.*) *This petition is our first step to earth:*—In the three former we made our ascents and approaches towards heaven; here our devotion flies at a lower pitch, and stoops at the world. By nature's rule, when things are at the highest, they must descend. When the sun hath climbed up to the remotest part of our tropic, and is placed at greatest distance from our hemisphere, he traverses his course, and by another tropic falls nearer to us again. In the three first petitions we were nearer the sun, nearer that place where the throne of God is fixed, and the sun of righteousness moves, heaven. Here we, as it were, cut the line, are in a new climate; the two globes of earth and heaven here divide themselves, this being the first side of the terrestrial. (*Archdeacon King.*) *Rescued from the curse:*—When Adam forfeited his obedience, and shut God out of his heart, the ear of God and the bounty of nature were at once barred against him; for at first the earth wore her commodities in her forehead, visible and eminent; but after man's fall, she, by God's command, called in her blessings, concealed her fruits, and instead of that plenty wherein once she was apparelled, now only wears that barren attire which God's curse cast upon her—thorns and thistles—from which curse nothing can rescue or redeem her but prayer and labour; prayer to open the ear of God, and labour to open the earth and search for those riches which lie hid within her bosom. (*Ibid.*) *Love before bread:*—We see in the common practice that till the custom be paid the trade is not free or open; so whilst the firstfruits, which are God's custom, rest unpaid, we cannot expect a profitable traffic with Him, or success in our own affairs. The story tells us that when Jacob, pressed by the famine which reigned in the land, sent to Egypt for victuals, he considered the dignity of the governor before his own necessity, and honoured him with a present, the best he could provide, before he asked for corn. We were not true Israelites if we more regarded meats and drinks than to do the will of God, or preferred *panem quotidianum*, " our daily bread," before the hallowing of His Name. Certainly to begin with God is a fair introduction to all other blessings. *Daily bread :*—A large provision for so short a voyage as life is a perplexity, not a help; and a burthen, not a supply. (*Ibid.*) *Our daily bread:*— As no part of the body was made only for itself, so no man. We are all one body, whereof Christ is head, and therefore one another's members. As we are all parts of that mystical body, so are we also of a political. Of which body, as the King is the head, and the counsellors the brain, so the rich man is the stomach that receives the good of the land. Now as the stomach receives the meat not to retain it still there, but to disperse it into all the parts of the body, which must be fed by that nourishment, so have rich men their wealth not to hoard up, but to disperse amongst the needy ; for *dispersit, dedit pauperibus*, is the rich man's office and commendation too. Do but observe how God waters the earth by several veins and channels. Shall the channel say to the dry ground, I will retain my waters, and shut up my banks from relieving your barrenness ? when the channel is but the conveyance of that blessing to the world. God oftimes reaches unto us His benefits by other's hands. He hath made the rich His almoner, his hand to contribute unto the necessities of his brethren ; for *per eum qui habet juvat egentem, per eum qui non habet probat habentem.* If then he be of such a cruel retention to close and shut up himself against the poor, he resists the ordinance of God, by withholding that good which He intended to convey to others by him. Christ teaches us to say " Our bread " and " Give us." (*Ibid.*) *This day :*—As it is the date of the petition, so must it also be the date of our solicitude. From whence I shall only raise these short lessons, and so end. First, we must know that our care of temporal blessings ought not to be prolonged so far as either to impede devotion or make life tedious. Care is a useless companion to Christians. (*Ibid.*) *A motive to quicken our piety, and invite us to a continual exercise of prayer :*—Do not thou, like a fortified town, because thou art victualled for many months, presume upon thy strength, or stand upon thy own guard, as if thou couldst hold out a siege against all necessities, like the rich man in the gospel, who, having filled his barns and storehouses, bid his soul rest securely in the confidence of his wealth. Know that God, with one fit of an ague, can shake thy strongest fortification, that He can cut off thy supplies, and break thy staff of bread, as He did Israel's, and by the battery of one hot disease even in a night's skirmish beat thy soul out of her frail citadel. Think it not enough to come to church upon Sundays, or serve God once a week, and forget Him till the next Sabbath's " All in " awake thee. As it was a constant daily sacrifice which the priest offered in the old law, so must thou offer up to God a sacrifice of prayer for the sanctification of this day, and each present day unto thee. Now as thou must not discontinue God's service, so neither must thou anticipate putting two days' devotions into one, or think to serve God so long at once as will serve for thrice. (*Ibid.*) *Every day :*—Let us not still look downward, lingering after the bread or the temporal benefits of this life, as Israel did after the fleshpots of Egypt; but address ourselves for a new voyage, remembering that when our strength and stomach shall fail, when age shall cast a general numbness over us, when this our bread shall grow insipid, and our palate tasteless, there is a new table and another kind of bread provided for us in the kingdom of Christ. Instead of this *panis quotidianus*, " our daily bread," *panis crastinus* (for so Saint Hierome writes that some Hebrews translated this place), a " future bread," which we shall eat the morrow after this world's day concludes. Such bread, which, when we have once tasted, will leave no more hunger to succeed it ; and such a morrow which shall have no new day apparent to inherit that light which died the evening before. For this life's *hodie*, which we call " to-day," shall be turned into a *quotidie*, " every day," in the next, but without difference, or vicissitude, or alteration. (*Ibid.*)

Ver. 4. And forgive us our sins.—*On the forgiveness of sin :*—I. THAT OUR SINS ARE OUR DEBTS. 1. How we come to be in debt to God, how this debt is contracted, and what is the ground of the action. That I may keep to the comparison, not forcing it, but fairly following it, you shall see that we fairly run in debt to God, as the children of men run in debt to one another. (1) We are in debt to God, as a servant is indebted to his master, when he has neglected his business, and wasted or embezzled his goods. (2) We are indebted to God, as a tenant is indebted to his landlord, when he is behind of his rent, or has committed waste upon the premises. (3) We are indebted to God, as a borrower is indebted to the lender. (4) Our debt to God is, as the debt of a trespasser to him upon whom he has trespassed. (5) Our debt to God is, as the debt of a covenant breaker, who entered into articles, and gave bond for performance, but has not made good his agreement, and so has forfeited the penalty of the bond, which is recoverable as far as the damage goes, by the non-performance of the articles. (6) Our debt to God is, as the debt of a malefactor, to the law and to the government, when he is found guilty of treason or felony, and consequently the law is to have its course against him. As the corruption of our nature makes us odious to God's holiness, so our many actual transgressions make us obnoxious to His justice ; and thus we are debtors to Him. (7) To make the matter yet worse, there is a debt we owe to God, which is as a debt of an heir-at-law upon his ancestor's account, of a son who is liable for his father's debts, as far as what he has by descent will go, and as far as he has any assets in his hand. (8) There are debts of ours, likewise, which are as the debt of a surety upon account of the principal. I mean the guilt we have contracted by our partaking of other men's sins. 2. Having opened to you the several ways how we come into this debt to God, let us next inquire what kind of debt sin is. (1) It is an old debt, it is an early, nay, it is an hereditary, encumbrance upon our nature. The foundation of this debt was laid in Adam's sin, we are in debt for the forbidden fruit he ate, so high does the account begin, and so far back does it look. (2) It is a just debt, and the demand of it highly equitable. (3) It is a great debt, more than we imagine. (4) It is a growing debt ; a debt we are still adding to, as a tenant who is behind of his rent, every rent-stage makes the debt more ; till we return by repentance, we are still running further upon the score ; still taking up upon trust, and treasuring up unto ourselves guilt and wrath against the day of wrath. 3. Having seen what kind of debt sin is, let us next see what kind of debtors sinners commonly are ; and we shall find them like other unfortunate debtors, that are going down in the world, and have no way to help themselves. (1) Bad debtors are oftentimes very careless and unconcerned about their debts ; when they are so embarrassed and plunged that they cannot bear the thought of it, they contrive how to banish the thought of it, and live merry and secure ; to laugh away, and drink away, and revel away the care and sorrow of it. Thus sinners deal with their convictions, they divert them with the business of the world, or drown them in the pleasures of sense. (2) Bad debtors are commonly very wasteful, and when they find they are in debt more than they can pay, care not how much further they run into debt. How extravagant are sinners in spending upon their lusts ! (3) Bad debtors are commonly very shy of their creditors, and very loth to come to an account. Thus sinners care not how little they come into the presence of God, but rather say to the Almighty, " Depart from us." (4) Bad debtors are sometimes timorous ; and though they strive to cast off all care about their debts, yet, when they are threatened, their hearts fail them, they are subject to frights, and are ready to think every one they meet is a bailiff. Thus sinners carry about with them a misgiving conscience, which often reproaches them, and fills them with secret terrors, and a bitterness which their own heart only knows. (5) Bad debtors are apt to be dilatory and deceitful, to promise payment this time and the other, but still to break their word, and beg a further delay. It is so with sinners ; they do not say they will never repent, and return to God, but not yet. 4. To affect you the more with the misery of an impenitent, unpardoned state, having showed you what your debt is, I shall next lay before you the danger we are in by reason of this debt. Many who owe a great deal of money, yet are furnished with considerations sufficient to make them easy, but they are such as our case will not admit. (1) An exact account is kept of all our debts. (2) We are utterly insolvent, and have not wherewithal to pay our debts. (3) We have no friend on earth who can or will pass his word for us, or be our bail. (4) We are often put in mind of our debts by the providence of God, and by our own consciences. (5) Death will shortly arrest us for these debts, to bring us to an account. (6) A day of reckoning will come, and the day is fixed. (7) Hell is the prison into which those debtors will at length be cast, who took no care to make their peace, and there are the tormentors to which they will be delivered. II. The sins we are to repent of, being our debts to God, THE MERCY WE ARE TO PRAY FOR IS THE FORGIVE-NESS OF THESE DEBTS. 1. Let us inquire what is included in this mercy of the forgiveness of sin as a debt, and what steps God graciously takes therein toward us, when we repent, and return, and believe the gospel. He acts as a merciful and compassionate creditor toward a poor debtor who lies at his mercy. (1) He stays process, and suffers not the law to have its course. Judgment is given against us; but execution is not taken out upon the judgment. (2) He cancels the bond, vacates the judgment, and disannuls the handwriting that was against us. (3) He gives an acquittance, and delivers it by His Spirit into the believer's hand, speaking peace to him, filling him with comfort, arising from a sense of His justification, and the blessed tokens and pledges of it. (4) He condescends to deal with us again, and to admit us into covenant and communion with Himself. 2. Having seen how much is included in God's forgiving us our debts, because it is so great a favour, that we may be tempted to think it too much for such worthless unworthy creatures as we are to expect, let us next inquire what ground we have to hope for it? How is it that a God infinitely just and holy should be thus readily reconciled to a guilty and polluted sinner upon his repenting? (1) We may ground our expectations upon the goodness of His nature. (2) We are to ground our expectations upon the mediation of our Lord Jesus. 3. What is expected and required from you, that you may obtain this favour, and that your debts may be forgiven? Christ, as a surety for us, has made satisfaction; but what must we do that we may have an interest in that satisfaction? (1) We must confess the debt, with a humble, lowly, penitent, and obedient heart. (2) We must acknowledge a judgment of all we have to our Lord Jesus, who has been thus kind to satisfy for our debt. This is one proper act of faith. (3) We must give to Christ the honour of our pardon, by relying entirely on His righteousness as our plea for it; acknowledging that other foundation of hope can no man lay, and other fountain of joy can no man open. (4) We must study what we shall render to Him who has loved us, who has so loved us. (5) We must engage ourselves for the future, that we will render to God the things that are His, and be careful not to run in debt again. (6) Our forgiving others is made the indispensable condition of our being forgiven of God. Concluding exhortations: 1. Do not delay to come to an account with your own consciences, but search diligently and impartially, that you may see how matters stand between you and God. 2. Be thoroughly convinced of your misery and danger by reason of sin; see process ready to be taken out against you, and consider what is to be done. 3. Agree with your adversary quickly, while you are in the way with him; make your peace with God, and do it with all speed. You need not send to desire conditions of peace; they are offered to you, if you will but accept of them; and they are not only easy but very advantageous. 4. In order to the making of your peace with God, make sure your interest in Jesus Christ, and make use of Him daily for that purpose: retain Him of counsel for you in this great cause on which your all depends, and let Him be not only your plea but your pleader, for that is His office. 5. Renew your repentance every day for your sins of daily infirmity, and be earnest with God in prayer for the pardon of them. Lastly, let those to whom much is forgiven, love much. (*Matthew Henry.*) *The forgiveness of sins:*—I. Notice the connection and dependence. Having prayed for our daily bread, we are next taught to pray for pardon. And this method is, indeed, most wise and most rational. For—1. The guilt of sin many times withholds from us those earthly comforts we stand in need of. 2. Without pardon of sin, all our temporal enjoyments are but snares and curses unto us. II. The words themselves. 1. The petition. (1) What our evangelist calls sins, St. Matthew calls debts. We stand indebted to God, both as we are His creatures, and as we are offenders. By the one, we owe Him the debt of obedience; and, by the other, the debt of punishment. (2) Now here to excite thee to a fervency in praying for the forgiveness of thy debts, consider—(*a*) The infinite multitudes of thy debts. (*b*) That God, who is thy creditor, is strict and impartial. (*c*) That the least of all these thy debts makes thee liable to be cast into the prison of hell, and to be adjudged to eternal death and punishments. (*d*) Consider, thou canst never pay God, nor discharge the least of thy debts for ever. (3) And, now that I have showed you our misery by reason of our debts, and you have seen the black side of the cloud which interposeth between God and us, so give me leave to represent to you our hopes and consolation, in God's free grace and the Divine mercy in dissolving this black cloud, that it may never more appear. And here let us—(*a*) Consider what the pardon of sin is. (*b*) The pardoning grace of God, in respect of us, is altogether free and undeserved. (*c*) The pardoning grace of God is not free, in respect of Christ; but it cost Him the price of blood. Let us consider unto whom this petition for pardon is directed. And that is, as all the rest are, **to** our Father, whose laws we have violated, whose justice we have offended, whose displeasure we have incurred, and to whose vengeance we have made ourselves liable and obnoxious, to Him we sue for pardon and remission. Hence we may collect this note: That it is the high prerogative of God alone to forgive sins. If, then, it be the prerogative of God alone to pardon sin, hence we may, for our abundant comfort, be informed—(a) That our pardon is free and gratuitous. (b) It is God that pardons, therefore our pardon is full and complete. (c) Is it God that pardons? Then, for thy comfort, know that He can as easily forgive great and many sins, as few and small. (4) Now, in this petition we pray not only for the pardon of sin, but likewise for all things that are antecedently necessary to obtain it. As—(a) We pray that God would discover to us the horrid odious nature of sin. (b) We pray that God would humble us under the sight and sense of our manifold transgressions; that, as our sins have made us vile in God's eyes, so they may make us vile in our own, to loath ourselves in dust and ashes for them. (c) We pray that God would give us His Spirit, to enable us to confess our sins cordially, and sincerely to pour forth our hearts before Him, and to acknowledge our manifold provocations with shame and godly sorrow, upon which God promised to grant us pardon and forgiveness. (d) We beg a more clear understanding of the sacrifice and atonement made by Jesus Christ, through which alone all pardon is purchased and procured; to know both what it is and why ordained; and, likewise, the knowledge of God's rich and free mercy; and the conjunction of this sacrifice and mercy together, in the great mystery of the freeness of Divine grace, and the satisfaction of Jesus concurring to the remission of our sins and the salvation of our souls. (e) We pray that we may have a high esteem of Christ, and may hunger and thirst more after Him and His righteousness, through whom alone pardon of our sins is to be obtained. (f) We pray that we may be brought over to close with the Lord Jesus Christ by a lively faith; that His righteousness thereby may be made ours, and we, by that righteousness, may obtain pardon of our sins, and an inheritance among them that are sanctified. 2. The condition or plea annexed to this petition. (1) The act: forgive. (2) The object: debtors. (3) The limitation of this object: our debtors. (4) The proportion or resemblance, in particle "as." Our forgiving of others must have these qualifications—(a) It must be unfeigned and cordial from thy very heart and soul; for so thou wouldst have God forgive thee. (b) Thou art obliged likewise to forgive freely, without any recompense or satisfaction from others. (c) We must forgive others fully and completely; for God doth so. (*Bp. Hopkins.*) *The forgiveness of sins:*—I. SINS ARE TRESPASSES AGAINST GOD. 1. Against the perfections of God. 2. Against the authority of God. 3. Against the express commandments of God. 4. Against the counsels and exhortations of God. 5. Against His warnings and threatenings. 6. Against His grace revealed to us in the gospel. 7. Against His patience. II. GOD IS WILLING TO FORGIVE US THOSE TRESPASSES, though very great, and daily repeated. This we may conclude— 1. From God's natural goodness and love to mankind. 2. From the declarations He has made of Himself, His mercifulness, and unwillingness that any should perish. 3. From His express promises. 4. From examples of His wonderful mercy recorded in the Scripture, for the encouragement of all truly humble penitents, though their guilt may be exceeding great, and they may have been sinners above others. 5. From the covenant made with Christ the Redeemer, that He should see the fruit of the travail of His soul, and justify many by bearing their iniquities. And as Christ the Redeemer was faithful to Him that appointed Him, and bare our sins, according to the counsel and command of the Father; so the Father will be fathful to Him: and whosoever believeth on Him shall be justified from all things, and shall never come into condemnation, never perish, but have everlasting life. III. QUALIFICATION OR DISPOSITIONS which must be found in all such as receive the forgiveness of sin. 1. In order to the forgiveness of sin, there must be repentance towards God, a confession of sin, and forsaking it; otherwise we have no ground (from anything that is written in the Scripture) to hope for mercy. 2. God requires, in order to a reconciliation, that we must believe in His Son whom He hath sent. 3. Our Saviour here mentions our forgiving those that trespass against us, as a qualification or disposition necessary to be found in us who hope to receive the forgiving grace of God to ourselves for our trespasses against Him: "Forgive us our debts, as we forgive our debtors." Practical reflections: 1. Let us seriously consider and admire the condescension and goodness of God, in proposing to be reconciled to us, when He can gain nothing by such a reconciliation, but all the advantage is ours. 2. Let us pray for the forgiveness of our daily trespasses. 3. If we would receive the remission of sin, let us pray, and labour, that we may have those dispositions which are found in all such as receive a pardon from God. (1) Let us labour to obtain, and pray earnestly to God for true repentance, a deep humiliation and godly sorrow for sin. (2) Let us pray for that great and absolutely necessary qualification for pardoning grace, faith in Christ Jesus; true, sincere, evangelical, justifying faith, by which we may be united to Christ, and made partakers of Him and His righteousness. (3) Let us forgive those that trespass against us; not seeking revenge; entertaining in our hearts no malice against them; doing them no harm, nor wishing them any; praying for them, and willing to serve them, and to do them good. Now, to close all—(4) Let us bless God for Jesus Christ, through whose blood we receive the forgiveness of sins; convinced and assured, that without an interest in Him, the wrath of God abideth on us, and will to eternity. (*John Whitty*.) *Unwillingness to acknowledge guilt :*—If left to our own proud blindness, how loth are we to acknowledge our guiltiness before God, and to sue in His courts for the boon of pardon, in the deep sense of our spiritual poverty and moral unworthiness. There was, in the early ages of the Christian era, a lying magician and philosopher, Apollonius of Tyanea, whom some of the ancients tried to set up as a rival, in wisdom and might and miracles, with our blessed Saviour. One of the speeches attributed to this Apollonius by his biographer is, " O ye gods, give me my dues." Instead of holding himself indebted to heaven, he regarded heaven as debtor to him, for what he supposed his blamelessness and eminent virtue. There bleated out the proud and impious folly of the unrenewed heart. But, as Coleridge beautifully said, in the later and more Christian years of his life, the men who talk of earning heaven by their own merits, might better begin by earning earth. Who of us really has deserved what he is daily enjoying of good, even chequered as that good may be, in this sublunary state, with mingling sorrow and joy? But, surely, in our more sober and meditative hours, even the unregenerate feel, more or less distinctly, their own guiltiness. This it is that makes solitude dreadful, and diversion so necessary, in order to kill time and drown thought. This it is that clothes death with terrors, and renders the image of a God—holy and the hater of sin—so irksome and formidable an idea to us. But how do men strive to lessen this irksome, yet inevitable, consciousness, by vain pleas and extenuations and criminations of their fellows, as these last have been their tempters, abettors, and accomplices. How do they seek to obliterate the record against them by flattering, and at times by bribing heaven. But can our richest gifts buy the All-rich, and our most lavish flatteries cheat the All-wise God? How can such a God be appeased, so that He shall efface the record of our moral indebtedness? We must recognize and confess our sin. And the devout mind, after every preceding petition in the Lord's prayer, prepares to drop in the utterance of the petition now before us, as into the dust of lowliest self-abasement. Is He our Father? this fatherhood has been spurned by His ingrate children. Is He in heaven, our native home and our proper end? We have lived as if we had sprung from earth and were ripening only for hell. His name, dread and pure, is it worthy, always and by all, to be hallowed? How have our daring levity and defiance profaned it; and trailed its sacred honours, as in the mire of our scorn and our filth ; and hung what is the dread blazonry of heaven over deeds and tempers sprung of the pit. Is His kingdom to be hailed and extended? How have we played, toward its glories and authority, the part of the rebel and the traitor. Is His will deserving of all obedience and study and conformity? How have we preferred to it our own will, and the will of the murderer and deceiver, Satan. Gives He still, kind and long-suffering, our daily bread? How have we "crammed and blasphemed our Feeder"! To subdue this sin, will it be sufficient to secure forgiveness for the past? Not—unless we staunch the fountain of evil, and provide against its out-gushings for the future. To this later work the succeeding petitions of the prayer refer. When Jesus came down to meet our debt, and to justify us by His righteousness and death, He also made provision and purchase of the Holy Spirit to renew and to sanctify. (*W. R. Williams, D.D.*) *The test of our spiritual state :*—God calls us to a daily and domestic scrutiny. We do not show a forgiving and generous spirit, in order that thus we may earn heaven ; but we are warned that the indulgence of a contrary spirit necessarily forfeits heaven. We test our spiritual condition, not by asking how our feelings are towards the dead—to our best friends—or towards angels. The Pharisees could praise dead saints, and canonise prophets, when once safe and mute in their graves. But we ask, What are my feelings towards the living prophets and witnesses of heaven—to my living neighbour, and rival, and enemy? When our Saviour healed the sick man of his long and sore infirmity, and bade him take up his bed and walk; the poor man's lifting of his couch and flinging its light weight on his rejoicing shoulders, was not the means of his cure, or the condition of his healing. It was the evidence, tangible and visible to himself and others, in the streets along which he passed, and in the home he re-entered, that he had encountered a great Prophet, and had received a miraculous healing. And so, when the leper, purged of his leprosy, was bidden to go and show himself to the priest, as he bared the skin now clear and white to the glance of the Levite, he was not fulfilling a condition of the cure, but receiving an authentication, a public and unimpeachable and official endorsement of it. And even thus is it, in this prayer. It is not our placability that purchases for us remission. Had the imperturbable countenance which Talleyrand was accustomed to wear, even when insulted, been the index of as imperturbable a soul, free from all malicious remembrances, it would not in itself have merited eternal blessedness. But God would furnish, as it were, in the forgiving spirit of His people, a portable crucible, so to speak, in which to try and purge daily the fine gold of our own heavenly hopes. To arm us against the selfishness which so clings to us, this petition, like all those preceding it, is not for the solitary suppliant. He asks not for himself, though like the prophet's penitents he "mourns apart"; but he implores in unison and sympathy with the absent. He says not, Forgive *me*, but forgive *us*. And then going beyond all the other petitions, he makes reference not to the absent only, but to the alienated— the injurious—the hostile. (*Ibid.*)   *The forgiving grace:*—We want from God a full and free forgiveness, that has mingled with it no grudges and no coolnesses; a forgiveness that blots out our transgressions, that takes away all our iniquity, and receives us graciously and loves us freely; and that mercy which we want from Him we must be ready to show to others. We stultify ourselves by asking our Heavenly Father to extend to us a measure of forgiveness that we are not willing to extend to our brother. Such a prayer is mockery, and we know that it is when we offer it. What is more, we cannot receive the fulness of the Divine forgiveness until we are ready ourselves freely to forgive—even to give ourselves for—those who have wronged us. The trouble is not with the phraseology of the prayer, but with the facts of the case. You say that the desert is a desert because no rain falls upon it; but that is only half the truth. No rain falls upon it because it is a desert. The heated air rushing up from its arid surface disperses the vapours that would descend in rain. Some moisture there must be on the earth, else there cannot be rain from heaven. So in your heart this forgiving disposition must be, else you cannot rejoice in the fulness of God's forgiving grace. The pardon may wait in the sky above you, but it cannot descend to you until that mind is in you which was also in Christ Jesus. (*Washington Gladden, D.D.*)   *Enmity is incompatible with profitable prayer:*—You have seen enmities and jealousies and grudges growing up between neighbours and brethren in the Church; and in every such case you have noticed that the spiritual life of these quarrelling Christians grew feeble and fruitless; that there was no fervour in their prayers, no joy in their praises, no sign of heavenly influence in all their holy convocations. And then you have seen a better mind take possession of them; mutual confessions and reconciliations followed; those who had been long estranged came together and forgave each other, and renewed the old bonds of charity and brotherhood. And then, how quickly, to the assemblies so long frigid and forlorn, the warmth of holy love and the consciousness of the Divine presence returned; how the pulse of the Church was quickened; and the new life from above issued in abundant fruits! Every great religious awakening is preceded by such works of reconciliation; and no wise servant of Christ expects any real spiritual growth or progress among those who are divided by petty feuds and contentions. It is not till we are ready to forgive that we find any profit in our prayers. (*Ibid.*)   *An unforgiving spirit:*—What would you think of one who prayed, "O Lord, forgive me the many sins which I have commited against Thee; but I will not forgive my fellow-creature who has offended me"? An unforgiving spirit will stand in the way of any one being pardoned who indulges it. While the good remember kindnesses, and forget injuries, the bad practise the opposite. There are too many who, even when they claim to have forgiven others with their lips, cherish in their hearts the spirit of the old Highland chief, in the days when clan met clan in deadly feud. A man of God, who visited him on his death bed, and urged him to make peace with his enemies, in order that he might receive the forgiveness of God, at last so far prevailed, that the word passed his reluctant lips.

Then, as if the death-chamber had been a stage, and the old chieftain an actor, who, having played his part, throws off the mask which he has for the time assumed, he turned his cold gray eye on one of his stalwart sons, and said, "I leave you a father's bitterest curse if *you* ever forgive them!" (*J. N. Norton, D.D.*) *Judgment without mercy :*—Between a mother and her daughter there had sprung up a serious quarrel. One house could not hold them. At length filial affection triumphed over pride, and the daughter repaired to her early home. No welcome met her at the door. She humbled herself to her mother—on bended knees imploring her forgiveness. She appealed to the bosom that had nursed her; but might as well have knocked on a coffin; there was no response. Nor—though imploring her by the mercies of God, and entreating her to forgive as she desired to be forgiven—could I, called in as a peacemaker, bend that stubborn will. By and by to this lonely house came another visitor. Death, who would not be denied admittance, arrived, summoning her to a bar where they shall have judgment without mercy who have shown no mercy. (*Ibid.*)   *Forgetting and forgiving :*—Prince Bismarck was once asked by Count Enzenberg to write something in his album. The page on which he had to write contained the autographs of Guizot and Thiers. The former had written, "I have learnt in my long life two rules of prudence. The first is, to forgive much; the second is, never to forget." Under this Thiers had said, "A little forgetting would not detract from the sincerity of the forgiveness." Prince Bismarck added, "As for me, I have learnt to forget much, and to ask to be forgiven much." *We must forgive, if we would be forgiven :*—During the Middle Ages, when the great lords were always at war with each other, one of them resolved to take signal vengeance upon a neighbour who had offended him. On the very evening when he had formed this bloody purpose, he heard that his enemy would pass near his castle, with only a few attendants, and this seemed an excellent opportunity for gratifying his revenge. He mentioned the plan in the presence of his chaplain, who tried in vain to persuade him to give it up. The clergyman said much about the sinfulness of revenge; but it was like talking to the wind. Seeing that his words had no effect, he added, "Well, my lord, since I cannot persuade you to give up this plan of yours, will you at least consent to come with me to the chapel, that we may pray together before you set off?" The duke agreed; and the two kneeled down before the altar. "And now," said the chaplain, "please repeat with me the prayer which our Lord Jesus Christ taught to His disciples." "I will do it," answered the duke. The prayer was said without hesitation until they reached the petition, "Forgive us our trespasses, as we forgive those who trespass against us." Here the duke was silent. "Will you be so good as to continue to repeat the words after me?" asked the chaplain. "I cannot," replied the duke. "Well, God cannot forgive you, for He has said so. You must, therefore, give up your revenge, or give up the use of this prayer. To ask God to pardon you as you pardon others, is to ask Him to take vengeance on you for all your sins." The iron will of the duke was broken, and he hastily exclaimed, "I will finish my prayer. My God, my Father, pardon me!" For the first time in his life he understood the Lord's prayer.   AND *forgive us :*—At this point of the Lord's prayer we get the first use of the conjunction, and there is a great deal of beauty in that word, "*and* forgive us." What was the former petition, and what is the use of the conjunction? "Give us our daily bread." This verbal link is itself a beautiful representation of the mysterious bond that actually unites body and soul. A man who simply had bread would be a poor creature indeed, who simply had the comforts of this life. It is quite right that you should pray to have bread; but the prayer must be conjoined to a prayer for some spiritual blessing. (*S. Coley.*)   There are two things which this text cannot mean. 1. It cannot mean that sinful man is to set an example by which the Divine administration is to be conducted.   2. It cannot mean that God's forgiveness of man is a mere equivalent for something that man himself has done. In suggesting an interpretation of this prayer, let it be observed that this is not the first petition in the prayer. Who are the men who can say, "Forgive us," &c.? They are the men who *have* said—1. "Our Father." 2. "Thy kingdom come." 3. "Thy will be done on earth. (*Dr. Parker.*)   *Of the fifth petition in the Lord's prayer :*— "And forgive us our debts, as we forgive our debtors" (Matt vi. 12). Before I speak strictly to the words I shall take notice—1. That in this prayer there is but one petition for the body—"Give us our daily bread"; but two petitions for the soul—"Forgive us our trespasses," "Lead us not into temptation, but deliver us from evil." Hence observe, that we are to be more careful for our souls than for our bodies; more careful for grace than for daily bread;

more desirous to have our souls saved than our bodies fed. In the law, the weight of the sanctuary was twice as big as the common weight, to typify that spiritual things must be of far greater weight with us than earthly. The excellency of the soul may challenge our chief care about it. If it be well with the soul, it shall be well with the body; if the soul be gracious, the body shall be glorious, for it shall shine like Christ's body. Therefore it is wisdom to look chiefly to the soul, because in saving the soul, we secure the happiness of the body. 2. From the connection in the text, as soon as Christ had said, give us "daily bread," He adds, "And forgive us." Christ joins this petition of forgiveness of sin immediately to the other of daily bread, to show us, that though we have daily bread, yet all is nothing without forgiveness. If our sins be not pardoned we can take but little comfort in our food. As it is with a man that is condemned, though you bring him meat in prison, yet he takes little comfort in it without a pardon; so, though we have daily bread, yet it will do us no good unless sin be forgiven. Daily bread may satisfy the appetite, but forgiveness of sin satisfies the conscience. Use 1. It condemns the folly of most people. If they have daily bread, the delicious things of this life, they look no further, they are not solicitous for the pardon of sin; if they have that which feeds them, they look not after that which should crown them. Use 2. Let us pray that God would not give us our portion in this life, that He would not put us off with daily bread, but that He would give forgiveness. This is the sauce that would make our bread relish the sweeter. Daily bread may make us live comfortably, but forgiveness of sin will make us die comfortably. In what sense is sin the worst debt? 1. Because we have nothing to pay; if we could pay the debt, what need we pray, "Forgive us"? 2. Sin is the worst debt, because it is against an infinite majesty. Sin wrongs God, and so it is an infinite offence. 3. Sin is the worst debt, because it is not a single, but a multiplied debt—forgive us "our debts;" we have debt upon debt. We may as well reckon all the drops in the sea, as reckon all our spiritual debts; we cannot tell how much we owe. A man may know his other debts, but we cannot number our spiritual debts. 4. Sin is the worst debt; because it is an inexcusable debt in two respects. (1) There is no denying the debt; other debts men may deny. God writes down our debts in His book of remembrance, and God's book and the book of conscience do exactly agree, so that this debt cannot be denied. (2) There is no shifting of the debt; other debts may be shifted off. We may get friends to pay them, but neither man nor angel can pay this debt for us; if all the angels in heaven should go to make a purse, they cannot pay one of our debts. In other debts men may get a protection, so that none can touch their persons, or sue them for the debt; but who shall give us protection from God's justice? (a) Other debts, if the debtor dies in prison, cannot be recovered, death frees them from debt; but if we die in debt to God, He knows how to recover it; as long as we have souls to strain, God will not lose His debt. Not the death of the debtor, but the death of the surety, pays a sinner's debt. (b) In other debts men may flee from their creditor, leave their country, and go into foreign parts, and the creditor cannot find them; but we cannot flee from God. 5. Sin is the worst debt, because it carries men, in case of non-payment, to a worse prison than any upon earth. Wherein have we the properties of bad debtors? 1. A bad debtor doth not love to be called to an account. There is a day coming when God will call His debtors to account. 2. A bad debtor is unwilling to confess his debt, he will put it off, or make less of it; so we are more willing to excuse sin than confess it. 3. A bad debtor is apt to hate his creditor; debtors wish their creditors dead; so wicked men naturally hate God, because they think He is a just judge, and will call them to account. The debtor doth not love to see his creditor. We would think it strange if writs or warrants were out against a man, or a judgment granted to seize his body and estate, yet he is secure and regardless, as if he were unconcerned. God hath a writ out against a sinner, nay, many writs, for swearing, drunkenness, Sabbath-breaking, yet the sinner eats and drinks, and is quiet, as if he were not in debt; what opium hath Satan given men? If sin be a debt—1. Let us be humbled. The name of debt, saith St. Ambrose, is grievous. 2. Let us confess our debt. 3. Labour to get your spiritual debts paid, that is, by our surety Christ. "And forgive us our sins, for we also forgive every one that is indebted to us" (Luke xi. 4). What forgiveness of sin is? 1. By opening some scripture-phrases—(1) To forgive sin, is to take away iniquity—"Why dost Thou not take away my iniquity?" (Job vii. 21.) (2) To forgive sin, is to cover sin— "Thou hast covered all their sin." This was typified by the mercy-seat covering the ark, to show God's covering of sin through Christ. (3) To forgive sin, is to blot it out—"I am He that blotteth out thy transgressions." (4) To forgive sin, is for God to scatter our sins as a cloud—"I have blotted out as a thick cloud thy transgressions." (5) To forgive sin, is for God to cast our sins into the depths of the sea; which implies God's burying them out of sight, that they shall not rise up in judgment against us. God will throw them in, not as cork that riseth again, but as lead that sinks to the bottom. 2. The nature of forgiveness will appear by laying down some Divine aphorisms or positions. Every sin is mortal, and needs forgiveness; I say, mortal, that is, deserves death. It is God only that forgives sin. To pardon sin is one of the royal prerogatives. That God only can forgive sin, I prove thus:—No man can take away sin unless he is able to infuse grace; for, as Aquinas saith, with forgiveness is always infusion of grace; but no man can infuse grace, therefore no man can forgive sin. He only can forgive sin who can remit the penalty, but it is only God's prerogative royal to forgive sin. But the Scripture speaks of the power committed to ministers to forgive sin—"Whose soever sins ye remit, they are remitted unto them." Ministers cannot remit sin authoritatively and effectually, but only declaratively. They have a special office and authority to apply the promises of pardon to broken hearts. As it was with the priest in the law, God did cleanse the leper, the priest only did pronounce him clean, so it is God who, by His prerogative, doth forgive sin; the minister only pronounceth forgiveness to the sinner, being penitent. Power to forgive sin authoritatively in one's own name was never granted to mortal man. Forgiveness of sin is purely an act of God's free grace. Forgiveness is through the blood of Christ. Free grace is the inward cause moving. Christ's blood is the outward cause meriting pardon—"In whom we have redemption through His blood." But if Christ laid down His blood as the price of our pardon, then how can we say, God freely forgives sin? If it be by purchase, how is it by grace? 1. It was God's free grace that found out a way of redemption through a mediator. 2. It was free grace moved God to accept of the price paid for our sins; that God should accept a surety; that one should sin, and another suffer; this was free grace. In forgiveness of sin, God remits the guilt and penalty. What is that remorse and sorrow which goes before forgiveness of sin? It is a holy sorrow, it is a grieving for sin, as it is sin, and as it is a dishonouring of God, and a defiling of the soul. The greatest sins come within the compass of forgiveness. Zaccheus, an extortioner; Mary Magdalene, an unchaste woman, out of whom seven devils were cast; Manasseh, who made the streets run with blood; yet these had pardon. Some of the Jews who had a hand in crucifying Christ were forgiven. God blots out not only the cloud, but "the thick cloud"; enormities as well as infirmities. When God pardons a sinner, He forgives all sins—"I will pardon all their iniquities": "having forgiven you all trespasses." The mercy-seat covered the whole ark; the mercy-seat was a type of forgiveness, to show that God covers all our transgressions. They whose sins are forgiven must not omit praying for forgiveness—"Forgive us our trespasses." Believers who are pardoned must be continual suitors for pardon. Sin, like Samson's hair, though it be cut, will grow again. We sin daily, and must as well ask for daily pardon as for daily bread. 1. From this word, "forgive," we learn that if the debt of sin be no other way discharged but by being forgiven, then we cannot satisfy for it. Sin being forgiven, clearly implies we cannot satisfy for it. 2. From this word "us," "Forgive us," we learn that pardon is chiefly to be sought for ourselves. What! will another's pardon do us good? Every one is to endeavour to have his own name in the pardon. In this sense, selfishness is lawful, every one must be for himself, and get a pardon for his own sins—"Forgive us." 3. From this word "our," "Our sins," we learn how just God is in punishing us. The text says, "Our sins"; we are not punished for other men's sins, but our own. Sin is our own act, a web of our own spinning; how righteous therefore is God in punishing us? When we are punished, we but taste the fruit of our own grafting. 4. From this word "sins," see from hence the multitude of sins we stand guilty of. We pray not forgive us our sin, as if it were only a single debt, but sins, in the plural. So vast is the catalogue of our sins, that David cries out, "Who can understand his errors?" Our sins are like the drops of the sea, like the atoms in the sun, they exceed all arithmetic. If pardon of sin be so absolutely necessary, without it no salvation, what is the reason that so few in the world seek after it? If they want health, they repair to the physician; if they want riches, they take a voyage to the Indies; but if they want forgiveness of sin, they seem to be unconcerned, and do not seek after it; whence is this? 1. Inadvertency, or want of consideration; they do not look into their spiritual estate, or cast up their accounts to see how matters stand between God and their souls—" My people do not consider." 2. Men do not seek after forgiveness of sin, for want of conviction. 3. Men do not seek earnestly after forgiveness, because they are seeking other things; they seek the world immoderately. When Saul was seeking after the asses, he did not think of a kingdom. The world is a golden snare. You would judge that prisoner very unwise, that should spend all his time with the cook to get his dinner ready, and should never mind getting a pardon. 4. Men seek not after the forgiveness of sin, through a bold presumption of mercy; they conceit God to be made up all of mercy, and that He will indulge them, though they take little or no pains to sue out their pardon. 5. Men seek not earnestly after forgiveness, out of hope of impunity. 6. Men do not seek earnestly after forgiveness through mistake; they think getting a pardon is easy, it is but repeating at the last hour a sigh, or a "Lord have mercy," and a pardon will drop into their mouths. But, is it so easy to repent, and have a pardon? Tell me, O sinner, is regeneration easy? Are there no pangs in the new birth? Is mortification easy? 7. Men do not look after forgiveness through despair. My sins are huge mountains, and, can they ever be cast into the sea? Despair cuts the sinews of endeavour; who will use means that despairs of success? Having answered this question, I shall now come to press the exhortation upon every one of us, to seek earnestly after the forgiveness of our sins. 1. Our very life lies upon the getting of a pardon; it is called "the justification of life." 2. There is that in sin may make us desire forgiveness. Sin is the only thing that disquiets the soul. (1) Sin is a burden, it burdens the creation; it burdens the conscience. And should not we labour to have this burden removed by pardoning mercy? (2) Sin is a debt—" Forgive us our debts"; and every debt we owe God hath written down in His book—" Behold it is written before Me," and one day God's debt-book will be opened—" The books were opened." There is no way to look God in the face with comfort but by having our debt either paid or pardoned. 3. There is nothing but forgiveness can give ease to a troubled conscience. There is a great difference between the having the fancy pleased, and having the conscience eased. Worldly things may please the fancy, but not ease the conscience; nothing but pardon can relieve a troubled soul. Suppose a man hath a thorn in his foot which puts him to pain; let him anoint it, or wrap it up, and keep it warm; yet, till the thorn be plucked out, it aches and swells, and he hath no ease; so when the thorn of sin is gotten into a man's conscience, there is no ease till the thorn be pulled out; when God removes iniquity, now the thorn is plucked out. 4. Forgiveness of sin is feasible; but, "There is hope in Israel concerning this." The devils are past hope; a sentence of death is upon them, which is irrevocable; but there is hope for us of obtaining a pardon—" There is forgiveness with Thee." 5. Consideration, to persuade to it: Forgiveness of sin is a choice eminent blessing; to have the book cancelled, and God appeased, is worth obtaining; which may whet our endeavour after it. That it is a rare transcendent blessing, appears by three demonstrations. (1) If we consider how this blessing is purchased, namely, by the Lord Jesus. There are three things in reference to Christ, which set forth the choiceness and preciousness of forgiveness. (a) No mere created power in heaven or earth could expiate one sin, or procure a pardon; only Jesus Christ—" He is the propitiation for our sins." No merit can buy out a pardon. (b) Christ Himself could not procure a pardon, but by dying; every pardon is the price of blood. (c) Christ, by dying, had not purchased forgiveness for us if He had not died an execrable death; He endured the curse. (2) Forgiveness of sin is a choice blessing, if we consider what glorious attributes God puts forth in the pardoning of sin. (a) God puts forth infinite power; when Moses was pleading with God for the pardon of Israel's sin, He speaks thus, "Let the power of my Lord be great." God's forgiving of sin is a work of as great power as to make heaven and earth, nay, a greater; for, when God made the world, He met with no opposition; but when He comes to pardon, Satan opposeth, and the heart opposeth. (b) God, in forgiving sins, puts forth "infinite mercy"—" Pardon, I beseech Thee, the iniquity of this people, according to the greatness of Thy mercy." (3) Forgiveness of sin is a choice blessing, as it lays a foundation for other mercies. It is a leading mercy. (a) It makes way for temporal good things. It brings health. When Christ said to the palsied man, "Thy sins are forgiven," this made way for a bodily cure—" Arise, take up thy bed and go into thine house." The pardon of his sin made way for the healing of his palsy. (b) It makes way for spiritual good things. Forgiveness of sin never comes alone, but hath other spiritual blessings attending it. Whom God pardons, He sanctifies, adopts, crowns. It is a voluminous mercy; it draws the silver link of grace, and the golden link of glory after it. 6. Consideration: That which may make us seek after forgiveness of sin is, God's inclinableness to pardon—"Thou art a God ready to pardon." We are apt to entertain wrong conceits of God, that He is inexorable, and will not forgive—"I knew that Thou art an hard man." But God is a sin-pardoning God. 7. Consideration: Not to seek earnestly for pardon is the unspeakable misery of such as want forgiveness; it must needs be ill with that malefactor that wants his pardon. (1) The unpardoned sinner that lives and dies so, is under the greatest loss and privation. (2) The unpardoned sinner hath nothing to do with any promise. (3) An unpardoned sinner is continually in danger of the outcry of an accusing conscience. An accusing conscience is a little hell. (4) All the curses of God stand in full force against an unpardoned sinner. His very blessings are cursed—"I will curse your blessings." (5) The unpardoned sinner is in an ill case at death. Luther professed there were three things which he durst not think of without Christ; of his sins, of death, of the day of judgment. Death to a Christless soul is the "King of terrors." But I am discouraged from going to God for pardon, for I am unworthy of forgiveness; what am I, that God should do such a favour for me? God forgives, not because we are worthy, but because He is gracious—"The Lord, the Lord merciful and gracious." "Free grace doth not find us worthy, but makes us worthy." Therefore, notwithstanding unworthiness, seek to God, that your sins may be pardoned. But I have been a great sinner, and sure God will not pardon me. David brings it as an argument for pardon; 'Pardon mine iniquity, for it is great." When God forgives great sins, now He doth a work like Himself. The desperateness of the wound doth the more set forth the virtue of Christ's blood in curing it. The vast ocean hath bounds set to it, but God's pardoning mercy is boundless. God can as well forgive great sins as less; as the sea can as well cover great rocks as little sands. God counts it His glory to display free grace in its orient colours—"Where sin aboundeth grace did much more abound." When sin becomes exceeding sinful, free grace becomes exceeding glorious. God's pardoning love can conquer the sinner, and triumph over the sin. Let us labour to have the evidence of pardon, to know that our sins are forgiven. A man may have his sins forgiven, and not know it; he may have a pardon in the court of heaven, when he hath it not in the court of conscience. The evidence of pardon may not appear for a time, and this may be—1. From the imbecility and weakness of faith. 2. A man may be pardoned and not know it, from the strength of temptation. But why doth God sometimes conceal the evidence of pardon? Though God doth pardon, yet He may withhold the sense of it a while—1. Because hereby He would lay us lower in contrition. 2. Though God hath forgiven sin, yet He may deny the manifestation of it for a time, to make us prize pardon, and make it sweeter to us when it comes. How then shall we know by the word whether our guilt is done away, and our sins pardoned? 1. The pardoned sinner is a great weeper. Have we been dissolved into tears for sin? God seals His pardons upon melting hearts. 2. We may know our sins are forgiven by having the grace of faith infused—"To Him give all the prophets witness, that whosoever believeth in Him shall receive remission of sins." In saving faith there are two things, renunciation, and recumbency. 3. The pardoned soul is a God-admirer—"Who is a God like Thee, that pardoneth iniquity?" 4. Wherever God pardons sin, He subdues it—"He will have compassion on us, He will subdue our iniquities." Where men's persons are justified, their lusts are mortified. 5. He whose sins are forgiven is full of love to God. He whose heart is like marble, locked up in impenitency, that doth not melt in love, gives evidence his pardon is yet to seal. 6. Where the sin is pardoned, the nature is purified. Many tell us, they hope they are pardoned, but were never sanctified; yea, but they believe in Christ; but what faith is it? A swearing faith, a whoring faith; the faith of devils is as good. 7. Such as are in the number of God's people, forgiveness of sin belongs to them—"Comfort ye My people, tell them their iniquity is pardoned." He whose sins are forgiven, is willing to forgive others who have offended him—"Forgiving one another, even as God for Christ's sake hath forgiven you." A king may pardon a traitor, but will not make him one of his privy council; but whom God pardons, He receives into favour. Forgiveness of sin makes our services acceptable; God takes all we do in good part. A guilty person, nothing he doth pleaseth God. Forgiveness of sin is the sauce which sweetens all the comforts of this life. As guilt embitters our comforts, it puts wormwood into our cup; so pardon of sin sweetens all; it is like sugar to wine. Health and pardon, estate and pardon, relish well. Pardon of sin gives a sanctified title! and a delicious taste to every comfort.

If sin be forgiven, God will never upbraid us with our former sins. Where God pardons sins, He bestows righteousness. With remission of sin goes imputation of righteousness—"I will greatly rejoice in the Lord, He hath covered me with the robe of righteousness." A pardoned soul needs not fear death. He may look on death with joy who can look on forgiveness with faith. To a pardoned soul death hath lost his sting. Death, to a pardoned sinner, is like the arresting a man after the debt is paid; death may arrest, but Christ will show the debt-book crossed in His blood. Now follow the duties of such as have their sins forgiven. Mercy calls for duty. Be much in praise and doxology. 1. "Bless the Lord, O my soul, who forgiveth all thine iniquities." Hath God crowned you with pardoning mercy? set the crown of your praise upon the head of free grace. 2. Let God's pardoning love inflame your hearts with love to God. 3. Let the sense of God's love in forgiving make you more cautious and fearful of sin for the future. O Christians, do you not remember what it cost you before to get your pardon! 4. If God hath given you good hope that you are pardoned, walk cheerfully—"We joy in God, through our Lord Jesus Christ, by whom we have received the atonement." Who should rejoice, if not he that hath his pardon? 5. Hath God pardoned you? Do all the service you can for God—"Always abounding in the work of the Lord." Let your head study for God, let your hands work for Him, let your tongue be the organ of His praise. The pardoned soul thinks he can never love God enough or serve Him enough. The last thing is to lay down some rules or directions, how we may obtain forgiveness of sin. We must take heed of mistakes about pardon of sin. 1. That our sins are pardoned, when they are not. Whence is this mistake? From two grounds. (1) Because God is merciful. (2) Because Christ died for their sins, therefore they are forgiven. 2. That pardon is easy to be had; it is but a sigh, or, "Lord have mercy." "As we forgive our debtors;" or, "As we forgive them that trespass against us" (Matt. vi. 12). I proceed to the second part of the petition, "As we forgive them that trespass against us." "As we forgive." This word, "as," is not a note of equality, but similitude; not that we equal God in forgiving, but imitate Him. 1. How can I forgive others, when it is only God forgives sin? In every breach of the second table there are two things; an offence against God, and a trespass against man. So far as it is an offence against God, He only can forgive; but so far as it is a trespass against man, so we may forgive. Let it persuade us all, as ever we hope for salvation, to pass by petty injuries and discourtesies, and labour to be of forgiving spirits, "forbearing one another, and forgiving one another." 1. Herein we resemble God. He is "ready to forgive," He befriends His enemies, He opens His hands to relieve them who open their mouths against Him. 2. To forgive is one of the highest evidences of grace. When grace comes into the heart, it makes a man, as Caleb, of another spirit. It makes a great metamorphosis; it sweetens the heart, and fills it with love and candour. When a scion is grafted into a stock it partakes of the nature and sap of the tree, and brings forth the same fruit; take a crab, graft it into a pepin, it brings forth the same fruit as the pepin; so he who was once of a sour crabby disposition, given to revenge, when he is once ingrafted into Christ, he partakes of the sap of this heavenly olive, and bears sweet and generous fruit; he is full of love to His enemies, and requites good for evil. As the sun draws up many thick noxious vapours from the earth, and returns them in sweet showers; so a gracious heart returns the unkindnesses of others with the sweet influences of love and mercifulness—"They rewarded me evil for good; but as for me, when they were sick, my clothing was sackcloth, I humbled my soul with fasting." This is a good certificate to show for heaven. 3. The blessed example of our Lord Jesus; He was of a forgiving spirit. 4. The danger of an implacable, unforgiving spirit; it hinders the efficacy of ordinances; it is like an obstruction in the body, which keeps it from thriving. A revengeful spirit poisons our sacrifice, our prayers are turned into sin; will God receive prayer mingled with this strange fire? 5. God hath tied His mercy to this condition; if we do not forgive, neither will He forgive us—"If ye forgive not men their trespasses, neither will your Heavenly Father forgive your trespasses." A man may as well go to hell for not forgiving, as for not believing. 6. The examples of the saints who have been of forgiving spirits. 7. Forgiving and requiting good for evil is the best way to conquer and melt the heart of an enemy. Our sins are innumerable and heinous; is God willing to forgive us so many offences, and cannot we forgive a few? No man can do so much wrong to us all our life, as we do to God in one day. But how must we forgive? As God forgives us. 1. Cordially. God doth not only make a show of forgiveness, and keep our sins by Him, but doth really forgive; He passeth an act of oblivion. 2. God forgives fully; He forgives all our sins. Hypocrites pass by some offences, but retain others. Would we have God deal so with us to remit only some trespasses, and call us to account for the rest. 3. God forgives often; we run afresh upon the score, but God multiplies pardon. (*T. Watson.*) *Our Father's forgiveness :*—" And forgive us our debts, as we forgive our debtors " (Matt. vi. 12). " And forgive us our sins; for we also forgive every one that is indebted to us " (Luke xi. 4). Ponder, first, the prayer for forgiveness—Forgive us our debts. This word " debts " first claims our attention. There are two senses in which man may be said to be a debtor to the Heavenly Father. First : Man is a debtor in the sense of dutifulness : a dutifulness unconditional, complete, unbroken, ceaseless, absolute; and this because God is Father, and he God's son. Of course, from a debt like this no son, so long as he remains loyal, can ever expect or even wish to be released. To owe the Father in heaven immortal obedience, thanks, trust, love, is man's blessedness and glory. But there is a second and terrible sense in which man may be said to be a debtor to his Heavenly Father : he owes Him arrears, or the debt of default in dutifulship. And this second debt is beyond the possibility of payment. And now, if Gabriel with all his spotless innocence and celestial strength is unable to outrun his duty or do a work of supererogation, what shall be said of poor, fallen, miserable man? A child of dust, conceived in sin and brought forth in iniquity, by nature, in the very fact of birth, a child of wrath, talking of making amends to God for past failures !

> " O Judgment ! thou art fled to brutish beasts,
> And men have lost their reason ! "

As well might the thief claim the watch he has stolen as the reward due to his knavery, or the assassin the love and esteem of the dead man's friends as the reward due to his deed of blood. But will God answer the prayer? Can He, will He, forgive our debts ? Most certainly He can and He will; and this precisely for the reason that He is what He is, our Heavenly Father. Were He something else, were He simply a Creator, or a Monarch, or a Judge, He might coldly say, " No ! My Government must be maintained. Justice must be satisfied. The law must take its course. Or, if I forgive, it can only be in view of a consideration, the payment of an equivalent." But precisely because God is something more than this, precisely because He is Father as well as Creator and Monarch and Judge, He says nothing of the kind. Overcoming us by a love so infinite that it must vent itself in a cross, He recreates our characters by subduing us into penitence, amendment, loyalty, sonship; and so He transfigures us from bankruptcy into sonhood. This is the way in which our Heavenly Father forgives us for His Son's sake our debts. And now let us ponder, secondly, the standard of forgiveness: " As we forgive " (or, as it probably should read, as we have forgiven) " our debtors." And, first, what does it mean to forgive our debtors ? Precisely what forgiveness means when our Heavenly Father forgives us our debts. And you know how He forgives us, at least those of us who have accepted His forgiveness ; for His pardon, as we have seen, does not really go into operation till we have actually accepted it. Recall, then, how the Heavenly Father has forgiven us. He has forgiven us freely, without stipulation or compensation. He has forgiven us fully, every one of our debts, and they are as countless as earth's sands : He has forgiven us infinitely more than we can ever be called upon to forgive others. He has forgiven us sincerely, from the depths of His own infinite Heart. He has forgiven us everlastingly, world without end. Most wonderful of all, He Himself has taken the initiative, offering us His forgiveness in advance of our even asking for it. And as He has forgiven us, so we are to forgive one another. Take, then, the initiative in forgiving thy brother. But while it is true that our Father's forgiveness of us is the model for our forgiveness of our brothers, yet this is not the point which the Lord sets before us in the pattern prayer. Elsewhere in Holy Scripture forgiveness begins in heaven and descends to earth ; here forgiveness begins on earth and ascends to heaven—"Forgive us our debts, as we have forgiven our debtors." Not that there is any merit in our forgiving one another. No, our Father does not forgive us our debts because we have forgiven our debtors; but our having forgiven our debtors is a condition of our Father's forgiving us our debts (Matt. vi. 14, 15; Luke xi. 4; Mark xi. 25; James ii. 13; 1 John iv. 20). For he shall have judgment without mercy that hath showed no mercy. Again : our forgiving our brother is not only a condition of our Father's forgiving us ; our forgiving our brother is also, so to speak, the standard or measure of our Father's forgiving us : Forgive us our debts, as, in the same spirit that, we have forgiven our debtors. It would be difficult to find in history, or in philosophy, or in Holy Writ, a more pregnant or more affecting sign of man's greatness than this little phrase, "As we forgive our debtors." Elsewhere in the Word we are taught to regard God as the standard of man's action ; but here we are taught to regard man as the standard of God's action. Here is a man who has been bitterly wronged by another ; he says to him, "I forgive you this, but I cannot forget it." He enters his closet and prays: "Father, forgive me, as I have forgiven him! Say to me in words that Thou forgivest me, but do not forget my offences! Blot them not out of the book of Thy remembrance! Do to me as I do to him!" Oh, how often does this prayer, if offered sincerely, mean a curse! Once more: our forgiving our brother is not only the standard or measure of our Father's forgiveness of us; not only a condition of His forgiving us; it is also a sign of our having been ourselves forgiven by our Father. In other words, our feelings towards those who have wronged us furnish us with a decisive test of our standing before our Father in Heaven. As a forgiving state implies a forgiven, so an unforgiving state implies an unforgiven. Ah, this is the meaning of these human relations of ours : this is the final cause of the incorporation of us into human society. The feelings we secretly cherish, as in the discharge of our daily duties we mingle among our fellows—these are the best interpreters of Christ's doctrine of forgiveness. Let us not waste our time in judging ourselves by theoretical, distant, shadowy tests. Let us deal with our own hearts as directly and practically as Christ's tests require. (*G. D. Boardman, D.D.*) *A confession before pardon :*—I. A CONFESSION. That naturally comes first. With God as with man, the confession must go before the pardon. But, more particularly, as bringing out the alarming nature of these debts, notice these things regarding them: 1. The countless numbers of them. 2. They are always increasing. If they were lessening, however slowly, there would be hope. But, so far from diminishing, they are growing. 3. They are all taken account of. God's eye sees them all. 4. They are all to be reckoned for. 5. We can do nothing to meet them. II. A PRAYER—"Forgive us our debts." The word "forgive" means remit, discharge, send away. The word is touchingly suggestive. About this forgiveness, and as a help to our asking it, I may make these three remarks. 1. It is free and gracious. 2. This forgiveness is complete; it takes in "all sin." It does not merely lessen it; it removes it, and leaves none remaining. I was once sent for, in great haste, to see a man who reminded me, more than any one I ever saw, of Bunyan's "man in the iron cage." He had at one time been on board a slave ship, and had taken part in the cruelties perpetrated against the poor negroes, and as the spectacle of their sufferings rose up before him, he was in utter despair. When I was shown into his room, he was dashing his clenched hands against the wall at the back of his bed, crying out, "Oh my sins! my sins! hundreds! thousands! If ye would but take away the half of them I could bear it. I've been worse than ever Paul was, and he said he was the chief of sinners," &c. I never felt more the blessedness of having God's free, immediate, complete pardon to offer, as I told him that God never pardoned the half of any man's sins, that His way was to pardon all or none, that He Himself had put the prayer into the sinner's lips, "Take away all iniquity," and that He offered him now this present and full pardon for the sake of His dear Son. 3. This forgiveness is everlasting: the sins, the debts, never come back. They are cancelled. They are covered. This is an intercessory prayer, that is, a prayer for others. "Forgive *us our* debts." We come now to look at another element in this petition of the Lord's prayer, which I stated thus: III. AN ENCOURAGEMENT, AND A PROMISE OR OBLIGATION—"As we forgive our debtors "; "for we also forgive." 1. It may be regarded as an encouragement to ask forgiveness from God. "Forgive us, as we forgive " : "for we forgive." In so far as there is anything good in us, it was God who put it there. In this respect, God has made us like Himself. If I might so speak, it is a little bit of God's image in us. On a May morning, as you are crossing a field, you see a little bit of glass, or a little drop of dew on a blade of grass, shining like a little sun. That reflection of it gives you some idea of what the sun is. 2. We may regard this clause as containing a promise, or obligation, under which we come when we pray this prayer. It is more than a promise, but it has that wrapped up in it. It is a declaration that we have forgiven all who have wronged us, for the verb is in the past tense—" as *we have* forgiven our debtors." I am not fit to be forgiven,—I am not capable of receiving forgiveness, if I am unforgiving. If a child has his hand filled with a stone, and you offer him gold, or food, or ought else that is desirable, he cannot receive the one without casting away the other. His hand cannot take it in. It is indispensable, in the very nature of things, that he part with the stone, in order to be able to take the gold, without attributing any merit to the casting away of what filled his hand before. And so, where an unforgiving spirit takes possession of any one—enters into and fills any heart—that heart cannot take in God's forgiveness. There is not the power to receive forgiveness. The unforgivingness must be cast out, that pardon from God may be a possibility. And after what fashion is it that this forgiveness must be exercised ? 1. Heartily. It is of no use merely to say it in words. " If ye from the heart forgive not," says Christ. 2. Universally—entirely. What kind of wrongs am I to forgive ? Every kind ; not only the lesser, but also the greater. 3. Habitually. Not only now and then, but constantly. Few things touch us more to the quick than unkind and abusive letters. Some Christian people have been sorely tried by these. The late Dr. Cotton Mather received many of them. After his death, they were found among his papers, tied up in a packet, with these words written on the cover, "Libels—Father, forgive them." (*J. H. Wilson, M.A.*) *Prayer for forgiveness :*—1. The most superficial view of the nature and objects of prayer cannot fail to teach us that such a request as this should be offered with great seriousness of mind. We would not go into the presence of an earthly prince, even though it were to solicit an ordinary favour, without forethought and preparation ; much less would we come as culprits to his throne to beg the interposition of royal prerogative in the exercise of the pardoning power, without respect and reverence. 2. There is also an honesty of intention, a simplicity and godly sincerity, in the man who offers this request, without which he may not hope to find access. A cold, formal, listless mind when the transgressor pleads for mercy, is in ill keeping with the object of his prayer. 3. There is earnestness in the man who, touched with his lost condition as a sinner, comes in sober verity to the foot of the throne, to crave pardon from a forgiving God, that bespeaks the struggles that are within. 4. To be offered either in seriousness or in sincerity, this request must also be offered in penitence. 5. It is a delightful thought, too, that associated as this request is with the name of Christ, it is offered in hope. Despair cannot pray. *A forgiving spirit :*—Our task is comparatively easy, therefore, as we proceed to show why the spirit of forgiveness in men is made a revealed condition of their obtaining forgiveness from God. The reason why a man of unforgiving spirit cannot obtain forgiveness is, that he is destitute of all true and genuine piety. The force of this remark may perhaps be the better perceived by something like the following observations. 1. Such a man has no true sense of his own sins. 2. Nor do we see how such a man can have any true sense of the Divine mercy. 3. It is equally true that a man of an unforgiving spirit has no love to God in his heart. 4. Nor may we overlook the thought, that where the spirit of forgiveness is wanting, there can be no honest regard for the interests of human society. The laws of Christ's kingdom do not allow any man to live for himself alone. History furnishes an affecting illustration of the need of a spirit of forgiveness, in order to the retaining of our evidence of forgiveness from God. There was in the Church at Antioch, in the third century, a minister by the name of Sapricius, and a layman by the name of Nicephorus, who after long intimacy had fallen into an unhappy quarrel, and carried it so far that they would not speak to each other when they met. After a while Nicephorus relented, and took every measure for reconciliation, but in vain. He even threw himself at the feet of his former friend, and entreated forgiveness for the Lord's sake, but without effect. About this time, a new storm of persecution arose, and Sapricius was marked out as one of the victims. The magistrates ordered him to obey the Emperor, and sacrifice to the heathen god. But he appeared ready to witness a good confession, and replied in an expression of his higher allegiance to the King of kings, " Perish idols, which can do neither harm nor good ! " The torture was applied, and he bore it firmly. The magistrate then commanded him to be beheaded, and while he was led out to execution, Nicephorus followed him, entreating his forgiveness. But it was in vain ; Sapricius's unforgiving temper remained to the last. At this juncture did the Saviour make good His word, " If ye forgive not men their trespasses, neither will your Heavenly Father forgive your trespasses." For at this trying period. all Sapricius's firmness forsook him ; the fear of death overpowered him, he recanted, and saved his life, while seemingly on the point of seizing the crown of martyrdom. While at the same time the Saviour's faithfulness was remarkably expressed towards the individual who had manifested a forgiving spirit. Nicephorus, annoyed at so unexpected a change in Sapricius, exhorted him to adhere to the faith, but in vain. And then himself flaming with zeal for the Christian cause, so dishonoured, turned to the executioners and said, " I believe in the name of the Lord Jesus, whom he has renounced." This was reported to the Emperor, and Nicephorus received the crown of martyrdom! We cannot rely upon the Divine mercy for ourselves while indulging an unforgiving and unchristian spirit towards others. (*G. Spring, D.D.*) *Sins ours:*—1. First, of them that shift the guilt of their sins upon Adam, and allege original corruption for an excuse of their transgressions. 2. But now, in the next place, if we cannot shift our sins upon Adam and that original weakness which we derived from his loins, we may perhaps upon the serpent, upon the devil. 3. We come now to the last complaint; which is most unjust of all, as being put up against the justice and goodness of God, " who giveth to all men liberally, and upbraideth not " (James i. 5). 4. And now, in the last place, as they are only ours, so they are fully and totally ours; and if we strive to make a defalcation, we add unto their bulk, and make them more mountainous than before. And as we do *minuendo numerum augere,* " by seeking to make our sins fewer than they are, sin more, and so increase their number "; so, by attempting to make them less, we make them greater. (*A. Farindon.*) *Called aboard again:*—Thus you see, like men set on shore for refreshment and provision of some necessaries for their voyage, we are called aboard again; Christ did only land us upon the world's shore in that middle petition, to refresh us in the midst of our travels, but He purposed not to afford us any long stay; for you may see man's meditations here embarked for the furthest point of life's voyage. For the clearing of which passage to his last home he uses all diligence in these three last petitions, which are, as it were, His harbingers to remove all impediments which might retard Him in the course of His future beatitude. See in this, man making his peace with God and the world, compounding with his creditor, God, and with his debtors, men, at one and the same rate—"Forgive us," &c., as " we forgive them," &c. There is nothing more dangerous to a Christian than to slight or diminish an offence. (*Archdeacon King.*) *No venal sins:*—The smallest leak which is sprung at sea may, if neglected, let in water to drown the tallest ship. Therefore, if the tide of sin have washed, though never so lightly, over thy bank, if a temptation have floated in upon thy soul by any of thy five ports, thy senses, make up the breach betimes, lest a tide or two more overwhelm, and lay thee quite under water. Despise not the smallest sin, for even that is a step to a greater. Remember thou mayest multiply pence till they come to a talent, so thou mayest link sin to sin, till they make a chain long enough to drag thee into perpetual bondage with the prince of darkness, long enough to reach from earth to hell, till the multiplication of those acts grow into a habit, become great and strong, and heavy enough to sink thee into the bottomless pit. Remember too, that as the least coins, even to the farthing, have their value, so also the least sins shall have their punishment. (*Ibid.*) *Our debts:*—There is not so naked, so penurious a thing as man. " Naked was he born, and naked shall he return," divested of all but his sins. We have no peculiar but this, nothing that we can call ours, but only our faults. Except that luckless patrimony, I know not what we can lay claim to, either that is without us, or in us. *Bona Fortunæ,* wealth acknowledgeth no sovereign but fortune, we are not masters of it; and though it abide with us as a hireling, perhaps till the end of our days, then it surely takes leave, often before that, becoming any one's save his whose it it last was. Nothing of all we had goes along with us but our winding sheet; for other things we have gathered, the Psalm says, " We know not who shall enjoy them"; sure we are, we shall not. And for that form which makes so many enamoured of themselves, can any call it theirs? when all the Parget's art hath invented are not able to coat it against the violence of time and weather, nor by all their fillings to repair those decays and breaches which sickness hath wrought upon it. The breath we draw, is that ours? Is it not sucked and borrowed from the next air? Our best part, the soul, is it any more than a loan, deposited for some years with the body, after whose expiration it reverts to Him that gave it. And, lastly, for our body, is it anything else but a lump of walking clay, a little earth inanimated; the certain restitution whereof we owe unto the dust from whence it was taken. What is there, then, of our whole selves which we can call ours, unless our sins? These are effects springing from our own depraved nature, the fruits of a vicious crooked will, our true legitimate issue, though born against all law, both human and Divine. They are *nostra*, " ours," by many assurances, ours by all titles both of right and possession. (*Ibid.*) *Of duties to be observed because every sin is mortal :*—The knowledge of the nature of every sin, and of the due desert thereof, ought to make us diligent in searching into the law of God, that thereby we may know what is sin, for " by the law is the knowledge of sin." And knowing sin, carefully and consciously to avoid it ; for " the wages of sin is death." And no way make ourselves accessories to the sins of others, for so we bring the blood of others upon our own heads. And if we have committed sins ourselves, or made ourselves accessory to the sins of others, not to soothe our consciences with the smallness thereof, and thereupon remain secure, not caring to repent thereof. "Except ye be born again ye shall perish." To work the more thorough repentance we ought thoroughly to search ourselves, and from time to time strictly to examine our thoughts, words, and actions. And as we discern any transgressions or alterations in any of them, instantly to crave pardon for them. Yea, because we cannot be ignorant that many sins unawares pass from us, to desire a general discharge of all other sins (which two points are expressly noted in this fifth petition). As we crave pardon for all sins past, so ought we to be watchful over ourselves for the time to come, even so watchful as to " abstain from all appearance of evil." Not regarding the common scoffs against preciseness, as the world termeth Christian, careful and conscionable watchfulness over a man's self. Commonly the wickeder sort do most justify themselves, and the upright most judge themselves. The upright use to judge themselves for their very ignorances and negligences. And surely sins of ignorance or negligence were better be judged, that they may be destroyed, then excused that they should be nourished. For " every thing must be brought to judgment," and " of every idle word that men shall speak they shall give an account in the day of judgment." Let not therefore the small sins be slighted. Floods are made with small drops. Water soaketh through small chinks, the ship is therewith filled, and if the pump be not plied the ship is drowned. (*W. Gouge.*) *Of the many debts wherein we stand bound to God's justice :*—1. Our souls will be the more wounded and humbled for them. The benefit whereof will be that God will be the more moved with pity and compassion towards us. 2. Our desire of discharge will be the more fervent. Whereby the Lord will the rather be moved to grant our desire. 3. The long-suffering of God in bearing with so many sins, so many ways committed against Him, and from time to time heaped one upon another will be the better discerned. 4. The riches of God's mercy in forgiving not a few pence, nor yet a few talents, but "many thousand talents" will be the more admired and magnified; and He Himself the more loved. (*Ibid.*) *Revenge is a kind of fire,* which if it be not presently quenched, will soon prove unquenchable. Nay, it is a deadly poison, which if it once seize on the soul will soon destroy it. No fire, no poison of a more increasing nature than revenge. Did men know what a wolf, what a tiger, what a viper wrath and revenge were, they would at the first sight thereof be startled, and get themselves as far from it as they could. If scorpions and apes were in men's houses, what pains would they take to cleanse their houses, that they might dwell securely? But they keep anger, wrath, malice, hatred, revenge, which are so many scorpions and serpents, and cleanse not the house of God, which is their heart. Yea, such a perverse disposition have many, as they use all the means they can to retain and nourish revenge, and to keep it in mind and memory. By oath, by imprecation, and other ways they will bind themselves not to forgive. They forbear not to say, " I may forget the wrong, but I will never forgive it." Hereby they provoke God to keep their sins in perpetual memory, and to bind Himself to execute vengeance on them. (*Ibid.*) *Of the force of this particle " as " in the condition annexed to the fifth petition :*—This note of resemblance, therefore, is not here used as it was in the third petition, for—1. There that from whence the resemblance is taken is more eminent. Here much meaner, It is there taken from those that are in heaven. But here from us on earth. 2. There it noteth a pattern for doing. Here, an evidence of doing. 3. There it is used for direction, to show what we should do. (*Ibid.*) *Pretences for not forgiving :*—1. He that hath wronged me is a base fellow. What more base to thee, than thou art to God? 2. The wrong done is unsufferable. What! more unsufferable than thy sins against God? 3. It is not the first time that he hath wronged me. Didst thou never but once sin against God? 4. He may wrong me again and again if I put it up. Why dost thou think so uncharitably of thy brother? But mayest thou not sin again and again against God? 5. It beseemeth not my place and honour to put up wrongs. Is God so accounted for bearing with sins? If God do thus, why art thou so much incensed with wrath, when any doth any wrong to thee? Thou shouldest rather behold thyself, how thou hast carried thyself against God. If anything will make thee forgive, surely this will. (*Ibid.*) *God's mind toward us :*—Learn hereby how to know God's mind towards thee. Thou needest not to climb up to heaven there to behold the face of God, whether He frown or smile, whether love or anger be seated in His eyes, but dive into thine own heart, and there observe what is thy mind towards thy brother. No looking-glass can give a truer representation of thy face than thine own heart a demonstration of God's heart towards thee. "We love, because He first loved us," and we forgive because He first forgave us. (*Ibid.*) *God's mercy is operative as fire :*—It warmeth that heart in which it abideth, and worketh mercy therein. Where, therefore, no mercy to man can be found, there is just cause to suspect no mercy of God hath been showed. The soul of an unmerciful man is no fit receptacle of the mercies of God. It abuseth, it perverteth them. (*Ibid.*) *The prayer for forgiveness :*—I. Let us consider THAT GOD IS THE SOURCE OF ALL FORGIVENESS. This is His right. It belongs to Him; it is His property; and He is jealous of it. "To the Lord our God belong mercies and forgivenesses." "It is God that justifieth; who is he that condemneth?" But not only is it the right and prerogative of God: it is His glory. It floweth out of His mercy. Forgiveness is but the stream, and it ariseth from the goodness and the mercy of God. And the reason why I lay stress on this, and I do it often, is because I see so frequently, and find so often in my own heart, this principle—a sort of harsh principle as it regardeth God; a loving principle as it regardeth Jesus, but some stern view as it regardeth the Father; whereas the glory of the gospel is, that if we have free forgiveness, it floweth out, like the bubbling stream from the overflowing fountain; it cometh forth from His glory; it is His glory. And yet it flows in a pure and unsullied channel; if you and I love God as we ought to love Him, we should say, I would not have mercy at the expense of Thy holiness. I want no exhibition of God's goodness upon the ruins of His holiness; I do not want to see the wreck of God's holy law, in order that He may exhibit His forgiving love. It emanates forth from the glory of God; and gloriously does He exercise it. It is indeed a bubbling fountain, ever full and ever running over. Hast thou ever seen the honeycomb drop honey out of its fulness? Did any argument of thine persuade it to drop? Why did it drop? Because it was full of honey. And why doth God forgive? Because He is God; and that which He doeth, He doeth like Himself, gloriously. Oh! yes, what God doth, He doth as God; and when He forgiveth, He forgiveth as God. And when one asks what are those sins that He forgives, see how the Holy Ghost describes them: sins deep as scarlet, and red as blood. II. HE LEADS THEM TO PRAY FOR THE FORGIVENESS OF THEIR SINS — "Forgive us our sins." And there seems, too, I think, involved in this petition, an imploring of God for all the blessings that spring out from forgiveness. III. THE PLEA WHICH OUR LORD PUTS INTO THE HEARTS OF HIS DISCIPLES—"For we also forgive every one that is indebted to us." (*J. H. Evans.*) **And lead us not into temptation.**—*Lead us not into temptation :*—I. WHAT SUGGESTS SUCH A PRAYER AS THIS? 1. Watchfulness. 2. Next, it seems to me to be the natural prayer of holy horror at the very thought of falling again into sin. I remember the story of a pitman who, having been a gross blasphemer, a man of licentious life and everything that was bad, when converted by Divine grace, was terribly afraid lest his old companions should lead him back again. He knew himself to be a man of strong passions, and very apt to be led astray by others, and therefore in his dread of being drawn into his old sins, he prayed most vehemently that sooner than ever he should go back to his old ways he might die. He did die there and then. Perhaps it was the best answer to the best prayer that the poor man could have offered. I am sure any man who has once lived an evil life, if the wondrous grace of God has snatched him from it, will agree that the pitman's prayer was not one whit too enthusiastic. It were better for us to die at once than to live on and return to our first estate and bring dishonour upon the name of Jesus Christ our Lord. He who has once been caught in the steel trap carries the scars in his flesh and is horribly afraid of being again held by its cruel teeth. 3. The third feeling, also, is very apparent; namely, diffidence of personal strength. The man who feels himself strong enough for anything is daring, and even invites the battle which will prove his power. "Oh," says he, "I care not; they may gather about me who will; I am quite able to take care of myself and hold my own against any number." He is ready to be led into conflict, he courts the fray. Not so the man who has been taught of God and has learned his own weakness; He does not want to be tried, but seeks quiet places where he may be out of harm's way. 4. This prayer seems to me to arise also somewhat out of charity. We should not be too severe with those persons who have done wrong, and offended us; but pray, "Lord, lead us not into temptation." 5. This prayer breathes the spirit of confidence in God. Of course He will lead me, now that I am His child. Moreover, now that He has forgiven me, I know that He will not lead me where I can come to any harm. This my faith ought to know and believe, and yet for several reasons there rises to my mind a fear lest His providence should conduct me where I shall be tempted. Is that fear right or wrong? It burdens my mind; may I go with it to my God? May I express in prayer this misgiving of soul? May I pour out this anxiety before the great, wise, loving God? Will it not be impertinent? No, it will not, for Jesus puts the words into my mouth and says, "After this manner pray ye." II. WHAT ARE THESE TEMPTATIONS WHICH THE PRAYER DEPRECATES? or say rather, what are these trials which are so much feared. 1. Men may be led into temptation by the withdrawal of Divine grace. 2. Another set of temptations will be found in providential conditions. 3. There are temptations arising out of physical conditions. Diseased livers, palpitating hearts, and injured brains are hard things to struggle against. 4. Mental conditions often furnish great temptations. 5. There are temptations arising out of personal associations, which are formed for us in the order of providence. III. LESSONS. 1. Never boast your own strength. 2. Never desire trial. 3. Never go into temptation. 4. Do not lead others there. (*C. H. Spurgeon.*)   *Temptation and deliverance:*—I. WHAT TEMPTATIONS ARE. Temptation, according to the proper signification of the word, is no other but a trial or probation. And this may be of two kinds—exploratory, or suasory. There is an exploratory temptation; to search out and to discover what is in man, what his graces and corruptions are. There is a suasory or enticing temptation, that inclines the will and affections to close with what is presented to them. 1. Now, in general, we may observe five several sorts of temptations: whereof some are of the former, others of the latter kind. (1) Some, whereby one man tempts another. (2) Some, whereby we tempt ourselves. (3) Some, whereby we tempt God. (4) Some, whereby God tempts us. (5) Some, whereby the devil tempts us. Now among these many various kinds of temptations which have been reckoned up, those temptations which we are to pray against are of three sorts—such as proceed from our own lusts and corruptions; such as proceed from other men's persuading us, either by motives or examples unto that which is evil; or, lastly, such as proceed from the devil. Or, else, they may be reduced to these two heads—the temptations which proceed from our own inbred lusts and corruptions and those which proceed from the devil; for, indeed, wicked men are but his agents and instruments, when they tempt us to that which is evil. 2. Now, that our Saviour Christ should make it the great matter and object of our prayers to beg of God that we may not be led into temptation, we may observe that it is a Christian's duty, not only to keep himself from sin, but also to endeavour to keep himself from temptation to sin. For—(1) It is a very ill sign of a rotten and carnal heart to be content to lie under a temptation, although it doth not consent to the commission of sin. (2) If you suffer a temptation to lodge in your hearts, you are in imminent danger of being prevailed upon by it. (3) Consider that, as all temptations are dangerous, and that we have great reason to fear lest, in the end, they should prevail upon us to commit the sin to which we are tempted; so most of them are not only temptations, but sins also. II. HOW GOD MAY BE SAID TO LEAD MEN INTO TEMPTATION. 1. God is said to lead us into temptation when He providentially presents outward objects and occasions which do solicit and draw forth our inward corruptions. 2. God is said to lead us into temptation when He withdraws the influences of His grace from us, and leaves us under the power of a temptation. 3. God is said to lead men into temptation when He permits Satan and wicked men his instruments to tempt us—yea, sometimes He gives them commission as well as permission; and appoints and sends them to do it. (1) He leaves these Canaanites to molest us, to teach us the wars of the Lord; to make us continually watchful; to breathe and exercise our graces; to administer matter for our conquest, and occasion for our crown and triumph. (2) To convince us of our own utter inability to stand of ourselves, without His help and assistance; thereby engaging us to depend upon His arm, and to call for Divine supplies and succours. (3) To glorify both His justice and mercy. His justice, in giving up wicked men to the rage of temptations; to be hurried by them from sin to sin, till at last they put an end to the succession of their sins in eternal damnation. And His mercy, in succouring of and supporting and delivering His children out of all their temptations. (4) God permits His own children to be tempted, that, by their victory over temptations, He may confound the malice of Satan, and commend the excellency of His own ways and service. III. DELIVERANCE FROM EVIL. 1. The thing here prayed against. (1) Satan. (2) All other evils are here meant; whether they be of sin or sorrow; whether they be transgressions or punishments; and that either temporal punishments, in those judgments which God inflicts upon sinners here, or eternal judgments, such as He hath threatened to inflict upon them hereafter. From all these we pray to be delivered—but the greatest of all these is sin. For— (a) It is greatest in the nature of it, as being the only thing that is contrary to the greatest good, even God. (b) It is the greatest evil, in the effects and consequences of it. 2. And whereas we are taught by our Saviour to beg this of God our Heavenly Father, we may observe that it is only the almighty power of God that can keep us from sin. 3. It now remains to show you the ways and methods that God takes to do it. (1) God delivers us from evil, by His restraining providence—putting a hook into men's nostrils, and a bridle into their jaws; and, by a powerful hand, reining them in when they are most fiery and furious. (2) God preserves from sin by His restraining grace. Now this restraining grace is that which is common, and vouchsafed to wicked men as well as good. Indeed, God by it deals in a secret way with the very heart of a sinner; and though He doth not change the habitual, yet He changeth the present actual disposition of it; so as not only by external checks laid upon men's lusts, but by internal persuasions, motives, and arguments, they are taken off the prosecution of those very sins which yet remain in them unmortified and reigning. (3) God hath another method of keeping men from sin, and that is by His special and sanctifying grace. And this is proper only to the children of God who are really sanctified and made gracious. Now, whatever sin God doth thus preserve any from, He doth it by exciting the inward principle and habit of grace to the actual use and exercise of it. There is a twofold grace always necessary to keep the best Christians from sin; habitual and exciting—and God, by the one, quickens and stirs up the other, which else would lie sluggish and dormant. Now that which we pray for in this petition is—1. That if it shall please God to lead us into temptation, yet that He would not leave us under the power of temptation; but, with every temptation, "He would make a way for us to escape, that we may be able to bear it." 2. That if, at any time, temptation should get the upper hand, and prevail over us to the commission of sin, yet that God would not leave us under the power of that sin; but raise us up again, by true repentance and godly sorrow, that so, at last, we may be delivered from the great and soul-damning evil of obduration and impenitency. 3. That God would not only deliver us from gross and self-condemning impieties; but from every evil way and work, and preserve us blameless to the heavenly kingdom of His Son. 4. That He would be pleased not only to deliver us from that which is in itself evil, but from all the occasions and all the appearances of evil—for these also are evil, if not in effect, yet in tendency. (*Bishop Hopkins.*) *The sixth petition :*—I. THE MEANING OF THIS PETITION. Keep us from all occasions of sin, such objects as would prevail upon us to commit it. Suffer us not to yield to temptation, and to fall into the sin to which we are enticed —let us not be left to ourselves when we are tempted. Permit us not to be brought into any temptation or snare. Suffer us not to be entangled in any dangers and difficulties which may not be easily supported by us. That God will give us a way of getting out of any temptation that befals us. That we may not be overcome by temptation; or that we may be kept from any such combat in which there would be great danger of our being vanquished. Such a request we are encouraged to offer up to God by these words in 1 Cor. x. 12, 13, "Let him that thinketh he standeth take heed lest he fall." It is our duty to watch and to take heed; this is required of us—but the grace of God alone is sufficient to keep us from falling. II. WHAT THIS PETITION SUPPOSES AND INCLUDES. 1. A real sincere belief of the particular providence of God, and especially towards His faithful servants. 2. Trust in God, His care, His wisdom and goodness to direct us. 3. Deliberate, firm, steadfast resolutions to follow the Divine conduct. 4. Fear of offending God, and of backsliding, and falling into a loose, careless way. 5. Watchfulness against temptations. 6. Courage to resist it, even the strongest temptation, such as falls in with our greatest infirmity, attacks us on our weakest side, such as promises us pleasure or worldly gain. 7. Fortitude to support us under troubles, to enable us to bear affliction for Christ's sake, and to suffer for Him rather than deny Him. III. WHAT GROUNDS WE HAVE to hope that God will answer this request, and not suffer us to be tempted (if we take proper care of ourselves, and do not provoke Him to forsake us, and leave us to ourselves ; which we may do, and which is actually too often done) ; or, that if we must fall into temptations and snares (which is unavoidable in the present life), God will concern Himself for our confirmation and establishment under all such trials of our faith and patience. The grounds of hope of a gracious audience and acceptance, in our humble petitions of this kind, are such as the following—1. That God is able to strengthen, stablish, and settle us, to deliver us from evil, and to secure us under the greatest dangers. 2. That there are some promises in the Word of God which encourage us (such at least as desire to be faithful) to hope that He will vouchsafe us this grace. 3. That we find in reading the Scripture, that such grace has been granted ; and why may not God be favourable to us, as well as to others, if we are not negligent and careless ourselves ? 4. You may derive hope (such of you as are the children of God, give me leave to use the Scripture style, you may derive hope) from your filial relation to God, that He will not suffer you to be seduced entirely from Him by any temptation that may befal you. 5. The intercession of Christ gives you such hope. Does He direct you to pray, "Lord, lead us not into temptation?" He Himself makes such intercession for you, "Father, keep through Thine own name those whom Thou hast given Me. I pray not that Thou shouldest take them out of the world, but that Thou wilt keep them from the evil." 6. You may go boldly to the throne of grace with this petition, because you are commanded to do it. IV. PRACTICAL SUGGESTIONS. 1. Let us pray that we may not be tempted above what we are able (by the grace of God with us) to bear ; that we may never enter into temptation, and—for our boldness and adventurousness, and want of a just sense of our own weakness, and a due fear of God—be there left ; left to ourselves, to the devil and his instruments to seduce us, and to lead us into sin and ruin. And let this petition in our prayer proceed from faith and trust in God. 2. Let us watch, as well as pray, against temptation. 3. When we are tempted to sin, and commit it, let us not say we are tempted of God ; either externally, by His putting us into such circumstances as to necessitate our sinning ; or internally, by corrupting our minds, raising sinful thoughts in us, and exciting us to sinful practices : this, I observed, is the devil's work, not God's. 4. When we pray that God will not lead us into temptation, but deliver us from evil, and the evil one, and not suffer the devil to lead us captive, let us not tempt one another. This would be no other than to be the instruments and servants of the grand enemy of mankind, the great seducer, who was the occasion of the first breach between God and man, and has found some to promote his interest ever since. 5. When we fall into temptation, let us with steadfast resolution resist it, and endeavour to keep ourselves from the evil to which we are tempted. 5. Let us succour them that are tempted, by good instructions, and serious advice and earnest persuasion ; so you may be instruments of delivering others from evil, and perhaps of saving them from death. All Christians should be like their Lord, and have compassion on them that are out of the way, or going out, seduced by temptation, and do what they can to prevent their error. (*John Whitty*.)　　*Lead us not into temptation* :—I. DOES GOD LEAD ANY ONE INTO TEMPTATION ? 1. God allows temptations which are devoid of the strictly moral element : trials (James i. 2). 2. God allows temptations which have in them some sinful suggestion, for the sake of our moral discipline. Job. Augustine's natural passions kept pressing him even after conversion, but drove him to hide himself more completely in God. A Christian lady was noted for the serenity of her disposition ; no one heard from her a complaint in whatever trial she might have been. She confessed to a naturally irritable temper which the Lord never took from her. She was so afraid of giving way that she ceaselessly prayed for restraining grace. It was the Divine peace that we saw, which descended about her like a halo sent down from heaven. 3. God allows sinful temptations to come against us as a consequence, and thus a punishment, for past transgression. But at the same time He saves all who call upon Him from their own undoing. III. OBSERVE THE CLOSE CONNECTION BETWEEN THIS AND THE FORMER PETITION, "Forgive us our debts." Only when the guilt of sin has been discharged at the Cross does the sanctifying influence follow. This will account for the failure of many of our cries, "Lead us not into temptation." We have not established a basis for help, because we have not yet been forgiven. III. WE ARE SAVED FROM TEMPTATION BY USE OF THE PRAYER. It would be a grand thing to withstand sin if we could do it in our own strength; but it is a grander thing to stand in God's strength, and to know that we have His and not our own keeping. (*J. M. Ludlow, D.D.*) *The danger of self-sought temptations:*—If we walk without care and without vigilance, if we acknowledge not God in our ways, and take counsel at Ekron, and not at Zion—leaving the Bible unread and the closet unvisited—if the sanctuary and the Sabbath lose their ancient hold upon us, and we then go on frowardly in the way of our own eyes, and after the counsel of our own heart, we have reason to tremble. A conscience quick and sensitive, under the presence of the indwelling Spirit is like the safety-lamp of the miner, a ready witness and a mysterious guardian against the deathful damps, that unseen but fatal, cluster around our darkling way. To neglect prayer and watching, is to lay aside that lamp, and then though the eye see no danger and the ear hear no warning, spiritual death may be gathering around us her invisible vapours stored with ruin, and rife for a sudden explosion. We are tempting God, and shall we be delivered? And if this be so with the negligent professor of religion, is it not applicable also to the openly careless who never acknowledged Christ's claims to the heart and the life? With an evil nature, and a mortal body, and a brittle and brief tenure of earth, you are traversing perilous paths. Had you God for your friend, your case would be far other than it is. Peril and snare might still beset you; but you would confront and traverse them, as the Hebrews of old did the weedy bed of the Red Sea—its watery walls guarding their dread way, the pillar of light the vanguard, and the pillar of cloud the rear-guard of their mysterious progress—the ark and the God of the ark piloting and defending them. But without God's blessing, and committed blindly to Satan's guidance—returning prayerless from a prayerless sanctuary to a prayerless home, and seeking a prayerless couch at night, and beginning on Monday a prayerless week, which is to find on Saturday evening its still prayerless end—you are like a presumptuous and unskilful traveller, passing under the arch of the waters of Niagara. The falling cataract thundering above you—a slippery, slimy rock beneath your gliding feet—the smoking, roaring abyss yawning beside you—the imprisoned winds beating back your breath—the struggling daylight coming but mistily to the bewildered eyes—what is the terror of your condition, if your guide, in whose grasp your fingers tremble, be malignant and treacherous and suicidal, determined on destroying your life at the sacrifice of his own? He assures you that he will bring you safely through, upon the other side of the fall. And SUCH IS SATAN. (*W. R. Williams, D.D.*) *In what sense we may pray against temptation:*—But you may say that if temptation is thus the lot of all men, we ought not to pray as in the text, "Lead us not into temptation." This does not follow: sickness is the lot of our race, and yet we may pray to God for health, and God will send it to us so far as He sees it to be good for us; indeed we may pray for all things, if only we use the proviso which our Saviour added to His prayer, "Nevertheless, not My will but Thine be done!" and thus we may pray against temptation, because it is a dangerous thing, and a thing painful to endure, even though we should come off victorious in the end. But after all, I conceive the spirit of the prayer against temptation is to pray quite as much for grace to withstand temptation as for freedom from it, quite as much for strength when temptation comes as for the happiness of its not coming at all: the man who prays against temptation, who fears to encounter Satan, who is always alarmed lest he should find his enemy at his elbow enticing him to sin, this man will in his prayer most certainly include another for grace and strength; he prays against temptation, at the same time he knows that it is not likely that he will be exempted from that which falls to the lot of all, and therefore he trusts that he may by God's grace be found ever ready for the conflict, armed with the shield of faith, the helmet of salvation, and the sword of the Spirit; he prays that no temptation may come upon him greater than he has strength to bear, but that God will make a way for him to escape that he may be able to bear it, and that however strong that enemy of his soul may be, there may be ever with him one stronger than the strong, even the Holy Spirit of God (*Bishop Harvey Goodwin.*) *The temptations that surround us:*—We carry about us an internal enemy, in that heart "deceitful above all things and desperately wicked," a traitor not plotting without and at the gates, but in the inmost citadel, cherishing even there his proneness to backslide from Shaddai to Diabolus, and but too eager to sell afresh the town of Mansoul to its old tyrannous usurper. We are surrounded by evil influences and ensnaring examples in the world which hems our path. "Ill-speech" is not only shouting his proclamations at "Ear-gate"; but in the frivolous and foul literature of our times, this orator and herald of Diabolus is sending his letters missive to "Eye-gate" as well, in ceaseless profusion. Then, let us remember the accursed alchemy of sin in us and in our tempters, both the visible and invisible—that hellish heart of corruption which can make God's works and choice gifts occasions of temptation to us, and render our very blessings a curse. Thus, a mother's kindness may injure the child on whom it is lavished. Friendship and kindred, and home and love, all may ensnare us. Wealth, in itself God's gift, how often is it made, by man's coveting, "filthy lucre." Knowledge, the food of the soul, how may it become the poisonous and baleful fruit of the forbidden tree; and worldly honour and worldly power, what crimes have they incited, and palliated, and protected. Life, may become—as in the case of many of the antediluvians it seems to have done —though its every hour throughout its long centuries were a new favour of Heaven—may become, in consequence of the treachery of man's heart misinterpreting its lessons, a fresh and stronger temptation to persevere in sin; and its extension may but serve to foster the hopes of prolonged impunity in wickedness. Our Bibles, and Sabbaths, and sanctuaries, and religious privileges, may be all so used or relied upon as to become but a seal of aggravation to our guilt, and of hopelessness as to our final conversion. The prophets' tombs, and Abraham for an ancestor, helped to make the Pharisees the more the children of hell. Social progress may become the watchword of revolt against revelation and God—liberty be perverted into an occasion of licentiousness—and the very ordinances and creeds of Christianity be transmuted into a veil and den for Antichrist. The power of immoral transmutation, of turning good into evil, possessed by our fallen nature, is most tremendous and appalling. Aye, the blood of a scorned Saviour, may be made, by your unbelief and mine, the deadliest element in our present sin and in our coming woe. Despite done to the Spirit of grace may convert His benign ministerings and proffered comfortings into the foundation of the sin that hath no remission before God, and no hope for all eternity. And in no scene of earth—in no condition—are we exempt from the incursions of temptation. If we flee to the desert, and brook not the sight of our fellow-creature's face, we bear thither the fiend within; we cannot build out or bar out the indwelling devil. The gratings of the monastery cannot exclude the wings of the fallen seraph, nor solitude sanctify the unregenerate heart. In the garden or the grove, the palace or the hermitage, the crowded city or the howling wilderness, sin tracks us, and self haunts us. If the poor is tempted to envy and dishonesty; the rich, as Augur testified, is equally endangered by pride and luxury. If the man of ten talents is puffed up with self-confidence and arrogant impiety; the man of one talent is prone to bury slothfully the portion intrusted to him in the earth, and then to quarrel with its Holy Giver. The great adversary has in every scene his snares, and varies his baits for every age and variety of condition and character. Each man and child of us has his easily besetting sin. (*W. R. Williams, D.D.*) *Temptation may be advantageous to us:*—Temptations drive the Christian to the grace and throne of Christ. And the victory of the plaintive, and feeble, and mortal disciple over the proud, and subtle, and mighty, but fallen archangel—notwithstanding all that archangel's talents and resources—illustrates to all worlds the wisdom, and faithfulness, and goodness of God. According to promise, "the worm Jacob" is made a brazen "flail to thresh the mountains." Our twining, pliant, and vine-like weakness, becomes in God's hand, rigid, piercing, and irresistible strength. Even here, we can see Paul profiting by the messenger of Satan, the thorn in his flesh, sent to buffet him. We see Luther towering into new boldness of faith, and shooting as from the pinnacles of temptation to a loftier height the rocket of his testimony; as, in Christ's strength, he goes to encounter the temptations of worldly wrath and Satanic hate, at the city of Worms, though, as he says, the devils he may meet there be many as the tiles on the roofs of its houses. You see Cranmer, out of the coil of the temptation that had once pinioned and thrown him, rising to a noble martyrdom, and thrusting resolutely into the blaze the guilty hand that had once denied his Lord's truths. And, as Luther said, such discipline, rugged and keen as it may for the time be, is necessary to Christian usefulness. "Prayer, meditation, temptation," said that reformer, make the true minister of Christ. Men learn the source of their strength, and the might of their Helper, and the love of their Heavenly Father; and "that the way of man is not in himself," but that our sufficiency is of God. (*Ibid.*) *The great salvation :*—This petition recognizes the fact that every man has his weakness and limitations, and that it is safer for him to be surrounded with good influences than with evil influences ; that character grows better in a congenial than in an uncongenial atmosphere. We must encounter evil, our daily duty will bring us often face to face with it ; but some paths are safer than others, some associations are less hostile to virtue than others ; and the prayer is that God will lead us into those paths where the danger is least ; that, so far as it is consistent with duty, His kind providence will keep us out of associations where our virtue will be assailed. To ask God that He will not lead us into such exposures is not to imply that He is likely to do this, and must be besought not to do it ; it means, simply, lead us out of and away from temptation. The petition contains something like what the logicians call a negative pregnant, in which the negative of one thing implies the affirmation of the opposite. 1. The petition implies that God will lead us if we ask His guidance. 2. It also implies that if we will follow Him, He will lead us into safe places, and away from the snares that are set for our feet. 3. It expresses our desire to be kept, so far as may be without neglecting duty, from exposure to the allurements of vice and sin ; to be surrounded with virtuous rather than with vicious influences. 4. It confesses our faith that God will so keep us if we put our trust in Him. (*Washington Gladden, D.D.*) *To the young :*— When you offer the Lord's prayer, do not forget to let your desire rest firmly and fervently on this petition. Ask the Lord to keep you away from bad company ; from the society of those who are vicious, and corrupt, and profane ; from association with those whose minds are filthy, and whose talk is vile ; from all communion with evil minds, and, so far as possible, from all knowledge of evil things. People talk about seeing the world, about getting their eyes opened, and all that ; but do you see just as much of the good of the world as you can, and just as little of the evil. Get your eyes open as wide as you can to behold the truth of nature and the beauty of the Lord, but shut them tight upon visions of sin and shame. I tell you, young people, that familiarity with evil words and evil ways bring no gain to you—nothing but loss and sorrow. There is one kind of ignorance you need never blush for—ignorance of the names, or of the arts, of vice and crime. If your too knowing associates jeer at you for such verdancy, thank God that you are not proficient in such knowledge. The less you know of the things that you are ashamed to speak of, the better for you. If by any possibility you have learned such things, forget them as soon as you can. And always remember, that, except as you seek to overcome evil with good, the safest way is to shun the evil. (*Ibid.*) *An intercessory petition :*—We must not overlook the plural form of this petition. It is not only a personal request, it is an intercessory petition. "Lead *us*; deliver *us*." Our thought takes in others besides ourselves ; the shelter and deliverance that we implore for ourselves, we ask for all our fellow-men. And surely if we ask the Lord to keep our neighbours out of temptation, we shall be careful how we ourselves do anything to place temptation in their way ; we shall do all that we wisely can to make the surroundings of their lives helpful, and not corrupting, to their virtue. (*Ibid.*) *To parents :*—When we pray that our children may not be led into temptation, let us do what we can to choose for them a place to live, and a manner of life in which they shall be exposed to the least possible temptation. Many a man prays at the family altar, "Lead us not into temptation," and then rises from his knees, packs his movables, and goes with all his family, where Lot went, straight down to Sodom. (*Ibid.*) *Parental folly :*—In modern days the first aim of all Christian parents is to place their children in circumstances where the temptations (which they are apt to call "opportunities") may be as great and as many as possible ; where the sight and the promise "of all these things" in Satan's gift may be brilliantly near, and where the act of "falling down to worship me " may be partly concealed by the shelter, and partly excused as involuntary, by the pressure of the concurrent crowd. (*John Ruskin.*) *Prayer against temptation :*—I have read in history that two men were condemned to die as martyrs in the burning days of Queen Mary. One of them boasted very loudly to his companion of his confidence that he should play the man at the stake. He did not mind the suffering, he was so grounded in the gospel that he knew he should never deny it. He said that he longed for the fatal morning even as a bride for the wedding. His companion in prison in the same chamber was a poor, trembling soul, who could not and would not deny his Master; but he told his companion that he was very much afraid of the fire. He said he had always been very sensitive of suffering, and he was in great dread that when he began to burn the pain might cause him to deny the truth. He besought his friend to pray for him, and he spent his time very much in weeping over his weakness and crying to God for strength. The other continually rebuked him, and chided him for being so unbelieving and weak. When they both came to the stake, he who had been so bold recanted at the sight of the fire and went back ignominiously to an apostate's life, while the poor trembling man whose prayer had been, "Lead me not into temptation," stood firm as a rock, praising and magnifying God as he was burnt to a cinder. (*C. H. Spurgeon.*) *The reach and worth of Christian intercession :—* "Lead us not into temptation." O strange and mysterious privilege, that some bedridden woman in a lonely garret, who feels that she is tempted to distrust the love and mercy of Him who sent His Son to die for the helpless, should wrestle with that doubt, saying the Lord's prayer; and that she should be thus asking help for those who are dwelling in palaces, who scarcely dream of want, yet in their own way are in peril great as hers ; for the student, who, in his chamber, is haunted with questions which would seem to her monstrous and incredible, but which to him are agonizing ; for the divine in his terrible assaults from cowardice, despondency, vanity, from the sense of his own heartlessness, from the shame of past neglect, from the appalling discovery of evils in himself which he has denounced in others, from vulgar outward temptations into which he had proudly fancied that he could not fall, from dark suggestions recurring often, that words have no realities corresponding to them, that what he speaks of may mean nothing, because to him it has often meant so little. Of all this the sufferer knows nothing, yet for these she prays—and for the statesman who fancied the world could be moved by his wires, and suddenly finds that it has wires of its own which move without his bidding ; for her country under the pressure of calamities which the most skilful seek in vain to redress ; for all other countries in their throes of anguish which may terminate in a second death or a new life. For one and all she cries, "Lead us not into temptation." Their temptations and hers, different in form, are the same in substance. They, like her, are tempted to doubt that God is, and that He is the author of good, and not of evil ; and that He is mightier than the evil ; and that He can and will overthrow it, and deliver the universe out of it. This is the real temptation, there is no other. All events, all things and persons, are bringing this temptation before us ; no man is out of the reach of it who is in God's world ; no man is intended to be out of the reach of it who is God's child. We must not crave quarter from the enemy : to choose for ourselves where we shall meet him, is to desert that guardianship in which is all safety. But we may cry, "Lead us not into temptation," and praying so we pray against ourselves, against our evil tendencies, our eagerness for that which will ruin us. Praying so, that which seemed to be poison becomes medicine ; all circumstances are turned to good ; honey is gathered out of the carcase ; death itself is made the minister of life. (*F. D. Maurice, M.A.*) *Lead us not into temptation :*—Dr. Talmage once stood on an anniversary platform with a clergyman who told this marvellous story : "Thirty years ago two young men started out to attend Park Theatre, New York, to see a play which made religion ridiculous and hypocritical. They had been brought up in Christian families. They started for the theatre to see that vile play, and their early convictions came back upon them. They felt it was not right to go, but still they went. They came to the door of the theatre. One of the young men stopped and started for home, but returned and came up to the door, but had not the courage to go in. He again started for home, and went home. The other young man went in. He went from one degree of temptation to another. Caught in the whirl of frivolity and sin, he sank lower and lower. He lost his business position. He lost his morals. He lost his soul. He died a dreadful death, not one star of mercy shining on it. I stand before you to-day," said that minister, "to thank God that for twenty years I have been permitted to preach the gospel. I am the other young man." *Temptation :*—1. It is not implied in the petition that God is our tempter. But—2. It does imply that, in some way, God has a control over the influences or the powers that tempt us. 3. The petition implies on the part of us who offer it—(1) That we feel our weakness ; (2) That we shall be watchful against the circumstances and conditions in which temptation is likely to find us ; (3) That we shall keep ourselves mindful of our particular weaknesses ; (4) That we shall quicken ourselves to watchfulness by keeping mindful of the sad results that can come from yielding to temptation ; (5) That we keep ourselves aware of the fact that temptation usually comes in some fair disguise; (6) That we are watchful against the first approaches of sin, the first steps in evil. (*G. W. Field, D.D.*) We must not flatter ourselves that this petition will be granted in its full extent. We must not flatter ourselves that God will enable us to go through life without being exposed to any sort of temptation. For this world is a place of trial and discipline. Now without some kind of temptation we should have no trials, and no opportunity of exercising several of the Christian graces. It is only in war and in battle that the soldier—and the Christian, remember, is God's soldier—can learn his duty thoroughly. He may learn to handle his arms in peace; but the coolness, the quickness, the watchfulness, the caution, the steady, unbending courage, which distinguish the veteran from the recruit, are only to be gained on actual service. So it is only by actual service against God's enemies, it is only by passing through temptations and trials, that the Christian can be trained to his work. He needs to be taught the lesson of his own weakness. He needs to be taught to watch and guard against the surprises and stratagems of the foe. He needs to be perfected in faith and patience. How is all this to be done, if he is kept, like a plant under a glass, from every breath and touch of temptation? No; we shall assuredly be led into temptation whether we pray against it or not; because there is no earthly road to heaven but has its own pitfalls and its own snares. This is a sad but certain truth; and I should only deceive you were I to tell you otherwise. (*A. W. Hare.*) *The sixth petition in the Lord's prayer:—* "Lead us not into temptation." Doth God lead· into temptation? God doth permit sin, but doth not promote it. He who is an encourager of holiness cannot be a patron of sin. God doth not tempt to that which He hath an antipathy against. What king will tempt his subjects to break those laws which he himself hath established? But is it not said, God tempted Abraham? Tempting there was no more than trying. God tried Abraham's faith, as a goldsmith tries gold in the fire; but there is a great deal of difference between God's trying His people's grace, and exciting their corruptions. Whence do temptations come? From ourselves. The heart is the breeder of all evil. The heart is a perfect decoy. 2. Temptations come from Satan. He is called "the tempter"; he lies in ambush to do us mischief, "he is always ready for battle"; the devil lays a train of temptation to blow up the fort of our grace. A saint's whole life, saith Austin, is a temptation. That we may see in what danger we are of Satan's temptations—consider (1) his malice in tempting. Satan envies man's happiness; to see a clod of dust so near to God, and himself, once a glorious angel, cast out of the heavenly paradise, this makes him pursue mankind with inveterate hatred. Consider (2) Satan's diligence in tempting—"he walketh about." He neglects no time; he who would have us idle, yet he himself is always busied. Like Marcellus, a Roman captain Hannibal speaks of, whether he was conquered, or did conquer, he was never quiet. More particularly, Satan's diligence in tempting is seen in this. (*a*) If he gets the least advantage by temptation, he pursues it to the utmost. If his motion to sin begins to take, he follows it close and presseth to the act of sin. (*b*) Again, Satan's diligence in tempting is seen in this, the variety of temptations he useth. He doth not confine himself to one sort of temptation, he hath more plots than one. He will tempt them to leave off ordinances; he will pretend revelations. Error damns as well as vice; the one pistols, the other poisons. Consider (3) Satan's power in tempting. He is called "the prince of the world," and the "strong man." He is full of power, being an angel; though Satan hath lost his holiness, yet not his strength. The devil's power in tempting is seen several ways. (*a*) He, as a spirit having an intellectual being, can convey himself into the fancy, and poison it with bad thoughts. (*b*) Satan, though he cannot compel the will, yet he can present pleasing objects to the senses, which have a great force in them. (*c*) The devil can excite and stir up the corruption within, and work some inclinableness in the heart to embrace the temptation; thus he stirred up corruption in David's heart, and provoked him to number the people. Satan can blow the spark of lust into a flame. (*d*) Herein lies much of his power, that he being a spirit, can so strangely convey his temptations into our minds, that we cannot easily discern whether they come from Satan, or from ourselves; whether they are his suggestions, or the natural births of our own hearts. A bird may hatch the egg of another bird, thinking it is her own; often we hatch the devil's motions, thinking they come from our own hearts. (*e*) Satan's power in tempting appears by the long experience he hath gotten in the art; he hath been a tempter well nigh as long as he hath been an angel. Who are fitter for action than men of experience? Who is fitter to steer a ship than an old experienced pilot? (4)

Consider Satan's subtlety in tempting. He hath several sorts of subtlety in tempting. (*a*) The devil observes the natural temper and constitution. The devil doth not know the hearts of men, but he may feel their pulse, know their temper, and so accordingly can apply himself. As the husbandman knows what seed is proper to sow in such a soil, so Satan finding out the temper, knows what temptations are proper to sow in such a heart. That way the tide of a man's constitution runs, that way the wind of temptation blows ; Satan tempts the ambitious man with a crown, the sanguine man with beauty, the covetous man with a wedge of gold. He provides savoury meat, such as the sinner loves. (*b*) Satan chooseth the fittest season to tempt in. As a cunning angler casts in his angle when the fish will bite best ; the devil can hit the very joint of time when a temptation is likeliest to prevail. There are several seasons he tempts in. In our first initiation and entrance into religion, when we have newly given up our names to Christ. The devil tempts when he finds us idle, unemployed. When a person is reduced to outward wants and straits, now is the devil's tempting time. Satan tempts after an ordinance. Why doth Satan choose this time to tempt in, after an ordinance? One would think this were the most disadvantageous time, for now the soul is raised to an heavenly frame. Malice puts Satan upon it. The ordinances that cause fervour in a saint, cause fury in Satan. As after a full meal, men are apt to grow drowsy, so after we have had a full meal at an ordinance, we are apt to slumber and grow secure, and now Satan shoots his arrow of temptation, and hits us between the joints of our armour. Satan tempts after some discoveries of God's love. Satan, like a pirate, sets on a ship that is richly laden ; so when a soul hath been laden with spiritual comforts, now the devil will be shooting at him to rob him of all. Satan tempts when he sees us weakest. He breaks over the hedge where it is lowest. A subtle policy of Satan in tempting is, he baits his hook with religion ; the devil can hang out Christ's colours, and tempt to sin under pretences of piety. Now he is the white devil, and transforms himself into an angel of light. Subtlety of Satan is, to tempt to sin gradually. The old serpent winds himself in by degrees, he tempts first to lesser sins, that so he may bring on greater. Satan's policy is to hand over temptations to us by those whom we least suspect. Some, like the spunge, suck in Satan's temptations. There are five sorts of persons that Satan doth most fit for brooding upon by his temptations. 1. Ignorant persons. The devil can lead them into any snare ; you may lead a blind man any whither. 2. Satan tempts unbelievers. An unbeliever will stick at no sin ; luxury, perjury, injustice. 3. Satan tempts proud persons ; these he hath more power of. None is in greater danger of falling by a temptation than he who stands high in his own conceit. 4. Melancholy persons. Melancholy is a black humour, seated chiefly in the brain. Melancholy clothes the mind in sable; it doth disturb reason; Satan doth work much upon this humour. Subtlety of Satan is, to give some little respite, and seem to leave off tempting a while, that he may come on after with more advantage. Satan, by feigning a flight, and leaving off tempting a while, causeth security in persons, and they think they are safe, and are become victors, when on a sudden, Satan falls on, and wounds them. Subtlety of the old serpent is, either to take men off from the use of means, or to make them miscarry in the use of means. Satan endeavours to discourage from duty by objecting want of success. Satan knows duties done superficially were as good to be left undone. That prayer that doth not pierce the heart will never pierce heaven. Satan can colour over sin with the name and pretence of virtue. The next subtlety of Satan is, he labours to ensnare us by lawful things. More are hurt by lawful things than unlawful, as more are killed with wine than poison ; gross sins affright, but how many take a surfeit and die, in using lawful things inordinately? Subtlety of Satan is to make the duties of our general and particular calling hinder and justle out one another. Subtlety of Satan in tempting is, to misrepresent true holiness, that he may make others out of love with it. He paints the face of religion full of scars, and with seeming blemishes, that he may create in the minds of men prejudice against it. Subtlety of Satan in tempting is, to draw men off from the love of the truth to embrace error, " that they should believe a lie." Satan is called in Scripture not only an unclean spirit, but a lying spirit. As an unclean spirit, so he labours to defile the soul with lust ; and as a lying spirit, so he labours to corrupt the mind with error ; and indeed this is dangerous, because many errors do look so like the truth, as alchemy represents true gold. Satan thus beguiles souls. Another subtlety of Satan is, to bewitch and ensnare men, by setting pleasing baits before them ; the riches, pleasures, honours of the world ;

"all this will I give thee." How many doth Satan tempt with this golden apple! Subtlety of Satan in tempting is, to plead necessity. The tradesman pleads a necessity of unlawful gain, else he cannot live; another pleads a necessity of revenge, else his credit would be impaired; thus Satan tempts men to sin, by telling them of the necessity. Subtlety of Satan in tempting is, to draw men to presumption. Presumption is a confidence without ground; it is made up of two ingredients, audacity and security; this temptation is common. Subtlety of Satan in tempting is, to carry on his designs against us under the highest pretences of friendship; he thus puts sugar upon his bait, and dips his poisoned pills in sugar. Subtlety is, when Satan hath tempted men to sin, he persuades them to keep his counsel; like them that have some foul disease, they will rather die than tell the physician. Subtlety of Satan is, to make use of fit tools and engines, for the carrying on of his work; that is, he makes use of such persons as may be likely means to promote his tempting designs. Subtlety of Satan in tempting is, he, in his temptation, strikes at some grace more than others; as in tempting, he aims at some persons more than others, so he aims at some grace more than others; and if he can prevail in this, he knows what an advantage it will be to him. If you ask, what grace is it that Satan in his temptations doth most strike at? I answer, it is the grace of faith; he lays the train of his temptations to blow up the fort of our faith. "Fight neither with small nor great, save only with the king." So faith is, as it were, the king of the graces; it is a royal, princely grace, and puts forth the most majestic and noble acts, therefore Satan fights chiefly with this kingly grace. 1. Because this is the grace doth Satan most mischief; it makes the most resistance against him—"whom resist steadfast in the faith." No grace doth more bruise the serpent's head than faith. 2. Satan strikes most at our faith, and would weaken and destroy it, because faith hath a great influence upon the other graces; faith sets all the graces a-work. Like some rich clothier, that gives out a stock of wool to the poor and sets them all a-spinning, so faith gives out a stock to all the other graces, and sets them a-working. Subtlety of Satan in tempting is, in broaching those doctrines that are flesh-pleasing. Satan knows the flesh loves to be gratified, it cries out for ease and liberty; it will not endure any yoke unless it be lined and made soft. The devil will be sure so to lay his bait of temptation as to please and humour the flesh. He who sells cheapest shall have most customers; the devil knows this is a cheap easy doctrine, which will please the flesh, and he doth not doubt but he shall have customers enough. Subtlety of Satan in tempting to the act of sin is, the hope of returning out of it by speedy repentance. Subtlety of Satan in tempting is, to persuade men to delay their repenting and turning to God. He saith, "the time is not come." Subtlety of Satan in tempting is, to infringe and weaken the saints' peace. If he cannot destroy their grace, he will disturb their peace. By what arts and methods doth Satan, in tempting, disturb the saints' peace? 1. Satan slily conveys evil thoughts, and then makes a Christian believe they come from his own heart. The cup was found in Benjamin's sack, but it was of Joseph's putting in; so a child of God often finds atheistical, blasphemous thoughts in his mind, but Satan hath cast them in. 2. Satan disturbs the saints' peace, by drawing forth their sins in the most black colours, to affright them, and make them ready to give up the ghost. From this subtlety of Satan in tempting, let me draw three inferences. 1. It may administer matter of wonder to us how any soul is saved. 2. Is Satan subtle? See then what need we have to pray to God for wisdom to discern the snares of Satan, and strength to resist them. Why doth God suffer his saints to be so hurried and buffeted by Satan's temptations? The Lord doth it for many wise and holy ends. 1. He lets them be tempted to try them. "Temptation is the touchstone of sincerity." By temptation God tries our love. 2. God suffers His children to be tempted that they may be kept from pride. The thorn in the flesh was to prick the bladder of pride; better is that temptation that humbles me, than that duty which makes me proud. 3. God lets His people be tempted, that they may be fitter to comfort others who are in the same distress; they can speak a word in due season to such as are weary. A man that hath rid over a place where there are quicksands, is the fittest to guide men through that dangerous way. 4. God lets His children be tempted to make them long more for heaven, where they shall be out of gunshot; there they shall be freed from the hissing of the old serpent. What rocks of support are there, or what comfort for tempted souls? 1. That is not our case alone, but hath been the case of God's eminent saints. 2nd Rock of support, that may comfort a tempted soul, is, that temptations, where they are burdens, evidence grace. 3rd Rock of support or comfort is, that Jesus Christ is near at hand, and stands by us in all our temptations. 1. Christ's sympathy in our temptations. 2. Christ's succour in temptation. Christ's agility in succouring. How and in what manner doth Christ succour them that are tempted? Several ways : (1) Christ succours them, by sending His Spirit, whose work it is to bring those promises to their mind, which are fortifying. (2) Christ succours them that are tempted by His blessed " interceding for them." (3) Christ succours His people by taking off the tempter. 4th Rock of support. The best man may be most tempted. 5th Rock of support. Satan can go no farther in tempting than God will " give him leave "; the power of the tempter is limited. 6th Rock of support. It is not the having a temptation makes guilty, but the giving consent. 7th Rock of support. Our being tempted is no sign of God's hating us. 8th Rock of support. Christ's temptation was for our consolation. 9th Rock of support. The saints' temptation shall not be above their strength. The lutenist will not stretch the strings of his lute too hard. 10th Rock of support. These temptations shall produce much good. See in what continual danger we are. See man's inability of himself to resist temptation. Here is matter of humiliation, that there is in us such an aptitude and proneness to yield to temptation. See hence, a Christian's life is no easy life ; it is military. Exhortation : Let us labour that we be not overcome by temptation. 1. Avoid solitariness. 2. If you would not be overcome of temptation, beware of the predominancy of melancholy. 3. If you would not be overcome of temptation study sobriety; " be sober, because your adversary walketh about." 4. Be always upon your guard ; watch against Satan's wiles and subtleties. 5. Beware of idleness; Satan sows most of his seed in fallow ground. 6. Make known thy case to some godly friend ; the hiding a serpent in the bosom is not the way to be safe. 7. Make use of the Word. This the apostle calls " the sword of the Spirit " ; a fit weapon to fight against the tempter. 8. Let us be careful of our own hearts that they do not decoy us into sin. 9. If you would not be overcome of temptation, flee the " occasions of sin." Occasions of sin have a great force in them to awaken lust within. 10. If you would not be overcome by temptation, make use of faith—" above all things take the shield of faith." 11. If you would not be overcome of temptation, be much in prayer. 12. If you would not be overcome of temptation be humble in your own eyes : such are nearest falling who presume of their own strength. 13. If you would not be foiled by temptation, do not enter into a dispute with Satan. 14. If we would not be overcome of Satan, let us put on Christian fortitude. 15. If we would not be overcome of a temptation, let us call in the help of others. 16. If we would not be overcome of temptation, let us make use of all the encouragements we can. (J. Watson.) " And lead us not into temptation " :—I. This, then, is the meaning of life: it is a probation. The real problem of every man's existence is his own character, what it is and how it shall issue. And to this end everything is probing him. Adversity is probing him ; prosperity is probing him ; and not only life in its generals, but life in every one of its details, is probing him. Every influence he feels, whether of the Holy Spirit, or of the angels, or of his fellow-men, or of demons, probes him. II. Observe now, that our heavenly Father, in His wise love, is sometimes pleased to subject us to unusual temptation, testing, probing. This is implied in the petition which His Son, our Lord, has taught us to offer : " Father, lead us not into temptation ! " There is in this word " lead " a distinct, emphatic recognition of the Father's administration, or, as we say, providence. Our circumstances in life are not the result of chance on the one hand, or of fate on the other. Thus He led Abraham when He commanded him to offer up Isaac. It came to pass that God did tempt, i.e., try, prove, Abraham. And all this explains the prayer which our Lord bids us repeat : " Father, lead us not into temptation." It is the prayer of genuine humility and profoundest self-distrust. III. Observe now, that each one is to offer this prayer not only for himself, but also for the whole world. Human society is a brotherhood of peril ; let it therefore also be a brotherhood of intercession and sympathy and mutual help. In drawing our meditation to a close, let me beseech you to keep away from temptation as well as to pray against being led into it. And yet our heavenly Father, for purposes of testing us, of revealing us to ourselves, of developing, fortifying, and perfecting our characters, of animating others by the example of our steadfastness, may deem it best not to grant the petition which His own Son has taught us : " Lead us not into temptation." " Prayer, meditation, temptation, make the theologian," said the great Augustine ; and, let us add, not the theologian only, but also the Christian.

Nothing so buttresses character as a great victory over a great foe. (*G. D. Boardman, D.D.*) *Temptation deplored :*—All the changes that men meet with are trials of their character. Nero was a very different man while the pupil of Seneca from what he was as the emperor of Rome. Solomon was a very different man in the early part of his reign from what he was in those voluptuous periods of his history during which he brought such reproach upon the throne. Men do not know themselves. Hazael the subject was a very different man from Hazael the prince. Who would have thought the youthful Mary, the Queen of England, the translator of the Gospels, would ever have deserved the appellation of the "bloody Mary"? Who would have supposed that Robespierre, once so sensitive to the sufferings of his fellow-men that he resigned a lucrative office under the government rather than condemn a culprit to the scaffold, would have filled Paris with blood ; or that William Dodd, once so celebrated for his usefulness as a minister of Christ, would have been executed at Tyburn for forgery? Sometimes a mere change of place, an unexpected conflict with an individual or a party, an unhappy alliance in business, or an unlooked-for alteration in public affairs, proves a touchstone to the character, before which truth and integrity wither, and gives a blow to the spirit of self-confidence, which is never so renewed that the sufferer can lift up his face before the world. Sometimes these very incidents result in a well-tested integrity and honour, prepare those who endure the trial for still severer conflicts, and furnish them for exemplary toil and sacrifices. They had this effect upon Abraham, Joseph, Nehemiah, Job, Jeremiah, Daniel, Paul, and thousands of others in later times. 1. The man who offers this request with a becoming spirit contemplates his exposure. The world is full of those who have been led away by temptation, who, before they were led astray, would have said that it could have had no influence upon them. Most of the boasting among men proceeds from the want of being tried. It should never be forgotten that a pardoned sinner is not past all peril. "Watch and pray," says the Saviour, "that ye enter not into temptation; the spirit indeed is willing, but the flesh is weak." This exposure to sin arises principally from the following sources : In every human being this side the grave there is a melancholy tendency to evil. There is a great deceiver, too, who is not only permitted to have the power, but is long practised in the arts of seduction. 2. This petition more especially contemplates as great an exception from this exposure as is consistent with the designs and will of God. While the petition, "lead us not into temptation," therefore, does not contemplate an entire exemption from temptation, it contemplates as great an exemption as is consistent with the will of our Father who is in heaven. (*G. Spring, D.D.*) *Of leading into :*—Our English maketh a manifest difference betwixt "unto" and "into," which is worth the noting in this place. The latter implieth a degree further than the former. A man that cannot swim may be led unto a deep pool, and yet be safe enough ; but if he be led into it he is in great danger of drowning except he be pulled out again. They who translate it, "Cast us not into temptation," do well express the sense. (*W. Gouge.*) *Of the many ways of delivering from evil :*—How may one be delivered from evil ? 1. By keeping away that evil which is ready to fall upon him. Thus were the Israelites delivered from the host of the Egyptians that eagerly pursued them. 2. By assisting him on whom the evil is fallen, so as he is not overwhelmed and overcome therewith. For this purpose read Psa. lxix. 14, 15. 3. By altering the nature of the evil, and turning it to a man's good. Thus God turned Joseph's abode in Egypt to much good. Herein this proverb is verified, "I had perished if I had not perished." 4. By taking away the force of the evil; as the force of the fire was taken away so as it burned not Shadrach, Meshach, and Abednego. This deliverance Christ promised to His disciples. 5. By removing the evil clean away. Thus God delivered Israel from the devouring pestilence. 6. By taking one away from the evil to come. Thus the good son of wicked Jeroboam, thus the good king Josiah, thus many righteous men have been delivered. (*Ibid.*) *Of the general points for which we are taught to pray in the last petition :*—What are we to pray for by virtue of the last petition ? Such things as concern the whole petition in general, or the distinct parts thereof in particular. 1. In regard of the whole, we ought to pray for sanctification. Thus doth St. Paul pray for the Thessalonians : "The very God of peace sanctify you wholly." As our own happiness moveth us to pray for justification, in the former petition, that we may be acquitted of sin, for which we should otherwise be damned, so the honour of God should move us to pray for sanctification. For this is the will of God, our sanctification, and thereby is the holy God much honoured. 2. In regard to the manner of setting down this petition negatively, we are taught to pray for freedom against the power of sin, as the Psalmist doth where he saith, "Cleanse me from secret faults: keep back Thy servant also from presumptuous sins; let them not have dominion over me." For in sin there is a guilt which maketh us liable to God's vengeance (this is prayed against in the fifth petition) and a power which holdeth us in bondage, and maketh us such slaves thereto as we cannot serve God. 3. For this end we are taught to pray for participation of the power of Christ's death; and—4. Participation of the Spirit of Christ. For in Christ's death there is distinctly to be considered a merit and a power. The merit thereof freeth from the guilt and punishment of sin; the power thereof from the dominion, yea, and by degrees from the very act of sin, which in the saints, after the death of their body, shall utterly cease. Of this power of Christ's death thus speaketh the apostle: "We are buried with Christ by baptism into death," &c. And again: "Our old man is crucified with Him, that the body of sin may be destroyed, that henceforth we should not serve sin." This power of Christ's death is conveyed into us by the Spirit of Christ. For we are "dead in sin." What are the particulars to be prayed for under the first part of the sixth petition? 1. Knowledge of our spiritual enemies. Without knowledge of them there will be no fear of them, no desire of help and succour against them, or of freedom from them. 2. Sight of the danger wherein we are by reason of them. When Elisha's servant saw the host of Aram that compassed the place where he was, then he cried out, "Alas, my master, how shall we do?" 3. Wisdom to discern their wiles, their many cunning stratagems, and kinds of assaults. David, who obtained such wisdom, undoubtedly prayed for it (Psa. cxix. 98–100). 4. Understanding of our own weakness. 5. Knowledge of the almighty power of God. Thus doth the apostle expressly pray in behalf of the Ephesians that they may know what is "the exceeding greatness of His power towards them that believe." 6. Restraint of Satan's power. This the angel intended when he said to the devil, "The Lord rebuke thee" (Jude, ver. 9). 7. Assistance from God; for though Satan be restrained, yet cannot we stand of ourselves, but shall fall, even through our own weakness. 8. Confidence and courage in God. 9. Sufficient grace to bear out assaults when we are tempted; for sometimes it is needful for us to be tempted. 10. Power over the flesh. 11. Contempt of the world. 12. Patience under all crosses. 13. Removal of judgments. 14. A blessed departure out of this world. So long as we are in this world we are subject to many evils, which lie and press sore upon us. (*Ibid.*) *Of the things for which we ought to give thanks in the last petition :*—What are the things for which thanks is to be given by virtue of the last petition. 1. Every sanctifying grace. 2. Freedom from the power of darkness. For both these we have the express pattern of the apostle. In regard of the former he saith: "I thank my God for the grace of God." Under this indefinite word "grace" he compriseth every particular sanctifying grace. Wherefore he addeth: "In every thing" (that is, in every grace) "ye are enriched." And "Ye are not destitute of any gift." In regard of the latter he also saith: "I give thanks to the Father, who hath delivered us from the power of darkness." We heard before that sanctification was the sum of this petition. But particular sanctifying graces—whereof nine are reckoned up together (Gal. v. 22, 23)—are the parts and members which make up that sum. Of these, therefore, we must take notice, and for these we must give thanks. Now, because that sum is implied under the negative, we are answerably to give thanks for freedom from the contrary, which the apostle styleth "power of darkness." Under darkness he compriseth sin, death, devil, and damnation. While we are under the power of these we are their vassals. It is therefore a blessing worthy of all praise to be freed from them. Other particulars generally concern the distinct parts of this petition. (*Ibid.*) *Of the particulars for which thanks is to be given by virtue of the first part of the last petition :*—What are the particulars for which the first part of the sixth petition requireth thanks to be given? 1. Understanding of the law, whereby we know what sin is when we are tempted thereto, how fearful a thing it is to yield to such temptations, how wretched their case is that are left to the power of temptation. "By the law is the knowledge of sin." That, therefore, which giveth us notice of so great danger is a thing praiseworthy, especially if we have understanding thereof. In way of thankfulness doth David oft acknowledge this. 2. Wisdom to discern our enemies and their assaults. This proceedeth from the former, and goeth a degree farther; and in that respect it bindeth us to more thankfulness. With thankfulness saith the Psalmist to God:

"Thou through Thy commandments hast made me wiser than mine enemies."
3. The victory which Christ hath gotten over our spiritual enemies. It is in praise
of Christ that the Psalmist saith to Him, "Thou hast led captivity captive." By
captivity he meaneth the world, the flesh, sin, death, the devil, and all other
enemies of our soul. Were not these by Christ made captives, and so chained,
restrained, and kept in, we could not stand against them; they would soon lead us
captives. For our sakes did Christ enter combat with them, and get victory over
them. We reap the benefit thereof; we therefore must give the thanks to Christ,
and say (as the heavenly spirits do): "We give Thee thanks because Thou hast
taken to Thee Thy great power,' and hast reigned, and destroyed them that destroy
the earth." 4. Strength to withstand our enemies. As Christ Himself hath overcome them, so by His Spirit He giveth us power to overcome, in which respect it
is said: "He hath given to us the spirit of power." On which ground saith the
apostle: "I thank Him who hath enabled me." 5. Resolution to yield to no
allurements, whether they come from the flesh or the world. A true, settled resolution is a great means to keep us safe. This comes from God; for by nature our
disposition is wholly inclined to the world and to the flesh. Wherefore, as David
blessed God for assuaging his passion, and keeping him from shedding blood, so
we must praise God (whensoever our mind is alienated from the world and flesh)
for that alteration of our disposition. 6. Patience to bear out all brunts. Afflictions to our weak flesh are sore temptations; but by patience we are kept from
being swallowed up by them. In which respect the apostle saw great cause to
thank God for the patience of the Thessalonians. 7. Power in all conflicts to
overcome. Such, though they be led *unto* temptation, are not led *into* temptation.
It is expressly noted of them that had gotten victory that they sang a song of
praise. (*Ibid.*)   *Of the particulars for which thanks is to be given by virtue of
the last part of the last petition :*—What are the things for which the second part
of the last petition requireth thanks? 1. Repentance after sin committed. This
is a sure evidence of deliverance from a great evil. Therefore the Church glorified
God because He had granted repentance. 2. Rescue out of Satan's clutches. If
Satan have at any time got any advantage against us, as he getteth great advantage against witches and sorcerers, yea, and against other impudent and audacious
sinners whom he hath fast in his clutches, to be rescued and recovered out of his
hands affordeth just cause of much thanks, which Mary Magdalene, out of whom
went seven devils, well knew to be most due, and therefore, in testimony of thankfulness, she followed Christ, and ministered to Him of her substance. 3. Recovery
out of the world. The apostle ascribeth glory to Christ for delivering us from this
present evil world. 4. Conquest of the spirit over the flesh. For by the spirit's
conquest are we freed from the dominion of the flesh. For this, therefore, the
apostle giveth express thanks. 5. Removal of judgments. Judgments and all
manner of crosses are in their kind evils; and removal of them is a deliverance from those evils; whereupon the saints have been thankful for such
deliverances. The Israelites give thanks to God for freeing them from the
Egyptian bondage; and David for causing the plague to cease; and Hezekiah for
taking away a deadly disease; and the Church for returning her captivity. 6.
Victory over death. Death in itself is a dreadful evil, the very entrance into
damnation. But by Christ the sting of it is pulled out, the nature of it is altered.
It is made a gate into eternal glory. This is that victory for which St. Paul giveth
thanks. 7. Hope of resurrection to life. 8. Hope of eternal glory. These are full
and final deliverances from all evil. God's promise of these to such as believe is as
a performance of them. Our hope, therefore, resting on God's promise for these,
affordeth just occasion of rejoicing and praising God, as St. Peter doth, and St.
Paul also. (*Ibid.*)   *Of duties required in the last petition :*—What duties are
we to endeavour after by virtue of the last petition? 1. To abstain from all sin;
for this is the main thing here prayed against. This is it which maketh temptation
so hurtful as it is. The more we forbear sin, the less damage shall we receive from
any temptations. Many, many, therefore, are the dehortations of Scripture against
sin. 2. To perfect holiness; for under the avoiding of any evil an endeavouring
after the contrary good is always in Scripture implied; yea, they are very oft
joined together. Now, holiness is perfected both by adding one grace to another,
and also by continual growth in every grace. These two duties arise from the
general sum of the last petition. 3. To be jealous over ourselves, fearing lest at
any time we should be overcome by any temptation; for we are not only weak, easy
to be overtaken and overthrown by every temptation, but also very prone to yield

to Satan's temptations, because they are either agreeable to our corrupt humour, or else we so fearful as to think we shall never stand out against them. This Christian jealousy will make us the more instantly and constantly to seek help of God. 4. To avoid all occasions of evil. Occasions of evil are temptations to evil. Should not they, then, who pray against temptations avoid them as much as possibly they can ? 5. To withstand beginnings. So did the apostle when he would not give place to false brethren (who were dangerous tempters), no, not for an hour. Thus much also he intendeth in this exhortation, " Give no place to the devil," which is as if he had said, " If Satan at any time tempt you, yield not an inch to him ; let him get no advantage at all, which he cannot but get if at the beginning ye yield any whit at all to him." Much good is got by a due observation of this duty, and much wisdom is manifested thereby ; for that evil which in the beginning is easily prevented can hardly, if at all, without very much damage, be redressed after it hath found some entrance. Instance poisonous and pestiferous diseases, fretting and festering sores, fires, breaches of water, and enemies entering within the walls of a city. 6. To watch continually. This is a duty whereunto in Scripture we are much exhorted, and that not without cause; for our spiritual enemies are always ready to tempt us, narrowly prying where to get any advantage against us. And soon they will get too great advantage if we be not the more watchful. To show that this duty is fitly inferred out of this petition, Christ expressly joineth it with prayer against temptation, saying, " Watch and pray that ye enter not into temptation." 7. To be sober and temperate. Where these are not, every tempter will rule as he list ; for intemperance and all excess blind the understanding, and open a passage to all manner of evil desires and filthy lusts, and make us unfit to pray, to watch, to fight, and to defend ourselves against our spiritual enemies. 8. To cast off every burden. By burdens are meant not only such things as are simply evil in themselves, but such also as being in their nature good, and may lawfully be used, yet through our weakness and inability to use them well, prove impediments to us in our spiritual combat; as the riches of that ruler whom Christ advised to sell all that he had, and to give it to the poor. Thus if honours, offices, recreations, companies which we frequent, or any worldly thing wherein we delight, prove a burden to us, and make us unfit to resist temptations—yea, rather make us yield to temptations—we are to cast them off, to avoid and forsake them. 9. To mortify our members on the earth. The flesh—that is, our corrupt nature— which containeth in it the mass of all sin, is styled a body. This body is made up of several particular lusts and evil motions, as a body of members. And as a body exerciseth all functions by the members, so the flesh executeth all mischiefs by particular lusts ; and one lust helpeth another, as one member another, and as dear are these lusts to the natural man as the members of his body. Those particular lusts are therefore fitly styled members, and they are said to be members on the earth. (1) In opposition to the spirit, and the graces thereof which come from heaven, and bring men to heaven. (2) In their own condition, which is, as the earth, base, filthy, corrupt, and vain. (3) In their operation, whereby they make men grovel and dote on the earth, and the things therein. By mortifying these, the foresaid body (which is a dangerous tempter) will in time be deprived of all strength, and we freed from the danger of the temptations thereof. Be diligent, therefore, in searching them out, and having found them, spare them not, as Saul did the fat beasts, but deal with them as Samuel did with Agag, and Joshua with the kings of Canaan. 10. To beat down our body. This is done by forbearing to pamper ourselves, and to satisfy our carnal desires, that so the flesh may not wax wanton, and, like a pampered jade, become unruly ; but that we may live within the compass prescribed and limited by God's Word. 11. To renounce the world. The world is such a tempter, as the friendship of it is enmity with God. " If any man love the world, the love of the Father is not in him." Demas, that old disciple Demas, by embracing the world, was brought to renounce his Christian profession. It is therefore most meet that " the world be crucified to us, and we to the world" ; that our hearts be clean alienated one from another, and that we have no more to do one with another than the living with the dead. Thus shall we be sure not to be overtaken by the temptations of the world. 12. To resist the devil. This is the only way to escape his temptations. He is like a wolf, which fiercely pursueth, and never leaveth such as fearfully fly from him, but flieth from such as manfully stand against him. So saith the apostle : " Resist the devil, and he will fly from you." 13. To put our trust in God. To what end do we else pray unto God ? 14. To suffer afflictions patiently. All crosses and afflictions are temptations. By a patient enduring of them we keep ourselves from being overcome by them. Let patience, therefore, have her perfect work. The last twelve duties arise from the first part of the last petition. 15. To avoid that which is any way evil. This we, praying against, must carefully avoid. The apostle exhorteth to " abstain from all appearance of evil." 16. To return from that evil whereinto we have fallen ; for they which pray to be delivered from evil must not lie in evil. All the exhortations in the Scripture to repent tend to this purpose. 16. To take heed of relapse. A relapse in bodily diseases is dangerous; much more in the soul's disease. (*Ibid.*)   *Of duties required in the last petition in regard to others :* —What duties doth the last petition teach us in the behalf of others ? 1. To consider one another. 2. To keep others from sin. 3. To edify others. They who are well built up in grace are well armed against all temptations. 4. To encourage others against their enemies. What a notable encouragement is this of the apostle: " Watch you, stand fast in the faith, quit ye like men, be strong." Another like, but more large encouragement, is set down (Eph. vi. 10–13, &c.). 5. To strengthen the weak. This did Christ expressly give in charge to Peter. 6. To keep others from falling from the grace of God. The apostle adviseth to look diligently hereunto (Heb. xii. 15). 7. To restore such as fall. 8. To save the obstinate with fear. 9. To receive the penitent. 10. To pray for others. (*Ibid.*) *Lead us not into temptation:*—My first task is to show God is no cause of sin. For is there any so far gone in error as to suppose the clear fountain of all goodness can be the foul sower of sin ? Can good and evil flow from the same head ? Or can the Judge of all the world play booty with His clients, receive a prayer with one hand and deal a curse with the other ? It is true the tongue can bless and curse with the same breath ; but God, who gave it motion, making it the organ of speech and interpreter of the heart, made not the perverse language which the tongue utters. Cursings were never stamped in His mint, but cast by him who is the author of lies and forgeries. Contraries never rose from one spring, nor do the brackish and sweet waters flow from the same rock. What a monster then should that man breed in his imagination that should pronounce God the author of sin ! If nature abhor to teem with opposites in one and the same womb ; if the grape and the thorn, the fig and the thistle, be births which one stock bears not ; if bitter and sweet be qualities which necessarily derive themselves from a different parentage ; then much more are good and evil births which the God of nature never yet reconciled in His acts. And sooner shall nature run counter to herself, inverting her even course ; sooner shall the congealed frost lodge with the fire, and winter become the preposterous mother of the harvest, than the true Father of Light be brought to father the spurious issue of night, sin, and error. (*Archdeacon King.*)   *Presumption :*—There is no ship so tall built or strongly ribbed which can be confident she will not founder in the next storm, nor is there any man of such a confidence who, if a tempest or temptation rise up against him, can be assured that at the instant he can call up so much reason and religion as to withstand it. Would you not judge him mad who, being come to an anchor in a safe road, would, like the dolphin, hunt the storm, and choose to ride it out at the main sea ? Is it not enough thou hast an antidote to expel poison, but thou must turn empiric upon thyself, hazard the empoisoning of thine own body, to try the power of thy medicine ? It is no discreet religion which seeks out dangers, and glories in temptations ; nor is he wise to salvation who presents himself to that hazard which Christ taught him to pray against. " Fateor imbecillitatem meam, nolo spe pugnare victoriæ ne perdam aliquando victoriam," saith St. Hierome. To hazard a set battle in hope of a doubtful victory is to outdare a man's judgment. It is possible that he who exposes himself to the danger of a fight may overcome, but it is probable he may fall. The peril is certain, the victory doubtful. In unneedful temptations I had rather distrust myself than make trial of my strength in apparent disadvantage. (*Ibid.*)   *Meeting temptations :*—Which are so many that, if we will compute our danger, we need not send out our wishes to meet temptations or bring them home to us ; they come too swiftly, and unbidden, like rough winds that blow from every corner of the sky ; and in that number, as if each minute were computed by them, so plentiful is the spawn of sin in our waters. (*Ibid.*)   *The devil lights his temptations :*—To make which more plausible it is ever his cunning practice to attire them in that dress and livery which best suits each man's humour and complexion. To the fantasy of the melancholy he whispers nothing but horror, plying him with all objects that may bring him to madness or despair. To the sanguine complexion he presents those wanton delights whereunto naturally it leans. The phlegmatic, like marshes which every tide overflows, he seeks to lay quite under water by the habit of that moist vice, which like a deluge covers the greater part of the earth—drunkenness. Lastly, the furious and choleric he prompts to quarrels, cherishing that unruly flame so long till he has made them believe that murder is the triumph of reputation; so causing them to purchase the opinion of an unhappy valour by bloodshed. At which luckless period he leaves them to the torture of a guilty conscience in this life and the fearful expectation of vengeance in the next. Thus doth the devil, like a politic engineer, besiege us in our own works, turning our passions, like daggers, upon our own breasts. (*Ibid.*)   But though the devil be the chief instigator of sin, the flesh is the instrument. Nay, saith Origen, "Etiam si, Diabolus non esset, homines haberent appetitum ciborum et Venereorum"—Were there no other devil, we have one at home, an invisible devil that lodgeth in the blood, the seditious appetite which urges us to perpetual mutiny against the good motions of God's Spirit. (*Ibid.*)   *Prayer the only protection:*—We are assured, though there be many windows and ports and doors for temptation to enter at, there is but one key to let us out or to lock us up against it, God's assistant or prevenient grace. (*Ibid.*) .   Which promise He performs either by giving us ability to decline them when they offer themselves at us, or by allaying them in such fashion that they become healthful medicines to cure, not poisons to corrupt us, and happy probations not to waste but to refine us. As gold runs purest from the furnace, finding no abatement of the substance, but the dross only, or by apportioning them to our strength that they do not overmatch us, so though He gives us not peace, yet He gives us means, by a fair defensive war, to hold out the siege against them. Be this then our comfort, that as temptation hath some ill in it, so it hath much good. It was said of the conspiracy against Julius Cæsar, "If in that action there were anything of glory, it belonged to Brutus, but all the malice and cruelty of the design was imputed to Cassius. I make a juster application: Whatsoever good is occasioned by temptation we must ascribe it to God, but the malignity which accompanies it belongs to the devil. (*Ibid.*)   *Fear of temptation:*—God has given to most of His creatures an instinct that leads them to fear, and as far as possible to avoid danger. If you lift your hand against any of the lower animals they will do their utmost to avoid the stroke. God has made that a part of their nature. If they see danger coming they try to get out of its way; and if that cannot be, they do their best to provide against it. You may have seen a flock of sheep, when a storm began to gather, all crowding together as if for mutual defence, and hurrying to that part of the field where they would be most likely to be safe from the fury of the blast. So common and natural is this fear of, and desire to avoid danger, that we wonder when we see anything else. When we see the moth fluttering about the evening lamp, attracted by its brightness, unwarned even after the flame has once and again taken the edge off its wing, darting at length into the very heart of the flame, and falling lifeless on the table, we wonder at that; and while we pity, we cannot help thinking and calling it a silly foolish creature. Now we, too, have got the same instinctive fear of outward danger. We fear disease, and do everything we possibly can to keep out of its way. We tremble at the thought of cholera coming among us. Fire-escapes, immense ladders, and other apparatus in towns, life-boats on land, and life-preservers on board ship, and many things else, tell how we fear, and will do the utmost we can to escape, approaching danger. One thing more dangerous and terrible than any of these we do not fear, we do not avoid. I mean that which is not necessarily sin in itself, though it so often leads to sin—temptation. I. A THREATENING DANGER—"temptation." When I speak of danger, you expect to hear of something alarming. When you were ill, and the doctor came to see you twice a day, you understood what was meant by there being danger. But when I speak of temptation, that alarms few or none. If you were to go over all the thousands that fill the cells of our prisons, they would all have something to say about having been tempted—that if they have not been tempted they would not have committed the crime, and so would not have been there. Every cell would re-echo the word "temptation," and, as you leave it, I can fancy I hear you saying, "What a dangerous and dreadful thing it must be to be tempted!" These temptations or solicitations to evil are so dangerous. 1. Because of the quarter from which they come—the devil, the world, and the flesh. 2. Their suddenness and unexpectedness make them dangerous. Ordinarily they give us no warning; they take us by surprise. During the mutiny in India, where warning was given, precautionary measures were at once taken; and when the enemy came our countrymen were ready for him, and, in more cases than one, were able to hold out. In this way the British Residency at Nagpore was saved through the instrumentality of that noble-hearted missionary, Stephen Hislop. But temptations, for the most part, give no warning. 3. Their power makes them dangerous. II. A CRY FOR HELP—"Lead us not into temptation." Perhaps some one asks, "Is it not interfering with God's providence to pray this prayer?" I answer, No. I am allowed to pray that I may be kept out of the way of other dangers, such as disease, or poverty, or death. And may I not ask that I may be kept from this danger as well as from these others? It may be needful and good that the temptation or the trouble otherwise should come, but I may lawfully pray to be kept from both. Perhaps some one asks, "Is it not cowardly to pray this prayer? Is it not shrinking back from the battle instead of manfully fighting it?" It is indeed an acknowledgment of weakness. It tells that I fear. But fear is one thing, and cowardice is another. Let us see, then, more particularly what this prayer asks. 1. It asks that we may be kept out of the way of objects that might entice to evil. To see certain things, to be in certain places, is enough, in many cases, to constitute a formidable temptation. There is a girl of dishonest tendency. The mere sight of money within her reach might again secure her fall. Surely she may well pray that things may be so ordered, that it may not be needful that she should go near them at all. 2. It asks that opportunities of evil may be kept out of my way. Oh, how much sometimes depends for my doing evil on my having the opportunity that favours it. 3. It asks that solicitations to evil may not come to us. I may be of a soft, yielding nature—very easily advised, very open to persuasion, not able to say, No. 4. It asks that examples of evil may be kept out of our way. How much the seeing of evil done influences others to do the like. (*J. H. Wilson, M.A.*) **But deliver us from evil.**—*The prayer for deliverance from evil:*—The Italian poet, in painting the world of woe, ranges its several dreary mansions along a narrowing and descending volute. The lower it sunk the narrower it grew in his vision. Escape from the influence of hell is, in the structure of the Lord's prayer, represented by an image the converse of the poet's. The higher the way of escape mounts, the broader it becomes. As by the winding pathway and the successive stages of this form of supplication we are borne upward out of the bowels of the pit into which the Fall had plunged us, so we find the path widening perpetually as it goes on ascending; as we proceed from one grade and platform of prayer to another the subject of request extends itself out more and more widely. As we climb the heavenly heights, new and broader prospects open around us. We begin by deploring sins within ourselves, and grope about the narrow and dark den of our own hearts; we then expand our petitions by reference to the temptations in the circle around and without us; and finally, in the words now before us, we look beyond the limits of sin in us and temptations around us, to the sorrow and pain which may remain, even where sin is renounced and where temptation is resisted. Beyond this state of probation we look to evil as it shall be recompensed and perpetuated in the world of retribution, and to yet another world, where all effects and traces of evil are effaced from the heart and lot of the blessed. Taken in this sense, then, the sentence includes a prayer for the repeal of the primal curse on man and earth. I. The cry of our text, STAMMERED, as by the unregenerate and heathen world, it universally is. The burden of the text is heard in the voice of the new-born babe, sending back the first draught of air which its tiny lungs have made, in wailing, as it lies back on its nurse's arm; and it is found in the death-rattle of the gray-headed grandsire, breathing his last after well-nigh a century's experience of life, and its toils and its woes. Each contest that sets man against his fellows—from wars like those of Tamerlane or Napoleon, that littered a continent with their millions of dead, down to the street-fray or the village lawsuit; each statute, tribunal, and prison, and penalty; each party-gathering and each party-badge; each form, and voice, and look of human anguish; the pauper's thin and trembling hand; the maniac's shriek, and the captive's asking eye; the sick man's hollow cheek; all the diseases that crowd the beds of the hospital, and perplex the physician's skill, and crowd the volumes of a medical library; all the remedies and diversions that seek to while away care or suppress thought; the drunkard's bowl, and the song of the reveller, and the gambler's dice-box—all the wild utterances of human revenge and hate; murder scowling on the brother whose presence it cannot abide, and jealousy and envy nibbling at character, and hinting dislike; all the ills of childhood, maturity, and age; each bead of sweat rolling from the brow of honest toil; each tear that falls from the eye, and each sigh that quits the burdened heart; every pang felt, and every complaint uttered? but waft upward to God or send around to our fellow-man the one sad, monotonous cry, "Deliver us from evil." II. That cry ARTICULATED, as by the penitent and Christian, now taught to know the plague of his own heart; it is—1. Taught of God's Word, he traces back all evil, social and physical, to moral evil, and finds the guilt of its introduction into our world resting on his race, and of its continuance resting on himself. 2. But who shall satisfy for past offences, and who uproot the strong tendencies for ill within him? Is there help in his fellows? They may aid and instruct and cheer him onward. The Christian Church, like travellers in arctic climes, watching to detect the first evidence of frost seizing the face of a fellow-traveller, its unconscious victim, and applying promptly the remedy, may aid him in watching against the frost of spiritual death, that unsuspected would else steal upon him. But they cannot make the atonement, or work the regeneration which he needs. May he look higher than earth and man? He must; for man and earth cannot solve his doubts or quell his fears. He is dying—who shall unsting death? He is to live and bide the doomsday? Oh, who shall give him acquittal there? God could, but will He? To Him he resorts. III. That cry answered, as it is, by God come down to our deliverance. (*W. R. Williams, D.D.*) *The great deliverance:*—"There is none righteous, no not one." Such is the Word of the Book. It is true. Rather startling to the moral man, who believes that he is doing the right thing; paying his way; just to all; owing no man; paying 20s. in the £. But it is true. Examine yourselves, and see what answer your conscience will give. " I am no worse than my neighbours," says one. Yes, there is a good deal of this negative goodness in the world. People are very anxious to declare what they have not done. But are they doers of good? Few, if they speak the truth, will dare to say, as did the Jewish Rabbi, "If there are ten righteous people in the world, my son and I belong to the ten; and if five, we belong to the five; and if two, we are the two; and if one, I am the one." No, the Scripture is true—"There is none righteous, no not one." "We have left undone those things that we ought to have done, and have done those things we ought not to have done." "All we like sheep have gone astray; we have turned every one to his own way." Well, then, we may pray—"Deliver us from evil." "Evil is ever present with us." Look around. It starts in loathsome guise from the pavements of our streets. It staggers from the glaring gin-palace at the corners of our highways. It rears its leprous form, sin-spotted, in palace as well as in hovel. It has left its mutilated wrecks in our hospitals and infirmaries. It lifts its hydra-head and horrifies us almost wherever we go. Nor need we go far to meet with it. It is near at hand. It is among our friends and acquaintances. It separates father from son, and son from father; mother from daughter, and daughter from mother. It comes between friends, who seemed made to cling together, and cleaves them asunder for the rest of their lives. It enters our very homes. It sits at our tables. It is at our firesides. Nay, it is in our very hearts. Well, then, may we pray—"Deliver us from evil." Evil has been said to be perversion of good. It has also been defined as absence of good. But if we accept either of these negative definitions, the question naturally presents itself—"What is good?" Goodness is obedience to God. Evil, then, must be disobedience. I. THE PRAYER IMPLIES THE NECESSITY OF DELIVERANCE. Sin springs from three causes. 1. From the influence of Satan or his emissaries over the hearts of men. Quaint old John Bunyan has well illustrated the power of Satan thus in his " Pilgrim's Progress." Christian is passing through the valley, close to the mouth of hell; and the evil ones step up to him, and whisper foul blasphemies into his ear, so insidiously that the poor pilgrim thinks they are the utterances of his own heart. May God deliver us all from this evil. 2. Another fruitful source of sin is our own lusts—our own passions. Man is, in his structure and his appetites, but a superior animal, moved by the same instincts, by kindred wants and wishes implanted in him, as in the inferior animals, for his own preservation, and the propagation of his species. But he has what is with them wanting—the moral control. God has breathed into his nostrils the breath of life. Man has become a " living soul." And that God who created him with these passions gave him power to control them, a power fatally weakened and largely lost by a long course of inherited sin, but which can be strengthened by the heartfelt wish expressed in the prayer— " Deliver us from evil." 3. Then there are the temptations afforded by the world. In our business, and in our pleasures, evil is continually present with us. The custors of business, the exaggerations of trade, the pushing manners of our own times, the very anxiety, laudable as it is, to be in the forefront in our walk in life, all these are fruitful sources of evil. And in the street, and in tram, and 'bus, and rail, on the way to and from our business, evil continually assails us, in the daily habits and customs of those with whom we are brought in daily contact. Our pleasures too often lead us astray. Amusements, innocent in themselves, cause us to neglect the serious duties of life, and thus become positive evils. II. THE PRAYER IMPLIES THE NECESSITY OF DELIVERANCE FROM ANOTHER SOURCE. We cannot deliver ourselves. (*The Weekly Pulpit.*)   *Deliver us from evil:*—I. A VERY GENERAL PETITION. 1. Evils not specified, because—(1) The catalogue would be endless. (2) Things evil in some circumstances are not evil in others, and therefore could not be classified in set phrases. (3) That which would be an evil by itself may work out its own compensation: storms that hasten the ship, sickness that brings the soul to religious faith, trials that have their reward in heaven, &c. 2. Anything sinful is a real evil in itself. II. ALL MORAL EVILS ARE ONE. 1. No such thing as a little evil. 2. No evil that belongs only to the individual. 3. No temporary evil coming from sin. III. THE POWER OF EVIL IS PERSONAL. IV. THE UNITY AND PERSONALITY OF EVIL A HOPEFUL FACT. Jesus has conquered the evil one. A "roaring lion" will be cowed by the glance of his conqueror. If we are with Christ, the devil will slink away. (*J. M. Ludlow, D.D.*)   *Deliver us from evil:*—The revelation of sonship is also the revelation of evil. Until we know God is Father, and we His dear children, we do not know how evil a thing is sin. You can see the reason of this. The slave, who has no idea of freedom, is content to wear his fetters. The man to whom this world is all does not feel it to be a prison. But let the revelation come: "Ye are not the son of the bondwoman, but of the free; ye have not received the spirit of bondage, but the spirit of adoption, whereby ye cry, 'Abba, Father,'" then how galling the fetters become, and what longing there is for the liberty of the children of God. Let the revelation of a man's true nature and destiny come to him, then the world is too little for him—it is stifling in its narrowness and closeness. His spirit wants a broader and loftier breathing-place. It is not the things God has made that can satisfy him. He wants God Himself. His heart and flesh cry out for God, for the living God. His prayer is, "Show us the Father, and it sufficeth us." And as long as evil comes between him and the light of his Father's face, his prayer must be, "Deliver us from evil." I. THE PRAYER OF GOD'S CHILD—"Deliver us from evil." 1. The evil God's child prays to be delivered from. It is necessary to have clear ideas upon this point. Many things we call evil are not so in reality. They may be but the hiding of some good, deeper than our poor minds can grasp, or the painful shocks that are bringing health and freedom for some captive child of God. The only real evil is sin. When we pray to be delivered from evil, we do not pray to be delivered from suffering, but from repining in suffering; from the blindness which does not see the hand of God in it. We do not pray to be delivered from poverty, or calamity, or death, but from the evil in us which would prevent us from turning every loss into gain, every trial into strength, and every vicissitude in our changing experience into a means of spiritual progress. In a word, we want to be delivered from the impulses and sway of the old nature, that we may enter into the life and freedom of the new. We want to escape the corruption that is in us, through becoming "partakers of the Divine nature." 2. This prayer is in perfect harmony with God's purpose in redemption. The student of the Bible and of history must see that deliverance from evil is the great object of the Divine discipline and culture of our nature. The Old Testament is a revelation of the righteousness of God. Its aim, from beginning to end, is to expose evil that men may know it and escape its thraldom. Even the judgment that followed swiftly upon transgression had at its heart a yearning desire for the deliverance of the sons of God. It was not because God delighted in vengeance, but in mercy, that departure from righteousness brought pain, and obedience, blessedness. And what is the purpose of the New Testament but emancipation from evil? Its light and its love—the revelation of the mind and heart of God in Jesus Christ—what is its aim if not salvation from the evil? The ideal of manhood as realized in Jesus shows you that you were not made to be the slaves of sin, but the free sons of God. The cross—the at-one-ment between humanity and God—shows you how through crucifixion of the evil your nature may be brought into complete and responsive harmony with God's, and so be delivered from the evil. 3. The desire of the prayer shall be completely realized. This is a blissful assurance to the man whose sense of evil is keen. He longs to be free from it, and would willingly die if so be he might become as stainless as the light, as pure as the heart of God. Now, use this prayer. Jesus would not have taught it you if He had meant to mock you. He would not have shown you the evil, if He had not intended to deliver you from it. He would not have carried light into your prison, and troubled you with a Divine discontent, if He had not intended to save. The same spirit which makes you cry, "Oh, wretched man that I am, who shall deliver me?" will put a new song into your mouth, "Thanks be unto God who giveth us the victory, through our Lord Jesus Christ." II. THE REASONS FOR USING THIS PRAYER. 1. The evil is within us. A man cannot flee from the plague of his own heart by going into a desert or shutting himself up in a cell. Doré, in his picture of the Neophyte, by a touch of genius all his own, has shown how the ideal the young man has chosen is failing to realize his hopes. In that beautiful face of his, so marvellously expressive, we see hope trembling between fear and disappointment; we see the shadows gathering over the beauty of the young man's ideal. The brutal countenances of some of the men that surround him, the stern scowl of others, the sensual look of most, these surely cannot express the purity and beauty of God's ideal. No; the young man has made a mistake. The picture says: The cloister is no more sacred than the world. Escape from the world is not escape from sin. See, these men still live in the old sensual nature. Escape from that. Come out of the old nature into the new. Live, not in the flesh, but in the spirit. Let Christ be formed in you, His spirit possess you, and then you shall be free. "For where the Spirit of the Lord is, there is liberty." 2. Then the evil is so subtle. Just here is our danger and our need of this prayer. 3. We must be delivered from evil before our salvation is complete. The evil destroys our peace, and comes between our souls and God. It dims our vision to all that is most beautiful in His character, and most Divine in His works. (*W. Hetherington.*) *Deliver us from evil:*—I. This petition implies THAT WE ARE LIVING IN A WORLD IN WHICH IS THE PRESENCE OF EVIL. II. This petition implies THAT THOSE WHO USE IT ARE UNDER A SENSE OF BEING IN BONDAGE TO EVIL. III. This petition implies THAT NOTHING LESS THAN THE OMNIPOTENT ARM OF GOD CAN DELIVER US FROM THIS EVIL. IV. This petition implies THAT NOTHING CAN BE SATISFYING TO THE CHRISTIAN BUT THE ENTIRE EXPULSION OF EVIL FROM THE WORLD. (*W. Dodsworth.*) *Deliverance from evil:*—The first of these three petitions asks for forgiveness; the next that we may be spared the grievous inducements to the sins which need such forgiveness; and the following and concluding prayer embraces deliverance from all the power and all the consequences of sin. Deliver us from evil—from all the wretched fascination and all the miserable results of sin, from its blindness and insensibility, from its unspirituality and rebellion, from its hardness and its punishment, from all that dishonours God and ruins the soul, from its guilt, its power, its shame and its doom. (*H. R. Reynolds, D.D.*) It is worth while to remark the difference between the notion of evil which the Bible teaches and that which the world teaches. If you ask a man of the world what evil is, he will tell you everything that gives you pain, or annoys you, or makes you uncomfortable. Bad health, for instance, he will say, is an evil; a lazy servant, a hard master, a quarrelsome neighbour, a damp house, poverty, afflictions of all kinds are evils. In short, evil, according to the worldly man, is whatever troubles the body, or interferes with our worldly comfort or prosperity. But is this the Christian's notion of evil? Is this the answer which St. Paul or St. John would have given if any one had asked them what evil is? They would tell you that the only evil of any consequence is what is against the will of God. So that the devil is above all the evil one; because he is the great opposer of that goodness which God wills and delights in. Worldly afflictions are indeed grievous so long as they last, so that we may indeed pray against them. But such a prayer must be offered up with a full sense of their comparative insignificance, lest we be troubled by them above measure. It must be offered up moreover in humble reliance on the wisdom and goodness of our Heavenly Father, lest peradventure we should be praying against a blessing. In a word, we must pray against them with an *if.* But our sins need no *if* in praying against them. Their danger, their burthen, their grievousness, their shame, their curse, we know too well from sad experience. God Himself has declared them to be evil. Therefore they should be the uppermost evil in our minds when we say, "Deliver us from evil." (*A. W. Hare.*) *Deliverance from evil:*—The wildest legends of the mediæval times usually contain within them an incrustation of fable, a precious germ of truth. Here is one which strikes us. A certain noble lady of Assisi had quitted her father's house by stealth, and had become a Franciscan. Her little sister Agnes, ten or eleven years of age, filled with love to her sister, and burn-ing with religious fervour, followed her into her seclusion. Naturally enough, the parents could not endure that a second child should be lost to their home. They gathered together a company of armed men, attacked the sister's retreat with rude violence, and tore the child away despite her tears and entreaties. As she would not accompany them of her own will, they began to drag her away by main force. Friends were helpless even to attempt a rescue; but the story tells us that she suddenly became heavy as lead in the arms of her captors, so that they could not carry her further, and were obliged to let her lie upon the ground. Despite their united efforts, she seemed to have become immovable, and they were com-pelled to leave her in the wood. When they were all gone, the child joyfully arose, and returned to her sister, never to be separated again. Strip the whole story of its unnaturalness, and its superstitious wonders, and you see what God does for His children when sin would make them its prey. At first the world would fain drag the young convert back to his former ways and pleasures. It comes with the rude force of persecution or temptation, and attempts to make a captive of one who has fled from it. When the young convert is utterly unwilling to be seduced from his consecration to his Lord, it is not long before he becomes "as a burden-some stone" to those who would bear him away. There is a weight of character, a solidity of grace, a sobriety of thought, and possibly a strangeness of manner about him, which is too much for them. He is not good company; even as a target for their jests he is a failure. They do not understand the reason, but they quit their hopeless work. Henceforth they admit the reality of the religion which at first they ridiculed as a temporary fancy. Right gladly delivered from the further solicitations of the worldly, the convert returns to his brethren, and rejoices in the liberty wherewith Christ has made him free. (*C. H. Spurgeon.*) *Temptation to be avoided :*—The writer saw at Chicago notices placed on several houses with the warning, "Smallpox is here"; "Fever is here." Only those having necessary business, or bound on errands of affection and philanthropy, would enter such a house. But may not the mark of moral pestilence be seen on the forehead of many a boon-companion, and over the entrance of many a saloon of pleasure? Is it not inscribed on every fascinating temptation to sin? Should we be less cautious regarding the health of the soul than of the body. (*Newman Hall.*)   *The devil's chief servants :*—The devil has a great many servants, and they are all busy, active ones. They ride in the railway trains, they sail on the steamboats, they swarm along the highways of the country and the thoroughfares of the cities; they do business in the busy marts, they enter houses and break open shops; they are everywhere, and in all places. Some are so vile-looking that one instinctively turns from them in disgust; but some are so sociable, insinuating, and plausible, that they almost deceive at times the very elect. Among this latter class are to be found the devil's four chief servants. Here are their names. "There's no danger." That is one. "Only this once." That is another. "Everybody does so." That is the third. "By-and-by." That is the fourth. When tempted from the path of strict rectitude, and "There's no danger" urges you on, say, "Get thee behind me, Satan." When tempted to give Sabbath up to pleasure, or to do a little labour in the workshop, or the counting-house, and "Only this once" or "Everybody does so" whispers at your elbow, do not listen for a moment to the dangerous counsel. If the Holy Spirit has fastened upon your conscience the solemn warnings of a faithful teacher or friend, and brought to mind a tender mother's prayers for your conversion, do not let "By-and-by" steal away your confidence, and, by persuading you to put away serious things, rob you of your life. All four are cheats and liars. They mean to deceive you, and cheat your soul of heaven. "Behold!" says God, "Now is the accepted time, now is the day of salvation." He has no promises for "By-and-by." (*Dr. Talmage.*) *But deliver us from evil :*—What evil do we pray to be delivered from? First, in general, "deliver us from evil": we pray to be delivered from the evil of sin. Not that we pray to be delivered immediately from the presence and in-being of sin, for that cannot be in this life, we cannot shake off this viper; but we pray that God would deliver us more and more from the power and practice, from the scandalous acts of sin, which cast a reflection upon the gospel. That sin is the most execrable evil, appears several ways. 1. Look upon sin in its original; it fetcheth its pedi-gree from hell. Sin is of the devil. 2. Look upon sin in its nature, and so it is evil. (1) See what the Scripture compares it to. Sin hath got a bad name. (2)

Sin is evil in its nature, as it is injurious to God.   It is a breach of God's royal law; " sin is a transgression of the law "; it is high treason against heaven. (3) Sin is evil in its nature, as it is a foolish thing. (4) Sin is a polluting thing. Sin is not only a defection, but a pollution; it is as rust to gold, as a stain to beauty; it is called " filthiness of the flesh and spirit." (5) Sin is a debasing thing, it degrades us of our honour. (6) Sin is an enslaving thing. A sinner is a slave when he sins most freely. (7) Sin is an unsavoury thing; " they are altogether become filthy "—in the Hebrew, they are become stinking. (8) Sin is a painful thing, it costs men much labour and pains to accomplish their wicked designs; " they weary themselves to commit iniquity." " Sin is its own punishment." (9) Sin is a disturbing thing; whatever defiles, disturbs. 3. Look upon sin in the judgment and opinion of the godly, and it will appear to be the most prodigious evil. The primitive Christians said, they chose rather to be devoured by lions without than lusts within. The godly testify sin is a great evil, in that they desire to die upon no account more than this, that they may be rid of sin. 4. Look upon sin in the comparative, and it will appear to be the most deadly evil. (1) Compare sin with affliction: there is more evil in a drop of sin than in a sea of affliction. Sin is the cause of affliction, the cause is more than the effect. Sin is the Phaeton that sets the world on fire. Affliction doth but reach the body, and make that miserable, but sin makes the soul miserable. Afflictions are good for us; " it is good for me that I have been afflicted." Thus affliction is for our good; but sin is not for our good, it keeps good things from us—" Your sins have withholden good things from you." A man may be afflicted, and his conscience may be quiet. Thus, in affliction, conscience may be quiet; but when a man commits a presumptuous, scandalous sin, conscience is troubled; by defiling the purity of conscience, we lose the peace of conscience.   In affliction we may have the love of God. Afflictions are love-tokens—" As many as I love, I rebuke." But when we commit sin, God withdraws His love; it is the sun overcast with a cloud, nothing appears but anger and displeasure. There are many encouragements to suffer affliction. Thus sin is worse than affliction; there are encouragements to suffer affliction, but no encouragement to sin. When a person is afflicted, only he himself suffers; but by sinning openly he doth hurt to others. Affliction can hurt a man only while he is living, but sin doth hurt him when he is dead. (2) Sin is worse than death. Were it not for sin, though death might kill us, it could not curse us. 5. Look upon sin in the manner of its cure; it cost dear to be done away; the guilt of sin could not be removed but by the blood of Christ; He who was God must die, and be made a curse for us, before sin could be remitted.   How horrid is sin, that no angel or archangel, nor all the powers of heaven, could procure the pardon of sin, but it cost the blood of God! 6. Look upon sin in the dismal effects of it, and it will appear the most horrid prodigious evil—" The wages of sin is death," that is, " the second death." Is sin such a deadly, pernicious evil, the evil of evils? See, then, what it is we are to pray most to be delivered from, and that is from sin; our Saviour hath taught us to pray, " deliver us from evil." Hypocrites pray more against temporal evils than spiritual. If sin be so great an evil, see, then, the folly of those who venture upon sin, because of the pleasure they have in it—" but had pleasure in unrighteousness." If sin be so great an evil, then, what wisdom is it to depart from evil? " To depart from evil is understanding." If sin be so great an evil, then, how justifiable and commendable are all those means which are used to keep men from sin? If sin be so great an evil, see, then, what should be a Christian's great care in this life, to keep from sin—" Deliver us from evil." Some make it all their care to keep out of trouble; they had rather keep their skin whole than their conscience pure; but our care should be chiefly to keep from sin. (1) Take heed of sins of omission. (2) Take heed of secret sins. (3) Take heed of your complexion-sin, that sin which your nature and constitution doth most incline you to. (4) Take heed of your sins which attend your particular callings. (a) The godly have something which may restrain them from sin. (b) The sins of God's people are greater than others, because they sin against more mercy. (c) The sins of the godly are worse, and have this aggravation in them that they sin against more clear illumination than the wicked — " They are of those that rebel against the light." (d) The sins of the godly are worse than the sins of the unregenerate, for, when they sin, it is against great experiences. (e) The sins of the godly are greater than others, because they sin against their sonship. Secondly, in this petition, " deliver us from evil," we pray to be delivered from the

evil of Satan. He is "the evil one." In what respect is Satan the wicked one?
1. He was the first inventor of evil; he plotted the first treason. 2. His inclination is only to evil. 3. His constant practice is doing evil. 4. All the evils and
mischiefs that fall out in the world, he hath some hand in them. (1) He hinders
from good. (2) He provokes to evil. The devil blows the fire of lust and strife.
Thirdly, in this petition, " deliver us from evil," we pray to be delivered from the evil
of the world. In what sense is it an evil world? 1. As it is a defiling world. It is
like living in an infectious air; it requires a high degree of grace to "keep ourselves
unspotted from the world." 2. It is an evil world, as it is an ensnaring world.
The world is full of snares. Company is a snare, recreations are snares, oaths are
snares, riches are golden snares. 3. It is an evil world as it is a discouraging
world. It casts scorn and reproach upon them who live virtuously. 4. It is an
evil world, as it is a deadening world. It dulls and deadeneth the affections to
heavenly objects. 5. It is an evil world, as it is a maligning world. It doth
disgust and hate the people of God—"Because ye are not of the world, therefore the
world hateth you." 6. It is an evil world, as it is a deceitful world. 7. It is an
evil world, as it is a disquieting world. It is full of trouble. The world is like a
bee-hive; when we have tasted a little honey, we have been stung with a thousand
bees. A man may abstain from evil, yet he may go to hell for not doing good—
"Every tree that bringeth not forth good fruit, is hewn down, and cast into the fire."
"Deliver us from evil," that is, from temporal evil. We pray that God will either
prevent temporal evils, or deliver us out of them. 1. We pray that God will
prevent temporal evils; that He will be our screen, to stand between us and
danger—"Save me from them that persecute me." 2. We pray that God will
deliver us out of temporal evils; that He will remove His judgments from us,
whether famine, sword, pestilence—"Remove Thy stroke away from me." Yet with
this we may pray to be delivered from temporal evils only so far as God sees it
good for us. In all the troubles that lie upon us, let us look up to God for ease
and succour—"Deliver us from evil." "Should not a people seek unto their God?"
(*T. Watson.*) *The dread of sin:*—One of the most effective means of deliverance
from this great evil, is prayer. Why do the children of God thus fervently pray to
be delivered from sin? 1. Sin is itself "exceeding sinful." It is "an evil thing and
bitter." It is the poisoned arrow; the dart that most bitterly wounds the soul.
2. When men are born of God, and become His children, they imbibe a portion of
His nature and spirit. Because sin is odious in itself, and hateful to Him, it is
hateful to them. 3. It is not like other evils which come upon them, and which
they mourn over, but which have no moral turpitude. 3. To this upward progress
sin opposes the most humiliating obstacles; it acts upon the mind just as a stupe-
fying or inflammatory disease acts upon the body. To a greater or less extent,
every sin does this; while habitual and aggravated sin does it to an alarming
degree. The heart, the great moral principle, the master impulse of the wondrous
machinery, itself disordered, throws into disorder all the natural faculties. True
religion, wherever it is felt in purity and power, always produces the most happy
effect upon the mind that embraces it. Nor is there anything that preventeth these
joys from being constant, unless it be the chilling, withering influence of sin. Sin
is the atmosphere of death. It is like returning winter to the soul when sinful
thoughts, sinful passions, and sinful pursuits agitate it. The Christian who is
even surprised into sin, finds it difficult to return to his wonted enjoyment of God.
Sin also diminishes, if it does not destroy the Christian's usefulness. True piety
is efficient and operative. Another reason for this request is found in the
fact, that sin is so universally destructive in its tendencies upon the happiness
and best interests of the world in which we dwell. There is still another
reason for this request: it is found in the claims of redeeming love. The
suppliant is one who addresses the God of pardon. He has become reconciled
to Him through that mighty Sufferer who hung upon the cross. God is His
Father now; He would not wound that heart of paternal love. (*G. Spring, D.D.*)
But deliver us from evil:—We must admit that it is an evil world. Look, first, at
the physical world. How many accidents there are in it! How many diseases
and deformities and agonies and deaths! What a world of sick-rooms and
infirmaries and graves! Is not that an evil world in which death is the inexorable issue of life? Again, look at Nature itself. Nature as a machine
is perfect. But among the products which the working of that perfect machine
turns out are the volcano and the earthquake, the morass and the desert, the
flood and the drought, the famine and the pestilence, deadly beasts and loath-

some vermin, painful accidents and misshapen forms, agonies and death. Again, look at the intellectual world. See how partial, unsymmetrical, are many of its judgments! With what sidelong, tortuous course does it approach truth, careening toward it under preponderant stress of self-bias. Again, look at the emotional world. What cares and apprehensions and silent griefs chafe and corrode and shrivel up the world's soul. How envy stings it, avarice cankers it, passion scorches it, hate chars it with coals of hell. How often purest affections are misplaced, most loving confidences betrayed. But it is when we enter the region of the distinctively spiritual world that the signs of evil are thickest and darkest. Man, although the son of God, is evidently, conspicuously, out of harmony with Him. He who is the all-pure and all-holy One is manifestly the object of human distrust and aversion. And the world's ceaseless prayer, whether consciously expressed or not, is this, "Deliver us from evil!" So, too, does the pagan stammer our prayer. Behold his pilgrimages and sacrifices and self-lacerations! Oh, what a cry for deliverance is that which goes up from the writhing dances and flaming suttees and gory Juggernauts of the heathen world! So, too, does the Christian articulate our prayer, oh, how distinctly and frequently and fervently! And now a momentous question comes up: Will the prayer be answered? Most certainly it will. For, first, it is the Son of God Himself who bids us offer it. Again: this prayer is to be offered to a Father—a Father, too, who is heavenly. And so did He once for all appear that He might put away sin by the sacrifice of Himself. And therefore, when He, the Son of God, was about to be born into the world, an angel bade Joseph call the name of the coming child Jesus, *i.e.*, Saviour; for His Saviourship would consist in this very thing, namely, He would save His people from their sins. And salvation from sins is salvation from sin's consequences as well as from sin itself, from grief as well as from guilt, from the evil of circumstances without as well as from the evil of character within. And this leads us to our last point, the completeness of the deliverance which the heavenly Father will give those who approach Him filially, in the name of His Son, our Divine next-of-kin or Elder Brother. It is a threefold deliverance. And, first, it is a deliverance of the spirit: that august part or side of man's three-fold nature, which links him with Deity, which can know Him intuitively, by sense of kinship, which can commune with Him who Himself is Spirit and the Father of Spirits. And the deliverance He offers is a full, complete, everlasting deliverance: the deliverance of the spirit from sin, from sin's penalty, from sin's dominion, from sin's guilt; in one word, from evil. Secondly, it is a deliverance of the Psyche, or soul, that mysterious principle within us which seems to be the centre and seat of our personality; that subtile bond of union which unites spirit and body; that inscrutable, undiscoverable pivot on which are suspended the conditions of life—life bodily and life spiritual; that seat of sensibility and thought and emotion; that mysterious thing which is life itself. And this life or soul, sharing as it does in the fortunes of the fallen spirit, operates and is operated on at every disadvantage. And the deliverance which the Son of God offers is a deliverance of the life and all its faculties from these unfavourable conditions: a deliverance of the judgment from all prejudice and perversion and blindness, of the imagination from all that is impure and untrue, of the memory from all unholy or bitter reminiscences, of the instincts from all sinful drifts, of the affections from all that is unheavenly or sorrowful; in short, from all evil. And, thirdly, it is a deliverance of the body: that wonderful structure in which life finds alike its home, its carriage, and its avenues. Sharing in the fortunes of the fallen spirit, the body shares its curse, and so is amenable to disease and anguish and death. And the deliverance which the Son of God offers is a deliverance of the body; its deliverance from imperfection and weakness and disease and mortality; in one word, from evil. In fine, the deliverance from evil for which the Son of God bids us pray is the repeal of the Eden curse. (*G. D. Boardman, D.D.*) *Deliver us from evil:*—We will show—1. What it is to be "delivered from evil." 2. That it is the work of God alone. 3. That being delivered we must offer up the sacrifice of praise and thanksgiving *Jovi Liberatori*, "to God our Deliverer," and give all the glory of the victory to Him alone. 1. When we hear of deliverance from evil, we may conceive perhaps such a deliverance as may set us at such a distance from it that it may not come near us. But there is a further deliverance, *ut prosit*, "that it may help us," that "out of this eater may come meat" (Judges xiv. 14, 15), even "sweeter than honey or the honeycomb" (Psa. xix. 10). We may truly say, "The very finger of God is here" (Exod. viii. 19). For it is the work of God to create good out of evil, and light out of darkness, which are heterogeneous and of a quite contrary nature. 1. First. When we pray to be "delivered from evil," we acknowledge that God hath *jus pleni dominii,* "such a full power over us," that He may, if He please, without any injustice deliver us up unto Satan, as He did Job, to be "smitten from the sole of the foot unto the crown" (Job ii. 7); that He may withdraw His blessings, and make us smart under the cross. 2. But, in the next place, because we are men, not angels, and converse on earth, where is *officina tentationum,* "a shop where the devil forgeth his terrors and his allurements, his fearful and his pleasing temptations," we send out prayers as in an humble embassage to crave God's aid and auxiliary forces. For as God hath His army to fight against His enemies—His locust, His caterpillar, and His palmer-worm (Joel ii. 25)—so hath He His army to defend those who are under His protection—His angels and archangels, who "are all ministering spirits, sent forth to minister for them who shall be heirs of salvation." 3. But further yet, in the last place, we beg God's immediate assistance, His efficacious and saving grace, that He will not only send His angels, but make us angels to ourselves. For no man can be "delivered from evil," *nisi in quantum angelus esse cœpit,* "but so far forth as he is become an angel," yea, *nisi in quantum Deus esse cœpit,* "but so far forth as he is become a God," "partaker," saith St. Peter, "of the Divine nature" (2 Peter i. 4), and endued with "wisdom from above" (James iii. 17). And as we pray for sight, so we do for foresight. (*A. Farindon.*) *Devout:*—'Tis sometimes seen that grief makes us eloquent; I am sure danger often makes us devout. Necessity prompts men to seek relief, and the apprehension of an ill, ready to fall upon us, sends us to God for shelter. (*Archdeacon King.*) *Deliver us from evil:*—I have heard of different kinds of animals—the timid hare as well as the sharp-toothed rat—when caught in a trap, actually gnawing through the unfortunate limb that had been seized, glad to escape with life, though they left a foot behind them, furnishing us with an illustration of a text of Scripture, the right meaning of which we would do well to keep in mind: "Wherefore, if thy hand or thy foot offend thee, cut it off: it is better for thee to enter into life halt or mained, rather than having two hands or two feet to be cast into everlasting fire." And so is it with men when danger of an outward kind threatens. They will try to keep as far as possible out of its way, and when they are face to face with it, in the very midst of it, what desperate efforts they will make to escape! I. WHAT THE PRAYER MEANS—what we ask when we offer this petition. The word "evil" is that upon which this head turns. If you ask me what I think is meant by this, I must give you my answer all at once, by saying, "It is sin and its consequences, in this life and the next." More particularly it asks—1. Deliverance from sin within. If I break my arm, or suffer from toothache, or am ill otherwise, I think it bad enough, but it is nothing like what is when I have sinned. Sin is the great destroyer of happiness. There is such a thing as a happy poverty, a happy sickness, but there is no happiness possible in connection with sin. Happiness and sin can no more agree together than light and darkness. Now where does sin have its seat—its dwelling-place? Is it not within? Is it not in the heart, so that you have it called in God's Word "an evil heart"? When I speak of evil, you think of something outside of you—some danger, or suffering, from which you need to be delivered. And yet the most dreadful of all the evils that you have to do with, and that you need to pray against, is the sin that is within you. In regard to the evil of it, this prayer asks deliverance from two things—the power of sin, and the love of it. A slave may love his chain, as well as be bound by it. He may like it, and be proud of it, as he looks at its gilded links, and hears the ring of it. He may cease to love it, and it may still be there: its power remains even when the love of it is gone. So, even when we have ceased to love sin—even when we hate it, as seeing what an evil thing it is—it may yet, more or less, hold us in its grasp, and get the advantage over us; and so we need to have its power broken, as well as the liking for it taken away. Both are included when we pray, "Deliver us from evil." 2. It asks deliverance from temptation without. 3. It asks deliverance from suffering and sorrow. These are what we oftenest think and speak of as "evil," and most earnestly seek deliverance from. II. HOW GOD ANSWERS THE PRAYER. 1. By granting the request, by delivering us from evil. He does this in a variety of ways. (1) By His providence; removing the opportunity or occasion of sin from us, or us from it, putting forth some providential restraint, creating some sudden diversion, so that the mind is turned to something else.

There is a young servant, fresh from her country home, where she has been brought up in the fear of God. Her fellow-servant is trying to lead her astray, is bringing influences no way for good to bear on her, and there is danger that the attempt will be successful. She prays, "Deliver me from evil." And she falls into bad health, or is not required any longer, or otherwise has to change her situation, to the regret of herself and her friends. It is the Lord's way of removing her out of the reach of harm, and answering her prayer. Sometimes the danger is escaped from by getting something else to do. You have seen a child amusing himself with a knife or razor, to the utter terror of his mother. He might not part with it otherwise, but she holds out to him a whistle or toy, and the dangerous weapon is thrown aside. Or he is engaged in mischief, and is cured of that by getting some useful work to do.

> "Satan finds some mischief still
> For idle hands to do."

The doing of good is the best preservative against, and cure for, the doing of evil. The best preservative against the love of evil is to have the heart occupied with the love of God. God, in His providence, sends the one in our way, and so delivers from the other. (2) By His grace. You remember how it was with Esau and Laban in the case of Jacob: God so wrought in their hearts that they were kept from sinning and carrying out their evil intentions. Sometimes we fear the evil, and are delivered from it in another way, by seeing it in its true colours, stripped of its mask. You have heard of men fighting duels. When one person wronged or insulted another, it used to be common to decide the matter with loaded pistols, and one or other was often wounded or killed. It was thought manly and brave; and the refusal so to fight was regarded as mean and cowardly. It was called an "affair of honour." How was the evil stopped? By seeing it to be murder. Sometimes He makes use of love, and this oftenest and best. He loves us out of our sin. I have heard of boys making an assault on an old lady's garden to steal the fruit, and being caught. She had them brought into her parlour, and when they looked for punishment, she told them she would "like them to get what they wanted in a right way." A plateful of cherries was accordingly brought in, they were kindly treated, and were told that the next time they wanted anything of the kind, they were to come in and ask for it. I need hardly say there was no more stealing. Kindness killed and cured these young thieves. The grace of God working in the heart is indispensable to any real and lasting deliverance. 2. God answers the prayer by refusing the request. I mean this, especially in the case of such apparent evil, but real good, as I spoke of before. A boy begins to learn Latin, and when he comes to find it so hard and difficult, he would give anything to get out of it again; pleads to be allowed to give it up, and thinks it very hard to be refused. By and by he becomes a famous doctor or scholar, and how often he thanks God he did not get his own way when he was a boy, for then he never would have been what he is. So we often ask deliverance from fancied evils, when it would not be good to get it. (*J. H. Wilson, M.A.*)

Vers. 5–8. **Which of you shall have a friend.**—*Importunity in prayer:*—I. A CASE SUPPOSED. If reluctant and hard-hearted men thus yield to the influence of importunity, how much more will the blessed God, who delights in bestowing benefits upon the needy, grant the requests of those who call upon Him! II. AN EXHORTATION ADDRESSED. 1. The true nature of prayer. It is simply a matter of asking and receiving. There are some who view prayer altogether in reference to its influence upon the minds of those who engage in it. That it has such an influence is undoubted; but over and above its soothing, elevating, purifying effects, there are direct and positive blessings to be looked for in answer to our requests. The labour of the husbandman is beneficial to him; in itself it is so; being conducive to his health and strength—to the invigoration of his powers both of body and mind. But it is not on that account that he labours. He expects an actual crop; and he goes forth and sees, first the blade, then the ear, and then the full corn in the ear. And so with prayer. 2. The proper spirit of prayer. Earnestness and importunity. "If the arrow of prayer is to enter heaven, we must draw it from a soul full bent." 3. The certain success of prayer. III. A TOUCHING ARGUMENT EMPLOYED. "How much more?" As much more as God is higher than man; as much more as God is holier than man; as much more as God is better than man—so much more will He give the Holy Spirit to them that ask Him. (*Expository Outlines.*) *Importunity in prayer :*—IMPORTUNITY WANTS SOMETHING. We have literally nothing in the house. Our only resource is to ask our friend to supply us, and, through us, our needy guest. God is our friend. Asking is prayer. II. IMPORTUNITY GOES TO GOD. Pray when you feel want. Do not put off. It would not answer for the host to wait until morning. It was midnight, true. But the traveller had come at midnight, at this unseasonable hour stood famished in the hall, might die before morning. He must go to-night. He must make haste. III. IMPORTUNITY CANNOT BE PUT OFF. At first it may seem to fail to get God's ear. But it calls still, until He answers. And having done this, it may seem to be rebuffed, as by a voice from within, " Trouble me not. . . . I cannot rise and give thee," so that it will be tempted to retire without its answer. But if it has an earnest, pressing case, it will not retire. The subject of delay in answers to prayer may not be fully understood by the wisest. By some it is most imperfectly apprehended. We have misconceptions of God. These may lead Him to delay. Such a misconception is seen in the form of the prayer in our parable, " Lend me three loaves." God does not lend, He gives. He is not a niggardly heart, grudging its bounty ; He gives freely. As it would wound a mother to have a child say, " Mother, lend me some bread," and she would, if she truly and wisely loved the child, devise some way to teach him that a mother's is not a lending but a giving love ; so it must be with God. Again, though there is true want in our hearts, it may not be as heartily expressed and as confiding as God wishes. Ask heartily. IV. IMPORTUNITY IS SPECIFIC. How specific this man is in stating his case ! He wastes no words. " A friend of mine, out of his way, is come to me, and I have nothing to set before him." It is well to pray for all mankind, for all the Church, for large and comprehensive objects, but pray specifically for "a friend of mine." He stands at your door. The petition here was as definite as the statement of the case. " Friend, lend me three loaves." It was a large supply. "One for the friend," says a quaint writer, " one for himself, and one to spare.' He meant to ask for enough. Fix the request at a large amount, but make it definite. If bread is what you want, ask for bread ; if you want three loaves, pray for three ; if you mean them for your friend out of the way, put in his name, tell who he is, and God will be pleased, if it is not lightly done, an irreverent smartness in prayer, but the fervent simplicity of an agonizing desire. V. IMPORTUNITY IS EXPECTANT. " Believe that ye receive, and ye shall have." This simple-hearted man knocking at his friend's door, has not admitted the idea into his mind of going home without the bread. Foster the high trust, which ever lives in expectation from God. Such faith He honours. A very worldly man was an object of prayer with his wife. Their little daughter became a Christian ; at once she entered into her mother's desires, and joined her in the prayer that her father might be converted. Her faith was remarkably simple. She read the direction to us to believe that when we ask for the Holy Spirit we shall receive. She believed ; she said to her mother, "Father will be converted." One evening he did not return home at his usual hour. An hour passed, two hours. His wife became anxious, then alarmed. The little girl said, " Why, mother, he's going to come home a Christian to-night. I prayed that he might." The mother smiled sadly at what she looked upon as the child's ignorant simplicity. The hour grew late, still he came not. The mother said, "I must sit up for him." The child replied, "Why, he's all safe, mother ; we ought to trust God and go to bed." She went to bed. When the father, at midnight, came, and told his wife how he had found Christ, and, later, they stood in tearful joy looking upon the sleeping face of their little daughter, the child waked and seeing them, before either could speak, with a glad cry exclaimed, "There, mamma, didn't he come home a Christian ? " Oh, for the spirit in us all of that praying child ! VI. FINALLY, IMPORTUNITY PREVAILS. All true prayer is answered. The Bible has but one teaching on this subject, experience but one trustworthy lesson. Thirty-four special prayers are given in the Scriptures ; every one was answered. It is not promised that the answer will come at once ; the tenor of Scripture is to the contrary conclusion. The answer is speedy from God's point of view ; with Him one day is as a thousand years. But we are taught to wait upon God, to wait patiently for Him, to be importunate. (*G. R. Leavitt.*) *Importunity in prayer :*— I. THE REASONABLENESS AND INCUMBENCY OF IMPORTUNITY. 1. The reasonableness and incumbency of importunity in prayer appear from the majesty and holiness of that Being whom we address, contrasted with our own weakness and sinfulness. The depth of feeling and anxiety for success with which we approach to ask a favour of a fellow creature, bear a proportion to his dignity and worth : what reverence, then, what fervour, what earnestness and perseverence of supplication, become us in drawing near to the King of kings, and Lord of lords ! 2. The reasonableness and incumbency of such importunity will further appear, if we consider the great value of the deliverances and positive blessings we implore. I speak here, of course, chiefly of spiritual deliverances and blessings. What more reasonable than that our anxiety and perseverance of pursuit should be regulated by the value of the objects we have in view ? We should, unquestionably, grudge that earnestness and continuance of application to avert a trifling evil, or to obtain a trifling advantage, which we should yet think well spent to save our life, or to gain a kingdom. But, let us only think of the importance of the spiritual deliverances for which we pray to God—deliverance from destructive ignorance, error, unbelief, guilt, and pollution—deliverance from the curse of God now, and from the wrath to come—deliverance from everlasting misery—and then let us ask ourselves with what importunity we ought to pray for such deliverances. How will the man cry for help who perceives the surrounding tide approaching to overwhelm him ! but how much more should we cry to God to save us from being drowned in eternal destruction and perdition ? II. ENCOURAGEMENTS TO IMPORTUNITY IN PRAYER. 1. It tends to prepare the mind for the blessings asked, and even is often the actual enjoyment of them. The Lord " prevents," that is, anticipates, " us with the blessings of goodness " ; and while we are praying, as well as when we are musing, the fire of devotion burns. 2. Again, such prayer has the promise of being answered. The general command to pray implies a general promise of a favourable answer. But there are many particular and express promises of this kind, especially to those who pray with earnestness and perseverance (see ver. 9). 3. Consider, too, for your further encouragement, some of the many scriptural examples of the success of importunate prayer. Suffer me now, in conclusion, solemnly to ask, Are you given to such importunity in prayer ? (*Jas. Foote, M.A.*) *Importunity in prayer :*—I. THE CASE STATED. 1. The appeal. (1) To whom made. To a " friend." (2) When made. " At midnight." (3) How made. Definitely. "Lend me three loaves." 2. The argument. (1) The fact of need. (2) The relationship implied. You are my " friend." 3. The response. (1) Most discouraging. (*a*) The attitude of the respondent discouraging. " He from within." (*b*) The spirit of the respondent discouraging. " Trouble me not." (*c*) The argument of the respondent discouraging. " The door is now shut," &c. 4. The appellant's success. (1) Negatively. (*a*) Not on the ground of friendly relationship. (*b*) Not on the ground of his need. (2) Positively. On the ground of his importunity. II. THE CASE APPLIED. 1. To every disciple. " And I say unto *you.*" 2. To the essential conditions of success in prayer. (1) Prayer itself essential. (2) To pray for what we need is essential. (*a*) Bread or fish are among the *necessaries* of life. (*b*) To ask these when *needed* is implied. (3) Importunity in prayer. 3. To the perfect assurance of success to those who thus pray. (1) " Every one " that thus "asketh." (2) This success is guaranteed on two grounds to the importunate pleader. (*a*) Our relationship. " Your heavenly Father." (*b*) God's infinite graciousness. " How much more?" Lessons : 1. The contrast in the parable heightens the believer's encouragement. (1) Our heavenly Father never answers " from within." (2) Our heavenly Father never says " Trouble Me not." (3) To the heavenly Father it is never " midnight." 2. Prayer as a Divine condition of blessing one of the most gracious evidences of the Divine love. 3. Importunity the only true evidence of the sincerity of our prayer, and the reality of our felt need, and actuality of our faith. (*D. C. Hughes, M.A.*) *Why we must be importunate in prayer :*—I think the meaning is, that Jesus would teach us in this way what we are learning in many other ways—that the best things in the Divine life, as in the natural, will not come to us merely for the asking ; that true prayer is the whole strength of the whole man going out after his needs, and the real secret of getting what you want in heaven, as on earth, lies in the fact that you give your whole heart for it, or you cannot adequately value it when you get it. So, " Ask, and it shall be given you ; seek, and ye shall find ; knock, and it shall be opened unto you," means—" Put out all your energies, as if you had to waken heaven out of a midnight slumber, or an indifference like that of the unjust judge." (*R. Collyer.*) *The midnight intruder :*—Why does the Lord fix upon " midnight " as the time when this transaction took place? 1. Because He would assure us that God is ready to hear us at any and every time of life, even the most unseasonable. 2. Because He would warn us of the obstacles in the way of a late application. The midnight intruder represents the sinner who only turns to God when overtaken by old age or severe sickness. Repentance long delayed is not easy work. (*J. Henry Burn, B.D.*) *Lessons :*—1. Our petitions never unseasonable. 2. No time unsuitable. 3. No spiritual mercy too great to ask. 4. No needed blessing exceeds God's power. 5. God never disinclined to hear. 6. God never unwilling to bless. 7. God is ready to answer. 8. God is able to grant. 9. God is willing to bestow. 10. God is waiting to be gracious. (*Van Doren.*) *Perseverance in prayer :*—God for a time withholds the answer to prayer. But the blessing is sweeter, when obtained. It is the Christian's duty to ask in faith, and to wait in hope. Perseverance in prayer effects no change in God, but effects a change in the petitioner. Miracles have ceased, wonders have not ; perseverance in faith and prayer will accomplish wonders. Diligence, perseverance, and importunity are honourable terms applied to prayer. They offend not God, but are enjoined by command, and taught by example. God is urgent with us, to make us urgent with Him. (*Ibid.*) *God giving His praying people bread for others :*— Because the word "importunity" occurs here, the parable is sometimes read as enforcing persevering prayer. Its lesson, however, seems not so much to be perseverance as intercession. So the subject is, God giving His people bread for others in answer to prayer. I. Here, first of all, we have, GOD'S FRIEND CALLED TO GIVE BREAD TO THE HUNGRY. Indeed it is more than the hungry. The traveller in the parable has lost his way ("out of the way," it is in the margin). That represents the call which, except he be sunk in deep spiritual indifference, the Christian hears. More urgent than any plea for the bread that perisheth is that for the bread that endureth unto everlasting life. Whilst he rests in the mercies which the gospel brings, outside are some who in darkness and sadness have lost their way, and pine for bread in the strength of which they shall press on to the light and home. The man of God hears their knock at his door, and their cry beneath his window, and in these a summons from a higher source to rise and give. 2. We hear it in the Divine pity wrought within us. For the desire to save a soul from death is "from above"; it is the spirit that led the Son of God to become incarnate and die. If He has made us pity the hungry wanderers in the dark, that pity is a Divine summons (it were criminal to refuse) to give. 3. And we hear it in the Divine direction of the hungry soul to us. For how often we can say "A friend of mine, out of the way, is come to me!" God makes some our special care : the children He has given us, the ungodly, the unconcerned, and the uncared-for. And they do ask; their look asks if not their speech. But why do they come to us? For the reason that Cornelius in his need sent to Simon in Joppa—because heaven told them to God who creates the hunger, does not leave them to satisfy it as they can, but tells them where to go for bread, and points to us, and that is why they come. 4. And we hear this summons in the method of the Divine working. Be sure it is of no use simply praying for our neighbours, nor for our friends and children ; God is ready to answer prayer, but it is His plan to answer it through us ; "Give ye them to eat," He says. If we lie self-indulgent in our spiritual repose, afraid to rise because of the cold and the tiredness, and only idly pray for the perishing without, the prayer will be of no use. God's very method is the solemn call to us to rise and give. II. But we have here next, GOD'S FRIEND WITH NO POWER TO FULFIL THIS CALL. We hear the call and desire to obey it, we rise and look into our store-room, but—there is nothing! "A friend of mine in his journey is come to me," we say, and alas, "I have nothing to set before him." Now that tends to the idea that God does not mean the supply to come through us ; He cannot, we think, expect us, who manifestly have nothing, to dispense something ; it must be a mistake for the hungry to come to our door ; at least, as we have no bread we may as well lie still, and leave others to do what we cannot. That reasoning makes idle, miserable Christians. Whilst their brethren work their life away in feeding the perishing, many Christians are useless, not always because they have no heart, but because they persuade themselves that they have no gift, and therefore no responsibility. Friends, have we not learnt that our responsibility is not measured by what we have, but by what we can get! We are sure to come to that if we try to obey God's call, for this conscious impotence is Divine preparation for the work. It is God preparing him who has nothing to receive something. One of the best signs when we know we are called to Christian service is the conviction of personal inability. But then we have here, GOD'S FRIEND TURNING TO GOD IN HIS HELPLESSNESS. From the thought that he has no bread he turns to remember a friend who has bread, and he goes to him : "Friend, a friend of mine in his journey is come to me, and I have nothing to set before him, lend me three loaves." Let this be the first thought of the helpless helper of others : God can give me what I need--the right truth, the right words, the right manner, and (far more than these) through them, unseen by me, He can impart Christ. God can do this. But the next thought is, God will ; with confidence we can turn to Him for " loaves " when we call Him, as in the parable, " Friend." And we prove that He and we are friends when, self-forgetting, we make another's wants our own. Never can we be more sure that God will show Himself our friend than when we are anxious about the necessities of our fellows, for He can look on nothing with greater friendliness. To plead for others is to please Him more than to plead for self. Oh, we cannot doubt, when we think thus, that God, who can give the bread we need for the traveller, will. Then the needy worker goes and asks Him. III. For we have here, GOD'S FRIEND SUPPLIED WITH WHATEVER HE WANTS. 1. This, then, is a call to prayer. God awakes to give when we awake to ask. 2. And our prayer is answered as we obey. 3. Then see what the praying friend of God may do ! The limit to God's giving is " as many as He needeth." (*C. New.*) *The setting of the parable :*—Like all such utterances of Christ, this draws its material from the ordinary life and incidents of the time. The deep stillness which settles upon an Eastern city soon after nightfall, is broken by the urgent call of a man under a neighbour's window. "Friend! friend!! lend me three loaves! a guest has arrived at my house." Not a strange occurrence in the East, where so many travel in the night to avoid the burning heat of the day. "Friend, lend me three loaves. My guest has taken me unawares. He is a hungry traveller. My larder is empty. I have nothing to set before him." And the answer is that of a man who cares chiefly for his own comfort ; a churlish answer enough : " Trouble me not. My door is shut and bolted. The household have gone to rest. I cannot rise and give thee." But the applicant is not so easily disposed of. The ungracious neighbour is not to be left so comfortably to his rest. Hardly has he settled himself on his couch when the knock at the door comes again, and the call is repeated; and again and again ; until, for very peace's sake, he is constrained to rise and give his persistent neighbour what he wants. (*Marvin R. Vincent, D.D.*)   *The naturalness of the illustration :*—The *curiosa felicitas* of the parable will best be made apparent by entering into a little detail, first in reference to the situation, and next in reference to the means by which importunity makes itself master of the situation. And in order to show how discouraging the situation is, it will not be necessary to lay stress on the hour of the night at which the petitioner for bread finds himself called on to provide for his unseasonable visitor. Travelling in the night is common in the East, and it may be said to belong simply to the natural realism of the parable that the incident related is represented as happening at midnight. One cannot but remark, however, in passing, that it belongs to the felicity of the parable to suggest what it does not expressly teach, viz., that the comfort it is designed to convey to tried faith is available to those who find themselves in the very darkest hour of their spiritual perplexities. But passing from this, we note the discouraging circumstances in which the man in need finds himself on arriving at his neighbour's door. The difficulty which confronts him is not a physical one ; that, viz., of finding his neighbour so profoundly asleep that it is impossible by any amount of knocking, however loud, to awaken him. His discouragement is, as the nature of the argument required it to be, a moral one ; that, viz., of finding his neighbour, after he has succeeded in arousing him to consciousness, in a state of mind the reverse of obliging, utterly unwilling to take the trouble necessary to comply with his request. The mood of the man in bed is most graphically depicted. It is the mood of a man made heartless and selfish by comfort. Comfortable people, we know, are apt to be hard-hearted, and comfortable circumstances make even kind people selfish for the moment. Jesus holds up to our view an illustrative example. And the picture is so sketched to the life that we cannot repress a smile at the humour of the scene, while fully alive to the deep pity and pathos out of which the whole representation springs. The man is made to describe himself, and to show out of his own mouth, what an utterly selfish creature he is. First, an ominous omission is observable in his reply. There is no response to the appeal to his generous feelings contained in the appellation " Friend " addressed to him by his neighbour. How true is this touch to human nature as it shows itself in every age ! The rich, who need nothing, have many friends, but the poor is hated even of his own neighbour. The first words uttered by the man in bed are a rude, abrupt, surly, " Don't bother me." For, so undoubtedly, ought they to be rendered.

It would be out of keeping with the whole situation to put a dignified speech into the mouth of a man irritated by unseasonable disturbance of his nightly repose. Next comes a comically serious detailed description of the difficulties which stand in the way of complying with the needy neighbour's request : " The door is already barred, and my children are with me in bed ! " Poor man, he is to be pitied ! If it were only the mere matter of getting out of bed, it would be no great affair, now that he is awake. But the unbarring of the door is a troublesome business, not so easily performed as the turning of a key-handle, which is all we Europeans and moderns have to do in similar circumstances. And then the dear children are in bed asleep; what if one were to waken them ; what a trouble to get them all hushed to rest again. Really the thing is out of the question. And so he ends with a peevish, drawling " I can't rise to give thee." His " I can't " means " I won't." The circumstances which hinder, after the most has been made of them, are utterly frivolous excuses, and it is simply contemptible to refer to them seriously as reasons for not helping a friend in need. But the very fact that he does this only shows how utterly unwilling he is, how completely comfort and sleep have deadened every generous feeling in his heart. But comfortable selfishness for once finds itself over-matched by importunate want. The situation is desperate indeed when the person solicited for aid finds it in his heart to refuse it on such paltry grounds. But the petitioner has the matter in his own hands; he can make the unwilling one fain to give him whatever he wishes, be it three loaves or thirty ; not for friendship's sake certainly, for of that there can be little hope after that contemptible " I can't rise and give thee "; but for very selfishness' sake, to get rid of the annoyance and be free to relapse into slumber. How then ? What are the means by which need is able to make itself master of the situation ? One word answers the question. It is shamelessness. Shamelessness, not in knocking at the door of a neighbour at such an hour, for that may be excused by necessity, and at all events it has failed. The shamelessness meant is that which consists in continuing to knock on after receiving a decided and apparently final refusal. (*A. B. Bruce, D.D.*)   *The struggle for attainment of spiritual good :*—In the interpretation and application of this parable, too much stress seems generally to have been laid upon one of the two persons presented to notice, and too little upon the other. To picture God as unwilling to hear and answer prayer, is wholly foreign to the spirit of our Lord's teaching and life ; but to emphasize the necessity of our acting as if the answer to prayer were not a thing to be easily obtained, is thoroughly in keeping therewith. The Master had just supplied His disciples with a most lofty and comprehensive form of prayer—a form embracing petitions which from their very nature could only be granted on condition of the petitioners themselves heartily co-operating with God; and now He utters this parable to enforce the truth that there are many obstacles in the way, and that we shall not succeed unless we prove ourselves to be very much in earnest, seeking as well as merely asking, and knocking in addition to both. Who that knows his own heart ever so little, can doubt that between prayer and its answer there are indeed many and serious obstacles ? First of all, there is the old man within— the traitor in the very heart of the citadel—urging us to give up the struggle and to swim with the stream. Then, there is all around us a cold and hostile world, ever tempting us to court its smile by the sacrifice of principle and (what so dear to us?) the indulgence of self. And, finally, the Evil One is always on the watch for an opportunity of blinding us to our own true interests, and keeping from us any suspicion of our danger until it is too late to turn back. Such are a few of the obstacles that confront the Christian when, rising from his knees, he day by day goes forth to contribute his share to the hallowing of God's name, the doing of God's will, and the advancement of God's kingdom. Nothing, surely, can be more certain than this ; that, so far as he himself is concerned, his petitions for those three primary blessings will go unanswered, unless he strive with might and main, with all the energy of which he is possessed, to bring about, first in his own heart, and then in the hearts of others, that complete surrender to God which is the absolute condition of all acceptable prayer. Then he may look for an answer, but not before.   *The parable of the importunate friend :*—This parable is meant to afford us effectual encouragement in prayer. Those who first faint in prayer, and then cease to pray, commonly do so from some kind of latent feeling that God does not regard them. Well, says our Lord, even supposing He does not regard you, do not give up asking, for even in the most unpromising circumstances persever-ing and importunate entreaty gets what it seeks. Take the most sluggish and selfish nature, the man who won't so much as get out of bed to do a friend a good turn, you can make him do what you want by the very simple device of going on knocking till you cause it to dawn on his slumbering brain that the only way to get the sleep he so much desires is first of all to satisfy you. (*Marcus Dods, D.D.*)   *The friend at midnight:*—This story is merely an illustration on which an argument is founded; and it is of immense importance that we have a correct idea of what that argument really is.   I. LET US HAVE THE CASE SUPPOSED CLEARLY BEFORE US.   The story.   Our Lord's comment upon it: "I say unto you, though he will not rise and give him because he is his friend, yet because of his importunity"—or rather, as it ought to be rendered, "shamelessness," or more strongly still, "impudence"—"he will rise and give him as many as he needeth."   Then the Lord proceeds to give the Magna Charta of prayer, in the familiar words, "Ask and it shall be given you," &c.   To this He appends a comparison between an earthly father's dealings with his children and those of our heavenly Father with His.   These last verses, as I believe, furnish the key to the argument in the parable.   Like them, it reasons from the less to the greater, or rather, from the worse to the better.   It does not mean to represent God as gruff and disobliging, like the neighbour newly roused out of his earliest sleep; neither does it recommend the suppliant to use with God such shamelessness or impudence as his friend employed with him.   But the suggested inference is this: If the impudence of that midnight knocker prevailed even with an angry and annoyed man so much that he arose and gave what was requested, how much more will the humble, reverent, believing, and persevering prayer of a true child of God prevail with the infinitely kind and loving Father to whom he makes petition?   Over against the irritated and reluctant man, only half awake, He places the calm, loving, heavenly Father, "who slumbers not, neither sleepeth"; while, in contrast with the impudence of his troublesome neighbour, He suggests such earnest pleading with a Father as that which they had just seen in Himself, or as He had recommended in the form which He had given them.   And the conclusion which He draws is: If the appeal in the former case was ultimately successful, how much more is it likely to be so in the latter!   He is far from encouraging us to trust in boldness or irreverence or impudence in prayer, as so many misunderstand His words.   We shall not be heard for our frequent speaking, any more than for our much speaking.   He would not have us trust in prayer at all, but in the loving, Fatherly heart of Him to whom we pray.   "Wait on the Lord"—that is the lesson. But some may say, "We have tried thus to wait on Him, and though we have waited long our prayers are still unanswered."   What answer can we give to these troubled spirits?   The answer will take us—II. Into the consideration of THE CONDITIONS OF SUCCESSFUL PRAYER.   1. The success of prayer is conditioned by the character of the suppliant.   (*a*) That which men desire for the gratification of malice, or the pampering of appetite, or the satisfying of ambition, or the aggrandizing of selfishness, God has nowhere promised to bestow.   (*b*) The wish that simply flits across the soul, as the shadow of the cloud glides over the summer-grass, is no true prayer. It must take hold of the spirit, and gather into itself all the energy and earnestness of the man.   (*c*) No one can long persist in such prayer without faith; and so at this point the Saviour's qualifying word, "believing ye shall receive," is appropriate.   (*d*) But more important than any of these conditions in the character of the suppliant is that laid down by Jesus, when He says, "If ye abide in Me, and My words abide in you, ye shall ask what ye will, and it shall be done unto you." We must not take the first part of that declaration and divorce it from the second. 2. A second class of conditions connect themselves with the nature of the thing requested.   That which we ask must be in accordance with God's will.   Beneath every genuine supplication there is the spirit of resignation.   3. This condition, connecting itself with the nature of the thing asked, is nearly akin to the third class of conditions which spring out of the purpose and prerogative of God Himself. This is a view of the case which has not been sufficiently attended to by Christians. "The hearer of prayer" is not the only relation in which God stands to His people.   He is their Father as well; and He is, besides, the moral Governor of the intelligent universe.   Therefore He uses His prerogative in answering prayer, for moral purposes; and the action which He takes on the petitions of His children is a portion of that discipline to which He subjects them.   Or, it may be that the kind of answers which He gives is determined by the influence which the suppliant's example may have on others.   III. If these views are sound and scriptural THERE MAY BE DEDUCED FROM THEM THREE INFERENCES OF GREAT PRACTICAL VALUE.   1. How impossible it is for us to discover the results of prayer by any merely human test.

2. To be successful suppliants we must be holy men.　3. How necessary it is that prayer should be characterized by entire submission to the will of God. (*W. M. Taylor, D.D.*)　**Because of his importunity.**—*Importunity :*—Why does our Lord connect the importunity needful to arouse the feeble affections of sleepy man with prayer to our Father in heaven, who sleepeth not, and who is love itself? The disciples said, "Lord, teach us to pray," and He taught them. He gave them a simple but sevenfold prayer. Each petition was as clear as the light of heaven. Together the petitions were like seven burning lamps of the spirit of prayer which remain ever before God's throne. But if they would pray well, they must be fervent —not faint. God does, indeed, give bread of heaven more willingly to His children than earthly parents give to theirs the bread of this world. But earthly parents do not get bread without husbandry, nor fish without tempestuous encounters with the weather, nor eggs without patient care for the fowls. And though God's Spirit is like the liberal air, the affluent sunshine, the multitudinous raindrops, yet as there must be seed in the ground for the rain to take effect, and lapse of days for the sunshine to mature the growth, and air, constant but changeful in its operation, that the living corn may abide and gain its sweetness, so only by patient working can God's spiritual gifts effect man's spiritual good. In our work God can only answer our effort through our patience prolonged; and after, in our prayers, He can only answer us by giving us work. You do not know the importunate effort your prayer implies. God is willing to give, and give at once; but He cannot give all things at once. (*T. T. Lynch.*)　*Importunity :*—The effects here ascribed to importunity are remarkable. Nothing is attributed to friendship or good neighbourhood, to the reasonableness of the request, the ease with which it could be granted, the benefit to be conferred, or what the necessity of the case required. The success is represented as owing to the nature and strength, and frequency of the importunity, or to troublesome, teazing, vexatious efforts long continued, and to the impatience and irritation which such conduct never ceases to produce. But is it possible to believe, that by such behaviour we can influence our Maker, that His patience can be exhausted, and that He can be induced to yield to clamour or unceasing repetition? No, certainly. But we are to consider what is common between the nature of the importunity described in the text, and that which is incumbent in a true Christian, when addressing his heavenly Father. Now, two things are requisite: 1. We ought to know what is declared in the Scriptures to be agreeable to the will of God ; and, consequently, what is proper for us to ask of God in prayer. 2. We ought to be as earnest in our petitions, and as incessant in making them, as the person here proposed for our example. (*J. Thomson, D.D.*)　*Need of importunity :*—Easiness of desire is a great enemy to the success of a good man's prayers. It must be an intent, busy, operative prayer. For consider what a huge indecency it is that a man should speak to God for a thing that he values not ! Our prayers upbraid our spirits when we beg tamely for those things for which we ought to die, which are more precious than imperial sceptres, richer than the spoils of the sea, or the treasures of Indian hills. (*Bishop Jeremy Taylor.*)　*There are three things in importunity :*—1. Fervency. This consists not in the loudness of the voice, albeit it be many times expressed by loud crying; the peacock hath a louder voice than the nightingale. Nor in long praying, for God doth not measure prayer by the length, albeit long prayers may be fervent prayers, but in the crying of the heart. 2. There must be frequency in it. We give not over at the first denial, no, nor at the second, if we be importunate. "One thing I have desired of the Lord, and I will seek after it" (Psa. xxvii. 4); that is, I have sought it, and will seek again and again. So Psa. lxix. 3 and Isa. lxii. 1. 3. As our suit is to be renewed, so we must persevere in it. So Jacob did not only wrestle, but continued all night and morning too. He gave not over till he had what he sought for. This is enjoined (Col. iv. 2; 1 Thess. v. 27). And that parable propounded for that very end that we should pray, and not faint (Luke xviii. 1). If importunate prayer be prevailing prayer, never marvel that so many of us pray and yet prevail not. The prayers of most are but lip labour, and lip labour is lost labour. Never think to be heard of God in mercy, or to obtain any blessing at the hands of God, by thy cold, careless, and customary prayer. David compares his prayers to incense, and no incense was offered without fire : it was that that made the smoke of it to ascend. But doth not this pass good manners to importune the God of heaven? Will it not be imputed impudence in the creature to press the great Creator to condescend to our requests. Princes love it not, mean men affect it not, and will God suffer it ? But God's ways are not as man's. With Him he is *magis importunus qui importunat minus*

—most troublesome, that is least troublesome, saith Gregory. But Austin speaks of some who pray, *nimis ardenter,* too earnestly. So that it seems to be a fault to be too importunate. There is a double importunity, one arising from an inordinate desire of that we crave, having no respect to the will and promise of God. This was in Israel desiring of a king. And there is another kind of importunity, joined with a subjection to the will of God, and this was in Christ (Matt. xxvi. 39, 42). But say we desire what is lawful, may we pray alike earnestly and importunately for one thing as for another, for small things as well as great, for earthly things as for heavenly? Our prayers are to be earnest as well for small things as for great, for things temporal as well as for things eternal, but yet not with the like degree of earnestness. The incense must smoke, and the pot boil; this cannot be without fire, yet we make not the like fire to roast an egg as to roast an ox. Other things are more common and transitory, being but mean and worthless in comparison of the other, scarce worth the naming, concerning which God is not well pleased that we should spend the heat of our zeal. It is worthy of your notice that our blessed Saviour, in that platform of prayer which He hath given us, puts daily bread before forgiveness of sins; not for that it is to be preferred, but for that it may sooner be despatched and more time spent about the other which concerns the salvation of our souls (there being two petitions of this nature for one of the other). For as it is in pouring out of some liquors that which is thinnest will first come forth and the thickest last, so is it oftentimes in pouring forth the soul to God. And thence it is that the faithful are usually more earnest and importunate with the Lord towards the end of their prayers (as it was with Daniel and David). This we often find. Albeit our earnestness is not to be alike in degree for small things as for great, yet our faith must be the same, let the thing be what it will be that we pray for, if lawful, small or great, temporal or eternal. It may yet be demanded, If it be not a fault to hasten God in the performance of His promises, are we not to wait His leisure? How then are we to importune Him, and be earnest with Him about them? Patiently to attend God's time, and yet earnestly to solicit the hastening of them, may well enough consist. Drexelius tells us of a vision that a religious man had at his prayers in the congregation. He saw a several angel at the elbow of every one present, ready to write down his petitions. Those who prayed heartily their angels wrote down their suits in gold; those that prayed but coldly and carelessly, their angels wrote too, but it was with water; those that prayed customarily, only from the teeth outward, had their angels by them, who seemed to write, but it was with a dry pen, no ink in it; such as slept had their angels by them, but they laid their pens by; such as had worldly thoughts, their angels wrote in the dust; and such as had envious and malicious spirits, their angels wrote with gall. If this be so, I fear few angels have wrote this day in golden letters; but the pens of the others have gone very fast. Have a care how thou prayest if thou wouldest have them written with the golden pen. (*N. Rogers.*) *Prayer made fervent by expression:*—Words add more force to our inward devotion; they stir up and increase the affection of the heart. As the beams of the sun wax hotter by reflection, so do the desires of the heart (saith one) by expression. (*Ibid.*) *Delay in answering prayer:*—If you desire to know the reasons of this delaying and putting off before He answers, they may be these. 1. God hath an eye herein to His own glory, which is exceedingly advanced hereby. 2. God doth thus delay us to quicken our appetites, inflame our desires, and make us the more earnest and fervent in prayer, dealing herein as the fisher doth in drawing back his bait to make the fish more eager of it. 3. God doth this for the trial and discovery of those graces that are in us, and to inure us to patience and obedience and submission of our wills to His. 4. Hereby the mercy is better prepared for us, for it becomes the greater and the sweeter; by delaying and putting off our suit we are brought to value the thing sued for the more, when things easily had are lightly esteemed: lightly come, lightly go. (*Ibid.*) *Prayer is the best means of provision:*—It is the surest course that can be taken to supply our wants. The best remedy in the day of our calamity. It must needs be so. 1. Because it is sanctified by God, and established by Divine wisdom for obtaining of all things needful that concern this life and the life to come (Psa. l. 15; Isa. xix. 20, 21; Phil. iv. 6; Heb. iv. 6). Now God having prescribed this (who is the Fountain of all blessing and Author of all help), it must needs follow that it is the best means that can be used. 2. This hath to do above. It comes to the throne of grace, lays hold on God's name (from whom alone all our help cometh), when as all other means and helps have to do below on earth, and with earthly things, and can go no further than men's counsels.

persons, or purses can reach. 3. This is a true catholicon, a general remedy for every malady (it is like the Indian stone that remedieth all diseases), as appears, 1 Kings viii. Whatsoever plague, whatsoever sickness or other misery doth befall us, prayer will remedy it. No such universal and general help in all extremities as this is. Physicians for divers diseases have divers remedies, but the Christian hath this one which is better than all—prayer. 4. It is the readiest remedy, evermore at hand ; in what place soever you are you may help yourselves and others by it (1 Tim. ii. 8). Jeremiah prays in the dungeon, Jonah in the whale's belly, Peter in the prison, Paul in the stocks. In the fields, on the leads, in the chamber, in the closet, in caves and dens of the earth, it may be taken and used. 5. It is the speediest remedy. No sooner are our prayers out of our mouths—nay, in our hearts, but they are in heaven, and no sooner are they in heaven but we shall find the benefit of them (Dan. ix. 21, 22, 23 ; Gen. xxiv. 15; Acts iv. 31). 6. It is an approved remedy. It hath its *probatum est* upon constant experience of God's saints, who have ever found it to be the best lever at a dead-lift (2 Sam. xxii. 4, 7 ; Psa. cxviii. 5). (*Ibid.*) *Interceding for others :*—They who love Christ love every member of Christ, to the lowest. Oh the happiness of a Christian who hath a stock going in every part of the Christian world. He is like some rich merchant, who hath his factors in all countries. Some in Spain, others in France, and where not where God hath a Church? The prayers of the saints are for the common good of the whole body, and the poorest member of that body is a sharer in all the prayers that are put up to heaven in the behalf of the Church. As when several ships go to sea, some traffic in one thing and some in another; some bring gold, others spices, and others other commodities; but all that is brought is for the common good of the country. So the prayers of the godly are like these ships that go to sea. Some request this of God, others that, but all that they bring home is for the good of the whole Church, whereof thou, being a member, shalt certainly be a sharer. If one Elijah can procure plenty, and prevail for a whole country, if one Isaac by prayer can make Rebekah fruitful, if the prayer of one righteous man can so prevail with God, what will so many eyes and hands reared up to heaven do ? Single prayers are like Sampson's single hairs, every one hath the strength of a man ; but the prayers of many are like his whole bush, or head of hair, able to overcome the whole host of heaven, and to bind the hands of God Himself, as appears by the passage betwixt God and Moses. And if men should fail me, yet Christ still loves me, and loving me, He will not be wanting in making intercession to His Father on my behalf. (*Ibid.*) *Storming heaven :*—We can see this principle at work, if we will, first in nature. It fills the whole distance between the paradise of the first pair and this common earth as we find it to-day. In that old Eden there was no barrier between the longing and its answer, and no effort needed to bring the answer, except the longing. The kindly, easy, effortless life went on, we suppose, as life might have gone on in the Sandwich Islands before Cook discovered them, had their inhabitants possessed the secret of how to live, in addition to their perfect climate, and the daily bread that came almost without the asking. In this life of ours, however, there is no such answer to our natural cry for what we need. The need may be, in its way, Divine, and the longing as Divine as the need; but before they can come to their full fruition, barriers have to be broken down that seem to have been put there by Heaven itself. We touch this principle again in a more personal way when we observe this striving in the experiences of men. Not to mention at this moment what is most purely spiritual in these conflicts, there is deep instruction in watching how some man is moved to do some thing that is to bless the world in a new and wonderful way when it is done ; but between the conception and the conclusion there are mighty barriers, that only the uttermost might of what is indeed a Divine persistence can finally overcome. It flashes on the soul with something of the nature of a revelation when it is done. Men say he must have been inspired to do it. Its blessing is so clear that we can almost see the shining track on which it has come from God to man. It would be natural to think then the way must be clear between the conception and execution of such a thing, not only because of the nobility of the thing itself, but of the urgent need of it among men. They knocked more than two hundred years for the locomotive before the door was opened, and if you have read this history of Mr. Goodyear, you will remember how at last the full revelation of the secret came in a flash, as when the diamond seeker watches for the sudden sheen of his treasure between the sand and the sun. But it was the eye that had been seeking patiently, persistently, and steadily through these long years that found the treasure, as when the apple fell;

if we had been there, we should have seen an apple fall where Newton saw the whole order of the sun and stars, because he had been wearying heaven night and day for years to open her doors to his beseeching about that matter. A true prayer must be the deepest and most painful thing a man can possibly do; may be so costly that he will give up, without a murmur, his very life, before he will give up that which his prayer has wrested, as it were, out of the heart of the heavens; and it may be so protracted, that twenty years shall not suffice to see it. For prayer, in its purest reality, is first the cry of the soul to God for His gift, and then it is the effort of the soul to make as sure of what it longs for, as if it were to come by its own winding. It is something in which the words we say are often of the smallest possible consequence, and only our unconquerable persistence under God is omnipotent. I went once to see the cathedral at Cologne. It is the most wonderful blossoming of Gothic art on the planet. Hundreds of years ago some man, now forgotten, found it all in his heart, and longed to make it visible in stone. But because it was so great and good, when the man died his work was still unfinished; it was still unfinished when his name was forgotten; at last, even the design of it was lost, and it seemed as if there was no hope that the cathedral would ever be done. But when Napoleon went storming through Europe, his marshals lighted on the old design, hidden in some dusty corner of a monastery; so it got back again to Cologne, and when I was there, all Germany was interested in finishing the noble idea. Now, since that church was begun, thousands of churches have risen and fallen in Germany, and no trace of them is left; but because the Dome Kirche is the grandest thing in its way that was ever done in stone, or ever conceived in a soul, two things follow: there must be a mighty span between the conception and the consummation, a striving through dark days and fearful hindrances to build it, and, at the same time, an indestructible vitality in the idea, like that which has attended it. It is but a shadow of this great fact concerning our spiritual life. The very worth of what we ask for from the heavens, because it is so worthy, is the deepest reason there is why the blessing cannot come until the full time—until it has had its own time. (*R. Collyer, D.D.*) *Earnestness in prayer:*—I have heard it said, and I fear it is true, that the worst performed work that we do in the day is our prayers: I fear that many of us, perhaps most of us, must confess this to be true. We are earnest in other things, our merchandise, our work, our studies; but how few of us are diligent in prayer, how few of us look upon this as our daily bread, how few of us live a life in any distant degree resembling that of our Saviour Christ. I fear the same thing is spoiling our communion with God which spoilt Adam's, a feeling of enmity to God, a consciousness of our wills not being wholly like His, of our having tastes which He does not approve, of our hearts being set upon the world. (*Bishop Harvey Goodwin.*) *Successful importunity:*—How often have I seen a little child throw its arms around its father's neck, and win, by kisses, and importunities, and tears, what had been refused? Who has not yielded to importunity, even when a dumb animal looked up with suppliant eyes in our face for food? Is God less pitiful than we? (*T. Guthrie, D.D.*) *Bounty after delay:*— When the householder is once roused by the importunity of his neighbour, he not only gives him the three loaves, for which perhaps he asked out of delicacy as the very least that would suffice, but "as many as he needeth"; enough to spread a bounteous repast. And when God delays giving, it is not only to encourage faith to press for that particular gift, but to introduce it to a larger range of gifts: to bring it to a better acquaintance with Himself, in whom are all gifts. A praying soul, in such circumstances, is like a thirsty man following up the windings of a clear, cold stream, but unable to get down to the water's edge because the banks are so steep. He walks mile after mile along the precipitous shores, and the sun is hot, and he is faint, and his thirst is aggravated by the sparkling water below; but by and by he finds himself among the springs, at the source of the stream, high up where the fountains are sheltered, and clear and exhaustless, and he bows down and drinks his fill. God is better than all His gifts, and the object of prayer is to make us acquainted with Himself. Your boy comes to you and asks you to buy him a fishing-rod; and he says, "I saw one to-day in a window, on such a street, which was just what I want. Can't I go down now and buy it?" And you say, "No, not to-day. Wait a little. You shall have your rod." And doubtless the lad is disappointed, perhaps a little sullen for the time, and a week passes and he hears nothing about his rod, and he begins to say to himself: "I wonder if father has not forgotten all about it." Then, just at the end of the week, you put into his hands a better rod than he has ever seen before, and with it a complete outfit for his sport, and the boy is overwhelmed with surprise and pleasure. And yet the main thing in all this is not that your son has received what he wanted. You meant he should have that ; but the gift won, through delay, has given him a new view of his father's wisdom, and a new confidence in his affection, which makes him say, " Hereafter, when I want anything of this kind, I will leave it all to father." That is the main point gained. And so the main thing which a man gains when God at last answers his prayer with the gift which he asked, is not the gift, but the clearer consciousness that God is better than His gifts, that he has all things in God. (*Marvin R. Vincent, D.D.*) *Power of earnestness:*—When a person told a story in a heartless way, Demosthenes said, " I don't believe you." But when the person then repeated the assertion with great fervour, Demosthenes replied, " Now I do believe you." Sincerity and earnestness are ever urgent. The prophetess at Delphos would not go into the temple once when Alexander wished to consult the oracle. He then forced her to go, when she said, " My son, thou art invincible " ; a remark which led him to believe he should always conquer in war. Luther was so earnest in his prayers that it used to be said, " He will not be denied." When Scotland was in danger of becoming Popish, John Knox prayed most mightily for its preservation in the true faith. " Give me Scotland," he pleaded, " or I die " ; and his prayers have been answered. Epaphras " laboured fervently in prayer." Christ " being in an agony, prayed the more fervently " ; and now, " the kingdom of heaven suffereth violence, and the violent take it by force." God has pleasure in holy importunity. " Ye shall seek Me, and find Me when ye seek Me with all your heart." We get fervour as we " continue instant in prayer," and our earnestness sends up our petitions to God through Christ, and brings down the blessings which God gives in His own time and way. Fervent and persevering prayer fits us to receive the blessings which God gives. Importunate prayer has divided seas, stopped the mouths of lions, raised the dead to life, and has secured all kinds of blessings. Cecil says of those who pray as they ought, " God denies them nothing, but with the design to give them a greater good." If our spirit " break with much longing," then " before they call, I will answer, and while they are yet speaking I will hear." (*H. R. Burton.*)

Vers. 9, 10. **Ask, and it shall be given you.**—*The law of prayer :*—This familiar text is usually quoted, and rightly so, as being one of the most precious promises and encouragements to prayer which the Bible contains ; but if you look at the text, it is far more than a promise encouraging prayer. It is a declaration of the condition of our receiving any good gift from God. For reasons which may not be fully intelligible to us, God has limited His mercy. There is the treasure-house full of grace. You go up to it ; the doors are locked. You must knock, or they will not be opened. There is the river of life open to all, but you may die from thirst on its banks unless you kneel. Ask, says Christ, then you will receive ; seek, and you will find ; knock, and it shall be opened unto you. This is really the final mystery of prayer. Why do we need to pray at all ? Can love that waits to be asked be perfect love ? And the mystery is deepened when you remember the very people that need God's grace most are those that never ask for it—wicked people, indifferent people, immoral people, unbelieving people, Godless people. They are the people that need the grace, and they will not ask for it. And yet God says, " No grace unless it be sought." Ye have not—why ? Not because you do not need it. Ye have not, because ye ask not. That, I repeat, is the great mystery of prayer. I. I do not pretend to be able to offer you any full explanation of the mystery, but there are three CONSIDERATIONS WHICH HELP TO ALLEVIATE THE DIF- FICULTY A LITTLE. 1. First of all, it is clear that prayer recognizes the sovereign freedom of the human will. Oh ! it is an awful thing, that human freedom of ours ! Why, my brethren, God lifts His little finger, and the stoutest heart would open its door. But if God entered a heart against its will, He would not enter a heart : He would enter a ruin. And to make prayer a condition of God's gift recognizes even in man's deepest sin the noble freedom of the human will. 2. Then, again, prayer at least implies some sympathy of the will of him who prays with God. You know that there are cables beneath the Atlantic which connect this country with America. Now and then you read in the papers that interruption has taken place in the cable. No messages pass, and the cause of the interruption is some defect in the conveying power in the wire ; some fault, as the electricians call it, in the cable itself. Well, now, just so there may be moral faults in the will which may make it impossible 'or God to give unless we are in sympathy with Him ; and to make prayer, there fore, the condition of God's gift is to imply inward sympathy of will with God. 2. And then, last of all, you cannot doubt—and I shall speak of that in a moment more fully—that whether we can understand the mystery of prayer or not, there is something in prayer, altogether apart from the answers which God gives to it, which justifies prayer. A great thinker once said : " I have conquered all my doubts, not with my books, but on my knees." " On my knees " : ah, yes ! And I have sometimes thought that if those golden gates of heaven were never opened for any answer to prayer to pass through, prayer would be enough by itself. There is something in the reflex attitude and influence and effect of prayer which makes prayer in itself a blessing. Ask, and the very asking is a grace. Seek, and before the answer comes you have found something worth finding. Knock, and that very knock is a blessing. But whether we can understand it or not, this is the law : I could almost put the law of prayer into a single sentence to which there is no exception—much prayer, much blessing; little prayer, little blessing ; no prayer, no blessing. II. Now, let me turn to the brighter side of this text, and ask you to consider for a few moments some of the BLESSINGS WHICH COME TO THOSE WHO OBEY THIS GREAT LAW OF THE KINGDOM. Let me encourage you to pray by these blessings. 1. First of all, I cannot find a word, though I have tried hard, to exactly express what I mean when I say that the first blessing of prayer is this: the unconscious check it imposes on the life. Any of you who spend half an hour every morning with God will know what I mean. You weave about your life a network of self-restraint never seen, most potent, most real, most felt when most needed. St. Paul had a word, a favourite word; and St. Paul was a very passionate man, a fiery man ; but there was a very favourite word with him; it is translated most inadequately in our version, "moderation." The Greek word means " high mastery of self " ; and that is what prayer gives a man. 2. The other day I was reading an article by one of our scientific men who has given up all belief in the supernatural in any answers to prayer, and yet he said these words : " If any one abandons prayer, he abandons one of the highest forces which mould and benefit human character." I do not wonder at it. You could not go into the presence of God, if God never answered prayer, without receiving a blessing. When Moses was on the Mount, we read that he came down from it, and his face shone, though he wist it not. There are shining faces in the streets of London to-day, if you have eyes to see them—men, women, not beautiful by nature, but beautiful by what is more than nature, beautiful with God's own beauty. You look at them, and you think of the words in Tennyson's " In Memoriam " :

" Her eyes were hymns of silent prayer."

You look at them, and you think of those better words, " They saw His face as it had been the face of an angel." 3. And yet the reflex blessing of prayer is as nothing, absolutely nothing, compared with its chief blessing—and with that I wish to close— that prayer has power with God. I do not shrink from the words. The prophet Hosea, describing that night of wrestling of Jacob with God, uses these words—you will find them in the Revised Version—" In his manhood he had power with God." Do you know what that power was ? It was the power of a lame man wrestling in prayer—" I will not let Thee go until Thou bless me." It was the power that every soul in prayer has with God to-day. (*G. S. Barrett, B.A.*) *Prayer certified of success :*—Our Saviour knew right well that many difficulties would arise in connection with prayer which might tend to stagger His disciples, and therefore He has balanced every opposition by an overwhelming assurance. I. OUR SAVIOUR GIVES TO US THE WEIGHT OF HIS OWN AUTHORITY. "I say unto you." 1. No laws of nature can prevent the fulfilment of the Lord's own word. 2. No Divine decrees can prevent the efficacy of prayer. 3. Notwithstanding God's majesty and thy weakness and sinfulness, thy prayer shall move the arm that moves the world. II. OUR LORD PRESENTS US WITH A PROMISE. 1. Note that the promise is given to several varieties of prayer. 2. Observe that these varieties of prayer are put on an ascending scale. " Ask "—the statement of our wants. " Seek " signifies that we marshall our arguments. " Knock "—importunity. 3. These three methods of prayer exercise a variety of our graces. Faith asks, hope seeks, love knocks. 4. These three modes of prayer suit us in different stages of distress. There am I, a poor mendicant at mercy's door, I ask, and I shall receive. I lose my way, so that I cannot find Him of whom I once asked so successfully ; well, then, I may seek with the certainty that I shall find. And if I am in the last stage of all, not merely poor and bewildered, but so defiled as to feel shut out from God like a leper shut out of the camp, then I may knock and the door will open to me. 5. Each one of these different descriptions of prayer is exceedingly simple. III. Jesus testifies to the fact that prayer is heard. (*C. H. Spurgeon.*) *It is sense of want that makes us to seek out :*—It was want that caused Abraham to go down into Egypt (Gen. xii. 10), Isaac into Gerar (Gen. xxvi. 1), Jacob to send his sons into Egypt (Gen. xlii. 2). For first, nature is proud, and loath to be beholding to any till needs must: every man naturally loves in the first place to be beholding to himself in any extremity; and if his own wit, or his own purse, or his own projects, or endeavours will help him, he will seek no further; he had rather pay than pray. Then again; life is dear, and nature is forcible to seek out for the preservation of itself, when it is necessitated and put to it, it will seek out before it suffer too much, and break through stone walls rather then famish. From hence we may conclude that there is some good comes unto us by want, some profit we may have by it. It teacheth us the worth of things most truly, and maketh us value the mercy as we should (at least far better than otherwise we would). It is the sharp winter that makes the spring to be sweet and pleasant; and the night's darkness that makes the light of the sun to be desirable: so sickness makes health more grateful; pain, pleasure more delightful; want, plenty more comfortable; and it makes exceedingly for the preservation of love and unity amongst neighbours, and towards the maintenance of civil society and commerce amongst Christians. And this is one reason why it hath pleased the manifold wisdom of God to enrich several countries with several commodities; divers gifts to several persons, not all to any one, that our wants may be supplied by their fulness, and one be beholding to another for a supply of his necessity, which otherwise would not be. Laish was a secure and careless people, and the reason is rendered to be this, "they had no want" (Judges xviii. 10). A fulness causeth us to contemn and scorn those whom in our wants we are glad to make use of. So we read (Judges xi. 6). (*N. Rogers.*) *True prayer must be accompanied with a sense of the want of those things we crave :*— When we come to God by prayer, a sense of those things we ask must be brought with us. This is required (James i. 5). "If any man lack wisdom," *i.e.*, if any be sensible of the lack of it and desire it. In the sense of want have God's servants come before Him continually. So Jehosophat, "We know not what to do" (2 Chron. xx. 12). So Hannah (1 Sam. i. 6–15). So David (Psa. lx. 11). So the Prodigal (Luke xv. 17). So all the godly from time to time. This is that that puts us in a praying condition; for first, no man will ask that which he supposeth he hath no need of (Matt. ix. 12); the proud Pharisee begged nothing, though he pretended thankfulness. Secondly, this is that that humbles us, and causeth us to be lowly in our own eyes; it is the having of some good that puffeth up, not the want of it. Thirdly, without a sense of the want of what we ask, we shall never earnestly desire it, nor use the means for the obtaining of it. It is want that makes us to seek out, as it did that man we heard of before, who went to his friend at midnight. Fourthly, should we have what we crave, yet without sense of want of the mercy, we should never prize it. Now there is a three-fold want that must be taken special notice of when we come to God by prayer. First of the blessing itself which we desire to have, be it outward or inward, corporal or spiritual, temporal or eternal; of what kind soever it be, we must be sensible, and have a feeling of it, and value it accordingly. A second want that we must take notice of is our own disability to help ourselves, and the disability of any other creature in heaven or earth to supply our wants. Thirdly, of our own unworthiness to obtain that we crave, we must be sensible. (*Ibid.*) *The efficacy of importunate prayer :*—I. What is importunate prayer? 1. It is restless. 2. Will not take either the privative "nay" of silence, or the positive "nay" of denial. 3. Nor will it take a contumelious repulse. 4. Impudent in a holy manner. I remember a story of a poor woman in Essex condemned to die: she falls to crying and screeching, as if she meant to pierce the heavens; the judge and those on the bench bid her hold her peace. "O my Lord," said she, "it is for my life I beg, I beseech you; it is for my life." So when a soul comes before God, and begs for mercy, he must consider that it is for his life. II. Why we must seek importunately. 1. God loves to be sought unto. 2. We should not be lukewarm in seeking mercy. It was a custom among the Romans, when any was condemned to die, if he looked for mercy, he was to bring father and mother, and all his kinsmen and acquaintance, and they should all come with tears in their faces, and with tattered garments, and kneel down and beg before the judge, and cry mightily; and then they thought justice was honoured. Thus they honoured justice in man, for a man condemned to die; and so the Lord loves His mercy should be honoured, &c., and therefore He will have prayer to be importunate, that it may appear by groans how highly we esteem of grace; our souls must pant and gasp after grace, the breath of the Lord being the soul of our souls, our hearts will die without it. This is to the honour of mercy, therefore the Lord will have us importunate. 3. As importunity must be in regard of God's mercy, so it must be in regard of ourselves, else we cannot tell how to esteem it. Soon come, soon gone; lightly gotten, suddenly forgotten; I have it, come let us be jovial and spend it, when this is gone, I know where to have more; but if he had wrought for it, and also must work for more, if he mean to have more, he would better esteem it. What then is the reason, may some man say, why so few are importunate in prayer? I answer—1. Because men count prayer a penance. 2. Men content themselves with formality. 3. Because they are gentlemen-beggars. Their hearts are full of pride. 4. Because they have wrong conceits of prayer. (1) They have high conceits of their own prayers; they cannot pray in a morning, between the pillow and the blankets, half asleep and half awake, but they think that they have done God good service; so that He cannot afford to damn them. Lord, how do I abuse the throne of grace? how do I abuse Thy sabbaths, Thy house, Thy name, and all the holy ordinances which I go about? A man that is importunate in prayer is ashamed; but when they think highly of their prayers, they are insolent, their prayers are damned, and they too. (2) As men have high conceits of their prayers, so they have mean conceits of their sins, they think not their sins so bad as they are. (3) As men have mean thoughts of their sins, so they have base thoughts of God. I cannot think God will be so strict. They think God will pardon them, and therefore because of this, men are not importunate with God. (4) Because they have wrong conceits of importunity. If a man knock once or twice, or thrice, and none answer, presently he will be gone; this is for want of manners; thou wilt knock seven times, if thou be importunate with them: they within may say, hold thy peace, begone, &c., but thou wilt not so be answered. Beloved, men are close-handed, they are loath to give; and they are close-hearted too, they are loath to take the pains to ask of God; they are loath others should be importunate with them, and therefore they are loath to be importunate with God. (*W. Fenner, B.D.*) *Importunate prayer:*—I. SIGNS OF IMPORTUNATE PRAYER. 1. The prayer of a godly heart. 2. The prayer of a pure conscience. 3. A prayer full of strong arguments. 4. A stout prayer. 5. A wakeful prayer. 6. A prayer that will not be quiet till it get assurance that God has heard it. II. PRAYERS THAT ARE NOT IMPORTUNATE. 1. A lazy prayer. That man that ploughs his field, and digs his vineyard, that man prays for a good harvest; if a man pray to God never so much, yet if he do not use the means, he cannot obtain the thing he prays for. Even so it is with grace; a man may pray for all the graces of God's Spirit, and yet never get any, unless he labour for them in the use of the means. God cannot abide lazy beggars, that cannot abide to follow their calling, but if they can get anything by begging they will never set themselves to work. So, many there be, that if they can get pardon of sin for begging, then they will have it; but let such know that the Lord will not give it for such lazy kind of praying. God gives not men repentance, faith, &c., by miracles, but by means. Thou must then use the means, and keep watch and ward over thine own soul, that so thou mayest get the grace thou prayest for. 2. A prayer that is not a full prayer, never speeds with God; but an importunate prayer is a full prayer, it is a pouring out of the heart, yea of the whole heart (Psa. lxii. 8). 3. Snatch-prayer is no importunate prayer; when men pray by snatches, because of sluggishness, or because their hearts are eager about other business. 4. Silent prayers are never importunate. Many go to God, and tell God they must needs have mercy, and fain they would have mercy, and yet they are silent in confessing the sin they should. Hast thou been a drunkard, and dost thou think that the Lord will forgive thee for crying, "Lord, forgive me," &c. No, no, thou must insist on it, and say, "Against Thy word I have been a drunkard, my conscience told me so, but I would not hear; I have felt the motions of Thy Holy Spirit stirring against me, and I regarded not; now if Thou shouldst turn me into hell, I were well requited; so many sermons have I neglected; I have wronged others in this kind, and I have been the cause why many are now in hell if they repented not. I have prayed for mercy, yet with the dog to his vomit have I returned, and therefore for all my prayers Thou mayest cast me into hell for ever; and now I have prayed, yet it is a hundred to one but I shall run into my old sin again; yet as I expect forgiveness, so I desire to make a covenant to give over all my sinful courses, and I am justly damned if I go to them again." Such a kind of prayer the Lord loves. 5. Seldom-prayer is no importunate prayer; when the soul contents itself with seldom coming before the throne of grace; an importunate soul is ever frequenting the way of mercy, and the gate of Christ; he is often at the threshold before God, in all prayer and humiliation. 6. Lukewarm-prayer is not an importunate prayer; when a man prays, but is not fervent, when a man labours not to wind up his soul to God in prayer. 7. Bye-thoughts in prayer keep prayer from being importunate; as when a man prays and lets his heart go a wool-gathering. I remember a story of an unworthy orator, who being to make an acclamation, O earth! O heaven! when he said O heaven, he looked down to the earth; and when he said O earth, he looked up to heaven. So, many when they pray to God in heaven, their thoughts are on the earth : these prayers can never be importunate. When a man prays, the Lord looks that his heart should be fixed on his prayer; for our hearts will leak, and the best child of God, do what he can, shall have bye-thoughts in prayer. Consider O Lord (saith David) how I mourn (Psa. lv.). There was something in the prophet's prayer that did vex him, and that made him so much the more to mourn before God. But as for you that can have bye-thoughts in prayer, and let them abide with you, your prayers are not importunate; the heathen shall rise up against you and condemn you. I remember a story of a certain youth, who being in the temple with Alexander, when he was to offer incense to his god, and the youth holding the golden censer with the fire in it, a coal fell on the youth's hand and burnt his wrist; but the youth considering what a sacred thing he was about, for all he felt his wrist to be burnt, yet he would not stir, but continued still to the end. This I speak to shame those that can let anything, though never so small, to disturb them, yea (if it were possible) lesser things than nothing; for if nothing come to draw their hearts away, they themselves will employ their hearts. III. How to GET IMPORTUNITY IN PRAYER. 1. Labour to know thy own misery. 2. You must be sensible of your misery. 3. Observe the prayers of God's people. 4. Get a stock of prayer. 5. Labour to be full of good works. 6. Labour to reform thy household. (*Ibid.*)   *The prayer of faith :*—The prayer of faith includes the following attributes : 1. Earnest desire. 2. Submission. 3. Dependence. 4. An earnest and diligent use of means. 5. Deep humility. 6. Faith. 7. Perseverance. 8. An absorbing regard for the glory of God. (*The Preacher's Treasury.*)   *The value of prayer :* — Undoubtedly, God's rule of action in nature we have every reason to regard as unalterable; established as an inflexible and faithful basis of expectation, and so far embodying the essential conditions of intellectual and moral life, and, for that reason, not open to perpetual variation on the suggestion of occasional moral contingencies. Petitions, therefore, for purely physical events other than those which are already on their way—*e. g.*, for the arrest of a heavenly body, the diverting of a storm, the omission of a tide—must be condemned, as at variance with the known method of providential rule. But a large proportion of temporal events are not like these, dealt out to us from the mere physical elements; they come to us with a mixed origin, from the natural world indeed, yet through the lines of human life, and as affected by the human will. The diseases from which we suffer visit us in conformity with the order of nature, yet are often self-incurred. The shipwreck that makes desolate five hundred homes is due to forces which may be named and reckoned, yet also, it may be, to the negligence which failed to take account of them in time. Wherever these elements of *character* enter into the result, so that it will differ according to the moral agent's attitude of mind, it is plainly not beyond the reach of a purely spiritual influence to modify a temporal event. The cry of entreaty from the bedside of fever will not reduce the patient's temperature, or banish his delirium ; but if there be human treatment on which the crisis hangs, may so illuminate the mind, and temper the heart, and sweeten the whole scene around, as to alight upon the healing change, and turn the shadow of death aside. The prayer of Cromwell's troopers, kneeling on the field, could not lessen the numbers or blunt the weapons of the cavaliers, but might give such fire of zeal and coolness of thought as to turn each man into an organ of Almighty justice, and carry the victory which he implored. Wherever the living contact between the human spirit and the Divine can set in operation our very considerable control over the combinations and processes of the natural world, there is still left a scope, practically indefinite, for prayer, that the bitter cup of outward suffering may pass away—only never without the trustful relapse, "Not my will, but Thine, be done." (*James Martineau, LL.D.*)   *Is the prayer of faith always answered ?*—I haven't time to answer that question as I should like to do ; but faith must have a warrant. A good many people think they have faith enough when they ask for certain things ; yet their prayers are not answered, and they wonder why. The trouble is, their faith had no warrant. For instance, if I should go out to meet the army of Midian at the head of three hundred men with empty pitchers I should probably be routed. Gideon had a warrant. God told him to go, and he went, and Midian couldn't stand. We have got to have some foundation for our faith, some promise of God to base our faith upon. Then again, if we don't get our prayers answered just as we want them it is no sign that God doesn't answer prayer. For instance, my little boy when he was eight years old wanted a pony. He got his answer ; it was "No." Was his prayer answered ? Of course it was. I got him a goat. A pony might have kicked his head off. A goat was a good deal better for a boy eight years old than a pony. It is a foolish idea to think that God has got to do everything you ask. You will notice that the people whose prayers are recorded in the Bible didn't always have their prayers answered just as they wanted them to be, but often in some other way. In all true prayer you will say, "Not my will, but Thine, be done" ; and all true prayer will be answered if you have made it in that spirit. God likes to have His children ask for just what they want, even though the answer He will give may be very different from what they expect. I want my children to ask me for what they want, but I don't give them all they ask for by a good deal. So make your requests known unto God, and the peace of God shall keep you. Look at those three men of Scripture that take up more room than any other three men in the whole Bible—Moses, Elijah, and Paul. Look at Moses and Elijah in the Old Testament. They didn't get their prayers answered in the way they wanted them, and yet God answered their prayers. You remember Moses wanted to go with the children of Israel into the goodly land, the promised land. You can imagine how strong that desire was after he had been with them for forty years wandering in the desert. He wanted to go into the promised land, and see his children settled in their home. But it wasn't the will of God that Moses should go. And that wasn't because God did not love Moses, for He took him up into Pisgah and showed him the whole country. A great many years later Moses did stand in the promised land, on the Mount of Transfiguration. His prayer wasn't answered in his way. God had better things in store for Moses ; and certainly I would rather be on the Mount of Transfiguration with Jesus Christ, and Peter, James, and John, than to have had to go over and fight as Joshua did. So we are not to think that God doesn't answer our prayers because He doesn't answer them just in the way and the time we want them answered. Take Elijah. If there ever was a man that knew how to pray it was Elijah. In the power of prayer he stood before Ahab and wrought wonders. After all that he prayed that he might die under the juniper tree. Was his prayer answered in his way ? Why, he was the only man under that dispensation who was to go to heaven without dying. I heard of a little boy, four years old, who asked his father to let him take a razor in his hand. His father said, "Oh, no, my boy ; you will cut yourself." Then that little fellow just sat down and cried as if his heart would break. A great many grown-up people are just like that— they are praying for razors. Elijah prayed for a razor—he wanted his throat cut. But his prayer wasn't answered that way. God wasn't going to take his life, or let him take it. He had something better for him. And now look at Paul. No one takes up so much space in the New Testament as Paul, and if there ever was a man that had power with God he had it ; and yet he prayed three times that the Lord would take the thorn out of his flesh. The Lord said, "I won't take it out, but I will give you more grace" ; and Paul said, "Thank God! I wouldn't have it taken out now if I could. I have got more grace by it." If you have got a thorn in the flesh remember that God has sent it for some wise purpose. God sends us tribulations for our good. Paul said he gloried in persecutions, because they lifted him nearer to God and made him more like Jesus Christ. (*D. L. Moody*.) *Revival always possible :*—A plain, shrewd man, in one of the daily prayer meetings, said that praying for a revival is "just like digging for water." Suppose a community as ignorant of the terms of obtaining water as we are of the conditions of revival. They apply to a scientific man, to know whether there is any way to obtain a constant supply of living water. They rather infer, from the fact that it rains tremendously sometimes without their help, that the supply of water is one for which they are ordained to wait passively, and that when it does not rain in their vessels, they must wait as patiently as they may. But if there is

water to be had otherwise in a dry time, they would make any exertion to get at it. "Certainly there is," their teacher responds, "water everywhere, water without limit, under your very feet." "How shall we get it?" "By digging for it." "How far must we dig?" "Five, ten, twenty, or even a hundred feet; in some places a thousand feet will not reach it. But no matter; if it is five thousand feet down, digging will invariably bring it. All you have to do is to dig till you find it."
Seeking and finding:—A young lady was seated in a cottage in the North-West of Spain, trying, in very imperfect and recently-acquired Spanish, to make plain the way of salvation to a group of poor villagers who had assembled to hear her. She had just said: "Jesus is able to save you to-day; is there any one here really wanting salvation?" Immediately a curious-looking little man rose from his seat, and throwing himself on his knees in the centre of the room, the tears streaming down his weather-beaten cheeks, cried out: "Oh, I do want to be saved! I would rather have the salvation of my soul than all the good things in this world." Unable to express herself as she would, she said: "Only Jesus can save. Seek Jesus." In his ignorance and superstition, the poor peasant took her words literally, and started off after the meeting to seek Jesus, climbing the mountains, hunting the pine forests and the sea-shore. He did this for three days and nights. At length, weary and disheartened, he threw himself on the ground, in a field, and, with his face on the earth, groaned out his agony of soul to the God of heaven. In His tender compassion He heard this poor man's cry, and filled his soul with joy and gladness, enabling him to trust in the unseen Lord. He had sought the bodily presence of Christ—a mistake very natural to a man always seeing images of the saints, while the living Saviour, by His Holy Spirit, lifted the veil from his understanding, and revealed Himself, the Light of life, more present and real than any earthly object. When he next appeared at the meeting, his face shone with the joy of heaven, as he told of the wonderful change God had wrought in his soul.
Adam's sons are a generation of seekers, but all are not happy in finding what they seek : but you must know that there is a two-fold seeking ; one right and true, when all due circumstances are observed therein ; that fails not. And there is another kind of seeking, which is unsound and hypocritical ; no marvel if that be unsuccessful. 1. Some there are that seek what they should not seek, but rather shun. 2. Others seek *recta*, but not *rectè* : right things, but they seek not rightly. 3. Some fail in the *quando* ; they seek, but out of season. 4. Some again seek, but not in the place right. 5. Others fail in the *sicut* ; it may be they seek in due time, and in the right place too, but they fail in the manner of seeking, they seek not as they should. Some seek without eyes ; they have the eyes of sense and reason, but that of faith is wanting ; they seek ignorantly, and unbelievingly ; their eyes are not opened, they know not what belongs to their peace. Some seek, but without a light. Some seek, but without humility, proudly and boastingly ; not upon their knees, but tiptoes. Some seek, but without sincerity ; fictitiously and hypocritically. Some seek, but not purely and chastely ; they seek not grace for grace's sake ; nor Christ, for Christ's sake (Hos. vii. 14 ; Isa. vi. 26). Some seek, but not fervently and earnestly : "They seek not as for silver" (Prov. ii. 4). Lastly, some seek not constantly and perseveringly : "Seek the Lord and His strength, seek His face evermore," saith David (Psa. cv. 4). Wherefore, be we encouraged to "set our hearts to seek the Lord aright" (1 Chron. xxii. 19). Seek what you should seek, seek where you should seek, seek when you should seek, seek as you ought to seek, and rest assured that your labour shall not be in vain ; you shall find. In seeking for earthly things at man's hands we often fail ; but if we seek the best at God's hands we always speed. We may go to the physician and seek health, but meet with death ; we may go to the lawyer and seek for law and justice, and meet with injustice and oppression ; we may seek to friends for kindness and favour, and find enmity and hatred from them ! All that seek to men speed not, though their requests be never so just and honest (as we find Luke xviii. 1). But whom did God ever send away with a sad heart that sought Him sincerely. Suetonius reports of Titus that he was wont to say that none should go away from speaking with a prince with a sad heart. God likes it not that we should go from Him with a dejected spirit : it is our own fault if we do. (*N. Rogers.*)
The subjective theory of prayer:—[That, namely, which restricts the value of prayer to the influence it exerts on the man who prays.] On this thing, Dr. Bushnell says, "Prayer becomes a kind of dumb-bell exercise—good as exercise, but not to be answered." Let the Saviour's words be carried out in the various figures used, on this theory, and its absurdity becomes at once apparent. 1. He

bids us "ask." Imagine a child asking for some favour, or for the relief of some want, and standing, hour after hour, repeating his requests, and being told by the father : "Go on asking, my child; it does you much good to ask. The longer you ask, the more good it will do you. Do not expect to receive anything, however, as the principal benefit of asking is that, by and by, you will not want anything, and will cease to make any request." 2. Jesus bids us "seek." Imagine a mother seeking a lost child. She looks through the house and along the streets, then searches the fields and woods, and examines the river-banks. A wise neighbour meets her and says : "Seek on ; look everywhere ; search every accessible place. You will not find, indeed ; but then seeking is a good thing. It puts the mind on the stretch ; it fixes the attention ; it aids observation ; it makes the idea of the child very real. And then after a while, you will cease to want your child. 3. The word of Christ is "Knock." Imagine a man knocking at the door of a house, long and loud. After he has done this for an hour, a window opens and the occupant of the house puts out his head, and says : "That is right, my friend ; I shall not open the door, but then keep on knocking. It is excellent exercise and you will be the healthier for it. Knock away till sundown, and then come again, and knock all to-morrow. After some days thus spent, you will attain to a state of mind in which you will no longer care to come in." Is this what Jesus intended us to understand? No doubt one would thus soon cease to ask, to seek, and to knock, but would it not be from disgust? (*W. W. Patton, D.D.*) *Urgency in prayer :*—The emphatic reduplication of the injunction marks what stress the Speaker laid upon it. So does the rising scale of intensity in the words employed : ask—seek—knock. To seek is a more industrious, and solicitous, and animated kind of asking. We ask for what we want ; we seek for that which we have lost : and this sense of loss sharpens at once our need and our desire. Again : to knock is a description of seeking at once most helpless and most importunate ; since he who seeks admission at his friends' door has nothing else to do but go on knocking till he be answered. The *asker* will study best how to state his plea when once he gains a hearing, but may never care to seek another opportunity. The *seeker* will make, or watch for, opportunities of access to the patron whose favourable ear he hopes to gain, but, often baffled, may grow weary in his efforts. The *knocker* must simply trust to the force of patience and of repetition, sure that if he knock long enough he shall be heard, and that, if he continue to knock long enough, he must be attended to. It would be impossible to teach with greater emphasis the idea that prayer is a laborious and enduring exercise of the human spirit, to which we need to be moved by a vivid, unresting, never-ending experience of our own need, and in which we ought to be sustained by a fixed certainty that God will hear us in the end. (*J. O. Dykes, D.D.*) *The reasonableness of prayer :*—The principal objection which the thought of our time makes to the efficacy of prayer is based upon the scientific idea of law. Law, it is said, reigns throughout the universe, and is unchangeable and deaf to all entreaty. The truth of all this must be ungrudgingly conceded. If it were not true, if the order of nature were not invariable, there could be no science. No stronger proof that there is an intelligent and benevolent Power, upholding and directing the course of nature, can possibly be given to a thoughtful mind, than its unbroken order and the invariable methods of the Divine will. Such, then, is the Reign of Law, and no man, it is said, can grasp the conception and enter into intelligent sympathy with it, without abandoning the fond conceit that God will grant a favour to one of His creatures on being asked to do so. It may have been pardonable to pray for rain, for health, for freedom from pestilence and famine, when these things were supposed to depend upon the caprice of an omnipotent will, but the scientific idea of law renders these prayers absurd. Well, now, I do not pretend to give a complete answer to this objection ; but I have a sufficient answer. It is the commonest fact of human life that man makes the forces and unchanging methods of nature the servants of his will. In this way he makes natural forces perform achievements which, when compared with any merely natural occurrences, might strictly be called supernatural. Now, if man, with his limited knowledge of the laws of the material world, can make them serve his turn in so many ingenious and surprising ways, while their order goes on unbroken, surely an Almighty and all-wise God, by skilful combinations of existing forces, and without departing from a single method to which His wisdom is pledged, can execute the behests of His own will. Surely He has not given man a greater liberty than He has left Himself. But this answer I have given is met by two objections. 1. It is said man's interference with the order of nature is obvious, it is a visible interposition, but who has ever marked the point where God interposes? If he counteracted one law of nature by another to meet the pleadings of His petitioners, would not science have detected His supernatural agency? Certainly not. No scientific man can explain what Force is, upon what its variations of intensity depend, or how its changes of form are brought about. 2. But then, there is another objection—that it is inconsistent with the wisdom of an omniscient God to suppose that He would ever alter His plan at the request of His creatures. Without pressing the answer that, as a God intent upon moral ends, it is part of His plan to leave room for answers to prayer, there is the obvious fact that God actually allows human beings to alter His plan, for His plan means here the original order of nature. The free will, the caprice, if you like, of human beings is constantly originating changes in nature which would not have been if *they* had not been, or would have been different if they had been other than they are. Now surely what man, for the purpose of his education and progress, has been permitted to do, God, having an eye to the same purpose, must be free to do Himself. The objections against the reasonableness of prayer from the point of view of the scientific conception of law, if valid at all, are valid for a great deal too much. They all imply that man is not free, that every thought of his mind and act of his will are as much determined for him by fixed laws as the course of the wind or the advance of the tide. And if this were true responsibility would be at an end; benevolence and murder would be simply different aspects of nature, like sunshine and storm. Religion would be a mere dream, resembling the fantastic forms of the mist as it catches the changing currents of the passing breeze. But there are very few who would not passionately reject a conclusion that contradicts our consciousness, and writes "vanity" over all the noblest and most pathetic passages of human history. (*E. W. Shalders, B.A.*) *Ask and it shall be given you :*—This is a very defective world. Everybody says so. We have here only the rudiments of things. There is beauty and there is blessing; but only in fragments. The consequence is that we hear endless murmuring and complaining. 1. "Ask and it shall be given you," is the reply of God. I have given you half; the other half is in My hand. You build a house, and one stone is wanting to complete it; you search everywhere, and are angry because you find it not. It is with Me; I have kept it purposely, that your house may not be built without Me. You build a ship; but the rudder is not forthcoming. I have kept it, that you may ask and receive, and discover that the whole is My gift." 2. Ask in the right quarter and it shall be given you. 3. Ask in the right way. Let God prescribe how we shall ask Him. 4. Ask for the most essential gifts first. Men on a wreck would ask for a sail, not for an embroidered garment. 5. Ask for regulated tastes and desires. This one gift will cut off at once a thousand occasions of murmuring. 6. Ask with importunity. 7. Ask in faith. (*G. Bowen.*) *Ask and it shall be given you :*—Perhaps you shrink from the very thought of mentioning your desires to God. You know enough of the character of God to be aware that the desires which occupy so large a place in your mind, are such as could not be communicated to Him without shame. After all, the best thing, in fact the only good thing you can do with these desires, is to take them to God and expose them to Him, and ask Him in infinite mercy to deliver you from them. Those wrong desires are your worst enemies, and until you be delivered from them there cannot be the dawn of salvation for you. Death came into the heart of Eve in the form of a desire for the forbidden fruit; and blessed would it have been for her if she had hastened to the tree of life seeking deliverance from that internal foe. Ask, then, for the Spirit of power and of truth to come into your heart, and subdue the vain desires that war against the soul. To have been brought to desire that which is good, is itself an infinite gain—far more to be esteemed than mines of gold and silver. Yes, a man with right desires and nothing else, is at the foot of a ladder leading up to a throne of life, light, and immortality; and bending angels hold out to him their friendly hands. Whereas a man with wrong desires, though a thousand camels fail to convey his riches, is wending a way that descends more and more precipitously to night and everlasting confusion. (*Ibid.*) *The principle of the text illustrated :*—" We want a railroad into Italy," cries the world, " and can go no farther for this mountain. What shall we do to find a way?" "There is no way," Heaven answers, "except to your persistency; but if you seek, you shall find; if you knock, it shall be opened unto you." And so the seeking of the answer to that prayer of the nations is entrusted to the keen sight of men whose searching will never tire until the way is found. The knocking is with hard steel at the hard rock, and it is only a question of persistence and endurance; then at last it has come to pass that even the heart of the unwilling mountain is won, and its midnight sleep driven away; and where for countless ages there has been only an utter and unutterable silence, there is now the mighty response of an answered prayer in the thunder of the locomotive. (*R. Collyer.*) *Every one that asketh receiveth :*—We have here no mere surmise on our part as to what becomes of the prayers which we present; it is a distinct affirmation concerning them on the part of God Himself to whom we present them. There is something very definite and precise about these words ; there is no explaining them away, or attaching to them any other meaning than the clearly obvious one, every one that asks *does* receive, and every one that seeks *does* find. Prayer, however, is necessarily a matter in which two are concerned ; and, as such, we have only heard what God has to say on it. What have we ourselves to say on it? Can we, from our hearts, echo God's words, and testify from our own experience to their truth ? Or, rather, is not the sad and perplexing experience of every praying man this : " How often have I asked and not received, sought without finding, and knocked without any door being opened to me ! " How, then, shall we reconcile these two utterances—that of God, to whom we address our prayers, and that of our own experience, as we vainly wait for an answer to our prayers ? We must remember that the words in verse 10 are God's utterance as to prayer, and not man's ; and we must admit the likelihood that God from the position from which He views prayer, may have laws relating to it which perhaps *must* be hidden from us. We must remember that in verse 10 we are not told that they that ask shall *see* that they receive ; that they that seek shall at once *have evidence* that they find; but simply that they *do* receive, they *do* find. Christ reveals this to us in order that, whatever our *experience* may be, we may *know* if we cannot *see*, that every one that seeks does find. He does not tell us that henceforth our experience shall no longer seem to be at variance with the great statement of the passage ; it must often seem to be at variance with it, so long as we live on this earth. What Christ does is mercifully to explain to us *how* this seeming variance may in reality cover an actual and bountiful answer to our prayers. (*W. F. Herbert.*)   *If a son shall ask bread :*— The illustration of the egg and the scorpion is not to be found in the parallel passage of St. Matthew. It introduces no new thought, but only strengthens the emphasis of what has been said already. It may be observed that the *stone* represents to us useless gifts, the *serpent* and the *scorpion*, things which are actually pernicious. If human fathers would not give either the one or the other to their children, it is inconceivable that our Father in heaven will mock the prayers of His children who call upon Him. And if He does not mock them, what will He give in answer to His children's prayers? In the Sermon on the Mount our Lord says that He will give " good things " ; here the language is more definite, " the Holy Spirit." The comparison of the two suggests that the best things which we can ask of God are spiritual blessings ; we may ask many things which seem good to us, and they may not really be good ; but the Holy Spirit is a perfect gift ; it must always be well for us to ask for it ; it can never be to our detriment to receive it ; therefore, while we are cautious how we ask for other gifts, we may always be instant in prayer for greater and still greater influences of the Holy Spirit upon our hearts. (*Bishop H. Goodwin.*)   You foolish, ignorant children of the great Father in heaven doubt and mourn because the things you pray for are often denied you ; but put yourselves, for a moment, in God's place, so far as to consider the prayers of your little children to you—children whose folly, as compared with your wisdom, is as nothing to your folly when compared with God's wisdom. 1. Your child comes to you one day hungry, and begging for bread, and, seeing a round, flat stone by your side which bears some resemblance to a loaf, he asks you for it, not for food, but for stone, supposing it to be bread. You do not give it him, but you take him by the hand and lead him home, where there is bread in plenty. The child is hungry, and as you lead him on he is not only hungry, but grieved and sad. " My father," he says, " whom I have been taught to love and trust, will not even grant me such a simple necessary as a loaf of bread to appease my hunger." You do not give him the thing he prayed for, but are you not fully answering the child's prayer? What he prayed for really was bread, and it is bread that you are about to give him ; the cause of the child's grief lies simply in his own childish mistake about the stone. 2. But Christ takes a further case, and not quite a parallel one. Your child, hungry again, comes to you as you wander through the meadow by the river, and asks you for a fish ; and seeing a shining thing by you which he takes to be a fish, he asks you for that, that he may get his hunger satisfied. Again you refuse him, and again he is grieved and perplexed at your refusal as you lead him to the well-spread table at home; but this time you have led your child not merely, as before, from a stone, which would simply have failed to satisfy him, but you have refused him a serpent, which would have poisoned him. 3. And now, Christ would say, these are just the kind of prayers which are constantly rising up from us to our Father in heaven, and the seeming want of answer to which awakens in us such constant doubt and murmuring and complaint. (1) A stone may look very much like a loaf to a little child, and health or wealth may look very like peace of mind to us; but what if God knows better than we do? (2) A serpent may look very like a fish to a child, and worldly prosperity in any form may look very much like well-being to us; but what if God knows that prosperity would be to us, not only like a hard stone to a hungry child, utterly unsatisfying and quite harmless, but like a venomous serpent that has a deadly sting? That is just what prosperity has been to many a man—it has poisoned his soul. And that, we may be very sure, is what prosperity would be to us, if God denied it to us. 4. We have been considering hitherto the denials of God to our prayers, for it is they assuredly which perplex us most. But does God merely answer our prayers by denying them? Is it His care merely to shield us from harm, without bestowing upon us any actual, positive good? Not so. "Every one that asketh *receiveth*." Not only is the foolish request denied, but some real and bountiful blessing is actually bestowed. If you refuse the stone or the serpent to your child, still you do not leave him to starve. "If ye then . . . Holy Spirit to them that ask Him?" "Yes," you say, "the Holy Spirit; but look at our manifold daily needs as they throng together in our morning prayers; will this one gift of the Holy Spirit supply and satisfy all these?" Not all your *desires*, for you desire stones and serpents, which would break your teeth and poison your life; but all your needs the Holy Spirit can supply; and, more than that, in no other way, except through the Holy Spirit, can your needs be supplied in that bountiful way in which God delights to supply them—in the way, that is, which enriches your spiritual life at the same time, and by the same means as your natural life is enriched. (*W. F. Herbert.*)   The common articles of food on the shores of the Lake of Tiberias were fish, bread, and eggs. The poor look for nothing else to-day. (*E. Stapfer, D.D.*) *A scorpion :*—This crab-like member of the *articulata* is very common in Palestine, where more than eight species are known. The most dangerous variety is the black rock-scorpion, as thick as a finger, and five or six inches long; others are yellow, brown, white, red, or striped and banded. During cold weather they lie dormant, but at the return of heat they crawl forth from beneath the stones under which they have lain hidden, or out of the crevices of walls and chinks of other kinds, and make their way, not only to the paths where men pass, but into houses, where they get below sleeping-mats, carpets, or clothes, or creep into shoes or slippers. They are carnivorous by nature, living on beetles, insects, and the like; but they sting whatever frightens or irritates them. Occasionally the sting causes death. (*C. Geikie, D.D.*)   *The commanding object of prayer :*—I have been thankful a thousand times that God does not absolutely and unconditionally promise in His Holy Word, any temporal, worldly, sensible blessing in answer to prayer, but only the gift of the Holy Ghost. The order of His kingdom would have been subverted if He had. I know not if there would have been in that case any true prayer for the Holy Ghost at all. The one great, unconditioned, unqualified promise of the gift of the Holy Spirit is purely personal, individual. No absolute promise anywhere that a saint shall receive the Holy Ghost for others by asking, or that on his praying acceptably, it shall be given to other than the one that prays. "To them that ask Him." (*G. F. Magorm, D.D.*)   *God's character viewed through man's higher nature :*—Consider the use which is here made of human nature by our Saviour in the interpretation of God. By direct analogy our Master taught us to infer the nature of God. If ye, then, being evil, being selfish, imperfect, give good gifts to your children; if parental love, poor as it is, is not so poor but that it will give to the child what the child wants and asks for, within the limits of his own benefit; if ye, being low down in giving power, do these things; if it is simply impossible for a child to appeal to a father or a mother for necessary things without a response, and without the benefit, how much more shall your heavenly Father, &c. Jesus stands and says, "Your Father is ineffably more a Father than you." Here, then, is our Master taking the great facts of human experience, and laying them as a part of the argument over against the Divine nature, and saying, "This which in you exists in miniature, in the imperfect condition, exists in God in transcendent measure, magnified, augmented, deepened, enriched, more fruitful and more powerful. If we have the products of the temperate zone out of our half-developed affections, God is tropical, eternal summer. (*H. W. Beecher.*) *The Holy Spirit :*—In the Greek of the New Testament the word rendered "Spirit" is the word constantly employed to denote "wind"; and the idea which it suggests is that of an influence in the realm of souls corresponding to the wind in the material world—subtle, untraceable, yet everywhere felt, all-penetrating, all-powerful—with a diversity of operations, too ; now a whispering breeze, then an air-torrent ; now breathing in calm contemplation, then inspiring a might before which the powers of evil are scattered and broken. Do you ask in what this Spirit is? Ask rather in what it is not. I. THERE IS A HOLY SPIRIT IN NATURE. Far be from us the theology which relegates creation to the mythical past. God as truly creates, as He created, the heavens and the earth. II. GOD'S SPIRIT IS ALSO IN HIS PROVIDENCE, and in our whole experience of life. III. THE HOLY SPIRIT OF GOD IS IN ALL THE PURE LIVES, GOOD EXAMPLES, AND BENEFICENT HUMAN INFLUENCES THAT ARE AROUND US. IV. THE HOLY SPIRIT IS IN JESUS CHRIST. The old liturgical formula, "The Holy Ghost proceeding from the Father and the Son," is not the mere dogma of a creed, but the fundamental truth of the Christian life. V. But this is not all. Between human beings presence is COMMUNION. Without word or act, influence, clearly felt and recognized, goes forth from one to the other, especially from the more powerful spirit of the two, if the weaker be confiding and loving, so that a revered and cherished presence is always felt to be a power. Thus must it be of necessity with the Divine presence, and so have all felt it who desire so to feel it. VI. If this Divine influence, this Holy Spirit, be not a mere dogma, but a vital and present reality, IT BELONGS TO US TO SEEK IT, TO PREPARE FOR IT, TO WELCOME IT. (*A. P. Peabody, D.D., LL.D.*) *The gift of the Holy Spirit :*—I. THE GIFT. The Holy Spirit is the essence of all good things; He is the highest good. This is the first promise of the gift to the disciples. II. THE GIVER. The heavenly Father is the Giver, and the one thing which I notice about Him is the great willingness with which our Lord says He gives this blessing. III. THE RECEIVER OF THE SPIRIT. 1. Who may receive into his soul the Holy Spirit? A man may be imperfect and in some respects "evil," and yet receive the Spirit. The disciples were "evil." The Saviour says so here. Yet He encourages them to ask for and expect the Spirit. Put away the thought from your minds that you must wait until you are holy before you can get the Spirit. You never will be holy until you receive the Spirit. 2. How is He to be received ! By simple asking. Let us say, "Lord, teach us how to pray," and, having learned how to pray, we shall only need to ask for the Spirit, and He will be given us. (*A. Scott.*) *The Holy Spirit in relation to missionary work :*—Let us try to realize our dependence upon the Holy Spirit for every spiritual power essential to the accomplishment of our missionary work. Consider our dependence upon the Holy Ghost. I. AS THE SOURCE OF ALL SPIRITUAL ILLUMINATION. II. AS THE IMMEDIATE SOURCE OF ALL HOLINESS. III. AS THE SOURCE OF OUR SPIRITUAL UNITY. IV. AS THE SOURCE OF SPIRITUAL JOY. And now there are three questions which I wish to put. 1. Are we filled with the Holy Ghost? 2. Is a new Pentecost possible to us ? 3. How is the fulness of the Spirit to be obtained? (*Griffith John.*) *Simply to ask :*—I was told lately by a young man who had been in Scotland, that he came one day to a gate, when the gate-keeper's little girl ran down and shut it, saying, "You have not to pay anything to pass; you have only to say, 'Please allow me to go through.'" The young man did as he was directed, and simply repeated, "Please allow me to go through," and the gate was immediately opened. The owner just wished to preserve the right of entrance; that was all. So, simply "ask, and it shall be given you ; seek, and ye shall find ; knock, and it shall be opened unto you." (*C. H. Spurgeon.*) *Answered prayers :*—If in a whole generation tens of thousands of men are praying to God for the things which they need, and if the result of their prayers, in long periods, is to give them larger judgment, better balance, more of those qualities which go to make manhood, then these results are an answer to their prayers. It may not be an answer to individual prayer; it may not be a specific answer to prayer ; but it is larger and better than that—it is an answer to prayer such as God sees to be best adapted to the wants of those who pray. I hold that his prayer is answered who rises into the presence of God in such a way that for the time being he feels that he is in the Divine presence. In other words, I think that the whole tone of a man's moral sense and of his intellectual life will be altered by having stood consciously in the presence of Supreme Wisdom, Purity, Goodness, and Power. One day when I was with Mr. Hicks, the painter, I saw on his table some high-coloured stones, and I asked him what they were for. He said they were to keep his eye up to tone. He explained that when he was working in pigments, insensibly his sense of colour was lowered or weakened, and that by having a pure colour near him he brought it up again, just as the musician, by his test-fork, brings himself up to the right pitch. (*H. W. Beecher.*)   *Our privilege to ask largely :*—There is not the slightest intimation that we can trespass by a too frequent application.   It is a challenge to our faith. " Ask "; and it looks out upon the infinite.   It is for our faith to extend it, and to apply it to what treasures of grace and goodness we please.   Can we not see that large asking and large expectation on our part honour God ?   Suppose some friend of ours, whose wealth is known to be practically unlimited, should declare his readiness and willingness to supply all our wants ; suppose he should put into our hand a book of " cheques," all signed by his own hand, and the amounts left blank for us to fill up in need with such sums as will meet every possible exigency ; and then suppose we go about half-starved, groaning with leanness and faintness, or only half-clothed, shivering in thin rags, and the shame of our nakedness bowing us down to the ground.   How such a demonstration on our part would shame the truth and generosity of our friend !   To ask largely of God (as Elisha asked of Elijah) will prepare us to receive a large blessing.   It will control our working ; it will shape our plans ; it will honour God.   (*A. L. Stone.*)   *Prayer an unfailing refuge :*—When I am out of heart, I follow David's example, and fly for refuge to prayer, and He furnishes me with a store of prayer.   I am bound to acknowledge that I have always found that my prayers have been heard and answered.   In almost every instance I have received what I asked for.   Hence, I feel permitted to offer up my prayers for everything that concerns me.   I am inclined to imagine that there are no *little things* with God.   His hand is as manifest in the feathers of a butterfly's wing, in the eye of an insect, in the folding and packing of a blossom, in the curious aqueducts by which a leaf is nourished, as in the creation of the world, and in the laws by which planets move.   I understand literally the injunction—" In everything make your requests known unto God," and I cannot but notice how amply these prayers have been met.   (*Fowell Buxton.*)

Ver. 13. **How much more shall your heavenly Father give the Holy Spirit.**— *The gift of the Holy Spirit :*—I. WHAT IS MEANT BY THE HOLY SPIRIT. 1. He is a person, and may be grieved. 2. He intercedes for believers. 3. He guides, hears, speaks, and shows things to come. 4. He is a Divine person, and truly God. (1) Sin against Him is unpardonable. (2) Lying to Him is lying to God. (3) Temples of the Holy Ghost are temples of God. 5. The Holy Ghost is enjoyed by all believers. (1) Proved from the apostle's declaration (Rom. viii. 9). (2) Evident from our Lord's promise (John vii. 37–39). (3) And from the method of communicating salvation (Tit. iii. 5, 6). II. FOR WHAT PURPOSE THE HOLY GHOST IS GIVEN. 1. As a Spirit of penitence and prayer. 2. As a Spirit of power. 3. As a Spirit of consolation. 4. As a Spirit of purity. 5. As a Spirit of wisdom. 6. As a Spirit of fruitfulness. III. THE MANNER OF ASKING FOR THE HOLY SPIRIT. " Your heavenly Father shall give His Holy Spirit to them that ask Him." 1. They must ask in sincerity. 2. They must ask evangelically. 3. Ask importunately. 4. Ask in faith. IV. THE WORDS OF OUR TEXT ARE ENCOURAGING TO HOPE. " If ye then, being evil, know how to give good gifts unto your children, how much more shall your heavenly Father give the Holy Spirit to them that ask Him." 1. Here we notice that mankind are evil. Yet, " they know how to give good gifts unto their children." 2. God is His people's Father. (1) He is their heavenly Father. (2) Covenant Father. (3) Good. (4) Wise. (5) Gracious. (*T. B. Baker.*)   *The efficacy of prayer for obtaining the Holy Spirit :*—The force of which argument depends upon a double comparison, of the quality of the persons giving, and of the nature of the gift. I. I shall show what is comprehended in this gift of the Holy Spirit, and how great a blessing and benefit it is. St. Matthew expresseth this somewhat differently : " How much more shall your Father which is in heaven give good things to them that ask Him ?" (Matt. vii. 11). Which, compared with the expression here in St. Luke, doth intimate to us, that the Spirit of God is the chief of blessings, or rather the sum of all good things. II. We shall in the next place consider what kind of asking, in order to the obtaining of this great blessing, is here required by our Saviour, when He says, " God will give His Holy Spirit to them that ask Him."   It must have these three qualifications : 1. It must be hearty and sincere, in opposition to formal and hypocritical asking. 2. It must be earnest and fervent, and importunate, in opposition to cold, and

faint, and careless asking. 3. It must be in faith, and a confident assurance
that God will hear us, in opposition to doubting and distrust. III. To confirm and illustrate the truth of this proposition, that God is very ready to give
the Holy Spirit to them that ask Him. 1. From God's free promise and declaration. And besides that here in the text, I might produce several others, but I shall
mention only one, which is very plain and express, and conceived in terms as large
and universal as can well be devised (James i. 5). 2. From the comparison here
used. It is a plain and undeniable argument, fitted to all capacities, because it
proceeds upon two suppositions which every man must acknowledge to be true. 1.
That earthly parents have generally such a natural affection for their children, as
does strongly incline them to give them such good things as are necessary and convenient for them, and which will not suffer them, instead of good things, to give
them such things as either are no wise useful, or any wise hurtful to them. This is
a matter of common, and certain, and sensible experience, which no man can deny.
2. The other supposition, which is as evident in reason as the former is in experience, is this : that God is better than men, and that there is infinitely more
goodness in Him than in the best man in the world ; because goodness in its most
exalted degree and highest perfection is essential to that notion which all men have
of God ; and this being a common principle, in which men are universally agreed,
no man can gainsay it. But, for the farther illustration of this argument, we will
consider a little more particularly the terms of the comparison which our Saviour
here useth ; our earthly and our heavenly Father ; temporal and spiritual good
things. 1. Our earthly and our heavenly Father ; in which terms the givers are
compared together. Now there are three considerations in a giver, which makes
him capable of being bountiful, and dispose him to it. (1) That he have wherewithal to be liberal, and can part with it without damage and prejudice to himself.
(2) That he be good-natured, and have a mind to give. (3) That he be related to
those to whom he gives, and be concerned in their welfare. Now all these considerations are more eminently in God, and with far greater advantage, than in any
father upon earth. 2. Let us compare likewise temporal and spiritual good things ;
in which terms you have the gifts compared together. So that the whole force of
the argument comes to this : that if we believe that earthly parents have any good
inclinations towards their children, and are willing to bestow upon them the necessaries of life, we have much more reason to believe that God our heavenly Father
is much more ready " to give His Holy Spirit to them that ask Him " ; whether we
consider the quality of the giver, or the nature of the gift. Application : 1. This
is a matter of great encouragement to us under the sense of our own weakness and
impotency. 2. Let us earnestly beg of God His Holy Spirit, seeing it is so necessary to us, and God is so ready to bestow this best of gifts upon us. 3. Let us take
heed of "grieving the Spirit of God," and provoking Him to withdraw Himself from
us. 4. God's readiness to afford the grace and assistance of His Holy Spirit to us,
to enable us to the performance of our duty, and the obedience of His laws, makes
all wilful sin and disobedience inexcusable. (*Archbishop Tillotson.*)   *Right replies to right requests :*—In this chapter there is an evident progress. It opens by
the disciples asking the Lord to teach them to pray. To that He gave a full and
sufficient reply ; He prepared them an outline of what complete prayer should be.
Then the chapter proceeds a little further to answer a question : we are shown how
to pray, but will God really answer us ? Is prayer only meant to do good to the
suppliant ? Does it end with the benefit which it works in us, or does it really
affect the heart of God ? The answer is given by our Lord with great clearness.
We have a parable to show that as importunity does evidently affect men, so importunity will also gain an answer from God, that He will be pleased to give us
what we need if we do but know how, with incessant earnestness, to come again and
again to Him in prayer. We are assured that asking is attended with receiving,
that seeking is attended with finding, that knocking will lead to opening, that it
is not a vain thing to pray. The truth here taught is not that God will refuse us
evil things if in our mistake we ask for them ; that is a truth, but it is not alluded
to here; the one statement of this verse is, that prayers for good things will be
answered, and that they will not be answered with gifts wearing the mere appearance of good, but with the actual good things desired. That simple thought I shall
endeavour to enlarge upon in this morning's discourse. I. RIGHT PRAYERS, RIGHT
ANSWERS. The child asks bread, his father does not give him a stone. We shall
have when we pray for needful things, the really needful things themselves, not the
imitation of them, but the actual blessings. And if our faith grows a little stronger,

and having obtained bread we ask for fish, not absolutely a necessary, but a comfort and a relish ; if we make bold to ask for spiritual comforts, consoling gifts and ennobling graces, something over and above what is absolutely needful to save us, our heavenly Father will not mock us by giving us superficial comforts which might be injurious as a serpent ; He will give us so much of comfort as we can bear ; and it shall be pure, holy, healthy comfort. And if, gathering more confidence still, we ask for an egg, which I take it was in Christ's day a rarer luxury, we shall not be deluded by its counterfeit. That is our first point—prayer for good things meets a good answer. II. Then the question will arise in every heart : "It seems then that I have only to ascertain that my prayer is for a really good thing, and I shall have it?" Just so, and hence, secondly, THE PRAYER FOR THE BEST THING IS SUREST OF AN ANSWER, for, saith the text, "How much more shall your heavenly Father give the Holy Spirit to them that ask Him?" 1. There is no doubt about the Holy Spirit being a good thing; when we therefore ask for Him, for His Divine presence and influence, we may rest assured that God will give it. Make that our first point under this head—God will give the Holy Spirit to them that ask for Him. 2. From the connection in which the text stands, I gather the following remark, namely, that it will truly be the Holy Spirit. Go back again to that first thought. The child asks bread, and does not get a stone ; you ask the Holy Spirit, and you shall receive the Holy Spirit. 3. But it appears plainly enough from the text that this Holy Spirit is to be given in answer to prayer. He will give you the real Spirit : no enthusiasm that might mislead you, no fanaticism that might injure you, no self-conceit that might become like a deadly scorpion to you, but His own gentle, truthful, infallible, Holy Spirit He will give to them that ask Him. III. Now for our last point. THE BEST OF PRAYERS, WHICH IS SURE TO BE HEARD, IS ALSO A MOST COMPREHENSIVE ONE. Turn to the parallel passage in the gospel of Matthew (chap. vii. 11). Now what does our text say, "How much more shall your heavenly Father give the Holy Spirit to them that ask Him?" Is it not clear then that the Holy Spirit is the equivalent for "good things," and that, in fact, when the Lord gives us the Holy Spirit He gives us all "good things"? What a comprehensive prayer then is the prayer for the Spirit of God. (*C. H. Spurgeon.*) *The good gift :*—I. THE FACT HERE TAKEN FOR GRANTED—that earthly parents, though evil, know how to give good gifts unto their children. It is not said that parents know how to choose always what is best for their children. Neither would our Lord assert that parental affection is never overpowered by other principles. Long misbehaviour has sometimes induced a father to disinherit his son. Such, and so strong, is natural affection : a principle, necessary indeed for the preservation of the species ; and so deeply implanted by our all-wise Creator, that it still survives the wreck of everything else that once was good in man. II. THE DOCTRINE, FOR THE ILLUSTRATION OF WHICH THIS FACT IS ALLUDED TO. The doctrine is, that your heavenly Father is much more likely to give the Holy Spirit to them that ask Him. Now, by following up the comparison which our Lord makes in the text, we shall see abundant reason for concluding, that God is not only as affectionate, but infinitely more so, than any human benefactor. For I may ask, in the first place, with Moses—1. "Is not He thy Father, that hath bought thee? hath He not made thee and established thee?" Has not Creation made you His children? and did He make you to destroy you? "But you think of your sins !" You do well ; but think also of the unfathomable mines of love, which those sins have brought to light. 2. What can this heavenly Father bestow on His children more worthy the name of a "good gift" than His Holy Spirit? He has given His Son ; yet even that gift avails us not, till the Spirit be added. 3. Is the spiritual bounty of our heavenly Father limited, like the affection of earthly parents, to those who can prove that they are His children? No—it is far more wide and expansive. It is offered to all that are His children by Creation ; without stopping to consider whether they are such by regeneration or no. For here again our Lord makes a change in His language. It is not—"How much more shall your heavenly Father give the Holy Spirit to His children"; but—"to them that ask Him." (*J. Jowett, M.A.*) *The best gift :*—I. The Holy Spirit is spoken of, in the text, as the best gift which God in His rich bounty can bestow on man. And, if we consider who the Holy Spirit is, and what He does for those who truly believe in Christ, we need not wonder that our Lord should thus speak of this unspeakable gift. He is our Guide, our Comforter, our Sanctifier. II. It is a plain and easy way which God has appointed for us, to obtain this precious gift : He will "give His Holy Spirit to them that ask Him." We are told "in everything by prayer" to "let" our "requests be made known unto God."

(E. Blencowe, M.A.)　　　*The gift of the Holy Spirit :*—I. OUR PRIVILEGE as the followers of Christ. 1. What is meant by the Holy Spirit. 2. The Holy Ghost is enjoyed by all real Christians. 3. For what purposes He is received by them. (1) As a Spirit of penitence and prayer. (2) As a Spirit of power. (3) As a Spirit of comfort. (4) As a Spirit of purity. (5) As a Spirit of wisdom. (6) As a Spirit of fruitfulness. II. OUR DUTY. To ask as God requires. 1. Sincerely. 2. Evangelically. 3. Importunately. 4. Believingly. III. These words also ENCOURAGE OUR HOPE. Application : 1. Recollect your privilege with suitable acts of piety. Such as—self-examination. Do you enjoy this gift as a Spirit of penitence, &c. (2 Cor. xii. 5). Humiliation : on account of your enjoying no more of it (James iv. 2, 8–10). Holy care : to cherish and improve what Divine influence you enjoy. By obeying Christ (Rev. iii. 2) ; and imitating St. Paul (Phil. iii. 13, 14). 2. Recollect your duty with perseverance in it (Col. iv. 2). 3. Recollect your encouragement with steadfast hope—of receiving the Holy Spirit in all His influences ; as a Spirit of prayer, penitence, power, &c. (*Theological Sketch - book.*) *The availability of the Holy Spirit :*—For every moral virtue, for the first germ of spiritual life, for growth, development, usefulness and increase we are dependent on the Holy Spirit. The great want of the times. I. IS THE HOLY SPIRIT AVAILABLE ? Can His presence be secured ? Surely. 1. If we consider the character of God, His universal beneficence, His desire to make His sentient and intelligent creatures happy, we need have no doubt. 2. This argument gains force in the light of God's great love in giving His Son for the reclamation of His lost race. If willing to make the greater sacrifice, will He not be willing to make the less ? 3. Our argument as to the availability of the Holy Spirit becomes absolutely conclusive when we consider that He is the promised and special gift both of the Father and of the Son. II. HOW SHALL WE CONSCIOUSLY REALIZE THE PRESENCE OF THE HOLY SPIRIT ? 1. Common interest and sympathy, and united prayer. 2. Avoidance of all known sins. 3. A sense of need, of dependence, of meekness, of unworthiness, of penitence, and an earnest heart-cry for help. (*S. D. Burchard, D.D.*) *The gift of the Spirit :*—Four central principles underlie this passage—in fact, underlie the Bible and all religion in the world. 1. Man has a capacity for God as truly as the stomach for food. God is as imperative a necessity to our spiritual nature as is bread for the body. 2. Man has a distinct need of God impressed upon him. The body is disquiet, if food be withheld. The soul is restless without God. 3. The Fatherhood of God is a pledge and guarantee that these deepest yearnings of man's nature will be gratified. A judicious parent prefers for his son character rather than fame, genius, or wealth. God also desires, above all things, our sanctification. 4. God gives the Holy Spirit to the eager, ardent, persistent, importunate soul. Do you really want it ? Honestly and earnestly asking, you shall receive. You must long for the Holy Spirit more than the hungry and thirsty long for food and water ; more anxiously than the storm-tossed sailor longs for the port. With this spirit you may be sure of an answer, and as much more sure as God is better than the best human parent. (*H. L. Thompson.*)　　*How God feels towards mankind :*—Here is what the Redeemer says to you, and me, and all : If you want to know how God feels towards you, and how ready God is to give you everything that is really good : here is something to go by. You know how much you would do for your children : you know how anxious you are to care for them in every way. You know how a father will work, and how a mother will watch, all for the good of their little ones. You know how much of the work that is done by men in this world, and how much of the care that is felt, is not for themselves at all, but for their children : all for them. After the dream of fame is past—after ambition is outgrown—the man toils on as steadfastly and earnestly as in his most hopeful and most aspiring days, that he may provide for his little ones ; that he may see them in comfort and happiness ; that he may push them on (as he trusts and prays) to be far better and happier than ever he was himself. The human heart is always the same : you do that now, my friends ; and so you may be sure that people did that long ago, in the days when Christ was here. Well, says Christ you know all that. You know all that, says His blessed voice : and now hear Me and believe Me when I tell you, that the great Father above is just like that ; only a thousand-fold better. If even you, sinful and evil, would wear your fingers to the bone, would lose your rest, would cut off every selfish indulgence, that you might see your children's wants supplied, that you might see the little things happy and good—then take this blessed truth to your heart, that in all you feel toward your children, you have a faint and far reflection of how the great God above feels

toward you. He feels for us just like that: cares for us, loves us, wishes us well, works for us. (*A. K. H. Boyd, D.D.*) *Prayer for the Spirit answered :*—1. Our privilege here exhibited. 2. Our duty prescribed. 3. Our hope encouraged. (*Anon.*) *God's care for His children far greater than man's :*—Let us now consider the truth that God differs from an earthly father by being far kinder, wiser, and better. O brethren, there is an immense deal suggested by that "how much more!" It would be an unspeakable comfort to us—it would be a glorious and comfortable truth—that God was just as willing to give us all we need as you kind-hearted people are to give what is needful to your little child. I think I know men and women who have hearts so good and kind; who are so ready to do what they can to make their own children happy, or to add to the happiness of any little child; that I should feel safe enough and sure enough in going, sinful, weary, to Almighty God, to ask for His mercy and His Blessed Spirit, even if I knew no more than this, that I should find such a welcome at His throne of grace as these good men and women would give to any suffering, helpless child, even if it were not their own. But "how much more!" What a silent reference to an inconceivable depth cf love and pity in the heart of God! It is as if Christ had said to those whom He addressed, You cannot understand the difference—words cannot explain the difference—here is the kind of thing, in yourselves; but in God "how much more!" Yet not a different kind of thing—the same kind of feeling you bear towards your children—only heightened up to a pitch you can never know. 1. God knows what is good for us, as no human parent can know what is good for his child. With the kindest intentions, we all know how injudicious parents often are; how often they err on the side of over-severity or of over-tenderness; how completely they sometimes mistake what is to conduce to the true good or happiness of their children; indeed it is not too much to say that a very great proportion of all the sorrow that is in this world arises from the mismanagement of parents in youth, or from the consequences of that mismanagement in after years. Now God knows us; knows what we are, and what we can do; knows what we are fit for, and how things affect us; knows all our peculiarities of temperament and disposition. He knows what we really need; He knows when to give us what we wish, and when to deny it; He knows how to make "all things work together for good" to such as love Him. 2. Another point in which appears the superiority of the great Father to whom Christ points us above all earthly parents, is His power. He is able to do all He wishes. He has all power to give us all good things; to help and save. You know how different it is with us; how well we often know what we should like to do for our children, to make them wise and good and happy; yet how very little we can do. 3. Then God is always kind. There are unnatural parents—let us hope, very few. There are people who repel their children's confidence; who from mistaken principle or from a bad heart do all they can to make their children miserable; who point out with pride in the misery of a child, that things have come just as they said they would; who so act as to make us wonder that a trace of natural affection shuold be left in their children's heart. I shall not dwell on a subject so miserable, save to remind you that our heavenly Father has anticipated such a case—"Can a woman forget her sucking child, that she should not have compassion on the son of her womb? Yea, they may forget, yet will I not forget thee!" 4. And now the last matter I shall name, as to which our heavenly Father excels the best earthly one, is that He is always near. Always within hearing; always within reach; never leaving, never forsaking; Father of the fatherless, Friend of the friendless; yea, "When father and mother forsake me, then the Lord will take me up!" O Father of mercies, remember this word unto Thy servants, upon which Thou hast caused us to hope! (*A. K. H. Boyd, D.D.*) *The gift of the Spirit :*—Cotton Mather, whose endeavours as a parent were highly blessed, says: "Let my prayers for my children be daily, with constancy. Yea, by name let me mention each one of them every day before the Lord. I would importunately beg for all suitable blessings to be bestowed on them; that God would give them grace and give them glory, and withhold no good thing from them; that God would smile on their education and give His good angels charge over them and keep them from evil, that it may not grieve them; that when their father and mother forsake them, the Lord may take them up. With importunity I would plead that promise on their behalf: 'The heavenly Father will give the Holy Spirit to them that ask Him,' Oh, happy children, if by asking I may obtain the Holy Spirit for them!"

Ver. 14. Dumb.—*The dumb spirit :*—There is a sense, and a very true sense, in which every natural man, every man who lets himself alone and lives practically without God, apart from Christ, in the world, has in him a dumb spirit, and can only lose that spirit under the healing touch of Christ. 1. I might speak—but it would not affect or be true of all who hear me—of that calamity, that curse, which we designate as a bad temper. Has any one here present a bad temper? Have you not been reminded sometimes, in that experience, of the dumb spirit spoken of in the text? That sullen silence; that overcast brow; that gloomy, morose, most irritating reserve; that gathering, threatening, overhanging cloud of dull, dark, speechless displeasure, by which a long evening has been rendered miserable, and upon which night and sleep have come without mitigation and without relief; that obstinate nursing and cherishing of an untold grudge, which wakens again in the morning to its last night's sullenness, and seems almost to pride itself upon its tenacity and its perseverence; was not this indeed an example of possession by a dumb spirit? 2. Mark that man—his name indeed is Legion—who lives what is called an entirely preoccupied and self-engrossed life; who has his business and follows it, has his interests and pursues them, has even his pleasures and enjoys them, but in all these has in reality no partner and no associate; looks to himself as to all that most intimately touches him, and himself only; excludes from his true confidence alike friend and brother, alike child and wife; gives out in social converse the merest superficialities of his thoughts, and in domestic intercourse the veriest dregs and refuse of his being; locks up in his own bosom the affections which God gave him for blessing, pre-supposes selfishness in others because he feels it in himself, and will trust no other soul with that confidence which he knows could have no reception and no reciprocity in his own. 3. It is made in Scripture both the duty and also the test of a Christian, that his speech be not only innocent, but beneficial; not only kind and frank, but consistent also and edifying. Now, if this be so, by what name can we designate that use of speech which altogether overlooks or refuses this high object? Let us all look back, my brethren, this morning upon our past employment of the gift of language. What shall we say of it? Is not the review most disheartening? To whom can we point as having been benefited by our possession of this marvellous thing? Nay—for effects are God's, not ours—when did we ever set ourselves seriously to do good by our conversation. Is it not true, alas! that as to any value, any worth, contained in the gift of speech, we might as well have been bereft of it. In the judgment of Him who heareth as well as seeth in secret, the spirit which has possessed us has been no better than a dumb spirit. 4. It has been so towards man. We have done no good with our speech. And how has it been towards God? The text stands in immediate connection with a passage of Holy Scripture about prayer. Strong encouragement has been given to our halting, failing faith, in reference to the duty of seeking God in prayer. A form of prayer has been given, in answer to the request of the disciples, Lord, teach us to pray; and words have been added, which show beyond all question that it is not in God but in ourselves that the work of prayer is straitened. Then follows immediately the brief narrative of the text: " Jesus was casting out a devil, and it was dumb." If the possession of the evil one makes us dumb (as to all that is valuable) towards man, so also does it towards God. (*Dean Vaughan.*)

Dumb :—Look at the Greek word here translated "dumb"; for, if it be considered that the mind of God is in any way breathed forth to us through the words of Scripture, those words will bear a careful investigation into their meaning. That Greek word means, in its first use, blunt, obtuse; and so a blunted or lamed man in tongue. Mark here, then, the first lesson enshrined in the little word. The power of speech was in that tongue, but that power was not presently available. The machinery of articulation was perfect, had once been used, but an intruding hand had grasped the driving-wheel, and the machinery was still. The power was there, I say, yet it was held in suspense; it needed some third stronger power to drive out the intruder and set moving the smoothly-going wheel again. Yet mark, what direction would the power take when the unloosed tongue told forth the thoughts within? Would the tongue burst forth into the direct ravings of impotent blasphemy, or speak praise from out of a convinced heart? It depended upon this, whether the intruding spirit within initiated the movement, or whether God again evoked the dormant power. Which should it be? (*Canon Wilberforce.*)

The downward course :—I can never forget a picture I once saw of Satan tempting Judas to betray his Master, a picture in which the painter had pourtrayed the face of the tempter as a hideous caricature of the tempted; as if the man, if only he could suddenly turn round and look over his shoulder, would be able to see in the face and the form of Satan what he himself would one day become if he gave way to temptation, and threw in his lot with devils. The painter had caught the lesson, I believe, that this miracle teaches. Are we alive to it? It is well sometimes to view one's self from the outside as well as from the inside—to climb a hill, as it were, and thence look down at yourself; just as we look at some great cathedral from a neighbouring hill, and from that elevation see a wholly different aspect from that which we gain by merely looking at it from the inside. Look, then, my brethren, very briefly at some of the causes which induce this terrible change, and at the remedies which God provides. The change is threefold : a blunted tongue, a defective hearing, a dulled mind—all these are implied in that one Greek word. A tongue that cannot speak to God, an ear that cannot hear His word, a mind too dull to receive Him—how do these come to you? How is it that the dumb spirit broods so heavily over many now? Brethren, it is because there is a great deception still kept up by the father of lies, because he finds an ally in our breasts " in that infection of nature which doth remain ; yea, in them that are regenerate." There is much outside business in religion in the present day ; there is much need for those who are thus busy to ask themselves, " Is my heart silencing or silent towards God?" There is nowadays much outside conformity to the Cross of Christ; there is surely much need for the conformers to ascertain whether their hearts and their lives are telling the story that their lips so often repeat. I speak to those who are struggling, however feebly; who are praying, however dumbly; who are turning to God, however uncertainly. Mark then, first, the silencing process employed by Satan, whereby he quenches the answering power of the spirit to the drawings of God. First, it is a gradual process—a slight impeding of the freedom of action—a little poison of sin which gently impedes the circulation of the spiritual life. So surely as the unused muscle or the long-bandaged limb loses strength, so does the impeded soul lose its power of communing with God. A neglected faculty becomes a withering faculty. A religion that becomes mechanical stops of itself. The power of faith towards God unused, unexercised, dwindles, decays, perishes, till at last one sometimes hears on a death-bed that awful self-pronounced sentence :—" I cannot pray—I have forgotten how : I cannot believe— it is so long since I thought of God." Again, all indulgence of tastes that lead us from God weakens the spiritual apprehension and warps the understanding, or there comes the loss of the power of all sound judgment which we see so remark-ably in sinners. The old words of Solomon are fulfilled. " They err who devise evil." They look upon all questions of morality from their own standpoint, which is an ever-lowering point. They now see no harm in that which would have once shocked them—no sin in that which once would have appalled them. They are satisfied ; and satisfaction with a low moral standard is one of the surest signs of a dumb spirit. They have no gratitude to God, and inability to thank our God is an unfailing symptom of a silenced tongue. And if so, brethren, in conclusion, what is the cure? The old heathen philosophy honestly confessed that it could find no cure. " Plato," said Socrates (we read), " perhaps the gods can forgive deliberate sin, but I do not see how." In the life and death of Christ the Saviour the mystery is solved, and the cure is made plain. The difficulty in this case is that the deaf cannot hear the words of Christ, the dumb cannot pray to Him, the blunted spirit cannot lift itself up towards Him. And yet, O my brethren, there is one sense that can be used even in the most extreme cases. Look once more at Christ as He is about to work the miracle of which I have spoken this evening. Mark how He has caught the mute appealing look in the eye of the voiceless man, as he turns instinctively to Christ for protection from the fearsome dweller within, from the tenant over whom he has long lost the power of control or the possibility of ejection. We, my brethren, can look up to Christ even when our spirits are most dull, even when our prayers are most heavy, even when the whole soul seems weighed down, oppressed, silenced by the sin in our nature. We can look up to Him when He began to struggle for the mastery with the bad habit of a lifetime, with the coldness of years, with the carelessness of a long duration. We can bring ourselves before Him (Oh, be His name ever blessed for it !), relying on His preg-nant words of faithful promise. " Him that cometh to Me I will in no wise cast out." If there be the will to be set free Christ will know it. He knows all the suffering, for the pangs that affect the member reach ever to the Head. By virtue of the mysterious sympathy which binds us to the incarnate God He knows it ; but, my brethren, as you are wrestling with your sin Christ your God knows it. He only wants you to place yourself completely under His charge; He only asks you to obey His every direction, and He will complete the cure in His own good time. He can do it, He can make this dumb spirit eloquent with praise; He can make this deaf ear thrill with the sweetest sound; He can make this obtuse spirit quick and attentive to the Word of God; He can set us once more free, so that we may understand by how much things Divine transcend things earthly; He can set us free, so that with St. Augustine we may understand that it is because God has created the human soul for Himself that that soul cannot rest until it finds its boundless rest in the bosom of God; set us free, so that with St. Bernard we may understand that men remain unconverted simply because they remain ignorant of the character of God, picturing Him to themselves as being like themselves. He can bid the untied tongue now confess the sin, and as the full confession wells up from out of the depths of a penitent heart, he does obliterate the guilt. (*Ibid.*) *A dumb devil cast out :*—A friend in London, who speaks now with a voice as clear as a bell, and preaches a full salvation, spoke to me in great trouble some years after his conversion. "You know I am such a fool; I am afraid to speak. The other day you called on some one to pray, and I shivered down to my shoes, I was so afraid you would ask me. I could not have prayed if you had paid me for it." This dumb devil was in full possession of him. He understood everything; you could not teach him much. I said, "You have a dumb devil. Do you believe the Lord Jesus can cast him out?" "Yes, I believe He can." "Yes, the devil himself believes that, but do you believe He *will?*" "I am afraid." "I am very glad of it; now let us kneel down and see whether the Lord will cast out the dumb devil." We were in a railway carriage together alone. We knelt down in the carriage and prayed. He could scarcely hear my voice for the noise; I think that was an encouragement to him. I went on praying to the Lord to loose the string of his tongue that he might speak plainly for the glory of God. He said, "Amen." "Thank God," I said, "the dumb devil is going." I began to pray again. He said, "Lord, answer prayer." "Amen," I said. "Hallelujah! the devil is going," and sure enough he began to pray for himself. I began to praise, and he was praising too. The train stopped, but we did not know anything about it; we went on praying and praising. The collector came to the door and said "Tickets," but we never stopped: we continued to praise God. Oh, we were happy! The guard shut the door and went away; he thought we were two madmen, I suppose! Oh, I wish there were more of such mad people. This man had got his liberty, and, glory be to God, he has used it since then. (*W. Haslam.*)　　*How devils may be expelled :*—In Charles Kingsley's Life there is a story of a madman who declared that the devil had got hold of him, and would not let him sleep. "The surgeon," says Kingsley, "came to me and said, 'As I cannot cure the man's mind by making his liver act, you must make his liver act by curing his mind.' So I went to the patient and agreed with him fully that the devil was in him. 'And I will tell you,' I said, 'why he is. It is because you have been a scoundrel. But if you will lead a new and honest life you may snap your finger at the devil.'" The "devil" left him presently, and the man was cured. So resolution may expel the devil of worry, even after the nerves are more or less broken. (*T. M. Coan, M.D.*)　　*Third Sunday in Lent :*—And as this miracle indicated the true nature of Christ's mission and appointments, it was at the same time a complete demonstration of His capacity and fitness for the work. And yet, it very differently affected different classes of witnesses. 1. There were some whom it greatly amazed. "It came to pass, when the devil was gone out, the dumb spake, and the people wondered." These were the commoner class of persons who saw what was accomplished. Common people with common sense are the world's best jury in nearly every case submitted to human arbitrament. God's truth is never fruitless. 2. A second class of persons who witnessed this miracle consisted of certain rebellious spirits, who were ready to grasp at any absurdity, and to commit themselves to any sort of inconsistency and self-contradiction, rather than admit that Jesus was the Christ. 3. There was a third class, however, who assumed an attitude of feigned modesty in the case, who were scarcely less reprehensible. They would not say whether the miracle was of God or of the devil, but assumed to be earnest inquirers, quite ready to believe if only the Saviour would show them some "sign from heaven." And very good and commendable did they evidently consider themselves in the attitude which they thus assumed. To them it was quite extreme and harsh to ascribe Christ's miracles to the devil. They would not be guilty of such daring opposition, or commit themselves to such ultraism. No, no; they would be moderate and reasonable in their course. True, they could not yet regard the question as sufficiently cleared up for decided action. Things were a little too inchoate and indistinct as yet. They wished to have them freer from embarrassment and objection before they moved. A great deal of bitter feeling and controversy existed, and they did not wish to be prematurely mixed up with it. They would therefore hold their decision in suspense, and wait for further developments, meanwhile siding a little with both parties, consenting with the worst, yet keeping up a fair show in favour of Christ and the truth. But the Lord knew their thoughts, tore off the painted mask, and gave them to understand exactly where their pretended neutrality placed them. "He that is not with Me is against Me: and he that gathereth not with Me scattereth abroad." The justice of this sentence is manifest. The evidence before these people was ample. 4. But there was yet another class represented among the witnesses of this miracle. "As He spake these things, a certain woman of the company lifted up her voice, and said unto Him, Blessed is the womb that bare Thee, and the paps which Thou hast sucked." She spake as a mother, and she spake well and truly. Her feeling toward Christ was of a very different sort from that which so basely aspersed Him, or so hypocritically put Him aside under cover of pious friendship. She had seen the miracle, and was moved with reverence and admiration by it. Quite too fleshly and sentimental were this woman's thoughts and emotions. Though well enough as far as they went, they did not penetrate to the true blessedness in Jesus, or to the right conditions on which its enjoyment rests. She did not rise to that evangelism which makes His truth in our hearts a far sublimer thing than to have our blood in His veins. And it is just here that the religion of many falls short. They have great admiration for Christ, the excellence of His spirit, the beauty of His teachings, and the beneficence of His works. And it is well as far as it goes ; but it is not religion. It is a mere earthly sentimentalism which fails of any saving effect. From this subject, then, let us learn the true glory and office of Jesus. He comes to us as verily the messenger and Christ of God. He comes to us with the great power of the heavens. In Him the potencies of the eternal kingdom are brought near to us. And it is all for our liberation from the thraldom and disabilities which Satan has inflicted upon us. He comes to us to open our blind eyes; to unstop our deaf ears; to loose our tied tongues; and to set us free. He comes to cast out of us the unclean and disabling spirit. From this subject let us also be admonished of the dangers that beset us of making our high privileges of none effect. The sublimest demonstrations of Christ's power and grace were the occasion of the deeper damnation to the Scribes and Pharisees; and we have in us the same sort of depraved hearts which they had. And, above all, let us learn from this subject what our great duty under the gospel is. It is not given by mere inference, but in plain and positive words, by the Saviour Himself. It is, to "hear the Word of God, and keep it." (*J. A. Seiss, D.D.*)

Ver. 16. **A sign from heaven.**—*Wishing a sign from heaven :*—I. "The Pharisees and Sadducees came, and tempting desired Him that He would show them a sign from heaven." They did not take what we would account a miracle on the human body as a sufficient sign, but in the presence of many great and marvellous works they still said to Jesus, "Show us a sign from heaven." Here we find the spirit which cannot see in Christ, or in Christ's religion, its own value, and which is always going outside of it for some token or evidence of its worth. There are people to whom all religion is a thing outside of them ; and they receive it, not because it meets any want in their hearts, or because they need it, but because it comes with an outside authority and show. What was there so far wrong in seeking a sign from heaven, that the people should be found fault with for demanding it ? Now there are many things which people might be justified in not believing until they had seen some sign from heaven. But the great truths which Christ taught were truths which came home to the hearts and consciences of men. These need no sign from heaven or earth ; they are their own witnesses to every man who hears them. When Christ taught the people, as He had just been doing, that the things which truly defiled a man were not the things he touched and ate, but the things which were in his heart, his thoughts and wishes, and the things he spoke and did, that teaching needed no sign, could have no sign, from heaven greater than itself. If you were to convince a man that he had done something wrong, and if you were to ask him to repent of the wrong, what would you say suppose he were to reply, "Show me a sign from heaven that I ought to repent "? Suppose, again, a man were taken out of darkness and allowed to gaze round on hill and sky and sea, how would you receive his demand, "Show me a sign from heaven that these things are what they are"? The light in which he is living is the standing sign from heaven, the only one, and the best. And in the same way, the only and the best sign from heaven in the things of the spirit, is the truth acting on the conscience and the heart. If a man can see nothing there, who can enlighten him? If a man is always asking you for an outward sign to prove that a moral or religious fact is true, if he has no touchstone in his own inner life to which he can bring it, how is he possibly to find such a touchstone outside of him? This was the condition of those persons who came to Christ demanding of Him a sign from heaven. And His reply to them proceeds upon the fact that they had signs all around them for their guidance in religion, as truly as they had signs for their guidance in the common affairs of life. Jesus Christ turns what is too often considered a secular object of inquiry into one of the most religious kind. It is too often taken for granted that the study of the signs of the times is not so much a religious as a political work. Christ's teaching was in itself a sign from heaven. It was a sign which no man who looked on human society could afford to despise. It came home to men's hearts; it brought new life, new comfort, new sources of hope and strength to mankind. II. On the part of disciples and friends, as well as enemies, there is often a misunderstanding of Christ's words. And this fact is illustrated here in a striking way. Jesus said to the disciples, "Take heed and beware of the leaven of the Pharisees and Sadducees." What words could be simpler or more intelligible? They did not at the moment connect His warning with any previous incident. "It is," said they, "because we have taken no bread." Their minds were on a very different level; they were engrossed with things of a very different kind from any which were troubling Christ, and naturally they regarded His words from their own point of view, and interpreted His teaching through their own state of mind and feeling. "Beware of the leaven of the Pharisees, and of the leaven of the Sadducees." Both Pharisee and Sadducee had lost the earnestness and sincerity which are essential to a true life; and our Lord warns His disciples against their hypocrisy, their insincerity, their shallow and outside religion, their inward contempt of all that was really good and worthy in religion and in human life. What is chiefly wanted to render religious teaching intelligible and valuable, is this spirit of sympathy between those who speak and those who hear. For want of this, much that would otherwise be plain is misunderstood altogether. Indeed you find often that it is not words, but thoughts and things, which are strange to men who do not enter into the spirit of them. There are numerous hindrances, perhaps, in our own life and in its general spirit to the reception of Christian teaching and the power of it. The impression which I wish to convey by all I have said is principally this—1. That we are to look for the great evidence of all religion in the religion itself. Believe that the light is its own best evidence, and that truth by its power on the human soul is enough. 2. And that sympathy with the Divine Teacher is required, in order to understand His teaching; and that this sympathy is best produced and kept strong by making the whole tone and spirit of His life the familiar tone and spirit of our own lives, and by taking to heart more than ever the great facts which are so prominent in the life and spirit of Jesus Christ. (*A. Watson.*)   *The gospel sign addressed to faith :*—Now what makes this a subject of interest to us is, that our Lord does expressly promise all Christians a certain gracious manifestation of Himself, which it is natural, at first sight, to suppose a sensible one : and many persons understand it to be such, as if it were not more blessed to believe than to see. Now, that this great gift, whatever it be, is of a nature to impart illumination, sanctity, and peace, to the soul to which it comes, far from disputing, I would earnestly maintain. And, in this indirect way, doubtless, it is in a certain sense apprehended and perceived; perceived in its effects, with a consciousness that those effects cannot come of themselves, but imply a gift from which they come, and a presence of which they are, as it were, the shadow, a voice of which they are the echo. But there are persons who desire the inward manifestation of Christ to be much more sensible than this. They will not be contented without some sensible sign and direct evidence that God loves them; some assurance, in which faith has no part, that God has chosen them; and which may answer to their anticipations of what Scripture calls "the secret of the Lord," and "that hidden manna" which Christ invites us to partake. Some men, for instance, hold that their conscience would have no peace, unless they recollected the time when they were converted from darkness to light, from a state of wrath to the kingdom of God. Others go further, and think that without a distinct inward assurance of his salvation, a man is not in a saving state. This is what men often conceive; not considering that whatever be the manifestation promised to Christians by our Lord, it is not likely to be more sensible and more intelligible than the great sign of His own resurrection. Yet even that, like the miracle wrought upon Jonah, was in secret, and they who believed without seeing it were more blessed than those who saw. All this accords with what is told us about particular Divine manifestations in other parts of Scripture. The saints reflected on them afterwards, and mastered them, but can hardly be considered as sensible of them at the very time. Thus Jacob, after the vision, says, "Surely the Lord is in this place, and I knew it not." Manoah said to his wife, after the angel had departed, "We shall surely die, because we have seen God" (Gen. xxviii. 16; Judg. xiii. 22, vi. 22; Acts xii. 9–11). Let no one think it strange to say that God may be holding communion with us without our knowing it. Do not all good thoughts come from Him? Yet are we sensible that they so come? Can we tell how they come? We commonly speak of being influenced by God's grace, and resisting His grace; this implies a certain awful intercourse between the soul and God; yet who will say that he himself can tell in particular instances when God moves him, and when he is responding this way or that? It is one thing, then, to receive impressions, another to reflect upon them and to be conscious of them. I have been speaking of the signs which He Himself promised; but others were announced concerning Him by His servants, and these, let it be observed, are secret also, and addressed to faith. The prophet Isaiah was commissioned to promise Ahaz a sign, "Ask thee a sign of the Lord thy God," he says, "ask it either in the depth or in the height above." When Ahaz would not speak, the prophet proceeded: "The Lord Himself shall give you a sign; behold, a virgin shall conceive, and bear a Son, and shall call His name Immanuel." Yet could there be a sign more secret, less exposed to the senses, less addressed to the reason, than the conception of Christ? It was a miracle, yet not an evidence. And so again, when our Lord was born, the angel gave the shepherds a sign; but which was the greater evidence, the angel himself, and the multitude of the heavenly host, or the sign itself which he sent them to see? "This shall be a sign unto you," he said; "ye shall see the Babe wrapped in swaddling clothes, lying in a manger." Was this an evidence of greatness or of meanness? Did it prove Him to be God, or was it a trial of faith? And so again, though it is not called a sign, yet it had been published in the manner of a sign, that the Lord should suddenly come to His temple, even the "Messenger of the Covenant," that "the glory of the latter house should be greater than that of the former," and that God would "glorify the house of His glory." But how did He come to fulfil these prophecies? As an infant in arms, recognized by one or two holy persons, and that by means of faith, without pomp, or display of greatness. Yet still Simeon said undoubtingly, "Mine eyes have seen Thy salvation; a light to lighten the Gentiles, and the glory of Thy people Israel." What is true in these instances is true of all the parts of our Lord's gracious economy. He was "manifested in the flesh, justified in the Spirit, seen of angels, preached unto the Gentiles, believed on in the world, received up into glory," yet what was the nature of the manifestation? The annunciation was secret; the nativity was secret; the miraculous fasting in the wilderness was secret; the resurrection secret; the ascension not far from secret; the abiding presence secret. One thing alone was public, and in the eyes of the world—His death; the only event which did not speak of His divinity, the only event in which He seemed a sign, not of power, but of weakness. Let us not seek then for signs and wonders, or ask for sensible inward tokens of God's favour; let us not indulge enthusiasm, or become the slaves of superstition, who are children of God by faith. Faith only can introduce us to the unseen presence of God; let us venture to believe, let us make trial before we see, and the evidence which others demand before believing, we shall gain more abundantly by believing. Almighty God is hidden from us; the world does not discover Him to us; we may go to the right hand and the left, but we find Him not. Opposed to this generous and vigorous faith are carnal blindness and grossness of heart, of which Scripture speaks so often. Whatever there is of spiritual light within us is quenched by indulging our natural tastes and appetites. Our Lord says, "Ye cannot serve God and mammon." He bids us watch and pray, and beware of eating and drinking, buying and selling, marrying and being given in marriage. We cannot have our eyes at once on this world and on the other. Those who live in the sun's glare, can see nothing in twilight; but those whose eyes are used to the shade, see many things which the others will not believe they can see. So is it with our souls; the minding of the flesh aiming at this world's goods, seeking to rise or succeed in life, gazing on greatness, rank, distinction, abundance, pomp and show, coveting wealth, measuring things by wealth, eating and drinking without restraint, placing no curb upon the passions, exercising no self-command, living without rule, indolently and weakly following the first idea which presents itself, the first impulse, the first temptation, all this makes the heart irreligious. Then it is that men ask for clearer evidence, and reject the truth; then they say, "How can these things be?" (*J. H. Newman.*)

Vers. 17–20. **Every kingdom divided against itself is brought to desolation.**— *The power of the King over the arch-enemy:*—I. THE CONDITION OF THE SINNER. What a condition it is! It is summed up in that twenty-first verse, "When the strong man armed keepeth his palace his goods are in peace." I will ask you to notice the five particulars here specified in that proud usurper's dominion—First, his personality; second, his power; third, his panoply; fourth, his palace; fifth, his peace. II. THE POWER OF THE SAVIOUR. Satan is strong, but the Divine Master is stronger. Upon that citadel the Lord Christ does not hesitate to advance. Man-soul is summoned. He effects an entrance, and more than that, He achieves the victory. He shall not only come upon him, but overcome him. And then a mighty transformation takes place in the soul of the believer. He divides the spoil. The faculties of the man are not to be destroyed; they are to be altered. What shall we say to it? Whatever it is, it teaches us that the whole powers of the restored man are to be laid at the feet of this Saviour. Mark what is said concerning Satan: .that he keeps his gates in peace. Blessed be God, when the transformation is effected, a greater, stronger one than he is also able to keep His gates in peace. III. I close with one word of WARNING. You know that warning word. He goes on immediately to say, "He that is not with Me is against Me, and he that gathereth not with Me scattereth abroad." He is saying to us, Beware of compromise; beware of half-and-half work in this matter of full surrender of your being to Him. What does He mean? I will endeavour by a story to illustrate what He says. Some years ago there was a rich man who possessed the whole of the town in which he lived, with the exception of one poor, small, and dirty hovel. He was greatly minded to possess the whole. He asked the price. The poor man, miserly and cunning, probably asked an exorbitant sum. "It is too much," said the would-be purchaser; "but I will tell you what I will do—I will cover this table with sove-reigns." "No," said the other; "no, I must have them on end!" "It is too much," said the purchaser. "No," said the other, "I must have them on end"; and so the bargaining went on, until the would-be purchaser gave up the business. As he left the room, the miser, looking at him with a leer on his face, said, "Re-member! the town belongs to thee and me." My dear brethren, Satan, if I may so express it, made a harder bargain with the Captain of our salvation than did that miser. We are redeemed, not with corruptible things as silver and gold, but with the blood of Christ. Shall it ever be that that cruel enemy shall come up to our Lord, and, pointing to the citadel of your or my heart, shall say, "Remember, the town belongs to me and Thee." But is there no lesson in that passage which follows? "When the unclean spirit is gone out of a man he walketh through dry places, seeking rest, but findeth none," and if he can find in you and me a foothold he will use it. It is my house, he says, and he comes back again; he comes seek-ing admission, and if he finds a place in our citadel he occupies it. He may be cast out as an unclean spirit, but he may return transformed as an angel of light, but an unclean spirit still. Is there no danger of this? I believe there is. Take heed that ye be not deceived. What is the remedy? I only know of one. It is to be God-possessed. It is to let that flag of Calvary float from roof to turret. It is to let God be in possession. Light expels darkness, health expels disease, God turns out Satan. (*E. W. Moore.*) *The personality and power of the devil:*—I. SATAN IS A PERSON. See how he is described. He is a man, active, intelligent, reso-lute, understanding his position, prepared to hold his own against all comers, to maintain his place at all hazards. Could there be anything more exactly in har-mony with the purposes and designs of the arch-adversary than that he should circulate a report that he does not exist? I remember years ago the late Rev. Canon Conway saying that, if a gang of housebreakers came into a neighbourhood, could there be any possible report more suited to their purposes than an announce-ment, which was generally believed, that there were no such persons as burglars, that if robberies occurred, or lives were lost, it was due exclusively to the folly and misguided character of the inmates of the houses, but that no blame could be attributed to housebreakers, for no such persons existed? II. But we will pass on to notice from his personality, HIS POWER. He is not only a man, but he is a strong man. My brethren, no good soldier despises his enemy. Satan is not a hobgoblin of the nursery, as some one has said—an easy name that we can utter in jest. Satan is a terrible being. Have you not experienced his power? I doubt not that I speak to hundreds who have. If you let him alone, it is most probable he will let you alone too. If you be in the attitude of hostility to him you will soon find out his power. In the fifth chapter of Mark's Gospel you will see the power of the demoniac, and the power which held that man. His power is backed by his panoply. You have it here; he is not only strong, but he is a strong man armed. He is not content with his own strength, so to speak, for the defence of his citadel, but he arms the poor citadel with defensive armour—the helmet of presumption, and the breastplate of pride, and the net-work shield of unbelief, and the coated mail of secret sin, and the fiery darts of venom and spite, and envy, and lust, and greed, which he hurls against all intruders. A palace is a dwelling-place for kings. Whose is this palace? What is this dwelling? My brethren, have we fully realized that you and I were intended to be nothing else than residences of Deity? Have we fully grasped the great thought that this is the culmination of God's dealing with us? Does God now fill His people's hearts with joy and the Holy Ghost? Satan can fill the heart of Ananias to lie to the Holy Ghost. The parallel is complete. Do you believe in haunted houses, ghost stories, and spectres with clanking chains? They may be fables, but there is terrible and solemn truth behind them. Has it ever occurred to you and me that unless this night we are possessed of God, as we sit in this room we are haunted houses—houses in which the devils live. It is one of the most startling descriptions that Scripture gives of the condition of the sinner, that Satan is not merely near him; Satan is in him. What an awful word is that in Luke xxii. 3, where we read that Satan entered into Judas surnamed Iscariot, being of the number of the twelve. What is this, a human being the house of an evil one? Every man can do what he will in his own house. An Englishman's house is his castle. What is this description that is given? Why, that Satan reigns and rules in the human heart of his slaves; that he goes in and out; that he opens and no man shuts, and shuts and no man opens. What an awful description! and the most remarkable thing about it all is the particulars with which it closes. While the strong man armed keepeth his palace, his goods are in peace. What peace? Peace, yes there is peace. It is the peace of death! Is that the peace that you and I desire? Only some half-hour ago, I heard a lady who had been travelling in the Riviera, the scene of the late earthquakes, say that before the rumble which brought the terrible disaster she felt that there was a stillness, a solemn stillness. It seemed as if nature held its breath; it seemed unnatural; it was unnatural; it was a presage of the coming storm. And this deadly slumber in which souls are left by the prince of darkness—slumber indeed, and peace-like it is—is a presage of the terrible awakening of the storm that shall burst some day upon a guilty world. (*Ibid.*) *Jesus refutes the Pharisees:*—How concisely and forcibly does He express His argument! It is impossible to exhibit it in a more striking manner. But, though it cannot be improved, it may, however, be otherwise stated. Thus, it presupposes absolute impossibilities in the character of Satan: 1. In the motives which influence him. For he is supposed, first, to wish to extend his power, and then to undermine it. 2. In the means which he employs, which are thereby calculated for accomplishing opposite purposes. 3. In the objects which he has in view, which presuppose a desire to do good and to do evil at the same time. These contradictions are happily expressed by our Saviour when He represents Satan casting out Satan, and divided against himself: in other words, as possessing two opposite characters, or forming two persons with contrary qualities. (*J. Thomson, D.D.*) "*Divided against itself*":—If two ships at sea, being of one and the same squadron, shall be scattered by storm from each other, how shall they come to the relief of each other? If, again, they clash together and fall foul, how shall the one endanger the other and herself too? It was, of old, the Dutch device of two earthen pots swimming upon the water, with this motto, "If we knock together, we sink together." And most true it is, that if spleen or discontent set us too far one from another, or choler or anger bring us too near, it cannot but that intendment or design, whatsoever it be, like Jonah's gourd, shall perish in a moment, especially if the viperous and hateful worm of dissension do but smite it. (*Spencer.*)

Vers. 21, 22. **A strong man armed.**—*The strong one driven out by a stronger one :*—
I. A PICTURE OF MAN IN HIS SINFUL STATE. Observe, that although man's heart
was intended to be the throne of God, it is now become the palace of Satan. It is
said of this strong man, moreover, that he is armed. Truly the prince of the power
of the air is never without weapons. His principal weapon is the lie. Then we
are told that he wears armour—for we read that the stronger warrior "taketh from
him all his armour wherein he trusted." Certain it is, the evil spirit is well
accoutred in that which is proof against all terrestrial steel. Prejudice, ignorance,
evil education—all these are chain-armour with which Satan girds himself. A
hard heart is the impenetrable breast-plate which this evil spirit wears ; a seared
conscience becomes to him like greaves of brass ; habitude in sin is a helmet of
iron. Notice, again, this strong man: besides being armed and plated with armour,
he is very watchful ; for it is said "he keepeth his palace"—keeps it like the faithful warder who with ceaseless tramp and sleepless eye holds watch upon the castle
wall. He does not put on the armour to sleep in it. You may find sleeping saints,
but never sleeping devils. We have in the text a good reason given why Satan
thus watches over the man whose heart he inhabits, because he considers the man
to be his property—"he keepeth his goods." They are not his in justice ; whatever goods there are in the house of manhood must belong to God who built the
house, and who intended to tenant it. But Satan sets up a claim and calls everything in the man his goods. The man's memory he makes a storehouse for ill
words and bad songs ; the man's judgment he perverts so that the scales and
weights are false ; the man's love he sets on fire with coals of hell, and his imagination he dazzles with foul delusions. He claims the whole man to be his own ;
and it is wonderful how readily his claim is allowed. Men fancy music in the
chains with which Satan binds them, and hug the fetters which he hangs upon
them. Nor is this all; Satan not only claims possession, but he claims sovereignty.
You perceive it is said, "his palace." A palace is usually the abode of a king, so
Satan considers himself a great king when he dwells in the human heart. I must
not leave this picture until you have observed that it is said, "while he keepeth
his palace, his goods are in peace." This is the most fearful sign in the whole
affair. The man is quite undisturbed—conscience does not prick him: why should
it ? God does not alarm him : who is God, that he should obey His voice ?
Thoughts of hell never disturb him. Men who are stupefied with laudanum may be
naked, but they are not cold ; they may have empty stomachs, but they are not
hungry ; they may be diseased in body, but they do not feel the torment : they are
drunken, and know not their misery: and so it is with the most of carnal men—
nothing awakens them. II. A REPRESENTATION OF MAN FOR A TIME REFORMED.
Observe, then, that in the case before us the unclean spirit goes out of his
own free will. Why does the evil spirit leave a man for a time ? Has he not
some hellish purpose in view ? Certainly he has. I think it often is because he
feels if he does not go out he will be driven out, but he thinks that by giving way
for a time he will satisfy the conscience till he gets it lulled to sleep faster than
ever. Thus he will stoop to conquer, retreat to draw his opponent into an ill position ; allow his throne to shake, that he may re-establish his dominion permanently.
Moreover, he thinks that by letting the man indulge in a little religion for a time,
and then turn aside from it, he will make him permanently sceptical so that he
will hold him fast by the iron chain of infidelity, and drag him down to hell with
that hook in his jaws. Now, after a time it appears that the evil spirit returned ;
he could find no rest for himself except in the hearts of the wicked, and therefore
he came back again. There is no opposition to his entrance, the door is not
locked, or if it be he has the latch-key. He comes in, there is no tenant, no man
in possession, no other proprietor. He looks round and cries, "Here is my house.
I left it when I took my walks abroad, and I have come back, and here it is ready
for me." The devil shouts his "Halloa!" and there is an echo through every
room, but no intruder starts up. "Is Christ here ?" No answer. He goes outside
and he looks at the lintel, for Christ's mark is sure to be there if Jesus is within.
"No mark of blood on the post, Christ is not here," says he, "it is empty, I will
make myself at home" ; for if Jesus had been there, though He had been hidden in
a closet, yet when He came out He would claim possession, and drive out the traitor,
and say, "Get thee gone! this is no place for thee; I have bought it with My
blood, and I mean to possess it for ever." But it is empty, and so Satan fills it
with stores of evil. The next thing the fiend notices is that it is swept ; as one
says, "Swept, but never washed." Sweeping takes away the loose dirt, washing

takes away all the filth. O to be washed in Jesus' blood! Here is a man whose house is swept—the loose sins are gone. He is not a drunkard; there is a pledge over the mantelpiece. He is no longer lustful; he hates that sin or says he does, which is as much as the devil wants him to do. The place is swept so tidy, so neat, you would not know him to be the same man as he used to be; and he himself is so proud to think he has got his house so clean, and he stands up at the threshold as he meets the devil with a "Good morning," and he says, "I am not as other men are—I am neither an extortioner, nor a drunkard; nor even as that Christian over yonder, who is not half what he ought to be—nor a tithe so consistent as I am." And as the devil looks round and finds the place swept, he finds it garnished too. The man has bought some pictures—he has not real faith, but he has a fine picture of it over the fireplace; he has no love to the cross of Christ, but he has a very handsome crucifix hanging on the wall. He has no graces of the Spirit, but he has a fine vase of flowers on the table, of other people's experiences and other people's graces, and they smell tolerably sweet. There is a fireplace without fire, but there is one of the handsomest ornaments for the fireplace that was ever bought for money. It is swept and garnished. III. A GRAPHIC PORTRAIT OF MAN ENTIRELY CONQUERED BY THE POWER OF THE GREAT REDEEMER. Now, observe here is a "stronger than he." This is not the man himself, the man is the house, the man is not so strong as the devil—who is this? This is Jesus Christ, who comes by His Spirit into the heart of man, and the Spirit of God is vastly superior to Satanic power, as much as the infinite Creator Himself must ever be superior to the finite creature. "He comes upon him," that is to say, He attacks him; and ah, how vehemently does Christ lay to at the great enemy of souls. One sword-cut cuts away the plume of pride; another blow takes away the comfort of sin; and another destroys the reigning power of sin. As soon as ever the stronger man has conquered the enemy, what does he do? He takes his sword of rebellion, snaps it across his knee, and pulls the armour from the back of the unclean spirit. Prejudice, ignorance, hardheartedness, all these are pulled off the old enemy. Christ Jesus then proceeds to divide the spoil. "There is the man's heart, I will take that," says He, "that shall be a jewel in My crown. The man's love I will set as a jewel upon My arm for ever. His memory, his judgment, his power of thought, utterance, and working—these are all Mine," says Christ. He begins to divide the spoil, He puts the broad arrow of the King upon every room in the house, upon every piece of furniture. The garnishing He pulls out; "I will adorn it far better than this," saith He. "There shall be no pictures of faith, but faith; there shall be no ornament in yonder grate except the ornament of the glowing fire of fervid zeal; there shall be no borrowed flowers, but I will train round this window the sweet roses and jessamine of love and peace of mind; I will wash what was only swept, with My blood I will make it white, and sweet, and clean; and I will strike the lintel and the two side posts with the hyssop, and with the blood mark, and then the destroying angel when he sweeps by shall sheathe his sword, and the black fiend when he would enter shall see the mark there, and go back trembling to his accursed den." This is conversion, the other was only conviction; this is change of heart, the other was only change of life. (*C. H. Spurgeon.*) *The strong man armed:*—I. LOOK AT THE DEVIL'S INFLUENCES FOR EVIL. 1. His possession may be more or less apparent. 2. His possession may be more or less oppressive. II. LOOK AT THE LORD'S APPLIANCES FOR GOOD. 1. The Lord Jesus comes upon Satan. Deliverance is from without, from above. 2. The Lord Jesus stands against Satan. 3. The Lord Jesus rises above Satan. (1) Strips him of his power. (2) Deprives him of his prey. (3) Expels him from his usurped authority in the soul. Lessons: 1. Whether men mean it or not, they do, and they must take sides. 2. Unless the expulsion of evil be by Christ, it will be a temporary relief followed by increased mischief. 3. When sceptical standers-by comment upon the seeming difficulties, the dispossessed soul knows and proves that the dumb spirit is gone. 4. When the unprejudiced observers witness what the Lord is doing, they know by whom it has been done. (*John Richardson, M.A.*) *Christ overthrowing Satan:*—I. CHRIST AFFIRMS THE ANCIENT DOMINION OF THE EVIL ONE IN ITS STRENGTH AND SECURITY. 1. Satan's kingdom was held by dint of great strength. 2. By means of many and various agencies. 3. With all the security of antiquity and custom. 4. And in consequence of the ignorance of the subjects over whom he reigned. 5. Yet this dominion was iniquitous. II. CHRIST DECLARES HIMSELF TO BE THE MIGHTY ONE, OVERTHROWING AND SPOILING MAN'S SPIRITUAL TYRANT. The figure is picturesque and vigorous. When you see a warrior in the palace of his foeman, capturing his arms and appropriating his goods, you know that the battle has been lost and won, that the strong man has yielded to the stronger, and is now either bound in the dungeon or dead upon the field. So, when you see such a victory as Christ's over the demon possessing this miserable sufferer, you know that the fight upon our behalf has been fought, that He who came to release the prisoners has already grappled with the grim foe who has made them captive, has demolished his power and humbled his pride. 1. Christ is stronger by reason of His own Divine nature. 2. Christ is proved to be stronger, as appears by the evidence of historical fact. The events of His ministry are witness; even then He saw Satan as lightning fall from heaven. 3. His victories upon earth were an earnest of His complete triumph over His foe and man's. Every foe must be put beneath His feet. Application: Each human heart is a battlefield between the two powers. Has Christ obtained the victory in our spiritual nature? (*Family Churchman.*)　　*Satan vanquished by Christ :*—I. THE STATE HERE DESCRIBED. 1. The description, "strong man armed," applies to Satan—(1) Because he was created a being of a higher order than man, and therefore superior to him in strength. (2) Because he has the strength of a numerous host available to the execution of his designs. (3) Because the skill he must have acquired by the long practice he has had, enables him to apply that strength, as it shall best serve to the accomplishment of his own designs. 2. The hearts of unregenerate men are the "palace" of Satan. (1) He keeps them in a state of dire captivity, aliens from the God who made them, and enemies of the Saviour who redeemed them. (2) He keeps them under the most powerful delusion. II. THE CONTEST. III. THE TRIUMPH. 1. Satan is rendered defenceless, with reference to all those who are made free from his dominion; so that the victory achieved for them may be maintained even by the weakest amongst them. 2. When Christ recovers His interest in man and His dominion over him, He disposes him, all that he has and is, for the destruction of sin, the good of the Church, and the glory of God. (*J. Fowler.*)　　*The conflict between Christ and Satan for the soul of man :*—I. THE NATURAL CONDITION OF THE HUMAN SOUL. Under the dominion of Satan; a dominion which is—1. Absolute. 2. Degrading. 3. Destructive. II. THE CHANGE WROUGHT IN THE CONDITION OF THE HUMAN SOUL BY—1. The character of the agent. 2. The method of the attack. 3. The victory of the Saviour involves the ransom of man from the guilt of sin; "there is no condemnation to them that are in Christ Jesus." III. THE DUTIES WHICH THE CONTEMPLATION OF THE CHARGE WROUGHT IN THE CONDITION OF THE HUMAN SOUL BY MEDIATORIAL GRACE SHOULD DEEPLY AND UNIVERSALLY IMPRESS. 1. There ought to be an humble acknowledgment of the supreme majesty of Christ. 2. Another duty must be regarded as being the formation of an impressive estimate as to the value of the human soul. 3. It is a duty earnestly to aspire after the application of delivering power to ourselves. 4. There is that of entire, absolute devotedness to Him by whom you are delivered. (*J. Parsons.*)　　*Resources of the adversary, and means of their destruction :*—I. THE DEFENCE AND RESOURCES OF THE ENEMY. 1. Idolatry. 2. Imposture. 3. Superstition. 4. Despotism. 5. Crime in its various forms. 6. False liberality in religion. 7. Corruption of religious revivals. II. HOW SHALL THE ENEMY BE VANQUISHED? 1. By the judgments of heaven, in which the Son of Man will come upon the strong man armed, and take away his armour. 2. By the universal propagation of the gospel; before the light of which, idolatry, imposture, and superstition, will retreat abashed. And—3. By frequent, and, at last, general revivals of religion; giving resistless power to the gospel, as it is preached to every creature. Conclusion: 1. There must be more faith in the Church of God. 2. There must be a more intense love for Christ in His Church. 3. There must be an era of more decided action, before the earth can be subdued to Christ. 4. For this glorious achievement, there is demanded more courage than has, in modern days, been manifested by the Church of God. 5. There must be new and more vigorous efforts to increase the number and power of evangelical churches in our land. 6. Special effort is required, to secure to the rising generation an education free from the influence of bad example, and more decidedly evangelical. 7. The vigour of charitable effort must be greatly increased. 8. The jealousies of Christians who are united substantially in their views of evangelical doctrine and religion, and who are divided only by localities, and rites, and forms, must yield, and give place to the glorious exigencies of the present day. 9. Let me add, that we must guard against the dangers peculiar to a state of religious prosperity. (*The Preacher's Treasury.*) *Lessons :*—Note here—1. That Satan is an unclean spirit, he hath lost his original purity, his holy nature in which he was created, and is by sin become universally sinful and impure; no means being allowed him by God for the purging of his filthy and impure nature; yea, he is a perfect enemy to purity and holiness; maligning all that love it and would promote it. 2. That Satan is a restless and unquiet spirit, being cast out of heaven he can rest nowhere; when he is either gone out of a man by policy, or cast out by power, he has no content or satisfaction, till he returns into a filthy heart, where he delights to be, as the swine in miry places. 3. That wicked and profane sinners have this unclean spirit dwelling in them; their hearts are Satan's house and habitation, and the lusts of pride and unbelief, malice and revenge, envy and hypocrisy, these are the garnishings and furniture of Satan's house: man's heart was God's house by creation, it is now Satan's by usurpation and judiciary tradition. 4. That Satan, by the preaching of the gospel, may seem to go out of persons, and they become sober and civilized; yet may he return again to his old habitation, and the latter end of that man may be worse than the beginning. (*W. Burkitt.*) *The division of spoil:*—The Divine conqueror is here represented as not destroying, but "dividing the spoil"—*i.e.*, employing for His own cause and glory everything that, before the conquest, Satan had been using for his own evil purposes. Now, this is the overlooked and apparently unimportant point in the parable we wish practically to consider as setting forth this simple proposition—That Christ Jesus, in the victories of His grace, whether individual or universal, turns to His own advantage, and employs for His own glory, all those physical powers and intellectual endowments—that whole array of influence and engine which previously the great adversary had perverted and made powerful for evil. I. We begin with the INDIVIDUAL, as certainly the most obvious reference of the lesson—the case of a sinful soul conquered by Christ in the process of regeneration. And thus it serves to rectify some wrong conceptions often entertained of the nature of regeneration. Here the representation of the great change wrought in the regenerated soul, is only a change in the sovereignty that overrules it. A change, not in the house's furniture and appointments, but in their uses and ownership. The stronger man has not come to destroy what was in the fortress, but to rescue it all from the hands of the strong man, and turn it to his own purposes. Those very endowments of reason, imagination, wit, wealth, power—acquirements which before were exercised sinfully, because without godliness—Christ would now employ for man's good and God's glory; not destroying but only "dividing the spoil." To be a Christian, is simply and truly to be the highest style of man—to have all the faculties and impulses of your nature lifted from the perishing things of earth. Oh, no; He would enter only to conquer and bind the despot that enslaves you—to unshutter the darkened windows, and let in heavenly airs, and odours, and sunshine; and, reviving in all their original beauty, and replacing in all their original glory, its magnificent adornments, transform it from the haunt of a demon to the home of a God! But now let us pass from the individual to consider—II. THE TEXT'S WIDER AND UNIVERSAL APPLICATION. This satanic despotism over the human heart is in exact analogy with his despotism over the earth as man's dwelling-place. The Bible everywhere represents this fallen spirit as practically "the god of this world." But there is a day coming when "the strong man" shall be mastered by "one stronger than he." The kingdoms and dominions under the whole heavens are to become Immanuel's, and this world become manifestly again the abode of a universally acknowledged Jehovah. All this we are assured of. But then, we do not believe that, as a result of this, earth is suddenly to be transfigured, as into another planet. Here, in the universal as in the individual, we look for this great law of conquest—that, having bound the strong man and taken away his armour, our glorious Redeemer will not destroy the spoil, but will only "divide the spoil." We judge that the world, under Messiah's reign, will be the world as it is, only redeemed from sin and re-established in, and filled with, all righteousness. Physically it will be the same world, but instead of working disobedience to the precepts of the Divine law, all natural agents and processes shall be consecrated to Christ; and holiness to the Lord "shall be written on the bells of the horses." Intellectually it will be the same world, and all sciences and arts flourish, and poetry see visions, and eloquence utter prophecies; but literature shall embalm with sweet spices the name of the Crucified, and science shall go forth along all its broad journeyings, only searching for God. Socially and politically, it will be the same; and though all despotisms shall cease, and every oppressor's rod be broken, yet, as under the old Hebrew theocracy different civil polities successively obtained, so then there may be all present forms of government. But high above finite magistracy shall rise one

Omnipotent enthronement, and monarchs, and princes, and presidents, and mighty men shall be mighty men, and presidents, and kings unto God. (*C. Wadsworth, D.D.*) *The strong man armed :*—What is it then? Why, the sinner's heart is Satan's house; the place wherein he dwells—not near it or round about it, but within it. Now, to make this clear, you all know what your own house is to you. You go to and fro in it at your own will and pleasure—you order everything in it, exactly after your own taste—you give commands to your servants or to your children, and they are compelled to obey you—you walk up and down its several chambers, and furnish them as suits your convenience—you take your ease and pleasure there, and none interrupts you—you knock at the door and it instantly opens to you—you close it, and none can have an entrance there, without your consent. In one word, which is better than the longest description that can be given, it belongs to you, it is your own ; you do what you like with it, it is a part of yourselves ; and you feel at once how much is contained in that! Even so is the heart of the sinner to Satan; just as much his property. Sinner! Satan is within thee! The ungodly heart is the very home of the evil spirit! But, it is well worth your remarking that our Lord describes the place wherein the strong man dwells, not as a mere ordinary house, but as a palace, a king's mansion. And yet certainly in one point of view, it is difficult to imagine anything less like a royal dwelling-place than the soul of the unconverted sinner. For who is it that lives in it? Take it, on his own showing—it is himself; he is master of it. Be it so : but what a vile thing this self is! Though men dress it up, as savages do their ugly idols, in order to give it some show of comeliness, and some appearance of beauty, it is truly a mean thing and a contemptible at the best. And as is the supposed master, so is everything about him. All the furniture of the dwelling is of the same description. Low thoughts—wretched passions—miserable ends and aims ; gild them and turn them as you will, they are all of the earth, earthy! No noble faith —no elevated hopes. It was intended to be a palace ; because, when Almighty God first framed it, He meant it for Himself to dwell in, and to put His glory there, and His purity, and His righteousness, and all the graces which attend upon His presence, and, like so many beams from the sun, are always issuing forth, and shining round about Him. And even the smallest dwelling that ever was, if a great king should make it his house, and live in it, would be fitly styled a palace. Nobody would think of the smallness of the place, but only the grandeur of its inhabitant. At any rate, the goods which are within this dwelling, and which furnish it, are the possession of him who resides there as lord and master, be it God or be it Satan. And magnificently did He who made you furnish you forth in this respect. There is a man's mind; a man's thoughts, which he can turn as he pleases ; directing them to things good or things evil. Again, there is what we call our affections, the power of loving, or feeling a strong attachment for this or that object. Then there is the power which all men possess, in a greater or less degree, of influencing the minds of other men, and persuading them by their words, or by their deeds and example, to serve God, or to serve themselves and the world! And, in very many cases, there is, all this time, a state of peace. Everything is quiet in the soul of the sinner ; Satan's reign is not disputed. How many solemn dispensations are sent to waken him, frequently in the shape of visitations on his friends and neighbours, sudden deaths, and so on! How is it he is neither moved nor changed, but is still the same? The man is not his own master! Satan has possession of him; and treats him as he will! The strong man keepeth his palace, and his goods are in peace, his own without difficulty or dispute. And, if you consider against how many workings and appeals of all kinds this possession is maintained, you will not and cannot doubt that a great deal of power is necessary to the strong man, to Satan with whom we have to deal. And he is strong in two ways. He is in himself powerful ; not able indeed, as yet, absolutely to destroy either body or soul, as he constantly desires to do, limited round about, in many ways, by the obstacles which God throws in his way, and by which he continually overrules him, but still very mighty to tempt and destroy. He is of no mean rank. He is the prince of this world, seducing men with riches and pleasures. 2. He is mighty too, not only in himself, but in the weaknesses and corruptions of those whom he sets himself to destroy, He winds himself into them. " Peace," he says to another ; "you are not open sinners—you do not pick, nor steal, nor slay. You are not drunkards, or swearers, or adulterers! Why should you trouble yourselves about loving God with all your heart, and making Him reign in all your thoughts?" Or again he says to others, " Peace! it is all true that God does require truth and holiness in the inward parts. It is true, as your alarmed heart testifies, that Almighty God is a consuming fire, and does exact obedience to His laws. But then, He is not so awfully strict and severe, as, in your first terror, you are inclined to suppose. I do not say cherish *all* sins, but *one* is not much to keep." If, I say, a man is clearly convinced that it is indeed the plain and unquestionable sense of Scripture, and the real counsel of God towards sinners, as any candid and reasonable man must be, why then, there would be danger of such a person's escaping his authority, if Satan directly denied what is undeniable to an awakened conscience. He therefore, wisely, does not attempt it. He says, " Peace—all this is true. But then there is abundance of time still left for it. You need not be in a hurry !" So there is peace again; the tempter is believed, and all becomes quiet in his house. Dear brethren, the first sign that the power of the strong man is about to give way, is this inward struggle. It is the Spirit from above, descending to the battle, and waking you out of your sleep, to put on your armour and to fight for your life. (*J. Garbett, M.A.*) *The strong man's armour :*—I. And, if you reflect for a moment upon that blessed being, in whom is our life ; the sinless man; the God in the flesh ; you will at once discern what peculiar fitness there is in Him for our deliverance from this spiritual battle! a fitness nowhere else to be found, or to be imagined. As the very and eternal God, He hath all power, equal to the Father, all brightness, and glory, and all unutterable perfections dwelling within Him, as in a fountain inexhaustible, and ever flowing over on the objects of His love. As man, again, one with us, He is our brother, united by ties unspeakable in any words which human nature can supply, with those for whose sake He came down from the bosom of the eternal glory. Christ for Himself has fought it all over before us, with the very same enemy, and against the very same arms and weapons which are directed against us. And right and well it is that so it should have been ordered. As Satan's first victory was gained over flesh and blood, in the same flesh and blood it seemed good to Almighty God that he should be conquered. Christ, then, is the stronger man who conquereth the strong for us and frees the soul from its captivity, which is the first point which the text suggests to our consideration. II. The next is the use which He makes of His victory. HE TAKETH FROM HIM, that is, from Satan, THE ARMOUR IN WHICH HE TRUSTED. The meaning evidently is, that He deprives him of those weapons of spiritual strength and spiritual delusion, by making use of which he was enabled to keep an uninterrupted dominion for so long a time. What is Satan's armour? to what, in fact, in the soul of the sinner, does he mainly trust, in order to prevent his escape into the liberty of the children of God? Evidently this is a most important point, necessary for us clearly to understand if we would enter into the secret wisdom of this mystery of iniquity, and put ourselves on an effectual guard against it. Now, I think, that those arms of Satan are mainly three. 1. Our self-love. 2. Our unbelief. And—3. Our indulgence in some one favourite sin. So long as we allow Satan possession of these weapons, it is impossible to expel him ; he keeps a fast and sure hold, in spite of any occasional struggle, of his house and all the goods that are therein. And I am sure you must confess that, wherever this is present, whichever essential doctrine of the truth as it is in Jesus it chooses not to credit, there Satan's possession is quite secure ! And it is, indeed, a powerful instrument of war in his hand, with which to repel the assaults of the gospel upon the heart, and to prevent Christ, the rightful owner, from entering in, and taking possession. (*Ibid.*) *The division of the spoils :*—And if it seems strange to any among you, that such things should give such delight, and if you ask the reason, it is precisely what I have been speaking about. The reason is, that the heart is in it, just as it might have been in the world, and in the service of Satan before. There is all the difference. Only imagine just as powerful a liking for the things of God, as some of you probably feel for the things of the world ; and just as strong a desire for God's favour and growth in all heavenly graces, and the full enjoyment of His presence, whether in heaven or earth, as sinners have for earthly vanities ; and the marvel is explained. Satan is spoiled, and what was once his, the heart, is now Christ's—that is all. And the consequence is, that the affections being engaged, the very same things, such as worshipping God in His holy house, which are practised alike by nominal and real Christians, are very different indeed in the feeling they produce, and the fruits they leave behind ! 1. Only look, then, at the practical difference which this produces. Is there an opportunity given us of promoting God's glory, and the spread of the gospel, say by giving somewhat out of our substance? We used to try to give as little as it was possible, and no more ; to invent all kinds of doubts, and difficulties, and scruples, and hesitations, full of worldly caution and worldly wisdom. Now we thank Him for such a privilege. We are filled with gratitude at being thought worthy to feed or to clothe the members of Christ, or to aid in the extension of the glorious gospel. It is only giving from what is not ours, but His. If we must give up anything, it must not be these deeds of love. Satan is spoiled, and we now do for God, what we once did for him. 2. Again—Is there laid before us, solemnly and affectionately, out of God's holy Word, some grace to be obtained, of which we never thought before; some holy temper which we have never cultivated, or some duty to ourselves, our families, or our neighbours, which has never been pressed upon us in former times. Is this the case, as it must be, with us all? Look at the result of our choice being on heavenly things. We no longer say, "No, the old ways were good enough for me; I take trouble enough in going to church and leading an upright life, and I shall do no more." No. We say, "It is well; this never struck me; but it is in scripture, it is in the practice of holy men, the saints of God. It is, I cannot deny it, a good and Christian thing to do, and such as the blessing of God will fall upon, if there is any truth in plain gospel words, and any reality in Divine grace. I am willing then to follow him whereso-ever He may lead me, and still to do more and more as increasing light shall guide me. By His aid I will do this good thing, and trust to Him to bless it." Here, again, the Christian is only doing in Divine things what he has done all his life in worldly ones; taking advantage of every new light, and every fresh instruction, and permitting no opportunity to pass, by which he could advance his interest or improve his chances of ultimate success. Satan is spoiled, and we now do for God what we used to do for him. 3. Again—It may be that, in the performance of this or that duty to God, and of obedience to one or other of the commandments which He has laid upon us, there may be inconveniences to encounter, difficulties in family arrangement, perhaps some labour to be undergone, some pleasure or relaxation to be abandoned, some worldly gain, or supposed worldly gain and advantage, to be sacrificed. We used not to scruple in such a case to sacrifice God instantly to the world or to ourselves. "I have pressing accounts upon my hands," a man says; "I cannot, therefore, come to church, or read the Bible, or meditate on my soul; business must be done whether or no, that is the main thing in the world, and God could not intend that I should so trouble myself to my own dis-advantage." "I shall have so much less at the end of the year if I give this or that, and what good will Christ's love do me in such a matter?" It is now; "God forbid that I should break His holy law, be it the Sabbath—be it prayer—be it almsgiving—be it what it may; how shall I do this wickedness, and sin against God? My soul is athirst for God, yea, even for the living God, and I am content if I can please and obey Him; where or what shall I be if I lose His love who is my all?" Here, again, you see, the Christian only does in the concerns of his soul, and in the service of God, what men of the world are always practising for earthly ends and objects. Satan is spoiled of his old weapons, that is all; we now do for God what we used to do for him. 3. Again—we encounter some grievous trial. We find, perhaps, when we least expected it, that something very dear to us must be given up, some grievous sacrifice be made, of something not in itself bad, perhaps; but not to be reconciled with a devotion of the soul to God in Christ. Formerly, it never would have entered into our heads to surrender it. But now it is, "Take it all, O Lord, lay this and everything else upon us, if it be Thy good will; Thy will, O Lord, and not ours be done." We give up the less for the greater, and trust where we know trust should be reposed, exactly as men do in the world. Satan is spoiled, and we now do for God what we used to do for him. (*Ibid.*)

Ver. 23. **He that is not with Me is against Me.**--*Neutrality in religion impos-sible:*—There is no device by which the god of this world more fatally deceives the souls of unwary men, than by leading them to suppose that they can take neutral ground in regard to the character and cause of Christ. Now, in proof of the asser-tion that neutrality in regard to the character and cause of Christ is impossible, let me—1. Adduce the testimony of the Word of God. The text is explicit. "He that is not for Me is against Me, and He that gathereth not with Me scattereth abroad." The same thing is taught in language not less explicit in our Saviour's sermon on the mount. "No man can serve two masters: for either he will hate the one and love the other; or else he will hold to the one and despise the other; ye cannot serve God and Mammon." Take another passage equally decisive. "The friendship of the world is enmity with God." Whosoever therefore will be a friend of the world is an enemy of God. 2. The same is evident from the nature of the human mind, and the laws under which it acts. Every man has some commanding principle of action, some supreme object of affection and pursuit; and he can have but one such object. 3. The truth of our doctrine is proved from the nature of the Divine requirements. These requirements are positive in their character, and cannot be satisfied with mere negative obedience. 4. The character and cause of Christ are in their nature such as render it impossible for any to feel indifferent or take neutral ground in respect to them. 5. The disclosures and decisions of the judgment day prove that neutrality in regard to Christ and religion is impossible. In conclusion, I am led to remark—1. It may be expected that those who assume neutral ground will take it unkindly when their deception and danger are exposed. 2. If all who are not for Christ are against him, then it is immensely important that this truth should be clearly set forth and fully known. (*J. Hawes, D.D.*) *Opposition to Christ :*—I. The DISGRACEFULNESS of being against Christ. In order to make this appear a little, you will observe—1. Nothing shows men more than their attractions and aversions. Mark the objects of their choice and of their preference; see with whom they most readily and pleasingly associate; and then call to remembrance the adage, "Tell me a man's company, and I will tell you his character." Congeniality is the inducement and the bond of union. To be against some individuals would expose you to general indignation. Which of you would like to be opposed to a Thornton, a Reynolds, a Howard, a Leighton, a Fenelon? But here we have the brightness of God's glory, and the express image of His person. 2. Again: nothing is more unreasonable, vile, and shameful than to oppose a Benefactor and Friend, who has laid you under peculiar obligations, upon whom you had no claim, and who has yet spared no expense, no pains, in order to serve you. II. The DANGER of being against Christ. 1. Can you overcome Him? 2. Can you endure Him? 3. Can you escape from Him? III. The POSSIBILITY of being against Him. 1. He has a people, and they that persecute them persecute Him. 2. He has a cause in this world: the gospel of our salvation. And how it has been opposed! It offends because it is the enemy of self and sin, and because of its sanctifying influence. 3. He has also a providential agency on earth; and the dispensations of His providence are designed to promote the purposes of His grace. Yet with some this is all in vain. They will have none of Him. IV. The evidence of being against Him. The question is, Are you with Him? Are you with Him in sentiment, in disposition, in action, in pursuit? Are you with Him as scholars are with their teacher, as servants are with their master, as soldiers are with their commander, as subjects are with their sovereign? Does He occupy the highest place in your regard? Does He dwell in your hearts by faith? Do you say, "Other lords besides Thee have had dominion over me, but henceforth will I make mention of Thy name"? And do you feel what is done against Him as done against yourselves? (*W. Jay.*) *Christian neutrality impossible :*—I. THE DESIGN CHRIST IS CARRYING ON. Redemption. II. THAT NO MAN CAN BE INDIFFERENT TOWARDS IT. 1. The design which Christ is pursuing is the greatest of all possible designs in every point of view. (1) It is great in its origin. (2) Great in extent. (3) Great in duration. 2. The great design which Christ is pursuing is totally opposed to all the selfish designs of mankind. 3. Christ, in carrying on His great, comprehensive, and benevolent design, employs all mankind as instruments in promoting it. 4. None of the inhabitants of the invisible world are indifferent towards the great and interesting design which Christ has undertaken, and is determined to accomplish. 1. If none can be indifferent towards the design which Christ is carrying on, then none have any ground to imagine that they are neuters in religion. 2. If none can be indifferent towards the design which Christ is carrying on, then all who do not act for Him, act against Him. As all must be for Him or against Him in their hearts, so all must be for Him or against Him in their conduct. 3. If all who are with Christ are united to Him in His great and glorious design, then all who are united to Him are more firmly united to one another than any other persons in the world. 4. If all who are not for Christ are against Him, then the most regular and amiable sinners may be as much against Him as any other sinners. 5. We learn from what has been said the great criminality of sinners. They are all against Christ in their hearts and in their conduct, without a single exception. And by opposing this great and glorious purpose they oppose the glory of God, and all the holiness and happiness in the universe. Is this a small error, or a mere venial fault? Is it not a sin of the first magnitude? Can they be guilty of a greater? 6. This subject shows the imminent danger of all who are against Christ and opposing His great and glorious design. (*N. Emmons, D.D.*) *No neutrality in religion:*—We are all either "gatherers" or "scatterers"; either workmen in the erection of a vast spiritual fabric, or destroyers who lay its honour in the dust. 1. We remind you, then, in the first place, that you are "scattering" Christ's seed in the world, if you are not "gathering" it. The absence of the Christian temper in your daily conduct, the absence of Christian charitableness in your judgment of your fellow-men—nay, the mere absence of all concern for the glory and spread of the Redeemer's triumphs, will all be, in effect, an absolute accession to the strength of His adversary; and that for this simple reason—that the war which Christ is carrying on is essentially aggressive. To stand still, therefore, in spiritual things is to help Satan. If you are "not with Christ," you are "against Him"; if you "gather not with Him," you are "scattering abroad." 2. Again: you are "scattering" Christ's flock in your families, if you do not "gather" them. 3. Again: you are "scattering" Christ's precious gifts in your own hearts, if you are not "gathering" them. Consider, then, what use you are making of the gifts which Christ hath given you. 4. But this text must have a more awful illustration still. Christ's scatterers and Christ's gatherers must have one more meeting yet; and only one. The gathered seed shall expand and ripen, till it becomes fit for the garners and the stores of heaven. The gathered flock shall rise from earth and sea, and pass under the portals of the everlasting dome. The gathered graces of the Redeemer shall be purged from their earthly dross, forming by their clustered brightness the "new name" upon His brow. But the scattered seed which you did not prize, the scattered flock which you would not feed, the scattered graces that you would neither seek nor keep nor bind up, shall all rise up in judgment against you, and in their turn shall scatter you. Christ Himself will be the only gatherer then. (*D. Moore, M.A.*) *What it is to be "with" Christ:*—What can the words mean for us? Not actual, personal, visible fellowship with Him. That is impossible now, or so long as we are in the flesh. Yet do we say, at times, to any teacher or leader who may have won our confidence, "I am with you in that," meaning that we accept the same doctrine, cherish the same convictions, have the same practical aims as he holds and is trying to reach. And that is substantially what is meant, I take it, by being "with" Christ: we are with Him, that is, if at all, in sympathy, in affection, and in active endeavour. Faith, love, obedience, in other words, constitute the triple cord which binds men to Christ. (*J. H. Rylance, D.D.*) *A half-Christian:*—"He that is not with Me." Such is our Lord's description of a half-Christian. Let us think what we are. And then let us consider why such a person not being with should be said to be against Him. Who then is not with Christ? Of course, and most obviously, he who never visits Christ, he who never seeks Christ, is not with Him. We may do both, and yet not live with Him. We may pray to Him and communicate with Him now and then, and yet not be with Him. That is quite possible. But it is too plain that, if we do not ever seriously pray to Him, or seek His presence, in our hearts by faith, we cannot be with Him. Those of us are not with Him who do not pray heartily and earnestly as well as regularly. Those of us are not with Him who, having been confirmed, do not habitually come to His holy table to have their faith strengthened and refreshed by His Holy Spirit. But this is not enough to explain the words. To be with Christ is to be on His side. It implies that there is a daily strife going on where we are, and that Christ is one of two parties in it. It implies that life, our own life, is a struggle, and that Christ is concerned in that struggle; interested in its progress, and interested in its end. And if this be the meaning of the words, "He that is with Me," we can all understand the meaning of their opposite, "He that is not with Me." You see that it does not necessarily imply active opposition to Christ. You need not have ever thwarted or ridiculed one of Christ's servants in order to expose you to the charge of not being with Him. It is a negative expression. It implies only that you have felt no deep interest in being yourself, or in inducing others to be, such as Christ would have you and them. It implies only that you have not taken pains to cherish the thought of God with reverence and love, to claim your position as His son, and to live up to it. It implies only that it has not been a great and constant object with you to get to heaven at last, and while upon earth to live as an expectant, as an heir, of heaven. But we were to inquire why those who are thus not with Christ are said to be against Him. The two ideas seem to be different. Surely there is a difference between a want of decision and an adverse decision ; between being a faint-hearted or even a cowardly soldier on the one side, and being positively enrolled and enlisted on the other? Yes, there is a difference ; we do not deny it. But what the text impresses upon us is this, that, for many practical purposes, and so far as the final personal issue is concerned, the faint-hearted, cowardly, treacherous soldier of Christ is rather an enemy to Him than a friend. (*Dean Vaughan.*) *Spiritual waste and wealth:—* In spiritual affairs we find we are subject to this condition in respect to one Supreme Spirit—that if we are not serving Him we are wronging Him ; if we are not gathering with Him—gathering wisdom and strength and purity and greater capacity for good and other "fruit unto everlasting life"—then we are wasting what belongs to Him. We are in a necessary stewardship, and this is one of its laws. The law may look exacting in the statement, but it is glorious in its operation. Neutrality, not only in the posture of our affections, but in the use of our active powers, is impossible. Not far from each of the great scenes of our Saviour's ministry there was a third party, taking no apparent share in the transaction. Those that sided openly with Him and publicly confessed their loyalty, on the one hand, and those that expressly opposed Him, on the other, became, of course, conspicuous in the conflicts that sprang up about Him. By their direct opposition to each other, Apostles and Pharisees, the family at Bethany and the Council at Jerusalem, John and Judas, Zaccheus and Herod, Joseph of Arimathea and Pilate, immediately suggest to us two distinct classes of people—the friends and the enemies of the Son of God. Decided convictions always throw men into definite positions. Near by, however, you might always find another class, more numerous, probably, than either of them. They are not brought forward into notice, because no real interest or choice brought them visibly into the struggle that was going on. Other things absorbed their attention. He speaks to that large third class among you to-day. If there is any question about that position—as to its rightfulness, or its safety, or where those that are trying to hold it really belong—does He not settle that question by the text? "He that gathereth not with Me scattereth." It is remarkable, in all the gospel, how invariable and how clear Christ makes this doctrine of absolute and necessary separation. There is *no* third party after all. There is no place for one. Non-profession does not make non-allegiance or neutrality. It makes allegiance to the enemy. It makes disloyalty. "He that is not with Me is against Me." The next truth to be remembered is our dangerous liability to be deceived just at that point—*i.e.*, to reckon as harmless or safe courses of life that are really anti-Christian. If there are any, here or elsewhere, who think they do enough because they are not positive opponents, mockers, or infidels ; who think that, because they never persecute, or revile, or take a traitor's silver, or meet to plot with scribes and Pharisees for Herod, therefore they are not secretly fighting against their eternal King, Christ here assigns them their place with terrible distinctness. Unlike the politic leaders of earthly kingdoms, He fearlessly casts this middle party from Him—that it may thereby become truly His. All are scatterers that are not gatherers with Him. There is a striking record, in the Book of Numbers, of a prophet who tried, in perilous days, to be on neither side, and paltered with a double tongue between the true God and His enemies ; but at last the issue between the two armies could be no longer evaded, and, after the battle, the body of this compromising neutral, Balaam, was found on the enemy's side, where it fell fighting against the Lord. It is in this sense that Christ comes to put men and families of men "at variance"—with one another—a strange thing to be written of Him. It is not for division's sake, but only that truth may not be confounded with a lie, darkness be called light, and the very foundations of all honour guilt. There can be no lasting harmony, no healthy peace, but in Him in whom all things in their unity consist. All is wasted then that is not done with a heart of love and that toward God ; all time that is not spent for Him—these days of busy labour in trades and professions ; these unsatisfying contortions of effort to be a little richer, or a little more noticed, or to climb one round more on the ladder that you will slip from the instant death touches your fingers ; these plans, schemes, travels, bargains, buildings—they look like gathering, but they are only scattering, unless in the midst of them all your character is daily built up, a spiritual house, Jesus Christ Himself being the chief corner-stone. Gather with Him and all the parts of your life which are yet alien or infirm He will steadily draw into the unity of His own body, making it strong and pure and immortal, knit together and making increase by the edifying of His love. (*Bishop F. D. Huntington.*) *Neutrality impossible in religion :*—" You don't mean to call me an enemy of religion, do you ? " said a farmer to a gentleman who was urging him to become a friend of Christ. "'He that is not for Me is against Me,' are Christ's words. Are they not decisive of your question ? " replied the gentleman. " But I am friendly to religion," rejoined the farmer. "Friendly ! How? You do not revile Christ, I know; but do you serve Him ? Do you avow yourself His disciple ? Are you His disciple ? Do you by your life and speech declare that faith in Christ is necessary to salvation ? " " I do not profess faith in Christ, sir," said the farmer ; " and, of course, I can- not consistently urge that faith on others." " Then, you see," replied the gentle- man, " that your influence is against the acceptance of Christ by others. Its voice is : 'Personal faith in Christ is not a very important matter ; if it were, I should seek it.'" The farmer was silenced. He felt that his friend was right. He saw that not to be on Christ's side was to be against Him ; not to be marching with His pilgrims to heaven was to be marching with His enemies to hell. He was right. There was no middle course.   *Impossible neutrality :*—Pythagoras, being asked what he was, answered that if Hiero were ever at the Olympian games, he knew the manner—that some came to try their fortune for the prizes, and some came as merchants to utter their commodities, and some came to make good cheer and meet their friends, and some came to look on ; and that he was one of them that came to look on. But men must know that, in this theatre of man's life, it is reserved only for God and the angels to be lookers-on. (*Lord Bacon.*)

Vers. 24–26. **When the unclean spirit is gone out.**—*The danger of losing convic- tions of conscience :*—I. The miserable condition of an impenitent sinner, before he is awakened to a serious conviction of his guilt. II. Convictions of sin con- stitute, in the eye of God, an important change in the state of man. III. We are here taught, that beings absolutely sinful find neither rest nor enjoy- ment but in doing evil. Wickedness is a spirit absolutely solitary. All its social character, all its sympathy, is nothing but the disposition which unites banditti in the fell purpose of plundering, pollution, and murder. With others it joins, solely because it cannot accomplish its foul ends alone. Even with these it has no union of heart, no fellow-feeling, no real sociality. It attracts nothing and nobody. Every thing it repels. Hell with all its millions is a perfect solitude to each of its inhabi- tants. IV. Persons under conviction are always in danger of falling anew into hardness of heart. V. The soul, from which convictions of sin have been finally banished, is more perfectly prepared to become the seat of absolute wickedness than before these convictions began. VI. The soul, from which con- victions are finally banished, becomes far more sinful than before its convic- tions began. Seven is here put for an indefinite number, and may be considered as standing for many. At the least, it denotes a greater number than one, and, in proportion, a greater series of temptations and dangers. These seven are also uni- versally more wicked than the original tenant of this impure habitation, more abso- lutely possessed of the fiendlike character than himself. From each, his danger is of course greater ; from all, how great, how dreadful ! Lessons : I. The immeasur- able importance of cherishing in the heart convictions of sin. II. We learn from these observations the high interest which persons in this situation have in being directed in their duty by sound wisdom. III. We also learn from this parable the miserable situation of unawakened sinners. (*T. Dwight, D.D.*)   *Description and danger of conviction when not followed by conversion :*—I. The first is the state of a man when the unclean spirit is gone out of him. All unconverted men are spiritually the slaves of Satan. II. "When the unclean spirit is gone out of a man, he walketh through dry places, seeking rest : and finding none, he saith, I will return unto my house whence I came out : and when he cometh, he findeth it swept and garnished." 1. Amidst all his convictions he has had no sense of the evil of sin. He has never seen it in its true colours, nor hated it for its evil nature. He has felt his misery ; but he has never heartily confessed his guilt. 2. He has given a farther proof that this is still the state of his heart, by the reliance which he has placed on his own strength and goodness. He has resolved, indeed, to forsake all sin ; but he has made this resolution, trusting entirely to his own strength. He has had no fear of his own heart, nor any notion of its utter depravity. It is plain that his heart remains unchanged ; the same impure habitation which it has always been. III. "Then taketh he unto him seven other spirits more wicked than himself, and they enter in and dwell there." These words describe the sinner's awful relapse under the power of Satan. Long-indulged habits call loudly for their usual gratifications. Unmortified lusts revive and renew their strength. Old companions in sin allure. IV. "The last state of that man is worse than the first." It is worse in three respects. 1. His guilt is greater. He has now more to answer for than he before had. He does not now sin in ignorance, as perhaps, he once did. 2. His misery will be greater. This consequence must naturally follow. They whose guilt is greater will justly receive a greater damnation. 3. His danger is greater. He may still be converted and find mercy. By turning to God in true faith and repentance, he may even yet be delivered from guilt and misery. But conversion is now less likely to take place than it formerly was. While you resist not conviction, beware of resting in it. You will not be saved by a conviction of your sins, but by a conversion from them. Mistake not one of these things for the other. (*E. Cooper.*) **The last state of that man is worse than the first.**—*On relapsing into sin :*—I. RELAPSING INTO SIN IS THE GREATEST INGRATITUDE. 1. It is the work of grace only, if our Lord, after we have committed a sin, receives us back into His house. 2. What should you say of the prodigal son if, shortly after the banquet, he had left his father's house again, thrown away the ring and shoes, and trodden under foot the best robe : if he had abused the presents of his father by new offences ? 3. As the physician is filled with scorn of a sick person, whom he had healed with great care, and who by disobedience had plunged himself into peril of death again : so the Heavenly Physician will depart from a soul which repeatedly commits the same sins again. II. RELAPSING INTO SIN IS THE GREATEST FOLLY. 1. Sin is like a disease which becomes more perilous by repeated attacks. 2. In proportion as the power of sin increases, the strength of man's will decreases. 3. The time for conversion is getting shorter and shorter. III. RELAPSE IS THE FORE-RUNNER OF ETERNAL PERDITION. Conversion depends partly on the good-will of the sinner, and partly on the grace of God. We have seen that the strength of will relaxes with every fresh sin, and therefore the relapsed cannot rely on it. And the greatest energy alone cannot perform the work of conversion. Without a full measure of grace the conversion of the relapsed is impossible. 1. It is to be feared that the ordinary graces will produce no effect upon him. God by His grace shows to the sinner the deformity of sin, terrifies him by its consequences and punishment, and endeavours to gain his affections by pointing out to him the infiniteness of the Divine charity. But if the man continually relapses into his old sins, are these motives likely to make a lasting impression on him ? 2. Or, are we entitled to expect from God extraordinary graces for the relapsing sinner ? Should God show greater mercy towards us, because we have been so ungrateful to Him ? When we continually tear open old wounds, think you the Heavenly Physician of our souls will prepare us a stronger remedy ? (*Bishop Ehrler.*) *The return of the evil spirit :*—A young man enters upon life in all the confidence of youth, and passion, and strength. He is borne along by the currents of the world, and he soon drinks deep into its polluted joy. First a spirit of gaiety, and then a spirit of uncleanness takes possession of his heart—and his soul, for awhile, is spell-bound by the fascination of the world, and he wraps himself in his forbidden pleasures. Presently it pleases God to arrest that young man. He is laid on a bed of sickness, and he eats of his own bitter sowing. He is brought very low in shame, and wretchedness, and remorse—he loathes his former courses—he turns from them with disgust—and he makes his resolutions, and he records his vows—the spirit that is in him is cast out, and the young man rises from his trouble a reformed character. Meanwhile, where is the evil spirit? Is he gone? For a little time he appears to let him alone ; but all the while he is but preparing himself for another temptation and a fiercer assault. He comes and he sees that young man abhorring the sins of his youth ; but uninfluenced by grace—untouched by the love of God ; he sees his heart silent in prayer, and his mind is still pointing to the world. And the evil spirit brings to bear upon that man a new and more powerful seduction. He is no longer to him the tempter to some sinful gratification ; but he enters into him a spirit of mercenary calculation—he becomes a man cold, secular, aspiring. Money, politics, greatness, argument, scepticism, occupy his mind—he is now for establishment and reputation—he grasps and he holds the world—he is not immoral, he is a formalist—he is not a profligate, he is covetous, Christless—his heart is further off from God than ever it was—he has not commenced anew—he feels no sins—he is a bitter censor of other men—he grows prejudiced—he is a practical infidel—he is sealed in his self-confidences—"and the last state of that man is worse than the first." (*J. Vaughan, M.A.*) *The seven-fold re-inforcement :*—It is not as the invaders of a country or besiegers of a city, that the evil spirit, with his sevenfold re-inforcement, rises up before the mind's eye in terrific grandeur. It is when we see him knocking at the solitary door from which he was once driven in disgrace and anguish. The scene, though an impressive one, is easily called up. A lonely dwelling on the margin of a wilderness, cheerfully lighted as the night approaches, carefully swept and garnished, and apparently the home of plenty, peace, and comfort. The winds that sweep across the desert pass it by unheeded. But, as the darkness thickens, something more than wind approaches from that quarter. What are the shadowy forms that seem to come forth from the dry places of the wilderness, and stealthily draw near the dwelling? One of the number guides the rest, and now they reach the threshold. Hark! he knocks; but only to assure himself that there is no resistance. Through the open door we catch a glimpse of the interior, swept and garnished—swept and garnished; but for whose use?—its rightful owner? Alas! no; for he is absent; and already has that happy home begun to ring with fiendish laughter, and to glare with hellish flames; and if the weal or woe of any man be centred in it, the last state of that man is worse than the first. Do you look upon this as a mere fancy scene? Alas! my hearers, just such fancy scenes are passing every day within you or around you, rendered only more terrific by the absence of all sensible indications, just as we shrink with a peculiar dread from unseen dangers if considered real, and are less affected by the destruction that wastes at noon-day, than by the pestilence that walks in darkness. Come with me and let me show you one or two examples of familiar spiritual changes which, if not the work of evil spirits, may at least be aptly represented by the images presented in the text and context. To the eye of memory or imagination there rises up the form of one who was the slave of a particular iniquity, which gave complexion to his character and life. It was perhaps an open and notorious vice, which directly lowered him in public estimation. Or it may have been a secret and insidious habit long successfully concealed or never generally known. But its effects were seen. Even those who were strangers to his habits could perceive that there was something wrong, and they suspected and distrusted him. He felt it, and in desperation waxed worse and worse. But in the course of providence a change takes place. Without any real change of principle or heart, he finds that his besetting sin is ruining his health, his reputation, or his fortune. "Strong" as the power of temptation, appetite, and habit is, some form of selfishness is "stronger" still. The man reforms. The change is recognized at once. He is another man. After the first painful acts of self-denial, the change appears delightful to himself. He seems once more to walk erect. A new direction has been given to his hopes and his desires, and, like Saul, he rejoices that the evil spirit has departed from him. At first he is afraid of its return, and keeps strict watch against the inroads of the enemy. By degrees he grows secure, and his vigils are relaxed. The temptation presents itself in some form, so contemptible and little to be feared, that he would blush not to encounter it. He does encounter it. He fights it. He appears to triumph for a moment, but is ultimately overcome. The next victory is easier. The next is easier still. He tries to recall the feelings which preceded and produced his reformation; but the spell is over. He knows that they have once proved ineffectual to save him, and he trusts in them no longer. Even the checks which once controlled him in his former course of sin are now relaxed; he is tired of opposition, and seeks refuge from his self-contempt in desperate indulgence. If you ask the evil spirit which at first has possession, what is thy name? you may receive for answer, drunkenness, or avarice, or lust. But ask the same after the relapse, and the response must be, My name is legion. Have you not seen in real life this terrible exchange of one besetting sin for several? Have you not known men, who once seemed vulnerable only at a single point, begin to appear vulnerable, as it were, at all points, perhaps with the exception of the one first mentioned? Now, when this is the case, besides the power exerted by each appetite and passion on the soul distinctly, there is a debasing and debilitating influence arising from the conflict which exists between them. Let the reformed libertine become at once ambitious, avaricious, and revengeful, and let these hungry serpents gnaw his soul, and it will soon be seen by others, if not felt by the miserable victim, that the evil spirit which had left him for a season has returned with seven others worse than himself; and as we see them in imagination enter the dwelling swept and garnished for their use, we may read, inscribed above the portal that shuts after them, "The last state of that man is worse than the first." (*J. A. Alexander, D.D.*) *The tendency of sin to increase if once admitted:*—These little sins, if they be so, will make way for greater. Little wedges open the way in the most knotty wood for bigger. As thieves, when they go to rob a house, if they cannot force open the doors, or break through the walls, let in a little boy at the window, who unbolts and unlocks the door, and so lets in the whole rabble ; thus the devil, when men startle at greater sins, and by them he hath no hopes to get possession of their souls, he puts them upon those sins which they think little, and by these insensibly enters ; for they, once admitted, open the doors of the eyes, of the ears, and of the heart too, whereby the whole legion enter, and rule and domineer in their souls to their ruin. Men do not, indeed they cannot, imagine the woeful consequences of neglecting their watch against the least sin. How many who have been so modest and maidenly at first, that they would not so much as give a lascivious person the hearing when he hath spoken wantonly ; yet by giving way to their own foolish thoughts, have at last prostituted themselves to their pleasure without any shame. Sinners increase to more ungodliness ; when they once venture down hill, they know not where nor when to stop. Workmen bore holes with little wimbles, which make way for the driving of great nails. When Pompey, saith Plutarch, could not prevail with a city to billet his army, he yet persuaded them to take in a few weak, maimed soldiers; but those soon recovered strength, and let in the whole army, to command and govern the city. Thus Satan, by sins of infirmity, prevails at length for sins of presumption. Great storms arise out of little gusts ; and clouds no bigger than the palm of a man's hand come in time to cover the whole heavens. The greatest river is fed with drops, and the biggest mountain made up of atoms. As Sylla said, when in his proscription time, that he slew so many, one pleaded for the life of Cæsar, *In uno Cæsare multi Marii :* " In one little youth, many old subtle men," so in one little sin, there may be many great ones. When one evil spirit hath got lodging in the heart, he prepares it, and makes room for seven more wicked and worse than himself. (*G. Swinnock.*)

Vers. 27, 28. **Blessed are they that hear the Word of God, and keep it.**—*Blessedness from the Divine point of view :*—I. THE WOMAN'S EXCLAMATION. 1. Implying, in an indirect yet very strong manner, the blessedness of our Lord Himself ; the idea being that from Him a blessedness was reflected on His mother. In this there is nothing but what is altogether commendable and deserving of imitation. 2. The exclamation was directly and chiefly intended to proclaim the blessedness of our Lord's mother. Neither is it, in this sense, to be condemned. Jesus Himself does not deny, and we ought not to question its truth. The happiness of parents is very much involved in the conduct and history of their children. The relation is most intimate and most tender. Their offspring are so closely entwined round their heart, as to occasion them, either most acute anguish, or most exquisite pleasure. But, if it is thus a general truth that parents are happy in the happiness of their children, how great must have been the happiness of such a woman as the Virgin Mary, in having such a son as Jesus Christ ! Vast indeed were the blessing and honour which were hers! And, as Mary was blessed in bringing forth such a son at first, so she was blessed in His future character and exploits. She was blessed in His dutiful conduct as a son: for " He went down to Nazareth, and was subject " unto His parents. She was blessed in the progressive improvement of His human nature, for, " Jesus increased in wisdom and stature, and in favour with God and man." She was blessed in the whole tenor of His holy life, as He was perfectly free from all taint of sin, and exhibited a pattern of every grace. She was blessed in hearing many of His delightful discourses, as she frequently attended His ministrations, and formed one of the many hearers who " bore Him witness, and wondered at the gracious words which proceeded out of His mouth." She was blessed in seeing many of the wonderful works which He performed : for on many other occasions of this kind it might have been said, as it was said on that at Cana in Galilee, that "the mother of Jesus was there." She was blessed in His glorious resurrection and ascension, when He rose a conqueror over death and hell, and when He was taken up into heaven, and sat down on the right hand of the Majesty on high, to wait till all His enemies be made His footstool. There she still continues to be blessed in contemplating His blessedness, and in hearing the blessings which are multiplied on His name. II. OUR LORD'S AMENDMENT ON THE WOMAN'S EXCLAMATION. He does not contradict what the pious woman had said. He only modifies and explains it, and makes an addition to it. Now, His amendment on the woman's words teaches us—1. That the happiness of Mary herself consisted rather in her being a believer in Christ, than in her being the mother of Christ. 2. That all true believers, as such, are more blessed than Christ's mother, as such. Was she honoured in her maternal relation to Him?—they are all connected with Him by a still closer relation, even by that union in consequence of which He and they are said to be one. They are blessed with light, pardon, sanctification, comfort, and every present privilege; and all these are sure pledges of the everlasting blessedness of heaven. There is still another idea included in this amendment of our Lord's; for, in its most extended meaning, it states a comparison, not only between the advantage of true religion, and that of having been the mother of Jesus, but also between the advantage of true religion and all other advantages whatever. We are here taught, then—3. That those who are believers, are more blessed on that account than on any other. Are you rich? or, at least, in easy circumstances?—then it is true that you may be, in some degree, happy in freedom from anxiety about your temporal wants, and in the moderate enjoyment of earthly good: but what are such possessions in comparison of your spiritual treasures, the unsearchable riches of Christ? "All things are yours." Other possessions are uncertain and temporary: but yours are the better, the "durable riches"; yours is the "inheritance incorruptible, undefiled, that fadeth not away." Are you learned in human knowledge?—so far well, for therein you may find much rational enjoyment. But rather blessed are you because you are taught of God in the wisdom which is from above, and instructed to know the Holy Scriptures, which have proved sufficient to make you wise unto salvation, through faith which is in Christ Jesus. (*Jas. Foote, M.A.*) *Believers as blessed as the Blessed Virgin:*—I. A BLESSEDNESS WHICH IS NOT TO BE DENIED. The Virgin Mother was blessed among women. To God alone we must render worship; but the memory of this saintly woman is to be revered. The angel made no mistake when he said, "Hail, thou that art highly favoured: blessed art thou among women." Nor was she in error when she said, "From henceforth all generations shall call me blessed." We call her blessed most heartily, for so she was. 1. The blessing which she received had been the desire of ages. 2. When at last the boon was bestowed upon the humble virgin of Nazareth, who was of the house of David, it came as a great favour. We must not, then, treat it as a light thing. The Saviour's "yea" was emphatic when the woman spake of His mother as highly blessed. 3. She herself received this honour as a great blessing. It was no vain thing to her to have charge of the infancy of our Lord. She felt it to be great blessedness to be placed in such a relation to the holy child Jesus. 4. She was, she must have been, blessed among women, and this woman who spake of her as such made no mistake; for think what blessings have come to all the world through the Virgin's wondrous child. "In Him shall all the nations of the earth be blessed." If all generations call Mary blessed, it is only because she brought into the world one who is a blessing to us all. And it was, it must have been, a great blessedness to Mary's heart to think that "that holy thing" which was born of her was the channel of such blessedness to all mankind. 5. I must, however, remind you that whatever the blessedness which this holy woman derived from being the mother of our Saviour's humanity, she needed it all, for she was called to a great fight of affliction because of it. II. That brings us to our second head: To hear the Word of God and keep it is A BLESSING PREFERABLE to having been the mother of our Lord. 1. We are sure of this, because in the weighing of the blessings the blessed Master of Beatitudes holds the balances. Jesus Himself adjusts the scales of blessedness. He who began His ministry with the word "Blessed," so often repeated, knows best which blessing is the best. 2. Happily this preference so truly given by the Master puts the highest blessedness within the reach of all of us who are here this morning. We are at this moment in a position to "hear the Word of God, and keep it." If grace be given, there are only these two steps to blessedness. 3. I now ask you to notice that this preferable blessing is found in a very simple manner. "Blessed are they that hear the Word of God, and keep it." The process is stripped of all ambiguity or mystery; there is nothing about it that is hard or difficult: "Hear the word, and keep it"—that is all." III. So now we close by considering this as A BLESSEDNESS TO BE AT ONCE ENJOYED. I breathe to heaven this earnest prayer, that we may now enter into this blessedness. Let us see if we cannot sit still in our seats for a while, and drink in this wine on the lees well refined. 1. This blessedness belongs to the present. Blessed are they that are hearing the Word of God, and keeping it. It is not a remote, but an immediate blessedness. While you are hearing and keeping God's Word you are then blessed. The blessedness is for

this world, and for you. " But I am so cast down." Yes, but you are blessed!
" Alas! I bear such a burden of afflictions." Yes, but you are blessed. " Alas!
I have not known a good time of late." No, but you are blessed! Your blessedness does not depend upon your fancies and feelings. If you hear the Word of God,
and keep it, you are at this moment blessed. Faith finds a present blessedness in
the Word of God, which she hears and keeps. 2. This blessedness lies, in a great
measure, in the very act of hearing and keeping God's Word. 3. This blessing is
not dependent upon outward circumstances. If you hear God's Word, and keep it,
you may be very ill, and yet in spirit you will be well; you may be very feeble, and
yet in spirit you will be strong; you may be dying, and yet you shall not die, for
he that heareth the Word of God shall never see death. In hearkening to the Lord
you have reached a region from which you look down upon the dust and smoke of
time and sense. (*C. H. Spurgeon.*) *Blessedness :*—I. THE WOMAN'S EXCLAMA-
TION. We may notice the cause of her exclamation, the speaking of Jesus. His
word, though powerful, is not a hurricane, but harmony. II. ON WHAT HER
ADMIRATION TURNED—" Jesus." The cold-hearted Pharisee might have felt disposed
to exclaim, " What irregularity! What a breach of order!" Jesus, however, was
in no danger of being disconcerted in His discourse from any casual interruption,
but was at all times fully at liberty to take advantage of every passing event. III.
OUR LORD'S REPLY. " Rather blessed are they that hear the Word," &c. This
reply naturally includes these particulars—1. His admission of the truth she
declared. 2. His assertion—" Blessed are they that hear the Word, and keep it."
3. The description—They that keep it. Unfortunately, many content themselves
with hearing (Ezek. xxx. 30, 32). I conclude—1. To hear the Word of God is not to
keep it. Many seem to believe religion consists in hearing. 2. Hearing is only instrumental to salvation. 3. The promise is not made to hearing, but to doing. Hear,
and your souls live. Be not a hearer, but a doer, otherwise—4. The blessing will prove
a curse. (*W. Jay.*) *The blessing of those who hear and keep the Word of God :—*
I. THE NECESSITY OF KNOWING THE WORD OF GOD. One great cause to which our
falling so frequently into sin may be ascribed is, a want of attention to the duties
incumbent upon us. Now it is evident that if we were to make it our daily
practice to meditate upon the Word of God, we should have our duty continually
before us. We should have the promises and the threatenings of the Almighty
ever before our eyes: this would necessarily produce such an impression upon our
hearts, as to make us fear and dread all iniquity, and to turn from the sins to
which we are naturally inclined, and most strongly addicted. II. HOW THE KNOW-
LEDGE OF THE WORD OF GOD, so necessary to our salvation, IS TO BE ACQUIRED. The
two chief means for the attainment of Divine knowledge are the reading of God's
holy Word, and the hearing of it preached. The sacred Scriptures are the great
means of converting sinners, and of building up saints in their holy faith. History
is full of conversions which the reading and hearing of God's Word have occasioned.
That eminent father of the Church, Augustine, tells us that he owed his conversion
to the reading of St. Paul's Epistle to the Romans, xiii. 11. Others have been
converted from the hearing and the reading of these words: " Repent ye, for
the kingdom of heaven is at hand." " In the beginning was the word." Another
in reading the Acts of the Apostles; and another from these words of St. Paul to
Timothy: " This is a faithful saying, and worthy of all acceptation, that Christ
Jesus came into the world to save sinners." If such be their mighty and magnificent effects, how necessary to be known, and studied, and understood of men!
Every part of Scripture, as being of Divine inspiration, ought to be thoroughly
studied, and inwardly digested; though, doubtless, there are some books and
chapters which claim our meditations, and require our studious perusal, more than
others. And then, in order that we may reap real benefit and advantage from the
perusal of the sacred Oracles, it is necessary that, like the Ethiopian eunuch, we
should read them with care and application, as containing the true knowledge of
salvation. III. THAT THE READING AND HEARING OF THE WORD OF GOD ARE NOT
SUFFICIENT FOR SALVATION, UNLESS IT BE REDUCED TO PRACTICE, is evident from these
words of our Lord Jesus Christ Himself (Matt. vii. 24). IV. THE BLESSEDNESS
AND HAPPINESS WHICH ATTEND THOSE WHO HEAR THE WORD OF GOD AND KEEP IT. The
blessedness of a true believer—of a faithful servant of Christ, is even greater than
that of the mother of the Saviour. How noble—how glorious a privilege is this!
In hearing and meditating upon the Word of God, believers experience a pleasure
and a satisfaction of which the men of the world can form no estimate, and entertain no idea whatsoever. (*J. Rudge, D.D.*) *The blessedness of obedience :—*I.

GOD INTENDS HIS WORD TO BLESS MAN. It is sent for this purpose. Truth is God's greatest boon to man. II. IF THIS BE SO, THEN THE BLESSING COMES OBVIOUSLY ENOUGH BY HEARING. The most natural way of conveying the truth is by speech. It is the earliest, the readiest, perhaps it shall be the latest. In many senses it will ever be the best. In simple, earnest speech you get all the requisites, truth itself in its appositeness, punctuation, emphasis, and, above all, the living soul transmitted by the living voice. III. EVEN WHEN THE WORD IS PURE, AND THE PREACHER A TRUE MAN, PREACHER AND TRUTH ARE NOT ENOUGH. TO HAVE THE BLESSING THERE MUST BE THE INWARD HEARING AS WELL AS THE OUTWARD. Nothing will serve but the actual contact of truth with the spiritual intelligence, the cordial reception of the quickening Word, and its verification in the stillness of the soul's depths. The Spirit quickeneth the Word by quickening the man, and, again, the man by the Word. Christ's words let in the Spirit to listening hearts, for they were spirit and life. IV. THE TRUTH MUST BE KEPT IN ORDER TO THE BLESSING. It must be kept, first, by spiritual means—by prayer, meditation, and constant endeavour of the soul to blend and assimilate the truth with itself, till they become, as it were, one. But nothing gives the truth a greater fixity in our nature and makes it ours so truly as embodying it in act and deed. It is at hand, it must be grasped; floating as sentiment and feeling, it must be secured, organized, converted into facts, and so into history. Truth is intended to be practised—it cannot otherwise pass into life. 1. When the heart has learned to endorse the truth, the outward doing is most natural and easy. 2. The nature that keeps the Word is blessed by being itself ennobled. As we learn to live by truth and for truth, we have sympathy with God. 3. And the blessing power of the truth thus heard and thus cherished is continuous. V. BUT WHAT ABOUT HEARING AND NOT KEEPING? One cannot conceive of anything sadder. For hearing prepares a man for a higher test. We go to be examined in our own class, and thence depart to our own place. And the most tragic of all earth's other tragedies appear to me necessarily to fall far short of this spiritual one. To have looked into the highest, and sunk to the lowest, to have had the noblest issues in our grasp, and to have preferred these miserable husks of self-indulgence and self-contentment! (*T. Islip*.) *A certain woman's commendation of Christ :*—These be the parts of my text; and of these in order. I. "Blessed is the womb that bare thee," &c., saith the woman. 1. And that which occasioned and moved her thus to lift up her voice was the power of Christ's works and words. Be not deceived—every good lesson should be unto you as a miracle to move you to give sentence for Christ against the Pharisees and all the enemies He hath; against the pride that despiseth Him, the luxury that defileth Him, the disobedience that trampleth Him under foot. Every good motion (for therein Christ speaketh to us) should beget a resolution; every resolution, a good work; every good work, a love of goodness; and the love of goodness should root and stablish and build us in the faith. 2. And so I pass from the motive and occasion to the person, who from what she saw and heard gave this free attestation. Truth doth not fail, though a Pharisee oppose it, but is of strength sufficient to make the weakest of its champions conqueror. For "the foolishness of God is wiser than men, and the weakness of God is stronger than men" (1 Cor. i. 25). Neither number nor sex hath so much power upon truth as to alter its complexion. And as it was no prejudice to the truth that she was but one, no more was it that she was a woman. For why might not a woman, whose eye was clear and single, see more in Christ than the proudest Pharisee who wore his phylactery the broadest? All is, not in the miracle, but in the eye, in the mind, which, being goggle or mis-set, or dimmed with malice or prejudice, beholdeth not things as they are, but, through false mediums, putteth upon them what shape it pleaseth, receiveth not the true and natural species they present, but vieweth them at home in itself as in a false glass, which returneth back by a deceitful reflection. And this is the reason why not only miracles, but doctrinal precepts also, find so different entertainment. Every man layeth hold on them and wresteth them to his own purpose, worketh them on his own anvil, and shapeth them to his own fancy and affections; as out of the same mass Phidias could make a goddess, and Lysippus a satyr. Prejudice will make a man persuade himself that is false which he cannot but know is most true. That which to a clear eye is a gross sin, and appeareth horror, to a corrupted mind may be as the beauty of holiness. The Pharisees saw it and the woman saw it : the one saw nothing but that which could not be seen, one devil casting out another; the other saw the finger and mighty power of God, and when she saw it, "she lifted up her voice, and said unto Him,

"Blessed is the womb that bare Thee, and the paps that Thou hast sucked." 3. And so we descend to that which we proposed in the third place, the vehemency and heat of her affection, which could not contain itself in her heart, but brake forth at her mouth. And herein we shall consider—(1) That she spake. (2) What she spake. "She lifted up her voice, and said unto Him, "Blessed is the womb that bare Thee, and the paps which Thou has sucked." (a) "Out of the abundance of the heart the mouth speaketh," saith our Saviour (Matt. xii. 34). "It evaporateth itself into the outward habit, breaks forth into voice, opens her shop and wares, that she may behold her own provision and riches abroad." The love of the truth tuneth the heart, and the heart the tongue. And this is the advantage that love hath of knowledge. Knowledge may be idle and unactive, but love is a restless thing, and will call up and employ every part of the body and every faculty of the soul to compass its end. Love is active, and will pace it on where knowledge doth but stand and gaze. Knowledge doth not always command our tongue; nay, many times we speak and act against our knowledge; but who speaks against that which he doth love? (b) Now, in the next place, what was it that begat her love but the admiration of Christ's person, His power, and His wisdom? She had heard of Moses and his miracles; but beholds a greater than Moses here. Application— 1. And, first, let us learn from this woman here to have Christ's wonderful works in remembrance, to look upon them with a steadfast and a fixed eye, that they may appear unto us in their full glory, and fill us with admiration. For admiration is a kind of voice of the soul. Behold, these are the wonderful things of Christ—to unite God and man, to tie them together by a new covenant, to raise dust and ashes to heaven: this is a great miracle indeed! 2. By her lifting up her voice, and blessing the womb that bare Christ, which was a kind of adoration (for admiration had not so shut up her devotion and love but that it was vocal and reverent), we are taught to magnify our Saviour with the tongue, and hand, and knee, and every member we have, as David speaketh. But I do but beat the air, and labour in vain. For now it is religion not to express it; and he is most devout who doth least show it. O when will this dumb devil be cast out? A strange thing it is that everything else, even our vices, should be loud and vocal, and religion should be the only thing that should want a tongue! that devotion should lie hid, and lurk and withdraw itself into the inward man! 3. Last of all: This woman's voice is yet lifted up, and calls upon us to lift up ours, even before the Pharisees. If our fear were not greater than our love, amongst these we should "lift up our voice like a trumpet," and put these monsters to shame, strike off their visor with noise, and bring in truth to tear off the veil of their hypocrisy. For, what! shall we not lift up our voice for truth but when she hath most voices on her side? Must truth be never published but in the times of peace? or must a song of praise be never chanted out but in a choir of angels? A Pharisee before us is a temptation, difficulty and danger are nothing else but a temptation, which is therefore laid in our way, to try if anything can sever us from the love of Christ and His truth. If we start back in silence, we have betrayed the truth to our fears, and left it to be trodden under foot by a Pharisee. He that can trifle with his God will at last blaspheme Him to His face. We have already handled the circumstantial parts of the text; we are now to treat of the substantial—the woman's speech and our Saviour's. 4. We begin with the woman's, "Blessed is the womb that bare Thee," &c. And that the mother of Christ was blessed we need not doubt. For we have not only the voice of this woman to prove it, but the voice of an angel, "Blessed art thou among women." "All generations shall call her blessed" (Luke i. 48). (1) Blessed, as the occasion of so much good. For when we see a clear and silver stream, we bless the fountain; and, for the glory and quickening power of the beams, some have made a god of the sun. Whatsoever presents itself unto us in beauty or excellency, doth not only take and delight us, but, in the midst of wonder, forceth our thoughts to look back to the coasts from whence it came. (2) Again: if it be a kind of curse to beget a wicked son, or, as Solomon did, "the foolishness of the people" (Ecclus. xlvii. 23). The historian observes that many famous men amongst the Romans either died childless, or left such children behind them that it had been better their name had quite been blotted out, and they had left no posterity. And speaking of Tully, who had a drunken and a sottish son, he adds, "It had been better for him to have had no child at all, than such an one." II. We come, next, to our Saviour's gentle corrective, "Yea rather." And this "Yea rather" comes in seasonably. For the eye is ready to be dazzled with a lesser good, if it be not diverted to a greater; as he will wonder at a star that never saw the sun. We stay many times and dwell with delight upon those truths which are of lesser alloy, and make not any approach towards that which is saving and necessary. 1. The philosopher will tell us that he that will compare two things together, must know them both. What a brightness hath honour to blind him that hath not tasted of the favour of God! What a paradise is carnal pleasure to him that a good conscience never feasted! What a substance is a ceremony to him that makes the precepts of the law but shadows! Therefore it is the method of wisdom itself to present them both unto us in their just and proper weight; not to deny what is true, but to take off our thoughts, and direct them to something better; that we may not dote so long on the one as to neglect and cast off the other. In my text the woman had discovered Christ's excellency; and Christ discovers to her His will, His Father's will, the doing of which will will unite her unto Him whom she thus admired, and make her one with Him, as He and His Father is one. "Blessed parents! yea, rather, Blessed thou, if thou hear My word and keep it." This is a timely grace, to lead her yet nearer to the kingdom of heaven; the lifting up of her voice was too weak to lift up those everlasting gates. This was a seasonable—"reprehension" shall I call it, or "direction"? 2. And now if we look into the Church, we shall find that most men stand in need of a "Yea rather"; who will magnify Christ and His mother too, but not do His will; will do what they ought to do, but leave that undone for which that which they do was ordained. "Blessed sacrament of the Lord's supper!" It is true; but, "Yea rather, Blessed are they that dwell in Christ." "Blessed profession of Christianity!" "Yea rather, Blessed are they that are Christ's." "Blessed cross!" The fathers call it so. "Yea rather, Blessed are they that have 'crucified their flesh with the affections and lusts.'" "Blessed church!" "Yea rather, Blessed are they who are members of Christ." "Blessed Reformation!" "Yea rather, Blessed are they that reform themselves." 3. This resolve of wisdom itself, as it doth cool and moderate our affections towards the outward and temporal favours and blessings of God, towards those of his right hand, and those of His left, so it doth intend and quicken them towards that which is blessedness indeed. It sets us up a glass, that "royal law" (James ii. 8), "that perfect law of liberty," which if we "look into, and continue in it, being not forgetful hearers, but doers of the work, we shall be blessed in it" (James i. 25). "Blessed are they that hear the Word of God," reacheth not home; and therefore there is a conjunction copulative to draw it closer, and link it with obedience, "Blessed are they that hear the Word of God, and keep it." For, first, God hath fitted us hereunto. For, can we imagine that He should thus build us up, and stamp His own image upon us, that we should be an habitation for owls and satyrs, for wild and brutish imaginations? that He did give us understandings to find out an art of pleasure, a method and craft of enjoying that which is but for a season? Was the soul made immortal for that which passeth away as a shadow, and is no more? Indeed, faith, in respect of the remoteness of the object, and its elevation above the ken of nature, may seem a hard lesson, yet in the soul there is a capacity to receive it; and if the other condition, of obedience and doing God's will, did not lie heavy upon the flesh, the more brutish part, we should be readier scholars in our creed than we are. Secondly. As the precepts of Christ are proportioned to the soul, so being embraced they fill it with light and joy, and give it a taste of the world to come. For as Christ's "yoke is easy," but not till it is put on; so His precepts are not delightful till they are kept. Aristotle's happiness in his books is but an idea, and heaven itself is no more to us till we enjoy it. The precepts of Christ in the letter may please the understanding part, which is always well-affected and inclinable to that which is apparently true; but till the will have set the feet and hands at liberty, even that which we approve we distaste, and that which we call "honey" is to us as bitter as gall. Contemplation may delight us for a time and bring some content, but the perverseness of our will breeds that worm which will soon eat it up. It is but a poor happiness to think and speak well of happiness, as from a mount to behold that Canaan which we cannot enjoy. A thought hath not strength and wing enough to carry us to bliss. But when the will is subdued and made obedient to the truth, then God's precepts, which are "from heaven, heavenly," fill the soul with a joy of the same nature, not gross and earthy, but refined and spiritual; a joy that is the pledge and the earnest, as the apostle calls it, of that which is to come. (A. Farindon, D.D.) The incarnation:—For, first, she knew at large that it was a blessed thing to be an instrument or conveyance of any great good unto others. "Blessed above women shall Jael the wife of Heber be, blessed shall she be above women in the tent" (Judg. v. 24). She had done her part to work deliverance for Israel. A cistern that contains the waters poured into it is much inferior to a fountain that sends them forth. It is nothing so laudable to be wrought upon, as to work that which is honourable. Even the parents that have enriched the world with such as are ornaments unto it, benediction reflects upon them for it, because they are conduit pipes of public felicity. Yet all those that have made others happy by their gifts and qualities had been for ever unhappy themselves if the child that was born this day had not sucked the breasts of a virgin. O happy parent! whose womb contained all the treasure that maintains the whole earth. Somewhat she collineated at this meaning that said unto our Saviour, "Blessed," &c. And each parent partakes in this reason, that it is joy and honour to them to have a renowned Son. All fruitfulness is to be congratulated, but hers especially—"Blessed is the womb," &c. I make no scruple to affirm it, that this was the very thought and fancy of the woman that uttered these words, that the mother was most honoured, full of fame and glory, who had a Son that spake so divinely, and wrought such heavenly miracles. It is a great recompense which God gives to careful parents upon earth when their offspring live soberly and temperately to be their comfort and honour. The fear of the Lord which is instilled into children from their infancy is not only the children's, but even the parents' happiness. The rare endowments that appeared in Christ made a certain woman here cast the praise of it upon the mother, "Blessed," &c. And thus far in the literal sense, as far as flesh and blood could reveal unto her; but if she could have seen into the Scriptures, as the Holy Spirit hath enabled us to see into them, there are other grounds of more evangelical observation. And first let it be noted, that the blessedness which is attributed to the womb that bore our Saviour redounds to all the members of His mystical body. Even as upon that saying of our Saviour to St. Peter, "Blessed art thou," &c. (Matt. xvi.). The eternal Father did more for us when He made Him flesh than when He made the heaven and the earth beside; without His incarnation the earth had been our curse, all the elements our plague, the heaven above our envy, and the hell beneath our portion for ever. One man in a family having a fortunate advancement makes his whole blood and kindred fortunate with him; how much more shall Christ make all mankind happy being made one of us. He is come near unto us all by that nature which He assumed of ours; and He hath redeemed us all by that glorious Deity which was ever His own. Finally, there was a concurrency of all sorts of blessedness in this most mysterious incarnation. II. I have done with the first general part of the text, the acclamation, both as a certain woman apprehended the words in her natural understanding, and in that prophetical sense which was above her understanding. Now it will be most material to observe how the Master of all wisdom corrected and refined it, "Yea rather, blessed," &c. O sacred Virgin, much more happy in entertaining the faith of Christ than in conceiving the flesh of Christ. I must not (and if I would I have no time) set forth before you what a fecundity of error there is in man's heart about the notion of blessedness. Our Saviour confines our straggling imaginations to this rule, that no good thing of a subordinate condition can style a man happy; it is a title to be given to that immense communication of good, when the soul shall enjoy the fulness of Him that filleth all in all. And this is tried by two particulars—First, if we treasure up the precious things of God in our ear, then if we transmit them to a more inward and a safer place, and treasure them up in our heart. So that the understanding of the law of God consists not in knowledge and speculation, but in practice and execution. We must be servants as well as disciples. (*Bishop Hacket.*) *Keeping the Word of God:*—The Rev. Mr. Erskine mentions a fact which may afford a very useful hint to every hearer of the gospel. A person who had been to public worship, having returned home perhaps somewhat sooner than usual, was asked by another member of the family who had not been there, "Is all done?" "No," replied he, "all is *said*, but all is not *done!*" How little is commonly done of all that is heard! "Blessed are they that hear the Word of God and keep it."

Vers. 29, 30. **The sign of Jonas the prophet.**—*The sign of the prophet Jonas:*—There is a peculiarity here which you ought carefully to consider. A sign was asked by an evil generation, that if Jesus were truly the Christ, they might receive Him as their King, and give Him their allegiance; but the sign which is proffered, even the sign of the Resurrection, presupposed the perpetration of that crime, the prevention of which was the great object for which the sign was solicited. A sign,

in short, is asked, which would prevent the rejection of Christ; a sign is propos
which would be no sign at all until He had been rejected. The Jews must crucify
the Christ in order to their obtaining the sign; whereas, they wanted the sign in
order that they might be withheld from the crucifixion. Let us look into this
matter. If, after all, an additional sign were to be given, why was such a sign
selected as could have no existence until the crime had been perpetrated which it
was the object of a sign to prevent? To this we reply, that it was not our Lord's
object to prevent the Jews from crucifying Him; but it was His object to leave
them inexcusable in so doing; and therefore did He ply them with miracles which
were fitted to convince all who had understanding, and with discourses which were
adapted to move all who had hearts. He gave proof enough of the justice of His
pretensions, for it was proof which prevailed to the bringing many to His side;
but when asked to carry proof to that extreme point where it becomes absolutely
irresistible, to crowd the landscape or the firmament with signs which should leave
the beholders no option, but compel them to receive Him as Messiah, why, He was
then solicited to a course not only inconsistent with the free agency of man, but
counter to the work which had brought Him down as a sojourner to earth. And
why marvel that Christ should have withheld that additional evidence which was
not necessary to make His countrymen inexcusable, and which would directly have
interfered with the completion of the scheme of redemption? "Yes," you may
say, "but the question is not why Christ should have refused all additional signs;
the answer to this is comparatively easy; but why, in consenting to give another
sign, He should have selected just that one, the sign of a resurrection, which must
necessarily have been ineffectual in withholding the Jews from the greatest of
crimes, and which could not exist unless and until they had committed that
crime?" Does it not almost seem a mockery of the Pharisees, that when they
asked a sign which might enable them to receive Jesus as the Christ, they were
denied all but one, which they could only obtain by rejecting Him as the Christ?
Remember, however, that sufficient evidence had been already vouchsafed; so that
the Pharisees would have had no ground of complaint had the demand for further
signs been met by unqualified refusal. And you are, moreover, probably quite
wrong in speaking of the sign of the Resurrection as though it must necessarily
have been too late to have been of service to the Jews, because undoubtedly too
late to prevent His crucifixion. The crucifying Jesus did not fill up the measure
of the guilt of the Jews; they did not touch the unpardonable sin, for they did
not withstand the whole amount of evidence until they had refused to be convinced
by the resurrection of Jesus and the miracles which evidenced the diffusion of the
Spirit. It was indeed such a crime as had never been committed on the darkened
stage of this fallen creation, that of putting to death as a malefactor the Being
who went about doing good, and in whose actions there was the power as well as
the loving-kindness of God. Yet—and there is no fact more glorious in the whole
range of theology—yet the blood of the crucified made atonement for the crucifiers.
Men had not sinned beyond the reach of mercy when they uttered the cry, "Away
with Him, away with Him"; they had not blocked up against themselves the
escape-path for eternity, when they buffeted the Mediator, and circled His forehead
with thorns, and nailed Him to the cross, and reviled Him in His agonies. We
will not indeed say that the Jews occupied so advantageous a moral position after
as before they had crucified their King. They had resisted a vast body of evidence,
and had therefore grown stronger in infidelity; they had perpetrated a most
atrocious crime, and their consciences must have been seared in the perpetration;
but if they had rendered themselves less accessible to the demonstrations of
evidence, less susceptible of the remonstrances of righteousness, they had not
rendered themselves one jot less the objects of the Mediator's regards, nor thrown
themselves beyond the reach of His extraordinary sacrifice. The blood upon their
hands, whilst it cried for vengeance on them as murderers, cried also—and oh!
the voice which spake of pardon was far louder and deeper than that which spake
of wrath—cried for mercy on them as the objects of redemption. And if that evil
and adulterous generation, moved by the sign of the Resurrection, overcome by
that most stupendous of all miracles, the breaking forth in His own might of the
Crucified One from the sepulchre—if they had discerned and acknowledged and
bewailed their iniquity, and flocking round the despised Nazarene had offered Him
with tears their allegiance, and besought of Him pardon, and bowed before Him
as a prince and a Saviour, who questions that this generation, eminent in guilt,
foremost in all that can make human nature infamous, would have gathered to

the succours of God, and that Jesus would have stood, the
who had scorned Him, and a life-giver to those who had slain
the sign of Jonas a sign which came too late, when the blood had
which blotted out the sin of the world? Call ye it too late, when
re proclaiming to their unbelieving countrymen, "Unto you first, God,
aised up His Son Jesus, sent Him to bless you!" Too late, when the
ation of the gospel and the resurrection is to "begin at Jerusalem," and the
men who with wicked hands had crucified and slain the Prince of Life are to
e entreated to look in faith to a Saviour waiting to embrace them, ere the tidings
of deliverance may be carried to the cities and the islands of the heathen? Oh!
no: all the aspect of strangeness disappears from our text; in place of manifesting
harshness, in place of giving a compliance of less worth than a refusal, Christ
displayed wondrously the graciousness of His character, and showed a still mighty
desire to win the Jews from infidelity, when in answer to a demand to show more
signs to an evil generation He said, "There shall no sign be given it, but the sign of
Jonas." You ask us to show that the sign of the Resurrection was in itself sufficient to work conviction in all fair inquirers, and we give you our reply by going
back over the waste of long ages, and leading you to Nineveh, that exceeding great
city, with its vast but impious population. We bid you mark how on a sudden the
sounds of revelry are hushed, how all the business and all the pleasures of the
stirring and luxurious metropolis come as in a moment to a stand, and how the
great and the mean, the king in his palace and the nobles in their halls, and the
poor in their hovels, as though shrinking from a wrath which rushed visibly on,
bow themselves to the earth, and cry mightily for deliverance. And why is this?
Hath God indeed come forth from the solitudes of eternity, and, riding the firmament in the chariot of His vengeance, hath He made bare His arm in the view of
the Ninevites? Have angelic beings, withering the eyesight of those who dared
gaze on their forms of fire, come down with the proclamation, that yet forty days
and the proud city shall be a ruin? Nay, a foreigner with no attendants, a poor
and unprotected stranger, a wanderer without a home and without a friend in the
magnificent capital, this is the being at whose bidding the tide of a nation's
wickedness has been stayed in its flowings. This is the being whose voice,
syllabling calamity, has put an arrest on the occupations and the joyousness of
hundreds of thousands. Then this foreigner, this stranger, this wanderer, must
have given striking evidence that he spake in God's name: and you will allow,
that if in any other case the like evidence be afforded, the effect wrought on the
Ninevites clearly shows that it ought to prove convincing. But this evidence was
the evidence of a resurrection. This prophet of disaster had been sepulchred
three days and three nights in the depths of the waters, and then rose up uninjured
from that strangest of tombs. This fact it is that the Ninevites knew; on this
fact it was that they received Jonas as a prophet. The evidence, then, of the
resurrection was sufficient, under the most unpromising circumstances, when it
stood absolutely alone, and the parties to be convinced were the idolatrous and
the profligate. It follows, therefore, that enough evidence is afforded, whenever
the evidence of a resurrection is afforded. When assured that a particular
evidence has overcome the infidelity of one people, I can be morally certain that
it is not owing to deficiency of proof that the like evidence failed to overcome the
infidelity of another people. There is a voice, then, in the history of Nineveh,
which proclaims the Jews inexcusable in their unbelief. The voice of weeping and
of wailing which issues from every house in that terrified capital is witness against
the wickedness of the haughty Jerusalem. A nation clothed in sackcloth, and
prostrating itself in spirit, and all because moved by the sign of a resurrection,
this is our proof that the sign of a resurrection is powerful enough to test the
pretensions of a prophet; and when, therefore, another nation resists the sign
which has thus shown its strength, continuing in unbelief, though the messenger
who declares himself authorized by God hath burst the bands of death and
mastered the grave, we can be persuaded of this nation that its infidelity is not
to be overcome by any evidence which consists with human accountability, and we
are convinced that Christ did all that could be done for "an evil and adulterous
generation," when He promised them as the last in the long series of proofs "the
sign of Jonas the prophet; for as Jonas was a sign unto the Ninevites, so shall
also the Son of Man be to this generation." Well, then, might the Redeemer,
when He had referred the scribes and the Pharisees to the sign of His resurrection
—well might He conjure up the scenery of the last judgment, and represent the

Ninevites as convicting the Jews and justifying their condemnation. "The men of Nineveh shall rise up in the judgment with this generation, and shall condemn it; for they repented at the preaching of Jonas! and, behold, more than Jonas"— for this is the true rendering, not "a greater than Jonas"—"behold, more than Jonas is here." The evidence granted to the Jews in the resurrection of Christ, in the preaching of the apostles and the gift of the Spirit, exceeded any that may be supposed to have been granted to the Ninevites in the preservation of Jonah. (*H. Melvill, B.D.*)   *A word with those who wait for signs and wonders :*—Reading the Old Testament, we observe that the Lord in the olden time condescendingly gave signs to His servants, when He saw that it would be for their good. Doubtless if again there should come a' necessity for signs to any of God's servants, such tokens would be given them. If there should ever be a time when it was not possible for Christians to walk by faith alone, or when it would be more to the honour of God that their confidence should be somewhat assisted by marvels and tokens, then would God go out of the ordinary way once again and His people should receive miraculous seals. In no case is such a thing at all necessary under the gospel dispensation, which is so enriched with plainest evidence, that to add more would be to hold a candle to the sun, or pour water into the ocean. In addition to this first remark, let us add that signs have been given, and yet have not wrought faith in those who have seen them ; and there is no necessary connection between seeing signs and believing that which the signs attest. I. I shall ask your attention while I DESCRIBE THE PERSONS who are an evil generation that seek after a sign. We have among us many individuals who are aware that they are sinners, and are conscious of their guiltiness to such an extent as to be very uneasy as to their condition. They clearly perceive that sin will be punished by the Great Judge, and they are much afraid of the wrath to come. They anxiously desire, moreover, to find salvation ; and, having long listened to the gospel, they are not ignorant of the way in which salvation is obtained; they understand the gospel in the letter of it to the highest degree. They are not unbelievers in any of the doctrines of the gospel; but illogical as their state is, they still remain unbelievers, with all this belief about them, and justify their remaining in unbelief by telling you that if they felt this, or if they saw that, or if this happened, or if the other thing occurred, then they would believe in Jesus, but not until then. They make different demands. There are some, and these are generally the most uneducated, who expect to experience remarkable dreams or to behold singular visions. Others we have met with, who suppose that in order to being saved they must feel some very peculiar physical sensation. Now you must not look for this. You must not put physical contortions or sensations as a test before the Lord, and say you will not believe in Him otherwise. These I hope are rare cases, but in very frequent instances I have met with people who will not believe in Jesus Christ to the salvation of their souls because they have not felt wretched enough. They have read in certain books of holy men who, when they were seeking a Saviour, were broken in pieces under the ponderous hammer of the law. They turn to such biographies, and they find the subjects of them uttering language similar to the book of Job, or to the words of Jeremy in the Lamentations. Ah! poor demented one, to desire misery, and to make your own wretchedness, and even your own unbelieving and wicked thoughts of God to be a kind of preparation for faith in Jesus Christ! It is a most insanely wicked thing, and yet many, many, many persist in unbelief because they think they are not wretched enough. Running to the other extreme, I have met with others who would not simply trust Christ because they were not happy enough. They have heard of the Christian's joys, and the peace, like a river, that evermore abideth, and they have said, " If I could get this peace, if this deep calm ruled in my spirit, then I could believe." As much as to say, "If I saw the wheat full grown in the fields of my soul, then I would begin to sow "; whereas the sowing must precede the reaping. I have met with some who would not believe in Christ because they could not pray eloquently. ''Oh,'' they have said, ''if I could pray like So-and-So, to whom we have listened with the greatest pleasure at the prayer-meeting, then I could put my trust in Christ, and there would be some hope for me!'' I have known others who must feel precisely like certain eminent saints have felt many years after their conversion, or else they cannot believe that they are saved. They will reach down the life of some holy man who had mastered his passions by long years of mortification, who had come to live near to God, and whose life was the heavenly life on earth, and they will mentally vow, " I must be just like this man," say they, " or else I cannot believe in Jesus." They say, in fact, to the Heavenly Physician, "I am sick and ready to die, but, Good Physician, Thou must make me as strong as Samson at once and on the spot, or else I will not receive Thy medicine," just as if the perfect spiritual cure of the soul were not a lifelong work of grace. II. I shall now, secondly, SHOW THE FOLLY OF SUCH CONDUCT. You are seeking a sign, one of these which I have described, or some other. 1. You seek what is quite unnecessary. What do you want a sign for? You want, you say, a token of God's love. What token of God's love to you can ever be wanted, now that He has given His only-begotten Son, first to live on earth, and then to die in pains extreme, the just for the unjust, "that whosoever believeth in Him should not perish, but have everlasting life"? I blush for you, that you should ask any token of God's love while Jesus Christ is before you, for herein is such love as nothing else can ever equal. What do you want a sign for? Why, to show, you say, that there is mercy for you. How do you need that? The very fact that you are alive shows how merciful God is! 2. You are also asking for useless signs. What evidence could there be now, for instance, in mere dejection of spirit? You want to feel miserable you say: what evidence would that be of your salvation? It seems to me that you are like a man who would say that he would catch hold of a rope if he could sink so many fathoms deeper in the ocean, or that he would avail himself of a dispensary if his disease were so much worse. How strange that a rational man should talk thus! Despair is no help to faith. Sinful doubts cannot assist you to Christ; they may most effectually keep you from Him. Are you not also seeking most unreasonable things? To ask a sign from God when He pledges His word seems to me to be out of all reason. You are a beggar, remember, and we have an old proverb that beggars must not be choosers; above all, how dare a beggar demand a sign before he receive an alms? III. I shall now want a few minutes more, and your very serious attention, while I now LAY BARE YOUR SINS, your grievous sins. 1. My dear hearers, in the first place, you make God a liar. Is not this the testimony of the Holy Ghost, "He that believeth not hath made God a liar"? 2. In the next place, you insult God's sovereignty. He has a right to give signs or not, as He wills; but you do, as it were, say, "Thou shalt give me a sign or else I will be damned. I will not have Thy mercy if I cannot have it in my own way: great God, I will not be saved unless I can feel as I want to feel." O fling away this accursed pride of yours, and kiss His silver sceptre, and say, "Lord, save me as Thou wilt. I believe, help Thou my unbelief." 3. I must tell you what is more, you are acting the part of an idolater. What does an idolater do? He says, "I cannot believe in an unseen God; I must have a golden calf or an image, that I can see with my eyes and touch with my hand." You say just the same. You cannot believe God's naked word, you demand something you can feel, something you can see. Sheer idolatry. 4. Do you not see, moreover, that you crucify the Saviour? Those who nailed His hands to the tree were not greater sinners, even if they were so great, as you are who say to Him, "Bleeding Saviour, I believe that Thou hast died on the cross; I believe that Thy blood could cleanse sin, but I cannot trust Thee to do it; I have no confidence in Thee; I cannot, will not trust Thee. I trust my husband, but I cannot trust my Saviour; I trust my child, but I cannot trust my God; I trust my minister, but I cannot trust the Son of God exalted in the highest heavens." Why, this is crucifying Him—this is treating Him as a dog only should be treated. IV. YOUR DANGER. In danger of death: you admit that, and now suppose you die in the state you are in. Why, you are almost saved; you are awakened, you are aroused, you have many good desires, but a man who is only almost saved will be altogether damned. There was a householder who almost bolted his door at night, but the thief came in; a prisoner was condemned to be hanged, and was almost pardoned, but he hung on the gallows; a ship was almost saved from shipwreck, but she went to the bottom with all hands on board; a fire was almost extinguished, but it consumed a city; a man almost decided remains to perish in the flames of hell. So is it with you; except you believe, all these things which you possess of good desire and emotion, shall be of no service to you at all, for "he that believeth not shall be damned." (*C. H. Spurgeon.*) *The demand for a sign:*—When Christ was on earth He was again and again assailed by this cry, "Show us a sign." "What sign showest Thou?" And there was an offer accompanying it. Show us this, and we will see and believe. If a man says to the holy and merciful Saviour, There is one proof which would satisfy me—which of us would not say, Surely Christ will grant it? Even if the thing asked he unreasonable, yet surely Christ will not be extreme to mark it—He will do what even prejudice asks—the end is good, and the means to it at least not evil. It is a natural question—we must not leave it without a word in answer— Why was Christ displeased, why is God silent, when this is the prayer? And I think we shall say—1. Because there is a radical fault in the prayer itself. It originates, where it ought to follow; it prescribes, where it ought to accept. There is a thorough upsetting and subverting, in such prayer, of the relationship of man to his God. In such prayer man goes first, and God is to go after. Man says, I will give the law to my God—I will tell Him what He ought to do—and then, if He does that, I will have Him; not else. The very prayer is presumption. 2. But again, Because the result thus reached is not the rest and the inheritance which God designs for us. A man who believes because he sees has not got at last the salvation which he came for. It is a poor inferior mechanical process altogether, this conviction by the help of signs. 3. We might add yet one other reason, and say, Because such proofs would hopelessly perplex and alienate the mind which expects the dealing of God to be uniform and consistent in all its provinces of operation. (*Dean Vaughan.*)

Vers. 31, 32. **A greater than Solomon is here.**—*Christ's superiority to Solomon:*— The superiority of Christ to Solomon may be traced in the following particulars. 1. In His origin. Solomon was indeed of honourable descent, being of the princely tribe of Judah, and of the family of David, who was one of the most illustrious monarchs that ever filled the throne of Israel. No one could claim a higher pedigree than Solomon, or receive a crown from the hands of a more honourable ancestor. Yet Jesus was David's greater Son, and to Him the pre-eminence belonged. With respect to His human nature, He was a rod from the stem of Jesse, and a branch growing out of his roots. With respect to His Divine nature, He is the eternal, co-existent, and co-equal Son of God, in a way mysterious and unknown. 2. In personal qualifications Christ obtains the pre-eminence, especially in that for which Solomon was so highly celebrated. Solomon with all his wisdom was weak and fallible, and liable to the greatest folly; but the Lord Jesus is wisdom itself, wisdom in the very abstract. He was liable to no mistake, to no error, either in judgment or in practice. He was the pattern of all excellence, and of all perfection. Even His enemies were astonished at His doctrine, and testified that never man spake like this Man. In two things especially He excelled all other teachers; He had the most perfect comprehension of His subject, and the power of making it effectually understood, not merely by outward instruction, but by internal illumination. 3. Christ exceeded Solomon in the purity of His life and the general excellence of His character. 4. Solomon sustained the two-fold office of prophet and king, and in both these Christ has the pre-eminence. 5. Christ exceeded Solomon in the mighty works which He performed as well as in His general character and dignity. 6. In the present glory which these illustrious personages possess, there can be no doubt which of them obtains the pre-eminence. Though Solomon was a partaker of Divine grace, and is now an inheritor of the invisible glory, it can bespeak no want of charity to suppose that his inconstancy and backslidings in religion have in some degree tarnished the lustre of his celestial diadem; but be it ever so bright and splendid, it falls infinitely short of that which is placed on the Redeemer's head, as the reward of His obedience unto death. (1) Let us contemplate the character of our Lord and Saviour with astonishment and delight, for a greater than Solomon is here. Let us consider the apostle and high priest of our profession, withdrawing our thoughts from every other object, and fixing them intensely upon Him. (2) As no object is so amiable and attractive, let us view the Saviour till our hearts are inflamed with love. (3) Let us view the Saviour by faith, saying with the prophet, "I will look unto the Lord, I will wait for the God of my salvation." (4) View His condescension with astonishment and love, that one so much greater than Solomon should have humbled Himself unto death, even the death of the cross, that He might raise us to dignity and honour. (*B. Beddome, M.A.*) *A greater than Solomon:*—Our first thought is that no mere man would have said this concerning himself unless he had been altogether eaten up with vanity; for Solomon was among the Jews the very ideal of greatness and wisdom. The second thought that comes to one's mind is this: Notice the self-consciousness of the Lord Jesus Christ. He knows who He is, and what He is, and He is not lowly in spirit because He is ignorant of His own greatness. He was meek and lowly in heart—" *Servus servorum,*" as the Latins were wont to call Him, " Servant of servants," but all the while He knew that He was *Rex regum,* or King of kings. I. BETWEEN CHRIST AND SOLOMON THERE ARE SOME POINTS OF LIKENESS. 1. And, first, in wisdom. He intermeddled with all knowledge, and was a master in all sciences. He was a naturalist; an engineer and architect; a politician, &c. He was everything, in fact. God gave Him wisdom and largeness of heart, says the Scripture, like the sand of the sea: "and Solomon's wisdom excelled the wisdom of all the children of the east country, and all the wisdom of Egypt. For he was wiser than all men; and his fame was in all nations round about." Yes; but our Saviour knows infinitely more than Solomon. I want you to-night to come to Him just as the Queen of Sheba came to Solomon, only for weightier reasons. You do not want to learn anything concerning architecture or navigation, agriculture or anatomy. You want to know only how you shall be built up a spiritual house, and how you shall cross those dangerous seas which lie between this land and the celestial city. Well, you may come to Jesus, and He will teach you all that you need to know, for all wisdom is in Christ. 2. Observe, next, that our Lord Jesus Christ is greater than Solomon in wealth. This was one of the things for which Solomon was noted. He had great treasures: he "made gold to be as stones, and as for silver it was little accounted of," so rich did he become. But, oh, when you consider all the wealth of Solomon, what poor stuff it is compared with the riches that are treasured up in Christ Jesus. 3. There was one point about Solomon in which every Israelite rejoiced, namely, that he was the prince of peace. His name signifies peace. His father, David, was a great warrior, but Solomon had not to carry on war. Those were halcyon days for Israel when Solomon reigned. Ah, but in that matter a greater than Solomon is here; for Solomon could not give his subjects peace of mind, he could not bestow upon them rest of heart, he could not ease them of their burden of guilt, or draw the arrow of conviction from their breast and heal its smart. 4. A fourth thing for which Solomon was noted was his great works. Solomon built the temple, which was one of the seven wonders of the world in its time. A very marvellous building it must have been. In addition to this he erected for himself palaces, constructed fortifications, and made aqueducts and great pools to bring streams from the mountains to the various towns. He also founded Palmyra and Baalbec —those cities of the desert—to facilitate his commerce with India, Arabia, and other remote regions. He was a marvellous man. And yet a greater than Solomon is here, for Christ has brought the living water from the throne of God right down to thirsty men, being Himself the eternal aqueduct through which the heavenly current streams. Christ has built fortresses and munitions of defence, behind which His children stand secure against the wrath of hell; and He has founded and is daily finishing a wondrous temple, His Church, of which His people are the living stones, and which God Himself shall inhabit. 5. Solomon was great as to dominion. He managed to bring various kings into subjection to him, and he was the greatest monarch that ever swayed the sceptre of Judah. It has all gone now. Poor, feeble Rehoboam dropped from his foolish hands the reins his father held. The kingdom was rent in pieces, the tributary princes found their liberty, and the palmy days of Israel were over. On the contrary, our Lord Jesus Christ at this moment has dominion over all things. God has set Him over all the works of His hands. II. BETWEEN CHRIST AND SOLOMON THERE IS MUCH MORE CONTRAST THAN COMPARISON—much more difference than likeness. 1. In His nature the Lord Jesus is greater than Solomon. 2. In His character. 3. In His influence. 4. In His power to bless. (*C. H. Spurgeon.*) *A privileged nation judged by the heathen :—* Mr. Johnstone observes that "When Japan was recently revolutionised, the inhabitants adopted Occidental customs, and many of them—chiefly their style of dress, social manners, and form of government—were taken from England. It was thought by those in authority in Japan that it would be well to look into the English religion, and see if it were better, and tended to the moral advancement of those professing it. A deputation was sent for that purpose, and beginning at London, set itself to study the Christian religion. I know not where they went to, nor from what standpoint they viewed it; but their report was unfavourable. They said that never in Japan had they seen such sin, such open licentiousness, drunkenness, selfishness, unkindness, and lack of sympathy as they had witnessed among the professed Christians of England, and they would advise that they adhere to their own religion, which was as good, if not better, than the Christian. Such was their report, after witnessing the life of the people of nominally Christian England.

Vers. 33-36. **The light of the body is the eye.**—*The single eye :*—The eye is evil when the vision is incorrect, double ; is single when it lays hold of one object with clearness and firmness. Shut the eye, or if the eye is diseased so as not to be able to see any one object distinctly, and we have the body full of darkness. This is true in the moral universe. 1. Intellectually. He whose judgment is uncertain, &c. He who has clear plans, &c. 2. Morally. He who has clear conceptions of right and wrong ; with what freedom and strength he walks forward. There is light in him ; there is light before him. 3. Spiritually. What does it mean to have a single eye in the religious world ? It means more than supreme love to God. It means that the whole mental and moral nature of the man must be right in its conceptions of religious truths. This may be summed up in five points. (1) Man must live for ever. The eternal, vital principle is in him. Suicide is not possible. (2) Man, as a sinner, needs transformation into God's character. (3) Christ has come from heaven to work the transformation—the atonement. (4) The necessity for a personal, affectionate faith. (5) The only way of safety is the exercise of this faith at once. (*R. S. Storrs, D.D.*) *Singleness of heart :*—Whatever a man regards as his chief good, on that, his heart—his supreme affections— will be fixed ; and by that will all his specific opinions, affections, desires, purposes, and actions be regulated and controlled. What, then, the eye is to the body, the practical estimate and regard which a man forms of his chief good is to the whole moral character. If the eye be incapable of vision, the whole body is doomed to all the evils of utter darkness. So, if the practical estimate which men form of their good be not according to the truth and reality of things, the whole moral man is doomed to error, to sin, and to ruin. To illustrate and confirm this truth I remark—I. THE PRACTICAL ESTIMATE WHICH EVERY MAN FORMS OF HIS CHIEF GOOD RESPECTS EITHER GOD OR THE WORLD AS ITS OBJECT. These are the only sources of good, of any kind or degree, which are opened to man. II. THIS PRACTICAL ESTIMATE DETERMINES ON WHICH OF THE TWO OBJECTS THE HEART IS FIXED. Here, it is necessary to distinguish carefully between a speculative estimate or judgment, and that which is practical. Let us consider the influence of this state of mind : 1. On a man's knowledge and belief of the truth. No one can have attentively considered human nature, without seeing how much the opinions of men are affected by the state of the heart ; and how much more perfectly they understand those subjects which it is for their interest to understand, than any others. If a man's heart, then, be right with God, the great truths which God has revealed to influence man to act up to this end of his being will be truths which he will especially wish to understand. It is on this principle that our Saviour has declared that if any man will do His will he shall know of the doctrine. 2. This state of mind, described in the text, decides the nature of all specific and subordinate affections. Light and darkness cannot be in the same place at the same instant. God and mammon cannot reign in the same heart. And when the glory of God is the light of the soul, like the splendours of the sun, it extinguishes the lesser lights which glitter before a worldly mind. The Lord and Creator of the heart there fixes His throne, and all the affections of the inner man bow to Him as their supreme Lord. 3. This state of heart will have the same influence on the external conduct. The man who has not the love of God in him may indeed be faultless in many points, but his conduct will be greatly deficient and erroneous in externals. He will do and he will neglect to do many things which it were impossible should be done or neglected, did he carry with him a continual sense of God's presence. But where the heart—the governing aim—is right, there is a principle which tends to bring everything right. There may indeed be some occasional deviation ; but deviation will be an interruption in the general course of conduct. There will be a principle of correction within, which will discover, regret, and reform what is amiss. For the principle is a universal principle ; a supreme regard to God will lead to one duty as well as to another—to acts of kindness as well as to acts of devotion. It will resist and correct little sins as well as great sins ; for the same authority reaches to one as to the other, and that authority is God's. It is also a uniform principle. It allows of no intermission of duty—sanctions no neglect of duty—admits of no indulgence of a beloved sin. For the authority which controls the man is God's authority, and it is ceaseless and eternal like Himself. It is a pure and holy principle. It tolerates no iniquity—no moral imperfections. It points to the highest purity ; it aims at God's perfect likeness. Concluding remarks : 1. Those whose hearts are supremely devoted to the world have reason to suspect that they embrace some serious practical error. 2. Our subject shows us the substantial difference between the saint and the sinner, and how great that difference. 3. Our subject shows the necessity of maintaining a right state of heart. 4. Our subject shows those who are destitute of true religion what they must do to obtain it. They must settle it with themselves that their false views of the world must be corrected, and their hearts taken from it and be fixed on God. Cost what it may, this must be done. (*N. W. Taylor, D.D.*) *Self-deceit :*—As the bodily eye is of great use and importance to the animal life, to the direction of its powers, and to the enjoyment of it ; so there is an interior eye of the mind of equal importance and usefulness to the direction of our highest capacity, and to the chief ends of our beings, which is the sense of good and evil, both natural and moral ; or, the judgment of the soul concerning their difference, and the methods of pursuing the one, and avoiding the other. Now we must remember, to begin with, that there is a great disparity between the case of the external sight and the distempers to which it is liable, and the judgment of the mind with which it is compared. External vision does not depend upon our own choice ; nor are we either to be praised or blamed for it ; an obstruction in the eye-sight may be a man's infelicity, it is not his fault ; but in the other case we are strictly and properly agents, charged with the care of ourselves, and with the improvement of our own powers and faculties, so that we may attain their true ends. Here, by the single eye, is meant the virtue of simplicity, without reserve or hesitation hearkening to, and following the pure voice of conscience, not using any artifice, colouring, or false disguise, nor suffering any bias or prejudice to rest on the mind whereby it may be imposed upon or misled. The evil eye is disease of the mind, very malignant, and extremely dangerous ; what less can be meant by total and most deplorable darkness ? but it is a voluntary contracted distemper. I. THE DANGER OF SELF-DECEIT. 1. This is plainly taught in Scripture (see Prov. xvi. 2 ; Isa. v. 20). 2. We can see instances of it within the range of our own observation. How common is it for men to make solemn professions of religion, and declare their confident hopes of acceptance with God, while yet it is notorious that they continue in a vicious course of life ? And how shall this be accounted for, without supposing the grossest self-deceit ? II. THE CAUSE OF SELF-DECEIT. In general, it is some prevailing corrupt affection or passion. The immediate result of vicious affections and unruly passions thoroughly possessing the hearts of men, is an unfairness in all their inquiries concerning their duty. III. THE MEANS whereby this fatal disease of the mind and error of the judgment is contracted and confirmed. 1. A false imagination. 2. Wrong notions respecting sin. 3. Feeble ineffectual purposes of future amendment and obedience. IV. THE EXTENT of this self-deceit. In some it affects the whole character and life. Such is the case described in the text, where the eye is supposed to be evil, the judgment totally perverted, the light turned into darkness which has got entire possession of the mind, and misled it in its chief concerns, its moral integrity and its future happiness. But, in some lower degree it is common to mankind ; and scarcely is there any one altogether free from it, that is, who is not in some particular instances misled in judging of himself and his own conduct, through remaining self-partiality and self-ignorance. (*Bishop Abernethy.*) *The effects of good and bad principles :*—I. SHOW THE INFLUENCE WHICH MEN'S PRINCI- PLES HAVE UPON THEIR PRACTICE. The judgment of the mind is the guide of life ; and for the most part, men's outward actions are governed by their inward senti- ments and opinions. They form to themselves some design, and lay down some principle or other ; and this, whatever it be, gets the ascendant of everything else, is most of all in their minds, and has the prevailing sway in their actions. And thus it must needs be, as long as men do not act by any natural necessity, by any blind instinct or impulse, nor are under the power of giddy chance, or overruling fate and destiny, but are rational and free agents, and left to their own liberty and choice : they cannot but be determined by their judgment and opinion of things, and square their actions according to the notions and principles they have imbibed. II. CONSIDER THE DIFFERENT EFFECTS OF GOOD AND BAD PRINCIPLES. 1. Of the good effect and influence of good principles. If our eye be single ; if we are free from all false notions and corrupt opinions ; if we have a true judgment of what is our chief happiness, and wherein it consists ; what is the great end of life, and what are the ways which lead to that end ; our whole body will be full of light. Discretion will then guide us, and understanding will keep us ; and our whole life and all our actions will be ordered right and have an uniform tendency to promote our true interest. We shall then be steady and constant in the pursuit of the " one thing needful," without ever standing still, or diverting to any other end. This will prove our best security both against the enticements of our own lusts, and **the** allurements of the world. 2. The ill influence and effect which bad principles have upon us. It is necessary for us to have some principles or other, if we would have our life answer any purpose. Without this, we are like the double-minded man, whom St. James describes, who " is unstable in all his ways " (James i. 8), who has no particular interest to serve, but is divided between several; between the interest of this world, and of the other. Such a man is always weak and wavering, unstable and inconstant in all his actions. He has several ends to serve, which many times cross one another; and so he pursues none of them vigorously; but while he is moving towards one, inclines to another ; and like a needle between two loadstones, is ever in a trembling posture, and doubtful state of mind. This is the condition of a man that has no principles at all. Next to this, it is as bad to have no good principles, no true principles of religion and virtue ; for without these we shall be exposed to every temptation, and liable to change with every wind. Having no fixed principle within us, we shall adhere to nothing upon any firm grounds ; but shall be ever varying, as the complexion of our body, or the temper of our mind, or the circumstances of external affairs happen to alter. We shall be superstitious at one time, careless or profane at another ; now a sceptic, and then a dogmatist ; of one religion to-day, and of another to-morrow, and the next day of neither ; and at last, perhaps, of no religion at all. As long as the world goes well with such a man as this, and he finds his interest in his duty, he will be loyal to his prince, true to his country, and faithful to his friend; but whenever the times alter, and these virtues are out of fashion, and become the object of scorn and reproach, and cannot be practised without apparent hazard to his own private interest, he will basely desert them, and will be sure to save himself, whatever becomes of everybody else. And this will put him upon any acts of treachery and injustice, of force or fraud, which are necessary to compass his self ends. III. How MUCH IT CONCERNS US TO FURNISH OUR MINDS WITH GOOD PRINCIPLES, and to take care that no ill principle whatever prevails over us. Application : 1. Hence appears the great usefulness and necessity of knowledge and understanding, especially in religion and matters of a moral nature. 2. From what has been said, it appears how cautious we should be in the choice of our principles ; as much as we should be in the choice of a guide to conduct us through an unknown and difficult way. 3. Hence appears the great evil and mischief, both the sin and the guilt, of imposing upon men's understandings, misinforming their judgments, and instilling false notions and principles into their minds, since this is to betray them to a guide that will assuredly mislead them, and instead of conducting them to heaven, will bring them into the pit of destruction. 4. And lastly, what has been said, should excite us to endeavour after this single eye, not only as it means in general a sound and impartial judgment, but in that literal sense which has already been hinted, as it imports singlemindedness, the having but one grand purpose and design, one ruling principle and affection, and that is serving God, and saving our own souls. (*Dr. Ibbot.*) *The universal influence of Christian principles :*—Consider the extensive influence of the state of heart described by the expression—" If thine eye be single." 1. As it respects a man's religious opinions. I do not assert, that if the state of a man's heart be right with God, his belief will be always right ; but this I maintain, that the state of his heart will very much influence his faith : so that if his heart be not upright with God he will be greatly disposed to error ; and, on the other hand, if the state of his heart be right it will tend gradually to correct what was erroneous in his creed, and to give him just views of religious doctrines. 2. The state of the heart will greatly influence the state of the affections. I mean, that if a man's real aim is to serve God, this will tend to bring all his affections and dispositions into a right state. For let a man be truly desirous of pleasing God, the tendency of this desire will be first to lead him to a better acquaintance with the character and perfections of that Being whom he now honours as his Supreme Master. And where the heart is thus turned to the frequent contemplation of Him whose attributes are infinitely glorious, what must be the result but an increasing conviction that He alone ought to be feared, and loved, and trusted? 3. The general conduct will be under a right influence wherever the heart is sincere towards God ; that is, if a man's grand aim is to please and serve God, it will produce a course of moral conduct worthy of a religious profession. 4. And lastly, the right state of the heart will influence, in a very remarkable degree, the future progress in religion. (*J. Venn, M.A.*) *The eye, the light of the body :*—What is the world, says one, without the sun, but a dark melancholy dungeon ? What is a man without eyes, but monstrous and deformed? The two eyes are two luminaries, that God hath set up in the microcosm, man's little world. When God would express His tender love unto His people, He calls them the apple of His eye. "He that toucheth you, toucheth the apple of His eye." And the like phrase St. Paul makes use of, when he speaks of the love of the Galatians unto himself: "I bear you record, that if it had been possible, ye would have plucked out your eyes, and have given them to me." The Emperor Adrian, with an arrow, by accident, put out one of his servant's eyes; he commanded him to be brought to him, and bade him ask what he would that he might make him amends. The poor man was silent; he pressed him again, when he said he would ask nothing, but he wished he had the eye which he had lost, intimating that an emperor was not able to make satisfaction for the loss of an eye. So the light of Divine truth is infinitely more valuable than all other blessings. If we come short of this, there can be no substitute found. If the soul should be lost, the whole world can afford us no relief. The Latin verses Adrian addressed to his soul, and translated by Pope ("Vital Spark," &c.) are well known. (*C. Buck.*) *Intensified light:*—Fresnel, by forming one vast reflector from many small ones, produced a glare eight times as intense as had previously been known. Shining out from a lighthouse, it could be seen as far as the earth's curvature would permit. Buffon, by collocating several hundred small mirrors, and causing the flame of a galvanic battery to play upon their focal centre, melted, in two minutes, the hardest metals, and set wood on fire at a distance of two hundred feet. The hostile ships of Rome, lying in the harbour of Syracuse, were wrapped in flames, we are told, by the fierce power of a compound sun-glass which Archimedes made. These facts are suggestive. If we unite in reflecting the rays of Him who is the Sun of Righteousness, stirring scenes will follow. It can but cause a sweeping revival; and the more flames there are, thus joined, the intenser will be the effect. Candles long hidden under bushels should, therefore, be uncovered. Their proper place is on a candlestick. "Ye are the light of the world," and should help illumine it. Candles should also be trimmed. Many smoke. They need snuffing. The wick of formality is too long. The flame is feeble, and flickers. It looks like a rushlight, and ought to flash like a star. It is dimly lighting a single home, and might brighten a whole street. With every blaze clear, and every candle in its place, uniting their light, "as flame plays with flame," a tremendous religious disturbance would speedily be heard of in all directions. Light never fails to make a stir. As sunrise rouses a sleepy world, so would a burst of "spiritual brilliancy" awaken the unconverted. (*J. S. Brecken-ridge.*) *Uncovering the light:*—Mrs. Godolphin testified to the truth at the corrupt Court of Charles II., and thus proved herself to be the worthy successor of the three Hebrew children and the saints in the household of Cæsar. Lady Huntingdon was a brave witness-bearer in the aristocratic circles of the eighteenth century. William Wilberforce carried his convictions with him whithersoever he went—whether to the drawing-room, to Parliament, or to the hustings. To Thomas Carlyle, in our own generation, a drawing-room meant only so many square feet of infinite space, and he was just as ready to speak forth the truth that was in him, and to protest against shams and make-believes, in the gilded saloons of nobles and princes as when he was seated in his own arm-chair. (*R. Abercrombie, M.A.*) *Seeing double:*—Be not like the foolish drunkard, who, staggering home one night, saw his candle lit for him. "Two candles!" said he, for his drunkenness made him see double, "I will blow out one"; and as he blew it out, in a moment he was in the dark. Many a man sees double through the drunkenness of sin. He thinks that he has one life to sow his wild oats in, and then the last part of life in which to turn to God; so, like a fool, he blows out the only candle that he has, and in the dark he will have to lie down for ever. *Peacefulness resulting from having a single eye:*—A South Sea Island preacher said: "In the olden time I had two wives; and what was the result? There was no peace for me, day or night, on account of the jealousy and scolding of these women. Christianity came, and I put away one of my wives. Now peace reigned in my home. It is even thus with a heart divided between Christ and the world. Choose one or the other. Don't strive to keep both. Be Christ's wholly; and then, as a spouse united to one Lord, you will dwell in perfect peace." (*"Jottings from the Pacific,"* by W. Wyatt Gill, B.A.) *Take heed of unillumined darkness:*—In France, every carriage, or cart, or waggon, must, after sundown, carry a light; and quite right too. On our mountain-roads, where should we be if our carriage encountered a hay-cart just at the turn of a road or at the edge of a precipice? It is very curious to see a little lantern gleaming out from a moving hill of hay, but it is in every way the correct thing. How we wish that all our acquaintances carried a light! Be they good or bad, we are glad to know where they are, and where they are going, for then we know how to deal with them. Your dark men are dreadful men. They seem to be afraid of discovering their own whereabouts, and we know not whether they are friends or foes. We are bound to drive warily when these people are about; and we should in their neighbourhood be doubly careful to keep our own lamp burning brightly. (*C. H. Spurgeon.*)   *Light in every part :*—We went one cold, windy day to see a poor young girl, kept at home by a lame hip. Her room was on the north side of a bleak house. It did not look pleasant without or cheerful within. " Poor girl," I thought, " what a cheerless life is yours, and what a pity your room is on the north side of the house." " You never have any sun," I said ; " not a ray comes in at these windows. It's too bad. Sunshine is everything. I love the sun." " Oh ! " she answered, with the sweetest of smiles, " my Sun pours in at every window and through every crack." I looked surprised. " The Sun of Righteousness," she said, softly. " Jesus—He shines in here, and makes everything bright to me." Yes! Jesus shining in can make any spot beautiful, and make even one bare room a happy home.   *A fountain of light :*—Men's experiences are too often like illuminated houses when a great victory or a great peace is celebrated. On such occasions men buy candles two or three inches long, and put them into little bits of tin sockets, and stick them up at every pane of glass, and light them, so that they may be seen by everybody that goes by in the street. And was there ever anything more beautiful ? That is just like folks under preaching, and often in revivals of religion. They have little bits of enthusiasm, little bits of candles, that will not burn an hour. And after they have gone out how much tallow there is on the window, and on the carpet, and all about! Now, if men, instead of having these petty illuminations, would establish in themselves a fountain of light, how much better it would be! (*H. W. Beecher.*)   **Take heed.**—*Cautions :*—1. Take heed of the great leading error of the worldly, who, in their practical judgment, prefer earthly to heavenly things, and thus are involved in spiritual darkness. Take eternity into account, if you would estimate things according to their real value, and would think and act as well-informed persons. 2. Take heed of shutting your eyes altogether against the light, of averting your thoughts altogether from the truth, and of resolving to persist wilfully in ignorance. There are none so blind as those who will not see. 3. Take heed of leaning to your own understanding. There are some persons who, being naturally uncommonly sagacious, or who, fancying themselves so, are so wrapped up in self-conceit as to undervalue the true light. Take heed of trusting in human learning, if you have had an opportunity of becoming learned. It is very melancholy that there are so many who rest in this to the neglect of the wisdom which is from above. Take heed of infidel and irreligious philosophy, falsely called philosophy. Reason is a noble endowment, and its right exercise is incumbent, but there are false reasonings of which you should be aware. 4. Take heed of the pride of self-righteousness; for it will blind you to your own demerit, and to the glory of Christ's finished work, and to the way of pardon and acceptance by faith alone. 5. " Take heed and beware of covetousness "; for it perverts the judgment and the affections. The love of money causes many " to err from the faith." 6. Take heed of the love of sin in general, and the indulgence of any particular sin. There can be no doubt that the love of sin exerts a fatal influence in perverting the understanding, and keeping men in darkness. There are many who " love darkness rather than light, because their deeds are evil." 7. Take heed of a spirit of envy, malice, and uncharitableness. This is called in Scripture an evil eye : " Is thine eye evil, because I am good ? " said our Lord. The indulgence of this spirit shows that the true light has not entered the soul, and tends still to keep it out. 8. Take heed of unfounded prejudice and partiality ; such a bias will lead you astray, and render your understanding as incapable of judging of truth as a jaundiced eye is of colours. Take heed of every sinister end, every improper design. This is, perhaps, peculiarly intended by an " evil eye." See that you have an honest, sincere, upright, single design. (*James Foote, M.A.*)   **The light which is in thee.**—*Of the light within us :*—I. THE EVIL WE ARE WARNED AGAINST. Turning the light within us into darkness. To help our understanding of this, let us consider with ourselves those intolerable evils which bodily blindness, deafness, stupefaction, and an utter deprivation of all sense, must unavoidably subject the outward man to. For what is one in such a condition able to do ? And what is he not liable to suffer ? And yet doing and suffering, upon the matter, comprehend all that concerns a man in this world. If such a one's enemy seeks his life (as he may be sure that some or other will, and possibly such a one as he takes for his truest friend) in this forlorn case, he can neither see, nor hear, nor perceive his approach, till he finds himself actually in his murdering hands. He can neither encounter nor escape him, neither in his own defence give nor ward off a blow; for whatsoever blinds a man, *ipso facto* disarms him ; so that being thus bereft both of his sight and of all his senses besides, what such a one can be fit for, unless it be to set up for prophecy, or believe transubstantiation, I cannot imagine. These; I say, are some of those fatal mischiefs which corporal blindness and insensibility expose the body to ; and are not those of a spiritual blindness inexpressibly greater? II. THE DANGER OF FALLING INTO THIS EVIL. It is as in a common plague, in which the infection is as hard to be escaped as the distemper to be cured ; for that which brings this darkness upon the soul is sin. And as the state of nature now is, the soul is not so close united to the body as sin is to the soul ; indeed, so close is the union between them, that one would even think the soul itself (as much a spirit as it is) were the matter, and sin the form, in our present constitution. In a word, there is a set combination of all without a man and all within him, of all above ground and all under it (if hell be so), first to put out his eyes, and then to draw or drive him headlong into perdition. III. HOW AND BY WHAT COURSES THIS DIVINE LIGHT COMES TO BURN FAINT AND DIM. 1. Whatever defiles the conscience, in the same degree also darkens it. 2. Whatever puts a bias upon the judging faculty of conscience, weakens, and, by consequence, darkens the light of it. 3. We now pass from these general observations to particulars. (1) Every single gross act of sin is much the same thing to the conscience, that a great blow or fall is to the head : it stuns and bereaves it of its senses for a time. (2) The frequent and repeated practice of sin has also a mighty power in it to obscure and darken the natural light of conscience, nothing being more certainly true, nor more universally acknowledged, than that custom of sinning takes away the sense of sin ; and, we may add, the sight of it too. For though the darkness consequent upon any one gross act of sin be, as we have shown, very great, yet that which is caused by custom of sinning is much greater and more hardly curable. (3) Every corrupt passion or affection of the mind will certainly pervert the judging, and obscure and darken the discerning power of conscience. (*R. South, D.D.*) *The nature of human actions :*—I. Consider the nature of human actions, and what dependence they have upon the directing principle, upon the light or understanding that is in the mind of man. II. Show what power men have over their own actions with regard to the influence of that light or understanding by which they are to be directed. III. Consider of what consequence it is in matters of religion that men fail not in this first and grand Foundation of all, in the Root, the Spring, the universal Guide and Director of their actions. " Take heed that the light which is in thee be not darkness." (*S. Clarke, D.D.*) *Light turned into darkness :*—If, in those days, which were not characteristically " days of light," Christ saw it necessary to urge this caution so strongly, we can conceive with how much greater force He would have pressed it now, when Daniel's prophecy is having such literal fulfilment on every side— "Many shall run to and fro, and knowledge shall be increased." Through the avenues of conscience, which is to the soul what the eye is to the body, communications from God are always pouring in. In nature, in providence, but still more by His Word, and by His own inward grace, He acts upon the man. The understanding is formed, the reason is directed, the affections are moved, the will is urged, holy influences stream in upon the inner being. And this process, up to a certain point at least, in every man's life, is continually going on. I believe that it is going on in every one of you at this moment. Hence your familiar acquaintance with Divine truth ! Hence your sense of sin ! Hence your frequent compunctions ! Hence your better desires and good resolves ! Hence your gleams of heaven ! Hence your appreciation and admiration of the real and the true ! To what a height that inner " light " is capable of being raised by culture it is impossible for us to estimate, seeing no man has ever cherished it as much as he might. But did we pray, and study, and listen, and obey the " still, small voices " as we ought, there would be no limit to the degree in which the judgment would be directed, the heart softened, the will conformed, the thoughts made sunny, the future assured, the love of God dominant, and heaven foretasted. For " if the eye be single, the whole body is full of light." If the openings

heavenward and Godward be all clear, and unchoked, and free, the whole man is
capable, and wise, and happy, and safe; and that is fulfilled which we read so
familiarly, and therefore so unintelligibly—" The path of the just is as the shining
light, which shineth more and more unto the perfect day." But it is a truth too
certain, that all this "light," with which God beams upon us, is capable not only
of being hindered, and resisted, and destroyed, but, worse than that, of actually
being converted into a deeper "darkness"—becoming a medium of spiritual blindness, or casting the soul into a more utter night. For there is no death so locked
as that which once lived the most; there is no blackness so black as the shrouded
day; there is no soul so dark as the soul that was once illumined! (*J. Vaughan,
M.A.*)

Vers. 37–39. **A certain Pharisee besought Him to dine with him.**—*The Pharisees
reproved:*—I. The invitation. 1. The prominence with which the Pharisees
figure in our Lord's life is noticeable. (1) In view of their profession of pre-
eminent piety. (2) In view of their scrupulous conformity to all the outward
forms of religion. (3) In view of their bitter emnity against Jesus, and their craft
and various forms of cunning used to ensnare Him. (4) What a commentary on
the powerlessness as well as hollowness of attention on the mere formalities of
religion. II. Our Lord's acceptance of the invitation. 1. Our Lord accepted
the invitation with full knowledge of the insincerity with which it was offered. (1)
But He knew it would give Him the opportunity of giving utterance to truths
which the occasion would naturally call forth. (2) May we appreciate the value of
opportunity. 2. Our Lord accepted the invitation with full knowledge of the
painful consequence that would follow His honest utterances on the occasion. We
must not shrink on account of consequences to speak the truth which God gives.
III. The surprise of the Pharisee. 1. This surprise was natural from the
Pharisee's standpoint. 2. And this ceremonial washing had a high moral design.
(1) To remind constantly of the need of inward purity. (2) But its spiritual
significance was lost sight of in the mere rite itself. 3. Our Lord's omission to
wash before the meal was premeditated. (1) That He did nothing that was not
premeditated, shows this. (2) The moral lessons He drew which the occasion
furnished Him, prove this. (3) In our Lord's life the lower was ever sacrificed for
the higher. IV. The practical lessons which our Lord drew. 1. From the folly
and wickedness of having a form of godliness while denying its power. 2. A
lesson on true cleanliness. V. The fearful judgments pronounced on religious
formalists. 1. Upon the formalists who made great pretensions to piety—the
Pharisees. 2. Upon the formalists who made great pretensions to Scriptural
knowledge—scribes. 3. Upon the formalists who made great pretensions to exact
analysis of the law—lawyers. Lessons: 1. In social life our Lord gives an
example of impartiality in His attention and interest: publicans, sinners, Pharisees
—invitations from all alike He accepted. 2. In social life our Lord gives us an
example of turning every incident to practical and spiritual account. 3. In social
life our Lord gives us an example of inflexible righteousness, conjoined with loving
sympathy. (*D. C. Hughes, M.A.*) *Pharisaical religion:*—I. The several signs
or developments of Pharisaical religion. 1. The substitution of external for
spiritual purity. 2. Attention to trifles may be compatible with neglect of great
duties. 3. Honour is sought from men; the honour which comes from God only
is despised. 4. Doctrines and practices may be taught by those who neither
believe their own doctrines nor observe their own precepts. II. The evil and
condemnation of Pharisaic religion. 1. It is misleading to observers. 2. It is
repugnant to God. 3. It is disastrous to the spiritual life of those who trust to it.
Men begin by deceiving others, and end by deceiving themselves. (*J. R. Thomson,
M.A.*) *Outward show and inward lack:*—It is unfortunately not difficult to find
illustrations of outward show and inward lack. The beautiful ivy-covered wall
which crumbles at a touch; the rosy apple worm-eaten at the core; the leafy
fig-tree which yet bears no figs; the luxuriant growth which covers the morass;
the poison-ivy, fair to look at but dangerous to the touch; the rustic seat, inviting
to rest, from which the serpent springs up,—may serve as examples. In mediæval
writings, mention is often made of poisonous rings. Outwardly they looked like
other rings, a narrow band of gold with a clear diamond set in it. But when the
ring was placed on the hand a slight puncture was made from behind the gem, and
a little poison injected into the finger, and so the death of the wearer was caused.
What an emblem of the Pharisee! Every child knows what a sham is. Perhaps

there is not one of them but has sometime received from a "funny" playfellow a pleasant-looking sweetmeat, which when taken into the mouth, nipped and burned the tongue. Or they may have taken up, in a friend's house, what they thought was a book, and found it to be only a box imitation of one. It will be easy then to show them how the same thing appears in human things. The merchant who sells oleomargarine under the name of butter is, like his goods, a sham. The church-member who stands up staunchly for Sabbath observance and regular attendance at church, and yet during the week tells business lies and makes dishonest profits, is a sham. And the boy or girl who is known at Sunday-school as one of the best scholars, but at home is ill-natured and selfish and revengeful, is also a sham. Teach the children to be sincere. An inconsistent person is like a sum in addition, with the wrong answer at the bottom. Everybody can run up the column of figures and see how wrong the summing up is. Show how the scholars may make the sum of their life-arithmetic correct. Or the insincere person may be compared to the baskets of peaches sometimes sold at the doors—a few large, ripe peaches at the top, but, when these are lifted away, nothing but unripe or decaying fruit beneath. Who would wish his life to be like that? (*Sunday School Times.*) *Hypocrisy branded :*—Hypocrites resemble looking-glasses, which present the faces which are not in them. Oh, how desirous are men to put the fairest gloves upon the foulest hands; and the finest paint upon the rottenest posts! To counterfeit the coin of heaven, is to commit treason against the King of heaven. Who would spread a curious cloth upon a dusty table? If a mariner set sail in an unsound bottom, he may reasonably expect to lose his voyage. No wise virgin would carry a lamp without light. O professor, either get the latter or part with the former. None are so black in the eyes of the Deity as those who paint spiritual beauty for spirit. . . . A false friend is worse than an open enemy. A painted harlot is less dangerous than a painted hypocrite. A treacherous Judas is more abhorred of God than a bloody Pilate. Christians! remember the sheep's clothing will soon be stripped from the wolf's back. The velvet plaster of profession shall not always conceal the offensive ulcer of corruption. Neither the ship of formality nor hypocrisy will carry one person to the harbour of felicity. The blazing lamps of foolish virgins may light them to the bridegroom's gate, but not into his chamber. . . . Oh, what vanity it is to lop off the boughs, and leave the roots which can send forth more; or to empty the cistern, and leave the fountain running which can soon fill it again! Such may swim in the water as the visible church; but when the net is drawn to shore, they must be thrown away as bad fishes. Though the tares and the wheat may grow in the field together, yet they will not be housed in the granary together. (*Archbishop Secker.*) *Hypocrisy sometimes difficult to discover :*—Formality frequently takes its dwelling near the chambers of integrity, and so assumes its name; the soul not suspecting that hell should make so near an approach to heaven. A rotten post, though covered with gold, is more fit to be burned in the fire, than for the building of a fabric. Where there is a pure conscience, there will be a pure conversation. The dial of our faces does not infallibly show the time of day in our hearts; the humblest looks may enamel the former, while unbounded pride covers the latter. Unclean spirits may inhabit the chamber when they look not out at the window. A hypocrite may be both the fairest and the foulest creature in the world; he may be fairest outwardly in the eyes of man, and foulest inwardly in the sight of God. How commonly do such unclean swans cover their black flesh with their white feathers! Though such wear the mantle of Samuel, that should bear the name of Satan. (*Ibid.*) *Conventional notions of sin :*—If you ask the Pharisee of old what sin was—"Well," he said, "it is eating without washing your hands; it is drinking wine without having first of all strained out the gnats, for those insects are unclean, and if you should swallow any of them they will render you defiled." His repentance dealt with his having touched a Gentile, or having come on the windside of a Publican. Many in these days have the same notion, with a variation. We have read of a Spanish bandit, who, when he confessed before his father-confessor, complained that one sin hung with peculiar weight upon his soul that was of peculiar atrocity. He had stabbed a man on a Friday, and a few drops of the blood of the wound had fallen on his lips, by which he had broken the precepts of holy church, in having tasted animal food on a fast day. The murder did not seem to arouse in his conscience any feeling of remorse at all—not one atom—he would have done the same to-morrow; but an accidental violation of the canons of mother church excited all his fears. (*C. H. Spurgeon.*) *Neglecting the inside :*—In Queen

Elizabeth's time, the way in which they cleaned out the hall of a castle, the floor of which might be covered with remnants of food and all manner of abominations, was to strew another layer of rushes over the top of the filth, and then they thought themselves quite neat and respectable. And that is what a great many of you do, cover the filth well up with a sweet smelling layer of conventional proprieties and think yourselves clean, and the pinks of perfection. (*A. Maclaren, D.D.*) *Heathen notions of sin :*—A missionary in India writes about what the people there call sin. He says : " Travelling across the country one day, I took shelter from the sun in a native hut. The man kindly spread a mat for me, and the shade of the thatched roof was very acceptable. Soon a large number of poor men, who had been working in the muddy road, came there to eat their mid-day meal of rice. A young man of a better class came a little afterwards. While the rice was cooking at the foot of a tree outside, I began to tell them about Jesus. But soon the young man interrupted me, saying, 'Sahib, I have not so much need of salvation as these men have,' and he pointed to their mud-covered legs, and thought of his own white clothes so free from mire. But I said again that all are sinners. ' There is none that doeth good, no not one.' At last he said, 'Ha! I made a mistake. We are all sinners.' Another day a man said to me, ' Sahib, you are a great sinner ;' as he said so he looked at my dusty boots and trousers, and then at my forehead streaming with perspiration. He had noticed how I had spoken to the people as though they were my brothers, and he concluded that if I were not a great sinner I should never be so poor, or have to work so hard, or mix so freely with the natives. Hindus, you see, think that God gives riches to the good and poverty to the bad. Once a man among the crowd said to me when I was preaching, ' Yes, that's true ; we may do anything to get salvation, even sin.' This was a strange mixture of ideas, was it not ? But it shows that they do not think of salvation as freedom from sin. We have to teach them this. They do not even know what sin is. How can they, if they know not the law of God ? If you ask a large crowd of Hindus the question, ' What is sin ? ' they will answer in a moment, ' Eating beef.' They say there are two unpardonable sins—killing a Brahmin and killing a cow. Sometimes we are asked, most seriously, ' Did Jesus Christ eat meat ? ' They think that if He did, He too was a sinner. From this it will appear how difficult it is to get natives to understand what sin is not." (*The Gospel in all Lands.*)

Ver. 41. **Give alms of such things as ye have.**—*Christian charity :*—In the Revised Version the translation is—"Give for alms those things that are within," and this preserves the point of the saying, which is obscured in the rendering of the Authorized Version. Our Lord had been invited to dinner by a certain Pharisee, and had sat down to meat without the customary ritual ablutions. In the eyes of His host He sat there defiled by His refusal of the outward cleansing ; and it was to teach the lesson that purity must be born within the soul and cannot come to it from without, that He spoke these words. I. IN ONE SENSE THIS PRECEPT MAKES CHARITY EASIER RATHER THAN MORE DIFFICULT. We do not all possess the things which are without—money, influence, rank, and the patronage they bring with them ; and if Christ had made charity to consist in the bestowal of such things He would have made charity an impossible virtue to a large number of His disciples. But when Christ enlarges His definition of charity, when He says almsgiving does not only consist in giving money or giving anything that is external, but in giving the " things that are within," He certainly seems to open this royal road to all who choose to enter it, for lives there the man so poor as to be unable to give a tear, a look, a kindly word, a touch of brotherly sympathy to his fellow-man ? II. Yet it needs but a moment's thought to discover that INSTEAD OF THIS COMMAND MAKING ALMSGIVING EASIER, IT REALLY MAKES IT MORE DIFFICULT. For which is the easier, to give what you may have in your purse to the poor, or to give yourself ; to bestow the coin that is hardly missed, or to bestow your thought, sympathy, personal interest on some sad case of misfortune and suffering ? 1. Among the "things that are within," we may certainly count the manner in which charity is bestowed. As John Morley remarks, "It is not enough to do good ; one must do it in a good way." There is more real value, both to God and man, in a little gift given in a good way, given with willingness, with cheerfulness, with gratitude for the privilege of giving, than in a great gift flung out from a stony heart, like honey out of the rock. 2. But manner is not everything. Sympathy is more than manner ; and of all the inner sources of wealth which confer value on our alms, sympathy is the chief. It is one thing to give a sovereign to a a poor widow overwhelmed with trouble; it is another thing to give ourselves, our time, our sympathy, to help to lift her to a happier life, and to make her feel there is one heart that cares for her. A little while ago a poor lost girl lay dying on some filthy straw in a London slum. I know not whether any relief had been sent from the great houses near by, but if it had been given it had not touched her heart or brought hope to that darkened life. One day a Christian lady heard of the dying girl, heard the sad story of her life, and mounting the rickety stairs that led to her miserable room, found her out. She went to her side. Her first act was to stoop down and kiss her. That womanly act—that Christlike act, rather let me say, the pure touching and loving the impure—brought a flood of cleansing tears to that girl's face; that act saved a lost soul. It was giving for alms of the "things that were within." 3. Once again, in illustration of the inner wealth which we are to bestow on others, there is our personal service in the relief of suffering, or the increase of human joy, or the saving of the lost. Neither the manner of almsgiving nor the sympathy of the heart is enough. We must do good as well as be good. From the service of God, as expressed in the service of man, there is no exemption. You may pay a substitute to take your place in the conscriptions of earth; in the war of God against sin and suffering and ignorance, there is no vicarious service. Christ gave Himself for us; and He asks us to give ourselves to Him and to His service on earth. The Church of Christ will never save the world until, following its Divine Lord, it goes out into the dark places of the earth to seek and to save that which is lost. There is no Christian charity worth the name without sacrifice. Its lowest form is the sacrifice of money; its highest is the sacrifice of ourselves—the giving without murmuring or grudging our best for the service of God in the service of man. 4. I cannot omit from the "things that are within," the inner life of Christ which He has imparted to the soul, the gospel of His redeeming love, which has made us what we are. Christ expects you to speak for Him, to be a gospel to those who know Him not. There is a preaching more eloquent than any sermon from the pulpit, and that is the message spoken, not by the minister, but by each individual Christian in his own life in the fitting season. (*G. S. Barrett, B.A.*) *The value of almsgiving:*—Instead of "such things as ye have," the words ought rather to be rendered, "give alms of that which is within the cup and platter," *i.e.*, of their contents: give food and refreshment to those who need it, and behold all things are clean unto you. This is one of those very many places which assign to almsgiving (of course if practised for the approval of God, and not for vainglory) an almost expiatory value (see Luke xvi. 9; Acts x. 4; Matt. xxv. 34, 35; 1 Tim. vi. 17, 18). Godet paraphrases it well: "Do you wish, then, that these meats and these wines should not be defiled, and should not defile you? Do not think that it is enough for you carefully to wash your hands before eating; there is a surer means: let some poor man partake of them." (*M. F. Sadler.*) *Offertorial gifts:*— When we read this verse in connection with those that immediately precede it, the meaning of it appears to become clear and unquestionable. The Pharisees, in whose company our blessed Lord was sitting at meat, had remarked upon His not first washing before the dinner; for they themselves, and all the Jews, by their example, except they washed their hands often (or to the elbow) ate not, "holding the tradition of the elders" (Mark vii. 3). Ye fools, do ye then hope to deceive God by cleansing the outside, while your inward hearts are thus full of all extortion and greediness? Nay, rather purify the inside; change ravening into mercy, and stinginess and grudging into almsgiving; and, behold, every part, both the inside and the outside, will become clean unto you. The praise of almsgiving, then, which is contained in this passage, seems to be that when it is duly done, it is better in the sight of God than all whole burnt-offerings and sacrifices; that it has a more cleansing efficacy than any ceremonial worship; that it is an inward cleanness, and as such is acceptable to God beyond any outward punctiliousness or exactness of service. I am led to select this topic of Christian instruction, my brethren, in addressing you to-day, in order to make a few observations on the benefits of the sacred offertory of the Holy Communion. 1. Let it be observed then, first, that the holy offertorial gift is a gift of peace. "If thou bring thy gift to the altar, and there rememberest that thy brother hath aught against thee, leave there thy gift before the altar, and go thy way; first be reconciled to thy brother, and then come and offer thy gift" (Matt. v. 23, 24). How shall any one, then, who is unkind, or quarrelsome, or unforgiving, be able to offer the sacramental gift? Be it ever so small, it is the token and symbol of peace. Think, then, my brethren, whether, even in this respect only, the offertorial gift have not a very strong and important reference to your own lives and habits. Think whether there be not many ways in which you are tempted to infringe the law of Christian charity and courtesy towards one another; whether mutual kindness and considerateness, in great and small things, in matters of all sorts, in deeds, in words, in nicknames, in insults, in injury of feelings or property ; whether such minute considerateness and kindly courtesy, be not a duty of which you greatly need to be sometimes reminded. And think again whether you are not apt sometimes, in treating those whom God has placed in a lower rank than yourselves in life, to offend against the same law.   2. Secondly, the offertorial gift is to be regarded as the first-fruit of alms.   Whatever a man may give in alms between communion and communion is to be considered as all offered to God in the offering of this the first-fruits.   Thus the little gift of the communion is, in fact, greater, even in amount, than it seems ; for it represents all that a man Christianly gives for similar pious and charitable uses till his next communion.   It is as the libation, sanctifying all the feast.   As Christian alms then, the offertorial gift may be of most various and unconceived effects.   Who knows what sorrows it may alleviate, what pains it may soothe, what wants it may supply?   Who knows again how many thanksgivings it may awaken, how many prayers for blessings on the giver, what hearts it may touch to repentance ?   Who knows what consequences, never to be known on earth, but surely to be declared in the Judgment, a little gift with God's good blessing on it may produce beyond our power to trace or think? how it may bring glory to God from men on earth and from rejoicing angels in the highest heavens?   Thus then, in the second place, I would urge you to prize the offertorial gift as opening to you the privilege of sacred alms-giving.   But I have hitherto spoken only of the outward aspects of the offertorial gift.   It is to the inward ones, if I may so express myself, that the text of St. Luke particularly refers, and to which I rather desire to direct your attention.   Consider, then, how many ways there are in which men need that money, in its various uses, should be sanctified to them.   You know in what remarkable terms the Holy Scriptures constantly speak of money : how they seem to identify it in a very particular way with evil and the powers of evil; how our Lord calls it by the name of the unrighteous mammon, and telling His disciples that they cannot serve God and mammon, seems to put the false god of money for the evil spirit ; and to say that he and his dominion are so separate and distinct from God and His kingdom, that whosoever is subject to the one cannot possibly be subject to the other also.   What, then, I desire to set before you is this : that you, too, in your present state of life are beginning to be tried in respect of money ; that the false god of money, the unholy mammon, solicits you in various ways, as well as those whose pecuniary trials are larger and more notorious ; that you have many such dangers even now, which you must learn to escape in these early days of springing Christian strength, and that the secret of your strength and safety is to be found in your communion offerings. There, while you dedicate the little first-fruits, you must intend to sanctify the whole.   There, while you directly consecrate a little, you must resolve that there shall be none unconsecrated; that Christian devotion and duty shall accompany you even in the most distant and secular uses to which the rest may be applied ; that the manner of spending the rest shall be appropriate to this beginning.   3. Consider, then, how entirely inconsistent with the offering of communion gifts is all incurring of debt.   How can any person venture to approach the altar of God with what he pretends to be a gift, while, in fact, the very piece of money which he offers belongs of right to another, and is not his own ?   Let no one, then, think that he shall honour God by making an offering at the altar of that which he owes. It is, according to the expressive idiom of the Latin, " another man's money "; and little indeed can we think that God will be glorified, or that blessing will follow on the gift, which is rather an additional sin than a manner of sanctifying our other actions.   And let all remember that to offer at the Holy Communion is, in fact, to forswear and abandon the practice of incurring debts.   2. Think, again, of waste-fulness and luxury, and consider whether you are not commonly tempted to spend money, often very hardly spared by those who supply it to you, in self-indulgence of the most wanton and needless kinds.   3. Again, how impossible it should be for one who offers a gift at God's holy altar to be dishonest, whether that dishonesty be shown in the coarser and more unquestionable ways of theft or cheating, or in the less obvious, but not less guilty devices, whereby advantage is often unfairly taken, and some enriched to their neighbour's loss !   4. And again, as connected with the last topic, consider whether it be possible for those who desire to make their offertorial gift in true earnestness and devotion, to endeavour to gain money in gambling or betting of any kind. And who that ever saw the gambling passion strongly exhibited in any person can doubt of what manner of spirit such a man is while the passion is on him—the Spirit of God, or the spirit of mammon ? 5. And, lastly, let me ask you whether it be possible for one who brings his offering to the altar, and desires thereby to make all his other pecuniary dealings clean unto him, to purchase any things that are themselves unlawful, whether they be unlawful by the universal law of God, or unlawful by the laws to which they are now subject, and which they must obey, as they hope to please God in the state of life to which He has called them ? Plainly, it is not possible. It would be an attempt to give God a little and Satan much. These, then, are some of the ways in which the Holy Communion offering ought to be of benefit to you in these years : so true is it that if we would act up to all the precepts and directions of the Church we should find that they bear in many unexpected ways upon our lives, and cannot be neglected without much and heavy loss. The offertory gives the sacred Church rule of spending money ; and there is no part of the subject, however remote or secular, to which the rule thence derived will not apply. (*(Bishop Moberly.)*

Ver. 42. **These ought ye to have done.**—*Spurious holiness :*—Rabbi Shammai, the narrow-minded rival of Hillel, was so scrupulous that he nearly starved his little son on the Day of Atonement, and made a sort of booth of his daughter-in-law's bed that his little grandson, just born, might keep the Feast of Tabernacles. Yet we are told that he was a luxurious and selfish man. It is easier to tithe mint than to live a holy life. (*Canon Farrar.*) *Neglecting the most important thing :*— A great French doctor was taking an English one round the wards of his hospital, all sorts of miseries going on before them, some dying, others longing for death— all ill. The Frenchman was wonderfully eloquent about all their diseases ; you would have thought he saw through them, and knew all their secret wheels, like looking into a watch or into a glass bee-hive. He told his English friend what would be seen in such a case when the body was opened! He spent some time in this sort of work, and was coming out, full of glee, when the other doctor said, " But, Dr. ——, you haven't prescribed for these cases." " Oh, neither I have ! " said he, with a grumph and a shrug ; " I quite forgot that " ; that being the one thing why these poor people were there, and why he was there too. (*John Brown, M.D.*) *Pardon desired for duties left undone :*—Dr. Samuel Johnson, in writing to his mother, says :—" You have been the best mother, and I believe the best woman, in the world. I thank you for your indulgence to me, and I beg forgive-ness for all I have done ill, and all that I have omitted to do well." So in the prayer he composed at the same time : " Forgive me whatever I have done unkindly to my mother, and whatever I have omitted to do kindly."

Ver. 45. **Thou reproachest us also.**—*Disputes reviewed :*—I. WE MUST ALL EXPECT TO BE CALLED TO AN ACCOUNT BY THE LORD JESUS. 1. We are all now in " the way "—travellers—following Christ in consort. 2. There will be a review of what passes in " the way." 3. The accounts in the great day must be given up to our Lord Jesus. God made the world, by His Son ; and by Him, as the fittest person, He will judge the world. Now this is a good reason—(1) Why we should judge ourselves, and prove our own work, and see that our matters be right and good against that day. Let us examine ourselves concerning our spiritual state, that we may make sure work for our own souls. (2) Why we should not judge one another, or be severe in our censures one of another. We thereby invade Christ's throne. II. WE MUST IN A PARTICULAR MANNER BE CALLED TO AN ACCOUNT ABOUT OUR DIS-COURSES AMONG OURSELVES. 1. If we talk anything which is good among ourselves, and which is to the use of edifying ; which manifests grace in the speaker, and ministers grace to the hearers ; Christ takes notice of that, and we shall hear of it again to our comfort, in that day when those who thus confess Christ before men shall be owned by Him before His father and the holy angels. 2. If we talk any-thing that is ill among ourselves ; if any corrupt communication proceeds out of our mouths, dictated by the corruption of our minds, and which has a tendency to corrupt the minds and manners of others ; Christ observes that too, is displeased with it—and we shall hear of it again, either by the checks of our own consciences, in order to our repentance, or in the day of the revelation of the righteous judg-ment of God, when, according to Enoch's prophecy, the Lord shall come to reckon with sinners, not only for all their ungodly deeds, but for all their hard speeches, spoken against Him. III. As our other discourses among ourselves by the way, so

ESPECIALLY OUR DISPUTES, WILL ALL BE CALLED OVER AGAIN, and we shall be called to an account about them.　1. Disputes commonly arise from difference of opinion, either in religion and Divine things (about which oftentimes the disputes and contests are most violent) ; or in philosophy, politics, or other parts of learning ; or in the conduct of human life.　These disputes (though not necessarily sinful in themselves, for men cannot be expected to agree on all points) are often such as we may justly be ashamed of, when we come to look back upon them.　(1) Upon account of the matter of them.　This may have been—(a) Something above us, with which we had no concern; or (b) something below us, not worth disputing about.　(2) Upon account of our management of them.　Our Master will be displeased with us if it be found that we have been hot and fierce in our disputes, and have mingled our passions and peevish resentments with them; if a point of honour has governed us more than a point of conscience, and we have contended more for victory and reputation, than for truth and duty ; if we have contended about things of small moment for, or against, them, and have neglected the weightier matters of the law and gospel ; if we have spent more of our zeal on matters in difference than they deserve; and have lost the vitals of religion in our heat about circumstantials, and have disputed away our seriousness and devotion—" What then shall we do when God riseth up ? and when He visiteth, what shall we answer Him ? "　2. Many disputes arise from separate and interfering interests in this world.　Neighbours and relations quarrel about their rights and properties, their estates and trades, their honours and powers and pleasures ; *Meum* and *Tuum*—" my rent " and " thy bond," are the great subjects of dispute, and engage people in endless strifes.　These disputes, as they are most common, so they are most scandalous, among relations, and those who are under particular obligations to love one another.　And whatever keeps brethren from dwelling together in unity, is very provoking to Christ, who has made brotherly love the livery of His family: and it is very hardly removed.　3. Some disputes, and hot ones too, arise merely from passion and clashing humours, where really there is nothing of judgment or interest in the case.　(1) As far as we are able to make a judgment, let us see to it that we have truth and right on our side, in all our disputes, and not be confident any further than we see just cause to be so.　We must not only never contend for that which we know to be false and wrong, but also never for that which is doubtful, or which we do not know to be true and right. (2) In matters of doubtful disputation.　While we are contending for that which we take to be right, let us at the same time think it possible that we may be in the wrong.　(3) Let us keep the full possession and government of our own spirits, in all our disputes.　Let us carefully suppress all inward tumults, whatever provocation may be given us ; and let our minds be calm and sedate, whatever argument we are engaged in.　(4) Let us never lose the charity we ought to have for our brethren in our disputes of any kind, nor violate the sacred laws of it.　(5) Let us often think of the account we must shortly give to our great Master of all our disputes with our fellow-servants by the way.　Let us consider how our disputes will look in that day, and what our own reflections will be then upon them.　IV. Of all disputes, Christ will be sure to reckon with His disciples for their DISPUTES ABOUT PRECEDENCY AND SUPERIORITY.　The prevalency of such a temper as this, as far as it appears, is very threatening.　But when the Spirit shall be poured out upon us from on high, there shall be no more such disputes as these ; and then the wilderness shall become a fruitful field.　Upon the whole matter, therefore, let our strife be, Who shall be best, not Who shall be greatest.　1. Let us never strive who shall be greatest in this world ; who shall have the best preferment ; who shall be master of the best estate, or make the best figure ; but acquiesce in the lot Providence carves out to us, not aiming at great things, or striving for them.　Consider what worldly greatness is. (1) What a despicable thing it is to those who have their eyes upon another world. (2) What a dangerous thing this worldly greatness is to those who have not their eyes upon another world ; how apt it is to keep their hearts at a distance from God, and from the consideration and pursuit of a future blessedness ; and to fix them to this world, and make them willing to take up with a portion in it ; and, especially, what a strong temptation it is to break through all the sacred fences of the Divine law to compass it.　2. Let all our strife be who shall be best, not disputing who has been best, that is a vain-glorious strife, but humbly contending who shall be so ; who shall be most humble, and stoop lowest, for the good of others ; and who shall labour most for the common welfare.　This is a gracious strife ; a strife that will pass well in our account, when all our disputes will be reviewed.　(*Matthew Henry.*)

Vers. 47, 48. **Ye build the sepulchres of the prophets.**—*Building the tombs of the prophets :*—The Jews, whilst honouring the prophets and reproaching their fathers, were flattering themselves that they could never have done the like. Would they not indeed? were they not at the very moment thirsting for the blood of Christ and contriving His destruction? Alas for the fatal facility with which those who are quick in discerning the faults of others can blind themselves to their own! Here was the fault of the Jews. They were the descendants of men who had persecuted and slain the prophets of God. But they themselves were ready to do the very same: they were plotting the death of the greatest Prophet, the greatest in all the signs or evidences of a prophet that had ever arisen in their land. And, nevertheless, they could see well enough how wrong their fathers had been, and could join in showing honour to the righteous persons whom they had treated so ill; but it does not seem to have struck them that they were closely treading in their steps, and were about to imitate, or rather far surpass, what they so loudly condemned. But is there no lesson here for ourselves? Let us first fix attention on the singular fact, that what is admired in the dead may be execrated in the living. There was no essential difference between the preaching of Christ, which excited the fierce anger of the Jews, and that of the prophets, which had similarly displeased and irritated their fathers. In both cases the preaching was that of the necessity of repentance, and of the certainty of vengeance, if not averted through the forsaking of sin. And the Jews, in the time of our Lord, could profess a high admiration of the preachers who had pressed these truths on their fathers, though, all the while, they were full of indignation against those who laboured to press them on themselves. The same takes place in our own day and generation. Call to mind the names of martyrs, and confessors, and preachers, who, whilst they lived, drew on themselves almost universal detestation by their zeal in the publication of truth and the exposure of error. Gather opinions as to these martyrs, confessors, and preachers, and you will obtain well nigh an unqualified verdict, pronouncing them amongst the worthiest of men, ornaments to their own age, and examples to every succeeding. Open a subscription for some testimonial in their honour; and money will flow in for the building their tombs and garnishing their sepulchres, just as though there were a general anxiety to evince a sense of their worth, and of the injustice of their contemporaries. But now go on to examine what the principles were which these dead worthies upheld, what the doctrines which they published, what the practices which they denounced. And do you think you will find that these principles are in general repute, these doctrines generally esteemed, these practices generally shunned? Oh, not so. The principles are still those which excite opposition, the doctrines are disliked, the practices are cherished. And it is by the feelings entertained towards the things taught, and not by those expressed towards the dead who were their teachers, that we are to judge whether men would have joined in persecuting the prophets. I care nothing for the stately mausoleum. I have no faith in the laboured panegyric. I am not to be persuaded, because sculpture and painting may devote themselves to the representing the magnanimous dead, or poetry consecrate its richest melodies to the story of their deeds and their wrongs. If the truth for which the dead died be not beloved by the living, there is no evidence that the living would not have aided in their destruction. But we may identify our own case yet more closely with that of the Jews. There is perhaps no more common feeling than that of amazement and indignation at the treatment which our Lord received from His countrymen. If ever there moved upon the earth the Being who seemed likely to disarm all enmity, and attract towards Himself universal affection, that Being undoubtedly was Jesus of Nazareth. He had so evidently no object but that of benefiting others, and He gave such evidences of ability to compass this object, that we might have supposed that all classes would have eagerly welcomed Him as a Prophet and Deliverer. And the apparent improbability of the rejection of Christ may easily induce a persuasion that, had we been in the days of the Jews, we could never have shared in their crime. But how ought such passages as our text to stagger us, showing us, as they do, that the Jews equally flattered themselves that they were incapable of the sin of putting a great Prophet to death! We make no doubt that, had we been contemporary with Christ, had we beheld His miracles and listened to His preaching, we should never have been of the number of those who sought His destruction. But what is this persuasion but the very persuasion of the Jews, who sat in judgment on their fathers as slayers of the prophets, and determined that they could never have joined them in their crime, and this too at the moment when they thirsted for Christ's blood, and bent themselves to compass His death? It may seem to me almost impossible that I should have conspired against Christ, that I should have helped to weave the crown of thorns and to drive the nails into His hands and His feet. But am I so unlike the Jew, is there any such radical difference between myself and the Jew, that I am warranted in believing that his wickedness could never have been mine? Ah, there is at least one point of similarity between us; and this ought to make me fearful of hastily concluding that there cannot be more. And what is this point? why, that the Jew and myself are equally ready to plead too much goodness to allow of joining in killing a prophet. My way of judging and deciding was precisely his, the reference to a crime which others committed, and determining against the possibility of any participation. And where there is the same assurance of inability to perpetrate a sin there is probably the same ability. Let us trust to no verdict of acquittal which we may be disposed to pass on ourselves after listening to that which the murderers of Christ so complacently uttered. So far, therefore, we may safely take the text, and give it as descriptive of what occurs amongst ourselves. But may we also denounce the woe which it contains? That woe is evidently denounced on account of the hypocrisy of those whose actions are described, on account of their conspiring against the living Christ, whilst joining to do honour to the murdered prophets. And is there anything parallel to this amongst ourselves? Indeed there is; for it is very easy to be indignant against those who put Jesus to death and all the while to overlook our own share in the guilty transaction. It is very easy to give up to universal execration the Roman and the Jew, and to be unmindful of the causes which brought round the Crucifixion. It is very easy to take the narrative of Christ's sufferings, just as you would the narrative of some doleful occurrence that happened in a remote age, and which has little more than its sadness to give it interest with your feelings. But who slew the Lamb of God? who drove the nails? who reared the cross? Not the Roman and the Jew. These were but agents and instruments. Christ died for the sins of the world: the sins of the world were really His murderers, though they used the Roman and the Jew as His executioners. And no man regards the death of Christ under a just point of view who does not charge himself with a share in the perpetration. He who does not make himself one of the murderers can scarcely have faith in the propitiation. And who will dare to assert that he is innocent of the blood of Jesus Christ? The Son of God is now virtually crucified afresh, whenever men turn away from the Redeemer, refusing to accept the mercy which He proffers, because they will not quit the sins which He abhors. It is virtually done by every wilful act of rebellion, by unbelief, by pride, by hardness of heart, by resistance to the strivings of the Spirit, by disobedience to the precepts of the gospel. The wilful transgressor does all which he can do towards rendering necessary a second crucifixion: he commits more and more of that which crucified Christ, and therefore, so far as his own guiltiness is concerned, may literally be charged with crucifying Him again. And, over and above this, you are to consider that Christ is continually coming to the impenitent and obdurate in and through the ordinances of religion, presenting Himself to them as their Redeemer, and beseeching them to receive Him, as they would hope to escape eternal destruction. But they treat Him with contempt. He calls, but they refuse: He stretches out His hand, but they will not regard. And what is all this if not the repetition of the Jewish denial and rejection of Christ? (*H. Melvill, B.D.*) *Ignorance of our own depravity:*—The Jews may have believed and boasted themselves incapable of taking part in the killing a prophet, little suspecting that they needed only the being placed in the same circumstances as their fathers in order to their imitating their crimes. And this is but the illustration of a general truth that, whilst men are not tempted to a sin, they cannot judge whether or not they would commit it if they were. With singular propriety are we instructed to pray, "Lead us not into temptation"; for only temptation may be needed to our perpetrating the worst crimes that disgrace human nature. They say that the earth contains varieties of seed, and that according to concurrent circumstances is there one production at one time and another at another. And this I am sure is the case with the heart, "out of which," according to Christ, "proceed evil thoughts, murders, adulteries, fornications, thefts, false witness, blasphemies." The seeds of all these iniquities are deposited in the heart; and a certain state, so to speak, of the moral atmosphere, or a certain combination of exciting causes, is all that is required to develop them in the practice. It does, therefore, but argue great ignorance of ourselves to suppose that this or that sin is too bad for us to commit. And the persuasion that we could not commit it is but an evidence of the likelihood of our being betrayed into the commission; for it shows a measure of self-confidence, as well as of ignorance, which God may be expected to punish by withdrawing His grace—and if that be withdrawn, where is human virtue? We are bound, as believers in Revelation, to believe that nothing of evil is beyond our power, and nothing of good within it, if we be left to ourselves, and are not acted on by an influence from above. And our only security against becoming perpetrators of crimes at whose very mention we perhaps shudder, lies in such a consciousness of our own depravity as leads to a prayerful, continual dependence on the preventing and restraining grace of God. (*Ibid.*) *The tombs of the prophets:*—I. THESE PHARISAIC WORTHIES DID CHEAP AND OSTENTATIOUS HOMAGE TO DEAD AND DISTANT VIRTUE. They "built the tombs of the prophets, and garnished the sepulchres of the righteous." Monuments of the illustrious and pious dead were common in Jerusalem. These memorials the Pharisees held in most officious veneration, repairing, ornamenting, or building them anew. Pious acts, one might deem. Could such grave-visaged votaries be other than God-fearing men? Alas for poor human nature! A certain homage to virtue it doubtless was, this rearing of monumental honours to prophets long dead. Even in the worst of men, such acts are not without their value in testifying to a conscience within them, and a God above them. We blame not the instinct for monuments, nor need we, for it is as deep as human nature, as old as history: witness the pyramids, Assyria, Egypt, Greece, Rome. We see it in the rude stone or cairn that marks some hard-fought field, or the spot where some old mailed king grimly bit the ground. It continues to fill our squares with statues, our graveyards with sculptures, our cathedrals with "storied urn and animated bust." Yea, it fills our houses with portraits and other relics of the dear departed, over whom memory contests it stoutly with the very grave, and makes it " give us back the dead, even in the loveliest looks they wore." Need I add that Christianity, too, which has a true and kindly side for everything natural, has its monumental institutions? But, with all this, monumental zeal is but a cheap, and often vulgar homage. Stone memorials may be projected and erected by very stony hearts. The tomb-building rage is often symptomatic of a degenerate time, in which the nation has passed its zenith, has stopped producing heroes, and now produces only their statues, or it may be, like Jerusalem, their persecutors and killers. Illustrations of this tendency are not far to seek, though we are very far from calling ours a degenerate age. In one of our minor capitals, any visitor may find in a certain spacious street, standing in a row, the express image of royal sensuality, supported on the one side by that of political tyranny, and on the other by that of political corruption. Some years ago, twenty-five thousand pounds were subscribed to erect a statue to a public person whose only known accomplishment was railway gambling, and whose only public virtue was success. The old prophets, persecuted through life, and at last stoned out of it, did come, in a future age, to get recognition. "The memory of the just is blessed," while " the memory of the wicked shall rot" ; and thus, even from foes, the good may get posthumous instalments of the honours that await them in full measure before assembled worlds. But this homage they never get till they are fairly out of the way. A dead prophet's tomb called only for the cheap surrender of a little pelf. The living prophet himself would have demanded the right hand or the right eye, the immolation of the darling lust, the consecration of the whole man. To deny due honour to the prophet, and pay mock honours to his tomb, was truly a lie in livery. So is it still. Wesley is lauded by many in our day who, were he alive, would brand him, as did even his pious contemporary Toplady, as "an inveterate troubler of Israel." Why? Because Wesley is out of their way—he has " ceased from troubling "; and thus he whom, living, men classed among troublers, may, now that he is dead, be enrolled among the saints. Thus death or distance lends enchantment to the view. The noblest monument we can rear to a prophet, is to gather up his teachings into our experience, and reproduce his character in our life. For the real monument of the heroes and martyrs that founded England's greatness —*circumspice!*—if you ask where it is, we answer, Where is it not? The true Wallace monument is not the rock-dwarfed thing which, under that name, disfigures a picturesque and memorable spot, but is seen in a nation of patriots who had the good sense to be indifferent to that structural anachronism, and who have often contributed many times its cost, in one of their cities alone, for modern patriotic objects common and dear to the United Kingdom. No tribute to such men as Watt and the Stephensons could equal that which thunders in every factory and steams on every sea.　II. THOSE PHARISEES BORE CHEAP AND OSTENTATIOUS TESTIMONY AGAINST DEAD AND DISTANT SIN.　They said, "If we had been in the days of our fathers, we would not have been partakers with them in the blood of the prophets."　Pious men!　Blushing crimson for being sons of prophet-murdering sires!　Such was their profession in regard to the dead.　What now was their actual practice in regard to the living?　You may read it here (verse 33) in the words "serpents," "vipers."　Our Lord thereby describes them as men whose hearts were venom-bags, whose mouths were open sepulchres, whose tongues were rooted, and floated, in the poison of asps.　There had already come among them a prophet, yea, and more than a prophet, even the Son of the Highest.　And how did those saintly tomb-builders receive Him?　"It is certain that a Herod and a Herodias to John the Baptist, would have been an Ahab and a Jezebel to Elijah."　Let this bring home to us the humiliating lesson of our fatal proneness to glide into the delusive persuasion that this or that sin is what we, for our parts, are wholly incapable of committing—that, though all men should fall into it, yet will not we.　Where is the Bible reading youth who has not in his inexperience marvelled at Israel's murmurings in the desert, and at the sad falls of some of the most eminent of the Old Testament saints?　But riper views, and deeper spiritual experiences, not only correct this mistake, but let us see in the very facts we once deemed so stumbling, striking evidence of the truth and divinity of the book that records them.　The holiest man will be the least disposed to declare himself incapable of this or that sin.　III. BY ALL THIS THESE PHARISEES EXPOSED AND CONDEMNED THEMSELVES (see verses 30, 31).　In conclusion, note one thing they ought to have done, but left undone; nay, did the opposite; that of humbly owning their oneness with the prophet-killing fathers.　Paradoxical as it may sound, this was the first step to standing out from their fathers' crime.　(*T. Guthrie, D.D.*)　*The vanity and wickedness of honouring dead saints, and persecuting the living :*—I. WHAT IS HERE MEANT BY "THE WISDOM OF GOD."　"Therefore also said the wisdom of God, I will send them prophets and apostles," &c.　In St. Matthew, our Saviour speaks this in His own name—"Wherefore, behold I send unto you prophets": for which reason, some think that by "the wisdom of God" our Saviour here designed Himself; as if He had said, Therefore I, who am the "wisdom of God," declare unto you.　But this is not very probable, our Saviour nowhere else in the Gospel speaking of Himself in any such style; though St. Paul calls Him "the power of God," and "the wisdom of God."　Others think that our Saviour here refers to some prophecy of the Old Testament to this purpose : "Therefore, the Wisdom of God hath said"; that is, the Holy Spirit of wisdom, which inspired the prophets in the Old Testament.　But this conceit is utterly without ground, for we find no such passage.　But the most plain and simple interpretation is this : "Therefore hath the wisdom of God said"; that is, the most wise God hath determined to send among you such messengers and holy men, and I foresee that ye will thus abuse them, and thereby bring wrath and destruction upon yourselves.　And whereas our Saviour says, in St. Matthew, "behold I send unto you prophets"; it is very probable He speaks in God's name, and that it is to be understood, Behold, says God, I send unto you.　By apostles is here meant all sorts of Divine messengers; for so St. Matthew expresseth it, "I send unto you prophets, and wise men, and scribes"; that is, several holy and excellent men, endowed with all sorts of Divine gifts.　II. WHO THIS ZACHARIAS WAS, HERE MENTIONED BY OUR SAVIOUR.　III. IN WHAT SENSE, AND WITH WHAT REASON AND JUSTICE IT IS HERE THREATENED, THAT "THE BLOOD OF ALL THE PROPHETS AND RIGHTEOUS MEN, SHED FROM THE FOUNDATION OF THE WORLD," SHOULD BE REQUIRED OF THAT GENERATION.　1. That it hath been the lot of holy and righteous men, in most ages of the world, to meet with very bad usage, to be "persecuted and slain."　The devil began this work early.　2. We may observe likewise, hence, how great a sin they are guilty of who persecute the righteous, and how terrible a vengeance from God waits on them.　3. From this whole passage of our Saviour, which I have been explaining to you, we may learn how vain it is for men to pretend to honour the dead saints, when they persecute the living.　(*Archbishop Tillotson.*)　*The world's treatment of its guides :*—Hannibal, the Carthaginian conqueror, when sailing from Italy to Carthage, suspected his pilot of treachery, and when the latter told him that a high mountain which appeared in the distance was a promontory of Sicily, believing himself imposed upon, he killed him on the spot, but afterwards buried him splendidly, and called the promontory by his name.　Thus he illustrated the way of the world with its true prophets. *Unique tombs :*—The tombs of Egypt are among the grandest and most striking of its monuments. The pyramids were tombs, and they are still wonders of the world. The rock-hewn sepulchres, however, which surround the pyramids, and which dot the mountain gorges of Thebes and Bene-Hassan, are now probably the most instructive. Their chambers are so many museums, containing not merely the embalmed remains, but, on the inscribed and sculptured walls, the whole history of the mighty dead. Nothing is overlooked or forgotten that would throw light on their lives and labours. In this way we have a most vivid picture of ancient Egypt; the victories of kings; processes in law courts; the building of cities; the hewing and transport of colossal statues and obelisks; the embalming of the dead; funeral rites and processions; marriage ceremonies; every department of household work and family life, such as cooking, washing, dressing, shaving the head and beard, eating; trades of all kinds—goldsmiths, painters, potters, glass-blowers, bakers, weavers; games and amusements—jugglers, music, dancing; tilling the soil; irrigating the fields; feeding and milking cows; watering flax, reaping, threshing, grinding—all these and many other things are delineated with singular, and not unfrequently amusing, minuteness of detail. In examining those unique tombs one can study the manners and customs, the private life and public acts, the religious rites and ceremonies, the features and dress of those who lived in cottage and palace in that country from three to four thousand years ago, with almost as much advantage as if he had lived among them. The perfect preservation of the paintings and papyri is astonishing. In this Western land of rain and frost half a century of neglect would destroy them; but in Upper Egypt rain and frost are unknown. The dry and equable climate is the grand curator; and this has been materially assisted by the desert sand, which has partially covered some of the monuments, and for long ages hermetically sealed many of the finest tombs. The figures and brilliant colouring on the walls, and written characters upon the papyrus have been thus preserved as fresh as if only finished yesterday. Looking at them one can scarcely believe that their age has to be reckoned by thousands of years. (*Cassell's Family Magazine.*) *Costly posthumous offerings :*—At the entrance are two sentry-box looking constructions with glass windows. These are lamps kept perpetually lighted, the flame not having been allowed to die out for many years. The sanctum is very splendid, the roofs and walls being lined with gold brocade, and the frames of the door inlaid with carved ivory. The air is oppressive with the perfume of flowers and spices. Flowers especially are a favourite offering at Buddha's shrine, and are always present in great profusion. On one occasion no less than 6,480,320 flowers were counted at the shrine, and it is recorded that in the fifteenth century a royal devotee sent 100,000 flowers a day for a considerable time, and each day the flowers were of a different kind. The karundua, or vessel containing the tooth, stands covered on a table of massive silver, richly chased, in the midst of a profusion of valuable articles of jewellery, which are either relics or offerings. The most beautiful in the collection is a bird with wings spread. It is formed entirely of diamonds, rubies, blue sapphires, &c., set in gold, which is hid by a profusion of gems. While we were all admiring this magnificent offering, the priests or monks removed several folds of muslin from the karundua, and discovered a sort of dome of gilded silver, about five feet high, studded with a few gems. When this was removed, another was found underneath, made of beautifully carved gold. This was festooned with jewelled chains, and literally incrusted with all the glittering gems for which Ceylon is so celebrated— sapphires and emeralds of extraordinary size, cat's eyes (much prized), rubies, amethysts, and pearls. Another similar covering, and still another, were taken off, when at last was reached a small case of gold, covered externally with rubies, emeralds, and diamonds, in which, resting on the leaves of a gold lotus, was the tooth itself. (*Ibid.*) *The hypocrisy of posthumous honours :*—I never saw the honours of this world in their hollowness and hypocrisy so much as I have seen them within the last few days, as I have been looking over the life and death of that wonderful man just departed, Charles Sumner. Now that he is dead the whole nation takes off the hat. The flags are at half-mast and the minute-guns on Boston Common throb, now that his heart has ceased to beat. Was it always so? While he lived, how censured of legislative resolutions, how caricatured of the pictorials, how charged with every motive mean and ridiculous; how, when struck down in Senate-chamber, there were hundreds of thousands of people who said, " Good for him, served him right!" O Commonwealth of Massachusetts! who is that man that sleeps to-night in your public hall, covered with garlands and wrapped in the stars and stripes? Is that the man whom, only a few months ago, you denounced as the foe of Republican and Democratic institutions? Is that the same man? You were either wrong then or you are wrong now—a thing most certain, O Commonwealth of Massachusetts! When I see a man like that pursued by all the hounds of the political kennel so long as he lives, and then buried under garlands almost mountain high, and amid the lamentations of a whole nation, I say to myself, "What an unutterably hypocritical thing is all human applause and all human favour!" You took twenty-five years in trying to pull down his fame, and now you will take twenty-five years in trying to build his monument. You were either wrong then, or you are wrong now. My friends, was there ever a better commentary on the hollowness of all earthly favour? (*Dr. Talmage.*)

Ver. 52. **Ye have taken away the key of knowledge.**—*The sin of perverting Scripture* :—The last woe pronounced by our Saviour against the Scribes and Pharisees, is for perverting the Holy Scriptures, and keeping the true sense and knowledge of them from the people: this St. Luke here calls, "the taking away the key of knowledge from men"; alluding to a custom among the Jews, in admission of their doctors. Those that had authority given them to interpret the law and the prophets, were solemnly admitted into that office, by delivering to them a key and a table-book; so that by the key of knowledge is meant the interpretation and understanding of the Scriptures, and by taking away that key is signified—1. That they arrogated to themselves the sole power of understanding and interpreting the Holy Scriptures. 2. That they kept the true knowledge of the Scriptures from the people, especially the prophecies which concern the kingdom and coming of the Messias; and so they hindered men from embracing our Saviour's doctrine, who were otherwise well enough disposed for it. Learn—1. That the written Word is the key whereby an entrance into heaven is opened unto men. 2. That the use of this key, or the knowledge of the Word of God, is absolutely and indispensibly necessary in order to salvation. 3. That great is the guilt, and inexcusable the fault of those who deny the people the use of this key, and deprive them of the knowledge of the Holy Scriptures, which alone can make them wise unto salvation. 4. That such as do so, shut the kingdom of heaven against men, endeavouring what in them lies to hinder their salvation. Men may miscarry with their knowledge, but they are sure to perish for lack of knowledge. (*W. Burkitt.*)　　*Hinderers* :—Some unpublished thoughts on "Hinderers and Hindrances," written by Frances Ridley Havergal, were forwarded by her sister Maria V. G. Havergal to the editor of *The Sunday Magazine.* We glean the following from the second paper, which appeared in the September, 1885, issue :— "A letter from Ernest at last! And the sister eagerly gives her father the morning budget at the breakfast table. Her mother watches, for gloom gathers on the father's face as he reads it. Silently the letter is given to the mother, and he passes through the open window to the pleasant terrace-walk beneath. The sister guesses in vain, 'What can Ernest have written?' The father paced up and down, thinking of the position he himself had won, and which he had hoped would be a stepping-stone for his son to one far higher, in which his many gifts of mind and heart would shine with no common effulgence. He had hoped his son would carry out and develop many schemes of benevolence he had set on foot. But that morning's letter was as a mighty crucible, wherein the man's devotedness to Him who had given him that darling son was to be tested and analyzed. What was that letter? '—— College, Cambridge. DEAR FATHER,—Will you listen to your son's request for your consent, your blessing, your prayers? Father, there is a burning impulse within me, a new life-pulse seems beating in my soul, a still deep voice ever sounding in my ears, "Go ye into all the world, and preach the gospel to every creature." Years ago that same voice called me, when I first heard stories about the heathen and their idols, and when standing by my mother I looked at the Church Missionary Society's green picture-book ("Juvenile Instructor"), of white men preaching to the heathen. Silently, but surely, has that call followed me. I have cried earnestly, "Lord, what wilt Thou have me to do?" and again the heavenly whisper comes, "Go ye." Therefore, though never before breathed to any but God, this is no sudden thought, no unconsidered plan. Father, let me go, let me take the cup of living water to him that is ready to perish. I should like to tread the very footsteps of Him who came to seek and to save that which was lost, to search in His name for the "other sheep, which are not of this fold." I know the hopes and the intentions which you have cherished for my future; but is not a missionary's joy a nobler gain, the missionary's crown a nobler ambition than any other? And what if the time came when, among the multitude out of all nations and kindreds and tongues, I might be permitted to recognize some who first heard a Saviour's name from my unworthy lips! My own dear mother! her heart will be with me in this; I know she lent me to the Lord. Dearest father, I believe Christ has called me; will you let me obey His voice? Your loving son, ERNEST.'" Reader, what would your answer have been? Would you have hindered? The father could not brook that the talents of his son, the pride of his ancestral hall, should go forth into the gloom and obscurity of distant shores. But who can tell how bitterly that question, "Father, will you hinder me?" returned to his mind when the bell tolled for the early death of that loved and devoted son! *Hindering* :—A young Savoyard, a poor little chimney-sweep, one day purchased a Testament, for which he paid ten sous (rather less than fivepence of English money), and set himself immediately to read it. Delighted to possess the Word of God, he, in his simplicity, ran to the priest to show him the good bargain he had made with his savings. The priest looked at the book, and told the young Savoyard that it came from the hands of heretics, and that it was a book forbidden to be read. The poor boy replied that everything he had read in the book told him about Christ; "and beside," said he, "it is so beautiful!" "You shall see how beautiful it is," said the priest, seizing it and casting it into the fire. The young Savoyard went away weeping. (*W. Denton.*) *Lamentable effect of hindering* :—Hume, the historian, received a religious education from his mother, but as he approached manhood confirmed infidelity succeeded. Maternal partiality, however, alarmed at first, came at length to look with less and less pain upon his declension, and filial love and reverence seemed to have been absorbed in the pride of philosophical scepticism; for Hume applied himself with unwearied, and, unhappily, with successful, efforts to sap the foundation of his mother's faith. Having succeeded, he went abroad, and as he was returning an express met him in London, with a letter from his mother informing him that she was in a deep decline. She said she found herself without any support in her distress; that he had taken away that only source of comfort upon which, in all cases of affliction, she used to rely; and that she now found her mind sinking into despair. She conjured him to hasten to her, or at least to send her a letter containing such consolations as philosophy could afford to a dying mortal. Hume was overwhelmed with anguish on receiving this letter, and hastened to Scotland, travelling day and night; but before he arrived his mother expired.

CHAPTER XII.

VER. 1. **The leaven of the Pharisees, which is hypocrisy.**—*Hypocrisy* :—I. THE HYPOCRITE'S CHARACTER. 1. A hypocrite may be known by the fact that his speech and his actions are contrary to one another. As Jesus says, "They say and they do not." Talk is easy, but walk is hard; speech any man may attain unto, but act is difficult. We must have grace within to make our life holy; but lip-piety needs no grace. 2. The next mark of a hypocrite is, that whenever he does right it is that he may be seen of men. To him virtue in the dark is almost a vice; he can never detect any beauty in virtue, unless she has a thousand eyes to look upon her, and then she is something indeed. The true Christian, like the nightingale, sings in the night; but the hypocrite has all his songs in the day, when he can be seen and heard of men. 3. Hypocrites love titles, and honours, and respect from men. There was another evidence of an hypocrite which was equally good, namely, that he strained at a gnat and swallowed a camel. Always suspect yourself when you are more careful about little than about great things. 4. These people neglected all the inward part of religion, and only observed the outward. As our Saviour said, they "made clean the outside of the cup and platter, but within they were full of extortion and excess." There are many books which are excellently bound, but there is nothing within them; and there are many persons that have a very fine spiritual exterior, but there is nothing whatever in the heart. 5· You may know a hypocrite by another sign. His religion depends upon the place, or upon the time of day. He rises at seven o'clock perhaps, and you will find him religious for a quarter of an hour; for he is, as the boy said, "saying his prayers to himself" in the first part of the morning. Well, then you find him pretty pious for another half-hour, for there is family prayer; but when the business begins, and he is talking to his men, I won't guarantee that you will be able to admire him. If one of his servants has been doing something a little amiss, you will find him perhaps using angry and unworthy language. You will find him, too, if he gets a customer whom he thinks to be rather green, not quite pious, for he will be taking him in. 6. There is another sign of the hypocrite, and now the lash will fall on my own back, and on most of us too. Hypocrites, and other people besides hypocrites, are generally severe with others, and very lenient with themselves. Have you ever heard a hypocrite describe himself? I describe him thus—"You are a mean, beggarly fellow." "No," says he, "I am not; I am economical." I say to him, "You are dishonest, you are a thief." "No," says he, "I am only cute and sharp for the times." "Well, but," I say to him, "you are proud and conceited." "Oh!" says he, "I have only a proper and manly respect." "Ay, but you are a fawning, cringing fellow." "No," says he, "I am all things to all men." Somehow or other he will make vice look like a virtue in himself, but he will deal by the reverse rule with others. Show him a Christian who is really humble, and he says, "I hate his fawning ways." Tell him there is one who is very courageous for Christ; "Oh! he is impudent," says he. Show him one who is liberal, doing what he can for his Master's service, spending, and being spent for Him; "Rash and imprudent," says he, "extravagant; the man does not know what he is about." You may point out a virtue, and the hypocrite shall at once say it is a vice. II. And now we are going to CAST UP THE HYPOCRITE'S ACCOUNT FOR HIM. Now, sir, bring us your ledger, and let us have a look at it. You are a hypocrite. Well, what is on the profit side? A good deal, I must confess. Here is, first of all, credit and honour. The next advantage is the ease which you enjoy. And, besides that, there are the honours you have received. That is the profit side of your account. Now turn to the other, and take note of what there is against you. In the first place, I see a black item down here. Some of the people of the world do not think quite as much of you as you imagine. The poor widow does not give you much of a character. You will have to be very careful, sir, or your base deeds will come out. The very first item I see down here is a fear that your hypocrisy will be discovered. It would take you only half as much trouble to be an honest man as it does to be a deceiver. A man who is in the habit of speaking truth need not mind how he opens his mouth, nor where; but a man who lies should be very careful, and have a very good memory, and recollect all he has ever said before, lest he should trip himself. But I see something worse than this; here is constant disquietude of conscience; hypocrites may seem as if they were at ease, but they cannot really be. The Christian who is true to God, and is really His child, can sometimes say, "I know that Jesus has taken away my sin." Assurance, vouchsafed to him by the Spirit, calms his fears, and he can rest in Christ. But the highest presumption to which the hypocrite can attain brings no such calm as that which is breathed upon the Christian by the lips of assurance. He can go to his bed, nay, he can go to his tomb in peace, but the hypocrite is afraid of a shadow, and fleeth when no man pursueth. And last of all, Mr. Hypocrite, I see an item here which you usually forget; it is this—that, despite of your profession, God abhors you, and if there is one man more than another who stinks in the nostrils of Jehovah, it is such as thou art—thou miserable pretender. Death shall find thee out, and hell shall be thy doom, for the hope of the hypocrite is as the spider's web, soon swept away; and where is he when God taketh away his hope? This, then, is the casting up of the hypocrite's account, and there is a deficit of an infinite amount. III. Now for the matter of the CURE OF THE HYPOCRITE. The thought of a present Deity, if it were fully realized, would preserve us from sin; always looking on me, ever regarding me. We think we are doing many things in secret, but there is nothing concealed from Him with whom we have to do. And the day is coming when all the sins that we have committed shall be read and published. (*C. H. Spurgeon.*) *How is hypocrisy discoverable and curable?*—The words naturally yield you this doctrine: Hypocrisy is a dangerous leaven, which ministers and people are chiefly and especially to beware of, and acquit themselves from. Hence you have a chapter of woes against it (Matt. xxiii.). And it is represented as that which renders odious to the Lord, and defiles, His choicest ordinances, and our best duties, if it cleave to them (Isa. i. 11, 12; lxvi. 3); and puts God to sad complaints and exprobations of such a people (Hosea vi. 4). I. WHAT HYPOCRISY IS. Much of the nature of a thing is many times discovered in its name; the name is a brief description. The word "hypocrite" properly signifies an actor or stage-player, a personator of other men in their speech, habit, and action. The Hebrew word signifieth both "a wicked man" and a "deceiver." And it is observed that those whom David, the devoutest man, called "wicked," Solomon, the wisest man, calls "fools," and Job, the most upright man, calls "hypocrites": all is but one and the same thing under divers names. Hypocrisy, then, is but a feigning of virtue and piety, which it seems to put on, and vice and impiety, which it conceals and would seem to put off. It is indeed vice in a vizor; the face is vice, but virtue is the vizor. The form and nature of it is imitation: the ends are vainglory, to be seen of men, or some gain or carnal respects. II. HOW IS HYPOCRISY RESEMBLED BY LEAVEN? Briefly thus: 1. Leaven is hardly discerned from good dough by the sight. And as hardly is hypocrisy distinguished from piety. 2. Leaven is very spreading. And so hypocrisy does a great deal of mischief; it spreads over all the man, and all his duties, parts, performances: and leavens all. 3. Leaven is of a sour taste and ungrateful smell. So is hypocrisy to God'sman. 4. Leaven is of a swelling nature: it extends and puffs up the dough. So hypocrisy is all for the praise of men. III. WHY IS IT CALLED "THE LEAVEN OF THE PHARISEES"? Because they were leavened with it to purpose; they were exact and super-eminent in this devilish art of personating and counterfeiting to the life. IV. WHEREIN IS THIS LEAVEN OF HYPOCRISY SO DANGEROUS THAT MINISTERS AND PEOPLE OUGHT FIRSTLY, CHIEFLY, TO BEWARE OF IT? There is great danger *of* it, and great danger *by* it. 1. There is great danger *of* it. (1) For we have the ground of the matter in ourselves. "Hearts deceitful above all things, and desperately wicked; who can know thy wickedness? I the Lord search the heart, I try the reins," &c. (Jer. xvii. 9, 10). As if none beside the Lord knew the bottomless depths and deceits of the heart! (2) The devil watcheth night and day to set fire to this tow. (3) And that we may not be secure, there are before our eyes and in our view dreadful examples. Balaam, a great prophet; Judas, an apostle familiar with Christ; Saul, Jehu, Herod, and Agrippa, famous kings. 2. And there is great danger *by* it. (1) The loss of all that is done. Christ will say, as to that young man, "Yet lackest thou one thing" (Luke xviii. 22), sincerity: wouldest thou have heaven too? Why then didst thou all things for the "praise of men? Thou hast thy reward," and art overpaid. "Depart from Me, ye that work iniquity" (Matt. vii. 23). (2) Frustrating of hopes, great hopes, hopes of glory and heaven, and escaping eternal misery. All these hopes must "perish" to the "hypocrite" (Job viii. 13); perish like a ship at the very mouth of the haven; perish while they are crying, "Lord, Lord"; perish into everlasting horror and eternal despair. (3) Full detection and manifesting of them in the sight and face of all the world. (4) And in hell the hypocrite shall be beaten with many stripes. For he knew his Master's will, and pretended he was doing it, and yet did it not. (*A. Bromhall.*)   *The leaven of hypocrisy :*—I. SOME WAYS IN WHICH THIS HYPOCRISY WORKS AND IS SHOWN. 1. Hypocrisy works in the bias of the mind. There is a secret end and aim with those in whom it works, apart from the glory of God. Self is always uppermost, even in religious acts and outward worship. 2. Hypocrisy shows itself in a resting in duties. Those in whom it thus works are satisfied to please self and others in them; they do not seek Christ in them; they go on in duties, but it is a bondage to them; their duties leave no savour on them; they are strict to a fault whilst engaged in them, and shame some gracious souls, who have not the self-command they show; but out of their duties they are light and frothy; there is nothing resting upon their spirits. View them at home, you see little or no difference between them and those who make no profession. 3. Hypocrisy shows itself in weariness of religion. Many, with all their outward zeal, are secretly weary of religious duties; they get nothing in them; they go away as they came, unwatered and unrefreshed; their inward spring seems dried up; Christ's yoke is often grievous to them. This is a far gone stage of the disease; it is the heart departing from the Lord. They slave and drudge on at duties, but are nothing bettered by them; they rather grow worse; their spiritual appetite seems departing. But for shame, many would give in at this stage, and walk no more as the open followers of Jesus. 4. Once more: hypocrisy works much in prayer, open and private. It regards choice of expression and fitting words more than the workings of desires in the heart, though the utterances are unconnected and broken. It depends on mental help more than spiritual assistance. II. THE KINDS OF CHRISTIANS WHO ARE MOST PRONE TO THIS SIN, AND WHO OUGHT, THEREFORE, TO BE MOST ON THEIR GUARD AGAINST IT. 1. Christians whose avocations bring them much into the world should guard against this sin. 2. Persons that are naturally crafty and subtle have great reason to watch against hypocrisy in their religious acts. 3. Those have great reason to guard against this sin who have been brought comfortably and calmly into peace with God, who have not been under great terrors of conscience, nor laid long, if at all, under a broken law—those who have come to Christ on the first motions of godly sorrow, and found peace with God. It too often happens that those who have been so gently dealt with do not value the blessing aright; they do not see what it cost the Son of God to procure. 4. Those who are naturally superstitious have need to be on the watch. It is a great advantage to Satan to meet with a superstitious person under the power of religion ; he will improve his advantage, and try to work upon their superstition, to bring them into bondage, and to make them hypocrites in numberless ways. He will try to give them too high an esteem for externals, to deaden, if possible, the power of religion in their souls. He will give them needless torment about little matters which in themselves are of no consequence or value, but he will try and magnify them in their eyes, and seek to persuade them to believe that much depends on them. They will be often led to believe that a scrupulous conscience is a tender one, whereas the two things are totally different ; and a man may have a very scrupulous conscience in religious matters that yet never hated sin or loved God. III. THE DANGER OF GIVING WAY TO THIS SIN, AND LETTING IT GAIN GROUND. This will also lead me to say a few words by way of caution how to prevent this. 1. It is a hateful sin in the sight of God. All hypocrisy is deception ; and God is a God of truth, and loves truth, and will have those who worship Him " worship Him in spirit and in truth." 2. Hypocrisy is a very deceiving sin. Hypocrites go on in duties, because the most of their religion lies in duties. Thus their duties deceive them. They judge well of themselves, because of their duties : but God judges of them by the state of their hearts. 3. Hypocrisy is a very dangerous sin. It works, as the Saviour says, like leaven ; it spreads over and taints, if unresisted and unchecked, all the healthy actings of the soul. It will, in the end, wear out all the sincere principles from which a professor once acted, and make him a confirmed hypocrite. There is danger of God giving up any who go on in this sin to a " reprobate mind " ; not all at once, but little by little, their spiritual strength will wax less and less, till it dries up altogether. They may be given up secretly to some corruption which will eat as a canker. Their souls will wither, because by their sin they cut themselves off from Christ. 4. But now, not to discourage any, it is good to have hypocrisy discovered ; the honest soul will be glad to know the worst, and never rest till he does. It is a bad sign to rest satisfied under uneasy feelings, hoping for a change, but without being stirred up to seek it. It is good to be severe with oneself, to sound our own hearts to the bottom, to beg of God and men to search and try us. It is only in this way—and that not now and then, or when pressed in conscience, but habitually—that hypocrisy will be kept under. (*H. M. Baker.*) *Different kinds of hypocrites:*—1. The worldly hypocrite, who professes godliness from worldly motives. 2. The legal hypocrite, who resigns his vicious practices to win heaven, but has no love to God. 3. The evangelical hypocrite, whose religion is an acknowledgment of sin, but with no desire to lead a godly life. 4. The enthusiastic hypocrite, who has an imaginary notion of the Saviour, and relies on impulses and feelings, and yet clings to vicious deeds. (*Van Doren.*) *Hypocrites in all ages:*—Cain in the first age ; Canaan in the second ; Ishmael in the third ; Esau in the fourth ; Saul among the prophets ; Judas among the apostles ; Nicholas among the deacons ; Ananias among the early Christians. (*Ibid.*) *Profession without possession:*—To profess a faith which you have not is to make yourself a deceptive trader, who pretends to be carrying on a very large business, while he has no stock, no capital, and is only obtaining credit on false pretences, and so is a thief. To make a profession, without having a possession, is to be a cloud without rain—a river-bed choked up with dry stones, but utterly without water ; it is to be a mere play-actor, strutting about for an hour with the name and garments of a king, to be exchanged, behind the scenes, for the garb of poverty, and the character of shame ; it is to be a rotten tree, green on the outside, but inwardly, as John Bunyan pithily puts it, " only fit to be tinder for the devil's tinder box." Be ye warned against fair pretensions where there is nothing to back them up. Above all things, eschew hypocrisy; stand aside from all mere pretence. Profess not to be what you are not, lest in that day when God comes to search the secrets of all hearts, you shall be condemned as reprobate silver, and consumed like dross. (*C. H. Spurgeon.*)　*Hypocrisy a common danger :*—An old English writer says :—"The Emperor Frederick III., when one said unto him he would go and find some place where no hypocrite inhabited, told him he must travel, then, far enough beyond the Sauromatæ or the frozen ocean ; for yet, when he came there, he should find a hypocrite if he found himself there. And it is true that every man is a hypocrite. Hypocrisy is a lesson that every man readily takes in. All are not fit for the wars; learning must have the picked and choicest wits; arts must have leisure and pains ; but all sorts are apt enough, and thrive in the mystery of dissimulation. *Pharisaic hypocrisy :*—That which was the disease of the Pharisee was the disease of the time. Our Lord calls that disease "hypocrisy." We have a reasonable horror of the name. We consider that it is applicable only to the worst men in the worst times. There is good excuse for that opinion ; yet it may rob us of the force of our Lord's warning—we may put it at a dangerous distance from ourselves. The hypocrite is the man who acts a part; there is no more evil significance in the word than that. And oh! how easy it is to be a hypocrite if that is his characteristic; how difficult it is not to be one! Do you not know with what terrible quickness a child becomes an actor or actress? Do you not know what we do to cultivate the acting talent, the acting habit in them? Do you not know what a number of social influences and contrivances are at work to convince men and women that it is their business to be masquers, that their skill is to be shown in the devising of masks? To strike at the root of this hypocrisy, to point out the remedy, this is the work which we ask from the King of men, from Him who knows what is in man. Jesus struck at the root of all social hypocrisy, of all personal hypocrisy, in Palestine, when He traced it to the religion which prevailed there. Then He pointed out the remedy in this sentence of everlasting might : "For there is nothing covered that shall not be revealed, neither hid that shall not be known." The religion of the Pharisees consisted in a series of attempts to please, flatter, and bribe the Ruler of the earth. If He could be persuaded not to look too curiously into the acts of His servants, not to probe the secrets of their hearts ; if He could be induced to accept a compensation for this evil, on certain conditions to tolerate that; if His commandments could be shown to bear different constructions for different persons; if cases might be imagined to which they did not apply, or applied with various qualifications and mitigations; if the creature could succeed in keeping the Creator at a distance from him, so that his secrets should not be brought to the light ; their religion had realized its highest objects. Such a religion was leavening the chosen people, as it was under other aspects, with the most dissimilar professions under heathen forms of worship, leavening the old Roman Empire. The priests and lawyers in Jerusalem, the Pontifiex and the Augur in Rome, were alike acting a part. They rehearsed their parts in private ; they performed them in public. The Pharisees were at once the consummate practisers of the art and the most systematic instructors in it. But what if the Ruler of the earth could not be flattered or bribed? What if *everything* that is covered *must* be revealed, if *everything* that is hidden *must* be known? What if the very act of the Creator is to reveal, if He is bringing all things to light, if He hates darkness? There is the whole question. Is it a God of light you serve, or a God of darkness? Acting hypocrisy is an impossible kind of service with the first, the only suitable one with the second. (*F. D. Maurice, M.A.*)　*Hypocrisy :*— Grace is the Christian's new nature, and hypocrisy is the art that counterfeits it. The hypocrite affects the innocence of the dove to hide the cunning of the serpent. By the hypocrite good men are oft deceived, for "Goodness thinks no ill where no ill seems." The hypocrite, like Judas, may salute Christ, but it is to betray Him. The hypocrite's life is a falsehood to heaven and to earth. The hypocrite gives his tongue to virtue, but his heart to vice. If there be "the head of gold," there are also "the feet of miry clay." Hypocrisy is the homage which vice pays to virtue. The more plausible hypocrisy is before men, the more detestable it is to God. The hypocrite serves Satan, and from Satan receives his reward. The religious hypocrite is at best a man of dark deeds, though clad in garments of light. He may approach the portals of heaven, but he does not enter. A hypocrite was discovered at a royal supper, but the king rejected him from the banquet. Man esteems him hateful, because he seems not what he is; and God hates him, because he is not what he seems. The Christian's heart oft speaks without the tongue, but the hypocrite's tongue always speaks without the heart. The hypocrite, like a bird of prey, although his course be towards heaven, yet is always looking and longing for something upon earth. The Christian gives to God the fruit of his labours; the hypocrite gives to God the fruit of his lips. The hypocrite is led by ostentation, and not by a sanctified conscience. Hypocrites may be " Christians in the skin, but they are demons in the core "; " their rhetoric may be pretty, their logic witty, but their practice is naughty." Hypocrisy is insulting to the virtuous, and cruel to the poor and afflicted. For he who hides his vices by hypocrisy, suspects the virtues of others to be hypocrisy. And the poor and afflicted remain poor and afflicted, because the sin of the hypocrite closed the hand of charity, and in consequence thereof genuine sorrow is oft suspected in place of being relieved. An impostor who asks for alms is a hypocrite in the lower grade. Hypocrisy may prevail in morals as well as in creed. Some men are hypocritical in both. Hypocrisy shall be detected, as in the case of Saul (1 Sam. xv. 14), Gehazi (2 Kings v. 26), Judas (Matt. xxvi. 50), Ananias (Acts v. 3), Simon Magus (Acts viii. 20, 21). Hypocrisy may be seen in the history of Jacob (Gen. xxvii. 20), Pharaoh (Exod. viii. 28, 29), Balaam (Num. xxiii. 10), Absalom (2 Sam. xv. 7), Hazael (2 Kings viii. 12, 13). Samaritans (Ezra iv. 2), Herod (Matt. ii. 8), High Priest (Matt. xxvi. 65), Pilate (Matt. xxvii. 24). Let the hypocrite tremble lest he perish by his own hypocrisy, for God is the God of Truth, Christ is the Word of Truth, and the Holy Ghost is the Spirit of Truth. " The hope of the hypocrite shall be as the spider's web " (Job viii. 13, 14). He is unwise who decries religion because some professing to be religious are hypocrites. None would take the pains to counterfeit pearls, if true ones were not of value. Men would not personate piety were it not of itself a noble quality. We best show our abhorrence of hypocrisy by holding the truth free from hypocrisy. (*Van Doren.*)

Vers. 2, 3. **Nothing covered, that shall not be revealed.**—*The revealing process :*— There is a tendency in things everywhere to manifest their natures, and make themselves known. Seeds that are buried, seek the light; shells deep in the sea grope their way to the shore; the processes of nature are to bring things to the surface. What is true in matter has certainly its counterpart in mind. Human character, notwithstanding all efforts to keep itself back, also tends to development; what is not seen at once is found out in a lifetime. The strong passions of the soul, like smothered fires or hidden springs, at last burst their way through, and become known. There is certainly going on around us in the operations of nature, and in the unfolding of events, a revealing process, as if creation and Providence had determined to let light into all dark places, and at last uncover human hearts. This, we suppose, is the general idea taught in the text. I. THERE ARE REVEALING PROCESSES GOING ON IN THE WORLD AROUND US, AND UNDER CIRCUMSTANCES WHICH MAKE IT EXCEEDINGLY PROBABLE THAT, IN THE WORLD TO COME, THEY WILL CONTINUE TO GO ON WITH ACCELERATED AND OVERWHELMING POWER. One fact often discloses a great deal, when brought into connection with another fact, which, when it stood by itself, told nothing. The ancient kings of the East were aware of this, when they sent messages from one to another on business which they wished to be kept secret from all but themselves. The message was written upon a piece of parchment, but so written that it could not be deciphered unless first bound upon a staff, which contained a counterpart and key to that which was sent, and each king kept one of these staffs; hence, if the messenger should lose the scrip, the secret would not be divulged, because not intelligible, unless wrapped round the wood: the one was read by the help of the other, though each spoke nothing by itself. So with events in human life; they throw light on each other when brought together. II. ALL THE HINDRANCES WHICH PREVENTED A PERFECT REVELATION OF THE CHARACTER IN THIS WORLD, WILL, IN THE NEXT, BE REMOVED. If even in such a world as this, where the body, and old associations, and friends, and forgetfulness, and ignorance of the consequences, contribute to quiet the goadings of conscience, men are still driven by remorse to give a detailed and minute account of the evil they have done, what may not be expected when, with conscience all alive, and memory quickened, the soul dismantled of its clay, stung by its sins, bereft of friends, and hindered by nothing, meets the eye of its Maker without a veil? Surely there is a provision in our nature, by reason of which every one shall give an account of himself unto God. III. MUCH OF THE BIBLE IS WRITTEN, AND ALL PROBATION ARRANGED, WITH REFERENCE TO A JUDGMENT IN THE MIDST OF MINUTE

AND AMAZING REVELATIONS. There is a foretokening all along our earthly way. If the wicked hear a " dreadful sound," what does he hear? If he sees a hand others do not see, what is it that he sees? The fear of God is not before his eyes, and yet he is afraid. There was a sound, a rustle of a leaf, yet to him a sound that spoke of discovery—a whisper of betrayal and development; he sees things around him working to the surface. Even a stain upon his robe, a paler hue upon his cheek, may have a voice to some one; many things have come out in ways most unexpected—and who shall say, after all, he may not have been observed! Perhaps the words of the aged preacher peal again upon his soul—" Every work into judgment, with every secret thing, whether it be good or whether it be evil." " For every idle word which men shall speak, shall they give account "; " Whatsoever ye have spoken in darkness shall be heard in the light "; and " The sea gave up the dead which were in it, and death and the grave the dead which were in them, and they were judged, every man according to his works," out of the things that were written in the books. IV. IF THERE WERE NO BOOKS WITH MAN'S DEEDS RECORDED IN THEM, NO CONSCIENCE IN THE SOUL TO URGE THEM FORTH, NO WITNESSES TO TESTIFY, AND NO FORMAL SENTENCE TO BE PRONOUNCED AND VINDICATED, STILL THE FUTURE CONDITION OF THE SOUL WILL ITSELF POINT BACK TO SPECIFIC ACTS OF SIN OR UNRIGHTEOUSNESS ON EARTH, AS THE GROUND OF ITS PECULIAR DESTINY. (*W. Neill.*) *The inner world:*—I. Now, we believe that God has dealt with man according to his temperament. He knows us far better than we know ourselves; and He would therefore work upon us in a manner most likely to produce a good effect. It may be, indeed, that the abstract idea of the Lord's coming to judgment, would have been in itself too lofty for a man fully to appreciate; so that in order to make man realize it, and thus to let it have a practical bearing upon our conduct, it has been necessary to enter into the detail, and describe one of the scenes connected with it. Or, to regard the subject in another light, it is noticeable that man feels no shame of God's knowledge of sin. This may be proved from the fact that we are guilty, all of us, of many secret sins, which we should blush to own to our dearest friend, but which we are ready enough to acknowledge to God. On the other hand, we are not often content that our good deeds should be known to God alone, but the majority of persons would seem to wish that men should regard them also. These considerations may lead us to understand, that it was from a complete knowledge of human nature that Christ warned His disciples by the announcement of the truth—that all secrets would eventually be brought to light. " Beware," He says, " of the leaven of the Pharisees, which is hypocrisy. For there is nothing covered, that shall not be revealed; neither hid, that shall not be known." II. By laying aside all further reference to God's perfect knowledge of human nature implied in the text, we would lead your minds to the doctrine which the text conveys—and, indeed, it is a most important one. Christ here speaks of the revealing at the last day, of all that we now hide in the closest secrecy. He tells us that there is nothing, hide it as we now may from the knowledge of others, which He will not reveal before the masses of the universe. The actions of a single day, who can number them? Go, examine your own hearts. Each man for himself must go down to the region of his own soul, and find out what is there going on. Thoughts and passions, motives and wishes, hopes and fears, hatred, lusts and affections, intentions of good, and designs of evil; these are the shadowy dwellers of that world within, whose name is legion, for indeed they are many. At one time they prompt us to external deeds; at another time, our external deeds are only the cloak beneath which they disguise themselves, so that men perceive them not. Oh, who can turn the mental eye inwards, and not marvel at, and fear the secret world which toils and burns in the heart? Yet we see it not all. He knows all things now, and there shall come a day when they shall be known no longer to God alone, but they shall be all declared to the gathered masses of the universe; for Christ has told us, that " there is nothing covered that shall not be revealed." III. And if this be true, does it not especially behove us constantly to regard the state of that heart which God so closely inspects? IV. And here we may notice a remarkable distinction between the judgment passed on our conduct by man on the one side, and by God on the other. Man takes into account our wicked actions only, while God often discerns matter of condemnation, long before the wicked action is committed. As viewed by an earthly tribunal, it is of little account what designs we may have had, if those designs have never been put into execution. If we are placed in positions where unavoidable circumstances really debar us often from those privileges which the gospel of Christ affords to man, we may safely commit ourselves to the hands of

God; He knows our hearts; and the day will come when it will be proved that, although debarred from many privileges, it was not really our own fault; our inclinations were good, and these inclinations shall be openly declared; for "there is nothing covered," no secret wish, no concealed desire, "that shall not be revealed; there is nothing hid that shall not be known." (*H. Palmer.*)　*Christians weighed in the balance:*—If we had eyes adapted to the sight, we should see, on looking into the smallest seed, the future flower or tree enclosed in it. God will look into our feelings and motives as into seeds; by those embryos of action He will infallibly determine what we are, and will show what we should have been, had there been scope and stage for their development and maturity. Nothing will be made light of. The very dust of the balances shall be taken into account. It is in the moral world as it is in the natural, where every substance weighs something; though we speak of imponderable bodies, yet nature knows nothing of positive levity: and were men possessed of the necessary scales, the requisite instrument, we should find the same holds true in the moral world. Nothing is insignificant on which sin has breathed the breath of hell: everything is important in which holiness has impressed itself in the painted characters. And accordingly "There is nothing covered that shall not be revealed; and hid that shall not be known." However unimportant now, in the estimation of man, yet, when placed in the light of the Divine countenance, like the atom in the sun's rays, it shall be deserving attention; and as the minutest molecule of matter contains all the primordial elements of a world, so the least atom of that mind shall be found to include in it the essential elements of heaven. (*W. Harris.*)　*No secrecy for sin:*—A man broke into a small church in Scotland, with the sacrilegious intention of stealing the communion plate. Hearing steps outside the building, and expecting that he should be discovered, he hurried to the end of the church, where, seeing a long rope depending to the ground, he laid hold of it for the purpose of climbing out of sight. But it proved to be the bell rope, and his weight rang the bell, which attracted his pursuers immediately to the spot. The man, of course, was caught; and thus wittily addressed the unconscious cause of his detection:—"If it had not been for thy long tongue and empty head I should not have been in my present predicament." This is the story as we get it from Mr. Gatty's book upon "the Bell"; but it has its lesson. Those who sin are pretty sure, sooner or later, to turn king's-evidence against themselves. There is a voice in wrong-doing; its long tongue will not always be quiet. All unaware, the offender puts out his hand and pulls the bell which tells against himself and summons vengeance to overtake him. Let no man dream that he can secure secrecy for his wickedness. Every timber in floor or roof is ready to cry out against him, and before he is aware of it, he will himself be ringing out his own infamy. What will be his dismay when he stands self-convicted before the assembled universe! (*C. H. Spurgeon.*)　*Guilt strangely revealed:*— Once, in a certain part of Germany, a box of treasure that was being sent by railway was found to have been opened and emptied of its contents, and filled with stones and rubbish. The question was, Who was the robber? Some sand was found sticking to the box, and a clever mineralogist, having looked at the grains of sand through his microscope, said that there was only one station on the railway where there was that kind of sand. Then they knew that the box must have been taken out at that station, and so they found out who was the robber. The dust under his feet, where he had set down the box to open it, was a witness against him. (*Clerical Library.*)　*The quickening of conscience:*—Just as the manipulations of the photographer in his dark chamber bring forth a picture which has been burnt into the plate by rays of light before, that when completed it may be brought to light again, and set before men that they may see what manner of persons they were; so, in the dark chambers of the dead, in the hidden spirit-world, there shall be a quickening of conscience. Many a dull picture, burnt into the mind amid the brightness of life shall be made terribly clear, the whole to be exposed as a finished view in the light of the judgment throne, and of Him who sits thereon. We are taught that we had better cultivate this photography of life ourselves. God has given to us the dark chambers of the night, no chambers of horror, but chambers in which, away from busy life, we may still be workers for Him, bringing forth the pictures of the day that are imprinted on conscience, and that may all be lost, unless we thus draw them forth. *Everything is recorded:*—It is related that, some time since, a gentleman visiting England called upon a gentleman there living in princely grandeur. After being passed from one liveried servant to another, with almost as much ceremony as if he were about to be brought into the presence of the Queen, he was shown into a large and elegantly furnished drawing-room, where he was received by the gentleman whom he sought. He saw that there were two other persons seated at a table in the room, but not being introduced to them, proceeded with his business. At the close of the interview, as he was about to leave, the gentleman remarked, " I am accustomed to have conversations with me recorded, and, that there may be no misunderstanding, these my amanuenses will read to you what you have said." The visitor was thunderstruck. He little thought, while sitting there, that two pairs of ears were catching up every word he uttered, and two pairs of hands were putting it into a permanent record. So with many in this world. They seem not to know that there is a Being about their path who hears every syllable they utter, and who, "when the books are opened," will bring everything to view. In a late work of fiction the Recording Angel is represented as dropping a tear, just as he enters the celestial gates, upon an oath uttered in haste by a favourite character, and blotting it out for ever. But that is fiction, and not truth. A greater than man declares that " whatsoever is spoken in darkness shall be heard in the light," and that " every idle word that men shall speak, they shall give account thereof in the day of judgment." (*W. H. Baxendale.*) *Eastern proclamations :*—Our Lord spent most of His life in villages ; and, accordingly, the reference here is to a custom observed only in such places, never in cities. At the present day, writes Thompson, local governors in country districts cause their commands thus to be published. Their proclamations are generally made in the evening, after the people have returned from their labours in the field. The public crier ascends the highest roof at hand, and lifts up his voice in a long-drawn call upon all faithful subjects to give ear and obey. He then proceeds to announce, in a set form, the will of their master, and demands obedience thereto.

Vers. 4, 5. **Be not afraid of them that kill the body.**—*The fear of God:*—I. What is that fear of God which the friends and disciples of Christ are expected to cherish? 1. We are sure that this fear is not, as some would have us believe, inconsistent with the enjoyment of the hopes and consolations of the gospel. 2. This fear blends itself with the other emotions of our mind, and gives a chastened character to them all. (1) Solemnity to our prayers. (2) Sobriety to our hopes. (3) Consistency to our conduct. (4) Intensity to our love. II. What considerations tend to promote this fear. 1. The greatness of His power. 2. The immaculateness of His purity and justice. 3. The constancy and greatness of His love. (*Anon.*) *Religious fear :*—I. Consider on what the fear of God, as it is a duty and a good disposition, is founded. 1. On a due sense of our own imperfections. (1) In practice. (2) In belief. 2. On a due sense of the perfections of God. God is most holy, and abhors iniquity as entirely opposite to His pure and undefiled nature. He is everywhere present, and from Him nothing can be hid. He is all-wise, and cannot be deceived. He is the just governor of the world, and as such He cannot but observe the actions of men, and will certainly render to every one according to his works. He is almighty, and can punish the rebellious many ways, by turning them out of being, or by making that being a pain to them for as long a time as He sees proper. He is also supremely good; and though this of all His perfections may seem the least suited to make us dread Him, yet whosoever judgeth so is much mistaken; for indeed there is not any one quality of the Divine nature so adapted to strike us with an ingenuous fear, with the fear of a child towards a parent, as this, and of such efficacy to deter us from sin, and to make us avoid incurring His just displeasure. Sin against God, as He is almighty, is the excess of madness and folly; but, as He is most kind and merciful, it is the basest ingratitude. II. The several degrees of this religious fear. A person is sensible that his practice is not at all suitable to his knowledge and judgment ; that he deliberately and continually offends God ; that he is not in His favour; that, according to the doctrine of the gospel, he shall be condemned at the last day, unless he amend; and yet he goes on in his evil ways. One who is in this situation and disposition, and who seriously reflects upon it, cannot help fearing God. He fears Him as his worst enemy ; he fears Him as a righteous and inflexible judge who will not spare the guilty. This fear is indeed well-grounded and rational and natural ; yet, producing no good effects, it hath no virtue in it, it is no act of religion. But, if it deter him from sin, it is then to him the beginning of wisdom, and it becomes another kind of fear, and truly religious, as will appear from a second instance. A wicked person becomes sensible of his dangerous state, resolves to deliver himself from it without delay, and begins a new course. He knows that this repentance, these good resolutions, and this change for the better, are things which God requires, which He approves, and which He hath promised to accept when they bring forth the fruits of a regular obedience. He hath, therefore, hopes of pardon, without which it is not possible for any one to amend : but these hopes are mixed with many and great fears lest he should relapse into his former vices, lest he should not accomplish all that is necessary for his salvation, lest he should be called out of this world before he has finished his important and difficult task. This is a religious fear, because it is mixed with hope, and honourable notions of God, and because it produces good actions. There is, further, a religious fear, which, bringing forth a regular obedience, and not being accompanied with so much dread and terror as that last mentioned, shows that the mind in which it is lodged is advanced to a higher degree of goodness. The fear of God, therefore, is a disposition of mind, different in degree, according as our state is with relation to God and to religion. There is a fear that God is offended at us, and will punish us ; which is the fear of a wicked person. There is a fear arising from a sense of our guilt, mixed and allayed with hopes that God will accept our amendment. This is the fear of a penitent sinner. There is a fear lest we ever should forfeit the favour of God, and fall short of that future reward which at present we may reasonably expect. This is the fear of a good man, and it is capable of increase or of diminution according to his behaviour. There is an awe and reverence which a due sense of God's perfections, and of the infinite distance between Him and His creatures, would excite in our minds, though we were secure of His favour, and had no fear of losing it. This is the happy state of those who have arrived as near to perfection as a good person can whilst he is on this side of heaven, and who are sensible that their course is nearly ended, and the time of their departure is at hand. (*J. Jortin, D.D.*)   *The reasonableness of fearing God more than man :*—I. CONSIDER THE POWER OF MAN, AND WHAT IT IS HE CAN DO. 1. He can kill the body, and take away our lives, which includes a power of doing whatever is less. 2. He can do not even this, however, without the Divine permission. 3. If permitted to do his worst, he can do but this. " After that they have no more that they can do." (1) " They can but kill the body," that is, they can only injure the worst and least considerable part of us. (2) When they have killed the body, by doing this, they do but prevent nature a little, they do but antedate an evil a few moments, and bring our fears upon us a little sooner ; they kill that which must die within a few days, though they should let it alone ; they do but cut asunder that thread which would shortly break of itself by its own weakness and rottenness. (3) " They can but kill the body " ; and what argument of power is this, to be able to kill that which is mortal? as if you should say, " They can break a glass ; they can throw down that which is falling." (4) The killing of the body does not necessarily signify any great mischief or harm in the issue and event. " They can kill the body," that is, they can knock off our fetters, and open the prison doors, and set us at liberty ; they can put us out of pain, thrust us out of an uneasy world, put an end to our sins and sorrows, to our misery and fears ; they can "give the weary rest," and send us thither where we would be, but are loath to venture to go. (5) " They can but kill the body " ; when they have done that, they may give over, here their proud waves must stop ; here their cruelty and malice, their power and wit, must terminate, for they can reach no farther. (6) " They can but kill the body," they cannot do the least harm to the soul, much less can they annihilate it, and make it cease to be. (7) And lastly, " They can but kill the body," that is, they can but inflict temporal misery upon us ; their power, as it is but small, so it is of a short continuance, it reacheth no farther than this life, it is confined to this world. II. CONSIDER HOW MUCH THE POWER OF GOD EXCEEDS THE POWER OF MAN ; which our Saviour declares in these words, " Who, after He hath killed, hath power to cast into hell." Which in general signifies, that His power is infinite and unlimited. 1. God's power is absolute, and independent upon any other. 2. His power reaches to the soul as well as the body. 3. In the other world He can raise our bodies again, and reunite them to our souls, and cast them into hell, and torment them there. 4. God can punish for ever. I proceed now to apply this serious and weighty argument, and to draw some useful inferences from it. I. That religion doth not design to annihilate and to root out our passions, but regulate and govern them ; it does not wholly forbid and condemn them, but determines them to their proper objects, and appoints them their measures and proportions ; it does not intend to extirpate our affections, but to exercise and employ them aright, and to keep them within bounds. II. We may infer likewise from hence, that it is not against the genius of true religion, to urge men with arguments of fear. No man can imagine there would have been so many fearful threatenings in Scripture, and especially in the gospel, if it had not been intended they should have some effect and influence upon us. Fear is deeply rooted in our nature, and immediately flows from that principle of self-preservation which is planted in every man; it is the most wakeful passion in the soul of man, and so soon as anything that is dreadful and terrible is presented to us, it alarms us to flee from it; and this passion doth naturally spring up in our minds from the apprehension of a Deity, because the notion of a God doth include in it power and justice, both which are terrible to guilty creatures; so that fear is intimate to our being, and God hath hid in every man's conscience a secret awe and dread of His presence, of His infinite power and eternal justice. Now fear being one of the first things that is imprinted upon us from the apprehension of a Deity, it is that passion, which, above all other, gives the greatest advantage to religion, and is the easiest to be wrought upon. III. THE FEAR OF GOD IS THE BEST ANTIDOTE AGAINST THE FEAR OF MEN. IV. IF GOD BE INFINITELY MORE TO BE DREADED THAN MEN, THEN, "WHO IS TO BE OBEYED, GOD OR MEN? JUDGE YE." I speak not this to diminish our reverence to magistrates and their authority; for by persuading men to fear God, who commands obedience to magistrates, we secure their reverence and authority; but when the commands of men are contrary to God's, and come in competition with them, shall we not hearken to Him who is supreme, the greatest and most powerful? Shall we not obey Him who hath the most unquestionable authority over us, and right to command us? Shall we not dread Him most who is to be feared above all, who can be the best friend and the sorest enemy, is able to give the greatest rewards to our obedience, and to revenge Himself upon us for our disobedience by the most dreadful and severe punishments? V. IF GOD BE THE GREAT OBJECT OF OUR FEAR, LET ALL IMPENITENT SINNERS REPRESENT TO THEMSELVES THE TERRORS OF THE LORD AND THE POWER OF HIS ANGER. This consideration, if anything in the world will do it, will awaken them to a sense of the danger of their condition, and of the fatal issue of a wicked life. (*Archbishop Tillotson.*) *The use of fear in religion:*—1. In the first place, the emotion of fear ought to enter into the consciousness of the young, because youth is naturally light-hearted. The ordinary cares of this life, which do so much towards moderating our desires and aspirations, have not yet pressed upon the ardent and expectant soul, and therefore it needs, more than others, to fear and to "stand in awe." 2. Secondly, youth is elastic, and readily recovers from undue depression. There is an elasticity in the earlier periods of human life that prevents long-continued depression. How rare it is to see a young person smitten with insanity! It is not until the pressure of anxiety has been long continued, and the impulsive spring of the soul has been destroyed, that reason is dethroned. The morning of our life may, therefore, be subjected to a subduing and repressing influence, with very great safety. It is well to bear the yoke in youth. The awe produced by a vivid impression from the eternal world may enter into the exuberant and gladsome experience of the young with very little danger of actually extinguishing it and rendering life permanently gloomy and unhappy. 3. Thirdly, youth is exposed to sudden temptations and surprisals into sin. The general traits that have been mentioned as belonging to the early period in human life render it peculiarly liable to solicitations. The whole being of a healthful hilarious youth, who feels life in every limb, thrills to temptation like the lyre to the plectrum. There are moments in the experience of the young when all power of resistance seems to be taken away by the very witchery and blandishment of the object. He has no heart, and no nerve, to resist the beautiful siren. And it is precisely in these emergencies in his experience—in these moments when this world comes up before him clothed in pomp and gold, and the other world is so entirely lost sight of, that it throws in upon him none of its solemn shadows and warnings—it is precisely now, when he is just upon the point of yielding to the mighty yet fascinating pressure, that he needs to feel an impression, bold and startling, from the wrath of God. Nothing but the most active remedies will have any effect in this tumult and uproar of the soul. 4. In the fourth place, the feeling and principle of fear ought to enter into the experience of both youth and manhood, because it relieves from all other fear. He who stands in awe of God can look down from a very great height upon all other perturbation. When we have seen Him from whose sight the heavens and the earth flee away, there is nothing in either the heavens or

the earth that can produce a single ripple upon the surface of our souls. 5. The
fifth and last reason which we assign for cherishing the feeling and principle of
fear applies to youth, to manhood, and to old age, alike ; the fear of God conducts
to the love of God. Our Lord does not command us to fear " Him who, after He
hath killed, hath power to cast into hell " because such a feeling as this is
intrinsically desirable, and is an ultimate end in itself ; it is in itself undesirable,
and it is only a means to an end. By it our torpid souls are to be awakened from
their torpor ; our numbness and hardness of mind in respect to spiritual objects is
to be removed. We are never for a moment to suppose that the fear of perdition
is set before us as a model and permanent form of experience to be toiled after—
a positive virtue and grace intended to be perpetuated through the whole future
history of the soul. It is employed only as an antecedent to a higher and a
happier emotion ; and when the purpose for which it has been elicited has been
answered, it then disappears. " Perfect love casteth out fear ; for fear hath
torment " (1 John iv. 18). But, at the same time, we desire to direct attention to
the fact that he who has been exercised with this emotion, thoroughly and deeply,
is conducted by it into the higher and happier form of religious experience.
Religious fear and anxiety are the prelude to religious peace and joy. These are
the discords that prepare for the concords. (W. T. G. Shedd, D.D.)   Lessons :—
1. An unwarrantable fear condemned, and that is, the sinful, servile, slavish fear
of man—" Fear not them that kill the body." 2. An holy, awful, and prudential fear
of the omnipotent God commended—" Fear Him that is able to kill both body and
soul." 3. The persons whom this duty of fear is recommended to, and bound upon ;
disciples, ministers, and ambassadors, all the friends of Christ ; they not only may,
but ought to fear Him, not only for His greatness and goodness, but upon the account
of His punitive justice, as being able to cast both soul and body into hell. Such a
fear is not only awful, but laudable ; not only commendable, but commanded, and
not misbecoming the friends of Christ. The ministers of God may use arguments
from fear of judgments, both to dissuade from sin, and to persuade to duty. It is
not unsuitable to the best of saints to keep in heaven's way for fear of hell ; it is
good to bid a friend fear when that fear tendeth to his good. (W. Burkitt.)
Warning words :—In verse 5 our Lord guards against the error of the soul's
annihilation. Also against the notion that the body will escape the ruin of the
soul. Perdition is not the destruction of the being of either, but of the well-being
of both. Learn, that to play false with convictions to save life will fail of its end.
God can inflict a violent death in some other and more awful way. 1. There is a
hell for the body as well as for the soul ; consequently sufferings adapted to the
one as well as the other. 2. Fear of hell is a divinely authorized and needed
motive of action even to Christ's " friends." 3. As Christ's meekness and tenderness were not compromised by this language, those ministers want their Master's
spirit who soften it to please " ears polite." (Van Doren.)   How far is it
to hell ?—A young man met the deacon of a church one Sunday morning, and
asked him the terrible question, " How far is it to hell ? " " Young man," was
the reply, " don't mock such a serious reality ; you may be nearer to hell than you
think." They had only just turned the corner of the road, and ridden a few yards,
when his horse threw him, and he was picked up dead.   Sweetness of life :—One
of the martyrs, when being led to the stake, was urged to recant ; and as a motive
to induce him to do so it was said, " Life is sweet, and death is bitter." " True,"
said the good man ; " life is sweet, and death is bitter ; but eternal life is sweeter,
and eternal death is more bitter."   Death cannot destroy the soul :—Methinks I
hear an accursed spirit in the nether world crying after death, and saying, " O
death, pause, turn back and quench my wretched existence ; in yonder world I
dreaded thee, I struggled hard against thee—I now invoke thy stroke, a stroke that
shall annihilate me for ever ! " And methinks I hear death, heartless as ever,
saying, " I cannot destroy thee ; I never had any power over thine existence ; I
could wither landscapes, breathe destruction into the face of every green field and
forest ; I could quench animal life, and have reduced all past generations of men
to dust ; but I could never touch the soul. The soul, secured in her existence,
' smiled at my dagger and defied the point.' I cannot paralyze memory, I cannot
extinguish the fires of conscience, I cannot destroy a soul." (The Homilist.)

Vers. 6, 7. **Not one of them is forgotten before God.**—God's universal oversight :—
You see the Bible will not be limited in the choice of symbols, and there is hardly
a beast, or bird, or insect which has not been called to illustrate some Divine truth

—the ox's patience, the ant's industry, the spider's skill, the hind's surefootedness, the eagle's speed, the dove's gentleness, and even the sparrow's meanness and insignificance. In Oriental countries, none but the poorest people buy the sparrow and eat it, so very little meat is there on the bones, and so very poor is it what there is of it. The comfortable population would not think of touching it any more than you would think of eating a bat or a lamprey eel. Now, says Jesus, if God takes care of such a poor bird that is not worth a cent, won't He care for you, an immortal? We associate God with revolutions. We can see a Divine purpose in the discovery of America, in the invention of the art of printing, in the exposure of the Gunpowder Plot, in the contrivance of the needle-gun, in the ruin of an Austrian or Napoleonic despotism; but how hard it is to see God in the minute personal affairs of our lives. We think of God as making a record of the starry host, but cannot realize the Bible truth that He knows how many hairs there are on your head. It seems a grand thing that God provided food for hundreds of thousands of Israelites in the desert, but we cannot appreciate the truth that when a sparrow is hungry God stoops down and opens its mouth, and puts the seed in. We are struck with the idea that God fills the universe with His presence; but cannot understand how He encamps in the crystal palace of a dewdrop, or finds room to stand, without being crowded, between the alabaster pillars of a pond lily. We can see God in the clouds. Can we see God in these flowers on this platform? We are apt to place God upon some great platform, or try to do it, expecting Him there to act out His stupendous projects; but we forget that the life of a Cromwell, an Alexander, a Washington, or an archangel is no more under Divine inspiration than your life or mine. Pompey thought there must have been a mist over the eyes of God because He so much favoured Cæsar; but there is no such mist. He sees everything. We say God's path is in the great waters. True enough; but no more, certainly, than He is in the water in the glass on this table. We say God guides the stars in their courses—magnificent truth!—but no more certain truth than he decides which ferry-boat you shall take to-morrow morning to New York. God does not sit upon an indifferent and unsympathetic throne, but He sits down beside you to-day, and stands beside me to-day, and no affair of our lives is so insignificant but that it is of importance to God. 1. In the first place, God chooses for us our occupation. I am amazed to see how many people there are dissatisfied with the work they have to do. I think three-fourths wish they were in some other occupation; and they spend a great deal of time in regretting that they got in the wrong trade or profession. I want to tell you that God put into operation all the influences which led you to that particular choice. You know a man having a large estate. He gathers his working hands in the morning, and says to one, "You go and trim that vine"; to another, "You go and weed those flowers"; and to another, "You plough that tough glebe"; and each one goes to his particular work. The owner of the estate points the man to what he knows he can do best; and so it is with the Lord. He calls us up, and points to that field for which we are best fitted. So that the first lesson coming from this subject is: Stay cheerfully where God puts you. 2. I remark, further, that God has arranged the place of our dwelling. What particular city, or town, or street, or house you shall live in seems to be a mere matter of accident. You go out to hunt for a house, and you happen to pass up a certain street, and happen to see a sign, and you select that house. Was it all happening so? Oh, no. God guided you in every step. He foresaw the future. He knew all your circumstances, and He selected just that one house as better for you than any one of the ten thousand habitations in the city. 3. I remark, further, that God arranges all our friendships. You were driven to the wall. You found a man just at that crisis who sympathized with you and helped you. You say: "How lucky I was." There was no luck about it. God sent that friend just as certain as He sent the ravens to feed Elijah, or the angel to strengthen Christ. Your domestic friends, your business friends, your Christian friends, God sent them to bless you; and if any of them have proved traitorous, it is only to bring out the value of those who remain. If some die, it is only that they may stand on the outpost of heaven to greet you at your coming. You always will have friends—warm-hearted friends—magnanimous friends; and, when sickness comes to your dwelling, there will be watchers; when trouble comes to your heart, there will be sympathisers; when death comes, there will be gentle fingers to close the eyes and fold the hands, and consoling lips to tell of a resurrection. Oh! we are compassed by a bodyguard of friends. Every man, if he has behaved himself well, is surrounded by three circles of friends; those on the outer circle wishing him well; those in the next circle willing to help him; while close up to his heart are a few who would die for him. God pity the wretch who has not any friends; he has not behaved well. 4. I remark, again, that God puts down the limit to our temporal prosperity. The world of finance seems to have no God in it. You cannot tell where men will land. The affluent fall; the poor rise. The ingenious fail; the ignorant succeed. An enterprise opening grandly shuts in bankruptcy; while out of the peat dug up from some New England marsh, the millionaire builds his fortune. The poor man thinks it is chance that keeps him down. The rich man thinks it is chance which hoists him, and they are both wrong. It is so hard to realize that God rules the money market, and has a hook in the nose of the stock gambler; and that all the commercial revolutions of the world shall result in the very best for God's dear children. My brother, don't kick against the Divine allotments. God knows just how much money it is best for you to have. You never lose unless it is best for you to lose, and you never gain unless it is best for you to gain. You go up when it is best for you to go up, and go down when it is best for you to go down. Prove it, you say. I will. "All things work together for good to them that love God." You go into a factory, and you see twenty or thirty wheels, and they are going in different directions. This band is rolling off this way, and another band another way; one down and the other up. You say—"What confusion in a factory." Oh, no, all these different bands are only different parts of the machinery. So I go into your life, and see strange things. Here is one providence pulling one way, and another in another way; but they are different parts of one machinery by which He will advance your present and everlasting well-being. (Dr. Talmage.) Of the providence of God:—I. THERE IS A PROVIDENCE. This appears—1. From plain Scripture testimonies (see Psa. ciii. 19; Eph. i. 11). 2. From the nature of God, who being independent, and the first cause of all things, the creatures must needs depend upon Him in their being and working. He is the end of all things, wise, knowing how to manage all for the best; powerful to effectuate whatever He has purposed, and faithful to accomplish all He has decreed, promised, or threatened. 3. From the harmony and order of the most confused things in the world. Everything appears to a discerning eye to be wisely ordered, notwithstanding the confusions that seem to take place. 4. From the fulfilment of prophecies, which could not possibly be without a providence to bring them to pass. II. Let us, in the next place, consider THE OBJECT OF PROVIDENCE, or that which it reacheth and extendeth to. And this is all the creatures, and all their actions—"Upholding all things by the word of His power" (Heb. i. 3). "His kingdom ruleth over all" (Psa. ciii. 19). III. I proceed to consider THE ACTS OF PROVIDENCE. They are two, preserving and governing the creatures and their actions. 1. God by His providence preserves all the creatures. 2. God does not only preserve the creatures, but governs and manages them, which is the second act of providence; whereby He disposes of all things, persons, and actions, according to His will; "The king's heart is in the hand of the Lord, as the rivers of water: He turneth it whithersoever He will" (Prov. xxi. 1). "The lot is cast into the lap: but the whole disposing thereof is of the Lord" (Prov. xvi. 33). "A man's heart deviseth his way; but the Lord directeth his steps" (Prov. xvi. 9). And this act of providence is also necessary: for as the creature cannot be or exist without God, so neither can it act without Him (Acts xvii. 21). God does not make man as the carpenter doth the ship, which afterwards sails without him; but He rules and guides him, sitting at the helm, to direct and order all his motions: so that whatever men do, they do nothing without Him; not only in their good actions, where He gives grace, and excites it, working in them both to will and to do of His good pleasure; but also in their evil actions, wherein they are under the hand of providence, but in a very different manner. (1) God permits sin, when He does not hinder it, which He is not obliged to do. (2) God leaves the sinner so far as He sees meet to the swing of his own lusts, and denies him restraining grace. (3) God bounds sin, and restrains men in their sins, as He does the raging sea, allowing it to go so far, but no further. (4) God overrules all to a good end. God has one end in wicked actions, and the sinner another. The sinner minds and intends evil, but God means and designs good by them all. IV. Our next business is to consider THE PROPERTIES OF DIVINE PROVIDENCE. 1. God's providence is most holy (Psa. cxlv. 17). 2. It is most wise (Isa. xxviii. 29). 3. Providence is most powerful. I shall conclude with an use of exhortation. 1. Beware of drawing an excuse for your sin from the providence of God, for it is most holy, and has not the least efficiency in any sin you commit. 2. Beware of murmuring and fretting under any dispensations of providence that ye meet with ; remembering that nothing falls out without a wise and holy providence, which knows best what is fit and proper for you. And in all cases, even amidst the most afflicting incidents that befall you, learn submission to the will of God. 3. Beware of anxious cares and diffidence about your through-bearing in the world. (*T. Boston, D.D.*) *Providence in our occupations :*—Hugh Miller says, " I will be a stone-mason " ; God says, " You will be a geologist." David goes out to tend his father's sheep ; God calls him to govern a nation. Saul goes out to hunt his father's asses, and before he gets back finds the crown of mighty dominion. (*Dr. Talmage.*) *Not forgotten by God :*—We talk about God's remembering us, as if it were a special effort, a laying hold by His great mind of something outside of Himself, which He determined to remember. But if we could only know how truly we belong to God it would be different. God's remembrance of us is the natural claiming of our life by Him as a true part of His own. When the spring comes, the oak-tree, with its thousands upon thousands of leaves, is alive all over. The great heart of the oak-tree remembers every remotest tip of every farthest branch, and sends to each the message and the power of new life. It is no harder work for the oak to feed and sustain and remember a million leaves than to feed and remember only one. The thrill of the common life is passed on, without effort, to each. Somewhat in this way we may think of God's remembrance of His millions of children. We may be no more than far-off leaves upon the great tree of His life. But we are remembered just as the heart remembers the finger-tips to which it sends the crimson blood. (*Victor Hugo.*) *Minuteness of God's care :*—It has been said, " God is great in great things, but He is very great in little things." This was illustrated by an incident which occurred in a room during a Scripture reading. There was a beautiful engraving on the wall of the Matterhorn mountain. It was remarked that the wondrous works of God were not only shown in those lofty, snow-clad mountains, but also the tiny mosses found in their crevices. A friend present said, " Yes, I was with a party at the Matterhorn, and, while we were admiring the sublimity of the scene, a gentleman of the company produced a pocket microscope and, having caught a tiny fly, placed it under the glass. He reminded us that the legs of the household fly in England are naked ; then called our attention to the legs of this little fly, which were thickly covered with hair " ; thus showing that the same God who made these lofty mountains rise, attended to the comfort of the tiniest of His creatures, even providing socks and mittens for the little flies whose homes these mountains were. (*Christian Age.*) *God's care for all creatures :*—It is interesting to look round the world, and note the various tokens to be seen everywhere of God's liberal hand in supplying the wants of His creature man. Dr. Livingstone, writing of some plants that grew in Kalahari Desert, mentions a plant called Leroshua, which he says " is a blessing to the inhabitants of the desert. We see a small plant with linear leaves, and a stalk not thicker than a crow's quill ; on digging down a foot or eighteen inches beneath, we come to a tuber, often as large as the head of a young child ; when the rind is removed we find it to be a mass of cellular tissue, filled with fluid much like that in a young turnip. Owing to the depth beneath the soil at which it is found, it is generally deliciously cool and refreshing." *Caring for a little bird :*—We are at a loss to conceive the infinite range of mind, thought, and heart that embraces alike the inconceivable magnitudes and the microscopic minutiæ of the universe. And yet this same phenomenon is witnessed in ourselves —minute images of God. While the great Gustavus Adolphus was in the midst of the dust, smoke, clangour, and excitement of a momentous battle, a little bird, dizzy and bewildered with the noise and wild atmospheric confusion, sank and lighted upon his shoulder. The battle, vast in its proportions, momentous in the interests it involved, still left room in his mind and heart for the distress and peril of that little bird, and he hid it in safety beneath the folds of his dress, and plunged again into the fight. The same trait appears—on a very small scale, it may be— in our own experience, and appearing there, pictures in miniature the all-embracing range of the Divine thought and providential care. *God may be safely trusted :*— An aged Christian who had long been an invalid, and was dependent on Christain charity for her support, on sending for a new physician who had just come into the place, and united with the same Church of which she was a member, said to him, " Doctor, I wish to put myself under your care, but I cannot do it unless you will trust my Father." " Well, Ma'am," replied the physician, "I believe your Father is rich ; I may safely trust Him." (*New Cyclopædia of Anecdote.*) *An ever watchful providence :*—A little error of the eye, a misguidance of the hand, a slip of the foot, a starting of a horse, a sudden mist, or a great shower, or a word unde-signedly cast forth in an army, has turned the stream of victory from one side to another, and thereby disposed of empires and whole nations. No prince ever returned safe out of a battle but may well remember how many blows and bullets have gone by him that might easily have gone through him; and by what little odd, unforeseen chances, death has been turned aside which seemed in a full, ready, direct career to have been posting to him. All which passages, if we do not ac-knowledge to have been guided to their respective ends and effects by the conduct of a superior and a Divine hand, we do, by the same assertion, cashier all provi-dence, strip the Almighty of His noblest prerogative, and make God, not the Governor, but the mere Spectator of the world. (*R. South, D.D.*) *Providence and individuals :*—Men talk in a general way about the goodness of God, His benevolence, compassion, and long-suffering ; but they think of it as a flood pour-ing itself out through all the world—as the light of the sun, not as the continually repeated action of an intelligent and living mind contemplating whom it visits and intending what it effects. Accordingly when they come into trouble, they can but say—"It is all for the best—God is good!" and the like, and it all falls as cold comfort upon them, and does not lessen their sorrow, because they have not accus-tomed their minds to feel that He is a merciful God, regarding them individually, and not a mere Universal Providence, working general laws. And then, perhaps, all of a sudden the new notion breaks upon them, "Thou God seest me!" Some especial providence, amid their infliction, runs right into their hearts ; brings it close home to them, in a way they never experienced before, that God sees them. (*J. H. Newman.*) *Man's fear and the Divine dissuasive :*—Our Lord, while instructing and preparing His disciples for future work as heralds of the kingdom, warns them that they will meet with many dangers and enemies; "but fear not," says the Master, "you are watched at every step, and come life, come death, you are safe." I. MAN'S FEARS. They are of two kinds—1. Those which respect this world. Some people go through life much more anxiously than others, though in outward circumstances there seems little difference in their respective lots. A good deal depends upon a man's temperament as to the way in which he will take things. Those on the lower ground have the least care. As we rise higher in the social scale, then it brings increasing solicitude. Provision has to be made not only for the wants of the day, but for appearances. It is right enough that men should look to appear-ances. God looks to appearances. He has made this world-house beautiful, and we are but following the Divine example when we try to make our life a thing of variety, largeness, and grace. But in doing so, the gates of anxiety are opened to us, and we are careful and troubled. 2. Fears respecting the world to come and our spiritual state and relation to that. The fullest victory over the cares and fears of this life is to be gained only by living for a higher world. Let us try to see Jesus standing as Lord of both worlds, and saying, "Fear not." II. THE DIVINE DISSUASIVE. "Fear not." This is supported and recommended by several argu-ments, as the limited power of man and of circumstances. Men may say and do a great deal which may be injurious to you, but you always come to the limit: "After that, there is nothing more they can do." Again, there is unlimited power with God, and if we are true trusting disciples of Christ this is a great dissuasive from fear. God will use all that infinite power to protect and save His trusting children. "He telleth the number of the stars," and has regard to every sparrow that flies. Why should we fear? Then our Lord teaches us that we are of more value to God than the inferior creatures. He has a higher care about us. (*A. Raleigh, D.D.*) *Divine providence :*—I. I SHALL ENDEAVOUR, IN THE FIRST PLACE, TO ILLUSTRATE THE SUBJECT OF A DIVINE PROVIDENCE. 1. Divine providence implies the preservation of all things. 2. Providence also implies the government of the world by its great and almighty Ruler. (1) Divine providence is particular in its government. A general providence must, in the nature of things, include a particular one. God cannot superintend the larger parts of the universe without taking care of the most minute parts. The all-wise and all-gracious Being who created all things, sustains all things. He is the Preserver as well as the Creator of everything that exists. As no part of His universe can be neglected or over-looked by Him, so no circumstance, however trivial, in the history of any individual is beneath His notice. No created thing can continue either to exist or to act independently of Him. He governs each individual with the same care and attention that He pays to the whole. (2) Divine providence is special in its regards. We know that God Almighty is the Father, the kind and gracious Father of all mankind; His providence is, consequently, exercised on behalf of all living things. He careth for the animal creation, every part of which is under His government; for " He giveth food unto the cattle, and feedeth the young ravens that call upon Him. The lions roaring after their prey do seek their meat from God; He openeth His hand, and filleth all things living with plenteousness." His providence is exercised also on behalf of the unholy and unthankful: to them He is kind and merciful, and for them He makes rich and constant provision. His love is not confined—" The Lord is loving unto every man, and His mercy is over all His works." We must, however, distinguish betwixt that general regard which the Almighty exercises towards the whole race of mankind, and that tender and special regard which He feels towards those who love Him, and constantly worship Him in spirit and in truth. (3) The administration of Divine providence, though often mysterious, is uniformly conducted by infinite wisdom, and with the most benign intentions. II. LESSONS WHICH FLOW FROM THIS REPRESENTATION OF DIVINE PROVIDENCE. 1. We are reminded of the supreme worth and importance of the friendship of God. 2. By this subject we are taught the duty of devout attention to the dispensations of Divine providence. 3. Reverential submission is another lesson that we derive from this important subject. 4. Finally, we derive from this representation of Divine providence a reason for cheerful and implicit confidence in God. This is the practical and consolatory use to which our blessed Lord applies the great truth now before us: " Fear not, therefore." If you truly fear God, you need fear none beside. (T. Lessey.) God's never-failing providence :— The little creature mentioned is one of the most insignificant that could be thought of; and the Lord selected it, just for that utter insignificance, to bring out thereby a truth which overwhelms the reason. He took out of His immense universe, an object so poor, so small, that nothing could be less important, to illustrate the doctrine on which the system of Christian morals is built; and the truth is this: that God is in intelligent relation with everything that exists; that there are, practically, no limits to His providence; that in the universe nothing is so minute as to be overlooked or forgotten. " Not one of them is forgotten." It is a striking phrase. It implies a knowledge which lasts, though the thing known may no longer exist; care, consideration, particulars retained in the faithful memory. And in the ephemeral history of the poor little bird, of which the great God and Saviour deigned to speak, not one item is forgotten; each tiny creature's life, in all its extent, is seen, and known, and borne in mind by Him to whom it owes that life. Now here is a truth, which may be called the beginning of the moral law, the foundation of Christian ethics, the Alpha and Omega of Christian practice. The doctrine of the never-failing providence of Almighty God is the sheet-anchor of man's safety. 1. The doctrine of God's providence is, at first, as terrible to contemplate as it is hard to realize; no one can bear to think of it, no one willingly admits it, who is leading an evil life. It means that there is nothing about you, or in you, or of you, but God knows and sees it all; the thoughts of your heart, the springs and motives of your acts, the vices of your blood. Then, also, those eyes sweep the entire circumference of the sphere in which you move; they see your friends and your foes, the tempting spirits which allure you, the guardians set for your defence; they mark the rise of the storms, as yet no bigger than a man's hand, which are coming up against you, and see, beyond, the sunshine which, after many days, may break out once more. You, just as you are, stand now before God, and simply for what you are, since there is no deceiving Him. 2. The truth of God's never-failing providence is awful indeed to those who know Him not, nor have Him in their thoughts; but to those who are near Him, and love to set Him ever before them as the Father and the Saviour, it is more precious than words can tell. To such it serves three purposes: it gives them guidance; it gives them strength; it gives the sense of safety. It shows them what they ought to do; it assures them of success; it blesses with the blessing of peace. That is the other side of the picture; and it shines in lovely light. If our sins are before Him, so also are our humble attempts to do right, our desires to win His approval, and regrets when we fear that we have failed. He follows us with merciful and tender consideration. When we go forth, the strong Hand is there to sustain us as we walk, and lead us through peril in safety. When we come in, the faithful guardian opens to us, and bids us rest in the quietness of perfect love and trust. We see Him in each event of life, and in the smallest particulars of each day, as the Friend who is near us all the time; we find Him in our rising up and in our lying down, in the home and its pure joys, in the loving faces there; we bless Him as the Author of every innocent pleasure; when the heart is glad we know that what filled it so full is the habitual sense that God is in our happiness, as the Author and Giver: all is of Him, and to Him do we give thanks. When we take up our daily work, it is with a song in the heart, because He worketh with us and will show us how our work should be done; and when we lay it down, it is with quiet satisfaction, because He has seen all, and remembers, and knows that though we may not have been perfect, we did what we could. His Holy Spirit, called the "Paraclete," the "Comforter," and the "Loving Spirit," is ever near us, and even within, since these mortal bodies are His consecrated temples; and the musical sounds often heard in the soul, like songs without words, are the voice of that Spirit, telling our spirit of the love of God for us and the reward of love for Him. 3. Its own reward follows on just and righteous doing; its reward follows surely on faith. It shall come to you along the three lines of warning, help, and comfort: the assurance of the Providence that never faileth, and never forgetteth, shall bring to you as its fruit, these precious results: A sober and awful sense of responsibility; a check and salutary restraint on action; a courage and energy above natural force; a constant sense of the Divine companionship; a transfiguration of your entire life; and, for the future, a settled restfulness and peace, the harbingers of eternal satisfaction in the likeness of Him whom now His children see by faith, but whom they shall know hereafter even as they are known. (*Morgan Dix, D.D.*) *God's wonderful care:*—When we think of the labour required to rear the few that are in our households—the weariness, the anxiety, the burden of life—how wonderful seems God's work! for He carries heaven and earth, and all realms, in His bosom. Many think that God takes no thought for anything less than a star or a mountain, and is unmindful of the little things of life; but when I go abroad, the first thing which I see is the grass beneath my feet; and, nestling in that, flowers smaller yet; and lower still, the mosses with their inconspicuous blooms, which beneath the microscope glow with beauty. And if God so cares for "the grass of the field, which to-day is, and to-morrow is cast into the oven," shall He not much more care for the minutest things of your life, "O ye of little faith"? (*H. W. Beecher.*) *The worth of sparrows:*—It is significant that Christ marked with so much interest the more lowly and homely of the creatures around us. He does not say, "Consider the eagle"—the monarch of the air, the symbol of empire and of victory; or, "Consider the nightingale," the sweet Eastern bulbul, that floods the Jordan banks and the shores of Gennesaret with its passionate music; but, "Consider the raven"—a fowl of ill-omen and unattractive to the eye, or draws attention to the sparrow, a very Pariah among the feathered tribes. It is like His preference for publicans and sinners over the lordly Pharisee and learned scribe. Who but Jesus would have dreamed of getting poetry and theology out of ravens and sparrows! Who but He would have compared Himself, as He did in the most pathetic utterance of His life, to a hen vainly calling her heedless brood to the shelter of her wings! But this fashion of speech became Him who was "meek and lowly in heart"; and who, moreover, being one with the Author of Nature, interprets best her deepest and simplest lessons. And what a revelation Christ's saying respecting the sparrows gives us of the working of God's providence! What an omniscience and omnipresence it implies! He declares that God actually notices and cares for every little feathered thing that flits twittering through the air, or hops from bough to bough in innocent and happy freedom, or pipes its solitary note "alone upon the housetop." And when the tiny creature falls, struck by stick or shot or stone, "it does not fall on the ground," He says, "without your Father." Nay, even as it hangs in the poulterer's stall, strung up with fifty others, waiting for the purchaser, poor almost as itself, who can find the farthing needed to buy two of them, still it is not "forgotten before God." The pitiful little tragedy, from beginning to end, is watched and recorded by the Supreme Mind! If He observes all that, what is there which He overlooks? If He "caters providently for the sparrow," and interests Himself in its fate, how solicitous His care for all His living creatures! How minute and delicate and sympathetic, as well as far-reaching and omnipotent, the oversight of His providence, which is not less special than general, not less particular than it is universal. Even a large-minded and noble-hearted man is distinguished above others by his freedom from contempt, by his insight into the meaning of little things, and his sense of the sacredness and the value of common life. His mind is superior to the mere bulk and splendour of outward things. And with God this must be so in the most absolute sense, to the most perfect degree. "He hath respect unto the lowly." And this "respect" extends in due measure to all His creatures. It is only when we believe that His care is thus universal that we can absolutely rely upon it for ourselves. (*G. G. Findlay, B.A.*) *Confidence in God's providence :*—After the battle of Manassas, Captain Imboden called upon General Stonewall Jackson, who was severely wounded, and found him bathing his swollen hand in spring water, and bearing his pain very patiently. In the course of their conversation Imboden said: "How is it, General, you can keep so cool, and appear so utterly insensible to danger, in such a storm of shell and bullets as rained about you when your hand was hit?" He instantly became grave and reverential in his manner, and answered in a low tone of great earnestness : " Captain, my religious belief teaches me to feel as safe in battle as in bed. God has fixed the time of my death. I do not concern myself about that, but to be always ready, no matter when it may overtake me." He added after a pause: " Captain, that is the way all men should live, and then all would be equally brave." *Remarkable deliverances :*—The celebrated author of the "Pilgrim's Progress" experienced several remarkable providential deliverances. Once he fell into the river Ouse, and at another time into the sea, and narrowly escaped being drowned. When seventeen years of age he became a soldier, and at the siege of Leicester in 1645, being drawn out to stand sentinel, another soldier in the same company desired to take his place. He consented, and his companion was shot in the head by a musket ball, and killed. *The doctrine of providence practically improved :*—I. To prove that the providence of God extends to all human affairs; and—II. To point out the practical uses we should make of this doctrine. I. Let us establish, by reference to the Scriptures, this great and important truth, THAT THE PROVIDENCE OF GOD IS UNIVERSAL; that it extends to all creatures and things throughout the whole world ; but, as that concerns us most, especially to all human affairs. By the providence of God, we mean His preserving and governing all His creatures, and all their actions. 1. This appears even from the light of nature. It seems necessarily to follow from His being the Creator of the world ; for it is reasonable to believe, that He who made all things, governs all things (Rom. i. 18–21 ; Acts xiv. 17). The existence of God, a Being of infinite power and wisdom and goodness, obliges us to believe that He will take care of His creatures. 2. But we have clearer light and fuller proof of this from the Bible, God's own revelation of Himself. There we read that God is the great Preserver. "What shall I do unto Thee," said holy Job, " O thou Preserver of men !" (Job vii. 20). And the psalmist exclaims, " How excellent is Thy loving kindness, O God! therefore the children of men put their trust under the shadow of Thy wings. O Lord, thou preservest man and beast" (Psa. xxxvi. 6, 7). And in the book of Nehemiah, the good providence of God is celebrated in these exalted strains : " Thou, even Thou, art Lord alone ; Thou hast made heaven, the heaven of heavens, with all their host, the earth, and all things that are therein, the seas, and all that is therein, and Thou preservest them all !" (Neh. ix. 6). The predictions of future events, and their fulfilment, of both which the Scriptures afford very numerous instances, furnish us with another proof of the reality of a Divine Providence ; for if God did not govern the world, He could not foretell what would come to pass. God forewarned Noah of the flood 120 years before it came. He foretold the bondage of Israel in Egypt ; how long it should last, and how they should be delivered. The captivity of Judah was foretold long before it happened ; how many years it should continue ; by whom, and by what means the people should be restored, and the temple rebuilt. All the circumstances relating to the birth, life, sufferings, death, and resurrection of Christ were exactly predicted. God, who preserves all creatures, governs them also. He does not commit the management of the world to deputies, as many of the heathen supposed. " The Lord reigneth." " He increaseth the nations, and destroyeth them : He enlargeth the nations, and straiteneth them again. He looseth the bond of kings, and girdeth their loins with a girdle. He leadeth princes away spoiled, and overthroweth the mighty " (Job xii. 18, 19, 23). The providence of God is to be owned in the affairs of families (Psa. lxviii. 6 ; cvii. 41). Nor are individuals beneath His notice, as the text plainly imports; not even the least of their concerns, " for the very hairs of their head are all numbered " ; consequently all their more important concerns. Even as to those events which we call contingent, or accidental, even they are under the direction and control of the Almighty (Prov. xvi. 33). This providence of God, the existence of which we have clearly proved. (1) It is sovereign and uncontrollable. Who hath resisted, who can resist, His will? (2) It is wise. " His work is perfect, all His ways are judgment." He cannot err: He cannot be deceived or mistaken. (3) It is mysterious. " Clouds and darkness are round about Him." (4) Always good. " Truly, God is good to Israel." " His eyes," directing all human affairs, " run to and fro throughout the earth "; and for what purpose ? " To show Himself strong " in behalf of all that fear and love His name. Yes, assuredly; for all " things work together for the good" of His people. II. We now proceed to the second part of the subject; namely, To POINT OUT THE PRACTICAL USES WE OUGHT TO MAKE OF THE DOCTRINE OF PROVIDENCE. This doctrine is, in truth, connected with the whole of practical religion. Take away providence, and you destroy the whole system of godliness, and leave no room for prayer or praise. 1. Let us stand in awe of the great Ruler of the world. Do His eyes behold, His eyelids try the children of men ? Is He in every place, beholding the evil and the good? In His hand is our breath and all our ways ? Who, then, shall not fear Him ? who shall not tremble at His presence ? 2. Let us rejoice that the reins of universal government are in the hands of Jesus Christ, our Saviour and our Lord—of Him who is our Mediator, our Redeemer, our Brother, and our Friend. 3. The doctrine of providence shows the propriety and utility of prayer; it affords the strongest motive, and the best encouragement to that duty. 4. The doctrine of providence shows the propriety of offering to God the sacrifice of praise and thanksgiving. 5. It shows the propriety of submission to the will of God. Does the Lord rule ? Submit to His government. 6. Improve the doctrine of Divine Providence, as a remedy against anxiety. 7. Finally: let this subject lead our minds forward towards the future and eternal world. (*G. Burder.*) *The Father's love for persons :*—He is the God of *all*, and yet He is *my* God. This view of God we all have a deep interest in impressing on our minds. We must strive to combine, in our conception of Him, the thoughts of a particular and a universal providence. On the one hand, we must not narrow His loving care, as if it were mindful of ourselves alone, nor think of Him only as doing us good. For this would be to rob Him of His infinitude, and darken the splendour of His boundless beneficence. Such a view would make religion the nurse of selfishness, and convert our connection with the Supreme Being into one of self-interest. Never let us try to monopolize God. Never let us imagine that God exists only as administering to our individual wants. Never let us for an instant forget His relation to the universe. But on the other hand, beware lest in thus enlarging your views of the Infinite One, you lose your hold of the correlative truth—that though all beings of all worlds are His care, though His mind thus embraces the universe, He is yet as mindful of you, as if that universe were blotted out, and you alone survived to receive the plenitude of His care. God's relation to you is not an exclusive one, but it is as close as if it were. Never conceive that your actions are overlooked and forgotten, because of the multiplicity of agents and beings who are to be guided and governed. Never fear that your wants are forgotten, because the boundless Creation sends up a cry to its common Father, and He has an infinite family for whom to provide. Never think that your characters are objects of little interest, because innumerable orders of beings of higher attainments and virtues attract the regards of this munificent King. Were you His only creature alive, He could not think of you more constantly and tenderly, or be more displeased with your resistance to duty, or feel more joy in your fidelity to right, than He does now. The human mind, apt to measure God by itself, has always found a difficulty in reconciling the two views which have just been stated. Through this propensity it fell into Polytheism, or the worship of many gods. Wanting a Deity, who would watch over their particular interests, and fearing that they would be overlooked by the Father of all, men invented inferior divinities—gods for each particular country and nation—and still more household gods, divinities for each particular dwelling, that they might have some superior power beneath which to shelter their weakness. I. BUT THERE IS NO INCONSISTENCY IN AT ONCE BELIEVING IN GOD'S PARTICULAR PROVIDENCE AND IN HIS UNIVERSAL PROVIDENCE. He may watch over all, and yet watch over each, as if each were all. There is a simple truth, which may help us to understand, that God does not intermit His attention to individuals in consequence of His inspection of the infinite whole. It is this. The individual is a living part of this living whole—vitally connected with it—acting upon it and reacted upon by it—receiving good, and communicating good in return, in proportion to his growth and power. From this constitution of the universe it follows, that the whole is preserved and perfected by the care of its parts. The general good is bound up in the individual good. So that to superintend the one is to superintend the other ; and the neglect of either would be the neglect of both.

What reason have I for considering myself as overlooked, because God has such an immense family to provide for? I belong to this family. I am bound to it by vital bonds. I am always exerting an influence upon it. I can hardly perform an act that is confined in its consequences to myself. Every new truth that I gain makes me a brighter light to humanity. I ought not then to imagine that God's interest in me is diminished, because His interest is extended to endless hosts of spirits. On the contrary, God must be more interested in me on this very account, because I influence others as well as myself. I am a living member of the great family of all souls; and I cannot improve or suffer myself, without diffusing good or evil around me through an ever-enlarging sphere. In these remarks we have seen, that from the intimate and vital connection between the individual and the community of spirits, God in taking care of each person is taking care of the whole, and that there is a perfect harmony between the general and the particular superintendence of God. From the same vital connection of beings, I derive another encouraging view, leading to the same result. I learn from it that God's attention to His whole creation, far from withdrawing His regard from me, is the very method whereby He is advancing my especial good. I am organically connected with the great family of the universal parent. Plainly then it is for my happiness, that this family should be watched over and should prosper. Suppose the Creator to abandon all around me, that He might bless me alone, should I be a gainer by such a monopoly of God's care? My happiness is manifestly bound up with and flows from the happiness of those around; and thus the Divine kindness to others is essentially kindness to myself. This is no theory; it is the fact confirmed by all experience. Every day we receive perpetual blessings from the progress of our race. We are enlightened, refined, elevated, through the studies, discoveries, and arts of countless persons, whom we have never seen and of whom we have never even heard. Daily we enjoy conveniences, pleasures, and means of health and culture, through advancements in science and art, made in the most distant regions. And in so far as we possess elevated, disinterested, and holy characters, or enlarged intelligence, have not these been cherished and encouraged by the examples, writings, deeds, and lives of far-spread fellow-beings, through all ages and nations? How much would each of us assuredly be advanced in happiness, wisdom, virtue, were the community around us—were all the persons with whom we hold intercourse—more humane and more heavenly! Is God, then, neglecting us in His care of others? How could He bless us more effectually than by carrying forward the great spiritual system to which we belong, and of which we are living parts? II. Thus having seen how consistent is the doctrine of God's care for the whole with the doctrine that He watches minutely over every individual, let ME NOW ASK YOU TO LOOK AT THIS DOCTRINE MORE CLOSELY, IN ITS PRACTICAL APPLICATIONS. Consider what affecting ideas it involves! According to this truth, we are, each one of us, present to the mind of God. We are penetrated, each one of us, instant by instant, by His all-seeing eye; we are known, every single person of us, more interiorly by Him than we are known to ourselves. Moment by moment the living God sustains us; and His own life continually flows into us through His omnipotent good-will. In fine, and above all, the Holy One never loses sight of our character and conduct. He witnesses and delights in our virtues. And He too witnesses and condemns every sin. Intimate and tender, beyond our highest conception, is our Heavenly Father's relationship to us! He is incessantly our creator and renewer, our upholder and benefactor, our witness and judge. The connection of all other beings with us, when compared with this, is foreign and remote. The nearest friend, the most loving parent, is but a stranger to us, when contrasted with God. No words can adequately express this living alliance of the Creator with His creatures. And knowing thus the intensity and the extent of this relationship, how is it possible that I can forget Him? My hearers, I have thus turned your attention to this sublimely affecting subject of our vital connection with God, not for the purpose of awakening temporary fervour, but that we may feel the urgent duty of cherishing these convictions. Were a person, who had lived in ignorance of all beyond mere sensitive existence, suddenly to receive a clear impression of God's all-embracing presence, he would undergo a greater change of condition, than if he were to awake some morning in a wholly new world, peopled by new beings, clothed in new beauty, and governed by laws such as he had never known by experience. He would be uplifted with the assurance, that at length he had found for his soul an all-sufficing object of veneration, gratitude, trust and love, an unfailing source of strength for every mortal weakness, an exhaustless refreshment of his highest hope, an ever-springing fount of holy emotion, virtuous energy, and heavenly joy, infinitely transcending all modes of good to which he had been wont to look. In a word, he would be utterly transformed. On the other hand, in degree as by faithlessness I lose sight of my intimate relationship with God, I am bereft of inward peace, of the desire for progress, of power to escape from myself. The future grows dim, and hope dies. A change comes over me like that which befals the traveller when clouds overspread the sky, when gathering mists obscure his path, and gloom settles down upon his uncertain way, till he is lost. The light of life is a constant consciousness of Divine fellowship. III. How THEN CAN WE ATTAIN TO AN ABIDING CONSCIOUSNESS OF LIVING RELATIONSHIP WITH THE LIVING GOD? How can we reach the constant feeling that He is always with us, offering every aid consistent with our freedom, guiding us on to heavenly happiness, welcoming us into the immediate knowledge of His perfection, into a loving fellowship with Himself? I shall confine myself to what seems to be essential, as the first step, in this approach to true communion with the Father of spirits. My belief is, that one chief means of acquiring a vivid sense of God's presence is to resist, instantly and resolutely, whatever we feel to be evil in our hearts and lives, and at once to begin in earnest to obey the Divine will as it speaks in conscience. You say that you desire a new and nearer knowledge of your Creator. Let this thirst for a higher consciousness of the Infinite Being lead you to oppose whatever you feel to be at war with God's purity, God's truth, and God's righteousness. Just in proportion as you gain a victory over the evil of which you have become aware in yourself, will your spiritual eye be purged for a brighter perception of the Holy One. (*W. E. Channing.*)

Ver. 8. **Whosoever shall confess Me before men.**—*The judgment-seat of Christ:*— I. For FINGER-POSTS that may guide our endeavour to come at the spiritual reality here symbolized, such thoughts as these may serve. 1. Evidently Christ here contrasts the seen and the unseen world as respectively small and great; here a petty vicinage, there a grand environment; here ignorant men, there high intelligences— the angels of God; here ourselves as affected by the examples and opinions of sinners, there ourselves as feeling the presence and the criticism of the pure; in dim light here, in dazzling light there. 2. Christ evidently contrasts the seen and the unseen world in their respective objects of honour and dishonour. 3. The next truth of which Christ here makes us certain is, that the future is simply the continuance of present relations to Him under changed conditions. Thus we approach a true and clear conception of what our Lord meant by confessing Him and being confessed by Him, &c. Not by what we say, but by what we are, is our present confession or denial of Christ most tellingly uttered before men. Likewise, by what He is, as compared with what we are, will His future confession or denial of us be most conclusively made known, to our glory or our shame before the heavenly witnesses—"the angels of God." II. From this look into the spiritual reality of our subject we draw some obvious and practical CONCLUSIONS. 1. Confessing or denying Christ is certainly no mere affair of words. Yet words, though weak, are not worthless. They can make their mark on character—our own and others' character. 2. Confessing Christ and being confessed by Christ are not to be separated in our thought, like work-day and pay-day, as if the confessing were all here, and the being confessed all there. What comes out there is simply the flash of an awakened consciousness of a judgment of Christ which has been going on here every day under the eyes of the invisible witnesses of many a negligent life. 3. Confessing or denying Christ here is not a question solely as to the totality or average of character, but quite as much a question as to the particulars of character. Point by point, the world compares the professed copy with its model, and recognizes agreements or contradictions in detail. No otherwise can it be in the presence of the angels of God. (*J. M. Whiton, Ph.D.*) *Confession of Christ:*—The confession of Christ by the apostles was before the heads of their religion, the chief priests who had crucified Him. It was before rulers and kings, before the philosophers of Athens, the libertines of Corinth. It was the bold, unflinching avowal that the world was saved by the cruel and disgraceful death of a Jew, one of a nation regarded with pretty much the same contempt as they are now. They who made this confession always made it at the risk of their lives. This confession of Christ is yet dangerous to life even in this nineteenth century. No man in a Mahometan country, brought up in the national faith, can embrace the Christian religion except at the risk of his life—at least it was so a very few years ago. In Christian England the confession of Christ has assumed a different form, but it equally requires sincerity and courage to make it; a Christian has now to profess the creating power of God amongst evolutionists, and the all-ruling providence of God in the company of unbelieving scientists. In some companies he has to brave the ridicule attaching to the belief in miracles. In the society of filthy-minded men he has to uphold the purity of Christ, and in the society of worldlings he may be called upon to uphold the rooted antagonism between the world and Christ. These may seem very poor and mild ways of confessing Christ compared to what our forefathers in the faith had to endure; but they all try the metal of the Christian. If he is faithful in confessing Christ in these comparatively little matters, he may have a good hope that God would, if called upon, give him grace to make a bolder and more public and dangerous confession if it was laid upon him so to do. Such is the confession of Christ; and the reward answers to it. "Before the angels of God," *i.e.*, before the court of God—before His special ministers. Notice the extraordinary reality with which the Lord here invests the unseen world of angels. To be honoured before them and receive their applause, infinitely outweighs the contempt and persecution of a condemned world. (*M. F. Sadler.*)   *Christian courage :—*I. Consider some of the OCCASIONS WHICH CALL FOR THE EXERCISE OF THIS GRACE. 1. It requires courage to be able to withstand persecution for conscience sake. 2. You will need courage to bear reproach for Christ's sake. 3. You will need courage to act up to your convictions of duty in your own family and in the world at large. 4. You will need courage to resist temptation. 5. Courage is necessary to confess Christ in the presence of the rich and powerful, and of all who are exalted above you in station and influence. "I will speak of Thy testimonies also before kings," said David, "and will not be ashamed." And what noble courage was displayed by Daniel, and by Shadrach, Meshach, and Abednego! 6. It may be that some of you will need courage to venture your life at the call of duty. You may need it for the right discharge of your business. You may need it to act vigorously in endeavouring to save the lives of others. 7. You will need courage to resist the mere apprehension of evil. 8. You will need courage to bear the evils of life while they are actually pressing on you. 9. You will need courage to meet the last enemy. II. In order, then, to the attainment of this necessary grace of courage, or, which is the same thing, in order to your preservation from sinful fear, let the following BRIEF DIRECTIONS be considered and followed: 1. Begin with a well-founded hope in God's mercy, through faith in the Lord Jesus Christ. Without this, though you may be free from fear, you must be exposed to the most awful danger; and, therefore, though you may be foolhardy, you cannot be rationally and scripturally courageous. But, if God be "on your side," as the Psalmist expresses it, then you need "not fear what man can do unto you." 2. Endeavour, next, after a very firm trust in God's providence. Remember that the slightest evil cannot befall you without your heavenly Father, and believe that He causes all things to work together for your good. 3. Reflect on the noble examples of courage which are recorded in Scripture. 4. Vex not yourselves with fears as to the future, but give yourselves to the duties of the present. 5. Consider the exhortations and promises of the Word of God, and have the substance of all, and the very words of many of them, in your memory. They abound to this effect throughout Scripture, especially in Isaiah, and the Psalms. 6. Think of the confession that awaits you from the Lord, and the crown of glory which will be yours, at last, if you be faithful. He assures you that He will confess you before His Father and the holy angels : and He says to each of you, "Be thou faithful unto death, and I will give thee a crown of life." Think often of this ; and the thought will far more than counterbalance any reproach, or opposition, you may meet with here. And, finally, mindful of your own weakness, and how certainly both your strength and courage would fail if you were left to yourselves, be much in prayer to God for this grace of holy courage. (*Jas. Foote, M.A.*) *Showing his colours :—*One day, as I sat in the barrack-room, I was thinking over in my mind the many difficulties with which I had to contend as a professing Christian, and how to overcome them. One thing, I said, I must do ; I must confess Christ, and not be ashamed of my colours. I had only recently been led to trust in the Lord Jesus as my Saviour, and had begun to pray and read all the books that were likely to help me to a better knowledge of the Lord Jesus. I had not the Bible to read ; that I had given away a few weeks previously to one of my comrades as a thing that I should never require in the future. There was but one thing that I had, up to the present, shrunk from doing, and that was kneeling down at my bed-side, and praying openly before my comrades, before going to bed. I felt dissatisfied with myself for being so cowardly, and had also made up my mind to do so that night. "You want to be seen of men," whispered Satan in my ear. "It is not for Christ's sake; you want the praise of man." I was fairly puzzled for a time, and was afraid of doing wrong. "If I were alone in this room to-night, what would I do before going to bed?" I asked myself. "Certainly, I should kneel down," I thought. "Then, if I do not do so to-night, it will be because I am ashamed to confess my Master before my fellow-men. Lord help me to do it to-night," I said, "for Christ's sake." The barrack-room in which I sat was a large one, capable of holding about one hundred men, and at night was lighted by four large oil lamps, which hung from the roof by chains. My bed stood right opposite one of these lamps, and there I sat waiting for nine o'clock, the time for all to go to bed. The scene around me was not a pleasant one, the men had but recently come from the canteen, where they had been liberally supplied with arrack (a native drink resembling rum, and which destroys more lives in India than the ravages of war or disease put together). Some of the men sat on their beds smoking, some stood in little groups discussing the topics of the day, others were singing popular comic songs, while a considerable number were quarrelling about something which had occurred at the canteen, and which ended in blows and blasphemy. Confusion and disorder reigned supreme. With the exception of a few who were so drunk that they were being put to bed by their comrades, all were contributing more or less to the general disorder. In a short time the bugles sounded the last post; it was nine o'clock at last. "Lord, help me," I said, and in the midst of all the confusion around me, I dropped upon my knees. For a few seconds the horrid din around me continued; it then ceased, and I knew that every eye was turned to where I knelt, right under the glare of that large oil lamp. Something strange had happened! Most of these men had been familiar with bloodshed in the Crimea, and in the still more recent and more deadly conflict of the mutiny. Of such things, the men were careless, but for things sacred they had a reverence. Many of them had praying mothers in old Scotland, who still prayed for them, and as I knelt before them now, not a hand was lifted against me, nor did a tongue speak a word! I say this to their credit, and for five years I continued to pray openly before them, without being molested in any way by them. I have had to reprove them for sin, but for this they honoured me, because I was not ashamed to show my colours. More than this, the Lord blessed my testimony, for He brought eight or nine of those men around me to bear witness for His name. Some are now in heaven, while others are preaching the everlasting gospel to their fellow men. (*A Soldier's Diary*.) *The reward of confessing Christ:*—There was a prince of right royal blood, who once upon a time left his father's palace and journeyed into a distant part of the king's dominions, where he was little known and cared for. He was a true prince, and he had about his face those princely marks—that strange divinity which doth hedge a king—that might have made the onlooker know that he was right royal. But when he came into the place, the people said, "This is the heir to the throne; let us insult him, let us hoot him!" Others said, he was no heir at all. And they agreed to set him in the pillory. As he stood there, every man did pelt him with all kinds of filth, and used all manner of hard words towards him; and they said, "Who dare acknowledge him for a prince? who dare stand by him?" There stood up one from the crowd, and said, "I dare!" They set him up in the pillory side by side with the prince; and when they threw their filth on the prince it fell on him, and when they spoke hard words of the prince they spoke hard words of him. He stood there, smiling, and received it all. Now and then a tear stole down his cheek; but that was for them, that they should thus ill-treat their sovereign. Years went by, the king came into those dominions and subdued them; and there came a day of triumph over the conquered city: streamers hung from every window, and the streets were strewn with roses. There came the king's troops dressed in burnished armour of gold, with plumes upon their glittering helmets. The music rang right sweetly, for all the trumpets of glory sounded. It was from heaven they had come. The prince rode through the streets in His glorious chariot; and when He came to the gates of the city, there were the traitors all bound in chains. They stood before Him trembling. He singled out from among the crowd one man only who stood free and unfettered, and He said to the traitors, "Know ye this man? He stood with Me in that day when ye treated Me with scorn and indignation. He shall stand with Me in the day of My glory. Come up hither!" said He. And amidst the sounding of trumpets and the voice of acclamation, the poor, despised, and rejected citizen of that rebellious city rode through the streets in triumph, side by side with his King, who clothed him in purple, and set a crown of pure gold upon his head. (*C. H. Spurgeon.*) *Power of confession :*—In relating his experience during the Peninsular war, Captain Watson says : " I was nominated to sit on a garrison court-martial. A number of officers of different ranks and regiments were present on the occasion, and before the proceedings commenced, some of them indulged in loose and sceptical observations. 'Alas,' thought I, 'here are many not ashamed to speak openly for their master, and shall I hold my peace and refrain when the honour and cause of Him who has had mercy on me are called in question?' I looked for wisdom and assistance from on high, and I was enabled to speak for a quarter of an hour in a way that astonished my hearers and myself. The Lord was pleased to give what I said a favourable reception, and not another improper word was uttered by them during my stay in that room." *Prompt confession :*—Dilawar Khan, formerly an Afghan robber, being convinced of the truth of the gospel, and having taken service in an English regiment at Peshawar, was, on the outbreak of the mutiny, ordered to Delhi. Separated from the missionaries before he had received baptism, and thrown among Mohammedans whose co-religionist he had been, he was determined to make his change of faith unmistakably known, and so, calling for a loaf of bread, he ate it with a European in presence of all. It was the only symbol of separation which the circumstances allowed. When baptized, he received the name Dilawar Messih = " Bold for Christ." *Confession of Christ unknown to nominal Christians :*—A Hindoo of rank was troubled in his conscience on the subject of a future state. He had heard of Christians, and longed to converse with them about their religion, and to know who Christ was. So he visited England, the Christian's land, supplied with introductions to some leading people. Being asked to a great dinner, he turned to his neighbour in the course of conversation, and said : " Can you tell me something about Christ, the founder of your religion? " " Hush," replied his new acquaintance, " we do not speak of such things at dinner parties." Subsequently he was invited to a large ball. Dancing with a young and fashionable lady, he took an opportunity of asking her who the founder of her religion, Jesus Christ, was. And again he was warned that a ball was no place to introduce such subjects. Strange, thought the Hindoo, are these Christians in England. They will not speak of their religion, nor inform me about Christ, its founder. *Confessing Christ :*—A great many years ago a Roman emperor said to a Greek architect : " Build me a Coliseum, and when it is done I will crown you ; and I will make your name famous through all the world, if you will only build me a grand Coliseum." The work was done. The emperor said : " Now we will crown that architect. We will have a grand celebration." The Coliseum was crowded with a great host. The emperor was there and the Greek architect, who was to be crowned for putting up this building. And then they brought out some Christians, who were ready to die for the truth, and from the doors underneath were let out the lions, hungry, three-fourths starved. The emperor arose amid the shouting assemblage, and said : " The Coliseum is done, and we have come to celebrate it to-day by the putting to death of Christians at the mouth of these lions, and we have come here to honour the architect who has constructed this wonderful building. The time has come for me to honour him, and we further celebrate his triumph by the slaying of these Christians." Whereupon, the Greek architect sprang to his feet, and shouted : " I also am a Christian." And they flung him to the wild beasts, and his body, bleeding and dead, was tumbled into the dust of the amphitheatre. Could you have done that for Christ ? Could you have stood up there in the presence of that great audience, who hated Christ, and hated everything about Him, and have said : " I, too, am a Christian "? (*Dr. Talmage.*) *Be not ashamed of the religion of Christ :*— If you go into a Mohammedan country, when the hour for prayer comes at three o'clock, you will see the Mohammedan kneeling down on his knees. He is not ashamed of his false religion. The only religion that gives a man victory over sin and the flesh, the only religion that gives a man spiritual power, is the religion of Jesus Christ, and yet it is the only religion that men are ashamed of. When Mr. Moody was at Salt Lake City he did not meet even one that was not proud of being a Mormon. Everywhere the fact was announced over their shops and places of business. If you meet a man who is possessed of an error he will publish it. Why should we, who have the truth, not publish it also? *Confession of Christ before men :*— If people are loud in the praise of the physician who has cured them of some deadly malady—recommending others to trust and seek his skill, why should not Christ's people crown Him with equal honours, commend Him to a dying world, and proclaim what He has done for them? Let them say with David, "Come, all ye that fear the Lord, and I will declare what He hath done for my soul"; and tread in the steps of the Samaritan who threw away her pitcher, and running to the city, brought them all out—crying, "Come, see a man who hath told me all things that I have ever done." It is a bad thing ostentatiously to parade religion; but it is a base thing for a Christian man to be ashamed of it: not to stand by his colours; by his silence, if not his speech, to deny his Master; to sneak away, like a coward, out of the fight. (*T. Guthrie, D.D.*) *Boldness in confessing Christ:*—I have no notion of a timid, disingenuous profession of Christ. Such preachers and professors are like a rat playing at hide-and-seek behind a wainscot, who puts his head through a hole to see if the coast is clear, and ventures out if nobody is in the way; but slinks back again when danger appears. We cannot be honest to Christ except we are bold for Him. He is either worth all we can lose for Him, or He is worth nothing. (*H. G. Salter.*) *The right kind of Christian:*—Not long ago an officer was accosted by a brother officer thus: "You're the right kind of Christian, not bothering people about their souls this way." The speaker himself made no pretensions to serious godliness; and the allusion was to certain officers who had a way of speaking out very intelligibly for Christ. Our friend had himself been converted; but, up to that time, he had been too timid to utter any articulate testimony. As his visitor left him that day, he began to reason with himself: "Well, if that man thinks I am the right kind of Christian, it is time I was looking about me and considering my ways." It was a somewhat novel point of departure; but from that hour, our friend has been another man, boldly confessing Christ and labouring to win souls. (*P. B. Power, M.A.*) *Speak for Christ:*—Brother—— was considered a consistent and by no means inefficient member of the Church. His seat was seldom vacant during divine service; and his place in the business meeting of the congregation, in Sunday-School and the prayer-meeting was seldom unoccupied. In short, his duties, public and private, as a member of the Church, were promptly, well, and faithfully performed. Yet on his death-bed he had his regrets. "I have," said he, "been a man of few words, and of a still tongue. Oh, if I had my life to live over again, I would speak for Jesus as I have never been accustomed to do." *Speaking for Christ:*—In a prayer-meeting at Boston I once attended, most of those who took part were old men, but a little tow-headed Norwegian boy, who could only speak broken English, got up and said: "If I tell the world about Christ, He will tell the Father about me." That wrote itself upon my heart, and I have never forgotten what that little boy said. (*D. L. Moody.*) *Confessing Christ:*—Jesus Christ expects that those who believe on Him should confess Him. I. WHAT IS MEANT BY THE WORDS "CONFESS CHRIST"? There is no great obscurity about them; still, a few words of explanation may bring out their meaning more clearly. Confessing Christ is an avowal of what He is in our esteem, of what He is to us. It assumes, of course, that there is an inward conviction that He is the Son of God, and the Saviour of the world. To confess Him is to let that conviction be outwardly expressed in some form or other, *i.e.*, it is a taking care that we do not stifle our convictions by keeping them to ourselves; but that we utter them, by letting it be known that we believe Christ, that we receive Him, that we worship Him, that we follow Him, as Teacher, &c. In a word, it is to say, "I am a Christian. I am Christ's man; 'for me to live is Christ!'" II. WHAT IS INVOLVED IN THE ACT OF MAKING THIS CONFESSION? It denies. It affirms. It opposes. Let us note each of these points. This confession denies that man is his own master. It is a practical declaration that we are under the authority of another, and it denies every other authority for man than that of the Lord Jesus Christ. Hence this confession affirms as well as denies. It avows the infinite right of Christ to rule over men because of His work for them! It is an avowal of His glory. Thus, this confession must needs oppose very much loose and wrong thinking of the present day. It is in opposition to the worldliness which would treat all religion and worship with supreme indifference. It opposes formalism, &c. And, by the terms of the expression, confessing Christ is as really *exclusive* as *inclusive*. It refuses to be cumbered with a host of commandments and doctrines of men. It declines to own any priestly intrusion between a man's conscience and the Lord Jesus, and hence is as much a confession of Christ only, as of Christ. III. IN WHAT WAY SHOULD THE CONFESSION BE MADE? 1. By letting it be seen that we are Christ's, by our light shining before men. The sun has no need to have the words, "I am a light," blazoned above or beneath him. Nor have even dim, artificial lights any need for this. They give light by shining. Now, though the parallel does not hold in every respect, yet in one point it indicates what we mean. Are you Christ's men, heart and soul? Then show it by being Christ-like. Not indeed that this is enough, but without it, nothing else can be enough. The importance of our unconscious influence can scarcely be overrated. So ought we to live that men can see that we are Christians by what we are, whether our conversation for the time being be on religious matters or no. 2. But the apostle Paul says: "With the mouth confession is made unto salvation." There is a saying, I am the Lord's, and this is a part of the confession—" speaking for Christ "—in the society in which you move. 3. Then, by acting for Christ we may confess Him. We may seek to spread His name among those who know Him not, and may make it a business of our lives to teach and train men for Him. 4. But let us not only passively endure, let us also take up the positive attitude of attack. We must not be content simply to receive rebuffs, we must give them, going forth without the camp, exposing error and rebuking sin. We can do this better in company than we can singly. I may go forth to work and witness alone, and succeed, but if a brother comes and stands by my side, and says, I am one with you, he makes me twice the man I was before. And out of this law of reciprocal influence, out of this power of combination—as being so much greater than that of isolation—there comes another means of making this confession, viz., joining the militant host of the people of God, or, to use a common phrase, joining the Church. IV. WHY SHOULD CHRIST BE THUS CONFESSED? For many reasons, each of which has some weight: but it is rather to the cumulative force of all of them that we desire to point attention. 1. Jesus Christ has definitely and expressly commanded it (Luke xii. 8, 9). 2. It is manifestly reasonable that we should avow our relation to such a Saviour, and His relation to us. For what are we, but sinful, dying men, owing our immortal life and eternal hopes to Jesus and His saving love? When the names of men whom a country loves to honour are often on our lips, as if we felt honoured by knowing something about them, shall it be that we keep silence only concerning the Man of Sorrows, as if it were aught but an honour to speak His name? God forbid. 3. It is assumed in the New Testament that Christ's men act as a corporate body. The institution that Christ intended to build up, He called "a Church"; and after He went to heaven, a group of one hundred and twenty were found meeting in an upper room, &c. 4. To avow your convictions, will help to give them definiteness and precision. So long as a conviction remains snugly lodged within, unexpressed, it need not be very sharply defined; but bring it out, put it into shape, set it in words, draw it forth to living action, and lo! it is at once a fuller and clearer conviction, owing to the very effort required to avow it! Yea, more, conviction unavowed becomes feebler. 5. Christ and the world are such opposites, that if a man has any adequate conception of the difference between them, he cannot help seeing the incongruity of a believer in Christ refusing to confess Him. When so many are opposed, or indifferent, does it not behove the friends of Christ to stand up for Him? 6. Jesus Christ confessed us. 7. Christ lives on earth in those who confess Him. By His Church He manifests Himself in living form to the world. His confessing ones are His mouthpiece by which He speaks to a dying world! And we want your voice and tongue, and hands and feet, and brain and heart, to be employed for Him in ringing out the grand testimony that the Father sent the Son, the Saviour of the world! 8. In confessing Christ we join such a blessed line of confessors. 9. The confession itself is such a glorious one. 10. The true confessors will be so blessedly confessed (Matt. x. 32, 33). "But," says one, "is there no medium between confessing and denying?" We reply, Christ puts none, therefore we cannot. Nor would we if we could. We would bid you turn away your eyes from all goals but the very highest of all! And suffer me to ask, Has not the promise of being confessed by Christ any charm for you? V. MANY DO NOT THUS CONFESS CHRIST. WHY IS THIS? 1. There is reason to fear that there are some who do not confess Christ because they know that if they were to do so, as things are now, they could but profess a regard for His name, which goes no further than outside reverence. They are not living in obedience to Christ; so that, even if they were to call Him "Lord, Lord," though there might be there a form of godliness, there would not be its power! 2. "That is not my reason," says one; "but it seems to me that in the Church you hedge round the open confession of Christ, which is involved in 'joining the Church,' with such difficulties, that many are thereby kept back." As might be expected, we find that the "difficulties," which Churches are supposed to put in the way, vanish in the course of friendly conversation with those who are kind enough and frank enough to state them. 3. Some do not confess Christ, on account of not seeing the importance of making such confession. But if Christ has commanded it, ought we not to obey orders without debating the question of its importance? 4. Some do not confess Christ owing to the feebleness of their personal conviction. When the heart beats feebly the whole frame languishes, and when brain nerve-power is lacking the heart beats feebly. Herein is one of the many parables of physiology. A lack of strength in the convictions of the soul is often a cause of holding back from avowing Christ. And this feebleness of conviction is often owing to confusion of thought, or to a lack of clear understanding with regard to the contents and mutual relation of religious truth. 5. Some are kept back from avowing their convictions through the fear of man (John xii. 42, 43, and others). 6. Others are kept back from confessing Christ, by a cause which is far less objectionable, because more reasonable, viz., a fear of themselves. Confession of Christ seems to them to involve so much, that they fear they can never come up to the high standard which is before their eye. They see, too, that there are some who, having confessed Christ, settle down at their ease, and they fear lest it should be so with them. 7. Some are deterred from confessing Christ by the warning of the apostle, " Whosoever shall eat this bread," &c. Whosoever is kept back by these words, should read the whole of the section of the chapter in which they stand ; he will then find that the persons there addressed were turning the Lord's Supper into a common meal, mistaking its nature and design. Hence they tarried not for one another ; some came hungry and feasted, and others were drunken. 8. "But look at the inconsistency of professors ! " Yes, we do look at it, and grieve over it, but how that should be a reason for not confessing Christ, it is not easy to see. 9. "Well, but I can be saved without making this confession." Do not be so sure of that. If you see it to be a duty which you owe to Christ, and then can leave a known duty unfulfilled, you are not a saved man ! None who continue in known disobedience to Christ are saved. Besides, look at the selfishness of the plea. It is as if all that a man had to think about was—being saved ! This may, indeed, be the first thing, but most assuredly it is not everything ! We would put another question : Suppose you refuse to confess Christ, can you do as much to save others as if you avowed Him as your Lord ? And to this we most decidedly answer, No ! VI. KEEPING BACK FROM THE CONFESSION OF CHRIST IS IN MANY RESPECTS A GREAT EVIL. Whether the reasons for keeping back be those which we have named or not, the non-confession of Christ is evil, though the kind and degree thereof may be varied according to the motives which lead to a secret rather than an open discipleship. 1. It is unworthy. Such a Saviour as we have ought to be confessed willingly, yea, joyfully. To keep silent on our tongues the name that angels love to sound forth through the realms of heaven, and for the one who thus keeps the name so still to be the one who owes to it all his hopes of eternal life, that is no worthy return for the suffering of the cross. Much reason had He to be ashamed of us, but why, oh ! why, should we be ashamed of Him ? 2. If any refuse to confess Christ they voluntarily lessen their own possibilities of usefulness. 3. For we have only to suppose this isolated working to be universally carried out, and then it is clear we should never hear of a visible Church at all ! The Church might remain, but her visibility would be gone. 4. Inactive convictions will be injurious. To have them and not act on them would be to our condemnation. 5. Another evil is, that not to confess Christ is to be disobedient to His direct command. 6. And still another evil in the non-confession of Christ on the part of those who are His, is that it may throw the balance of their personal influence on the wrong side. VII. WHAT SENTIMENTS AND FEELINGS SHOULD MOVE US TO THE CONFESSION OF CHRIST ? 1. Gratitude. 2. Love. When once it is clear that He has commanded it, and that He is infinitely worthy of being so confessed, then love to Him for His infinite worthiness should leave us without hesitation as to the course to pursue. And there is this distinction between being moved by gratitude and being inspired by love. Love is the higher affection of the two. Gratitude is the desire to recompense, or at least to acknowledge, a favour received. Love is the passion which cleaves to One who is in Himself surpassingly glorious. 3. Loyalty. Gratitude has respect to what Christ has done for us ; love to what He is in Himself ; loyalty, to His relation to us as Leader and Commander. 4. The feeling of brotherhood should impel to the confession of Christ. 5. Compassion for men who are out of Christ should lead us to confess Christ. VIII. IN WHAT SPIRIT SHOULD THE CONFESSION BE MADE ? This we may gather from the notice already given of the feelings which move us to make it. Evidently it should not be made without much thought, care, and prayer. The essential qualifications for such a confession are—sincerity and truth; without these there must be an unreality about the confession, which would not only render it null and void, but would bring greater guilt on the individual making a merely hollow confession. This, of course, must be the prime matter. When any one says, I am Christ's man, he should say it because it is true, for to say it cannot make it true, if it is not so otherwise. But this being the case, any one contemplating a step so important will be anxious to put into it all the meaning that he can do. To help such in so doing, let us observe—1. The step should be taken humbly; not in a spirit of boastfulness or self-sufficiency, nor yet with the notion uppermost of "becoming a professor." 2. The confession should be made with fear and trembling. 3. At the same time that fear should not be so disproportionate, as to prevent a hallowed joy in confessing Christ. 4. We should always bring with us to the confession, a sense of the great and undeserved honour put on us in having such a Christ to avow. If a king should have pity on a pauper, and should translate him from a workhouse to a palace, and clothe him with royal robes, and make him partner of his throne, and should then educate him up to his dignity, and all out of pure regard to that pauper, without his having done aught to deserve it, might he not in his elevated position glory in the honour put upon him, and with a sense of the honour might he not well proclaim his deliverer and friend? 5. Making the confession of Christ should be attended with a spirit of entire devotion to the interests of the kingdom. 6. There should be the desire to gain such an amount of Christian intelligence as shall give him the right kind of influence in the Church of God. 7. But, if possible, even more eagerly intent should the individual confessing Christ be on "adorning the doctrine of God" his "Saviour in all things," by pureness, lowliness, meekness, and long-suffering. 8. To all this, let us add—There should be a reliance on Divine aid and on the indwelling of the Holy Ghost. These, the Saviour whom we confess has received for us, and will impart them to us. And no one who has an approximately adequate sense of the grand destiny of the Christian life will ever dream of attaining it by his own unaided power. IX. THERE ARE SPECIAL REASONS JUST NOW FOR SUCH A CONFESSION OF CHRIST AMONG THE INDIVIDUALS COMPOSING OUR PROTESTANT CONGREGATIONS. Certain features in the several epochs of time may furnish reasons which would make a specially urgent duty of what would be a duty at any time. Such features show themselves now in the ecclesiastical movements and theological conflicts of the day. This may appear more clearly as we proceed. 1. A special reason for this confession is found in the fact, that only by banding together as Christian people can we give practical effect to Christ's own law, that those who love Him should uphold His cause. 2. It is important to hold up to the view of men another principle: viz., that Christian men, when associated together in their corporate capacity, are empowered by Christ with authority to carry on His work. 3. It is important, at a time when so many are denying and disobeying Christ, that hearts which are loyal to Him should cheer on each other in their witness-bearing for Him. 4. It is important that each Christian man should bear a testimony for the doctrine and polity which he believes to be most in accordance with Christ's will, and most effective for Christ's service. 5. Whatever we can do to leaven public sentiments with the truth of Christian doctrine, and to show the relation of that doctrine to the well-being of a nation, it is our bounden duty to do, and towards this, it is no unimportant contribution for us to band together with those who uphold the cause of our Lord. (*C. Clemance, D.D.*)

Ver. 9. **He that denieth Me before men.**—*On denying Christ :*—I. How MANY WAYS CHRIST AND HIS TRUTHS MAY BE DENIED ; AND WHAT IS THE DENIAL HERE CHIEFLY INTENDED. Here, first, in general I assert that we may deny Him in all those acts that are capable of being morally good or evil; those are the proper scene in which we act our confessions or denials of Him. Accordingly, therefore, all ways of denying Christ I shall comprise under these three. 1. We may deny Him and His truths by an erroneous, heretical judgment. 2. We may deny Christ verbally and by oral expressions. Now our words are the interpreters of our hearts, the transcripts of the judgment, with some farther addition of good or evil. He that interprets, usually enlarges. 3. We may deny Christ in our actions and practice ; and these speak much louder than our tongues. To have an orthodox belief and a true profession, concurring with a bad life, is only to deny Christ with a greater solemnity. Belief and profession will speak thee a Christian but very faintly, when thy conversation proclaims thee an infidel. Many, while they have preached

Christ in their sermons, have read a lecture of atheism in their practice.   As for
the manner of our denying the deity of Christ here prohibited, I conceive it was by
words and oral expressions verbally to deny and disacknowledge it.   This I ground
upon these reasons—1. Because it was such a denial as was " before men," and
therefore consisted in open profession ; for a denial in judgment and practice, as
such, is not always before men.   2. Because it was such a denial or confession of
Him as would appear in preaching ; but this is managed in words and verbal profession.   But now, if we take the words as they are, a general precept equally
relating to all times and to all persons, though delivered only upon a particular
occasion to the apostles (as I suppose they are to be understood), so I think they
comprehend all the three ways mentioned of confessing or denying Christ, but
principally in respect of practice, and that—(1) Because by this He is most
honoured or dishonoured.   (2) Because without this the other two cannot save.
(3) Because those who are ready enough to confess Him both in judgment and
profession are for the most part very prone to deny Him shamefully in their doings.
Pass we now to a second thing, viz., to show—II. WHAT ARE THE CAUSES INDUCING
MEN TO DENY CHRIST IN HIS TRUTHS.   I shall propose three. 1. The seeming supposed absurdity of many truths.   Upon this heresy always builds.   The seeming
paradoxes attending gospel truths cause men of weak, prejudiced intellectuals to
deny them, and in them, Christ; being ashamed to own faith so much, as they
think, to the disparagement of their reason. 2. The second thing causing men to
deny the truths of Christ is their unprofitableness.   And no wonder if here men
forsake the truth and assert interest.   To be pious is the way to be poor.   Truth
still gives its followers its own badge and livery, a despised nakedness.   3. Their
apparent danger.   To be resolute in a good cause is to bring upon ourselves the
punishments due to a bad.   III. We proceed now to the third thing, which is to
SHOW HOW FAR A MAN MAY CONSULT HIS SAFETY IN TIME OF PERSECUTION WITHOUT DENY-
ING CHRIST.   This he may do two ways. 1. By withdrawing his person. Martyrdom is an heroic act of faith ; an achievement beyond an ordinary pitch of it; "to
you," says the Spirit, " it is given to suffer " (Phil. i. 29).   It is a peculiar additional gift ; it is a distinguishing excellency of degree, not an essential consequent
of its nature. "Be ye harmless as doves," says Christ; and it is as natural to them
to take flight upon danger, as to be innocent. Let every man thoroughly consult the
temper of his faith, and weigh his courage with his fears, his weakness, and his
resolutions together, and take the measure of both, and see which preponderates ;
and, if his spirit faints, if his heart misgives and melts at the very thoughts of the
fire, let him fly, and secure his own soul, and Christ's honour. 2. By concealing
his judgment.   A man sometimes is no more bound to speak than to destroy himself ; and as nature abhors this, so religion does not command that.   In the times
of the primitive Church, when the Christians dwelt amongst heathens, it is
reported of a certain maid, how she came from her father's house to one of the
tribunals of the Gentiles, and declared herself a Christian, spit in the judge's face,
and so provoked him to cause her to be executed.   But will any say that this was
to confess Christ or die a martyr? He that, uncalled for, uncompelled, comes and
proclaims a persecuted truth for which he is surely to die, only dies a confessor to
his own folly, and a sacrifice to his own rashness.   Martyrdom is stamped such
only by God's command ; and he that ventures upon it without a call must endure
it without a reward.   Christ will say, " Who required this at your hands ? "   His
gospel does not dictate imprudence; no evangelical precept justles out that of a
lawful self-preservation. He, therefore, that thus throws himself upon the sword,
runs to heaven before he is sent for ; where, though perhaps Christ may in mercy
receive the man, yet He will be sure to disown the martyr. IV. Having thus
despatched the third thing, I proceed to show WHAT IT IS FOR CHRIST TO
DENY US BEFORE HIS FATHER IN HEAVEN.   Hitherto we have treated of men's
carriage to Christ in this world ; now we will describe His carriage to them
in the other.   These words clearly relate to the last judgment: and they are a
summary description of His proceeding with men at that day.   And here we will
consider—1. The action itself—" He will deny them." 2. The circumstance of the
action—" He will deny them before His Father and the holy angels." (R. South,
D.D.)   Some ways of denying Christ:—1. We deny Christ when we advocate
opinions which tend to lessen the authority of His religious teachings. 2. It is
denying Christ to represent Him as a mere man.   He Himself said, " I and My
Father are one.   He that hath seen Me, hath seen the Father."   And He commended Thomas for addressing Him as " my Lord and my God."   How can any

one affirm that He was only a man without the guilt of denying Him ? 3. We may often deny Christ by silence. No doubt some well-meaning people at times do harm by introducing religion into conversation under unsuitable circumstances, or by harsh polemical replies to what some unbeliever has said. But most of us are in far greater danger of a culpable silence when Christ's truth ought to be vindicated, and Christ's own claim to reverence and trust ought to be earnestly and lovingly declared. 4. We may deny Christ by appearing at places and engaging in pursuits which irreligious people themselves recognize as unsuitable for an earnest Christian. 5. We deny Christ by neglecting efforts to spread the saving knowledge of Him at home and abroad. The Confederate general, Albert Sidney Johnston, in the last letter he wrote before he fell at Shiloh, said, " The popular test of a military man's merit is success. It is a hard test, but it is the true one." We do not believe that success is always the true test of merit, but beyond question it is the popular test. Now, many irreligious people consider that Christianity is upon the whole a comparative failure. Large portions of the world it has never even nominally conquered. Some countries in which it once existed, including the Holy Land, have long been Mohammedan. And in the countries called Christian, a large proportion of the people are not really the subjects of Christ's spiritual reign. The hasty observer is wrong in concluding that Christ's work in the world is a failure ; but must we not feel grief and shame at the thought that he has right plausible ground for such a conclusion? Just in proportion as we fail of any effort to spread Christ's spiritual reign, we give men an excuse for rejecting His authority and neglecting His salvation. And thus to act is in a distressing manner to deny Christ. 6. In fact, a Christian is always and everywhere either confessing Christ or denying Him. Every wrong act performed, every duty disregarded or imperfectly discharged, every indication of a character not conformed to His will and likened to His image, is, by the very necessity of the case, a denial of our Lord and Saviour. (*J. A. Broadus, D.D.*) *Denial of Christ :*—Note here—1. That not to confess Christ is, in His account, to deny Him and to be ashamed of Him. 2. That whosoever shall deny or be ashamed of Christ, either in His person, in His gospel, or in His members, for any fear or favour of man, shall with shame be disowned and eternally rejected by Him at the dreadful judgment of the great day. Christ may be denied three ways—doctrinally, by an erroneous and heretical judgment; verbally, by oral expressions; vitally, by a wicked and unholy life—but woe to the soul that denies Christ any of these ways. (*W. Burkitt.*) *David Straiton, the Scottish martyr :*—In the seventeenth century, David Straiton, a Scotchman, was one day in a solitary place where the New Testament was being read. When the words of this verse sounded in his ears, he threw himself on his knees and said, " For Thy mercy's sake, Lord, let me never deny Thee or Thy truth for fear of death or corporeal pains." At his trial he firmly defended the truth, and not only died for it himself, but greatly cheered his fellow-martyr, Norman Gourlay. *Ashamed of Christ :*—What would the Queen think of her soldiers, if they should swear they were loyal and true, and were to say, " Your Majesty, we prefer not to wear these regimentals, let us wear the dress of civilians! We are right honest men and upright, but do not care to stand in your ranks, acknowledged as your soldiers; we had rather slink into the enemy's camp, and into your camps too, and not wear anything that would mark us as being your soldiers." Ah! some of you do the same with Christ. You are going to be secret Christians, are you, and slink into the devil's camp and into Christ's camp, but acknowledged by none? (*C. H. Spurgeon.*)

Ver. 10. **Blasphemeth against the Holy Ghost.**—*Blasphemy against the Holy Ghost :*—I. First, the OCCASION on which this declaration was made requires our particular attention ; for it does not appear that it was ever repeated or applied to any other subject. II. Let us, then, inquire into THE NAME AND NATURE OF THE CRIME TO WHICH OUR SAVIOUR SO SOLEMNLY REFERS. 1. It is necessary to attend to the name, for it is often applied erroneously. Thus we often hear of the sin against the Holy Ghost ; whereas it is called in Scripture by no name except blasphemy against the Holy Ghost. This distinction, however, is highly important ; for there may be other sins against the Holy Ghost, though less criminal than blasphemy, and therefore not liable to the same terrible punishment. Thus the Apostle Paul said to the Thessalonians, " Quench not the Spirit," and to the Ephesians, " Grieve not the Holy Spirit." 2. We must, therefore, next consider the application of the word blasphemy here. In the original language of the New Testament it signifies detraction, or calumny, or slander, and is frequently mentioned as a crime committed against man. Thus, in the Acts of the Apostles, the Jews accused Stephen, saying, " We have heard him speak blasphemous words against Moses and against God." But, in our language, blasphemy is never used in a general sense, or is said to be committed against man ; it always denotes a crime committed against God. 3. Another observation deserves particular attention. The word blasphemy is never applied by our Saviour or His apostles to opinions formed in the mind, or to mere errors of judgment. 4. To prevent mistake it is necessary that we should define the nature of this crime with the utmost correctness and precision. (1) Now as it is to be remembered that it is called blasphemy against God, or against the Holy Ghost, so it is necessary to remember that though the crime may be conceived and planned in the mind, yet it cannot be completed till it be uttered in words ; for speech is essential to it, as the word blasphemy strictly and properly signifies hurtful speech. (2) There was, however, a part of the crime of the Pharisees which was committed in their minds. It consisted in the malignant desire and intention of using words for the purpose of producing on the minds of others feelings of contempt or aversion, and disbelief, in relation to the miracles of Jesus. Still the crime was not completed till it was committed in words. III. We come now to a very important question, WHY IS BLASPHEMY AGAINST THE HOLY GHOST DECLARED TO BE UNPARDONABLE ? 1. It was not a crime to which the Pharisees were led by unforeseen accident, by sudden surprise, by laudable or even excusable feelings. On the contrary, it was deliberate, it was the result of reflection, it was a plan cautiously formed ; for it was the consequence of a consultation among the scribes and Pharisees ; and it formed the ground of a conspiracy against Jesus. 2. It showed, in this particular case, a total disregard of truth. It indicated a high degree of depravity, a complete want of principle, no fear of God, and a contempt for supernatural evidence, though of the strongest kind. In fine, it proved that their minds were closed against conviction ; and that no proof, however powerful, nor means of improvement, however perfect, would be effectual. 3. But the strongest reason which can be given for declaring blasphemy against the Holy Ghost to be unpardonable, is, that it seems to be a crime for which there is no repentance. There are cases in which repentance becomes impossible. For repentance presupposes the existence of some good principles ; it presupposes a disposition to discover truth, to examine evidence, to see our faults, and to be ready to acknowledge them, to feel shame, regret, and remorse for offending God. But there is nothing that we know which could produce repentance in men who have, for a long life, wilfully, stubbornly, and habitually rejected the most powerful means of conviction. Repentance supposes a sense of guilt capable of being roused on account of faults which we have discovered. But this cannot be when the understanding is perverted, and the conscience seared, and when the evil passions have expelled the pious and benevolent affections. It is true that the dread of future misery may still remain ; but when the mind is reduced to so deplorable a state, the fear of future misery plunges men into despair. Now, where there is no repentance, we are not taught to expect pardon. Hence we may see why blasphemy is unpardonable. (*J. Thomson, D.D.*) *Of the sin against the Holy Ghost :*—First : What this sin against the Holy Ghost is, for people are very ignorant of it. Secondly : How and in what respect this sin against the Holy Ghost is above all other sins the unpardonable sin. I. IF YOU ASK, WHAT THIS SIN IS ? I answer both negatively and affirmatively. Negatively. 1. It is not that sin, whereby men do barely deny the personality, or the deity of the Holy Ghost. Possibly a man may deny the personality or the deity of the Holy Ghost, and yet not sin the sin against the Holy Ghost. For as Chrysostom observes, in his time there were divers heretics that did deny the personality and the deity of the Holy Ghost, and yet afterwards repented, and were received into the bosom of the Church. As it doth not consist therein, so neither doth it consist in every opposition, or in a bare opposition unto the work of the Holy Ghost, as distinct from the Father and the Son. Unto God the Father belongs power ; unto the Son, wisdom ; unto the Spirit, holiness. The work of the Father is to create ; the work of the Son, to redeem ; the work of the Spirit, or the Holy Ghost, to sanctify. And hereupon some have thought that opposition unto holiness is the sin against the Holy Ghost. But you find here it is a blasphemy, therefore not every opposition. As it doth not consist therein, so it is not necessary that every man that sins the sin against the Holy Ghost, should be an universal apostate, backsliding from the profession of the gospel, and the power thereof. I know it is ordinarily thought so; but I say, it is not necessary that whosoever doth sin the sin against the Holy Ghost, should be a gospel apostate, backsliding from the gospel, and the power thereof, once professed: for these Pharisees, who sinned against the Holy Ghost, never professed the gospel, neither do we read of any backsliding in them, from the power of the gospel once professed; and yet they sinned against the Holy Ghost. Surely, therefore, such a gospel apostasy is not of the essence of the sin against the Holy Ghost. Some think that this sin doth consist in final unbelief and impenitency; but final impenitency and unbelief is not the sin against the Holy Ghost, for by final unbelief and impenitency, they either understand that impenitency and unbelief which a man lives and dies in, or that which he purposeth to continue in to the last. The latter cannot be the sin against the Holy Ghost, for many have purposed to continue in their unbelief to their death, and yet have been converted and pardoned. And the first cannot be the sin against the Holy Ghost, for—1. The Jews whom Christ spake unto did then commit this sin, and yet they had not continued in it to their death. 2. Final unbelief is rather a sin against the Son; but the sin against the Holy Ghost is distinguished from that. 3. Our Saviour saith, "Those that commit this sin shall not be forgiven in this world, nor in the world to come." Not in this world. If, therefore, final unbelief or impenitency be this sin, then Christ should threaten that he that dies in his sin shall not be forgiven whilst he lives. 4. If a man sin against the Father or Son, and die impenitently in that sin, he shall not be forgiven either in this life or in the life to come: but herein the sin against the Holy Ghost is worse than the sins against the Father or the Son, and therefore it cannot consist therein. 5. The apostle saith, "There is a sin unto death, I say not that you pray for it" (1 John v. 16). Doth he say that we must not pray for a man, and for the forgiveness of his sin when he is dead? 6. It is that sin for which there lies no remission, but a man may sin such a sin whilst he lives: for if any man sin wilfully, there remaineth no sacrifice for sin, and wilfully a man may sin before his death. 7. It is such a sin as a man may know another man is guilty of whilst he lives, for saith the apostle, "There is a sin unto death, I say not that you pray for it": but final unbelief and impenitency is not known till death. 8. Our Saviour saith, "He that speaketh a word against the Holy Ghost shall not be forgiven." But a word may be spoken against the Spirit long before a man dies, and therefore surely this sin against the Holy Ghost doth not consist in final impenitency and unbelief; final unbelief and impenitency is not this sin against the Holy Ghost. 9. For then all wicked men living under the gospel, and dying impenitently, should sin the sin against the Holy Ghost, which is false. You will say, then, What is this sin against the Holy Ghost, and wherein doth it consist? Affirmatively. It is that wilful sinning against God, whereby a man doth maliciously oppose and blaspheme the proper and peculiar work of the Holy Ghost, and that after he hath been convinced thereof by the Holy Ghost. I say, It is a wilful sinning against God; and so the apostle speaks, saying, "If any man sin wilfully, after he hath received the knowledge of the truth, there remains no more sacrifice for sin" (Heb. x. 26). So that the sin for which there is no sacrifice, and of which there is no remission, is a wilful sin. Now a man is said to sin wittingly, willingly, and wilfully: wittingly, in opposition to ignorance; willingly, in opposition to force and constraint; wilfully, in opposition to light, knowledge, and reason; and so he that sins against the Holy Ghost doth sin; for says the apostle, "If any man sin wilfully, after he hath received the knowledge of the truth," &c. He that commits this sin doth also oppose and blaspheme the proper and peculiar work of the Holy Ghost; for it is called here, a blasphemy, and a blaspheming of the Spirit, as distinct from the Father and the Son. Suppose that some ignorance in the understanding be the remote cause of the sin, yet malice may be the next and chief cause. As for example: suppose that a man hath taken up some prejudice against another, through a mistake and error; yet now he hates him, and out of hatred kills him; shall not this murderer be said to kill him out of malice, because the malice was founded upon a mistake or error? Yes, surely. But why is he said to kill him out of malice? Because malice was the next cause of this murder. So that though ignorance be the remote cause of a sin, yet malice may be the next cause thereof; and being so, he shall be said truly to sin *ex malitia*, though with some precedent ignorance, as the remote cause thereof. Yet if you ask, how it can be that the will should be always carried out upon what is good, and yet a man sin maliciously? Plainly thus:

from what hath been said, the will of man is an universal appetite, willing that which is naturally good, as well as that which is honestly good. If it be carried out upon that which is naturally good, it will hate all that spiritual good which is contrary to the obtainment of it, and the man will oppose and blaspheme what the will hates. Now because the hatred and malice of the will is the cause of that blasphemy and opposition, the man is truly said to oppose and blaspheme out of malice, though the will be carried on upon that which is naturally good at the same time; which was the case of these Pharisees: for they sought their own honour and greatness; Christ and the truth opposing, they did hate Him and the truth; and because they hated Him, the truth, and that light which reproved their sins, they did oppose and blaspheme, and that out of malice, and so the sin against the Holy Ghost is a malicious sin, or that sin whereby a man doth oppose and blaspheme the proper and peculiar work of the Spirit out of malice. Yet this is not all. But, it is that sin against God, whereby a man doth maliciously oppose and blaspheme the peculiar work of the Holy Ghost, after he hath been convinced thereof by the Holy Ghost; for possibly a man may oppose and blaspheme, even maliciously, the work of the Holy Ghost, and yet not be convinced of it by the Holy Ghost, but otherwise; but those that sin this sin, are such as are enlightened, and made partakers of the Holy Ghost in the gifts and common graces of it (Heb. vi.). And so these Pharisees were convinced by the Spirit which did work that great work before them; and yet after such a convincement wrought by the Spirit, they did maliciously oppose and blaspheme this work of the Spirit. So that I say, the sin against the Holy Ghost is that wilful sinning against God, whereby a man doth maliciously oppose and blaspheme the proper and peculiar work of the Holy Ghost, and that after he hath been convinced thereof by the Holy Ghost. II. BUT WHY IS THIS SIN, ABOVE ALL OTHER SINS, UNPARDONABLE? Not in regard of difficulty only, or because it is hardly pardoned, as some would; for many sins are hardly pardoned, and yet are not the sins against the Holy Ghost; for, as Zanchy doth well observe, if this sin were only unpardonable, because it is hardly pardoned, then a man might pray for those that sin this sin: but the apostle saith, "There is a sin unto death, I do not say that ye shall pray for it" (1 John v. 16). Therefore, the unpardonableness of it doth not lie here. Neither is it unpardonable only in regard of event, because in event it shall never be pardoned, for there are many sins which in event shall never be pardoned, which yet are not the sins against the Holy Ghost. There is many a wicked man that goes to hell, whose sins in event are not pardoned, and yet he did never sin against the Holy Ghost. Neither is it unpardonable because it is so great as doth exceed the power and mercy of God; for God's mercy and power, in forgiving sins, is like Himself, infinite. Neither is it unpardonable because it is against the means of pardon; for then the sin against the free love of the Father, and the sin against the Son, should be unpardonable. Neither is it unpardonable because a man doth not repent thereof; for then all sins unrepented of should be sins against the Holy Ghost. It is true, that those who commit this sin cannot repent, as the apostle speaks— It is impossible that they should be renewed to repentance (Heb. vi.), because God doth give them up to impenitency: but we do not find in Scripture that their not repenting is made the reason of the unpardonableness of this sin. But the sin is unpardonable because there is no sacrifice laid out by God's appointment for it— "If any man sin wilfully, there remaineth no more sacrifice" (Heb. x.), and without blood and sacrifice there is no remission. And thus now ye have seen what the sin against the Holy Ghost is; in what respects it is not, and in what respects it is unpardonable; and so the doctrine cleared and proved, That the sin against the Holy Ghost is the unpardonable sin, which shall never be forgiven, neither in this world, nor in the world to come. The application follows: If the sin against the Holy Ghost be the unpardonable sin, then surely the Holy Ghost is God, very God, true God, as the Father is: for can it be a greater evil, or more dangerous, to sin against a creature, than against God the Father? It is God that is sinned against, now the Holy Ghost is sinned against; yea, the unpardonable sin is against the Holy Ghost. But I am afraid I have sinned this sin, and the truth is I have often feared it: and my reason was and is, because my sins are so great, so exceeding great. Great, say ye; how great, man? I have sinned against my light, I have sinned against my knowledge, I have sinned against my conviction; and therefore I fear I have sinned the unpardonable sin. But I pray, for answer, did not Adam sin against light, when he ate the forbidden fruit? Did he not sin against his knowledge, and against conscience? Yet he sinned not against the Holy Ghost, though he brought all the world under condemnation by his sin; for the Lord Himself came and preached mercy to him, "The seed of the woman shall break the serpent's head." And I pray did not Jonah, when he run away from God, sin against his light; and did he not sin against his conviction, and against his knowledge? yet he did not sin against the Holy Ghost, for the Lord pardoned him and wonderfully delivered him. Possibly this therefore may be, and yet not a sin against the Holy Ghost. It is true indeed, that those who sin against the Holy Ghost do sin against their light, knowledge, and conscience; but whoever sins against light and knowledge, though he sins greatly, doth not sin against the Holy Ghost. Oh, but I fear that I have sinned this sin, for I have fallen foully into gross sins. That is ill. But I pray did not David sin so; were they not great and gross and foul sins that David fell into, such as one of your civil, moral men would abhor? yet he did not sin against the Holy Ghost, for the Lord pardoned him, and Nathan said from the Lord, "The Lord hath forgiven thee." Oh, but yet I fear that I have sinned this great sin, for I am much declined, I have lost my former acquaintance and communion with God; I have lost my former heat and affections to good, and in duty; and I fear upon this account that I have sinned this great sin. Be it so: yet did not the Church of Ephesus lose her first love? yet this Church of Ephesus did not sin the sin against the Holy Ghost: why? for the Lord saith unto her, "Repent and do thy first works." She could not have repented thus if she had sinned this sin. Oh, but yet I fear that I have sinned this great sin, because that I have sinned directly against the Spirit; I have quenched, I have grieved, I have resisted the Spirit: the Spirit of the Lord hath come and fallen upon my heart in preaching, and I resisted and grieved it; the Spirit of the Lord hath fallen upon my heart in prayer, and I have grieved that; therefore I fear I have sinned this great sin that shall never be pardoned. This is ill too; but those that you read of in Acts vii., resisted the Holy Ghost, yet they did not sin the sin against the Holy Ghost, for then Stephen would not have prayed for them. But I am afraid that I have sinned this great sin, the sin against the Holy Ghost, because I have not owned, but denied the truth. The work of the Spirit is to enlighten and to lead into truth, and I have not owned, but denied the truth rather, therefore I fear that I have sinned this great sin against the Holy Ghost. This is evil, very evil. I remember a speech of Godteschalchus, worthy to be written in letters of gold: I am afraid, said he, to deny the truth, lest I should be for ever denied by the truth, that is, Christ. But I pray, did not Peter deny the truth when he denied Christ; and did he not do it again and again, and did he not do it openly, with scandal; and did he not do it after admonition; and did he not do it with cursing and swearing? and yet he did not sin against the Holy Ghost, for the Lord pardoned, and took him into His bosom, and made him a blessed instrument in the Church. Thus far yet a man may go possibly, and yet not sin this sin. Oh, but I am afraid yet that I have sinned it, for I have been an opposer of goodness, I have been an opposer of the people of God, and I have been a blasphemer; therefore I fear I have sinned this sin. This is ill indeed. But, I pray, tell me, was not Paul an opposer and blasphemer of the saints and ways of God; and yet he did not sin against the Holy Ghost; for I did it ignorantly, saith he: "I was a blasphemer and a persecutor, but I obtained mercy, for I did it ignorantly." Oh, but yet I fear I have sinned this great sin, for I have forsaken God, and God hath forsaken me; God is gone, Christ is gone, and mercy is gone. Oh, what freedom once I had, but now God is departed from me, God hath forsaken me: and I fear it is upon this account, because I have sinned this great sin. But doth not David say, "How long, O Lord, wilt Thou forget me, forsake me?" and our Saviour Himself saith, "My God, My God, why hast Thou forsaken Me?" There is a gradual forsaking, and there is a total. As with a man that goes from his house; possibly he goes a voyage, or is from home a quarter, half year, or a year; but he doth not leave his house; for his wife, his children, and goods are there still: but another man goes from his house, the house is let, and he carries away all his goods: this is a total departure, the other gradual. So now it is with the Lord: He doth sometimes forsake His own children for a time; but He doth not pull down His hangings, or carry away His goods; He doth not go away, but returns again; this is gradual. But there is a total forsaking of a man, and then He gives him up to his sin. Now this is not the burden that you lie under; for if God had thus forsaken you, you would be given up to your sins, and you would give up yourselves unto all uncleanness. Oh, but I am afraid, yet, that I am under the worst forsaking, and that therefore I have sinned this great sin ; for I do lie despairing, saying, God is gone, and mercy gone ; I am in the dark. Oh, I despair, I despair, and upon this account I fear I have sinned this great sin, the sin against the Holy Ghost. But, now, whosoever you are that have laboured under this fear, as indeed this fear I know hath oppressed many, give me leave to ask you four or five short questions. The first is, Whether canst thou not find in thy heart to forgive men that do trespass against thee ? Do not you find a disposition in your own heart to forgive others ? Yes, I praise the Lord that I do. Now if you can find in your heart to forgive others, I am sure God can find in His heart to forgive you, and therefore you have not sinned this great sin, which is unpardonable. Secondly, Whether, aye or no, have you ever opposed the ways of God, the people of God, and that out of malice ? No : I confess I have opposed them, but the Lord knows I did it ignorantly, it was not out of malice ; then remember the description of this sin. Thirdly, Whether, aye or no, do not you desire to be humbled for every sin, though it be never so small ? Yes, for though I know that my greatest humiliation cannot make an atonement for my sin ; yet I know that the least humiliation in truth doth please God, and it is my duty to be humbled for every sin ; for the least sin is a great evil ; and He that commands humiliation for the one, commands it for the other also ; and through grace I desire to be humbled for every sin. Why, then, you cannot have sinned against the Holy Ghost, for it is impossible that they that sin this sin should be renewed to repentance. Fourthly, Whether, aye or no, do not you desire above all things the breathings of the Spirit of God upon your heart ? Yes : oh that God would come and breathe upon my poor soul in duty. But those that sin against the' Holy Ghost do despite to the Spirit of grace (Heb. x.). Fifthly, Where do you find in all the Bible that those that sin this sin against the Holy Ghost are afraid that they have sinned it ? Those that sin against the Holy Ghost are never afraid that they have sinned against the Holy Ghost. But again, If the sin against the Holy Ghost be indeed the unpardonable sin, what cause have we all to look to our steps, to our words, to our actions ? Beloved, this sin against the Holy Ghost is the professor's sin ; a man less than a professor cannot sin this sin against the Holy Ghost ; this sin against the Holy Ghost is the knowing man's sin, a man less than a knowing man cannot sin the sin against the Holy Ghost : and, as I said before, a man may possibly go very far in sin, and yet not commit this great unpardonable sin : so now, on the other side, I say, possibly a man may go very far in religion, and yet he may sin this sin. These Pharisees that committed it had the key of knowledge : knowing they were, and very knowing in the Scriptures ; as for zeal, they travelled sea and land to make a proselyte ; for their practice, they fasted twice a week, exceeding strict in observing the Sabbath day ; the lights of the Church, and the eyes of all the people were upon them for their guides ; and yet these men sinned this sin against the Holy Ghost. Oh, what care should there be in all our souls ; how had we all need to look to our ways ! The more truth revealed, the more danger of sinning this sin, the more great works of God are done by the very Spirit and finger of God ; if men do oppose and blaspheme, the more danger of sinning this great sin. But you will say, We grant indeed that this sin against the Holy Ghost is the unpardonable sin, and woe be to them that do fall into it, and it cannot be committed but by a knowing man ; but what shall we do that we may be kept from this great transgression ; that whatsoever sin we do fall into, yet we may be kept from this great evil, and this unpardonable sin ? I would that you would mind and consider the description which you have heard, and think of it. But I will tell you what David did. Saith David, "O Lord, keep back Thy servant from presumptuous sins, so shall I be free from the great transgression." It seems then that presumptuous sinning makes way to this great transgression. Again : Be always humbled for lesser sins. He shall never fall into the greatest, that is always humbled for the least ; he shall never fall into the worst that is always humbled for the smallest. Besides, fear is the keeper of innocency ; fear is the guard of innocency. If you always fear to commit it, you shall never commit the same. In case that you do at any time fall into sin, say, Well, but through the grace of God, though I commit what is evil, I will never oppose what is good ; by the grace of God I will carry this rule along with me : Though I commit what is evil, I will never oppose what is good. In case any great work be done before you that lies beyond your reach and beyond your fathom, say, Though I do not understand this work, I will admire ; and though I cannot reach it, yet I will not blaspheme and speak against it. And if heretofore, Christian, thou hast found God breathing upon thy heart in any ordinance, public or private, or in any way of God, take heed, as for thy life, that thou dost never speak evil or blaspheme that way of God wherein thou hast found the Spirit of God breathing. And if, indeed, you would be kept from this great transgression, then take heed of all declinings, and the steps thereof. (*W. Bridge, M.A.*)   *Blasphemy against the Holy Ghost :*—I. First, then, let us see what the text does not mean. We may, I think, feel quite sure that it does not mean that there is some particular form of words of the kind generally known as " blasphemous," which, once uttered, leave him who has spoken without hope. "By thy words thou shalt be justified, and by thy words thou shalt be condemned." But the intervening context shows us that He is speaking of words as the expressions of the heart, and as indications of its fixed habit and its settled attitude. They were the symptoms of disease, not the disease itself. They marked, not merely local affection, but constitutional derangement. The same principle applies to our good words, which I am apt to think may in the end prove more condemning than our bad ones. That we shall go to heaven for pious ejaculations which are unreal, or go to hell for impious ejaculations equally unreal, is altogether contrary to the tenour of Scripture and to its revelations, and our own ideas of the character and attributes of Him whose judgment is according to truth. 2. Again, the sin spoken of in the text cannot be a sin of which men have ever repented. Because wherever there is repentance there is pardon through the Saviour. This, if I understand anything about the gospel, is its great message. Let us go on to Manasseh, king of Judah (2 Kings xxi.). It is not easy to imagine anything worse than we are told about him. He undid the work of Hezekiah, his father. And now, as I get near to saying what seems to me the meaning of the text, I am sorry that I must set aside the opinion of some great and good men ; of Wesley amongst them. He thought, and others thought also, that this sin is neither more nor less than "the ascribing those miracles to the power of the devil which Christ did by the power of the Holy Ghost "—in short, that it was only possible during the Saviour's ministry. I cannot think a warning so solemn and striking, recorded in three of the four Gospels, should relate wholly to a past kind of sin. No : the outward part of sin perpetually shifts and changes : its principle and essence remain the same. Nor should we escape the terror of the text by adopting what I may call the " obsolete " interpretation as regards the sin. There are other passages, not quite so well known perhaps, but as awful when we think of them. "There is," says St. John, "a sin unto death : I do not say that he shall pray for it." St. Jude writes of some who " were before of old ordained to this condemnation "—" twice dead "—" plucked up by the roots "—" to whom is reserved the blackness of darkness for ever." In the Epistle to the Hebrews we are told of some for whom " remained no more sacrifice for sin," and of some whom "it was impossible to renew unto repentance." St. Paul, writing to Timothy, mentions some who " should proceed no further," who " resisted the truth as Jannes and Jambres withstood Moses." All these passages remain, even though we succeed in removing the text to the region of the past. All these, as well as the text, must, I think, be read in the same light ; and all must be thought of in connection with what I said at the outset—that what can never be forgiven must be something of which men have never repented. What can this be ? It can scarcely be anything less than deliberate, conscious resistance to acknowledged truth ; persistent choosing of darkness rather than light. You will say, perhaps, that there cannot be such a thing. Are you so sure ? Think for one moment. Do you not see something like it—apart from religion altogether—every day ? Does not the drunkard, or the spendthrift, or the gambler know his end—I mean in this world—as well as you do ? And still he goes on. What can you do for him ? Nothing. At least nothing except in the way of " hoping against hope." You do your very best : and you are right ; but while you cannot prove it, you feel that there is failure before you. Come to the Bible. Take that wonderful case of Ahab and Micaiah. Ahab did not believe that there was *no* God. Nor did he doubt the mission of Micaiah. Nor did he once hint that he thought him untruthful. He had one objection, and only one : " I hate him because he doth not prophesy good concerning me, but evil." Micaiah exposes to him the deceitfulness of the other prophets : and he still has nothing to say but to repeat his old objection. After which he goes on deliberately to death. Take two instances from the New Testament. What effect was produced by the raising of Lazarus ? Some of the Jews " sought to put Lazarus also to death." When Peter and John performed what the Jewish rulers admitted to be a " notable miracle, which they could not deny," they did what ? Threatened them, and tried to hinder the further spread of the gospel thus attested. All these, surely, are cases which—if we merely reflected, without reading the Bible at all—we should be obliged to own were verging on and tending to something unforgivable. This view will be confirmed if a well-supported reading of St. Mark's account be the true one. It makes him say —not is in danger of eternal *damnation* or judgment; but is in danger of eternal *sin.* The depth of condemnation is only for the depth of sin; and by resisting grace, shutting the eyes to light, we are surely sinking into that depth. It is not that God arbitrarily marks out a sin or even a course of sin, which He will not pardon. But He warns us that we may bring ourselves to a state in which we will not have pardon, and reach the Satanic condition of consummated sin, and seem to say, as he alone can say, "Evil, be thou my good." (*J. C. Coghlan, D.D.*) *The sin that shall not be forgiven :*—Taking this sentence with the rest of the passage, I cannot doubt that it tells us what the sin of the Pharisees and of the nation was; why they were cast out of their stewardship in that age; why the sentence upon them remains still. We say, "They rejected Jesus; they would not believe all the evidence which He brought from prophecies and miracles to attest His divine mission." He says, "All words spoken against the Son of Man will be forgiven"; but there is a blasphemy against the Spirit of God—there is a confusion of good with evil, of light with darkness—which goes down far deeper than this. When a nation has lost the faculty of distinguishing hatred from love, the spirit of hypocrisy and falsehood from the spirit of truth, God from the devil, then its doom is pronounced—then the decree must go forth against it. I believe that is the natural sense of these awful words here and elsewhere; if we give them that sense we are delivered from imaginations which have darkened the gospel to a number of souls, and the warning to ourselves becomes much more tremendous. (*F. D. Maurice, M.A.*) *The unpardonable sin :*—Aretius, a godly and eminent author, speaking of the sin of the Holy Ghost, "I saw," saith he, "and knew the man myself, and it is no feigned story. There was a merchant in Strasburg whose whole life was abominable for whoredom, usury, drunkenness, contempt of God's Word; he spent his life in gaming and whoring to his old age. At last he came to reflect on himself, and be sensible of the dreadful judgments of God hanging over his head. Then did his conscience so affright, and the devil accuse and terrify him, that he fell into open and downright desperation. He confessed and yielded himself to the devil as being his. He said the mercy and grace of God could not be so great as to pardon sins so great as his. Then what horror was upon him, gnashing of teeth, weeping, wailing; yea, he would challenge Satan, and wish the devil would fetch him away to his destined torments. He threw himself all along upon the ground: refused both meat and drink. Had you seen him, you would never have forgot him while you had lived; you had seen the fullest pattern of a despairing person. Yet, after the many pains of godly and learned men who came to him, watched with him, reasoned with him, laid open the word and will of God, and after many prayers, public and private, put up for him, at length he recovered and became truly penitent; and having lived piously for certain years after, he died peaceably." Wherefore, he concluded, it is not an easy matter to determine of any man sinning against the Holy Ghost, and incapable of mercy so long as he live. *Delivered from despair :*—The Puritans were wont to quote the remarkable experience of Mrs. Honeywood as an instance of the singular way in which the Lord delivers His chosen. She for year after year was in bondage to melancholy and despair, but she was set at liberty by the gracious providence of God in an almost miraculous way. She took up a slender Venice glass, and saying, "I am as surely damned as that glass is dashed to pieces," she hurled it down upon the floor, when, to her surprise, and the surprise of all, I know not by what means, the glass was not so much as chipped or cracked. That circumstance first gave her a ray of light, and she afterwards cast herself upon the Lord Jesus. (*C. H. Spurgeon.*)

Vers. 11, 12. The Holy Ghost shall teach you.—*Divine help for ministers in discharging their duties :*—The advice and promise contained in these verses were very suitable to the disciples, many of whom were soon to be called before Jewish and Roman courts of various kinds for the sake of Christ. Plain and illiterate as the disciples generally were, they would be ready to be much alarmed at the thought of appearing before civil and ecclesiastical rulers and judges, not only from the apprehension that they might be condemned if they did not plead their cause aright, but still more from the apprehension that from some failure in judgment, or memory, or eloquence, on their part, the cause of the gospel might suffer—which was dearer to them than their life. Their Lord, therefore, wisely and graciously counselled and encouraged them in that prospect. "Take ye no thought," said He; not that prudent thought was unbecoming, or that they were to be rash, and speak unadvisedly with their lips: but they were forbidden to take anxious, perplexing, and disquieting thought, as the word might be rendered, and as He said on another occasion, "Take no thought for the morrow." Such thought as that, at the time they were speaking, would have argued distrust in God, and would have thrown them into such confusion as would have incapacitated them from speaking as they ought. They were not to be studious of making a fine appearance; nor were they to be apprehensive that the Lord would allow either them to be put to shame, or His own cause to suffer. Nay, as spoken to those who were under the influence of plenary inspiration, these words forbade them to spend time in premeditation on their defence of themselves, or on their declaration of the gospel, for it is thus expressed in Mark, "Take no thought beforehand what ye shall speak, neither do ye premeditate." "Take ye no thought," as it is in Luke, "how, or what thing," that is, either as to the manner or matter of what "ye shall answer," or say in defence of yourselves; "or what ye shall say," that is, what ye shall say in declaring the truth before your accusers and audience, be they what they may. And to encourage them to this, He assures them that the Holy Spirit would suggest to them at the time whatever was proper to be said, and would direct and strengthen them to say it in the best manner. Now, all this is often exemplified very strikingly in the Acts of the Apostles, in which we read of several of the disciples being carried before different courts, where they trusted in God, and had this promise so fulfilled to them as to enable them to speak, and in every way to conduct themselves, in the most becoming and noble manner. As to the application of these words to the succeeding ages of the Church; it becomes all Christians, and especially Christian ministers, neither presumptuously to abuse them, nor unbelievingly to neglect the legitimate encouragement which they contain. It would certainly be a gross perversion of this passage, if any preachers were now to imagine that it would countenance them in ordinary cases in coming forward to preach without previous study. Now that miraculous inspiration has ceased, they have to seek their knowledge from the Word of God, and in the way of diligent, persevering, and prayerful application of mind; that they may bring forward abundance of suitable matter, in the best way of which, all their other duties being considered, they are capable. Whatever might be the rule in cases of emergency, even the inspired teachers themselves were required thus to "stir up the gift of God that was in them"; and therefore much more is such diligence necessary in those who have no such inspiration. It is no difficult matter, indeed, for a man who abounds in self-confidence and readiness of expression to speak often and long, in a certain way, of the things of God with little or no preparation, but it is a poor boast to boast of such a habit; it is a poor compliment to the intelligence of his audience to indulge it; there will be no need for him or his admirers to proclaim that his effusions are extemporary, for that will be but too evident. In many cases this is, doubtless, under the guise of zeal, the refuge of indolence; and it would be well for him to consider whether he be not labouring under an error in imagining that there is anything peculiarly spiritual or praiseworthy in offering to God that which costs him nothing. The words which were addressed to inspired Timothy are surely at least as suitable in this view to ordinary teachers: "Give attendance to reading, to exhortation, to doctrine. Neglect not the gift that is in thee, which was given thee by prophecy, with the laying on of the hands of the presbytery. Meditate upon these things, give thyself wholly to them, that thy profiting may appear to all. Take heed unto thyself, and unto the doctrine; continue in them; for in doing this thou shalt both save thyself and them that hear thee." In a different sense, David "prepared with all his might" "for the house of his God." "Because the preacher, too, was wise, he still taught the people knowledge, yea, he gave good heed, and sought out, and set in order many proverbs." If due diligence be not used, to expect the help of the Spirit is not faith, but presumption. At the same time there is much direction and encouragement here to ministers when they are in the way of duty. The spirit of this passage teaches them not to fail to declare the will of God when they are suddenly called on to do so in the course of providence. They are not to hang back or to hesitate then, but are to discharge the duty in the best way they can under God. On extraordinary occasions they may expect, though not miraculous, yet extraordinary, assistance. They may expect that their strength will be as their day; that their Master's grace will be sufficient for them, and that His strength will be made perfect in their weakness. Nor need they be afraid to speak, in any circumstances, however trying or dangerous, into which their Lord brings them. (*Jas. Foote, M.A.*) *Martyrs inspired by the Spirit :*—You will be struck in reading " Foxe's Acts and Monuments " to find how many of the humblest men and women acted as if they were of noblest blood. In every age the line of martyrs has been a line of true nobility. When the King of France told Bernard Palissy that, if he did not change his sentiments, he should be compelled to surrender him to the Inquisition, the brave potter said to the king, " You say I shall be compelled, and yet you are a king; but I, though only a poor potter, cannot be compelled to do other than I think to be right." Surely the potter was more royal than the king. The cases are numberless, and should be as household words among you, in which humble men, feeble women, and little children have shown a heroism which chivalry could not equal. The Spirit of God has taken the wise in their own craftiness, and answered the learned out of the mouths of babes. The answers of uneducated persons among the martyrs were frequently so pat to the point, and hit the nail so well on the head, that you might almost suppose they had been composed by an assembly of divines ; thay came from a better source, for they were given by the Holy Spirit. The bearing of the bleeding witnesses for our Lord has been worthy of their office, and right well have they earned the title of " The *noble* army of martyrs." (*C. H. Spurgeon.*) *Providential prompting :*—Some time ago a town missionary had in his district a man who never would suffer any Christian man to come into his house. The missionary was warned by many that he would get a broken head if he ventured on a visit. He therefore kept from the house, though it troubled him to pass it by. He made a matter of prayer of it, as was his wont, and one morning ventured into the lion's den ; when the man said, " What have you come here for ? " " Well, sir," he said, " I have been conversing with people in all the houses along here, and I have passed you by because I heard you objected to it ; but somehow I thought it looked cowardly to avoid you, and therefore I have called." " Come in, then," the man said ; " sit down. Now you are going to talk to me about the Bible. Perhaps you do not know much about it yourself. I am going to ask you a question, and if you can answer it, you shall come again ; if you do not answer it, I will bundle you downstairs. Now," he said, " do you take me ? " " Yes," said the other, " I do take you." " Well, then, this is the question : Where do you find the word ' girl ' in the Bible, and how many times do you find it ? " The city missionary said, " The word ' girl ' occurs only once in the Bible, and that is in the Book of Joel, the third chapter and the third verse : ' They sold a girl for wine.' " " You are right ; but I would not have believed you knew it, or else I would have asked you some other question. You may come again." " But," said the missionary, " I should like you to know how I came to know it. This very morning I was praying for direction from God ; and when I was reading my morning chapter, I came upon this passage : ' There shall be boys and girls playing in the streets of Jerusalem ' ; and I found that the word ' girl ' did not occur anywhere else but in Joel." The result of that story, however odd it seems, was that the missionary was permitted to call ; and the man took an interest in his visits, and the whole family were the better, the man and his wife and one of his children becoming members of a Church some time afterwards. Is not God the answerer of prayer ?

Vers. 13, 14. **Who made Me a judge or a divider over you ?**—*Christ not a civil judge, but a Redeemer :*—At first sight, Christ's refusal to interfere between these brothers seems astonishing. Is there not a question of justice to be decided ? And who is so competent to deal with it as the Holy and Just One ? I. THE REASON OF THIS STRANGE REFUSAL. It is sometimes said that Jesus Christ only seeks the eternal salvation of the soul, and does not concern Himself about other human interests. This explanation is specious, and is eagerly accepted by infidelity. But we cannot leave such a weapon in the hands of unbelief. Our Lord assigns the highest importance to the soul's redemption from sin, and yet sympathizes with human nature in its entirety. Why, then, does Christ refuse to interfere in this dispute ? There are two ways of reforming men—an external one and an internal one. The first method pronounces decisions, formulates laws, changes governments, and thus settles all moral and political questions. The second seeks, before everything else, to renovate the heart and the will. Jesus Christ chose the latter plan. He remained steadfast to it, and this alone evinces the divinity of His mission and the permanent value of His work. Observe here one or two results. Christ's refusal determines the relation of Christianity—1. To political questions. I believe in the profound influence of Christianity on the political destiny of nations—it can help them to become free, great, and prosperous. But on what condition can it elevate them? Like Jesus Christ, it must act in a purely spiritual manner; it must free souls; it must preach justice, holiness, love. 2. To social problems. Christ's work consists in uniting in common respect and affection those who are divided by their interests. This mission should be ours. Let us oppose selfish pride and levelling envy; let us summon all men to prayer, to humiliation and to mutual pardon and love—to that sanctuary of spiritual equality where rich and poor meet together, remembering that God has made them both. II. THE PRINCIPLE WHICH CHRIST ENUNCIATED. (*E. Bersier, D.D.*) *Christian socialism:*—There is no doubt that the greatest question of the day in Europe and even in America is Socialism. Socialism ought to be carefully distinguished from Communism; but the two words are often indiscriminately used, and this confusion renders Socialism odious to many, for—

> "What is a Communist? One who hath yearnings,
> For equal divisions of unequal earnings.
> Idler or bungler, or both, he is willing
> To fork out his penny and pocket your shilling."

"The magic of property," says Arthur Young, "turns sand into gold." It has done more in this country to produce a spirit of self-help than State aid for the whole planet ever could do. In thus teaching the duty and necessity of self-help, the Church proves herself to be the chief friend of the poor. Not so Communism. By destroying the right of personal ownership in the means of production, and by fostering dependence on State-help, it undermines the energy and self-help of all classes, and is the enemy of the poor quite as much as of the rich. But was there not, many ask, a community of goods, and were not all things in common, in the primitive Church at Jerusalem. Certainly, but this community of goods was not compulsory, but purely voluntary. It did not come about by any sort of confiscation. "While it remained, was it not thine own?" were the words addressed to Ananias; "and after it was sold, was it not in thine own power?" It was a voluntary act of love rather than a duty. Still less was it a right which the majority might assert against individuals. The estimate of comparative needs recognized when these Jerusalem Christians parted their possessions to all men, as every man had need, shows clearly that property was not alienated beyond control. This, then, was very different from the Communism taught at the present day, which demands an equality enforced by a central authority, and which, so far from inculcating a spirit of self-denial, looks for the self-indulgence of all. Modern Communists affirm that Communism was the natural outcome of the Liberty, Equality, and Fraternity implied in Christ's teaching. That the principle did not hold its ground is ascribed by them to the ambition and worldliness of the Church as she increased in power, especially after her official recognition as the State religion of the Roman Empire. On the other hand the defenders of the principle of individual property as opposed to Communism (which in their opinion is a "mutiny against society") deny that the Church ever sanctioned officially, or that her Founder ever recommended, such a custom as that of "having all things in common." As a matter of fact, we may say with an able Church historian, that the community in Jerusalem growing out of the society of the apostles, who were accustomed already to the common purse system, hit upon the daring plan of establishing a community of goods. And this was fostered by the first outburst of enthusiastic brotherly love, being all the more readily accepted in consequence of the prevailing expectation among the disciples of the approaching subversion of all things. Nowhere out of Jerusalem do we find any other early Christian community of goods. The arrangement at Jerusalem was not intended to be permanent, and perhaps those political economists are not far wrong who assert that it did more harm than good, and produced the chronic state of poverty that existed among "the poor saints at Jerusalem." The Master Himself had left no definite instructions as to the future social organization of His "little flock." It had been His plan all along to lay down general principles, leaving them to be worked out in the course of time, rather than to prescribe definite lines of conduct under given circumstances. The ideal of a perfect society was ever held up by Him to His most intimate disciples. He formed no plan, however, for realizing this ideal in a political polity. The working out of His principles was left to the "new leaven" which was to reform character, and thus indirectly society. The "patrimony of the poor" is not to be restored by means of violent social changes, but by moral influences working upon rich and poor alike. Christ's sympathy was with *all* classes, and He applied remedies to individuals in preference to propounding revolutionary theories for the construction of society. Happily the rich are beginning to recognize this truth. There is obviously an immense outgrowth in the generous distribution of wealth. But the rich have difficulties as well as the poor, and one of these lies in determining how to expend their money in a way that will prove beneficial to society. The question, "To whom or to what cause shall I contribute money?" must be a very anxious one to conscientious men of wealth. "How are we to measure," we may suppose rich men to ask, "the relative utility of charities?" The fact is, riches must now be considered by all good men as a distinct profession, with responsibilities no less onerous than those of other professions. And this very difficult profession of wealth ought to be learned by studying social science and otherwise with as much care as the professions of divinity, law, and medicine are learned. When in this way the rich accept and prepare themselves for the duties of their high calling, it will cease to be a cause of complaint that in the nature of things money tends continually to fall into the hands of a few large capitalists. The spirit of brotherly love which underlies Christian Socialism is being more and more understood in the present day. The great communistic principle, "All for each and each for all," is practically gaining ground. (*E. J. Hardy, M.A.*)   *Worldliness vitiating spiritual teaching:*—A camp-meeting incident taught us what manner of spirit was in this man. An honoured preacher was closing a moving sermon; his appeals to sinners were full of spiritual power; his voice was husky with deep feeling; the tears were streaming down his face as he urged sinners to repent and penitents to believe. A slight movement near by attracted our attention. Just outside the railing around the communion-place were two men deeply engaged. A life insurance agent, on one knee, ciphering out his arguments to his victim, who leaned toward him. The scene brought up the man who interrupted the sermon of Jesus. What would people think of a man who should, from his pew, cry out to the preacher in the midst of a mighty discourse, "What is the price of cotton to-day?" "What is gold worth?" He would perhaps be put out. Certainly he would deserve it. Such a man was he who broke in upon the sermon of Jesus with his request for the Master's intervention in the matter of a contested inheritance. How humiliating a thing it is that a man's mind could be so filled and saturated with business that the most solemn and awful words of even Jesus were heard as an idle, meaningless voice—heard and not feared. Mark our Lord's answer. He dismissed the man with one sharp word: "Man, who made Me a judge or a divider over you?" But the lesson must not be lost. This wickedness of utter worldliness is instructive. Turning to His disciples, Jesus "said unto them, Take heed and beware of covetousness." See what covetousness can do to the heart of man; see what it does in this man! It has consumed him! (*Christian Age.*)   *Missionaries and litigants:*—Mr. Richards, missionary in India, on his journey to Meerut, halted under the shade of a tree, in the outskirts of a large village, by the roadside. As he sat there two of the Zemindars of the neighbourhood came up, and respectfully saluting him, entreated him to act as an umpire between them, and settle a dispute in which they had been long involved about the boundaries of their respective lands. Mr. Richards declined interfering in the matter, but intimated his readiness to give them information respecting the important concerns of salvation. Having read and explained the Scriptures, they listened with attention and delight. The disputants embraced each other with apparent cordiality, and avowed that they would dispute no more about their lands, but love each other, and strive to seek and serve God. (*W. H. Baxendale.*) *Christ's refusal to interfere:*—It may seem strange that to so natural a request Christ should return so discouraging an answer, and, withal, apply it with such a parable. But there are two things to be considered. 1. That it was not Christ's mission to reorganize society immediately, nor by a demonstrative act, but that He undertook to reorganize society by implanting those principles which should work in us reorganific wisdom. Certain great influences were to be infused into the heart, which gradually but surely would work out all needed changes, and work them out

in the order of their proper succession and growth. It was for Christ to prepare
the great influences and principles that the world needed, but for us to carry them
out into practical execution. It is for God to bring forth the spring, and all its
genial influences, upon the earth; but men must avail themselves of these influences,
and by the plough, and by the seed, and by the ready hand of tillage, prepare the
harvests that they are to reap. And so, in the New Testament, there are authoritatively established principles of love and justice, which, if practised, would evolve
the world's harmony. And it is our business, each in his own place, and with
reference to the age in which he lives, to apply these principles, and to change the
face of society, and the administration of affairs in the world. This was the reason
why our Saviour did not undertake that which He was asked to do. 2. But, in the
case in hand, although there might be a matter of great injustice in the partition
of the estate, the elder and stronger and shrewder, perhaps, getting advantage of
the younger, and defrauding him; yet it was quite possible that both of these
brothers might be alike under the influence of corroding and hateful avarice. A
man may demand his dues with a spirit just as selfish as that which withholds
them. A man may be just as selfish in seeking his rights as another man is in
withholding them from him. Both the despot and his victim—the evil-doer
and the evil-sufferer—may be in a like selfishness, in a common bitterness,
and in a common guilt. Human life is full of such cases and scenes. Every
day, men that are hard, coarse, selfish, avaricious, envious, contentious, are
striving together, and in full conflict, each sometimes wronged and sometimes wronging; but either way, and always, actor or recipient, of a worldly spirit, of a
corrupt nature, of an intense selfishness, of a despotic pride, unjust and unlovely.
While Christ refused, then, to assume the office of civil justice, or to interfere
even by advice, He gave to both of these men, and to all upon that occasion, the
instruction which the motive of the petitioner seemed to suggest. (*H. W. Beecher.*)
Christ's judgment respecting inheritance:—I. THE SAVIOUR'S REFUSAL TO INTERFERE.
1. He implied that it was not His part to interfere. " Who made Me a Judge or a
Divider? " He stands aloof, sublime and dignified. It was no part of His to take
from the oppressor and give to the oppressed, much less to encourage the oppressed
to take from the oppresser himself. It was His part to forbid oppression. It was
a Judge's part to decide what oppression was. It was not His office to determine
the boundaries of civil right, nor to lay down the rules of the descent of property.
Of course there was a spiritual and moral principle involved in this question. But
He would not suffer His sublime mission to degenerate into the mere task of deciding casuistry. He asserted principles of love, unselfishness, order, which would
decide all questions; but the questions themselves He would not decide. He would
lay down the great political principle, "Render unto Cæsar the things that be
Cæsar's, and unto God the things which are God's." But He would not determine
whether this particular tax was due to Cæsar or not. So, too, He would say, justice,
like mercy and truth, is one of the weightier matters of the law; but He would not
decide whether in this definite case this or that brother had justice on his side. It
was for themselves to determine that, and in that determination lay their responsibility. And thus religion deals with men, not cases; with human hearts, not
casuistry. 2. In this refusal, again, it was implied that His kingdom was one
founded on spiritual disposition, not one of outward law and jurisprudence. That
this lawsuit should have been decided by the brothers themselves, in love, with
mutual fairness, would have been much; that it should be determined by authoritative arbitration was, spiritually speaking, nothing. The right disposition of their
hearts, and the right division of their property thence resulting, was Christ's kingdom. The apportionment of their property by another's division had nothing to do
with His kingdom. Suppose that both were wrong—one oppressive, the other
covetous. Then, that the oppressor should become generous, and the covetous
liberal, were a great gain. But to take from one selfish brother in order to give to
another selfish brother, what spiritual gain would there have been in this? Suppose again, that the retainer of the inheritance was in the wrong, and that the
petitioner had justice on his side—that he was a humble, meek man, and his petition only one of right. Well, to take the property from the unjust and give it to
Christ's servant, might be, and was, the duty of a judge. But it was not Christ's
part, nor any gain to the cause of Christ. He does not reward His servants with
inheritances, with lands, houses, gold. The kingdom of God is not meat and
drink, but righteousness, and peace, and joy in the Holy Ghost. Christ triumphs
by wrongs meekly borne, even more than by wrongs legally righted. 3. He

refused to be the friend of one, because He was the friend of both. He never was the champion of a class, because He was the champion of humanity. We may take for granted that the petitioner was an injured man—one at all events who thought himself injured; and Christ had often taught the spirit which would have made his brother right him; but He refused to take his part against his brother, just because he was his brother—Christ's servant, and one of God's family, as well as he. And this was His spirit always. The Pharisees thought to commit Him to a side when they asked whether it was lawful to give tribute to Cæsar or not. But He would take no side as the Christ—neither the part of the government against the taxpayers, nor the part of the taxpayers against the government. II. THE SOURCE TO WHICH HE TRACED THIS APPEAL FOR A DIVISION. He went to the very root of the matter. "Take heed and beware of covetousness." It was covetousness which caused the unjust brother to withhold; it was covetousness which made the defrauded brother indignantly complain to a stranger. It is covetousness which is at the bottom of all lawsuits, all social grievances, all political factions. The true remedy for this covetousness He then proceeds to give. "A man's life consisteth not in the abundance of the things which he possesses." Now observe the distinction between His view and the world's view of humanity. To the question, What is a man worth? the world replies by enumerating what he has. In reply to the same question, the Son of Man replies by estimating what he is. Not what he has, but what he is, *that*, through time and through eternity, is his real and proper life. He declared the presence of the soul; He announced the dignity of the spiritual man; He revealed the being that we are. Not that which is supported by meat and drink, but that whose very life is in truth, integrity, honour, purity. (*F. W. Robertson, M.A.*)   *The bearing of the gospel on every-day life:*—The Word of God, my friends, affords men direction in all the circumstances of life, inasmuch, at least, as it contains general rules which may be applied to particular cases. I. INJUSTICE AND QUARRELS BETWEEN NEAR CONNECTIONS REGARDING THE PROPERTY OF DECEASED RELATIONS ARE VERY UNSEEMLY AND UNCHRISTIAN. It sometimes happens that the head of a family, or a very near relation, is no sooner laid in the grave, than the survivors, who expect to benefit in their substance by his decease, begin to strive about what he leaves behind him. How unbecoming, in the very face of such a memento of the vanity of earthly things, to be carried away by the desire of having, and that in such a way as to overlook the ordinary proprieties of life! Common feeling, not to speak of any higher principle, should at least teach them to keep such disputes to themselves (if they do at all arise), and not to outrage decency by making them public. II. We may remark, from this passage, that those WHO HAVE ANY PROPERTY TO LEAVE BEHIND THEM SHOULD BE CARE-FUL TIMEOUSLY TO SETTLE THEIR AFFAIRS BY A LATTER WILL, SO THAT JUSTICE MAY BE DONE AND DISPUTES PREVENTED AFTER THEY ARE GONE. In some cases the law of the land may be sufficient to divide an inheritance as justice and a man's own reasonable inclination might desire. In most cases, however, there would be room for litigation; and in many cases, especially where there is much property, something that equity or mercy requires will be neglected if there be no distinct testament. How far a man is at liberty to consult his own particular wishes on such an occasion, independently on the general principles of nearness of kindred, which are usually observed, is a very difficult question. No particular rules can be laid down to meet every case. The Christian should consult conscience, the Word of God, and, perhaps, also a judicious friend or two. III. THE GOSPEL OF CHRIST DOES NOT INTER-FERE WITH CIVIL RIGHTS OR HUMAN LAWS. No doubt it is intended and fitted to influence them indirectly, for everything ought to be managed in a way consistent with its holy precepts; but it gives no countenance to its adherents to disregard existing institutions or to usurp the places assigned to others. Dominion is not founded on grace. The provinces of civil and ecclesiastical government are quite distinct. Not but that they may, and should, be so managed as mutually to assist each other; but still, their office is distinct, and relates to quite different things. IV. Once more here, THIS PASSAGE IS UNFAVOURABLE TO MINISTERS ENGAGING IN SECULAR BUSINESS, AND ESPECIALLY IN PUBLIC CIVIL OFFICES. (*Jas. Foote, M.A.*)   *A warning against worldliness and covetousness:*—I. A RUDE INTERRUPTION. 1. This suggests a sad but common occurrence. Worldly thoughts obtruding themselves at unseasonable times. 2. This suggests a constantly-needed but oft-neglected duty. To take heed how we hear. II. A FITTING REBUKE. 1. It rebuked the man for his gross view of our Lord's mission. 2. It rebuked the man for the worldliness of his spirit. III. A MORAL LESSON. 1. The subject—covetousness. (1) Covetousness is "an inordinate desire for gain"; "an avaricious disposition"; "a disposition to have more than others." (2) Covetousness is foolishness. (a) For after it has attained its object there is no satisfaction. (b) It unfits the soul to enjoy spiritual things. 2. The elucidation of the subject. (1) A parable. (2) A very instructive parable. (a) It shows God's goodness to the wicked (ver. 16). (b) It shows the inadequacy of worldly prosperity to inspire gratitude (ver. 18). (c) It shows the degrading influence of worldly thoughts. (d) It shows the shortsightedness of worldliness. (e) It shows that God's eye is on all. (f) It shows the uncertainty of life. (g) It shows the relation of time to eternity. 3. The Divine application. (1) Selfishness and godliness incompatible (ver. 21). (2) Anxiety a sin (ver. 22). (3) The great duty. To be "rich toward God." (*D. C. Hughes, M.A.*) *Covetousness :*—I. COVETOUSNESS IN ITS BEARING UPON THE RECEPTION OF TRUTH. 1. Consider for a moment the truths which Jesus had just been uttering. (1) The sin of hypocrisy. (2) The sin of the man-fearing spirit. (3) The comprehensiveness of God's care. (4) The blessed consequences of confessing Christ, and the dreadful consequences of denying Christ. (5) The appalling sin—the blasphemy against the Holy Spirit. (6) The Divine help promised in times of persecution. 2. In the midst of utterances such as these, this man, filled with worldly thoughts, interrupted our Lord in His address. (1) Of how many in our day is this man a representative! (2) The most solemn truths uttered in the sanctuary, or spoken by friends, often fall as seed upon a hard-beaten road. II. COVETOUSNESS IN ITS BEARING UPON THE SOUL'S TRUE JOY. Two things are here stated. 1. That our Lord's mission was not to interfere in secular affairs. 2. That "a man's life," in the sense of true joy, does not arise from wealth or position or fame. III. COVETOUSNESS IN ITS BEARING ON OUR FINAL DESTINY. 1. The parable shows that the most selfish of men may be prospered in worldly affairs. 2. The parable shows that the most abundant prosperity of the worldly-minded only intensifies their selfishness and blinds their spiritual vision. 3. This parable shows that, however farsighted and shrewd worldly-minded men may be in their business affairs, it is by their spiritual condition that God judges them. 4. This parable shows that the uncertainty of the time of death should have its legitimate weight with them. Lessons: 1. The sin to which our attention is here called is the crying sin of our age. 2. This is one of the most subtle and unconscious of all classes of sins to which we may be exposed. 3. It is a sin the most difficult to be reached by truth. 4. It is no less heinous and damning, because it is so subtle and unconscious. (*Ibid.*)

Ver. 15. **Take heed and beware of covetousness.**—*Business life :*—I shall try to keep in view the chief risk to the moral and religious nature which are incident to a business life, and my aim will be to show you where the best safeguard against it is to be sought. I. THE CHIEF DANGERS, WHAT ARE THEY? It is a misfortune in the path of a commercial trader to be kept in perpetual contact with the purely material value of all possible substances. The public sentiment of great business centres is apt to reckon a man's worth by his business profits. It is always tempted to erect an ignoble or defective ideal of success in life. I do not speak of the vulgar dangers to honesty and truthfulness which indeed beset men in all professions and classes. II. WHAT ARE THE SAFEGUARDS? 1. Cultivate to the utmost a youthful thirst for truth, and a youthful sympathy with what is ideal, unselfish, grand in conduct. 2. Cultivate a sympathizing contact with men and women in other than mere business relationships. These are safeguards of the secondary order. 3. The only primary and sufficient safeguard for any of us is the religion of Jesus Christ. See how the Christian man is guarded against settling down into a selfish worldling. (1) Religion opens the widest, freest outlook for the mind into the eternal truth, enlarging a man's range of spiritual sight, and enabling him to judge of all things in both worlds in their true proportion. (2) It supplies us for that reason with the only true and perfect standard by which to test the value of things, and so corrects the one-sided materialistic standard of business. (3) It transforms business itself from an ignoble to a noble calling, because it substitutes for the principle of mere profit the ideal of service. (*J. O. Dykes, D.D.*) *On covetousness :*—1. It is not wrong to amass wealth. It is not wrong to increase it if you have the beginnings of it. Neither is it wrong to make provision for its safety. There is no moral wrong in the ownership and administration, or in the increase of wealth. It is not wealth that ever is a mischief. It is what it does to you that makes it injurious or beneficial. It is what you do with it that makes it injurious or beneficial. 2. It is not wrong, either, to be richer than other men. The essential difference of power in different individuals settles the question as to the Divine economy in this regard. Men are made of different executive forces, of different acquiring powers. And in the fact that men are made relatively weak or strong, that they are in ranks and gradations of inferiority or superiority with respect to natural endowments, there is the most unequivocal evidence that human society was not meant to be one long, flat prairie-level, but that it was meant to be full of hills and valleys and gradations of every kind. And there is no harm in that. I am not injured by a man that is superior to me, unless he employs his superiority to tread me down. I am benefited by him if he employs it to lift me up. Superiority is as powerful to draw the inferior up as to pull them down, and it is comprised in the Divine plan of beneficence. And the same is true of wealth. 3. All the roads which lead to wealth that are right to anybody are right to Christians. What a Christian has not a right to do nobody has a right to do. Moral obligations rest on grounds which are common to me and to you. If there is any distinction here, the Christian has rights which the infidel has not. As a son of God, and as one who is attempting to carry himself according to the commands of God, the Christian may be supposed to have rights of premium. Therefore, if it is right for you to sail a ship, it is right for me to sail a ship ; if it is right for you to traffic, it is right for me to traffic ; if it is right for you to loan money on interest, it is right for me to loan money on interest. The circumstance of a man's being a Christian does not change his relations in any whit, except this, that if possible it gives him higher authority than others have to do whatever it is right for any man to do. All things are yours because you are a son of God. 4. Nay, the gift of acquiring wealth, commercial sagacity, creative industry, financial ability—these are only so many ways by which one may bring his gifts to bear upon the great ends of life and serve God. Some men, who are capable mechanics, capable artists, capable business men, wish to do good, and they say, " Do you not think I had better preach ? " I think you had. I think every man ought to preach. If you are a banker, behind the counter is your pulpit, and you can preach sermons there which no man in any other situation can. By practising Christian integrity in a business where others take permissions of selfishness, you can preach more effectually than in any other way. Every man must take his life, and serve God by it. If God has given a man literary capacity, genius for poetry, or the power of eloquence, it is to be consecrated and employed for the glory of God and the good of his fellow-men. He is to serve, not himself alone, but the cause of beneficence with it. If you have the skill of an artist, it is not given to you for your own selfish gratification and delight. These men that are made seers of truth through eyes of beauty are under the most fearful responsibilities and the most sacred obligations. If a man has given to him the skill of achieving results, the skill of conducting business, or pecuniary skill, he can serve God by that, if not as well, yet as really, as by any other consecrated power. Therefore a man is not forbidden either to have riches or to increase riches, or to employ any of the ordinary ways by which it is right to increase riches. If he have a gift in that direction, he is bound as a Christian man to develop it; and it is a talent for which God will hold him accountable. 5. It is the godlessness of selfishness, then, that is so wicked in wealth, in the methods of getting it, in the methods of keeping it, and in the methods of using it. It is selfishness that leads a man to undertake to procure wealth by means that disregard duty ; it is selfishness that leads a man to set up wealth as the end of his life, for which he is willing to sacrifice all the sweet affections, all the finer tastes, all the sensibilities of conscience. The curse of wealth consists in the getting of it in a way which emasculates a man, and degrades his moral nature. The curse of wealth-getting is seen where a man amasses wealth only that it may shut him in from life, building himself round and round with his money, until at last he is encaverned with it, and dwells inside of it. Geologists sometimes find toads sealed up in rocks. They crept in during the formation periods, and deposits closed the orifice through which they entered. There they remain, in long darkness and toad stupidity, till some chance blast or stroke sets them free. And there are many rich men sealed up in mountains of gold in the same way. If, in the midst of some convulsion in the community, one of these mountains is overturned, something crawls out into life which is called a man ! This amassing of wealth as only a means of imprisonment in selfishness, is itself the thing that is wicked. The using of wealth only to make our own personal delights more rare, without regard to the welfare of others—this it is that is sinful. The Divine command is, "Beware lest ye be rich and lay up treasure to yourself, and are not rich toward God." If you have a surplus of one thousand dollars, this command is to you; if you have a surplus of ten thousand, it is to you; if you have a surplus of ten hundred thousand, it is not a whit more to you. Now, my Christian brethren, are you rich toward God in the proportion in which you have been increasing your worldly wealth? I can tell you, unless your sympathies increase, unless your charities increase, unless your disposition to benefit your fellow-men increases, in the proportion in which your riches increase, you cannot walk the life you are walking without falling under the condemnation of this teaching of Christ. Your life is one of getting, getting, getting! and there is but one safety-valve to such a life; it is giving, giving, giving! If you are becoming less and less disposed to do good; if you are becoming less and less benevolent; if you are less and less compassionate toward the poor; if you say, "I have worked myself almost to death to get my property, and why can I not be allowed to enjoy it?" if you hug your gold, and say, "This is my money, and my business is to extract as much pleasure from it as I can"—then, my friend, you are in the jaws of destruction; you are sold to the devil; he has bought you! But if, with the increase of your wealth, you have a growing feeling of responsibility; if you have a real, practical consciousness of your stewardship in holding and using the abundance which God is bestowing upon you; if you feel that at the bar of God, and in the day of judgment, you must needs give an account of your wealth—then your money will not hurt you. Riches will not hurt a man that is benevolent, that loves to do good, and that uses his bounties for the glory of God and the welfare of men. But your temptations are in the other direction. I beseech of you, beware. (*H. W. Beecher.*) *The nature and evil of covetousness:*—I. THE MANNER OF THE CAUTION. 1. The great danger of this sin. (1) How apt we are to fall into it. (2) Of how pernicious a consequence it is to those in whom it reigns. 2. The great care men ought to use to preserve themselves from it. II. THE MATTER OF THE CAUTION. The vice our Saviour warns His hearers against is covetousness. 1. The nature of this vice. The shortest description that I can give of it is this: that it is an inordinate desire and love of riches; but when this desire and love are inordinate, is not so easy to be determined. And, therefore, that we may the better understand what the sin of covetousness is, which our Saviour doth so earnestly caution against, it will be requisite to consider more particularly wherein the vice and fault of it doth consist; that, whilst we are speaking against covetousness, we may not under that general word condemn anything that is commendable or lawful. To the end, then, that we may the more clearly and distinctly understand wherein the nature of this vice doth consist, I shall—First, Endeavour to show what is not condemned under this name of covetousness, either in Scripture or according to right reason; and—Secondly, What is condemned by either of these, as a plain instance or branch of this sin. I. WHAT THINGS ARE NOT CONDEMNED UNDER THE NAME OF COVETOUSNESS, either in Scripture or according to right reason, which yet have some appearance of it; namely, these three things: 1. Not a provident care about the things of this present life. 2. Not a regular industry and diligence for the obtaining of them; nor—3. Every degree of love and affection to them. I mention these three, because they may all seem to be condemned by Scripture, as parts or degrees of this vice, but really are not. II. I COME NOW TO SHOW WHAT IS CONDEMNED IN SCRIPTURE UNDER THE NAME OF COVETOUSNESS; and by this we shall best understand wherein the nature of this sin doth consist. Now covetousness is a word of a large signification, and comprehends in it most of the irregularities of men's minds, either in desiring, or getting, or in possessing, and using an estate. 2. The evil and unreasonableness of this sin. (1) Because it takes men off from religion and the care of their souls. (2) Because it tempts men to do many things which are inconsistent with religion and directly contrary to it. (3) Because it is an endless and insatiable desire. (4) Because the happiness of human life doth not consist in riches. (5) Because riches do very often contribute very much to the misery and infelicity of men. III. I come now, in the last place, to make some application of this discourse to ourselves. 1. Let our Saviour's caution take place with us, let these words of His sink into our minds: "Take heed and beware of covetousness." Our Saviour doubles the caution, that we may double our care. It is a sin very apt to steal upon us, and slily to insinuate itself into us under the specious pretence of industry in our callings, and a provident care of our families: but however it may be coloured over, it is a great evil dangerous to ourselves, and mischievous to the world. Now to kill this vice in us, besides the considerations before mentioned taken from the evil and unreasonableness of it, I will urge these three more: (1) That the things of this world are uncertain. (2) That our lives are as uncertain as these things; and—(3) That there is another life after this. 2. By way of remedy against this vice of covetousness, it is good for men to be contented with their condition. 3. By way of direction, I would persuade those who are rich to be charitable with what they have. (*Archbishop Tillotson.*)   *The evil and folly of covetousness :—* I. TO EXPLAIN THE ARGUMENT BEFORE US, AND TO JUSTIFY IT, that is, to show the meaning of the assertion, "that a man's life doth not consist in the abundance of his possessions," and to show that it is strictly true. 1. That the being and preservation of life doth not consist in nor hath any dependence on these things, every one must be sensible. No man imagineth that riches contributed to his existence, or that they are essential to the human constitution; not one power of nature is either the more or the less perfect for our having or wanting them. 2. As the being and the preservation of a man's life do not consist in nor depend on the abundance of the things that he possesseth, so neither do the highest and best ends of it. 3. The enjoyment of life doth not consist in riches; and as this is the only end which they have any pretence or appearance of answering, if upon a fair inquiry it shall be found that they come short of it, then it must be owned they are what our Saviour calleth them, deceitful; and His assertion in the text is true, that life doth not in any sense consist in them, which therefore is a strong argument to the purpose He applieth it to, namely, against covetousness. It is necessary to observe here, what every man must be convinced of upon the least reflection, that riches are not the immediate object of any original desire in the human nature. If we examine our whole constitution, with all the primary affections which belong to it, we shall find that this hath no place among them. And yet it is certain that the love of riches is become a very powerful lust in the human nature, at least in some minds, and they are thought of great importance to the comfortable enjoyment of life. Whence doth this arise? How doth happiness consist in them? It is plain that the total amount of their usefulness to the purposes of enjoyment is only this, that when other circumstances concur to render a man capable, they afford the larger means of it in various kinds. 1. Of sensual gratifications. 2. The pleasures of the fancy or imagination. 3. Of doing good to his fellow-creatures, either his own near relations or others, as his disposition inclineth him. This is, I think, stating the case fairly, and allowing all to riches which can be demanded for them. Let us now consider each of these particulars, that we may see of what importance they are to happiness, so far, I mean, as they are supplied, and the opportunities of them enlarged by riches. And, first, the pleasures of sense are of the very lowest kind, which a man considering as common with us to the brutal species cannot but think far from the chief happiness of a reasonable nature, and that the advantage of furnishing us with great plenty and variety of them is not extremely to be valued or gloried in. Besides, there are certain bounds fixed by nature itself to the appetites, beyond which we cannot pass in the gratification of them without destroying enjoyment and turning it into uneasiness. Another sort of pleasures are those of the imagination, arising from the beauties of nature or art, of which we have an internal sense, yielding delight, as we have the sensations of colours, sounds, and tastes, from external material objects, by our bodily organs which convey them. These, it is certain, afford great entertainment to the human life, though in various degrees, according to the different measure of exquisiteness or perfection in the sense itself, which is improved in some beyond others by instruction, observation, and experience; and according to the knowledge men have of the objects. Yet we must remember that these pleasures are not appropriated to the rich, nor do depend on riches, which are only the means of acquiring the property of them, in which the true enjoyment doth not consist. The beauties of nature are unconfined, and every man who hath a true sense of them may find objects enough to entertain it. The last, and indeed the truest and highest, enjoyment of life, is in doing good, or being useful to mankind. And of this riches affords the largest means, which enjoyeth life in the best manner, maketh the best provision for his own comfort in this world. But as this is not the case of the covetous man, it is perfectly agreeable to the text, which declareth that life, that is, enjoyment, doth not consist in abundant possessions; not that it doth not consist in parting with those possessions for the uses of charity. To set this matter in a just light, let it be observed, that the moderate desire and pursuit of riches is not at all inconsistent with virtue; so far from it, industry is a virtue itself, as being really beneficial to society, as well as to the person who useth it, furnishing him with the conveniences of life, and especially with the means of being useful to his fellow-creatures. But when a man hath used honest industry, so far he hath discharged his duty, and laid a foundation for all the true enjoyment which can arise from riches; for that doth not depend on success, or the actual obtaining of large possessions, but principally on the inward dispositions of the mind. III. Having thus explained our Saviour's assertion in the text, and showed the truth of it, let us next consider THE PURPOSE TO WHICH HE APPLIETH IT, NAMELY, AS A DISUASIVE FROM COVETOUSNESS. All that covetousness aimeth at is, the obtaining of large worldly possessions. Now supposing them to be obtained, which yet is very uncertain, but supposing it, and it is the most favourable supposition for the covetous man, what is he the better? If neither the being and preservation of life, nor the ends, nor the enjoyment of it, dependeth on this. (*Bishop Abernethy.*) *Christ's warning against covetousness :—*I. Covetousness is an INNATE sin. It was a principal part of the first transgression. In this first preference of temporal good to spiritual obedience and the favour of God may be seen, as in a glass, all after covetousness. From that fatal hour to the present, mankind universally have, "by nature," "worshipped the creature more than the Creator," proving themselves to be influenced by an innate propensity to grasp at earthly things, and to follow them in the place of God. II. Covetousness is a DECEPTIVE sin. The same may be said indeed of all sins; but of this more especially, because it is a decent sin. Other sins alarm, because of their interference with the passions and interests of our neighbours; and have, on that account, discredit and shame attached to them. Lying interrupts confidence, and weakens the bonds of society; murder lays its hand on the persons, and theft on the property of men; adultery invades the most sacred rights and breaks the dearest ties; even drunkenness, by its brutality and offensiveness to peace and order, is regarded with general disgust and odium. But where is the disgrace of covetousness? How regular a man may be, how sober, how industrious, how moral, and yet be the slave of this vice! III. Covetousness is a MULTIPLYING sin. This also may be said of most other sins, but eminently so of covetousness. It leads to prevarication and falsehood. Then comes hardness of heart. He that sets his affections on money, will love it more than he will love his fellow-man. He will have little pity for the sufferings of the poor, or if he have a little he will stifle it, lest his pity should cost him something. Still less will he compassionate the spiritually wretched. IV. Covetousness is an AGGRAVATED sin. It is not merely an omission of duty, or a transgression of law; but it is an abuse of much mercy. For who gives a man power to get wealth?— whence come health, ability, and labour, skill, opportunity, success;—come they not from God?—could any man earn one shilling if God did not enable him?—and if any man have property, not of his own earning, could he have been possessed of it but for the kind providence of God? And we know that He bestows it that it may be employed in His service and for His glory. But covetousness refuses so to employ it. V. Covetousness is a GREAT sin. It originates in mistrust of God, and unbelief in His word. VI. Covetousness is a DESTRUCTIVE sin. Other sins slay their thousands, but this slays its ten thousands. Many other sins are confined to the openly ungodly, and have their victims exclusively from among those that are without; but this sin enters into the visible Church, and is the chief instrument in the hands of Satan of destroying the souls of professors. (*Essex Remembrancer.*) *Warning against covetousness :—*I. COVETOUSNESS BREEDS DISCONTENT, ANXIETY, ENVY, JEALOUSY. And hence it comes about that covetousness takes all the sweetness and peace out of our life. It makes us dissatisfied with our homes and surroundings. It keeps us for ever anxious as to our relative position. It sets us continually on comparison. It underestimates the pleasures and joys of life, and overvalues and magnifies its troubles. It makes the poor man wretched in his poverty, and hardens his heart against the rich. It energizes the man of competence with new vigour to compass overflowing abundance, and pushes forward the wealthy in the struggle for pre-eminence and power. In the prosperous it naturally develops into greed or reckless extravagance; in the disappointed, into hawking envy or green-eyed jealousy. It invades and spoils our religious life. It embitters us during the week by thoughts of our inferiority. It frets continually at the ordering of Providence. It destroys sweet confidence in God's wise and loving care. It sees evidences of the Divine partiality in the inequalities of the human lot. The good graciously granted turns to ashes on the lips because another has it in greater abundance. It keeps many a one from the house of God. It follows many another to the sanctuary to spoil the worship, and, through the sight of the eyes, to gangrene the soul more perfectly, and send it home burning with a deeper envy. II. COVETOUSNESS MISLEADS AND PER-

VERTS THE JUDGMENT. Covetousness is to the mind what a distorting or coloured medium is to the eye. Just as everything in a landscape seen through such a medium is out of proportion or falsely coloured, so everything in life seen through the medium of covetousness appears under fearful distortion or most deceptive colouring. It breaks up the white light of truth into prismatic hues of falsehood and deceit. III. IT HARDENS THE HEART AND DESTROYS THE BENEVOLENT AFFECTIONS. A cherished covetousness gradually crystallizes into habit and principle. It narrows and pinches the entire being. It grows strong by indulgence. The more it has the more it wants. The more it gets the tighter it grasps it. An avaricious millionaire will haggle for a halfpenny as quickly as a day labourer. No meaner or more metallic being can be found than he in whom covetousness has done its legitimate work. And hence comes much of the heart-ache of individuals, the misery of families, and the trouble of society. It leads men to deprive themselves of the comforts of life. It is deaf to the voice of natural affection. IV. IT TENDS TO AND ENDS IN CRIME. A strong desire to get confuses the judgment as to the proper means of getting, and gradually becomes unscrupulous in the use of means; ultimately all hesitation is overcome, all restraints broken through, all dangers braved. Get, it will at all hazards. Not that every covetous man becomes a criminal; but this is the tendency in every case. And when we remember that all overreaching, all petty deception and cheating, is in reality crime, it will go hard with the covetous man to clear his skirts. There is a vast amount of crime unseen by the law, but perfectly open to the view of heaven. "There's no shuffling there." But much of the known crime of the world—some of it the most atrocious and unnatural—springs directly from covetousness. Whence comes the reckless speculation, the stock-jobbing and gambling, which agitate the markets and unsettle trade? Whence the defalcations, breaches of trust, the forgeries which startle us by their frequency and enormity? Whence the highway robberies, burglaries, murders, which have affrighted every age, and still fill our sleeping hours with danger? The answer is plain: From a desire to get, cherished until it would not be denied. Such a desire in time becomes overmastering; it balks at nothing. Out of it spring crimes of every name and form, from the littlest to the most colossal, from the murder of a reputation to the murder of a nation, from the betrayal of a trust to the betrayal of the Son of God. V. IT RUINS THE SOUL. In aiming to get the world, man loses himself. Every consideration heretofore urged tends to this. The real life is neglected; God and His claims are forgotten. In sensual enjoyment the soul is drowned, and suddenly the end comes. (*Henry S. Kelsey.*) *Wealth not necessary to an ideal life:*—"He became poor." My brethren, what a thought is this! The Lord of heaven, God the Almighty, the All-rich, the All-possessing, chose, when He came among His creatures, to come as a poor man. He who is in the form of God, "took upon Him the form of a servant." Earthly poverty, in the fullest sense of the word, He accepted as His own. Born more hardly than the very poorest peasant among us, even in a stable, cradled in a manger, brought up in a poor mechanic's cottage, His food rough barley loaves, His sleeping-place ever uncertain, His disciples poor men like Himself, hard-working fishermen—finally, stripped of His very garments, and left absolutely naked, to die! Surely, if riches and possessions were indeed the highest end of man's being, He who came to restore man to dignity and happiness would have come among us rich and great. So far as our human minds can fathom, the work of our salvation might have been accomplished by one who was rich in earthly things, as well as by One who was poor. The sacrifice might still have atoned. It is even possible to imagine an aspect under which the contrast of the sacrifice itself would have been heightened, had a rich man rather than a poor man died for his fellow-men. Yet, at a time when riches and the good things which riches procure abounded in the world, He chose, deliberately and willingly chose, the lot of the poor, and is among His own creatures "as He that serveth." All "the kingdoms of the earth, and the glory of them," He deliberately cast aside. And since, indeed, He, the typical Man, the Head of the new Creation, the "Firstborn of every creature," chose thus to be stripped, and bare, and poor, does He not, I pray you, teach this lesson, that the highest condition, the very perfection of man's nature is even such as this? Nay, more. I hesitate not to say that from the moment Christ came thus among us, poverty—yea, poverty—has its own special blessing. (*W. J. Butler, M.A.*) *Covetousness:*—I. THE NATURE AND GENERAL CAUSES OF COVETOUSNESS. 1. It does not consist in a lawful care about the things of this life, or in a proper regard to the principles of prudence and frugality. But it consists in too eager a desire after the things of this life. Setting our hearts upon them. 2. It may be known by the tenacity with which we hold the things of this life. Treating them as our chief good. 3. The general causes of covetousness are principally these: (1) A corrupt and perverted state of mind. (2) Discontent with, and distrust of, the providence of God. (3) Forgetfulness of the soul, and those things which are eternal. II. Its EVIL AND PERNICIOUS EFFECTS. Consider—1. Its effects personally. It is the source of many vices. "They who will be rich," &c. (1 Tim. vi. 9). It tempts men to base and unjust means to get money. It hardens the heart, blunts the feelings, and renders the soul callous and sordid. It fills the mind with distraction, and prevents all true and solid enjoyment. It keeps out Christ and salvation. 2. Its effects on society. A covetous man is a misanthrope to his species. 3. Its effects in reference to God. 4. Its effects as exhibited in the examples revelation furnishes. Let us then notice the means necessary. III. FOR ITS PREVENTION AND CURE. 1. Serious consideration of the shortness and uncertainty of life. How madlike, inordinately to love what must so shortly be taken from us! 2. A reflection on our responsibility to God for all we possess. Stewards. Day of reckoning will arrive, God will judge us. All give an account, and receive according as our works shall be. 3. A renewal of our hearts by the grace and Spirit of God. 4. Imitation of Christ's blessed example. 5. Repeated and prayerful examination of our hearts before God. (*J. Burns, D.D.*) *The warning against covetousness* :— Covetousness is like a dangerous rock in the sea of life, over which we have to sail. Multitudes of wrecks are scattered all around it. The warning of our text is like a light-house, which God has caused to be built upon this rock, to give us notice of the danger to be found here, in order that we may avoid it. I. COVETOUSNESS WILL DESTROY OUR HAPPINESS. II. COVETOUSNESS WILL INJURE OUR USEFULNESS. III. COVETOUSNESS WILL LESSEN, OR LOSE, OUR REWARD. Two Christian friends called on a wealthy farmer one day, to get some money for a charitable work in which they were engaged. He took them up to the cupola, on the top of his house, and showed them farm after farm, stretching far away, on the right hand, and on the left, and told them that all that land belonged to him. Then he took them to another cupola, and showed them great herds of horses, and sheep, and cattle, saying, as he did so—"Those are all mine too. I came out here a poor boy, and have earned all this property myself." One of his friends pointed up to heaven, and said—"And how much treasure have you laid up yonder?" After a pause, he said, as he heaved a sigh, "I'm afraid I haven't got anything there." "And isn't it a great mistake," said his friend, "that a man of your ability and judgment should spend all your days in laying up so much treasure on earth, and not laying up any in heaven?" The tears trickled down the farmer's cheeks as he said—"It does look foolish, don't it?" Soon after this, that farmer died. He left all his property for others to use, and went into the presence of God only to find that his love of money, and the wrong use he had made of it, had caused him to lose all the reward which he might have had in heaven. Some years ago, near Atlanta, in Georgia, there lived a man who was a member of the Church. He was a person of some influence in that neighbourhood. But he was a covetous man, very fond of money, and always unwilling to pay his debts. He had a little grand-daughter, about nine years old, who was living with him. She was a bright, intelligent young Christian. She had heard of her grandpa's love of money, and his unwillingness to pay his debts, spoken of, and it grieved her very much. One morning, as they were sitting at breakfast, she said—"Grandpa, I had a dream about you, last night." "Did you? Well, tell me what it was." "I dreamed that you died last night. I saw the angels come to take you to heaven. They took you in their arms, and began to go up till they were almost out of sight. Then they stopped, and flew round awhile, but without going any higher. Presently they came down with you, and laid you on the ground, when their leader said—' My friend, you are too heavy for us. We can't carry you up to heaven. It's your debts that weigh you down. If you settle with those you owe, we will come for you again before long.' " The old gentleman was very much touched by this. He saw the danger he was in from his covetousness. He resolved to struggle against it. The first thing after breakfast, he went to his room, and in earnest prayer asked God to forgive his sin, and to help him to overcome it. Then he went out and paid all his debts; and after that was always prompt and punctual in paying what he owed. So he minded the warning of the text, and was kept from losing his reward. (*R. Newton, D.D.*) *Covetousness* :—I. THE NATURE OF COVETOUSNESS. It is the love of money. A passion that grows upon men. We begin by loving it for the advantages it procures, and then we learn insensibly to love it for its own sake, or perhaps for some imaginary uses to which we flatter ourselves we shall apply it at some future time. We avoid certain extremes, and thus escape the imputation of covetousness, but we are not on that account the less influenced by the greediness of filthy lucre—we have given our hearts none the less to it on that account. And this passion grows in a most remarkable manner. Men encourage it in one another, and many a look seems, even without a word, to say, "Taste, and see how good money is." Thus, by degrees, the love of money manifests and extends itself, making of him who cherishes it, in the words of our Lord, "a servant of mammon." Verily He was wise who said, "Take heed, and beware of covetousness." Further, this love of money takes different forms and changes its name among men, without however being in any respect changed in the sight of Him who knoweth the heart. 1. One man loves money to keep—this is the covetous man properly so called—the covetous man according to the true meaning of the word. He may possibly succeed in avoiding the odium of the title, but to separate him from his treasure would be to separate him from a part of his existence, and he could willingly say of money what God has said of blood, "Money, it is the life." 2. Another man loves money to spend it. This is the prodigal. A man may be at the same time covetous and prodigal. These two dispositions, instead of excluding one another, mutually encourage each other. Thus a Roman historian who knew human nature well, mentions this trait among others in the character of the notorious Cataline: "He was covetous of the wealth of others, lavish of his own." 3. A third man loves money for the sake of power. This is the ambitious man. It is not the desire of hoarding that rules him—it is not the love of spending which possesses him, but the delight of his eyes and the pride of his heart is to witness the influence which money gives him. Of these three forms of covetousness, miserly covetousness is especially the vice of old age; prodigal covetousness that of youth; and ambitious covetousness that of manhood. But covetousness belongs to all ages and conditions. II. THE SIN OF COVETOUSNESS. I imagine we too generally underrate the judgment which God passes upon covetousness. We think that we are at full liberty to enrich ourselves as much as we can, and then to do what we please with the wealth that we have acquired. Thus we give ourselves up to covetousness. We should not act thus with respect to intemperance, to theft, but it seems that covetousness is quite another sort of sin. Whilst these vices disgrace those who are guilty of them—whilst they entail consequences injurious to the peace and tranquility of society, covetousness has something more plausible, more prudent, more respectable about it. It generally lays claim to honest worthy motives, and the world will dignify it by the name of natural ambition, useful industry, praiseworthy economy. I may even go a step further. A covetous man may be in a certain sense a religious man. He may be quite an example in his respectful attention to the worship and ordinances of God. In fact, the love of money is almost the only vice a man can entertain while he preserves the appearance of piety. And there is great reason to fear that of all sins, this one will ruin the greatest number of those who profess to serve God. Instances: Balaam, Achan, Gehazi, Judas, &c. In fact, a man cannot turn to the Lord but covetousness must perpetually oppose him, from the earliest preception of religious impressions, to the most advanced period of his faith. Has he only just been called by the Lord and bidden to the feast? Covetousness persuades two out of three to excuse themselves on the plea: "I have bought a piece of ground, and I must needs go and till it"—or, "I have bought five yoke of oxen, and I must needs go and prove them." Has he begun to listen with interest to the truth and received the good seed in his heart? Covetousness plants thorns there also: "soon the cares of this world, and the deceitfulness of riches, choke the Word, and it becomes unfruitful." Has he advanced still further in the way, and gone some time in the paths of piety? Covetousness still despairs not of turning him out of them, and of including him amongst the number of those who, "having coveted money, have erred from the faith." Happy indeed is he, if, "taking the whole armour of God," he knows how to "withstand in the evil day, and having done all to stand." Happy if he does not imitate those imprudent travellers. whom Bunyan describes as leaving, on the invitation of Demas, the way to the holy city to visit a silver mine in the hill Lucre. "Whether," says this truly spiritual writer, "they fell into the pit by looking over the brink thereof; or whether they went down to dig; or whether they were smothered in the bottom by the damps that commonly arise—of these things

I am not certain; but this I observed, that they were never seen again in the way."
Ah! dear brethren, "take heed, and beware of covetousness!" III. We have now,
however, to consider THE CONDEMNATION GOD RESERVES FOR COVETOUSNESS. And this
condemnation and punishment begins in this life. There is no passion which
renders its victims more truly miserable. Solomon tells us that the lover of money
cannot satisfy himself with money. His cares increase with his wealth. Every
one enjoys it except himself. (*J. Jessop, M.A.*) *A warning against covetousness :*—The great point of instruction in this chapter is, dependence on God; that
He is all-sufficient for the happiness of the soul, and that He will give what is
needful for the body. The particular point of the text is, a warning against
covetousness; and never was there a day in which the warning was more needed,
when a most inordinate thirst of money-getting is abroad, when speculations
of the most extensive kind are afloat, and when money-crimes of the most
extravagant kind have shocked the public mind. I. THE WARNING. Covetousness
is like a fire, one of the four things which are never satisfied (Proverbs xxx. 15).
You may heap fresh fuel upon it, but it only burns the higher, and its demands are
greater. Let me ask, does your present prosperity lead you to regard the warning
of the text more? to believe that there is danger in your present position? If your
soul be in a healthy condition you will pay more attention to the text. But you
may say, "Oh! my gains as yet are very slight, I have made but little money, I
scarcely feel the warning can be applicable to me; when I have made a fortune,
then I will consider." "Take heed, and beware of covetousness," saith the Lord.
But suppose your success in business should continue, that you reach the very
point at which you aim, would you then be more likely to accept our Lord's warning
than now? Nay, less likely; for you would then be more confirmed in disregard of
what He says than you are now; you would be less a believer in His Word than
now. Take heed *now.* II. THE REASON FOR THIS WARNING. 1. Because money
cannot save the soul, and therefore cannot secure happiness in the next life. 2.
Because riches make to themselves wings and fly away, and a man may thus be
deprived of what he builds on for happiness. 3. Because of the uncertainty of life.
The parable which succeeds the text illustrates this. Although this rich man had
ample provision for the body so long as it lasted, yet his goods could not ward off
death; still less could they provide for the happiness of the soul when God required
it in another state of existence. These considerations are enough to show us that
"a man's life consisteth not in the abundance of the things which he possesseth."
You may ask, then, What does a man's life consist in? 1. In a heart at peace with
God through Jesus Christ our Lord; in pardon of sin; in acceptance with God; in
the knowledge that this poor dying life is not all, but that there is a life beyond the
grave, blessed and everlasting, purchased by the blood of Christ, and to which
believers shall be kept by the power of God through faith. 2. In a well-founded
hope of eternal life; in the knowledge of what Jesus Christ has done for sinners;
in a spiritual understanding of the value of Christ's obedience unto death, His
resurrection and ascension; in the assurance that all the promises of Scripture are
"Yea and Amen in Christ," and will be fulfilled to all who trust Him. 3. In being
contented with the station in which God has placed us, and the means which
God has given us, feeling assured that if we could have served God better in
another station there He would have placed us, and if we could have used more
means rightly and for His glory, He would have given them to us; in a heart which
recognizes God's hand in all dispensations, and which is able to say "Amen" to
all He does in the way of submission, and "Alleuia" in the way of praise
(Philippians iv. 11, and Revelation xix. 4). 4. In an earnest desire to serve God
and our neighbour. There is no real happiness without a desire and endeavour to
do good and to obey God's Word; and, as I have already said, our usefulness will
ever be in proportion to our conformity to the image of the Son of God. This is
true happiness: not exemption from trial and discipline, but the assurance of the
sympathy of Christ under it, and the belief that "all things shall work together for
goo l to them that love God"—the confidence that my Father, the Father who loves
me, rules all. This will be the greatest safeguard against the love of money, and
the crimes which spring out of it; this will keep a man humble, moderate, prayerful, holy, and happy, and enable him better to resist temptation in whatever shape
it may present itself. (*W. Reeve, M.A.*) *On covetousness :*—I. CAUSES OF
COVETOUSNESS. 1. A corrupt and perverted judgment. We form a false opinion of
the world, and think more highly of it than it merits. 2. Distrust of the providence
of God. 3. Involving ourselves too much in the world. 4. Neglecting to look at

things unseen and eternal. II. Bad effects and consequences of co
1. It tempts men to unlawful ways of getting riches.   2. It tempts men
sinful ways of keeping what they have thus procured.   3. It fills the sou
quietude and distraction. 4. It prevents all good, and is an inlet and encou
to evil. Nothing so soon and so effectually stops the ear and shuts the hear
religious impressions.   5. It excludes from the kingdom of God. III. Co
tions for the prevention and cure of covetousness.   1. Endeavour to
vinced of the vanity of all worldly possessions. They are insufficient and unc   .....
2. Seek Divine grace to enable you to set bounds to your desires. 3. Learn to
order your affairs with discretion. 4. Cast all your cares upon God. (*S. Laving-
ton.*)   *Our Lord's warning against covetousness :*—Here observe—1. The manner
of our Lord's caution ; He doubles it ; not saying, " Take heed " alone, or " beware "
only ; but, " Take heed," and " beware " both. This argues, that there is a strong
inclination in our natures to this sin ; the great danger we are in of falling into
it, and of what fatal consequence it is to them in whom this sin reigns. 2. The
matter of the caution, of the sin of which our Saviour warns his hearers against,
and that is covetousness : " Take heed, and beware of covetousness "; where, under the
name and notion of covetousness, our Saviour doth not condemn a provident care
for the things of this life, nor a regular industry and diligence for obtaining of
them, nor every degree of love and affection to them ; but by covetousness is to be
understood an eager and insatiable desire after the things of this life, or using
unjust ways and means to get or increase an estate ; seeking the things of this life,
with the neglect of things infinitely better, and placing their chief happiness in
riches.   3. The reason of this caution ; " because a man's life consisteth not in the
abundance of the things which he possesseth." Human life is sustained by a little ;
therefore abundance is not necessary, either to the support or comfort of it. It is
not a great estate and vast possession that makes a man happy in this world ; but
a mind suited to our condition, whatever it be. (*W. Burkitt.*)   *Sin masked by
wealth :*—What could be more natural, they would ask, than that he should make
arrangements for the accommodation of the vast increase of his wealth ? Why
should he not make the most of what he had ? Why should he not spend time and
thought on a matter of so great importance ? Alas ! this is exactly what our Lord
calls " the deceitfulness of riches."   " Some sins are open beforehand, going before
to judgment." Every one admits their sinfulness. It is not so with riches.
Neither the possessors of riches nor those about them perceive in them danger, or
the possibility of sinning in their use. Often rich men actually know not that they
are rich. There is a respectability in being rich which masks a hundred forms of evil.
Most of the sins which are admitted to be sins are such as are injurious to society.
But the habits which wealth brings are exactly those in which society most delights,
and therefore no warning voice, no hand of chastisement, are lifted against the selfishness, unthankfulness, self-satisfaction, vanity, pride, which follow too often in the
train of riches. Against drunkenness, dishonesty, falsehood, and the like, we all
hold up our hands and eyes, but *these* may pass. (*W. J. Butler, M.A.*)   A
man's life consisteth not in the abundance. *A man's life :*—I. What a man's life
is not. " A man's life consisteth not in the abundance of the things which he
possesseth." It is a very common mistake to suppose that a true life is a successful life, a prosperous and wealthy man is said to have succeeded in life. But that
is not the sort of life to which Jesus refers in the text. He shows us in one place
the picture of a man who had been prosperous, one who wore purple and fine linen,
and fared sumptuously every day ; one whom many had envied. Yet his life was
not a success, and there are none of us who would care to change places with him.
The gospel also shows us another example of a mistaken life. It shows us a young
ruler who had great possessions, and many good qualities, yet his life was not a
success : he went away from the true Life, he went away from Jesus. No, " a
man's life consisteth not in the abundance of the things which he possesseth. II.
What a man's life is. It matters not whether we are rich or poor, successful or
unfortunate, clever or dull ; the secret of a true life consists in trying to do our
duty towards God and our neighbour in that station of life to which it has pleased
God to call us. This is the only true life, the only life worth living, the only life
which brings comfort here, and happiness hereafter, since " the path of duty is the
way to glory." Some one has said very truly, " The word duty seems to me the
biggest word in the world, and is uppermost in all my serious doings." When
Lord Nelson lay dying, in the hour of his last great victory, at Trafalgar, his last
words were, " Thank God, I have done my duty." Believe me, brethren, his is the

only true life who can say at the last, feeling all his failures and mistakes, and humbly conscious of his weakness, "Thank God, I have *tried* to do my duty." There is only one path for us to tread in as Christian people, and that is the path of duty marked out for us by God. 1. This life, if truly carried out, will be an earnest life. To do work well, we must be in earnest. If a labourer is set to clear a field of weeds, and if he is in earnest, he takes two hands to his work. So if we are to get rid of the weeds of evil habits and besetting sins, if we are to sweep the house, and search diligently till we find the precious treasure which we have lost, we must put two hands to the work. Every man who wants to live a true life must have a definite object, and be in earnest in reaching it. Those who succeed are those who aim high. The schoolboy who is contented with the second place in his class will never be first. The man who is content to sleep in the valley will never reach the mountain-top of success. A true life is one of duty towards God and our neighbour, done earnestly and with our might; a life which aims at heaven, a life whose ruling principle is the will of God. 2. And again, the true life is not only an earnest life, but also an unselfish life. God will not only have us good ourselves, but will have us make others good. We all influence our fellow-men for good or evil, just as we ourselves are good or evil. A bad man in a parish or community is like a plague-spot, he is not only bad himself, but he makes others bad. A good man in a similar place is like a sweet flower in a garden, beautiful in himself, and by shedding sweetness around him making the lives of others beautiful. Believe me, the best sermon is the example of a good life. (*H. J. Wilmot Buxton, M.A.*) *Covetousness :—* I. WHAT COVETOUSNESS IS. Mainly an inordinate respect and desire for earthly property. Its worst form is the desire for earthly goods at the expense of others. II. WHERE COVETOUSNESS HAS ITS ROOTS. Love of creature more than Creator. A vice which degrades human nature; and a sin which dishonours God, and violates His law. III. HOW COVETOUSNESS SHOWS ITSELF. A grasping habit. Dissatisfaction with present possessions. The covetous man's sole interest in life lies in his accumulations. IV. WHITHER COVETOUSNESS IS PRONE TO LEAD. Hardened heart. V. THE END TO WHICH UNREPENTED COVETOUSNESS BRINGS THE VICTIM AT THE LAST. (*J. R. Thomson, M.A.*) *Money valued at more than money's worth :—* I. THE AILMENT :—THE SPIRITUAL CONDITION OF MEN, WHICH DRAWS DOWN THIS REPROOF FROM THE LORD. The precise point with which we are at present concerned is this: An erroneous estimate of wealth pervades this community. Money is valued at more than money's worth. This lies at the root of the evil. The high esteem in which money is held, gives impetus to the hard race with which it is chased. The aim follows the estimate. Whatever is in a community by common consent accounted most valuable, will be practically followed with the greatest eagerness. A false reckoning has been cast up as to where the chief good of a country lies, and the mass is moving on in a direction many points aside from the course of safety. They give away for it that which is far more precious than it. One of the oldest memories of my mind relates to a case entirely analogous. The event lies far back in childhood—I might even say infancy. The French prisoners in a Government depôt (now the general prison at Perth), were allowed to hold a kind of fair, where they sold from within their railings a variety of curious articles of their own manufacture, to visitors whom curiosity had attracted to see the strangers. Thither I was taken one day, with all my money in my pocket, to see the Frenchmen. During a momentary absence of the person in charge, I set my heart upon a rude bit of wood daubed with gaudy colours, and called Napoleon. The man who possessed it, seeing me alone, accosted me, told me in broken English that nothing could be more suitable for me, and offered to sell it : at once I gave him all the money I possessed, and carried off my prize. Search was made for the man who had cheated me, but he had disappeared behind his comrades, and we never saw him more. I was obliged to return home with a sad heart, and an empty hand, destitute of sundry useful articles which I had been led to expect, and which my pence would have purchased, if they had rightly been laid out. I distinctly remember yet the deep melancholy that came over my spirit, as the reality came home to me that the money was gone, and that there was no remedy. It is lawful to obtain a lesson by comparing great things with small. Men are like silly children in the market-place of life. They are taken by the glitter of a worthless toy. They buy it. They give their all for it. If you give your time, your hands, your skill, your heart for wealth, you are taken in. Even the wealth you have obtained cannot be kept. This habit of accounting money the principal thing, a habit caught up in childhood from the prevailing tone of society, and strengthened by the example of those whom the world honours—it is this that lays bare our defences, and makes us an easy prey to the destroyer. Those who have money usually plume themselves upon the possession of it, without reference to any other claim on the respect of mankind. Simply in virtue of their gold, they take a high place, assume an important air, and expect the homage of the multitude. A rich man will despise a poor man, though the poor man inherits a nobler genius and leads a better life. The claim made might expose the folly of a few; but the claim conceded fastens folly down as a general characteristic of the community. How few there are who will measure the man by his soul—who will neither fawn upon wealth, nor envy it—who on account of it will neither set its possessor up nor down—who, in judging of his character, will ignore altogether the accident of his wealth, and award the honour which is due to the man, according as he fears God and does good to his brethren! In the practical estimation of this community, riches cover a multitude of sins. Oh, if men would learn to weigh it in the balance of the sanctuary, to see it in the light of eternity; if we could get now impressed on our minds the estimate of money which we will all have soon, it would not be allowed to exercise so much effect in our lives. II. THE WARNING WHICH SUCH A MORAL CONDITION DREW FORTH FROM THE LORD, AND THE REASON BY WHICH IT IS ENFORCED: "Take heed and beware of covetousness, for a man's life consisteth not in the abundance of the things which he possesseth." The best method of applying the caution will be to expound the specific ground on which it is here made to rest. There are three different senses in which "a man's life" may be understood, all of them obvious, and each charged with a distinct practical lesson. 1. Life in its literal and natural sense—the life of the body—does not consist in the " abundance " of the things which one may possess. The life is in no degree dependent on the " surplus " over and above the supply of nature's wants. A very small portion of the fruit of the earth suffices to supply a man's necessities. The main elements are, a little food to appease hunger, and some clothing to ward off the cold. In this matter, God has brought the rich and the poor very near to each other in life, and at death the slight difference that did exist will be altogether done away. As a general rule, it may be safely affirmed that the life of the rich is as much endangered by the luxuries of their abundance, as that of the poor by the meanness of their food. The air and exercise connected with his labour go as far to preserve his health as the shelter and ease which the rich man enjoys. Looking simply to life—mere animal being and wellbeing—we are justified in affirming that abundance, or overplus of goods, is no advantage to it. This is a wise arrangement of our Father in heaven. He is kind to the poor. He has protected them by laws that men cannot touch—laws imbedded in the very constitution of the universe. In this view of the case, it is not consonant with right reason to make the acquisition of wealth the main object of desire and effort. 2. "A man's life" may be considered as the proper exercise and enjoyment of a rational, spiritual, immortal being—that use of life which the all-wise Creator manifestly contemplated when He arranged the complex constitution of man. Hitherto we have been speaking of animal life merely, common to us with the lower orders of creatures; now we speak of such a life as becomes a creature made in the image of God, and capable of enjoying Him for ever. To this life, how very little is contributed by the surplus of possessions over and above what nature needs! Indeed, that surplus more frequently hinders than helps the highest enjoyment of man's life. The parable which immediately follows the text bears, and was intended to bear, directly on this subject. Besides the folly of the rich man, in view of death and eternity, he made a capital mistake even in regard to his life in this world, when he said to his soul, "Soul, thou hast much goods laid up for many years, take thine ease, eat, drink, and be merry." The increase of riches does not increase a soul's enjoyment. In proportion as a rich man is indifferent to his wealth, his enjoyment of life does not spring from it, but from other sources. In proportion as his heart is given to his wealth, his enjoyment of life decreases. It is a law—a law of God which misers feel—that, if a man loves money, then the more money he gets, the less he enjoys it. 3. Life in the highest sense, the life of the soul, obviously does not depend in any degree on the abundance of earthly possessions. The whole world gained cannot prevent the loss of the soul. Consider the first object, a man's life. It is the life of the dead in sin, the life by regeneration, the life quickened by the Spirit and sustained in Christ, the life which, being hid with Christ in God, shall never die. This is a great thing for a man. Hear the word of the Lord—that abundance is not your life. It is not so needful as your life. If you take it too near your heart, it will quench your life. Ye cannot serve two masters. Expressly, ye cannot serve these two, God and Mammon. Money, like fire, is a good servant, but a bad master. It is this surplus, this superabundance, that is the dangerous thing. When it is sought as if it were life to a soul, it becomes to that soul death. When a man falls into deep water, he could easily preserve his life if he would permit his whole body to lie beneath the surface, except so much of his mouth and nostrils as is necessary for the admission of air. It is the instinctive, but unwise, effort to raise portions of the body above the water, that sinks the whole beneath it. It is the weight of that portion which has been, by a convulsive effort, unnecessarily raised, that presses down the body, and drowns the man. It is by a similar law in the province of morals that avarice destroys the life of the soul. The whole amount of money that a man obtains for the purpose of using, and actually does legitimately use, does no harm to the interests of his soul. It may be great, or it may be small, while it is kept beneath the surface, so to speak— kept as a servant, and used as an instrument for legitimate objects—it is as to spiritual matters indifferent. So far as money is concerned, the man is in equili- brium, and his spiritual character will depend on other influences. But when some portion is raised above the line—when it is taken from a servant's place, and raised to that of a master—when a surplus is sought, not for use but for its own sake—when the love of money begins—when it is set up by the man above himself, as an object of his affection—then that surplus, whether great or small, presses down the soul, and the man sinks in spiritual death. It is this lust that " drowns men in perdition " (1 Tim. vi. 11). (*W. Arnot.*)   *The miser's misery :*—There was once a nobleman living in Scotland who was very rich. But his covetousness, or love of money, was very great. Whenever he received any money, he turned it into gold and silver, and stowed it away in a great chest which he kept in a strong vault, that had been built for this purpose down in the cellar. One day a farmer, who was one of his tenants, came to pay his rent. But when he had counted out the money, he found that it was just one farthing short ; yet this rich lord was such a miser that he refused the farmer a receipt for the money, until the other farthing was paid. His home was five miles distant. He went there, and came back with the farthing. He settled his bill, and got his receipt. Then he said, " My lord, I'll give you a shilling if you'll let me go down into your vault and look at your money." His lordship consented, thinking that was an easy way to make a shilling. So he led the farmer down into the cellar and opened his big chest, and showed him the great piles of gold and silver that were there. The farmer gazed at them for awhile, and then said : " Now, my lord, I am as well off as you are." " How can that be? " asked his lordship. " Why, sir," said the farmer, " you never use any of this money. All that you do with it, is to look at it. I have looked at it too, and so I'm just as rich as you are." That was true. The love of that selfish lord for his money, made him think of it day and night, and the fear lest some robber should steal it, took away all his comfort and happiness, and made him perfectly miser- able.   *The terrible evil of covetousness :*—Three men, who were once travelling together, found a large sum of money on the road. To avoid being seen, they went into the woods near by, to count out the money, and divide it among themselves. They were not far from a village, and as they had eaten up all their food, they con- cluded to send one of their number, the youngest in the company, into the village to buy some more food, while they would wait there till he came back. He started on his journey. While walking to the village, he talked to himself in this way : " How rich my share of this money has made me ! But how much richer I should be if I only had it all ! And why can't I have it ? It is easy enough to get rid of those other two men. I can get some poison in the village, and put it into their food. On my return I can say that I had my dinner in the village, and don't want to eat any more. Then they will eat the food, and die, and so I shall have all this money instead of only having one-third of it." But while he was talking to himself in this way, his two companions were making a different arrangement. They said to each other : " It is not necessary that this young man should be connected with us. If he was out of the way, we could each have the half of this money instead of only a third. Let us kill him as soon as he comes back." So they got their daggers ready, and as soon as the young man came back they plunged their daggers into him and killed him. They then buried his dead body, and sat down to eat their dinner of the poisoned food which had been brought to them. They had hardly finished their dinner before they were both seized with dreadful pains, which soon ended in their death. And here we see how the happiness and the lives of those three men were destroyed by the love of money. *Covetousness:*—Two students had been competing at a university for the same prize, and one gained it by a few marks. The defeated candidate had set his heart on the prize, and was bitterly disappointed. In his room that evening, along with two friends, he began to speak of his defeat, and as he spoke such a look of anger and greed came into his face that one of his friends said in an undertone to the other, " See! the wolf! the wolf!" This exclamation did not hit far from the truth. Covetousness brings a man to the level of the beasts. That a man's life consists not in the abundance of the things he has is well brought out in the classic fable of King Midas, who found from bitter experience how fatal a gift was the touch that converted all things into gold. There is an Arabian story which tells how, at the sack of a city, one of the rulers was shut up in his treasure-chambers, and starved to death among bars of gold and sparkling gems. True as this is of the physical nature, it is more true of the spiritual. The man with the muck-rake in Bunyan saw nothing of the golden crown that was offered him. Many a man, intent on gathering his grain into his barns, forgets therewith to lay hold of the better bread of life! (*Sunday School Times.*) *Oriental covetousness:*—To beware of covetousness is a lesson that has always been specially needed in the East. The grasping for more is fearful. It is usually considered the only worthy object in life. The ordinary Oriental simply cannot comprehend how a European can travel for pleasure, or spend money for archæological investigation, or in any of the pursuits we think higher than that of money. Yet, on the other hand, the declaration that "a man's life consisteth not in the abundance of the things which he possesseth" is one that is taught the great mass of the Orientals by a hard experience. Abundance they cannot know. Conceding that "the things which he possesseth" are necessary for his life in this world, whether higher or lower, the life is not in their superfluity. An Oriental is rich who is not in danger of immediate want, who knows where he can get all his meals for to-morrow. Though the Greek of this clause seems difficult to many, it seems to the writer difficult only in its capability of rendering into English; especially because one who wishes to turn it into *good* English must choose at the start which of two allowable idiomatic forms he must choose. But Oriental conditions throw upon it a beautiful light: " For not in their superfluity to any one is his life (does his life come) from his possessions"; or, not in having superfluity does a man have his life out of his goods. It may be admitted that the grammatical government of one word is not altogether certain; but there are many cases, nearly or quite parallel, in classic Greek, where the author, for greater piquancy, has purposely left the construction of a word thus in suspense, to be governed by either of two others; the canon of the iron-bound grammarians, that every word in a given sentence has a fixed construction, to the contrary notwithstanding. (*Ibid.*) *Covetousness:*— The Rev. R. Gray tells of a certain duke that has a passion for costly diamonds; and what is the consequence? His house resembles a castle rather than a mansion, and is surrounded with a lofty wall, one which no one can climb without giving alarm. His treasure is kept in a safe let in the wall of his bedroom, so that it cannot be reached without first waking or murdering the owner; the safe is so constructed that it cannot be forced without discharging four guns, and setting an alarm-bell a-ringing in every room. His bedroom, like a prisoner's cell, has but one small window, and the bolt and lock of the massive door are of the stoutest iron. In addition to these precautions, a case, containing twelve loaded revolvers, stands by the side of his bed. Might we not inscribe over it, " Diamonds are my portion; therefore do I fear "? *Possessions do not constitute life:*—Does a man's life consist in "the abundance of the things which he possesses?" Does amplitude of possession necessarily confer happiness? and is it such happiness as is sure to last? Nay; try abundance of possessions by this test, and you will find that it miserably fails. Wealth, or large possessions, may bring happiness—this we do not deny; it may confer splendour, of which men are proud; power, which they delight to exercise; comforts, which they cannot but cherish; and luxuries, which they undoubtedly enjoy. But are all these things so necessarily and uniformly the results of affluence, as that they always follow from it?—or, rather, does not splendour sometimes become overpoweringly irksome, and do not men sometimes shrink from the responsibilities of power as a burden almost intolerable? And may there not be other concomitants of wealth or of ample possessions, which tend to make the comforts or the luxuries which affluence confers but a very poor compensation for counter trials to which it exposes ? Riches will not ward off pain or disease; the owner of immense property may be racked with pain, or he may languish in sickness, alike with the humblest menial or the poorest peasant. Let us, however, suppose a different case; let there be nothing to disturb the enjoyment of those pleasures which result from affluence; nay, I will even imagine, that, in addition to those already mentioned, the owner of vast possessions has other blessings poured into his lap, such as money alone will not purchase. God has given to him wealth freely to enjoy, and he has around him the costlier and more precious possessions—children by whom he is revered and loved—the esteem and respect of his fellows—and, what no man can afford to despise, the good-will and affection of the humblest and the poorest who live in his neighbourhood. And had we the power of sketching vividly such a case as this—could we delineate to you the owner of some ample property, whom, nevertheless, ancestral honours have not made proud, but who demeans himself alike to all with the gentle courtesy and condescension, which are the true elements of real nobility; who employs what God hath given him, not merely for his own selfish gratification, but finds happiness in diffusing around him what may minister to the comfort of others—could we picture to you that man, around whom his children and his children's children delight to cluster, with feelings of veneration and affection; or who, when he walks abroad, receives the unbought benediction of the poor, because they respect him for his virtues, and love him for his charities—even in a case like this, there would be no contradiction to the truth that " his life "—his real life—" consisteth not in the abundance of the things which he possesseth." And supposing Christianity to have exerted its influence on this man's heart, and brought him as a penitent suppliant to sue for mercy at the feet of the Redeemer, and led him to rejoice in the hope which is laid up for a believer, oh! he will be the very last to deem that his real life could consist in the abundance of his possessions. He might lawfully thank God, who had conferred upon him means of scattering so many blessings around him, and sources of so much comfort to himself; but, above all, he would rather thank God for having taught him to " use this world without abusing it "—to regard himself as no more than the tenant at will, with but a passing interest in the possession confided to his trust; to recollect, and to act upon the recollection, of a coming period, when every earthly possession, be it howsoever costly or large, will have to be forsaken—and thus he would be foremost to confess, that " a man's life consisteth not in the things which he possesseth." Alas! he might well say, for those who act as though it doth; a thousand causes may arise to embitter the enjoyment which springs from possession; or, if these in God's providence are warded off, then the more unsullied the temporal happiness, the more confounding is the thought that death will interrupt it. And surely this is enough to vindicate the accuracy of what is declared in our text. (*R. Bickersteth, M.A.*) *Covetousness a tyranny:*—The muscles of the arm if you never exert them except in one fashion, will become set, so that you cannot move them, like the Indian Fakir, who held his arm aloft so long that he could not take it down again. Man, continuing in sin, becomes fixed in its habit. Only the other day we read of a great millionaire in New York, who once was weak enough to resolve to give a beggar a penny. He had grown old in covetousness, and he recollected himself just as he was about to bestow the gift, and said, " I should like to give you the penny, but you see I should have to lose the interest of it for ever, and I could not afford that." Habit grows upon a man. Everybody knows that when he has been making money, if he indulges the propensity to acquire, it will become a perfectly tyrannical master, ruling his own being. (*C. H. Spurgeon.*) *The vice of covetousness:*—It is a vice that increases in those who harbour it, making them miserable and utterly mean. A very wealthy French banker, worth many hundred thousand francs, would not purchase for himself a little meat when he was almost dying for want of the nourishment. A Russian miser used to go about his house at night barking like a dog, to prevent robbers coming to get any of his great wealth, and because he would not be at the expense of keeping a dog. Are not covetous people punished as the dog in the fable was, which, in snatching at the shadow in the water, lost the meat he had in his mouth? or as Tantalus was, of whom the ancients said he was up to the neck and surrounded with all good things, but he could never get or enjoy one of them? Covetous persons are also like the old man of whom Bunyan tells, who spent his life in raking together dirt, straw, and worthless things; whilst he never heeded the immortal crown an angel offered him. Rowland Hill said, " Covetous persons should be hung up by their heels, that all their money might fall from their pockets, for it would do them good to lose it, and others good to get it." (*Henry R. Burton.*)   *The danger of covetousness :*—A shepherd boy, of small experience, was one day leading his little flock near the entrance of a mountain cavern. He had been told that precious stones had often been discovered in such places. He was, therefore, tempted to leave his charge, and turn aside to explore the dark recesses of the cavern. He began to crawl in, but as he proceeded his face took on a veil of cobwebs, and his hands mittens of mud. He had not gone far when he saw two gems of a ruby glow lying near each other. He put forth his eager fingers to seize them, when a serpent bit him. In pain and fear he crawled quickly back to the light of day, and ran home to the chief shepherd to obtain some remedy for the bite. The good man, who was also his elder brother, sucked the poison from the wound, and applied to it a healing balm. Never afterwards did that shepherd covet the treasures which may lie concealed behind mountain rocks. (*Hervey's Manual of Revivals.*) *No profit in possessions :*—What is Alexander now the greater for his power? What is Cæsar the higher for his honour? What is Aristotle the wiser for his knowledge? What delight hath Jezebel in her paint? Or Ahab in his vineyard? What is a delicious banquet to Dives in hell? Or, what satisfaction can the remembrance of these transitory delights bring? All the beauty, honour, riches, and knowledge in the world will not purchase one moment's ease. All the rivers of pleasure, which are now run out and dry, and only flow in our remembrance, will not cool a tongue (Col. ii. 22). (*A. Farindon.*)   *Riches cannot purchase satisfaction:*—Think you that great and rich persons live more content? Believe it not. If they will deal freely, they can but tell you the contrary; that there is nothing but a show in them, and that great estates and places have great grief and cares attending them, as shadows are proportioned to their bodies (Eccles. ii. 1–11). (*Abp. Leighton.*)   *The true standard of riches :*—No man can tell whether he is rich or poor by turning to his ledger. It is the heart that makes a man rich. He is rich or poor according to what he *is*, not according to what he *has*. (*H. W. Beecher.*)   *Avarice, a fearful disease :*—Cortes was asked by various Mexican States, what commodites or drugs he wanted, and was promised an abundant supply. He and his Spaniards, he answered, had a disease at their hearts, which nothing but gold could cure; and he had received intelligence that Mexico abounded with it. Under the pretence of a friendly conference, he made Montezuma his prisoner, and ordered him to pay tribute to Charles V. Immense sums were paid; but the demand was boundless. Tumults ensued. Cortes displayed amazing generalship; and some millions of the natives were sacrificed to the disease of his heart. (*Percy.*)   *Greed of avarice :*—We see the most rich worldlings live the most miserably, slaved to that wealth whereof they keep the key under their girdles. *Esuriunt in popina*, as we say, "they starve in a cook's shop." A man would think that, if wealth could do any good, it could surely do this good, keep the owner from want, hunger, sorrow, care. No, even these evils riches do not avoid, but rather force on him. Whereof is a man covetous but of riches? When these riches come, you think he is cured of his covetousness: no, he is more covetous; though the desires of his mind be granted, yet this precludes not the access of new desires to the mind. So a man might strive to extinguish the lamp by putting oil into it; but this makes it burn more. And as it is with some that thirstily drink harsh and ill-brewed drinks, have not their heat allayed, but inflamed; so this worldling's hot eagerness of riches is not cooled, but fired, by his abundance. (*T. Adams.*)

Vers. 16–21. **The ground of a certain rich man brought forth plentifully.**— *A successful worldly policy :*—I. THE PICTURE OF A SUCCESSFUL WORLDLY POLICY. 1. No sin in worldly success. 2. No sin in wise and thoughtful provision for worldly goods. 3. The sin consisted in his regarding the possessions as his own absolute property. II. THE PICTURE OF A DISASTROUS WORLDLY POLICY. 1. A foolish life because of the narrowness of its aims and purposes. You have seen some little ant-hill with its teeming life, a miniature world of employment and duty; its busy inhabitants absorbed and careless of any world beyond their own. So this man spent his life, and spent it, perhaps, happily enough, getting and spending, and gathering and consuming, and pulling down and building up again; until that other life and that other world thundered in upon him and would not be forgotten. For mark what is the great lesson after all. It is the fatal want in the man's character and life to which Christ would call our attention. Not what he had, but what he lacked was his undoing. He was rich toward man, but he was not rich toward God, and so while men called him "a success," God called him "a fool." 2. Again, this policy is a disastrous one, and this life is called a foolish life, because of its hopes and expectations. The man evidently calculated upon finding happiness some time or other in the future. Like most of us, he had never been exactly at ease, but now that he is to retire from active life—what promises men do make themselves when they have given up business!—when his new barns are built, then he will eat and drink and be merry. How human this is, for "man never is but always to be blessed." 3. A foolish life because of its false security. The one flaw was there. He calculated on a long life. The door was fastened against poverty, and the time of undue labour and anxiety was past, and the house of feasting was ready; but there was one visitor against whom he could not bar the door. "All men think all men mortal but themselves," and the danger which haunts us through life is of all things most unreal to us. Years ago among the Swiss mountains there was a village over which an avalanche had hung threateningly for nearly half a century. It was only a question of time, sooner or later it must come down and bury all beneath. Travellers warned the inhabitants of that village, but apathy only grew stronger with familiarity. Grey-headed men who had played as boys underneath the awful crags, now gathered in their harvest contentedly with scarcely a glance at the threatening danger. So all went on until one calm summer day, when, with scarcely a warning sound, down came the overwhelming mass, bringing destruction and death upon all beneath. III. Lastly, we have here THE PICTURE OF THE END OF A MERELY WORLDLY POLICY. Suddenly, unexpectedly, with no other warning than this of the text, the last hours of life have come. Like that avenging angel who passed over the households of Egypt, so with this man, the death angel is coming amid the shadows and with the darkness. How the hours of that terrible night must have worn on slow as centuries! He began it with pleasant promises, in health, and strength, and hopefulness, a reaper and a gatherer in the harvest fields; and lo! he, too, feels the sharp thrust of the sickle, and that amid the unripe grain which yields no promise of fruitfulness. He ends it, and with this one short, thrilling, awful night, the tragedy of life is over. I have read of one hanging over a fearful precipice who, looking up, saw the rope by which he hung jagged and worn against the sharp rock to a single thread which could hold out but a moment longer. So this man's spirit must have hung over eternity that night. Consider it! God's salvation, the teachings of wisdom, were with him as with all. Yet thus it was, that a life of privileges, and great worldly prosperity, and multiplied blessings, ended thus disastrously amid overwhelming confusion. With God so near, and infinite mercy never afar off, life darkened and darkened until the last glimmer of hope was gone, and the man was left to grope his way amid the shadows of an everlasting night. (*W. Baxendale.*) *Of the deceitfulness of riches:*—Riches deceive the worldly-minded—1. In regard to their earthly felicity—for—(1) They fill the heart with cares. (2) They occasion much trouble and solicitude. (3) They prove but a short-lived possession. (4) They delude with the hope of a long life. 2. In regard to true felicity; for—(1) They can provide no true satisfaction to the soul. (2) They sink it into utter sensuality. (3) They foreclose the heart against any solemn care for salvation. (4) They prevent the inheritance of better goods. (*F. G. Lisco.*) *The rich fool:*—I. A GOOD CULTI-VATOR. 1. He was rich. So is God. So were Abraham, Job, David. "The *love* of money" (not money itself) "is the root of all evil." 2. His investment was wise. Land cannot be consumed by fire, or removed by foe. 3. His farm was prosperous. He understood his business. II. A BAD CALCULATOR. He undertakes to solve the problem of life, and proves a wretched bungler in the use of figures. 1. He omits the greatest factor in the problem. God forgotten, the problem works out wrong. 2. He makes a wrong estimate of the soul. 3. A wrong distribution of his goods. 4. Wrong calculation of time. (*Anon.*) *The rich man—where right and where wrong:*—I. WHERE RIGHT. 1. It was right that his ground should bring forth plentifully. Industry, &c. 2. It was right that he reflect, "What shall I do?" Common sense. II. WHERE WRONG. 1. He was wrong when he said, "I have no room." Not barn-room, but soul-room, life-room. He measured his room by measuring his barn. 2. He was wrong when he said, "*My* fruits and *my* goods; *my* soul." That was all wrong. He was not his own. 3. He was wrong when he said, "And I will say to my soul, Soul, thou hast much goods laid up for *many years.*" He had the *goods*, but not the *years*. 4. He was wrong when he said, "I will say to my soul . . . Take thine *ease.*" Here the man was all animal. The mistake was, that he had left God out of account in his calculations. (*Homiletic Review.*) *A business man's mistake :*—I. Let us in the outset look at some of the ATTRACTIVE CHARACTERISTICS which this man exhibited. 1. For one thing, he was wealthy. Observe the Bible never is found joining in with any wild tirade against riches. Inspiration has not even said, as some quote it, that money is the root of evil. On the whole, it is a good thing to be rich ; great usefulness can be attained by silver and gold. 2. This man in the parable was successful in business. That shows well as an evidence of his shrewdness and industry. He is considered a benefactor to the world at large, who makes two spears of grass grow where only one grew before, for he thus augments the general wealth. 3. Furthermore, this was a prudent man. He shows himself in the recorded soliloquy here as being thoughtful concerning the future. II. But now let us consider some EXTRAORDINARY MISTAKES which this wealthy man made. 1. To begin with, he made a mistake in thinking there was no place for produce except in barns. It is a fool's question to ask where one can stow away money ; it is the part of a wiser man to ask how he can do God service with the use of it. Just that is what this man did not think of doing. 2. So we see another mistake he made : he supposed his riches would be a comfort to him when they were hoarded. Whereas they became then only a care and a burden. Money is our instrument, not our end. When it goes beyond that, it owns us, instead of our owning it. The nearest approach to the old disease of the possession of devils that we have in modern times is exhibited when a man is possessed of the money he think he possesses. 3. The third mistake this man made was worse than any one of the others : he left out of his thoughts all consideration of the infinite God who made and owned him. He says "my" barns, "my" goods, "my" fruits, and even "my" soul. It would seem that he imagined he was the absolute proprietor of all he touched in two worlds. He fell into the radical error of forgetting he was at the best only the steward of God who had sent him his unusual harvests. 4. But this mistake inevitably led to another : he seems to admit that his soul has no higher needs than his body (see ver. 19). The word here is "dialogued" ; he is pictured as holding a sort of complacent conversation with himself. To us there is an intense impression of sadness in his use of such expressions as are recorded. He talks to his immortal soul in terms of the grossest familiarity, as if that soul ought to be grateful to him for his generous foresight in having made quite sufficient provision for all its future. Do souls need luxurious ease ? Are they to be for evermore content with having enough to eat and to drink ? Are souls to be congratulated by rich people in this unctuous way just because there is much fodder stored now in the new barns ? Is being merry what the image of God in man has been hankering after all these years ? Most of us have read the story of the shipwrecked mariner on an inhospitable island perishing with famine. One day a box was suddenly swept ashore, and he rushed eagerly to loosen its fastenings ; but he fell back in fainting disappointment and consternation, saying, " Alas, it is only some passenger's pearls ! " When this soul of ours is at last off upon the eternal shore, unready and unfurnished, will its undying hunger be appeased with indigestible jewels of earthly opulence alone ? And will it be merry then ? III. We must come back to the parable now once more, in order to consider THE SEVERE REBUKES WHICH THIS RICH MAN RECEIVED. 1. In the first place, God summoned his soul away from him. Opulent men grow old just like other people. Some of them also die young and in middle life just like other people. As life is running on in our great American wear and tear of money-getting, it is coming to be more and more observable that they are apt to die suddenly. The strife of the street saps the vitalities of many human constitutions. There are vast solicitudes bred by unusual increase of property, and the work often does much, while the worry does more, to shorten life. Death sometimes comes in the night. 2. In the second place, this man's property was ignominiously scattered. Those new barns were never builded, after all. There is a striking rhetorical power here in the use of the question rather than of the assertion. The vagueness of the certain distribution of hoarded fortunes is what constitutes its worst unwelcomeness to the owner. Oh, what stores of enforced wisdom this reluctant old world has been obliged to acquire on this its most sensitive point ! It actually sounds like irony to raise such a question in times like ours. How have we seen wills broken, legacies diverted, fortunes squandered, and all the favourite plans of the year thwarted on the instant, by some unwise and unanticipated heir ! (see Eccles. ii. 18, 19). It was the wisest man in the world that said that ; and his son was a fool—or a knave, which was undoubtedly worse.

Mark, then, the conclusion of the whole matter (see ver. 21). Will the thousand daily histories never teach men wisdom? Think over Hugh Miller's words: "The climax is a favourite figure in the book of Providence. God speaks to us in His dispensations; and in the most eloquent terms of His discourse, piles up instance upon instance with sublime and impressive profusion." (*C. S. Robinson, D.D.*) *The foolish rich man :*—I. The folly of this man appears in the fact that HE COMPLETELY IGNORED HIS RESPONSIBILITY TO GOD IN THE MATTER OF HIS POSSESSIONS. 1. He speaks throughout as if he had all the merit of his prosperity, and gives God no praise; while the idea that any portion of the increase of his fields belonged to God seems never to have entered into his mind. But does this man stand alone in this particular? Are we not all too prone to take to ourselves the sole credit for any prosperity we have acquired, or for any eminence we have reached? 2. The destriction to himself of the honour of his success led directly to the complete appropriation by this man of its fruits. He never thought of consulting God about the disposal of his property. And there are multitudes among us, who never pray to God about their business at all. Some may pray that He would send them prosperity; but when the prosperity comes, how few there are, comparatively speaking, who lay their wealth at His feet, and ask Him to direct them in disposing of it! II. The folly of this man appears in the fact that HE IGNORES THE CLAIMS OF OTHER MEN UPON HIM FOR HIS HELP. He had no idea, apparently, that there was any other possible way of bestowing his goods than by storing them in his barns. As Augustine has replied to his soliloquy: "Thou *hast* barns, the bosoms of the needy, the houses of widows, the mouths of orphans and of infants"; these are the true storehouses for surplus wealth. It is right to provide for those who are dependent upon us; it is prudent to lay up something in store against a possible evil day; but after that, the storehouse of wealth should be benevolence. I have somewhere read that a lady once went to call upon a friend near the close of autumn, and found her emptying her closets, and exclaiming, "Oh, these moths! these moths! that have consumed almost everything that I laid away in the beginning of the summer." The visitor expressed her sorrow, but said she did not know what it was to have a garment moth-eaten. Whereupon her friend asked for the specific which she used, and to her surprise received for answer, "I gave away to the poor, months ago, all the garments for which I had no longer use; and there was no difficulty in preserving the remainder from the moths." III. The folly of this man is seen in the fact that HE IMAGINED THAT MATERIAL THINGS WERE PROPER FOOD FOR HIS SOUL. True riches—or, in other words, the true food of the soul, by which alone it can be nourished and satisfied—are to be found in God alone. Reconciliation to God, peace with God, likeness to God, and fellowship with God, that alone can fill the heart of man. God for us in the work of His Son, God with us in the orderings of His providence, God in us in the indwelling of the Holy Spirit, and God before us in the hope of heaven, that is the true food of the spirit of man; and to think of sustaining it with material fruits and goods and possessions, is as absurd as it would be to try to satisfy the hunger of the body with a diamond, or to quench the thirst of the body with a pearl. IV. The folly of this rich man is apparent from the fact that HE HAD ENTIRELY IGNORED THE TRUTH THAT HIS MATERIAL POSSESSIONS WERE NOT TO BE HIS FOR EVER. "There are no pockets in a shroud." "How much did he leave?" asked one man of another, in the street-car, as they were talking of a millionaire whose death had been announced in the morning paper. "All he had," was the solemn and suggestive reply. (*W. M. Taylor, D.D.*) *Unsanctified riches :*—I. THE OCCASION OF THIS PARABLE. II. THE INCIDENTS IT DESCRIBES. 1. The circumstances in which this person was placed. 2. The anxieties of which he was the subject. 3. The projects upon which he resolved. 4. The spirit by which he was actuated. (1) Ungodliness. (2) Earthliness. (3) Selfishness. (4) Presumption. 5. The fearful doom which awaited him. A person once said on his death-bed, "I have gained thirty thousand pounds." A very decent sum, many may be disposed to remark; it is not the lot of every adventurer to be so successful. But there was something he lost as well as gained; and, in general, the losses and the gains are placed one against the other. "I have gained," was his language, "thirty thousand pounds, *but* I have lost my soul." These were the two sides of the balance sheet which he was now, at the close of life, making up: thirty thousand pounds on the one side, the soul lost on the other. The separate items on both sides of the sheet might have been numerous. He did not gain the sum specified all at once, nor was the soul lost at once. But the winding up of the whole affair, after adding to this and deducting from that, presented the conclusion which has been given. But was it a good speculation? We should like to put the question to men of judgment, of practical wisdom, of cool and calculating habits, who can turn a matter over, looking first at one side, and then at the other, and ask them, whether it really was? But whatever their opinion might be, we have the verdict of One, whose competency to judge in such a case cannot be questioned. His language is, "What shall it profit a man if he gain "—not thirty thousand pounds, but—" the whole world, and lose his own soul ; or what shall a man give in exchange for his soul ? " III. THE LESSONS IT INCULCATES. The attainment of heavenly riches should be our great concern. 1. They are durable. 2. Their possession is unattended with any danger. 3. They are accessible to all. 4. They should be sought earnestly, and without delay. (*Expository Outlines.*) *Christ's picture of a worldly life :—*I. THE PROSPERITY OF A WORLDLY LIFE. 1. This man prospered by means of a legitimate calling. 2. His prosperity was largely the outcome of his industry and good management. 3. To his own industry had been added the blessing of God, without which a man must toil in vain. II. THE PERPLEXITY OF A WORLDLY LIFE. When the heart is set on material wealth, it will become burdened with care. There is a state of mind in which it is possible to be happy and rich with little. III. THE SELFISH SCHEMING of a worldly life. " This will I do," &c. His ruling spirit is selfishness ; he lives and moves in the little world of self. " Get all you can and keep all you get," seems to be the motto of his life. He was a close-fisted man of the world, whose earthly soul had been hardened by the sun of prosperity. 1. He forgets his relation to his fellow-men. He acts as if he had no connection with the race. He has no thought of brotherhood. 2. He does not recognize his obligation to the Divine. No thankoffering for the Giver of all good. He sacrifices only at the shrine of self. IV. THE MISTAKE OF A WORLDLY LIFE. 1. Forgetfulness of God. 2. The underrating of his spiritual nature, and the overrating of his material possessions. 3. Forgetfulness of death, and presuming on "many years." V. THE DIVINE JUDGMENT ON A WORLDLY LIFE. 1. A revelation of character. 2. Startlingly sudden. 3. Upsets all plans. 4. Seals worldling's doom. (*W. Smith.*)　*A wise fool :—*I. Let us look at him simply in the light of this world, and try to ESTIMATE HIS CHARACTER ACCORDING TO THOSE PRINCIPLES BY WHICH WE ORDINARILY GAUGE THE WISDOM AND WORTH OF OUR FELLOW-MEN. 1. It is evident that he was an industrious man. 2. It is pretty clear, too, that this was a careful, frugal man. He not only made money, but knew how to save what he made. 3. Then this man was a thoughtful, judicious man. 4. This man was a rich man. 5. It may be taken for granted that this man was highly respected in the neighbourhood in which he lived. 6. It is pretty evident that this man was influential, as well as respected. II. Let us shift our point of observation, and LOOK AT THIS MAN IN THE LIGHT OF ETERNITY. 1. His folly appears in his total misapprehension of the true end of life. 2. His folly is seen in his total misapprehension of the nature and the necessities of the soul. 3. His folly is seen in the mistaken notion which he has respecting the right use of wealth. 4. His folly is seen in the proposals which he makes to himself in respect to time, without any reference whatever to Him to whom alone time belongs. (*W. S. Blackstock.*)　*Unsanctified riches :—*I. THE CIRCUMSTANCES IN WHICH THIS MAN WAS PLACED. He was prosperous, and increasingly so. Just in such circumstances as most people long for. There are several interesting inquiries connected with the acquisition of riches ; such as, how far the desire of acquisition may be indulged—where is the point at which it becomes criminal—and what are the consequences of its excess and abuse. It would much assist, did such maxims as the following meet with due acknowledgment. 1. That riches, with their attendant comforts and influence, are to be regarded as the bestowments of Providence. 2. That riches, with their attendant comforts and influence, furnish means for extended usefulness. 3. That riches with their attendant comforts and influence, involve the pressure of a solemn responsibility. II. THE MEDITATIONS IN WHICH HE INDULGED. Observe the different aspects of imperfection and sin which the recorded meditations comprehend. 1. In the state of his mind as to the source of his possessions. There is no allusion to God, as the giver of the good in which he delighted (Hosea ii. 8 ; Prov. xxx. 8, 9). 2. In the intended application of property. Ought there not to have been some act of charity to man, or some gift to the temple of God ? 3. In the mode of calculating on futurity. " This will I do : I will pull down my barns." And then—" I will say unto my soul, Soul, thou hast much goods laid up for many years " (Prov. xxvii. 1 ; James iv. 13, 15). 4. In the nature of desired and anticipated enjoyment. " Take thine ease ; eat, drink, and be merry." (*a*) There is indicated a fondness for indulgences, in themselves utterly unworthy of the intellectual nature with which man is endowed. (*b*) There is a careful and an entire exclusion of all that belongs to the interests and redemption of the soul. III. THE REPROOF BY WHICH HE WAS ARRESTED. 1. As to the event announced in the message of God—how momentous? "Thy soul shall be required of thee." Besides the separation of the individual from worldly riches, the event announced comprehends his appearance before God for judgment (Luke xvi. 19–26). 2. As to the time when this event was to be fulfilled—how soon it was to come!—"This night!" Ere another sun arose, his destiny would be sealed. (*The Preachers' Treasury.*)　　*The rich fool :*—A rich man. Look at him. He is what almost all would like to be, and are striving to be. Or, if not striving to be, it is because they despair of success, and not because they would not be rich if they might. A rich man! who would not be glad to stand in his lot? Take heed, and beware. Mark the effect of this man's wealth upon him. 1. It increased his covetousness. 2. It made him anxious. 3. Selfish. 4. Atheistical. 5. Sensual. (*Ibid.*)　　*The rich fool :*—I. THE RICH MAN'S POSSESSIONS. II. HIS ANXIETIES. Riches and cares are inseparably wedded together. III. HIS DETER- MINATIONS. 1. He resolves on the means of accumulation. 2. He forms his arrangements without any reference to the providence of God. 3. He reckons on his riches as the joy and portion of his soul. 4. He confidently calculates on an extended existence. IV. HIS SUDDEN AND FATAL ARRESTMENT. 1. Observe how he is disturbed by the voice of Deity. "God said"—either by some deep, unmistakable impression on his heart and conscience, or by some sudden infliction of disease. 2. Mark the sudden termination of his career. 3. The eternal ruin of his soul. (*J. Burns, D.D.*)　　*The rich worldling :*—I. HIS CIRCUMSTANCES. Rich, prosperous. A state of imminent danger. It is difficult to be prosperous and rich—1. Without loving riches. The love of money, &c. Whoso loveth the world, &c. 2. Without thinking ourselves the better and greater for these. How they puff up the mind. How men glory in their professions. 3. Without trusting in them, and not in God. There is danger when full, of denying Him. II. HIS CHARACTER. God gives it, therefore must be correct. "Thou fool." Now, his folly is seen in the following particulars: 1. In being anxious amidst profusion. 2. Because he expected his soul to be happy with temporal things. He tried to make an earth-worm of his soul. He wished to grovel in the dust. 3. Because he pre-sumptuously calculated on years to come. III. HIS END. 1. Sudden and unexpected. 2. Unprepared. 3. Dreadfully momentous. Application: 1. Do not idolize, and trust in riches. 2. Be anxious for your soul's welfare. 3. Come to Jesus. He will make you wise to eternal life. 4. Do not presume. Do not calculate upon the future. (*Ibid.*)　　*The character and end of a sensualist :*— I. THE FOLLY OF THE PERSON MENTIONED. The man's folly consisted in—1. His making the things of this life his chief good. 2. His supposing that worldly goods would satisfy his soul. The folly of such conduct will appear, if we consider (1) The nature of the soul. It is a spiritual and a rational principle (Gen. i. 27, and ii. 7 ; Job xxxii. 8). Can the gross materials that feed the body satisfy the soul? (2) The capacities of the soul. They, on account of its very nature, are so vast, that no measure of created good can possibly satisfy them. (3) The duration of the soul. It is immortal, everlasting (Eccl. xii. 7 ; Matt. x. 28). Can perishable things—such as earth affords—earth that will itself be destroyed, satisfy the immortal soul of man? Such foolish conduct, as that already described, naturally leads to another species of folly, that of—3. Presuming on continued, on long life. He said, "Soul, thou hast much goods laid up for many years." How infatuated must that man have been, who could thus calculate! (see Psa. xlix. 11–13). Do we not see mortals arrested, and borne to their graves, at every stage of life! II. THE MANNER IN WHICH GOD TREATED THE SUBJECT OF THIS FOLLY. 1. He was called away suddenly. 2. Unexpectedly. 3. Amidst a profusion of worldly goods. 4. By language that strongly expressed the Divine displeasure. Reflections: 1. Worldly prosperity is so far from being a proof of personal goodness, or of the Divine favour, that the subjects of it may be so wicked as to incur sudden and severe destruction. 2. The proper enjoyment of life does not depend on large possessions (ver. 15). 3. Rich men are, on account of their riches, in peculiar danger—of living without God—of indulging in sensual gratifications—of presuming on long life—and of neglecting their souls. 4. Life is uncertain. It is therefore our highest wisdom to be living for eternity. (*Theological Sketch-book.*) *God and the sensualist :*—I. THE SENSUALIST'S ADDRESS TO HIS SOUL. 1. Converse with the soul is proper and necessary. 2. Converse with the soul should be adapted to its nature as immortal, and should regard its eternal felicity. 3. Converse with the soul should have a tendency to excite its instant and ardent attention to everlasting happiness. But the rich sensualist in the text converses in a way altogether different. 1. He discovers erroneous ideas of true enjoyment, and represents the uncertain things of this world as capable of conferring happiness on an immortal mind, endeavouring to satisfy that which is spiritual with that which is material, and that which is undying with that which is perishable. 2. He over-rates worldly substance by giving it a durable and satisfying quality. 3. He degrades his soul, and endeavours to persuade it to compromise its eternal interests, and to seek that in gluttony, drunkenness, and the allurements of pleasure, which can be found in God only. II. THE VOICE OF GOD TO THE SENSUALIST. 1. God takes notice of the conduct of sinners in regard to their souls. 2. The Almighty interrupts his schemes, and annihilates his ideas of enjoyment. "But God said unto him." I will darken thy perspective, and suspend thy enjoyments —thy building, founded in delusion, shall suddenly vanish—thy soul shall depart, and thy goods be the portion of another. And, when thou art spoiled, what wilt thou do? 3. The rich man is charged with folly. 4. He is summoned to surrender his soul. (*R. Cope, LL.D.*)   *On worldly-mindedness:*—1. The EVIL of this rich man's conduct. Nothing whatever of a criminal nature is laid to his charge, as to the manner in which his abundant wealth had been acquired. No oppression, no avaricious extortion, no "grinding of the faces of the poor," nothing unfair or dishonest, nothing even ungenerous, is alleged against him; and what is not so much as insinuated in the narrative, we are not entitled to suppose. Nothing appears in the simple statement, but the blessing of Providence upon lawful industry—the luxuriant productiveness of his fields : "The grounds of a certain rich man brought forth plentifully." For this, surely, the proprietor was not to blame. What, then, is the grand error, what the leading and predominant sin, of this poor rich man? I answer, in one word, worldliness; or in another, which, though negative in its form, will be found of much the same positive amount, ungodliness. There is a total absence of God. In receiving, calculating, resolving, anticipating, "God is not in all his thoughts." Let us trace out a little this general observation in a few particulars. 1. There is, then, in the first place, the deliberate choice of the world, and the things of the world, as his portion, not only in preference to God, and the things of God, but without even a thought of the Divine favour and blessing as any essential ingredient in the cup of felicity, or as at all necessary to the legitimate and full enjoyment of his "good things." This did not enter into his estimate. 2. In the second place, he forgot God as the giver of all that he enjoyed, and the object of his gratitude. He received the gift, and forgot the Giver. He rioted in the unrestrained enjoyment of a profusion of good, and overlooked the hand from which it came. He "gave not God the glory." 3. In connection with the absence of gratitude for the past and the present, there was, in the third place, no proper sense of dependence on God for the future. This appears, both in regard to his wealth, and in regard to his life. The continuance of both depended every moment on the Divine will. But this is entirely out of mind: "I will say unto my soul, Soul, thou hast much goods laid up for many years; take thine ease, eat, drink, and be merry." While he forgot that God had given, he forgot also that God could take away. 4. In the fourth place, he over-looks the authority of God as his rule, and the glory of God as his end, in the use of his riches. He lives but for himself. Selfishness is his law, selfishness is his aim. 5. He forgets, too, in the last place, the account which he had to render to God of the manner in which he used His bounties. II. The FOLLY of this rich man's conduct. 1. His folly consisted, in the first place, in seeking his happiness from unworthy and inadequate sources. 2. The folly consisted, secondly, in depending upon the greatest uncertainties; yes, on known, acknowledged, proverbial uncertainties. We have formerly seen how he reckons on the continuance both of property and of life. This was impious. It was ungodly presumption— practical atheism in one of its various forms. But the folly of it was not less egregious than its impiety. It is the very extreme of infatuation, to calculate and to proceed upon what we know to be in the highest degree precarious. "Be wise to-day." To-morrow you may never see. Even of to-day, the present moment alone can be called your own; and every moment you delay the preparation for a coming eternity is a moment of folly—folly, of which the unutterable amount will be felt, when it is too late to redeem your guilty error, at the judgment-seat of

God. 3. This leads me to notice more particularly a third ingredient in the folly —that, namely, of minding time, and forgetting eternity; occupying himself with the enjoyment (according to his unworthy conceptions of it) of the life that now is, and making no provision for the life that is to come. How striking, how awakening, how mortifying the question, " Then, whose shall those things be which thou hast provided ? " He had provided them for himself, but in a few hours they were to cease to be his. He had provided them for many years, storing them up with anxious and self-applauding care, as a portion for a long life; but the years on which he counted he was never to see. (*R. Wardlaw, D.D.*) *Covetousness :*— I. A SOLEMN WARNING AGAINST COVETOUSNESS AS OBSCURING OUR VIEW OF, AND LEADING US TO DISREGARD, THE TRUE PRINCIPLE OF LIVING. II. THE PROCESS BY WHICH A MAN MAY BECOME COVETOUS. The instance given by our Saviour is not an extreme one. It is one adapted rather for a standard example of a process subtle and gradual, from whose operation no man is exempt. The successive steps of the process, as here delineated, are : 1. Prosperity (ver. 16). His prosperity was not culpable. It was a blessing of God. It may have been creditable to the rich man. His good husbandry may have been thus rewarded. No gain could be more legitimate. He was rich in the crop, not through speculation in it, or in an exorbitant price put upon it, as it stood in the field. 2. Calculation (ver. 17). To plan, again, is not sinful. It is a duty rather. But, natural and right though the question (" What shall I do. . . . ? ") is, it is dangerous. One needs to guard vigilantly, lest he make so much of the question, " What shall I do to save ? " that he shall make too little of the question infinitely more pressing, " What shall I do to be saved ? " 3. The decision to increase his investments (ver. 18). In this decision, again, there is no necessary guilt. The purpose formed by the rich man was not of necessity a covetous one. True, he might, as one of the Fathers suggests, have made barns of the houses of the poor, the mouths of orphans and widows. But these are not the only lawful storehouses. Men may accumulate, may increase accumulations. We do right to broaden our plans, to tear down and build greater. All social and material progress would cease if this spirit of enterprise should be quenched. All improvements in our modes of travel, of business, of living, are results of this spirit, which grasps the significance of prosperity, wisely forecasts the future, and at critical junctures says, " I will tear down and build greater." It is a grand trait in man or nation, this of making large, bold plans for the future. Through it God is subduing the world. Nevertheless, be on your guard against this spirit. It can only be safely exercised under the most vigilant observation, lest we become selfish in our plans, making them centre in ourselves. This was the grand mistake which the rich man actually made, viz.: 4. The appropriation of his goods (ver. 19). Before, he had pressed the limit of innocency; now he passed it. This was more than a dangerous choice; it was a guilty one. It became manifest now that he had long been suffering his sense of accountability to decline; it had died out; and, with atheistic hardihood, he erased the name of God in the deeds and bonds, and substituted his own. Such a process may have with us a similar result. III. THE FOLLY OF THE COVETOUS MAN AS SEEN IN HIS FATE. He made at least three fatal mistakes : 1. He assumed that what we have is ours. This is not the reasonable or the natural view of property. The parable of the pounds is intelligible to children. The conception it presents, viz., that we hold our property in trust, is agreeable to our natural conviction. 2. That the soul is richer the more goods one has (ver. 19). " Soul, thou hast much goods." We shrink from the coarse suggestion that a man's life consists in his goods. But may it not consist in the abundance of his goods? No. Possessions are not life; cannot give it, cannot sustain it. It is true for every human being. Young man, or woman, seeking possessions and not life—you who have gained a little of earth's treasure, and are setting your heart upon it unawares—remember, oh, remember ! that possessions are not life. This house, this stock, this land are not your life. Remember that you may make these things your life. They may become *you* by an unconscious process of transfer. Are your goods you ? Consider. Subtract from your thoughts, your imagination, your affections, your purposes, your property, what will be left ? Will your very life be gone? Will it make no substantial difference ? Will you be rich toward God ? 3. The rich man assumed that he could reckon on the future. This was a terrible mistake : God waked him from it. He stands transfixed. He listens to the terrible voice: " Thou fool, this night thy soul shall be required of thee." " This night." Can it be? In the very midst of his hopes and plans, with the barns unbuilt, the fields unreaped, the figs untasted ?

May he die to-night? **Is it** fixed? Must he die to-night? Can it be possible that with his fortune secured his life is insecure; not merely that, is doomed? Whether he lies down upon his bed, or sits and watches, with all the house alight, or flees from God, will death come to-night? And to-morrow morning will they be whispering, "He is dead"? Will another master stand here in the dewy field and see the skimming swallow, and hear the droning bee? Will all his wealth be another's to-morrow? Will another build the barns, another store and spend the harvest? Who was this fool? May it be you? Among the human remains exhumed at Pompeii are those of a woman laden with treasure, hastily seized and still hugged tightly in her arms. She was evidently caught on the very threshold of her own dwelling by the avalanche of ashes. Her sudden fright remains upon her face, indelibly printed there, an awful suggestion of the horrors of the unexampled tragedy. What figure could more fitly illustrate our Saviour's warning! Well might it be placed in every square of the city, with mutely eloquent dissuasion, to admonish us of the danger of a covetous love of this world. Look upon this ill-fated woman. Look upon the rich fool. Listen to the Saviour's words. Take heed, and beware of covetousness. (*G. R. Leavitt.*) *The rich fool :*—Of this man nothing ill is actually said, nothing bad really appears. If we look at him as he is described, it is hard to say how he was worse than most of us. It is true that he spoke overmuch of *my* this and *my* that: "I have no room," he said, "to bestow *my* fruits; I will pull down *my* barns, and build greater, and there will I bestow all *my* fruits and *my* goods." But do we not all do the same? The crops which have rewarded long toil, the profits yielded to patient enterprize, the little hoard painfully earned and saved, do we not call them ours, and think them ours too? Do we not talk of *our* corn, of *our* earnings, of *our* balance in the bank—and this not merely for convenience of speech, but because we regard ourselves as the actual independent owners of them? Do we not very generally forget that, in truth, all that we have is not ours, but God's—lent to us by Him, that part may be given back directly for His service, that the rest may be profitably spent to His glory, and that all may be given account of at the last day? It is true, also, that he spoke too rashly of the future, as if that also were his own: "I will pull down my barns, and build greater"; and yet more, "Soul, thou hast much goods laid up for many years." But do not we for the most part do the same? When things have prospered with us, when our returns come in, do not we too make pleasant plans, and promise ourselves so much ease, so much enjoyment for the future? Do we not make promise to ourselves of building this new house or setting up that new carriage, of taking a pleasant journey here, or making a happy home there, and have no thought of God in it all? Yea; and though we should add a D.V. or a "God willing" to it, is it not generally a mere pretence of submission—as much as to say, we are aware that He can prevent it, if He chooses, but we do not at all suppose He will? Again, it is true that the man was profane in addressing such words as he did to his soul: "Soul, thou hast much goods laid up for many years; eat, drink, and be merry." Souls do not eat or drink, neither can they rest and enjoy themselves on the strength of so many hundreds a year, and when he used the word it should have reminded him that the higher part of his nature required other and better provision for the many years to come. But no doubt he spoke ignorantly, meaning only to address himself, and regarding himself on the whole as a being whose chief end was to eat and drink and amuse himself—as an organization mainly capable of enjoying meats and drinks, of welcoming cessation from toil, and of delighting in the good things of this world. Have we, as a rule, attained any higher view? Do not we, with far less excuse than he, commonly speak and think of ourselves as if we lived and moved and had our being in the things of this life—as if eating and drinking, ease and merriment, were sufficient to satisfy us? Or, if we rise above these things, do we not seek others equally inappropriate to the true life of the soul—intellectual delights, social pleasures, high positions—gifts of civilization to our modern days, good and noble in their way, but transitory, earthly, and therefore incapable of sustaining those immortal souls, which can only be filled with the love of God, which can be satisfied with nothing less than Him. "Soul," we say to ourselves, "thou art very well off; the world hath gone well with thee; thou hast enough and to spare; thou hast no cause to envy anybody, while many have reason to envy thee; thou hast done well, and art decidedly to be congratulated." This is no untrue fancy, as your heart and mind know well: thus does the soul whisper to itself, as it surveys its position; thus does it speak, and thus does God answer it—"Fool, fool that thou art, with all thy silly self-complacency and self-satisfaction; fool, with all thy worldly wisdom and temporal success; fool, with thy well-dressed person and well-filled purse, with thy well-furnished house and well-stored mind; fool, that congratulatest thyself on the possession of these things, and rememberest not that they must perish in an hour, and that thou hast nothing else." "Fool"—it is God that says it, not I; it is His verdict on me, just as much as on you, when I begin to glory in earthly things. He *is* a fool that takes comfort in a well-fed body while his soul is starving, that regards with satisfaction his well-dressed person while his soul is still unclad in righteousness, that gazes with complacency upon the length and richness of his rent-roll while his tale of good works remains short and poor, that prides himself on the beauty of his earthly habitation while he is preparing for himself no goodly mansion in the world to come,—a fool, in short, who suns himself in the momentary warmth and sunshine of to-day, and recks not of the eternal darkness which must begin for him to-morrow. It may be that we are all fools together, minding earthly things out of all reasonable proportion to the heavenly things. If so, let us endure to be convicted of folly now, that we be not branded as fools before the universe; let us accept the rebuke now, while our souls are our own, lest we meet with it then, when they shall be demanded of us. (*R. Winterbotham, M.A.*) *The rich fool:—* 1. He was a fool, because he gave not God the glory. 2. He was a fool in God's account, for the use he intended to make of his possessions. 3. He was a fool, because he confounded body and soul together. 4. He was a fool chiefly in this—that he so confidently and surely reckoned on many years to come. (*E. Blencowe, M.A.*) *The folly of worldly men:—*I. Consider THE THINGS WHICH THEY REFUSE. 1. The things which they refuse are of inconceivable value, the very best things of heaven and earth; things did I say? consider what is comprehended in them, viz., God the chief good to be their God, and Jesus Christ; they refuse Him, an interest in Him; they see nothing in Him to desire Him; and now doth not this show them fools? They know not what is good, know not how to choose, they discern not a precious pearl from a worthless pebble. 2. They refuse incorruptible things, such riches that are durable treasure that neither moth nor rust can corrupt. 3. They refuse (though they are ready to perish with hunger) that which is bread, nay, Bread of Life, most rare, sweet, delicious, and soul-nourishing, fattening and satisfying Bread, and all else that is good and proper food for their souls; which except they eat of they must die and perish for ever; and doth not this show they are fools? 4. They count those things not worth one serious thought or regard, which all that were truly wise esteemed above all the treasures, riches, and glory of the whole world; nay, more worth than ten thousand worlds. Secondly, Let us consider what things they are which worldly men choose, and the nature of them, instead of those things, or before those things which they refuse. 1. They choose things unlawful, or such things that are forbidden, and in their choice incur the wrath and displeasure of God, and are thereby proclaimed enemies and rebels, and such that God's soul abhors, for by an inordinate love of riches they are idolators: and the covetous God abhorreth. 2. They choose such things that are the portion of reprobates. My brethren, God gives the riches of this world to his enemies, and to such who have their portion in this life, to whom He denies His choicest and chiefest blessings and favours. 3. They are corruptible things, things which perish in the using, things also that are uncertain. 4. They choose the riches, pleasures, and grandeur of this world, which ruin the souls of all trust in them, or set their hearts upon them. The world, in its riches, is a cruel enemy to poor mortals, and such who over-prize them do but hug a viper or serpent in their bosoms, and is not this one article of our faith, that the world (as well as the flesh and the devil) is a mortal enemy to the soul? What, harbour a thief, a treacherous and cruel murderer, in our house, who will soon, if not overcome, lay all the family in their blood, and dead at his foot! what folly greater than this! Ah! how many thousands are now in hell, that the love of this world sent thither, or brought eternal ruin upon. 5. The things wicked rich men choose are but mere vanity or a shadow. "Vanity of vanity, all things are vanity" (Eccl. i. 2); not vain, but vanity in the abstract, the worst of vanities, and therefore no folly greater than to esteem the riches of this world as a man's best and chiefest happiness; they weary themselves for very vanity; should you see a man pursue, or run after, and strive to catch or take hold of a shadow, would you not say he was a lunatic, or a natural, or mere fool? Such fools are the rich men of this world. Moreover, empty things that cannot satisfy, gold and silver can satisfy no man: "He that coveteth silver shall not be satisfied with silver, nor he that loveth abundance with increase, this is also vanity" (Eccl. **v.** 10). This shows his folly; he hath abundance, and yet desires more as if he had nothing, and is never content and satisfied with what he hath, and yet counts these things the best of all good; which shows he is a fool. 6. The love of riches is the root of all evil; and such "that will be rich fall into temptations and a snare, and into many foolish and hurtful lusts, which drown men in destruction and perdition" (1 Tim. vi. 9). Now if such are the nature and dreadful effects that attend riches, what fools are they that set their hearts upon them! They do but "heap up treasure against the last day" (James v. 3), or treasure up wrath and Divine vengeance. (*B. Keach.*)　　*Unsanctified riches:*—I. The circumstances in which he was placed. 1. That riches, with their attendant comforts and influence, are to be regarded as the bestowments of Providence; not to be considered as the recompence of independent human effort, but ever subject to the superintendence and arrangement of Him who is the author of every good and perfect gift. 2. That riches, with their attendant comforts and influence, furnish means for extended usefulness, and place in the hands of the possessor a power which he should employ in promoting the temporal and the spiritual welfare of his fellowmen. 3. That riches, with their attendant comforts and influence, involve the pressure of a solemn responsibility. They are granted, on a principle of stewardship, and with an obligation to account. II. The meditations in which he indulged. 1. Imperfection and sin existed in the state of his mind as to the source of his possessions. There is no allusion to God, as the giver of the good in which he delighted; there is no acknowledgment of dependence, there is no aspiration of gratitude. He looks with complacency on the amount of his possessions; and then, in the inflation of vanity, and in the calculating spirit of worldly wisdom, he proceeds to arrange his plans, as if perfectly independent of all obligations and of all responsibility to a superior Being. 2. Imperfection and sin existed in the intended application of property. A portion of his wealth was to be expended in enlarging his accommodations, and then his possessions were to be accumulated in one vast hoard, to remain in the treasure-house untouched, except for the purpose of securing some additional advantage. Ought there not to have been some act of charity to man, or some gift to the temple of God? 3. Imperfection and sin existed in the mode of calculating on futurity. The rich man, you will perceive, assumed, with a strong and an undoubting confidence, that no event would happen, to interfere with the accomplishment of his plans, and that he should possess a long period of existence, and of happiness. 4. Imperfection and sin existed in the nature of desired and anticipated enjoyment. "Take thine ease; eat, drink, and be merry." The guilt connected with the intention thus expressed as to the pleasure of future life, is twofold. First there is indicated a fondness for indulgences, in themselves utterly unworthy of the intellectual nature with which man is endowed; and secondly, there is a careful and an entire exclusion of all that belongs to the interests and redemption of the soul. III. The reproof by which he was arrested. 1. As to the event announced in the message of God—how momentous! "Thy soul shall be required of thee." It comprehends his removal from the substance on which he had doated. His toil, his scheming, his rising early, his sitting up late, his eating the bread of carefulness, were now to end, and to be discovered as having been rendered in vain. 2. As to the time when this event was to be fulfilled—how soon it was to come!—"This night!" Almost as soon as he had uttered his grovelling dreamings, was his last change to be undergone. It was a brief space indeed! The poison of death was circulating rapidly within him; the shadows of the evening portended the deeper darkness of the grave; and ere another sun arose, his destiny would be sealed. (*J. Parsons.*)　　*The folly of the worldly man:*—I. The character of a worldly man. 1. He makes the pursuit of the world his chief business. (1) Sacrificing to it the duties of religion. (2) Pursuing it merely for his own gratification, and not for the glory of God. 2. He finds in this world his chief happiness. 3. He sets upon the world his chief affections. II. Every such man, Christ says, is a fool. 1. He gives up certainty for uncertainty. The world is most uncertain in its (1) attainment; (2) retainment. 2. He prefers his body to his soul. The body is the casket which encloses the precious immortal jewel—the soul which God has given us. Now, suppose any man, having an exceedingly precious jewel enclosed in a casket, bestowed all his care on the casket, watched over it day and night, regularly went to see that it was secure, but allowed the jewel to be a plaything to his children, would he not be a fool indeed? 3. He prefers time to eternity. (*John M'Lean.*)　　*The sinner summoned:*—I. The first thing to be remarked in the text is the expression "thou fool." This pattern of a worldly-minded man is called a fool on many accounts. 1. He abused the leisure given him for studying the nature of heavenly wealth. 2. Again, whereas the plentifulness of his stores should have set his heart entirely at rest about all such worldly matters, he was perplexed concerning the manner of bestowing his goods; he vexed his mind about room for his fruits; when he had doubtless many poor neighbours whom he might have fed out of his abundance. He determined to pull down his barns, and build greater, when he should rather have been employed in pulling down the worldly vanity of his heart, in rooting out his sins, and building up the hope of his salvation on the foundation of Jesus Christ. And still more on these accounts he is justly called a fool. 3. But above all other reasons, he is called a fool, because he reckoned, with such unfounded security, on the continuance of a long life. II. Observe, in the second place, HOW SUDDEN IS THE SUMMONS! HOW IMMEDIATELY THE FOOLISH LOVER OF THIS WORLD IS REQUIRED TO LEAVE HIS GOODS AND POSSESSIONS, AND TO YIELD UP HIS SOUL TO JUDGMENT. "This night." The summons does not say to-morrow. That word, with which he had doubtless put off many a good resolution, is not now spoken to himself. What would he give now for one of those many hundreds of days which he once wasted in thoughtless indolence! III. THE PARTICULAR SEASON OF THE SUMMONS IS NO LESS REMARKABLE THAN ITS SUDDENNESS. "This night." He is called away, not in the light of day, but in the darkness and gloom of night. IV. CONSIDER WHAT WAS REQUIRED OF THIS UNHAPPY MAN. Not his goods and fruits, he had better never have hoarded them. Not his spacious barns, he had better never have built them. Not his worldly accomplishments, they are now of no value. All these things in which he once took such delight and pride, all these if he used them not to God's glory, how glad would he be now, had he never had them. The memorial of their possession must accompany him to judgment; and they are not what will be there required. No, it is his soul. (*C. Girdlestone, M.A.*) *The last night:*—1. This man's exit from the world was in strong contrast with his life. When visitors came to that house, the master, no doubt, would take them out, and say, "There are twenty acres of grain; ten acres of corn; fifteen acres of grove. See those sheep down in that valley. See those cattle on that hill. All mine! Come and look at those fig-trees. There are some figs ripe. Help yourself. Plenty of them. See how those grape-vines thrive—and these pomegranates!" Abundance of everything. Plenty to eat, plenty to wear, and plenty to congratulate. Yet, amid all that, he dies! How impudent death is! 2. The man of the text made sudden exit. So removal from this world is always sudden. I have heard of rare cases where persons said, "Such a day of such a month will be my last," and it was so. But the man of the text was not more amazed than most people. Even the most confirmed invalids expect to get well. They expect some new effect of medicines, or a new style of doctor, or a change of climate will help them. It is while men are calculating on long days that that decisive hour comes—while they are expecting an enlargement of business accommodations, or are getting in their crops, or are trying to draught a new barn—suddenly! And why not? Hold that glass of exquisite ware, and let it drop on the pavement. How long does it take to shiver it? Wonder not that the delicate bowl of life was broken at the fountain. Our life is of such delicate mechanism, so finely poised, so hair-strung, that the least collision is fatal. The wonder is that, with such exquisite machinery, the pivots do not oftener slip, and the spring break, and all the works instantly crash. The vast majority of the race go out of this life without a physical pang. They flash away. You cannot calculate the brevity of the time between when the arrow leaves the bow and when it strikes the target. A minister of Scotland, at breakfast, asked for something more to eat, and a child started to get it, but he cried out, "Hold! hold! my Master calleth me. I have breakfasted with you, and shall sup with my Lord Jesus to-night." And as quick as that he was gone. The rail train rushes along towards Norwalk bridge. The draw is off. Down the train plunges. In Wales, a miner, not aware of the foul air of the mine, strikes a match. Instantly two hundred souls are in eternity. 3. It was night when the man of the text went. So it is night when most of the race depart. A vast majority of the race die between eleven and three o'clock at night. There seems something in the atmosphere at that time to loosen the grasp of body and soul. Nearly all my friends have gone away in the night. The most of those who die by accident die in the night, because then the impediment on the track is not seen. Then it is that the flame gets headway before it is discovered. Then the burglar and the assassin are assisted by the darkness. The first-born of Egypt perished in the night. Sennacherib's host fell in the night. 4. But the most remarkable thing about the exit was that he was unprepared for it. It was not a lack of brain that kept him in unpreparedness. A man who could make money as fast as he could was not lacking in sharpness. He knew what to plant, and how to culture what he had planted. He was not one of the dead-and-alive men who make no progress. His barns were large enough before, but they are too small now, with crops all the time growing. He was what Americans would call "smart," and what the English would call " clever." Now a man who knows enough to do business, knows enough to save his soul. All of the idiots will be saved at last. He was not an idiot. But alas! how many men are wise for time, and foolish for eternity! They know enough, when they sell a thing, to get the worth of it, but they barter away an immortal soul for nothing. They have everything insured but their souls. They are careful to have all their titles good except that for heaven. (*Dr. Talmage.*) *The rich fool:*—I. The parable first invites to some remarks upon WORLDLY PROSPERITY, AND SOME OF THE ANXIETIES BY WHICH IT IS NOT UNFREQUENTLY ATTENDED. " The ground of a certain rich man brought forth plentifully," the parable begins. " The ground"; the man did not owe his wealth to any success in commercial adventures, to a judicious plying of his business in the great waters, or to any of those forms of rising in the world which too often lead men to give their own skill all the praise. Not that in regard of our obligation to the Giver of all good it makes any difference whether our wealth come to us in one way or in another—by the blessing of God upon our industry, or in the gift of God in the sunshine and in the shower—for every way it is true that " the Lord thy God, He it is that giveth thee power to get wealth." Still, I think, it does lay an added weight upon our gratitude, and should make the sense of debt and dependence to be felt more keenly, when God prospers almost without making use of our own exertions at all. As when we come into possession of a fruitful land, or succeed to a business already made to our hands; in such cases we feel the blessing comes to us so straight and direct from heaven, that the temptation to say, "my power and the might of my hand hath gotten me this wealth," is utterly taken away. Even the world allows us nothing to be proud of in such instances; we thrive upon the labours of those who have gone before, or perhaps upon a mere accident of the soil. " The ground of a certain rich man brought forth plentifully." But "a man's life consisteth not in the abundance of the things which he possesses"; the ground that brings forth plentifully is seldom free from some roots of bitterness. In the parable of the sower and the seed, our Lord makes cares and riches go together. And they do very often ; for with more wealth, we take more servants, and that is a care. The more treasure we have, the more fear of losing it; and that is a care. The larger the produce of our fields, the more room we want to put it away; and that is a care. II. Let us proceed to the second view of this parable, or that which sets before us SELFISHNESS AND ITS PROJECTS. The man's debatings were soon over, for he called to his counsels neither God nor man, seeing that for the glory of the one he had no concern, and with the wants of the other had no sympathy. He was a law unto himself, he had none to think of, and none to obey; his goods were his own, his length of days was his own, his very soul was his own; so at least he reasons, for this is the plan of life to which he tells us his mind is made up—"And he said, ' This will I do,'" &c. Many things press for notice here. First, his language, " my barns, my fruit, my goods," although agreeable to the common usage of men, yet taken in connection with what follows, is a plain ignoring of God's hand in his prosperity, or God's right in regard to its proper use. One would think he had been beholden to God for nothing; neither for seed nor soil, nor clouds, nor genial suns; so completely is the idea of stewardship lost sight of, and the Creator's loan viewed as the creature's right. Then, there is a strange and presumptuous covenant with the future—future harvests, that they shall not fail; future years, that he shall live to enjoy their fruits. They are the most obvious truths which men are most slow to learn—how feeble is our hold on prosperity—a blight, a shipwreck, a credulous trust in some new and fraudulent speculation, a dishonest servant, or a perfidious friend, let any of these befal us, and what becomes of our many goods? And many years—he has made sure of this also; he has entered into a covenant with sickness, and accident, and the marching pestilence, with the waters that they shall not overflow him, and with the flames that they shall not kindle upon him ; he had only not made a covenant with God. But, besides all this sinful bargaining for a long series of morrows, we should not fail to observe with what resolute intenseness and determination of purpose his heart is set upon the enjoyment of the world. " Soul, take thine ease. While my wealth was accumulating, and my diligence was needed, and there was a possibility that the tide of success might turn against me, I had my unavoidable anxieties; but I am past all this now, I am beyond the reach of reverses, hence-forth I will fling myself upon the soft lap of prosperity, and without an apprehen-sion or a care sleep the rest of life's hours away." " Soul, take thine ease "; eat, drink, and be merry too, steep the senses in a blithe forgetfulness, forbid the entrance of every intruding monitor who comes to tell you that you have an eter-nity to live for, or an offended God to meet. And then, observe that awful stroke of irony with which the Saviour makes the man address language like this to his soul—"Soul, thou hast much goods "—thou, the eternal, the changeless, thou who art sprung from a nobler ancestry than the angels, and fashioned in the mould of God, see here the portion I have provided for thee, meats that debase, drinks that stupefy, luxuries that sensualize—" eat, drink, and be merry." The world abounds with these epicurean Christians; who, instead of nourishing their souls with proper sustenance, with holy thoughts, with sacred joys, with hopes that centre in God and ambitions which point to heaven, turn God's image into dust again, and try to satisfy the cravings of an immortal mind with ashes, with wind, with meats, and drinks, and mirth. " Soul, thou hast much goods, take thine ease." III. But the parable we have been considering takes its most solemnizing and striking form when we view it as setting forth GOD'S ARREST ON WORLDLY PRESUMP-TION AND THE RECOMPENSE THAT SHALL FOLLOW. The man's plans are formed; he is at agreement with death; he has pledged the seed-time and the harvest, and the couch is laid smooth on which his soul is to have many years of ease, when in a moment, in the twinkling of an eye, he finds all this baseless fabric crumbled to the dust. Let me conclude with two applications of our subject. The first, bearing on the duty of securing the true riches; and the other, on the turning of perishable riches to a wise and sanctified account. The first of these duties is set forth in one weighty and emphatic sentence by the Great Teacher Himself; may we all remember it, if we remember nothing else. " So is he that layeth up treasure for himself, but is not rich toward God." " So is he "; that is, as this man, with the fiat of heaven against him made out, the messengers of wrath half on their way, with just one short night between his soul and a wretched immortality. " So is he "; that is, so is every one who layeth up treasure for himself, comforts for himself, ease, mirth, worldly happiness for himself, while as to the true riches he is a mere beggar, for he is not rich towards God; has not provided himself with bags that wax not old, has no treasure laid up there, where no rust nor moth can corrupt, and where theives do not break through and steal. But the parable also suggests a caution as to the right use of perishable riches; the duty of making them subser-vient to the highest ends, and the certainty that sooner or later they will be taken from us, if we spend upon self or upon self's fancied wants that which God designed either for advancing His own glory or for mitigating the sufferings of mankind. (D. Moore, M.A.) Christ's portrait of folly:—I. GODLESSNESS IS FOLLY. The conversation between this man's soul and himself shows the bent and make of his mind. There was no room for God in his plan of life. His godlessness was very bad in him, for he was a successful Jewish farmer. As a Jew, he had drunk in the name of God with his mother's milk. His one book was full of the great name, and every one around him believed in God. The Temple, the Sabbath, and a thousand things besides were always speaking to him of God. But though a Jew, he was a perfect heathen at heart. He did not profess to be an atheist, yet he lived the atheist's life. A thoughtful farmer in Palestine was like the islander who said, " Other people may forget God, but the St. Kilda man never can." In no other country are the crops so plainly in God's hands. The wind, the rain, and the locusts every year make them a success or a failure. His plains waving with God's great bounty should have melted his heart. Strange that to receive a blessing often and regularly makes a man unmindful of God. Every plan of life is folly in which God is not first, midst, and last. Without this, all other wisdom is vain. He only is wise who begins, carries forward, and ends all in and with God. II. GREED IS FOLLY. This rich farmer was very greedy, and his greed was of the meanest kind, and had no excuse. For he was rich, and growing richer, and embarrassed with riches, and in that genial climate and simple age he needed little money. His was greed without need. He was a mere money-maker, and the slave of the money he possessed. His wealth was like a glacier in midwinter, which feeds no river and gladdens no valley. His soul died of self-love. His is the most perfect and vulgar selfishness, the meanest of all the vices. His greed for money was like the greed of the drunkard, whose drinking puts an end to the drinker, but not to his thirst. Like a wild beast, he will retire into his own corner and gorge himself. All need this warning against greed. But there is a greed which can never grow too great. Every child of the kingdom is a child of boundless desire. " Blessed are they that hunger and thirst." You may pull down the barns of your knowledge and love, and build greater without blame. III. To MISTAKE HAPPINESS IS FOLLY. He thought that bigger and fuller barns would make him happy. His full barns were a paradise for mice, but not for men. 1. Length of life cannot be secured by riches. The farmer could lay up goods enough in his barn for many years, but not years enough for the enjoyment of his goods. A French writer says that most successful merchants die about the time when the paint is drying in the splendid villas in which they were hoping to find their ease. Wealth cannot buy an extra hour. " Millions of money for a minute of time," was the vain offer of England's dying Queen. All history shows that men and nations perish from plenty rather than from poverty. 2. A man's happiness, the life of life, does not consist in the abundance of riches. Bigger barns don't give fuller life. 3. The eternal life does not consist in plenty of earthly goods. A golden key cannot open the gate of heaven. The treasures of grace are as free to the beggar as to any man under heaven. IV. To FORGET THE FUTURE IS FOLLY. The great Greek writers often picture the rich man. His heart grows haughty and he forgets God. He then becomes an eyesore to heaven ; he must be abased ; and a certain train is laid for his destruction. At last a thunderbolt, without any sign of its coming, leaps out of the blue sky and strikes him down. Such a fate overtook this poor rich man. He forgot the uncertainty of time and the certainty of eternity. The words, " This night," startle and solemnize us. His soul is required of him as a trust or deposit which he had abused, and it is taken from him by main force. His life was an utter failure. It was like a well-carved stair, "ascending, winding, leading up to nought," and good for nothing. True wisdom takes in the whole of our life in time and eternity. It chooses the life that lives and fashions the everlasting man and woman. As eternity is greater than time, faith is the highest wisdom. How different from this rich man's is the death of one whom Christ has made wise unto salvation, even when the death-sickness comes as suddenly as the summons came to him. A little boy was laid down with cholera. The minister visiting him paused at the cottage door, for he heard the voice of prayer. The dying boy repeated the Lord's Prayer, and then added, " Now I am ready, Lord." (*J. Wells, M.A.*)　　*Self the wrong centre :*—My fruits, and *my* goods, and *my* soul, and *my* barns. That is all wrong. He has narrowed down things to a point. He has made himself the centre of reckoning; he has constituted his own individuality into the standard of life. But surely a man may say "my soul"? No. Only in a secondary sense, at least, may he say that. "For all souls are Mine," saith the Lord. The fundamental error in life is that a man should call himself his own. And until that deadly, fatal reasoning is driven out of him, he will never take hold of life by the right end. The discussion is not, "Is what I have in my hand my property or not?" My friend, your hand itself is not your own. Why, then, be wasting your life in some little peddling debate about what you hold in your hand? No man can live wisely, deeply, truly, until he has got out of the notion that he is his own property. Herein is the great mystery of the Christian faith: Ye are not your own; ye are bought, ye belong to another. Glorify God in your body and your spirit, which are God's. I do not, therefore, follow a man into any debate, when he says, " My barns, my fruits, my goods." I let him chatter on; but when he says, "My soul," I arrest him! He may fight all day long about his barns and his fruits and his goods, and no useful result would testify to our wordy debate. But if I can convince a man that his soul is not his own, except in a secondary sense; that it is God's; that it is a bought soul; and that it must take its law and its way from the utterances of God—I shall have brought the man to the right point from which to start all the courses and all the discipline of his life. Is not selfishness at the root of all evil? Is not a man little in proportion as he debates everything in the light of his own personality? (*J. Parker, D.D.*)　　"*Thou fool*" :—Why use this expression? The man was very wise, on one side of his nature. So many of us are clever in little points ! So many people are prudent and sagacious and wise in one aspect of their nature, and are utter and irredeemable fools in others. If the light that is in us be darkness, how great is that darkness ! Few men are foolish altogether. The man in the parable talked wisely up to a given moment, and from that time he went down into the utterest and worst imbecility. What does God say? "This night." God sometimes gives but short notice to His tenants. (*Ibid.*) "*This night*":—The man had forgotten the nights! He talked about years in whole numbers; about the bright spaces called day; but did not think of those black lines called night. Between to-day and to-morrow there rolls the black night-river, and we may fall into it, and never step on the shore of the morning. " Whatsoever thy hand findeth to do, do it with all thy might." (*Ibid.*) *Worldly things to be used gratefully :*—Make your ground bring forth plentifully; be the best farmers in the neighbourhood; be successful in all kinds of business or profession; and, if you possibly can, rise to the very top of the line along which you are working. But all the while hold all these things loosely; hold them in a spirit of stewardship. Then you will hold them rightly, and when God says, " Let go ! " it will be but a step into heaven! The only things we can carry out of this world are our thoughts, our feelings, our impulses, our desires—all the elements which make us spiritual men, and invest us with moral character. We take out of this world our moral and spiritual condition, and as the tree falleth, so must it lie ! What, then, do I find wanting in the speech of the foolish man? I find no grateful heart in it all. The man never blessed his banquet in the name of God. Not a word do I hear to this effect: " God hath dealt bountifully with me; praise God from whom all blessings flow. He hath put all these things into my care; He hath entrusted me with all this large estate that I may administer it in His name. Lord, teach me how to use it, so that not one crumb be wasted, but that the whole be so ordered and dispensed as to bring honour to Thy name, and satisfaction and gladness to Thy children that are round about me." He doubles his enjoyment of worldly things, who uses them gratefully; he drinks the best wine, who drinks out of the goblet of thankfulness; he has most who gives most; and he grows most truly, who, for Christ's sake, expends himself for the good of others most fully. (*Ibid.*) "*To-night I shall want you !* " And we cannot say Him, No. You may say No to your best friend; you can refuse the invitation of your most importunate associate; but when God says, " I shall want you to-night," you cannot write a note of excuse ! When God says, " Thy soul shall be required of thee to-night," you cannot say, " Lord, let it stand over for a week." See, then, our weakness, as well as our strength; and know this, oh man, as a matter of dead certainty, whatever our religious faith may be, though we are the vilest, vulgarest, and most stubborn atheists, that we cannot escape the final day—the great deed—the deed of death ! (*Ibid.*) *How, then, am I to become prepared for the last great scene?*—As a wise man, I think I shall be doing right in turning this over in my mind, and making some reflections upon it; and thus have I resolved, by the strength and grace of God to do, now that the year is closing round me and bidding me farewell : "I will put my confidence in God—in God as revealed in the person and ministry of Jesus Christ; in God as known to me through the Cross, as the one Saviour; God the Son, who loved me and gave Himself for me. I will walk in the way of God's commandments, and I will diligently study His precepts; I will make His Book the man of my counsel and the light of my way. All that I can do I shall do according to the strength He gives me, and I will praise Him for the power with which He may invest my life. This I will do; and I think it is the right thing." (*Ibid.*) *Prosperity to be distributed :*—When God's goodness was showered upon him in such abundance, he should have opened his treasures and permitted them to flow: for this end his riches had been bestowed upon him. When rain from heaven has filled a basin on the mountain-top, the reservoir overflows, and so sends down a stream to refresh the valley below; it is for similar purposes that God in His providential government fills the cup of those who stand on the high places of the earth—that they may distribute the blessing among those who occupy a lower place in the scale of prosperity. But self was this man's pole star : he cared for himself, and for none besides. Self was his god; for to please himself was practically the chief end of his existence. (*W. Arnot.*) *The method of reserving all for self is as unsuccessful as it is unamiable :*—The man who should hoard in his own granary all the corn of Egypt, could not eat more of it than a poor labourer —probably not so much. It is only a very small portion of their wealth that the rich can spend directly on their own personal comfort and pleasure : the remainder becomes, according to the character of the possessor, either a burden which he is compelled to bear, or a store whence he daily draws the luxury of doing good. (*Ibid.*) *Stewardship not ownership in property :*—Our stewardship and our dependence on God ought always to be silently, if not verbally, recognized. The captain talks of "*my* craft," but he knows that it is only entrusted to him for a season, and he returns it to its owners at the proper time. The soldier speaks of "*my* gun," but he knows that it is a government weapon, and is to be used in fighting the government's battles. So it is right to speak of "*my* money," "*my* possessions," provided God's supreme ownership is recognized. That was not how the rich man did in the parable. He grasped everything, recognized no higher ownership. He acted like the child who snatches the toy or the fruit thanklessly from the hand of its parent, and huddles it up in its pinafore lest some other should see and share the enjoyment. When the bubble is gained it bursts. Show the children how that is true, illustrating it from the common stories of Mazzini, Lord Chesterfield, Queen Elizabeth's death-bed, &c.; and make clear how all too eager seeking, whether for wealth or pleasure or fame, is overshadowed by God's calm judgment: "Thou fool." (*Sunday School Times.*)　　　*Material things cannot feed the soul:*—Do you suppose that a man can feed his soul in that way? Can a soul be fed with silver or gold? Can a soul be made merry because outward goods increase? How beggarly the conception! How stultified the man appears by this very address to himself! He proposed to feed that which was divine with that which was essentially animal. He had no holy thoughts, no merciful inclinations; he had no chastened and purified aspirations! he had no sweet and loving affections; he had nothing that was glorious in holiness, or beautiful in any wise. But, "O, my soul," said he, "take thine ease." How many men there are that try to quiet their souls. How many men there are that say to their uneasiness, "Why art thou disquieted in me, O my soul? Art thou not rich?" A man's soul rich because his pocket is rich! How many men say, "Oh, soul, what wilt thou? What have I not done for thee? Look abroad and behold the fields. They are all thine. Look upon all these harvests. They are thine. Glance up the mountain side, and measure all the stately trees thereon. All these things are thine, and all these mansions, and all these titles and bonds, and all this silver and gold." And the poor smothered soul says, "I will have none of them." The soul—has it a mouth? Can it eat, as a man's body can? The soul—is it a broker and exchanger of money? Does it love to hear the clink of gold and silver? Is that the soul? (*H. W. Beecher.*)　　　*Oriental ideas of enjoyment* :—"Eat, drink, and be merry," is the sum and substance of true Oriental enjoyment, as it generally appears among the rich. The covetous are not necessarily misers in self-indulgence; but how better does he know how to spend his money who has looked upon gain as the sole end of labour and thought? The poor scholar enjoys literature and grammatical disputes; the moderate people meet every evening at the coffee-houses, and take their *finjans* of coffee with their long pipes, and discuss politics or listen to the teller of romances; but the rich feast, with hired dancers and much mirth; sometimes even using the appliances of the old Roman glutton to multiply the enjoyments of their appetite and the capacity of their stomach. (*Sunday School Times.*)　　　**Thou fool.**—*The rich fool* :—I. THE SINFULNESS OF THE RICH MAN. Notice the remarkable fact that he addressed his *soul*, when forming his plan for a long course of selfishness. Now, what had the soul to do with the indulgencies and enjoyments which he thought his riches would procure? Is it the soul which eats? Is it the soul which drinks? Is it the soul which luxuriates in voluptuous ease? Had he addressed his body, and thus seemed forgetful or ignorant of its being immortal, we must have wondered at him less, and had thought him less degraded; but to confess that he had a soul, and then to speak to that soul as though it were material, a mere animal thing, with fleshly appetites and passions, this marked him, at the very outset, as the creature of sensuality; as though he knew no higher use of faculties which distinguished him from the brute, than to give a zest to gratifications which he had in common with the brute! But, nevertheless, there was truth in the address of the sensualist; he was not so mistaken as at first he may appear. He spake, indeed, to the soul as though he had reckoned it a part of the body, and thus seemed strangely to confound the corporeal and the spiritual; but was he actually guilty of an absurdity? With such a speech to make, ought he to have addressed himself exclusively to the body? Nay, he was more candid, rather than more ignorant, than the great mass of sensualists. Our accusation against men in general is, that they have made themselves all body. Through the corruption of human nature, and through the habits and practices of unrighteousness, the soul is so debased, and so surrenders the ascendency to the flesh, that man becomes as literally a mere animal, living only to gratify animal propensities, and looking not beyond the present scene of being, as though the immortal principle were extinguished, in place of dormant, and death were to be annihilation. We want to know whether, with the great body of unconverted men, it would virtually make much perceptible difference if they had no souls. What is there in their conduct which indicates the workings of an inextinguishable principle, or which would necessarily be much altered, if, in place of being inextinguishable, it were declared of this principle, that it should be quenched at death? So that the rich sensualist was not far wrong in speaking to his soul, as though it were his body. True, indeed, the soul could not literally eat, the soul could not literally drink ; but the soul might have no taste, no relish, for spiritual things, the whole man might be given up to corporeal indulgencies, and the soul might be in such subjection, such slavery, to the flesh, as to think of nothing but how to multiply its gratifications or to increase their intenseness. And the case is thoroughly the same, when a man is not given up to mere animal pleasures. But now we wish to point out another thing to you—that the very essence of idolatry is discernable in this address of the rich man to his soul. It may justly be said, that the rich man substituted his stores for God, put them in the place of God, or looked to them to do for him what God alone could do. Capital is to this man in the place of Divinity ; and he is virtually saying to his soul, not as the Christian ought to say, " Soul, thou hast a never-failing Guardian, who will be sure to provide for thee through the shifting scenes of life," but, as a worshipper of his own possessions might say—" Soul, thou hast much goods laid up for many years ; take thine ease, eat, drink, and be merry." But we do not suppose that we have even yet reached the extreme point of this rich man's offence. He must have greatly provoked God by his materialism, and probably still more by his idolatry, but it was to neither of these that God pointedly referred when He interfered in just judgment, and we therefore conclude that it was in another particular that the chief offence lay. And this particular seems to have been his reckoning on many years of life. If it had been his idolatry which had specially provoked retribution, it would probably have been on the immediate object of idolatry that vengeance would have descended. God might have said, " I will fatally blight thine harvest ; I will utterly burn up thy crops : where then will be thy sustenance, where thy boasted security against want ? " But the judgment is evidently directed against the insolent expectation of long life. The speech is virtually, " Thou hast assumed, or taken for granted, that thou hast many years to live, utterly forgetful that the times of every man are in My hand, and for this I will instantly visit thee. ' O fool ! this night thy soul shall be required of thee.' " The rich man is called a fool, and is upbraided as a fool, on the ground of his having supposed himself quite sure of life ; so that evidently the reckoning on the distance of death is given as what, more than anything else, had displeased God in his conduct. It is as though God could have borne yet longer with his voluptuousness, though he had actually confounded the material with the spiritual, and debased the soul into a mere slave to the flesh ; it is as though God could have borne yet longer with his idolatry, though he had substituted his own storehouses for a presiding Deity, and given to the hoarded corn all the confidence which should have been given to an ever-active providence ; but when he presumed to make sure of life, to reckon, not only that his goods would last many years, but that he should have many years in which to enjoy them, then it seems as if the provocation were complete, and vengeance could no longer be deferred. And there is evidently a peculiar invasion, as it were, of the prerogatives of God, whensoever a man calculates that death is yet distant. Life is that of which, even in appearance, no man can have a stock in hand. The life of to-morrow cannot be stored up to-day ; though, in a certain sense, the supply of to-morrow's wants may be, supposing that we live till to-morrow. There is not, therefore, that shadow of an excuse for reckoning on the prolongation of life, which there may be for reckoning on a provision for its wants. The man who has a large stock of corn shows himself indeed unmindful of the sovereignty of God, if he conclude that on that account he cannot live to be needy ; but he is infinitely outdone by another, who, because he believes himself in strong health, confidently concludes that he shall not soon die. We want very much to press this on your consideration. Every man who is not labouring earnestly to save the soul is reckoning on long life. We care not whether or not he acknowledge this to others, we care not whether or not he acknowledge it to himself : he may profess a thorough belief in the uncertainty of life, but the fact is that he makes sure of life, and the proof is that he takes no pains to secure his salvation. If he knew that he should die in a-week, if he knew that he should die in a month, he would not keep the next world out of sight, but would labour with all earnestness to prepare for the change which could not be deferred.　And what, then, can it be, but a secret persuasion that he shall not die in a week, or that he shall not die in a month, which makes him altogether neglectful of the soul's interests?　He would not be thus neglectful if persuaded that " in the midst of life we are in death," and it is fair to conclude that he is neglectful because not so persuaded, or rather because persuaded of precisely the reverse.　And the fearful thing is, that this very reckoning upon life, which men would hardly perhaps think of classing amongst their sins, may be the most offensive part of their conduct in the eye of the Almighty, and draw upon them the abbreviation of that life, and thus the loss of the expected opportunities of repentance and amendment.　A man determines that he will taste a little more pleasure, or accumulate a little more wealth, before attending to the high duties of religion. Now the great provocation may not be, as you might at first sight suppose, in the preference of worldly pleasure or worldly wealth to what is celestial and enduring, but in concluding that he shall have the time in which to eat or to drink or to gather in money.　God did not strike down the rich man whose history is before us, so much because he was a sensualist, as because he was a fool—a fool in making sure of life when there was nothing to assure him, and in reckoning on life as a fixed term when it is only held from moment to moment.　Oh ! how easy to overlook this ! how easy to keep out of sight the sin of reckoning upon life, whilst we are quite aware of the sin of mis-spending life !　(*H. Melvill, B.D.*) *A fool in God's sight :*—God did not call this man a fool because he looked well after his worldly interest.　So far as it appears, he was an honest, industrious, and enterprising man, who did not make his money by speculation or fraud, but in an honest way.　I don't know any occupation that is more honest than that of a farmer.　Up in the morning, whilst others lie in bed.　Active, persevering, and diligent, I dare say he looked sharply after his cattle and his men too ; but God did not find fault with the man for that, on the contrary, I find in this Bible that God applauds our being " diligent in business, fervent in spirit, serving the Lord," which means that we can serve the Lord as well in business as in devotion.　The Apostle Paul speaks plainly of those who want to eat without doing any work.　" If there be any man," says Paul, " who will not work, he shall starve ; and these things command and exhort, &c."　And Jesus always selects His disciples when they are busy.　We have a good many instances of Christ calling men to be His disciples ; but I challenge any present to point to one who was not busy.　One is draining fish ; another with his pen over his ear ; another making tents.　Christ calls men when they are busy ; Satan when they are idle.　Don't suppose, then, that God called this man a fool because he was busy in his worldly interests ; he who does not do so is worse than an infidel.　I. He called him a fool because he took no account of God.　We are told in this story, what the man thought within himself, and what he said within himself.　You will notice there is not a single whisper of God in the whole. God was not in all his thoughts.　David describes the fool as the man who says in his heart there is no God ; but David does not say, " the fool hath said with his lips."　There are many who say it in their hearts that have not the courage to do it with their lips, and I challenge the Holyoakes and the Bradlaughs, who deny God's being, to say that their understanding leads them to this conclusion ; it is the heart—" the fool hath said in his heart," not in his brain but in that rotten heart that hates what is holy.　And because this man lived as if there was no God, God calls him a fool.　II. Because he took no account of the people.　He never thought of anybody but himself—selfish to the backbone.　And the text describes him laying up a treasure for himself.　That little word "I," occurs six times—what *I* am to do.　I.	He had just one idea in his head, and not a very big one—to make himself as rich and as jolly as he could be.　He made a god of himself, and had not a thought of any living outside of himself.　Hoarding up from time to time, and all for number one.　Lest it be supposed we speak hardly of this man, let us admit that we all have a touch of this.　Some men are better at " raking than pitching," better at raking in than pitching out to other people.　What a fool is that man who does not make good use of his money when living.　He is like a hog, that is good for neither draught like the horse, nor for clothing like the sheep, nor for milk as the cow, nor for watch as the dog, but only, after he is dead, to be cut up and parcelled out amongst his friends ; and because he was such, God called him a fool.　III. Because he took no account of his own soul. In one sense he did, for he says, "Soul, thou hast much goods" ; but was not that just what showed what an outrageous fool he was; he thought his his immortal soul could subsist upon what money could bring—he was content with a mere brute existence. There is no greater folly than to suppose you can fill the soul with what satisfies the body. Your barns cannot hold what the soul demands any more than you can fill a wooden box with virtue. It was an old custom among the Romans, when at the bar and pleading as an idiot and not responsible (but many plead this, and have their senses), to place upon the table an apple and a nugget of gold—a beautiful tempting apple and a dull heavy golden nugget; if an utter idiot he was sure to seize the apple, if he had his senses he would touch the gold. Now the farmer, judged by this test, was a fool, for he chose the apple—not the imperishable treasure, but the short-lived pleasures of this world. Perhaps, we have some like this here to-day. You can scarce give a thought to the world that is to come. Every day in the week, Monday, Tuesday, and Wednesday, finds you immersed in business, all for this world, all for the poor dying body; and the more you get, the more impatient you are to get more, for prosperity is like salt water, the more you drink the thirstier you become. Some live only to get rich and pamper this poor dying body, but God says to you this afternoon, "Thou fool." IV. ONCE MORE, HE WAS A FOOL BECAUSE HE TOOK NO ACCOUNT OF ETERNITY. The idea of death never entered into his mind, only of enjoying what he had laid up. I ask any sensible man if this was not folly. Suppose you are about to go to New York, and you make provision for the distance to Liverpool and no farther; is that not folly? But this man had started on an everlasting journey, and all the preparation he made was for a few steps this side of the grave; he was struck down that night, as thousands have been since, and, doubtless, as some here to-night may be. Jesus never took a brush or painted a picture like this without meaning us to learn a solemn lesson from it. We are all ready to say what a fool that man was to take no account of these things. But, stay, hear what Jesus adds: So many are there "that layeth up treasure for himself and is not rich toward God." And this is the question with which I close now. Are you laying up treasure for this world, or are you rich towards God? Have you accepted the riches of God's grace in Christ Jesus, as a guilty sinner? Have you thrown yourself into the Saviour's arms, and found pardon and peace for your soul? My message to-night is, that if you have not, you are lost; believe in Him and you are saved. (*J. T. Davidson, D.D.*) *The rich fool*:—It is an awful thing to be a fool! When any other calamity befalls a man he is conscious of his misery. But the fool does not know that he is a fool. That one fact makes a lunatic asylum the most saddening place in the whole wide world. To see one in the form of man gathering sticks and stones about him, and believing that he has great possessions; or one in the form of woman bedecking herself with bits of ribbons and faded flowers, as if to attract your admiration, or aimlessly giggling—she knows not at whom; another nursing a doll; another crowned with a mock crown—it is more pitiable than to see them wild or moody, or than it is to visit a hospital. And to be truly wise—wise not in our own opinion, for the fool is that; not in the opinion of others, for "men will praise thee when thou doest well to thyself"; but in the judgment of One who can neither deceive nor be deceived,—can there be any greater blessedness attainable by man? How then shall we know whether we are fools or wise? Can there be a truer standard to test ourselves by than Christ's? How shall we know what His judgment of us would be? There is no better way of finding out than by looking at the cases with which He came in contact on earth, and seeing how He judged them. Here is one of those cases. In a parable He draws the picture of a man whom we would have called wise, and whom He calls "fool." How do I know that we would have called him wise? Because of what is not said and because of what is said about him. Nothing is said against him. Had he been an open sinner, Jesus would have told us, for that would have been the ground on which He called him a fool. As nothing is said against him, we are bound to assume that he was a moral, respectable, law-abiding Jew; a man in full communion with the Church of God on earth. And note, on the other hand, how much is positively said in his favour—fairly put down to his credit, to enable us to judge him aright. In the first place, he was rich. Now, there is a natural presumption in a man's favour when he is rich. If he has made the money himself, it is implied that at least he has been industrious, economical, prudent, capable of sacrificing the present to the future. All these are good qualities. They may not be the highest, but surely, as far as they go, they are good. If he has inherited the money, he has proved that he is able to take care of it, and that implies the possession of qualities good in their way also. Then the rich man in our parable had evidently gotten his riches in a legitimate way—not by cheating others, not even by speculation, or in any way at the expense of others; but from the soil, directly from the bounty of God. No way more honourable than this, all will admit. Again, we see in the man no boasting of his industry or skill; no foolish talking to others about his wealth; no indications of any rash action to be taken. We are simply told that when his great abundance came, through his ground bringing forth plentifully, "he thought within himself." Admirable! That is just what we would advise our friends to do in like circumstances. Fourthly, this man was not one of those penurious, close-fisted creatures, who are too mean to spend anything, even on the permanent improvement of their property. Many a farmer would have been content with the old barns, adding an unsightly addition perhaps, or building one new barn that would hold all his overplus. But this was a spirited, enterprising business man. He saw that the time had come for acting with energy, and he at once decided on doing so. He would pull down these old barns and build others that would hold all that the land was ever likely to yield. Lastly, he was not one of those restless, avaricious mortals who give themselves up to the sole task of increasing their store; who define "enough" as "a little more than what we have." Had he been one of those human beavers, he would have said, "I am on the high road to be a millionaire; I can buy out my neighbour on the right of me, and next year I shall buy out my neighbour on the left; and who knows but that I may die the owner of the whole county!" Such a thought never entered into this man's mind. He was satisfied with his portion, and he aimed now at dignified repose and enjoyment. "I will say to myself, 'Soul, thou hast much goods laid up for many years; eat, drink, be merry.'" Is it possible to avoid thinking well of such a man? How fairly Christ draws His picture! not prejudicing us against him, taking him at His own estimate, describing him in his own language. When such a man is in our community, how anxious we are to get him into our society and our congregation. He is one of your typical, solid, model men. And yet—the one only name that the living God gives to him is "Thou fool!" Why? The narrative supplies reasons enough for one who looks beneath the surface of things. He was a fool because he forgot—as most of us forget—and, in forgetting, he practically denied, the four great facts of life—God, his neighbour, his soul, and death. He forgot God. His language is "my goods," "my barns," "all my fruits and my goods." Very like the language we use, but that only shows that he is not alone in his practical atheism. There is no recognition of the Giver; no gratitude; no longing after Him who never wearies in His loving-kindness towards us. His very gifts hide Him from us. Instead of making us grateful they foster pride. They make us say or feel, "How wise, how strong, how industrious, how deserving we are!" And we—fools and blind—see Him not, who should be the object of all our love. He forgot his neighbour. This folly—common enough though it is—was more surprising than the former. A man who is accustomed to go entirely by his senses may think himself excusable for not seeing Him who is invisible. But how can he help seeing his neighbour? And, seeing him and his needs, what occasion was there to go to the expense of building new barns? Were there not barns enough ready made to his hand? What an honour God put upon him when He gave him the opportunity of taking His own place to those bereaved ones! God had built barns for him. He did not see them, poor man! The chance was given him of being as a god to the poor. He lost it, and he never got another chance. Was he not a fool? And yet what a countless number of followers he has! How many of us use our money, our intellectual power, our time, our education, our opportunities, as under law to God for our brothers, for the country, for the Church, for future generations, for the purifying, sweetening, ennobling of the life of the community? He forgot his soul. This is folly still more inexcusable. A man may say, "I cannot prove that there is a God." He may also say, "As for my neighbour, am I his keeper? Every man for himself!" But how is it possible to forget his own soul? And yet this forgetting or unbelief springs from the previous forms of unbelief. Deny God, and you will soon deny your neighbour; and then you are not far off from denying yourself. He that knows not God and man knows not himself. I do not wonder that such a man thought that when money was provided all had been provided. Inexcusable as it is, this has always been the common form of infidelity, and the form that brings the most certain nemesis. He forgot death. This was the crowning proof of folly. We have seen that a man may give reasons for forgetting God and his neighbour. And philosophers nowadays rather ridicule the idea of there being a soul or anything but matter in man. But even a philosopher can hardly deny that there is such a thing as death. The reality comes home to all of us. The old and the young are taken; the light of our eyes and the strength of our life. And death forces us to think. No matter how immersed we may be in the affairs of the world, it drags us away to a silent room, and forces us to look beyond the present and the visible. It opens a door, and shows us this little inch of time and sense girdled by the immensities and the eternities—

> " Now at my back I always hear
> Time's wingèd chariots, hurrying near,
> And yonder all before me lie
> Deserts of vast eternity."

And yet, inexcusable as the folly is, we are all guilty of it. In forgetting death we forget eternity, and what folly can be compared to that? (*Principal Grant.*) *God's interruption of the rich fool's soliloquy :*—I. THE INTRODUCTORY PREFACE. " But God said unto him." 1. God interrupts him. He speaks to him while he is speaking to himself. Thus it pleases the Lord to deal with men many times in such cases as these are: He graciously interposes Himself in their sinful courses, and in their vain projects, and in their foolish imaginations; He puts them out of their track; He lays a rub in their way; He will not suffer them to go on; He so sweetly guides and overrules them by the hand of His providence, that He prevents their commission of those sins which their hearts lust after, and in a manner takes them off. And happy were it with us if we would observe His dealings in this kind. God's interruptions are promotions. The more He hinders us, the more He puts us forward; and so we should make account. There cannot be a greater mercy than to be stopped and interrupted in sin, as there cannot be a greater judgment than not to observe this interruption. 2. God opposes or contradicts him in this his speech. (1) The rich man spake to himself by way of applause; God spake to him by way of reproach. (2) The rich man so spake to himself as that he did promise himself ease, and pleasure, and contentment; God so spake to him as that He threatened him with dissolution. (3) The rich man promised himself ease, and pleasure, and contentment for many years; God threatened him with dissolution that very night. (4) The rich man did appropriate all this provided peace, and comfort, and contentment to his own soul; God questioned who should have the things which he had provided. We see the opposition before us. II. THE DISGRACEFUL APPELLATION. " Thou fool." With men honesty is folly, and conscience is folly, and plain dealing is folly, and preaching is folly. These are foolishness with men; but they are not so with the Lord. God calls fool, as one that can judge of folly; God calls fool, as one that will punish folly. 1. Fools peremptorily conclude upon that which is uncertain. 2. Fools absolutely neglect that which is necessary. 3. Fools altogether prefer and provide for that which is superfluous. III. THE THREATENING TIDINGS. " This night thy soul shall be required of thee." 1. The punishment. Not the loss of his goods, but the loss of his soul. 2. God does not tell him who should do it; but, by a Hebraism, leaves it indefinite—" they." It is no matter to thee who. It may be these very goods of thine, it may be thy barns, it may be thy servants, it may be thy friends. 3. The manner of the execution. Thou shalt not give up thy soul unto them; they shall snatch it from thee, and take it away by force. 4. The time—" this night." It is not, as Jeremiah to Hananiah, Thou shalt die this year; nor is it, as Hosea of the revolting Israelites, A month shall devour them; nor is it as the Lord to Adam, Thou shalt die this day. But different from all these, it is *this night*. This *night*, in opposition to this day; not at noon, but, for greater horror, at night. *This* night, in opposition to another night; not to-morrow night, not the next night, nor the night after, but this very night, which follows thine applauding of thyself. IV. THE EXPOSTULATORY INFERENCE. " Then, whose shall those things be, which thou hast provided?" 1. They shall not be thine. A man's wealth lasts no longer than his life, neither has he longer comfort from it. (1) Seeing men have their wealth for no longer time than their lives, it concerns them then to enjoy it, and use it to the best advantage. There is a vanity and a curse which God has laid upon many men, that they shall be rich, and nothing the better for it. They are not the better for it here, because they do not use it; and they cannot be better for it hereafter, because the nature of the things will not permit it. They vex themselves to get their wealth, they vex them-selves to keep it, and yet have no comfort by it. Who would provide such things, as for which he should never be the better? (2) And again, let us then learn to provide for a better estate, to lay hold on eternal life, and to lay up in store for ourselves a good foundation against the time to come. 2. Thou shalt not know whose they shall be. The wealthiest man that is cannot be sure who shall be his heir. No man when he goes out of the world can tell whose his goods shall be; this is another affliction. For a man might be ready to say, " Though I shall not have the benefit myself, yet I shall leave them to those that shall, my children and my posterities after me "; nay, but, says God, "Thou knowest not whose they shall be"; neither whose, if ye take it numerically, for the particular individual persons ; nor whose, if ye take it qualitatively, for the nature and con-dition of the persons ; neither of these persons dost thou know. (*Thomas Horton, D.D.*) *An unexpected requisition :*—I. WHAT IS THE SOUL ? It is the real life, because—1. It is the seat of all life's motives. The soul uses intellect and will as hands and feet. It really does all that we consciously do. 2. It is the seat of all feelings. 3. It is the seat of all responsibility. 4. It is the only enduring part—immortal. II. THE SOUL REQUIRED. 1. Its motives exposed. No more conceal-ment from others, from ourselves. 2. Its feeling unchecked. Like an exposed nerve. 3. Its accounts audited. Engrossed in eternal records. 4. Its immortal character and destiny fixed. III. The man A FOOL, because he did not realize that—1. His soul was his real life. 2. His soul might at any moment be required of him. (*Anon.*) *The soul required :*—Not a gracious summons, but by force of an arrest. Painfully rendered up, to God's inexorable demands. Terrible angels, like pitiless exactors of tribute, shall seize thee. Not as a vessel, when the signal is given, joyfully lifts anchor and departs ; but torn by winds and dragged from its moorings. Death to the righteous comes as the dawning of the morn-ing (Amos v. 8), sinking to sleep (Acts vii. 60 ; 1 Thess. iv. 14); but to the wicked it is the approach of a tempestuous night (Job xxvii. 20). (*Van Doren.*) *Whose shall those things be which thou hast provided ?*—Ah, me ! if some of those wealthy men who have gone in recent years from this busy, bustling city into the world beyond, could come back for a moment, and see what fightings there have been over their fortunes; how the details of their own idiosyncrasies have been dragged out into the light, to prove, if possible, that they had not sense enough to make their wills ; how the most painful secrets of their lives have been proclaimed upon the housetop ; how the skeleton in their closet has been handled and laughed over by the profane and unfeeling crowd ; and how their sons and daughters and relations, out to the farthest limit of consanguinity, have wrangled over their por-tions—I think they would say within themselves, "What consummate fools we were to spend our days on earth in laying up treasures to be squandered thus in the courts, and to be quarrelled over by a hungry crowd, as wolves howl over carrion ! " And if they had to live again, they would try, I think, to be their own executors, and to use their possessions in a way that would bless the world and glorify their God. There has been, as I cannot help thinking, a grim irony in God's providence in cases like these ; and, as I read the reports of the surrogate's court from time to time, I am reminded of the words, "He that sitteth in the heavens shall laugh ; the Lord shall have them in derision." At all events, they prove conclusively the short-sightedness and folly of those whose sole delight in life was the adding of dollar to dollar. But a deeper thought is here suggested: "Whose shall those things be ? " Whose were they all along? They were God's, and should have been used for God. You remember, in that most glorious scene in David's glorious reign, when he brought out what he had gathered for the building of the temple, and consecrated it all to God, and his people willingly followed his example, he used these remarkable words, " All things come of Thee, and of Thine own have we given Thee; *for* we are strangers," &c. Mark the force of that " for " in this con-nection. Men come and go, but God is the immortal Owner of all things ; and in giving to Him of our possessions, we but give Him of His own. (*W. M. Taylor, D.D.*) *Presumption punished :*—A minister, who was visiting from house to house, met on his walk three young men with axes on their shoulders. He stopped and conversed with them. Two appeared somewhat serious ; the third, a gay, frank young man, replied, "You see, sir, that splendid white house on that farm yonder ? " " Yes." " Well, sir, that estate has been left to me by my uncle, and we are now going to do chopping in the woodland that belongs to it. There are some heavy debts on the estate which I must settle before the farm can be fully mine, and as soon as I have cleared it of these I mean to become a Christian." "Ah, young man," said the pastor. "beware! you may never see that day; while you are gaining the world you may lose your soul!" "I'll run the risk," said he, and they parted. The three young men went into the woods, and this daring procrastinator and another commenced felling a tree. A dry, heavy limb hung loosely in the top, and, as the tree was jarred by the successive strokes of the axe, it quitted its hold, and fell crashing through the branches on the head of the young heir, and stretched him on the ground a lifeless corpse! *A sudden call :*—Mr. Wilcox, in a sermon, mentions the following incident. A young man, in the vigour of health, with the fairest prospect of a long and prosperous life, was thrown from a vehicle, and conveyed to the nearest house in a state that excited instant and universal alarm for his safety. A physician was called. The first question of the wounded youth was, "Sir, must I die? must I die? deceive me not in this thing!" His firm tone and penetrating look demanded an honest reply. He was told he could not live more than an hour. He waked up, as it were, at once to a full sense of the dreadful reality. "Must I, then, go into eternity in an hour? Must I appear before my God and Judge in an hour? God knows that I have made no preparations for this event. I knew that impenitent youth were sometimes cut off thus suddenly, but it never entered my mind that I was to be one of the number. And now, what shall I do to be saved?" He was told that he must repent and believe on the Lord Jesus Christ. "But how shall I repent and believe? there is no time to explain the matter. Death will not wait for explanation. The work must be done. The whole business of an immortal being in this probationary life is now crowded into one short hour, and that is an hour of mental agony and distraction." Friends were weeping around, and running to and fro in the frenzy of grief. The poor sufferer, with a bosom heaving with emotion, and an eye gleaming with desperation, continued his cry of "What shall I do to be saved?" till, in less than an hour, his voice was hushed in the stillness of death. *Not ready for death :*—A woman was in the habit of attending the place of worship in which I preached, who occupied a seat on the stairs, and who was very tenacious of her sitting, not allowing any other person to occupy it. She was observed by her friends, who sought occasion to converse with her on the important subject of religion, but she was very shy and evasive. All they could extract from her was this appalling reply: "Oh, I shall only want five minutes' time when I am dying to cry for mercy; and I have no doubt God Almighty will give it me." It was in vain to remonstrate with the woman; this was always her reply. Time passed on. One day I was walking down the street, when a young woman ran up to me in a state of great agitation and excitement, exclaiming, "Oh, Mr. East, I have found you; do come to my mother, sir; come this minute, sir; she is dying, she is dying!" I hastened with her to the house, and was astonished to find in the dying sufferer the poor unhappy woman who had attended my place of worship. She was evidently expiring, but, turning her dying eyes towards me, she cried out, "Oh, Mr. East, I am lost, I am lost!" and expired. *The uncertainty of earthly things :*—I was travelling in the South lately, and a circumstance came to my knowledge, affectingly illustrative of the great uncertainty of the things of time. A gentleman, with great labour and perseverance, had secured for himself and his family a princely fortune, and built a fine house in the country. It was several years in preparing for his reception; and, after having got it finished, he purposed taking his family, and there enjoying himself, saying, as the man before us, "Soul, thou hast much goods laid up for many years; take thine ease, eat, drink, and be merry!" The mansion was prepared; and, no doubt, full of anticipation, with his family he went into it; but scarcely had they occupied it, when his wife was cut off by a stroke, two of his daughters were summoned into eternity, and, when I was there, three of them were confined to their chambers, in a state of entire helplessness, and utterly incapable of enjoying those good things which God in His providence had bestowed upon them! The old gentleman himself, however, had secured the pearl of great price; his heart, having discovered the vanity of the earth, had been raised to the things that are above, where Christ sitteth on God's right hand. It seemed to me a most striking illustration of the complete vanity and uncertainty of this world, and the consummate folly of any man giving up his interest in religion for the sake of anything which the world can yield. (*John M'Lean.*) *"And then" :*—"Oh, if I were lucky enough to call this estate mine, I should be a happy fellow," said a young man. "And then?" said a friend. "Why, then I'd pull down the old house, and build a palace, have lots of prime fellows round me, keep the best wines, and the finest horses and dogs in the country." "And then?" "Then I'd hunt, and ride, and smoke, and drink, and dance, and keep open house, and enjoy life gloriously." "And then?" "Why, then, I suppose, like other people, I should grow old, and not care so much for these things." "And then?" "Why, then, I suppose, in the course of nature I should leave all these pleasant things—and—well, yes—die!" "And then?" "Oh, bother your 'thens'! I must be off." Many years after, the friend was accosted with, "God bless you! I owe my happiness to you!" "How?" "By two words spoken in season long ago—'And then?'" *Selfishness unsatisfying :*—Of all that have tried the selfish experiment, let one come forth and say he has succeeded. He that has made gold his idol—has it satisfied him? He that has toiled in the fields of ambition—has he been repaid? He that has ransacked every theatre of sensual enjoyment—is he content? Can any answer in the affirmative? Not one. And when his conscience shall ask him, and ask it will, "Where are the hungry, whom you gave meat? The thirsty, whom you gave drink? The stranger, whom you sheltered? The naked, whom you clothed? The prisoned, whom you visited? The sick, whom you ministered unto?" How will he feel when he must answer, "I have done none of these things—I thought only for myself"? (*Dr. Johnson.*) *Death cannot be evaded :*—Carlyle, in his "History of the French Revolution," tells us of a Duke of Orleans who did not believe in death; so that when his secretary stumbled on the words, "The late King of Spain," he angrily demanded what he meant by it. The obsequious attendant replied, "My lord, it is a title which some of the kings of Spain have taken." In all this assembly I have not such a lunatic ; for you unanimously believe that the entire race of men await alike the inevitable hour. We know that all our paths, wind as they may, will lead to the grave. A certain king of France believed in death, but forbade that it should ever be mentioned in his presence. "And if," said he, "I at any time look pale, no courtier must dare, on pain of my displeasure, to mention it in my presence"; thus imitating the foolish ostrich, which, when pursued by the hunter, and utterly unable to escape, is said to hide its head in the sand, fancying that it is secure from the enemy which it cannot see. (*C. H. Spurgeon.*) *An agonizing question:*—At an early hour in the morning a few of the citizens of the town of G——— might have been seen hastening towards the depôt. A run of twenty minutes brings the dashing train to a bridge, sixty feet below which, as in a channel cut through the rock, runs the now swollen waters of Lee's Creek. The recent freshet had undermined one of the principal piers. There is a fearful crash, and, as the coaches fall through the awful space, one is heard to exclaim, "My God, where are we going?" Whether these words were uttered by lips devout or profane will probably never be known. A moment longer and the wreck is in flames, and so dreadful is the burning, that of the twelve or fifteen persons fatally involved, the charred remains of but few could be identified even by their friends. My God, where are we going? Reader, where are we going? We are going! Another incident in connection with this same railway disaster—for these are facts, as the writer has occasion to believe. Amid the wreck, some coin was spilled upon the floor of the broken car. As the fire progressed, one poor sordid soul was seen gathering the pieces of gold in his hand. Whether he escaped, or whether he was overtaken by the flames and perished grasping his treasure in his fist, we know not. (*The United Presbyterian.*) *A fool in God's sight :*—My text introduces us into a fine farm-house. The occupant has been wonderfully successful. He has not made his money by business dodges. He has never "cornered" anybody in stocks. He never lent money on a mortgage with the understanding that it might lie quiet for several years, and then, as soon as the mortgage was recorded, went down to begin foreclosure. He never got up a bogus company, sold the shares, and then backed out in time to save himself, leaving the widows and orphans in the lurch, wondering why there were no dividends. As far as I can tell, he was an honest, industrious, enterprising man. The crops were coming in. The mow and the granary were full, and the men and oxen tugged away at other loads. The matter was a great perplexity. After you have gone to the trouble to raise a crop, you want some place to put it. Enlargement is the word. I see him calculating, by the light of a torch, how much extension of room is needed. So many loads of corn, so many of wheat. It must be so many feet front, and so many feet deep. He says, "When I get the new building done, I shall have everything. Nothing then for me but to enjoy myself." In anticipation of the barn enlarged, he folds his arms and says, "If anybody in all the world is prosperous and happy, I am that man." But his ear is stunned with the words, "Thou fool!" "Where did the voice come from?" "Who dares say that to me, the first man in all this country?" It was the voice of God! "Thou fool, this night thy soul shall be required of thee!" What was the malady that took him immediately away?—whether apoplexy, or some mysterious disease that the doctors could not account for—I know not. But that night he expired. He never built the extension. Before the remaining sheaves had been gathered he was himself reaped. They hauled in no loads of grain on the next day, but a long procession (for successful men always have big funerals) followed him out to burial. If the world expressed its sentiments in regard to him, it would put over his grave, "Here lies interred a successful man, of great enterprise and influence, and he departs mourned by the whole neighbourhood. Peace to his ashes." God wrote over his grave, and on his barn-door, an epitaph of four letters—"Fool." That the Divine epitaph was correct, I infer from the fact that this man had lived so many years and made no preparation for the future, and because he was postponing everything until he got larger barns. Additional barn-room could not make him happy. Show me the man made happy by worldly accumulation. He does not exist. (*Dr. Talmage.*) *A man's own thought about himself, and God's :—*Do you take notice how in the light of imagination are contrasted here a man's convictions and thoughts respecting himself, and God's thoughts about him? Was there a single man that lived within a day's journey of this man that did not praise him? Was this man's name ever mentioned in all the region round about but that men said, "Ah! one of the richest and most honourable men in the community"? When men were speaking of prosperity and thrift, was not he spoken of? Were there not pleasing titles addressed to him when men would gain his friendship? Did not the man weave his own title out of these expressions of men's thoughts respecting him? If you had asked him, What is thy name? he would have said, My name is The rich man. What is thy name? Prince among my fellows. What is thy name? The abounding man; The prosperous man; The eminent man; The great man of the neighbourhood; The much-talked-of man. What is his name, O Lord? Fool. He knew every name but the right one. The probability is that no man had ever addressed him by his true title. He had been called by the name of his childhood; but that was not his name. He had been called by names bred of wealth; but these were not his names. He had been called by names that came from men's flatteries; but these were not his true names. When God spoke to him out of eternal truth, He said to him, "Thou fool!" and that was his name. It is very strange that a man should live to be forty or fifty years of age and not know his own name. Oh, how many there are in this congregation who have not the slightest conception of their nature and name. If I were to call out, "Fool, come hither," who of you would stir? But when God comes to call men, by-and-bye, with that irresistible voice, "Fool," oh, my soul, is it thou that then wilt be obliged to hear and answer? Are there not many of you that walk in honour, and are girded about with praise, who, if God were to launch your title through the air and fix it quivering in you, would be obliged hereafter, by this strange baptism of God, to wear the name "Fool"? What a contrast there was between the apparent and the real position in which this man stood! We read in the Bible of men's walking in a vain show. We read the exclamation of him of old, "How are they cast down, as in a moment!" Here was a man in the very focus of prosperity, and yet he stood within a hand's-breadth of his own grave. He seemed to defend himself from the intrusion of misfortune, and yet he was soon to be cast down. He had all that men usually covet. He had wrapped himself round and round with many coverings of wool, and silk, and fine linen, and supplied himself with abundant stores of things pleasant to the eye, and of things pleasant to the palate, and was honoured and respected; and now, having accomplished the purposes of his life, he began to lay himself back, as it were, and say to himself, "Now the toil is over; now the accomplishment is reached; now take thine ease." And what sort of an ease was it? "Eat, drink, and be merry." Self-indulgence and lust, which is the end and outcome of very much of the prosperity of this world. Self-indulgent pampering, selfish luxury—this was it. And he seemed to himself, he seemed to men, to have reached the very climax at the very moment the hand of God was extended to smite him down utterly and for ever. (*H. W. Beecher.*) *A fool brought to his senses :—* Some time ago, when passing along one of the crowded streets of London, a gentleman was attracted to a corner where, in the midst of some two hundred people, his eye rested upon a man in the dress of a clown, who drew the attention of all the passers-by. Moved with tender pity for the man, whose daily bread was earned in such a way, and lifting up his heart in prayer, he pressed through the crowd, and gave him a carefully selected tract. The clown contemptuously took it, and, to the astonishment and dismay of the giver, held it up and commenced reading it aloud. Word after word he read, with wonderful distinctness, till at length his eye rested on its closing sentence: "Thou fool! this night thy soul shall be required of thee." His whole frame shook with emotion, and with instant speed he left the crowd. While the people around were looking on in amazement, the gentleman followed, and, finding him, drew him aside, and tried to enter into conversation with him; but the only answer he could obtain was, "I'm lost! I'm lost!" Who can describe the joy that filled his soul when he found that God had by his Holy Spirit brought home to this man's heart and conscience the truth and power of that word which he had despised hitherto! In love and gentleness was the saving power of Jesus set before him. Every word he drank in as living water; all hardness was gone. He had been led to the foot of the cross as a repentant prodigal, and found forgiveness through a crucified Saviour. "Blessed are they who sow beside all waters." *The foolish farmer:*—A rich farmer once said to the Rev. John Cooke, "I don't like religion, and I told you so." "You are not the only farmer of the kind," replied Mr. Cooke. Then referring to this text, he said, "Do you think that this man was a fool?" "I shall not say, sir." "To me he appears to have been one—(1) Because he preferred his body to his soul; (2) Because he preferred the world to God; (3) Because he preferred time to eternity; (4) Because he lived as if he were never going to die." *Selfishness:*— "I have seen a woman," said a writer in the *Christian* (American), "professing to love Christ more than the world, clad in a silk dress costing 75 dols.; making up and trimming of same, 40 dols.; bonnet, or apology for one, 35 dols.; velvet mantle, 150 dols.; diamond ring, 500 dols.; watch, chain, pin, and other trappings, 300 dols.; total, 1,100 dols.—all hung upon one frail, dying worm. I have seen her at a meeting in behalf of homeless wanderers in New York wipe her eyes upon an expensive embroidered handkerchief at the story of their sufferings, and when the contribution box came round, take from a well-filled portemonnaie of costly workmanship twenty-five cents to aid the society formed to promote their welfare." *A scoffer taken at his word:*—A Christian man once occupied a desk in the same counting-room on the wharf with a man much older than himself, who was a coarse, profane atheist, quite disposed to make others like himself. One night, as they were about shutting up, this man took our informant by the jacket, and said, flippantly, that he was surprised "such a clever fellow as he should believe in religion"; using some very blasphemous expression. To a request that he would abstain from such language, he repeated some of his profane slang; and to a remark, that, "if such notions might do to live by, they would not do to die by," he said, "I'll venture it!" "I think you would have some fears if it should be said to you, 'Thou fool! this night thy soul shall be required of thee,'" said the friend. "I am ready," said the scoffer, pointing and looking upward. They parted. The profane man turned the corner of the street to go one way, and his friend went in the opposite direction. Within one minute after they separated, the scoffer fell dead upon the sidewalk. **So is he that layeth up treasure for himself.**—*The insane rich man:*—My brethren, if the busy stir and activity around us were for a subsistence, it would not be necessary that a preacher should select such a text as this; nor, indeed, would the Saviour have uttered this parable. But, in fact, a very small part of this hum and bustle, this hustling and jostling, is for a competency. It is the absorbing love of money, it is the insane lust of accumulation, above all—in this country, where everybody is crying out "equality!" and everybody dreading nothing so much as equality —it is the eager strife of social rivalry which is driving on the machinery, and keeping in an eternal whirl all this restless and articulate vitality. I. "So is he"; so insane. The conduct marked here is not simply folly; the word translated "fool," means madman. The case is one of real insanity; the man before us is a confirmed moral lunatic; and if he be not in an asylum, it is simply because the people around him are as infatuated and deranged as himself. The insanity in the text is neither the desire to have nor to enjoy wealth, but it is the absorbing possession of the mind by a single engrossing passion which monopolizes every thought, and shuts out other objects, even the most noble and important. Here are some of the symptoms of this man's insanity. 1. He forgets that he is immortal—that he has eternal interests to secure. 2. He does not consider the brevity and uncertainty of human life. 3. A third and still more glaring proof of "madness in the heart" of this rich man, is the material estimate, the purely money value, which he puts upon everything, even upon his soul. 4. So mad upon his idol is this man, that he not only misinterprets his own nature, but entirely forgets that there is a God to whom he is accountable. "So is he that layeth up treasure for himself"; treasure for himself. All the aims and purposes of this owner of broad lands centre in himself, nor need we go far to find the original of this portrait. Select any one of the busy throng you see in the world (I had almost said, I blush to own it, in the church); observe his conduct, penetrate his bosom, what are all his thoughts and wishes but a constant repetition of these words, myself, myself? In losing sight of God and his soul, this monomaniac has lost sight of the purpose and end of life, he has missed entirely the object of his creation. What, indeed, is the happiness he promises himself? It is indolence, feasting, mirth, riotous living. "Take thine ease, eat, drink, and be merry"—this is all he proposes, all his wealth can secure. And is this all for which he was created? Is man made in the image of God, that he may "take his ease, eat, drink, and be merry"? Is it for this that he is ennobled with those glorious gifts which place him only a "little lower than the angels"? Is this the happiness for which God has formed such a being? Not only his enjoyment. His work, his employment, his ambition, what are these? "I will pull down my barns and build greater." His hands can find nothing more important to do, his intellect nothing more noble to design, his heart nothing more worthy of its loftiest aspirations. II. But the folly and madness of this rich man are not the only things which the parable illustrates. His disquietude and trouble are also most strikingly portrayed. So IS HE; SO RESTLESS AND UNHAPPY. This is our next topic. "What shall I do?" cries this rich man, and why? What is the matter? What aileth him? "What shall I do, because I have no room to bestow my fruits?" "What shall I do?" Well, and what will he do? He is rich, he is prosperous, he "has more than heart could wish," and his great concern is to know what it is best for him to do. Let us now see what his determination is. What he ought to do is plain; he ought to be grateful to God; he ought not to "trust in uncertain riches, but in the living God"; he ought to abound in deeds of charity— "that they do good, that they be rich in good works, ready to distribute"; he ought to watch and pray lest riches prove a fatal snare, lest, like another rich man, he have "his good things in his lifetime;" he ought to tremble as he thinks "how hardly shall a rich man enter the kingdom of God"; in fine, he ought to be "laying up in store for himself a good foundation against the time to come, that he may lay hold on eternal life"—making to himself "friends of the mammon of unrighteousness, that when he dies they may receive him into everlasting habitations." This is what this man ought to do, this is what the Bible charges the rich to do, but the rich seldom consult the Bible on this or any other duty. The Bible apart, however, ought not common sense to instruct the rich? ought not reason to cure a sane man of this restlessness and anxiety? On a certain day, says the historian, Pyrrhus the king, elated by victory, was detailing to Cineas, his prime minister, all his projected triumphs. "I will next conquer Sicily." "What then?" "Then I will subdue Africa." "What then?" "Then I will make myself master of Spain." "And what then?" "Why then," said the monarch, "we can take our ease and be happy." "And why," replied Cineas, "why cannot we do that now?" So with this rich man; what happiness can wealth purchase, which he may not enjoy now? But the admonitions of reason have as little influence as those of conscience upon a man whose heart is debased by covetousness. Look where we will, we see this truth, that men are more intent on possessing than enjoying; and when the desire to accumulate becomes the ruling passion, rest, contentment, all real happiness, are sacrificed to this monopolizing vice. Everybody tells you, indeed, that he wants only a competency; but by a competency, everybody means a little more than he happens to have at present. A few have too much, many too little, but nobody was ever yet found who had just enough. III. The last admonition which the Saviour designs to convey in this parable has reference to THE FEARFUL PERILS TO WHICH WEALTH EXPOSES THE SOUL. Danger from the absorbing influence over the heart; "where your treasure is, there will your heart be also"; the prodigal is soon disgusted with sensual pleasures, but the love of money only becomes more deeply rooted and engrossing as other passions are destroyed by age; it is quickened and invigorated by their ashes. Danger from the insuperable obstacles to conversion; "he went away sorrowful, for he had great possessions"— strange cause for sorrow, but never sorrow more reasonable. Danger, because, with the possession of wealth, pride is almost invariably insinuated into the heart; "Charge them that are rich in this world that they be not high-minded"; where can we look without seeing men, once poor and humble, and bidding fair for heaven, but now rich, inflated with self-importance, filled with ambitious thoughts for themselves and their families; an ambition which changes not only their style of living, but their style of worshipping God—changes their Church, changes their preacher, changes their creed; Mammon making a revelation, in the light of which truth is seen to be falsehood, and falsehood truth; and thus Christ, and faith, and salvation are immolated to pamper a contemptible vanity? Danger from that utter selfishness which increasing wealth fosters; "layeth up treasure for himself," is elated with a feeling of independence; cares nothing for others; is occupied only with his own ease, and pleasure, and aggrandizement. (*Richard Fuller, D.D.*) *The folly of laying up earthly riches:*—This man's folly was toiling for treasures he could not use. He gathered treasures, but lost them, his soul, and God. Enriching himself outwardly, he impoverished himself inwardly. Linking his being with perishable things, he perishes with them. Thus he became poor, blind, naked, in one hour (Rev. iii. 17). A wise man desires no more than what he may get justly, use soberly, distribute cheerfully, and leave contentedly. Love and faith of the heart are "the unsearchable riches" (Eph. iii. 8). A believing beggar dying, quits his poverty, and goes to his riches. Millionaires oft in time are beggars in eternity (Luke xvi. 23). (*Van Doren.*)   *The true riches:*—When we come to define riches, we find it difficult to give preciseness to the idea attached to the word. The man who has gold enough for all his wants is rich. Money is but a means to an end, that end being the convenient attainment of things requisite for comfortable existence. The soul has wants as well as the body, and the means by which its necessities are to be supplied may be called "riches," the true riches. I. WHAT ARE THESE RICHES? He is rich who has a good conscience, a will in unison with God's, and emotions of happiness in the contemplation of God; God Himself is the true wealth of the soul. We are all originally poor, for we have sinned and wandered from God. But we all, if we will, may become spiritually wealthy through Jesus Christ our Lord. II. HOW CAN WE ACQUIRE THESE RICHES? James has given us the answer—"rich in faith." It is by faith that we become rich toward God. III. HOW ARE WE TO KEEP AND INCREASE THESE RICHES? Paul enlightens us here when he bids Timothy charge his hearers to be "rich in good works." The riches of personal deliverance may be regarded as the one pound which Christ gives to all who will take it; his own good works are the improvement which the believer makes on that original gift. This improvement is both personal and diffusive. IV. THE EXHORTATION TO "LAY UP FOR YOURSELVES TREASURES IN HEAVEN." 1. The pursuit of this wealth is attended with no danger to the character. 2. In the search every one may be successful. 3. This spiritual treasure is abiding. (*W. M. Taylor, D.D.*)   *Treasure misplaced:*—To set the heart on the creature is to set a diamond in lead, or to lock coals in a cabinet and throw jewels into a cellar. (*Bishop Reynolds.*)   *The Christian's treasure:*—There is a saying in Plutarch recorded of a rich Roman (Crassus), that he did not think that man rich who knew all that he had." Truly in this man's account a Christian is truly rich; he hath laid up more treasure than himself knows of; yet, although a Christian knows not how much he hath, yet he shall lose none; it is safe, being laid up in heaven; every star is as a seal set upon the treasure-door. (*Bishop Hopkins.*)   *Business all absorbing:*— The captain of a whaling ship said, "I cannot attend to religion. My mind is occupied with other things. If you looked into my heart, I believe you would find a whale there." (*H. R. Burton.*)   *The heart with the treasure:*—I was much struck, writes one, the other day, in reading about a nobleman who died a few days since. He had an iron safe, or chest, all locked up, but marked, "To be removed first in case of fire." When he died, his friends opened the chest, supposing, of course, that some valuable document, or deed of property, rich jewellery, or costly plate would be found in it. But what did they find? They found the toys of his little child, who had gone before him. Richer to him were they than all the world's wealth, richer than his coronet; brighter than all the jewels that sparkled on his crest. Not his estate, not his jewels, not his equipage, nothing glorious and great in this world; but the dearest objects to him were the toys of his little child.

Vers. 22–28. **Take no thought for your life.**—*Reasons for banishing vexatious care:*—1. It is needless; "your heavenly Father knoweth that ye have need of these things"; and will certainly provide for you; and what need you take care, and God too? Cast your care upon Him. 2. It is fruitless; "which of you, by taking care, can add one cubit to his stature?" We may sooner, by our carping care, add a furlong to our grief, than a cubit to our comfort. All our care, without God's help, will neither feed us when we are hungry, nor nourish us when we are fed. 3. It is heathenish; "after all these things do the Gentiles seek" (Matt. vi. 32). The ends and objects of a Christian's thoughts ought to be higher and more sublime than that of heathens. 4. Lastly, it is brutish, nay, worse than brutish. The birds of the air, the beasts of the field, the ravens of the valley, all are fed and sustained by God, without any care of their own, much more His children. Has God a breakfast ready for every little bird that comes chirping out of its nest, and for every beast of the field that comes leaping out of its den, and will He not much more provide for you? Surely, that God that feeds the ravens when they cry will not starve His children when they pray. (*W. Burkitt.*)   *The body of less import-ance than the soul :*—The body is but the husk or shell, the soul is the kernel; the body is but the cask, the soul the precious liquor contained in it; the body is but the cabinet, the soul the jewel; the body is but the ship or vessel, the soul the pilot; the body is but the tabernacle, and a poor clay tabernacle or cottage too, the soul the inhabitant; the body is but the machine or engine, the soul that ἐνδόν τι, that actuates and quickens it; the body is but the dark lanthorn, the soul or spirit is the candle of the Lord, that burns in it. And seeing that there is such difference between the soul and body, in respect of excellency, surely our better part challenges our greatest care and diligence to make provision for it . . . Some philosophers will not allow the body to be an essential part of man, but only the vessel or vehicle of the soul; *Anima cujusque est quisque.* The soul is the man. Though I would not be so unequal to it, yet I must needs acknowledge it to be but an inferior part : it is therefore so to be treated, so dieted, and provided, as to render it most calm and compliant with the soul, most tractable and obsequious to the dictates of reason; not so pampered and indulged, as to encourage it to cast its rider, and to take the reins into its own hand, and usurp dominion over the better part, the τὸ ἡγεμονικὸν, to sink and depress it into a sordid compliance with its own lusts, *atque affigere humi Divinæ particulam auræ* (xv. 17; Eccles. xii. 7; Gal. vi. 7, 8; Rom. xiii. 14; 1 Cor. ix. 27). (*Ray.*)   *Vanity in dress :*—It is enough to make one weep to think of the multitudes who are only living for the frivolities of this life. I read lately that the Emperor of Brazil had given the Queen a dress made of spiders' webs; it took 17,000 webs to make it. What a curiosity! No doubt the Queen would keep it all her life. Oh, what an amount of time and labour to make this dress! It reminded me of the way we cover our-selves with vanities, wasting a life over it. Oh! give it up, and take the beautiful robe of Christ's righteousness.   *The spirit of content :*—I once engaged in dis-course with a Rosicrucian about the great secret. He talked of it as a spirit that lived in an emerald, and converted everything that was near it to the highest per-fection it was capable of. "It gives a lustre," said he, "to the sun, and water to the diamond. It irradiates every metal, and enriches lead with all the properties of gold. It heightens smoke into flame, flame into light, and light into glory. He further added that a single ray dissipates pain and care and melancholy from the person on whom it falls. In short," said he, "its presence naturally changes every place into a kind of heaven." At length I found that his great secret was nothing else but content. (*Addison.*)   *Do not borrow trouble :*—There is no one who acts more unwisely than he that "borrows trouble." He that borrows money may invest it to great advantage. The borrower of a good book may be a great gainer by its study and perusal. But who gains by "borrowing trouble"? Is trouble so joyous and enriching that we shall be happier if we can only enjoy it a few days before it comes? Does it not withdraw the light of joy from our counten-ance? Does it not withdraw our thoughts from the present, and unfit us for its joys and pleasures? Where, then, is the wisdom of prophesying evil that we may "borrow trouble" from it? (*Alliance News.*)   *The folly of caring more for the body than the soul :*—The body is to the soul as a barren turf to a mine of gold, as a mud wall about a delicate garden, as a wooden box wherein the jeweller carries his precious gems, as a coarse case to a fair and rich instrument, as a rotten hedge to a paradise, as Pharaoh's prison to a Joseph, or as a mask to a beautiful face. (*T. Adams.*)   *The soul foremost :*—I do not approve the sullenness of that soul which wrongs the body; but I worse like to have the body wrong the soul, to have Hagar tricked up in Sarah's garments and set at upper end of the table. If the painted popinjay that so dotes on her own beauty, had an eye to see how her soul is used, she would think her practice more ill-favoured and unhandsome than per-fuming a putrefied coffin, or putting mud into a glass of crystal. For shame, let us put the soul foremost again, and not set heaven lowest and earth uppermost. (*Ibid.*)　　*Both body and soul lost :*—There is a parable of a woman, who, having twin children, and both being presented to her, she falls deeply and fondly in love with the one, but is careless and disrespectful of the other : this she will nurse herself, but that is put forth.　Her love grows up with the child she kept herself · she decks it fine, she feeds it choicely ; but at last, by overmuch pampering of it, the child surfeits, becomes mortally sick, and when it was dying she remembers herself, and sends to look after the other child that was at nurse, to the end she might now cherish it ; but when the messenger came she finds it dying and gasping likewise, and examining the truth, she understands that through the mother's carelessness and neglect to look after it, the poor child was starved ; thus was the fond, partial mother, to her great grief, sorrow, and shame, deprived of both her hopeful babes at once.　Thus, every Christian is this mother, the children are our body and soul : the former of these it is that men and women fall deeply and fondly in love with, whilst indeed they are careless and neglect the other ; this they dress and feed, nothing is too good or too dear for it ; but at the last the body surfeits, comes by some means or other to its deathbed, when there is very little or no hope of life ; then men begin to remember the soul, and would think of some course to save it : the minister he is sent 'for in all haste to look after it ; but, alas! he finds it in part dead, in part dying ; and the very truth is, the owner, through neglect and carelessness, hath starved the soul, and it is ready to go to hell before the body is fit for the grave.　And so the foolish fond Christian, to his eternal shame and sorrow, loseth both his body and soul for ever.　(*Spencer.*)　　*God is the universal Provider :*—There is no such thing recognized in Scripture as "laws of nature," by which the various creatures are sustained.　God is here and elsewhere represented to us as feeding them Himself : "He giveth food to all flesh."　He may employ secondary means, but He must Himself be present with these secondary means, or they would not continue in action for a single day.　And in this respect the Bible is infinitely more philosophical than modern books of science : for these books represent the present state of things as carried on by laws themselves, whereas a law, being an unconscious rule or limitation, can do nothing of itself.　It must be kept in action by a will, *i.e.,* an Intelligence, which, considering the boundless field it has to occupy, we can hold to be nothing less than the Supreme Will.　(*M. F. Sadler.*)　　*A lesson from the birds :*—Luther had a quick eye to detect and read the lessons of nature.　Thus, on a certain calm summer evening he happened to be standing at a window, when he observed a small bird quietly settle down for the night.　"Look how that little fellow preaches faith to us all !" he exclaimed.　"He takes hold of his twig, tucks his head under his wing, and goes to sleep, leaving God to think for him."　　**Add to his stature one cubit.**—*Limitations :*—It is well for men to think that there are some things which, with all their power, they cannot do.　Some of these things are apparently very simple, yet even though simple and easy as in some cases they appear to be, cannot be done, even when men give the whole stress and pith of their minds to the attempt.　This is implied in the phraseology of the text : Which of you by taking thought, by anxiously considering, by most perseveringly endeavouring, by straining his wit and strength to the very utmost, by spending his days and nights in the effort, can add one cubit unto his stature?　There are some difficult things which we can do by putting out all our strength.　There are others which mock the fulness of our power, and the tenacity of our patience. We resolve to do them, and we are beaten back, and taught a lesson of self-impotence which otherwise we never could have learned.　Can you add one cubit unto your stature?　You may wear high-heeled boots, you may order the tallest hats, but the height of your stature you are utterly unable to increase.　God Himself sovereignly draws certain boundary lines.　In some instances God allows us to a large extent to draw our own boundaries ; in others He presently gives the final and decisive word, "Hitherto—no further."　It is important to know the difference between quantities which are variable and quantities which are fixed.　This knowledge may save us a great deal of trouble, and prevent very much pain.　Can your teeth bite the rock?　However hungry you are, is there strength in your jaw to bite the granite?　Can your feet stand upon the flowing river?　Can you lay your finger upon the lowest of all the stars that shine in heaven?　A thousand such questions show that we are hemmed in by the impassable ; we walk upon the edge of a gulf ; and our mightiest endeavours show us that after all we are only beating ourselves against the bars of a great cage !　A painted cage, but a cage still

—a cage lamplit, but a cage still. Now this limitation of our power must have some meaning. Jesus Christ makes use of it in illustrating not only the sovereignty, but the goodness of God. He teaches us to trust the Father, who has determined the height of our stature. He shows that if we cannot do such apparently little things as He has specified in His sermon, it is absurd to suppose we can do things which are infinitely greater; checks our anxiety by showing that our keenest solicitude about earthly concerns boots nothing when it gets beyond trust, and becomes practical atheism. This argument is as beautiful in its simplicity as it is universal in its application. Wherever there is a man, whatever his colour, language, age, he can understand this challenge, "Can you add one cubit unto your stature?" Why are you not taller? There seems to be room enough above you to admit of growth. Why don't you grow? You would not shut out the light of the sun even if you were half an inch taller! You would not imperil the stars if you did stand half a hair's breadth higher! Why do you not add to your stature? You can scheme, and arrange, and plot, and suggest. Sir! why not add to your stature? You cannot. Then consider—ask yourself a few plain searching questions. See how God rules in all the things—in your height, in the bounds of your habitation, in all the limits which He has set to your life. This great fact of the Divine limitation of human power is to rule us in the deepest of our studies, and in the profoundest of our worship. If we lay hold of this truth, and have a clear, deep, tender conviction of it, and of all the truths which it represents, three great effects ought to be produced upon our life. I. It should foster the most loving and confident trust in the goodness of God. There is a point where we cannot go one iota further, where we are compelled to one of two things—reverent and intelligent trust, or the ostrich blindness which seems to proceed upon the principle that to shut the eyes is to escape all observation and all control. The course of reasoning in our minds ought to be this: "I cannot add one cubit unto my stature; God has determined my height." If He has been mindful of such a little thing as that, will he be unmindful of great things? II. In the next place, this truth should moderate our tone respecting opinions which are not decisively settled by revelation. If a man can't increase his stature, how can he increase the volume of God's truth? If a man can't increase his stature, who gives him authority to speak where God has been silent? III. In the last place, this truth should encourage us to cultivate with fuller patience and intenser zeal the powers which we know to be capable of expansion. We see some things most sharply by contrast. Here we have a point which challenges contrast of the most practical and instructive kind. For example: You cannot add one cubit unto your stature, yet you can increase the volume and force of your mind. See the truthfulness of the doctrine we have laid down, that in some things God sharply gives the final line, in others He leaves great liberty, and calls men to growth that seems to have no end. See how apparently arbitrary is Divine sovereignty in some of its workings A man can't increase his height one inch, and yet I find nowhere a limit to intellectual supremacy and to the expansion of intellectual power. Your body has done growing, but your mind may just have began to look at the alphabet of truth. When the animal has reached the utmost limit of its capability, the intellectual, the Divine may go on increasing, expanding, refining, for God constantly says to the faithful servant, "Thou hast been faithful over a few things, I will make thee ruler over many things." Whatsoever a man's mind legitimately attains, God still says, "Come up higher." IV. Again, though you cannot add one cubit unto your stature, you may relieve the pain of a thousand hearts. V. Again, though you cannot add one cubit unto your stature, you may cultivate an ever-deepening acquaintance with the will of God; you may know God more perfectly, read His Word with a clearer eye, receive the suggestions and instructions of His Holy Spirit more lovingly, more loyally and trustfully, so that you may be men in understanding. Let us go to them, then, knowing that we are limited in our little sphere; that there are marked and positive limitations in some cases; and that everywhere—excepting when we are growing up into the likeness of God—there is limitation. Let that rebuke human reason—let that curb human selfishness—let that stand by us when we read the Holy Word and try to solve its mysteries. And when we become weary of looking at our littleness, our experiments, and our impotence, and turn round in other directions, we find that we may take wings—strong, great, unwearying pinions—and fly away right up to the very heart and heaven of God! Though we be little we are great. Though we are shut in and confined and mocked in some directions, in other directions we are citizens of the universe, freemen of the whole creation. Blessed are they who know alike the limit and the liberty of human life ! (*J. Parker, D.D.*)

Ver. 27. **Consider the lilies.**—*Lessons from the flowers : to children :*—There are three virtues which Jesus was endeavouring to teach when He told His disciples to consider the lilies. They are, contentment, obedience, humility. I. FLOWERS ARE NOT ONLY BEAUTIFUL, BUT THEY ALWAYS SEEM CONTENTED AND GLAD. Did you ever think how little they have to make them so? They live on other people's leavings. The air gives them only what finer folks reject and call poison. When the birds and the beasts have taken from the atmosphere all they want, the flowers, like poor Lazarus, desire what is left, the crumbs that fall from the rich man's table. Then, too, if there is any dreadful filth from the sewers or the barnyard, of which men do not know how else to be rid, they give it to the flowers; just as I have seen certain children send ragged clothes and broken toys to the Christmas poor-box. But the flowers are grateful, and though they cannot talk they blush with gratitude, pink or blue or yellow or white, according to the colour of their blood. Then the poor flower-folk, out of these odds and ends which nobody else will have, make for themselves such splendid clothes as King Solomon could not get, though he had first choice of everything, and all the weavers and tailors and jewellers in the world to dress him. So our first lesson from the flowers is to get all the good out of the things you have, before you wish for more things. II. FLOWERS HAVE NO WINGS AND NO FEET. They must stay in one place. Therefore they never do anything which they cannot do at home. If a boy will stick to that, he will grow up like a flower into a noble and beautiful man. When the Lord Jesus was asked to do wrong, He said : "I and My Father are one." It was His way of saying, "That is not as they do at home; therefore I cannot do so here." If boys use their feet to get away from home, they are worse off than the flowers, which have no feet. But if they use them to carry their homes wherever they go, they are far more blessed then the fairest flowers. III. THE FLOWERS HAVE NO TONGUES. I do not mean that you must not talk. God has given us tongues, and means us to use them. But let the silent beauty of the flowers teach us to do all the good we can and make no fuss about it. Never be in a hurry to tell people you are Christians, but act so that they cannot help finding it out. Did you ever watch beans grow? They come out of the ground as if they had been planted upside down. Each appears carrying the seed on top of his stalk, as if they were afraid folks would not know they were beans unless they immediately told them. But most flowers wait patiently and humbly to be known by their fruits. Sometimes boys get laughed at because they think they must tell everybody that they are Christians. They talk about their piety, and never show it in any other way. But no boy gets laughed at for being a Christian; for being true and brave and kind and humble and pure, like the Lord Jesus. (*W. B. Wright.*)   *God's care for the lilies :*—The Lord's argument requires that these should be the wild lilies, the lilies of the field, as we read in the parallel place in St. Matthew. As they spring up spontaneously, man, by his cultivation, has added nothing to their perfection. They are creations of God on which He has lavished such splendour of form and colour that Solomon's jewelled robes were not to be compared to them, and yet God has thus gorgeously clothed them for no apparent purpose except to exhibit profuseness of beauty; they last but a day, and the next day their withered stalks are gathered for fuel for the oven. Not one in one million delights the eye even of a child ; and yet each particular one serves its purpose in creation. Each one is observed and its beauty noted by God—by Him who numbers the grains of sand and the drops of dew— each particular one, though never to be seen by man, is as perfect of its kind as if it had been destined to adorn the temple of God. (*M. F. Sadler.*)   *Nature set against manufactures :*—"Consider the lilies how they grow . . . . Solomon in all his glory was not arrayed like one of these." There is nature set against manu- factures, and set so as to throw them into pitiable contrast. Solomon was all as to his decorations, manufacture—the decorations were hand made; and the lily is lifted up, and declared to be his superior in tender delicacy of beauty to all the colour that flamed on the shoulders of the king. How are they made? Look at them and you will know. Compare anything which you have made with anything which you find in nature; and you will see that you have either been copying nature or travestying by mean and impotent imitation what nature has done so infinitely well. Can you show me anything so delicate as the bloom upon the cheek of the peach? Touch it. Now put the bloom back again! Look at the meadow in the morning when brightened with dew, and tell me if the hand of man ever made such a scene as that dewy field presents when the sun shines upon it? What gleaming diamonds—what glowing rubies—what glittering emeralds—what a blazing of living and all but speaking colour! How made? "Not made with hands!" Touch one of the jewels. It is gone! Restore it! No angel could! (*J. Parker, D.D.*) *Considering the flowers:*—Dr. Chalmers luxuriated among the plants and flowers of the season, and delighted to examine minutely the structure and the beauties of some humble production that would have escaped the notice of a less practised eye. He said to a friend one day—after he had been rapt in admiration of nature and nature's God—"I love to dwell on the properties of one flower at a time; to fix my mind on it exclusively until I feel that it has taken complete hold of my mind. This is a peculiarity of my constitution. I must have concentration of thought on any given thing, and not be diverted from it." The friend's attention was arrested in the garden by a sunflower of large dimensions and exquisite colouring. He (Dr. Chalmers) said, with deep emotion, "Oh, that we could so open our hearts to the beams of the Sun of Righteousness!" It was in such scenes that one not only saw but felt that the train of thought was heavenward—that his heart and his treasure were in heaven. *Christ and the lilies:*—Our Lord reminds us by such words as my text of the profound teaching that lies in the simplest objects strewn before us in the world. As the flowers expand their whole being to the light; as every wave upon the sea reflects the arched heavens above it; as the mountain peaks point ever upward to the skies; as the world of nature leads up to God; so should we be flower, sea, mountain, unfolding our whole nature to the light of God, mirroring back in happy response the glory of heaven encircling everywhere our lives, pointing by our steadfastness and rectitude directly up to Him. Let us listen to nature's teaching, and from it learn what God would have us learn about our life. I. LILY-LIFE AND GROWTH TEACH US FREEDOM FROM CARE. The lily builds itself up from within. Like the primrose and crocus, the flower springs directly from the root. The sweet lily of the valley, which is, perhaps, the best known plant that bears the name of lily, pushes its way up step by step from the creeping root-stock. The leaves open out, and from their sheath the slender stalk rises. Tiny knots of pale green fibre form round its head; they droop; the stem arches itself, and the little knots open into white and regularly formed bells, brimming with richest fragrance. The wonder is how so much fragrance can be compressed within so small a thing. Watch how it grew. It made no fuss. It never paused as if in uncertainty. It was never divided in its plant-mind whether it should go on trying to be a lily, or whether it should try to be something else. It just went on as it had started from the root, growing, being itself, without hurry, and presently the bells formed, the sweetness and beauty came. It was that which God intended it to be—a lily. Consider it. Ours is to be the pure lily life. The one thing we have to do is to persevere in being what we are— Christians. 1. We suffer from temptation. It harasses and baffles us. Is not the simple solution for all temptations, great or small, to go back to the very root of our life? "I am Christ's. I cannot do this thing. My Master gave up ease, comfort, and life also, on the Cross. I can give up my desires and likings for Him. He would not do this thing. He would not argue or parley. 'Get thee behind me, Satan,' would be His word. It must be my word also." Temptations lodge themselves in our fancy. They haunt our imagination. Well, though they do, go on with life's true work just the same. The lily pauses for no fancy. It goes on growing. So, in spite of fancies and imaginings, go on being, and living, and doing as Christ would were He in your place. Go back to the root. Be Christ's, in spite of your state of mind, your inclinations and fancies. 2. Disappointments and sorrows hinder us. They lodge in our fancy. They people our brain with vague fears. I think if we went to a lily and plucked off one of its tiny bells, or tore away the leaf that sheathes the stem, the lily would still struggle bravely, and rear its head as proudly as it could. It would strive still to fulfil its life, because it grows from the root, and the root is not gone. Shall we be stripped of something we hold dear—wealth, bodily vigour, the friends we love tenderly—and therefore cease to grow? Christians cannot give up. II. THE LILY GROWS EVERYWHERE. And so do Christians. God has planted some of us in bare desolate places. We are not happy and contented. We believe we should lead a more useful and a nobler life if our environment were changed. It is impossible to say what any of us might do or become if we were in different positions from those we occupy. Let me remind you, however, of one great fact. For the present you are in one particular spot, and no other; working at this particular calling and no other; possessed of just this particular amount of education and knowledge, and no more. And this being the case, God requires of you to reverence and reveal Him, to witness for Him, in the particular place in which He has at present established you; and to use there the talents, the opportunities and grace He has given you. Try and brighten life where you are. In the narrowest sphere, as a subordinate or a servant, be true to your Christian nature. Perform the lily's part. Let one little corner of the world, at any rate, be more pleasant and heavenly because you are in it. III. THE SPECIAL UTILITY OF THE LILY. Many of the larger varieties of the lily can exist where herbage at first cannot. The soil is very dry, and grass would be scanty were it not for the function discharged by the lily. There is no continuous greensward in Palestine, such as is seen in the parks and around the homesteads of our native land. The lily, however, can exist in the dry soil, for it carries in its bulbous root its own store of nourishment. Fixed in the ground, but sustaining itself in large measure from the bulb, it grows into the perfect flower. As vegetation always attracts moisture, the lilies draw from even that dry atmosphere the humid particles it contains. Their broad opaque leaves screen from the sun plants that come to nestle under their shade. The lilies create the conditions under which herbage can exist and thrive. The flocks of the shepherd always wend their way to the spot abounding with lilies. The gazelle and other wild deer are found grazing there, not cropping the slender flowers, but luxuriating in the succulent grass which grows beside them—a scene of which the inspired poet in the Canticles has availed himself: the bride comparing her spouse to a roe or young hart feeding among the lilies. "I am my beloved's, and my beloved is mine; he feedeth among the lilies." "Consider the lilies!" How useful they are! We are to be like them in this. We are to make it more possible for others, by our influence and example, to live a holy and a spiritual life. IV. THE LILY IS BEAUTIFUL. Its adornment is most rich and sumptuous. Its colours—white, scarlet, and gold, glow in splendour over the whole landscape. And yet it simply grows; it attends to its life, not to its raiment. Why take thought for raiment? Yet many people are vain enough and unwise enough to perplex and trouble their whole lives simply and mainly about dress and furniture—about the adornment of their persons, the garniture of their houses. The law the Saviour gives us is most plain. Live first. Think most about life. And He means soul-life, the life in God, the life of a child of God, which is the only real and worthy human life. Be earnest about purity, holiness, spirituality of character. (*A. J. Griffith*.) *The lessons derived from the plant :*—"Wherefore, if God so clothe the grass of the field, which to-day is, and to-morrow is cast into the oven, shall He not much more clothe you, O ye of little faith?" (Matt. vi. 30). The inspired writers are in the way of employing all the objects in nature with which we are familiar, in order to illustrate spiritual truths. Solomon sends the slothful man to the ant : "Go to the ant, thou sluggard." Isaiah makes the ox and ass rebuke the ingratitude of the professing people of God : "The ox knoweth his owner, and the ass his master's crib, but Israel doth not know, my people doth not consider." All this exercised a most beneficent influence on pious men in ancient Israel. Living as they did, much in the open air, and in perpetual view of the wondrous works of God in earth and sky, nature was seen by them to be full of God. The grass sprang, the flowers bloomed, the wheat and barley yielded their increase, and the vine and the fig and the olive-trees their rich fruit, all in obedience to God's command; and as they did so they showed forth the glory of God as well as furnished nourishment to His creatures. Would that the example set by Hebrew shepherds and husbandmen as they tended their flocks or pruned their vineyards would induce those who live much among the works of nature to take like elevated views. The plant in particular has been much employed by the inspired writers to convey spiritual lessons. The life of the plant seemed to them like the spiritual life in the soul; the rain and dew that nourished it reminded them of the grace which comes down from heaven; the flowers which adorned it taught them that the soul should be adorned with heavenly graces; and the fruit which it yielded admonished them that they too must bring forth fruit unto God. I. WE ARE TO CONSIDER THE WORKS OF GOD, AND IN PARTICULAR THE PLANTS, THE LILIES, AND THE GRASS OF THE FIELD. "Consider," says he, "the lilies of the field." There are many who do not consider them. Some of these persons are fond of seeing or possessing fine specimens of human workmanship in dress or furniture or houses or paintings, but they " regard not the works of the Lord, nor the operations of His hands." " And yet I say unto you, that even Solomon in all his glory was not arrayed like one of these." We are to mark them ; we are to mark how they grow. We need no scientific knowledge, no learned terms, to enable us to do this. All persons who have eyes to see may see it with or without book learning, whether they have or have not been at schools or colleges. They may in particular observe two things. 1. Every part of the plant is made to serve an end. " They toil not, neither do they spin " ; yet every organ of the plant has its use. Look at the swelling tree that overshadows us, or at this graceful lily at our feet. Consider it. It has roots which serve a purpose. These roots penetrate into the soil and draw nourishment from it. These spread out downwards as the trunk and branches mount upwards, and enable the tree, the oak for example, to stand the storms of a hundred winters. The form of the bole of a tree, and the manner in which it fixes itself in the ground, is said to have yielded some suggestions to a celebrated engineer in the construction of a famous light-house (Eddystone). You may remark how the tree springs up from the ground as a stem or trunk, on which hang all the branches and flowers and seed and fruit. This trunk, as it mounts upwards, spreads out all around into the air as branches and branchlets. These are covered with leaves rejoicing in the sunshine, and the moisture of dew and rain, and drawing in nourishment from the atmosphere. Upon these, at the proper season, you may look for and find flowers to delight the eye, and seed wherewith to propagate other plants after their kind, and fruit for the sustenance of God's creatures. It is obvious to every reflecting mind that in this Divine workmanship every part has its use and its end. The architect of a famous palace (Sydenham) confesses that he derived some of the ideas embodied in that structure from observing the wonderful provision made for bearing up the very broad leaf of one of the most beautiful of lilies. But there is another principle to be observed in the plant. 2. There is visible in the plant an order, an ornament, a beauty. Special reference is made to this by Him who made them, and who now uses them to teach us lessons. God is said not only to have made, but to have clothed the grass of the field. While every part of the plant has its use, it has also a clothing ; it is clothed with beauty to minister to our delight and manifest the Divine glory. It can be shown that every plant and every organ of the plant is, as it were, constructed upon a model or pattern in the Divine mind. Look at the full-formed tree growing apart from all other trees, and you see at once that it is made to grow up into a particular form, and this form is beautiful to look upon. It can be shown that every tree takes its own peculiar form—a form after its kind ; and if not interfered with, that form is lovely. Look, too, at the flower of the lily, or any other plant, and in every part of it—its stalk, its petals, and inner organs, in their forms, and in the way in which they are placed—there are obvious order and ornament to call forth our admiration and our praise. Then, what richness of colouring in the flower. First of all, every colour is beautiful in itself ; and then, colours which are accordant are placed alongside of one another in pleasing melody or exciting harmony. It needs science to explain all this, to show how it arises, and point out the causes of it ; but it needs no science to enable us to observe it or enjoy it ; the eye perceives it spontaneously, and drinks in the beauty, and it needs only piety to enable us to turn all this into an anthem of praise. This clothing of the plant meets us everywhere. Take the commonest plant—the furze that grows on the common, the seaweed that cleaves to the rocks washed by the ocean, or the fern that springs up in the mountain glen—and you may observe in its structure, in its leaves, and all its pendicles, a wonderful correspondence of side to side, and a counterbalancing of one part by another. Let the eye travel over nature, as we walk among the cultivated fields, or on the grassy slopes and valleys of our upland districts, or among the thick woods where the winds have sown the seeds, and bush and tree of every kind spring up, each eager to maintain its place and show its separate form and beauty, and we discover an order and a grace in every branch and blade and leaf and colour. Pluck the leaf and flower and consider it, and observe how one edge has the same number of notches in it as the other edge, and what nice balancings and counterpoises there are, and how nicely the lines and dots and shadings suit one another, and recur each at its proper place, as if all had been done by the most exact measurement and under the most skilful and tasteful eye. Enter the rich arbour or the cultivated garden, and observe how the flowers have been enlarged or improved by the care which has been taken of them ; and in this gayer colour and in that fuller expanse and more flowing drapery and richer fragrance mark how God, who rewards us for opening our eyes and looking abroad upon His works, holds out a still greater reward to those who in love to Him, or in love to them, take pains with them and bestow labour upon them. Now, all this fitness and all this order and beauty testify of the wisdom and goodness of God. All these objects point upward to their God and to our God. But these works of God can also serve other religious ends. They may be used as lesson-books; they are thus used by Christ to instruct us in great spiritual truths. Nature may thus be sanctified, and be made to teach us the very same lessons as the inspired Word. II. SECONDLY, WE ARE TO CONSIDER THE GROUNDS WHICH WE HAVE FOR TRUSTING IN GOD THAT HE WILL PROVIDE FOR OUR TEMPORAL WANTS. "Wherefore, if God so clothe the grass of the field, which to-day is, and to-morrow is cast into the oven, much more shall He clothe you." This is a specimen of Bible reasoning. The Bible speaks as "unto wise men," and calls on us to "judge" what "it says." Its reasonings are all brief, all very conclusive, but at the same time easily followed. Take, as an example, "If God spared not His own Son, but gave Him freely to the death for us,"—here is the premise, and the inference follows—"how will He not with Him also freely give us all things?" The argument is irresistible. The lesson comes home at once to us. Every bird we hear carolling its song, for the very pleasure of it, on the tree or in the air; every flower that we see expanding its petals in the fields or garden, is rebuking our want of faith and confidence in God, and, as it were, saying, "If God take such care of me, will He not much more take care of you?" "Ye are of more value than many sparrows," of more value than all the grass of the field. Ye have a body that is fearfully and wonderfully made, made with even a more amazing skill than the lilies of the field. The lilies are arrayed in greater splendour than Solomon ever was; and Solomon's body and every man's frame is more wondrously made than the loveliest plant that ever adorned meadow or mountain. Surely the God who made that goodly frame will also feed and clothe it. We are warned against a spirit of unbelief; we are exhorted to cherish a spirit of confidence. Christ would deliver us from a spirit of anxiety. The fowls of the air gather their food, but they have no feeling of anxiety while they do so. III. THIRDLY, WE ARE TO CONSIDER THAT IF GOD SO CLOTHE THE GRASS OF THE FIELD, THAT IF HE SO CLOTHE THE BODIES OF HIS PEOPLE, MUCH MORE WILL HE CLOTHE THEIR SOULS. This is not the direct lesson taught in the text, but it arises very directly out of it. If God does thus clothe the bodies of His people, much more will He clothe their souls with heavenly graces. And ah, these souls of ours need to be clothed! The plant once of a graceful form and clothed with the richest hues, but now bent, broken by the wind, bemired in the dust—this is the emblem of the soul, once in the very image of God, and arrayed with a brighter glory than the lily, but now fallen from its first estate, broken and torn and polluted by sin! Ah, how like is that soul to the grass which has been cut down, and which is about to be cast into the oven! That soul has been cut off from its God, the source of all spiritual life; already has the life ceased to circulate in it, and it is ready to be cast into the fire that is not quenched. Can it indeed be that this soul is to grow and to flourish once more upon its stalk? Christ's work when on earth was a work of salvation. They brought to Him the sick, the maimed, and the blind, and He healed them all. Not only is the soul once dead made alive in this work—it is beautified and adorned. Yes, if you have faith but as a grain of mustard-seed, you will, by the vital power which is imparted, be clothed with graces of many a hue, each lovely in itself, and lovely in the place which it has to occupy: there will be the brighter colours, the blue, the pink, and the orange of faith and confidence and hope, mingling with the darker but not less lovely colours—with the red, the purple, and the olive of penitence, humility, and patience; and the whole lightened and brightened by what is, after all, the pure beam of heaven, by the pure white light of love, coming direct and unbroken from Him who is light and love. Yes, brethren, our souls need to be beautified. They need not only to be renewed, they need to be adorned. There are some Christian men and women who are under the influence of true faith and steady principle, but they are not amiable. They are cross or peevish or violent or stubborn. Such persons need to be clothed, that they become not only good, but lovely—as the lily is lovely. My friends, this world of ours is but a nursery, a place of nurture, where we are to be reared and then transplanted—transplanted into the paradise above. These flowers around us have their beauty but for a day; but it is different with the souls which are being adorned by the spirit of God. They are to bloom for ever in a better land, where are no winds to blight, no storms to destroy.

(*J. McCosh, D.D.*)   *Lessons from the lilies*:—1. The great characteristic of spring plants is the production of their blossoms direct from the root, and not, as in the plants of summer and autumn, from the sides and extremities of leaf-covered shoots.   And is not what is thus true in the physical world true also in the world of human nature?   All the spring-growths of human life come direct from the root of our being.   The blossoms of faith, hope, and love that are fairest and freshest are impulses and intuitions of the heart, and not slow growths elaborated by the foliage of experience.   First thoughts, that seem to come like inspirations directly from the Source of all good, are better than second thoughts that result from careful calculations and long processes of balancing of reasons.   The summer and the autumn of life teach us caution and reserve, and we produce our blossoms half concealed among the cloud of leaves that have nourished them.   But the spring gives confidence and openness, and loves to display its beauties with a charming candour and simplicity.   Happy are we if—when the snows of those dreary winter trials that have blighted our life have passed away—our souls have been so restored —made so fresh and young in the new spring life that has come upon us from on high, as that we shall put forth the beauties of holiness and the fruits of righteousness directly from hearts that are rooted and grounded in the love that passeth knowledge.   2. While sitting one day in a musing mood on the summit of a lofty mountain, I noticed growing in the crevices of the rock beside me a few plants, which are usually found only in the thick grassy sward of cultivated fields.   In that bare, bleak spot they were removed from the competition and pressure of their fellows, and had to struggle only with the elements for existence.   But instead of becoming more luxuriant in consequence, they were dwarfed and stunted, and miserable looking in comparison with their lowland brethren.   So is it, I thought, with human beings.   We all long at times to escape from the cares and fierce competition of our complicated social life, and to find our happiness in the primitive simplicity of nature.   But the evils of the wilderness are in reality worse than those of the crowd.   Better far the struggle for existence among our fellows, which helps to make us patient and self-denying, and fruitful in every good word and work, than the struggle with the loneliness and monotony of the hermitage, which makes the mind morbid, and leaves so much of our nature undeveloped. 3. To the plant growing in the dry, parched land, the cloudless sun is a foe that blasts and destroys.   But let its thirsty root have access to water in the irrigating channel, and immediately the withering sun is converted into the best of friends. The scorching rays that formerly caused the leaves to droop and languish now fill them with strong and vigorous life.   So the fierce rays of the world blight and wither the soul that has no counteracting and restorative principle of faith.   But let the root of our being reach the river that maketh glad the city of our God—let it drink from the heavenly well-springs—and immediately the blighting power of the world is overcome; the afflictions which are not joyous but grievous, help us to bring forth the peaceable fruits of righteousness; and all things minister to our faith and growth in grace.   4. In the midst of the everlasting snows of Mont Blanc—surrounded on every side by glaciers, and elevated many thousands of feet above the valley—there is a solitary projecting rock, where the scanty soil is covered in July with rare Alpine plants.   The rays of the sun, reflected by the snow and ice around, shine with double power upon this favoured spot, and create a warm, genial climate, in which the flowers bloom with unexampled beauty and luxuriance; while the frozen peaks shelter them from all the storms as in a kind of natural conservatory.   Thus the very inhospitable forces of nature minister to the welfare of these flowers.   When first I saw this summer garden in the midst of eternal winter, my heart was touched with the peculiar pathos of the sight.   It was an emblem to me of the blessedness to be found even in the midst of a sorrow that blights and chills the whole life.   The things that seem to be against us are in reality working together for our good.   5. After the creamy blossoms of the mountain-ash or rowan have passed away, a time succeeds in which the tree has no special beauty or brightness.   It lingers during the summer months in dull, cold, uniform greenness.   But all through this dormant season it is silently and unmarkedly preparing for the rich crop of scarlet berries with which it is crowned in autumn.   So the mind has periods of dullness, which usually occur after periods of much fertility and creative power.   It sheds its intellectual blossoms, and sinks into a state of languor and inaction.   But this dreary time is the herald of renewed activity and increased brightness to come.   6. Leaves work for the whole tree ; no part of it is independent of them, or could exist without them.   Blossoms, on the other hand, have a higher and more special function to perform. They elaborate honey, and perfume, and sweet juices not derivable from the leaves, and having special relation to the fruit. So is it with the human tree. Our existence and welfare depend upon those who till the soil and reap the fields. Our whole social economy is based upon the labour of their hands. They produce the food and work for the maintenance of the whole community. But poets and artists have higher functions assigned to them. They are the blossoms of humanity, whose creations impart colour and fragrance, light and sweetness to our life. To them we owe the most precious and enduring fruits of our civilization. 7. The seeds of a begonia taken from the same pod will germinate, some in a few days, some at the end of a year, and some at various intermediate times, even when they are all placed in the same external circumstances and exposed to the same conditions of growth. Similar differences of mental development and moral character are often exhibited by members of the same family, brought up around one mother's knee, and trained and educated in the same loving school of home. 8. Every one knows the beautiful downy head that succeeds the gaudy yellow of the common dandelion. It is composed of the delicate feather-winged seeds which the wind carries from place to place, so as to spread the plant as widely as possible in situations suitable for its growth. To country children it often serves as a rustic clock. They blow away the little feathery seeds in order to find out the time of day from the number of the ones that remain behind on the cushioned summit of the stem. Let us take heed, lest while we are only amusing ourselves, we should be scattering ignorantly the seed of evil influences, which may take root in other hearts, and lead to their undoing. The idle breath that blows away some airy trifle, merely to mark and pass the time, may have results as wide as the world, and as lasting as eternity. 9. Wet places generally produce fragrant plants. The sweet-gale, or Dutch-myrtle, grows in myriads among the moorland bogs; and the Eucalyptus, or gum-tree of Australia, thrives best in marshy soil. These, and such-like plants, exhale an agreeable balsamic odour, which has a most salubrious effect upon the moist atmosphere, and neutralizes the miasma of the swamps by its antiseptic qualities. When such aromatic plants predominate, the climate becomes healthy, and intermittent fever is unknown. There are similar compensations and counteractives in the moral world. There are Christians whose lives exhale the fragrance of holiness, and neutralize the noxious influence of the ungodly around them. 10. The favourite flower of the late French emperor, the third Napoleon, was the violet. Bouquets of it were always in his private chambers, and wreaths of it decked his bier and tomb. We should have fancied that a man so full of ambition, whose whole public life was one of much pomp and display, would have selected some prouder and gaudier flower. Perhaps it was the sense of contrast that led him to set his affections on a lowly plant, which has always been regarded as the emblem of humility; that made it refreshing for him to turn his eye, wearied with the glare and the loud-asserting grandeur of life, on this meek dweller in the shade, creeping over the mossy ground, and hiding its modest purple head among its own green leaves. Or was it because there was something of the violet-nature in the man's own character—because something in the heart of the great man corresponded to something in the nature of the lowly flower? Did he find a sympathy in this mute creature of God for a part of his being which was unknown to his fellow-creatures? The witness of the heart is not always written in the living epistle of the life, known and read of all men. A man is known as a hard, dry, logical writer, in whose works not a trace of sentiment or of feeling is seen; and yet this man in his secret heart has a passion for poetry, and in his private moments it forms his favourite reading. The great metaphysician, Sir William Hamilton, had a special delight in the fairy literature of little children, and returned to it with relief after the loftiest flights into the rare regions of abstruse philosophy, as the lark returns to its nest in the meadow from the blue fields of heaven. Probably more of the real man is told us by Napoleon's unexpected love of a little lowly flower, than we learn from all the grand successes and mournful reverses of his wonderfully chequered life. 11. In tropical countries the aspect of the vegetation is drooping, hanging down; in temperate countries it is upright, self-supporting. How characteristic of the difference between the inhabitants of the tropics, and those of the northern zones—the langour of the one and the energy of the other! 12. A beautiful little daisy grows by the side of a path in the outskirts of a large city. It follows with its golden eye all day the march of the sun through the heavens. Like a miniature sun it expands its white luminous petals—

and revolves in its little orbit on earth—as its great prototype revolves in its magnificent orbit on high. When the sun sets, the daisy closes its little eye and sinks into sleep. That daisy read me a lesson, which it would be my highest happiness to learn and practise. What it does will-lessly and unconsciously, I should do willingly and consciously, "Whom have I in the heavens but Thee, O God, and there is none upon the earth whom I desire beside Thee." God alone is co-natural with my spirit; all influences that own Him not are foreign and un-congenial; they have no true relation to my higher being. The True Light that lighteth every man that cometh into the world, is alone the element of life. (*H. Macmillan, D.D.*) *The lessons of the lilies :*—The works of God are words of God ; they speak to us. The works of God are mirrors, reflectors of God ; they show God to us. 1. The lilies of the field, as God's workmanship, reveal the fountain of life and being. Flowers taken alone cannot make manifest to us the depth and breadth of that fountain, but they may show us its quality. A cup of bright and sparkling water brought to us from a well tells us nothing of the quantity of water in that well, and nothing concerning the force of the spring or springs constituting the well ; but even a cup of cold and pure water may demonstrate that the well is pure. In like manner, flowers show nothing of boundless might and of high wisdom, but they do reveal the calm beauteousness of the source whence all living things flow. It is often said that there cannot be gross vice in a man who, delighting in flowers, cultivates them. May we not, in harmony with this remark, observe that there can be nothing harsh or hard or repulsive in the God who has made the lilies of the field ? 2. The lilies of the field embody and express Divine conceptions—thoughts and ideas of God. The image of every flower was in the mind of the Creator before creation. He designed the lilies of the field and the glorious company of their kindred. If this be accident, and if so-called accident can produce this, then verily accident is God. Not more certainly have paintings and sculpture been preconceived by the artists, and buildings of renown designed by architects, than flowers have been in the first instance mental creations by God. 3. The lilies of the field are God's workmanship. In the fine arts the conceiver is the worker. In other departments one designs and plans, and others execute. Flowers are the work of God's fingers. The first of every kind is a distinct creation, with seed in itself, and the rest the offspring of this seed. The seed is the second cause. God is the first cause. The laws of life and growth are God's mode of working, but in these laws there is a strong, skilful, living hand. There are rules of working in every handicraft, but no man denies the existence of the craftsman, because his productions are made by the established and recognized laws of his craft, and by tools adapted to the materials upon which he works, and to the object which he has before him. 4. The lilies of the field are God's care. This is not manifest to the eye of the body. And sometimes things happen which tend to exclude the idea and sense of God's care. The scythe of the mower cuts down the flowers. The wind passes over the flower and it is gone, and the place thereof knoweth it no more. The flower is consumed by some animal. A careless foot treads it down. Some hand—perhaps a wanton hand—plucks it. The flower has not grown without human culture. And thus, that which has reared the flower, and that which has cut short its day, alike hide the care of God. But care does not involve perpetual existence, or freedom even from that kind of injury which terminates being. In the providential sense there are no wild flowers. There are children without father and mother, or with evil fathers and mothers, who are destitute of human care ; but there are no flowers without Divine care. And the proof of Divine care is in their perfection. 5. The lilies of the field exhibit God's bountifulness. All flowers alike of the field and of the garden render some ordinary service—are of some use. They furnish food, medicine, clothing, shelter, to innumerable living things. And they render in part this service to man. God does not provide for us according to the rigid rule of that which is necessary. He adds to that which is necessary that which is pleasant to the senses and agreeable to the soul. The cup of supply is not only filled, it runs over. 6. The lilies of the field are propagated and developed by the working of various natural laws. There is a tendency in some minds to look only on the hard and rigorous side of law. But law is good. It secures many and great advantages. And we may transfer our remark to moral law. The law is holy, and the commandment holy and just and good. The morning dawns, the sun shines, spring takes the place of winter, the earth is fruitful, flowers bloom, and the lilies of the field grow, according to law. Some men magnify natural laws into a god, and others degrade moral laws into an irksome and unrighteous yoke. The moral law of God obeyed will bring forth nothing but love. To speak evil of any laws which God has made is to speak evil of God. 7. The lilies of the field are parts of a perfect whole. They sustain a relation with the whole earth, and with all that therein is, and they are in harmony with the entire creation. Their life, their growth, their form, their colour, are all in concord. There is nothing which they contradict, nothing with which they clash. The key-note of creation is in the flowers, a note neither too high nor too low for us men, but adapted to allure into singing the heart of every human child of God who has been reconciled unto his Father. 8. The lilies of the field show us a sense of beauty in the nature of God, and a satisfaction in its expression. To God, objects which are capable of being beautiful would not be "very good" unless they were clad in beauty. This is one reason of sin being so hateful to God. It is moral deformity, spiritual hideousness and ugliness. There is a beauty in holiness which is one of the Divine attractions to it. 9. The lilies of the field are what they are through various affinities and relationships. They are the children of the sun. His beams travel more than ninety millions of miles to cherish and to colour them. They are the children of the earth, and are brought up on her lap, and are nourished at her bosom. They are the children of the rain and of the dew and of the air. The flowers have several subordinate parents, each of which hath its service, and performs its part. In this condition of floral life we see one of the conditions of our own existence. We have a Divine Father, and we have human parents— mother and father. We have intercourse with heaven, and are resident on earth. We have to do with things spiritual and material, temporal and eternal. We are moved from within, and we are influenced from without. Various agencies and influences work together to array the lilies of the field, and several forces are ever working upon our human nature. A true Christian is a pilgrim on earth with citizenship in heaven, a child of God while a son of man, the workmanship of God, though instructed and comforted and helped by his fellows. As sun and earth and rain and dew work together to produce the lilies of the field, so all things work together for good to them that love God. 10. The lilies of the field are supposed to find in the nature of man that which will respond to their attractiveness. They are made, in part at least, for man's eye and for man's soul. If we were that which we ought to be, we should need no voice to bid us "consider the lilies." Discipleship to Jesus Christ does not shut our eyes to the earth, or close our hearts to the material works of God. 11. The lilies of the field may teach us freedom from care, and from morbid self-consciousness. That which God has to do for us He does perfectly, without our thought and care. Let us not direct our mind to that which belongs to God's thought. Let us not try to touch with our hands that which is the exclusive work of God's fingers. Anxiety can do nothing that is good, but it may effect much mischief. It cannot produce anything that is good. "Which of you by taking thought can add one cubit unto his stature?" It cannot beneficially alter anything. "Thou canst not make one hair white or black." It is not in itself a power of good. It is not power to pray. It is not power to work. It is not power to think. It is not power to judge. It is not power to discriminate and determine. But it is power for much mischief. It blinds the eye, so that there is no seeing of God, nor is there any vision of heaven. It makes the ear deaf, so that the voice of God's promises, and the voice of the Holy Ghost the Comforter, cannot be heard. It palsies the tongue in the direction of praise. It destroys all taste and relish for the abundant provisions of God's mercy. It spoils all present blessings. It wastes the passing moment. It encumbers to-day with that which belongs to the morrow. It forms unwise projects, and begets scaring dreams. It is as foolish as though the lilies were to begin to spin. O, ye anxious ones, consider the lilies. (*S. Martin.*) *The preaching of the lilies :*—I. Consider, how MIRACULOUSLY they grow. How wonderful, is it not ? to meditate upon it a little ; that wonderful process by which the hard, inorganic soil and rock are absorbed and assimilated, so that they become converted into organic forms ; yet the germ was there, otherwise no organization could have been developed. Surely nowhere is God more visible, I say, than in the flower. If the spirit of adoration does not descend upon a man by a bed of flowers, or by a single flower, it will descend nowhere ; Why, "Consider the lilies—how they grow." Is not this a miracle ? Is not this a mystery ? Consider who originated the beautiful type, and who perpetuates the beautiful race, and who adjusted the root to the soil and to the stem, and who broke open the seed, and bade the imprisoned spirit spring forth. II. Consider, WITH WHAT BEAUTY AND LOVELINESS they grow. Children of fashion and vanity, "consider how they grow!" They do not seek to deck themselves with gay and gaudy attire from without; all their adornment and ornament are from within; this is beauty, not of the silken robe, nor the cataract of the diamond; nor the sparkling jewel; this is beauty, and it resembles that "whose adornment is not of the plaiting of hair, nor the putting-on of apparel; but even the ornament of a meek and quiet spirit." That is how they grow; they show the obviousness of inner beauty; they have no fawning fashions; it is all very calm, and sweet, and quiet, and all from within; indeed, we know that all flowers are alike in this; the gaudy tulip and the flaunting holly-hock; their life, too, is from within; they all attract to themselves essences and helps from the whole earth; but they must be in harmony with the proper spirit of the plant. Pride assimilates to itself pride; and chastity, chastity. "Consider how they grow." "Yes, look to us," they seem to say, "we are as God clothed us; we are but grass of the field; but God clothed us; He gave us these white bridal vest-ments, and placed us in this conservatory of vivid green. You, children of men, run to and fro in search of the draperies you call your own; you heap adornment on adornment; until adornment becomes deformity; you are not clothed like the lily, and you never will be until your soul and your clothing shall have the same visible unity; a pure mind is seen even in the pattern and the fashion of its attire, and how can the lily-vestments suit you, whose souls are so soiled? But when you shall be pure within, then shall you be even as the angels, and then shall be given to you the garments pure and white, "which are the righteousness of the saints"; and then the Church, the "King's daughter, all glorious within," shall be like unto us; and the graces of the inner nature shall exhibit themselves in a life holy, harm-less, and renewed. III. Consider, BY WHAT IMPROBABLE AUXILIARIES they grow; by what a hidden life they grow. Is it not strange that such purity should spring from the black earth?—strange that such whiteness should shoot up from the soiled ground? It is a mighty miracle, and it is ever going on. Thus God is constantly transforming mineral darkness into floral light; thus He is constantly taking up the very miry clay itself, and moulding it and perfecting it into forms of beauty; and that which He is able to do in nature, shall I dare to think He cannot do in grace? IV. Consider, HOW YIELDINGLY AND COMPLYINGLY they grow. "Blossoms," says Pliny, the Latin naturalist, "are the joy of trees"; and wherever these beautiful vegetative creatures are found, they seem to say to us poor care-worn creatures: "Yes, be joyful too. The darkness of thy lot is only the avenue through which thou art passing. God, who is good to the flower and to the blossom of the tree, will not forget thee." V. Consider, TO WHAT DIVINE USES they grow. Legible lessons of Almighty wisdom, love, and power. (*E. Paxton Hood.*) *Consolation from flowers:*—There is, without a doubt, a profound human truth involved in this direction of our Lord. Biography furnishes us with some lessons, sublime in their simplicity, and consolations won by human suffering, only from the consideration of plants inferior in their beauty to lilies. Who is not acquainted with that memorable passage in the life of the great African traveller, Mungo Park, where, in the wilderness—robbed, stripped naked, five hundred miles from the nearest European settlement—surrounded by savage animals and savage men—in the depths of the horrible rainy season of Africa—in the very last and lowest extremity of human destitution and misery—he says: "I reflected that I was indeed a stranger in a strange land, yet I was still under the protecting eye of that Providence who has condescended to call Himself 'the stranger's friend.' At this moment, painful as my reflections were, the extraordinary beauty of a small moss irresistibly caught my eye. I mention this," he says, "to show from what trifling circum-stances the mind will sometimes derive consolation; for, though the whole plant was not larger than the top of my finger, I could not contemplate the delicate con-formation of its root, leaves, and capsule, without admiration. Can that Being, thought I, who planted, watered, and brought to perfection, in this obscure part of the world, a thing which appears of so small importance, look with unconcern upon the situation and sufferings of creatures formed after His own image? Surely not. Reflections like these would not allow me to despair. I started up, and, disregarding both hunger and fatigue, travelled forwards, assured that relief was at hand; and I was not disappointed. In a short time I came to a small village, where I overtook the two shepherds who had come with me from Kruman." Thus the little flower was the salvation of the great traveller, and the poor moss became to him what our Lord intended the lily should be to us. The stories of the consolations of the flowers are very numerous. The venerable and the holy Henry Martyn, in a well-known passage, describes the feelings existing in his mind by the discovery of a little flower, growing on the rocky summit of the Table Mountain at the Cape. " The road was steep, but the hope of soon being at the top encouraged me to ascend very lightly. As the Kloop opened, a beautiful flame-coloured flower appeared, in a little green hollow, waving in the breeze. It seemed to me an emblem of the beauty and peacefulness of Heaven, as it shall open upon the weary soul, when the journey of life is finished." And James Montgomery, in some very sweet verses, has commemorated the joy of Dr. Carey in India, at Serampore. In one of his letters, he says, " I don't know that I ever enjoyed, since leaving Europe, a pleasure so simple and exquisite as the sight of this English daisy afforded me ; not having seen one for upwards of thirty years, and never expecting to see one again." And I should think there are few of you with whom Picciola, is not a well-known and household story ; you remember the Italian Patriot—confined in an Austrian dungeon in the horrors of Spielberg ; when the last torments of the most petty, and disgusting, and loathsome tyranny were harassing the heart—when the cold stone walls, and the cruel bars, and the iron guards shut out all hope from the poor exile—a flower became an angel, and its delicate beauty, creeping through the chinks of the court-yard stones, awoke all grateful considerations, and became a missionary and messenger of peace and rest to the breaking heart. Yes, this is a guide to what our Lord meant, when He directed His disciples to the flowers. (*Ibid.*) *Trust in God taught by the lilies :*—This is the lesson of the lilies ; this is what they are saying to the doubting man. They keep hope, and trust, and faith alive in the world of the human heart. We need to stoop to the things which are beneath us, rather than to soar to things which are above us, to learn confidence in God ; and we gain that confidence more by glancing at the infinite expenditure of Divine purpose in the small and evanescent flower, rather than in the majestic and the transcendent mountain or star. Hence it is that they keep the heart fresh and cool from the fever of passion. You carry a flower to a sick room ; what a sweet power it sheds over the heavy airs of the chamber ; it will keep the heart of the poor invalid meditating the whole day, the primrose or the early spring violet. And I passed the other day by a poor widow, in a close London street, putting out of her window her bough-pot, and tenderly watching and watering it ; and methought her poor bereaved heart was drinking blessings beyond all her power to know, from those sweet flower-children bending their heads so meekly to her tending. Thus they are watched, these children of God. " And why art thou cast down, oh thou of little faith ? " (*Ibid.*) " *Consider the lilies !* "—In the English graveyard at Florence stands a broken column entwined by a lily carved in marble. It is erected to " Lily Nye, aged 21," and bears this inscription :

> " There was a lily once, most purely white,
>   We watched it daily, 'twas so fair a sight,
>   For she was purer than a driven flake
>   Of snow ; and in her grace most excellent,
>   The loveliest flower that death did ever take,
>   The tale—for tale there is—of this white stone,
>   Are these fair letters. While she lived she shone."

May it be ours, like the lily, while we live, to shine and brighten the world with heavenly beauty and heavenly blessing. (*A. J. Griffith.*)   *Grass :*—No natural object gathers around it so many scriptural associations, and suggests so many spiritual analogies, as the grass of the field. The wailing sibylline voice, borne on every breeze, has never ceased to echo over the earth, " All flesh is grass." This burden of Nature's prophecy is true literally as well as metaphorically. It is one example among innumerable others of what has been often observed, that the poet is the real philosopher, and the truest language necessarily what we call figurative. The lesson which the perishable form of the grass teaches, is rendered more impressive still by the enduring part which its structure performs in the economy of nature. It is the first organized agency that extracts, by its living energies, nutritious particles from the hard inorganic soil. In its tissues the dust of the earth first becomes vital. Day and night, season after season, it is unceasingly purveying for the wants of the animal kingdom, gathering the materials of nourishment and strength from the air and earth, reducing the impalpable and evanescent forces of light, heat, and moisture, into solid and enduring forms, which can be eaten and transformed into complicated organisms and vital powers. Man cannot live upon grass, properly so called. He cannot derive a direct subsistence from it. The experiment was once made in notable circumstances, but it turned out a deplorable failure. During the disastrous campaign of Napoleon's army in Russia, the soldiers, in the absence of all other food, were obliged to boil and eat the common grass of the field, which they dug out from beneath its covering of snow and ice; and in every case where this wretched food was partaken of in sufficient quantity to allay the intolerable cravings of hunger, delirium and racking pains were the results. But, though grass eaten directly would prove injurious to man, inasmuch as his digestive organs are not adapted for its assimilation, it forms the support of domesticated animals, which he rears exclusively for their use as human food. The materials of his structure are first derived from the air, earth, and water, by means of grass; they are still further organized and prepared by the agency of graminivorous animals; and they reach him at last in a proper condition for his nourishment in the shape of animal food. The grass of the field is thus indirectly, but most truly, man's stay and support. But there is a way in which even directly grass forms human food. The stem and blades, and other inferior parts of the vegetation, are intended for the support of the inferior animals; but the fruitful ear, the more highly-organized seed, the crown and consummation of the plant, the "flower of grass," into which its vital powers and nourishing qualities are drawn up and concentrated, is reserved for food to man. How strange to think that the most highly-organized of the inhabitants of the earth, created in the image of God, should thus depend for his subsistence directly and indirectly upon the lowest and simplest of all herbs! "He maketh the grass to grow upon the mountains." The wild grasses are taken, as it were, under the special providence of God. In their perennial verdure in regions above the zone of man's cultivation, we have a perpetual proof of God's care of the lower animals that neither sow nor reap. The mountain grasses grow spontaneously; they require no culture but such as the rain and the sunshine of heaven supply. They obtain their nourishment directly from the inorganic soil, and are independent of organic materials. Nowhere is the grass so green and vigorous as on the beautiful slopes of lawn-like pasture high up on the Alps, radiant with the glory of wild flowers, and ever musical with the hum of grasshoppers and the tinkling of cattle-bells. Innumerable cows and goats browse upon them; the peasants spend the summer months in making cheese and hay from them for winter consumption in the valleys. This exhausting system of husbandry has been carried on during untold centuries; no one thinks of manuring the Alpine pastures; and yet no deficiency has been observed in their fertility, though the soil is but a thin covering spread over the naked rocks. It may be regarded as a part of the same wise and gracious arrangement of Providence, that the insects which devour the grasses on the *Kuh*, and *Schaf Alpen*, the pasturages of the cows and sheep, are kept in check by a predominance of carnivorous insects. Were the herbivorous insects allowed to multiply to their full extent, in such favourable circumstances as the warmth of the air and the verdure of the earth in Switzerland produce, the rich pastures which now yield abundant food for upwards of a million and a half of cattle would speedily become bare and leafless deserts. Not only in their power of growing without cultivation, but also in the peculiarities of their structure, the mountain grasses proclaim the hand of God. Many of them are viviparous. Instead of producing flowers and seeds, as the grasses in the tranquil valleys do, the young plants spring from them perfectly formed. They cling round the stem and form a kind of blossom. In this state they remain until the parent stalk withers and falls prostrate on the ground, when they immediately strike root and form independent grasses. This is a remarkable adaptation to circumstances; for it is manifest that, were seeds instead of living plants developed in the ears of the mountain grasses, they would be useless in the stormy regions where they grow. They would be blown away far from the places they were intended to clothe, to spots foreign to their nature and habits, and thus the species would speedily perish. The more we think of it, the more we are struck with the wise foresight which suggested the creative Fiat, "Let the earth bring forth grass." It is the most abundant and the most generally diffused of all vegetation. It suits almost every soil and climate. It forms pastoral landscapes under the weeping skies of Europe; it forms bamboo forests and cane-brakes under the glowing skies of the tropics. It ministers to the food of man in mild climates; it ministers to the luxuries of man in hot climates. It may, however, be said to cover with a uniform green mantle the whole surface of the globe. And this mantle is not only ornamental, but eminently useful. It protects the roots of trees and flowers from the scorching effects of the summer's sun and the blight of the winter's frost. I began this paper with the assertion that man lives, both directly and indirectly, upon grass; I close it with the inevitable antithesis, that grass lives upon man. The melancholy words of Scripture, "All flesh is grass," are equally true whether we read them backwards or forwards. Strange mysterious circle of relations within which all organized nature is contained, and in which man himself, in common with the beast and herb of the field, has to perform his part and exchange offices and duties! The particles which circulate through his system must be again reduced to the inorganic state, out of which they were first formed, and restored to the tissues of the grass from which he derived them. The debt of nature must be paid; the obligations which for threescore years and ten had been accumulating must be discharged at last. The body, that had been sustained in life by the yearly produce of the fields, must return again to the dust to fertilize and enrich the produce of future fields, and keep the great vortex of life continually in motion. Grass forms the beautiful and appropriate covering of the grave. As it is the earth's first blessing, so it is her last legacy to man,

> " Whose part in all the pomp that fills
> The circuit of the summer hills
> Is—that his grave is green."

The body that it fed when living, it reverently covers when dead with a garment richer than the robe of a king. When all other kindness in food, and clothing, and emblematic teaching is over, it takes up its silent Rizpah-watch beside the tombstone, and forsakes not what all else has forsaken. Gently does it wrap up the ashes of the loved and lost, wreathing like a laurel crown the cold damp brow with its interlacing roots, drawing down to the darkness and the solitude the warm bright sunshine and the soft dews of heaven. (*H. Macmillan, D.D.*) *Christ, the interpreter of Nature*:—To the filial eye of Jesus Christ the moral world always shone through the natural world and glorified it. He saw all the beauty of Nature; nothing of all its great riches was lost on Him; and in a multitude of parables and other pictorial touches, He has set Nature in her endless operations and aspects before us. But our Lord could never for a moment rest in Nature, or look on her as an end in herself. To him the whole visible universe was eloquent with meanings and lessons, with reminiscences and presages that ennobled and glorified her, because they came through her from a better world out of which she too had sprung, and for the sake of which she was daily sustained and administered. The cornfields, the vineyards, the flowers, the birds of the air, the flocks of sheep in the meadows, the sky, the clouds, the times of ploughing and sowing and reaping, the starry nights, and the all-enriching sun—all the powers, provisions, and aspects of Nature were dear and beautiful to Him; and all the more so, that their beauty and beneficence were not their own, but were all so many manifestations of the wisdom and power and goodness of His Father. The sun that rose on the evil and on the good was "His sun"; the rain fell on the just and the unjust from His windows; His Father fed all the fowls of the air, and clothed all the grasses of the field. Jesus Christ was the only true Minister and Interpreter of Nature she has ever had. He alone fully understood her place and appreciated her plan. He alone could reveal her, and set forth her whole message, because He saw her and rejoiced in her as the manifestation of His Father's wisdom, and the operation of His Father's hands. I suppose the beasts of the field see the greenness of the grass and the lustre of the flowers among which they feed their fill and lie down to rest. I suppose the eagle also sees the vast landscape over which he sails; but no one supposes that the brute cattle have any knowledge or enjoyment of the beauty amid which they browse, or that a ravenous bird is at all tamed by being bathed daily in the glorious sunlight. They have no eye wherewith to see the beauty of earth and sea and sky; Nature has no revelation of that kind to make to them. And there are too many men who are as beasts are before the beauty of Nature: they have eyes, but they see not; and ears, but they hear not. There are other men, again, who are entranced and enraptured with the glory of creation, but who are all the time as dead as a stone to the glory of God. But the immediate aim of Christ in this most exquisite passage is to lead us all to trust ourselves and all that concerns us to the Fatherly providence of Almighty God. These cabinet-pictures of animate and inanimate nature are not works of pure art, that is to say, they are not pure

art in the sense of being without practical application to the needs and wants
of men. They are as beautiful as if they stood here for their beauty alone; and
they are as useful, as instructive, and as full of moral ends, as if they were barren
of every other quality. We are so limited in our gifts and in our scope, that we
have often to shut out all thought of use when we aim at a perfect work of art;
just as, on the other hand, we are often compelled to neglect the pursuit of beauty
when we are bent on utility. But both Nature and Art, with the language that
best exhibits them, are all plastic and harmonious in the hands of Jesus Christ.
He is not instructive at the expense of beauty; nor, when most beautiful in His
words and works, is He less rich to those who sit at His feet. Pointing in the
most perfect words to the fowls of the air as they are fed from the hand of God,
and then at the lilies of the field as they outshine Solomon in all his glory, our
Lord says to us, " So, only in better ways, does your Heavenly Father care for, and
take all needful thought for you. Leave, then, all your over-thoughtfulness and
anxiety to Him; He alone can fulfil all your thoughts and without anxiety make
them good. Torture not yourselves with what is above your strength and beyond
your scope. Take all thought for that part in your life and in His providence
which He has appointed you. Do your daily task with all fervour and fidelity, but
after your allotted thought has been taken and your appointed part accomplished,
leave the issue with Him who holds all issues in His own hand. Plough your field
to its utmost furrow; sow your seed with a liberal hand, and when the harvest
comes put in the sickle and store up the hundredfold fruits. Sow your seed with
all thoughtfulness in the seedtime, and leave it without more thought till the harvest. With the sowing of the seed your work is, for the time, done. Take your
well-earned rest, and thus you will be the more ready for the arduous labours of
the harvest. Do not wade about among the sprouting corn as if your restless feet
would make the blade fill better, or the shock ripen sooner. The plough, and the
seed-basket, and the sickle, and the threshing instrument, and the winnowing fan
are all yours to make use of with all due thought and care, each at its proper
season; but the former and the latter rains, the filling sun and the mellowing winds,
are all in your Father's hand. 'I have planted,' said Paul, 'and Apollos watered;
but God gave the increase.' Leave, then, your husbandry in His hands also.
Take you no thought where He takes all." But the best thing in this rich and
beautiful passage, and the thing to which it all leads up, is yet to come, and it
comes in these noble and inspiring words: "But seek ye first the kingdom of God,
and His righteousness." Having taught and illustrated in the happiest and wisest
way the religious observation and use of Nature, and having by means of Nature
risen above Nature and entered the all-embracing economy of Divine Providence,
Christ now comes to that for which both Nature and Providence exist and operate,
namely, for man, and for his pursuit and possession of righteousness. This is the
end, this is the goal, this is the crown of all. He has already warned His disciples
in never-to-be-forgotten words that their righteousness must far exceed the
righteousness of the scribes and Pharisees; must indeed be a righteousness of
another kind and quality altogether. Seek first, He would say, the solid righteousness of the ten commandments. "Think not that I am come to destroy the law
or the prophets; I am not come to destroy, but to fulfil." Then seek the yet more
spiritual righteousness of this sermon I am now preaching unto you. And if there
be any other righteousness yet to be revealed, God will ere long open up and make
offer of that also unto you. Sufficient for the Sermon on the Mount is the
righteousness thereof. (*A. Whyte, D.D.*) *The beauty of the grass*:—To get a
good idea of the beauty of the grass, endeavour, in imagination, to form a picture
of a world without it. It is precisely to the scenery of Nature what the Bible is to
literature. Do you remember that idea of Froude's, that the Bible had been
obliterated, and every other book had thereat lost its value, and literature was at
an end? Take away this green ground colour on which Dame Nature works her
embroidery patterns, and where would be the picturesque scarlet poppies or white
daisies, or the grey of the chalk cliffs, or the golden bloom of a wilderness of
buttercups? Its chief service to beauty is as the garment of the earth. It
watches night and day, at all seasons of the year, " in all places that the eye of
Heaven visits," for spots on which to pitch new tents, to make the desert less
hideous, fill up the groundwork of the grandest pictures, and give the promise
of plenty on the flowery meadows where it lifts its silvery and purple panicles
breast-high, and mocks the sea in its rolling waves of sparkling greenness. (*C.
Hibberd.*)

Ver. 29. **Neither be ye of doubtful mind.**—*A new parable :*—Our Lord here crushes a whole world of meaning into a single word, which, as we study it, resolves itself into a bright, impressive picture or parable. The phrase really comes to this : " Do not toss about in the windy offing, when you may ride safely in the sheltered haven." And if we take it in connection with what goes before and what comes after, we find that the complete parable runs thus : " Do not toss about on the wide dangerous sea of Care, on which so many make shipwreck, but rather take shelter in the safe and tranquil harbour of Trust in God." Had our Lord paused to expand the parable, and had He thrown it into the form which most of His parables assume, He might have used some such words as these : " The Kingdom of God is like unto a large and tranquil harbour, into which all who sail across the stormy sea of life may enter and be at rest." Now the calm and simple ideal of life which Christ here holds up before us is one that has a special claim on us, and a special charm, in days such as these when most men are seeking outward good—seeking wealth and worldly advancement—with a passionate and feverish eagerness. Who does not long, at least at times, to escape

> The heavy trouble, the bewildering care
> That weighs us down who live and earn our bread?

Who is not weary of the strain, the waste, the ungenerous rivalry, the intense and protracted drudgery which what men call " success in life " demands? Who does not see that the pursuit of what we call " comfort " is well-nigh taking all comfort out of our days? Who does not admit, in any moment of cool reflection, that the general homage to wealth is becoming a degrading and unmanly idolatry, inducing false estimates of character, and leading men to value the means of living above the true ends of life? What we should admire in our neighbours, what we should chiefly aim at for ourselves, is not a gay and wealthy outside of circumstance, but noble character—virtue, wisdom, piety, inward worth. And this is the aim, the ideal, which the Lord Jesus sets before us. He bids us seek first the Kingdom of God ; and the Kingdom of God is *within* us, not without. He would have us cultivate those graces of spiritual character which fit us both to meet any circumstances and changes of circumstances in this life, and to enter with the joy of a foreseen triumph on the dark and narrow avenue which leads to the life to come. If we take His counsel, He promises us an absolute freedom from care. He assures us that we shall ride safely in a sheltered port instead of tossing on the heaving storm-swept sea. Not that He prohibits care and thought. A man *must* take thought, must study and plan and contrive, if he is to be a wise man. We *may* make the voyages which the necessities of life demand, and bring home much store of merchandise ; but then, we are to *have* a home, " a city of the soul " to which we may repair ; and when we reach it, we are not to cast anchor in the windy offing, but to take refuge in the tranquil haven. That is to say, we are to attend to the duties and labours of life, attend to them with diligence, give our best thought and care to them ; but, when these duties and labours are discharged, we are not to vex our souls with an incessant anxiety as to the issue of our toils ; we are to leave that with God, and not to be careful because He cares for us. So, again, *forethought* is no more forbidden than thought. A wise man, a man with " discourse of reason," *i.e.*, a man in whom reason is not dumb and inert, must " look before and after." There would be no unity in his life, no continuous development and activity, no linking on of month to month and year to year, if he did not look forward and scheme for the future as well as for the present. What Christ forbids is so looking onward to to-morrow as to cloud to-day, so anticipating the future as to darken the present. And this is the very point at which we commonly fail. To-day may be well enough, we admit ; or, at the worst, we could get through its tasks and endure its trials. But what of to-morrow? What of the future? How shall we meet the toils and losses and troubles we foresee? Now it is from this pernicious habit of " borrowing trouble from the future," as though we had not enough of it in the present, that Christ would save us. " Trust in God for the future," He says ; " Do your duty to-day, and leave to-morrow with Him. And let this trust be your tranquil haven, your harbour of refuge, whenever the waves of Care run high." Rest and refit in the harbour to-night ; and if, when the morning breaks, you have to sail out into a stormy sea, you will at least be in a better condition to meet it. (*S. Cox, D.D.*)   *Possessions and prospects :*— Perhaps I am speaking to some child of poverty. I remember a beautiful story applicable to you. The late Lady Huntingdon, passing by a low, mean-looking cottage one day, heard a faint, soft sound inside, and drew up to the door, when she heard a voice uttering these words, " O my God, I thank Thee that I have all this—the Lord Jesus now and heaven at last." Thought the listener, what can this mean? Curiosity is strong; and giving the door a little touch, she saw an aged one—a poor woman, eighty years of age—with a pitcher of water and a crust, and her hands raised in the attitude of thanksgiving, and her words were, " O Lord, I thank Thee that I have all this, and the Lord Jesus Christ, and heaven at last." Rest in His word. "My God shall supply all your need." Oh, sweet the scant supply where there is a confiding, joyous heart! Birds of song sing as merrily just before their breakfast, though they don't know where it is to come from, as they do when they have got it. And the God who watches over the bird will not neglect you. "Lacked ye anything?" said the Lord to the seventy, who had been sent out without any worldly emoluments; and they answered, "No, Lord." Many a saint at the close of his pilgrimage can say the same; can say, "Notwith-standing all the vicissitudes and changes and losses that I have endured, God has given me food and raiment, and I have, not wanting much, wanted for nothing." (*J. Denham Smith.*) *Confidence in God :*—" Never did man die of hunger who served God faithfully," Cuthbert would say, when nightfall found them supperless in the waste. "Look at that eagle overhead! God can feed us through him if He will "—and once, at least, he owed his meal to a fish that the scared bird let fall. A snowstorm drove his boat on the coast of Fife. "The snow closes the road along the shore," moaned his comrades; "the storm bars our way over sea." "There is still the way of heaven that lies open," said Cuthbert. (*J. R. Green, " Short History."*)

Ver. 31. **Seek ye the Kingdom of God.**—*Manner of sanctifying our exertions for daily bread :*—The Lord gives us continually our daily bread, multiplying for this the grain in the field; yet are we contented with it? The reason of our discon-tentedness is, because we are inclined to make our daily pursuits for a livelihood the main point, and the Kingdom of God a secondary one. Perhaps we go so far even as to separate one from the other, although religion, like the leaven, should penetrate all our works and bring God's blessing upon all we do. This blessing will be given to us if we endeavour to sanctify our solicitude for our daily bread, by performing our employments—I. IN OBEDIENCE TO GOD. 1. It is God's will that I work. By this truth we should be induced—(1) To consider and esteem labour as a sacred duty. (2) To avoid idleness, which is not only sinful in itself, but also the source of sin and poverty. 2. I work for God's honour. This truth renders labour—(1) Consoling, though hard. (2) Meritorious. II. IN THE SPIRIT OF PENI-TENCE. I must work, because I am a sinner. 1. This reflection will reconcile you to your work. As the heart is wounded by undeserved punishment, so a generous mind finds satisfaction in a consciousness of justice being done. 2. It ennobles man : imparting to him—(1) Deep humility. (2) True wisdom. III. IN ORDER TO FULFIL A DUTY TOWARDS OTHERS. Only he that has lost all sense of duty can refuse to work. For—1. Labour is a duty of justice. God's wrath is challenged by—(1) Idlers. (2) Squanderers. 2. Labour is a duty of charity. (1) You are bound to provide for your family. (2) And for the poor. (*Bishop Galura.*) *The wisdom of attending to God's business :*—Your business—you cannot neglect that. Call to mind the story of the rich English merchant to whom Elizabeth gave some com-mission of importance, and he demurred to undertake it, saying, "Please your Majesty, if I obey your behest, what will become of these affairs of mine?" And his monarch answered, "Leave those things to me, when you are employed in my service, I will take charge of your business." So will it be with you. Do but sur-render yourself to Christ, and He, of His own free will, takes in hand all your affairs. (*C. H. Spurgeon.*) *God's promise to be relied on :*—I was once crossing the Atlantic, and had come within three days' sail of the Irish coast. Fog and darkness shut out the sun by day and the stars at night. We had to trust to dead reckoning—that is, to the log, the compass, the chart, and other nice nautical com-putations. Standing by the captain, I heard him say on the last of these days, "We ought to see Fastnet Light in *twelve minutes !* " I took out my watch and waited. We saw the welcome light in just *eleven !* " There, thought I, is a triumph of nautical skill and calculation, to push on so steadily and surely through the darkness day after day to the point aimed at. We justly confide in one who has proved himself trustworthy in human affairs, but the witness of God is greater.

Why ever distrust Him? He has not only fixed the movements of the stars and the tides, but His promises of grace are unchangeable. (*R. S. Storrs, D.D.*) *Seeking God's Kingdom for children also :*—" Few things are looked back on by me with less satisfaction than my own conduct in respect to my children, except in one particular, which appears to have been the grand secret ; and that is, that I have always sought for them, as well as for myself, in the first place, the Kingdom of God and His righteousness." (*T. Scott.*) *Admonition addressed to the young :*— Let us press the seeking God's kingdom first on those who are yet in the springtime of their days. And we will just tell you what we believe would constitute a thorough submission to the precept of our text, and what, therefore, entitles a man to depend on the fulfilment of the promise. We will suppose that, from his youth upwards, an individual has proposed to himself the salvation of his soul as the prime object to engage his solicitudes and occupy his strivings. We may suppose that, so soon as he could discern the evil and the good, so soon as the will had the power of making an election, he decided in favour of the paths of righteousness, and set out on the heavenward course ; and, ever afterward, we may regard him as holding on in one uniform course of faith and obedience ; so that, whatever the other objects which may demand and obtain some share of his attention, he keeps ever uppermost, as the great end of his being, that attainment of God's favour to which he had devoted himself at the outset of life. Of such an individual it may be asserted, in all the extent of which the expression admits—he has " sought first the Kingdom of God and His righteousness." He has sought it first, as having begun with this seeking ; he has sought it first, as having never permitted another object to take precedence : and to the doing this is what we would earnestly exhort the younger of our hearers. " Seek ye first the kingdom of God and His righteousness " : seek ye first this kingdom—first, before ye seek the wealth of the world, which cannot satisfy you, or the honours of the world, which will only mock you, or the pleasures of the world, which like the Dead Sea fruits, wear a bloom to the eye, but are ashes to the taste—first, before the strength has been impaired, and the spirit has been broken, and the eye has lost its fire, and the hope is sick with disappointment. "*First !* " Will ye give the bounding pulse, and the soaring thought, and the eager glance, and the rushing purpose, to the slavery of time and created things, and think of bringing the jaded energies, the thin grey hairs, the emaciated limbs, and consecrating them to the service of God? We know that even in old age the kingdom may be sought, the kingdom may be found ; we dare not, therefore, and we thank God that we dare not, regard any individual, be he ever so old, be he ever so hardened, as having outlived the opportunity of being saved. We preach to the man of four-score years ; and though, in the expressive language of Solomon—"the daughters of music are brought low, and the grasshopper is a burden, and the silver cord is almost loosed, and the golden bowl broken," we still say to him, " Now is the accepted time; now is the day of salvation." And yet it is impossible not to feel, that where there has been, for forty, or sixty, or seventy years, a determined resistance to all the proffers of the gospel, the case is growing comparatively hopeless. We may go on with our work ; but it is impossible to go on with a very light heart. And never does the minister of Christ seem charged with a commission in which success is so doubtful, as when sent to the infirm and worn-out sinner, who, having given the strength of life to Satan and the world, has at last only the dregs with which to make an offering to his God. We say, indeed, it is our duty, ay, and it is our privilege, to say, even to the old person who has been hardening for half a century under faithful sermons —It is not too late to " seek " ; " seek," therefore ; " the Pearl of great price " may even yet be found—even yet, though the last streak of light is fading from the sky, though the film is gathering on the eye, and the cold and rough wind threatens to put out the lamp ; we say to him, " Seek ! " But now tell me, my brethren, can we do otherwise than feel, that even if he seeks he seeks last. And where is the promise to those who seek last ?—last, inasmuch as heaven is not sought until earth is sliding from the grasp? Where is the promise to those that " seek " *last* " the kingdom of God and his righteousness ? " We remember the words which, in the Book of Proverbs, are placed in the mouth of Eternal Wisdom—" I love them that love Me ; and those that seek Me early shall find Me." " Those that seek Me *early !* " Here is an express promise. It is a promise that does not exclude those who seek late, but certainly it does not include them. We have, however, better hopes of the young. We know, indeed, that you feel tempted to delay and put off the giving heed to the solemn things of eternity. And why so ? Because you regard religion as a melancholy thing—as circumscribing your pleasures and curtailing your enjoyments; and you feel that it will interfere with many things in which you delight—the gewgawry of fashion, and the revelry of life. There are certain things which you wish to keep a little longer, and which you perceive that true religion will require you to surrender. So you make the calculation—you shall run but little risk in giving a year or two more to the world; you shall have time enough left for the care of the soul. Ah! thus, to speak the unvarnished truth, you are balancing the chances of destruction against another draught of the intoxicating cup; you loiter round the edge of the pit, to pluck flowers which fade in the gathering. And yet all the while the true pleasure is in religion. Yes, that it is—the elevation of soul—the companionship with beings of the invisible world —the filling up with God the immeasured voids of a human spirit—the beatings of a large philanthropy—the sense that, "all things are ours, for we are Christ's, and Christ is God's"—life curtained by lovingkindness—death abolished by the Mediator—eternity studded with the rich and the radiant,—these are ours; we know them, we feel them to be ours. What! then, has religion no pleasures? Nay! "seek ye first the kingdom of God, and His righteousness." It is seeking peace; it is seeking comfort; it is seeking happiness. Seek ye this "*first*," assured that—oh! for the testimony that might be given from above! oh! for the testimony that might be given from beneath!—assured that, though thousands have wept bitter, scalding tears because they sought late, none have ever found that they began too soon. (*H. Melvill, B.D.*)   *God's people not forgotten by Him:*—Many years ago, when in my country charge, I returned one afternoon from a funeral, fatigued with the day's work. After a long ride, I had accompanied the mourners to the churchyard. As I neared my stable door, I felt a strange prompting to visit a poor widow who, with her invalid daughter, lived in a lonely cottage in an outlying part of the parish. My natural reluctance to make another visit was overcome by a feeling which I could not resist, and I turned my horse's head towards the cottage. I was thinking only of the poor widow's spiritual needs; but when I reached her little house, I was struck with its look of unwonted bareness and poverty. After putting a little money into her hand, I began to inquire into their circumstances, and found that their supplies had been utterly exhausted since the night before. I asked them what they had done. "I just spread it out before the Lord!" Did you not tell your case to any friend?" "Oh no, sir; naebody kens but Himsel' and me! I kent He wadna forget, but I didna ken hoo he wad help me till I saw you come riding ower the brae, and then I said, There's the Lord's answer!" Many a time has the recollection of this incident encouraged me to trust in the loving care of my heavenly Father. (*J. H. Norton.*)

Ver. 32. **Fear not, little flock.**—*Christians forbidden to fear:*—I. An agreeable resemblance. A flock (Psa. lxxix. 13; John x. 27). The flock of Christ is—1. A purchased flock (1 Cor. vi. 20; 2 Pet. ii. 1; Acts xx. 28). 2. A flock washed in the blood of Jesus (1 John i. 7; Rev. i. 5). 3. A chosen flock (Matt. xx. 16; Mark xiii. 20). 4. A marked flock (2 Tim. ii. 19; John xiii. 35). 5. A patient flock—under provocations, and amidst sufferings and delays (Job i. 22; Rom. xii. 12; Luke xxi. 19; Heb. x. 36, xii. 1, 2, vi. 12; Rom. ii. 7). Christ an example (1 Peter ii. 21–25). 6. A harmless flock (Matt. x. 16; Philem. ii. 15). 7. A flock exposed to troubles and enemies (Eph. vi. 11, 12, 13). 8. A useful flock. II. A distressing truth. A little flock. 1. Small at its commencement. 2. Small at the present day, when compared with the great bulk of mankind. III. A benignant engagement. "It is your Father's good pleasure to give you the kingdom." 1. The kingdom of His power (Psa. cv. 12, 13; Dan. iv. 3). 2. The kingdom of His grace (2 Cor. iii. 18). 3. The kingdom of glory (1 Cor. vi. 9). This is heaven, and in this view of it conveys—(1) The idea of power. A kingdom implies a sceptre, authority, and dominion. (2) The idea of glory. It is the abode of glorified spirits. It is the abode of the celestial hierarchy. It is the abode of Jesus. It is the abode of God the Father. (3) The idea of felicity (Rev. vii. 9–17). It is our Father's good pleasure (Isa. lxiii. 16). He is our Father — 1. By right of creation (Mal. ii. 10). 2. By right of preservation. 3. By right of redemption (Gal. iii. 13; Job xix. 25). 4. By right of adoption (Rom. viii. 15, 16). It is His good pleasure to give us the kingdom. It is not a debt but a gift—a free gift. IV. A prohibition. "Fear not." What is it that true believers are not to fear? 1. They are not to fear God with a slavish fear (Rom. viii. 15; 1 John iv. 18). A filial fear they must have

(Psa. lxxxix. 7 ; Heb. xii. 28 ; Psa. xxxiv. 9). 2. They are not to fear man (Isa. lvii. 11 ; Matt. x. 28). (1) The wrath of man (Psa. cxxiv. 1–3 ; lxxxii. 29). (2) The power of man (Heb. xiii. 6 ; Isa. xxxvi. 29). (3) The policy of man (Job v. 12, 13 ; 1 Cor. i. 25). 3. They are not to fear the instruments of human cruelty (Isa. liv. 17). 4. They are not to fear suffering under affliction (John xiv. 33 ; Job v. 19–22 ; 2 Cor. iv. 17 ; Rom. viii. 10). 5. They are not to fear Satan (Rom. vi. 20). 6. They are not to fear death (Rom. viii. 38, 39 ; 1 Cor. xv. 55 ; 2 Cor. v. 5). 7. They are not to fear hell (John iii. 18, v. 36 ; Isa. liv. 9). The reason why they ought not to fear—1. It dishonours God. 2. It slanders His power (1 Chron. xvii. 24). 3. It slanders His faithfulness (2 Tim. ii. 13 ; 1 Thess. v. 24). 4. It slanders His wisdom (1 Tim. i. 17). 5. It slanders His care (1 Pet. v. 7 ; Matt. vii. 11 ; Isa. xxvii. 3). 6. It slanders their calling—they are called to be saints (Isa. li. 2). 7. It slanders their cause, viz., religion, the cause of God (Deut. xxiii. 29). 8. It is hurtful to them—it distracts their minds (Luke viii. 22–25). 9. It produces hypocrisy and dissimulation (Isa. lvii. 11 ; Gen. xx. 2–11 ; xxvi. 19). 10. It enfeebles the soul (Isa. vii. 2). 11. It strengthens the enemy (Jud. iii. 2). 12. It discourages the saint (Deut. xx. 8). APPLICATION. 1. Are you comprised in this little flock? 2. Go on with undaunted courage, knowing that God will help you, and afterwards give you the kingdom. (*J. Blackmore*). *Fear not, little flock :—* I. THE PERSONS ADDRESSED. "Little flock." 1. Separated by eternal election. 2. Bought by particular redemption. 3. Effectually called. The word "flock" denotes — 1. Their patience. 2. Meekness. 3. Humility. 4. Harmlessness. 5. Comparatively few in number. 6. And little in the estimation of the world. II. THE EXHORTATION. "Fear not." 1. Fear not the body of sin. "Thine iniquity is taken away, and thy sin purged" (Isa. vi. 7). 2. The oppositions of Satan. "Through death He might destroy him that had the power of death, that is, the devil" (Heb. ii. 14). 3. The besetments of the world. "We are chastened of the Lord, that we should not be condemned with the world" (1 Cor. xi. 32). "Fear not," for—1. Temporal mercies. 2. The efficacy of grace. 3. The faithfulness of God. 4. For Christ is all love. 5. The Spirit constant. 6. And heaven sure. III. THE REASON ASSIGNED. "It is your Father's good pleasure to give you"—1. The kingdom of grace here. 2. The kingdom of glory hereafter. It implies that it is — 1. Their Father's gift. 2. By His soverign pleasure. 3. Delighting in them. 4. Rejoicing over them. 5. And supplying all things to them. (*T. B. Baker.*) *The privileges of Christ's flock :—*I. WHY THE LORD'S PEOPLE ARE CALLED A LITTLE FLOCK. 1. They are called a "flock," principally from the peculiar regard shown them by the Lord. 2. They are called a "little flock," because they are but few in number. II. WHAT THEY HAVE TO FEAR. They are not exempt from the common calamities of life. In some respects they are more exposed to them than other people. They have reason therefore to fear—1. Wants. Though man may provide for to-morrow, he cannot secure what he has provided. Hence all are so desirous of placing themselves as far as possible out of the reach of any disastrous contingencies. In making such provision the true Christian labours under many disadvantages. He cannot use those means of acquiring wealth which the generality of the world employ without any scruple. He cannot devote all his time and all his attention to secular engagements. On these accounts he may at times be tempted to indulge excessive care, and to harbour fears of want and embarrassment. 2. Sufferings. The flock of Christ are not only subject to the trials incident to our present state, but are liable to many sufferings peculiar to themselves. They are "as sheep in the midst of wolves." III. WHY, NOTWITHSTANDING THEIR DANGERS, THEY SHOULD NOT FEAR. God has "provided for them a kingdom." God condescends call to Himself their "Father." And deals with them as His children. He has "prepared for them a kingdom" that is infinitely superior to all the kingdoms of this world. The glory of it cannot be expressed or conceived ; nor will the duration of it ever end (Heb. xii. 28). This He has given to them for their inheritance. It is His determination to invest them with it, and His delight to preserve them for it. His almighty power is ever exercised for this purpose (1 Pet. i. 4, 5). Yea, His whole heart and soul are engaged in accomplishing His gracious intentions (Jer. xxxii. 41). This is a very sufficient antidote to all their fears. (*Theological Sketch-book.*) *The antidote of fear :—* Each word of the text is full of encouragement and strength for weak and timid hearts. I. THE CHURCH OF CHRIST, BE ITS MEMBERS MANY OR FEW, IS VERY DEAR TO HIM. II. THE FUTURE OF THE CHURCH IS NOT TO BE JUDGED BY ITS PRESENT CIRCUMSTANCES AND SURROUNDINGS : THE POSITION IS THAT OF AN HEIR IN EXPECTATION OF HIS

INHERITANCE. III. THE NECESSITY OF BANISHING FEAR FROM A HEART THAT HAS SUCH KINGLY PROSPECTS. (*J. Kay.*) *Encouragement to Christ's flock :*—I. INQUIRE INTO THE REASONS WHY THE DISCIPLES OF CHRIST ARE CALLED "A FLOCK," AND WHY "A LITTLE FLOCK." They are called a flock to show the peculiar regard which the Saviour has to them. They are a "little" flock, as compared with the multitude of the ungodly. Three reasons why it remains "little." 1. Because the method of admission into this flock is contrary to the enmity of the human heart. 2. The laws of this flock are too holy and self-denying for the generality of mankind. This therefore tends to keep it small. 3. Another reason why the flock of Christ is small, is the opposition and persecution it meets with from a sinful world. II. POINT OUT THE VARIOUS SOURCES OF FEAR TO THIS, AT PRESENT, LITTLE FLOCK. They are not exempt from the common calamities of life ; yea, in many respects, and for wise reasons, they are more exposed to them than other people : "Many are the afflictions of the righteous." III. ENDEAVOUR, UNDER THE INFLUENCES OF THE SPIRIT, TO REMOVE ALL NEEDLESS FEARS FROM THE FLOCK OF CHRIST, BY REMINDING THEM OF THE PROPERTIES OF THAT KINGDOM WHICH CHRIST HAS PROMISED. 1. A peaceful kingdom. 2. A holy kingdom. 3. An eternal kingdom. (*Essex Remembrancer.*) *The little flock comforted by their Shepherd :*—I. WE REMARK THE DISCIPLES OF CHRIST ARE COMPARED TO A FLOCK OF SHEEP. The property of the ancients consisted for the most part in the number of their cattle, especially in their flocks of sheep. And the Lord's portion is His people ; Jacob is the lot of His inheritance. His people are the purchase of a Saviour's blood, and the called of His grace. He is the great Shepherd, who gave His life for the sheep. Like sheep, moreover, they are meek, and inoffensive, and harmless ; they imbibe the Spirit of the Shepherd, which is a Spirit of peace and love ; imitative of Him, "who when He was reviled, reviled not again ; when He suffered, threatened not, but committed Himself to Him that judgeth righteously." These are they which follow the Lamb whithersoever He goeth. In their collective capacity, as a flock, they do not bite and devour one another, like wolves among sheep ; but feed and lie down together in green pastures, as the property of the same master, the partakers of the same privileges, and the expectants of the same immortal happiness. II. THIS FLOCK OF CHRIST IS FOR THE PRESENT COMPARATIVELY SMALL. III. THE FLOCK OF CHRIST ARE AT TIMES THE SUBJECTS OF DISTRESSING ANXIETIES. They sometimes fear lest their temporal wants should not be supplied. At other times they fear they should not hold out to the end, but make shipwreck of faith and of a good conscience ; and that having begun in the spirit they should end in the flesh. They are at times anxious lest they should bring a reproach upon their profession, and cause the good ways of the Lord to be evil spoken of. And never do their fears rise higher than when they witness some professors, who seemed to be pillars, depart from Zion's ways, and either embrace pernicious errors, or fall into many foolish and hurtful lusts which drown men in destruction and perdition. IV. A GLORIOUS KINGDOM AWAITS THE FLOCK OF THE REDEEMER AFTER DEATH. V. THEIR HEAVENLY FATHER GREATLY DELIGHTS IN HIS FLOCK, AND WILL TAKE A HOLY SATISFACTION IN PUTTING THEM INTO POSSESSION OF HIS ETERNAL KINGDOM AND GLORY. VI. IT HIGHLY BECOMES THE FLOCK OF CHRIST TO DISMISS THEIR FEARS, AND TO BELIEVE THAT GOD WILL NOT PERMIT THEM TO WANT ANY GOOD THING IN THEIR WAY TO THE KINGDOM. (*Ibid.*) *The little flock :*—I. AN ENDEARING APPELLATION. II. A SALUTARY CAUTION. 1. Fear not suffering. 2. Fear not affliction. 3. Fear not the temptations of Satan. 4. Fear not death. III. A CHEERING ASSURANCE. (*W. J. Brock, B.A.*) *Fear not, little flock :*—I. Consider HOW CHRIST'S PEOPLE CAME TO BE HIS FLOCK. 1. By the express commandment of God. 2. By the purchase of His atoning death. 3. By actually bringing His people into His fold. II. Consider THE DESIGNATION HERE GIVEN OF CHRIST'S PEOPLE. "Little flock." Let it be considered, not as a point of dry arithmetic, or of dogmatical and uncharitable condemnation of others, but as a melancholy fact, that should awaken yourselves. Is it so that Christ's flock is a little flock ? then the way of the multitude of mankind is not the way for you to follow if you would be saved, but you must follow the way of the peculiar people. III. THE ENCOURAGING EXHORTATION here addressed by Christ to His little flock. "Fear not." 1. Believers have no reason to fear want. It is one of the offices of the Good Shepherd to feed His flock. They shall, in general, have whatever degree of worldly prosperity may be conducive to God's glory and their own good. 2. But want is not the only thing which they may be ready to fear : they may fear the various other afflictions and calamities of life ; and yet they have no reason to fear them. He will keep them from all troubles that would be injurious to them, and He will assist them, and bear them safe through those through which He has determined that they shall pass. 3. Nor need Christ's people fear that they shall be overcome by their spiritual enemies, or be left to fall finally from grace. They are, indeed, beset with many spiritual dangers, but they have a mighty and faithful helper. 4. Nor need they fear death. 5. Nor need they fear coming short of heaven. (*Jas. Foote, M.A.*) *The little flock encouraged:*—If you were asked, my dear children, what commandment in the Bible comes the most often, do you think you should know? Shall I tell you which commandment God gives most frequently? "Fear not." He says this more than eighty times—I believe eighty-four times; this is much oftener than any other commandment. "Fear not." You know if we are afraid, it looks as if we did not trust God. If anybody is afraid in the dark, if anybody is afraid of thunder, if anybody is afraid of going to bed alone, if anybody is afraid of robbers, if anybody is afraid of wild beasts, if anybody is afraid that God will not forgive him (when he asks Him), if anybody is afraid that God will not guide him all along till he gets to heaven—then he does not trust God. Now we must look to see to whom it is that God says, "Fear not." It is called, what? "Little flock." Now, why is it called "little"? 1. Perhaps it is because there are so few in it, there are very few. A young man told me the other day that he was seven years at Eton, and he did not believe all the time that there was one real Christian there. Now, he could not tell. Very often religious boys are to be found where you do not think they are, and he might have made a great mistake. Very often God's people are hidden people. We cannot tell; but I am sure there are very few,—and I never knew a school yet, where there were a great many. There are but few, and so it is a "little flock." If you turn to Jeremiah, you will see how God makes a "little flock,"—you will not wonder it is "little" when you read that. "I will take you one of a city, and two of a family, and I will bring you to Zion" (Jer. iii. 14). So you see there are only to be "two" or "three." Nobody naturally tries to love God; and if nobody seeks to love God, or to care about his soul, he must not wonder at "the flock" being so "little." 2. Do you not think the reason is, not only because so few love God, but because there are so many "little" lambs in it? there are so many children in it (Isa. xl. 11). Do you not think they are called "a little flock" because everybody in that "flock" thinks so "little" of himself? Everybody who is a Christian thinks "little" of himself, or ought to do so. If anybody thinks much of himself he is by no means a Christian. "It is your Father's good pleasure to give you the kingdom." What a good God must that great God be in heaven, who made the sky and stars, and who sits upon that beautiful throne in glory, and gives to such poor creatures as we are "the kingdom"! There was once a great Roman emperor going through Rome in grand triumph, surrounded by all his attendants,—his courtiers and his soldiers; he himself was riding in a chariot, accompanied by sound of trumpets,—oh! so grand! The emperor was in the midst of that great procession, when a little child came out of the crowd, ran up to this great man, and of course he was put back,—they cried out, "Go back, little child—go back—go back! He is your emperor!" And the little child said, "Yes, he is your emperor, but he is my father." Oh! how beautiful it is to say of the Lord, "He is my Father!" "Your Father!" How did He become your Father? (See Jer. iii. 19.) God has one child; that is, Jesus. Nobody can be God's child who is not joined to Jesus—a member of Jesus —united to Jesus. Then you become indeed God's child. When we are joined to Jesus, then He is our Father in a sweeter sense. So that if you wish to be able to say, "Our Father, which art in heaven," you must love Jesus, follow Jesus, be like Jesus, and be united to Jesus. And oh! what a pleasant thing to have God's eye upon you. Now we must look at the last thing. What is He going to "give us"? Do you know? He will "give us the kingdom." Then I suppose He gives us everything—the greater and the less. In Romans xiv. 17, it is said, "For the kingdom of God is not meat and drink; but righteousness, and peace, and joy in the Holy Ghost." Thus we have "the kingdom of heaven" in our hearts when we have "righteousness, and peace, and joy in the Holy Ghost." If we have that, then we have good hope, and when we die we shall go to heaven. And, my dear children, do you know you are all trained to be "kings"? I wonder how the Prince of Wales is trained. I should think he must be always thinking, "Oh, I am going to be a king." And that is what you ought to be thinking. "You should say, "I am going to be a king." Yes, every child, who is a Christian, is going to be a "king." "Fear not, little flock, it is your Father's good pleasure to give you the kingdom." You have heard of Charlemagne,—he ordered that when he died, there should be a chapel built just like the chapel of the Holy Sepulchre at Jerusalem; and that he should not be buried like other men, but like a king, and so he said, "Do not lay my body down, but set me upon a throne, and bury me like a king." He was to have a room set apart for him at the side of the chapel, and there was to be a Bible opened and laid by his side when he was dead, and the sword of Charlemagne was to be laid on the other side—and upon his head a crown of gold, and a robe over his shoulders. So he was buried. Years afterwards, the Emperor Otho went to see how Charlemagne looked; the chapel was opened, and he went in to see him,—and what did he see? He was crumbled up into dust. There was the cowl; the crown was not destroyed, but was saved. There was Charlemagne, one of the greatest kings that ever lived—there he was, all dust. Now I will tell you of another man. There was a poor miserable-looking old man, who lived in an almshouse—I will not say where—and the poor old creature had the palsy, and if you had seen him you would have heard his shoes knocking together with the palsy; and he was sitting in his chair when a gentleman went to see him, and said, "Well, my friend, how do you do?" "Oh! I am waiting—waiting." "Are you waiting for me?" "No, I am waiting for my Master; for Him to bring me my crown." "Bring you your crown?" "Yes, I am going to be a king." "How do you know that?" "Because Christ has said it—' Fear not, little flock; for it is your Father's good pleasure to give you the kingdom.'" (*J. Vaughan, M.A.*) *The people of Christ exhorted to lay aside their fears :*—I. THE EXHORTATION: "Fear not, little flock." If it had not been expressly said by St. Luke, that Jesus spake these words to "His disciples," we should have had no doubt to whom they were addressed, from the title which He gives them, "little flock." Let us then represent to ourselves a little flock of sheep travelling through a wide and barren wilderness; and let us suppose that, thus circumstanced, they could be sensible of their situation, and of the wants and perils to which they were exposed. Would they not have many causes of alarm? Would there not be many things which would excite their fears? 1. In the first place, they would be terrified at the thought of the cruel and ravenous enemies with which they were surrounded. Every moment they might be surprised by the roaring lion, or the prowling fox, or the hidden serpent, without any means on their part of escape or defence. Beset by such adversaries, they might reasonably fear that every day would be their last. 2. Again, ignorant of the road by which they must travel through this wilderness, and arrive at those rich and fertile pastures, after which they were seeking, they could not but fear being entangled and lost by the way. Here would be a continual source of anxiety and apprehension. 3. Once more, the apprehension of want and famine would be another fruitful source of uneasiness. Such we may reasonably conclude would be the fears and anxieties of the "little flock," in the circumstances supposed: and now let us apply these things to the spiritual flock, to the people of Christ, the sheep of His pasture, and the lambs of His fold. And let us see whether they have not like grounds and causes for fear. The world is to them a wilderness; a wilderness through which they are travelling towards a better country, that is, a heavenly; a land of heat and drought, beset with dangers, and filled with their enemies. Another ground of fear to the people of Christ is their ignorance and unacquaintedness with the way in which they should go; their readiness to be discouraged at the difficulties in their road; and their propensity to turn aside, and to wander into other paths. How often do they find themselves in such situations, that they can scarcely discern the path of duty, and see the course which they ought to follow! The failure of provision by the way, of those means and accommodations which are necessary for the support and comfort of the present life, is still another fruitful cause of anxiety and alarm. II. THE ARGUMENT BY WHICH IT IS ENFORCED: "For it is your Father's good pleasure to give you the kingdom." Surely there is enough in this passage to allay the fears and to comfort the hearts of the most timorous and desponding. 1. In the first place, let the people of Christ call to mind, that God is their Father. Our Lord, speaking to them in the text, says, "your Father." Being members of Christ, they are children of God. 2. In the second place, let them recollect that this their Heavenly Father has prepared an inheritance for them; and what kind of an inheritance is it? Such an inheritance as the children of such a Father might well expect to receive; a royal inheritance; a "crown," a "kingdom." Suffice it in one word to say, that the inheritance is such as their Heavenly Father, the God of all power and love, has prepared for His dearly-purchased and His dearly-beloved children. 3. In the third place, let them reflect, that with respect to this kingdom, great and glorious as it is, beyond all our thoughts and conceptions, yet it is their Father's " good pleasure to give it them." He has prepared and provided it for them. He has promised it to them : and it will be His delight and His joy to put them into possession of it. It is His good pleasure that they should have it ; and that, not because they have deserved it, not because they have done anything to purchase it, or can ever do anything to make Him an adequate return for it— no ; but because He delighteth in mercy, and hath pleasure in the felicity of His chosen. " It is His good pleasure to give them the kingdom." It is a royal gift. Now, then, my brethren, let us see how the argument, thus opened, applies to the case before us, and enforces the exhortation in the text. "Fear not, little flock"; fear not that you shall be left to wander in the wilderness without protection, guidance, and provision by the way. Have you not in heaven a Father—an Almighty Father, who loves you with the tenderest love; watches over you with the most anxious care; and desires your happiness with even more than a Father's heart? And will He ever leave you or forsake you ? Besides, hath He not provided an inheritance for you ? Hath He not designed, hath He not promised, to make you inconceivably blessed with Himself for ever ; and is it possible that He will not bring you safely into the possession of this inheritance ? Oh ! be ashamed of your unbelief. Be ashamed of your fears. (*E. Cooper.*)   *God's flock :*—The true followers of Jesus Christ have always been a little flock, compared with the rest of mankind. I. Then the majority may be on the wrong side. II. Then weakness does not of necessity involve danger or defeat. III. Then heaven is God's gift, and not the reward of works. IV. Then God does not judge by appearances. V. Then God, who promises the kingdom, will surely keep His word. VI. Then the Christian should be hopeful and happy. In life's fiercest tribulations, we should never forget that God's promises are worthy of our strongest confidence, and our constant trust. (*T. Kelly.*) *The Christian's sense of security :*—A sense of security seems indispensable to happiness. A habit of foreboding, of thinking something evil is ever about to happen cannot but seriously mar our comfort and satisfaction. This constant dread of impending ill is by no means an uncommon, but a very common thing. We cannot well avoid a natural looking ahead for danger when travelling, but perhaps the less we have of that the more perfect our enjoyment. To be in the presence of one who is continually imagining something ill is near, is very trying to our own peace of mind. For a mind once habituated to foreboding becomes very fertile in its imaginings and will create a great danger from some very trifling occurrence. For such a mind there would seem to be no rest night or day. Constant anxiety is eating up its vitality, which soon becomes exhausted, involving, too, the body in its terrible progress towards dissolution and death. A cure for this harassing temper of mind is the cultivation of a sense of security by a constant looking unto God for guidance and strength. A reliance on Him and a willing obedience to Nature's laws will do far more for our happiness than ought beside. Even the dearest friends will fail us at times, yea often, and the truest source of joy must be ourselves purified and lifted by a constant looking unto our Heavenly Father. (*Christian Age.*)   *Going to the kingdom :*—Mrs. G—— was one day visiting an aged man, a friend of her father, and one who was associated with him in early life. Though differing widely in sentiment, the two old men still felt a deep interest in each other. Mr. S—— had been one of those who ran after the world to overtake it. All that it can give, he had obtained. Now he inquired after the state of his friend, whom he knew to be in circumstances of far less external comfort than himself. As he listened to the story of his patience and suffering, and of his cheerfulness with which he could look forward, either to a longer pilgrimage in this world, or to the hour of death, his conscience applied the unexpressed reproach, and he exclaimed, " Yes, yes, you wonder I cannot be as quiet and happy too : but think of the difference ; he is going to his treasure, and I—I must leave mine ! "

Ver. 33. **Sell that ye have, and give alms.**—*Sell all :*—Do not hoard it for yourself; do not, like the rich fool, call them *your* fruits. Do not consider yourselves proprietors of your goods. Regard them not as yours, but as God's. Sell them to God, and dispose of them in mercy for the wants of others. This is not a command that no money be kept for our own use, but that righteousness should not be neglected through fear of poverty. They make the best of bargains, who secure eternal life. They obtain the best of treasures who carry them through the grave. Self-righteous, lazy, mendicant friars, a burlesque on the text. Men may part with all, only to be more covetous than before. The command was given in good earnest to the young man. It demands the soul to be unfettered of earth-born weights. It requires a consecration of all our means to God. Mariners save the vessel by throwing the cargo into the sea. Possessions cease to be harmless the moment they acquire the mastery. Esteem it no loss if your all is destroyed for Christ's sake. No sacrifice of treasure meritorious in purchasing heaven. Some give their all to the poor, and still lose heaven (1 Cor. xiii. 3). (*Van Doren.*) *Noble self-sacrifice :*—The present Queen of Sweden, in a spirit of the noblest self-sacrifice, sold her jewels to provide for her people hospitals, orphanages, and convalescent homes, such as we possess in this country. Visiting on one occasion in person a convalescent home of her own founding, a poor bed-ridden woman thanked her for her kindness and her care. As she spoke one or more tears of gratitude fell on the queen's hand, who was sitting by her side. The queen sweetly said, as she saw the glittering tokens of a thankful heart, " God is sending me my jewels back again."

Vers. 35–40. **Men that wait for their Lord.**—*Of the believer's readiness for the coming of Christ :*—This readiness stands in watchfulness and fidelity. I. WATCH-FULNESS. 1. Its nature. 2. Its ground. The servant's relation of dependence toward his Lord. 3. The motive to it. The glorious reward. 4. The difficulty of it. The long delay. 5. Its necessity. The uncertainty of the time. II. FIDELITY. 1. Motives to it. (1) The confidence reposed in him by the Lord ; (2) who intrusts to him a large sphere of operation ; (3) in which much good may be done. 2. Its nature. (1) That is, deals justly. (2) And in proper season. 3. Its consequences. (1) The internal joy of a good conscience. (2) The Lord's approval and recompense. 4. Exhortation to fidelity from the mournful conse-quences of the opposite. 2. Source of faithlessness. Security and unbelief. 2. Nature of faithlessness. (1) Abuse of power. (2) Ill use of means entrusted to it. 3. Mournful consequences of faithlessness. (1) He finds himself surprised in his security. (2) He is severely punished. (3) And the punishment, whether more lenient or more severe, is perfectly just. (*F. G. Lisco.*) *Watching for the Mas-ter :*—I. CONSIDER OUR EXPECTATION. 1. We expect Christ's second advent as King and Judge. Or—2. We expect our own decease, which will take us into His presence, to give an account of ourselves. II. OUR PRESENT POSITION. 1. We are His servants. We belong to Him, and are subject to Him ; He has given us work to do in His absence—work which should occupy all our time, and engage all our powers. Specifically, there is the work of our own sanctification ; and there is the work of Christian beneficence and labour in the world. 2. We are left to ourselves for a season. We have it in our power to refuse doing His work. We may use His property and gifts for our own pleasure or profit. We may be indolent, selfish, and sensual, and lull ourselves to sleep and carelessness. 3. But He will return, and call us to account. We expect a day of reckoning. III. ITS ISSUES. 1. If found faithful, what joy and honour will be ours ! (See verse 37.) 2. If found unfaithful, what discomfiture and ruin ! (See verse 45, &c.) IV. OUR TRUE INTEREST AND DUTY. 1. It is, to live wholly for eternity—for Christ. 2 It is, to be prepared for death and judgment every moment. (See vers. 35, 40.) 3. It is, to stir up others to the same wakefulness and zeal. (*The Congregational Pulpit.*) *The nature of Christian watchfulness :*—1. Alertness. 2. Activity. 3. Circumspection. (*Van Oosterzee.*) *The motive of Christian watchfulness :*—1. Certainty. 2. Suddenness. 3. Decisiveness of the coming of the Lord. (*Ibid.*) *What does the Lord demand of His faithful servants ?*—1. An eye that is open for His light. 2. A hand that carries on His work. 3. A foot that is every instant ready to go to meet Him and to open to Him. (*Ibid.*) *What does the Lord promise to His faithful servants ?*—1. Honourable distinction. 2. Perfect content-ment. 3. Beseeming elevation. (*Ibid.*) *Watchfulness in its true character :*—1. Its inner essence. 2. Its blessed consequences. 3. Its indispensable universality. (*Arndt.*) *Irresistible grace :*—I. THE REPRESENTATION WHICH IS HERE GIVEN OF GOD'S MODE OF DEALING WITH MEN. " He cometh and knocketh." Where? At the " door " of our hearts. Then the door is by nature closed against God. And this applies equally to all. We allow all that can be asked of us, in regard to a vast difference between man and man ; but only with reference to their characters and their conduct as members of society. When we try them by their love to God, by their willingness to submit to Him, by their desire to please Him, we contend that there is no difference whatever, but that all must be equally included under one emphatic description—" Enemies in your minds by wicked works." This truth it is which we derive from the words of our text—the truth that the heart of every one amongst us is naturally barred against God, so that though it will be readily opened at the touch of friendship, or the call of distress, yet does it obstinately exclude that Creator and that Benefactor, who alone can fill its mighty capacities. And, if the text thus pourtray to you the natural condition of the human heart, it shows you, with equal accuracy, by what kind of manner Christ tries to gain the entrance which is wickedly denied. We speak not yet of the mode, in which it may be said, that Christ " knocks " at the door of the heart. We confine ourselves simply to the representation that no kind of violence is employed; there is nothing like forcing the door; but when Christ has "knocked," it still rests with man to determine whether he will obey the summons, and let in the guest. You will all admit that there is nothing in the text which looks like what is called IRRESISTIBLE GRACE; nothing to favour the opinion that there is any inteference with the free will of man, in order that he may be compelled or induced to renounce what is evil, and embrace what is good. The representation is purely that of such an appeal to man as man is quite at liberty to withstand. There is a " knocking " at the door; perhaps a loud knocking, and a continued knocking, but still it is left with man to decide whether he will hear the voice and throw open the door. It is very clear from this, whatever we may hold as to human corruption and disability, that none of us can be excusable in being still unconverted and at enmity with God. If Christ have only "knocked" (and this can hardly be denied by any who have ever heard the sound of the gospel), the whole blame is chargeable on themselves, if He have not also entered, and taken possession of the heart. And how does Christ knock? We might almost say that He knocks by every object in creation, and by every provision in redemption. Every feature of the landscape, every tree of the forest; every flower of the garden, every joint and every muscle of my frame—all are gifted with the same energy, an energy in proclaiming that there is a Supreme Being, infinite in wisdom and goodness, as well as in might. And through each, therefore, this Being may be justly affirmed to " knock " at the door of the heart, demanding its love and its allegiance. And there are modes yet more personal than these, in which God may be said to " come and knock " at the human heart. Does He not often inflict fatherly chastisements—removing objects of deep love, and startling those who were sunk in lethargy, and living as though they had here an " abiding city " by sudden and distressing dispensations? And if God may be said to knock at the heart by the visitations of His providence, will you not allow the same in regard of all those actings on men, which are especially to be referred to the Second and Third Persons of the Trinity? We are bold to declare of every sermon that you hear, and every chapter which you read, that it knocks at the heart. The written word and the preached word are the exhibitions of what has been done for you by the Lord your Redeemer; and in resisting these, you resist the strongest possible appeal to every charity of the heart, to every susceptibility, to every hope, and to every fear. When Christ is evidently set forth " crucified amongst you," the throes of His agony and passion; the instruments of shame and torture, the crown, the nail, the cross, the spear, the indignities endured without resentment, the griefs sustained without a murmur; the contumely poured on the Lord of Glory, the death submitted to by the Lord of Life, and all " for us men and for our salvation";—each of these may emphatically be said to rush against the heart, pleading against its indifference, and worldliness, and pride, and soliciting admission for a Saviour who longs to enter it, only that He may purify and bless and fill it with lasting happiness. And to this must be added what must occur to every one of you, that the suggestions of conscience, and the strivings of the Spirit, are means through which Christ often " knocks " at the heart, and that too, with a violence which will scarcely permit inattention. Who is there of you who will presume to say that he never heard this knocking? II. THE PROMISE MADE TO THOSE WHO YIELD TO HIS SOLICITATIONS. We will not insist upon that point of the representation which sets before us Christ as actually ministering— ministering as a servant to such as open when He knocks. We must not give too literal an interpretation to such sayings, though we may certainly understand our blessed Lord as affirming that He will graciously condescend to employ all His power and authority in advancing the honour and happiness of those who hearken to His call. Whilst waiving this, let us consider only the representation of " sitting down to meat " in association and company with the Lord our Redeemer. It has often been said, and we suppose with much truth, that heaven would be no scene of enjoyment to the wicked if they could be admitted within its gates without having the heart first changed by Divine grace. There cannot be happiness unless our faculties and desires have their counterpart objects. This is only saying that we must have our faculties rectified and receive a new set of desires ere we can possibly find happiness in the occupation and pleasures of the invisible world. And such a remark is specially in place with regard to the promise made by Christ in our text. It is not a promise which can wear much attractiveness to men who are wholly strangers to vital religion. There is not much in it to excite them, because it addresses itself to feelings which they do not yet possess and presupposes desires of which they are not conscious. They may see that the promise refers to close intimacy and rich communion between Christ and the soul, but they are disposed to resolve all such things into idealism and enthusiasm: they cannot profess to understand how they can be, nor if they be real, how they can also be valuable. But let us all add, that if unconverted men find no relish for the blessing to which the promise refers, this alone is sufficient to make them earnest in obeying Christ's summons and opening the door. Certainly we do not know a more startling truth if we be impenitent and indifferent, than that heaven would be no heaven to us, even if we could gain entrance within its precincts; and it is going far beyond all ordinary descriptions, whether of mental or corporeal tyranny, to say that there is such a thorough unfitness for every pleasure which has God for its author, such a thorough incapacity for enjoying the blessings which God delighteth to secure to those whom He loves, that they would carry, as it were, hell into heaven, and be unspeakably miserable, even where there is to be "no more death, neither sorrow, nor crying, neither shall there be any more pain." That man indeed, must have wretchedness woven up with all the elements of his being, so that he must be his own tormentor, his own accuser, his own executioner, who could be translated from hell to heaven, and find the purities of the heavens a burden with the infirmities of earth. We will not, therefore, hear that there is no stirring motive to the unconverted amongst you in these words of the Saviour—"he shall gird himself, and make them to sit down to meat, and will come forth and serve them." That you do not feel their force; that you do not see their beauty; this alone is argument enough why you should labour to fulfil the conditions and "open immediately," upon hearing the knocking of Christ. To have no relish for what Christ has to bestow, proves such incapacity for happiness as is more formidable than the mere accumulation of misery. Therefore should the unconverted be as much roused by a promise whose worth they do not feel as by one which should actually address itself to their hopes and their wishes. If the "door were to be opened" that wealth might pour in, and that carnal pleasure might abound, what alacrity would there be in obeying the summons and withdrawing the bolt! But if the door is to be opened, that the Mediator may enter, and if this seem in no degree an inducement; why, this very fact ought to furnish the strongest possible inducement! for, unless I can learn to be happy in God's way, how unspeakably wretched must I ever be in my own! But we may well believe that there are others in this assembly who have appreciated the worth of the promise in our text. To such we need not say that there is a communion and intercourse between Christ and the soul, which if not capable of being described to a stranger, is unspeakably precious to those by whom it is experienced. It is no dream of the enthusiast; it is the statement of soberness and truth. The Redeemer so manifests Himself to those who believe in His name that He communicates to them such a sense of His presence, and brings them into such intimate companionship, that He may be said to enter in and "make them sit down to meat." There is what I may venture to call a social and family intercourse; not indeed an intercourse in which the majesty and the dignity of the Mediator are ever forgotten, but nevertheless one which is as cordial and unreserved as it is actual, the soul opening all her capacities that she may be filled with all the fulness of the Saviour, and the Saviour deigning to impart himself in His various offices. (*H. Melvill, B.D.*) *The kind Master:*—First let us glance at the form of the parable. A certain Oriental gentleman, or "lord," has gone to the wedding of a friend. The festivities connected with an Eastern marriage were spread over many days, a week at least, sometimes a month. All the friends of the family were expected to put in an appearance, but only a select few remained to the end. The rest might come and go at any hour, on any day, that suited their convenience or pleasure. So that when this Hebrew gentleman went to his friend's wedding, his servants could not tell to an hour, or to a watch, or even to a day, when he would return. But, however long he delayed his coming, they kept a keen look-out for him. When night fell, instead of barring up the house and retiring to rest, they girt up their long outer robes, that they might be ready to run out at any instant to greet him; they kindled their lamps, that they might run safely, as well as swiftly, on his errands. They even prepared a table for him; for, though he was coming from a feast, he may have had to ride far and long, and, in any case, a little fruit and a cup of pure water or of generous wine might be very acceptable to him. In this posture, with these preparations, they await his coming. And when he comes, he is so pleased with their fidelity and thoughtfulness that, instead of sitting down to meat or hastening to his couch, he girds up his loins, bids his servants sit down to the very banquet they had prepared for him, and comes forth from his chamber to wait upon them. I. THE WATCHFULNESS OF THE SERVANTS. As they waited for the coming of their master, so are we to wait for the coming of ours. If we take the great promise of the New Testament—the second advent of Christ—if we divest it of all mere accidents of form and date, and reduce it to its most simple and general terms, what does it come to? It comes at least to this: that, somewhere in the future, there is to be a better world than this—a world more wisely and happily ordered, a world in which all that is now wrong will be righted, a world of perfect beauty and growing righteousness; in a word, a world in which He who once suffered for and with all men will really reign in and over all men, His spirit dwelling in them, and raising them towards the true ideal of manhood. And is not that a reasonable hope? Does it not make a vital difference to us whether or not we entertain it? If in this world only we have hope, we are of all creatures most miserable. If the tragedy of human life be pregnant with no Divine purpose, if there be no better time coming, no golden age of righteousness and peace—if, in short, we can no longer believe in the advent and reign of Christ, then surely every thoughtful spectator of this vast tragedy must say, "It were better for men that they had never been born!" But if we believe in this great promise, if we cherish this great hope, then can we with patience wait for it. And this is the very posture which our Lord here enjoins. II. THE FRIENDLY AND BOUNTIFUL KINDNESS OF THE MASTER. Whatever we have done for God, He will do for us; when He reckons with us, we shall receive our own again, and receive it with usury. It is but a metaphorical expression of that great law of retribution which pervades the whole Bible, but the happier face of which we are too apt to overlook—that whatever a man sows, that shall he also reap, *that*, and all that has come of it. The Divine reward will be at once equitable and bountiful. If in this present life we have shown some capacity for serving God in serving our fellows, we may be sure that in the life to come we shall receive the harvest of our service; we may be sure that God will do for us all that we have done for Him, and a great deal more. But what, after all, is the best part of a man's reward for a faithful and diligent use of any faculty here? It is that his faculty, whatever it may be, is invigorated, developed, refined by use. If, then, I have here used my faculty and opportunity for serving God in serving my fellows, I may hope and believe that hereafter my best reward will be an enlarged faculty of service and ampler opportunities for exercising it. If I love righteousness here, and pursue it, I find all righteous men and influences on my side, and so get my reward; but my best reward is that I myself am ever growing in righteousness, in the power of teaching and serving it. (*S. Cox, D.D.*) *Preparation for death :—* I. THE DESCRIPTION OF DEATH WHICH CHRIST HERE GIVES. 1. Death, you perceive, is here represented as the coming of Jesus Christ. In His capacity of Mediator, He comes at death, to terminate that "space for repentance" which He has allotted to each individual; He comes to demand an account of our stewardship. 2. But our text refers, with peculiar emphasis, to the uncertainty in which we are left, as to the time when our Lord will come. That He will come, we are distinctly and impressively assured: and the time, the place, and the manner of His coming, are all foreknown to Him, and appointed by Him. But they are all unknown to us; the year, the day, the hour are unknown; whether it shall be "in the second watch, or in the third watch"; whether it shall be in the morning, or in the evening, or at noonday; "for in such an hour as ye think not, the Son of Man cometh." II. THE PREPARATION FOR DEATH WHICH CHRIST ENJOINS. 1. Preparation for death is founded on a belief of the gospel of Christ. 2. It includes a devout anticipation of death, and a reference to it amidst the concerns and engagements of life. 3. Preparation for death includes also a holy and habitual perseverance in the service of Jesus Christ. III. THE BLESSEDNESS WHICH CHRIST HERE ENSURES TO THOSE

WHO DIE IN THIS STATE OF PREPARATION. 1. They are blessed with peace and hope in the prospect and in the act of dying. 2. They are blessed with an entrance into heaven immediately after death. (*J. Alexander.*) *Waiting for the Lord :*—Our dear friend, Mr. James Smith, whom some of you remember as preaching the Word at Park Street, and afterwards at Cheltenham, when I saw him, some little while before his departure, described himself thus : " You have seen a passenger that has gone to the station, taken his ticket, all his luggage brought in, all packed up, strapped, directed ; and you have seen him sitting with his ticket in his hand, waiting till the train comes up. That," said he, " is exactly my condition. I am ready to go as soon as my Heavenly Father pleases to come for me." And is not that how we should always live—waiting for the Lord's appearing ? Mr. Whitefield used to say, of his well-known order and regularity, " I like to go to bed feeling that if I were to die to-night, there is not so much as a pair of my gloves out of their proper place." (*C. H. Spurgeon.*) *Always ready :*—When war was declared between France and Germany, Count von Moltke, the strategist, was fully prepared for it. The news was brought to him late one night at Kreisau : he had already gone to bed. " Very well," he said to the messenger, " the third portfolio on the left," and went to sleep again until morning. (*H. O. Mackay.*) *Watching is essential :*—A general, after gaining a great victory, was encamping with his army for the night. He ordered watch to be kept all around the camp as usual. One of the sentinels, as he went to his station, grumbled to himself, and said, " Why could not the general let us have a quiet night's rest for once, after beating the enemy ? I'm sure there's nothing to be afraid of." The man then went to his station and stood for some time looking about him. It was a bright night, with a harvest moon, but, as he could see no sign of danger anywhere, he said to himself, " I am terribly tired, I shall sleep for just five minutes, out of the moonlight, under the shadow of this tree. So he lay down. Presently he started up, dreaming that some one had pushed a lantern before his eyes, and he found that the moon was shining brightly down on him through the branches of the tree above him. The next minute an arrow whizzed past his ear, and the whole field before him seemed alive with soldiers in dark green coats, who sprang up from the ground, where they had been silently creeping onward, and rushed toward him. Fortunately the arrow had missed him ! so he shouted aloud to give the alarm, and ran back to some other sentinels. The army to which he belonged was thus saved, and the soldier said, " I shall never forget, as long as I live, that when one is at war, one must watch." (*Christian Age.*) *Preparation for death :*—The Rev. Dr. Kidd was a Scotch minister of some prominence, and very eccentric, and one who had his own way of doing things. One of his parishioners says: " I was busy in my shop, when, in the midst of my work, in stepped the doctor. ' Did you expect me? " was his abrupt inquiry, without even waiting for a salutation. ' No,' was my reply. ' What if I had been Death ? ' he asked, when at once he stepped out as abruptly as he came, and was gone almost before I knew it." What a question ! What a thought for every one of us ! Does not Death come to most, if not to all, as unexpectedly as this ? And does not the inquiry impress the lesson from our Saviour's lips, " Be ye also ready ; for in such an hour as ye think not, the Son of Man cometh." " *Be ready !* "—In the early part of 1875, a young minister, desirous to see the working of the railway signals, points, and telegraph, entered a signal box on a branch line (where the road crossed the metals) for that purpose. The man in charge was most affable, and willing to supplement his limited knowledge of it, by showing him the working of the various branches of trust committed to his charge, as the respective trains came through. Only a few moments elapsed when the sharp ring of the gong attracted both signalman and his visitor to the telegraphic instrument, and the signal " Be ready " was given for a fast through train. The answer returned, the signal lowered, the points righted, and, like the rushing of a mighty wind, on came the ponderous engine and its train of human life. Fast went that train, but the " Be ready " flew before it from station to station, preparing for it clear metals and a safe journey. A few days elapsed, and the same train was again due ; the " Be ready " had been received and forwarded ; the signals lowered, the points righted ; but one of the gates had somehow got unlocked, and hung across the road. The signalman rushed to the gate hoping to fling it back, but was too late. The train dashed on, and the mangled corpse of the poor man told of his sudden exit from this world to the next. Have you not received the " Be ready " again and again ? Look well to your signals, look well to your points, and see that you *are* ready. The Apostle Paul once got the signal "Be ready," and his reply was this: "I am now ready to be offered up, for the time of my departure is at hand." (*Christian Age.*) *Waiting and watching:*—Faith without works has no testifying and authenticating fruit. They are the two extremes of the one tree, viz., the root and the fruit; they are the two halves of the one whole—together they make up the complete Christian. In the text, this completeness is brought out and illustrated in a forcible manner, in the three aspects in which our Lord presents the Christian, viz., a servant, a light-bearer, and a watchman. I. In the first direction which our Lord gives, "Let your loins be girded about," we have before us the picture of A SERVANT GIRDED FOR DUTY. I need not tell you what the position and duties of a servant are; how it is expected of him that he should know his place, and humbly and faithfully discharge the duties of his station. He should, if possible, identify himself with his master's interest, and conduct himself in a manner which will sustain his master's honour. The servant of Christ has the noblest of all masters—the holiest of all services—the most honourable of all positions. The servant of a king ever bears about him the reflected honour of the king, and the amount of this honour is in proportion to his nearness or remoteness to the throne. So the servant of the King of kings borrows dignity from the Being whom he serves. He wears no outward insignia of that dignity, as earthly courtiers do in stars or ribbons; but it is a glory which reflects itself in his daily life, and evidences his relation to Jesus by the fidelity and zeal which he shows in His service. The fact that what he does, he does for Christ, lifts it out of the plane of menial duty, and places it in the higher region of holy privilege. Such a service ought to call out prompt obedience, loving devotion, unwearied effort, and thorough sympathy with the aim and purpose of God in the work of man's salvation. II. But, secondly, the text tells us that the Christian is to BE A LIGHT-BEARER as well as a servant. Not only must his loins be girded, but his lights must be burning, The Christian lives in the midst of moral darkness. Sin is darkness, and he lives in a world of sin; a world in which men love darkness rather than light, because their deeds are evil. Error also is darkness. If Christ is in you His light will shine out through you; and if none shines out through you, it will be because there is none in you. Where the light is, there will be the shining. The absence of light proves the absence of Christ; for you cannot cover up His light or smother His beams. The necessity for these lights being ever burning arises from the personal need of the believer himself; and from the necessity of showing forth to others the light and truth which he has found in Jesus. The personal security of the disciple, then, requires that he should let his lights be burning. His spiritual comfort also depends on this. St. John, after declaring that "God is light, and in Him is no darkness at all," immediately adds, "If we say that we have fellowship with Him, and walk in darkness, we lie, and do not the truth; but if we walk in the light, as He is in the light, we have fellowship one with another." The holier the life, the brighter the light. The more the light shines for others, the greater is the inner glow of our own hearts, and the greater the outer glory given to God. The absence of light where we expect to find it, often produces most disastrous results. III. Lastly, the text tells us that the Christian is to be a WATCHMAN: "and ye yourselves like unto men that wait for their Lord." The watchman-like character of the Christian is to show itself in two ways. First, by watching over himself; and secondly, by waiting for his returning Lord. Over himself he must watch, lest he become careless in duty, remiss in keeping his light burning, and be overtaken with drowsiness and indifference. Self-watchfulness is the necessary pre-requisite to spiritual peace and growth. Only the self-confident and the self-ignorant are unwatchful; and the unwatchful always become an easy prey to the spoiler. All that the great deceiver asks of us is, not that we should openly abandon our religion, but simply ungird our loins—let our light go out and cease to watch. He will finish the work which we thus by carelessness and unwatchfulness begin. In addition to this self-watchfulness there is the other position to be taken, viz., waiting for our returning Lord. This may imply that outlook which all true Christians like to take in reference to the Second Advent of Christ, when He shall come again to judge the world. (*Bishop Stevens.*) *The lamp of the soul ever burning:*—I. CONSIDER THE EMPTY, UNTRIMMED LAMP AS THE EMBLEM OF THE NOMINAL PROFESSOR. A lamp is a very serviceable thing, serviceable for lighting our stormy coast, and guarding against shipwrecks; serviceable for lighting our homes; but it is of little service unless it is trimmed, and unless it has oil in it. Now a hollow professor is like a lamp of this kind, a lamp with no oil in it, that cannot be lighted when you want it ; as useless, though more dangerous. He lets not the lamp of his profession shine before men with the light of practice, with the light of good works, because the lamp of his profession is destitute of the oil of Divine grace. The oil is the emblem of Divine grace in the Christian profession. And as it is impossible to light a lamp without first putting oil into it ; so is it impossible for a hollow professor to shed around on this dark world the beautiful and refreshing light of good works, unless, first, the oil of Divine grace is poured into the empty receptacle of his unconverted heart, by the unseen hand of the Holy Spirit. II. CONSIDER THE LAMP, WITH OIL IN IT, BUT NOT LIGHTED, AS AN EMBLEM OF THE TRUE CHRISTIAN, BUT NOT EXACTLY SO WELL PREPARED FOR THE SECOND COMING OF THE SON OF MAN AT AN HOUR UNEXPECTED. It is an easy thing for the lamp of the Christian to grow dim, or to go out. If the Christian is not watchful, the slightest blast from the insidious temptations of the world, the flesh, and the devil, will blow his lamp out. Want of prayer, irregularity in prayer, coldness in prayer, will put the Christian's lamp out, or make it burn very dull. Neglect of the Scriptures, neglect either in not searching them, or in searching them in a self-righteous and careless spirit, will extinguish the bright light of the lamp. Or irregularity, or formality, in attending the Sacrament, and the other Divinely appointed means of grace, will cause the lamp to emit a dim and unhealthy light. Yielding to the besetting sin will put the lamp out ; yielding to any wilful sin will put the lamp out. Remissness in self-examination will put the lamp out. Want of zeal for Christ will put the lamp out. Want of faith in Christ will put the lamp out. Want of hope in Christ will put the lamp out. Want of love for Christ will put the lamp out. Want of an abounding stedfastness in the work of the Lord, will put the lamp out. III. CONSIDER THE LAMP BURNING, AS AN EMBLEM OF DUE PREPARATION FOR CHRIST'S SUDDEN COMING. Brethren, it is a hard thing in a world like this, and with an old evil nature that clings to the new man, for the Christian to keep his lamp burning. There are few Christians, indeed, whom sudden death has found, or the second advent will find, not only with lamps, and the oil in the lamps, but the lamps themselves burning. "Sudden death, sudden glory," has been the noble motto of a very distinguished minority, and death has not had power to make them retract. Absent from the body, present with the Lord ; so said St. Paul in life, and so he felt in death. Come, Lord Jesus, come quickly, are among the last glorious words on record of St. John. They shed a burning and shining light upon this dark world of sin and woe to the very last. Their whole eventful lives were spent in being good, or doing good. "To them to live is Christ, to die is gain." When their lamps grow dull, and seem threatening to go out, they immediately brighten them up, and make them burn again, by betaking themselves to the throne of grace. IV. To each of these three classes of Christians, denoted by the lamp, WE WOULD OFFER A WORD OF EXHORTATION BY WAY OF WARNING OR ENCOURAGEMENT. 1. To the first we would say, yours is a sad case, indeed. You trust in the lamp of a hollow profession to save you in the great, and awful, and searching day of your Lord's second coming. You trust to a lamp without oil to light it. If you put confidence in any refuge of lies of this description, what a miserable end yours will be when Christ cometh. The God that seeth not as man seeth, the God that searcheth the hearts and trieth the reins, is to be your Judge, and pronounce your final doom. 2. To the second class of Christians we would say, guard against all those things that tend to put the lamp out. Every Christian knows what has the influence of deadening the light of the Spirit in his soul, and such a course ought to be strenuously avoided. 3. To the third class of Christians here designated, let us offer the word of encouragement. Often seated amid nights of terrible darkness, on the rock that is higher than we, on the rock of ages, have you been looking patiently, and in faith, over Time's troublous sea, for the glad day of Christ's coming to arrive, watching for the day-star to rise. Let your lamps be thus burning, till He comes. It will not be long before He does come. Yet a little while, and He that shall come, will come, and will not tarry. Then your soul's vigils will come to an end. (*R. Jones, M.A.*) *What do you keep a lantern for ?*—A blind beggar sat by the side-walk on a dark night with a bright lantern by his side. Whereat a passer-by was so puzzled that he had to turn back with—"What in the world do you keep a lantern burning for ? You can't see ! " "So't folks won't stumble over me," was the reply. We should keep our lights brightly burning for others' sakes, as well as for the good of being "in the light" ourselves. *Christian preparedness :*—A Christian must stand in a posture to receive every message which God shall send. He must be so prepared as to be like one who is called to set off on a sudden journey, and has nothing to do but to set out at a moment's notice ; or like a merchant who has goods to send abroad, and has them all packed up and in readiness for the first vessel that is to sail. (R. Cecil.)   Ready :—We should always stand " with our lamps burning, and our loins girt." A Christian should always be as a ship that has taken in its lading, and is prepared and furnished with all manner of tackling, ready to sail, only expecting the good winds to carry him out of the haven. So should we be ready to set sail for the ocean of eternity, and stand at heaven's gate, be in a perpetual exercise of faith and love, and be fittingly prepared to meet our Saviour. (H. G. Salter.)   The expectant servant :—I. WHY IS THERE SUCH A CONTRAST IN THE PRESENT STATE OF THE CHURCH AS COMPARED WITH THE CHURCH IN APOSTOLIC TIMES? 1. Christ predicted this apathy. 2. The narrow views prevalent as to the idea of "judgment" have much to do with this indifference. Christ is to establish a rule of equity, to establish righteousness in the earth, let us remember. 3. In saying "It is expedient for you that I go away," the Lord did not say that it was expedient to stay away. We seem to act as if He said so. But He said, "I will come again." II. THE BLESSEDNESS OF WAITING FOR CHRIST. 1. It shows our real affection for Him. 2. It shows that we entertain right views of the work of Christ, and are in sympathy with that work. 3. This expectant attitude testifies to our supreme desire for spiritual blessings : those gifts of His grace which prepare us for His work here, and for the glorious vision of His face at the Marriage Supper of the Lamb. (H. G. Weston, D.D.)   Christian watchfulness :—Let the duty of watchfulness engage your most careful attention. How vigilant is he who is appointed to keep watch at sea ! " The watchful mariner," says one, " is ever on the look out. His eyes and ears are both open. Be the prevailing fear an enemy's force, or a sunk rock, or concealed bank, or shelving coast, he discerns the smallest symptoms, observes the motion of the waves sounds with the line, and gives the alarm on the most minute alteration. Without such watchfulness, the most precious merchandise, and the lives of men, would be each hour in jeopardy. Much the same is the case in warfare by land. The sentinel on the outpost is heedful of the most inconsiderable object within his station ; and in the darkness of the night, his ear listens to every noise. Nothing can divert his attention from fidelity to his charge. Such also is the case with the watchman in the besieged city. From the walls, as far as he has light, he marks each change and alteration in the posture of the enemy, draws a judgment from the nicest circumstances ; and, in the night, discerns even the rustling of the leaf moved by the breath of heaven ; and at every suspicious noise he gives the alarm to the guards of the city. Without this the cry of havoc would oft be heard in the town, when drowned in heaviness and slumber." Thus it is that you should watch for your own souls. Be watchful lest ye make shipwreck of faith and a good conscience. Be watchful against your spiritual enemies. " Be sober, be vigilant; because your adversary the devil, as a roaring lion, walketh about seeking whom he may devour." Watch over your words and actions, and your very thoughts. " Keep your hearts with all dilligence, for out of them are the issues of life." Beware of those things which are contrary to watchfulness, such as sloth, inconsideration, worldliness, and sensuality. And see that you join prayer to watchfulness. (Jas. Foote, M.A.) Found well employed :—Philip Henry, the father of the commentator, called upon a tanner, who was so briskly employed in tanning a hide that he did not notice the minister's approach, and on looking round he apologized for being found thus employed. Philip Henry replied, " Let Christ, when He comes, find me equally well employed in the duties of my calling." Many other ministers have made the same reply to similar excuses.   All watched :—" A story that I read when a boy," says one, " made a great impression on me. At a lonely country house a pedlar asked permission to leave a large pack of goods. Some one looking at it in an out-of-the-way room, thought they saw it move. A man in the house fired at it : a groan was heard, and blood issued. Inside the pack was the accomplice of coming robbers, with food, and a wind-call. Neighbours were got in, guns were loaded, and all watched. In the night they sounded the call ; the robbers came, were welcomed with a volley, and fled, taking their dead and wounded with them."   Waiting for the Lord :—Two centuries ago, Andrew Gray, the M'Cheyne of his time, and who, like him, was early called home, once said at a communion season, "Oh, when shall these blue heavens be rent, and we be admitted to the marriage supper of the Lamb? I long for the day when all the language of heaven and earth shall be, 'Come, come, Lord Jesus.'" But, in a more marked degree still, this was the theme in which Samuel Rutherford ever specially delighted. "All is night that is here," he said; "therefore sigh and long for the dawning of the morning, and the breaking of that day of the coming of the Son of Man! Persuade yourself the King is coming: read his letter sent before him, 'Behold, I come quickly.' Wait with the wearied night watch for the breaking of the eastern sky, and think that ye have not a morrow." (*J. H. Norton.*) *The coming of Christ:*—I. THE PERSONS TO WHOM THE COMMAND WAS ADDRESSED WERE ORIGINALLY THE AUDIENCE TO WHICH OUR SAVIOUR WAS SPEAKING. These, as St. Luke informs us, were an innumerable multitude of people, gathered, as it would seem, to hear him preach the gospel. A part of them were His disciples, a part of them were His enemies, and a part, probably including the greatest number, could scarcely have known anything of Him, unless by report. To all these classes of men the command is addressed in the written gospel. To him who reads it, and to him who hears it, it is addressed alike; and that whether he be a Christian, or a sinner, acquainted with Christ, or unacquainted. II. IN EXAMINING THE COMMAND ITSELF, I SHALL BRIEFLY MENTION— First, What that is for which we are to be ready; and—Secondly, What is included in being ready. First, We are required to be ready for the coming of Christ. There are several senses in which this phrase may be fairly understood, as used in the Scriptures. (1) When it is applied to individuals it particularly denotes the day of death. Death to every man is the time in which Christ will come, which will terminate every man's probation, and put an end to the necessity and duty of watching, so solemnly enjoined in the text. (2) We are also required to be ready for the judgment; (3) and for eternity. Secondly, I will now proceed to inquire what is included in being ready. 1. Profaners of the Lord's Day are not ready for the coming of Christ. 2. Prayerless persons are not ready for the coming of Christ. 3. Those who do not profess the religion of Christ, and enter into His covenant, are not not ready for His coming. 4. Those persons also are unprepared for the coming of Christ who prefer the world to Him. 5. All persons are unprepared for the coming of Christ who have hitherto put off their repentance to a future season. 6. All those persons also are unready for the coming of Christ who in their schemes of reformation reserve to themselves the indulgence of some sinful disposition, or the perpetration of some particular sin. 7. Those also are unready for the coming of Christ who do not continually and solemnly converse with death, judgment, and eternity. 8. Careless Christians are also unprepared for the coming of Christ. III. I WILL NOW PROCEED TO THE CONSIDERATION OF THE REASON BY WHICH THE DUTY OF PREPARING OURSELVES FOR THE COMING OF CHRIST IS ENFORCED IN THE TEXT—"For the Son of Man cometh in an hour when ye think not." How solemnly ought we to remember that death will not wait for our wishes, that the judgment is now hastening, that eternity is at the door? Disease, unperceived, may now be making progress in our veins, and may be preparing, without a suspicion on our part, to hurry us to the grave. How absurd, how deceitful, how fatal is our procrastination! (*T. Dwight, D.D.*) *Proper preparation for death:*—I. THE SOLEMN EVENT FOR WHICH WE ARE EXHORTED TO PREPARE. Death. II. WHAT CONSTITUTES A PROPER PREPARATION FOR DEATH? 1. The justification of our persons by a true and lively faith in Christ. 2. The sanctification of our souls by the effectual operation of the Holy Spirit. III. WHY SUCH A PREPARATION BECOMES IMMEDIATELY NECESSARY. 1. Because the time of His coming, or (what is substantially the same thing to us) the time of our death is awfully uncertain. 2. Because delay may be fatal and irretrievable. (*D. Ruell, M.A.*) *Signs and preparations of the last judgment:*—I. REMOTE SIGNS. 1. The coming of Antichrist (2 Thess. ii. 3, 4). 2. The coming of Enoch and Elias, and the spread of faith (Rev. xi. 3–12). II. PROXIMATE SIGNS. 1. Tribulations on earth (Luke xxi. 9, &c.). 2. Signs in heaven (Matt. xxiv. 29). 3. The standard of the cross of Christ (Matt. xxiv. 30). It shall appear—(1) As token of Christ's victory. (2) As the key of heaven. It is the cross that re-opened heaven, and it is our cross carried after Jesus that will open heaven to us. (3) As a measure of our works. (4) As a reproach to all the enemies of Christ (John xix. 37). III. IMMEDIATE PREPARATIONS. 1. The bodies of the dead will rise. 2. All men must appear before the tribunal of Christ. 3. The wicked shall be separated from among the just. (*J. Marchant.*) *Ready, or not ready?*—I. JESUS CHRIST WILL COME AGAIN. 1. Not in humble guise, but in His glorious majesty. 2. Not to procure salvation, but to inquire who among men have sought His salvation and accepted His offers, and to pronounce sentence accordingly. II. CHRIST WILL COME WHEN WE DO NOT EXPECT HIM. 1. The world generally will be unprepared. 2. For each of us, death is the coming of the Son of

Man. III. THE NECESSITY OF BEING PREPARED TO MEET OUR GOD WHEN HE COMES. 1. Are you forgiven? 2. Are you growing in holiness? (*A. Bibby.*)   *Ready!—* Anxious thought misdirected only secures misery. Supreme efforts of thought, involving the greatest tension of heart-strings, should be spent on objects worthy of themselves. We were once shown a crossing-sweeper who had received a university training. What a waste! Men who spend their lives in seeking the daintiest food to eat, and the costliest dress to wear, waste time and talent, energy and substance, on the inferior parts of their being. Where, then, should anxious thought be exercised? "But rather seek ye the kingdom of God." "Let your loins be girded about, and your lights burning." "Be ye therefore ready also." These are the objects worthy of our anxiety and prayer. 1. BE READY—BE RECONCILED TO GOD THROUGH JESUS CHRIST. IT IS HERE THE PREPARATION BEGINS. No one is ready to die who is not justified by faith and has peace with God. We do not wish to limit the power of God to save, even at the last moment, but we must say that it is a hazardous practice. Life at the longest is but brief to prepare for a world which has no end. For a long journey, and for a long stay from home, more elaborate preparations are made than for a short stay. When one intends to quit his native land for ever to reside in some distant colony, every preparation possible is made for that event. Observe also that the preparation is made with a view to the future. We who are hastening towards the judgment-seat need remember the exhortation—"Prepare, O Israel, to meet thy God." Our sins must be pardoned, and our hearts cleansed by the blood of Jesus. Without this we shall encounter the frown which will strike an eternal shudder through the soul. "Now, then, we are ambassadors for Christ, as though God did beseech you by us : we pray you in Christ's stead, be ye reconciled to God." II. BE READY—BE ON YOUR GUARD AGAINST THE ALLUREMENTS OF THE WORLD. Let neither prosperity nor adversity steal our opportunities, but let our heart be fixed on heavenly things. The stag is swift of foot, but it is often caught by its own horns in the thicket of the forest. Men who pride themselves on their business capacities are drowned in the pleasures of wealth-getting. This world is full of enticements, and as Calypso would have detained the hero in her beautiful grotto, so these exert an influence prejudicial to the growth of heavenly desires. Let us cultivate the spirit of prayer, and commune often with the opposite shore. Every prayer reminds us that there is a happy land yonder where the saints stand in bright glory. III. BE READY—BE IN CONSTANT EXPECTATION OF HIS COMING. Of all thoughts this is the sweetest. The Apostolic Church was fired daily with the hope that the Master was at hand. A lieutenant who had been mortally wounded was asked if he had a word he wished to be conveyed to his wife, replied, "Tell my wife that there is not a cloud between me and Jesus." It was a triumphant death. Be ready to welcome the Saviour when He comes, that no earthly entanglements may detain you one moment. (*The Weekly Pulpit.*)   *Preparation for death and judgment:*—To die! This is the sure end of earthly life. However long our life may be, it must terminate in death. We may struggle as we will, but the stream of time is carrying us onwards, and we must be swept away ; strong swimmers though we be, we cannot contend against the flood, but onward we must go, each day bearing us upon its bosom to the boundless Sea of Eternity. Since, then, death is so certain to each of us, what is it to die? To die is to stand in the presence of the King of kings. Is no preparation required to appear before the Majesty of Heaven? And to die is not only to appear before the King, but to stand before a Judge. Moreover, to die is to stamp our lot with eternity. Now if we look at death in this light, as appearing before a King, as standing before a Judge, and as the settling and consolidation of our future existence, what arguments might we draw from these facts that we should be "ready also." Many men say, "Oh! when I come to die I shall say, 'Lord, have mercy upon me' ; and will then get ready to go to heaven." Dressing for heaven, my friends, is not done quite so rapidly as that. Besides, how do you know that even five minutes will ever be given to you? I have heard of such a man, who often made it his boast that he would so prepare for heaven ; but, alas! coming home one night, drunk, his horse leaped the parapet of a bridge, and he was heard cursing as he descended to his doom. Such may be your lot ; sudden death may smite you, and there will be no time for preparation—there will be no time for you to prepare to meet your God. And now what is the preparation that we require to make? If death be what I have said it is, it is needful that we should be prepared for it ; but what is the preparation? My hearers, there are two things necessary before a man can face his God without fear. The first is, that his sins should be pardoned. When an unpardoned sinner shall come into the presence of God, he shall not stand in the Judgment, for the burning wrath of God shall consume him like stubble. "Depart"—says God—"depart, ye cursed; ye have lived in sin against Me; go and reap the harvest ye have sowed; inherit the reward of your own works." Sin unpardoned clothes a man with rags; and shall a man stand in rags before the King of Heaven? Sin unpardoned defiles a man with filth and loathsomeness; and shall filth and loathsomeness appear before perfection, or blackness stand in the presence of light and purity? Sin unpardoned makes man an enemy of God, and God an enemy of man. Sinners, lay hold of Christ. Ye doves, ye who are timid, and fear the tempest of God, hide yourselves in the cleft of the Rock of Ages, so shall ye be sheltered in the day of the fierce anger of the Lord. Now, as I have said, the first thing necessary for salvation is pardon of sin, and that is to be had through faith in Christ. But, secondly, even if a man's sins are pardoned, he would not be prepared to die if his nature were not renewed. If you could blot out all your sins in a moment, and if it could be possible for you to go to heaven just as you are, you could not be happy there; because heaven is a prepared place for a prepared people. An unconverted man in heaven would be like a fish out of water—he would be wholly out of his element. Holy Mr. Whitfield used to say, that if an ungodly man could go to heaven as he is, he would be so miserable there that he would ask to be allowed to run to hell for shelter! Ye who find our places of worship dreary prisons, and Sundays dull days, how could you bear everlasting worship? How could you bear to have eternal Sabbaths, and continual songs of praises morning, noon, and night? Why, you would say, "Let me out; Gabriel, let me out; this is not the place for me; let me be gone; I am not happy here." Verily, verily I say unto you, ye must be born again. Well, cries one, "I will change my nature." My dear friends, you cannot do it; you may alter your habits, but your nature you cannot; there is only One that can alter nature, and that is the Holy Spirit. Christ blots out sin, and the Holy Spirit renews the heart. You may reform, but that will not take you to heaven. It is not being reformed; it is being reborn; made new creatures in Christ Jesus. (*C. H. Spurgeon.*) *Prepare at once:*—I was preaching in Essex but a few months ago, and the sermon was scarcely finished, when a Christian woman, who was hearing it, dropped dead in her pew. It was but a little while ago, in Kent, that during a sermon, a poor man who had bent forward, and listened with all his ears, fell forward on his face, and then and there appeared before his God. Sudden deaths are not such common things as perpetually to keep us in alarm, yet they are common enough, I hope, to make both young and old arise and hear the voice of God—"Prepare, prepare, to meet your God." Oh! my hearers, it is but a short time with the very longest lived amongst us. I see here and there a hoary head. Is that grey hair yonder a crown of glory or a fool's cap? It is either the one or the other. There are young persons here too, O let them look forward to the longest time that we may live, and how brief the period! Time—how short! Eternity—how long! Well, since die we must, I do beseech and intreat you to think of death. Why should all your time be spent in thinking of the things of this world, when there is another world beyond the present? Why, why, is this short life to have all your thoughts, and the life to come to have none of them? I have heard of a monarch who, having a fool in his court, gave him a walking-stick, with an injunction never to part with it, until he should meet with a bigger fool than himself. He kept it for many a day, until at last, the monarch dying, the fool (who was a wise man, after all) came, and said, "Master, where are you going?" "Well," said he, "I am going to die." Said the fool, "How long are you going to be there?" "Oh!" said the monarch, "for ever and ever." "And have you not made any preparation for the journey; have you no house to live in when you get there; have you nothing ready?" said the fool. "No," said the monarch, "I never thought of it." "There," said the fool, "take the walking-stick; I play the fool in this world, but you have fooled away the next: you have entirely neglected the world to come, and are a fool in very deed." And is not that the English after all of what those men are who are so careless of the world to come? (*Ibid.*) *Death a surprise:*—1. Death is a surprise in the time of its coming. 2. It is a surprise in the way of its coming. 3. It is a surprise, as it finds the sinner unprepared. He meant to be ready, but death was too quick for him. OBSERVATIONS: 1. God has wisely hidden from us the day of death, that we may be always ready and watching for His coming. 2. There is never but a step, a breath, a heart-throb, between any man and death! While the citadel is guarded, and the walls and gates are watched day and night with sleepless vigilance, an unseen foe lurks within, and with noiseless tread, at the midnight hour, enters the chamber of the sleeper, and life is extinct. Be ready, O man! The Son of Man may come at any hour, in any place, by any agency, along any one of a thousand unseen avenues. (*Homiletic Review.*) *Danger of unwatchfulness :*—A great commander was engaged in besieging a strongly fortified city. After a while he concentrated his forces at a point where the fortifications were stronger than at any other, and at 2 p.m., under a bright sun and a clear sky, ordered an assault. When expostulated with by an under officer, the commander replied, " At this point such a general is in command. At this hour of the day he is invariably accustomed to retire for a long sleep. When informed of our approach he will deny the fact, and send a messenger for information. Before the messenger returns we shall gain possession of the fortress." The facts turned out exactly as predicted. " Yonder weak point," said the commander, " is held by General ——. There is no use in attempting to surprise him ; he is never for a moment off his guard." *A sudden call :*—The following story is by an Indian officer :—It was the height of summer, and a tropical sun had just set, and a cool, refreshing sea-breeze was blowing, which we were inhaling with delight. A fever peculiar to the climate had prostrated many of all ranks, and proved fatal in some instances ; and among the convalescents was a young officer in whom I had taken a great personal interest. His strength, however, not recruiting as rapidly as could be wished, the medical authorities advised his return to England for a short furlough ; and just as the mess bugle had sounded, and I was preparing to dress, he came in in high spirits, but with tottering steps, to tell me that, as that very evening a steamer was expected, he had obtained leave to embark, and he heartily wished me good-bye. His last words were : " I am going home to-night, and perhaps the steamer will come in before you leave the mess ; if not, see me off." It was midnight before we left the mess-room ; and on walking to my quarters I found a lamp burning in my friend's room. I looked in and found him sleeping soundly, but breathing very loudly. I went up to him, and found all my efforts to waken him unavailing. I immediately summoned the doctor, and to my horror he pronounced him to be dying. In three hours, and just as the signal-gun was fired to announce the arrival of the steamer in which he had engaged his passage, his spirit passed away. He was gone home. He had lived to Christ on earth, and by his bedside lay the Bible which he had just read before he slept that fatal sleep. " Watch ye, therefore, for ye know not when the Master of the house cometh."

Vers. 42–44. **That faithful and wise steward.**—*Our stewardship :*—I. HERE IS REPRESENTED A SITUATION OF WEIGHTY RESPONSIBILITY. A stewardship. All responsibility on the part of man is owing to God. 1. And first, my brethren, let it be remarked that God, on this principle and in this relationship of responsibility, or of stewardship, has endowed us with natural faculties : faculties which impart to us a dominion and empire over the various orders of that material creation by which we are surrounded ; faculties which enable us to distinguish between right and wrong, between good and evil ; faculties which therefore entitle us to comprehend the purposes for which moral government is formed ; and faculties which permit our assimilation to the attributes and image of our Maker, that assimilation by which, most of all, He is dignified and honoured. There are, my brethren, you observe in these cases, entrustments which are committed to all, and the improvement of which is required from all, excepting, indeed, in cases of sad and mysterious affliction, or where it is usurped by madness. And those who, from time to time, have conceived, whether truly or falsely, that they have received an amount of natural faculties greater than the ordinary measure, must always remember, with deep and with prayerful solemnity, that what remains for them is nothing but humility, and seriousness, and diligence, and prayer. 2. Secondly, let it be observed that upon this principle and assimilation of stewardship God has also endowed us with many advantages and blessings. The comforts that men derive from their measure of worldly substance and competency, whatever it may be, and the comforts which they derive from the intimacies of friendship and the sweet and tender endearments of private and domestic life, ought not to escape enumeration, and ought not to be meanly esteemed. 3. God, on this principle of stewardship, has also endowed us with many religious privileges. He has endowed us with many religious privileges : that is to say, those means that are eminently adapted to instruct His creatures in the knowledge of His will, and to prepare them and guide their feet into the ways of quietness and peace. II. Here is presented AN IMPORTANT CHARACTER BY WHICH THIS SITUATION IS DISTINGUISHED. The Redeemer, you observe, speaks of the faithful and wise steward's love to the cause of his master. What we intend now to remark on this is, that these are the attributes which it is desirable that every human being should sustain with respect to that stewardship under which he is placed. 1. To be faithful and wise stewards, men must ascertain the nature of the duty which is imposed. 2. To be faithful and wise stewards, men must love the duty which is imposed. 3. To be faithful and wise stewards, men must practically perform the duty which is imposed. 4. To be faithful and wise stewards, men must habitually contemplate the account to be rendered of the duty which is imposed. III. THE DELIGHTFUL RESULTS IN WHICH THE MAINTENANCE OF THAT CHARACTER IN THAT SITUATION IS TO TERMINATE. 1. The public approbation of the Divine Master. 2. The introduction to substantial honour, and perfect and eternal happiness. (*J. Parsons.*) *A faithful steward:*—The other day I [Rev. F. S. Cook, D.D., in "Altering the Gospel"] received a communication from a lawyer, who says that a very large owner has discovered that a very small piece of property belongs to him, and not to the small proprietor in whose possession it has for a very long time remained. The matter seemed a trifling one. We had a conference, and there came the steward with the lawyers, and he was furnished with maps, and, putting on his spectacles, examined them with great care. Why? It was a small matter to him, but because he was a steward he was expected to be faithful. And when he found that this small piece of ground belonged to his lord he was determined to have it. So let me say—as stewards of the gospel of God— never give up one verse, one doctrine, one word of the truth of God. Let us be faithful to that committed to us, it is not ours to alter. We have but to declare that which we have received. *Christian devotedness:*—Did you never read Henry Martyn's life, a polished scholar, a man of learning and repute, giving up all for Christ to go to Persia and there to die without having seen a convert, perhaps, and yet content to live, content to die, in far-off lands for his Master's sake? Did you never read of Brainerd far away among the Indians, toiling on, and in his old age teaching a poor black child its letters, and thanking God that when he could not preach, he could yet teach the child its letters, and so do something for his dear Lord who had done so much for him? Ay, did you never read and think of even St. Francis Xavier, papist as he was? Yet what a man, how consecrated, how zealous! with all his errors, and all his mistakes, and all his faults, yet passing over sea and land, penetrating forests, and daring death a thousand times, that he might spread abroad the poor misguided doctrines which he believed. As much as I hate his teaching, I admire his all but miraculous zeal. When I think of some such men; when I would fain censure their mistakes, I can only censure myself that I cannot even so much as think, or cannot do more than think of living such a life as they lived. (*C. H. Spurgeon.*) **Blessed is that servant.**—*The blessedness of the well-employed servant:*—I. WE ARE ALL OF US SERVANTS AND STEWARDS, and ARE TO BE IN EMPLOYMENT. We must be "doing." Religion is no idle and lazy thing, it is not sluggish and sleepy, it is not drowsy and lethargic, but it is lively and active, vigorous and operative, and always puts us upon holy endeavours and enterprizes. A Christian is not made to stand still and do nothing. His soul and all its faculties were given him for some great design, and fitted for some excellent use and work. II. IT IS NOT ENOUGH TO BE EMPLOYED AND TO BE DOING SOMETHING; WE MUST BE "SO DOING"—doing our Master's work. We had better be doing nothing than not be *so* doing—"so run, that ye may attain," saith the apostle. The racer may run, and with full speed, and yet never reach the goal, never obtain the prize, for he may run out of the way, and make haste from the mark. And though he keeps the way, he may not be swift enough. The manner as well as the matter of religion is to be minded, and the latter of these chiefly. I shall endeavour, then, to explain this duty of a Christian in my text; I will show you what it is to be so doing, and I pray God the several particulars, which are all plain and intelligible, may have influence on our lives and practices, that when our Lord shall come, we may be found employed about these following things. 1. Meditating and examining ourselves, serious consideration and reflection on our ways. The Christian is to be busied within doors; he is to be rifling his own breast, and taking account of the inward frame and disposition of his heart. 2. Watching is another exercise meant here by the "so doing," as you may see in verses 37 and 38 of this chapter. You are, then, to watch over your hearts, and to keep them with all diligence. And moreover, you are to watch over your actions and lives; you must avoid the occasions of every vice, and keep a strict guard over your senses, which are the common inlets to sin, and betray you to the commission of the greatest follies. "Behold! I come as a thief" (saith Christ), "blessed is he that watcheth" (Rev. xvi. 15). 3. Praying is another good and laudable posture to be found in when our Lord cometh. "Watch and pray" go hand in hand together, and they are never more seasonable than when we are expecting the coming of our Lord. 4. Lamenting and sorrowing for our sins is to be "so doing"; and is another good work to be found in when we are to depart hence, and appear before the impartial tribunal of heaven. Our sins and failings are very numerous, our slips and offences are many and frequent, and we cannot sufficiently lament and bewail our folly, and implore the Divine pardon, and invoke the assistance of the Holy Spirit, but let us resolve to do it with all our might, and with sincere and upright hearts, that our present sorrows and lamentations may give us an entrance into undisturbed joy and felicity. 5. Whilst we have opportunity, let us reckon it our duty and interest to be constantly attending on God's holy ordinances, not only that of prayer (before mentioned), but that of reading and hearing God's Word; also the Holy Communion. 6. Doing of works of charity to the souls and bodies of our brethren is an acceptable employment, and will render our last accounts easy to us. 7. Serving God in the several particular callings and places wherein He hath set you is a work which you should endeavour to be found doing. Let me tell you, you serve God by your secular vocations; you may bring glory to Him even by your worldly employment, though it be never so mean and contemptible. The poorest labourer, by a conscientious discharge of his proper trust, by diligence and honesty, is in a capacity to honour his Maker and the religion which he professes. Every one in the sphere and orb wherein Providence hath fixed him must act, move, and influence. Serve God with constancy both in your general and particular calling. This is Christianity, and this will bring a blessing upon you and yours. III. OUR LORD WILL COME AND TAKE AN ACCOUNT OF WHAT WE HAVE DONE. The Master will come and visit His servants whom He hath set on work. My brethren, our Lord observes and minds what we do; He takes notice whether we be idle or watchful, whether we busy ourselves about His work or Satan's. And it will not be long before He comes and reckons with us for all our past demeanour. The days of accounting are these two, death and the last judgment. These are the set times of our Lord's coming, and none can reverse and escape them. The voluptuous and debauched person must appear before that great tribunal, and give an account of his wild and brutish deportment; the unclean person who shunned the light, and thought to conceal his folly by darkness and retirements, must then appear and stand out in the open view of the world, and be accountable for his lewd and lascivious practices. The profane swearer, who blasphemed the holy name of God and His Son Jesus, must then bow and prostrate himself to Him whom he before profaned. The mighty oppressor, who escaped here the earthly judge, and by his wealth and power made himself too great for human judicature, must stand at that great bar and submit to the fatal sentence. The hypocrite, who thought to deceive God as well as his neighbours, shall appear then in his true shape, which he never did before. The uncharitable man, the fomenter of strife and discord, the man that haled others before the judge, must himself appear before the Judge of heaven and earth, and answer for all his unchristian and unbrotherly behaviour. IV. THOSE SERVANTS WHOM CHRIST AT HIS COMING SHALL FIND ABOUT HIS WORK AND BUSINESS ARE IN A BLESSED AND HAPPY CONDITION. 1. How comfortable must it needs be to a holy person that he hath not only all his lifetime endeavoured sincerely to serve his God, and to do all the good he could in the world, but that, by God's grace assisting him, he hath persevered in the same course until death; and now that he is to depart this life he is not employed in the works of darkness, he is not displeasing God, and offending good men, but he is about his Master's business, and he expires his last breath in the discharge of his duty. Blessedness is entailed on the servant who thus behaves himself. If you consider the nature of the thing itself it cannot be otherwise, for he being made by God to serve Him, and to be wholly at His beck and disposal, it must needs be that his satisfaction and happiness should consist in conforming himself to God's will, and in acting according to His laws and commands. I may add likewise that God will protect His servants in the discharge of His own work. They are safe whilst they are doing what He sets them about. Come what will, they cannot be miserable. The summary application of all may be that of 2 Peter iii. 11. " Seeing, then, that all these things shall be dissolved " (seeing that the day of the Lord approaches, and Christ will come to judge thee speedily, either at death or at the last judgment), "what manner of persons ought ye to be in all holy conversation and godliness?" how exemplary should your lives and conversations be? how zealous should you show yourselves in all the exercises of religion. Give me leave to direct you (as to this great matter) in these few words: 1. Pray more fervently. Unite all your forces now and wrestle with God, and cry mightily unto Him for yourselves, for this place where you inhabit, and for the whole land of your nativity. 2. Disengage your affections more resolvedly from the world. You are convinced by this time, surely, that the world is vain and uncertain. Dote not on its enjoyments, sink not your souls into earth, plunge them not into the mire, be indifferent as to all things here below, and be ready to part with any of this world's goods. 3. Oppose vice more vigorously than ever, and the rather because of those many strong temptations you meet with in this degenerate and corrupted age. 4. Breathe after heaven more passionately. Let the ill things which you behold here below be the occasion of raising your thoughts and desires toward those mansions above where nothing inhabits but what is pure and holy. 5. Let your lives and actions acquaint the world how mindful you are of that great account which you are to give at the coming of the Lord. Desire to be found doing your Master's work, and then be not solicitous about the wages, but assure yourselves that that will be a recompense far beyond your thoughts and wishes. Wherefore comfort one another with these words. (*John Edwards, D.D.*) *The faithful servant:*—I. The faithful principles of the true servant of God. 1. He views God as an ever-present Master. 2. He acknowledges God as the Giver of life and salvation to his perishing soul. II. The honourable occupations of the true servant of God. He considers himself to be entrusted with various gifts; not for his own pleasure, but for God's glory; not for selfish ends, but for the highest good of his fellow-creatures. All that he possesses he considers as being his Lord's goods ; and he does not dare to waste any part of them. He takes an inventory of what is committed to him, and " occupies " or trades therewith. He turns everything to good account; he squanders nothing. To this end, more-over, he often reviews his own proceedings ; and these self-examinations are pre-paratory to that last solemn hour when it shall be said, " Give an account of thy stewardship ; for thou mayest be no longer steward." See how he dedicates his talents to the Most High, and employs all his mind for God! What poor, ignorant sinners, whether at home, or heathen abroad, can I bring to the knowledge of Christ? What afflicted person can I comfort? What tempted servant of Christ can I succour? What neighbour, or friend, or relative, that is unconverted, can I win to Christ? Thus, moreover, he lays out his time ; his years, his days, his very hours are engaged for God. III. The generous dispositions of the true servant of God. In one word—love. Therefore, nothing is irksome, nothing burdensome. IV. The reward which shall be given to the true servant of God. 1. He is commended. 2. He is promoted. 3. He is admitted to joys inconceivable. (*W. Jowett, M.A.*) *The blessedness of the faithful servant:*—I. The honourable occupation described is that of a servant diligently employed in his Master's work. 1. Labour is not necessarily and essentially a curse. Adam in Eden. Labour in itself is invigorating, promoting the welfare of the body and the cheer-fulness of the mind, while it tends to keep the heart from the power of those temptations which find in the idle and unoccupied an easy prey. It is idleness in all its forms against which the displeasure of our God is expressed with repeated emphasis in the sacred Scriptures. And labour is honourable, whether in the lowly engagements of those who tread the humbler walks of life, or in the more imposing pursuits of those who occupy the prominent stations of society ; whether the miner who labours in the bowels of the earth, or the author who with his pen records the processes and results of laborious thought for the guidance of his fellow-men. God has prescribed labour as one of the lasting arrangements of the social world. Everything is full of labour, from the glowing seraph, who flies through boundless space, the willing agent of Almighty will, down to those mysterious laws which keep the universe in being and secure its destined aims ; and man is to be no exception, his varied powers of body and of mind were bestowed, not to evaporate in listless, dreamy idleness, to be prostituted for the needs of selfishness and pleasure, but to be employed in active, healthful toil; hence we say labour is honourable. And if prescribed and honourable in the social world, much more so is its relation to the religion of Jesus. He would have no idlers in His kingdom. The idea of our text is that of a servant diligently engaged with his work. Now this, you know, is not the case with all; by some it is done partially, sluggishly, grudgingly, fitfully; but the character here described is supposed to recognize his obligation, without which no one will prove a faithful servant; to carry out his obligations with perseverance, feeling that every day has its claim, and every hour its demand; and further, seeking his Master's approbation, and thus making his labour his delight, as will always be the case when the smile of approbation is felt to be a coveted reward and a gratifying recompense. This we have described as an honourable position, and contrast justifies the representation. How unlike the trifler and the profligate is the course of the faithful servant! 2. Such a character is honourable in the unprejudiced estimate of the world. To whom do we look back with reverence and esteem? To the men who lived solely for selfish ends, either that they might amass a fortune or obtain a name? or to those who spent their all in riotous living? Oh no, they have passed into a silence as complete as the destruction they have secured, or are remembered only as warnings to others to avoid their folly and escape their doom. It is the patriot toiling or suffering for his country's good. A Howard or a Fry risking the infection of disease in their efforts to alleviate the sufferings or restrain the progress of guilt—the humble, devoted instructor of youthful ignorance—the faithful pastor—the sanctified intellect—the self-denying philanthropist—these are they whom the world, with all its evils, yet delights to honour—whose names are embalmed in fragrant recollection, who are looked upon as men who are held up for the admiring imitation of succeeding generations—these, the servants diligently and faithfully engaged in their work, are the lights of the world and the salt of the earth. 3. Such characters are honourable in the approving representations of God's own Word. II. CONSIDER THE BLESSEDNESS WITH WHICH SUCH A COURSE SHALL BE CROWNED. "Blessed is that servant, whom his Lord when He cometh shall find so doing." 1. Here we are referred to a solemn event, the coming of the Master. 2. And yet further, the form of our text suggests to us the uncertainty of the mode and the moment of the Master's arrival. Uncertainty—not with Him, for known unto God are all things from the foundation of the world, but uncertainty as respects ourselves; the moment is hastening on, but we know it not—the mode is arranged and fixed, but it is not revealed. Nor can any careful induction of facts lead us to any reliable conclusion as to what awaits us—under what circumstances, or at what time, the Master will come to us. Sometimes we see the servant left to toil on through the whole extent of the wilderness, like Joshua and Caleb, while others enter the promised land in the springtide of their youth or in the full yet undecayed maturity of advanced years: wearisome sickness sometimes makes the exhausted traveller cry, "Come, Lord Jesus, come quickly," while others, spared the struggle and the dying strife, drop the coil of mortality and soar away on more than eagle's wings, and find themselves at rest. None, none can tell the hour or foresee the mode by which he shall be summoned to the final interview, yet the event with all its details is determined and known to Him in whom we live and move and have our being. The time is settled when, by the slow process of decay, or suddenly without previous notice, amid scenes of pleasure, the occupations of business, or in the solitude of retirement, we shall hear the Master's voice, and be called to appear before Him. (*Henry Madgin.*)

Vers. 45, 46. **My lord delayeth his coming.**—*Emboldened by delay:*—History says that long ago it had been announced that the world was coming to an end, and there was great excitement in London. It was said that the world would perish on a certain Friday. On Tuesday, Wednesday, Thursday, and Friday the people were in the cathedral, praying and weeping. It seemed as if the whole English nation was being converted to God, for it was announced as certain by philosophers that on the coming Friday the world would perish. Friday came, and there were no portents, no fires in the air, no earthquakes. The day passed along just like every other day, and when it was past and the night came, it is said that in London there was a scene of riot, and wassail, and drunkenness, and debauchery such as had never been witnessed. They forgot their vow, they forgot their repentance, they forgot their good resolutions. Oh, how much human nature in that! While trials and misfortunes come to us, and we are down deep in darkness and trouble, we make vows. We say: "Oh Lord, do so, and I will do so." The darkness passes, the peril goes away. We are as we were before, or worse; for oh, how often I have seen men start for the kingdom of God, come up to within arm's reach of it, and then go back farther from God than they ever were before, dropping from the very moment of their privilege into darkness for ever. (*Dr. Talmage.*)

Ver. 47. **Beaten with many stripes.**—*Many stripes :*—Our Lord in the context urges His disciples to diligence, watchfulness, and fidelity. This is important, for we are stewards, servants, and are responsible to Him who will one day say unto us, "Give an account of thy stewardship." I. THE CHARACTER SUSTAINED—"That servant." In many passages of Scripture true believers are called the servants of God. Called so by God—by Christ—by believers themselves (see John xii. 26). "Paul a servant of God"; "James, a servant of God," &c. 1. The servant's Master. This is Christ. He is the Head of the Church—the Divine Sovereign —Lord of all. He issues His commandments — appoints His ordinances— gives His rewards (John xiii. 13; Matt. xxiii. 28). 2. The servant's origin. Once servants of sin, of Satan—the world—pleasure—self. Now enlightened to perceive the superiority of Christ—translated from the kingdom of darkness (Rom. vi. 16–22). 3. The servant's character. (1) Must be faithful, give up all for his master. (2) Patient. His work will require self-denial. (3) Enduring, day after day he must toil on in an evil and difficult world. (4) Anxious to please, out of love and affection, not from fear or dread. II. THE SERVICE REQUIRED—"The will of the Master." What is the will of our Master? 1. Faith and repentance. These duties are desired in order that they may accomplish the servant's salvation (John iii. 16; Mark xvi. 15, 16). 2. The advancement of His Kingdom. This is to be brought about by the servant's labour. It is an unspeakable honour to be so employed. 3. Internal sanctification. Humility for failings. The acquisition of holiness. Piety of life. Sanctification of spirit. 4. Zeal in duty. Love is not to wax cold—the voices of prayer and praise are not to be silent—the hands are not to hang down—the voice is not to be silent. III. THE CONSEQUENCES ATTENDANT. On doing this duty depends reward or punishment. If it is faithfully performed, the servant shall have the approval of his Master; if neglected, His blame. 1. This is natural. It is the way of the world. A bad servant is soon discharged. A dishonest one is disgraced. 2. It is also just Wages would not be given unless they were earned. Slaves were obliged to obey. 3. It is for the good of the just. If careless, ignorant, evil men were admitted to heaven, it would be a place of misery. IV. THE PUNISHMENT PROPORTIONATE. An ignorant servant may be awkward without intentionally transgressing. But for those who know what is right, and deliberately sin, there will be many stripes. It is those who transgress against light and privilege and mercy, who will have to bear the full brunt of the law. Therefore—1. How great was the guilt of the Jews. They had God's oracles. Special revelation. Continuance of guidance. 2. How much greater our guilt if we offend. We have not only the light of the Jews, but the full blaze of Christ's revelation, and light, and work. All things made plain. All prophecies fulfilled. All directions given. If we neglect our duty, how many will be the stripes we shall receive! (*The Preachers' Analyst.*) *Practice in religion necessary in proportion to our knowledge :*—I. THAT IGNORANCE IS A GREAT EXCUSE OF MEN'S FAULTS, AND WILL LESSEN THEIR PUNISHMENT; "but he that knew not, but did commit things worthy of stripes, shall be beaten with few stripes." 1. There is an ignorance which doth wholly excuse and clear from all manner of guilt, and that is an absolute and invincible ignorance, when a person is wholly ignorant of the thing, which, if he knew, he should be bound to do, but neither can nor could have helped it, that he is ignorant of it; that is, he either had not the capacity, or wanted the means and opportunity, of knowing it. In this case a person is in no fault, if he did not do what he never knew, nor could know to be his duty. For God measures the faults of men by their wills, and if there be no defect there, there can be no guilt; for no man is guilty, but he that is conscious to himself that he would not do what he knew he ought to do, or would do what he knew he ought not to do. 2. There is likewise another sort of ignorance, which either does not at all, or very little, extenuate the faults of men; when men are not only ignorant, but choose to be so; that is, when they wilfully neglect those means and opportunities of knowledge which are afforded to them ; such as Job speaks of—"Who say unto God, depart from us, for we desire not the knowledge of Thy ways" (Job xxi. 14). But our Saviour here speaks of such an ignorance as does in a good degree extenuate the fault, and yet not wholly excuse it; for he says of them, that they knew not their Lord's will; and yet that this ignorance did not wholly excuse them from blame, nor exempt them from punishment, but they should "be beaten with few stripes." 3. There is an ignorance which is in some degree faulty, and yet does in a great measure excuse the faults which proceed from it; and this is when men are not absolutely ignorant of their duty, but only in comparison of others, who have a far more clear and distinct knowledge of it; and though they do not grossly and wilfully neglect the means of further knowledge, yet, perhaps, they do not make the best use they might of the opportunities they have of knowing their duty better; and therefore, in comparison of others, who have far better means and advantages of knowing their Lord's will, they may be said not to know it, though they are not simply ignorant of it, but only have a more obscure and uncertain knowledge of it. Now this ignorance does in a great measure excuse such persons, and extenuate their crimes, in comparison of those who had a clearer and more perfect knowledge of their Master's will; and yet it does not free them from all guilt, because they did not live up to that degree of knowledge which they had; and perhaps if they had used more care and industry, they might have known their Lord's will better. II. THAT THE GREATER ADVANTAGES AND OPPORTUNITIES ANY MAN HATH OF KNOWING THE WILL OF GOD, AND HIS DUTY, THE GREATER WILL BE HIS CONDEMNATION IF HE DO NOT DO IT. "The servant which knew his Lord's will, and prepared not himself, neither did according to it, shall be beaten with many stripes." "Which knew his Lord's will, and prepared not himself"; the preparation of our mind to do the will of God, whenever there is occasion and opportunity for it, is accepted with Him; a will rightly disposed to obey God, though it be not brought into act for want of opportunity, does not lose its reward: but when, notwithstanding we know not our Lord's will, there are neither of these, neither the act nor the preparation and resolution of doing it, what punishment may we not expect? For, after all the aggravations of sin, there is none that doth more intrinsically heighten the malignity of it, than when it is committed against the clear knowledge of our duty, and that upon these three accounts: 1. Because the knowledge of God's will is so great an advantage to the doing of it. 2. Because it is a great obligation upon us to the doing of it. 3. Because the neglect of our duty in this case cannot be without a great deal of wilfulness and contempt. (*Archbishop Tillotson.*) *The enlightened, yet disobedient servant, beaten with many stripes :*—I. THE LORD JEHOVAH IS OUR JUST AND LAWFUL MASTER, AND LEGITIMATELY CLAIMS OUR SUPREME AFFECTION FOR HIS EXCELLENCIES, AND OUR ENTIRE OBEDIENCE TO HIS LAWS. He makes His claims, and He has a right to them. 1. Has He not a right to our supreme affection, and our entire devotedness to His will, as our Creator? 2. The claim will increase when we consider that He is not merely our Father in giving us existence, so that we derive our being from Him, but that we receive our wellbeing from Him. 3. His claims are still higher, and we may say, resistless, on the ground of redemption. II. THE LORD JEHOVAH HAS AFFORDED YOU AND ME, AS HIS SERVANTS, THE CLEAREST KNOWLEDGE OF HIMSELF, AND OF HIS RIGHT OVER US, AND OF HIS WILL TOWARDS US, AND OF HIS EXPECTATIONS FROM US. 1. By a letter—a book. 2. By His servants—the persons who bear the letter. 3. By the unction of His Holy Spirit imparted to us. III. IT IS EVIDENT, FROM THE CHOICE AND CONDUCT OF MANY, THAT, THOUGH THEY MUST AND DO KNOW THEIR MASTER'S WILL, YET THEY DO NOT "PREPARE THEMSELVES NOR DO ACCORDING TO IT." IV. THE SIN OF SUCH MEN, THEREFORE, IS STAMPED WITH PECULIAR MALIGNITY, AND, WITHOUT PARDON, WILL BE FOLLOWED BY THE SEVEREST PUNISHMENT. You that know your Master's will, and do it not—remember, your sin is stamped with peculiar malignity. The malignity of a crime always bears proportion to the known dignity of the character insulted. To insult a constable, in the exercise of his official capacity, is a crime; to insult a magistrate on the bench is a greater; to insult a monarch on his throne is rebellion. Therefore, the gradation of crime always rises in proportion to the known dignity of the character offended. Then what must be—what *must* be the black aggravation of your crime, who know your Master's will, and know who that Master is, and yet do not "prepare yourselves nor do according to it"? You sin against God the Father in His laws—and you know Him to be so; you "trample under foot the blood of the Son of God"—and you know Him to be so; you "do despite unto the Spirit of Grace"—and you know who it is that you are doing despite unto. Remember, also, there is an aggravation in the case. It is not one sin committed once; it is the same sin committed again and again, under growing aggravations. Human laws say—for the first offence the penalty shall be light, for the second it shall be doubled, for the third it shall be trebled, and so on, so that punishment always bears proportion to the multitude of the offences. Very well; then, pray what sort of a sinner must you be? You know your Master's will, and do it not; and that is not in one instance—one sin once committed, or one duty once omitted, or one blessing once neglected—it is the same sin committed again, and again, and again, a thousand times repeated with increasing aggravations. Judge, then, "wicked and slothful servant," of such a Master! what must be the malignity of your sin. And then, again, it is not one sin committed a thousand times even, but a multitude of sins committed again and again with those magnifying aggravations. (*W. Dawson.*)   *God's penal law :*—I. ALL MEN EXIST IN A STATE OF OBLIGATION TO GOD. They are His servants; He, their Master. II. THE RESPONSIBILITIES OF MEN, CONNECTED WITH THEIR STATE OF OBLIGATION, VARY IN PROPORTION TO THEIR OPPORTUNITIES OF KNOWLEDGE AND OF IMPROVEMENT. 1. There exist in the world very different degrees of opportunity for knowledge and improvement. 2. We are placed in circumstances which afford to us the highest degrees of opportunity for knowledge and for improvement. 3. Possessing as we do such opportunities, we are under a special call to eminent devotedness to the service of God. III. THE PUNISHMENT OF MEN FOR THE VIOLATION OF THEIR RESPONSIBILITIES, IS REGULATED ACCORDING TO THE VALUE OF THE OPPORTUNITIES WHICH THEY HAVE POSSESSED, AND HAVE ABUSED. There are two remarks under this part of the subject to which your attention will be called. 1. You will observe, first, that punishment is to be inflicted upon all by whom their original obligations have been forgotten and violated. The desert of punishment is presented under the phrase of "committing things worthy of stripes." A certain period is stated to be appointed by the master, or lord of the household, for the purpose of returning, in order to inflict punishment, or grant rewards, according to the characters of those by whom he has been professedly served. 2. But, what we principally intend to insist on, on this part of the subject, is, that the punishment to be inflicted on those whose opportunities have been many, will be far more grievous than the punishment to be inflicted on those whose opportunities have been few. "Many stripes," or larger and heavier inflictions, are to be the portion of him who knew his lord's will and did it not; but "few stripes," or minor inflictions, are to be the portion of him who knew not his lord's will, and did it not. In this infliction of stripes there seems an allusion to the law, which you observe to be contained in Deuteronomy xxv. 1-3. The deduction of the Saviour, in connection with this law, appears to be this: that those whose opportunities have been few shall receive a certain amount of punishment, limited in some mode analogous to that which is contained in the announcement of the law; but that those whose opportunities have been many, and who yet have abused and slighted them, are to be subjected to a punishment to which no limit and no measure are to be assigned: they are to endure the keenest inflictions which the wrath of an Almighty and Infinite Being can pour upon them. (*J. Parsons.*)   *The penalty of disregarded duty :*—I had an aged friend who knew Robert Pollock, the celebrated Scotch poet, and he told me that Pollock lost his life through too vivid views of the great future. It seemed as if he walked amid the realities of the eternal world. It was too great for his physical strength, and he died in early life. Robert Pollock one day caught a glimpse of the destiny of those who miss heaven. I can recollect here and there a sentence: "And as I listened I heard these beings curse Almighty God, and curse the Lamb, and curse the earth, the resurrection morn, and seek, and ever vainly seek for utter death. And to the everlasting anguish still the thunders from above, responding, spoke these words which, forlornly echoing through the caverns of perdition, fall on every ear: 'Ye knew your duty, but ye did it not.' Then back again recoiled a deeper groan—a deeper groan! O what a groan was that!" (*Dr. Talmage.*)   *Result of sinning against the light :*—A few weeks ago, a poor woman came to my surgery, and said, "A young woman is lodging in the same house with me, who is wretchedly poor, in great suffering, and, I fear, near her end." I accompanied the woman home. She led me to the bedside of the dying girl, and left us together. It was a dreadful scene. A girl of three or four and twenty lay on a wretched pallet, with scarcely any covering. A single chair and a broken table was all the furniture the room contained. Near the bed was hanging, on a few pegs, the girl's finery. Yes, alas! finery. Dresses of gaudy material, and showily made up, were flaunting their gay colours in this chamber of death, looking in that girl's eyes as she lay dying, as witnesses of her sin and folly, and reminding her that, as soon as she was dead, these things, which had cost her so dear, would become the property of the landlady, as payment of the debt she had not money to discharge. I leaned over the bedside, and took her hand in mine. I told her that Jesus had sent me to her with an offer of peace and pardon. "No," she said, hoarsely—"no, I was brought up in a Sunday-school; I knew the right, but I did it not. There is no pardon for me now." I knelt down, I prayed for her—prayed, as she had not confidence to pray for herself—her sinful self. I besought Him that she might repent and find peace. But, even as I talked with her, she died, uttering the fearful cry, "Too late! too late!" (*Dr. Raynor.*)   *Disregarding the light :*—It is said that off the coast of New Zealand a sea-captain steered his vessel directly toward the light, and, thinking himself safe, fell asleep. His vessel dashed upon the rocks at the very foot of the lighthouse. The beacon-light shining out upon the deep for protection and guidance furnished no help to the slumbering mariner. Indeed, his culpability was greater because of the abuse of the friendly gift. *Degrees of punishment :*—The legend of St. Macarius of Alexandria runs thus: "One day as Macarius wandered among those ancient Egyptian tombs, wherein he had made himself a dwelling-place, he found the skull of a mummy, and turning it over with his crutch, he inquired to whom it belonged; and it replied, 'To a pagan.' And Macarius, looking into the empty eyes, said, 'Where, then, is thy soul?' And the head replied, 'In hell.' Macarius asked, 'How deep?' And the head replied, 'The depth is greater than the distance from heaven to earth.' Then Macarius asked, 'Are there any deeper than thou art?' The skull replied, 'Yes: the Jews are deeper still.' And Macarius asked, 'Are there any deeper than the Jews?' To which the head replied, 'Yes, in sooth! for the Christians whom Jesus Christ hath redeemed, and who show in their actions that they despise His doctrine, are deeper still.'"

Ver. 48. **For unto whomsoever much is given.**—*The law of accountability :*—These words are rendered as a reason why those servants that know their master's will are beaten with more stripes than those that knew it not, because they did not improve their advantages. And Christ pleadeth the equity of it from the custom of men, expressed in their common proverbs or sentences, that go from hand to hand among the people. A beneficiary that hath received much from his benefactor is obliged to a greater gratitude. A factor that hath his master's estate in his hands must make a return according to the degree of the trust. These things being evident by the light of nature, and granted among all men, our Lord accommodateth them to His purpose, which is to show God's proceedings with men are according to the degree of their advantages—"For unto whomsoever," &c. In the words observe four things: 1. A double conveyance of benefits to us. Whatever a man receiveth, it is either given as a gift or committed as a talent. For, first, He saith, "To whomsoever much is given"; and presently, "To whomsoever men have committed much." 2. These things are not given to all in the same measure; there is a difference in the distribution; some have "much," others have "little." 3. Whether men have received much or little, it is all in reference to an account; this is signified in the words, "required," "asked." 4. Answerable to their mercies shall their account be; much for much, and little for little. To whom anything is given, of him something shall be required and asked; but to whom "much is given" and "committed," of him shall they "ask the more"; not more than is committed, but more than is required and asked of another; as where the soil is better and more tilled, we look for the better crop, and we expect that he should come sooner that rideth on horseback than he that goeth on foot. (*T. Manton, D.D.*)   *Privilege the measure of responsibility :*—The husbandman, the more he improves his ground the greater crop he looks for; the more completely the soldier is armed, the better service is required of him; the scholar that is well instructed must show great fruits of his proficiency. Thus the earthly part of man drinks in the sweet showers of grace that fall upon it. The blessed Spirit of God puts upon us that panoply, the whole armour of God. And the same Spirit teacheth us all things, leads us into all truth, and brings all things to our remembrance which Christ hath spoken for our good. Shall we then, being thus cultivated, thus armed, thus instructed, not bring forth fruits in some measure answerable to so great indulgence? Shall such blessings of God be received in vain? (*T. Stapleton.*)   *Gifts entail responsibility :*—The husbandman looks for more fruit from some of his fruit-trees than from others; those upon which he bestows most time, cost, and labour, from these he expects most fruit; and is displeased if his expectation be not answered accordingly. This shadows out unto us that God expects greater returns of duty from some persons than from some others, and neglect thereof provokes God against them. In the ceremonial law God required more sacrifices from the rich than from the poor : such as had great store of oxen, sheep, and other things to be offered in sacrifice, should not have been accepted had they offered " a pair of turtle doves, or two young pigeons," which yet were accepted from the poorer sort of persons. So also under the gospel, " to whom much is given, of them doth He require the more." God had done great things for Eli and David, and expected (accordingly) greater returns of duty and obedience all their lives after ; but they failing in some great particulars, God is sore displeased with them, and reckons up the great benefits and particular engagements they had received, and tells them He expected other returns from them. So also Hezekiah received much, and God looked for answerable returns; but he rendered not according to the benefits received, and God was displeased with him upon that account. God planted a vineyard, and bestowed much care and pains about it, and looked for an answerable return of good fruits, but because it brought forth wild grapes instead of good and pleasant grapes, He laid it waste. Some have received more, and lie under greater engagements from God than others, therefore God looks to receive more. This shows us the great danger such persons lie under who have received much from God, and return but little ; having received many talents, and not making an answerable return by improving of them to the honour of God and advantage of His people ; nay, who perhaps use all against God and His people. God gives to some many gifts of nature and common graces, much knowledge, learning, wisdom, great riches, honours, offices, places, much time, liberty, great and choice means of grace, special providences and dispensations, and many other talents which others have not : of these God requires more than of those who have fewer and less of these things, and the not making suitable returns provokes God against them. If God spared not His choice servants, Eli, David, Hezekiah, &c., if judgment begin at the house of God, how shall the ungodly and sinner escape ? Let every one of us consider what we have received, that so we may make unto God some answerable returns: God looked for more (and received more) from him that had the five talents, than from him that had received but two. No one (not the lowest, or meanest) is freed from making returns of duty to God : though God requires much from those who have received much, yet the mean person, who has but a little, must return of that little. " Let him work with his hands, that he may have something to give to him that needeth " ; and it will be " accepted according to that a man hath, and not according to that he hath not." So, also, of the use and improvements of all other talents, gifts, graces, liberty, power, and the rest. (*Austen.*)   *Duty measured by ability :*—In Xenophon's " Memorabilia " it is recorded of Socrates that, " when he offered small sacrifices from his small means, he thought that he was not at all inferior in merit to those who offered numerous and great sacrifices from ample and abundant means; for he said that it would not become the gods to delight in large rather than in small sacrifices ; since, if such were the case, the offerings of the bad would oftentimes be more acceptable to them than those of the good; nor would life be of any account in the eyes of men, if oblations from the bad were better received by the gods than oblations from the good ; but he thought that the gods had most pleasure in the offerings of the most pious. He used also to quote with approbation the verse, ' Perform sacrifices to the gods according to your ability,' and used to say that it was a good exhortation to men with regard to friends, and guests, and all other relations of life, to perform according to their ability." (*Biblical Things Not Generally Known.*)   *Responsibility according to knowledge :*—Richard Knill was one day talking to some military officers in Madras, when one of them asked : " What do you missionaries mean ? Do you think that poor black fellow will be damned ? " " I hope not," replied Knill, " but if he is, I think his punishment will be very light compared with yours if you neglect God." The words so struck home that the officer lifted up his hands and said: " I believe it ; I have long thought so."

Ver. 49. **I am come to send fire on the earth.**—*The fire of contention ; or, the trouble that follows the gospel :*—1. There may be dissension betwixt the good and the good ; and hereof is the devil the author. It is the enemy that sows those tares. Christ came not to send this fire, yet He wisely tempers it to our good. 2. There may be dissension betwixt the wicked and the wicked ; and hereof also is Satan author. He sets his own together by the ears, like cocks of the game, to make him sport. Hereupon he raised these great heathen wars, that in them millions of souls might go down to people his lower kingdom. Hereupon he draws ruffian into the field against ruffian, and then laughs at their vainly spilt blood. All the contentions, quarrels, whereby one evil neighbour vexeth another, all slanders, scoldings, reproaches, calumnies, are his own damned fires. 3. There is a dissension between the wicked and godly; nor yet is Christ the proper and immediate cause of this. For "if it be possible, as much as lieth in you, live peaceably with all men" (Rom. xii. 18). 4. There is an enmity betwixt grace and wickedness, a continual combat between sanctity and sin; and this is the fire Christ came to send. He is to some a living stone, whereupon they are built to life; to others a stone of offence, whereat they stumble to death. 1. The FIRE is discord, debate, contention, anger, and hatred against the godly. (1) Debate is like fire; for as that of all elements, so this of all passions, is most violent. (2) Contention is like fire, for both burn as long as there is any exustible matter to contend with. Only herein it transcends fire—for fire begets not matter, but consumes it; debate begets matter, but not consumes it. (3) As a little spark grows to a great flame, so a small debate often proves a great rent. (4) As fire is proverbially said to be an ill master but a good servant, so anger, where it is a lord of rule, is a lord of misrule; but where it is subdued to reason, or rather sanctified by grace, it is a good servant. That anger is holy that is zealous for the glory of God. 2. The FUEL whereon this fire works is the good profession of the godly. LESSON 1. That we have need of patience, seeing we know that the law of our profession binds us to a warfare; and it is decreed upon that "all that will live godly in Christ shall suffer persecution." When fire, which was the god of the Chaldeans, had devoured all the other wooden deities, Canopis set upon him a caldron full of water, whose bottom was full of holes artificially stopped with wax; which, when it felt the heat of that furious idol, melted and gave way to the water to fall down upon it, and quench it. The water of our patience must only extinguish this fire; nothing but our tears, moderation, and sufferance can abate it. But this patience hath no further latitude than our proper respect; for in the cause of the Lord we must be jealous and zealous. 2. That we must not shrink from our profession, though we know it to be the fuel that maintains this fire. 3. That we think not much of the troublous fires that are thus sent to wait upon the gospel. 4. That we esteem not the worse of our profession, but the better. It is no small comfort that God thinks thee worthy to suffer for His name. This was the apostles' joy, not that they were worthy, but "that they were counted worthy to suffer shame for Christ" (Acts v. 41). 5. Seeing the fuel is our integrity—and this they specially strike at—let us more constantly hold together, confirming the communion of saints, which they would dissolve. (*T. Adams.*) *The gospel a fire:*—We must look for a Scriptural use of "fire" which shall have some bearing upon the subject of division and discord as caused by the gospel. We find such a use in the very idea of kindling. If the gospel was a mere tame and spiritless influence, a mere soothing and stroking down of human faults and passions, a mere palliative and balsam for the wounds and sufferings, for the wrongs and woes of fallen nature, it would have differed in many other respects from the thing which Jesus Christ brought us from heaven; but certainly and most evidently in this, that it would have caused no strifes and no contentions, no violences and no discords. It is because the gospel is first and above all else a "fire," enkindled and sparkling, pervading and transforming the whole body and substance of the being to which it is effectually applied, that it brings with it this irritating, this provoking, this exasperating influence upon every bystanding and surrounding being which repudiate, and "we will have none of it." It needs but a little reflection to make all hearts echo the statement. There are those in this day who tell us that the real gospel is a mere enforcement or suggestion, or, if you will, revelation of charity. We ask what is meant by "charity," and we find that it is a sort of easygoing tolerance for all creeds and all religions, a good-natured "live and let live" for all the philosophies, and all the philanthropies, and all the superstitions, and all the idolatries which have entered into the heart of man, as the truth and the whole of truth, the duty and the whole of duty, whether toward God or toward man. Now at present we are only concerned to say so much as this, that if the gospel had thus entered the world, if this had been the idea of it as Christ and the apostles preached it, it would have raised no hostility; it could not possibly have had the history which we know Christianity has had, as flinging abroad upon the earth "division" or a "sword"; and for this simple reason that it would not have had in it one single characteristic of "fire." Men would have been perfectly willing under Nero or Domitian to let Christians alone, if they would only have glided about among their contemporaries as men whispering peace and safety, hinting at a new divinity, one among many, each having some claim, and none having an exclusive claim to the belief and faith of mankind; a new divinity to occupy one niche of a crowded and world-wide pantheon—"Jesus and the resurrection." Athens would have let this alone; Rome would have let this alone; human nature would have made room for this, because it would have put oil or water in the place of fire; because it would have been a mere religion of negatives and platitudes, stirred by no storm and brightened by no ray. "I came to cast fire upon the earth," and although fire has many beautiful and many comforting aspects, this is in virtue of a quality which makes it also, and before all else, penetrating and exploring, consuming and purifying, a power, first, formidable and destructive; then, secondly, an influence brightening and warming, cheering and comforting. It is thus with the sign, it is thus, also, with the thing signified. I. THE GOSPEL A FIRE IN THE HEART. The gospel, entering a heart, begins with kindling. There is much in that heart. We speak not only of hearts which the Lord suddenly opened at Philippi or Corinth to listen to the preaching of a new faith, when all round and all antecedent had been Jewish or Pagan; we speak of hearts to which gospel sounds, whether of word or of worship, are but too familiar, and we say that, even in these, if a new reality is ever by the grace of God given to the gospel, there is much fuel ready for the burning, much as to which the gospel would be nugatory if it did not burn up—probably many known sins, certainly a multitude of frivolities and vanities, which to let alone would be to say "peace" where there is none; which to let alone would be to live the life in the sleep of death, but which to assail is to bring a "sword" between soul and spirit, to proclaim war to the knife against many inveterate habits, and to cause a revolution in the most cherished tenacities of the being; and it is just in proportion as this first office of fire is faithfully and effectively done that any other can be safe or even true. Thoroughness in yielding ourselves to the purifying, is the condition alike of the illuminating and the warming, and the comforting. It is just where the fire is not allowed to consume that it refuses to burn brightly for companionship or for cheering. II. THE GOSPEL A FIRE IN THE WORLD. This, which is the real struggle of the gospel in the heart, is also its real struggle in the world. If the gospel would begin and end with comforting, it would be welcomed everywhere; if it would settle down as a mere pleasant guest in the chamber and at the social table, making all easy all round, saying or sounding as if it said, "Live as you list and all shall be peace at the last," nothing could be more popular; then it would have the promise, in commonest parlance, of two worlds—the life that is and the life that shall be. It is this uncompromising character, this call for decision and for a whole heart, this demand for a life wholly given, in purpose and affections to the Lord who bought it, which makes the gospel a "sword" for such as will not have it for a "fire"; and yet, brethren, it is just this uncompromising character which makes it a power, and which makes it a charm, and which makes it a gospel. Oh, we could any of us construct a religion which should cry "peace" when there is none; we could any of us make a gospel, using a few phrases and elements of the real one, which should be accommodating, and which should be complimentary, and which should be plausible, and which, therefore, should be fashionable; and which, just in the same degree, would leave every sore festering, and every woe desolating, and every vice and crime destroying, of the old Adam and of the fallen and of the sin-spoilt man. But what should we have done, when we had done all this to perfection? We should not have evoked one grand heroism such as lies at the bottom even of the ruined humanity; we should not have evoked one echo from the slumbering temple of the God-made man; we should have done nothing whatever towards the actual want, and the real hunger, and the one despair of the soul, which feels that its true wretchedness is separation from God, and that its true cure would be the getting back home. "I am come to send fire on the earth." So Jesus speaks; and we, who have one breath of God in us, feel that "fire" is the element wanting. We want the water of cleansing, and we want the wind of scourging, and we want the earthquake of demolishing; and oh, what we want above all, is the "fire" which does all these things, and which yet adds to them all the grace of transforming, and the grace of kindling, and the grace of inspiring, and the grace of enabling, and the grace of the new life. It is the "fire" which has made Christianity great; it is not the mere washing with the water of a new innocence; it is not the light of the lamp of information even as to the mysteries of grace and redemption: it is the enkindling of Christian souls with the fire of love, and the fire of zeal, and the fire of an outspoken boldness, and the fire of even an impatient and intolerant hatred of misery and wickedness. It is this which has done great things in the earth in the name of Christ and God; it is this which has demolished idols; it is this which has at last toppled down slavery; it is this which has made missionaries strong, and martyrs brave, and churches militant; it is this which has provoked indeed the rage of the world and devil; but it has also shown enemies, open and secret, that "greater is He that is with us than he that is in the world." "I am come to send fire upon the earth, and what would I, but that it were already kindled?" It is kindled now. Ages and generations have lived in the blaze of that fire, and Christ, who knows what is in man, loves that "fire" better than the tame sluggishness, the lifeless torpor, the false peace which prevails everywhere where that "fire" comes not. "Already kindled!" Is it kindled round us? Is it kindled in us? Are we a stagnant, torpid, lifeless multitude? or, are we of the kindled, inspired, living, and life-breathing few? For few still are they in whom this Spirit of God is, not for selfish comfort, but for inspired power. Let us hazard some little, let us encounter some little, that we may please Him who said—"Oh, that it were already kindled," because He loved the "fire" rather than the chill, because He loved the enthusiasm rather than the half-heartedness. (*Dean Vaughan.*)　*The fire which Christ kindles on earth :*—1. A fire which warms what is cold. 2. Purifies what is impure. 3. Consumes what is evil. (*Van Oosterzee.*)　*The controversy which Christ has brought on earth :*—1. How we are to wish for it. 2. How we are to fear it. 3. How we are to endure it. (*Schenkal.*)　*Suffering, a baptism :*—For the Christian a threefold baptism is necessary. 1. The water baptism of sprinkling. 2. The spiritual baptism of renewal. 3. The fire baptism of trial. (*Van Oosterzee.*)　*The discord which Christ has brought upon earth :*—1. A surprising phenomenon, if we look at—(1) The King (Psa. lxxii.). (2) The fundamental law of the kingdom of God (John xiii. 35). 2. An explicable phenomenon if we direct our eye to—(1) The severity of the gospel. (2) The sinfulness of the human heart. 3. A momentous phenomenon. This strife is a proof of the high significance, and means for the establishment, the purification, and the victory of Christianity. (*Ibid.*)　*The truth in the Church :*—I. Let us consider THE DESIGN OF OUR LORD'S ADVENT, AS HERE ANNOUNCED BY HIMSELF. Indeed, each peculiar aspect in which our Lord's work is viewed by Him is a characteristic variety, which tends both to enlarge and rectify our views on the subject. When He contemplates His work in relation to the fallen condition of our race, His announcement of His design is this—"I am come to seek and to save the lost." When He views it in relation to the redemption He was to accomplish, He speaks of it as being "a ransom price for many." When He views it in its relation to God, His exclamation to the Father is "I have come to glorify Thee on the earth." When He viewed it in regard to Himself, His representation was, that He had come into this far country "to get Himself a kingdom." And when He viewed it in relation to the world at large, He announced Himself as the Light of the world—as "a light to lighten the Gentiles "—as "the Bread that came down from heaven, of which if a man eat he will never die"—as having living Water to bestow, of which "whosoever drinketh shall never thirst "— as Him who had come "not to call the righteous but sinners to repentance." In all these representations the same great idea is either expressed or shadowed forth— namely, that the mystery of our Lord's incarnation and life and passion had no other design, nothing less than the undoing of all that sin had produced in our world—that out of that dark and formless chaos into which the whole spiritual creation here had been thrown, He might produce a new order of things, where for man there should be purity, dignity, and joy; and for God, the re-establishment in glory and in majesty of His full authority over the heart and the conscience of man. The announcement of our Lord's passion and work given in the passage before us, belongs to the last of the classes above enumerated; those, namely, in which its general bearings on the ignorant, the guilty creatures of our race, is proclaimed. In the Old Testament prophecy, the advent of the Messiah had been described as an event which should result in the purging away from the Church of God of all filth, "by the spirit of burning"; in the utterance of the prophetic voice it had been foretold of the Messiah, that He "should sit as a refiner and purifier of silver, to purify the sons of Levi, and purge them like gold and silver, that they should offer unto God an offering in righteousness." In these passages the idea of purification and refinement is most distinctly brought before us by the symbolic language in which the design of the Messiah's mission is described; and it is in reference apparently to the same idea, applying to Himself this description of the

Messiah, that our Lord uses the words now before us. By some interpreters, indeed, their application has been restricted to those dissensions and fiery controversies which the religion of Christ has, through the hostility of mankind, been instrumental in producing in our world. And to this they have been led by the allusion our Lord Himself makes to these dissensions in subsequent verses of this chapter. But this interpretation can hardly be admitted, for these dissensions and controversies are not necessary, far less essential, parts of our Lord's work, but clearly the results springing out of the evil state of man's heart, and it cannot be to the collateral and accidental results of the circumstances among which He comes, that our Lord alludes "I am come to send fire on the earth." It does appear a very weak and impotent interpretation of such an assertion to represent it as meaning nothing more than the quarrels among men, which may be its result. By the fire here spoken of, which our Lord had said He came to send on the earth, is to be understood that purifying, remodelling, renovating power which He came to diffuse through the mass of our race. He came not merely to deliver a message, and to do by it an appointed work, but by means of that message and in consequence of that work, to set the world on fire. He came to revolutionize the world by infusing into it a new element of spiritual life and activity. In short, to melt and fuse the whole fabric of earthly relations, that out of its elemental parts His plastic hand may construct a more perfect form of being, and thereby cover this earth which God has made with a race of beings worthier of Him who made them, and of that fair and fertile world which He has given them to inhabit. This great change which our Lord had come to commence finds its basis in His sacrificial work; and the means by which it is to be carried forward are the promulgation of the mighty truths connected with that work. So long as sin remains, evil, and gloom, and sorrow, must overhang our earth : but let sin be removed, and the removal of the cause will be followed by the cessation of all the evils the presence of that cause has occasioned and perpetuated. Now the only way in which sin can be removed from the conscience of the man by whom it has been committed, is by his being fully forgiven all the guilt of sin, and perfectly cleansed of all the pollution of sin, by God. But will God, can God, thus purify the sinner ? The answer comes to us from the cross of Christ. The fire which consumed the sacrifice upon that mystic altar was fiercer than the fire of Tophet; but it was a fire that cleanses, that brings renovation and purity to a world of polluted and perishing sinners. As it was necessary that this fire should be kindled first on the altar of atonement, so it is only as our torch is irradiated on that altar, that we can spread the sacred flame through the world. The only means by which we can hope to ransom and purify our fallen race, is by making known to each individual of it the great facts and doctrines connected with the sacrificial work of Christ. All other means will prove inefficient. Thus is this doctrine adapted to the great objects for which it was designed. The religion of Jesus Christ has been sent forth by its great Author, as a mighty fire, to purify and remodel the world. In accomplishing this great work, Christianity begins with individuals, and by successive conquests over the corruptions and guilt of individual souls, advances to the salvation of multitudes, and the renovation of the race. The "fire" which Christ sent into the world is to enwrap the whole world in its purifying blaze; but then it is to do so only by being kindled in heart after heart, and warming and sanctifying home after home. And wherever this sacred fire is experienced, it will stretch forth its lambent flame to fasten on new objects, and accomplish new transformations. It comes not like the lightning, appearing suddenly in the east, and darting instantaneously to the west. It comes with a slow, steady, and advancing flame. At first its light falls amidst the corruptions of some solitary path; but gradually it extends its light, and heat, and purifying influence, until, passing into a mighty conflagration, it encircles whole countries and continents. As she advances to the accomplishment of her purpose, and attainment of her triumph, she must, of necessity, come into collision with much that men have been accustomed to value and to revere. Many of the forms of social life, many of the bulwarks of earthly policy, many of the institutions of human intercourse, are the mere offspring of sensual taste and habits, or, at the best, mere artificial contrivances for the effecting of a compromise between the good and the evil that are strangely mixed up in the tissue of our mortal life. Every advance Christianity makes in our world must be connected with conflict. Not a single bosom is surrendered to her occupancy without a struggle. II. I have now to direct your attention for a little to OUR LORD'S EXPRESSION OF ARDENT DESIRE FOR THE COMMENCEMENT OF THAT WORK WHICH HE THUS CAME INTO THE WORLD TO

ACCOMPLISH : " I am come to send fire on the earth : I would that it were already kindled !" If you examine the chronology of the gospel history, you will find that the discourses of which my text forms a part were delivered by our Lord within a very short time—three or four weeks, at the very utmost, of His crucifixion. As He uttered these words, then, He had His sufferings full in view, and was in the immediate prospect of entering upon those scenes of unparalleled agony through which He passed to the accomplishment of His work. With the feelings that then occupied His bosom these words are in full harmony. The considerations which thus induced our Saviour so ardently to desire the accomplishment of His work are to be sought, doubtless, in the consequences that were to result from the accomplishment of that work ; and though these can never be present to our minds with the force that occupied His, yet it may be permitted to us without presumption to institute an inquiry into these considerations, and the effect it may be supposed they would have in causing Him thus to long for their realization. Allow me, then, to refer to a few of the consequences of the kindling of that fire the Saviour came to send upon the earth. 1. And first, the diffusion of Christianity stands closely connected with the promotion of the Divine glory in the world. In consequence of the prevalence of sin, the glory of God, as manifested in this portion of His universe, has been fearfully obscured. 2. In the diffusion of Christianity, our Lord traced the fulfilment of His own gracious purpose to men, and the success of His own work in their behalf ; and this prospect naturally prompted the desire expressed in the words before us. When our Lord became incarnate, and entered on the work of His humiliation, it was in order that by means of that work He might bring to pass the design and purpose which had eternally occupied the Infinite mind. Is it to succeed, or is it to fail ? He anticipated the joy of the angels, as they witnessed sinner after sinner converted unto God. He foretasted—a foretaste peculiar to Himself— the joy of bringing many sons unto glory. And as all these prospects in bright manifestation and in firm assurance pressed on His view, who can wonder that His bosom should have thrilled with ardent desire, and His cry should have been with regard to that fire, by which these results were to be secured—" I would that it were already kindled "? 3. Our Lord saw in the extension of Christianity, a vast increase to the purity and moral goodness of the world ; and this filled His mind with delight and intense desire that the work were already begun. To a mind possessing any degree of intellectual vigour, and not altogether destitute of right moral feeling, the state of a thinking, accountable, and immortal being like man, lying under the polluting, degrading, destroying power of sin, cannot fail to raise emotions of the deepest pain. And knowing that in that purifying fire He had come to send on the earth was to be found the only real and effectual remedy for this sad state of things, who can wonder that His sacred bosom should have expanded with an ardent desire which gave itself vent in the exclamation—" I would that it were already kindled ! " 4. The bearing of His religion on the happiness of mankind must also have actuated the Saviour in desiring its speedy and steady diffusion. When we cast our eye over the condition of our race, we behold man universally engaged in the eager pursuit of happiness, often baffled in the pursuit, and constrained in disappointment of spirit to exclaim—"Who will show us any good ? " But in the gospel of Jesus Christ there is a panacea for man's ills, and an antidote for man's sorrows. Wherever it spreads, the people that " sat in darkness see a great light," and upon them that dwelt in the region of the shadow of death, a light shines. 5. The force of these considerations is greatly enhanced by the fact, that the triumphs of Christianity are progressive, and that her conquests are perpetual. " All nations shall be blessed in Christ, and all nations shall call Him blessed." Nor shall this continual extension of territory in any degree endanger the stability of the kingdom itself. With many earthly empires the shouts of their victorious arms have passed into the knell of their approaching doom. Rome fell through the vastness of her dominions, and the very multitude of her conquests. Spain fell from her proud pre-eminence among the nations of Europe, from the time that her chivalry gained for her new empires on the other side of the Atlantic. And Britain, invincible within her own sea-bound shores, has ere now found the same defeat in consequence of the wide extent of her foreign possessions. But no such contingencies threaten the empire of Christ. However vast, or however far it spreads, the eye of Omniscience watches over it, and the arm of Omnipotence secures its safety. It is emphatically and absolutely " an everlasting kingdom." All things else with which man has to do are destined to decay. Amidst the ruins of earthly kingdoms, amidst the dissolution of the terrestrial system, amidst the wild crash of worlds it shall remain unshaken and unharmed; "the Lord thy God, the Lord thy lawgiver, the Lord thy judge, He will save thee!" How glorious the prospect thus expanded before us! What a gush of exhilarating and triumphant emotion is it calculated to excite in every renewed and holy mind! With what feelings of unutterable delight must it have been associated in the mind of the Redeemer, who could view it in all its vastness, and appreciate it in all its glory! and with what earnestness must He have entertained the desire that the fire by whose sacred flame all this was to be effected were already kindled! Oh, my hearers, let us see to it that the fire burns in our own bosoms, and that there it is carrying forward its salutary work. God forbid that we who are seeking the spread of the gospel throughout the world, should either be destitute of its power, or but slightly influenced by its spirit. The times in which we live, demand that we should be men of earnestness, energy, and perseverance. These, sirs, are not times for the mere idleness of religious profession, for the mere refinements and enjoyments of Christian association. (*W. L. Alexander, D.D.*)　　*The fire of contention :*—Upon a close examination of the text, and a comparison with the following verses, there can be no doubt whatever, that the sending fire upon earth, indicates nothing less than what it at the first glance appears to import, namely, the production of great and violent contention and animosity. When the religion of a crucified Saviour was originally made known to the world, greatly varied, even within a single family circle, was the reception which it met with. Some, when they had heard the word, received it with joy, and cried out, with the Ethiopian, "See, here is water; what doth hinder me to be baptized?" While others, only observing of the preacher of Jesus and the Resurrection, "He seemeth to be a setter forth of strange gods," persisted in their ancient course, and loved darkness rather than light, because their deeds were evil. Placed in such circumstances, it was almost impossible for the Christian members of a household, with whatever circumspection and caution they might walk, to avoid giving offence. Though they kept silence, and refrained even from good words, their conduct was a tacit reproach to their connections. When they refused to offer the drink-offerings of those dumb idols, or to make mention of their name with their lips, they sufficiently declared their opinion of those that did it, as of men labouring under gross delusion. Now we may observe how sensitive to the slightest apparent contempt of their opinions the spiritually ignorant and superstitious are. Again, the Christians could not, on any terms, partake of the pleasures which their unconverted friends chiefly esteemed; many of them were unclean, and many of them were cruel, teeming with all abomination and pollution. They were compelled, therefore, to stand aloof in their festivities, and as children of light, to have no communion with the works of darkness. This must, according to all experience and observation of the characteristics of weak and vicious men, have contributed in no small degree to engender a spirit of bitterness. The slave of vice cannot bear the eye that looks mournfully on his evil indulgences. Finally, Christianity incapacitated the professor from attaining to many worldly honours and emoluments, and hence another struggle while a parent's ill-judging affection endeavoured to impose upon a child conformity to existing iniquities, that his prospects in this life might not be blighted, and the other as resolutely persisted in the determination to witness a good confession before men, lest his prospects in eternity should suffer a much more fatal blight. How soon such contentions might call into action the most malignant passions of the heart, may be judged from examples nearer to our own times, in which a rational resistance to unreasonable, though originally kind desires, has stirred up the most inveterate hostility. But in all this we only see the natural consequences of a pure and undefiled religion coming in contact with the evil passions of man's unconverted heart. There was nothing hostile to the peace of the world in Christianity itself, and it became the innocent cause of much disquietude and tumult, merely because man would not suffer man to enjoy liberty of conscience. (*W. H. Marriott, M.A.*)　　*The gospel as a fire :*—How often we have found the air on a summer's day hot, oppressive, and stagnant. Not a breath of wind stirs the leaves which hang parched or weltering in the burning rays of the sun. The very birds are silent, as though unable to breathe. Suddenly the thunder peals, and the great rain-drops patter upon the ground. Then the storm bursts forth in all its fury. Flash succeeds flash with startling rapidity, the thunder rocks the very buildings in which we are sheltered, and the rain descends in a fierce deluge. At length the storm ceases, and then what a change has passed over the scene! Before, there

was a peace; but it was the peace of inanimation and death; now there is a
peace, but it is the peace of blessed life. The air is cool and fresh, the trees
assume their verdant hues, the flowers give forth their sweetest fragrance, the birds
make the groves echo again with their glad melody; in a word, all nature is
peaceful with a deep exuberant vitality. And so with the gospel; it arouses men
from their deadly lethargy, producing sorrow, distress, and anguish; but after this
there comes a peace, even "the peace of God, which passeth all understanding."
(*O. Spenceley.*)   *Fire purifies:*—I remember, some years ago, when I was at
Shields, I went into a glass-house; and, standing very attentive, I saw several
masses of burning glass of various forms. The workman took a piece of glass and
put it into one furnace, then he put it into a second, and then into a third. I said
to him, "Why do you put it through so many fires?" He answered, "Oh, sir, the
first was not hot enough, nor the second; therefore we put it into a third, and
that will make it transparent." (*G. Whitefield.*)   *An agressive gospel:*—Fire is
the life and the light of the world, and, as a symbol, deserves to be studied. Its
power has never been ascertained. Every effort made to subdue it is attended with
the consciousness of its unconquerable nature. It melts iron, burns marble, changes
granite into dust, feeds on wood, evaporates water; and yet, when properly used
and ministered unto, it is the health and life of the world. Such is the gospel.
Receive it into the soul, and it changes the miser into the benefactor, the slothful
into the diligent, and the lukewarm into the fiery apostle who, like Jeremiah, finds
a fire in his bones which will consume if it finds not vent. 1. The purpose is
avowed—"I am come to send fire." Not to bring, but "send." 2. This fire is
sent. It is here, and is yet to be more manifest. 3. The outlook is one of
endeavour. Christ is organizing for victory. 4. The urgent need of the Church
to receive this fire. 5. Instead of being alarmed when the gospel produces excitement, we are to look for it. 6. Christ longs to have the fire kindled. 7. Behind
every fervent prayer is the unreached desire of Christ. 8. The plan is fixed, the
fire is to be kindled in the individual heart. (*J. D. Fulton, D.D.*)   *The question
of Christian missions stated and explained:*—I. THE MISSION OF CHRIST WAS UNDER-
TAKEN FOR THE MOST IMPORTANT ENDS. 1. To present an atonement to the Divine
government for the sin of man. 2. To overthrow the rebellious power which had
usurped the dominion of this world. 3. The redemption of innumerable multitudes
of our race from the consequences of their apostasy. 4. The formal assumption
and complete discharge of His mediatorial characters. II. THESE ENDS COULD
ALONE BE PROSECUTED AT A MOST PAINFUL EXPENSE. 1. We cannot conceal the fact
that Christianity may affect political systems. 2. It is further admitted that
Christianity must produce a variety of innovations. 3. Very unnatural divisions
in society have apparently been fomented by Christianity. 4. Christianity must be
viewed in connection with those persecutions which it has experienced. 5.
Christianity has drawn forth some acts, on the part of its adversaries, which have
more effectually exposed the depravity of human nature than any other occasion
could have admitted. 6. The religion of Jesus Christ has very frequently been perverted to designs most estranged from its character, and abhorrent to its spirit. 7.
The augmentation of moral responsibility has necessarily attended the establishment of Christianity. III. THE IMPORTANCE OF THESE ENDS JUSTIFIED THE VAST
EXPENSE NECESSARY TO THEIR ACQUISITION. 1. Here, then, we find an apology for
our warmest zeal and firmest courage, in extending Christianity. We but imbibe
the spirit and follow the steps of our Exemplar. 2. And here, too, we learn that
this unconquerable temper, this inexpressible ardour, is of the first importance in
every department of missions. Nothing half-hearted should be betrayed in our
institutions at home, or efforts abroad. 3. In this spirit of unshrinking courage,
and unabating ardour, let us proceed. We carry the commission of Him who
"came to send fire on the earth." We may blow the flame, we may spread the
conflagration; what will he, if it be already kindled? All must yield to the gospel
of Christ or be consumed by its progress. (*R. W. Hamilton, D.D.*)   *Fire—the
want of the times:*—I. CONSIDER THE HISTORY OF THE GOSPEL. 1. It begins with a
revelation, contained in the Bible. Bending over the page, we are struck with the
extraordinary doctrines herein revealed. As we believe the doctrine of Divine love,
we feel it to be a truth which sets the soul on fire with joy, gratitude, and love. 2.
I have commenced the history of the gospel with the book; but, remember, the
gospel does not long remain a mere writing; it is no sooner thoroughly read and
grasped than the reader becomes, according to his ability, a preacher. We will
suppose when a preacher whom God has truly called to the work proclaims this

gospel, you will see for a second time that it is a thing of fire. Observe the man! If God hath sent him, he is little regardful of the graces of oratory; he counts it sheer folly that the servants of God should be the apes of Demosthenes and Cicero; he learns in another school how to deliver his Master's message. He comes forward in all sincerity, not in the wisdom of words, but with great plainness of speech, and tells to the sons of men the great message from the skies. The one thing of all others he abhors, is to deliver that message with bated breath, with measured cadence, and sentences that chill and freeze as they fall from ice-bound lips. I would not utter too sweeping a sentence, but I will venture to say that no man who preaches the gospel without zeal is sent of God to preach at all. 3. In tracing this history of the gospel, I would have you observe the effect of the preaching of such a one as I have described. While he is delivering the truth of a crucified Saviour, and bidding men repent of sin and believe in Christ, while he is pleading and exhorting with the Holy Ghost sent down from heaven, do you see the fire flakes descend in showers from on high! One of them has dropped just yonder and fallen into a heart that had been cold and hard before; observe how it melts all that was hard and iron-like, and the tears begin to flow from channels long dried up. 4. Opposition is aroused next. There is no good doing if the devil does not howl. II. Secondly, LET US STUDY MORE CAREFULLY THE QUALITIES OF THE GOSPEL AS FIRE. 1. First, fire and the gospel are notable for ethereal purity. 2. The gospel is like fire, again, because of its cheering and comforting influence. He that hath received it finds that the cold of this world no longer pinches him; he may be poor, but the gospel's fire takes away the chilliness of poverty; he may be sick, but the gospel gives his soul to rejoice even in the body's decay; he may be slandered and neglected, but the gospel honours him in the sight of God. The gospel, where it is fully received into the heart, becomes a Divine source of matchless consolation. Fire, in addition to its warmth, gives light. The flaming beacon guides the mariner or warns him of the rock: the gospel becomes to us our guide through all the darkness of this mortal life; and if we cannot look into the future, nor know what shall happen to us on the morrow, yet by the light of the gospel we can see our way in the present path of duty, ay, and see our end in future immortality and blessedness. Life and immortality are brought to light by the gospel of Jesus Christ. 3. A third likeness between the gospel and fire is its testing qualities. No test like fire. That piece of jewelry may seem to be gold; the colour is an exact imitation; you could scarcely tell but what it was the genuine metal. Ay, but the melting pot will prove all; put it into the crucible, and you will soon see. Thus in this world there are a thousand things that glitter, things which draw admirers, that are advocated in the name of philanthropy and philosophy, and I know not what beside; but it is wonderful how different the schemes of politicians and the devices of wise men appear when they are once put into the fining pot of the gospel of Jesus Christ. 4. A further parallel between the gospel and the fire lies in their essential aggressiveness. 5. Our religion is like fire, again, because of its tremendous energy and its rapid advance. Who shall be able to estimate the force of fire? Our forefathers standing on this side the river, as they gazed many years ago upon the old city of London wrapped in flame, must have wondered with great astonishment as they saw cottage and palace, church and hall, monument and cathedral, all succumbing to the tongue of flame. It must be a wonderful sight, if one could safely see it, to behold a prairie rolling along its great sheets of flame, or to gaze upon Vesuvius when it is spouting away at its utmost force. When you deal with fire, you cannot calculate; you are among the imponderables and the immeasurables. I wish we thought of that when we are speaking of religion. You cannot calculate concerning its spread. How many years would it take to convert the world? asks somebody. Sir, it need not take ten minutes, if God so willed it; because as fire, beyond all reckoning, will sometimes, when circumstances are congenial, suddenly break out and spread, so will truth. Truth is not a mechanism—and does not depend upon engineering. God may, when He wills it, bring all human minds into such a condition that one single text such as this, "This is a faithful saying, and worthy of all acceptation, that Christ Jesus came into the world to save sinners," may set all hearts on a blaze. Vainly do we reckon the missionary costs so much, and only so many can therefore be sent. Ay, but God works most by weakest means full often, and sometimes achieves by his poorest saints works which He will not perform by those who have every visible appliance. 6. Once more, the gospel resembles fire in this, that it will ultimately prevail. III. Lastly, if the gospel be thus like fire, LET US CATCH THE FLAME.

1. If this fire shall really burn within us, we shall become from this very moment fearless of all opposition. That retired friend will lose the strings which bind his tongue; he will feel that he must speak as God shall bid him; or if he cannot speak, he will act with all his might in some other way to spread abroad the savour of Immanuel's name. That coward who hid his head, and would not own his profession, when the fire burns, will feel that he had rather court opposition than avoid it. 2. If we catch this flame we shall, after having defied all opposition, weary utterly of the mere proprieties of religion which at this present time crush down like a nightmare the mass of the religious world. 3. If we shall catch this fire, we shall not only become dissatisfied with mere proprieties, but we shall all of us become instant in prayer. Day and night our soul will go up with cries and moanings to God, " O God, how long, how long, how long? Wilt Thou not avenge Thine own elect? Will not Thy gospel prevail? Why are Thy chariots so long in coming? Why doth not Christ reign? Why is not the truth triumphant? Why dost Thou suffer idolatry to rule and priestcraft to reign? Make haste, O God, grasp Thy two-edged sword and smite, and let error die and let truth win the victory!" It is thus we shall be always pleading if this fire burns in our spirits. 4. This will lead us to eager service. Having this fire in us, we shall be trying to do all we can for Christ. (*C. H. Spurgeon.*)　　*The fire Christ kindles:*—I. Here we have one of those statements of Christ which have been and still is made use of by superficial, ill-disposed unbelievers, IN ORDER TO BRING HIM AND HIS RELIGION INTO DISCREDIT. If all His many statements, declarations, and utterances, which inculcate love and good-will to mankind, leave them cold and indifferent; those which speak of the destructive tendency of His religion inflame them with hatred and malice towards Him, and the object of His life and work. As soon as they hear that Christ Himself said, " I am come to send fire on the earth," and again, " Think not that I am come to send peace on earth, I am come not to send peace, but the sword," their anger is uncontrollable. With an air of righteous indignation, they exclaim, " All this Christ's followers have faithfully carried out to the detriment of mankind." To justify their assertion, they refer us to the persecution and blood-shed instigated and perpetrated by those who bore His name, and strenuously maintain that all was done in His name and by His authority. These implacable enemies of Christ and His religion do not shrink from making Christ Himself responsible for all the cruel and barbarous deeds wrought at one time or other by professing Christians. They have indeed the testimony of history on their side, where all such cruelties and inhumanities have been recorded and transmitted to posterity. But we have a right to demand of those who sit in judgment over others, not to be so unjust as to make Christ and His religion responsible for them. We shall, no doubt, at once be told to read our text, for in it Christ expressly says that He came to send fire on the earth; and we shall be asked to read further on, where He says that He did not come to send peace on earth, but the sword. Of course Christ speaks of fire and the sword, but by no means in the sense His enemies or mistaken friends would have it. In the ordinary life fire need not be a destructive element, nor the sword a weapon with which to kill others; for fire has also many very useful qualities, it imparts heat and light, and the sword is wielded to defend and uphold justice. That Christ employs these figuratively, and as such representing forcibly great and important spiritual truths, there is not a shadow of doubt. The fire He means is no other than His holy love, kindling within man a sacred flame of devotion for everything good, true, and just; and the sword He speaks of is no other than the Spirit of God, who wields the mighty word of God. II. CHRISTIANITY IS FIRST OF ALL A DESTRUCTIVE POWER BEFORE IT CAN BE THAT WHICH IT IS IN REALITY AND TRUTH, viz., A DIVINE POWER TO RENEW AND SANCTIFY MAN. It would not have been a Divine power for the spiritual good of man had it not such a twofold tendency and effect; for as man has become despoiled by sin, God's holy love manifested in Christ has first of all to destroy this pernicious element in him before it can effectually accomplish its Divine mission for him. The fire Christ kindles in the heart of fallen, sinful man is meant to consume all ungodliness and unholiness, all the idols that may be enshrined there; and if our own will and consent allow this work to be effected, the sacred fire of love, of devotion to God and our fellow-men, will be kindled in the purified and sanctified temple of our heart. If Christ's love is, however, obstinately resisted, the unholy fire will remain burning within man, never to be extinguished. Christ's fire, however, destroys, in order to rebuild within us a glorious temple crowned with the inscription, " Holiness unto the Lord." III. If Christianity were only a destructive power, we could have

gladly dispensed with it, for there are enough of such powers and agents at work in nature and society, in the individual and among nations. THE PRIME OBJECT OF CHRISTIANITY IS, FORTUNATELY FOR THE HUMAN RACE, NOT TO DESTROY MAN'S LIFE, BUT TO SAVE IT ; not to separate man from man, but to unite all men closely and intimately by one bond of love as brothers of one common Father in heaven. Christianity, as a new life-giving power, only destroys that which hinders man's growth in holiness, godliness, and righteousness, thus retarding his spiritual development and progress heavenwards. The holy fire burning on the altar of a believing Christian's heart not only consumes all impurity in him, but kindles a sacred flame of love and devotion in him towards God and the true well-being of his fellow-man. (*A. Fürst, D.D.*) *Missionary enthusiasm :*—This fire which our Lord came to send was a Divine enthusiasm inspired by His Spirit for the glory of God, for the highest good of man—an enthusiasm enwrapping like flame the faculties of soul and body, transfiguring weak and commonplace natures by the purifying and invigorating energy of a supernatural force. " I can do all things," said St. Paul, "through Christ that strengtheneth me." This enthusiasm has, undoubtedly, many other outlets, many other effects. The missionary spirit is one of its chief, its noblest manifestations—the spirit which burns to carry the name and kingdom of Christ wherever there are souls to be saved and blest. What, then, let us ask, are the elements which go to make up the missionary spirit ? Or, rather, what are the convictions by which the sacred flame is kept alive within the soul? There are, I apprehend, three main elements, three ruling and inspiring convictions, at the root of missionary enthusiasm. 1. Of these, the first is a deep sense of the certainty and importance of the truths of the gospel. The apostles were the first missionaries, and we see in their writings how deeply they felt both the importance and the certainty of their message. St. Paul speaks of "preaching among the Gentiles the unsearchable riches of Christ." St. Paul prays that the Ephesians may have the eyes of their understanding so enlightened as to "know what is the hope of their glory, and what the riches of their calling and their inheritance among the saints." St. Paul's language has sometimes been spoken of as hyperbolical and inflated, but only so because the great living facts which were so present to the apostle's soul are hidden from the soul of the speaker. If, my brethren, it be indeed true that the everlasting Son of God left the glory which He had with the Father before the world was, and took our poor nature upon Him, and had a human mother, and lived on this earth for thirty-three years, and then died in pain and shame to rise from death, to rise from the grave in which He was laid, to return, still robed in the nature in which He had died and risen, to the glories of His heavenly home—if this be a fact, it is trivial to speak of it as " an important fact." It distances in point of importance everything else that has occurred in human history. What in the world are all the triumphs, all the failures, all the humiliations, all the recoveries, of which human history speaks, in comparison with this ? What heart have we to dwell on them when we have really stood face to face in spirit with the incarnation and the passion of the Son of God? This is what men like Xavier or Martin have felt ; and this sense of the overwhelming importance of the facts of redemption has not, in the cases of these eminent missionaries, been weakened by any suspicion whatever, created by a sceptical atmosphere of thought around them, about the truth of the facts. The apostles had had no doubts about the facts. "I know whom I have believed," cries St. Paul. "We have not followed cunningly devised fables," protests St. Peter. " We were eye-witnesses of His majesty." " That which we have seen and heard," says St. John, " declare we unto you, for the life was manifested, and we have seen it, and declare unto you that eternal life which was with the Father and was manifested unto us." In the mind of the apostles the truths of the Christian revelation centred, every one of them, in the living person of Christ—God and man ; and an utter devotion to His person, based on a profound conviction of the reality in detail and as a whole of those truths, was at the root of that spirit of enterprising charity which went forth to convert the world. In the heart of those first missionaries, as so constantly since, the crucified Son of God whispered daily, hourly, that He might keep alive within them the sacred flame :

> " Behold what I have borne for thee !
> What hast thou done for Me ? "

2. And the second conviction which goes to make up missionary enthusiasm is a

sense of the need which man has of revealed truth. The apostles were possessed by this element also of that sacred flame which Christ came to send upon the earth. The apostles did not invest contemporary heathenism with that halo of false beauty which has been more or less fashionable in Christendom ever since the renaissance. They saw in heathendom the kingdom of darkness. Its material civilization, its splendid literature, its vast organizations civil and military, its social and political traditions, were nothing to them or less than nothing. "We know," said St. John —"we know that we are of the truth, and the whole world lieth in wickedness. All that is of the world, the lust of the flesh and the lust of the eyes and the pride of life, is not of the Father, but is of the world, and the world passeth away and the lust thereof." The highest civilization, so termed, was in St. Paul's eyes just as much in need of the gospel as the rudest types of savage life. He had as much to do for the cultivated heathens who listened to him on the Areopagus of Athens as for the wild heathens of the Mediterranean islands, who after their rude fashion showed him no little kindness when he was saved from his shipwreck, for he saw everywhere error and sin—error which obscured the real nature of God and the true destiny and the highest interest of man—and sin which made man God's enemy, the antagonist of God's uncreated nature as the perfect being. The conviction that those who were not in Christ were lost—lost unless they could be brought to Him to be illuminated, to be gifted with a new nature, to be washed, to be sanctified, to be justified before the presence of the All-holy—this was the second element of conviction which urged the apostles onwards through the world to convert it—which urged them on even to martyrdom. 3. And the third conviction that goes to make up the missionary spirit is a belief in the capacity of every man for the highest good—for salvation through Christ. Intellectual dulness, want of imagination, want of what people have taken to calling lately "sweetness and light," want of moral fervour and quickness—these are not barriers. Doubtless some minds, some natures—I would rather say some souls—present more points of contact with the gospel than do others. Some, I admit, present very few indeed ; but no child of Adam is so constituted as to be incapable of receiving the truth which is necessary to his highest good; and the true missionary knows that if he can only get deep enough beneath the surface, beneath the crust of habit formed by sensuality, by indifference, by prejudice, he will at length find a home for truth —he will at length find that which will respond to it in the secret spring of the soul. Nelson used to tell young midshipmen who were entering the navy that they ought to look forward, every one of them, as a matter of course, to commanding the channel fleet, or at least to commanding a line-of-battle ship. And this faith in general capacity for success is still more necessary in the Christian missionary. He looks upon every child of man as bearing within him capacities for the highest greatness—capacities which have only to be roused and developed by the assured grace of God. Now, this faith in humanity—in what it may be made by grace—is assailed in our days on the ground that character and circumstances are, after all, too imperious to be set aside—that they, as a matter of fact, make us what we are—that it is folly to think of overruling them by any doctrine or secret influence that can be brought to bear. And this is not a new idea. The learned physician Galen, who wrote in the third century of the Christian era, and who as a heathen was strongly prejudiced against the Church of Christ, remarks with reference to the education of children, " The cultivator can never succeed in making the thorn bear grapes, for the nature of the thorn is, from the first, incapable of such improvement." And then he goes on to say that if the vines which are capable of bearing such fruit be neglected they will either produce bad fruit or none at all. Here Galen marks out what, in his opinion, could really be done with human nature—certainly we must remark, within very narrow limits indeed—and what, in his opinion, it is folly to attempt. Tertullian, an eminent Christian writer of the period, in his treatise on the human soul, admits that the bad tree will bring forth no fruit if it be not grafted, and that the good tree will produce bad fruit unless it be cultivated. So much for nature, but then Tertullian proceeds, "And the stones will become the children of Abraham if they be formed to the faith of Abraham, and the generation of vipers will bring forth fruits meet for repentance if they expel the poison of malignity. For such," he says, "is the power of Divine grace which, indeed, is more powerful than nature." The heathen Celsus probably expressed a general opinion among his friends when he said it was literally impossible to improve a man who had grown old in vice before his conversion. Cyprian, who was afterwards Bishop of Carthage and a martyr for Christ, had taken, he tells us, exactly the same view of the impossibility of changing natural habit. How he learnt the power of God's grace he tells us in a most remarkable passage of one of his extant letters. "Receive," he says to his correspondent, "that which must be experienced before it can be understood. When I lay in the darkness, in the depths of the night, when I was tossed hither and thither by the billows of the world, and wandered about with an uncertain and fluctuating course, I deemed it a matter of extreme difficulty that any one could be born again —could lay aside what he was before, while his corporal nature remained what it was. How, said I, can there be so great a transformation as that a man should all at once lay aside what is innate from his very organization, or, through habit, has become a second nature? How should a man learn frugality who has been accustomed to luxuries? How should he who has been clad in gold and purple condescend to simple attire—the man who has been surrounded with public honours take to privacy, or another exchange admiring troops of dependents for voluntary solitude? The allurements of sense, I said to myself, are surely very tenacious. Intemperance, pride, anger, ambition, lust—these must, when once indulged, they must perforce, retain their hold. So I said to myself, for I was, in truth, entangled yet in the errors of my former life, and did not believe that I could be freed from them; and so I complied with the vices that still cleaved to me, and in despair of amendment submitted to my evil inclinations as if they were part of my nature. But when the stain of my former life had been washed out by the laver of regeneration, a pure and serene light was poured into my reconciled heart. When the second birth received from heaven through the Spirit had changed me into a new man, things formerly doubtful were confirmed in a wonderful manner. What had been closed before became open before my eyes; what had been dark was now illuminated; power was given to do what had seemed difficult; the impossible had become possible. I can see now that my former life, being of fleshly origin and spent in sin, was a life of earth. The life which the Holy One has kindled in me is a life from God." This testimony has been re-echoed since by thousands and thousands of Christians and, therefore, the barriers of habit enshrined within venerable traditions which the Christian missionary encounters to-day in China or in India, however serious they may be as practical obstacles, are not really insurmountable. By and by the gospel leaven will surely begin to ferment, and then these vast, ancient, complicated societies will heave and break till they open a way to the influences of the gospel, if not so swiftly, yet as surely, as do the uncultivated New Zealanders and Polynesians. To doubt this is to lose faith, if not in the gospel, at least in humanity—in the capacity of every being for coming to the highest truth, for coming to God in Christ. (*Canon Liddon.*)

Ver. 50. **I have a baptism to be baptized with**—*Intensity in Christian service:*— I. OF THIS INTENSITY CHRIST HIMSELF WAS THE PERFECT EXAMPLE. Fervour reached white heat in the Son of Man, and the service of the kingdom received the whole of it. Do you think these words were spoken calmly? As we listen to the Speaker, we are conscious of the strain, the tension of spirit, the travail of soul! And what was it that moved the Saviour so profoundly, that made His soul "exceeding sorrowful"? His death on the cross, and burial in Joseph's tomb; but not these things regarded by themselves; death and the grave had less terror for Him than for the saintliest of His followers; but He thought of these in their august and solemn relations to His redeeming work. In His cross and passion, love to God and love to man were mysteriously and perfectly blended; His surrender to God was absolute and entire, wanting nothing; while the appeal of His love to man, unsurpassed in tenderness, maintains to-day its unrivalled influence and power. St. Paul used Christ's word—"straitened," in another and most significant connection: "The love of Christ constraineth us." Christ was Himself "constrained," that He might "constrain" His servants by His own great love to the end of time. This revelation of love to God and man in the death of Christ by no means adequately accounts for the agitation of the Saviour's soul. We must go deeper; unless we do so we have no sufficient clue to the mystery of this hour. The beginning of Christ's passion was reached; already He is the Sinbearer. Our text, then, is not the cry of the hireling, bent only on accomplishing his day, longing eagerly for the last hour and the close of his task; it is something infinitely nobler, the cry of the "only-begotten of the Father," shut up, urged, pressed, filled with pain, panting as one oppressed in breathing, till His Father's will is done. Behold the perfect Example! If we wish to gauge this intensity, and know how great it is, let us place it side by side with our own low aims, calculating love, measured efforts, and frequently barren lives. Strangers to devotion, to intense devotion, cannot properly serve under such a King. II. CAN WE, WITH THIS PATTERN BEFORE US, GET ANY HINTS RESPECTING THE SPRING OF SUCH INTENSITY? How is the fire kindled? What is the secret? When Christ spoke, He was in close touch with His Father. The Baptism was appointed; not self-chosen, not accidental, but set down in the Father's will; recognized as being there, and accepted in the teeth of natural shrinking. Surely this is evidence of fellowship without a break, high and habitual; fellowship with God, therefore, is one secret of intense life in souls. A second secret of intense life, then, is familiarity with Holy Scripture. Men of the Bible may be furnaces, icebergs they can never be. And the passage, taken as a whole, indicates clear insight into the sins and sorrows of men, and a true estimate of our needs. The Speaker "knew what was in man"; was in close contact with man; saw our ruin, accepted the risks, and rendered at all costs the needed help. A third secret of intense life is, keep touch with men. We want to kindle the holy fire and keep it burning—then brethren, we must hold much converse with Christ. The planets get light and heat from the sun; we from the Sun of Righteousness. We must look into the face of Christ and gain power for work by habitual, sustained, and abundant communion with Him. III. We are now in a position TO APPRECIATE SOME OF THE SALIENT FEATURES OF THIS INTENSITY IN CHRISTIAN SERVICE. It is not concern about our own safety; by the whole diameter of the globe it is divided from that. How much solicitude we expend on ourselves! Are we God's sons? Are our evidences clear and bright? Definite answers to such inquiries we ought to get. Till we get them this holy passion can find no sufficient room within us. The intense spirit, the Christ-spirit, only possesses souls that can swing out of self. All Christ's anxiety and travail of soul was about others—about God, His Father, the revelation of His mind, the establishment of His rule, and the winning of men to obedience—about man, His brother, his waywardness and misery; the remedy, how it could be provided and how applied. We must be like Him! The noblest in us is impossible while we are occupied with ourselves. The mother at the bed-side of her fever-stricken child forgets self, so does the fireman as through flame and smoke he rushes to the rescue. Then heroism grows sublime, and becomes an inspiration. This intensity is not distinguished by exemption from trial, even the trial of apparent failure. Certain discoursings on earnestness in Christian work are depressing. We see how the purest are often most tried, and the best and most skilful husbandmen have longest to wait for the fruit. "It is enough for the servant to be as his Lord." What equipment was His—wisdom, stature, favour with God and man; and the Holy Spirit without measure. What Divine patience! The crown of enduring influence and ultimate success intensity like our Master's will assuredly wear. When Christ spoke, it appeared as if His was the only soul fired by this passion. Like Pompey's pillar, He was solitary, conspicuously alone! Then the good soil received the precious grain of wheat; it died, and from that moment was no longer alone! Paul's letters are rich in passages which breathe the intense spirit of our text. The case of John, the beloved disciple, is, if possible, more remarkable. He caught fire early; the holy passion was aglow in him. After the Council at Jerusalem he disappeared from view. For fifty years we hear nothing of him; but in the calm, loving utterances of his Epistles, and the penetrating light of his profound Gospel, we have evidence of the strength of a long hidden fire. It glowed till the century ended, when other fires were extinguished. Thus Christ reproduced Himself—the fire-circle enlarged; candidates for this baptism multiplied; and to-day no power is so fresh, so vigorous, and so aggressive as the power of Jesus Christ. Enduring influence and final triumph still lie with intense earnestness. It brings into line every power we possess, and allies each with the power of God. "Why could not we cast him out?" cried the humiliated disciples. "Because you didn't believe you could," was Christ's startling reply. The intense man ever believes he can; faith in God renders all things possible. The man of faith " burns his way when he cannot bore it "; and while the calculating halt in the initial stages of their task and cannot succeed, he stands radiant with the joy of an accomplished work. Everywhere we have machinery; power is the thing wanted. "I gained no theology from Dr. Chalmers," said Robertson, of Irvine, "but I gained enthusiasm." (*J. R. Wood.*) *The Surety's baptism:*—The baptism of the Son of God, here spoken of by Himself, was the baptism of wrath; for He who was made sin for us must be baptized with this baptism. It is the knowledge of this fiery baptism of our Divine Surety that gives to us the reconciliation and the peace which, as sinners, we need. It was of this fiery baptism that He Himself spoke when He said, " Now is My soul troubled." This baptism the Son of God must undergo; and He knew this. It was appointed Him of the Father, and arranged in the eternal covenant. " I *have* a baptism to be baptized with." He knew it; He knew the reason of it; He knew the result of it; and He knew that it could not pass away from Him. He had come to fulfil all righteousness; He had come to be made a curse for us. In this awful utterance of our Substitute, as He looked forward to the cross, we have—I. A LONGING FOR THE BAPTISM. He desired its accomplishment. He knew the results depending on it, and these were so divinely glorious, so eternally blessed, that He could not but long for it—He could not but be straitened till it was accomplished. The cup was inexpressibly bitter, but the recompence for drinking it was so vast, that He could not but long for the hour when it should be put into His hands. II. THE CONSCIOUSNESS OF FEAR AND BITTER ANGUISH IN CONTEMPLATING IT. He was truly man, both in body and soul. His Divine nature did not relieve Him of one grief, or make His sufferings mere shadows. It fitted Him for being filled with more sorrow than any man could be. It conferred on Him an awful, we may say a *Divine*, capacity of endurance, and so made him the subject of sharper pain and profounder grief than otherwise he could have been. III. THE STRAITENING IN REGARD TO ITS ACCOMPLISHMENT. Like Paul, He was in a strait between things which pressed in opposite ways, and which must continue to press till the work was done. 1. He was straitened between the anticipated pain, and the thought of the result of that pain. 2. He was straitened between grace and righteousness. Till the great sacrifice was offered, there might be said to be conflict between these two things. Between His love to the sinner and His love to the Father there was conflict; between His desire to save the former and His zeal to glorify the latter there was something wanting to produce harmony. He knew that this something was at hand, that His baptism of suffering was to be the reconciliation; and He pressed forward to the cross, as one that could not rest till the discordance were removed—as one straitened in spirit till the great reconciliation should be effected. (*H. Bonar, D.D.*) *The sense in which Christ was "straitened"*:—The manner in which our Saviour here expresses Himself, fully evinces that His heart was greatly set upon this important baptism. He was straitened till it was accomplished! The word *sunechomai*, which is here translated " straitened," will admit of the following variations or different readings of our Lord's words: 1. How am I pressed together, and under a ponderous weight of imputed sin, and its dreadful concomitants! The Lord laid on Him, as the Head of the Church, and Surety of the covenant—the iniquities of us all. And He bore our sins in His own body on the tree. To be thus straitened was no way inconsistent with the final accomplishment of the work in which He stood engaged: for His work of suffering is over, and Jesus our Saviour is straitened no more! His being thus straitened in His human views of the work, and in the feelings of human nature, does not suppose Him to be *merely* human, though it certainly proves Him to have been *really* human. Each nature operates in Him, according to its essential properties. The Divine nature knows all things; upholds all things; rules all things; and acts, by its presence, everywhere. The human nature was born, yielded obedience, died, and rose again. But it is the same person, the same Christ, that acts all these things; the one nature being His, no less than the other. 2. How am I straitened, may be read thus—How am I held fast in the grasp of almighty justice, and bound fast with cords (Psa. cxviii. 27) of legal authority, and bonds of covenant engagements! Infinite love to His people, and to the honour of Deity as demanded by the person of the Father, bound Him fast in bonds, which secured eternal salvation. Justice held fast the bondsman, till all demands were fully paid. But when His baptism was accomplished, His person was free, and His people redeemed. Immanuel is straitened no more; He is held under judgment no more; when He became innocent (as the mediator of His people) or free from all sin, and had wrought all righteousness, justice could demand no more. He was delivered for our offences, and rose again for our justification. That baptism which so straitened our Lord, my brethren, hath made us for ever free indeed! O Thou immortal Deliverer of sin-bound captives, accept and maintain in Thy free people, perpetual hallelujahs to Thy redeeming name! 3. Again, How am I straitened, may be understood—how am I afflicted and distressed in mind. My soul is exceedingly sorrowful, said our agonizing Lord. O what love is here ! He took our sorrows, He bore our stripes, He endured the curse for us ; and thus He made our peace for ever. 4. Once more. How am I urged and constrained. For this sense of the word, see 2 Cor. v. 14. Jesus was first bound with His people in union indissoluble. He could not but feel the strongest desire for their redemption, whose persons and welfare lay so near His heart. He was urged by the desire of having the work accomplished. Justice called upon Him for her right ; and the joy set before Him excited Him to His important baptism, out of which He knew He should surely emerge, and ascend to the enjoyment of the glory which He had with the Father before the world was. His baptism is now accomplished, and He is straitened no more ! Who, then, shall bind the members, since the Head is free ? (*J. Stevens.*) *Christ's baptism of suffering* :—The phraseology is by no means unusual which represents afflictions and trials as a baptism with which an individual must be baptized. In addressing the sons of Zebedee, Christ had asked, " Can ye drink of the baptism that I drink of, and can ye be baptized with the baptism that I am baptized with ? " In the Old Testament, moreover, the Psalmist speaks of "entering into deep water," which is manifestly the same imagery as that employed in the New. There is a peculiar beauty in this form of expression, when the party to whom it is applied is a righteous and God-fearing man. Baptism is the being dipped in the water, the being sprinkled with the water, and not the being drowned or completely over-whelmed. The form of expression denotes that, however tremendous the affliction may be, it shall not be finally destructive ; nay, that it shall issue in addition to what has already been attained. For the word " baptism," in its very essence, has reference to some essential change, so that the man when baptized is presumed to enter on a state from which he had been previously excluded. It will be needful that you carry with you this general view of baptism, as rightly introductory to, and symbolical of, an alteration in circumstances or state, if you would enter fully into our Lord's meaning when He speaks in our text—" But I have a baptism to be baptized with ; and how am I straitened till it be accomplished ! " The whole structure of the sentence is in exact keeping with the common notion of baptism, seeing that a condition of greater freedom is evidently looked forward to by Christ, as certain to result from those waves of fire through which He had to pass. He laboured under a species of bondage prior to His agony and death ; and the con-sequence of the agony and death would, He knew, be deliverance from this bondage. There is, therefore, peculiar fitness in His describing that agony and death as a baptism with which He should be baptized. A change was to take place ; and for the bringing about of that change, immersion in a deep ocean of trouble was actually indispensable. I. CONSIDER CHRIST'S AGONY AS A BAPTISM. Now, it was a stupendously great work which our blessed Lord undertook in His mission to earth. He had assumed human nature in union with the Divine, and thus stood in the attitude of the representative of mankind. He was no solitary and isolated being acting out for Himself the duties which, as a creature, He owed to the Creator ; He was the Surety of the whole of our race ; and in the very minutest cir-cumstance of His life we have a close and important concern. He took our transgressions just as well as those of all others living on the earth, and cast them into the waves, and then they rolled on an immensity of wrath, and the innocent Surety bowed down, and trembled, and sank beneath the impetuous torrent. Not, however, that this is the only reason why our Lord's agony and passion may be characterized as a baptism. We have spoken to you of baptism as introductory to some alteration in state or condition. The word only applies to cases in which some change is presumed, as the result of immersion, to have taken place either literally or symbolically. But, with respect to the sufferings of Christ, they agree in every point with the declaration which limits the applicability of the phrase. The baptism of our Lord was such, that length of time was not needful in order to give effect to endurance. Each instant of our Surety's anguish, seeing that He was God as well as man, was equivalent to such countless ages of human punishment, that it was enough for justice that he should be immersed in the water, and then quickly emerge. This fallen creation, tottering under the curse, was then plunged into an abyss of wrath, and sparkled as a renovated thing so soon as He arose above its surface. The agony in Gethsemane was only for a brief season ; the ignominy of the crucifixion was soon brought to a close ; the imprisonment of the grave quickly gave way ; and then He who " bore our sins in His own body on the tree," was literally baptized with the baptism of bitterness. The woe, infinite in extent, was but finite in duration—" Thou wilt not leave My soul in hell ; neither wilt Thou suffer thine Holy One to see corruption." He must descend into darkness, that the waves and the storms might go over Him. Anguish—He must endure it; contumely—He must submit to it; the hidings of His Father's face—even this, the bitterest and most grievous of all, must be encountered. But then this enduring, this wrestling, they were but for a brief season. He did not tarry in the waters, though it was needful He should be covered by them. And thus the emerging and immersion follow so closely one on the other, that you cannot better describe the great work than by saying of our Lord, that He had "a baptism to be baptized with." II. CONSIDER IN WHAT RESPECTS IT WAS THAT THE SAVIOUR WAS STRAITENED TILL THIS BAPTISM WAS ACCOMPLISHED. The work of redemption was not complete, and Christ therefore was "straitened," as unable to exhibit a finished deliverance. The Spirit was not yet poured out on His followers; and therefore was He "straitened," inasmuch as He could not preach the deep mysteries of His gospel. Conflict with Satan was not concluded, and therefore was he "straitened" in His human nature, being still exposed to all his attacks. And, lastly, He had not yet won the headship over all things, and therefore was He "straitened" by being circumscribed in Himself, in place of expanding into myriads. These, with like reasons, serve to explain, in a degree, the expression of our text; though we frankly confess that so awful and inscrutable is everything connected with the anguish of the Mediator, that we can only be said to catch glimmerings of a fulness which would overwhelm us, as we may suppose, with amazement and dread. III. LET US COMMEND TO YOU, IN CONCLUSION, THE NOBLE DESIRE OF ST. PAUL. "That I may know Christ, and the power of His resurrection, and the fellowship of His sufferings, being made conformable unto His death." There is to be wonderful analogy between the firstborn and His people, and we call on you to examine whether you find it realized in your own experience. Unto each of us there remains the baptism of death; a baptism in the truest and most literal sense; for we do but pass through the Jordan, and not stay in the waters. But are we "straitened?" Do we feel ourselves "straitened" till this baptism is accomplished? Let us have no evasion and no subterfuge. We are predestined to be conformed to the image of God; and as He was "straitened," so, if we belong to Him, shall we also be "straitened." Who can be a real Christian and not feel "straitened?" It is our very profession that we are but strangers and pilgrims below; that our home is above. There is "a law in our members warring against the law of our mind—the good that we would we do not—the evil that we would not we do"—"we bear about with us a body of sin and death"—"we see only through a glass darkly"—"it doth not yet appear what we shall be." Are we not then "straitened?" I would give my soul to heavenly music, to communings with the glorious beings of the invisible world; but the flesh clogs the spirit, weighs it, and presses it down, and thus am I "straitened." I would love God with all my heart, with all my soul, and with all my strength; abstracting myself from things that perish in the using, and centring myself on the joys that are laid up for the faithful; but my affections are seized on by the creature; the visible prevails over the invisible, and thus I am "straitened." I would mount even now on the wings of faith, realizing the promise that "they who wait on the Lord shall renew their strength; they shall mount with wings as eagles." I would walk to and fro through the inheritance of the saints, but the things of time hang lead on the pinion, and thus I am "straitened." I would have my thoughts by day and my dreams by night coloured by the pencil of Christian hope; but indwelling corruption throws a stain on the picture, and thus I am "straitened." (*H. Melvill, B.D.*) *The Lamb of God hastening to the altar:*—Christ's eagerness for the consummation of His sacrificial mission sublimely pathetic and heroic. I. The cross loomed up in His thought with increasing vividness and more absorbing interest toward the last. II. Eager for the suspense to be changed to certainty. For the Father's glory to be magnified. For the ending of the curse, and the beginning of the blessing. III. Eager to make the supreme proof of His love to sinners, and to see the result. "I, if I be lifted up," &c. IV. Eager to return by the gateway of the cross to the Father's bosom. (*Homiletic Review.*) *Christ's longing for the completion of His work:*—The great truth which the text exhibits, is the entire and intense devotedness of Christ to the completion of His mediatorial suffering, with a view to its subsequent and sublime results. I. We have to show, first, THAT THE SAVIOUR UNIFORMLY EXHIBITED THE DEEP CONCERN WHICH THE TEXT EXPRESSES FOR THE COMPLETION OF HIS MEDIATORIAL WORK ON EARTH. 1. To say that He had not been beguiled or surprised into the work of our redemption would be saying but little. He had undertaken it intelligently, and with the distinct foresight of all the liabilities which it involved. He had looked into the darkest recesses of depravity in the human heart, and had sounded the lowest depths of human misery, before He came to expiate the one or relieve the other. 2. To say that He had not been forced into the great undertaking, would be saying but little. 3. To say that the ardour evinced in the text for the completion of His work was not of new or sudden growth, would be saying but little. A large and interesting class of Scriptures exist to prove that there never was a moment in which, even prior to His incarnation, He did not anticipate its completion with similar intensity of desire. 4. To say that He did not neglect the work which was given Him to do, would be saying but little. "My meat," said He, "is to do the will of Him that sent Me, and to finish His work"—in other words, His devotedness was entire. "For their sakes," said He, "I sanctify Myself"—and He did so. 5. And not only was His devotedness entire, including the consecration of all His powers, it was eager and intense, not allowing the unnecessary delay of a moment, nor admitting of the slightest increase. To say that four thousand years were allowed to elapse prior to His advent, is no objection whatever to this statement. It only reminds us that His devotedness, ardent as it was, was yet regulated by wisdom—that His zeal was not the zeal of improvident precipitation—that He did not sacrifice one interest to another. II. But why this eager and intense desire to reach the goal of His humiliation? Surely He was not in love with suffering! Let us proceed, secondly, to specify some of the reasons which account for it, and we shall find that it was not only explicable and justifiable, but infinitely necessary—well for a guilty world that His zeal was not a particle less. 1. For what? He had undertaken to minister to the relief of a world groaning in its misery—and all that misery was before Him. He did not—by necessity of nature He could not—content Himself, as we do, with vague impressions of human woe. He saw it with a distinctness and felt it with a power which made it all His own. He felt that its every sigh and its every struggle was, in effect, a distinct appeal that He would hasten the work of deliverance, and He was straitened until the work was accomplished. 2. But there was more than misery to be remedied—there was guilt, the cause of it all—and that He had undertaken to atone for. He knew the history of sin. 3. But more still. There was more than the misery of man to be remedied—more than the rights of justice to be satisfied; there was the character of God to be embodied and made manifest as the God of love—and He had undertaken that. And hence the anxiety of Christ to perform the act which should prove it. For to wipe off every stain from the character of God, and to present it in its real glory, infinitely outweighed with Him every other consideration. 4. And this reminds us of another reason to account for His eagerness to reach the cross—the glory which should accrue to God in the salvation of mankind. III. But we have to show, thirdly, that though the great crisis is passed, the concern of Christ for the salvation of man is undiminished. True, as far as that concern involved suffering it has ceased. 1. Would you admit that a person discovered urgency for an object if he lost not a moment in arranging for its attainment? No sooner had the Saviour emerged from the tomb than He summoned His disciples, and began to prepare them for their missions to the ends of the earth. 2. Does a person discover intense concern for an object, if he consecrates all his power to its attainment? The Saviour did this. As soon as He could say in His mediatorial capacity, "All power is mine," He added, "Go preach the gospel to every creature." 3. Does a person discover intense concern for an object if he not only consecrates all his own power to it, but if the first use which he makes of that power be to secure and employ the agency of others? In the loftiest sense, the Saviour did this. The first agency which He engaged after He ascended the mediatorial throne was that of the Holy Spirit—the great agent of the universe. 4. Does a person discover intense concern for an object, if he commands and lays under tribute the instrumentality of every one belonging to him for its attainment? 5. But speak we of the fact that Christ has thus laid all the members of His Church under solemn obligation, as a proof of His unabated solicitude for human salvation; from the concluding Book of Scripture, the Book of the Revelation, there is reason to believe that He has engaged the agency of every angel in heaven for the same object. 6. "But why this continued solicitude on the part of Christ?" it may be asked. Has not His great sacrifice been not only offered, but accepted? and is He not now exalted in consequence to the right hand of God?" Yes; but His concern relates now to the proclamation of His atoning sacrifice throughout the world, and to the salvation of those who rely on it. Having provided the means of salvation, He is now for pressing on to the end. IV. Brethren, WHAT SHOULD BE THE PRACTICAL APPLICATION OF THIS SUBJECT? If the devotedness of Christ to the salvation of man was such that He not only agonized on the cross, but even agonized for it, and if His Divine solicitude be still undiminished—then, surely, the Christian cannot render less than entire devotedness to the same object. Accordingly, the Saviour claims every Christian here for Himself. Your character is to be a reproduction of the character of Christ. The disinterestedness which appeared in Christ is to reappear in you. The tenderness of Christ—His untold solicitude for human souls—is to live over again in your tones of entreaty, your wrestling prayers for their salvation. The blood of the cross itself is, in a sense, to stream forth again in your tears of anguish, your voluntary and vicarious self-sacrifice to draw men to Christ. 2. But if we thus sympathize with Christ, we shall see the importance of everything calculated to promote the object of His solicitude. Viewed in connection with these objects, nothing we do is insignificant—an act apparently trivial, a word, a look, acquires a character of infinite moment. 3. But this reminds us, next, that if we truly sympathize with Christ, we shall not be satisfied with merely providing the means of usefulness, or with putting them into action—we shall be deeply anxious to see the end of all such means accomplished. The Saviour was not only straitened till He had reached the cross—till He had provided salvation; all the solicitude which He then felt for the means, He now feels for the end. 4. But this subject reminds us, brethren, finally, that if we truly sympathize with Christ, we shall be conscious of deep humiliation at our past apathy, and of holy impatience and concern to see the designs of His death realized in the salvation of our fellow-men. And ask we for motives to this? Is it nothing that Christ expects it? Is it nothing that He has turned His whole self into a sacrifice, compared with which nothing else deserves the name? and that He has devolved it on us to multiply as far as we can the copies of His character in our own? Is it nothing, again, that others have felt this? Yes; the duty is not only obligatory but practicable, for others have felt it. And should it not urge our languid movements into zealous activity when we reflect that "the time is short"? 5. And achieved it shall be. How should the prospect quicken our activity and inflame our desire! To think that the scene of the Saviour's humiliation shall be the scene of His ultimate triumph. (*J. Harris, D.D.*) *The shadow of the coming cross :*—Those who maintain that the crucifixion was an afterthought in the mind of Christ: that no vision of it clouded His pathway, and no place was assigned for it when He began first to preach and to teach, have read those narratives to very little purpose. Holman Hunt, the modern "evangelist of art," was much nearer the truth on this matter when he painted his celebrated picture, "The Shadow of Death," in which he clearly reveals his opinion that, whilst yet a horny-handed workman in the obscure carpenter's shop at Nazareth, making yokes and ploughs for the husbandmen of Galilee, the shadow of the coming cross fell upon the pathway of Christ, and gave an unwonted solemnity to a young manhood, in all else so natural. (*J. Cuttell.*)

Vers. 51–53. **Suppose ye that I am come to give peace on earth ?**—*Strife engendered by the gospel :*—We try to soften this terrible prophecy by our comments. As if we could explain facts which are notorious to every reader of history, to every one who has had experience of what is passing in his own time! As if we could convince any reasonable persons that there have not been, that there are not, these strifes in families ; that the gospel of Christ has not provoked them, and does not provoke them still! Or as if our Lord, supposing He is the Prince of Peace, as we say He is, wanted our help to vindicate Him from the charge of being the Author of war! Surely we may trust Him with His own character. All that is required of us is, that we should let His words come to us in the fulness of their power and their condemnation. Goodness and gentleness do stir up what is opposed to them in us ; we know that they do. Our sectarian animosities are kindled by the message of God's goodwill to men ; we know that they are. Can we not understand then, how, coming among a set of hostile factions, which abhorred one another, but observed a conventional decency in their strife, Christ stirred up their rage to its very depths ? Cannot we understand how the fury of both burned for awhile against Him—a hollow truce being established between them by the presence of a common enemy ? Did it not revenge itself for that restraint afterwards ?

Did not every hearth and household become a battle-field in that war? This was the state of Jerusalem, as its own historian describes it in the latter days. He can give us the narrative calmly, Jew though He was. When Jesus looked forward to it, He was straitened with agony. He felt in every fibre of His own being what was coming upon His land. There may have been moments when the evil spirit thrust the thought full upon Him : " Would it not be better to shrink from Thy task ? If this is the effect of the peace which Thou proclaimest, why not let them welter on without any announcement of God's kingdom ? " Such suggestions have been continually made to His followers, when they have spoken of peace, and when those to whom they have spoken have made them ready for the battle. If He was tempted in all points like them, He cannot have been free from this kind of anguish. Nor will He have overcome the tempter with any other weapons than those with which He has furnished them. He must have said, for Himself and for them, " My work is with the Lord, and My judgment with My God. In His own time My Father will accomplish His purpose. The hollow alliances of sects will end in more fierce and frantic war. But through that war will come the discovery of the peace which passeth understanding, the peace which lasts in the midst of the world's tribulations ; that peace will be established through the whole creation." (*F. D. Maurice, M.A.*)   *Religious divisions* :—I. Let us inquire, then, into THE SCRIPTURE DOC-TRINE WITH REGARD TO THE EFFECTS OR CONSEQUENCES OF THE MISSION OF CHRIST. Christ's mission into our world has two sets of effects. There are its effects upon the Christian believer, and its effects upon human society. 1. There are its effects upon the true believer of the gospel. These are manifold and great. (1) Let us take, in the first place, the effect upon the believer in respect of his relation to God. That effect is peace. Our text was never meant to deny it. " We have peace with God through our Lord Jesus Christ." But such as are in Him have "peace from God the Father." He gives them that peace. "Peace," He has said, " I leave with you ; My peace I give unto you : not as the world giveth, give I unto you. Let not your heart be troubled, neither let it be afraid." (2) Consider, in the second place, the effect upon the believer as regards his own dispositions and feelings. Here also it is peace. " The fruit of the Spirit is peace." " The kingdom of God is righteousness, and peace, and joy in the Holy Ghost." Christ came to take the bitterness and enmity out of our hearts, and to reconcile us to God. (3) In the third place, attend to the effect upon the believer with reference to his fellow-believers. Again the effect is peace. He is united to them in love. (4) Notice, lastly, the effect upon the believer with reference to them that are without. True it is that Christ came to draw a people for Himself out of the world. " Come out from among them, and be ye separate," is indeed His call to every sinner to whom the gospel is preached. Let us go on to consider its effects upon human society. 2. The effects, or consequences upon human society may be divided into ultimate and immediate. (1) Those that are ultimate. They are of the happiest kind. The description in the passage from which our text is taken does not suit them at all. Scripture pourtrays them in most attractive terms. " The mountains," we are told, " shall bring peace to the people, and the little hills, by righteousness." " He shall come down like rain upon the mown grass ; as showers that water the earth. In His days shall the righteous flourish, and abundance of peace, so long as the moon endureth " (Psa. xxxii. 3, 6–7, 10–11, 17 ; Isa. ii. 4, xi. 6–10). The prediction of the angels shall be verified, and on earth there shall be peace. (2) The immediate consequences. When we look into these, far different scenes present themselves. But we must distinguish. (*a*) An immediate consequence of the mission of Jesus is the very opposite of division. Wicked confederacies are occasioned by it. " The kings of the earth set themselves, and the rulers take counsel together, against the Lord, and against His Anointed, saying, Let us break their bands asunder, and cast away their cords from us." Pharisees and Sadducees cry together, "Away with Him ; crucify Him." Herod and Pontius Pilate join hands over His grave. (*b*) But, secondly, and to come at last to the doctrine of the text, division and strife among men are also immediate results of the mission of our Lord. II. Having thus arrived at the subject which the text brings before us, and having ascertained what place, among the effects of Christ's mission, belongs to that particular effect of it which we have now to consider, we go on to advert to SOME SCRIPTURE EXAMPLES OF THE FEUDS AND BROILS WHICH JESUS FORETOLD. The schisms and dissentions which our Lord sends on the earth may be classified. 1. In families. An example is furnished in the family circle of Jesus Himself. His brethren, we are told, did not believe in Him (John vii. 1–10). His own kinsmen took umbrage at His doctrine and claims. An instance of alienation in its earliest stage occurs in the case of the man who was born blind (John ix.). 2. Christ makes strife among friends and companions. An instance occurred in the case of Himself and His disciples (John vi. 60-66). Then, again, what a breach did Christ make between Saul of Tarsus and the allies at Damascus, to whom the former had letters from the authorities in Jerusalem. We are told that they took counsel to kill Him, watching the gates day and night (Acts ix. 19-24). 3. Christ makes strife in the general community. There are many examples of this. Paul's preaching at Antioch in Pisidia (Acts xiii. 42-50; xviii. 12-17; xix. 23-34). 4. Christ sends division into the visible Church. Take the following practical illustrations of the fact. (1) There is the controversy which arose at the time of the feast of tabernacles, as recorded (John vii. 40-53). (2) We have the history of the labours of Paul and Barnabas at Iconium (Acts xiv. 1-7). (3) Next, let us attend the great apostle to Corinth, and consider his eventful sojourn there. The record is in Acts xviii. 1, 4-8, "After these things Paul departed from Athens, and came to Corinth." "And he reasoned in the synagogue every Sabbath, and persuaded the Jews and the Greeks. And when Silas and Timotheus were come from Macedonia, Paul was pressed in the spirit, and testified to the Jews that Jesus was Christ. And when they opposed themselves, and blasphemed, he shook his raiment, and said unto them, Your blood be upon your own heads; I am clean: from henceforth I will go unto the Gentiles. And he departed thence, and entered into a certain man's house, named Justus, one that worshipped God, whose house joined hard to the synagogue. And Crispus, the chief ruler of the synagogue, believed on the Lord with all his house; and many of the Corinthians hearing believed, and were baptized." What was it that fell out at Corinth on this occasion? There was a disruption of the Church. Paul, as his manner ever was, began by addressing himself to those to whom belonged "the adoption, and the glory, and the covenants, and the giving of the law, and the service of God, and the promises." A disruption ensued, as we have said. (4) Let us attend the Apostle of the Gentiles once more, and consider what befel during his ministry at Ephesus :—"And it came to pass, that while Apollos was at Corinth, Paul having passed through the upper coasts, came to Ephesus." "And he went into the synagogue, and spake boldly for the space of three months, disputing and persuading the things concerning the kingdom of God. But when divers were hardened, and believed not, but spake evil of that way before the multitude, he departed from them, and separated the disciples, disputing daily in the school of one Tyrannus. And this continued by the space of two years; so that all they which dwelt in Asia heard the word of the Lord Jesus, both Jews and Greeks (Acts xix. 1, 8-12, 18-20). III. Thus have we examined the successive schisms and feuds that sacred history shows to have arisen from the mission of our Lord. It is now time that we shortly advert to THE PROPER CAUSES TO WHICH THESE ARE TO BE TRACED. We have just said that Paul was not blameworthy in regard to the divisions with which he had to do. Although, however, Paul did not do wrong, it by no means follows that wrong was not done. Strife and separation, especially in the worship and service of God, are not good, and blame must lie somewhere on account of them. Where, then, ought the blame to be laid? We shall specify some causes which reason and Scripture point to, as lying at the foundation of all religious strife, and you will then be better able to judge in the distribution of the blame. 1. There is the existence of sin. "From whence come wars and fightings among you? Come they not hence, even of your lusts that war in your members?" The first, the greatest, and the worst division of all, was produced by sin. It was sin that set God and man at variance. Next came division between man and his fellow, and this was the native effect of sin. The fatal schism between Cain and his brother, had sin at the root of it. Sin must create discord. There never will be peace in the world or in the Church, until it is cast out. 2. There is Satan's rule in the world. Satan, my brethren, has his dark kingdom amongst us. And is he the friend of peace? Delighting in strife for its own sake, he delights in it also as an instrument of gratifying his malice against Christ, and of injuring the kingdom of Christ. We say, then, that the rule of the crafty god of this world is a cause, and a prime one, of the divisions that take place. 3. There is the enmity of the wicked. Is it not true that the Church of God everywhere is hated by the world? This hatred is not unfruitful. It has raised persecutions of every form; and its emissaries have gone forth, alas! too seldom in vain, to create envyings, strifes, heresies, schisms in the Church! IV. It remains to say somewhat on THE RELATION BETWEEN THE DIVISIONS WHICH ARE **FOUND TO BE IMMEDIATE CONSEQUENCES OF CHRIST'S MISSION ON EARTH, AND THOSE**

ULTIMATE RESULTS WHICH HAVE BEEN PROMISED. We have already adverted to the nature of the latter, and given specimens of the glowing language of Scripture concerning them. To the former they bear no resemblance—they are not only different—they are contrary. But God, who makes all things helpful to His designs, and the very mischiefs that flow from sin, the world, and the devil, and are meant to thwart Him, conducive to the execution of His plans, has established an important relation between the two. 1. Present divisions will enhance the enjoyment of the final unity and peace. The sweetness of pleasure is increased by the recollection of pain that preceded it. The memory of disease heightens the relish of health. 2. Divisions now prepare the way for the peace and unity that are to come. Divisions testify of the existence of evils of which they are the natural fruits. By their means the attention of the Church is turned to these evils and fixed down upon them. And believers will err much if they seek to heal divisions in any other way. Let them beware of patching up a premature peace. The outward form of unity is a mockery, and the maintenance of it a hypocrisy and a sin, when unity of heart and principle does not exist. It is only a pernicious semblance of peace that can be reached, so long as the roots of discord and schism are not pulled up. (*A. Gray.*) *Variance caused by the gospel :*—Among a low caste people at Ellenpur near Gondah in Northern India, there has been a great struggle to draw the converts back into heathenism. The following case, as described by Mr. B. H. Badeley, an American missionary, we give as an illustration. In the jungle lived a man and his wife who had several children, and a young girl eighteen years of age. This uneducated village girl was very brave in her endurance of persecution for Christ's sake. She had learned to love the Saviour by attending the services at the house of the native preacher and noticing the conduct of his wife. Several months before her baptism she told her relatives that it was her purpose to become a Christian ; but they would not hear of it, and threatened to kill her if she dared to take such a step. She continued, however, to attend the preaching, and the Lord Jesus drew her towards Himself. One Sunday after the service, her relatives came in a body to take her away. Her infuriated mother fell upon her, and made several attempts to harm her, but was prevented. The native teacher told the people that if the girl wished to go with them they could take her, but if she chose to stay among the Christian families she was at liberty to do so. They then used every effort to make her willing to go, promising her fine clothes, jewels, presents, and rich food, but in vain. They besought her not to disgrace them by becoming a Christian, but she only answered that she had become a Christian in heart and could not change. At last, on their promising not to do her any harm, the native preacher, fearing a disturbance, let her go. Then they carried her to another village some miles away, shut her up, threatened to kill her, endeavoured to change her purpose by incantations ; but all in vain : she remained firm. At last they decided to give her up, and brought her to the native preacher, saying : "Here, take her ; we can do nothing with her." Shortly after this we had the pleasure of baptizing her.

Vers. 54–57. **How is it that ye do not discern this time ?**—*Signs of the times :*—
I. CONSIDER THE RELIGIOUS ASPECT OF OUR OWN AGE. 1. The times are sadly darkened with superstition. 2. A parching wind of unbelief is sweeping over the Churches. 3. Religious apathy abounds. The remedies for this are—(1) Prayer. (2) Personal activity. 4. There is an evident withdrawal of the Holy Ghost from this land. The earth has her harvest, but where is the harvest of the Church. Where are revivals now ? The Spirit is grieved, and is gone from the Church ; and why is it ? Have Christian men become worldly ? It is true that you can scarcely tell a Christian from a worldling, nowadays ? O for more holiness, then ; this is the demand which the times make upon us. Ye men of God, be holy, yea, be ye perfect even as your Father which is in heaven is perfect. Has unbelief restrained the dew and rain of the Spirit ? Is it true that He cannot do many mighty works among us because of our unbelief ? O for more faith, then. Put up the prayer, "Lord, increase our faith," and rest not day nor night till the prayer be heard. II. Now, I have to use the text in reference to THE TIMES WITHIN US. There is a little world within our bosom, which has its winds and its clouds, and if we are wise we shall watch. First, I shall speak to believers. Believers, there are times with you when the "cloud rises out of the west, and straightway ye say, There cometh a shower." Times of refreshing—you have had them ; look back upon them, they are choice memories. You must have the Spirit of God, or how can

you live? Much more, how can you bring forth fruit unto perfection? Watch for these showers, then, and when they come, use them. Open your heart, as the earth opens her furrows after a long drought, when there are great gaping cracks in the soil ready to drink in the shower. Let your heart be receptive of the Divine influence. Wait upon the Lord, and when the Lord comes to bless you, be like Gideon's fleece, ready to imbibe and retain the dew, till you are full of it. Believers, we have to speak to you also about spiritual drought, for you have such seasons. "Ye see the south wind blow, and ye say, There will be heat; and it cometh to pass." You have your droughty times—at least, I have mine. They may be sent in chastisement. We do not value the blessing of the Spirit enough, and so it is withdrawn. Sometimes they may be intended to try our faith, to see whether we can strike our roots deep down into rivers of waters which never dry, and tap the eternal springs which lie beneath, and yield not to the summer's drought. Perhaps our times of drought are sent to drive us to our God, for when the means of grace fail us, and even the Word no longer comforts us, we may fly to the Lord Himself, and drink at the well-head. Perhaps, however, this drought has been occasioned by ourselves. Worldliness is a south wind, which soon brings a parching condition upon the spirits of men. My last and most solemn work is now to come. I have to speak to sinners. Ungodly men are fools before God, but they are very often the reverse of fools in common life. They know what weather there will be, they can read the signals of the skies. Now I ask them to use the wit they have, and of themselves judge that which is right. If you lived in Palestine, when you saw a cloud you would expect a shower. When you see sin, do you not expect punishment? (*C. H. Spurgeon.*)　　*Sign of a coming shower:*—Miss Rogers, in her "Domestic Life in Palestine," says:—At Haifa, I was sitting one day in the oriel window at the British consulate, with the Rev. Dr. Bowen (the late lamented bishop of Sierra Leone); black clouds came travelling quickly from the west over the lead-coloured sea. Dr. Bowen observed, in the words of Christ, "When ye see a cloud rise out of the west, straightway ye say, There cometh a shower; and so it is." He had scarcely uttered the words, when the clouds spread, and fell in a tremendous torrent; the sea swelled, and rolled heavily to the shore; the ships looked as if they would break away from their anchors, and loud peals of thunder made the casemented recess in which we sat tremble violently.　　**Why even of yourselves judge ye not what is right?**—*Christ appealing to the man within the man:*—To judge what is right, in the matter here under notice, is to form a right conclusion as to the question of questions, "What think ye of Christ?" And, you observe, our Lord speaks of a possibility of drawing the true answer, not from "evidences" commonly so called, not from "signs of the times," not from miracles, not from proofs of power exhibited to the senses, but from within—from something inside the man, saying to him, God is here. A distinction is made in the text between a discernment of truth by "signs," and a judgment upon it exercised from within. It is quite clear that the words "of yourselves" express something more intimate, more essential to the man, than that action of the mind upon external evidences for the want of which He has just reproved them. The "signs" are clear, He says, but you ought not to want them. There is that in you which ought to have "judged what is right," as to Me and My gospel, without waiting for other evidence of wonder or sign. Brethren, there is something in us to which Jesus Christ appeals, besides the mere intellect. It is quite clear that Jesus Christ, when He was upon earth, placed not one part but the whole of the man in the judgment-seat before which He pleaded. If He had been satisfied with a formal assent to His revelation; if His object had been to reckon His followers by millions, and to cover the inhabited world with churches, without further question as to the state of hearts towards God, or as to the character of lives in the view of eternity; He might have said, "How is it that, with evidence so conclusive, ye do not discern this time?" but He would never have gone on to say, "Yea, and why even of yourselves judge ye not what is right?" This addresses that compound thing, that complex being, of which intellect is but one element, and not the noblest. Jesus Christ stands upon earth, and, seeing us as we are, as such speaks to us. When He has gained our first attention, if so it be, by miracles, He goes on to reason with us concerning ourselves. He reminds us that there is that in us which makes us first rebels against duty, and then cowards before conscience; rovers in pursuit of satisfactions which come not, and slaves in the prospect of inevitable death. He deals with us as persons not all intellect; persons whose life is lived in many homes and many regions, of thought and feeling, of memory and hope, of companionship and affection, making it indispensable that one who comes to us with an effectual treatment of our actual condition should not only convince our understandings as to his claims and his credentials, but also (and much more) draw our hearts towards himself as the very rest and home and satisfaction of our being. And as this is His aim, so this is His method. He stands here in the midst of us, and His first words are, " When ye pray, say, Our Father." Say it, whosoever you be, and whatsoever. It is a revelation, pure and simple—He brings it to us out of the great heaven—and yet He is able to appeal to us, His audience, as to the self-evidencing character of this which He says. " Even of yourselves," He says, judge what I say. Is it not good? is it not true? is it not verified within? And so of the rest. " Come unto Me, all ye that labour and are heavy laden, and I will give you rest." Does not He who thus speaks bring His own witness with Him? Well must He know us. " Never man spake like this man." Try whether this word, which is so good, so pure, so lovely, has not, in the very being so, its evidence of Deity in the speaker. Is there not here the very knowledge of the Omniscient? Is there not here that very Fountain of goodness, whose thoughts are at once ours and not ours? Is not this what I mean by God? Shall I not rest and nestle at once under the shadow of this wing? (*Dean Vaughan.*)   *The meanness and falseness of the common excuses for irreligion and immorality :*—These words appear, by the parallel places in the other evangelists, to have been originally designed against those amongst the Jews, who from dislike of the strictness of our blessed Lord's morality, pretended ignorance of His Divine mission, after He had given abundant proofs of it; when yet, without any separate proofs of it at all, the main things which He taught carried their own evidence along with them, and every man's heart bore witness to their truth. " The Pharisees came forth, with the Sadducees also, tempting Him, and sought of Him a sign from heaven" (Matt. xvi. 1; Mark viii. 11). But He, with no less dignity than prudence, refused to gratify a curiosity, both ill-meaning and endless; and " sighing deeply in His spirit," as St. Mark informs us, at this perverse disposition of theirs; told them, with a kind, because needful, severity of speech, where the defect lay. " A wicked and adulterous generation seeketh after a sign " : your sinful inclinations and lives, not the want or the desire of sufficient evidence, prompt you to this demand: and " verily I say unto you, there shall be no sign given," no such visible manifestation of Divine glory as you insolently require, vouchsafed " to this generation:" nor is it requisite. " When ye see a cloud rise out of the west, straightway ye say, there cometh a shower, and so it is. And when ye see the south wind blow, ye say there will be heat, and it cometh to pass. Ye hypocrites, ye can discern the face of the sky and of the earth: but how is it that ye do not discern this time?" That is: on other occasions you appear very able to judge of things by the proper indications of them. How can you then, with any colour of sincerity, pretend, that amidst so many prophecies fulfilled, and so many miracles performed, you have not, after all, sufficient conviction, that this is the season when the Messiah should appear, and that I am He? Nay, as to the principal part of My doctrine, which is the real cause of your antipathy to the whole; as to the great precepts of pure religion and uniform virtue, and your need of repentance and faith in God's mercy; what occasion is there for any farther demonstrations of them, than your own hearts, if honestly consulted, will not fail to afford? " Yea, and why even of yourselves judge ye not what is right?" Now this method of reasoning is equally applicable to unbelievers and cavillers in all ages. It is in vain for them to invent new difficulties, or magnify old ones, concerning the authority of our religion; while the reason of things, the truth of facts, and the nature of God and man continue to exhibit so full proof of those fundamental articles of it, the eternal obligation of moral duties, the sinfulness of every one's nature and life, the necessity of repentance, and humble application for pardon and grace. And, since the true quarrel of such persons is against these doctrines, and these cannot be shaken; they had much better reconcile themselves to the whole, than make fruitless attacks upon one part; in which, if they were to succeed (as they never will), they would, in point of argument, be almost as far from their favourite scheme, of liberty to do what they please, and think highly of themselves notwith- standing, as they were before. For the whole of their case is: they perplex things on purpose, in order to complain that they are not clear: walk with their eyes wilfully shut, and then insist that they cannot be blamed if they stumble, for it is quite dark, and they do not see a step of their way. For the confirmation of this, let us take a view of the fundamental parts of practical religion—those which men are most apt to fail in—and see which of them all any one can fairly say he was ignorant of, or doubtful about, and had not the means of sufficient light to direct his steps. 1. To begin with the belief and worship of Almighty God. Is not every man capable of seeing, let him be ever so little acquainted with nature, that the heavens and the earth, the order of the seasons, the returns of day and night, the whole frame of things in general, is full of use and beauty; and must be the work of amazing power, wisdom, and goodness? And what He hath made, no doubt but He governs and superintends. This is the plain obvious account of things, that one should think must almost offer itself of course to every common mind, without any learning at all; and the deepest learning gives it the strongest confirmation. And what, then, hath any one to plead for himself, if he lives regardless of Him "in whom he lives, and moves, and hath his being"; without gratitude to His bounty. 2. Let us now proceed to the duties which we owe to our fellow-creatures. The sense of these, because they are of more immediate importance to the good of society, God hath imprinted with greater strength on our minds than even that of our obligations to Himself. As it must be the will of Him, who is so just and good to us all, that we should be just and good to one another, and from this principle, as the root, every branch of right behaviour springs; so He hath planted in our hearts a natural love of equity, a natural feeling of kind affection; a natural conscience, applauding us when we act according to these dispositions, condemning us when we violate them; and seldom do we deserve its reproaches, but either at the time, or soon after, we undergo them. 3. The third part of our duty is the government of ourselves, according to the rules of sobriety, temperance, and chastity. Now who doth not know, that the observance of these virtues is right and fit: that the violation of them is prejudical to the reason, the health, the reputation, the fortunes, the families of men, and introduces riot and madness, confusion and misery into the world? 4. But further yet: Doth not every man know in his conscience, that, plain as his duties to God, his fellow-creatures, and himself are, he hath more or less transgressed them all; that he hath a nature continually prone to transgression; that, therefore, he needs both pardon for what is past, and assistance for the time to come; and that he can have neither but through God's undeserved mercy? Upon the whole, since most of the main branches of our duty are thus obvious to our understandings of themselves; and all of them are constantly taught us, by the holy scripture, by the laws of our country, by the opinion and consent of the wisest and best of mankind, by the instructions of persons appointed for that purpose; what account do we imagine we shall possibly be able to give, why religion, so easily apprehended, is so little practised by us! If any doubt of the reality of the command; the reason is, that they desire to doubt: and how can we flatter ourselves that anything is excusable, which proceeds from a disposition of mind so grossly and wilfully wrong? Suppose a servant of ours had purposely kept out of the way of receiving our orders, or invented perplexities and cavils about the meaning of them, or the certainty of our having delivered them, because he had no mind to obey them: would that justify him? Should we not immediately tell him, that what he easily might and clearly ought to have known and understood, he was inexcusable, if he would not know and understand? And what must we think of our great Master in heaven, if we try to impose on Him with devices and tricks, that will not pass amongst ourselves? But in reality men have not this excuse, if it were one. They do know how they ought to behave; they do know that they ought ",to live soberly, righteously, and godly in this world, looking for" the recompences of another; and they well know in the main what particulars this obligation comprehends; how grievously they have fallen short of them, and what need they have to repent and humbly beg forgiveness and strength, through Him who hath procured us a title to both. We can easily deceive ourselves; we can make specious pleas one to another for our failings; which the occasion that we have for allowances in our turn incline us often to look upon very favourably in our neighbours. But, in the sight of God, supposing a thing incumbent on us, and supposing it easily known to be so; what can be said to the purpose why we did not perform it? "We were poor and ignorant." But we were not, or we needed not to have been, ignorant in this particular. "We were suspicious and doubtful." But our doubts were affected, not real; or partial, not honest and upright. Still there are some, especially in some circumstances, who are to a much greater degree excusable for the sins they are guilty of than others. But yet all excuse is not a justification; and will least of all prove such to those who, instead of endeavouring to act right, set themselves to contrive reasons why their acting wrong should be dispensed with. It is true, the very best have their faults, and faults not indulged shall be forgiven us; if we are truly sorry for them, and earnestly apply to God's mercy through Christ for pardon, and carefully watch against the return of them. (*T. Secker.*)

Vers. 58, 59. **When thou goest with thine adversary.**—*Agreeing with the adversary* :—This solemn exhortation of our Lord's may be viewed in different points of light, as intended to subserve various purposes, both in civil and religious life. 1. It may refer to the case of debtor and creditor .If in a way of trade, or for the support of ourselves and families, we owe anything to any man, the debt ought to be honourably paid, or at least compounded to the satisfaction of the creditor, lest, if he proceed to extremities, we suffer by our delays, and fall victims to our own stubbornness and obstinacy. The apostle's command is, that we should owe no man anything, but love one another, and render to all their dues. 2. The text may refer to persons offended and injured, and those especially on whom the offence or injury may justly be charged. 3. If not originally intended, the text may at least be applied to the case of a sinner, who is exposed to the displeasure of an offended and justly incensed God. I. Observe WHAT IS IMPLIED IN OUR AGREEING WITH OUR OFFENDED MAKER, CONSIDERED UNDER THE IDEA OF AN ADVERSARY. 1. In order to our coming to an agreement with our holy and righteous Adversary, we must be thoroughly sensible of our alienation from God, of the enmity of our hearts against Him, and be led to view with deep distress the breach and the separation which sin has made. Mourning and humiliation are the forerunners of joy and exaltation, and a lively hope arises out of holy despair. 2. Being thus awakened and convinced, the eye of faith must be directed to the Saviour, who is the great peace-maker betwixt God and us. Jesus is both the wisdom of God, and the power of God, the man of His right hand, whom He hath made strong for Himself. Hence the language of God to the sinner is, " Let him take hold of My strength, that he may make peace with Me; and he shall make peace with Me" (Isa. xxvii. 5). 3. The eye of faith being fixed upon the Saviour, as the only medium of reconciliation, we must next implore forgiveness and acceptance in the sight of God. II. CONSIDER THE TIME AND MANNER IN WHICH WE ARE REQUIRED TO AGREE WITH OUR ALMIGHTY AND RIGHTEOUS ADVERSARY. 1. It must be done " quickly," without delay, and " whilst thou art in the way with Him." The utmost solicitude is required in a matter of such high importance. 2. Reconciliation with God must be sought immediately; because the present opportunity is the most favourable. Now thou art " in the way with Him," in the way of obtaining mercy, and of finding favour in His sight. Now that He affords us means of grace, and especially when He gives us a disposition to improve them, it becomes us to hearken to the first calls of His Word, and fall in with the first motions of His Spirit. III. Briefly notice THE MOTIVES BY WHICH THE EXHORTATION IS ENFORCED. 1. If this agreement be not speedily effected ; He that was an adversary will remain an adversary still ; and of all enemies God is the most powerful, and the most dreadful. In His favour is life, and His loving-kindness is better than life; His displeasure therefore is worse than death, even in its most hideous and terrific forms. 2. This awful Adversary will deliver over the incorrigible to the " Judge," to whom all judgment is committed, and whose office it is to pass the final and irrevocable sentence. Before Him shall be gathered all nations, and we must all appear before the judgment-seat of Christ, to receive according to the deeds done in the body, whether they be good or whether they be evil. Our God shall come, and shall not keep silence : a fire shall devour before Him, and it shall be very tempestuous round about Him. 3. The Judge having passed sentence on the offender, will deliver him to the " officer " whose business it is to carry the sentence into full effect. In the last great day the angels will be employed in gathering together the elect from the four winds of heaven, in gathering the wheat into the garner, and binding up the tares in bundles to burn them with unquenchable fire. 4. The officer will " cast into prison," where the evil angels are already reserved in chains of darkness unto the judgment of the great day, and where the disembodied spirits of wicked men are still waiting their final doom (Jude 6 ; 1 Pet. iii. 19). (*B. Beddome, M.A.*) *The controversy between man and God* :—Here is a high controversy between man and God. This is not one of those disputes in which plaintiff and defendant are working one against the other with all those subtleties and chicaneries which, in the hands of ingenious advocates, can place the best rights in peril. The court is one in which every one of us is quite sure of justice, and nevertheless in which every one of us is quite sure of condemnation. Come, and let us weigh well the excellence of the counsel which would urge us to an immediate endeavour to the settlement of our quarrel, and that, too, on the principle that if our adversary once bring us before the judge there will be no alternative to our being "cast into prison," and our remaining there till we have "paid the last mite." Now, when you have once given a spiritual character to the passage before us—when, that is, you have abstracted your thoughts from litigation in a mere human court, and settled that our Lord was speaking of a controversy between man and God—it will become evident that our text announces the chief truths both of the law and of the gospel; of the law which brings us in as guilty, of the gospel which proposes to us a method of deliverance from our adversary whilst we are yet "in the way." The position of every one of us—whether he be duly alive to it or not—is that position which gives him God for his adversary. But, still further, he is actually on the way with this adversary—on the road with him, to bring the cause before the magistrate. For this of which we affirm that it could hardly take place, except the party were all awake to his condition of having some cause about to come on at a human tribunal, holds good of every living man who (whether he heed it or not) is daily drawing nearer to the judgment-seat of Christ. So that there is the most thorough accuracy in the description of our text, when applied without exception to every child of man. It is not in this life that he will be brought to that trial by which his state for eternity shall be unalterably fixed; but he is on his way to the trial. Let him walk what path he will out of the many which present themselves to the steps of wandering man, it is a path which inevitably conducts him direct to the court and to the bar. He may swerve from all that is right; he may change the precise line, and be continually deviating to the one side or the other; but he is always advancing to the dreaded tribunal, where on His throne of light sits the anointed Judge of humankind; for there is no escape from this universal enactment—"It is appointed unto men once to die, but after this the judgment." Neither in all these wanderings—wanderings which must lead to the same termination—is there any escaping, even for a solitary moment, from the adversary whom our sins have called up. Go what winding or intricate way you may towards the court in which you have been cited to appear, as though it were your own shadow inseparable from you whilst there is nothing to interrupt the fierce blaze of the sun, the adversary is with you that you may not suddenly make your way to the bar, and there find no accuser. Oh, awful condition of every one of us! And we cannot forbear from dwelling for a moment on one peculiar word in the text, the peculiarity of which may have escaped your attention; that is, the word "hale." "Lest he hale thee to the judge." The word implies the being dragged violently, by main force. Up to this word the description is almost that of two parties, who though they have a dispute are walking quietly together, as if they had agreed to refer it to the judge, and to abstain in the meanwhile from any altercation. There is no evidence of anything like struggle between the two; the accuser is using no violence with the accused. But at this word there passes a total change over the picture; as though on the very threshold of the judgment-hall, just when the two were about to enter, the accused drew affrightedly back—made desperate resistance—but seized as in an iron grasp by his accuser, were thrown down before the judge. May not this indicate what otherwise we have no means of positively asserting—that often at the very last moment of a life of worldliness and indifference; aye, and when, so far as bystanders can judge, the departing man is going off the scene without a fear and without a struggle, there is an awful trepidation and repugnance—the soul being roused into a sense of its tremendous position, shrinking back as though it would find some mode of escape, and passionately pleading if but for an hour's delay. Such an expression would seem to admit us as spectators of the final fearful struggle, exhibit to us, whilst there is externally every appearance of quietness, that shuddering attempt at retreat when retreat is impossible, which must prove beyond all power of description, what a tremendous thing it would be the being found unprepared to die. If anything can make you dread the being unprepared to die, it is that. If anything can scatter the delusion which is often caused by the apparent composedness of the dying, though they have lived careless of religion, it is that. You may not mind the having your adversary always at your side; you may walk as unconcerned as though you were not thus compassed, until—ah! until the foot is on the theshold of the court, and then—O God, look graciously upon us, and spare us the ever knowing the grief, the strife, the more than mortal agony, which make up the one expression "hale thee to the judge." But is there, then, no possibility of escape for the accused, if he once come with his accuser before the judgment-seat? Evidently not. The whole stress of our Lord's representation lies upon this. Without giving any reasons for the fact, it is assumed as incontrovertible. You are exhorted, you observe, to "give diligence as thou art in the way"; it being most distinctly implied that there is no place for diligence afterwards. But how long shall we be "in the way"? I know not where this mysterious threshold is; I know only that it may be everywhere. The man who is standing at my side one instant may have crossed it the next. One finds it in the crowded street; another on the solitary mountain; a third upon the waters. This man reaches it after years and years of painful walking; that whilst his step has lost nothing of its youthful spring. Where is this mysterious threshold; where the precincts of this terrible court? Anywhere— everywhere! Then it is only for this one moment that we can pronounce ourselves "in the way." (*H. Melvill, B.D.*) *Lessons:*—Note here—1. That God and man were once friends. 2. That God and man are now adversaries. 3. That man, and not God, is averse to reconciliation and agreement. 4. That it is the wisdom, the duty, and interest of fallen man, speedily to accept of terms of peace and reconciliation with God. 5. That an eternal prison will be their portion who die in their enmity against God. (*W. Burkitt.*)   *Fatal result of delaying to come to agreement:*—William III. made proclamation when there was a revolution in the north of Scotland, that all who came and took the oath of allegiance by the 31st of December should be pardoned. Mac Ian, a chieftain of a prominent clan, resolved to return with the rest of the rebels, but had some pride in being the very last one that should take the oath. He consequently postponed starting for this purpose until two days before the expiration of the term. A snow-storm impeded his way, and before he got up to take the oath and receive a pardon from the throne, the time was up and past. While the others were set free, Mac Ian was miserably put to death. In like manner, some of you are in prospect of losing for ever the amnesty of the gospel. He started too late and arrived too late. Many of you are going to be for ever too late. Remember the mistake of Mac Ian! (*Dr. Talmage.*)

CHAPTER XIII.

VERS. 1–5. **The Galileans, whose blood Pilate had mingled.**—*Teachings from tragedies:*—We shall miss the very point of Christ's teaching if we suppose that He meant to lessen our sense of the inseparable connection between sin and punishment. What, then, did He mean? He meant this: That every personal visitation, whether by violence or by accident, is not to be regarded as a retribution for a personal sin; that we are too short-sighted to judge, and that we are too sin-stricken ourselves to overlook, in our condemnation of others, our own need of repentance. The main purpose of such startling events is to arouse individuals and society at large to a recognition and to a repentance of their own sins. He appears to me to have opposed on the one hand the levity of those who ignore the connection between natural and moral evil: and, on the other hand, He rebuked the narrowness of those who connected individual sorrows befalling others with individual sins. In all ages and in all lands this hydra-headed fallacy has asserted its power. The ordeal in mediæval times was based on it (the noble having the ordeal of fire and the bondman the ordeal of water), and the "wage of battle" has not yet lost its hold on the nations, and even Christians regard war as a decisive appeal to the Lord of hosts, to show on which side right lies, though history abundantly shows that often might has won and right has lost. This is the principle on which people have constantly based their judgments, and do so still, though in different form. If you clamber the hills at the back of Penmaenmaur you will see the stones which are said by the people to be quoit players, who were petrified by the judgment of God for playing the game on Sunday. You smile at that; but there are multitudes now who, hearing of a disaster on the railway, will call it a judgment if it happens on Sunday, an accident if it happens on Monday. I. THINK OF THE FOLLY OF THIS SHORT-SIGHTED JUDGMENT. 1. It presupposes that this is the world of punishment, whereas Scripture and experience alike testify that it is the world of probation. 2. The folly of these hasty judgments of ours also appears from their constant contradiction by unmistakable facts. It was of the wicked, not of the righteous, that the Psalmist said: "They are not plagued as other men." Indeed, we should lose faith in a righteous God altogether if this world were the only stage on which His purposes are worked out. There is a good story told of John Milton which will illustrate this point, though I do not vouch for its accuracy. It is said that when the great poet was living in Bunhill-fields, forsaken and blind, old and poor, one of the despicable sons of Charles I. paid him a visit, and said : " Do you not see, Mr. Milton, that your blindness is a judgment of God for the part you took against my father, King Charles." "Nay," said the poet of the Commonwealth, "If I have lost my sight through God's judgment, what can you say of your father, who lost his head ? " Well, that is a fair example of the confusions and contradictions which arise from endeavours to interpret, by our short-sighted notions, the far-reaching purposes of God. 3. And what will be the result if men are taught to look for Divine decisions now, before the appointed revelation of the righteous judgment of God ? Why this : that wicked men will be emboldened in wickedness so long as they seem to escape all rebuke and disaster—and they often do. They are profligate, but not punished : prayerless, yet crowned with blessings ; dishonest, yet succeed all the better in their ventures ; cruel and hard, yet make money faster because they are so ; and soon they will call darkness light and light darkness ; and will go on recklessly, amid the sunshine of prosperity, to a hell they do not believe in ! Well might our Lord rebuke the hasty judgments of men on account of their folly. II. But, apart from its folly, THERE IS SIN IN THIS HABIT TOO OFTEN, IF NOT ALWAYS. 1. It leads even religious people to a kind of untruthfulness which the King of truth always and everywhere condemns. They cannot help seeing the contradictions and anomalies I have alluded to, and they naturally shut their eyes to those which do not fit in with their theory. If, for example, helpless people are crushed in a theatre, it is a "judgment," but if in a church, it is an "accident." If an evil happens to themselves, it is a "trial"; but if it comes to another, it is a "warn-ing." But all this is untrue and unreal, and, therefore, it is abhorrent to our Lord. Yes, and it is detected by a sharp-eyed world, which adduces it as a proof of the unreality and unfairness of religious people, and so our testimony for the King of truth is weakened. Jesus meant what He said when He uttered those memorable words : "He that is of the truth heareth My words." 2. Besides, there is often harshness in those judgments of ours on other people. We think and say that they are sinners above all others because they suffer such things. This hard con-demnation of others was one of the chief sins of the Pharisees, and it called forth some of the sternest words our Lord ever uttered. 3. I am not sure but what the thought of other people's sins is comforting and pleasant to us ; presenting a con-trast by which we may throw up into relief our own virtues. And such self-com-placency was a third sin Jesus saw in His hearers. (*A. Rowland, LL.B.*) *A direct application :*—I. OCCURRING INCIDENTS SHOULD TEACH US SPIRITUAL TRUTHS (vers. 1, 4). II. IT IS THE TENDENCY OF THE HUMAN MIND TO JUDGE RASHLY (ver. 2). III. THE SPIRIT OF CHRISTIANITY RESTRAINS THE RASHNESS OF HUMAN JUDGMENT. "I tell you, Nay." IV. WE SHOULD AT ALL TIMES LOOK AT HOME. "Except ye repent, ye shall all likewise perish." (*A. F. Barfield.*) *Judgments and repentance :*—I. We are to speak on the common, but erroneous idea, that THE SINFULNESS OF AN INDIVIDUAL MAY BE CONCLUDED FROM THE JUDGMENTS BY WHICH HE IS OVERTAKEN. We can affirm it to be an axiom received by the men of every generation, that punish-ment and sin are so near relatives, that to perform the one is to incur the other. And the axiom is a true axiom, though in certain instances it may be wrongly applied. It is a truth, a truth to which hereafter the unrolled history of the universe shall bear witness, that human guilt provokes God's wrath ; and that the greater a man's offences the sterner shall be the penalties with which he is visited. And we think it altogether a surprising thing that this truth should have retained its hold on the human mind ; so that in the worst scenes of moral and intellectual degeneracy it hath never been completely cashiered. We think it a mighty testi-mony to the character of God as the hater and avenger of sin that even the savage, removed far away from all the advantages of Revelation, is unable to get rid of the conviction that guilt is the parent to wretchedness, and that, let him but see a fellow-man crushed by an accumulation of disaster, and he will instantly show forth this conviction by pointing to him so branded with flagrant iniquities. But whilst the common mode of arguing thus leads to the establishment of certain truths, it is in itself an erroneous mode. This is the next thing which we go on to observe. The Jews concluded that the Galileans must have been peculiarly sinful, since God had allowed them to be butchered by the Romans. They showed, therefore, that they believed in an awful connection between sinfulness and suffering, and so far they were witnesses to one of the fundamental truths of Revelation. But, nevertheless, we gather unquestionably from Christ's address, that it did not follow that because these Galileans were massacred they were sinners above all the Galileans. Now, if we would attend to the course and order of God's judgments, we should presently see, that although wherever there is suffering there must have been sin, still nothing can be more faulty than the supposition that he who suffers most must have sinned most. There is no proportion whatsoever kept up in God's dealings with His creatures between men's allotments in this life, and their actions. On the contrary, the very same conduct which is allowed to prosper in one case entails a long line of calamities in another. II. Now this brings us to our second topic of discourse. We have shown you the erroneousness of the inference drawn by the Jews; AND WE GO ON TO THE REPROOF WHICH THEY MET WITH FROM THE REDEEMER. We bid you, first of all, observe that Jesus, in no degree, denies the actual sinfulness of the murdered Galileans. He only sets himself against the idea which had been formed of their relative sinfulness. What they had suffered was, undoubtedly, a consequence of sin in the general—for if there were no sin, there could be no suffering. But the calamity which overtook them was no more necessarily the produce of particular sin, than was the blindness of the man concerning whom the disciples asked, "Who did sin, this man or his parents, that he was born blind?" Sinful, then, the Galileans were, and, because sinful, they also suffered. But of their sinfulness we all partake, and, what then is to exempt us from partaking of their suffering? We are taught by our text that if we repent we shall be delivered; if we repent not, we must perish. And I just wish to set before you, with all plainness and simplicity, THE EXACT PLACE WHICH REPENTANCE OCCUPIES IN THE BUSINESS OF OUR RECONCILIATION TO GOD. There has been much mistake abroad on this matter, and both repentance and faith have been wrongly exhibited by a diseased theology. A man is not pardoned because he is sorry for his sins. A man is not saved because he believes upon Christ. If you once say that it is because we do this or that, that we are accepted of God, you make the acceptance a thing of works, and not one of grace. If we say to an individual, Repent and believe and thou shalt be saved, the saying is a true saying, and has the whole of God's Word on its side. But if we say, Repent, and because penitent, thou shalt be forgiven, we represent repentance as the procuring cause of forgiveness, and thus do fatal violence to every line of the gospel. Repentance is a condition, and faith is a condition, but neither the one or the other is anything more than a condition. In itself there is no virtue in repentance—in itself there is no virtue in faith. That repentance must precede pardon is clear from every line of the scheme of salvation; but that repentance must precede coming to Christ is a notion fraught with the total upset of this scheme. We deny not that a legal repentance, as it may be termed, is often beforehand with our turning to the Mediator; but an evangelical repentance is not to be gotten except from it. It is a change of heart—it is a renewal of spirit—it is the being translated from darkness to light, the being turned from dead works to serve the living and true God. And if all this mighty renovation is to pass upon man, ere it can be said of him that he has truly repented, then he must have betaken himself to the Redeemer's fulness in order to obtain the very elements of repentance, and this is distinctly opposed to his possessing those elements as qualifications for his drawing from that fulness. Of all things, let us avoid the throwing up ramparts between the sinner and the Saviour. I am bold to say that, if the gospel be conditional, the only condition is a look. "Look unto Me, and be ye saved." (*H. Melvill, B.D.*) *The judgments of God:*— This story is often used, it seems to me, for a purpose exactly opposite to that for which it is told. It is said that because these Galileans, whom Pilate slew, and these eighteen on whom the tower of Siloam fell, were no worse than the people round them, that therefore similar calamities must not be considered judgments and punishments of God; that it is an offence against Christian charity to say that such sufferers are the objects of God's anger; that it is an offence against good manners to introduce the name of God, or the theory of a Divine Providence, in speaking of historical events. They must be ascribed to certain brute forces of nature; to certain inevitable laws of history; to the passions of men, to chance, to fate, to anything and everything, rather than to the will of God. No man disagrees more utterly than I do with the latter part of this language. For as surely as there is a God, so surely does that God judge the earth ; and every individual, family, institution, and nation on the face thereof ; and judge them all in righteousness by His Son Jesus Christ, whom He hath appointed heir of all things, and given Him all power in heaven and earth ; who reigns, and will reign till He hath put all enemies under His feet. Our Lord does not say—Those Galileans were not sinners at all. Their sins had nothing to do with their death. Those on whom the tower fell were innocent men. He rather implies the very opposite. We know nothing of the circumstances of either calamity ; but this we know—that our Lord warned the rest of the Jews, that unless they repented—that is, changed their mind, and therefore their conduct, they would all perish in the same way. And we know that that warning was fulfilled, within forty years, so hideously and so awfully, that the destruction of Jerusalem remains as one of the most terrible cases of wholesale ruin and horror recorded in history ; and—as I believe—a key to many a calamity before and since. Like the taking of Babylon, the fall of Rome, and the French Revolution, it stands out in lurid splendour, as of the nether pit itself, forcing all who believe to say in fear and trembling—Verily there is a God that judgeth the earth—and a warning to every man, class, institution, and nation on earth, to set their houses in order betimes, and bear fruit meet for repentance, lest the day come when they too shall be weighed in the balance of God's eternal justice, and found wanting. But another lesson we may learn from the text, which I wish to impress earnestly on your minds. These Galileans, it seems, were no worse than the other Galileans ; yet they were singled out as examples, as warnings to the rest. It is as if they were punished, not for being who they were, but for being what they were. History is full of such instances ; instances of which we say and cannot help saying—What have they done above all others, that on them above all others the thunderbolt should fall ? Was Charles the First, for example, the worst, or the best, of the Stuarts ; and Louis the Sixteenth, of the Bourbons ? Look, again, at the fate of Sir Thomas More, Bishop Fisher, and the hapless monks of the Charterhouse. Were they sinners above all who upheld the Romish system in England ? Were they not rather among the righteous men who ought to have saved it, if it could have been saved ? And yet on them—the purest and the holiest of their party—and not on the hypocrites and profligates, fell the thunderbolt. What is the meaning of these things ?—for a meaning there must be ; and we, I dare to believe, must be meant to discover it ; for we are the children of God, into whose hearts, because we are human beings and not mere animals, He has implanted the inextinguishable longing to ascertain final causes—to seek not merely the means of things, but the reason of things ; to ask not merely How ? but Why ? May not the reason be—I speak with all timidity and reverence, as one who shrinks from pretending to thrust himself into the counsels of the Almighty—but may not the reason be that God has wished thereby to condemn not the persons, but the systems ? That He has punished them not for their private, but for their public faults ? Looking at history in this light, we may justify God for many a heavy blow, and fearful judgment, which seems to the unbeliever a wanton cruelty of chance or fate ; while at the same time we may feel deep sympathy with—often deep admiration for—many a noble spirit, who has been defeated, and justly defeated, by those irreversible laws of God's kingdom, of which it is written—"On whomsoever that stone shall fall, it will grind him to powder." We may look with reverence, as well as pity, on many figures in history, such as Sir Thomas More's ; on persons who, placed by no fault of their own in some unnatural and unrighteous position ; involved in some decaying and unworkable system ; conscious more or less of their false position ; conscious, too, of coming danger, have done their best, according to their light, to work like men, before the night came in which no man could work ; to do what of their duty seemed still plain and possible ; and to set right that which would never come right more : forgetting that, alas, the crooked cannot be made straight, and that which is wanting cannot be numbered ; till the flood came and swept them away, standing bravely to the last at a post long since untenable, but still—all honour to them—standing at their post. When we consider such sad figures on the page of history, we may have, I say, all respect for their private virtues. We may accept every excuse for their public mistakes. And yet we may feel a solemn satisfaction at their downfall, when we see it to have been necessary for the progress of mankind, and according to those laws and that will of God and of Christ, by which alone the human race is ruled. And we shall believe, too, that these things were written for our example, that we may see, and fear, and be turned to the Lord. (*C. Kingsley, M.A.*) 　　 *Accidents, not punishments:*—I. First, LET US TAKE HEED THAT WE DO NOT DRAW THE RASH AND HASTY CONCLUSION FROM TERRIBLE ACCIDENTS, THAT THOSE WHO SUFFER BY THEM SUFFER ON ACCOUNT OF THEIR SINS. Now, mark, I would not deny but what there have sometimes been judgments of God upon particular persons for sin; sometimes, and I think but exceedingly rarely, such things have occurred. Some of us have heard in our own experience instances of men who have blasphemed God and defied Him to destroy them, who have suddenly fallen dead; and in such cases, the punishment has so quickly followed the blasphemy that one could not help perceiving the hand of God in it. The man had wantonly asked for the judgment of God, his prayer was heard, and the judgment came. And, beyond a doubt, there are what may be called natural judgments. You see a man ragged, poor, houseless; he has been profligate, he has been a drunkard, he has lost his character, and it is but the just judgment of God upon him that he should be starving, and that he should be an outcast among men. You see in the hospitals loathsome specimens of men and women foully diseased; God forbid that we should deny that in such a case—the punishment being the natural result of the sin—there is a judgment of God upon licentiousness and ungodly lusts. And the like may be said in many instances where there is so clear a link between the sin and the punishment that the blindest men may discern that God hath made Misery the child of Sin. But in cases of accident, such as that to which I refer, and in cases of sudden and instant death, again, I say, I enter my earnest protest against the foolish and ridiculous idea that those who thus perish are sinners above all the sinners who survive unharmed. Let me just try to reason this matter out with Christian people; for there are some unenlightened Christian people who will feel horrified by what I have said. To all those who hastily look upon every calamity as a judgment I would speak in the earnest hope of setting them right. 1. Let me begin, then, by saying, do not you see that what you say is not true? and that is the best of reasons why you should not say it. Does not your own experience and observation teach you that one event happeneth both to the righteous and to the wicked? It is true, the wicked man sometimes falls dead in the street; but has not the minister fallen dead in the pulpit? 2. The idea that whenever an accident occurs we are to look upon it as a judgment from God would make the providence of God to be, instead of a great deep, a very shallow pool. Why, any child can understand the providence of God, if it be true that when there is a railway accident it is because people travel on a Sunday. I take any little child from the smallest infant-class form in the Sunday-school, and he will say, "Yes, I see that." But then, if such a thing be providence, if it be a providence that can be understood, manifestly it is not the Scriptural idea of providence, for in the Scripture we are always taught that God's providence is "a great deep"; and even Ezekiel, who had the wing of the cherubim and could fly aloft, when he saw the wheels which were the great picture of the providence of God, could only say the wheels were so high that they were terrible, and were full of eyes, so that he cried, "O wheel!" If—I repeat it to make it plain—if always a calamity were the result of some sin, providence would be as simple as that twice two made four; it would be one of the first lessons that a little child might learn. 3. And then, will you allow me to remark, that the supposition against which I am earnestly contending, is a very cruel and unkind one. For if this were the case, that all persons who thus meet with their death in an extraordinary and terrible manner, were greater sinners than the rest, would it not be a crushing blow to bereaved survivors, and is it not ungenerous on our part to indulge the idea unless we are compelled by unanswerable reasons to accept it as an awful truth? Now, I defy you to whisper it in the widow's ear. And now, lastly—and then I leave this point —do you not perceive that the un-Christian and unscriptural supposition that when men suddenly meet with death it is the result of sin, robs Christianity of one of its noblest arguments for the immortality of the soul? Brethren, we assert daily, with Scripture for our warrant, that God is just; and inasmuch as He is just, He must punish sin, and reward the righteous. Manifestly He does not do it in this world. I think I have plainly shown that in this world one event happeneth to both; that the righteous man is poor as well as the wicked, and that he dies suddenly as well as the most graceless. Very well, then, the inference is natural and clear that there must be a next world in which these things must be righted. If there be a God, He must be just; and if He be just, He must punish sin; and since He does not do it in this world, there therefore must be another state in which men shall receive the due reward of their works ; and they that have sown to the flesh shall of the flesh reap corruption, while they that have sown to the Spirit, shall of the Spirit reap life everlasting. Make this world the reaping place, and you have taken the sting out of sin. II. Now to our second point. WHAT USE, THEN, OUGHT WE TO MAKE OF THIS VOICE OF GOD AS HEARD AMIDST THE SHRIEKS AND GROANS OF DYING MEN ? 1. The first inquiry we should put to ourselves is this : "Why may it not be my case that I may very soon and suddenly be cut off ? Have I a lease of my life ? Have I any special guardianship which ensures me that I shall not suddenly pass the portals of the tomb ? " And the next question it should suggest is this : "Am not I as great a sinner as those who died ? If in outward sin others have excelled me, are not the thoughts of my heart evil ? Does not the same law which curses them curse me ? It is as impossible that I should be saved by my works as that they should be. Am not I under the law as well as they by nature, and therefore am not I as well as they under the curse ? That question should arise. Instead of thinking of *their* sins which would make me proud, I should think of *my own* which will make me humble. Instead of speculating upon *their* guilt, which is no business of mine, I should turn my eyes within and think upon *my own* transgression, for which I must personally answer before the Most High God." Then the next question is, "Have I repented of my sin ? I need not be inquiring whether *they* have or not : have *I ?* Since I am liable to the same calamity, am I prepared to meet it ? Do I hate sin ? Have I learned to abhor it ? For if not, I am in as great danger as they were, and may quite as suddenly be cut off, and then where am *I ?* I will not ask where are *they ?* And then, again, instead of prying into the future destiny of these unhappy men and women, how much better to inquire into our own destiny and our own state ! 2. When we have used it thus for inquiry, let me remind you that we ought to use it also for warning. " Ye shall all likewise perish." " No," says one, " not likewise. We shall not all be crushed ; many of us will die in our beds. We shall not all be burned ; many of us will tranquilly close our eyes." Ay, but the text says, " Ye shall all likewise perish." And let me remind you that some of you may perish in the same identical manner. You have no reason to believe that you may not also suddenly be cut off while walking the streets. You may fall dead while eating your meals—how many have perished with the staff of life in their hands ! Ye shall be in your bed, and your bed shall suddenly be made your tomb. You shall be strong, hale, hearty, and in health, and either by an accident or by the stoppage of the circulation of your blood, you shall be suddenly hurried before your God. Oh ! may sudden death to you be sudden glory ! But it may happen with some of us, that in the same sudden manner as others have died, so shall we. But lately, in America, a brother, while preaching the Word, laid down his body and his charge at once. You remember the death of Dr. Beaumont, who, while proclaiming the gospel of Christ, closed his eyes to earth. And I remember the death of a minister in this country, who had but just given out the verse—

> " Father, I long, I faint to see
> The place of Thine abode ;
> I'd leave Thine earthly courts and flee
> Up to Thy house, my God,"

when it pleased God to grant him the desire of his heart, and he appeared before the King in His beauty. Why, then, may not such a sudden death as that happen to you and to me ? (*C. H. Spurgeon.*) *Lessons :*—1. We may hence learn to beware of rashly judging others. Let us think of the guilt which we should thus incur, and also of the retribution in kind, which we should thereby prepare for ourselves. 2. We may hence learn not to be too hasty in interpreting afflictive dispensations of Providence against ourselves. We may sometimes hear a person who is labouring under great reverses, or heavy bodily distress, express himself thus, " Surely I must be a very great sinner, else such things could never have been laid on me." If his meaning, in expressing himself thus, be that he is a great sinner in himself, that he suffers less than he deserves, that he might justly be cast off altogether, and that he ought to humble himself under the rod, and consider well what ought to be amended in his feelings and character—nothing can be more proper. But if his meaning be, that such sufferings are a proof that he is a sinner beyond others, and that he is still unpardoned and unrenewed, and that God is treating him as an enemy, and probably will cast him off for ever—nothing can be more hasty. The truth of the case may be the very opposite; and, if his humility be real, probably is the very opposite. Let all afflicted souls learn to seek to God for the sanctified use of their trouble, and support under it; and let none vex themselves with dark surmises whose trust is in the God of mercy. 3. We may hence learn to be thankful for our own preservation. When we hear of the heavy calamities, and the sudden removal of others, let us bless God for our own safety. What but His kind care has preserved us? Let us be thankful for our ordinary and daily preservation, and especially for signal deliverances. Let us be thankful, too, for our quietness and safety during our solemn religious services. When we think what blindness, unbelief, wandering of thought, and varied sinfulness, mix even with our very best services, and especially with our worst, how thankful should we be that the Lord has not broken in and made a breach on us, and mingled our blood with our sacrifices. 4. We learn from this passage, that it is our duty to mark and improve calamities, and especially violent and sudden deaths. It is right to speak of them to each other, with a view to our mutual benefit. When God's judgments are abroad in the earth, the inhabitants of the world should learn righteousness. "Be ye also ready : for, in such an hour as ye think not, the Son of Man cometh." 5. But there is one other lesson from this passage, on which I am especially desirous of fixing your attention, namely, the necessity of genuine repentance. Our Lord Himself, here says twice, "Except ye repent, ye shall all likewise perish." Consider, then, what is implied in repentance unto salvation; and seek to become possessed of it. (*Jas. Foote, M.A.*) *The massacre of the Galileans :*—There is no account in Josephus, the only Jewish contemporary historian, of this massacre of the Galileans. The oldest account of it is in Cyril of Alexandria, about four hundred years after it occurred, and runs thus : "For these [Galileans] were followers of the opinions of Judas of Galilee, of whom Luke makes mention in the Acts of the Apostles, who said that we ought to call no man master. Great numbers of them refusing to acknowledge Cæsar as their master were therefore punished by Pilate. They said also that men ought not to offer to God any sacrifices that were not ordained by the law of Moses, and so forbade to offer the sacrifices appointed by the people for the safety of the Emperor and the Roman people. Pilate, thus being enraged against the Galileans, ordered them to be slain in the midst of the very victims which they thought they might offer according to the custom of their law, so that the blood of the offerers was mingled with that of the victims offered." It is also conjectured that this interference of Pilate in slaying these Galileans was the cause of his quarrel with Herod, who resented his interference until a reconciliation took place by his sending Christ to him as one under his own jurisdiction. (*M. F. Sadler.*)   *An accident wrongly described :*—I remember that terrible accident which occurred on the Thames—the sinking of the "Princess Alice" steamboat. It appalled everybody, and we called it a "mysterious providence." I remember reading in the newspapers that when the collision occurred the boat "cracked and crumbled like a matchbox"—that was the sentence used. Why did it do so? Not by a special providence, but because it was built like a matchbox—as slim and as flimsy : and the providence that ended so fatally was, as usual, not the providence of God, but the reckless greed of man. (*J. Jackson Wray.*)   *Scrutable providences :*—Modern science has brought the world a fifth gospel. In it we read that God commands us to give Him our whole heads as well as our whole hearts, for that we cannot know Him nor obey Him till we discern Him in every minutest fact, and every immutable law of the physical universe, as in every fact and law of the moral. It is barely two hundred years since the great Cotton Mather preached a famous sermon called "Burnings Bewailed," wherein he attributed a terrible conflagration to the wrath of God kindled against Sabbath-breaking and the accursed fashion of monstrous periwigs! For years after his time the Puritan colonies held fasts for mildew, for small-pox, for caterpillars, for grasshoppers, for loss of cattle by cold and visitation of God. They saw an Inscrutable Providence in all these things. But when their children had learned a better husbandry and better sanitary conditions the "visitations" ceased. When, in Chicago, a night's fire undid a generation's toil, spreading misery and death broadcast, was that horror in the least degree inexplicable? Every man who, within thirty years, had put up a wooden house in a city whose familiar breezes were gales, and whose gales were hurricanes, solicited that rain of fire. They who, hasting to be rich, fell into the snare of cheap and dangerous building, digged, every man, a pit for his neighbour's feet as well as for his own. The inscrutable aspect of the calamity was that it had not come years before. And the Providential lesson would seem to be that laws of matter are laws of God, and cannot be violated with impunity. When the earthquake well-nigh swallowed up Peru, five or six years ago, men stood aghast at the mysterious dispensation. But heaven has not only always declared that tropical countries are liable to earthquakes, but had taught the Peruvians through hundreds of years to expect two earthquakes in a century, travelling in cycles from forty to sixty years apart. The citizens of Arica have not only this general instruction, but that special warning which nature always gives. A great light appeared to the south-east. Hollow sounds were heard. The dogs, the goats, even the swine foresaw the evil and hid themselves. But the simple men passed on and were punished. Before the Alpine freshets come the streams are coffee-coloured. Even the tornadoes of the tropics, which are instantaneous in their swoop, so plainly announce themselves to old sailors that they reef sails and save ship and life, while only the heedless perish. The simoon gives such certain and invariable warnings that the caravan is safe if it be wary. Herculaneum and Pompeii were built too far up the mountain. And that the builders knew quite as well as the excavators of the splendid ruins know it now. But they chose to take the risk. And to-day their cheerful compatriots gather their heedless vintage and sit beneath their perilous vines still nearer to the deadly crater. St. Petersburg has been three times inundated, and after each most fatal calamity processions filled the streets and masses were said to propitiate the mysterious anger of God. Peter the Great, who built the city, was the successor of Canute. He ordered the Gulf of Cronstadt to retire, and then set down his capital in the swamps of the verge of the Neva. Whenever the river breaks up with the spring floods, the trembling citizens are at sea in a bowl. Only three times has the bowl broken, so much money and skill have been expended upon it. But when a March gale shall drive the tide back upon the river, swollen and terrible with drifting ice, drowned St. Petersburg will be the pendant for burned Chicago. (*Ibid.*) **Except ye repent, ye shall all likewise perish.**—*True repentance :*—True repentance is a change of mind, accompanied by a sincere renunciation of sin. Its evidences are— 1. A consciousness of the evil of sin. 2. Self-condemnation. 3. A sense of unworthiness. 4. Great grief on account of the sin committed. 5. A truthful confession before God. 6. Prayer for power to resist temptation. 7. A mind open to good impressions. 8. Its emblem among plants is a "bruised reed." 9. Its model among men is Christian weeping before the Cross, but afterwards Christian rejoicing in hope. This is "repentance that needeth not to be repented of." "I desire to die," said Philip Henry, "preaching repentance; if out of the pulpit, I desire to die repenting." (*Van Doren.*) *A faithful warning :*—A young woman, being requested to join a Christian Society, stated that she had a tract given her when a scholar in a Sunday-school, in which tract an account was given of a young woman who died happy. This girl in her illness called her sister to her, and affectionately said, "Sister, if you do not repent of your sins, and turn to Jesus Christ, where God is you can never come." This so impressed the young woman that she never forgot it. She added, "Wherever I was, whatever I was doing, this was always on my mind, ' where God is you can never come.' I was very much distressed at my situation, and could find no peace." She eventually came to Jesus, became happy in the enjoyments of the pardon of her sins, through faith in the atonement of Christ Jesus, and lived in the expectation of realizing what her faith anticipated. ALL *sin must be repented of :*—If seven robbers were to get into a man's house, even though six of them were discovered and made prisoners, and sent off to jail, yet, as long as the seventh was known to be concealed in some secret corner, the master of the house could not well feel himself out of danger. Or, if a bird has fallen into a snare, and is only caught by a single claw ; or, if any animal has been caught in a trap, though it should be only by the leg, yet they are both in as much danger as if their whole bodies were entrapped. Thus it is that certain destruction awaits us, unless *all sin*, even the *very least*, be repented of. Pharaoh, after having been smitten with many plagues, at last consented to let the people go, provided they left their sheep and cattle behind them. But this would not satisfy Moses. He, acting for God, says, "All the flocks and herds must go along with us ; not a hoof shall be left." So Satan, like Pharaoh, would keep some sin in us as a pledge of our returning to him again ; and even though sin be taken away, he would wish the occasion of sin to remain. For instance, he might say, "Leave off gaming ; but still there is no occasion to burn the cards and throw away the dice." "You

must not do your enemy any injury, but there is no occasion for you to love him."
But God's language is of a different sort. He says that the occasion of sin, though
it be dear as a right hand, must be cut off; if we retain an eye for Satan to put his
hook into, he will be sure to insinuate himself, and the latter end may be worse than
the beginning. (*F. F. Trench.*)   *What repentance cannot do :*—Suppose I should
preach the gospel in some gambling-saloon of New York, and suppose a man should
come out convicted of his wickedness, and confess it before God, and pray that he
might be forgiven. Forgiveness might be granted to him, so far as he individually
was concerned. But suppose he should say, " O God, not only restore to me the
joys of salvation, but give me back the mischief that I have done, that I may roll
it out." Why, there was one man that shot himself; what are you going to do for
him? A young man came to Indianapolis, when I was pastor there, on his way to
settle in the West. He was young, callow, and very self-confident. While there
he was robbed, in a gambling-saloon, of fifteen hundred dollars—all that he had.
He begged to be allowed to keep enough to take him home to his father's house,
and he was kicked out into the street. It led to his suicide. I know the man that
committed the foul deed. He used to walk up and down the street. Oh, how my
soul felt thunder when I met him! If anything lifts me up to the top of Mount
Sinai, it is to see one man wrong another. Now suppose this man should repent?
Can he ever call back that suicide? Can he ever carry balm to the hearts of the
father and mother and brothers and sisters of his unfortunate victim? Can he ever
wipe off the taint and disgrace that he has brought on the escutcheon of that
family? No repentance can spread over that. And yet how many men there are
that are heaping up such transgressions! (*H. W. Beecher.*)   *Repentance :*—I.
THE CIRCUMSTANCES THAT LED TO THIS IMPORTANT TEACHING ABOUT REPENTANCE.
II. THE NATURE OF REPENTANCE. 1. The relation of repentance to faith. In
order of time they spring up together in the soul. In order of nature faith must
precede repentance. We cannot turn from sin without Christ, and we cannot come
to Christ without faith. 2. Repentance consists of three elements. (1) Godly
sorrow for sin. 1. Not mere sorrow for sin, for there is much sorrow because sin is
an evil and brings punishment, yet no godly element in it. 2. It is the sorrow of
a man more concerned for his guilt than his misery, whereas worldly sorrow is more
concerned for the misery than the guilt, and would plunge into deeper guilt to
escape the misery. 3. Illustrations of worldly sorrow (Pharaoh, Ahab, Judas).
4. The true spirit of godly sorrow is that of the prodigal—" I have sinned before
heaven, and in Thy sight." Also David's sorrow (Psa. li. 1–4). (2) Confession of
sin. 1. This is an essential part of repentance. (Often a relief to guilty men to
confess their crime.) 2. It must be very thorough and humbling and heart-
searching. 3. It is connected with the continuous forgiveness of believers (1 John
i. 7). (3) Turning from sin to God. 1. The godly sorrow must have a practical
result, in the way of proving its genuineness and attesting itself by fruits. 2.
Necessity of reparation recognized by civil law (cases of libel). But there are
injuries in which no reparation can be made (murder). 3. In cases of Pharaoh,
Ahab, Judas, no turning from sin to God, though there may have been sorrow and
confession of sin. 4. There must be a turning from all sin—from the love and
the practice of that which is sinful. III. THE NECESSITY OF REPENTANCE. 1. Jesus
spoke the words of the text in a spirit of prophecy. (Forty years after, at siege of
Jerusalem, the Jews felt the meaning of the " likewise " of the text.) 2. Preachers
cannot now say that, but they can say that if you do not repent you will perish
everlastingly. (*T. Croskery, D.D.*)   *The necessity of repentance :*—1. That those
who meet with more signal strokes than others, are not, therefore, to be
accounted greater sinners than others. The Lord spares some as great sinners, as
He signally punisheth. I tell you, nay. Reasons of this dispensation of Providence: 1. Because of God's sovereign power and absolute dominion, which He will
have the world to understand—" Is it not lawful for Me to do what I will with Mine
own?" (Matt. xx. 15.) 2. Because we are now under the mixed dispensation of Providence; not the unmixed, reserved to another world, when all men shall be put into
their unalterable state. 3. Because the mercy of God to some is magnified by His
severity on others. 4. Because in very signal strokes very signal mercies may be
wrapped up. 5. Because this dispensation is in some sort necessary to confirm us in
the belief of the judgment of the great day. USE 1. Then learn that unordinary
strokes may befall those that are not unordinary sinners; and therefore be not rash
in your judgment concerning the strokes that others meet with. 2. Then adore the
mercy of God to you, and wonder at His sparing you, when ye see others smart

under the hand of God. 3. That the strokes which any meet with, are pledges of ruin to impenitent sinners. But "Except ye repent, ye shall all likewise perish." Reasons of this are—1. Because they show how hateful to God sin is, in whomsoever it is (Isa. xlii. 24). 2. Because they show how just God is. He is the Judge of all the earth, and cannot but do right. 3. Because whatever any meet with in the way of sin is really designed for warning to others, as is clear from the text (see 1 Cor. x. 11, 12). 4. Because all those strokes which sinners meet with in this life are the spittings of the shower of wrath that abides the impenitent world, after which the full shower may certainly be looked for. USE 1. Be not unconcerned spectators of all the effects of God's anger for sin going abroad in the world; for your part and mine is deep in them. There is none of them but says to us, as in the same condemnation, "Except ye repent, ye shall all likewise perish." 2. Consider, O impenitent sinners, how can ye escape, when your ruin is insured by so many pledges thereof from the Lord's hand, while ye go on in sin? 3. The strokes that others meet with are loud calls to us to repent. That is the language of all the afflicting providences which we see going on in the world. To confirm this, consider—1. God does not strike one for sin with a visible stroke, but with an eye to all. 2. Thereby we may see how dangerous a thing sin is to be harboured; and if we will look inward, we may ever see that there is sin in us also against the God of Israel. 3. How much more do strokes from the hand of the Lord on ourselves call us to repent? (Hos. ii. 6, 7). USE 1. We may see that none go on impenitently in a sinful course, but over the belly of thousands of calls from Providence to repent, besides all those they have from the Word. 2. Impenitency under the gospel cannot have the least shadow of excuse. The calls of Providence common to the whole world, are sufficient to leave the very heathens without excuse (Rom. i. 20); how much more shall the calls of the Word and Providence, too, make us inexcusable if we do not repent? I come now to the principal doctrine of the text. I. EXPLAIN THE NATURE OF REPENTANCE. 1. What it is in its general nature. 2. How it is wrought in the soul. 3. The subject of true repentance. 4. The parts of repentance. I come now to the application of the whole. And here I would sound the alarm in the ears of impenitent sinners, to repent, and turn from their sins unto God. O sinners, repent, repent; ye are gone away to your lusts and idols, turn from them; ye have turned your back on God, turn to Him again. In prosecuting this call to repentance, I shall—1. Endeavour to convince you of the need you have to repent. 2. Lay before you a train of motives to repentance. 3. Show you the great hindrances of repentance. And—4. Give directions in order to your obtaining repentance. (1) Labour to see sin in its own colours, what an evil thing it is (Jer. ii. 19). What makes us to cleave to sin is false apprehensions we have about it. To see it in itself would be a means to make us fly from it. For this end consider—1. The majesty of God offended by sin. Ignorance of God is the mother of impenitency (Acts xvii. 30). 2. The obligations we lie under to serve Him, which by sin we trample upon. 3. The wrath of God that abides impenitent sinners. 4. The good things our unrepented-of sins deprive us of. 5. The many evils which are bred by our sin against the honour of God, our own and our neighbour's true interest. (1) Be much in the thoughts of death. Consider how short and uncertain your time is. (2) Dwell on the thoughts of a judgment to come, where ye shall be made to give an account of yourselves. (3) Meditate on the sufferings of Christ. (4) Pray for repentance, and believingly seek and long for the Lord's giving the new heart, according to His promise (Ezek. xxxvi. 26). (*T. Boston, D.D.*) *Nature and necessity of repentance:*—I. NATURE. 1. Repentance implies godly sorrow for sin. 2. Repentance involves hatred of sin. 3. Repentance includes reformation. This, as it respects both the affections of the heart and the conduct of the life, is the crowning excellence of this evangelical virtue. II. NECESSITY. "Except . . . perish." 1. This is the decision of God respecting all men. 2. The facts point this way. Sinners have perished—sinners distinguished by no peculiarity of guilt—sinners, therefore, in whose case there was no more reason to anticipate the righteous judgments of heaven than there is to anticipate it in other cases. What God has done in these instances, there is every reason to believe He will do in others like them. This is the argument of our Lord, and it comes to us in unabated force. 3. The moral government of God requires it. 4. Also the moral character of God. Sin is abhorrent to His nature. As a holy God, He must regard it with absolute abhorrence and ceaseless displeasure. To suppose otherwise is to suppose God either to approve or to be indifferent to what is directly opposite to Himself, and worthy of His eternal rebuke. It is to suppose

God to hate, or wholly disregard His own perfections and glory. But can a spotless God hate Himself? Can His own infinite perfection become an object of indifference to Himself? Can He fail to abhor sin with a measure of indignation proportioned to the purity and infinitude of His nature? (*N. W. Taylor, D.D.*) *Of repentance :*—We should labour to make good use to ourselves of God's judgments on others. Why? God expects it; this is the way to prevent the execution on ourselves. How? 1. "Learning righteousness" (Isa. xxvi. 9); faith, seeing Him execute threatenings; fear, beholding His severity; obedience, sure want of that is the cause; love, whilst we escape. 2. Forsaking sin: "Sin no more" (John v. 14). All sin, because every sin is pregnant with judgment; therefore it summons to search and try, &c., especially those sins which brought wrath on others. Observe providences; use means to discover what is the Achan, &c. We have great occasion to practise this. Wrath is kindled and burns, &c.; the cup of indignation goes round; the sword has had a commission, &c.; the scars and smarting impressions continue in bodies, estates, liberties. Let us learn to believe, to tremble, to love. Let us forsake sin, our own; the sins that have unsheathed the sword, mixed this bitter cup. Make not this warning ineffectual with the Jews' supposition. Rather hear, believe, apply what Christ says, Except I repent, &c. I. FROM THE ADMONISHER, CHRIST, IN THAT HE TEACHES REPENTANCE. Repentance is an evangelical duty; a gospel, a new-covenant duty. This should not be questioned by those who either believe what the gospel delivers, or understand what it is to be evangelical; but since it is denied, let us prove it. And first from this ground. 1. Christ taught repentance. But He taught nothing but what was evangelical. 2. It is excluded by the covenant of works. No room for repentance there. 3. It is required in the gospel (Acts xvii. 30). 4. It was preached by the apostles (Luke xxiv. 47; Acts ii. 28, iii. 19). 5. It was the end of Christ's coming (Matt. ix. 13) to call sinners. 6. It was purchased by Christ's death (Acts v. 31). 7. It has evangelical promises. 8. It is urged upon evangelical grounds (Matt. iii. 2; Mark i. 14, 15). 9. It is the condition of the prime evangelical mercy. God offers, gives remission of sins, upon condition of repentance. What Christ commands us, Himself does practise (Luke xvii. 3). If he repent, forgive him. So Acts iii. 19, and ii. 38. 10. It is confirmed by the seal of the covenant of grace. Baptism is the seal of repentance. 11. It is a fundamental of Christianity (Heb. vi. 1). 12. It is the way to life (Acts xi. 18). 1. It reproves those who reject this duty as legal. Certainly those who find not this in the gospel, have found another gospel besides that which Christ and His disciples preached. 2. Exhort. To practise this duty evangelically, that is most congruous. Directions: (1) Undertake it for evangelical ends. The end gives nature and name to the action. If your aims be legal, mercenary, the act will be so. Go not about it only to escape hell, avoid wrath, satisfy justice, remove judgments, pacify conscience. Ahab and Pharaoh can repent thus, those who are strangers to the covenant of grace. How then? Endeavour that you may give God honour, that ye may please Him, that you may comply with His will, that you may never more return to folly. Confess, to give honour, as Josh. vii. 19, get hearts broken, that you may offer sacrifice well pleasing. (2) Let evangelical motives lead you to the practice of it. Act as drawn by the cords of love. The goodness of God should lead you to it (Rom. ii.). (3) In an evangelical manner, freely, cheerfully, with joy and delight; not as constrained, but willingly. (4) Repent that ye can repent no more. This is an evangelical temper, to be sensible of the defects and failings of spiritual duties. (5) Think not your repentance is the cause of any blessing: it is neither the meritorious nor impulsive cause; it neither deserves any mercy, nor moves the Lord to bestow any. (6) Think not that your repentance can satisfy God, or make amends for the wrongs sin has done Him. (7) Ye must depend upon Christ for strength, ability to repent; all evangelical works are done in His strength. (8) Ye must expect the acceptance of your repentance from Christ. (9) Think not your repentance obliges God to the performance of any promise, as though He were thereby bound, and could not justly refuse to bestow what He has promised to the penitent; for He is not obliged to fulfil it till the condition be perfectly performed. Imperfect repentance is not the condition; God requires nothing imperfect. If He accomplishes His promise upon our weak defective endeavours, it is not because He is by them engaged, but from some other engaging consideration. Now our repentance is defective, both in quantity and quality, measure and manner, neither so great nor so good as is required. Why, then, does God perform? How is He obliged? Why, it is Christ that has obliged Him; He makes good the condition. When we cannot bring so much as is required, He makes up the sum; He adds grains to that which wants weight. He has satisfied for our defects, and they are for His sake pardoned, and therefore are accepted, as though they were not defective. (10) Expect a reward, not from justice, but mercy. II. Thus much for the admonisher, "I tell you." PROCEED WE TO THE ADMONITION. And in it—1. The correction, "nay." Hereby He corrects two mistakes of the Jews : (1) Concerning their innocency. They thought themselves innocent, compared with the Galileans, not so great sinners (ver. 2). (2) Concerning their impunity, grounded on the former. Because not so great sinners, they should not be so great sufferers, nor perish as they in the text. From the first. 1. (1) Impenitent sinners are apt to think themselves not so great sinners as others ; to justify themselves, as Pharisees in reference to others ; like crows, fly over flowers and fruit, to pitch upon carrion ; say as Isa. lxv. 5, "Stand by thyself," &c. (*a*) Because never illuminated to see the number, nature, aggravations of their own sins, how many, how sinful; examine not their hearts and lives ; judge of sins according to outward appearance, not secret heinousness. (*b*) Self-love. They cover, extenuate, excuse their own; multiply, magnify others. (*c*) Ignorance of their natural sinfulness. In which respect they are equally sinful as others. Seed-plots of sin ; have a root of bitterness, an evil treasure of heart; a disposition to the most abominable sins that ever were committed, such as they never thought of, nor will ever believe they should yield to (2 Kings viii. 11, 12); want nothing but temptation, a fit occasion. Take heed of this. It is a sign of impenitency. Paul counts himself the chief of sinners : "If you judge yourselves," &c. (1 Cor. xi. 31). (2) From their conceit of impunity. Sinners are apt to flatter themselves with the hopes they shall escape judgments. If they can believe they are not so great sinners, they are apt to conclude they shall not perish : "Put far from them the evil day" (Amos vi. 3), threatened (ver. 7); cry Peace, &c. Satan has blinded them. Beware of this. It has been the ruin of millions. Those perish soonest who think they shall longest escape (Amos vi. 7 ; 1 Thess. v. 3; "Be not deceived, God is not mocked," &c. Believe the Lord threatening rather than Satan promising. 2. The direction—"Repent." Repentance has such a relation to, such a connection with, life and salvation, as this cannot be expected without that ; for though it be neither merit nor motive, yet consider it as it is, an antecedent and sign, qualification, condition, or means of life and salvation, and the truth will appear. (1) An antecedent. So there must be no salvation till first there be repentance. Sown in tears before reap in joy. (2) Sign. A symptom of one being an heir to salvation. (3) Qualification. To fit for life. He that is in love with sin is not fit for heaven. No unclean thing enters there. Neither will God Himself endure him to be there. (4) Condition. For that is, without it, never see God : "Except ye," &c. This is the condition, without which ye shall not escape. (5) Means and way to life : Christ's highway. "Repentance to life" (Acts xi. 18). Peter directs them to this (Acts ii. 38). What is it to repent? Why must they perish that do not? To repent, is to turn ; to return from former evil ways (Ezek. xiv. 6). 1. Sorrow for sin. To repent, is to mourn for sin (2 Cor. vii. 9, 10). (1) Hearty, such as greatly affects the heart. Not that of the tongue, which is usual, I am sorry, &c. ; nor that of the eyes neither, if tears spring not from a broken heart; not verbal, slight, outward, superficial, but great, bitter, cordial humbling; such sorrow as will afflict the soul. (2) Godly sorrow (2 Cor. vii. 9, 10), sorrow for sin, as it is against God ; not as it is against yourselves, prejudicial to you ; as it brings judgments, exposes to wrath, makes you obnoxious to justice, brings within the compass of curses, and in danger of hell. 2. Hatred of sin. This is an act of repentance, and that indeed which is principally essential to it. This hatred is (1) well-grounded ; (2) universal; (3) irreconcileable. 3. Forsaking sin. Terror to impenitent sinners. Hear the doom in the text: "Except ye repent," &c. Those that do not, will not repent, must perish, shall perish. There is no way without repentance to avoid perishing, and these will not repent, mourn, hate, forsake sin. What will become of them? Christ, the righteous Judge, gives sentence, they shall perish, certainly, universally, eternally. 1. Certainly. For Christ has said it. He speaks peremptorily ; not they may, but they shall. 2. Universally. All, and every one, without exception, whatever he be, have, do, or can do, "Except," &c. Christ speaks to the Jews, and to all without exception —all perish. If any people in the world had any ground to plead exemption, sure it was the Jews ; no people ever in greater favour, none ever had greater privileges. Whatever you can plead why this should not concern you, they had as much ground to plead. 3. Eternally. Soul and body, here and hereafter, now and for ever, must perish without redemption : For who shall redeem from it but Christ? and

Christ cannot do it except He will act against His own Word, except He will deny Himself. The sentence is passed, and none in heaven will, none in earth can, recall it. Exhortation: To the practice of this duty. Christ urges it, and under such a penalty. These should be sufficient enforcements. But there are many more considerations to stir up to this duty. I shall reduce them to three heads: some concerning—1. Sin to be repented of. 2. Christ that urges repentance. 3. Repentance itself, the duty urged. 1. Concerning sin. (1) No creature ever got, nor can get, any advantage by sin. (2) The least sin is infinitely evil. When I say infinite, I say there is more evil in it than the tongue of men or angels can express, than their largest apprehensions can conceive. When I say infinite evil, I understand it is a greater evil than the greatest in the world besides it. (3) The least sin deserves infinite punishment, *i.e.*, greater than any can endure, express, or imagine. (4) The least sin cannot be expiated without infinite satisfaction. (5) It is the cause of all the evils that we count miseries in the world. Whatsoever is fearful, or grievous, or hateful, owes its birth to sin. Were it not for sin, either no evil would be in the world, or that which is now evil would be good. (6) It is the soul's greatest misery. Those evils which sin has brought into the world are lamentable, but the miseries wherein it has involved the soul are much more grievous. (7) It is God's greatest adversary; it has done much against the world, more against man's soul; aye, but that which it does against God is most considerable, as that which should move us to hate, bewail, abandon it, above all considerations. It has filled the world with fearful evils, the soul with woeful miseries; but the injuries it does to God are most horrible. (8) Consider the multitude of your sins. If any one sin be so infinitely evil in itself and in its effects, oh how evil is he, what need to repent, who is guilty of a multitude of sins! 2. Considerations from Christ, who enjoins repentance. If our sins were occasion of sorrow to Him, great reason have we to mourn for them. But so it is; our sins made Him a man of sorrows. The cup which He gives to us, He drank Himself; He drank out the dregs and bitterness, the wormwood and gall, wherewith this sorrow was mixed. That which He left to us is pleasant. The cup which Christ gives us, shall we not drink it? Nay, the cup which Christ drank, shall we refuse to taste? Our sins made Him weep and sigh, and cry out in the anguish of His spirit; and shall we make a sport of sin? 3. Considerations from repentance, the duty enjoined. That is the time when all happiness begins, when misery ends, the period of evils; the time from whence ye must date all mercies. Till then, never expect to receive the least mercy, or have the least judgment, evil, removed without repentance. (*D. Clarkson, B.D.*) *Take heed to thyself:*—There is a peculiar point and pregnancy of import in these words, which may be wholly overlooked in making them a simple basis for the general affirmation that all sinners must repent or perish. This, true and awful as it is, is rather presupposed than positively stated. To confine ourselves to this, as the whole meaning, is to lose sight of two emphatic words—"ye" and "likewise." Assuming, as a truth already known, that all men must repent or perish, the text affirms that they whom it addresses must repent or perish likewise, that is, like those particularly mentioned in the context. Another feature of the passage which is apt to be neglected is, that it not only teaches the necessity of repentance to salvation, but presents a specific motive for its exercise, or rather teaches us to seek occasions of repentance in a quarter where most of us are naturally least disposed to seek them; nay, where most of us are naturally and habitually prone to find excuses for indulging sentiments as far removed from those of penitence as possible; uncharitable rigour and censorious pride. 1. That suffering is a penal consequence of sin seems to be a dictate of reason and conscience no less than of revelation. At all events, it is a doctrine of religion which, above most others, seems to command the prompt assent of the human understanding. They who acknowledge the existence of a God at all, have probably no impressions of His power or His justice stronger than those which are associated with His providential strokes, and more especially with death as the universal penalty. War, pestilence, and famine are regarded by the common sense of men not merely as misfortunes, but as punishments, and nothing more effectually rouses in the multitude the recollection of their sins than the report or the approach of those providential scourges. In all this the popular judgment is according to the truth. 2. What is thus true in the aggregate must needs be true in detail. If all the suffering in the world proceeds from sin, then every Divine judgment in particular must flow from the same source. Wherever we see suffering we see a proof not only that there is sin somewhere to account for and to justify that suffering, but that the individual sufferer is a sinner. 3. And yet it cannot be denied that there is something in this doctrine thus presented, against which even the better feelings of our nature are disposed to revolt. This is especially the case when we contemplate instances of aggravated suffering endured by those who are comparatively innocent, and still more when the sufferings of such are immediately occasioned by the wickedness of others. Can it be that the dying agonies of one who falls a victim to the murderous revenge or the reckless cupidity of others are to be regarded as the punishment of sin? Against this representation all our human sympathies and charities appear to cry aloud, and so intense is the reaction in some minds that they will not even listen to the explanation. 4. This feeling of repugnance, though it springs from a native sense of justice, is mistaken in its application because founded upon two misapprehensions. In the first place it assumes that the sufferings, in the case supposed, are said to be the penal fruits of sin committed against man, and more especially against the author of the sufferings endured. Hence we are all accustomed to enhance the guilt of murder, in some cases, by contrasting the virtues of the victim with the crimes of the destroyer. And in such a state of mind not one of us, perhaps, would be prepared to hear with patience that the murder was a righteous recompense of sin. But why? Because at such a moment we can look no further than the proximate immediate agent, and to think of him as having any claim or right of punishment is certainly preposterous. But when the excitement is allayed, and we have lost sight of the worthless and justly abhorred instrument, we may perhaps be able to perceive that, in the presence of an infinitely holy God, the most innocent victim of man's cruelty is, in himself, deserving only of displeasure; or, at least, that no difficulties hang about that supposition, except such as belong to the whole subject of sin and punishment. 5. If any does remain, it probably has reference to the seeming disproportion of the punishment to that of others, or to any particular offence with which the sufferer seems chargeable in comparison with others. But there is no authority for holding that every providential stroke is a specific punishment of some specific sin, or that the measure of men's sufferings here is in exact proportion to their guilt, so that they upon whom extraordinary judgment seem to fall are thereby proved to be extraordinary sinners. 6. The effect of this last error is the more pernicious, and the cure of it more difficult, because the doctrine which it falsely imputes to Christianity is really maintained by many Christians as well as by many who make no such professions. It often unexpectedly betrays itself in a censorious attempt to trace the sufferings of others back to certain causes, often more offensive in the sight of human censors and inquisitors than in that of a heart-searching God. But even where the sin charged is indeed a sin, its existence is hastily inferred from the supposed judgment, without any other evidence whatever. This uncharitable tendency can be cured only by the correction of the error which produces it. 7. But in attempting this correction there is need of extreme caution, as in all other cases where an error has arisen, not from sheer invention or denial of the truth, but from exaggeration, or perversion, or abuse of truth itself. Let us not, *e.g.*, attempt to vindicate the ways of God to man by denying the doctrine of a particular providence. No distinction can be drawn between the great and small as objects of God's notice and His care, without infringing on the absolute perfection of His nature by restricting His omniscience. 8. Nor must we deny any penal or judicial connection between particular providential strokes and the sins of the individual sufferer. To deny that the bloated countenance, the trembling limbs, the decaying mind, the wasted fortune, and the blasted fame of the drunkard or the libertine, are penally consequences of sin, of his own sin, of his own besetting, reigning, darling sin, would be ridiculous, and all men would regard it in that light. And the same thing is true of some extraordinary providences. When a bold blasphemer, in the act of imprecating vengeance on his own head, falls down dead before us, it would argue an extreme of philosophical caution or of sceptical reserve to hesitate to say, as the magicians said to Pharaoh when they found themselves confronted with effects beyond the capacity of any human or created power, "This is the finger of God." What, then, it may be asked, is the error, theoretical or practical, which Christ condemns, and against which we are warned to be for ever on our guard? If it be true, not only that suffering in general is the fruit of sin, and that every individual sufferer is a sinner, but that particular sufferings may be recognized as penal retributions of particular sins, where is the harm in tracing the connection for our edification or for that of others? 1. Even if the general rule be granted the exceptions are so many and notorious as to render it inapplicable as a standard or criterion of character. 2. This is a matter which God has not subjected to our scrutiny. 3. The tendency of such inquisitions, as shown by all experience, is not so much to edify as to subject—not so much to wean from sin as to harden in self-righteousness, by letting the censorship of other men's sins and other men's punishment divert our thoughts entirely from those which *we* commit, or those which *we* are to experience. Here, then, is the use which this instructive passage teaches us to make of the calamities of others, whether those which fall on individuals in private life, or those which strike whole classes and communities. The whole secret may be told in one short word— Repent. As the goodness of God to ourselves ought to lead us to repentance, so ought His judgments upon others to produce the same effect. Every such judgment should remind us that our own escape is but a respite—that if they who perish in our sight were guilty, we are guilty too, and that unless we repent we must all likewise perish. The words are full of solemn warning and instruction to us all. They give a tongue and an articulate utterance to every signal providence, to every sudden death, to every open grave, to every darkened house, to every scattered fortune, to every blighted reputation, to every broken heart in society around us. They command us, they entreat us to withdraw our view from the calamities of others as proofs of *their* iniquity, and to view them rather as memorials of our own, of that common guilt to which these manifold distresses owe their origin, and in which we, alas! are so profoundly and so ruinously implicated. (*J. A. Alexander, D.D.*) *The naturalness of God's judgments :*—Now the principle that every judgment of God is connected, in the way of ordinary cause and effect, with the sin or error therein condemned, destroys at once the notion that plague or famine are judgments upon us for infidelity, or rationalism, or sabbath-breaking, or our private sins, for there is plainly no natural connection between the alleged sin and the alleged punishment. For example, the town which takes due sanitary precautions may refuse to give one penny to missions, but it will not be visited by a virulent outbreak of cholera. The town which takes no sanitary precautions, but gives £10,000 a-year to missions, will, in spite of its Christian generosity, become a victim to the epidemic. The lightning will strike the ship of the good man who chooses to sail without a lightning-conductor, it will spare the ship of the atheist and the blasphemer who provides himself with the protecting rod. There is, then, always a natural connection between the sin and the punishment, and the punishment points out its own cause. It is my intention this morning to show the truth of this principle in other spheres than that of epidemic disease. If we can manifest its universality, we go far to prove its truth. Take as the first illustration the case of the moral law. The commandments have force, therefore, not because they are commanded by a God of power, but because they are either needful for, or natural to, human nature. Nor is the judgment which follows on their violation any more arbitrary than the laws themselves. As they have their root in our nature so they have their punishment in our nature. Violate a moral law and our constitution protests through our conscience. Sorrow awakes, remorse follows, and remorse is felt in itself to be the mark of separation from God. The punishment is not arbitrary, but natural. Moreover, each particular violation of the moral law has its own proper judgment. The man who is dishonest in one branch of his life soon feels dishonesty —not impurity, not anything else but dishonesty—creep through his whole life and enter into all his actions. Impurity has its own punishment, and that is increasing corruption of heart. Take, again, the intellectual part of man. The necessities for intellectual progress are attention, perseverance, practice. Refuse to submit to these laws and you are punished by loss of memory or inactivity of memory, by failure in your work or by inability to think and act quickly at the proper moment. Again, take what may be called national laws. These have been, as it were, codified by the Jewish prophets. They were men whose holiness brought them near to God and gave them insight into the diseases of nations. They saw clearly the natural result of these diseases and they proclaimed it to the world. They looked on Samaria, and saw there a corrupt aristocracy, failing patriotism, oppression of the poor, falsification of justice, and they said, God will judge this city, and it shall be overthrown by Assyria. Well, was that an arbitrary judgment? It was of God ; but given a powerful neighbour, and a divided people in which the real fighting and working class has been crushed, enslaved, and unjustly treated— and an enervated, lazy, pleasure-consumed upper class, and what is the natural result? Why, that very thing which the prophets called God's judgment. God's judgment was the natural result of the violation of the first of national laws—even-handed justice to all parties in the State. The same principle is true in a thousand instances in history; the national judgments of war, revolution, pestilence, famine, are the direct results of the violation by nations of certain plain laws which have become clear by experience. For these judgments come to teach nations what is wrong in them, and the judgments must come again and again while the wrong thing is there. We find them out by punishment, as a child finds out that he must not touch fire by being burnt. The conclusion I draw from this is, that all national judgments of God come about naturally. But there are certain judgments mentioned in the Bible which seem to be supernatural—the destruction of Sodom, of Sennacherib's army, of the Egyptians in the Red Sea, the plagues sent upon the Israelites, and others. These are the difficulty. How shall we explain them? or shall we seek to explain them at all? First, we must remember that the writers had not the knowledge capable of explaining them; that nature to them was an insoluble mystery. They naturally, then, referred these things to a direct action of God, or rather, because they were out of the common, to an interference of God with nature. They were right in referring them to God, but it is possible that, owing to their ignorance of nature, they were wrong in their way of explaining them. Secondly. There is a thought which goes far, if it be true, to explain these things —it is that the course of human history may be so arranged, that, at times, healing or destructive natural occurrences coincide with crises in the history of a nation. For example, we might say that the sins of Sodom had reached their height at the very period when the elastic forces which were swelling beneath the plain of the Dead Sea had reached their last possible expansion. Or that the army of Sennacherib lay encamped in the way of the pestilential wind, which would have blown over the spot whether they had been there or not. Thirdly. Whatever difficulty these things present to us in the Bible, the same difficulty occurs in what is profanely called profane history. There is not the slightest doubt, were our English history written by a Hebrew of the time of the kings, that the eclipse and the thunderstorm at Creçi, and that the storms which broke the Armada on the rocks of England and Scotland, would have been imputed to a miraculous interference by God with the course of nature. We do not believe these to have been miraculous; but we do believe them, with the Jew, to be of God. But we must also believe that they are contained in the order of the world—not disorderly elements arbitrarily introduced. That is, while believing in God as the Director and Ruler of human affairs, we must also believe in Him as the Director and Ruler of the course of nature. We see in all things this law holding good—that God's judgments are natural. There is another class of occurrences which have been called judgments of God, but to which the term judgment is inapplicable. There are even now some who say that the sufferers under these blows of nature suffer because they are under the special wrath of God. What does Christ say to that? He bluntly contradicts it! "I tell you nay"—it is not so. There are not a few who still blindly think that suffering proves God's anger. Has the Cross taught us nothing better than that, revealed to us no hidden secret? There is no pain, mental or physical, which is not a part of God's continual self-sacrifice in us, and which, were we united to life and not to death, we should not see as joy. But, say others, God is cruel to permit such loss. Three thousand souls have perished in this hurricane. Is this your God of love? But look at the history of the hurricane. "Could not God arrange to have a uniform climate over all the earth?" We are spiritually puzzled, and, to arrange our doubts, God must make another world! We know not what we ask. A uniform climate over all the earth means simply the death of all living beings. It is the tropic heat and the polar cold which cause the currents of the ocean and the air and keep them fresh and pure. A stagnant atmosphere, a rotting sea, that is what we ask for. It is well God does not take us at our word. When we wish the hurricane away, we wish away the tropic heats in the West Indies and along the whole equator. What do we do then? We wish away the Gulf Stream and annihilate England. How long would our national greatness last if we had here the climate of Labrador? Because a few perish, is God to throw the whole world into confusion? The few must be sometimes sacrificed to the many. But they are not sacrificed without due warning. In this case God tells us plainly in His book of nature, that He wants to keep His air and His seas fresh and clear for His children to breathe and sail upon. The West Indies is the place where this work is done for the North Atlantic and its borders, and unless the whole constitution of the world be entirely changed, that work must be done by tornadoes. God has made that plain to us; and to all sailing and living about warm currents like the Gulf Stream it is as if God said, "Expect my hurricanes; they must come. You will have to face danger and death, and it is My law that you should face it everywhere in spiritual as well as physical life; and to call Me unloving because I impose this on you, is to mistake the true ideal of your humanity. I mean to make you active men, not slothful dreamers. I will not make the world too easy for My children. I want veteran men, not untried soldiers; men of endurance, foresight, strength and skill for My work, and I set before you the battle. You must face manfully those forces which you call destructive, but which are in reality reparative." Brethren, we cannot complain of the destructive forces of nature. We should have been still savages had we not to contend against them. (S. A. Brooke, M.A.)　*The case of passing judgment concerning calamities examined: What kind of judgment on such occasions is innocent and just ascertained; and the culpable extremes noted and censured:*—I. I shall observe WHAT KIND OF REFLECTIONS OR CONCLUSIONS WE MAY JUSTLY RAISE UPON ANY CALAMITIES WHICH BEFALL OTHER MEN. 1. In the first place, we need not be scrupulous of thinking or saying that the persons so visited are visited for their sins. Our blessed Lord finds no fault with the Jews for suggesting or supposing that the Galileans were sinners, and were punished by God for their sins. All mere men are sinners, and all afflictions whatever have a retrospect to sins committed, and are, in strictness of speech, punishments of sin. 2. That all calamities whatever are to be understood as coming from the hand of God. The Jews looked upwards to a higher hand than his, supposing Pilate to be the minister or executioner only of the Divine vengeance; and in this they judged right. II. TO TAKE NOTICE OF THOSE EXTREMES WHICH MANY SO RUN INTO, BUT WHICH WE OUGHT ABOVE ALL THINGS CAREFULLY TO AVOID. There are two noted excesses in this matter: one the text expressly mentions, the other is omitted, or only tacitly pointed to. That which is mentioned, is, the drawing rash and uncharitable conclusions from greater sufferings to greater sins; as if they who have suffered most must of consequence have been the worst of sinners. The other, which is not mentioned, but yet is tacitly condemned, is, the being positive and peremptory as to the particular sin, or kind of sin, that draws down God's judgments upon any particular person or persons. That which I now intend to treat of, is the pointing out, or specifying the particular sin or sins, for which we suppose God's judgments to have fallen upon any particular person or persons. The motives for doing this are many and various, as circumstances vary, though all centering in self-flattery, or partial fondness to ourselves. Sometimes it is vanity and ostentation, while we affect to make a show of more than common sagacity in discovering the hidden springs of events, and in interpreting the secrets of Divine providence. Sometimes party prejudices and passions have the greatest hand in it; while we are willing to measure God by ourselves, and to fancy that He takes the same side that we do. If our opposers or adversaries fall into troubles or disasters, how agreeable a thought is it to imagine that it was a judgment upon them for their opposition to us. But the most common and prevailing motive of all for censuring others in this manner on account of their afflictions, is to ward off the apprehension of the like from our own doors, and to speak peace to ourselves. Observe it carefully, and you will scarce find a man charging a judgment of God upon others for any particular sin, and at the same time acknowledging himself guilty in the like kind. No, he will be particularly careful to pitch upon some vice, which he himself, in imagination at least, stands clear of, and is the farthest from. The designs of providence are vast and large; God's thoughts are very deep, His judgments unsearchable, His ways past finding out. 1. Sometimes the primary reasons, or moving causes of the Divine judgments, lie remote and distant in place or in time; several years, perhaps, or even generations, backwards. God may "visit the sins of the fathers upon the children, unto the third and fourth generation of them that hate Him. He has at any time full power and right to take away the life which He gives, or any worldly comforts which Himself bestows; and if He sometimes chooses to exercise this right and power on account of things done several years or ages upwards, there can be no injustice in so doing; but it may more fully answer the ends of discipline, and God may show forth His wisdom in it. This I hint, by the way, as to the reason of the thing: the facts are evident from the sacred history. When King Ahab had sinned, God denounced His judgments against him, but suspended the execution, in part, to another time; assigning also the reason for deferring it: "Because he humbleth himself before Me, I will not bring the evil in his days, but in his son's days will I bring the evil upon his house": which was accordingly executed, in the days of his son Jehoram, about fifteen years after. 2. It may further be considered that sometimes the best sort of men are permitted to fall a sacrifice to the rage and violence of the worst ; and this either because the world is not worthy of them, or because God gives them up, that their malicious persecutors may fill up the measure of their iniquities. In either view the thing is rather a judgment of God upon the wicked who remain, than upon the righteous so taken away. 3. Supposing we were ever so certain that any person is visited for his own sins only, without any respect to the sins of his ancestors, or of any man else ; yet great mistakes may be committed in conjectures made about the particular sins. We have a very remarkable instance of it in Shimei's censure upon King David. III. To POINT OUT THE PRACTICAL USE AND APPLICATION OF THE WHOLE. 1. Let it be observed that religious and righteous men are often grievously afflicted. In which case it is most evident that, though they may and do deserve as great temporal afflictions as can be laid upon them, yet they do not deserve them more, nor so much as those worse men that escape. God, for many wise reasons, may sometimes punish good men in this life, and spare the ungodly. The sins of the former, being of a smaller size, may be purged away by temporal calamities ; while the greater transgressions of the latter are reserved for an after-reckoning, a more solemn and dismal account. Good men may retain some blemishes, which want to be washed away in the baptism of afflictions. Or, God may sometimes serve the interest of His Church, and set forth the power of His grace, and the efficacy of the true religion, by the sufferings of good men ; which is the case of martyrs or confessors who have been persecuted for righteousness' sake. 2. Suppose we certainly knew that any person who is under trouble, or who has remarkably suffered, and died by the hand of God, had been a wicked and ungodly man ; yet we cannot justly conclude, that he was at all worse than many who had not so suffered. For in some cases it may be an argument rather in his favour, to prove that he was not so bad as others. First, I observe, that in some cases the afflictions which a bad man suffers may be an argument in his favour, as affording a probable presumption that he is not so bad, but rather better, than those who escape. Now, I say, when God punishes a sinner in such a way as affects not his life, with a view to his amendment (whether it be by extreme poverty or disgrace, or bodily hurts or diseases, or whatever else it be), in these cases it may serve for an argument in his favour, to prove that he is somewhat better than many others that are spared. For God, who sees into the hearts of all men, may know what effect His visitation will have upon him ; and may therefore mercifully mark him out for sufferings, as foreseeing of what use they will be towards the bringing him to a sense of his sins and to be a serious repentance : whereas others, who are more hardened in their vices and follies, He may totally reject as past cure ; and so may let them go on and prosper for a time, until death comes and brings them a summons to a higher and more dreadful visitation. But here, perhaps, you might ask, Why should such or such sinners be singled out for examples rather than others, and refused the privilege of a longer time to repent in, if they were not greater and more grievous sinners than the rest ? To which I answer : First, supposing them to have been all equally guilty (which was indeed the supposition I have proceeded upon), yet it might be necessary to cut off some, and some rather than all ; and, in such a case, God might choose to single out such as He saw proper to animadvert upon, while His mercy is free to pass by others. But further, it should be considered that those who are spared, except they repent, are in a worse condition than those who have already suffered ; their judgment is respited only, and deferred for a time, to fall the heavier at the last. So that, though they have some favour shown them, in being spared so long, they have the more to account for ; and, without repentance, will at length pay dear for their privilege. But, I must add thirdly, that, supposing the offenders not to be equally guilty, yet God may, if He pleases, and very justly too, cut off the best first, and spare the worst, for two very plain reasons : one, because the best may sufficiently deserve it, and God may do as He pleases. The other, because that, if it were His constant method always to take vengeance upon the worst first, many would be thereby encouraged to go on in their sins, as long as they should imagine there were yet any men left alive more wicked than themselves. (D. Waterland, D.D.) *Thorpe's repentance :*—In the days of Whitfield, Thorpe, one of his most violent opponents, and three others, laid a wager who could best imitate and ridicule Whitfield's preaching. Each was to open the Bible at random, and preach an extempore sermon from the first verse that presented itself. Thorpe's three competitors each went through the game with impious buffoonery. Then, stepping upon the table, Thorpe exclaimed, "I shall beat you all." They gave him the Bible, and by God's inscrutable providence, his eye fell first upon this verse, "Except ye repent, ye shall all likewise perish." He read the words, but the sword of the Spirit went through his soul in a moment, and he preached as one who scarce knew what he said. The hand of God laid hold upon him, and, intending to mock, he could only fear and tremble. When he descended from the table a profound silence reigned in the company, and not one word was said concerning the wager. Thorpe instantly withdrew; and after a season of the deepest distress, passed into the full light of the gospel, and became a most successful preacher of its grace. *Love in warning :*—That father who sees his son tottering toward the brink of a precipice, and, as he sees him, cries out sharply, "Stop, stop!"—does not that father love his son? That tender mother who sees her infant on the point of eating some poisonous berry, and cries out sharply, "Stop, stop! put it down!"—does not that mother love that child? It is indifference that lets people alone, and allows them to go on every one in his own way. It is love, tender love, that warns and raises the cry of alarm. The cry of "Fire! fire!" at midnight, may sometimes startle a man out of his sleep, rudely, harshly, unpleasantly. But who would complain if that cry was the means of saving his life? The words, "Except ye repent, ye shall all perish," may seem at first sight stern and severe. But they are words of love, and may be the means of delivering precious souls from hell. (*Bishop Ryle.*) *Terror not necessary to repentance :*—There are those who will not come into God's kingdom unless they can come as Dante went into paradise—by going through hell. They wish to walk over the burning marl, and to snuff the sulphurous air. If a man has done wrong, his own thoughts should turn him to reparation; but if they do not, the first intimation from the injured friend should suffice. (*H. W. Beecher.*) *Repentance :*—1. Repentance is a difficult work, God must work it. It is not in man's power (2 Tim. ii. 25). And He peradventure will give it, no man is certain of it. It is a supernatural grace not only above nature corrupted, but nature created; for man in innocency had no need of it. 2. It is a necessary work. Our Saviour before showed the necessity of it—"Except you repent, you shall all perish" (vers. 3, 5). So Matt. iii. 10. Turn or burn, there is no remedy. 3. And it is a most excellent grace. A fair daughter of a foul mother. She looks backward, and moves forward; is herself a dark cloud, yet brings a fair sunshine. Is this a riddle to you? I will read it. Sin is the mother, repentance is the daughter, the mother is black and ugly, the daughter fair and lovely: God is the Father of repentance, and He could never endure the mother sin, but hates her society; being born, she slew her mother, for by repentance sin is slain, and in so doing God doth bless her; she no sooner receives breath, but she cries for pardon and forgiveness. Miracles she works. The blind eyes are by her made to see the filthiness of sin; the deaf ear she causeth to hear the word of truth, the dumb lips to cry out for grace, and the heart that was dead, becomes now alive to God, and the devil that ruled in it is now expelled. She looks backward to sins past, and is humbled for them, yet she moves forward to holiness and perfection. In short, repentance is herself cloudy, and made up of sadness, yet everlasting joy and happiness doth attend it. (*N. Rogers.*) **Or those eighteen.**—*Errors respecting the providence of God :*—It is probably in part the cause, and partly the effect, of the idea of gloom and sadness that we are far too apt to associate with religion, that we regard God so much as if He were only the sender of evil and not of good, as if He indeed sent the dark cloud that occasionally casts its shadow across our path, but had no concern with the bright and gladsome sunshine that habitually enlivens it. Judge for yourselves. Suppose that some being that knew nothing of God were to become an inmate of one of our dwellings, and were to derive all his knowledge of Him from our conversation, is not the probability that he would first and oftenest hear His name mentioned in connection with some calamity, and that he would form the idea that we regarded Him as some mysterious power who had to do only with sickness, and death, and funerals? Now, it is doubtless well that we should recognize the hand of God in the evils that befal us; and a most blessed thing it is that we can resort to Him in the day of sore distress, when our hearts are ready to sink within us, and we feel that all others than He are miserable comforters; but surely it is not well that we should shut Him out from our thoughts when all goes well with us. We treat God very much as an unkind husband treats his wife, giving her the blame of all that goes amiss in the domestic affairs, forgetting that it is to her prudence and good management that he is indebted for innumerable and often unthought-of comforts.

Another misconception into which we habitually fall respecting the Divine Providence is to think of it as only having to do with the great and striking events of our lives, and not with the daily and hourly occurrences, which are individually small and scarcely thought of, but which, in the aggregate, make up very nearly the whole of our lives. It may have happened to some of us to be delivered from great and imminent danger, in circumstances in which it was almost impossible to avoid recognizing the finger of God ; and it is well if we have felt due gratitude for such a deliverance. But if we viewed the matter aright, ought we not constantly to be filled with gratitude to Him for keeping us from falling into danger ? Is the continuance of health not as great and as special a blessing as the recovery from sickness ? When some harrowing calamity occurs in our neighbourhood, we feel that those who have been in the midst of it, and who have escaped unscathed, have a loud call addressed to them for thankfulness and praise ; but does it ever occur to us, that if there be any difference, the call is still louder to us for gratitude, because we have been kept out of the danger itself ? Depend upon it, that for one great event in our lives in which we see the hand of God's providence visibly at work, there are ten thousand small events in which it is not less really, though less manifestly, at work. It was a received maxim amongst a particular sect of the old heathen philosophers, that Jupiter had no leisure to attend to small affairs ; but it is our blessed privilege to know regarding Jehovah, that, whilst He counts the number of the stars, and calls them all by their names, He superintends the fall of every raindrop, and directs the course of every sun-ray, and clothes the lilies of the field with glory, and feeds the young ravens when they cry to Him ; that, whilst He rules over the destinies of states and empires, He watches over the flight of every sparrow, and numbers the very hairs on the heads of His people. (*T. Smith, D.D.*) *The bad and good use of God's signal judgments upon others :*— I. The wrong use which men are apt to make of the extraordinary and signal judgments of God upon others ; and that is, to be uncharitable and censorious towards others, which is commonly consequent upon a gross and stupid neglect of ourselves. For men do not usually entertain and cherish this censorious humour for its own sake, but in order to some farther end ; they are not so uncharitable merely out of spite and malice to others, but out of self-flattery and a fond affection to themselves. This makes them forward to represent others to all the disadvantage that may be, and to render them as bad as they can, that they themselves may appear less evil in their own eyes, and may have a colour to set off themselves by the comparison. It is the nature of guilt to flee from itself, and to use all possible art to hide and lessen it. II. More particularly consider some of the rash conclusions which men are apt to draw from the judgments of God upon others, whether upon public societies and communities of men, or upon particular persons. 1. It is rash, where there is no Divine revelation in the case, to be peremptory as to the particular sin or kind of it ; so as to say, that for such a sin God sent such a judgment upon a particular person, or upon a company of men, unless the judgment be a natural effect and consequent of such a sin ; as, if a drunken man die of a surfeit, or a lewd person of a disease that is the proper effect of such a vice, or if the punishment ordained by law for such a crime overtake the offender ; in these and such-like cases, it is neither rash nor uncharitable to say, such a mischief befel a man for such a fault ; because such an evil is evidently the effect of such a sin : but in other cases, peremptorily to conclude is great rashness. Thus the heathens of old laid all those fearful judgments of God, which fell upon the Roman empire in the first ages of Christianity, upon the Christians, as if they had been sent by God on purpose to testify His displeasure against that new sect of religion. And thus every party deals with those that are opposite to them, out of a fond persuasion that God is like themselves, and that He cannot but hate those whom they hate, and punish those whom they would punish, if the sway and government of things were permitted to them. 2. It is rash, likewise, for any man, without revelation, to conclude peremptorily, that God must needs in His judgments only have respect to some late and fresh sins, which were newly committed ; and that all His arrows are only levelled against those impieties of men which are now upon the stage, and in present view. This is rash and groundless ; and men herein take a measure of God by themselves, and because they are mightily affected with the present, and sensible of a fresh provocation, and want to revenge themselves while the heat is upon them, therefore they think God must do so too. But there is nothing occasions more mistakes in the world about God and His providence than to bring

Him to our standard, and to measure His thoughts by our thoughts, and the ways and methods of His providence by our ways. Justice in God is a wise, and calm, and steady principle, which, as to the time and circumstances of its exercise, is regulated by His wisdom. 3. It is rash to conclude from little circumstances of judgments, or some fanciful parallel betwixt the sin and the punishment, what sinners, and what persons in particular, God designed to punish by such a calamity. There is scarce anything betrays men more to rash and ungrounded censures and determinations concerning the judgments of God, than a superstitious observation of some little circumstances belonging to them, and a conceit of a seeming parallel between such a sin and such a judgment. In the beginning of the Reformation, when Zuinglius was slain in a battle by the papists, and his body burnt, his heart was found entire in the ashes ; from whence (saith the historian) his enemies concluded the obdurateness of his heart ; but his friends, the firmness and sincerity of it in the true religion. Both these censures seem to be built upon the same ground of fancy and imagination : but it is a wise and well-grounded observation which Thuanus, the historian (who was himself of the Roman communion), makes upon it—" Thus " (says he) " men's minds being prejudiced beforehand by love or hatred (as it commonly falls out in differences of religion), each party superstitiously interprets the little circumstances of every event in favour of itself." Everything hath two handles ; and a good wit and a strong imagination may find something in every judgment, whereby he may, with some appearance of reason, turn the cause of the judgment upon his adversary. Fancy is an endless thing ; and if we will go this way to work, then he that hath the best wit is like to be the best interpreter of God's judgments. 4. It is rash, likewise, to determine anything concerning the end and consequence of God's judgments. 5. And lastly, It is rashness to determine that those persons, or that part of the community upon which the judgments of God do particularly fall, are greater sinners than the rest who are untouched by it. And this is the very case our Saviour instanceth here in the text. And this brings me to the—III. Third particular I proposed, which was to show HOW UNREASONABLE IT IS FOR MEN TO DRAW ANY SUCH UNCHARITABLE CONCLUSIONS FROM THE JUDGMENTS OF GOD UPON OTHERS, THAT THEY ARE GREATER SINNERS THAN OTHERS ; AND LIKEWISE, HOW FOOLISH IT IS FROM HENCE TO TAKE ANY COMFORT AND ENCOURAGEMENT TO OURSELVES, THAT BECAUSE WE ESCAPE THOSE CALAMITIES WHICH HAVE BEFALLEN OTHERS, THEREFORE WE ARE BETTER THAN THEY. Our Saviour vehemently denies that either of these conclusions can justly be made from the remarkable judgments of God which befall others and pass by us—" I tell you, Nay : but except ye repent, ye shall all likewise perish." 1. It is very unreasonable for men to draw any such uncharitable conclusions concerning others, that because the judgments of God fall upon them, that therefore they are greater sinners than others. For—(1) What do we know but that God may inflict those evils upon those particular persons for secret ends and reasons, only known to His own infinite wisdom, and fit to be concealed from us ? What do we know but He may afflict such a person in a remarkable manner, purely in the use of His sovereignty, without any special respect to the sins of such a person as being greater than the sins of other men ; but yet for some great end, very worthy of His wisdom and goodness? (2) What do we know but that God may send these calamities upon some particular persons in mercy to the generality ; and upon some particular places in a nation out of kindness to the whole? It is foolish likewise to take any comfort and encouragement to ourselves that, because we have escaped those sore judgments which have befallen others, therefore we are better than they are ; for (as I have shown) these judgments do not necessarily import that those upon whom they fall are greater sinners, and that those who escape them are not so : but suppose it true, that they were greater sinners than we are, for any man from hence to take encouragement to himself to continue in sin, is as if, from the severe punishment which is inflicted upon a traitor, a man should encourage himself in felony ; both these sorts of criminals are by the law in danger of death, only the circumstances of death are in one case more severe and terrible than in the other ; but he that from hence encourageth himself in felony, reasons very ill, because he argues against his own life. The only prudent inference that can be made, is, not to come within the danger of the law, which punisheth all crimes, though not with equal severity. Thus I have done with the first thing I propounded to speak to from these words, viz. : The wrong use which too many are apt to make of the signal and extraordinary judgments of God upon others. I proceed to the second thing I observed in the text, viz. : The right use we should make of the judgments

of God upon others; and that is, to reflect upon our own sins, and to repent of
them, lest a like or greater judgment overtake us. This our Saviour tells us in the
next words, "But except ye repent, ye shall all likewise perish." I shall only draw
an inference or two from what I have already discoursed upon these two heads.
1. Let us adore the judgments of God, and instead of searching into the particular
reasons and ends of them, let us say with St. Paul (Rom. xi. 33). 2. Let us not
be rash in our censures and determinations concerning the judgments of God upon
others; let us not wade beyond our depth into the secrets of God: for "who hath
known the mind of the Lord, or who hath been His counsellor?" (*Archbishop
Tillotson.*) *Lessons from accidents :*—I. THE CONTRADICTION OF A GREAT ERROR
IN JUDGMENT. Our blessed Redeemer here teaches us by example to seize upon the
events which transpire around us, and to turn them to the improvement of those
who hear of them. Some ungenerous Jews informed Him of the barbarous and
impious way in which Pilate had taken vengeance upon some Galileans, "mingling
their blood with their sacrifices"; in reply to whom Jesus referred them to another
case, not of Galileans, but of "dwellers at Jerusalem," not by the hands of man,
but by the hand of God; that from these two together He might draw two very
important lessons. 1. The accident which befell those eighteen. They were
buried alive beneath the ruins of a falling tower. A melancholy end! Death,
come at what time and in what form it may, is dreadful, except to those who by
grace are raised above the fear of it—a very few. The approach of it is most appalling to human nature. It is not natural to man to die; it is no part of the original
constitution of his being; and nothing can reconcile most men to it. And it
becomes still more revolting as it is aggravated by circumstances not common. 2.
The inference drawn from this accident. The Jews argued that their sufferings
were the proof of their sins; that their rare doom was evidence of their rare guilt.
This was a common notion among them; and there was some reason in it, for if
left to argue out our own principles, without information or experience, we should
conclude that God would always reward men according to their deserts, and that,
as all suffering is the offspring of sin, the one would be proportioned to the other,
so that the amount of one would indicate the amount of the other. This notion
was greatly confirmed in the mind of the Jew by the peculiar government which
God exercised as the King of Israel, under which His providence did often indicate His pleasure or displeasure, dispensing present blessings and curses according
to His promises and threatenings by Moses. And though this was with the nation
rather than with individuals, there were on record in their Scriptures particular
instances of evident reward both of evil and good which led them to make the
general rule. We, in the same way, knowing that "the curse of the Lord is in
the house of the wicked, but He blesseth the habitation of the just," are apt to
come to their conclusion, and to regard the death of those who perish miserably
as a marked punishment. Therefore we must ponder the third thought in the
text—3. The denial which our Lord gives to this inference. We are not expressly
told what was the intention of those who related to Jesus the cruel assault of
Pilate upon the Galileans at the very altar of God. But we can gather it from the
answer of the Great Teacher, which is evidently not the answer that they desired.
He plainly showed their supposition to be that which I have assumed, by His
direct contradiction of it. "Suppose ye," He said (meaning "Ye suppose") "that
these Galileans were sinners above all the Galileans because they suffered such
things? I tell you, Nay"—which He confirmed by the parallel question and
answer in our text. And if there were any triumph of party spirit in these bearers
of evil tidings, Jesus took it away well by thus turning their attention from the
despised Galileans to their fellow-citizens—teaching them that if the inference
were just in the one case it would be so in the other, yet with Divine impartiality
denying it in both. And this forbids all to draw such an inference, even in
thought. Which prohibition let me strengthen by a fourth consideration—4. The
reasons which there are against such conclusions. It ought to be enough to know
that the principle upon which they are founded is often false, and that it is not in
our power to ascertain whether it be true or false in most cases. Yet I would
deepen the impression by reminding you that such inferences are apt to harden
our feelings and take away our pity—a great evil for us. We cannot but have
more sympathy with an innocent sufferer than with one who is guilty; yet should
human misery in every form and in any man at once awaken our unfeigned and
generous compassion, and keep this alive as long as it lasts. II. THE SUGGESTION
OF A MOST IMPORTANT PERSONAL THOUGHT. Some might suppose from the line of

argument which I have now followed that I do not believe in the special providence of God (though I have really asserted it), and ask, "Is there evil in the city, and the Lord hath not done it?" or if not, does He act without reason? Then I reply, that my unwavering faith is, that whether there be good or evil done in this way, it is the Lord's doing; but persuaded that every event which transpires is the appointment of His providence, I perceive also that He does not make His appointments known to us to gratify our curiosity or to justify our censures; "for He giveth not account of any of His matters," not willing that we should judge His servants in the present state of our ignorance. Moreover, I have followed, not the dictate of my own mind, but the course indicated in the text, the great object of which is to teach us to consider ourselves rather that to censure others; for in it Jesus says, "Except ye repent, ye shall all likewise perish." Awful as was their end, such an end awaits you if you avert it not. In which saying there are three things worthy of notice. 1. The solemnity of this warning. The catastrophe to which our Lord referred was both instant and terrible; and it was the type of that which befel the hapless multitudes dwelling in Jerusalem at the time of its utter destruction. We tremble at the tale, and should have grown sick and faint at the sight, like so many stout men who witnessed it. And does any such doom await any among us? Many, ay, all, but for the grace of God. 2. The reasonableness of this warning. Whether we see it or not, there is reason in everything that God does, and in everything that Christ says. In the last great day, however, the reason shall be evident why some perish and others are preserved; all men shall discern it. It is intimated in our text; they will perish who would not repent, though space was given them for repentance. But where is the necessity for this? One short word is the answer—Sin. 3. The universality of this warning. (*J. Williams.*) ◦ *Sudden and signal calamity improved :*—I. Now, first, let us inquire what are those FALSE CONCLUSIONS which men are apt to draw from the stirring and startling events of providence. 1. The first feeling in the mind of man, when God sends afflictive dispensations, is to lose sight of Divine providence altogether. This is to drive God out of His own world—to refer the thing altogether to second causes. "Oh! it was an accident; it was some chance event; it was some unfortunate circumstance; or it was something which occurred from carelessness, want of watchfulness, want of circumspection, want of foresight and provision"; forgetting a Divine hand, losing sight of an almighty Providence. 2. And this is the second remark I have to make—that when the event which occurs is so marked and peculiar that man cannot altogether lose sight of Divine providence or of the Divine hand, he then is disposed to attribute some special guilt or some special misfortune to the sufferers themselves. He tries to find out some particular circumstances in the case which has occurred that may apply peculiarly and expressly to the parties concerned. II. But now I come, in the second place, to inquire into those SOLID AND IMPORTANT LESSONS which these events are really designed to teach us. 1. Now, of the lessons which this solemn event is intended to teach, the first is this—that we are all standing on the brink of an eternal world. Beloved brethren, it does not require any mighty effort of Jehovah, any vast convulsion of nature, to destroy us or to carry us out of the world. A single spark will do it; a little smouldering spark getting amongst combustible matter, or thrown into any other circumstances in which these accidents by fire occur, is a sufficient agent in the hand of your God to destroy life. A little disorder in any part of the animal frame can do the same. The air you breathe is impregnated with disease. The very ground on which you walk may prove your death. A fall, a stumble—a thousand minute accidents—may kill you. 2. This event reminds us of the punishment due to sin. 3. A loud and most solemn call to repentance. (*D. Wilson, M.A.*)

Vers. 6–9. **A certain man had a fig-tree.**—*The barren fig-tree :*—I. THE FAVOURABLE POSITION IN WHICH THIS TREE WAS PLACED. In a "vineyard"; not on some neglected waste-ground. Under culture and care. This is the condition of those favoured with the privileges and blessings of the gospel dispensation. This is especially the condition of those who are members of the Christian Church. 1. Who have been professedly brought out of the world into the Church. 2. Who are favoured with the spiritual means and ordinances of the gospel. 3. Who are the subjects of the especial and rich promises of the new covenant. 4. Unto whom the graces and blessed influences of the Holy Spirit are freely imparted. 5. Who are the objects of the Divine care and complacency. We are directed—II. To THE EXPECTATIONS OF THE PROPRIETOR. He came seeking fruit (ver. 6). This expectation was reasonable. God expected this from the Jews. He required them to be more wise, and holy, and obedient, than the heathen who surrounded them. God requires this from all favoured with the privileges and blessings of the gospel economy. He particularly requires and expects it from His own professing people—the members of His Church. He expects—1. Their hearts to yield the fruits of holy graces. 2. Their lips to yield the fruit of thanksgiving and praise. 3. The fruits of obedience in the life. 4. The fruits of usefulness, by the employment of their powers and talents in His service. III. THE PROPRIETOR'S DISAPPOINTMENT. IV. THE COMMAND THE PROPRIETOR ISSUES. "Cut it down; why cumbereth it the ground?" (ver. 7). 1. This sentence was not a hasty one. There had been three years' care, and labour, and forbearance. God exercised His great long-suffering towards the Jews. So to men in general. So to fruitless professors in the Church. To all God manifests patient and enduring forbearance. 2. A sufficient reason is assigned for the order given. "Why cumbereth it the ground?" It was worthless in itself. It occupied precious ground. It took up the nutritive portions of the soil, that useful fruitful trees required. V. THE REQUEST THE VINE-DRESSER PRESENTS. "He said, Lord, let it alone this year also," &c. (ver. 8). He denies not the allegations of the owner. He vindicates not the final continuance of the tree. But he entreats—1. For a short period of suspense of the sentence. One year. One year only! One round of the seasons. One year's showers and sunshine. 2. He engages to give it special attention. "I will dig about it, and dung it" (ver. 8). I will try and search out the cause, and use all reasonable means to remedy it. He further adds—3. His willingness then to obey the order of the proprietor. This is not only implied, but directly stated. "If it bear fruit, well"—well for the tree, the proprietor, and the vine-dresser; "And if not, then thou shalt cut it down" (ver. 9). This pleading for the cumberer has often been verified in the prayers of the parent, the friend, the minister; but it is true in the highest and best sense of the Lord Jesus. He ever lives to intercede. (*J. Burns,* *D.D.*) *The barren fig-tree:*—I. Notice THE SITUATION OF THE TREE, the place where it stands. It is in God's vineyard, and our Lord tells us how it came there. The vineyard was not its natural situation. It did not spring up there, nor was it brought there by accident. God Himself had it planted there. An emblem, brethren, of our situation at this hour, and of the way in which we came into it. II. See next WHAT IS EXPECTED FROM THIS TREE. Is it that it shall take root and grow where it is planted, and receive the showers of heaven as they fall on it? We may say, "Yes"; but God says, "No, this will not satisfy Me; what I want of it is fruit—not wide-spreading branches and luxuriant foliage; the wild fig-tree of the desert will give me these. I must have of that tree something answering to the situation in which I have placed it, and to the care and pains I have bestowed on it. I come to it seeking fruit." And what is this fruit? It is not those things which some of us perhaps have now in our minds, the social and moral virtues, charity, honesty, and such like. These are all good in their way, but these are fruits of nature's growth. The wild fig-tree will produce them. The heathen and idolater will bring them forth. The tree our Lord speaks of is a tree in a vineyard, a planted and cultivated tree, and something more than fruit of this common kind is expected from it. God wants fruit from us corresponding to the privileges He has bestowed upon us; not only more fruit than any heathen could render Him, but fruit of another kind—Christian fruit, such fruit as nothing but the gospel of Christ can produce, and none but men planted in His Church, and brought under the influence of that gospel, ever yielded Him. III. And now go on to another point in the parable—THE SCRUTINY THIS FIG-TREE DRAWS ON ITSELF. Observe, the owner of the vineyard does not forget the tree when he has planted it, nor does he sit at home waiting for his servants to bring him the produce of it when there is any; he is described as coming again and again into his vineyard, and going up to this tree and examining it. "He came and sought fruit thereon"; he was anxious about the matter, anxious, not only to gather the fruit if he could find any, but also not to overlook it if there should be some. None watch us like God. We do not see Him as He stands by our side; the great Observer of us is invisible and His scrutiny a silent one; we think no more of Him perhaps than a tree in our garden thinks of us as we walk by it; but He marks every one of us every hour with the most searching attention. He listens to our words, He acquaints Himself with our doings. IV. Observe THE MARVELLOUS PATIENCE OF GOD WITH THIS UNFRUITFUL TREE. "Behold, these three years I come seeking fruit on this fig-tree, and find none." There is surprise, you observe, expressed in this language; surprise, it may be, at the unfruitfulness of such a tree in such a place; but still more, it is surprise at God's patience towards Him, that these words seem chiefly to express. The Lord speaks in them as though He Himself were wondering at His own patience. V. But mark THE DISPLEASURE EXPRESSED AT LAST AGAINST THIS UNFRUITFUL TREE. It is a displeasure which has long been kept under. It comes upon us after long forbearance with us. It is something which has triumphed over great love and great patience; not the flowing of a stream that has always had a free course, moving along in an unobstructed channel, it is a river bursting through barriers which have long damned it up, and pouring forth its accumulated waters in a desolating heap. Look here. The patient owner of this tree becomes all at once determined on its destruction. For three years he goes up to it, searching among its leaves for fruit; he comes away disappointed, but yet silent. There is no blaming of the tree, no complaining of it. The people in the vineyard, who have witnessed all this, may have ceased to notice it, or if they still notice it, they may say, "That tree is safe. Unfruitful as it is, for some strange reason our master loves it, and so well does he love it that he will never remove it." But all at once comes the command, "Cut it down; why cumbereth it the ground?" And what follows? Is the tree at once levelled? No; for notice—VI. THE INTERCESSION MADE FOR IT. The dresser of the vineyard answering, said unto him, "Lord, let it alone this year also, till I shall dig about it and dung it; and if it bear fruit, well; and if not, then after that thou shalt cut it down." Here, doubtless, a heavenly scene is laid open to us. There is but one Mediator who can interpose effectually between God and man. Ministers, parents, and friends, may say concerning this or that sinner, "Lord, let him alone"; but Christ is not thinking here of any of these. He has Himself in His thoughts; He is anticipating His employment at His Father's right hand whither He is going. He is the vinedresser who pleads for this worthless tree to save it from destruction. And how natural and touching are the terms in which His intercession is made! Not one word does He utter against this barren tree. Not one word does He say of all the labour He has bestowed upon it. With a wonderful pity and condescension, He seems to trace its long unfruitfulness to His own neglect. "Lord, let it alone. The fault may be mine. I have not done for it all I might. Henceforth I will do more. It shall become the special object of My labour and care." And then comes in these words a glance at all the glorious consequences that would follow. "If it bear fruit, well," our translators say, but there is no word answering to "well" in the original. Our Lord does not say what would follow the fruitfulness of this tree. He breaks off as though He could not say. It seems as though all the glory and delight resulting to His Father and Himself from a sinner's salvation had rushed into His mind and silenced Him. "If it bear fruit— O, the happiness for that poor sinner, and O, the unutterable joy for Thee and Me!" But, mark you, it is only a year that the Intercessor asks for this tree, one year, a limited season. After that, He says, He will interpose no longer; and more—He will acquiesce in the sentence of its destruction; "Thou shalt cut it down." I know not, brethren, how this language may strike some of you, but there seems to me something very fearful in it. Who is it that promises here to acquiesce after a little in the entire destruction of every unfruitful hearer of God's truth among us? It is none other than He who has shed His heart's blood for our salvation, and who has all our life long been pleading that we may be spared. It is painful to have a kind earthly friend give us up, but to be given up, and given up to certain destruction, by the blessed Jesus, the kindest of all friends, One who bears with and loves us as none but Himself can bear and love—think what we will of it, there is something appalling in this. It is like a father who has cherished fondly a son, a worthless son, while all around have been calling out for justice on him—it is like that father's being at last forced to say, "I can hold out no longer. I can do no more. Let justice have him." (*C. Bradley, M.A.*) *The parable of the barren fig-tree:*—I. FROM THE SCOPE OF THE PARABLE WE MAY NOTE—1. That temporal judgments inflicted on some should excite others to fear God's Divine wrath and vengeance. 2. No person ought to be rash to censure others on whom temporal judgments befall: there is no knowing either love or hatred by anything that is under the sun. II. EXPLAIN THE TERMS. 1. By "a certain man," is meant the great God. 2. By "vineyard" is meant the Church of God. (1) The Church is taken out of the field of this world. (2) Walled or fenced in. (a) Defended by special providences, &c. (b) By holy angels. 3. But why does our Lord compare professors of religion to fig-trees? (1) He may allude to the practice of those who had vineyards in the land of Canaan, in which they frequently planted not only vines, but fig-trees. (2) It may be because a fig-tree that brings forth good figs requires much heat of the sun. So professors of Christianity cannot thrive so as to bring forth good fruit, but under the Divine and warm influences of the Sun of Righteousness, and the blessed gospel of God's grace. (3) Because no tree is commonly more fruitful than the fig-tree. (4) A fig-tree bears choice fruit. (5) Fig-trees bear fruit all the year (see Jer. xvii. 7 ; Psa. xcii. 12-14). (6) There are some barren fig-trees ; they are not of the right kind, but seem a bastard sort of plants. So some professors, who, though they are planted in Christ's vineyard, yet are barren or fruitless; they are not true believers, but mere counterfeits, professors, that have the name of spiritual fig-trees, but not the nature. 4. "Came and sought fruit thereon." (1) God takes notice of every particular person that is planted in His vineyard. (2) God expects fruit from each. (3) If there be but one member in the Church that is fruitless, God will soon find him out. 5. By " three years," I understand to be meant that time God is pleased to afford to a people, a certain time being here mentioned to denote an uncertain. (1) The first year may denote the beginning of the means of grace, which God affords to men. (2) The second year, the proper time that fig-trees bear fruit, if not the first year, then it is expected that it brings forth fruit the second. (3) Or it may imply that God expects sinners should bring forth quickly after they sit under the means of grace. (4) Moreover, it may denote that the means of grace may not be of long continuance. (5) Also it may signify God's patience. 6. "Cut it down," &c. God will not always bear with fruitless professors. (1) God may direct His speech to His Church, and to the subordinate vinedressers. " Cut it down " by excommunication. (2) Or God may speak to Jesus Christ. Smite his root, let him wither. (3) Give him up to his own heart's lust. (4) Leave him to delusions. (5) Death. Inferences : 1. Let such as are planted in God's vineyard tremble if not fruitful in grace. The Church will be no sanctuary to such. 2. Some who are in Christ's vineyard were never planted there by God. 3. Men may have leaves, and even the appearance of fruit, and may seem to grow and flourish for a time, yet, nevertheless, may not bring forth the true and saving fruits of the Spirit. 4. The barren soul shall not stand long in God's vineyard. 7. The reason why this barren fig-tree is cut down. (1) It is good for nothing. (2) Another tree might grow where it stands. (a) Barren professors cumber poor ministers by their cross and peevish spirits. (b) They cumber the spirits of their pious parents. (c) They cumber the minds of serious Christians, members of the same Church, who are ashamed to hear of their pride, passion, idleness, &c. (d) They are a sad incumbrance to the whole vineyard. (e) They are cumbersome to God Himself (Isa. i. 14). (f) They grieve and afflict the Spirit of the Lord Jesus Christ. (g) They grieve the Holy Spirit. 8. "Let it alone this year also." (1) Barren souls are spared through Christ's prayer and intercession. (2) God is slow to anger, unwilling immediately to cut down unfruitful professors. 9. Why does Christ intercede for sinners? (1) Because He died for them. (2) Because He ever lives to make intercession with the Father. (3) Because He knows that if He interceded not, no sinner could live a moment longer. (*B. Keach.*) *The fig-tree spared another year :*—I. OF THOSE WHO HAVE A PLACE IN THE CHURCH OF CHRIST, SOME ARE BUT BARREN PROFESSORS. Even among the twelve there was a traitor ; and Christ has forewarned us that there will always be hypocrites mingled with His people. By the barren fig-tree, however, is meant, not only the plausible hypocrite, but all merely nominal Christians ; all who, having the means of grace, do not improve them. Yes, my brethren, all of you are included, who, while you attend in this house of God ; while you bend the knee before Him ; while, sabbath after sabbath, you hear the gospel-sound, listen to its warnings, its invitations, its free and gracious promises ; to whom, monthly, are offered the sacramental pledges of redeeming love : still continue far from the kingdom of God ; by your life and conversation show, that you are none the better for the opportunities you enjoy ; still live in indulged sin, or, at least, bring forth no fruit to the glory of God ; are still careless, irreligious, worldly, vain. II. THE BARREN PROFESSOR CANNOT ESCAPE THE SEARCHING EYE OF GOD. He sees the heart and inmost thoughts. He cannot, and will not, be mocked. III. GOD EXPECTS FRUIT FROM US. And justly so. 1. Ask yourselves, then, brethren, do you bear fruit answering to your profession of repentance? Are you risen from an unconverted state, and walking in newness of life? 2. Do you bear fruit answerable to your profession of faith? You profess to believe in Him who has bought you with His blood. Are you living no more to yourselves, but to Him who died for you? 3. Is the fruit you bear suitable to the opportunities and means of grace which you enjoy? Highly are you favoured, brethren; you are members of a pure Church; you assemble to a pure form of worship. The Word of God, the sacraments are yours; to you is the gospel preached. Might not the Lord of the vineyard have laid the axe to the root? Why is it thou art spared? Because God is patient long suffering, merciful, and He would have thee repent. IV. OBSERVE THAT IN JUDGMENT GOD REMEMBERS MERCY. Well might justice say, "Cut it down." But there is an Advocate in heaven. Behold One interceding at God's right hand: "Let it alone this year also, till I shall dig about it and dung it: and if it bear fruit, well." Blessed be God, for us mercy hath rejoiced against judgment. We are yet spared; and to what end hath Christ Jesus been thus long-suffering? It is that He may show yet richer goodness; that He may try more abundant means. "Let it alone, till I shall dig about it, and dung it." "And if it bear fruit, well." All care and pains will have been well bestowed, if, after all, the sinner bear fruit to God. God's mercy will be magnified; His grace exalted. V. And now, lastly, OBSERVE THE SURE DOOM OF THOSE WHO CONTINUE STILL UNFRUITFUL:—"If not" (if the tree then bear no fruit), "then after that thou shalt cut it down." It is, then, possible to weary out the patience of God Himself. It is possible, by a hard and impenitent heart, to let the day of grace go by. There may, there will come a time, when mercy shall cease to plead, and leave room for judgment only; when Christ Himself will give up His intercession. O, awful state! when the Saviour Himself withdraws; when His Spirit, grieved, resisted, quenched, finally quits the stony heart. Then follows death-like insensibility—a fearful apathy to all spiritual things, or, it may be, a daily growth in all iniquity, till at length the sinner's cup is full. (E. Blencowe, M.A.)   The barren fig-tree:—I. THE PLANTATION OF THE FIG-TREE. 1. This "certain man" denotes God. To Him everything belongs. "The earth is His, and the fulness thereof; the world, and they that dwell therein." But the Church is peculiarly His, as it is called by His name, and formed to show forth His praise. 2. But who is intended by the fig-tree? It cannot be a real Christian. All the truly regenerate are fruitful. They are not equally, but they are really, fruitful. The character here intended is a man placed in the external and visible Church, and enjoying all the privileges of such a favoured situation. It was once the highly favoured Jew. It is now the highly favoured Christian, blessed with all the religious advantages of Judaism, multiplied, improved, perfected: it is now the highly favoured Briton, born not only in a land of freedom and science, but of gospel grace. It is thou who wast brought up in a godly family, and favoured with the prayers, the instructions, the examples, the tears, of pious parents. It is thou who hast a name and a place in His sanctuary, from Sabbath to Sabbath, where "thine eyes see thy teachers: and thy ears hear a voice behind thee, saying, This is the way, walk ye in it, when you turn to the right hand, and when you turn to the left." II. THE COMPLAINT OF THE PROPRIETOR. 1. His observation. 2. His disappointment. 3. His patience. "These three years." Why did He not complain the first year? Why did He not destroy it the second year? Why does He bear with it to the end of the third? Why?—To teach us that judgment is His strange work—that He delighteth in mercy; that He waiteth to be gracious; that He is longsuffering to us-ward, not willing that any should perish, but that all should come to repentance. III. THE SENTENCE OF DESTRUCTION—"Cut it down; why cumbereth it the ground?" Here we see—1. That they who derive no benefit from the means of grace are detrimental. 2. Unprofitableness under the means of grace is exceedingly provoking to the Most High. And can we wonder at this when we consider what a waste it is of time; what an abuse it is of privilege; what a contempt it is of the Divine goodness; what a disregard it is of the soul and eternity! Sin is to be estimated not by its grossness, but its guilt. And what aggravates guilt? The light we possess; the obligations we are under; the restraints we break through. 3. God possesses justice as well as mercy; and though He bears long, He will not bear always. "Sentence against an evil work is not executed speedily"; and, as the consequence, the heart of the sons of men is often fully set in them to do evil. But how absurd, as well as dangerous, is such perverse reasoning! Is forbearance forgiveness? No. IV. THE INTERCESSION OF THE VINE-DRESSER. 1. He pleads for the suspension of the stroke. "Let it alone this year also." Thou hast borne with it long, I own, already; oh! bear with it a little longer. And why is He so desirous of sparing the sinner a little longer in this world? Because, in order to our having the grace *of* repentance, it is necessary that we should have space *for* repentance : because while there is life there is hope; but "when once the master of the house is risen up, and hath shut to the door," opportunity is over, importunity vain. 2. He engages to use additional means to produce fertility—" Till I dig about it, and dung it." The Word shall be preached with more fervour than before. The minister shall be particular in describing his case, in alarming his fears. Friends shall warn, admonish, invite. Conscience shall awake and reprove. Disappointments shall show him the vanity of the world. Sickness shall invade his frame. Death shall enter his family, and smite a connection by his side. The day in which he lives shall be dark and cloudy. He shall hear of "distress of nations with perplexity; the sea and the waves roaring ; men's hearts failing them for fear, and for looking after those things which are coming on the earth: for the powers of heaven shall be shaken." And can he retain his ungodliness through such a year as this? 3. Here is the supposition of future produce. "If it bear fruit, well." Well for the owner (John xv. 8). Well for the vine-dresser, as his labours will be rewarded. Well for the vineyard ; it will be adorned, enriched, and replenished. Well for the tree itself, as it will escape the punishment of barrenness, and obtain the blessing of fruitfulness. 4. Here is the doom of final impenitence. Even the patience of the Saviour may be exhausted. (*W. Jay.*) *Judgment threatening, but mercy sparing :*—I. To all unprofitable, untruthful sinners, we utter this hard, but needful sentence: TO CUT YOU DOWN WOULD BE MOST REASONABLE. It is right and reasonable to fell barren trees, and it is just as right and reasonable that you should be cut down. 1. This will appear in the first place, if we reflect that this is the shortest and the surest way to deal with you ; it will cost the least trouble, and be most certainly effectual in removing you from the place to which you are an injury rather than a benefit. 2. Another reason makes the argument for judgment very powerful, namely, that sufficient space for repentance has already been given. 3. Sinner, I argue thy case somewhat harshly, thou thinkest. All this while there has been no sign of improvement whatever in thee. 4. But there are other reasons why " Cut it down " is most reasonable, when we consider the owner and the other trees. (1) First of all, here is a tree which brings forth no fruit whatever, and therefore is of no service. It is like money badly invested, bringing in no interest ; it is a dead loss to the owner. What is the use of keeping it ? The dead tree is neither use nor ornament ; it can yield no service and afford no pleasure. Cut it down by all manner of means. And even so with thee, sinner ; what is the use of thee ? (2) But there is a worse consideration, namely, that all this while you have been filling up a space which somebody might have been filling to the glory of God. Where that barren tree stands there might have been a tree loaded with fruit. (3) Moreover, and to make bad worse even to the worst degree, all this while ungodly men are spreading an evil influence. II. Our second most solemn work is to remind thee, O impenitent sinner, that FOR GOD TO HAVE SPARED YOU SO LONG IS A VERY WONDERFUL THING. That the infinitely just and holy God should have spared you, unconverted man, unconverted woman, up till now, is no small thing, but a matter for adoring wonder. 1. Let me show you this. Consider, negatively, God is not sparing you because He is insensible towards your sins : He is angry with the wicked every day. 2. It is not because the offence is at a distance, and therefore far from His observant eye. 3. Mark, sinner, He has spared you not because He was unable to have destroyed you. He might have bidden the tiles fall from the roof, or the fever might have smitten you in the street ; the air might have refused to heave your lungs, or the blood might have ceased its circulation in your veins. The gates to death are many. The quiver of judgment is full of sharp arrows. The Lord has but to will it, and your soul is required of you. You will be no more missed than one sere leaf is missed in a forest, or one dewdrop in a thousand leagues of grass. Judgment needs but a word to work its utmost vengeance, and withal you are so provoking that the marvel is that Divine severity has spared you so long. Admire and wonder at this longsuffering. 4. Remember that this wonder is increased, when you think of the fruit He deserved to have had of you. A God so good and so gracious ought to have been loved by you. 5. And ah, my hearers ! I have to touch upon a very solemn part of the business now, when I notice again that some, perhaps, here present have been guilty of very God-provoking sins. Shall God be always provoked ? Shall mercy be preached to you for ever in vain ? It is a marvel, it is a wonder that these God-provoking sins have so long been borne with, and that you are not yet cut down. III. And now, WHAT ɪꜱ ᴛʜᴇ ʀᴇᴀꜱᴏɴ ꜰᴏʀ ᴀʟʟ ᴛʜɪꜱ ʟᴏɴɢꜱᴜꜰꜰᴇʀɪɴɢ? Why is it that this cumber-ground tree has not been cut down? The answer is, because there is One who pleads for sinners. But what has been the secret cause that you have been kept alive? The answer is, Jesus Christ has pleaded for you, the crucified Saviour has interfered for you. And you ask me "Why?" I answer, because Jesus Christ has an interest in you all. (*C. H. Spurgeon.*)   *Lessons from the fig-tree:*—1. This parable cuts up all pleas of negative goodness. Unproductiveness is decidedly criminal. 2. This parable calls on you to examine yourselves, whether you be barren or fruitful; and to follow out the result aright, whatever it may be. 3. This parable calls on us all to be thankful to the Lord for sparing us hitherto. It gives this call to us without exception, and especially if any of us have been spared in the time of great danger, restored from severe sickness. 4. Let none of us so abuse God's sparing mercy as to presume on it for the future; but let us all improve the present season without delay, and hold ourselves in constant readiness for death. (*Jas. Foote, M.A.*)   *The barren fig-tree:*—The principles underlying this parable are, briefly, these : That much will be required of those to whom much has been given; that, if those to whom much has been given fail to meet that which is required of them, sentence of destruction will be pronounced against them ; and that, though the execution of this sentence may be deferred at the intercession of Christ, it will certainly be carried out if there be no repentance and amendment manifested. I. Gᴏᴅ ʜᴀꜱ ᴘʟᴀᴄᴇᴅ ᴜꜱ ɪɴ ᴛʜᴇ ᴍᴏꜱᴛ ꜰᴀᴠᴏᴜʀᴀʙʟᴇ ᴄɪʀᴄᴜᴍꜱᴛᴀɴᴄᴇꜱ ꜰᴏʀ ᴛʜᴇ ʙʀɪɴɢɪɴɢ ꜰᴏʀᴛʜ ᴏꜰ ꜰʀᴜɪᴛ. The privileges of the Jews were small in comparison with those which we enjoy. They had the prophets; we have the Son of God. Let us never forget that responsibility is proportional to privilege. II. Gᴏᴅ ᴇxᴘᴇᴄᴛꜱ ᴇxᴄᴇᴘᴛɪᴏɴᴀʟ ꜰʀᴜɪᴛ ꜰʀᴏᴍ ᴀ ᴛʀᴇᴇ ᴏɴ ᴡʜɪᴄʜ Hᴇ ʜᴀꜱ ʙᴇꜱᴛᴏᴡᴇᴅ ꜱᴜᴄʜ ᴇxᴄᴇᴘᴛɪᴏɴᴀʟ ᴀᴅᴠᴀɴᴛᴀɢᴇꜱ. If we *have* so much more than others, we ought to *be* just so much better than they. The fruit in this case is that of character—what we are rather than what we do: what we do only in so far as that is the genuine outcome and spontaneous revelation of what we are. Righteousness, meekness, fidelity—in a word, moral excellence springing from our faith in Christ, and our devotion to Him—that is the fruit which God expects to find in us as the occupants of His vineyard. III. Gᴏᴅ ᴘʀᴏɴᴏᴜɴᴄᴇꜱ ꜱᴇɴᴛᴇɴᴄᴇ ᴏꜰ ᴅᴇꜱᴛʀᴜᴄᴛɪᴏɴ ᴏɴ ᴀʟʟ ᴡʜᴏ, ʜᴀᴠɪɴɢ ʜᴀᴅ ꜱᴜᴄʜ ᴘʀɪᴠɪʟᴇɢᴇꜱ, ʙʀɪɴɢ ꜰᴏʀᴛʜ ɴᴏ ꜰʀᴜɪᴛ (see John xv. 6; Matt. vii. 19). The Jews are one example of this ; the seven Churches in Asia are another. If we wish to secure permanent prosperity, we must remember that we can do so only by maintaining constant fruitfulness in works of faith and labours of love, and holiness of character. When these disappear, and barrenness sets in, then there will come the sentence, "Cut it down." IV. Tʜɪꜱ ꜱᴇɴᴛᴇɴᴄᴇ, ᴘʀᴏɴᴏᴜɴᴄᴇᴅ ᴏɴ ᴛʜᴇ ʙᴀʀʀᴇɴ ꜰɪɢ-ᴛʀᴇᴇ, ɪꜱ ɴᴏᴛ ᴀᴛ ᴏɴᴄᴇ ᴄᴀʀʀɪᴇᴅ ɪɴᴛᴏ ᴇxᴇᴄᴜᴛɪᴏɴ. For all such respite as interposes, in any case, between evil desert and its immediate punishment, men are indebted to the intercession of Christ. V. A ʀᴇꜱᴘɪᴛᴇ ɪꜱ ɴᴏᴛ ᴀ ᴘᴀʀᴅᴏɴ. Only a postponement. Take care not to regard God's forbearance, which is meant to give space for repentance, as an actual manifestation of indifference, or approval. Guilt after such forbearance, and against it, will be greater than before.(*W. M. Taylor, D.D.*) *Of Christ seeking fruit, and finding none :*—Those who enjoy the means of fruitfulness should bring forth fruit ; those who are planted in the Lord's vineyard, and have a standing under the means of grace, should be fruitful. This is clear in the words, and indeed in every part of this parable. 1. They are planted in the vineyard for this purpose. That is the proper place for fruit-trees ; another place than the vineyard would serve them, if they were not set there for fruit. 2. The Lord, who gives them place here, expects it. He is said to come and seek fruit (vers. 6, 7). It is that which he has just cause to look for. 3. He heinously resents it when he finds no fruit, and expresses his resentment to the dresser of his vineyard. It is an abuse of his patience; the longer he bears with such barrenness the more it is abused. It is a provocation that he will not bear long with. After three years' forbearance, he passes that severe sentence, "cut it down." 4. It is an injury to the place where they stand. They cumber the ground, that is the reason of the sentence (ver. 7). It takes up that room which might be better employed ; it sucks away that moisture which would make others fruitful ; it over-drops the plants that are under it, hinders the spreading and fruitfulness of others. A better improvement might be made of the ground ; it is a loss to the owner of the vineyard, when such a plant is suffered, καταργεῖ ; which may signify the spending the heart of the ground to no purpose (ver. 7). 5. Those who have most tenderness for such, can have no ground to seek a long forbearance of this barrenness. The dresser of the vineyard will venture to beg no more forbearance than one year, after that he yields it up to excision (vers. 8, 9). 6. All labours and pains, all care and culture, in digging about and dunging it, is lost upon it. Those whom the Lord employs to use all means for their improvement, have nothing left them in the issue, but occasion of sad complaint, that they have laboured in vain, spent their strength for nought (Isa. xlix. 4). 7. Such will certainly be ruined. Where fruit is not found, nothing can be expected but cutting down. The lord of the vineyard will not spare them, and the dressers of the vineyard will not longer intercede for them. All in a little while agree in that fatal conclusion, "cut it down." All these, and each of them, make it evident, that those who are planted under the means of grace, are highly concerned to bring forth fruit. The most pertinent and profitable inquiry, for further clearing of this truth, will be, what fruits it is they should bring forth? What we are to understand by fruit, and that fruitfulness which is so much our duty? And of this I shall give you an account by the quality, quantity, and continuance of it. To these heads we may reduce those severals, whereby the Scriptures express to us what this fruit is. I. For quality. It must be *good* fruit. Grapes, not "wild grapes." 1. Real. A show, an appearance of fruit will not suffice. If it be not real, it has not a metaphysical goodness, much less a moral or spiritual. The fig-tree in the gospel made some show of fruit; but Christ finding none upon it really, He cursed it, and it withered (Matt. xxi. 19). It must not be like the apple of Sodom, which has nothing to commend it, but only a fair outside. Fair appearances may delude men, and pass for better fruit with them than that which is good indeed. But God is not, cannot be mocked; it is He that comes to seek fruit, and it is not the fairest shows will satisfy Him, it must be real. 2. It must be such as imports a change of the soul that brings it forth. 3. It must be distinguishing fruit; such as no trees can bring forth but those that are good, and such as will make their goodness apparent (Matt. vii. 16, 20); such as may approve ye to God and your own consciences to be trees of righteousness, the planted of the Lord, and such as may make this known to men too, so far as by visible acts it may be known; such as may carry a conviction with them to the consciences of others, that you are indeed what you profess yourselves to be, such as will leave them no just exception against it (1 Pet. iii. 16). 4. Seasonable. That it may be good fruit, it must be brought forth "in due season" (Psa. i.; Matt. xxi. 41). The lord of the vineyard looks for fruit in his season (Mark xii. 2; Luke xx. 10). There is a season for everything (Eccles. iii. 1), and then, if ever, it is good. 5. Sound. A fair skin is not enough to commend fruit for good, if it be rotten within. And so is our fruit, if the inward temper and motions of the heart be not correspondent to the outward actions and expressions. II. For the quantity. It ought to be much (John xv. 5, 8). There should be—1. A fulness of fruit. Those that enjoy the means, must not only bring forth fruit, but be fruitful; should bear abundance. Heart and life should be filled with it (Phil. i. 11). 2. A proportionableness to the means of fruitfulness, to the plenty and power of them. So much as will answer the care and pains is taken with them. If a man take more pains, and be at more charge in opening the roots of a tree, and dunging it, and pruning it, in fencing and watering it, and it bring forth less or no more fruit than another that has no such care and pains taken with it, it will scarce pass for a good, a fruitful tree. That is barren ground, which brings forth less, after all care and culture, than that which has less tillage. 3. An increase. Those who enjoy the means of fruitfulness, must grow more and more fruitful. The longer they stand in the vineyard, and continue under the means of grace, the more fruit they should bear. You expect not much of a tree the first year; but after it is of standing to bear, you expect that it should every year increase in fruitfulness, and bring forth more and more. So the Lord expects from us. 4. Variety. Their fruit must not only be much of some sort, but of every sort. They must not only abound in some kind of fruit, but must bring forth fruits of all kinds. III. For continuance. It must be *lasting* fruit. Of which in three particulars. 1. The fruit they bear must continue. It must not wither and come to nothing before the Lord of the vineyard come to reap it. 2. They must continue bearing fruit. The good ground did approve itself to be good, because it brought forth fruit "with patience" (Luke viii. 15). They only are good and fruitful ground, who persevere and hold out in bearing fruit. 3. They must be bearing it always; not only *semper*, as a tree that fails not of fruit once a year, but *ad semper*, as if a tree should bear fruit all the year long. Use 1. This leads us to take up a lamentation for the barrenness of the place, the unfruitfulness of the people of this land. Use 2. For exhortation.

If those that enjoy the means of fruitfulness ought to bring forth, then are you highly concerned to take notice of it as your duty, to be fruitful, and to comply with the Lord herein. (*D. Clarkson, B.D.*) *The parable of the fig-tree :*—I. Those whose lot it is to live within the pale of the visible Church, are a highly favoured people. Compared with the rest of mankind, they are like an enclosed field or garden, in the cultivating or adorning of which the proprietor lays out great pains and expense. II. God requires, and has a right to expect, that those who are so highly favoured should bring forth fruits of a corresponding kind. It is the peculiarity of the gospel that privilege precedes duty, but it is always taken for granted that duty shall follow. III. There is often great ground for lamentation and complaint, that those who are favoured by God, in point of privilege, fail in rendering Him homage. How many are there who despise the goodness, and long-suffering, and forbearance of God! How many are there who know not this the day of their merciful visitation! IV. God is justly and sorely provoked by such conduct. " Cut it down," says He, " why cumbereth it the ground ? " What is the use of its remaining longer, but to fill up room in that garden on which I have bestowed so much pains, to intercept the light of the sun from the other trees that are bearing fruit, to draw away the sap from them ? V. God is pleased to spare unprofitable members of the Church, and to extend their day of grace, notwithstanding all their provocations. (*T. McCrie, D.D.*) *Bringing forth fruit :*—Every man is expected to be fruitful in some way or other ; there is no situation in which a man cannot bring forth some good fruit. Servants may bring forth good fruit before their superiors. I heard, the other day, of a servant, a godly person, who wished to change her place. " Has your master been unkind ? Did he not give you wages enough ? " " No ; he gives more than I shall have elsewhere ; but they are so wicked, I can't bear their ways. I would rather work harder, with less wages, than stay to see their evil doings." Dear brethren, I pray this for you—that God would teach you to hate sin wherever you see it, and that you would not jest at it, or wink at it. I wish to make you all good Christians under the influence of that grace that can alone make you wise to salvation. Masters, you may do much good. I once heard an anecdote of a poor servant maid. She went to live in a house, but after some time wanted to leave her place. She was recommended to stay, as they were religious people. " Oh," said she, " I will go to no such house as this again ; for, while master and mistress pretend to be very pious when they are out, they are devils at home. Let me rather go where the righteous are a sneer, and where righteousness is utterly despised." I tell you that true righteousness creates heaven in men's houses ; and where the fear of God is there is righteousness in every department, and it is the glory of the family circle. (*Rowland Hill, M.A.*) *The figless fig-tree :*—In regard of God, we ought to be fruitful. First, for that He hath deserved it. Secondly, He seeks for it. Thirdly, and when He finds it, He counts Himself honoured and glorified by it. First, HE HATH DESERVED FRUIT FROM US, in that He hath bought us at a dear rate from our vain conversation, to serve Him all our days in holiness and righteousness; He hath chosen us to be " a peculiar people unto Himself, zealous of good works," and make choice of us before others, that we should be fruitful, and that our fruit should abide and abound. He hath made us His own workmanship, by the effectual calling of grace, and " created us to good works to walk in them." He hath planted us, hedged us about, manured us, watered us with the sweet dews of His Word and gospel from heaven; trimmed us with His pruning hook of judgments and corrections. " And what could He do more for us that He hath not done ? " God hath set in hope, planted in hope, watered in hope, of some answerable return, and shall it be denied? or canst thou imagine that God hath took all this pains with thee, and bestowed all this cost upon thee, that thou shouldest bear green boughs or gay blossoms only ? Secondly, HE HATH SOUGHT IT OF US, as our text speaks. Now seeking implies divers things : First, an earnest desire to find the thing sought for, as Luke xv. 4 ; Matt. xiii. 45. Such an earnest desire hath God to find fruit on us, whom He hath planted in His Church, as appears by those pathetical speeches which He uses, Deut. v. 29, xxxii. 29; Psa. lxxxi. 13 ; Hos. vi. 4. And in this chapter, Luke xiii. 34; xix. 41, 42. By all which, and many such like, it appears that He doth seek seriously and fervently for fruit, and is much grieved when He is deceived in His expectation. Secondly, Seeking imports diligence and frequency. It is no rare but a continued act. So Cant. iii. 1–4 ; Luke xv. 8 ; 2 Tim. i. 17. Thus God comes and seeks for fruit, not once, not twice, and then gives over, but He comes often. Thirdly, Seeking implies mildness and gentleness. Thirdly, WE SHOULD BRING FORTH FRUIT, FOR THAT GOD HOLDS HIMSELF

GLORIFIED BY IT. "Herein is My Father glorified" (saith Christ) "that you bear much fruit" (John xv. 8). Secondly, We ought to have a special regard to the credit of the gospel, which is the doctrine of God's grace, and teacheth men to be fruitful, "in denying all ungodly lusts, and in living soberly, righteously, and godly in this evil world" (Tit. ii. 11, 12). Thirdly, God will have a special care of us. The Israelites in their conquests were forbidden to lift up an axe against any tree that bare fruit (Deut. xx. 19, 20). God will provide for all fruitful Christians in public calamities (Ezek. ix. 4). Fourthly, "It shall be unto us according to our fruit" (Jer. xvii. 10). We read that Xerxes adorned the plane-tree, and hung it with many rich and precious jewels, because He delighted in the shade thereof ; much more will God adorn fruitful trees, for that He delights in the fruit thereof. In this life He will reward with glory and honour. A fruitful Christian carries a heaven in his heart, joy and comfort (Cant. vii. 17), a happy and blessed communion that is between Christ and him ; and hereafter there is a blessing abides him for ever (Heb. vii. 8). And thus you have heard what reason we have to be fruitful, both in respect of others, and of ourselves as well as others. Lastly, If we cast our eyes upon the whole creation, and every creature therein that God hath made, we may be stirred up and provoked to fruitfulness. The heaven, the earth, the sea, and all therein, are fruitful in their kind ; and shall man be barren and fruitless, for whom all these are fruitful? (*N. Rogers.*) *God the Owner of the vineyard :*—Now briefly of the owner's peculiar interest and propriety therein. It is His vineyard. How His? Is He the owner and possessor of no more but that? and the fig-tree mentioned thereon growing? "The whole earth is the Lord's and the fulness thereof ; the round world, and they that dwell therein," saith the Psalmist (Psa. xxiv. 1), and yet in regard of the affection that He bears unto the Church, He doth in a manner count Himself owner of nothing but this. The Church is the peculiar inheritance of the Lord, He doth more respect it than He doth all the world besides. "The Lord's portion is His people, Jacob is the lot of His inheritance," saith Moses (Deut. xxxii. 9) ; they are His peculiar ones (Exod. xix. 5, 6) ; His glory (Isa. xlvi. 13) ; His ornament (Ezek. vii. 20) ; His throne (Jer. iv. 21) ; His diadem (Isa. lxii. 3) ; His Hephzibah (Isa. lxii. 4) ; His only delight is in her. 1. He hath chosen them from the rest of the world. "Only the Lord hath a delight in thy fathers to love them, and He chose their seed after them, even you above all people, as it is this day," said Moses to Israel (Deut. x. 15). The Lord "hath chosen Zion, He hath desired it for His habitation " saith David (Psa. cxxxii. 13, 14). "Ye are a chosen generation" saith Peter (1 Pet. ii. 2). God chooseth for His love, and loves for His choice ; they are called His by election. 2. He hath purchased His inheritance with a great price ; the whole world cost Him not so much as His Church did, it was bought with blood. He hath entered into a league and covenant with His Church, to become their God, and take them for His people, and so He hath not with the world besides (Hos. ii. 13 ; 1 Peter ii. 10). Man is frequently resembled to a tree in Scripture ; so Job xix. 10 ; Dan. iv. 10, 11, 14, 20 ; Isa. xliv. 23 ; Jer. xi. 19 ; Ezek. xvii. 24 ; Matt. iii. 10, vii. 17, 18, 19, xii. 33. The resemblances are many ; take we notice of some. 1. In respect of shape, a tree hath its root, trunk, or body, boughs, branches, and smaller twigs issuing from thence. Man's head is his root, his body answereth the trunk or stock of a tree, his arms and legs are his boughs and branches, his fingers and toes the smaller twigs. Only here is the difference, man is *arbor inversa*, a tree turned upside down, saith the philosopher. For the root or head of a tree standeth on the earth, and extendeth itself towards heaven in the stock, boughs, and branches of it. But man (this mystical tree) hath his head upwards, as his root ; and his branches and boughs grow downward to the earth : to teach us (saith one) whence we have our sap, moisture, and nourishment, not from the earth below, as the tree hath (which was Esau's blessing), but from the dew of heaven, which was the blessing of Jacob (Gen. xxvii. 28, 29). 2. In respect of growth, there is some good resemblance. A tree is first tender in the twig, then stiff in the stock ; and lastly, withered and doating in the age of it. So man in his childhood and infancy is flexible, easily inclining to virtue or vice, as he is taught and instructed. Like wax, he is apt to receive any impression that shall be put upon him, and (as Pliny speaketh of the fir-tree) the nearer it is to the root, the more smooth it is, and less knotty. So the nearer man is to infancy and childhood, the less sinful and freest from vicious courses ; but when he once comes to be stiffened, and confirmed in the strength of his stock by man-age, then he waxeth more tough and violent in his courses (as did Rehoboam and Joash): the elder we grow, usually the worse we are. Adam was worse in his breeches than he was before; so is it with his sinful posterity. And as man grows thus in his youth, so he is drooping in his age. Let him be as strong as the oak, as tall as the cedar, as straight as the pine-tree, as green and flourishing as the laurel or bay-tree; when age seizeth on him, his strength is weakened, his tallness abated, his straightness crooked, his greenness withered. 3. There are several sorts and kinds of trees; some greater than others, and some taller; some straighter, some broader; some younger, some elder; some barren, some fruitful; so is it amongst men. All are not of the same rank and quality, some are of high degree, others low (Psa. lxi. 9). Some exalted, others brought down. Saul was a tall tree, "higher than others by the head and shoulders." Zaccheus was a low tree, lower than the people by head and shoulders. Absolom was a goodly green, straight tree, none in Israel to be compared with him for beauty. Mephibosheth was a tree lame and crooked from his childhood, by a fall that he got out of his nurse's arms. Some are fruitful, others unfruitful. Of which more hereafter. 4. In respect of outward state and condition the resemblance holds. High trees are subject to greatest dangers, being exposed to the violence of the winds, blasts of lightning, the dints of thunderbolts, and usually the higher the less fruitful. Low trees are subject to the browsing of beasts, trampling down with feet, and twenty other annoyances. The tree of a middle stature is chiefly safest, and beareth the best fruit. Thus it is with man. Those in high place lie open to the winds of alteration, to the lightnings of disasters, to the thunderings of envy and malice. "How are the mighty overthrown" (said David in his epitaph for Saul). Oh! "how are they fallen?" how often are they split with the weight and greatness of their own boughs? 5. Trees are not without their diseases, as Pliny showeth, nor is man without his. The same author tells us that, to that time, three hundred several diseases were discovered, which man was subject unto (some philosophers say two thousand, and that there is two hundred to which the very eye of man is incident). Sure I am, there is no tree subject to so many diseases as the body of man is. 6. In respect of the use, man may be resembled unto a tree; some trees are for building, others for burning, being once felled. So it is with all mankind, being felled by death; some are for the building up of "that house which is not made with hands" (2 Cor. v. 1), others for fuel in hell, "their end is to be burned" (Heb. vi. 8). Other resemblances we might acquaint you with, but I must observe measure. Let not this that hath been said be passed over without some useful application. (*Ibid.*) *A fig-tree:*—It was no ordinary nor trivial tree, but of a noble and generous kind (called upon by other trees to be king over them), and brought forth sweet and delicious fruit (Judg. ix. 10). Why a fig-tree should be mentioned rather than any other tree, some reasons may be rendered, as this in general: The fig-tree was very common in Judea, and frequently planted in their vineyards, for that the vine delighteth much in its neighbourhood and shade; and thence is it that we so frequently find them joined together in the Scripture (Deut. viii. 8; 1 Kings iv. 25; Psa. cv. 33; Joel i. 7 and ii. 22; Amos iv. 9; Hag. i. 19). More particularly, in reference to the synagogue of the Jews, and that state, the fig-tree, above other trees, did best set forth their condition. The fig-tree is a succulent plant, full of leaves and luxuriant branches; so did that nation come out, and spend its sap in outward observations and ceremonies, contenting itself with the fair leaves of outward profession, crying out, "The temple of the Lord, the temple of the Lord," drawing near with their lips when their hearts were far off. Again, the fig-tree is the first that buddeth, but the last whose fruit is ripe; the Jews budded long before the Gentiles (and it is to be prayed for that the time of their ripe fruit may be hastened), but the fulness of the Gentiles must come in before their ripening can be expected, as the apostle shows (Rom. xi. 25, 26). In reference to the Christian Church under the New Testament, the fig-tree is named in respect of sundry properties, wherein it doth hold resemblance. 1. The fig-tree is full of sap and moisture, it is the most juiceful of any tree, the root of it doth abundantly feed it; so doth Christ His Church, He is the Root of it, and on the Root depends the firm standing thereof, and the life of every branch; from this Root we have our radical moisture, from His fulness we derive grace, and grace for grace (John i. 16). 2. The fig-tree is fruitful above other trees. It hath fruit one under another, insomuch that one fig thrusts off another, through its abundance. The Egyptian fig-tree (saith Solinus) bears fruit seven times in a year; pull off one fig, and another breaks forth in the place thereof very shortly after. So fruitful is the Church of God and every sound member of it; they are "filled with the fruits of righteousness"

(Phil. i. 11). 3. The fruit of the fig-tree is a most delicious fruit: "Shall I leave my sweetness?" said the fig-tree (Judg. ix. 11). And such is the fruit of every good Christian, acceptable and pleasing both to God and man. What the apostle speaks of the works of charity (Phil. iv. 8; Heb. xiii. 16) may be said of every other gift and grace, "it is an odour of a sweet smell, a sacrifice acceptable and pleasing unto God"; we are "a sweet savour unto God" (saith the apostle). The fruits of our graces are God's dainties (Cant. vi. 2). 4. The fig-tree is forward in putting forth; it foretells a summer, as our Saviour shows (Matt. xxiv. 32). God's people are "a willing people" (Psa. cx. 3). Forward to every good work that God requires to be done (Gal. i. 16; 2 Cor. viii. 10, and ix. 2). Even in this sense the godly may be said to be *Primitiæ Dei*, the first-fruits of God. And this their forwardness promiseth a summer; it brings a blessing upon a nation. 5. The fig-tree makes not so glorious a show as do other trees, it neither blooms nor blossoms, and yet bears abundantly: so is it with the sound Christian, he makes not that show that the hypocrite doth, but he is more fruitful (Matt. vi. 3, 4, 6; Luke xviii. 11–14). The harlot exceeds the chaste matron in gaudy attire, as the Church of Rome doth ours. 6. The fig-tree best bears the brunt of winter storms, and is freest from summer's thunder (saith Pliny), that never strikes it. Sure it is that the godly Christian is best armed for hard weather, and best enabled to go through variety of conditions (Phil. iv. 12, 13). Nor do the thunderbolts of an angry God ever strike him; that thunder and lightning which comes from the throne comes through the rainbow, the covenant of grace and mercy, before ever they come at him (Rev. iv. 5). 7. Amongst all trees there is none whose leaf doth so much resemble the hand of a man as doth the fig-tree's. The leaf of the asp resembles the tongue, but the leaf of the fig-tree, man's hand. Christianity sets us to work; it stands, not in a verbal profession, but in action (Matt. xxi. 28; John xiii. 17; James i. 22). (*Ibid.*) *Trees:*—The heathens of old were idolatrous in multiplying gods to themselves, even to the number of thirty thousand (saith Hesiod); whatever they best liked, that they created a god, and so of whatever they most feared. Of a clap of thunder they made a Jupiter, of a tempest at sea they made a Neptune, of an earthquake they made a Pluto, &c. And to these their created gods they erected temples, altars, and consecrated the goodliest and fairest trees that they met withal; which ancient practice of dedicating this and that kind of tree to several gods as proper and peculiar to them was always observed (saith Pliny), and yet remaineth to this day. Thence Lucian took occasion to deride the practice of those times, feigning their idol-gods to sit in Parliament, and every one making choice of that tree which he most fancied. Jupiter makes choice of the oak for its strength, Apollo of the bay-tree for its greenness, Neptune of the poplar for its length, Juno of the eglantine for its sweetness, Venus of the myrtle tree for its beauty. Minerva sitting by, demanded of her father Jupiter what might be the reason, that seeing there were so many fruitful trees, they all made choice of those trees which were fruitless. He answered her, *Ne videamur fructu honore vendere*, that we may not be thought to chaffer our honour away for fruit. "Well," said Minerva, "do you what you please; I, for my part, make choice of the olive for its fatness and fruitfulness. All commended her choice, and were ashamed at their own folly. This you will say is but a fiction; and it is no other, but it discovered the folly of men of that generation, and so it may do of ours. In elections and choices fruitful trees are least of all regarded. The ambitious he seeks after unprofitable honour, high place, rule, and government, and would be advanced above the rest of his brethren; he affects the cypress for its tallness (a tree that great men much esteem of, and nourish in their walks, but it is hardly made to grow), and when it is come up, the fruit is good for nothing, the leaves of it are bitter, the scent strong, neither is the shade thereof wholesome. The young gallant is for the double-coloured poplar, all for form and compliment. Oh, there is much of a gentleman in that, the leaves of this tree are soft, and full of down, which soon flies away like the down of the thistle into the air; this tree is an emblem of dissimulation. The flattering courtier likes well the clasping ivy, which yet is an enemy to all trees and plants, it undermineth walls, and is good only to harbour serpents and venomous creatures, insomuch that Pliny wonders it should be honoured by any, or counted of any worth; and yet heathen emperors have used to make them garlands of it, and wear them on their heads. Rehoboam too much affected these ivy codds (1 Kings xii. 8). And it is the fault of greatness. The covetous worldling prefers the ash to all other trees; he loves to bear the keys, and delights in being the jailer of his wealth. The body and bulk of this tree is hard and tough, and the leaves unwholesome to any beast that doth not chew the cud. In short, some choose for beauty, some for sweetness, some for greatness, some for greenness, but where is he or she that makes Minerva's choice, to choose for fruitfulness? As Samuel said of the sons of Ishai (one having a goodly stature, another a goodly countenance), " Surely now the Lord's anointed is before me." So we think of these goodly and tall trees (but fruitless in grace), if honour comes, wealth comes, beauty comes, &c., This is the anointed of the Lord ; this must be he. But "God seeth not as man seeth "; man looketh on the outward appearance, but the Lord looketh on the heart, as was told Samuel. (*Ibid.*) *Acceptable fruit :*—Others there are that bring forth fruit as well as buds and leaves, and yet their fruit shall not be accepted. 1. For that it is not natural and kindly fruit, but degenerate. In the creation every seed and plant brought fruit after its kind ; so it is in the regeneration, good trees bring forth fruit answerable to the stock wherein they are engrafted, and the sap they thence receive, and the profession that they make ; but these men walk after the lusts of the Gentiles, and bring forth the fruits of the flesh (such as those mentioned, Gal. v. 19), no manner of way answering to the seed that hath been sown in them by the ministry of the Word, which they have heard, and the doctrine which they have been taught. 2. Say it be fruit of a better kind, yet it is not seasonable fruit. It may be that they are ten or twenty years in blooming, so long before they come to any good resolution to leave their vicious ways and courses ; and then they trust to latter springs and showers for the perfecting and ripening of it, and so neglecting the due season of fruit, it happens that, with Esau, they find "no place for repentance, though they seek it carefully with tears." 3. Their fruit is not sound fruit, but rotten at the core (however it be goodly and fair to look upon), like those apple-trees in Assyria (of which Solinus writes), the fruit whereof is yellow as gold, but being touched is rotten ; or like the apples of Sodom, beautiful to the eye, but being touched they fall to cinders. Zealous they seem outwardly, when they are cold at heart or else lukewarm. Their aims and ends in all their devotions is self. 4. Their fruit is not fair, it is shrivelled up, either in some few duties of the first table, as hearing, reading, praying, &c., but in the duties of the second table they are very tardy (Isa. lviii. 3, 5, 6). So the Pharisees made long prayers, and under that pretence "devoured up widows' houses" (Matt. xxiii. 14), and such is the fruit of all hypocrites. Or else they are observant in the duties of the second table, with neglect of the first (as Matt. xxiii. 23), and such is the fruit of the civilian and moral man. 5. Their fruit is not lasting ; it holds good for the summer season of prosperity, but when the winter of adversity and persecution comes, it fails (Luke viii. 13). And such is the fruit of the temporary believer and time-serving Christian ; his fruit lasts not all the year, not during term of life, when, as a good fig-tree is never without some figs hanging on the tender boughs, winter nor summer, a good Christian, like the palm-tree spoken of, Psa. xcii. 12, grows fat and flourishing even in old age. Let these and all such other be advised not to flatter themselves nor suffer themselves by vain pretences to be undone. It is not a fair blossom, a green leaf, nor fruit of outward profession, external reformation, common illumination, or any of the like nature, that will satisfy God's expectation. He looks for fruit, and good fruit too, from every fig-tree, and at your hands He will require it. Wherefore, be exhorted to be fruitful Christians, that you may answer God's expectation. Let your fruit be the " fruit of righteousness" (Phil. i. 11), "fruit unto holiness" (Rom. vi. 22), "fruit unto God" (Rom. vii. 4), that is, to the glory and praise of God, and such as He will accept of. Now that this use may be the more profitable, I shall acquaint you with three particulars. 1. With the properties or qualifications of that fruit that shall find acceptance. 2. With the means that must be used for the producing of fruit so qualified. 3. With the motives that may stir us up to the bringing forth of such fruit. Of each of these briefly, and in order. (*Ibid.*) *A fig-tree planted in his vineyard :*—That the Church is a spiritual vineyard is a truth that hath strong confirmation from Scripture. In the Old Testament we find it so styled (Psa. lxxx. 8, 9, 15 ; Cant. viii. 11, 12 ; Isa. v. 1, 7 ; Jer. ii. 21). The like in the New (Matt. xx. 1, 2, and xxi. 28, 33 ; Mark xii. 1 ; Luke xx. 10). But why is it resembled to a vineyard, rather than to another thing? It is compared to many other things in Scripture, besides a vineyard, as to a house, to an orchard, to a garden enclosed, to a field in tillage, to a threshing-floor, &c. But of all other resemblances of earthly things none doth so fully express and set forth the nature and condition of the Church as this of a vineyard, which, that it may appear the better, let us take notice of some particulars, wherein this spiritual vineyard, the Church, doth hold resemblance with the other.

1. A vineyard is a place separated and enclosed from other grounds. No vineyard is naturally a vineyard; hand and heart must go to make it so. The Church is called and separated from the world, both in life and conversation, as appears, Lev. xx. 24, 26; Num. xxiii. 9; Deut. xiv. 2; John xv. 19. 2. No vineyard is in its perfect glory so soon as it is taken in. Her plants being set, come not presently to perfection and growth, but by degrees. So it is with the Church (Eph. iv. 11, 12). Divers workmen and labourers are ordained to be employed about it, for the perfection of it, even after it is planted. 3. A vineyard, when it flourisheth and is come to some perfection, is a place of great delight, both in respect of the pleasant smell that it yieldeth, and comfortable shadow that it affordeth; so is the Church (Hos. xiv. 6, 7). "The smell of it is like unto a field that the Lord hath blessed." Her vines and tender grapes give a good smell (Cant. ii. 13, 14). Her graces are compared to things most sweet (Cant. iv. 13, 14). 4. To a vineyard it may be compared in respect of the fertility or fruitfulness thereof. It bears much fruit, and fruit of the best kind. A vineyard is stored with divers plants (one plant maketh not a vineyard); and those plants are laden with fruits, they bring forth in bunches and clusters, and not a berry here and another there, but the load is such that the branches bear, that it seems many times to exceed the strength of the branch that bears them. The Church is fertile of children; there are multitudes of them that believe. So fruitful is the Church of children as that she wonders at her own increase, and saith, "The place is too strait for me: give place to me that I may dwell. Who hath begotten me these, seeing I have lost my children and am left desolate" (Isa. xlix. 19, 20; liv. 1). And as a vineyard is more fruitful than any other plantation, so it yieldeth the best fruit of any other. No fruit is more delectable to the taste, nor more comfortable to the heart, than that which comes from the grape. And what fruit can be compared with the fruit that a Christian bears? All other fruit that grows without this fence is but sour and bitter, seem it never so fair and glorious to the eye, yet it is but hedge fruit, or like unto the grapes of Sodom and clusters of Gomorrah (Deut. xxxii. 32). 5. A vineyard is a well-ordered place, there the hillocks may be seen equally swelling, the stakes pitched in a good height and distance, the vines handsomely pruned, the ground cleanly kept, and well hoed, all things are well ordered in it. And so is it in the Church, insomuch that Balaam himself could not but admire at it, and in a rapture cry out, "How goodly are thy tents, O Jacob, and thy tabernacles, O Israel! As the valleys are they spread forth, as gardens by the river's side," &c. (Num. xxiv. 5, 6.) 6. To a vineyard the Church may be compared, in respect of the imbecility and weakness of it. No possession, said Cato, requires more pains about it than a vineyard doth. Corn comes up and grows alone of itself, without the husbandman's care (Mark iv. 17). But the vine is a frail kind of plant, it must be supported, sheltered, daily dressed and attended, else it soon waxeth luxurious, and is in danger to grow wild, after it once waxeth wanton. 7. A vineyard is very subject to be annoyed and wasted by the beasts of the wood and foxes of the field, which love to burrow under it, and delight to be cropping and pilling of her plants, and eating of her grapes, as Solomon intimates (Cant. ii. 15). So is the Church, her enemies are many that conspire against her (Psa. lxxxiiii. 2-13). (*Ibid.*) *Man's ingratitude:*—The ill requital that we have made to God for all the good we have received from Him hath been in part discovered. Now give me leave to discover unto you the vileness of this vice, ingratitude, that we may shun it and hate it; and the rather, because we have been foretold that it is one of those sins that renders these times perilous. And so, first, take notice that it is a compounded sin; it hath many poisonous ingredients in it which makes it extremely evil, and amongst others these—1. Ignorance, and such an ignorance as whereunto mercy is denied (Isa. xxvii. 11). He that made them will show them no favour, being a people of no understanding, it being wilful and affected. Thus God complains of Israel, "Israel doth not know" (Isa. i. 3), and Hos. ii. 8. 2. Idolatry. Ingratitude doth not only pass by without notice-taking of good bestowed, but ascribes all to others. Thus Israel ascribed all their plenty, their bread, their wine, their wool, their water, &c., to their lovers or sweethearts, that is, to their idols and false gods (Hos. ii. 5). 3. Pride is another sinful ingredient that goes to the composition of it. "Their hearts were exalted," saith God of ungrateful Ephraim, "therefore have they forgotten Me" (Hos. xiii. 6). And this is rendered as the reason why Hezekiah returned not to God according to that he had received—"His heart was lifted up in him" (2 Chron. xxxii. 25). 4. Envy, that is the daughter of pride, and will wait upon her mother; where the one is the other will be; we grudge no men the praise of their kindness but whom we envy

and hate. And by experience we have found that true, which Tacitus saith of extraordinary favours, which, lighting upon ill minds, cause hatred instead of love. 5. There is much of sacrilege in it. The ungrateful man robs God of that honour which is due unto Him, and which He hath reserved to Himself, nor will He give it to any other. God is content that we should have the good of all, but the praise of all He looks to have Himself. 6. There is atheism in it. Thus those ungratful wretches, mentioned by Job, whom God hath blessed with temporal abundance, ask, "What is the Almighty that they should serve Him" (Job xxi. 25). Secondly, it is a sin that all law condemns. The law of nature is against it. For naturally every effect is brought back to its cause (as all waters come out of the sea, so all return thither again). Now God is the cause of all things and persons, therefore, whatsoever we have and whatsoever we are must be ascribed unto Him. (*Ibid.*) *The dressing of the vineyard :*—For the better accomplishing and perfecting whereof there are three principal virtues (as implements) which are necessarily requisite in these dressers of the Lord's vineyard. 1. Skilfulness and ability to do this work that he is called unto. This is required (2 Tim. ii. 2 ; 1 Tim. iii. 2).· 2. Faithfulness and sincerity—"He that hath My word, let him speak My word faithfully," saith God (Jer. xxiii. 28). 3. Care and vigilancy—"Be diligent to know the state of thy flocks, and look well to thy herds," saith Solomon (Prov. xxvii. 23). (*Ibid.*) *Cumberers of the ground :*—Barren professors are cumbersome ; unprofitable burdens they are to the vineyard of the Lord. 1. They are sterile and barren in themselves, and in that respect cumbersome, and a burden to the earth. 2. As they do no good, and are cumbersome in that respect ; so they do much harm, and so become unprofitable burdens, and that many ways. (1) To the soil whereon they grow, the very earth is the worse for a fruitless fig-tree. It was the sin of man, at first, that caused God to curse the earth to thorns and thistles, and ever since He hath turned "a fruitful land into barrenness, for the wickedness of those that dwell therein." The sins of those within the pale, are they for which a land doth mourn (Hos. i. 4). So is it in the vineyard of the Lord. Let a barren and unprofitable fig-tree have his standing, wheresoever the ground shall be the worse and not the better for him. Let Rehoboam be rooted among the kings in the land of Judah, and the shields he finds of gold he will leave of brass. Let Balaam be numbered among the prophets, and Judas among the apostles ; and the vineyard of the Lord shall find cause enough to say of such a fig-tree, that it cumbers the ground. The Church suffers by the growth of such trees ; it loseth her heart and fatness. Her beauty and glory is much blemished by the growth of such plants in it. (2) Such barren trees are cumbersome and burdensome to other trees and plants that grow, or might grow, in the vineyard ; and that divers ways. (*a*) A barren tree possesseth the place of a better, and by its good will would not suffer any to grow near it. The best rooms at feasts, the chief seats in synagogues, proud Pharisees will take up ; nor is there any place for better guests till they be removed lower, and commanded to give place, and so room made, by their removal, for others that are invited. The like may be seen in David's case, who was annointed to be king over Israel long before his instalment. Saul sat yet upon the throne, and David must be content to stay a while for that, till Saul be removed ; and, that being done, then he shall be planted and seated in his room, in Hebron. So whilst Judas supplies the place of an apostle, honest Matthias shall be kept out ; his place must be voided, before another take his bishopric (Acts i. 20). The Jews they must be broken off before the Gentiles be grafted in (Rom. xi. 9). And whilst those ungrateful farmers of the vineyard held their lease it could not be taken by others, who would gladly have hired it, and "rendered the fruit thereof in due season" (Matt. xxi. 43). (*b*) Such as are barren and unprofitable in their places, devour not only equal nutriment with him that beareth, but many times starve other inferior plants within their reach ; drawing away the heart and fat of the soil with their suckers and feeders. What a breadth beareth some great ash or oak ! How far do their roots spread, albeit underground and unseen ? Yet it may be perceived by their soaking of the ground and drawing away nourishment from corn and plants that are near unto them. It is thus with many an unprofitable and barren Christian, he is a soaker, and that in respect both of things that concern this life and a better ; and so cumbersome. Such are to be found in the Church. In private families likewise there are many such burdensome plants to be found ; many a fair estate is consumed by pride and luxury, voluptuousness and prodigality. (*c*) They are troublesome and cumbersome to other plants by their unprofitable shade, over-topping and over-dripping them, and keeping the influence of heaven from them, so that they cannot enjoy the warm beams of the sun, which brings healing with it under its wings. (*d*) They are cumbersome, in harbouring under their branches things hurtful to other plants. None shall be harboured under their shade unless it be a stinging nettle, or some sullen weed, or some venomous and poisonous creature. (*e*) They are burdensome to the Lord of the soil, and owner of the vineyard, who complains of such barren plants (Isa. i. 14, 24, vii. 13, xliii. 24; Amos ii. 13). God complains of their burden; they are cumbersome unto Him; He finds a pressure under them; He is dishonoured by them and cannot long endure it. (*f*) The dressers of the vineyard are burdened and cumbered by them. Christ, the principal Dresser, laments the barrenness of Jerusalem (Luke xix. 41; Matt. xxiii. 34; John xi. 38). Christ groaned, as it seems, under the Jews' malice. (*Ibid.*)   *The patience of God :—* Be persuaded to make the right use of the patience and long-suffering of the Lord, as the apostle directs (Rom. ii. 4), and let it lead thee, as it were by the hand, to true repentance, remembering—1. How long God hath trusted thee with His patience, and given thee time to make thy peace, and sue out thy pardon. Should a traitor that is condemned as thou art have a reprieve granted him for half so many years as thou hast lived (albeit he had no promise granted of a final pardon), upon his good carriage and behaviour; how thankful would he be, and how happy would he think himself in that. 2. Forget not how many have suffered for those sins that thou art guilty of long since; who had not that patience showed unto them that thou hast had, but were taken away and carried to execution, upon the very act of their sinning, as Zimri and Cosbi, who were smitten in the act of their lust; Ananias and Sapphira in the very act of lying, &c. 3. In not making the right use of God's patience and profiting by it thou despiseth it; and in despising it thou despiseth goodness. (*Ibid.*)   *God's patience not inexhaustible :—* God's patience hath a period; it hath its bounds and limits beyond which it will not pass. For proof, read Amos viii. 2—"The end is come, I will not pass by them any more"; that is, I will have no more patience towards them. So Jer. i. 11, 12—"I will hasten My word to perform it"; that is, to make good the judgments that I have denounced. And that text should still be sounding in our ears —"An end is come, an end is come; behold it watcheth for thee, behold, it is come, it is come" (Ezek. vii. 5-16). Should God always bear with sinners, He should suffer in all His attributes; His justice would be wronged and blemished, which by no means will endure that the wicked should be held as innocent (Exod. xxxiv. 7; Jer. xliv. 2). "He is a jealous God" (Exod. xx. 5; Deut. iv. 26). Now, should God perpetually bear with sinners, it would be a disgrace unto Him. His jealousy will not endure that sin should ever go unpunished (Psa. l. 21; Mal. iii. 15). He is a most wise God, "God only wise" (1 Tim. i. 17). Albeit, He bears and spares and shows mercy to sinners, it is ever moderated with wisdom. He forbears as long as there is hope (Jer. li. 9). But when men become incurable, His wisdom will not suffer Him to bear any longer (Isa. i. 5). He is a good God; and being good, He must needs love goodness and hate iniquity (Psa. xlv. 7). Now, God should not be good, if He should be ever good to those that will never be good; His goodness will not suffer Him ever to spare those that hate and despise goodness. So we might show of His other attributes. (*Ibid.*) *Privilege not prescriptive right :—*However legal or usual the presence of a fig-tree in a vineyard may be, it is not, as in the case of a vine, a matter of course, and Christ must have had a reason for introducing it, and the reason can only be found in the didactic significance of the emblem. What, then, was the reason? On our view of the drift of the parable it is not difficult to answer the question. The fig-tree is chosen to represent Israel as a tacit yet effective protest against the notion of her possessing a prescriptive right to occupy in perpetuity the place she held in God's favour. The supposition is directed against the pride and self-importance of an elect race, prone to think that Israel and God's kingdom were synonymous, or as intimately and essentially related to each other as are vineyard and vine. To have used the vine as an emblem of Israel might have seemed to concede this claim, but by selecting the fig-tree as an emblem Christ said to His countrymen in effect, "Ye have no natural or necessary place in the sphere within which God's grace manifests itself, like a vine in a vineyard, without which the vineyard can hardly be conceived: Ye are but a fig-tree in the vineyard, legitimately, suitably enough there, yet there by accident, or by free choice of the owner, and there only so long as ye serve the purpose for which He put you there." (*A. B. Bruce, D.D.*)   *One vineyard :—*It was one; not vineyards, many; and from hence we may conclude that the Church of Christ is one, and but one. The multiplicity of particular churches do not hinder the unity of the catholic; all these are but parts of it, as one tree that hath several arms and branches. Many stones make but one house, many houses one city, many cities one kingdom; so, many men one particular congregation, many congregations one visible Church, many Churches one catholic one. Or as the ocean-sea is but one in itself, yet running by divers countries and coasts, hath the name according to the coast it runs by; as the English Sea, the Irish Sea, the German Sea, &c., yet all but one sea. So we distinguish of Churches, yet all is but one and the same, one catholic Church and no more. It is very true, that God is resembled to man in Scripture. He likeneth Himself to man, and speaks after the manner of men unto us. Yet we have somewhat more to take notice of, for God is pleased not only to liken Himself to man, but He takes upon Him the profession of an husbandman, resembling Himself to a careful and painful vinitor, that had a fig-tree planted in his vineyard, &c. (*Ibid.*) *The fruitless fig-tree:*—I. THE FIG-TREE WAS FAVOURED. No other fig-tree was so favoured. For it was not there by chance like a berry-bush in the woods, or a tree on the top of an old tower, the seed of which had been carried on the wings of the wind, or by a bird that, on the way to its nest, frightened by a hawk, had dropped its mouthful. The owner had deliberately planted this tree in his vineyard. You are planted, not in the open unsheltered waste, but in the Church of Christ, and in a Christian home. You are not like a little dying boy, who said to the Christian friend visiting him, " O sir, do ye think I would hae ony chance wi' God? ye see I canna read ony "; or like an untaught carter I knew, who used to give a boy a penny to read to him "blads o' the Bible." That dying boy, that carter, was like a fig-tree growing on the road-side. You are like a fig-tree planted in a vineyard. What could have been done for you that has not been done? II. THIS FIG-TREE WAS FRUITLESS, THOUGH SO FAVOURED. III. THIS TREE, FAVOURED THOUGH FRUITLESS, IS YET SPARED. Many poets speak of trees as having life, as thinking, feeling companions, for whom they cherish an almost human attachment. The trees of our boyhood are dear to us, because interwoven with memories of bright days. I have known a wood spoiled, because the proprietress would not permit the cutting down of trees which she regarded as the friends of her girlhood. She seemed afraid of "wronging the spirit in the woods." The feeling is natural. The keeper of the vineyard had planted the fig-tree, and watched its growth. It is his own, and he has a longing, lingering feeling for it. He won't give up hope of it. President Garfield, when a boy, was wonderfully saved from drowning. " Providence thinks it worth while saving my life," he said to himself, when he stood panting and dripping on the deck of the canal boat, and the fire of noble resolve then began to burn within him. Lord Clive and Wallenstein, in boyhood, made some wonderful escapes, and burst forth into an exclamation that surely they were reserved for something great. Many have had the same feeling. IV. THE FIG-TREE, FAVOURED THOUGH FRUITLESS, AND SPARED, IS YET TO BE JUDGED. God's patience is most wonderful, it goes far beyond all our thoughts and dreams, but it has limits. To be fruitless is a greater calamity than befell those slain by Pilate at the altar, or buried under the tower of Siloam; it is the only real calamity; for it is to be an eternal failure. (*J. Wells, M.A.*) *The penalty of ignoring the end of existence:*—Just as when any article, as a pen, a watch, an engine, or anything else which will not work, or answer the end for which it was made, is thrown aside as useless; or as a fruit-tree which will not bear fruit is cut down as a cumberer of the ground, so those who do not answer this end of their existence—glorifying God—may be set aside or otherwise punished. (*H. R. Burton.*) *A warning to useless lives:*—I. CONSIDER THE COMPLAINT ALLEGED: IT IS THAT OF UNFRUITFULNESS. Fig-trees are generally three years before they bring forth any fruit to perfection; but this was perpetually barren, and likely to remain a cumberer of the ground. 1. Observe the patience and forbearance of God in His conduct towards the barren fig-tree, the barren and unprofitable professor. He endures with much longsuffering the vessels of wrath fitted for destruction. 2. Though the Lord suffers long and is kind, He strictly observes all our conduct, and keeps an account of the advantages we enjoy, and the use we make of them. 3. Great as is the danger of unfruitfulness, nothing but heavenly culture, nothing but Divine influence can produce in us the fruits of righteousness. 4. Divine forbearance, though long continued, will finally have an end. Though He bears long, He will not bear always. The longer the storm has been gathering, the heavier it will fall; the longer the sword has been whetting, the sharper it will cut, and the deeper it will wound. Longsuffering on God's part, if it do not lead to repentance, will be followed by more grievous suffering on our part. II. THE DOOM THAT IS PASSED UPON THE BARREN FIG-TREE: "Cut it down, why cumbereth it the ground." 1. A sentence like this is sometimes passed against unprofitable characters, even in the present life. 2. The barren fig-tree is cut down at death, when it is not only cast out of the Church, but out of the world. 3. The stroke will fall still heavier in the day of judgment, when the barren tree shall not only be cut down, but cast into the fire. III. THE REASON GIVEN FOR THE AWFUL SENTENCE: THE FIG-TREE WAS NOT ONLY UNPRODUCTIVE, BUT INJURIOUS; it "cumbereth the ground." 1. It was unprofitable, and so is every sinner that does not bring forth fruit unto God. 2. The fig-tree was injurious, as well as unprofitable; for it encumbered the ground, and occupied a place which might be filled to more advantage. (*B. Beddome, M.A.*) *Unfruitful professors cut down as cumberers of the ground:*—I. To SHOW WHO ARE THE UNFRUITFUL IN GOD'S VINEYARD, TO BE CUT DOWN. 1. Dead trees. They being still in their natural state, are spiritually dead in trespasses and sins. The gospel is the means of life to a dead world, called therefore the word of life (Phil. ii. 16). It is by it that the Spirit of life is conveyed into the dead soul. This Spirit is received by the hearing of faith. Thereby faith comes whereby the soul is united to Christ the fountain of life. But alas! many continue dead under quickening means, destitute of the Spirit and of faith. So they cannot bring forth the fruits of holiness, they can do nothing that is truly good, more than a dead man can move and act. 2. Rotten trees. Dead souls are spiritually rotten also. "They are altogether become filthy." This speaks reigning vanity and worthlessness, as the rotten tree is light. How many such are in God's vineyard, whose mind is vain. 3. Withered trees. When the tree has lost all sap and is withered away, it cannot bring forth fruit, but must be cut down. Many that sometimes looked green and promising under the means of grace, have lost all now. Their convictions are stifled, their affection to the things of God is gone, and the gospel is become tasteless to them. 4. Barren trees, that have leaves but no fruit. 5. Degenerate trees bringing forth evil and noxious fruit. To such God says, "Yet I had planted thee a noble vine, wholly a right seed: how then art thou turned into the degenerate plant of a strange vine unto me?" These bring forth the fruits of the flesh in abundance, that are deadly like the wild gourds of the wild vine. II. How AND IN WHAT RESPECTS DO THESE CUMBER THE GROUND. 1. They take up room, precious room, that might be better occupied. 2. There is no advantage to the owner from that part of the ground which they occupy. 3. There is no comfort to the vine-dressers from that part of the ground such occupy, though otherwise much might arise from it, if it was planted with other trees. The pains of the labourers is lost upon such trees. 4. The sap of the ground which barren trees draw to them, of which they are yet nothing the better, might nourish fruitful trees. Lastly, they hinder the fruitfulness of other trees in the vineyard; drawing the sap from them. So they are not only not profitable, but hurtful. III. INQUIRE WHY CUMBERERS OF THE GROUND ARE SPARED SO LONG. 1. For to try if they will mend. 2. For the prayers of the godly. 3. For the sake of their seed designed for vessels of mercy. 4. That impenitent sinners may be wholly inexcusable. There is a measure of iniquity to be filled up, and so long the Lord will bear with sinners, and no longer (Rom. ii. 5; Gen. xv. 16). It remains—IV. To CONSIDER THE IMPORT OF CUTTING DOWN. It denotes—1. Patience at an end. 2. Never fruit more to grow upon them. 3. The sharpness of the stroke. 4. The suddenness of the stroke. 5. The destructiveness of it. 6. The casting of it out of the vineyard. 7. That the barren tree is to be cast into the fire. Uses. 1. The unfruitfulness under the gospel prevailing in our land, forbodes a time of hewing and cutting down. Our privileges have been signal ones, our misimprovement signal; so will our stroke be likewise. 2. Impenitent sinners have a dangerous station in God's vineyard. A barren tree may be much safer in the wood than in the garden. 3. Take heed what part ye act in God's vineyard. Be concerned to know for what use you are in it. Beware of being cumberers of the ground. 4. Lay no more weight upon external Church privileges than they will bear. Happy are they that dwell in God's house, if they learn the true manners of the house. But if in God's house they live ungodly lives, it had been better for them they never had known it. Lastly, consider what fruit ye bring forth under the means of grace; and do not overlook the privileges which you enjoy. Ministers sow the seed, Christ Himself will look after the fruit, and will notice who bring forth the fruit of a preached gospel, and who cumber the ground. (*T. Boston, D.D.*) **These three years.—** *Three years:*—He comes to particular man three years. First, in youth. I have planted thee in My vineyard, given thee the influence of My mercies ; where is thy fruitfulness ? Alas ! the young man sends him away with a *Nondum tempus ficorum*—It is too early for me to fall to mortification ; would you put me to penance before I have had the leisure and pleasure to offend ? He is ready to send Christ away in the language of that foul spirit, " Art Thou come to torment me before my time ? " But whose charge is it to " Remember thy Creator " *diebus juventutis ?* Then the conquest is most glorious, because then it is most difficult. You say, It is never too late ; but I am sure it is never too soon, to be gracious and holy. Secondly, in middle age ; and now the " buying of farms," and " trying of beasts," the pleasures of matrimony, the cares for posterity, take up all the rooms of the soul. Men rather busy themselves to gather the fruits of earth than to yield the fruits of heaven. Here is strength of nature and fulness of stature, but still a defect of grace. Perhaps Christ hath now some fair promises of fruits hereafter, " Let me first go bury my father, then " (Luke ix. 61). Thirdly, in old age. Now the decay of body should argue a decay of sin. The taste finds no relish in riot, the ears cannot distinguish music, the eyes are dim to pleasing objects, very " desire fails " : now all things promise mortification. He that cannot stir abroad in the world, what should he do but recollect himself, and settle his thoughts on the world to come ? Now fruits, or never. Not yet ; morosity, pride, and avarice, are the three diseases of old age. Men covet most when they have time to spend least ; as cheating tradesmen then get up most commodities into their hands when they mean to break. Still He comes seeking fruit, and is returned with a *Non inventus*. But doth He forbear all trees thus long ? No ; some are snatched away in the flower and pride of their life ; yea, they be not few that will not allow themselves to live, but with riot and intemperance hasten their own ends, before they have well begun or learned what life is ; like bad scholars, that slubber out their books before they have learned their lessons. That instead of *Non est fructus*, we may say, *Non est ficus*, the tree itself is gone. And that goodly person, which like a fair ship hath been long a-building, and was but yesterday put to sea, is to-day sunk in the main. We do not eat, drink, and sleep, and take such refections of nature, *ut non moriamur*, that we might not die—that is impossible—but that we should not die barren, but bear some fruits up with us to Him that made the tree. (*T. Adams, D.D.*)　　*God and man dealing with unfruitfulness :*—A farmer, who had turned his attention to the raising of fruit, said to a friend as they sat at table, " I have cut down over fifty peach-trees to-day." " Why is this ? " " Because the fruit was not good. The peaches were too small." Afterwards, walking through the orchard, the friend saw where the trees had stood, and also the spot where, after being cut down, they had been burned. This procedure brought to his mind at once the Saviour's parable of the fruitless fig-tree. Oh, if God dealt with men as they deal with the trees in their orchards, what a fearful destruction of our race would ensue.　　*Fruit :*—Nothing is created for itself, but so placed by the most wise providence, that it may confer something to the public good, though it be but as the widow's two mites to the treasury. The poorest creature yields some fruit, wherein it doth imitate the goodness of the Maker. We know not readily what good serpents and vermin may do ; yet certainly they have their fruit, both in sucking up that poison of the earth, which would be contagious to man ; in setting off the beauty of the better pieces of creation—for though the same hand made both the angels in heaven and the worms on earth, yet the angels appear the more glorious, being so compared — besides their hidden virtues abstracted from our knowledge. Of stones they make iron, rubbish serves to raise bulwarks, the small pebble for the sling, worms and flies are baits for fishes ; everything is enabled with some gift for the universal benefit, and so to produce those fruits is their natural work. The sun comes forth of his chamber like a bridegroom, fresh and lively ; and rejoiceth as a giant, to run his diurnal course, to lighten us with his refulgent beams, to generate, cheer, and mature things with his parental heat : this is his fruit. In his absence, the moon and stars adorn the canopy of heaven, reflecting their operative influence to quicken the lower world : this is their fruits. The curled clouds, those bottles of rain, thin as the liquor they contain, fly up and down on the wings of the wind, delivering their moist burdens upon the earth, teats whereon the hungry fields and pastures do suck ; yet they expect no harvest from us : this is their fruits. The subtle winds come puffing out of their caverns, to make artificial motions, wholesome airs, and navigable seas ; yet, neither earth, air, nor sea return them recompense : this is their fruits. The earth, in a thankful imitation of the heavens, locks not up her treasures within her own coffers; but without respect of her private benefit, is liberal of her allowance, yielding her fatness and riches to innumerable creatures that hang on her breasts, and depend upon her as their common mother for maintenance. Of the beasts that feed upon her, kine give us their milk, sheep their wool; every one pays a tribute to man, their usufructuary lord: this is their fruits. Fruit-bearing trees spend not all their sap and moisture upon themselves, or the increase of their own magnitudes; but the principal and purer part of it is concocted into some pleasant fruits, whereof neither they nor their young springs ever come to taste; but they proffer it us, and when it is ripe, they voluntarily let it fall at their masters' feet. Never did the olive anoint itself with its own oil, nor the vine make itself drunk with its own grapes, nor the tree in my text devour its own figs: yet they all strive to abound with fruits. Let me raise your meditations from earth to heaven: the holy angels there are called "ministering spirits"; those royal armies fight for us against our enemies; like nurses, they bear us up in their arms, and, though unseen, do glorious offices for us: this is part of their fruit. The blessed Trinity is always working: "Hitherto my Father worketh, and I work" (John v. 17). The Father by His providence and protection, the Son by His mercy and mediation, the Holy Ghost by His grace and sanctification; all dividing the streams of their goodness for the best behoof of the world. The more anything furthers the common good, the more noble is its nature, and more resembling the Creator. The earth is fruitful; the sea, the air, the heavens are fruitful; and shall not man bring forth fruits, for whom all these are fruitful? While all the armies of heaven and earth are busied in fructifying, shall man, of more singular graces and faculties, be idle, a burden to the world and himself? Both the Church of God for the propagation of piety, and the world itself for the upholding of His state, require our fruits. If happiness consisted in doing nothing, God, that meant Adam so happy, would never have set him about business; but as paradise was his storehouse, so also his workhouse: his pleasure was his task. There is no state of man that can privilege a folded hand. (*T. Adams.*) *No fruit:*—None? Haply not so thick with fruits as the "vines of Engedi"; every land is not a Canaan, to flow with milk and honey. But yet some competent measure, enough to pay the landlord rent for the ground it stands on; no, "none." If there be none to spare, whereof the owner may make money, yet *sufficiat ad usum suum, ad esum suum*—that he may eat the labours of his own hands; no, "none." If the number be not "as the sand," yet let there be "a remnant" (Rom. ix. 27). If there cannot be a whole harvest, yet let there be "a tenth" (Isa. vi. 13). If not a tenth, yet let there be some "gleanings" (Micah vii. 1); and that is a woeful scarcity. If the gleanings be not allowed, yet let there be here and there a fig, a grape, a berry, "on the outmost branches" (Isa. xvii. 6), that the planter may have a taste. It is too defective, when *non florebit ficus*—the tree doth not flourish; but *quando non erit uva in vitibus, non ficus in ficulneis* (Hab. iii. 17)—when there shall not be "a grape on the vine, nor a fig on the tree" (Jer. viii. 13), this is a miserable sterility. Something hath some savour, but none is good for nothing. Indeed, all trees are not equally loaden; there is the measure of a hundred, of sixty, of thirty; an omer and an ephah; but the sacred dews of heaven, the graces of the gospel, bless us from having none! "I find none." None? Peradventure none such as He looks for, no fruits delicate enough for the Almighty's taste. Indeed, our best fruits are never perfect and kindly ripened; still they relish sour and earthly, and savour of the stock from which they were taken. They are heavenly plants, but grow in a foreign and cold climate; not well concocted, not worthy the charges and care bestowed upon us. Set orange or fig-trees in this our cold country, the fruit will not quit the cost of the planting and maintaining. But the complaint is not here of the imperfection or paucity of fruits, but of the nullity: "none." Some reading that text with idle eyes, that after all our fruits, we are still "unprofitable trees" (Luke xvii. 10), because they can find no validity of merit in their works, throw the plough in the hedge, and make holiday. But shall not the servant do his master's business, because he cannot earn his master's inheritance? Shall the mason say, I will share with my sovereign in his kingdom, or I will not lay a stone in his building? Yet good fruits have their reward; though not by the merit of the doer, yet by the mercy of the accepter. Sour they be of themselves, but in Christ they have their sweetening; and the meanest fruits which that great "Angel of the Covenant" shall present to His Father, with the addition of His own "precious incense" (Rev. viii. 4), are both received and rewarded. In their own nature they may be corrupt;

but being dyed in the blood of Christ, they are made pleasing to God : yea, also profitable to the Church, and useful to men, seem they never so poor. Even a troubled spring doth often quench a distressed soldier's thirst; a small candle doth good where the greater lights be absent; and the meanest fruit of holy charity, even a cup, though it be not of the juice of the grapes out of the vineyard, but of cold water out of the tankard, in the name of Christ, shall have its recompense (Matt. x. 42). But here the complaint is not of the meanness or fewness, but of the barrenness—none at all. (*Ibid.*) *Unfruitfulness aggravated by privilege* :—Howsoever God may endure barrenness out of the Church, in want of means, yet He will never endure it under means. It is better for a bramble to be in the wilderness than in an orchard; for a weed to be abroad, than in a garden, where it is sure to be weeded out, as the other to be cut down. If a man will be unprofitable, let him be unprofitable out of the Church. But to be so where he has the dew of grace falling on him, in the means of salvation, where are all God's sweet favours, to be a bramble in the orchard, to be a weed in the garden, to be noisome in a place where we should be fruitful, will God, the great Husbandman, endure this? Whatsoever is not for fruit is for the fire (Matt. iii. 10). (*R. Sibbes.*) *Nominal Christians* :—A gentleman once entered a hall with his little son, when they saw a number of well-dressed people, some of them standing together in groups, while others sat at their ease. The lad's attention was arrested by a pleasant-looking man, in gaudy dress, and he inquired of his father who it could be. " Ask the gentleman who stands near you," answered the father, with unmoved gravity. " If you please," said the boy, addressing the stranger, " can you tell me who that gentleman opposite is?" No answer was given, and the lad looked amazed. At last the father said to him, " Those things which so much resemble men and women are only wax figures. There is no life in them, natural as they appear. Fair to look upon, they are without soul; all outside, and nothing else." Are mere nominal Christians much more than these wax figures ! We may admire the artistic skill which can fashion matter into forms of beauty; but what are all the outside appearances of religion in the deceitful Pharisee compared with the holiness of life in the heart of the true believer? Happy would it be for us if we all sought for " the fruit of good living" in our own lives before God Himself comes to seek it. The ancient Greeks used to quote the proverb that " The feet of the avenging deities are shod with wool," intimating thereby the noiseless and unexpected manner in which they approach their victims. Thanks to God's tender forbearance, He always gives us timely warning before the fatal blow is struck. The parable of the barren fig-tree, from which the text is taken, was designed by our blessed Lord to be a warning to the Jewish nation, whose mercies had been so many, but whose day of grace was so soon to end. It is, however, no less applicable to all, of every age and country, who have the opportunity of receiving the means of grace, and of securing the hope of glory. (*J. N. Norton, D.D.*) *Fruitless lives* :—How many who are called Christians live lives so utterly fruitless that they might have such obituaries written of them as this : " While professing to be followers of Him ' who went about doing good,' they were never known to go out of their way to speak kindly to the poor and the friendless, or to invite any stranger to church. Fields of usefulness close to their own dwellings were often pointed out to them, but they showed no ambition to be imitators ' of them who through faith and patience inherit the promises.' An enlarged charity may hope that theirs is the blessedness of those who ' die in the Lord,' but we cannot add (in the apostle's expressive words of commendation) that they ' rest from their labours,' and that ' their works do follow them.' " (*Ibid.*) **Lord, let it alone this year also.**—*The sentence suspended* :—I. THE INTERCESSION OF JESUS—ITS MERCIFUL NATURE. 1. The ground of the plea is in Himself. God spares the sinner for Jesus' sake. 2. The prospective efficacy of the plea lies in what the Saviour has done for the sinner. Thoughts of peace concerning him have revolved within His breast. He has laid down the plan of his recovery. A life of the sweetest virtue, and the most complete self-sacrifice, has been expended to work out the plan. II. THE INTERCESSION OF JESUS—ITS SPECIAL END. The roots are at fault; the sinner's heart must be changed. 1. The power of the means. Historically the record is grand; intrinsically the power is the same to-day. The stoutest hearts have been broken, and the most guilty consciences have been washed. 2. The stubborn heart may relent. Unprolific trees have been started, some by a very hard winter, others by a very warm summer, to yield fruit. Once the sap was thrown into its proper channel the tree continued to bear. So

God's dealings with men are means to move the heart. Even Ahab is not beyond His reach. The furnace of affliction has melted many. God sent His people to Babylon, and said, "Behold, I will melt them, and try them; for how shall I do for the daughter of my people"? All other means had failed. There are, therefore, probabilities of side influences producing such changes in men's condition, so as to leave with us possibilities that the truths of the gospel will in the end produce the greater changes unto life. III. THE INTERCESSION OF JESUS—LIMITED AS TO ITS TERMS. "But if not, thou shalt cut it down." This is the solemn voice, not of righteousness, but of the intercession itself. 1. Such a state of impenitence is fearful to contemplate. The end of it is the hardest part. The uninterrupted course of wickedness leads to inevitable destruction. 2. The sentence carried out. "Cut it down." We would gladly close our eyes and not witness the scene, but the authority of the text bids us still look on. God ceases to be a Father, Christ is no longer a Brother, the light is put out for ever, the soul is cast into outer darkness, and the heart pierced with a thousand regrets. "Cut it down," being fruitless; burn it, being useless. Let such a warning as this serve to quicken thought, so that we may observe the time of mercy. (*The Weekly Pulpit.*) *Mercy in sympathy with righteousness :*—The restriction of the intercession of the vinedresser for a prolongation of the experiment to a single year indicates Christ's own sympathy with this Divine rigour. He is the vinedresser, and His ministry of grace and truth is the means whereby it is faintly hoped Israel may yet, at the eleventh hour, be made spiritually fruitful. But, full of grace though He be, He neither expects nor desires an indefinite extension of Israel's day of grace. He knows that though God is long-suffering, yet His patience, as exhibited in the history of His dealings with men, is exhaustible; and that in Israel's case it is now all but worn out. And He sympathizes with the Divine impatience with chronic and incurable sterility. For though He preaches with enthusiasm a gospel of grace, He does so with the aim of producing in the recipients of the good tidings holiness, and in the conviction that belief in the gospel is the most efficient cause of holiness. A kingdom of God must be a kingdom of righteousness, and if Jesus presented it to view as a kingdom of grace, it was because He believed that was the most direct way of reaching the ideal. It was made a kingdom of grace to begin with, that it might become a kingdom of righteousness to end with. In this respect there is absolute agreement between Christ and Paul. The Herald of the kingdom, not less energetically than the apostle of the Gentiles, repudiates the idea that men might sin with impunity because grace abounded. The intercession put into the mouth of the vinedresser is a solemn act of repudiation, similar in import to Paul's protest in the sixth chapter of his Epistle to the Romans. "Let it alone this year also, till I shall dig about it, and dung it; and if it bear fruit next year, well; and if not, thou shalt cut it down." (*A. B. Bruce, D.D.*) *The mercy of new probation :*—I. HERE ARE SET FORTH THE CONDITIONS AND RESPONSIBILITIES OF LIFE UNDER THE GOSPEL. 1. The individuality of God's gracious dealings. 2. A picture of gracious provisions enjoyed. 3. The responsibility involved in the possession of gospel blessings. II. THE MISUSE OF GOSPEL PRIVILEGE AND OPPORTUNITY AS IT IS HERE DECLARED. Instead of fruitfulness there was barrenness. The gospel grace proves in many instances to have been all in vain. Faults are not corrected. Sins are not put away. The new life is not lived. Salvation is not enjoyed. 1. Now this resultlessness of the ministry of the Word does not imply any necessary defect in its human presentation, especially where barrenness is seen side by side with growing strength and abundant fruitfulness. Neither does it imply any withholding of any single gracious or Divine element necessary to the result. Neither does it imply any decree or principle limiting the application of what is admitted to be an adequate and universal remedy. When we ask why men are and remain unsaved under the sound of a faithful and full gospel ministry, we cannot find refuge either in the Divine intention, in the character of the provision, in the mode of its presentation, or the absence of the power of the Holy Spirit of God. We exhaust all possible reasons, and have to come back to one, and one only—human wilfulness. The will-not of unbelief makes the grace of God of none effect. 2. The second thing here is the Divine patience with these unfruitful hearers. 3. The mischiefs which attend the unfruitful and are wrought by them. "Why cumbereth it the ground also?" The "also" was left out of the older version, and the sense thereby weakened. The idea expressed is not only that the tree is useless, but that it is also baneful. The word "cumber" means now to occupy a place disadvantageously. But it had a more extensive sense of old, and the word here really means that it marred, poisoned, did mischief to the soil. Its shade was injurious. But also it drew to itself the fatness of the soil, the nourishment which other trees needed, and impoverished both them and it. III. THERE IS A SPECIAL TIME OF GRACE, WITH A CERTAIN CATASTROPHE IF IT BE NOT IMPROVED TO GOOD PURPOSE. 1. The benefits of intercession on behalf of those who are unbelieving and fruitless. 2. The extended season and increased facilities for fruitful growth which are thus afforded. (*The Preachers' Monthly.*)   *The secret orderings of the soul's life :*—O could there be laid out before our eyes the secret and wonderful workings, the incessant and anxious care, of which the inner life of any one soul is the object, how should we be lost in amazement at the unmerited, the marvellously constant, love of God! Who can speak as he should of the intricate, the minute ordering of the events of daily life, so disposed and governed that each may do its part in training us for our true rest? Who can tell of the secret drawings of love, the hidden inspirations, the discipline of sorrow, the lessons of chastisement, which are brought to bear upon us one by one? God speaks to us at one time amid the sweet breath of heavenly consolation, at another in the midst of the furnace of affliction ; He multiplies around us the means of grace ; He brings us within the influence of holy seasons, or places, or persons ; He presents to us motives which are strong enough to overcome anything but the most hardened impenitence; He pursues us with the solicitations of His love ; He does everything short of taking from us our freewill, that will whose power freely to choose its own highest happiness of necessity involves the alternative of rejecting it. And when apparently nothing more remains to be done, when even the energies of Divine love seem to have exhausted themselves in vain upon the hardness of a heart which is resolutely bent upon sin ; even in that supreme moment, that crisis of the soul's destinies, when the cry goes forth from the Eternal Justice, "Cut it down, why cumbereth it the ground?" there rises up from the depth of Divine compassion which dwells in the heart of the Redeemer the pleading petition for a yet further extension of the day of grace, "Lord, let it alone this year also." Some healing remedy may yet be found, some appeal may even yet obtain an entrance—the door before which the Lord has been so long standing and knocking in Divine patience and sorrow may even yet be opened to Him, that He may enter in and sup--the dresser of the vineyard will once more dig about the fruitless tree and dung it—and if it bear fruit—well. If it bear fruit—well. Yes, my brethren, but there is an alternative, a possibility, terrible to dwell upon, but which yet forms an important part of the teaching of this parable, and one which we may not overlook. "If not, then after that thou shalt cut it down." Yes, there arrives a moment hidden in the eternal councils of the Most High, at which even the voice of the Great Intercessor ceases to plead, and acquiesces in the righteous judgment of God. (*S. W. Skeffington, M.A.*)   *This year also :*—The interceding vine-dresser pleaded for the fruitless fig-tree, "let it alone this year also," dating, as it were, a year from the time wherein he spoke. Trees and fruit-bearing plants, have a natural measurement for their lives: evidently a year came to its close when it was time to seek fruit on the fig-tree, and another year commenced when the vine-dresser began again his digging and pruning work. Men are such barren things that their fruitage marks no certain periods, and it becomes needful to make artificial divisions of time for them ; there seems to be no set period for man's spiritual harvest or vintage, or if there be, the sheaves and the clusters come not in their season, and hence we have to say one to another, "This shall be the beginning of a new year." I. The beginning of a new year SUGGESTS A RETROSPECT. Let us take it, deliberately and honestly. "This year also"—then there had been former years of grace. The dresser of the vineyard was not for the first time aware of the fig-tree's failure, neither had the owner come for the first time seeking figs in vain. God, who gives us "this year also," has given us others before it ; His sparing mercy is no novelty, His patience has already been taxed by our provocations. 1. Years of great mercy. 2. Years of sharp affliction. 3. Opportunities for usefulness, which have come and gone. 4. Unfulfilled resolutions. II. The text MENTIONS A MERCY. "This year also"—a grant from infinite grace, as the result of love's pleadings, and in pursuance of love's designs. 1. The wicked man should count that the Lord's longsuffering points to his salvation, and he should permit the cords of love to draw him to it. O that the Holy Spirit would make the blasphemer, the Sabbath-breaker, and the openly vicious to feel what a wonder it is that their lives are prolonged "this year also"! Are they spared to curse, and riot, and defy their Maker? Shall this be the only fruit of patient mercy? The procrastinator who has put off the messenger of heaven with his delays and half promises, ought he not to wonder that he is allowed to see "this year also"? The believer is kept out of heaven "this year also" in love, and not in anger. There are some for whose sake it is needful he should abide in the flesh, some to be helped by him on their heavenward way, and others to be led to the Redeemer's feet by his instruction. Surely, for the sake of souls, for the delight of glorifying our Lord, and for the increase of the jewels of our crown, we may be glad to wait below "this year also." III. "This year also" IMPLIES A LIMIT. Even when Jesus is the pleader, the request of mercy has its bounds and times. There will come a last year to each one of us : therefore let each one say to himself—Is this my last? (*C. H. Spurgeon.*)   *Another year granted :*—I. PROLONGED LIFE IS MAINLY VALUABLE FOR THE ENLARGEMENT OF SPIRITUAL OPPORTUNITY. II. THE NEGLECTED OPPORTUNITY FURNISHES REASON WHY THE VERY INTERCESSOR HIMSELF WILL ACQUIESCE IN OUR CONDEMNATION. (*S. Robins, M.A.*)   *God's forbearance of the barren fig-tree :*—I. THE VINE-DRESSER'S PETITION AND REQUEST. 1. The matter of the request—"Lord, let it alone." It is the special duty of faithful ministers and pastors and labourers in God's vineyard, to divert and keep off that wrath, vengeance, and judgment which He threatens, and which is near to their people (see Joel i. 13, ii. 17 ; Isa. lxii. 6, 7). The ground hereof is this— 1. Because ministers are middle persons, as it were betwixt God and the people : they mediate and deal betwixt both; as it is declared expressly of Moses (Exod. xix. 1). This is one thing which makes for this work to be performed by them ; and then, which we may add hereunto, the affection which does belong unto them from this relation. This it makes for it also. When a child is in any danger, who should sooner speak for it than the father? When a sheep is ready to be swallowed up, who should sooner interpose than the shepherd? When a city is ready to be betrayed, who should sooner bestir himself than the watchman and governor of it? Why thus it is now with those who are ministers and pastors of the Church. They are fathers, they are shepherds, they are spiritual watchmen, and what not to work them, and to engage them hereunto. This very expression in the text carries an argument with it, wherein they are called dressers of the vineyard, who are much concerned in the safety of those trees that belong unto it, as a piece of their own handy-work. This it first of all shows us, how that ministers not only serve to instruct God's people, but to protect them ; not only to show them their duty, but to keep off their ruin. 2. The determination of the time for the exercise and continuance of this forbearance—"This year also." (1) This implies that He had for some time let it alone already (see Gen. vi. 3 ; 2 Chron. xxxvi. 15, 16). This the Lord is pleased to do upon divers considerations. (*a*) Out of His nobleness, and royalty, and generosity of mind, as we may so express it. To show that He does not take pleasure or delight in the death of sinners, as He hath sometimes told us. He loves not to destroy there where He can any way spare. (*b*) The Lord does thus with many people, that thereby He may leave them so much the more inexcusable, and may be justified in His proceedings against them, when He comes to judgment indeed ; that all men's mouths may be stopped, and that they may believe so much the more fully in God. (*c*) Sometimes, to exercise this patience of the vine-dressers themselves, which labour and take pains about these fig-trees, God will hereby sometimes prove them, and God will sometimes hereby trouble them ; as St. Paul observes it in himself, from the non-proficiency and impenitency of the Corinthians (2 Cor. xii. ult). And by His own patience and forbearance of such persons, God will leave them His ministers to a spirit of patience and forbearance in themselves, in conformity to God's own example. (2) This implies a further desire of continued patience and forbearance ; which proceeds upon these grounds. (*a*) That speech, love, and affection, which they bear unto them. Hatred is all for destroying ; and that out of hand. But love, it is desirous of sparing, and preserving of the party beloved, as long as it can. (*b*) There is ground for this desire and request of ministers in the behalf of their people, from that hope which they are willing to conceive of their amendment and reformation. (*c*) This disposition in ministers proceeds out of respect to themselves, and a holy jealousy and suspicion which they may conceive of their own neglectfulness. II. THE CONDITIONS WHICH THIS PETITION PROCEEDS UPON. These are twofold. The one is taken from himself— "Till I shall dig about it, and dung it." And the other is taken from the fig-tree, upon supposition, either of amendment or incorribleness. "If it bear fruit, well; if not, then after that thou shalt cut it down." We begin first of all with the former, viz., that which is taken from himself—"Till I shall dig," &c.   Where there are two things observable of us. 1. The phrase or expression. 2. The doctrine or notion which is contained under it, and is exhibited to us from it. For the First : The phrase or expression. We may here take notice of the nature and condition of a minister's work and employment; which, because it is expressed to us by digging and dunging, is hereby signified to be a very difficult and laborious service. Now, Secondly : For the thing itself, or notion. Taking this passage in the scope and connection of it, there is so far hereby signified and intimated unto us the efficacy and advantage of the ministry to such a purpose as is here expressed. "Till I shall dig about it, and dung it"; as who shall say, that would do it. From whence we may note thus much : That the labour and pains of the ministers is a means whereby God hath sanctified and appointed for the good and edification of the people. If anything do them good, and make them to be that which they should be, this is that which must do it—preaching and taking pains with them. The second is taken from the fig-tree, by way of a double supposition. Either, first, of future fruitfulness. "If it bear fruit, well"; or, secondly, of further incorrigibleness; and, "if not, then," &c. First, to speak of the former; to wit, the supposition of future fruitfulness. "If it bear fruit, well." This word, "well," it is not expressed in the original text, but it is necessarily supplied here in our English translation, to make the sense complete. First, "Well" : that is, well for the Lord and Master of the vineyard : well for thee; it shall be well. So, when the fig-tree bears fruit, it is well for him that owns it (Prov. xxvii. 18). And so it is here; when a people prove fruitful, God Himself is so much the better for it. This must not be taken strictly and rigorously, but by way of dispensation. God reckons and accounts Himself profited when we do that which is our duty before Him; when we are active and fruitful in goodness, and answer those gracious opportunities and advantages of being better which God in goodness affords unto us, we do thereby the more honour God and express His grace in us, as it becomes us to do. "Herein is My Father glorified, in that ye bear much fruit," says Christ Himself to His disciples (John xv. 8). Secondly, "Well" : that is, well for the husbandman and dresser of the vineyard. "Well," that is, well for thee. It is well for the minister when the people thrive in goodness, and are fruitful in every good work : namely, upon this account; because he sees some good success and effect of his labour amongst them. Thirdly, well for the vineyard, and the rest of the trees in it. One barren and unfruitful fig-tree may spoil a whole set and row of trees besides. It prejudices other plants which are near it. On the other hand, when any are fruitful, and active, and zealous in goodness; their zeal, it provokes many others so much the more to piety. And so it is well for the vineyard. Lastly, and more especially; well, for the fig-tree itself. It is well for every particular person, when of barren, he comes to be fruitful in every good work (Psa. cxxviii. 2). And so much may suffice to be here spoken of the first supposition mentioned; to wit, of future fruitfulness, in these words, "If it bear fruit, well." The second is, of further incorrigibleness; in these; "and if not, then, after that, thou shalt cut it down." Which words, "after that," seem to carry a double reference and respect with them. The one is to the Lord of the vineyard; patience and forbearance towards it. "After that "; that is, after that thou hast let it alone for one year longer, as I desire of thee; if after that it shall still prove unfruitful, then do thus and thus with it. The second is, to the vine-dresser's pains and labour about it. "After that," that is, after that I have digged about it, and dunged it; if after that it shall yet prove no better, but remain barren and unfruitful still; then, I say, no more of it, but this; that "thou shalt cut it down." And here, again, this expression—"Thou shalt cut it down," it hath a double emphasis with it. First, an emphasis of prediction; and secondly, an emphasis of permission. An emphasis of prediction— "Thou shalt cut it down," that is, thou wilt cut it down : there is nobody that can hinder thee. An emphasis of permission—"Thou shalt cut it down"; that is, thou mayest cut it down; there is nobody will hinder thee. From both together, we have these two points observable of us : First, that a people's continued unfruitfulness, after God's long expectations from them, and forbearance of them, makes His judgments to fall unavoidably and irrecoverably upon them. After that, thou wilt cut it down; it is a word of prediction or commination. Secondly, that a people's continued unfruitfulness, after long enjoyment of the means and labours of the ministers amongst them, it takes off the prayers and intercessions of the ministers for them. After that, thou mayest cut it down. And so it is a word of permission, or submission, to the will and mind of the Lord of the vineyard. (*Thomas Horton, D.D.*)   *The use of prolonged discipline :*—I think something may be gained here by descending into the particulars. One of these agricultural operations imparts to the tree the elements of fruitfulness, and the other enables the tree to makes these elements its own. Digging gives nothing to the tree; but it makes openings whereby gifts from another quarter may become practically available. The manure contains the food which the plant must receive, and assimilate, and convert into fruit; but if the hardened earth were not made loose by digging, the needed aliment would never reach its destination. Similar processes are applied in the spiritual culture: certain diggings take place around and among the roots of barren souls, as well as of barren fig-trees. Bereavements and trials of various kinds strike and rend; but these cannot by themselves renew and sanctify. They may give pain, but cannot impart fertility; the spirit much distressed may be as unfruitful as the spirits that are at ease in Zion. These rendings, however, are most precious as the means of opening a way whereby the elements of spiritual life conveyed by the Word and the Spirit may reach their destination. The Lord, who pours in the food for the sustenance of a soul, stirs that soul by His providence, so that grace may reach the root and be taken in. As the constituents of fruit, held in solution by air and water, cannot freely reach the plant whose roots lie under a long unbroken and indurated soil, so the grace of God contained in the preached gospel is kept at bay by a carnal mind and a seared conscience. It is when afflictions rend the heart, as a ploughshare tears up the ground, that the elements of life long offered are at length received. It is thus that providence and grace conspire to achieve the purpose of God in the salvation of men. In this work mercy and judgment meet; and saved sinners, on earth and in heaven, put both together in their song of praise (Psa. ci. 1). (*W. Arnot.*) *Pleading for a respite:*—"If any particular circumstance might be considered as making a more deep, lasting, and serious impression than others, it was a dream which I had when at school. I felt the apprehension of the approach of the last great judgment day. After I had perceived vast multitudes of the human race appearing before the throne of Christ, some being approved, and others rejected, I at length beheld my beloved father and mother, and several of the family. I heard them distinctly examined, and as distinctly heard the Judge say, 'Well done.' At this period my whole soul was filled with horror, being conscious that I was not prepared to pass my final scrutiny. At length my name was announced, and I felt all the agonies of a mind fully expecting to be banished from the presence of God. The Judge, then, in language which struck me with mingled shame and hope, said, 'Well, what sayest thou?' I fell at His feet, and implored mercy, and prayed, 'Lord, spare me yet a little longer, and when Thou shalt call for me again, I hope to be ready.' With a smile, which tranquillized my spirits, the Lord replied, 'Go, then, and improve the time given thee.' The extreme agitation awoke me; but so deep was the impression, that I have never forgotten it." (*Herbert Mends.*) *More time for repentance:*—John Hardonk, while on shipboard, dreamed one night that the day of judgment had come, and that the roll of the ship's crew was called except his own name, and that this crew were all banished; and in his dream he asked the reader why his own name was omitted, and he was told it was to give him more opportunity for repentance. He woke up a different man. He became illustrious for Christian attainment. (*Dr. Talmage.*) *Fruit sought by God:*— The first thing which strikes us, perhaps, in the transaction, is ITS INDIVIDUALITY. There must have been many vines and many fig-trees in the vineyard; but the story is told as if the whole vineyard were for that one tree alone; and as if the great Proprietor concerned Himself only with it. Whether we recollect how soon He began, or how often or how long He has been, He does not forget, He has catalogued it, and registered it. "Behold"—it implies that the person addressed is very conscious how lengthy the time has been, and how very anxious and very patient the Dresser has been—"Behold, these three years I come seeking fruit on this fig-tree, and find none: cut it down." Oh! it is a very humbling recollection— those years of love and care—it is very humbling, if it is not more, those years of unfaithfulness and emptiness which God all along has been counting. And observe it—it is the Dresser who has been the searcher, and He who did all for you is the one who has been looking for something from you. And the true measure of the emptiness is the extent of the culture. Had the dressing not been what it is, the wonder would have been less. WHAT IS "FRUIT"? What is it which is to a man what the figs are to the fig-tree? I answer, first, it would be something appropriate to his nature, accordant with his being. "For men do not gather grapes of thorns, or figs of thistles." And what is the nature of the being of a man?

Physical, intellectual, impassioned, spiritual. Such, then, must fruit be, real and tangible, visible and felt, reasonable, thoughtful, balanced, affectionate, earnest, spirit going forth to spirit, assimilating itself to God. And it must be "fruit" in its season. We do not expect man's fruit at child's age. There may be separate fruit for a man, and separate fruit for a woman. And every man has his own special fruit, which he ought to bear. And next, it must be in the man as it is in the natural tree. The tree takes up of its own soil, and by a strange process of transformation, what it took up in one form, earthy, comes out at last in another—for beauty and for usefulness—heavenly. So must it be in a man. What he is to give to God is not angelic service, but human. He must draw it from the earth, but it assumes a character different, not its own. How does that take place? The sap flowing from the root through the stem, runs into the branches, and there diffusing itself to every tendril, makes a deposit, and so forms fruit. Just so, the Holy Ghost, flowing from the eternal love of the Father, through the Son, the Lord Jesus Christ, makes His way to every grafted member in the mystical body, and goes out into every, the weakest, the minutest, part of man—each feeling, each thought, each word, each motion, making holiness. But many a storm, and many a sunshine; many a dark night, and many a bright day; many a wind, and many a rain, and many a chill, go to do each their own proper work, till the blossom is set; and when it is set, on and on, till the bud becomes "fruit," and this fruit, till it is sweet. It must have its own true, proper flavour. So it is with you. You must pass through all the changes of your moral atmosphere, you must know various discipline, till, little by little, by that sap, which is the Spirit of God, coming to you through Jesus Christ, you get love, the love of God, the sweet savour of love, without which nothing is fruit. (*J. Vaughan, M.A.*) *Fruit, or no fruit :*—Now supposing the predestined interval pass away, and you are not a fruit-bearer? There will be no more notice, it will come quietly, solemnly, instantaneously, abrupt, irrevocable, "Cut it down." Then "the axe will be laid at the root," and you will go up to your bed, and you will begin to decline and fade away. Or a blow will do it in a moment, and you will lie down, a thing that has never fulfilled its intention of life; then how is it to live for ever? But if otherwise, if you begin now, in any degree, really to live for God, and repay God's care, and honour Him, what will you have then? There is no answer given in the original. We have put in "well." God had left it a blank, for every one to fill in just as he likes; and we cannot fill it in with too much. But let it stand, "well." "If it bear fruit, well." "Well," all health, all joyous health for the soul, "well." "Well" will it be to live well, to die well, to meet God well. "Well" will it be to go on bearing more fruit for ever and ever. "Well" will it be for you to be eternally happy, and Christ to "see of the travail of His soul in you, and to be satisfied." "Well." Then what is the conclusion? Do not go on living a useless life. Let God have some satisfaction in you. Begin at once. Do something. Let there be some "fruit" seen—at home, in your temper, in your intercourse, in your daily conduct, in your own family. Let there be more "fruit" in your own closet, in more real communion with God in private. Let there be a "fruit" in the world, in something taken up and done definitely for the Lord Jesus Christ. Let there be a "fruit" in the Church—truer worship, more frequent use of ordinances, more sympathy and love shown to all the brethren. And let there be a "fruit"—fruit best of all, in your own soul—more of Jesus there—a humility, a tenderness, a holy singleness, which shall show Jesus, just as the grapes shows the vine. (*Ibid.*) *Fruitfulness the gauge of value :*—Years ago in Mentone they estimated the value of land by the number of olive trees upon it. How many bearers of the precious oil were yielding their produce? That was the question which settled the value of the plot. Is not this the true way of estimating the importance of a Christian Church? Mere size is no criterion; wealth is even a more deceiving measure, and rank and education are no better. How many are bearing fruit unto the Lord in holy living, in devout intercession, in earnest efforts for soul winning, and in other methods by which fruit is brought forth unto the Lord? Jesus looks for fruit (Mark xi. 13), His operations upon us are intended to produce fruit (Luke xiii. 9), and if there be none in a Church we may expect to hear Him say of it as He did of old—"And now go to; I will tell you what I will do to My vineyard: I will take away the hedge thereof, and it shall be eaten up; and break down the wall thereof, and it shall be trodden down: and I will lay it waste: it shall not be pruned, nor digged; but there shall come up briers and thorns: I will also command the clouds that they rain no rain upon it. (*C. H. Spurgeon.*)

Vers. 10–17. A woman, which had a spirit of infirmity eighteen years.—*Two pulpits :*—I. Observe one thing at the outset: HOW MANY ANONYMOUS BELIEVERS THERE ARE IN THE BIBLE RECORD WHO GIVE HELP ALL ALONG THE AGES. Put alongside of this story the account previously given of the man healed of leprosy, and the other man at the same time cured of palsy. Of this last we have precisely the same record—"And immediately he rose up before them, and took up that whereon he lay, and departed to his own house, glorifying God." In close connection with these cases there are mentioned "multitudes," but no personal particulars are furnished. The pages of God's Word are crowded with such incidents. The woman of Samaria, the man of God that came to Eli, the lad who gave his bread and fishes at Tiberias—all these have had a mention, but nothing more to identify them in the inspired annals. It is really of little consequence who we are; it matters more what we are. II. Observe, in the second place, THAT EVEN IN EXTREME HOPELESSNESS OF DISEASE ONE MAY EXHIBIT A SUPREME AND ILLUSTRIOUS FAITH. This woman was evidently in a most deplorable condition; she was actually doubled up with deformity. When a believer is smitten terribly, he is not always just in the mood to be reasonable. Every nerve is quivering with agony ; he cannot see the wisdom nor the fairness of its infliction. The more common danger for a Christian under trial is that he shall sink into a state of stupor, of listlessness, or despair. A great numbness settles upon the soul. There are pains which lie a great distance lower than the bottom of the grave. The poet Cowper, tearing out a leaf from his own awful experience, says, "There are as truly things which it is not lawful for man to utter as those were which Paul heard and saw in the third heaven; if the ladder of Christian life reaches, as I suppose it does, to the very presence of God, it nevertheless has its foot in the very abyss." Now against both of these baleful postures of mind, the passionate and the listless, does this thought of preaching the gospel from a pulpit of patient suffering for the great glory of God array itself. It is wise to keep in mind the fact that souls may be won to the Cross by a life on a sick-bed just as well as by a life in a cathedral desk. Pure submission is as good as going on a foreign mission. III. Right here, therefore, observe, in the third place, AN EXPLANATION IS OFFERED OF THE MYSTERY AND THE PURPOSE OF SUFFERING. Pain is a sort of ordination to the Christian ministry. It furnishes a true believer with a new pulpit to preach from. A wise man will do better to learn this lesson early. I am anxious now to bring this thought close to our own minds and hearts at once. In the rooms of the American Tract Society, in New York, were until lately standing two objects which I studied for some meditative years, once a month, at a committee meeting. One is a slight framework of tough wood, a few feet high, so bound together with hasps and hinges as to be taken down and folded in the hand. This was Whitefield's travelling-pulpit ; the one he used when, denied access to the churches, he harangued the thousands in the open air, on the moors of England. You will think of this modern apostle, lifted up upon the small platform, with the throngs of eager people around him ; or hurrying from one field to another, bearing his Bible in his arms ; ever on the move, toiling with herculean energy, and a force like that of a giant. There, in that rude pulpit, is the symbol of all which is active and fiery in dauntless Christian zeal. But now look again : in the centre of this framework, resting upon the slender platform where the living preacher used to stand, you will see a chair—a plain, straight-backed, armed, cottage-chair ; rough, simple, meagrely cushioned, unvarnished, and stiff. It was the seat in which Elizabeth Wallbridge, "the dairyman's daughter," sat and coughed and whispered, and from which she went only at her last hour to the couch on which she died. Here again is a pulpit ; and it is the symbol of a life quiet and unromantic and hard in all Christian endurance. Every word that invalid woman uttered—every patient night she suffered—was a gospel sermon. In a hundred languages the life of that servant of God has preached to millions of souls the riches of Christ's glory and grace. And of these two pulpits, which is the most honourable is known only to God, who undoubtedly accepted and consecrated them both. The one is suggestive of the ministry of speech, the other of the ministry of submission. IV. Hence, WE MAY EASILY LEARN WHAT MIGHT BE ONE OF THE MOST PROFITABLE OCCUPATIONS OF A CHRONIC INVALID. No one can preach from any pulpit without the proper measure of study. Sick people are always in danger of becoming egotistic and selfish, and the best relief from that is for each child of God to busy himself in labouring for others' salvation. Said the intelligent Doddridge, even while he was lingering in the last hours of his life, " My soul is vigorous and healthy, notwithstanding the hastening decay of-this frail and tottering body; it is not for the love of sunshine or the variety of meats that I desire life, but, if it please God, that I may render Him a little more service." Such a purpose as this will lead a Christian to thoughtful examination of what will make his efforts most pertinent. He will study doctrine. He will study experience too. V. SOME PEOPLE RECOVER FROM LONG ILLNESS ; CHRIST HEALS THEM, AS HE DID THESE MEN IN THE STORY. So there is one more lesson for convalescents—what are they going to do with their lives hereafter? (*C. S. Robinson, D.D.*) *The lifting up of the bowed down:*—I. Our first subject for consideration is, THE BOWING DOWN OF THE AFFLICTED. We read of this woman that "she had a spirit of infirmity and was bowed together, and could in no wise lift up herself." 1. Upon which we remark—first, that she had lost all her natural brightness. Alas, we know certain of the children of God who are at this moment in much the same condition. They are perpetually bowed down, and though they recollect happier days the memory only serves to deepen their present gloom. 2. This poor woman was bowed towards herself and towards that which was depressing. She seemed to grow downwards; her life was stooping; she bent lower and lower, as the weight of years pressed upon her. Her looks were all earthward, nothing heavenly, nothing bright could come before her eyes; her views were narrowed to the dust, and to the grave. So are there some of God's people whose thoughts sink evermore like lead, and their feelings run in a deep groove, cutting evermore a lower channel. You cannot give them delight, but you can readily cause them alarm. "All these things are against me," say they, for they can see nothing but the earth, and can imagine nothing but fear and distress. We have known certain prudent, but somewhat unfeeling, persons blame these people, and chide them for being low-spirited ; and that brings us to notice next— 3. That she could not lift up herself. There was no use in blaming her. Of what use is it to advise a blind person to see, or to tell one who cannot lift up herself that she ought to be upright, and should not look so much upon the earth ? This is a needless increase of misery. Some persons who pretend to be comforters might more fitly be classed with tormentors. A spiritual infirmity is as real as a physical one. 4. Note further about this poor woman, that bowed down as she was both in mind and body, she yet frequented the house of prayer. Our Lord was in the synagogue, and there was she. II. I invite you, secondly, to notice THE HAND OF SATAN IN THIS BONDAGE. We should not have known it if our Lord had not told us, that it was Satan who had bound this poor woman for eighteen years. 1. He must have bound her very cunningly to make the knot hold all that time, for he does not appear to have possessed her. You notice in reading the evangelists that our Lord never laid his hand on a person possessed with a devil. Satan had not possessed her, but he had fallen upon her once upon a time eighteen years before, and bound her up as men tie a beast in its stable, and she had not been able to get free all that while. The devil can tie in a moment a knot which you and I cannot unloose in eighteen years. 2. Satan had bound the woman to herself and to the earth. There is a cruel way of tying a beast which is somewhat after the same fashion. I have seen a poor animal's head fastened to its knee or foot, and somewhat after that fashion Satan had bound the woman downward to herself. So there are some children of God whose thoughts are all about themselves ; they have turned their eyes so that they look inside and see only the transactions of the little world within themselves. They are always lamenting their own infirmities, always mourning their own corruptions, always watching their own emotions. The one and only subject of their thoughts is their own condition. If they ever change the scene and turn to another subject it is only to gaze upon the earth beneath them, to groan over this poor world with its sorrows, its miseries, its sins, and its disappointments. Thus they are tied to themselves and to the earth, and cannot look up to Christ as they should, nor let the sunlight of His love shine full upon them. 3. This poor woman was restrained from what her soul needed. She was like an ass or an ox which cannot get to the trough to drink. She knew the promises, she heard them read every Sabbath day; she went to the synagogue and heard of Him who comes to loose the captives ; but she could not rejoice in the promise or enter into liberty. So are there multitudes of God's people who are fastened to themselves and cannot get to watering, cannot drink from the river of life, nor find consolation in the Scriptures. They know how precious the gospel is, and how consolatory are the blessings of the covenant, but they cannot enjoy the consolations or the blessings. Oh that they could !

They sigh and cry, but they feel themselves to be bound. 4. There is a saving clause here. Satan had done a good deal to the poor woman, but he had done all he could do. He can smite, but he cannot slay. The devil may bind you fast, but Christ has bound you faster still with cords of everlasting love, which must and shall hold you to the end. That poor woman was being prepared, even by the agency of the devil, to glorify God. III. I want you to notice in the third place THE LIBERATOR AT HIS WORK. We have seen the woman bound by the devil, but here comes the Liberator, and the first thing we read of Him is that—1. He saw her. His eyes looked round, reading every heart as He glanced from one to another. At last He saw the woman. Yes, that was the very one He was seeking. We are not to think that He saw her in the same common way as I see one of you, but He read every line of her character and history, every thought of her heart, every desire of her soul. 2. When He had gazed upon her, He called her to Him. Did He know her name? Oh, yes, He knows all our names, and His calling is therefore personal and unmistakable. 3. When the woman came, the great Liberator said to her, "Woman, thou art loosed from thine infirmity." How could that be true? She was still as bent as she was before. He meant that the spell of Satan was taken off from her, that the power which had made her thus to bow herself was broken. 4. Our Lord proceeded to give her full enlargement in His own way : He laid His hands on her. She suffered from want of strength, and by putting His hands upon her, I conceive that the Lord poured His life into her. The warm stream of His own infinite power and vitality came into contact with the lethargic stream of her painful existence, and so quickened it that she lifted up herself. The deed of love was done : Jesus Himself had done it. IV. I will not linger there, but invite you now to notice THE LOOSING OF THE BOUND. 1. She was made straight we are told, and that at once. Now, what I want you to notice is this, that she must have lifted herself up—that was her own act and deed. No pressure or force was put upon her, she lifted up herself ; and yet she was "made straight." She was passive in so much as a miracle was wrought upon her, but she was active too, and, being enabled, she lifted up herself. What a wonderful meeting there is here of the active and the passive in the salvation of men. 2. The most remarkable fact is that she was made straight immediately ; for there was something beyond her infirmity to be overcome. Suppose that any person had been diseased of the spine, or of the nerves and muscles for eighteen years, even if the disease which occasioned his being deformed could be entirely removed, what would be the effect? Why, that the result of the disease would still remain, for the body would have become set through long continuance in one posture. But this woman was cured entirely, instantaneously, by the power of the Lord. 3. The cure being thus perfect, up rose the woman to glorify God. What did she say? It is not recorded, but we can well imagine. It was something like this : "I have been eighteen years in and out among you ; you have seen me, and know what a poor, miserable, wretched object I was ; but God has lifted me up all in a moment. Blessed be His name, I have been made straight." What she spoke with her mouth was not half of what she expressed. No reporter could have taken it down ; she spoke with her eyes, she spoke with her hands, she spoke with every limb of her body. V. Fifthly, let us reflect upon OUR REASON FOR EXPECTING THE LORD JESUS TO DO THE SAME THING TO-DAY as he did eighteen hundred years and more ago. What was His reason for setting this woman free? 1. According to His own statement it was, first of all, human kindness. Tried soul, wouldst thou not loose an ox or an ass if thou sawest it suffering? "Ay," sayest thou. And dost thou think the Lord will not loose thee? Hast thou more bowels of mercy than the Christ of God? 2. More than that, there was special relationship. He tells this master of the synagogue that a man would loose his ox or his ass. Perhaps he might not think it his business to go and loose that which belonged to another man, but it is his own ass, his own ox, and he will loose him. And dost thou think, dear heart, that the Lord Jesus will not loose thee? He bought thee with His blood, His Father gave thee to Him, He has loved thee with an everlasting love : will He not loose thee? 3. Next, there was a point of antagonism which moved the Saviour to act promptly. He says, "This woman being a daughter of Abraham, whom Satan hath bound." Now, if I knew the devil had tied anything up I am sure I would try to unloose it, would not you? We may be sure some mischief is brewing when the devil is working, and, therefore, it must be a good deed to undo his work. But Jesus Christ came into the world on purpose to destroy the works of the devil ; and so, when He saw the woman like a tied-up ox, He said, " I will unloose her if for nothing else that I may undo what the devil has done." 4. Then think of her sorrowful condition. An ox or an ass tied up to the manger without water would soon be in a very sad plight. Pity it, poor thing. Hear the lowing of the ox, as hour after hour its thirst tells upon it. Would you not pity it? And do you think the Lord does not pity his poor, tried, tempted, afflicted children? Those tears, shall they fall for nothing? Those sleepless nights, shall they be disregarded? That broken heart which fain would but cannot believe the promise, shall that for ever be denied a hearing? Hath the Lord forgotten to be gracious? Hath He in anger shut up the bowels of His mercy? Ah, no, He will remember thy sorrowful estate and hear thy groanings, for He puts thy tears into His bottle. (*C. H. Spurgeon.*) *The infirm woman in the synagogue :*—I. Our first reflection, as we look at this brief narrative, is that it furnishes us, on the part of the woman, with an illustration of ATTACHMENT TO THE PUBLIC WORSHIP OF GOD. A characteristic of devout and earnest religion in all ages. Public worship bears on it the stamp of Divine approval. See you neglect it not. II. Our second reflection is, that the text supplies an illustration of THE COMPASSION AND POWER OF JESUS CHRIST. Not only was the woman in the synagogue with her ailments; the Lord was there also with His wondrous grace. He did not neglect external ordinances. Jesus, then, was in this synagogue, and as usual He was on the look-out for some good work to do. He had a quick eye for suffering and sorrow. No sooner did He see this woman, than He healed her. What power, and what compassion! He exercises the same to-day. Earth has no sorrow that He cannot heal. And besides curing diseases, He can heal sins. III. I observe, next, that the text supplies an illustration of THE BLESSED ADVANTAGES OF BEING FOUND IN THE WAY OF DUTY. To the synagogue, at the time of worship, this woman went. Likely enough she was tempted to absent herself for one reason or another, just as we are tempted now; but she refused to listen to the temptation. She chose the better part of obeying God's law, and in doing so she was blessed beyond all expectation or hope. Little did she think, when she left home, what mercy was in store for her. Had she stayed in the house, or gone to see her friends, or been anywhere but where she was, she would have missed it all. So may we always, when in the way of duty, expect a blessing. IV. I remark, once more, that the text supplies an illustration of THE GRATITUDE OF A HEART ALIVE TO THE BLESSING BESTOWED ON IT. As soon as the woman was made straight, she "glorified God." Even if she had never spoken a word, she would have been a monument to the Divine praise. Sun and moon and stars, as they shine in the heavens, declare the glory of God. All great productions glorify their author. So this healed woman glorified her Healer. And not only so, but also audibly, there and then, before all. (*W. Walters.*)　　*An infirm woman cured on the Sabbath :*—I. THE STATE OF THE WOMAN. Diseased in an extraordinary degree, and for a very long period. II. THE CHANGE PRODUCED BY THE POWER OF JESUS. This case presented no difficulty to Him. Yet, to new-model the diseased frame, to make straight what was crooked, to relax what had been rigid for many years, required a power as great as that of creation. III. THE MEANS EMPLOYED. He used no resources of art, no remedies whatever; He even employed no means to astonish or surprise; He made no display of His power. He said nothing of the violence or inveteracy of the disorder; nothing to influence the imagination either of the woman herself or of the spectators. Conscious of possessing the power of curing all diseases, He exercised it by merely declaring the simple fact that her disorder was removed; while she exhibited the most undeniable proofs of complete restoration, by standing in a firm and erect position. IV. We have next to observe THE IMPRESSION PRODUCED BY THIS MIRACLE, first, on the woman, and then upon the ruler of the synagogue. 1. The effect on the woman was highly pleasing. She was delighted with the change which she instantly experienced; and her heart rose in gratitude to God, who alone, she was convinced, could have effected so wonderful a cure. 2. How different was the effect of this miracle on the mind of the ruler of the synagogue! Instead of directing his attention to the display of power, such as he had never witnessed before; instead of thinking of the goodness which had voluntarily removed so distressing a disease from a person so helpless; instead of sympathizing with the unexpected and rapturous happiness of the woman, he thought only of the captious objections which an enemy might raise. V. We have, lastly, to inquire, WHY THIS MIRACLE WAS DONE ON THE SABBATH? Our Saviour graciously condescended to reason, and He reasoned, as upon all other occasions, in the clearest and most conclusive manner. His mode of reasoning is always best adapted to the object which He had in view. Here it was sufficient to show, that the ruler of the synagogue, and all other Jews, did actions every Sabbath deliberately and intentionally, which, though humane and unavoidable, were not more so than the relief which He had just conferred upon the unfortunate woman. "Hypocrites," said He, "who is there among you, that doth not on the Sabbath loose his ox or his ass from the stall, and lead him away to watering? And must not this woman, a daughter of Abraham, whom Satan hath kept bound these eighteen years, be released from this bond on the Sabbath-day?" Thus our Saviour argues from the practice which they themselves sanctioned, which led to the conclusion that the action He had done was still more laudable, because an act of greater humanity. (*J. Thomson, D.D.*) *The crooked woman made straight :—* I. THE AFFLICTED WOMAN. 1. The nature of her complaint. Probably her spine was affected, so that she could not stand erect. Such a deformity, while humiliating to all, would be particularly trying to a female. 2. Its duration. A sharp affliction, if short, is much easier borne than a lighter one that is long continued, as in this instance. II. THE UNEXPECTED CURE SHE RECEIVED. 1. Where she was cured. In the synagogue. In spite of her deformity, she did not absent herself from the sanctuary. Well for her that she did not! 2. The manner in which she was cured. Two things are mentioned. (1) The gracious words which our Saviour uttered. As in the case of the ten lepers, she is declared to be cured before the act was performed. But with Christ, purpose and accomplishment, willing and doing, are identical. When He speaks, the thing is as good as done; when He commands it is sure to stand fast. (2) The condescending act He performed. 3. How she felt when cured. It is said that "she glorified God," by which is meant that she adored and magnified His holy name for the wonderful deliverance she had experienced. There are many ways in which we are to glorify Him, and this is one of the most important. It might have been supposed that all present would have joined with her in praising God; such, however, was not the case. Other feelings than those of grateful homage and adoration were called forth, which leads us to the next particular, namely—III. THE REFLECTIONS WHICH HER CURE OCCASIONED. In this, the concluding part of the narrative, we have—1. The charge. 2. The defence. 3. The result. It is shown in regard to two classes. (1) The ruler and his party. "And when He had said these things all His adversaries were ashamed." They felt that no answer could be given to what Jesus had been saying; they were therefore speechless and confounded. (2) The multitude. "All the people rejoiced." The miracle had been so signal, and the subsequent vindication had been so complete, that they gave unequivocal demonstrations of their gladness and delight. In applying this subject there are three classes to which it more especially speaks. 1. The wretched vassals of sin and Satan. The condition of this poor sufferer may be regarded as emblematic of every individual who is tied and bound with the chains of his iniquities. Let the sinner's cry therefore be, Lord, loose this miserable soul of mine, which Satan hath so long bound in his slavish fetters. 2. Those whose minds are too much enthralled by earthly affections. It was the misfortune of this woman that her eyes were bent downward, but what was her unavoidable calamity is our wilful sin. Our souls cleave to the dust, and we seek, not the things above, but the vain and perishable objects of time and sense. O how important is it that we should be lifted up from such a grovelling condition, and be liberated, in order thereto, from the thraldom of this present evil world! 3. The downcast and sorrowful. (*Expository Outlines.*) *A daughter of Abraham :*—Set me to look at a downright extraordinary creature, not merely plain but positively ugly—like the woman whom Christ healed, who had been plagued with a devil of infirmity eighteen years, and was now doubled up, hideous—and tell me whether if you look at that woman long enough you will see her beauty. No! The more I look at her, the less I like her—the longer I behold her, the faster I run away from her. But I am called back to her by one little touch. Christ claims for her no beauty, invests her with no fancied fairness. "She, too, is a daughter of Abraham." This is all. But this was enough; for Christ knew that by this appeal He lifted the poor, stricken, bowed creature of infirmity, and gave her a place with the rest of Abraham's children. He called upon the patriotism of the Jews—and they had a patriotism, though but a narrow one. Their cavilling was put an end to at once. This is the secret. The only way to conquer natural disgust at ugliness and sickness and disease, is to set these unsightly objects in the light of Divine Love. "One is your Master, even Christ, and all ye are brethren." Bring these poor degraded wretches, and ask us to love them individually, and we fail to do it. To lift them out of the misery in which they rest, and to make them lovable, you must set them in the light of the great Fatherhood of God and His passionate love of humanity. A man goes into a sick-room, and there poor humanity is at its worst; there you may find the bottom of all man's meanness, his cowardice, his want, and his weakness; there you may see nature in decay, as ugly as the working of a continual want and weakness can make it, But as you cross the threshold of the sickroom, the great need of the patient is more than all; and if you come as the angel of healing, as the angel of true service, the heart is too full and the hand too busy for you to stop to look either for beauty or for ugliness, and that love which prompts to the duty makes labour light. The poor sick person is not less tiresome, or less offensive, or less tedious, but the feeling which prompted disgust has gone. When men declared the possibility of walking on hot iron if the heart were pure and the conscience unstained, they did but figure the great power of Innocence. Una with her lion is but weak, but Una in her innocence is strong. And that which Innocence is thus so truly fabled to do, Divine Love surely does, overleaping difficulty and overcoming disgust. Christianity does not ask us to believe that ugly things are lovely; but, filling man with true love and holy enthusiasm, makes him able to endure the sight of foulness and meanness, that he may cleanse and raise the foul and mean. Thus "one touch of nature makes the whole world kin." Is not this poor woman a daughter of Abraham? Is not this poor degraded wretch a brother? I remember that before England got rid of her great disgrace of slavery, the abolition people used to distribute handbills, headed with a picture of a chained negro ; the poor thick-lipped black asking, "Am I not a man and a brother?" We all acknowledged the claim. But if he had said, "Am I not a beauty?" I should have answered, "No, my brother; you are certainly not a beauty. I decline to admire you." Should he reply, "This is all a matter of taste," I should answer in turn, "I don't believe a word of it. To my eyes you are very particularly ugly." But when he kneels there before me, amd lifts up his poor chained wrists, and puts up that plea for his own humanity—"Am I not a man and a brother?" then, poor, scourged, broken, jaded as he is, I own him. He has a spark of true manhood in him, and shall be scourged, reviled, and sold in bondage no longer. Thus the scheme of the Christian religion completes itself. It has the manliest scorn for meanness, and the manliest pity for weakness. (*G. Dawson, M.A.*) *Freedom realized through believing* :—Once the Emperor of Russia had a plan by which he was to liberate the serfs of that country. There were forty millions of them. Of some of them, their whole time was sold; of others, only a part. The emperor called around him his council, and wanted to have them devise some way to set the slaves at liberty. After they had conferred about it for six months, one night the council sent in their decision, sealed, that they thought it was not expedient. The emperor went down to the Greek Church that night and partook of the Lord's Supper, and he set his house in order, and the next morning you could hear the tramp of soldiers in the streets of St. Petersburg. The emperor summoned his guard, and before noon sixty-five thousand men were surrounding that palace. Just at midnight there came out a proclamation that every slave in Russia was for ever set free. The proclamation had gone forth, and all the slaves of the realm believed it. They have been free ever since. Suppose they had not believed it? They never then would have got the benefit of it. *The highest emancipation* :—A very old Greek myth represents Prometheus chained to a rock by command of Jupiter, who then sent an eagle to feed upon his liver in the daytime, which the god caused to grow again at night. Hercules, however, it was said, killed the eagle, and set suffering Prometheus at liberty. Let this fable, or the narrative in your lesson, remind you that naturally you and all are bound by Satan to his slavery and drudgery, by evil tempers and passions, by bad habits, and in other ways. How the drunkard is enthralled by his craving for drink; the miser by his thirst for gold ; and others by their minding of earthly things ! And how disappointments and anguish, like evil birds, prey upon their spirits. But Christ looses from every infirmity of the soul caused by sin or Satan. And just as a freed bird warbles its joy-throb in the note of thrilling gladness, so we should praise God with joyful lips, as well as glorify Him by our life and best service. "Massa, me will be your slave for ever," said a negro to the kind Englishman who, at great cost, had emancipated him. What shall we do for Jesus, who delivers us from such greater evils? (*Henry R. Burton.*)

Vers. 18, 19. **Unto what is the kingdom of God like ?**—*On the kingdom of God :*—The kingdom of God is an expression of various significations in the sacred volume. Sometimes is meant by it the universal dominion of the Deity; sometimes the final blessedness to which the saints are heirs; and in a more confined sense it frequently signifies the gospel state, or Church of Christ. In this last sense, it is used in the text; and the thing signified is illustrated by a comparison, remarkable for that aptness and beauty, with which all our Saviour's parables are distinguished. I. We are first led by the resemblance, to which our Saviour likens His kingdom, to remark THE SMALLNESS OF CHRISTIANITY IN ITS BEGINNING. Seeking for the symbol with careful consideration, He chooses one, proverbial among the Jews for littleness, the smallest object possessed of life and expansive force. Small as is the symbol, it is not smaller than the thing it was designed to represent. An obscure prophecy was the first germ of Christianity, and its only label, a simple rite : the prophecy—God's promise to the woman, and sacrifice—the rite. We have ever to bless our God that as early as death laid claim to our race, the seed, whose fruit is to nourish us into immortality, was sown by His hand; and in due season made to spring up into lively appearance before an expecting and wondering world. II. This brings me to remark, from the image which Christ furnishes in the text of "the kingdom of God," ITS PROGRESSIVE CHARACTER. In the visible ministry of the Messiah and promulgation of the gospel it assumed its definite appearance. This took place under the most unfavourable circumstances. The soil in which it appeared was incongruous with its nature, and the clime inclement. In its genuine state Christianity had to withstand many a blast; to endure both chilling cold and scorching heat; to encounter everything which could threaten to check its growth, and crush it in the dust. But it was a plant of an inherent vigour, which no climate could kill, nor rudeness impair; and, under the fostering care of Him who rules all seasons and disposes all events, it grew daily, it rose in height, and spread the wonder of the world; it became established. III. This brings me to observe, THAT THE PARABLE CARRIES US FORWARD TO A PERFECTED GROWTH AND TRIUMPHANT STATE OF THE GOSPEL KINGDOM. Though now it presents the sure refuge to all people, its branches are not filled; there is room for much further growth, and dread occasion for much pruning. As yet, defiling vines cling to the stately tree, obstructing its spread, and defacing its beauty. As yet, the Jews "look" not " on Him whom they pierced "; and to many Gentile tribes, the Cross is " foolishness." As yet, there is need to cry to the children of men, " Know the Lord "; and many of them are fluttering wildly, and wandering into dangers, for want of the places in which they may find rest and shelter. But the figure by which the Church is described, and which has appeared hitherto so apt and exact, apprises us of a mature and triumphant state of our Redeemer's kingdom. The plant of the little seed, through its progressive growth, is to attain to a perfect height, and strength, and greatness. It is to become a " great tree "; yea, greater than all the trees that are in the earth. Its root is fixed; and it shall continue to extend its growth till all the inhabitants of our world rejoice in the shadow of the branches of it. The Christian religion is composed of such elements; there are in it such principles and arrangements as suggest of themselves that if it be true it is designed for universal extension and perpetual duration. We have now considered the beautiful and exact resemblance furnished by Christ of " the kingdom of God." There are inferences from this subject of great weight and variety. Let me entreat your patience while I adduce only a few which are too instructive to be omitted. 1. The first is, that this is one of those singularly important comparisons or parables which are not only illustrative but prophetic. 2. Another important inference from what has been said is, that the gospel is the object of constant providential care. 3. The last inference I shall make from our Saviour's lively representation of His kingdom is, the encouragement it is calculated to afford to His pious people. (*Bishop Dehon.*) **It is like a grain of mustard-seed.**—*The mustard-seed :*—" The kingdom of heaven is like to a grain of mustard-seed—which indeed is is the least of all seeds." It is no exception to the law of growth which prevails throughout nature, and exemplifies how what is mightiest is often the product of what is apparently feeblest. Not only the giant oak, capable of defying the fiercest storms, but whole forests which yield materials for a nation's fleets, may have lain wrapped up within a single tiny acorn. In history, whatever has been most enduring and has exerted most influence, has been born in obscurity and feebleness, and grown up by almost imperceptible stages—whereas, whatever has, like the gourd of Jonah, arisen to its full height of a sudden, has withered and died away with the same rapidity that it arose. But Christianity is the most striking instance of the kind. Its fountain-head is the manger of a stable in a small Judean town. There is a strange unobtrusiveness about the character and mission of the Author and Finisher of our faith. When we know who He was, the only begotten Son of God, and what His purpose was—the salvation of the world—we might expect to see Him take up a position full in the world's view, attracting to Himself man's whole attention, making kings His deputies, and philosophers His apostles, and orators His heralds, and armed captains His attendants. But no! the manger of a stable was His cradle—poverty, hard labours, great sorrows, keen sufferings, were His constant companions. It was the little seed-corn which had to be dropped into the ground and die ere the earth could bear a harvest of righteousness and peace. It was that by the preaching of which a few poor, illiterate Galilean fishermen were called upon to brave and overcome the opposition which all the wealth, authority, antiquity, military force, taste, and philosophy, as well as ignorance and sin, of the world, could muster against them, to conquer the prejudices of the Jews, to undermine the superstitions under which Rome had grown up to be the mistress of the world, to confound the subtleties and wisdom of the Greeks, and to dispel the darkness of heathenism. It looked the most hopeless of tasks. There are instruction and warning for us in that. The gospel is the most emphatic protest against judging of things by their outward appearance. It is the solemn and decisive testimony of God to the superiority of spiritual principle over material magnificence. It casts down power and might to exalt spirit and truth. Many persons have an eye only to behold external and worldly greatness. There is no hope for any one, however, so long as he persists in looking at things with that dull, unspiritual eye. The gospel, in all that is distinctive of it, is spiritual, and can only be spiritually discerned. The parable having told us that the gospel in its origin is small, weak, and apparently insignificant, proceeds to speak of its growth, of its amazing progress. From the least of seeds it becomes the greatest of herbs; from an almost invisible grain it rises into a tree, where the birds of the air find shelter. It is unnecessary to insist that the history of the last eighteen hundred years has amply verified this representation. The Church, which at Pentecost only numbered a few score of persons, soon counted its adherents by thousands, burst the trammels of Judaism, and, even in the lifetime of its first apostles, established itself, without any other instrumentality than the foolishness of preaching, in all the large towns of the civilized world. All Europe and America are now more or less under its sway, and it is advancing with slow but sure steps to the conquest of the entire earth. It is more important to observe, as the text specially calls on us to do, that this long history is throughout a growth—that it may be fitly likened to a seed becoming a tree. Let us so look at it for a little, and see what lessons it has for our profit. 1. This is the first. The whole of Christianity, in so far as it is true, once lay in a small compass. All the truths, all the institutions, all the virtues which it embodies, may be traced back to a single life as their germ. The mustard-tree was wholly in the mustard-seed. The oak, great although it now is, once lay wrapped up entire in the acorn. All that properly belongs to it lay folded there. Nothing save what is foreign and hurtful, nothing save excrescences and parasites, have come from any other source. The influences of light and heat, and wind and dew, have only brought out what was there from the first. It is so, likewise, with Christianity. It has grown up through eighteen hundred years, it covers now a very large portion of the earth, but all that truly belongs to it even at this hour has sprung from the lowly life of Jesus. All that is good in its creeds, its institutions, the conduct it inspires, has germinated from some word of His—has lain as a thought in His mind or an affection in His heart; and whatever man has introduced of his own into religious belief or practice is only an excrescence, a parasite, a cause of weakness and decay. The lowliest life ever lived on earth has thus been infinitely the most fruitful. The least of all seeds has become the greatest among herbs. 2. The seed has not only all the rudiments of the future tree within it, but the life which unfolds them and sends out first the root and trunk, and then the branches, leaves, blossoms, and fruit. And the word of the gospel has likewise an indestructible principle of vitality, which cannot be repressed, cannot be arrested. It grows by the very necessity of its nature, under the influence of grace, just as the living seed, by the very necessity of its nature, under a genial sky cannot remain in the ground, but sends up blade and bud and branch. There is in this assertion no latent fatalism. Although the gospel has indeed been in history like a tree growing out of a living seed, it follows not that human will has had nothing to do with its progress. There is nothing in history, properly so called, with which human will has not had to do. Every improvement it tells of has been effected by human self-denial and toil. The country we live in was once covered with putrid morasses and gloomy forests, and yielded only a scanty and impure subsistence to a few hordes of wandering savages. Now its morasses are dried up, its forests cleared away, large cities stand thick strewn over it, its well-cultivated plains yield food enough for millions, and its industry produces an annual revenue the most enormous. What has wrought the change? Labour, and labour alone—labour of mind and of body. Not an inch of conquest has been won without mental exertion and physical toil, without anxious thought and an active hand. Religion is no exception to this rule, but its most striking example. It has had nobler and more numerous martyrs and missionaries—has called forth more heroic labours and costlier sacrifices—than all other causes together. And this is quite consistent with the fact that the gospel grows by a life of its own—that though man's labour is needed to apply and diffuse it, he neither makes it nor puts life and fruitfulness into it—that he receives it with these in itself, so that if he cast it into the ground it will spring and grow up of its own Divine energy, and according to its own Divine laws. 3. Growth implies increasing divergence and definiteness of parts and functions. It is a separation of the one into the many, a change from the simple to the complex, from the vague to the distinct. The seed out of which a plant issues is at first uniform in tissue and composition, but soon it divides into two parts, afterwards new contrasts appear in each of these, and it is by endless such changes that the complex combination of tissues and organs in a perfect plant is produced. While the parts are thus increased in number, each of them becomes more prominent in itself, more sharply distinguished from others, and more strictly confined to its own special use. Wherever growth takes place, this is the process traceable. It is what we see in every herb, in every animal, in civilization, in government, language, science, and art. Different as all these are in themselves, there is only the one way in which they can grow, in which they can truly progress. The kingdom of God conforms to the same conditions. Its history has consisted throughout in the evolution of doctrines, institutions, and modes of life, out of a very simple germ. Our elaborate systems of theological science so far as true, our manifold institutions for religious and benevolent purposes so far as good, our endlessly diversified modes of social being so far as right, are developments of the living word of the gospel, in which, however, they lay enfolded only as the tree in its seed, as results in their principle, as special and definite dogmas in broad and general statements. Those who say, "Let us cast to the winds our creeds, our systems, our definite dogmas, and return to the primitive simplicity of apostolic men," forget that God has not left it to the world's own will to return of a sudden, or to return at all, to the point from which it has taken eighteen centuries for it to advance. They might as well counsel us to throw off all the laws and institutions, all the countless arrangements of the elaborated civilization in which we live, and retrograde to the rude and simple life of the earliest dwellers in Asia and Europe. We are where we are, where long ages of thought and toil have placed us, and, even if ungrateful enough to desire it, there is no going back for us now. 4. The growth of the kingdom of God has been continuous. We may fail to measure its progress from day to day, because it is not rapid, but slow, not with observation, but without it. There is still another truth involved, and it is one which we must not despise because it is simple. Growth requires time. God has everywhere placed that as an inevitable separation between germination and maturity, between the seed and the perfect tree. Let us conform, then, to the condition. When we are despondent or angry because our labours in a Christian cause are not crowned with immediate success, we are no wiser than the little child who deposits a seed in the ground and is grieved not to see it springing up on the very day it has done so. (*R. Flint.*) *The mustard-seed and the leaven:*—I. THE GERM OF THE KINGDOM. 1. It is something new. Watch that sower: he takes the seed and plants it in his garden. The seed suits the soil, but it was not in the soil at first. It came from above, out of the sower's hand. 2. The germ is small at first: "like to a grain"—a very small particle—" of mustard-seed, which a man took." II. ITS GROWTH. III. THE GLORY OF THE KINGDOM. 1. The kingdom is one, though it belongs to all ages and nations. Christ speaks of a kingdom, never of kingdoms. A tree is a unity, for though it has many leaves and branches, it has but one root and one life-sap. Those who are sundered by seas, and ages, and thousands of influences, are all made one by Christ. 2. It is a world-wide kingdom. As the tree is for every bird from any quarter of heaven that wishes its shelter, so Christ's religion is for all sorts of people. 3. And it blesses, and only blesses. It creates and increases all that is bright and joyous. Christ's is a kingdom of love, of help, of grace, of salvation, and heaven is its end. 4. It will become very great though very small in its beginnings. (*J. Wells, M.A.*) *The external progress of the kingdom as illustrated by the growth of the mustard-seed:*—It is ever important to remember that Christianity, at first like a small grain of seed, spread throughout the world, until the nations of the earth came to flock like birds to its protecting shelter, by no aid except its own inherent spiritual power. There was nothing to help it in the character of its early teachers. There was nothing to make its progress easy in the conditions of the Jewish and Gentile worlds. It came to the Jewish world, and found it saturated with thoughts of Jewish exclusiveness, and full of hopes of an earthly Deliverer. There was nothing in the teaching of this Messiah to appeal to the one, or to pander to the other. It told the Jew that his dreams of a temporal Messiah were futile, that it was a kingdom of spiritual power—not supported by external force or conquering by arms—which it had come to establish amongst men. Thus, though it appealed to no religious or national instinct in the Jew, though it was hostile to both, Christianity triumphed. Nor, again, in the Gentile world, represented by the two great nations of Greece or Rome, was there any congenial soil for the little seed of early Christendom to take root in, and find its sustenance. The Greek world was full of the pride of intellect, and the worship of sensuous beauty, and to it Christianity came with no scheme of a new-fangled philosophy, with no subtleties of scholastic ethics. The preaching of the Cross of Christ, the teaching of a religion of self-sacrifice and love, so simple that the child could understand it, was its message. It presented as the object of their adoration and worship no incarnation of physical beauty, no image of physical strength, but a Nazarene upon a cross—His features so marred with sorrow that there was no beauty in Him that they should desire Him. And yet this Christianity had an inherent force of its own, before which the intellectual pride and the philo-sophic genius of Greece had to bow at last in submission. St. Paul preached at Athens, and not a few but felt as they listened, within sight of their own Academy, and beneath the shadow of honeyed Hymettus where the sages had trod, that this new preacher taught, with a power not of this world, a grander faith, which must outlast even the city of the Violet Crown. The wave spread still westward to Rome —proud mistress of the world. It fared as ill with her material and political strength as it had done with the intellectual force of Athens. To those who wor-shipped force and were glutted with military conquests, this new faith came preaching tenderness, forgiveness, charity. To Rome, who saw her eagles swoop in the farthest east and west, it proclaimed the supremacy of spiritual triumphs— it preached the deliverance of the captive—the brotherhood of nations. At first only whispered in prison cells, or flung to the beasts of the arena, or its holy symbol grasped in feeble hands, and pressed to dying breasts of martyrs, the religion of Christ soon won its way over every obstacle, and at last Christianity entered the imperial palace, and wore the diadem of the Cæsars. Now, when we turn from these triumphs of Christianity to examine what means she employed for her propagation, we can find nothing, humanly speaking, to account for it. Twelve men—Jews, without hereditary distinc ion; without political influence; without (except in one or two cases) intellectual acquirements—these were the men who —without any aid on earth; with a gospel that was opposed to every national, and philosophic, and religious prejudice of Jew, and Greek, and Roman; which was hostile to every feeling of pride and selfishness in the human heart—accomplished the grandest and most stupendous revolution the world had ever seen. People say sometimes that they find it hard to believe the miracles on which Christianity is based—surely the grandest, greatest miracle is the existence of Christianity itself. If, then, there were nothing in the outside world to which it appealed; nothing in the natural hearts of men which it came to satisfy: if we cannot discover in the characters of those who preached it any human reason to explain its progress— how are we to account for the spread of Christ's kingdom, except by attributing it to some spiritual power of its own? (*T. T. Shore, M.A.*)

Vers. 20, 21. **It is like leaven.**—*The hidden leaven:*—The kingdom of heaven, or the work of God in the soul, is like leaven. 1. It at once occurs to us that leaven is something foreign to and different from the meal in which it is hidden;

that it does not spring from or arise out of any fermentation in the meal; for, if left to itself, the meal would decay, and would never become leavened. Leaven has therefore to be introduced. It must be inserted, or, as the word here expresses it, "hidden." And this implies that "the kingdom of God cometh not with observation." Yet it comes, it is not there, it does not grow in a man, it does not come in the natural birth, it is not born "of blood, nor of the will of the flesh, nor of the will of man, but of God"; therefore, wherever there is the work of holiness in the soul of the sinner, it is "a new birth unto righteousness," he is "delivered from the power of darkness and translated into the kingdom of God's dear Son." 2. Then, it is clear, in the next place, that grace in the heart will be an abiding work—it will be energetic and permanent. Howsoever and wheresoever a man receives grace, whether in regeneration, at baptism, in approaching God's table, in the reading or the preaching of the Word, through the instrumentality of sickness or tribulation; whatever the time, or the date, or the circumstance, it will be active, and it will put forth energy in the soul. The very purpose and object of it is that it may leaven and produce a revolution, a rejuvenation, a transformation in the heart in which it is lodged. Therefore, brethren, we have no saving grace, unless it is working in our souls, and working mightily and effectually. 3. Next, it is clear that the result will be in those in whom it is hidden that it will be assimilated, and that it will produce effects similar to itself. Though the leaven be a foreign infusion into the meal, yet the leaven acts upon the meal, and makes it partake of its flavour, and like the leaven in taste, and action, and result; so that it assimilates. And is it not so in regard to grace got into a man's heart? It is not to be *upon* him as a mere scion—tied to a tree, but not incorporated with the tree; but it is to be *in* him, as a graff inserted in the stock and incorporated with the stock, so that it is no longer the old graff, but it is producing genuine fruit; instead of the crab, the apple from the garden of Eden shall be the result. Even so the grace of God in the soul of man works in him. 4. But it is a comfort to think, in the next place, that the assimilating operation of this leaven is gradual and progressive. It is not all at once. It is what may be in existence some time before it is discoverable in its results. Its progress is slow, but certain. 5. And it is pervasive. The leaven leavens on until it pervades the whole mass. A man, if he has the grace of God, cannot be good in one week and bad in another. 6. And then, brethren, the crown of the whole is, that the leaven shall ultimately pervade the whole mass. Before it is complete the whole mass is assimilated, and prepared, and so the kingdom of heaven is like unto leaven hid in meal. Yes, brethren, this is indeed the ground of our encouragement. He is faithful, "who also will do it"; and again, "God is faithful" who will "perform"; and again, it is said, God "worketh in you both to will and to do"; and, if He works in you, can the work fail?" (*R. Hall, M.A.*) *The growth of the kingdom :*—You tell your child that this pine-tree out here in the sandy field is one day going to be as large as that great sonorous pine that sings to every wind in the wood. The child, incredulous, determines to watch and see whether the field-pine really does grow and become as large as you say it will. So, the next morning, he goes out and takes a look at it, and comes back and says, "It has not grown a particle." At night he goes out and looks at it again, and comes back and says, "It has not grown a bit." The next week he goes out, and looks at it again, and comes back and says, "It has not grown yet. Father said it would be as large as the pine-tree in the wood, but I do not see any likelihood of its becoming so." How long did it take the pine-tree in the wood to grow? Two hundred years. Then men who lived when it began to grow have been buried, and generations besides have come and gone since then. And do you suppose that God's kingdom is going to grow so that you can look at it and see that it has grown during any particular day? You cannot see it grow. All around you are things that are growing, but that you cannot see grow. And if it is so with trees, and things that spring out of the ground, how much more is it so with the kingdom of God! That kingdom is advancing surely, though it advances slowly, and though it is invisible to us. You will remember our Master's beautiful parable, where He says, "The kingdom of heaven is like unto leaven, which a woman took and hid in three measures of meal till the whole was leavened." I suppose you know what that means. I go into your kitchen when you are baking bread, and ask, "What is that you are stirring into that flour?" You say, "It is yeast." I ask, "What is it for?" You say, "It is to raise the bread." I imagine that it is to raise it in a way that shall be perceptible to my senses, and say, "Let me see it do it." You set the bread away in a warm place, or at the south, in a cool place, if you can find one, and you say, "Now it will rise." After watching it closely for a while, I say to you, "I do not see that it has risen at all." You say, ' Bless you, my child, you cannot see it rise!" I go away, and stay till I think it will have come up, if there is any such thing as its coming up, and then go back, but I cannot see that it has undergone any change. I wait and wait and wait, and at last say, "I do not believe it is going to rise." And you say, "It has risen already," and tear it open ; and lo! it is full of holes ; and you say, "Now do not you believe that it has risen ? It has been rising all the time, only you could not see it rise." Christ says that His kingdom is just like that. It is a great kingdom, which extends all over the world, and into which He has put the leaven of Divine grace. That grace is like yeast, and it works in this kingdom of Christ. You cannot see it, even if you watch for it ; but there it is ; and if, after a while, you go and look at it, you will be convinced that it has been working, by the results which it has produced. You will find that things have been done, though you could not see them done. Men are becoming better the world over, though you cannot trace the process by which they are becoming better. Christ's kingdom goes forward from age to age, though you cannot discern the steps by which it is going forward. While men, as individuals, pass off from the stage of life, God's work does not stop. (*H. W. Beecher.*) *The leaven :*—I. THE KINGDOM OF GOD IN THE HEART IS LIKE LEAVEN HID IN MEAL. It is so, first of all, because something which does not belong to human nature, something which does not originate there, is introduced into it. The leaven was not in the meal from the first, did not inherently belong to it ; on the contrary, a woman took the leaven and hid it in the meal. The meal did not change itself : and no more does man change himself. It is only a power not his own which can change him. But the doctrine of the Cross is indeed in a heart as leaven in meal. It is as if *hid* in the heart. You cannot see it. You cannot touch it. It ferments within, concealed from feeble human sense; a secret power of life at the centre of the soul ; a silent, unobtrusive power slowly but surely working its way outwards. Before the gospel can change the heart in any degree, before it can act either quickly or slowly, it must of course be *in* the heart, actually in it, and not outside of it, however near to it. The leaven did not, and could not, produce any change in the meal until the woman opened the mass of meal and put the leaven into the midst of it. Leaven in one corner of a room will not leaven meal in another ; and no less absurd is it to suppose that, if the gospel be merely in your intellects, and the world be in your hearts, the gospel so placed will renew your hearts and sanctify your lives. The manner, also, in which leaven acts on meal illustrates singularly well the manner in which the gospel of the kingdom, the truth as it is in Christ, acts on the heart and life. Leaven changes the nature, yet does not destroy the substance of meal. Meal leavened remains meal, but endowed with new properties, and adapted for new uses. It acquires another character, another appearance, another fragrance and taste. So the gospel does not destroy any inherent power or faculty of the mind, but gives to all its powers and faculties a different character, a new direction. It does not even destroy the natural peculiarities distinctive of individuals. Again, different men have been endowed with intellect, sensibility, and will, in very different proportions. In one man intellect greatly preponderates; in another sensibility ; and in another will. There are some who seem, as it were, all intellect, who analyze everything, reason out everything—who can find no rest until they see clearly the naked truth—who must have their grasp firmly on principles before they can proceed at all, but who are exceedingly self-contained as to the expression of feeling, and from whose lips anything like sentiment or poetry would sound unnatural and unreal. There are others whose minds, although far inferior in closeness of intellectual grasp and keenness of intellectual penetration, yet possess a delicacy and depth of feeling which render them, perhaps, still more worthy of admiration. There are others who with very moderate endowments, either intellectual or moral, command the greatest respect, and win implicit confidence through their force, decision, and rectitude of will. Now, one of these forms of character may be more desirable than another, and a better form than any of them, an ideally best form, might be one in which the three elements— intellect, sensibility, and will—were equally mingled. But certain it is that all the forms exist, and that their distinctive features have their ground in the original constitution of individuals. Certain it is also that the gospel does not reduce these forms to one common type. It has no tendency even to lessen any of their characteristic peculiarities. Again, the gospel acts like leaven, because it works from within outwards in all directions. Leaven diffuses itself through the mass in which it is hid equally all round until the whole is leavened. So the gospel is a power which does not exert itself, as it were, only in one straight line, but in every direction all through the nature. It does not seize on one faculty of the soul and change it, and then advance to another faculty and change it, and so on till the whole man is changed. It does not deal with the will at one time, with the feelings at another, and the intellect at another, waiting until it has effected a complete conquest in the one region of human nature before it proceeds to the others ; but it grasps all the elements and faculties of the soul at once, and works on all simultaneously. This diffusion of the gospel through the life is like that of leaven in meal, secret, gradual, and complete. It is secret. The operation of the Spirit in the regeneration of man is as invisible as the operation of leaven in the conversion of meal into bread. No eye but that of God can trace it. II. Having thus endeavoured to show that the gospel works in the heart of the individual like leaven in meal, I have now to show THAT IT WORKS AFTER THE SAME MANNER IN SOCIETY. It is a twofold process—special and general. There is a special action of part on part, and also a general action of the whole on each part. There is a special action of part on part. Christ, when He had communicated of His life and Spirit to His apostles, for instance, enabled them too, poor and despised and unlearned as they were, to communicate of the same to others, and so to become in their turn the leaven of the world. In a mass of meal subjected to the action of leaven, each leavened particle acts upon all those in immediate contact with it, leavening more deeply the only partially leavened, and conveying the leaven to those which have not previously come under its power ; and not otherwise is it in society, where every individual who has experienced in himself the efficacy of the gospel becomes for the circle of his influence, as leaven, to work still farther. He communicates of the grace which he has received. Besides this special action of part on part, of individual on individual, there is also, as I have said, a general action of the whole on each part of society, on the individual. The gospel is not without influence even where it is not closed with as the power of God unto salvation. It so far imbues, or at least modifies, by its spirit all the laws, institutions, and usages of society, that none, not even those most hostile to it, live as they would have done if it had not been. It improves both the characters and conduct of men in every case, although it may be only seldom that it works a genuine conversion in them. It demonstrates its energy more or less even on those who count themselves unworthy of eternal life. Let us draw from history an illustration or two. The civilizations of antiquity rested on force. Slavery was their central fact. It is only slowly, only step by step, that society has emancipated itself from this condition of things. St. Paul sent back a fugitive slave to his master, the runaway convert Onesimus, to Philemon ; and neither in the Old Testament nor the New is there any explicit statement against slavery. The spirit of the gospel condemns it, but not the letter. The spirit of the gospel, however, gradually put forth its Divine power. Little by little the slave of antiquity gave place to the serf of the Middle Ages, attached to the soil, but also protected by it ; little by little feudal Europe ripened into industrial Europe, and the serf became the hired labourer ; little by little free labour and commerce rose into importance, and brought with them security of person and property, the spirit of independence, the sense of human equality, the power of self-government, a truer conception of justice, the arts of peace, a new and broader and far more Christian civilization. Our own day has seen the ancient tyranny of man over man, in its double form of pure slavery and of serfage, receive two signal and heavy blows, one on the old continent and the other on the new, and on both, in Russia and in America alike, the present has proved itself stronger than the past— what is pagan has had to succumb before what is Christian. Take another example. See what the gospel has done in the domestic circle. The pagan family, with its deplorable degradation of the woman, continued for generations within the Church. That was cast off at length, but the grave error of despising and depreciating domestic life was introduced. The Reformers were gradually led to perceive that the family required not to be suppressed, but only to be sanctified ; yet their views of it were pervaded by a narrow and legal spirit which has borne bitter fruits, and which society has been ever since outgrowing. The true conception of the family is of far more recent date than the Reformation, and is still vague and imperfect. If we ask to whom this progress is due, no one can distinctly tell us, for it is a silent and secret movement which has been little if at all associated with individual and party names. It comes of that unceasing purpose which runs through the ages, widening the thoughts and sympathies of men. It comes of that invisible power which dwells in the gospel and works through humanity, leavening it more and more, transforming it more and more into the holy, beautiful, and glorious kingdom of God. (*R. Flint.*) *The leaven :*—I. GRACE OUT OF US. The leaven was not in the meal to begin with, but was put into it by the woman. And so we must go out of ourselves to find the source and supply of grace. We are glad to know that this leaven is sometimes in young hearts very early, before they can remember, even from their birth; but in every case it is the same heavenly leaven. It brings a new life into the soul. II. GRACE FOR US. The leaven is for the meal: anywhere else it is useless, lost. Planted in the soil, it decays; left in the open air, it wastes. As God has made leaven for the meal, so all His grace is for the soul of man. And God's grace is for the sinful only. God the Father does not need it; Jesus Christ does not need it; the Holy Ghost does not need it; the angels in heaven do not need it—they have no sins to be forgiven, no wants to be supplied; the angels who fell have it not in their offer. The riches of God's grace are all to be used, and to be used by sinners like us. III. GRACE IN US. The woman in baking opens up the meal with her hands, puts the leaven in the centre, and covers it over. The Roman Catholics seem, many of them, to forget that the leaven must be in them. The Italian brigand wears carefully on his breast a cross and charms which the priest has blessed. He must have the sign on the breast, though he has not a particle of the thing signified within. You have heard of "the Holy Stairs" at Rome. They belonged, it is said, to the house of Pontius Pilate, and were mounted by our Saviour on the last day of His life. One of the popes granted nine years of indulgence for each of the twenty-eight steps, to every one who climbed them on his knees, with a contrite heart. Pius VII. in 1817 "renewed this indulgence, but perpetually, and declared that it may be applied also to the souls in purgatory "; and the last pope approved of that declaration. It is most humbling to see hundreds at the present day climbing these stairs on their knees and kissing them, and fancying that their souls have somehow got much profit by the exercise. The marble steps have been covered three times with wood to protect the marble from being worn away ! and you notice that the marble in the centre has been worn down two or three inches. Luther was climbing these stairs, when the words flashed upon him, " The just shall live by faith." Filled with shame, he rushed off, and from that day remembered that grace is something within and not without the man. In the Middle Ages wicked kings often gave orders that they should be buried in a monk's frock. Wearing such a dress, they hoped that Peter would be deceived, and would let him into heaven. And Popish errors often lurk among Protestants; for all the errors of Romanism have their origin in fallen human nature. Lord Macaulay tells that a Colonel Turner was hanged for burglary fully two hundred years ago. At the gallows he told the crowd that he had received great comfort from one reflection: he had never entered a church without taking off his hat. Ah ! you may find traces of such mistakes nearer home. There is room in your little heart for the whole kingdom of heaven; but it must be in your heart, else all the outward observances in the world won't profit you. For the leaven never leavens till it is hid *in* the meal. So grace has no power till it is planted in your inmost part. IV. GRACE SPREADS IN US. It has been found out quite lately how the leaven spreads. It grows like a plant with the most amazing rapidity. When the meal has enough of water and warmth, the leaven multiplies itself on every side. Though it seems dead and small, it is yet a living thing with an enormous greed of growth, which is one of the greatest wonders in the wonder-world of chemistry. Leaven does not spread in unground grain, for the hard covering resists its entrance. And so the coatings of our pride must be taken away, and our spirits must be made contrite, and then shall the leaven spread. O my God, is Thy leaven in me? Is it spreading within me? V. GRACE SPREADS, OR SHOULD SPREAD, THROUGH AND THROUGH US. For it is like leaven hid in three measures of meal till the whole was leavened. Your tea-table yields a good illustration of a spreading power like that of leaven. The melted sugar goes through every drop of your tea and sweetens it; the cream mixes itself with the whole cupful, and colours it. God's grace should likewise give a heavenly sweetness and colouring to the whole life. It does more than touch, it influences; it does more than influence, it controls all. We may take the three measures of meal for the three chief parts of our nature—the body, the mind, and the heart. Our nature is not diseased as an apple or a potato is diseased, but as the blood is diseased when poison courses through the whole. Nor is our nature like those newly-built ships, which have many watertight compartments, one of which may be filled with the inrushing sea, while the rest remain dry. The parts of our nature lie together like the three measures of meal, so that the leaven can pass easily from the one to the other, and so through all. Grace will thus mix itself up with your home-life, your school-life, and by and by, with your public life. Spreading silently through the whole, it will, by uniting all the graces upon you, make your character gracious and graceful. VI. GRACE SHOULD SPREAD THROUGH US INTO OTHERS. The leaven wins over all the meal to its own side, and makes it like itself. A clerk who hated swearing entered one of our large offices where nearly all were profane. Soon not an oath was heard. His example, by a happy contagion, prevailed among all his associates. A minister, whose church was situated near the barracks, one day said to a soldier, " I wonder at you soldiers ; you can go up to the cannon mouth, and you have not courage to pray before your comrades." "You are mistaken," was the reply. "A recruit lately came into our room, and the first night he knelt down to pray. A shower of pillows, belts, and shoes fell upon him. He did so for five nights. On the fifth night, one of the wildest men in our company shouted, 'Halt, lads! that's enough ; he can stand fire !' That wild man knelt down by his side, and now most of the men in our room engage in prayer, and several of us have become professors of Christ." (*J. Wells, M.A.*)

Vers. 23, 24. **Lord, are there few that be saved ?**—*Unpractical questions about religion :*—The man that asked this question has long been dead, but the character lives, and it is not among the rarest exhibitions that we see. We carry to the Bible, if not the very same question he put to the Saviour, yet questions as unpractical and irrelevant, or if not in every sense irrelevant, yet premature and of minor importance ; and so it is when you have the opportunity of conversing with clergymen and others, for whose theological knowledge and science in the Scriptures you have some respect. Your questions are such as these, "What is likely to be the future condition of such as die in infancy?" Cannot you trust them in the hands of God? Are you afraid that He will do them injustice? "What is the probability of the salvation of the heathen?" And why do you wish to estimate that? Is not this one thing clear, that their condition for the present life, and their prospects for the life to come, would both be far better, provided they had the gospel? And is it not manifestly your duty to do all that is in your power to send them the gospel? What, then, do you want more? Why expend all your charity in wondering, and wishing, and hoping, and pitying? Let it rather flow forth in its appropriate channel, in action. Do something. Promote foreign missions. That is the way to care for the heathens. Another is curious to know if we shall recognize each other in heaven. That is taking it for granted that we shall get there. Let us make sure of heaven, before we agitate the question of recognition. And then let us be satisfied with this, if our heavenly Father sees that it will be conducive to the happiness of the children whom He has adopted from earth that they should recognize each other and recollect the relations and renew the intimacies of life, it will be so, and if not, it will be otherwise. There are those who investigate the Scriptures primarily for some historical purpose, or to resolve some prophetical question. Others consult these oracles but as critics ; and still others, only as cavillers, anxious to see how much they can discover to find fault with. They wonder what this passage means, or how it is possible to reconcile this part of the Bible with that, or what could have induced our Saviour to express Himself as He is reported to have done on certain occasions which they will specify ; and the conclusion to which they come, perhaps, after all, is that this is a very strange and unintelligible volume ; they can make nothing out of it. Ah! and is it so that they can make nothing out of it? Can they not make out of it what their duty is? Do they not but too plainly perceive that it is something, which they have no disposition to do, and is not this the secret of their fault-finding? (*W. Nevins, D.D.*)   *Silence of Scripture on irrelevant questions :*— Thus, a Government sends forth a colonist ; but gives him just information enough to enable him to perform his particular work. A general charges an inferior officer with a special duty ; but here, too, there is silence as to whatever does not belong to this duty. To enlarge the official directions given in either case, so as to include all the knowledge the superior may possess, would perplex the agent and withdraw his attention from that which concerned his work to that which did not concern it.

And if we are to expect such silence in a parent's dealings with a child, and in a Government's dealing with a subaltern, how much more reason have we to expect it in the dealings of God with man! God knows all things, and endures from eternity to eternity! Man comes into the world knowing nothing, lives at the best a life which endures for a few years, and in this short life is charged with the momentous work of preparing for the eternity to come. Silence, then, on all irrelevant questions is what we would expect in the revelation of an all-wise God, and of the irrelevancy He is the sole Judge. *Prying into the secret things of God reproved :*—I. THE QUESTION PROPOSED. II. THE ANSWER GIVEN TO IT. I. The question is put in very general, and seemingly inoffensive, terms; yet probably a great deal of Jewish pride and uncharitableness couched under it. This busy man's inquiry proceeded from an ill-natured hope of being confirmed in the national persuasion, that God was not the God of the Gentiles; but had reserved future happiness for the Israelites alone. But supposing there was no ground for imputation either of ill-will or vanity; still all such questions—for this is a leading one to many others—are useless and irreverent. Since, then, God is just, He will make none miserable farther than they deserve; since He is good, He will both pardon and reward in such degree as is fit; and since He is wise, what appears disorder and confusion to our short sight will appear in the end perfect regularity and proportion. But why was our nature formed so liable to fall short of it, in the sad degree that we often do? II. Part of the text, to which I now proceed, REFUSE TO GRATIFY THE QUERIST'S CURIOSITY, AND RETURN AN ANSWER ENTIRELY PRACTICAL : that it was not the business of mankind to pry into what God had hid, but mind what He had revealed, and to master another kind of difficulty, that of fulfilling His commands; that multitudes indeed, who professed religion, would finally appear to have professed it in vain; but this was a matter not to raise idle speculations upon. One fatal mistake of believers in religion hath always been an absurd notion that their steady faith in it, their zeal to support and spread that faith, their punctilious observance of certain forms, their constant practice of some precepts, and their periodical pretences of sorrow for having wilfully lived in the neglect of the rest; that one or other of these things would be accepted, instead of true piety and virtue. Immediately after the text He declares, that neither acknowledgment of His authority, nor attendance on His teaching, nor anything else, shall avail the workers of iniquity. They who have not been thus forewarned go on indeed with great ease; but it is not in religion that they go on. Doubtless common decency and outward regularity are very valuable things—would God more attention were paid to them! But still with these there may be little true sense of duty to God, or even man; little care that the heart and affections be such as they ought; nay, much indulgence of very criminal actions, either concealed from the world or approved by it. In short, almost everything may be right in the opinion of those around us, perhaps in our own: and almost everything wrong in the eyes of our Maker. That most men act wickedly is no more an objection against religion, than that most men act unwisely is against common prudence. That so many fail by taking a wrong course is only a warning to make sure of taking the right. And if in that several duties are painful, it is not Christianity that hath made them so. All its peculiar precepts are easy in themselves, and assistances to the practice of the rest. (*T. Secker.*)   *The number of the saved :*—A natural question to any one who thinks seriously of the destiny of human life. 1. Probably prompted in this instance merely by curiosity. This Jew, educated from childhood under a creed in which the most rigid aspects of the doctrine of election were taught, came to Christ in the hope that he might get some authoritative statement of the mystery of predestination from this One whom he regarded as a prophet of God. Christ replies, "Strive," &c. Whether there be few or many saved is no business of yours; what you have to do is to make your own calling and election sure; that cannot be accomplished by indulging in idle speculations about other people, but by struggling yourself with your whole energy, to enter into and be within the narrow door that leads to salvation. Not easy work, but difficult; not a question about your opinions, but a question of action. Agonize as wrestler, and be content with nothing but admittance. 2. Another sense in which we may put the question. Are there few or many who show in their lives that they are being delivered, because of their faith and love towards Christ, from their sins, and that the gospel they profess is producing in them the Christian spirit—the spirit of love, purity, truth, gentleness, considerateness, kindness, righteousness? This seems to have been the very light in which Jesus

Christ Himself viewed the matter of salvation, for He goes on, after this man puts his question, to cast discredit upon the religion of opinions and observances, and to insist upon doing the will of God as being the only security. It is when we put the question in this sense, that we may discover ground for some serious reflections. Are there many whose lives are savingly affected by the religion they profess? Is the Christian spirit being realized in Christian society? Are there few or many of whom you can confidently assert that there is a deliverance from sin actually going on, and of goodness being attained, which is the fruit of their faith and love towards Christ? For my own part, the sad conviction is frequently borne in upon me that, when thus tested, the question admits almost of only one reply. How seldom is it that when we go to Church we expect to be made spiritually better, to be saved from our everyday sins, and to get such convictions and strength as may make us liker and liker the Master in life and character? (*N. Macleod.*)

Ver. 24. **Strive to enter in at the strait gate.**—*Christ's warning against formalism:*—This has been called "a serious answer to an idle question." The answer is not only serious, but rendered with striking skill and power. The questioner was a single Pharisee. The answer is directed to the whole sect. The question related to the "few" that might be saved. The answer emphasizes the "many" who are in danger of being lost. The question was idle and speculative. The answer is an appeal to immediate action and earnest endeavour. I. The material tastes of men. It is undeniable that men love forms for their own sake. It is self-evident also that some degree of form is indispensable to spiritual religion. "I am from above, ye are from beneath." Here is the gulf opening at every point between God and men. Hence to bridge this gulf some visible forms become necessary. These forms are harmless as long as they fulfil their end. But the moment when, for any reason, the form becomes more attractive than the spiritual fact for which it stands, when the bridge detains rather than forwards the seeking faith of the soul, when for any reason a man begins to love the road more than the communion to which it leads, the altar more than the name that sanctifies it, the cross more than the Crucified, then he begins to pervert needed means of worship into unlawful ends. He is ministering to worldly tastes, and though he still call it religion, he is in fact a formalist, a promising Pharisee. II. The speculative tendency of the mind is another broad road to formalism. The philosophic formalist is like a man standing on the bank of a stream, whose passage is his only salvation; but he has no thought of crossing. He is engaged in calmly trying the depth of the channel at different points. He surveys the scenery of the opposite shore with a critical eye. He measures the swiftness of the current, and carefully estimates its force per cubic foot. He notes the colour and density of the water, and asks with considerable interest about how many make the crossing safely. All this information he shuts away in his note-book, and seems rather well content with the result. It would seem farcical if it were not sadly true that multitudes of men and women, in our own day, imagine this to be religion; or more exactly, they live and die in the hope that through these processes of inquiry they are drawing nearer to a rational faith. The progress of the intellectual formalist is a sheer delusion. He only circles round and round the holy mystery. He is ever learning, but never coming to a knowledge of the truth. III. The self-righteousness of the natural heart is another fertile source of formalism in religion. It was on this road that the questioner in the text had gone astray. Now, our Lord's treatment of this many-headed evil was sharp and brief. "Strive to enter in at the strait gate." Here is, at once, the knell of all false hopes and the cure of all wrong methods in religion. See how much these words contain. 1. The genuine spiritual life has a single gate of entrance. It is *the* gate. Many shall seek to enter in by other gates—gates imagined or invented—but they shall not be able. There is but one gate. 2. This one gate is a "strait gate" also. It was too narrow for the swelling robes and expanding phylacteries of the Pharisee. It is too narrow still for the routine of the formalist or the philosophy of the intellectualist. It is too strait for inflated self-righteousness. If these shall enter, it must be by some other gate; yet there is but one, and this is strait. But this strait gate is wide enough for repentance and faith. It is high enough for humble sinners who will stoop to enter. 3. The gate is not only one gate, and narrow, but a deadly effort is required to pass it. *Strive* to enter in. A better word would be "agonize." *Agonize* to enter in at the strait gate. (*J. B. Clark.*) *Earnestness in seeking salvation:*—We know that more than seventy thousand immortal beings pass daily into their fixed eternal state, and that for six thousand years nearly thirty millions a year have gone to the unseen world ; and the thought must unavoidably force itself upon every mind, Are the largest portion of them lost? Must we believe a great part of these myriads live here but to acquire a title to everlasting woe ? Such inquiries are natural, and we can scarcely resist the impulse to make them. Jesus Christ was perfectly able to answer them. Let us, then—I. In the first place, ENDEAVOUR TO ASCERTAIN HOW HE REGARDED THEM. It has generally been thought that our Lord's reply was a tacit censure upon all such questions ; but it may have been a censure upon the spirit and motives of the man rather than upon his inquiry. Our Saviour took no notice of *him*, but directed His answer to all around, and said unto *them*, " Strive to enter in at the strait gate." The Jews supposed that all of their nation would be saved, and all the Gentiles lost ; and if the inquirer asked in this uncharitable spirit, we may conclude that this was the reason why our Lord took no notice of him. Or the person who put the question may have been himself a wicked man, neglecting his own salvation, and actuated by an idle curiosity concerning the fate of others, and therefore unworthy of a reply. We need not suppose, then, that our Lord meant to condemn all such inquiries. We cannot well avoid them. We cannot look upon the thronging multitudes around us without having the question forced upon us, What is to be their future fate ? We must cease thinking before we can cease asking, " Are there few that be saved ?" And, indeed, it seems necessary to ask, in order to form some judgment respecting the eternal destiny of others, for how can we make any efforts for their salvation if we cannot estimate their danger ? The Bible itself gives us aid in such inquiries. It tells us that a vast multitude, which no man can number, shall stand before the throne ; and yet it teaches that of those who grow up to years of maturity there are few that go in at the strait gate, and many that enter the broad way to death, and thus, in fact, replies to the question in our text. II. Again we may observe, THAT THERE IS ANOTHER VERY COMMON MISTAKE WITH REGARD TO THE MEANING OF OUR TEXT. Our Saviour says, " Many shall seek to enter in, and shall not be able." Some understand this to refer to the gate of salvation ; that is, many shall seek on earth to enter that gate, or to become Christians, but shall not be able ; and accordingly they proceed to give us many reasons why they shall not be able ; as, for instance, they seek, but do not seek earnestly enough, or they seek for a time and then fall away. But the true meaning seems to be, many at the last day shall seek to enter into the gate of heaven, but shall not then be able. III. Having noticed these erroneous views of our text, we may now observe, in the third place, THAT THE GREAT POINT OF IT IS, TO URGE UPON US EARNESTNESS IN THE WORK OF OUR SALVATION. The straitness and difficulty is in ourselves not in anything of God's imposing. The entrance upon eternal life is like a narrow gateway, wide enough to admit every individual, but nothing more. If a man comes to it with a great bulky burden upon his shoulders, he will find it impossible to force a passage ; but if he will lay down his load of pride and worldliness, his lusts and pleasures, instead of attempting to carry them with him in the way to heaven, there will be nothing to impede his entrance ; he can slip through easily, and travel in that narrow way comfortably. Just in proportion as we renounce sin will the pathway to heaven become plain and easy. IV. But here, my brethren, is difficulty enough ; God has revealed the way of life clearly ; Jesus, by His work on earth and in heaven, smoothes that way, and renders it accessible to all ; BUT THE GREAT MATTER IS TO PERSUADE MEN TO OVER-COME THAT IN THEMSELVES WHICH WOULD HINDER THEIR SALVATION. V. But, my brethren, if ye will not do what yourselves must acknowledge to be reasonable now, HEAR WHAT CHRIST SAYS YE MAY DO HEREAFTER—" Many, I say unto you, will seek to enter in, and shall not be able." How vividly does the Bible describe the awful disappointment of those who are to be thrust out of Christ's presence at the judgment day ! One would think that when they found themselves on the left hand of the Judge, that would convince them that there was no room for hope. But no ; our Lord represents them as pleading still for admission, " Lord, Lord, open unto us." And when He answers, " I know you not," still they will not give over, but plead, " When saw we Thee an hungered, and fed Thee not, or thirsty, and gave Thee no drink ?" and long after the fatal word, " Depart from Me, ye cursed," has been uttered, their pleadings may follow their ascending Judge to move His compassion. Vain cries ! but dreadful ! (*W. H. Lewis, D.D.*) *On the obtaining of salvation :*—I. THOSE ALONE WHO STRIVE ENTER IN AT THE STRAIT

GATE. Every part of redemption is connected with striving, and the Christian under its influence must work out his salvation with fear and trembling. Within his own household there are enemies, for his "heart is deceitful above all things, and desperately wicked," and he must watch and be sober. Is he on a race? to reach the goal he must lay aside every incumbering weight, and with his eye steadily fixed on the prize, he must not faint by the way, nor cease to strive till he has secured the end of his labour. From fears without and fightings within, the Christian is kept ever active, and through much tribulation he must enter the kingdom of God. The heart of a Christian is a field of action in which two powerful armies are engaged—grace and corruption. New strength in acquired by resistance, and day by day opposing powers wax feebler and feebler; and the Christian retiring from a well-sustained conflict exclaims, "Oh, death! where is thy sting? oh, grave! where is thy victory?" "Thanks be to God for His unspeakable gift." II. FEW THUS STRIVE, AND THEREFORE FEW ARE SAVED. Many wish salvation, but few strive to enter in at the strait gate. The word "many" in our text may either refer to a great number or to mankind generally. Few are to be found who do not seek in one way or other, or at some time of their life, to enter in at the strait gate; but they do not strive, and thus are excluded. Conscience accuses, fears alarm, and they seek salvation; but their hearts are either too much carnalized or they do not value sufficiently the salvation of the soul. Hence they merely seek, and do not strive. They would have no objection to enter in at the strait gate by seeking when they found it convenient; but to strive, and that for a continued time, is out of the question. They would willingly enter into heaven; but to take it by violence requires too much exertion for their dispositions. (*A. Robertson, M.A.*) *The dangers of formality, and the difficulties of salvation :*—I. THE OBJECTIONABLE NATURE OF THE QUESTION PROPOSED. 1. Objectionable, as indicating an exclusive and self-righteous spirit. 2. Objectionable, as indicating an undue curiosity upon a subject which God has concealed from human view. II. THE SOLEMN EXHORTATION TO WHICH IT GAVE RISE. The Christian is exposed to the ridicule of the scoffer, the contempt of the scorner, and the sneers of the profane. His conduct is misrepresented, his words misinterpreted, and his motives misunderstood. His religion is termed hypocrisy, his faith presumption, his holiness self-righteousness, his strict walk with God an arrogant assumption of superiority over men, and his diligent attendance on the means of grace and ordinances of religion a mere observance of useless forms and ceremonies. His wisdom is called folly, his patience pusillanimity, his meekness cowardice, his sobriety avarice, his almsgiving an ostentatious display of benevolence; and his zealous exertions for the temporal and spiritual welfare of man and the honour and glory of God are stigmatized as unhallowed attempts to promote his own worldly interests and to advance his own worldly reputation. These oppositions from without are abetted by the corruptions of the heart within, which "is deceitful above all things, and desperately wicked," and is ever inventing excuses for indulging in forbidden gratifications and for resting in a mediocrity of spiritual attainments. Add to these considerations the devices and stratagems of the arch enemy of God and man, by which he deludes men into a false security and seduces them into the commission of sin, exaggerating the enjoyment and concealing the danger of the forbidden fruit, and saying, as he did of old, "Ye shall not surely die," and who does not see the necessity of vigilance, circumspection, and active exertion to secure the favour of God, according to our Saviour's exhortation, "Strive to enter in at the strait gate"? III. Such being the difficulties which beset the path of life, we are at no loss to account for THE APPALLING TRUTH WHICH CHRIST BRINGS FORWARD TO ENFORCE THAT EXHORTATION—"For many will seek to enter in, and shall not be able"; the meaning of which is, that many have thoughts and faint desires of heaven who will never be found among the heirs of glory. The spectators might wish the happy lot of the successful racer or the victorious combatant in the public games of Greece, and sigh for the laurels which crowned his brow and the acclamations which awaited his return home; but such idle and empty wishes could never secure the prize. Even the prophet who "loved the wages of unrighteousness" could exclaim, "How goodly are thy tents, O Jacob, and thy tabernacles, O Israel! Let me die the death of the righteous, and let my last end be like his." But desires like these may be felt without the slightest approximation to the object desired. It is to covet a treasure and refuse to dig for it. It is to know of a "pearl of great price" and grudge the expense of buying the field where it is deposited. It is to wish for the abundance of the harvest and decline the labour of cultivating the soil. Alas! how great is the number of those who in regard to the kingdom of heaven put the wish for the act, who idle away their time, and "spend their strength for nought," through all the stages of an unprofitable existence, and then sink down, astonished and confounded, into that gulf of endless perdition from which they have never made any real effort to escape. (*H. Hughes.*) *Warning against formalism :*—I. A CURIOUS QUESTION. 1. This question, though curious, is very natural. (1) Natural to pry into the future. (2) To desire to know the future spiritual condition of mankind is most natural. 2. If such an inquiry was proper at all, it was proper to make it of Christ. (1) Because He knew all about it. (2) Because He would readily answer it if best. II. THE MASTER'S ANSWER. 1. Not satisfactory to the curiosity-seeker. (1) This fact deserves careful notice. (2) This fact a direct rebuke to all mere curiosity-seeking. This applies to science, art, literature, and religion. · 2. Christ's answer most satisfactory to the real inquirer after truth. (1) Because of its eminently practical character. (2) Because of its stirringly earnest character. (3) Because of its solemnly warnful character. This warning implies (*a*) the possibility of self-deception on the part of professing Christians; (*b*) that self-deception will not exonerate any from condemnation in the day of judgment; (*c*) that the condemnation of all workers of iniquity will be irreversible. (4) Because of its delightfully encouraging character to all true Christians. Lessons : 1. Christ ever raised the practical above the theoretical. So should we. 2. Christ ever raised the spiritual above the secular. So should we. 3. Christ ever raised the substance above the form. 4. Christ here reveals the reason of men's aversion to true godliness. 5. Christ here plainly declares the irretrievable misery to which such aversion inevitably leads. (*D. C. Hughes, M.A.*) *Strive to enter in :*—1. A weighty requirement. 2. A just requirement. 3. A beneficent requirement. 4. A practicable requirement. (*Van Oosterzee.*) *The broad way and the narrow :*—MOVEMENT. Certain, inevitable movement of human beings is implied in the whole passage. Our Lord regards the multitudes around Him as all in motion—none quiescent, none fixed and centred. We are not dwellers, we are travellers. We are all on the way—we are not stopping even here and now. I see the staff in your hand! I see the dust on your sandals! I hear the tread of a thousand feet! Onward and away each one goes, by the way that he chooses, and he shall never rest—not in deepest sleep, not in stillest midnight—for one moment, until he passes through the gate of death to some way everlasting. MORAL PROGRESS IS ALSO CONSTANT. This is a far more serious and important kind of progress. If we could stay our spirits amid this universal vicissitude, and keep them in fixed conditions, the outward change would be of less moment. But the moral progress is as constant, and infinitely more important, than any change that can be apprehended by the senses. It is a solemn thought that the one process or the other is going on in every one of us, without the intermission of a day or an hour. True, many a man does not *feel* himself to be growing either better or worse sometimes for a long time; and therefore he yields to the delusion that it is really so. Vessels that are in the habit of trading on the great rivers, going up and coming down, stay at this port or that, sometimes for days, trading or waiting. The waters sweep past them, but they are motionless, anchored in the river or moored to the quay. So some men are under the delusion that they can moor themselves, as moral beings, to certain circumstances and states, in such a manner that there shall be no difference between yesterday and to-day, between to-day and to-morrow. They seem to think that they can anchor moral character in the stream of life, and hold it in the same place for months or years. It can never be done. THERE ARE ONLY TWO WAYS. The broad and the narrow. Along one or other of these has every mortal pilgrim gone. By one or other of these is every living man travelling now. Let us look now at these two ways. Take the broad way first, if for no other reason because it *is* the broad way. It is the most manifest and obtrusive, and the nearest to us naturally. Begin at the beginning of it. It has a gate. A gate is a place of entrance—to a city, or a field, or a country. As a religious term it means the beginning of a course or onward career. There are critical and decisive points in life to which men come. There are gates of decision, narrow or wide, through which they pass into the course which lies within. He is speaking to reasonable and responsible men of their acts of choice, in the decisive times and places in life. He is speaking of the entering in at either gate of those who know that they so enter. And yet the knowledge may not be very express or clear. From want of reflection, from want of observance of the real character and consequences of things, men may go on from youth to age without being aware that they pass through "gates" at all. They live as they list, or as they can. All this is consistent with the spirit of the passage, "wide is the gate!" One may go through it and hardly know it is there. And the way is broad. All kinds of persons may walk in it. The man of the world may work out his schemes, gather his money, and achieve his position. The pleasure-seeker may eat and drink, and dance, and sleep, and sing. The sensual man, who kills his moral life and vilifies the Divine image within him, may pass on unchecked. The formalist may count his beads, and say his prayers. These persons are not all alike. Some are much worse than others, some are on the darker side of the road, some are on the side nearest the narrow way, "not far from the kingdom of God." They cast many a look to that better way, and perhaps some day they may enter it. In saying that there are but two ways, we do not abolish the distinctions of morality. Let them all stand. They do not touch the essence of the truth that a man is going in the main one way or another. As a moral being, having in him the element of progressiveness, he must, on the whole, be either rising to life or sinking to ruin. Again, following our Lord's description, we come to a gate, and He calls it a "strait gate." There is thus an undisguised difficulty in salvation. The way is narrow, but the gate that gives entrance to it is narrower still. The beginning of some great enterprises among men is sometimes very easy and imperceptible. A great palace is to be built. The beginning of the work is, that a man lays a measuring line quietly to the ground, or a workman with a spade turns up a piece of turf. A company of men start for the ascent of Mount Blanc. But they do not go up at first, they go down by a river side, then their path slopes gently up through the pine woods, and it is not at the beginning of their undertaking that they find hardship and toil. But *this* work of returning to God, in the case of one who has not kept the narrow way from the first, is most difficult at the beginning. The most miserable and agonizing moment to the prodigal son must have been that which preceded the resolution to arise and to go to his father. The question occurs : How is this? Is it by Divine arrangement? In one sense it is not. "God will have all men to be saved." "He is not willing that any should perish." The way, which *to us* has a strait gate and is practically narrow, is, in fact, as made by Him, wide in its gate and broad as a way; while, on the other hand, the way, which to us is so broad, seen from the heights will seem narrow. So much depends on the point of view! The angels looking down on the broad way may see that it is really narrow. They may say : "How strait the gate! What a pressure upon conscience to get through! How narrow the way! Girded with penalty, overhung with danger, ending in death!" Looking at the narrow way they may say : "How wide is the gate! Wide as the Divine nature. How broad is the way! Broad as the everlasting love of God—penalties all exhausted, promises hanging like ripening fruit, and helps ready at every step of the progress!" But our point of vision is not the angelic one. We need to know what the way is *to us*. Christ stands on our own plane of life when He describes the way; to us, practically, it is narrow, and the gate of entrance to it is strait. To lay aside figure, the gate can be none other than repentance—the leaving of one life behind and entering on another. Therefore, the gate is strait! O how strait, when a man sees that he cannot pass in with one allowed sin, not even a little one! "Narrow is the way." True, it is not so narrow to most Christian people as it ought to be. It is not so narrow to *any* traveller on it as it ought to be. We shall close by naming three inducements to walk in this narrow way. 1. The gate is strait, but it is always open. You come to a nobleman's park, and you look in through the gate. The gate is massive, high, broad, and beautiful. But it is shut. You can look through the bars of it, but you cannot get in. All its width and magnificence avail you nothing as a means of entrance. Passing on, you come to a little wicket-gate which opens into a narrow footpath over rugged ground, but which leads up and away to the hills where the light is shining. That little wicket-gate is open, day and night! 2. The narrow way is narrow; but it grows wider as you go on. It grows wider, lighter, pleasanter, easier—that is the law of the road. The very opposite result takes place on the broad way of self-indulgence. That becomes narrower and darker and more full of peril as men go along in it. 3. The end is everlasting life. Who can tell the meanings, hidden in the heart of God, that these words contain? It "leadeth unto life." Ah, is not that enough to reconcile us to it all—its straitness, its narrowness, all its steeps and roughnesses? Is not that enough to draw us into it as by the gravitation of eternity—the end is "everlasting life"? (*A. Raleigh, D.D.*) *Earnestness in religion, recommended and enforced:*—I. THE DIFFICULTIES WHICH OBSTRUCT THE ENTRANCE INTO HEAVEN. 1. An object, when viewed under different aspects, assumes different hues, and presents itself in different forms. 2. But while the gospel is humbling, it is also holy in its tendency. It is a doctrine according to godliness. II. I ADVERT TO THE CAUSES OF THAT DISAPPOINTMENT WHICH MANY IN THE MOMENTOUS CONCERN OF THEIR SOUL WILL EXPERIENCE. 1. One obvious reason why many seek to enter in and are not able is that they seek not in the appointed way. 2. Another cause of that disappointment which many will experience is the unseasonable time at which they commence the attempt of entering in at the strait gate. They make no preparation for the coming of the Bridegroom till His approach is actually announced. 3. Another reason why many will fail in their attempt of obtaining admission into heaven is the irresolute and indecisive manner in which that attempt is prosecuted. Consider the magnitude of the object for which you are exhorted to strive. It is the life of your soul. 2. Consider the consequences of not complying with this admonition. 3. Consider, lastly, the certainty of success which awaits your compliance with the admonition. "Your labour shall not be in vain in the Lord." Strive, and ye shall enter in. (*E. Cooper.*) *Striving for heaven:*— Look for a moment at the nature of these difficulties—at the magnitude of these obstacles. They may be arranged under three heads. I. EXAMPLE. Who has power to breast himself against the influence of popular sentiment, ever flowing in one direction, and always with an urgent and resistless tide? The spirit of the world, which is antagonistical to that of the gospel, moulds its habits, and manners, and opinions, which, though they be not always opposed to the outward forms of religion, are always at variance with its inward and humble spirit. Religion has never acquired such an ascendency in the world, that there was not always a heavy balance in the scale of popular influence against it ; so that almost the first difficulty which presents itself to the mind of that man, who is beginning seriously to ponder the question of a personal consecration to God, is that which rests in the contempt that awaits such a change, and the overpowering influence of that scornful sentiment and adverse example which prevail around him. Men are enslaved by the power of example. Its influence over them is like a mighty spell, which it requires a superhuman power to break. Need I say that he who goes to heaven must go there in the face of this influence? Not a soul ever entered the strait gate but he came in direct conflict with this power, and, through grace, triumphed over it. II. But let us look at the influence of PERSONAL HABITS AND CUSTOMS. The sinner is accustomed to sin. Every one of his habits, of a moral nature, has been formed under its influence. It is the atmosphere in which he has lived, and moved, and breathed. It has encircled him from the first dawn of life. From such a heart have our habits sprung, and in such a soil have they taken root. Who is ignorant of the power of habit? Even where it holds no relation to the moral feelings, it is often so strong as to produce involuntary action. Now, these habits, so deeply rooted, so long cherished, so undisputed in their sway, and so ascendent in their power, are every one of them, like so many cords, binding us to our idols and our lusts. Under their mighty impulse the sinner is rushing on to ruin. I ask, if anything short of that great, and determined, and desperate struggle, indicated in the word "strive," agonize to enter, can give us emancipation from this dreadful power?—freedom from this debasing thraldom? III. There is a still more serious difficulty than any which I have yet named. The sinner, to enter the strait gate, MUST CONTEND AGAINST THE FORCE OF NATURE ITSELF, AND WITH A POWER THAT SHALL SUBDUE IT. The moral nature of man is wholly corrupt. There is not a single chord in the heart that vibrates to the love of God. Now, you will observe, that it is this state of the heart that renders man susceptible to temptation. It is this which gives to the world such a mighty power over him— which renders him so easy a prey to its allurements, its fascinations, its deceitfulness, and to the wiles of the devil. But it is necessary that I should say a word upon the nature and extent of that aid which God proffers us. Do you not know that there are many who suppose that God offers to remove these difficulties Himself, and exempt the sinner from all responsibility in reference to them? God makes no such offer to any sinner. The Saviour says, "Strive to enter in at the strait gate." Would He address such language as this to the sinner if there were no difficulties in his way, or if He expected to remove them all Himself? By no means. The truth is, God does not propose to take one of these difficulties out of the way. He simply offers to help the sinner to overcome them. If a man, launching his bark from the shore at Chippewa, should row vigorously till he had reached the centre of the Niagara, and should then haul in his oars, and commit his frail vessel to the power of the current, would he have any reason to expect that he should reach the opposite shore ? If he had the energies of a giant, would that prevent his being carried down the cataract, and buried in the gulf below ? An expectation of reaching the opposite shore entertained by that man, when folding his arms and whistling to the fury of the current, would be just as reasonable as an expectation of reaching heaven entertained by the sinner who sees himself borne down on the current of worldliness and sin to the gulf of perdition, and yet will make no resolute efforts to resist the tide and bear himself to a place of safety. Of what avail is it that the Spirit of God, omnipotent in His power, tenders His aid to the sinner, and visits his heart, if, after all, that sinner cannot be roused to such a state of feeling and effort as are indicated by the emphatic language of our Saviour used in the text ? Believe me, dying sinner, the Spirit of God has not come into the world that He might leave you to slumber while He fights your enemies, and through mighty obstacles opens to you the way to the kingdom of heaven. This is not the manner in which He teaches us to fight the good fight of faith. But it is time to conclude. 1. From our subject, thus discussed, we see why it is that so few, even of those who have some solicitude about their salvation, and are strictly moral in their deportment, and always respectful towards religion, ever attain to a satisfactory and well-established confidence of their interest in God's love. They have never made thorough work of religion. They have rested in its forms. They have shunned its crosses. 2. Again : Is it not clear from our subject that there are many in the Church on earth who will never enter heaven ? (*J. W. Adams, D.D.*) *The strait gate :*—" But we thought," perhaps some one may say, " that the message of the gospel which preachers have to deliver was a smiling invitation ; these words sound like grave, urgent counsel." That is what they are—grave, urgent counsel. If any one said to you in a soft, sentimental tone, " Make money," you would be ready even to laugh ; rot because you consider money-making an unattractive occupation, which indeed it is not, but because you know that it is not easy to make money. You do not need to be told to do this thing, but only *how* to do it. There are many things we are willing enough to do, if we only knew how to do them. But there are others we do not like to do, although we ought to do them ; partly because of difficulties, which might nevertheless be overcome, and partly because the ends proposed, the rewards offered, are not attractive to us. Of course every one to whom we should say, " There is another life after this : would you like it to be a happy one ? " would answer, " Certainly I should." But if no one expects to get a comfortable place here without taking trouble ; why should any one expect to get a comfortable place hereafter without taking any ? Still, when we say, " Enter ye in at the strait gate," if one word disheartens, another comforts. The word " strait " perhaps brings us to a pause ; but the word " enter " beckons us forward. We should not be urged to " enter " were entry impossible. If the entrance looks narrow, it is less difficult than it looks. Every one feels a truth in our Lord's words about the two ways ; the one, easy and crowded, yet neither safe nor honourable ; the other, difficult and unfrequented, and yet the best way, indeed the only right one. But though we all feel we have truth here, yet we may treat this old Scripture saying very much as we do an old weapon of which, when we look at it, we cry, " Ah, you were sharp and strong once ; you have been wanted in the world ; but you are not needed now : rest where you are ; ours is a quiet time ; and should we ever have to fight, we will find new weapons, of a better make." And even if we do not thus treat our Lord's saying, we may yet feel some perplexity as to its application. We must look about, then, to find a gate into the meaning of these words ; and when we have found one, we must go along the pathway of our thought with care and steadiness. Who shall help us to the meaning of Christ's words ? He Himself shall help us. He Himself travelled on the narrow path, when He might have taken the broad one. And did He not call Himself both a door and a way, saying, " I am the door," " I am the way " ? He who, quickened and strengthened by another's example, walks as that other walked, does as he did, hopes as he hoped, and leaves the crowd as he left it, makes that other his " way." On the one hand, then, we have a Teacher who invites us to trust in and follow Him as a Saviour ; and, on the other, a Saviour who offers us life, and yet, as a Teacher, instructs us that we must overcome many difficulties if we would gain it. How can we reconcile these things? He who spoke of the strait gate, we say, Himself went into the way of righteousness thereby. He who told us of the narrow way, walked therein, knew its sorrows, was acquainted with its griefs. He chose the narrow way when He might have taken the broad one and have travelled it with a most able guide and companion by His side, and a most brilliant end before Him. We often speak of a brilliant career. What career so bright with outward victory as Christ's would have been, if He had accepted the magnificent proposals of the devil? His way would have been broad, and thronged with admiring attendants. But He took the way of goodness instead of the way of greatness. He went down among the poor instead of up among the proud. He sacrificed Himself to others instead of others for Himself. And the mighty work He did was this: He made "the way" that was impassable to any but Himself, passable to others who should follow in His footsteps. By taking the way, He became the way; by taking the way of righteousness, He became the way of salvation. Even in the perils of ordinary life, if any one man will dare to take a new course, and it prove a successful one, many will dare to follow him. And he usually benefits us in two manners; he makes our obstacle less, and our courage greater. When, then, Jesus Christ says invitingly to all, "Follow Me," speaking as a Saviour; but says also to each, "Take up your cross, and, carrying that, follow Me"—teaching us that the way is hard, we do not feel that urgent counsel is inconsistent with cheering invitation. We can reconcile the words that seem discouraging with the words that so much encourage. For every one of us there still remains his own difficulty; but our Saviour has so encountered and overcome the great difficulties that beset human nature in its progress to perfection and blessedness, that every one of us has a good hope of success through Him. Not only are obstacles removed and courage imparted, so that we *can* do what we could not, and *will* dare what we would not; but we are assured of an enabling power, even Christ's Spirit bestowed on us by God, and an unfailing protection, even an Almighty Providence ever working around us. Christ is more than an Example shining from the past; He is a Power working in the present. (*T. T. Lynch.*) *The narrow leads to the broad:*—Through the narrow we come into the broad; by a narrow intricate channel into the wide sea full of riches; by a narrow and perilous pathway into the great city, so stately, so secure. The attainment of true knowledge, the performance of true work, fidelity to "pure religion," are not easy. Commencement and continuance have alike their difficulty. The gate is strait; the way narrow. But in order to obtain many a state of advantage in which we may "walk at liberty"—find, that is, our path pleasantly wide and the country round us pleasantly open—is anything more requisite than exact careful attention at the outset of our endeavour, and exact careful regard to our own course as we go along? No: often this is enough. Perhaps all of us can read a printed page as easily as if we were rolling in a rapid chariot upon a broad level road. But the Alphabet was our "strait gate," and along the "narrow way" that our Spelling-Book opened before us we had to go, for a long time, slowly and carefully. If we have learned a handicraft, we had our "strait gate" and our "narrow way," skilful as we may now be. In most courses of life we have our special first troubles; but our trial is not over when our entry has been made—we cannot proceed without a steady purpose, a good courage, and a staff. And no man can be, or can reasonably expect to be, a Christian, without the same attention at the outset, and considerateness on the course as are demanded of him if he would be merchant or mechanic, artist or man of science, discoverer or patriot, or even if he would learn to read a book. But more than attention at first and care afterwards are required for the spiritual life—to be a true Christian, and indeed to be a true man in any worthy department of human activity. The renunciation of much that others accept, and even the abandonment of much that, but for the work in hand, you would retain, may be required of you. This renunciation is a "strait gate"; and "separateness," though it be separateness from sinners—and some sinners are pleasant people—is a "narrow way." Christ was alone amid the crowd in His unruffled wisdom, before He was alone on the cross in the grasp of death, man's enemy. His "narrow way" lay through the populous city before it entered the valley of the shadow of death. There are other narrow ways along our streets than the pavements. One man riding in his coach may be travelling on the narrow way of honour and duty, and the foot-travellers may be hastening on at rapid pace upon the broad road. Now it may be the poor, and now the rich, that is in the wrong way, or in the right. The confession of an error, the avowal of a conviction, economy of money or time, abandonment of habit, are often " strait gates," which stand quite plainly before us, and need no finding. But our Saviour speaks of men " not finding " the strait gate. And He Himself, as the Teacher of Israel, was a gate that many of His countrymen failed to find. They could not see that He would lead them to welfare. Had He been a strong soldier, He would have seemed to them the broad plain way to prosperity! He that notices a yellow stain in the rocks, and does not perceive that it means gold, misses a gate. A suggestion comes, a proposal is made, tidings are brought: " There is a gate here," says one man; but another "cannot see it." For all of us there are gates we cannot miss seeing; and for all of us there are gates which we may overlook, and so miss a great good, even the greatest. Many fail to find their gate because they are looking for the grandly difficult rather than the humbly difficult. (*Ibid.*) *Difficulty of religion:*—It appears, then, that it is not an easy thing to enter in; that it is a hard and difficult matter for a man to be saved. Now let us see some particulars in which it is difficult. Let us observe some of those points of religion, in which if we would succeed, we are bound to strive; and where if we strive not, we shall not enter in. 1. One thing which is of very frequent occurrence, and in respect of which men are very commonly mistaken, is their attendance on the worship of God. You think it perhaps enough to attend when it is convenient, to come when you can spare time from business or pleasure; once on the Sunday, or not even thus often. But is this striving to enter in? Many of you know well that if you were really to strive you could attend more frequently, more regularly. Be not, then, deceived. The way is narrow, the gate is strait; strive to enter in, or you approach in vain. 2. Or consider now the doctrines of Christianity. Many of you perhaps think very little about them, deem them above your comprehension, and never take pains to understand them. Or if you do, you complain that they are hard to discover, and difficult to understand. And so indeed they are, to the natural man, to the mind that is unenlightened by the Spirit of truth. But never imagine that this excuses you from the duty of searching into them, or that here you may safely walk in the broad path, neglecting to learn what God has thought fit to teach. 3. If there be any here who spend no time, take no anxious thought, give no diligent attention to know the things that belong to their peace; to them I say, you are mistaken, you are in danger, you must strive, or you will not enter in. 4. Or take the account which the Scriptures give of what a Christian ought to practise. Is it not a constant warfare, a continual effort, to mortify the flesh, to renounce the world, and to resist the devil? It is when we fail, to renew the contest; when we faint, to recover strength; when we succeed, still to press forward; to seek ever more and more excellent gifts; and to run as in a race, every day of our lives, unto the very hour of death, that we may win the prize. Is this a hard saying? Is this view of our duty as Christians difficult and discouraging? It may be so. But the question is not whether it be a difficult one, but whether it be the true one. Could it be the true one, unless it were difficult? Could any view of the way to be saved be correct, unless it pointed to a narrow path, to a strait gate, and bid us strive, in order to enter in? (*C. Girdlestone, M.A.*) *The strait gate:*—I. A GATE WHICH IT IS MOST DESIRABLE TO ENTER. 1. Because it is the gate of the city of refuge. Outside of Christ the sword of fire pursues us swift and sharp. From God's wrath there is but one escape, and that is by a simple faith in Christ. Believe in Him, and the sword is sheathed, and the mercy and the love of God will become your everlasting portion; but refuse to believe in Jesus, and your innumerable sins, written in His book, shall be laid at your door in that day when the pillars of heaven shall reel, and the stars shall fall like withered fig-leaves from the tree. Oh! who would not wish to escape from the wrath to come? 2. It is desirable to enter this gate, because it is the gate of a home. What sweet music there is in that word "home"! Jesus is the home of His people's hearts. We are at rest when we get to Christ. We have all we want when we have Jesus. 3. Moreover, it leads to a blessed feast. Happy the man who believes in Jesus, for he becomes at once content, complacent, and at ease. Not only does he find rest in Christ, but good cheer and great delight, halcyon peace, and hallowed satisfaction are the portion of his lot. 4. It is the gate which leads to Paradise. And who would not wish to pass through it when he considers the lot of those outside the gate? II. THERE IS A CROWD OF PEOPLE WHO WILL SEEK TO ENTER AND WILL NOT BE ABLE. 1. Some are unable to enter because the pride of life will not let them. 2. Some are unable to enter because they carry contraband goods with them. When you land in France, there stands the gendarme who wants to see what you are carrying in that basket. If you attempt to push by you will soon find yourself in custody. He must know what is there; contraband goods cannot be taken in. So at the gate of mercy—which is Christ—no man can be saved if he desire to keep his sins. He must give up every false way. 3. Not a few are unable to enter in because they want to postpone the matter until to-morrow. 4. Others, and these are in the worst plight of all, think that they are in, and that they have entered. They mistake the outside of the gate for the inside. Conclusion : Thus it is that a crowd—I had almost said a countless crowd—of people nowadays seek to enter in, but for manifold reasons they are not able to do so. And yet there is a more appalling aspect to the same fact. " Many, I say unto you, will seek to enter in, and shall not be able." Panic-stricken, the dying man sends for the minister whom he never went to hear when his health was good and hours hung heavy on his hands. Some years ago I was awakened about three o'clock in the morning by a sharp ring of the door-bell. I was urged without delay to visit a house not very far from London Bridge. I went; and up two pair of stairs I was shown into a room the occupants of which were a nurse and a dying man. There was nobody else. " Oh, sir," said she, " Mr. So-and-so, about half-an-hour ago, begged me to send for you." " What does he want ? " I asked. " He is dying, sir," she replied. I said, " I see that. What sort of a man was he ? " " He came home last night, sir, from Brighton. He had been out all day. I looked for a Bible, sir, but there is not one in the house ; I hope you have got one with you." " Oh," I said, " a Bible would be of no use to him now. If he could understand me I could tell him the way of salvation in the very words of Holy Scripture." I spoke to him, but he gave me no answer. I spoke again ; still there was no reply. All sense had fled. I stood a few minutes gazing at his face, till I perceived he was dead. His soul had departed. That man in his lifetime had been wont to jeer at me. In strong language he had often denounced me as a hypocrite. Yet he was no sooner smitten with the darts of death than he sought my presence and my counsel, feeling no doubt in his heart that I was a servant of God, though he did not care to own it with his lips. There I stood, unable to help him. Promptly as I had responded to his call, what could I do, but look at his corpse and go home again ? He had, when too late, sighed for the ministry of reconciliation, sought to enter in, but he was not able. There was no space left him then for repentance ; he had wasted the opportunity. (*C. H. Spurgeon.*) *The two ways :*—I. THERE ARE BUT TWO ROADS in which all mankind are travelling ; in the one or the other of which each of us is at this moment. These two roads are called, from the ends to which they severally lead, the way of destruction and the way of life. The Scriptures speak of no other. If we go on in the way of destruction, we shall surely come to destruction ; if we walk in the way of life, we shall as surely attain eternal life. Accordingly, the Scriptures speak of men under two names only ; as believers or unbelievers ; as servants of sin, or servants of holiness ; as children of God, or children of the devil. They recognize no middle state ; no path running between the two great roads, in which we may walk without the fear of hell, even though we may have no very bright hope of heaven. II. THE WAY OF DESTRUCTION IS DESCRIBED IN THE TEXT BY THE FOLLOWING MARKS. 1. The gate is wide. There is no difficulty in entering in. There needs no self-denial, no striving, no mastery over ourselves. Our own hearts naturally carry us towards it. 2. And as the gate of entrance is wide, so is the way broad. It is broad, because it admits of many paths, all forming, however, but one road, and all leading but to one end. The ways of sin are various ; the devices of Satan for man's destruction are manifold. Moreover, it is easy travelling there. Smooth and pleasant to the flesh. 3. As the gate is wide, and the way broad, so there are many that go in thereat. This is another mark of the way of destruction. It is well trodden ; it is thronged with travellers. III. Now turn to consider THE WAY OF LIFE. See what are its marks. In every respect we find it the very opposite to the way of destruction. 1. In the first place, the gate is strait, that is, narrow and confined. The gate of the way of destruction is wide, and stands open before us, inviting us to come in. But the gate of life is not so easy to enter. And why ? Has God made it hard ? Is He unwilling that we should find the path of life ? Surely not. But our own corrupt hearts love it not. 2. And after we have entered, we find that the way is narrow. There are many paths leading to destruction ; there is but one that leads to life. " Without holiness no man shall see the Lord." And what is holiness ? It is to believe in Jesus Christ, to love God, and to have His Holy Spirit dwelling in us ; to deny ourselves, that we may do His will ; to raise ourselves by faith and prayer above the world, and to set our affections on things above. 3. No wonder, then, that the other mark of the way of life is this, " Few there be that find it." It is a way but little travelled. Men love ease; they naturally care for the pleasures of the body which are at hand. It is hard to be persuaded to think of spiritual joys. (*E. Blencowe, M.A.*) *The strait gate :*—In proportion to the importance of any kingdom is the stringency of the conditions of entrance. In the meantime we shall forget that there is a kingdom of heaven. We shall look into the kingdoms of the earth which men account important, imperial, worthy of possession; and I guarantee to find upon the portals of all such kingdoms these words : " Strait is the gate, and narrow is the way." It will be something to find that inscription above the gates which open upon all the kingdoms which men who sneer at religion think important. Then, if we can read this inscription in their own handwriting upon the gates which open on their petty empires, what if we shall find the same words written—only written by the hand of God—over the portals which open on the city of the Great King? We shall thus be enabled to see that Divine revelation, though often above human reason, is not always opposed to it; and that God will have a judgment against us—irresistible, penetrating, and terrible—on account of the very principles which we ourselves have laid down in those departments of life which we considered important. Here is the kingdom of human learning: Knowledge, critical acquaintance with letters, ample and accurate information about history, power of scientific inquiry, collation, analysis, all that is known by the name of learning; and over the gate of that kingdom I find this inscription, " Strait is the gate, narrow is the way." A man does not by shaking his little arms shake himself into scholarship; it is not done by a wave of the hand. It is done in yonder way :—See! where the man gets up before the lark, before the sun calls him with its voice of light, who trims his lamp, and goes over yesterday's lesson in critical review before he begins to-day's study; pulls himself up by every variety of discipline; cudgels his memory, stores his mind with all kinds of literature; who works after the sun has gone away, to take the morning with him to some distant clime, turning over the pages of his book—not as you turn over the pages of your light reading—but reading every word, studying every sentence, extracting the gold from every book. We say, " Why are you doing this?" "Because," he says, " I am determined to be a subject in the kingdom of learning, and the motto over the gates is this, ' Strait and narrow is the gate, the road.' " So we begin already to admit the principle of the text, that in proportion to the scope and importance of any kingdom is the stringency of the conditions of entrance. Here is a little kingdom, which we shall characterize as the kingdom of merely muscular competition. Men are going to try muscular force with their fellow-men—they are going to have a boat race. You and I cannot walk along the river-side and instantly take into our heads the notion that we will have a spin with these men and beat them all. That can't be done. Strait is the gate and narrow is the way that leads even to athletic supremacy. A man who has been drilled, disciplined, exercised, will beat you, except a miracle be wrought for your advantage. So we are getting nearer and nearer to the principle that in proportion to the importance of any object, the scope of any kingdom, the consequence of any condition of affairs, is the narrowness of the road, is the straitness of the gate. It is the same with all kinds of intellectual supremacy. Granted that there may be inspired geniuses here and there—let us allow that some men may have had a short and easy road to intellectual power and supremacy—still the rule holds good : That he who would be highest must toil most perseveringly and conscientiously. Here, for example, is a man who wishes to excel in authorship. You read his book. You don't see all that lies behind the book. You don't see the rough outline which he first sketched—writing off-hand, as it were; on, and on, and on—blotting, and interlining, and erasing. There it is; just a rough manuscript, with hardly any shape—a line of thought running through it which he alone can see. He lays it aside and takes up another sheet; brings then the rough draft, writes over many parts with care, compression, condensation, that he may give it point and pertinence. He burns the first draft; lays the second aside, lays it by for six months, until he has become another man, viz., a critic of his own productions. He takes up his manuscript again for the last time—goes through it, striking out everything that is opposed to taste, inserting, improving, refining, curving, enriching, and expending himself upon it. Ask why? He says, " I mean this book to live after I have been taken away. I mean this to be a testimony. I mean this to be the last, richest, best expression of my attainments and my convictions ; therefore I have expended myself fully upon its preparation." What is it that is written over the man's study and over the man's desk ? This : " Strait is the gate, narrow is the way." No doubt there are men who can write beautiful nothings by the mile, sell them in the morning, and have them forgotten at sundown. But the writers who wish to enrich all coming generations, to stimulate the most distant posterity, have not the knack of shaking out of their coat sleeves the standard literature of the country. It is a question of preparation, self-culture, self-control, and putting out the stress of the whole being upon it. Then, at least, a man deserves to succeed. The effort after all may not be masterly, the man may fail to attain the position at which he has aimed; but " in all labour there is profit," and the man himself is fuller and stronger for the very industry which he has put forth. We are thus enabled to say that the entrance to the kingdom of heaven is necessarily the straitest, narrowest of all. What are other kingdoms to the Kingdom of Life ? When you have learned all that books can convey to you, what is your kingdom ? When you have obtained all the money that you can possibly own, what is the kingdom of pecuniary means ? When you have sharpened, quickened, stimulated, and enriched your brain to the highest possible point, what is the kingdom of mere intellectual force and supremacy when compared with the kingdom of Life in God ? As, therefore, this is held to be the highest kingdom of all, where is the unreasonableness of making the conditions of entrance into this kingdom the most exacting and stringent of all ? We are thus prepared to say, that by so much as men have the power to strive for inferior kingdoms will they be witnesses against themselves if they fail to strive after the highest kingdom of all. Men are continually getting up evidence which will be used for them or against them in the day of judgment. The day of judgment may be the shortest day that ever dawned, may be but a moment, because every man will judge himself, and one look at God's face will mean destiny ! By so much as we have the power to strive and have admitted the principle of striving, in relation to inferior kingdoms, are we preparing a judgment against ourselves if we have not accepted the conditions of entrance into the Divine empire. Let us now have a judgment day. There is no occasion to wait ten thousand years for the day of judgment. We can have it now ! Let the eloquent man be judged, the man who has made the uses of speech his study from his earliest days. Hear his statement, but fail to follow his example : " I copied with my own hands six times the most voluminous histories of my country, that I might attain to what I supposed were the excellencies of their style. I disqualified myself for appearing in ordinary society by disfiguring my personal appearance, in order that I might bind myself to study by day and practice of speech by night. I have put pebbles in my mouth to cure my stammering ; I have run up the steepest hills in the country that I might strengthen my lungs ; I have harangued the sea that I might obtain power over tumultuous elements ; if you would follow me along the road, walk it as I have done, inch by inch." And he has never thought about God's kingdom—kingdom of light, and life, and truth, and beauty ! Hear God. " Thou wicked and slothful servant, thou knewest, thou didst understand all about care and pains and discipline and culture, thou oughtest therefore—" And the man has no answer. No man can answer God when he comes face to face with his Maker ! He may chaffer with Him now ; he may utter his little speeches against his Maker now. But when it comes to the last reckoning of all, when a man takes up his life in his hand and says, " This is what I have done," God will point out to the man in his own life the things which will damn and consume him ! What is this kingdom of which we have been speaking ? It is called the Kingdom of Life. There are two gates, and only two. Two roads, and only two. Two destinies, and only two. The gate, the way leading to destruction—the way leading to life. (*J. Parker, D.D.*) On *striving to enter in at the strait gate* :—I. EXPLAIN THE EXHORTATION. By the strait gate, we are to understand the entrance into that way which leads to life ; and to enter in at the strait gate denotes the commencement of holiness in the heart of man. The same thing is denoted by conversion—by making a new heart —by giving God the heart—by reconciliation to God—by repentance for sin—by faith toward our Lord Jesus Christ. The gate is said to be strait or difficult, on account of the difficulties of entering it. The expression is designed to show us that to commence a religious course is difficult. The difficulty arises, not from the nature of religion, but from the depravity of the heart. Hence the text requires us to " strive to enter in at the strait gate." The sinner must summon all the powers of his soul to the performance of his duty, and to put himself upon the utmost exertion, of which as a moral being he is capable, in the work of turning to God. 1. The understanding must be duly employed. 2. Conscience must perform its appropriate part in connection with all the moral sensibilities of the soul. 3. The will or the heart—that faculty of the soul by which man chooses and refuses, loves and hates—is also to be properly exerted. II. ENFORCE THE INJUNCTION. 1. It is a command of God. 2. The command is perfectly reasonable. The requisition is, that man should do that, neither more nor less, which, as a moral being, he is qualified to do; that he should put those moral faculties which God has given him upon their appropriate exertions; in a word, that he summon all the faculties of his soul to the single point of doing as well as he can do. 2. It is only by compliance with the precept in the text, that man will perform his duty, and secure his salvation. All who shall seek the favour of God and eternal life without striving, *i.e.*, seek these blessings without that full, and vigorous, and appropriate exertion of all the moral faculties of the soul, must fail of final salvation. This is plain from the nature of the case. If duty is not seen, if obligation is not felt, if the will or heart does not comply, no obedience is, or can be rendered. 4. I would further enforce the injunction, from the case of those who make no efforts to perform the duty, and the manner in which the Divine Spirit converts the sinner. It is a momentous fact—a fact which, in one respect, even after all the displays of mercy in the work of redemption, saves this guilty world from the midnight of despair— that the Spirit of God renews the heart of man through the truth. "Of His own will begat He us with the word of truth." The very object, and the only object, for which the Spirit strives with sinners, is to give truth its proper effect on the mind, the conscience, and the heart; and the thing, and the only thing, which He does, in regeneration, is actually to secure this effect. But how? Does the Spirit of God give effect to truth, when that truth is unthought of; and when the sinner effectually shuts it away, alike from his understanding, and his conscience, and his heart? Has such a thing ever been known or heard of, in all the earth, that God has converted a stupid sinner, continuing stupid? Is there one such on earth—one such among the redeemed in glory? Not one. Remarks: 1. This subject shows us that the sinner may become a Christian soon, and how he may do so. Religion, whether it be called repentance, faith, a new heart, or love to God, is action—mental, moral action. The sinner, to become the subject of either, must act it. What the Holy Spirit does, is not to impart a gift merely to a passive subject, a mere receiver, but to move a free moral agent to act—to act as a moral agent. 2. We see what a fearful condemnation awaits the impenitent sinner. (*N. W. Taylor, D.D.*) *The wrong and the right anxiety* :—I shall take occasion, from the question and the exhortation before us, to speak to you to-day of a wrong and a right anxiety. Let us consider—I. THE QUESTION, AS EXPRESSIVE OF A WRONG ANXIETY—"Lord, are there few that be saved?" Why, in the case before us, and in most others in which it is entertained, does this inquiry indicate a blameworthy solicitude? I answer—1. Because it bespeaks the absence of a due regard to a man's personal interests. He from whom it proceeds has his mind drawn off from that which vitally concerns himself and his own destiny, and absorbed in the affairs of others. His individual relations and responsibilities are merged in those of his fellow-creatures. He is forgetful of obligations that press urgently upon his own being, in his extreme desire to know how men in general will be found to have fulfilled theirs, when the end shall come. With a work of overwhelming magnitude, demanding from him the whole energy of his whole nature, he is allowing that energy to dissipate itself in the prosecution of a vain curiosity. 2. Because it relates to a point which God has not chosen to determine positively in His holy Word. The attempt to solve it is an effort to be wise above what is written. The presumptuous individual would fain place himself on a level with the Infinite and Omniscient; he would read with his weakling eyes the sublime secrets of the eternal records; he would rashly plant his feet where angels fear to tread. And, brethren, it is not difficult to find the counterpart of this man in our own day. We everywhere see, and in almost every one, the same disposition to pry into matters beyond the ken of humanity; to seek to understand subjects which the short plumb-line of our reason is incompetent to fathom. II. THE EXHORTATION, AS SUGGESTIVE OF A RIGHT ANXIETY—"Strive to enter in at the strait gate: for many, I say unto you, will seek to enter in, and shall not be able." "Strive"—that is, be anxious, be supremely concerned about this. Look on smaller matters with indifference: do not let them absorb you; regard them as subordinate, and comparatively trivial. But in reference to the end of which I speak to you now, let your solicitude be all-absorbing; let it lay hold of your whole being; let it colour and modify all your thoughts and actions. You will not err in doing so, for this is a right and laudible anxiety. But let me now, by two or three remarks, show that the solicitude which our Lord thus commends and enforces is indeed right. 1. And first, I may say, this is a right anxiety, because it is necessary. Entrance into life, personal salvation, which is what is meant by going in at the strait gate, is not to be attained without it. We must "agonize," as the word is, " to enter in at the strait gate," or we shall never reach the celestial home at the end of the narrow way. This anxiety is indispensable, and therefore it is right. But I call this anxiety a right one—2. Because it respects an object of paramount importance and worth. This object I have already described, in general terms, as being our personal salvation. 3. Because it is an anxiety that will be abundantly rewarded in the attainment of its end. Now, you need hardly be told, my brethren, that there are innumerable solicitudes of men which never yield anything but disappointment ; myriads of earnest and persevering endeavours that altogether fail in realizing the object for which they are put forth. In worldly matters, I believe it is the few only who succeed. The majority are, more or less, the victims of blasted aims and abortive projects. Yonder, in a bare and unfurnished attic, is a man who began life as an aspirant for literary distinction. The early stages of his journey were bright with hope, and fruitful of plans ; but soon its aspect changed. Discouragement, failure, neglect, followed each other in quick succession in the progress of his life-story, and though he burnt on the midnight oil, and wrought out in the laboratory of his brain beautiful and clever productions, they have never come to light. The public that was to admire and laud them has never even learnt his name, and his gray hairs are being brought down with sorrow to the grave. There, among the humblest in yon pauper's home, is another, who made wealth the grand aim of his being ; sought for it with a mad eagerness that robbed him of peace by day and rest by night ; sought for it by fair means and foul ; but fortune showed him no favour. Riches never came, or if they did, soon took to themselves wings, and flew away, and now his last days are dragging out in poverty, and his only remaining pleasure is to recount, with drivelling simplicity, to those around him, the astute schemes he conceived without results, and the numberless efforts he made in vain. And here is a third man, whose self-elected sphere in life was that of statesmanship; he aspired to rule ; he thought himself born to command. He dreamt of parliaments swayed by his eloquence, and borne down by his arguments, until all made way for him as a leader. And what is he now ? See him yonder, haranguing with the garrulity of second childhood, an ignoble and ignorant crowd, whom only the hope of amusement could induce to listen to him for a moment. He has sown to the wind, and has reaped the whirlwind. Such are the disappointments that wait upon human anxieties and aims. In reference to them, possibility, or, at most, probability of accomplishment, is all that can be calculated on. But it is not so in relation to the anxiety which I am seeking to awaken in you all to-day. Religious aims never come to nought. Endeavours after salvation, of the right sort, cannot fail of their object ; here is certainty to build upon. If then, mere possibility, or probability, will inspire and sustain effort, ought not this much more to do so ? If for an uncertain possession you willingly endure such toil, and submit to such patient plodding, as many of you do, will you not much more give diligence, by prayer, and faith, and effort, to obtain a certain inheritance ? Will you do so much for a corruptible crown, and refuse to do it for an incorruptible? (*C. M. Merry.*) *A time to strive :*—It is said that the question proposed in the text, "Lord, are there few that be saved ? "—or, as the words stand in the original, "are the saved few?" —was at the time of Christ's ministry upon earth vehemently debated in the schools of the Jewish doctors ; and therefore, when the speaker now referred it to the Lord Jesus, it was either for the confirmation of a judgment already formed, or from conscious incompetency to form any judgment of his own aright. While, however, the inquiry is that of an individual, more curious, it may be, about the future destiny of others than concerned about his own, the Lord addresses the answer to the whole company of the disciples. It was one who said to Him, " are the saved few ? "—it was to many that He said, severally as well as collectively, "Strive," each of you, "to enter in at the strait gate : for many, I say unto you, will seek to enter in, but shall not be able." I. First, then, THERE IS AN END PROPOSED, WHICH IS SALVATION. "Lord," one said unto Him, " are there few that be saved ? " But the Lord not only, as we have observed, addressed His reply to all, but He adapted it to what the question ought to have been, rather than to what it was. It should have been, " What must *I* do to be saved ? " II. And THE MEANS OF ATTAINING TO

SALVATION, which form the second point proposed for our consideration, are compre hended and condensed by our Lord in one single emphatic word—" Strive "—ye who would be saved—" strive to enter in at the strait gate." This word " strive " is indeed in the original most significant and impressive. It implies the concen tration of all the energies, faculties, and powers of the understanding and the heart in one great object, which must be attained at any cost ; it supposes the exertion of every member, the straining of every nerve, the union of body and soul putting forth all their vigour and determined to succeed òr to perish. The Lord has Him self expressed the same idea elsewhere, in language striking and impressive. " The kingdom of heaven suffereth violence, and the violent take it by force." The general meaning of this must certainly be, if it is to have any meaning at all, that in the concerns of the soul we are to be in earnest. We are not to take counsel with flesh and blood ; we are not to conpromise principle for pleasure, or to oscillate between interest and duty. There stands the gate ; strait it is ; and strait it ever will be ; all the skill and all the subtlety of man cannot extend it by a span, or widen it by a hair-breadth. The gate of eternal life is as God has fixed it from the beginning, and as He will maintain it to the end. But, my dear brethren, while it is a strait or narrow gate, blessed be God, it is also an open gate. If all earth cannot widen it, all hell cannot close it ; open it is, open it stands, night and day, and the voice of mercy is ever heard to issue from within—" I am the Door ; by Me if any man enter in, he shall be saved." What is it, then, you will ask, to strive, as the Lord enjoins ? and against whom, or against what, is the strife to be maintained ? To this I answer, generally and primarily, the strife is against the flesh, with its affections, appetites, and lusts. III. This, then, is the reason—to be considered in the third and last place—WHY WE ARE TO BE PROMPT, AS WELL AS EARNEST, IN THE EMPLOYMENT OF THE MEANS, THAT WE MAY NOT BE DISAPPOINTED OF THE END. A day will come, when " many shall seek to enter in, but will not be able." And why will they not be able ? Because " light came into the world, and they loved darkness rather than light " ; because they were laden with incumbrances which they would not lay aside, and fettered by chains which they would not even attempt to burst ; because they " troubled and vexed His Holy Spirit, until that He was turned to be their enemy, and fought against them." They would not when they could ; and when at length the error of their perverseness is made clear by dread experience as the sun at noon-day—when the death-bed comes, which is " the detector of the heart "—they cannot when they would. (*T. Dale, M.A.*) *The strait gate :*—I. THE GATE. That of which our Lord here speaks is not the gate of repentance, or of faith, or of conversion ; but the gate of complete sanctifi cation, of glory, of the kingdom of God, not at the lower end, but at the higher ; not the gate at the beginning of Christian experience, but at the end of its earthly career ; not Bunyan's wicket-gate, but the gate of the city celestial. A different gate from that mentioned in Matt. vii. 13, to enter which no effort is required, but simply believing. Here a battle has to be fought, and it is he that overcometh who enters in (2 Tim. iv. 7 ; 2 Pet. i. 5-7). We start from a strait gate ; we run on to another strait gate. The one is at the cross ; the other before the throne. II. THE STRIVING TO ENTER. " Agonize." The gate is hard to enter. Why ? Not in the sense of admitting only a few ; but, because everything that is un Christlike is refused admission. How much, then, we have to take off and lay in the dust ! Self. Pride. Worldliness. Moreover, the gate is strait in another sense. The porter is particular. Certain positive qualifications are necessary. Only the workers of righteousness are admitted : those who bear the image of Christ. (*A. Scott.*) *The two ways :*—Painting the difficulties and hardships attendant on a course of life does not seem to be the best way to attract men to it. And yet it frequently is so. Many a boy has been made a sailor by stories of shipwreck and suffering, and the martyr's fire has often lighted new converts to the faith for which he died. The appeal to the lower motives, which says, " Do this because it is agreeable," is a very feeble and a very shabby one, as compared with that which says, " You will have a great many difficulties on this road, but do the thing because it is right, and, therefore, in the long run, best." So our Lord here, in these solemn and familiar words, exhorts us to discipleship, not because it is easy, but because it is hard ; and warns us against the other path because of its con venience. He does not say, " *Although* the one gate is wide and the other narrow, yet enter," but He says, " *Because* the one gate is wide, do not go in at it, and because the other is narrow, do !" Or, to put it into other words, this text exhorts us to be Christians because of the difficulties in the path, and warns us against the other road because of its seeming immunities and comforts. I shall best, I think, carry out the spirit of the words before us if I simply try to dwell upon these four particulars, and see how all of them enforce the exhortation. I. Look then, first, at THE TWO GATES. The gates come into view merely as the means of entrance upon the path. To put into plain English the meaning of our Lord's words, He says to us, "Be Christians because it is a great deal easier to begin to be evil than to begin to be good." All evil things are easily commenced. It is not difficult to begin to be bad; the difficulty comes afterwards. But the gate of discipleship is narrow, because you have to make yourself small to get in at it, like Milton's angels that had to diminish their size to enter the council chamber. It is narrow, inasmuch as you have to leave outside wealth, position, culture, righteousness, self-help, everything that is your own, or you will stick in the aperture like a loaded mule in some narrow doorway. You cannot drive through there in a carriage and pair; you must alight and walk. The surest way to get in is to go down on your knees. As in those narrow passages for defence which you find in the pre-historic houses on many a Scotch moor, where there is only a little aperture leading to a tortuous avenue, along which a man has to crawl on his face; so, if you want to get into the road that leadeth to life you have to go down very low, and abandon self, and leave ever so much rubbish outside, for it will let you in, and it will let nothing in but you. Fancy a king, like that German emperor that stood outside the gate of Canossa, in the snow, coming up to the door with all his robes on, and his crown on his head. He has to take off the crown, for the gate is not high enough to admit that. He has to strip himself of his robes, for the gate is not wide enough to admit their stiffened velvet and gold; he tries again and again to force himself through its narrowness, until he stands stripped of all but the hair shirt of penitence, and then he can get through. "Strait is the gate," letting in one at a time, like a turnstile that admits single people and takes in none of their belongings. These are the conditions on which we become Christ's disciples. II. Now, CONSIDER THE SECOND CLASS OF ENFORCEMENTS OF THE EXHORTATION DERIVED FROM THE CONTRAST OF THE WAYS. "Broad is the way," in the one case, narrow in the other: which, being put into plain English, means that to the natural man, to flesh and blood and all that belongs to it, not only is the initial step, which makes a Christian, hard, but that to be a real Christian continues hard right along. So, be suspicious of easy roads, and turn a deaf ear to the world that says to you, "Come, and eat of my bread, for it is pleasant, and drink of the wine that I have mingled." If you are ever in doubt about two courses, choose the unwelcome and the hard one; and in ninety-nine cases out of a hundred you will have chosen the one that God meant you to walk in. The road is broad, therefore avoid it; the way is narrow, therefore walk ye in it. III. Again, OUR LORD DRAWS ANOTHER ARGUMENT FROM THE POPULARITY OF THE ONE PATH AND THE SPARSE TRAVELLERS UPON THE OTHER. "Many there be that go in thereat." That is a reason for your not going in. "Few there be that find it." That is a reason for your trying to be one of the few. "What everybody says will be true." If you can get a perfectly unanimous vote you may rely upon it; but what the majority says is generally false. So it is in matters of opinion; so it is in conduct. The sombre thing about the world is, not that men are miserable, or that men are mortal, but that the mass of men choose to be foolish and bad, and they do so because it is easiest. The sluggard's motive of saving trouble shapes the lives of most of us. It is easy travelling in the ruts. A cabman will always try to get his wheel on the tram rail. It goes smoothly. We are ever disposed to swallow what everybody round about us declares to be food, even though we, in our inmost hearts, know that it is poison. Tell a man that ten thousand people go to see something, and he is sure to make the ten thousand and first as soon as he can. Tell him that nobody goes that road and he will not go it. Jesus Christ comes to us, and says—therein echoing the words and consciences of all true teachers and guides —"Be suspicious of what most people believe, and avoid what most people do." The road is traversed by crowds. Well, that is a presumption against it. Dead fish go down the stream, living ones swim the other way. Where you are called to go, never mind though you have to go alone. IV. Our Lord's final argument is from THE CONTRAST OF THE ENDS. "Life"—"destruction." The one path has an inclination upwards, while the other steadily descends. (*A. Maclaren, D.D.*) *The strait gate—a sermon to children:*—I. THE GATE. You have gone to another part of the country to spend your holidays, or to visit friends. There is a noble castle in the neighbourhood, with beautiful grounds, trees and shrubs and flowers, and lakes with swans and all sorts of water-fowl, and other attractions which I cannot describe. You have heard much about the place, and have been told, if ever you are within reach, to be sure to go to see it. But when you go, the very first thing that meets your eye is the gate. That stands between you and what you so much desire to see, and your very first question is, "How am I to get in? How is the gate to be passed? Whom shall I get to open it for me?" The first thing with which you have to do is—the gate! Or, there is to be some special treat for children, nearer home. It is a gala-day. Crowds of young people in holiday dress, and all merry and in high spirits as can be, are hurrying along. All are pressing forward to a common meeting-place. You follow the crowd. You would like to get in. As they come up, they show their ticket of admission, and pass on. And as you look in wistfully after them, your thought is—the gate! the door! How could *I* get in? Now, it is just so with other and higher things. As to all that is good in God's house and kingdom here, and all that is good in God's heavenly kingdom and home yonder—the great question with each of us is, "How shall I get at it? How shall I get in?" The great question is, about the gate—the door. Now, I might get many answers to the question, "What is the gate?" Some might answer, prayer is the gate, quoting such a passage as that, "Ask, and ye shall receive; seek, and ye shall find; knock, and it shall be opened unto you;" or, "Whosoever shall call upon the name of the Lord shall be saved." Some might say, faith is the gate: "Believe on the Lord Jesus Christ, and thou shalt be saved." Some might say, repentance is the gate: "Except ye repent, ye shall all likewise perish." Some might say, conversion is the gate: "Except ye be converted, and become as little children, ye shall not enter into the kingdom of heaven." Some might say, regeneration—being "born again"—is the gate: "Except a man be born again, he cannot see the kingdom of God." All these are correct, so far as they go. But I believe the best of all answers to the question, "What is the gate?" is—Christ. Christ is the gate. So you find Himself saying, "I am the Way; no man cometh unto the Father but by Me." And again, "I am the Door; by Me, if any man enter in, he shall be saved." And again it is written, "Through Him we have access," or entrance. I shall try to explain to you how Jesus is the Gate, the Door, the Way. If you had offended some one, and he were to say that he would have nothing to do with you, would hold no communication with you except through me; that he would not listen to your application for pardon, except as it came through me; that I was the only person to whom he would listen, as seeking help for you, then *I* would be your "way"— "your door"—so far as he was concerned. And just so, I cannot get access to God the Father, except as coming through the Lord Jesus—in His name—making mention of Him. He is the only Mediator between God and me. I shall suppose you to be in prison, sentenced to lie there for months, or years, or for a whole lifetime, on account of some crime or for debt, or, it may be, condemned to death. I offer to take your place and become the prisoner in your stead, undertaking, as your substitute, to lie there for you as long as you should have lain, or to die for you, and you accept my offer, change places with me, and are set free. If you were asked, how you got out, you would say that you got out through me; that I opened the door for you; that I was your door out. Now that is what Jesus is and does. II. THE STRAITNESS OF THE GATE. It is called the "strait" or narrow gate. That does not mean, as we have seen, that there is any gate of wood or iron, and that it is so small that your bodies can hardly get through, push as you will. It just means that the way of salvation is difficult—is hard—that entering in by Christ as our door of salvation, our way of life is, in many views of it, very difficult, though, in other respects, it is most simple, most easy. I might speak of "the strait gate" in other matters. For instance, you have, in some way, been misbehaving, and you cannot bring yourself to say you have done wrong, to confess your fault, and own yourself sorry for it, and promise never to do the like again. You are shut up in your room. You hear your mother's footstep in the passage. You saw the tear in her eye, as you not only did the wrong, but refused to acknowledge it; and as you hear her at your door, and know that she is waiting there for the needed confession, it is as if a voice within cried out, "Yes; do it!" but your pride, your temper, your high spirit, will not let you, and you don't. It is a "strait gate." 1. There must be the giving up of your sin. You cannot come to Christ without this. You must let your sins go. Here is a narrow entrance. A blind man comes up to it with a great bundle on his back. It would let him in, but it will not let in his bundle. Either he must let go his load, and leave it behind him, or else he must stay outside with it. Now, your sins are just such a bundle. And then they have got such a hold on you—they so cling to you—they seem a part of your very self! To give them up is like leaving an arm behind you, and that is not easy. These dear sins of yours!—who shall tell what the giving of them up is?—forsaking your bad habits, bad companions, bad books— those silly, exciting, polluting novels, and story books, and tales, which used to have such an attraction for you; renouncing your bad tempers, pride, vanity, love of dress, indolence, resentment, talebearing, selfishness, greed, and such like things. Oh, it is hard to part with these!—it is a "strait gate." Ay, the gate is so strait, that it will not let in one consciously spared sin; and it is often one— just one—that keeps people out. They will not give it up, and the strait gate will not let it through. 2. There must be the giving up of your self-righteousness— your own goodness. By that, I do not mean that you are to cease to do any good thing that you have ever done—that you must give up doing good, just as you must give up doing evil. But I mean, that you must no more trust to your good-doing than to your evil-doing as a ground of acceptance with God. At a funeral one day I heard a minister thank God on behalf of an old saint, that, "by God's grace, she had been enabled to give up self—sinful self and righteous self." Now, the giving up of sinful self, as we have seen, is difficult enough; but it is not nearly so hard as the giving up of righteous self. 3. You must enter in at this gate alone. Part of the "straitness" consists in the solitariness of it. The crowd do not go that way—they do not like it. And it is not easy to differ from other people in anything. It is not easy even to wear an article of dress unlike our neighbours. It requires a great deal of courage even to do that. Now, one must be very much alone in entering this gate. Hence one of the difficulties of it. There are two remarks, however, which I must make here, by way of encouragement, and as so far an offset to the straitness of which I have spoken. The first is, that although the gate is strait, it is open—always open. You don't need to open it: it is open already. The second is, that though the gate is always strait, it is not so strait for children. Children can get in at small openings more easily than older and bigger people can. III. The need of ENTERING IN. It is not enough to know about it, to think about it, to promise, to intend, to resolve. None of all these will do. You must enter in. There is a ship at sea, beating about—the wind blowing hard, the waves breaking over it. A leak is discovered—all hands are at the pumps; the water is making; darkness comes on; guns of distress are fired. There are piteous cries for help. At length, yonder is the harbour! The cry bursts forth from a hundred voices, "The harbour! the harbour! Yonder are the lights! Listen! don't you hear the voices?" And yet they may sink in sight of the harbour, at the very mouth of it, almost in, knowing all about the entrance. And next morning it will be all the sadder to see the ship lying at the very harbour's mouth—touching it—a wreck, and all on board perished. They did not "enter in." IV. The need of STRIVING, in order to enter in. That is to say, there must be earnestness, thoroughgoing earnestness—throwing ourselves with our whole heart into it, resolving never to give up, but with God's help to win the day. And now let me ask one or two questions ere I close. 1. Are you striving? If such earnestness is needful, if the kingdom of heaven suffereth violence, if without this there is no hope, no chance of being saved—what are you doing in order to be saved? Are you striving? 2. Are you letting anything keep you back? A man who had climbed up a tree overhanging a river, lost his hold. As he was falling down he caught hold of a twig, by which he hung. A boat put off for his rescue, and came alongside, just beneath him; but there he still hung, and save him they could not. Their cry was, "Let go the twig, or we cannot save you!" and only when he let go was salvation possible. Perhaps you are holding by some "twig," some sin, some fancied goodness, refusing to give it up. I would leave this word to ring in the ear of such: "Let go the twig! Let go the twig! Let nothing keep you back!" 3. Are you putting off? You have no security for to-morrow. No day is yours but to-day. What a bitter thought it will be, that you might have entered in, and you would not, and so are for ever shut out! (*J. H. Wilson, M.A.*) *The difficulties of a Christian life considered:*—I. THE DUTY ENJOINED. 1. The course of a holy and Christian life, in order to the obtaining of eternal happiness, is here represented to us by a way, which every man that would come to heaven, must walk in. For so St. Matthew (who expresseth this more fully) makes mention of a way, as well as a gate, by which we must enter into it—"Strait is the gate, and narrow is the way, that leadeth to life." And this, though it be not expressed by St. Luke, is necessarily understood—" Strive to enter in at the strait gate"; that is, into the way that leads to life. 2. The first difficulties of a holy and religious course of life are here represented to us by a strait gate. For the gate at which we enter, and the way in which we walk, can signify nothing else, but the beginning and progress of a holy and religious course. Now these difficulties are either from ourselves or from something without us. (1) From ourselves; from the original corruption and depravation of our nature, and the power of evil habits and customs, contracted by vicious practices. Our natures are vitiated and depraved, inclined to evil, and impotent to good; besides that, being habituated to sin and vice, it is a matter of infinite difficulty to break off a custom, and to turn the course of our life another way. Now, because this is the difficulty of our first entrance into religion, it is represented by a strait gate, which is hard to get through. (2) There are, likewise, other difficulties from without; as, namely, the opposition and persecution of the world, which was very raging and violent in the first beginnings of Christianity. And this our Saviour represents by the ruggedness and roughness of the way, as St. Matthew expresseth it (Matt. vii. 14). 3. Our diligence and constancy in this course are represented by "striving," a word which hath a great force and emphasis in it, ἀγωνίζεσθε, a metaphor taken from the earnest contention which was used in the Olympic games by those who strove for mastery in running or wrestling, or any of the other exercises which were there used. And to the business of religion, if we will set upon it in good earnest, these three things are required : (1) A mighty resolution to engage us in a holy and Christian course. (2) Great diligence and industry to carry us on in it. (3) An invincible constancy to carry us through it, and make us persevere in it to the end. 4. The difficulties of a holy and a Christian life are not so great and insuperable as to be a just ground of discouragement to our endeavours. (1) Consider the assistance which the gospel offers to us. By the assistance of the Holy Spirit, which is promised to us, we may conquer all difficulties. (2) Consider, that the greatest difficulties are at first; it is but making one manful onset, and sustaining the first brunt, and the difficulties will abate and grow less, and our strength will every day increase and grow more. The gate is strait; but when we have once got through it, "our feet will be set in an open place." (3) Consider that custom will make religion easy to us. (4) Consider the reward that religion propounds, and this must needs sweeten and mitigate all the troubles and difficulties that are occasioned by it. This "strait gate" through which we must enter, and this "craggy way" which we are to climb up, leads to life, and he is a lazy man, indeed, that will not strive and struggle for life. II. Here is a REASON ADDED TO ENFORCE THE EXHORTATION or duty; "for many shall seek to enter in, and shall not be able": that is, there are a great many that will do something in Christianity, and make some faint attempts to get to heaven, who yet shall fall short of it, for want of such a firm resolution and earnestness of endeavour, as it is necessary to the attaining of it. 1. Some trust to the external profession of the true religion. 2. Others have attained to a good degree of knowledge in religion, and they rely much upon that. 3. There are others that find themselves much affected with the Word of God, and the doctrines contained in it. 4. Others are very strict and devout in the external worship of God. 5. Others confide much in their being members of the only true Church, in which alone salvation is to be had, and in the manifold privileges and advantages which therein they have above others of getting to heaven. 6. Others think their great zeal for God and His true religion will certainly save them. 7. Others go a great way in the real practice of religion. 8. Others rely much upon the sincerity of their repentance and conversion, whereby they are put into a state of grace, and become the children of God, and heirs of everlasting life; and being once truly so, they can never fall from that state, so as finally to miscarry. 9. Others venture all upon a death-bed repentance, and their importunity with God to receive them to mercy at the last. (*Archbishop Tillotson.*) *The Christian's journal :*—The thing that I will chiefly labour in, is (according to the drift of the place) to show what things ought of necessity to be in every one that would be saved. It will be excellent matter of direction to all those that are yet unconverted, and of resolution and confirmation to such as have truly cared to walk the way that leadeth unto life. 1. The first thing which by authority of this text of Scripture ought to be in every one that desireth salvation, is a right understanding and a true acknowledgment of his own wandering. Reason itself must needs yield to this in other things, and it must needs be true in this. How shall I persuade a man to enter into the strait gate, if he do not feel and perceive himself to be in a way in which it is not safe for him to continue? If we look into the Scripture we shall see good proof for this point, namely, that the acknowledgment of our by-past error is the very first degree unto sound conversion. Deceive we not ourselves, either we must begin here at the sight of our old errors, or else we can never tread the path that leadeth unto life. 2. The next thing which by the rule of my text must be in every one that would be saved, is, care to seek out the true way, and that path, which leadeth and bringeth the goers in it unto life. This is plain also (as to me seemeth) by this Scripture; for as the light of a man's ancient wandering must go before his entrance into a new course, so of necessity when he perceiveth his errors, the right way must be sought out, and certainly understood, before he can enter thereinto; so that He which bids me enter into the gate of life, bids me withal to seek where that gate is, for otherwise my desire of entrance is in vain. If a master do will his servant to go to such a house, it is presupposed that either he doth know the way to it, or else must make inquiry for it. And this care to inquire out the true way in this particular, is the plain doctrine of the Scripture (Jer. vi. 16; 1 Thess. v. 24; Acts xvii. 11; 1 Kings xviii. 21). 3. The third thing which this text necessarily commendeth unto us, if we would be saved, is a resolution when we have felt our error, and found the right way and the true gate, all delays laid aside to make a present entry. If you ask how I prove this by my text, I thus make it manifest. So here, the commandment and charge being given indefinitely, without any express limitation of any set time, it followeth that it is presently to be performed. Our Saviour saith not, enter hereafter when thou art more at leisure; or to the young man, enter when thou art old; or to the old man, enter when thou art a-dying; or to the covetous man, enter when thou hast glutted thy desire with wealth; or to the drunkard, enter when thou art utterly disabled that thou canst be drunk no longer: but He saith to all, at the instant "Enter"; do it presently, do it straightway, defer not to do it. And this is also the plain doctrine of the Scripture—"I made haste," saith David, "and I delayed not to keep Thy commandments." It is commended in Peter and Andrew, that when Christ called them, they left their nets straightway. When Christ called Zaccheus, the text saith, that he " came down hastily." The reason why there must be a resolution of present entrance is, because as there is a time of grace, in the which the gate of mercy stands open, so there is a time of judgment, in which this gate will be shut up, and all hope of entry utterly removed. 4. The fourth thing which now followeth to be treated of, is the entrance itself; our former wandering must be felt, the right and true way must be sought for; when it is found, a resolution of present entrance must be put on; and then next we must put forward. " Enter in at the strait gate." To this act of entrance there are two things required, the first is (that I may use terms agreeable to my text) stooping; the second, a stripping of ourselves of whatsoever may hinder our entrance. First, there must be a kind of stooping, because the coming in is low. It is said of heaven in the Scripture, that " it is a house not made with hands." Now, as in the matter thereof it is differing from our earthly buildings, so is it in the framing and contriving of it. In great men's houses, it is a great eyesore to see a little, low, and pinching entry to a large and spacious dwelling; but to the end all things may be answerable, as the house is of great receipt, so the gates must be high and lofty, and the coming in according. But now in this house which is eternal in the heavens it is otherwise. Indeed it is large within, " For in My Father's house " (saith Christ) "are many mansions"; but yet the gate unto it is exceeding low, the entry narrow, the passing in very strait. It is the gate of humility. Well, it followeth, together with this stooping, there must go (as I said) a certain stripping of ourselves also; he that would go through a strait way, a narrow entry, it is no wisdom for him to clog himself with many things about him; he had need rather to lighten himself, that he may go through with the greater ease. The covetous man with his bags, the swearer with his great oaths, that malicious man that swells with his malice, the ambitious with his high thoughts, the vicious with his minions, the drunkard with his full cups; these and the like to these can never enter here with their dependances. What sin soever thou hast formerly delighted in, if it were to thee as thy right hand, or thy right eye, thou must cut it off and cast it from thee, thou must strive to strip thyself of it, or else this gate is much too little for thee to go in at. This is like the hole the snake creepeth through, where he leaves his old skin behind him. If thou mean to come here, thou must then say with St. Peter, "It is enough for me that I have spent the time past of my life, after the lusts of the Gentiles, walking in wantonness, lusts, drunkenness, gluttony, drinkings, and in abominable idolatries." Other things, better things, are now expected of me; even that henceforth, "I should live, not after the lusts of men, but after the will of God." It is an excellent place. I could bring in a cloud of witnesses to make good this point, that old sins must be stripped off, when we once put our foot to the threshold of this strait gate. 5. The fifth thing, then, which by the authority and strength of this text ought to be in every one that desireth salvation, is a continual proceeding and going on in good things. I doubt not but you shall see this plainly proved to be comprehended in the text. Our Saviour here compareth heaven to a place from which by nature we are all estranged; true religion is the way leading unto it, humility (the denial of ourselves, and the renouncing the bypast pleasures of sin) is the gate entering us into this way. Now the use, you know, of a way, is for travellers, not for idle loiterers, or vain gazers, or time-deluding triflers; such is this spiritual way, it is a way leading to life, and therefore requireth a continual proceeding, from step to step, from grace to grace, without desisting, without tiring, until the journey's end be reached unto : and this is the express doctrine of the Scripture. The enterers into this gate of life must not stand (as it were) about the door, and sit them down as soon as they have begun to taste of good things, but there is a way before them to be travelled in; and, as through the necessity of nature, they come every day nearer to the end of their days, so by the power of grace they must strive to come every day nearer to the end of their faith, the salvation of their souls. Let us apply it. (1) To reprove that which hath been reproved often, but is not yet reformed, and that is our slackness, and our sluggishness in spiritual things. (2) Well, for a second use; if it be so dangerous a thing not to go forward, what is it, think we, to go backward, to decay, and grow cold in our love to good things? "Their last state" (saith our Saviour) "will be worse than their first." And, "it is better not to have known the way of righteousness, than after they have known, to turn from the holy commandment given unto them." The evil spirit that is once cast out, bringeth with him "seven devils worse than himself." Now to this going on and proceeding in the way to life there are sundry things belonging which it is very meet that we should be made acquainted with; they are impertinent neither to the matter nor to the text. 1. The first is, continual guidance and direction. A man that is to journey in a way unknown will not be satisfied with this alone that he is set into the right way, but considering the possibility of erring, he will furnish himself with as many directions as he can, glad he will be of any man's company that understandeth the way; sometime he will be at the charge rather than fail to hire a man that may conduct him. The way of peace which leadeth unto happiness, is a way which flesh and blood is not acquainted with, and the nature of man is of itself very subject to mistaking; therefore his duty that would grow in godliness is to get unto him the direction of some sure guide, which will not deceive him, that so he may not fail of the end and mark which he desireth. The head guide is the Lord Jesus, He hath recommended His directions unto us in His Word; and for the common benefit and instruction of His Church, He hath given gifts unto men, and enabled them to lay open the mystery of the Scripture, and by this His ordinance He guides and directs those that are in His eternal counsel ordained unto life. 2. The second thing that must accompany our purpose of going on in the way to happiness, is circumspection and an earnest heeding of our course. So much is very manifest by the text. You see here, that as the gate of entrance is termed "strait," so the way of progress is called "narrow." Now a narrow way requireth heedfulness, a little slipping, or going to this side or that, may breed a great deal of inconvenience. And if we examine the Scripture we shall see the like heed-taking required in this spiritual journey. The third thing which must accompany our purpose of going on in the way of happiness is a resolution and preparation for such encumbrances as may meet us on the way. It is wisdom, we know, in travelling to be prepared for the weather, to be armed against such as lie in wait to spoil, and do many times make a prey of the goods, nay even of the lives, of the passersby : so in this case, inasmuch as a man intending to proceed in the ways of God shall be assaulted with many grievances, it is good policy both to put on a resolution to wrestle with them, and to be armed so that he may prevail against them. The last thing which must accompany our purpose of going on, is an often calling the course passed to an account, to see whether it be right and straight, yea or no; he who journeyeth in a way which he is not acquainted with, it is wisdom for him ever and anon to be mindful of the directions which were given him, and to remember the marks which were told him, the turnings and the by-paths which he was warned of, to the end that by thinking hereupon, if he finds he is right, he may proceed with comfort; if he be deceived, he may return quickly before he has wandered too far and erred overmuch. So it must be in this way. (*S. Hieron.*) *The narrow way, and the broad way* :—To insist in virtuous courses, and to attain at length to everlasting bliss, is no easy achievement. To be saved is a very difficult matter. There must be great pains and labour in getting through the gate. In which words you may observe these two general parts. 1. An exhortation to an important duty—" Enter ye in at the strait gate." 2. The reasons and arguments to enforce the practice of this duty, and they are two. The first is taken from the easiness of the contrary performance, and the multitude of those that perish by it. " For wide is the gate, and broad is the way that leadeth to destruction, and many there be that go in thereat." The second argument is taken from the difficulty of this duty, and the paucity of those who perform it aright, and consequently attain to life and happiness. " Because strait is the gate, and narrow is the way, which leadeth unto life, and few there be that find it." I. IT IS FAR MORE HARD AND DIFFICULT TO BE TRULY HOLY, AND TO ENTER INTO HEAVEN AND HAPPINESS, THAN MEN COMMONLY IMAGINE. This is founded upon these positive words of our Saviour, " Strait is the gate," &c. This happens thus upon this twofold account. 1. By reason of the great things which are to be done by us in order to salvation. 2. Because of the great things which are to be suffered by us. 3. (and which comprehends the former) In regard of the great and powerful enemies that we are to encounter with. II. My second proposition (which is indeed the consequent of which I have been insisting upon) is this, that OF ALL THE MEN IN THE WORLD THERE ARE BUT FEW THAT ATTAIN TO HEAVEN AND HAPPINESS. The number of them that shall be saved is very little in respect of those that shall be damned. Our Saviour not only tells us that " Strait is the gate and narrow the way which leadeth unto life," but He adds this also, " Few there be that find it." Absolutely speaking, many are saved ; but speaking comparatively, very few. The New Jerusalem hath more gates than one (as it is described in Rev. xxii.), *i.e.*, as I conceive, many enter into it. But, notwithstanding this, it is likewise an undeniable truth that vast numbers are shut out of the New Jerusalem—yea, many more are excluded than are let in. The greatest number of men are wicked, and follow their evil courses, and perish everlastingly. Weeds and briars grow apace, and fill every field and hedge, but useful flowers and plants are more scarce. Godliness is rare, and hath few followers ; but the wicked are very numerous. Sinners go by whole troops to hell. You may behold multitudes of men and women posting with all haste in the broad way. That road is beaten and frequented. The number is very great of scandalous and ungodly men, but there are very few that live according to the rules of the gospel, and attain to celestial bliss and glory. 1. To begin with that which was the sad beginning of all our miseries, it must needs be that the number of those who are saved is but little in comparison of those that are damned ; and also that it is a very difficult thing to attain to salvation and happiness ; it must needs be so, I say, because of the great shipwreck at Adam's fall. Many were cast away in that bottom. For that first man carried our concerns and effects in his vessel, and when this split on the rock we were all shattered and plunged into misery. Truly it is a wonder that any escaped and got to shore safe. 2. There is in most men a wilful ignorance of the way to salvation, and of their own good and welfare ; and this may be assigned as a main cause why so few are saved. How many ignorant souls are there who content themselves with their dark road that they are in ? They see others striving to enter in at the strait gate, and they observe that they put themselves to a great deal of trouble and pains ; wherefore they, for their part, continue in the blind and obscure path which they have taken, and there they live at ease, and indulge their follies, and are not solicitous to correct them. A considerable part of the Christian world is ruined by this means. 3. Unbelief damns a great part of the world, and causes the number of the blessed to be so scarce. A fault of the will, as well as of the understanding. 4. This may be assigned as another reason why the number of those that are saved is but small, in comparison of the great multitudes that are damned, namely, because men nourish insensibleness and security, and will not be affected with the wretchedness of their condition. There are few that have a sense of the burden of their sins ; and how then can it be expected that they should have a desire to be eased of it ? Where sin lies light, the salvation by Christ Jesus is ever vilified and disrespected. 5. Pride and self-conceit are another cause why so great multitudes of men fall short of salvation and happiness, and why the number of those that are saved is so rare. It is no wonder that the gospel salvation is everywhere slighted, since it so directly crosses the grain of our nature—I mean, our high opinion of ourselves. 6. The way to life must needs be difficult, and few there be that find it, because men wilfully deceive themselves. This is an undeniable truth (though the generality of the world will not acknowledge it) that there is a cheat in every sin, and that men are grossly deluded and imposed upon by the commission of it. Hence in Scripture you read of the "deceitfulness of riches" (Matt. xiii. 22), and "deceitful lusts" (Eph. iv. 22), and the "deceivableness of unrighteousness" (2 Thess. ii. 10), and the "deceitfulness of sin" (Heb. iii. 13). All which acquaints us that when a man breaks God's laws, and acts contrary to his duty, he deceives and cozens himself. The spirit of folly and vanity reigns in him; his judgment of things is nothing but fond mistake and dotage. False propositions are entertained by him, and his whole life is a delusion. It remains now that I make some inferences from both the propositions which I insisted upon—1. From the difficulty of being saved. 2. From the paucity of those that are saved. Is it so hard a thing to be saved?—then make it not harder. Is the way to heaven so narrow, and the gate strait?—then do not make it straiter than it is. Stop not up the way by your own fault. You have no need to render heaven and happiness more difficult than indeed they are. Take it in these two particulars, straiten not the gate—(1) By limiting the grace of God. (2) By imposing unnecessary austerities on yourselves. 2. In the second place, then, is the gate so strait, is the way to heaven so difficult?—then the fond opinion of those men is baffled and confuted who persuade themselves that the purchase of heaven is cheap and easy. They need not take much pains, they say, to attain to happiness. God made man for it, and He will be sure to bestow it on him. Hence they take no care how they act; they sit still, and carelessly look about them, but never mind their proper duty and concern. They hope to get to heaven as well as the best, but they are never solicitous about the way to it. This is a sign indeed that they think it an easy thing to get thither. They must take it with all its hardships. 3. Seriously sit down, and think how few there are in the whole heap and herd of mankind that attain to heaven. This is a seasonable inference from the foregoing doctrine. Your thoughts and meditations cannot be exercised about a more important subject than this. 4. This doctrine which I have been discoursing of to you reproves the guise and manner of life which most men addict themselves to. 5. This doctrine which I have treated of is encouragement to those that are reproached for singularity and preciseness, and because they will not do as others do, because they will not swim with the stream, but bear up against it, and go cross to the sinful world. Let this comfort them that they are not in the broad way, the way which is trod by most, which leads to destruction; but that they have chosen the narrow way, which certainly conducts them to life and bliss. 6. Then I may add this, in the next place, as a proper inference, make not multitude or number an argument in actions of religion. It is reported of a certain pagan king that, being persuaded to be baptized, standing at the font, he asked to what place his predecessors, or most of them, were gone. It was answered they went to hell. To which he replied, "It is best to follow the most rather than the fewest"; and so refused to receive baptism and persisted still in his paganism. The very same argument induces men generally to perish eternally rather than to walk in the way of holiness, and be everlastingly happy. They will do as the most do, whatever comes of it. But do not you think that to be best which is done by the most, and think not that it is safest to go with the crowd. For as multitude excuses not a man from sin; so neither will it privilege him from punishment. 7. Bless God that you are in this way; magnify His holy name, that you have been directed by the spirit of grace to leave the wide path of sin, and to walk in the narrow and strait way which leads to life and happiness. 8. You that have this singular favour conferred upon you, you that have been directed into the narrow way which conducts you to life and happiness, you that are so eminently distinguished from others, you that are so few in number—see that ye be kindly and friendly to one another. You are but a little flock, you are a poor remnant, you are despised and hated by the world; let this remind you of loving one another more. 9. If so few are saved, then you who doubt whether you be of those few, examine yourselves. Search and try your state and condition. Many are called, but few are chosen. There are many in the Church, but few true saints. Therefore suspect yourselves, be anxious and solicitous to know what you are. 10. Then, if there be but few that shall be saved, be sure that you be of that number. When a fatal pestilence enters into a city or town, and begins to spread itself and to infect the neighbourhood, you may take notice how busy men are at such a time in providing for their safety, and in securing themselves from the spreading contagion.

Should you not be much more busy and solicitous when sin, the worst of plagues, spreads itself far and near, and disperses its contagion in all places, and amongst all sorts of persons, and when so many die of it, and everlastingly perish? Should you not be very careful to provide for your safety and security, to avoid the fatal infection of sin? Should you not labour to be of that small number who shall not be destroyed by it? And how is this to be done? Take it in brief thus—Live the life of those few that shall be saved. Act, and walk, and behave yourselves in all things as those that are the small elect number of true Christian believers. Let your conversation be as becomes the gospel of Christ. III. The third and last proposition grounded on the words, and that is this, THOUGH THE GATE BE SO STRAIT AND THE WAY SO NARROW, YET IT IS OUR INDISPENSABLE CONCERN TO ENTER INTO THEM, AND IN ORDER TO THAT TO STRIVE. There is no entering into the gate of life without striving; therefore make it the business of your whole life to strive that you may enter. 1. I say, it must be early. "Seek ye first the kingdom of God, and His righteousness." We must make our religion our first care and business. Go into the narrow way speedily, enter into the strait gate presently, before thou art old and decrepid, and canst not be able to get through. Observe how wicked men make haste and delay not to follow their evil ways, and to provoke God, and to act all things unworthily and basely. They crowd so fast into the broad way that one would believe they thought there would not be room enough to hold them unless they made haste. But in the way of life you move slowly, you rid no ground, but you fondly hope that with your soft and easy pace you shall arrive in good time at heaven and happiness. But be not mistaken. This dull pace will not reach heaven. 2. Your striving must be earnest. It must be with great intenseness, vigour, and zeal. "The kingdom of heaven must suffer violence; and the violent take it by force." The Kingdom of Heaven is got by those that "thrust": so the Greek properly is to be rendered. If you would enter in at the strait gate, you must thrust and push forwards, you must make your way with violence and force. It was the resolve of that famous Punic general in his march over the Alps to find, or make way. 3. Your striving must be constant and persevering. Our striving, as it must begin betimes, so it must continue to the end. As it must be earnest, so it must be frequent and lasting. Assiduity must be joined to earnestness and fervency. No time is to be omitted and neglected, you must in season and out of season, night and day, prosecute this great design. It is said that if a man has once learned to swim he can never forget it, or lose it by long disuse. I am sure it is not so with any moral and spiritual actions. They must be repeated and renewed by constant exercise, or else they will fail. Wherefore the apostle's exhortation is seasonable (1 Tim. iv. 7). I will now offer to you two weighty considerations, which you must always have before you, and by the influence of them you will be moved to strive, and that with great zeal, although the greatest difficulties lie in your way. The considerations are these: 1. Take notice how men strive for the world. 2. Observe how they strive and take pains in the pursuit of sin. 1. I say, consider how men strive and contend, work and take pains, sweat and toil, to purchase the riches, delights, and honours of the world. And shall they be so solicitous and laborious for their worldly and secular advantage? And wilt not thou strive and labour for the true riches, durable pleasures, and heavenly honours? You must make their practice your example and pattern, *i.e.*, you must strive as much for heaven as they do for earth. It was, I remember, the saying of Cardinal Wolsey, that great and rich prelate, when he grew out of favour, and was sent for, and seized in the king's name, "Had I served God," said he, "as truly and carefully as I have served my master, my sovereign, He would not have forsaken me as this doth." This will be a sad and forlorn reflection to any of you, that you took more pains to please man than God; to purchase the favour of some great one rather than His whose favour is better than life. It will be grievous to remember that you toiled and laboured, and disturbed your rest, and incurred innumerable hazards to become wealthy and gain an estate in the world, and yet that you were unconcerned in the business of your immortal souls, that you never took any pains, or lost an hour's sleep about it. This will be a killing reflection to you when you come to die. Be persuaded, therefore, to prevent it by your speedy care and endeavours, by employing your chief time and labour in working out your salvation. 2. Now I will pass to the second, which is this: Consider how men strive and take pains in the pursuit of sin and wickedness, and in the ways of hell and destruction; and let this excite you to be as laborious and diligent in the pursuit of good-

ness and blessedness. The kingdom of darkness (as well as the kingdom of heaven) suffers violence, and the violent take it by force. Men sweat and toil to purchase damnation. Let this make you ashamed, when you are apt to complain of the strait gate. Remember, that vice as well as virtue hath its hardships, yea it hath many more. To gratify a vain lust, how strangely sometimes do men deprive themselves of all their ease and peace, all their rest and quiet, and plunge themselves into unspeakable sorrows, disturbances, and distractions? Quit not then the way of holiness because of some difficulties which you meet with in it; but consider that there are more difficulties that attend a sinful life. The narrow way is more easy than the broad one. When thou art once used to it, thou wilt find it to be such. And now, in the last place, I have several plain and practical directions to offer to you, by the help of which your striving to enter in at the strait gate will certainly be effectual and successful. The first help is earnest prayer; the second is seriousness, and being in good earnest; the third is to resist the first beginnings of sin; the fourth is to make a conscience of the least sin; the fifth, to avoid the appearance of evil; the sixth, to be always fearful. (*John Edwards, D.D.*) **Will seek to enter in, and shall not be able.**—*Disappointed seekers:*—Many seek to enter in, but are not able. 1. When they will enter in through another door than the narrow one. 2. When they will enter in through the narrow door indeed, but only if they have made it somewhat wider. 3. When they will enter in through the narrow door indeed, but without leaving behind what cannot be taken along. (*Van Oosterzee.*) *The grand disappointment:*—
I. THE WAY OF ENTRANCE INTO THE STRAIT GATE. The way of entering on a truly religious course, and the way of entering into heaven, are precisely the same. We must enter the former by faith in Christ, and by the same means must we enter the latter. 1. A few remarks occur here. One is, that Christian diligence and labour can only be effectual through the aid of the blessed Spirit of God. 2. Another remark is, that labour is quickened by prayer. This strengthens our feeble hands, and calls down those supplies which raise the feeble efforts of nature into the powerful efforts of grace. 3. A still further remark which occurs here is, that the Christian's labour will not extend beyond this life. The Scripture teaches us to conceive of heaven by a few simple ideas. One of those ideas which is particularly soothing and delightful is that of rest. There may be active employment in heaven, but there will be no toil. Be patient then, brethren, under all your labours, whether of the body or of the mind. II. WE ARE TO CONSIDER THE CHARACTERS, WHO, SEEKING TO ENTER INTO THE STRAIT GATE, SHALL BE REFUSED. "They shall seek to enter in, and shall not be able." 1. The negligent. 2. He who contents himself with mere desires for his religious good. 3. The scorner. 4. He who criminally mistakes the path of life. By this subject—1. We are taught the personal and individual character of true religion. 2. We are taught how groundless are the fears which our text may sometimes have occasioned in the minds of the sincere and upright. (*Essex Remembrancer.*) *Self-delusion:*—I. MANY PROFESSORS ARE DECEIVED. So the text teaches us. It does not say, "a few may be misled," but "many shall seek to enter in, and shall not be able." That many professors are deceived is clear enough from the language of Christ Himself, both here and in other places. II. IT IS NOT SURPRISING THAT THERE ARE FALSE PROFESSORS. There is an imitation of the externals of godliness which it is not easy to detect. Art can carve a statue so that it almost breathes; and some of us in looking at very skilful paintings have mistaken them for realities. In a notable picture in the exhibition, you will have noticed an imitation of sunlight shining under a door, so well effected, that many go up to it to ascertain if it be not really a gleam from the sun. We know that men can counterfeit coins and notes so well that only the most experienced can detect them; and in all commercial transactions men are so well aware of the subtlety of their fellows that they look well lest they be deceived. The vital mysteries of godliness are mysterious: the inner life cannot be perceived by the carnal eye, and the outer life of the godly seemeth to most men to be but morality carried out with care; and hence it becomes but a very simple task for a man to make himself look just like a Christian, so as to deceive the very elect. To learn by heart that which others say *from* the heart—to get the outline of a believer's experience, and then to adapt it skilfully to one's self as our experience —this is a thing so simple, that, instead of wondering that there are hypocrites, I often marvel that there are not ten times more. And then, again, the graces—the real graces within — are very easy to counterfeit. There is a repentance that needeth to be repented of — and yet it approaches near as possible to true

repentance. Does repentance make men hate sin? They who have a false repentance may detest some crimes. Does repentance make men resolve that they will not sin? So will this false repentance; for Balaam said, "If Balak would give me his house full of silver and gold, I will not go beyond the word of the Lord." Does true repentance make men humble themselves? So does false repentance; for Ahab humbled himself before God, and yet he perished. And as for faith, how easy it is to counterfeit this! Even in Christ's day, there was a faith which wrought miracles but did not save the soul; and Paul tells us that if we had a faith which could remove mountains, yet if we had not charity, it would profit us nothing. Dear friends, let us remember, too, that there are so many things which help a man to deceive himself. He himself is naturally disposed to be very partial. "Let well alone," is a proverb which most men have learned. Very few men 'care to look at the worst of their own state; they would rather say, "Peace, peace," than think too harshly of themselves. What man ever gave himself a bad character? or if he did, what man could not abundantly excuse himself for having such a character? Then there is the devil, who never wants us to be too careful, for heedlessness is one of the nets in which he takes his prey. III. THIS DELUSION MAY CONTINUE THROUGHOUT LIFE, EVEN TO THE LAST MOMENT. IV. The next point is this—that this delusion, even to the last, MAY SEEM TO HAVE THE MOST EXCELLENT ARGUMENTS TO SUPPORT IT. I shall prove this from Scripture. A man may be a deceiver, and he may accomplish his task all the more readily because he can say, "I have made and I have maintained a very respectable profession in the Church. I do not know that I have ever tarnished my character; I believe I am looked upon by most people as a pattern and example." Yes, this may be all correct, and yet you may be shut out at the last. Again, some may bring a very careful outward observance of religion as an excellent argument, and think the conclusion to be drawn therefrom to be very satisfactory. "Lord, we have eaten and drank in Thy presence, and Thou has preached in our streets." You have been baptized; you are always at the Lord's table; your pew always sees you in it whenever the doors are opened. All this is very proper and right; but it may all help to make you more easily deceived. You may conclude that you must be right because of this; and yet, the Master may say, "I never knew you." If means of grace could raise men to heaven, Capernaum would not have been cast down to hell. O friends, your preachings, prayings, almsgivings, tract distributings, unless grace be in you, help you in your delusion, and make it the more difficult to arouse you from it. V. And now to the last point, this delusion may last through life, and be sustained by many specious arguments, but IT MUST ALL BE DISPELLED. (C. H. Spurgeon.) Philip Henry's dying advice:—Mr. Philip Henry said to some of his neighbours who came to see him on his death-bed, "Oh, make sure work for your souls, my friends, by getting an interest in Christ while you are in health! If I had that work to do now, what would become of me? I bless God, I am satisfied. See to it, all of you, that your work be not undone when your time is done, lest you be undone for ever." The one journey through the world:—"When I was a young man," says James Simpson, "there lived a man in our neighbourhood who was universally reported to be uncommonly liberal in his dealings. When he had any of the produce of his farm to dispose of, he made it an invariable rule to give good measure—over good, rather more than could be required of him. One of his friends, observing his frequently doing so, questioned him why he did it, told him he gave too much, and said it would not be to his own advantage. Now mark the answer of this man: 'God Almighty has given me but one journey through the world, and, when gone, I cannot return to rectify mistakes.' Think of this, friends—but one journey through the world." Heaven is worth striving for:—The difficulty of obtaining shows the excellency; and, surely, if you consider but what it cost Christ to purchase it; what it costs God's Spirit to bring men's hearts to it; what it costs ministers to persuade to it; what it costs Christians, after all this, to obtain it; and what it costs many a half-Christian that, after all, goes without it; you will say, that here is difficulty, and therefore excellency. Trifles may be had at a trivial rate, and men may have damnation far more easily. It is but to lie still, and sleep out our days in careless laziness. It is but to take our pleasure, and mind the world, and cast away the thoughts of sin, and grace, and Christ, and heaven, and hell, out of our minds; and do as the most do, and never trouble ourselves about these high things, but venture our souls upon our presumptuous conceits and hopes, and let the vessel swim which way it will; and then stream, and wind, and tide, will all help us apace to the gulf of perdition. You may burn a hundred houses easier than build one; and kill a thousand men, than make one alive. The descent is easy, the ascent not so. To bring diseases is but to cherish sloth, please the appetite, and take what most delights us: but to cure them, will cost bitter pills, loathsome potions, tedious gripings, abstemious, accurate living, and perhaps all fall short too. He that made the way, and knows the way better than we, hath told us "it is narrow and strait," and requires striving; and they that have paced it more truly and observantly than we, do tell us it lies through many tribulations, and is with much ado passed through. Conclude, then, it is surely somewhat worth that must cost all this. (*R. Baxter.*)

Vers. 25–30. **When once the Master of the house hath risen up.**—*False dependence on Church privileges :*—In the eyes of Him who "seeth not as man seeth," who readeth the heart and weigheth actions in the balances of the sanctuary, the worker of iniquity is not only the man who disregards religion and commits open wickedness; but also he who, if he avoid certain sins, avoids them not because he fears God or is constrained by Christ's love, and who, if motives were analyzed, would be found to have regard to the good opinion of the world, rather than to the will and the glory of Him who called him into being. You must search your hearts. You must see whether God be first in your hearts; whether your great fear be the fear of offending Him—your great desire, the desire of pleasing Him; whether "old things have passed away," and "new things"—new tendencies, new hopes, new dispositions, have been communicated; so that you can declare "your conversation," your citizenship, to be "in heaven." Above all things, do not rest upon outward privileges. "The kingdom of God is within you." I do not depreciate the means of grace. The "workers of iniquity" may be those who delight in sermons and never miss a sacrament. This is not my assertion; I draw no picture from imagination; I ask you not to conjecture a case. But I may suppose the judgment past; the Son of Man hath appeared in the clouds of the heavens; He hath gathered to Himself a great company from the east and west, from the north and south; yea, with "a multitude which no man can number, out of every people and tribe and tongue," He hath sat down to the banquet, to which, from the beginning, He had invited our race. And there are numbers excluded: some "speechless," as though conscience-stricken, forced to own to themselves the justice of their exclusion. But there are others who press on with a bold front, as though they believed that "the door" had been closed by mistake, and would be opened to them so soon as they knocked. Who are these? Are these the open despisers of religion—the extortionate, the adulterer, the profane, the neglecter of ordinances, the scorner of mysteries, the scoffer at righteousness? Nay, not so. I never read of such as knocking for admission. Such may be of those who cry passionately to the rocks and to the hills to cover them; but not, so far as we are told, of those who expect entrance when the door has been closed. These are rather persons who lived in the profession of Christianity; whom the Sabbath saw regular in attendance on the ordinances of the Church; of whom ministers were hopeful, because they always found them using the means of grace; who, nevertheless, were uncircumcised at heart, and had not given themselves up for "a habitation of God through the Spirit." Yes, ye diligent hearers, ye constant communicants! take ye this on the authority of the Judge Himself; ponder this when ye go hence; be heedful that ye rest not satisfied with your state if ye have no better evidence than is thus to prove worthless at the last. The parties who shall "knock," and who shall then be rejected as "workers of iniquity," shall be those who can say—and that too without being contradicted—"We have eaten and drunk in Thy presence, and Thou hast taught in our streets." (*H. Melvill, B.D.*) *Almost saved, yet rejected :*—There are multitudes who will go a long way towards heaven and then stop short. They will give up everything but one thing for Christ, and therefore are they near heaven; but they keep that one, and therefore must they be excluded at the last. And it will be their having been so near which shall give such terror and fearfulness to the final exclusion. Almost believers upon earth, they are almost guests at the marriage-supper above. Oh! that voice—the known voice of the Redeemer—the voice which had often been heard in the proclamations of the gospel—how thrillingly will it come from the midst of the rejoicing assembly! how terrible will be the utterance, "I know you not, whence ye are!" Any voice rather than that voice. It will remind the almost Christian of what had been once in his power. His very recognition of the voice will so force on him the conviction that he might have made a covenant with Christ, that perhaps the bitterest thing of all in his banishment from heaven will be that the sentence proceeds from such lips. He could bear it better if an angel or an archangel syllabled the decree—though the voice might be awful as that of "many waters" when the fierce storm has roused them. But the voice which he had been wont to hear in the sanctuary, the voice which had spoken to him of pardon, the voice which even from the Cross had breathed the touching words, "Father, forgive them, for they know not what they do"—the voice which, as he was used to think, had addressed him in friendship, and promised him immortality—to hear *this* voice, too well remembered, bidding him "depart" when he knocks for admission—terror of terrors! keenest, hardest thing of all! What shall torment a man in hell like the consciousness that he had been almost in heaven? Thus it is to be. The men who "have eaten and drunk in Christ's presence" are to go to the very gate, to see Abraham and Isaac and Jacob admitted to the banquet, to distinguish the voice of the Redeemer as answer is made to them from the celestial hall, and then they are themselves to "go away into outer darkness!" Well may our Lord add, as He does, "There shall be weeping and wailing and gnashing of teeth." I would that this might warn you; that this might startle you. If there are any of you who are resting on outward duties and privileges, and have not given your hearts to the Lord, oh! do not shrink from self-examination; be not afraid to know the worst. The "Master of the house" hath not yet "risen up and shut to the door." You may still secure for yourselves admission at the last. (*Ibid.*)   Depart from Me.— *Exile from God:*—This world basks in the sunshine of Deity, and it scarcely knows the genial summer which it thereby enjoys. We would attempt to measure the extent of the blessing by considering the consequences of its withdrawal. When the solemn words, "Depart from Me," shall have died away upon the ears of the banished multitudes, in what state of being will they find themselves? What sort of existence will stretch out before them? "Absence from God," this is their sentence. We would inquire into what that sentence carries with it. We may sometimes have fancied that the wicked will hurry from the Divine presence with a feeling of relief in escaping from the Omniscient eye. Such is the traditional representation, in painting, of the flight of the condemned from the face of the Judge; yet more true perhaps would be that which should depict them as standing without power of motion, struck and chilled to the very heart at the doom, the miserable consequences of which may then just begin to be foreboded, "that they should henceforth see Him no more." Let us, then, endeavour to deduce some of these consequences, and hence argue back to the blessings which we now enjoy and so little appreciate. I. THERE IS A SENSE IN WHICH GOD CANNOT BE SAID TO BE ABSENT FROM ANY PART OF HIS DOMINIONS. A being may be termed present in a place either by inclusion of person or by manifestation of his face. Now as God cannot be confined personally in any single locality, so therefore must He be present personally everywhere; there can be no spot from which He is essentially shut out. This is what is expressed by the Psalmist, "If I ascend up into heaven Thou art there; if I go down to hell Thou art there also." He speaks, you observe, of a presence of God even in hell. Yet does the text make the doom of the impenitent a doom of exile from God. Depart from Me! what a banishment is this! It tells of a land where the heavens are as brass, and the earth as iron; where the prospect is bound in on every side by adamantine rocks, which allow no sight of better things beyond, no voices from holier shores to penetrate; where, never for one single moment, may the spirits of the inhabitants escape beyond the barriers of what they see and touch and hear, to the imagination of beings more pure and gentle and powerful than themselves; where the idea of good can never arise; but within and without, above and around, evil continually shall be the one overwhelming vision. Depart from Me! Who can picture the loneliness and desolation of the soul thus cut off from God? We have heard how prolonged solitary confinement issues in the overthrow of reason, in the prostration of all mental and bodily powers. But if the absence of man, and the voice of man, and the companionship of man, be so disastrous to his fellow-man, who shall measure the consequences of the entire withdrawal of God from His creature, who delineate the terrific desolation of that prison-house where God is not? II. We have reasoned that the absence of God from the future world of the lost will be a source of infinite sorrow, as being the immediate destruction of religion; AND TO WITHDRAW RELIGION FROM A WORLD IS TO WITHDRAW A MAIN ELEMENT OF HAPPINESS. We would add that in departing from God we shall leave behind all that is beautiful in art or ennobling in knowledge. Now it is very observable in the history of mankind how the arts and sciences have been connected in their origin and growth with religion. Astronomy was early mixed up with the worship of the sun and stars. The colossal remains of ancient days are, in almost all cases, those of fabrics designed for purposes of religion. Similarly, since the Incarnation of Christ, it has been the Church of Christ which has been the mother and fosterer of learning. Poetry, music, sculpture, painting, architecture, have been inspired in their loftiest efforts by religion. Again, the history of civilization is the history of Christianity; where-ever true religion prevails, wherever the Church of Christ is planted, there do you find human life in its most secure and refined state. We owe whatever is noble in literature, or beautiful in painting, or sublime in science, not to the natural develop-ment of our secret powers unassisted by Divine grace, but all these things are the result of a working of the Spirit of God in the spirit of man. It is not unaided human intellect which has produced those glorious works which are the heirlooms of the world, but human intellect, warmed, quickened, supported—in a word, inspired by the great God Himself. Thus God is to man's mind what the sun is to the physical world. It is the bright shining of the sun which draws out the vegetation of the ground, which ripens the fruit, and paints the flower. The more potent the rays of the sun, as in tropical climates, the more gigantic are the products of the soil, the more luscious the fruit, the more gorgeous the plumage. Even so with the world of mind. The more clear the vision of God, the more exalted is the development of the creature. Hence the angels are more excellent than man, because they see more of God. Hence the purer our religion, the less clouded our knowledge of God, the more rapid will be the growth of our own mental powers. It is the presence of God which educates the soul of man, ennobles its conceptions, enlightens its understanding, inflames its imagination, directs its judgment. You may call it the religious sentiment. But what is a religious feeling but the presence of God felt sensibly in the depths of our nature? And, if so, you will at once perceive another dread result of man's banishment from God. To command the wicked to depart from God is to command all the powers of man's mind to stand still for ever. Away from God men will be able neither to think or to do ought that is excellent or attractive. To send him away from God is to freeze all the currents of man's soul. No goodly invention, no sound of melody, no line of beauty can ever be known in that world where God is not. Who has not felt how a cloud passing athwart the sun upon a summer day takes all the loveliness from the landscape, all radiance from the sky, all sparkling from the waters, all balm from the air, and causes a chill to run through the limbs, which a moment before exulted in the sensation of life? And even such a coldness is that which will pervade the whole moral being of those from whose world God shall in His wrath withdraw Himself. Conclusion: The doctrine which we would enforce is, that religion is to be looked at and represented as a joy and solace, not as a yoke of bondage. Our great fault is that we do not sufficiently strive to render our most holy faith attractive. Surely it has in it the capacity to vanquish opposition by its very sympathies with our common requirement. Let us then, one and all, cast away the idea of religion as a yoke, a bondage, a work, and take it to ourselves as (what God intended it) a foretaste of the pleasures at His own right hand. (*Bishop Woodford.*) *The sinner in presence of the judgment:*—I. THE SINNER WILL BE ENCOMPASSED BY THE MULTITUDE OF HIS SINS. If, during this earthly life, an evil conscience is the most cruel tormentor, a two-edged sword for the sinner, he will feel its stings the most—1. At his departure from this life. (1) All self-delusions will vanish when the fragile body breaks down, the world with its possessions disappears, and time will be no more. (2) All terrors attack the soul of the sinner—his sinful past, his helpless present, and an inevitable and hopeless eternity. 2. At the approach of judgment, when the sinner's conscience will be—(1) Its own witness, because in the presence of Divine omniscience it will understand how useless it is to tell a false-hood, or to bring forth excuses, and how utterly impossible to conceal anything. (2) Its own accuser, as it will be obliged to make a sincere self-accusation con-cerning many faults and heinous crimes which were concealed in life. (3) Its own judge, as it will condemn the folly of its aberrations, the vanity of worldly attach-ment, the perversity of delaying conversion, &c., and it will itself approve the sentence pronounced by God. II. THE SINNER WILL BE STRAITENED BY THE SEVERITY OF JUDGMENT. 1. Jesus Christ, to whom the Father has committed all judgment, will, as God, avenge the insulted Divine dignity because of contempt and ingrati-tude, and His grieved humanity, because the sinner refused to give alms, and com-mitted so many unjust actions against his neighbour. 2. As Man. He who was before the mild Mediator and Intercessor in behalf of the sinner will be now the inexorable Judge. 3. As Redeemer He will demand an account, because the sinner has scorned His precious blood, and has slighted the graces offered to him; and because he has been the cause of the ruin of other souls. 4. As Model of a virtuous life, He will convict and confound the sinner. III. THE SINNER WILL BE UTTERLY CONFOUNDED BY THE SENTENCE PRONOUNCED AGAINST HIM. 1. This sentence will be as dreadful as hell itself. (1) Deprived for ever of the Beatific Vision. (2) Condemned—the creature by its Creator, man by his God, the Christian by his Redeemer. (3) Cursed—the soul, the body, all the senses and faculties. 2. This sentence will be perfectly just, for the punishment will be—(1) Proportionate to the multitude of sins, and to the wickedness, knowledge, and position of the sinner. (2) The portion of the infidel and reprobate sinner only, who, as he was not willing to believe and repent in time, ought to suffer in eternity. 3. The sentence is irrevocable. 4. It will be forthwith executed. (*De la Rue.*) *The disappointments which will take place at the day of judgment:*—I. SOME OF THE HUMAN RACE WILL BE SHUT OUT OF THE KINGDOM OF GOD WHO HAVE CONFIDENTLY EXPECTED ADMISSION. 1. Of this number will be all those who leave the world relying upon their own righteousness. 2. Of this number are all those persons who place their reliance on external religious services. 3. Of the same number is the enthusiast. Enthusiasm is a reliance for religious knowledge, dispositions, and duties on immediate and supernatural communications from God. No such communications exist in fact. Those which are mistaken for them are only the suggestions of a wild and heated imagination. 4. Of the same number also are those persons who rely upon a decent and amiable behaviour. 5. Of the same number also are they who rely upon what are called the moral duties of life. 6. Another class of men who will be exceedingly disappointed hereafter, will consist of those who rely on what may be called a religious character. 7. Persons who believe themselves to be religious because others believe them to be of this character constitute another class of those who will experience this dreadful disappointment. 8. Another class of these persons is composed of those who place their religion in the knowledge, and not in the obedience of Divine truth. 9. Another class of the same persons is formed of those who place their reliance upon their zeal. "It is good," saith the Apostle Paul, "to be zealously affected always in a good thing" (Gal. iv. 18). A cold, stupid, heartless professor of religion, absorbed in the concerns of this world, gives little evidence that his profession is sincere; and, if he be a Christian, is a disgrace to the name, and a spot upon the character of religion. Yet there is a zeal which is not according to knowledge. 10. Another class of the persons under consideration is formed of those who place their hope in a faith which is without works. II. OTHER PERSONS, WHOM THESE EXPECTED TO SEE SHUT OUT, WILL BE ACCEPTED. 1. Of this number there will be a multitude of such as, in this world, have lived in humble and despised circumstances. 2. In this number will be found great multitudes who have been our own friends, companions, and equals in the present world. 3. In this number will be included also a multitude of persons who, in this world, appear to be religious, and are, on that account, despised by others. 4. Of this number also will be found those whose acknowledged characters and opinions have, in many respects, been different from ours. III. THAT THE DISTRESS OCCASIONED BY THIS DISAPPOINTMENT WILL BE VERY GREAT. Weeping and gnashing of teeth are glowing images of extreme anguish; and this anguish is, by our Saviour, attributed to the two-fold disappointment mentioned in the text. What less can be believed from the nature of the subject? The disappointment will follow strong and high-raised expectations, and, in many instances, undoubting confidence. It will be a final disappointment. It will be a disappointment of every object for which we can hope, of every good which we are capable of enjoying. Concluding remarks: From these solemn and affecting considerations we can hardly fail to derive many, and those most important, practical lessons. 1. We are strongly urged by them to the most watchful care in determining what the genuine religion required by the gospel is. 2. With these solemn considerations in view, let me also urge every member of this assembly to examine the ground of his own hope of salvation. 3. These considerations strongly urge us to entertain very humble apprehensions of our own character. 4. These considerations powerfully compel us to exercise charitable thoughts towards others. (*T. Dwight, D.D.*) *The doom of self-deceivers :*—I. THE CHARACTERS SPOKEN OF. SELF-DECEIVERS. II. THEIR CONDITION. Thrust out of the kingdom. III. THE SIGHT THEY WILL WITNESS. The joy of the redeemed. IV. THE SORROW WITH WHICH THEY WILL BE OVERWHELMED.

" Weeping and gnashing of teeth." (*A. F. Barfield.*)   *Thrust out of the kingdom of heaven :*—" One day," says a lady, speaking of her early years, " when I was returning home, I saw my dear mother sitting on a bank in the orchard weeping bitterly. I thought she was weeping on account of my father's death. I went to her, and asked her why she wept so ? Her answer was, ' I may well weep to see my children taking the kingdom of heaven by violence; while I myself shall be shut out.' As well as I was able I pointed her to the Lamb of God which taketh away the sin of the world; from that time the work of grace in her soul began." *The heathen entering the kingdom of God :*—An Indian chief who had aided in the missionary work in his own tribe, the Ojibwa tribe, related this incident :—" An Indian boy of his tribe was taught to read, and presented with a New Testament, of which he became very fond. From that he learned to love the Saviour of whom he read such wonderful things in that wonderful book, and became a devout and sincere Christian. His chief passed many an hour with him in religious conversation. One day the boy sent for the chief who had instructed him, to come over to his father's cabin, for he was sick. On going there he found him in bed, suffering under a burning fever. Taking out from under his blanket his New Testament, which he had loved to read, he gave it to the chief and said : ' Here, I want you to take this, and when they bury me, please put this under my head.' ' Why,' asked the chief, ' do you wish it put there ? ' The dying lad replied : ' I want it there, so that as I rise in the resurrection I can give it to Jesus as I see Him come.' Not long after the young Christian spirit left the fevered body, and the cabin in the wilderness, for a palace on the plains of glory." So dies many a missionary convert just learning the rudiments of the gospel.   **There are last which shall be first.**—*Reversings :*—I. Some who are first in natural gifts are last in spiritual gifts. II. Some who are first in opportunity are last in improvement. III. Some who are first to start in the race are last at the goal. IV. Some who are first in privilege at one time are last in it at another. 1. The fall of the race itself is a case in point. 2. The casting away of the Jews and the calling of the Gentiles is another case. 3. The extinction of the Christian Church in many Eastern lands is a fact of the same kind. Concluding remarks : 1. These spiritual transpositions are the exception, not the rule. Other things being equal, the first will remain first. First in means, first in results; first in asking, first in receiving; first in faith, first in righteousness; first in self-culture, first in self-conquest; first in well-doing, first in well-being. When it is otherwise, something is wrong. The first place is not lost till it is abused. 2. Whilst this action of God is sovereign, it is never arbitrary. Men reap what they sow, and as they sow. (*J. E. Henry, M.A.*) *Lessons :*—1. Let us mark the authority of this passage in favour of strictness in religion. There is, indeed a spurious strictness about trifles which neglects the weightier matters of the law, and which is worthless ; but there is a proper and commendable strictness in adhering faithfully to all the duties of religion, which is required by the command to enter in by the strait gate. Let who may call it preciseness, but let us be steady to our principles and to our duty. 2. Let us neither over-rate nor under-rate the difficulties which lie in our way to heaven. But let us view them exactly as they are, that we may neither be inactive nor disheartened. 3. Let us remember, that whatever these difficulties may be, they must be overcome, else we are undone. Necessity will make the sluggard toil, and the coward fight ; but what necessity is equal to this ? 4. Let us carefully improve the present season. If we knock now, it shall be opened unto us ; but we shall knock too late after the door is finally shut. 5. Let us not trust in Church privileges. Let us not say, " The temple of the Lord, the temple of the Lord, the temple of the Lord are we " ; but let us so improve the means of grace here, that we may be prepared for glory hereafter. 6. Let us realize to our minds the separation which will take place when men shall either be admitted into heaven, or cast off for ever ; and, in doing so, let us follow the one party in the path of faith and holiness to glory ; and let us sedulously avoid the course of the other, saying, each of us, " O my soul, come not thou into their secret ; unto their assembly, mine honour, be not thou united." 7. As we are among the very first in point of privileges, let us not be the last in point of improvement. Much having been given to us, much will be required of us. 8. Finally, while we give ourselves diligently to the business of salvation, let us look for success in the way of dependence on Divine grace implored by prayer. This alone can enable us to overcome the difficulties which lie in our way ; and this will enable us to do so effectually. (*Jas. Foote, M.A.*)   *The reversal of ordinary judgments :*—Probably all thoughtful and religious people have often been disgusted at the readiness of the unthinking to pass judgment on their fellow-men, and to assign them their due praise or blame. And thoughtful spirits have longed for real justice, and have consoled themselves by thinking of that great reversal of human judgments which assuredly awaits us when we shall stand before the judgment-seat of the All-seeing and All-just. In order to bring home forcibly to our minds the full conviction that God will judge His creatures hereafter far differently from the way in which we commonly judge them now, it may be well for us to consider a few plain facts bearing on the case, facts which make it quite inevitable that God should set aside our hasty and ill-considered verdicts concerning good and bad people. 1. We forget that the sources or roots of holiness and of sin are often the same in great measure. Vices are often virtues run to seed. Prudence in its old age often turns into miserliness. Virtues, by their exuberant and luxuriant growth, often dig their own graves. "Be not righteous over-much: why shouldest thou destroy thyself?" seems often a very needful warning. And it very commonly happens that decayed virtues appear worse than born vices. *Corruptio optimi est pessimum.* For instance, scarcely any misanthropy is in a way so savage as that of disappointed faith in mankind. Misanthropy, if it be chiefly discontent with the actual condition of men, and hopeless yearning for their improvement, is not altogether far from the kingdom of God. As it surveys the meanness and the paltriness of mankind, it may well exclaim in the language of Jesus, "My God, my God, why hast Thou forsaken us?" In general it is perfectly plain that the sources of sanctity and sinfulness are often in great measure the same. This is the grain of truth in the common saying, "The greater the sinner, the greater the saint." Force of character tells in *either* direction. A very vivid nature is the source of both good and evil. Depth of feeling gives a man a great tendency to go wrong in this bewildering world, and also a great recuperative power when he has gone wrong. At the final judgment we can well understand that there must be a great reversal of ordinary human judgments. God will look to the roots of character in us; and we shall then see that the foundations of heroic virtues have been laid in many a forlorn soul which we thought overpowered and slain by evil in this life. And perhaps they will rank higher in the celestial kingdom, who have thus in grief and shame laid the foundations of a glorious temple of God, than those who have, with but little trouble, built for God a poor, common, little meeting-house of decent respectability. "Many that are first shall be last, and the last first." Perhaps the truest of the elect may be saved the last in point of time, the last to leave the wrecked ship of a storm-beaten humanity. 2. Further, we must remember that some sins which from an external point of view seem equally great, are in reality very different in their importance and significance. Of some sins we may say that they express the real and true nature of the man committing them. He is, as it were, *totus in illis*, wrapped up in them. They are the outcome of his truest and most permanent self; whereas, in other cases, like that of David, sins often seem quite transient phenomena, as it were eclipses of a man's real nature, hardly so much a man's own doing as that of some alien or hostile spirit which has seized him; instances of demoniacal possession, and not of natural or innate wickedness. Such assuredly was the sin of the minister, Arthur Dimmesdale, in Hawthorne's "Scarlet Letter." Such sinful actions form an exception to the general rule; they do not help to form a persistent habit of sinning. On the contrary, they are like the exacerbations and paroxysms which often precede recovery in the case of bodily maladies; they are the work of the evil spirit tearing the soul with especial fury just before it is cast out. Thus it sometimes happens that a man's whole after life is the better for a fall, which has shown him the hatefulness of sin, and also his own weakness. 3. Again, sins which admit of high aspirations are in reality far less dangerous than less gross Pharisaic sins, which are not clearly recognized as sins, and which in consequence do not seem to call for repentance. Publicans and harlots are more likely to repent and change than those Pharisees whose sins are so intensely respectable that they seem almost virtues. Baptized or consecrated selfishness is the greatest hindrance to true goodness. 4. Again, in trying to forecast the future judgment of God, we must take account of the terrible mystery of inherited evil tendencies—tendencies which are often much increased by bad education. Many people are born blind spiritually, because their parents have sinned. Just as Nature often produces bodily abortions, so no doubt does it often produce spiritual abortions. There are myriads of hapless souls which never had any real probation at all in this life. 5. Lastly, in the case of the more strictly religious virtues our judgments are often glaringly false—*e.g.*, concerning reverence and the merits of faith. Much that passes for reverence is merely irreligious indifference. Men do not wish to be troubled by religion in their daily life, so they erect for it a shrine far remote from all the feelings and actions of ordinary life. And this banishment of their Creator they call reverence for Him. To talk of God as if He were an unmeaning abstraction is often considered reverent; to talk of God as if He were our Father, our Guide, and our unfailing Friend, is often considered irreverent. Moreover, some men are so entirely reverent in heart, so utterly filled with an abiding sense of the reality of religion, that they are comparatively careless of their manner. Pierced through and through by a sense of God's presence, it never strikes such men that they need prove their reverence. And so reverence itself sometimes causes apparent irreverence. Probably Elijah would be reproved for irreverence if he were to worship in a ritualistic church; for the true altar of the Eternal was deep down in the prophet's awe-struck heart, and he would probably care but little for any external altar. Again, we err greatly in our ordinary judgments of doubters in religion. Doubt is often a really hopeful sign, just as pain of body is often a sign that paralysis is passing away. Doubt is often only a sort of moulting in the spiritual world, the moulting of the soaring eagle wings of faith. Hence it often has a very real value. (*A. H. Craufurd, M.A.*)

Vers. 31, 32. **Go ye and tell that fox.**—*"That fox":*—The attempt of the Pharisees to frighten Jesus Christ out of Perea drew from Him a prompt and sharp rejoinder. The answer was to the effect that no such threats could influence the purpose or in the least degree accelerate the movements of the Nazarene. His work was near an end, but He would have no hurry or panic. He would cast out demons and perform cures to the last day that His predestined stay in Perea would permit. If Herod wished to put a hasty stop to such works, so much to the discredit of Herod. As for the menace to His life, Jesus despised it. He was going up to Jerusalem, knowing that He would be killed. But Herod could not kill Him. At the outset of His ministry an angry crowd in Galilee had tried to make an end of Him, but they could not. The Prophet could not die but at Jerusalem. The metaphor here was in the opprobrious epithet applied to Herod Antipas—" that fox." Evidently it expressed, and was meant to express, that the Lord Jesus saw through and despised the cunning wiles of the Tetrarch. Many writers on the Gospels, both in Germany and among ourselves, have been anxious to protect our Saviour from the charge of speaking disrespectfully of a ruler, and have therefore tried to show that this epithet was in reality hurled against the Pharisees, who had affected so much solicitude for His life. In the present case, it is as plain as words can make it that Jesus stigmatized Herod as " that fox." The man was a selfish intriguer, neither good nor strong, but cunning, subservient to those above him, a sort of jackal to the imperial lion at Rome, but ruthless to any who were beneath him and within his grasp. Probably it was this metaphor that suggested to Jesus that of the hen protecting her brood, which immediately follows. He looked on Herod and men of his stamp as devourers of the people. As for Himself, He might seem to be weak and unable to save Himself, but He was the best friend of the people; and if they would only gather to Him, He would cover them with the wings of His protection, so that no fox could do them hurt. But the Pharisees, and ultimately the misguided people too, took part with the fox against Him. And why should it be thought strange that Jesus could entertain and express a feeling of scorn for what is mean and wicked? Some of our moralists assert too roundly that mortal man has no right to feel contempt. There is a contempt that is ignoble, and there is a contempt that is noble. The ignoble is that which rests on mere conventionalism and prejudice, as when one despises another for being less highly born or less richly provided than himself. It flourishes among conventional professors of religion who yet sing the praises of humility. Such hauteur could not find place in the breast of our Saviour, and ought not to be harboured by any Christian. Wherever it enters it hardens the heart, dries up the sympathies, inflates the sense of self-importance, and induces a cold indifference to the wants and woes of others. But there is a noble scorn that may dwell in the heart along with tender compassion and fervent love. If there be a genuine appreciation of what is good and true, the obverse side of it must be a healthy contempt for what is wicked and false. (*D. Fraser, D.D.*)   *Righteous reproach:*—He does not hesitate to call Herod a fox—a mere cunning, designing man, only courageous when there is no danger at hand; scheming and plotting in his den, but having no true bravery of heart; an evil-minded person, whose whole character is summed up in the word "fox." What! did Jesus Christ, then, call men names? Not in the usual sense of that expression. Did He call Herod a fox out of mere defiance or spite? He was incapable of doing anything of the kind. When Jesus Christ spoke a severe word, the severity came out of the truth of its application. Is it not a harsh thing to call a man a liar? Not if he be false. Is it not very unsocial to describe any man as a hypocrite? Not if he be untrue. Wherein, then, is this wickedness of calling men names? In the misapplication of the epithets. It is wicked to call a man true, if we know him to be untrue. There is an immoral courtesy; there is a righteous reproach. We do not use harsh words when we tell men what they really are. On the other hand, it is a matter of infinite delicacy to tell a man what he really is, because, at best, we seldom see more than one aspect of a man's character. If we could see more of the man, probably we should change our opinion of his spirit. In the case of Jesus Christ, however, He saw the inner heart, the real and true quality of the Tetrarch; and, therefore, when He described Herod as a fox, He spoke the word of righteousness and of truth. It was not an epithet; it was a character in a word; it was a man summed up in a syllable. Let us, therefore, be very careful how we follow this example, because we ought to have equal knowledge before we take an equal position in this respect. On the other hand, let us beware of that simulation of courtesy, which is profoundly untrue, which is despicably immoral—the kind of thing which sets itself to catch the favour and the flattery of the passing moment. (*J. Parker, D.D.*)   *Christ's work cannot be stopped:*—We thought that Jesus Christ's labour would be cut short by this message from Herod. Jesus Christ must finish what He has begun. But is it not in the power of the great and the mighty to say to Christ, "You must stop at this point"? It is in their power, truly, to say it, and when they have said it they may have relieved their own feelings: but the great, the beneficent, the redeeming work of the Son of God proceeds as if not a word to the contrary had been said. The kings of the earth set themselves, and the rulers took counsel together against the Lord, and against His anointed; and behold their rage came to nothing, and their fury recoiled upon themselves! "He that sitteth in the heavens shall laugh; the Holy one shall have them in derision." Are we opposing Jesus Christ? Are we in any way setting ourselves against the advancement of His kingdom? It will be an impotent rage. Go and strike the rocks with your fist—perhaps you may batter down the granite with your poor bones. Try! Go and tell the sea that it shall not come beyond a certain line, and perhaps the hoary billows will hear you, and run away and say they be afraid of such mighty men. Try! You have nothing else to do, you may as well try. But as for keeping back this kingdom of God, this holy and beneficent kingdom of truth—no man can keep it back, and even the gates of hell shall not prevail against it. Men may rage; men do rage. Other men adopt another policy; instead of rage and fury and great excitement, they set themselves against the kingdom of God in an indirect and remote way. But both policies come to the same thing. The raging man who pulls down the wooden cross and tramples it underfoot, and the man who offers a passive resistance to the progress of the kingdom of heaven, come to the same fate. The light shines on, noontide comes, and God gets His own way in His own universe. (*Ibid.*)   *Perseverance in the path of duty:*—An example of the marvellous power to be found in the motive of duty is afforded in the seven years' march of David Livingstone from the coast of Zanzibar toward the courses of the Nile. What else, indeed, could have so well sustained him in his trials with savages, and noxious insects, and nearly impassable jungles, and starvation, and prostrating disease, and prospective death? "In this journey," he writes, in the calmest style of self-examination, "I have endeavoured to follow with unswerving fidelity the path of duty. . . . The prospect of death in pursuing what I knew to be right did not make me veer to one side or the other." And so this sublime hero struggled on until, while apparently engaged in the act of prayer, he passed from a kneeling posture on earth to an enthroned position in heaven.

Ver. 33. **I must.**—*Reconciliation with life:*—Sooner or later we all of us have to learn to say those words, "I must"; and our whole character, good or evil, saved or lost, will depend upon the way in which we learn to say, "I must." How we should learn to say, "I must," is the subject of this morning's sermon. "Nevertheless, I must walk to-day, and to-morrow, and the day following." Not to the Son of Man alone, but to every man there come inevitable days of life. No human will can escape the necessity of saying at some hour, "I must." Even Napoleon has his St. Helena. We say, " I will " ; and the next day find ourselves saying, " I must." God never suffers us to say the one for many hours without compelling us to say the other. Thoughtlessly we go our way, and look up to find ourselves facing the inevitable. There it is, steadily confronting us. It is hard as the face of a precipice. We cannot go around it. We cannot climb over it. We must stand still before it. There is no word of our English speech which we more cordially dislike than this same short word "must." We will not brook it when spoken to us by other men. Any friendship would be broken by it. Love knows nothing of it. Liberty consists in refusing to speak it when kings proclaim it, or any foreign might commands it. Men have died rather than yield to it. Yet consider how large a portion of our daily life is put before us, and how much of our own personality is given to us under some form of necessity; and how large consequently is the work of reconciliation to be accomplished, if it be possible, between the "I wills " and the " I musts" of our lives. There is, to begin with, the "must " of heredity. We cannot vacate our inherited individuality and choose another and a happier. We have to accept ourselves as we were born. Besides this primal necessity of our birth, there are the fixed grooves of natural law in which our lives must run, and all the forms of circumstance to which our individualities must be fitted. In the midst of these physical, industrial, and social necessities our space of spirit and freedom seems small as the cage of a bird, and hard sometimes as the treadmill of a beast of burden. Every day, every hour, has its limitations and thraldom of spirit for us. Pain is an insult to the spirit. Sickness is humiliation of the soul. Death is the triumphing as of an enemy over us. I have been expressing thus our common feeling of irreconcilableness to much that seems inevitable in human life. In order that we may learn to say " I must " in any true and free way, we should look more intently into the nature of this great compulsion which is laid upon us all. What is it ? It wears ofttimes a face of fate. Is that its only and eternal countenance ? Is there any thoughtfulness for us behind it ? What or whose is this will which must be done on earth as in heaven ? Our tone and temper when we say "I must " will depend very vitally upon our belief concerning the character of the Power whose grasp is the inevitableness of human life. To what voice, and to what voice alone, in the universe may a man answer, " I must," and " I will"? For this also is true that there can be no reconciliation for us with the inevitable, no happy harmony of our spirits with our circumstances and our necessities, until in some way we have learned to answer, " I will," from within our own free hearts, whenever that Voice from without speaks to us its inevitable " You must." The two voices from without and from within must become one, keyed to the same note and making one music, before life can be harmony and peace. I might say that it is religion which does this blessed work; that I have seen religion reconciling men and life ; and that religion has joined soul to life so happily that henceforth no man can put them asunder. I might urge that only when we gain clear perception that every inevitable thing is a Divine thing, every word " You must " in our life a word of God, only then can we begin to answer with good heart, " I will." I might set in order the reasons for believing that beneath this whole appearance of inevitableness in human life and history there is a will of Divine righteousness, and a heart of infinite love. When we feel the touch of the love of God in the hand of fate, our hearts can say through all our tears, " Thy will be done." I might urge further that our present life, with its civilized temptations, and its polite lies of the devil, and its fashionable demons of unbelief and unrighteousness, lays upon all true men an urgent necessity of realizing the presence of the living God on this earth, if indeed we would keep the faith and the hope of a man's spirit amid the shams, and shames, and tumults of our world. I might urge you to try this religious way of reconciliation with life, to seek for some sign of God's presence, and to wait for some revelation of God's pure will, in all the events which come to you, and which you must meet in your way of life. But there is a nearer argument than this. There is clearer proof of this one true way of happy and harmonious life than even these evidences of our reason and conscience. It is shown to us—the true life, in its full strength, its noble harmony and peace, is all revealed to us—in the Christ of the Gospels. That was the life of perfect reconciliation with the world. When only twelve years old, what must be as His duty and His ministry was already Jesus' will of life. " I must " and " I will " strike one note in His Diviner speech. When He said, " I must be about My Father's business," it was with no cheerless tone, with no heartless voice of resignation. It was His meat to do the will of Him that sent Him. Knowing this world to be God's world, and perceiving life in it to be God's will, what He must do was what He would do, and every necessity of His ministry was welcome as a messenger from God's presence. The tragic inevitableness of His life—that dark shadow which He saw stealing over His path long before the disciples noticed any sign of its approach—the need of His sufferings and death, which even when He went down His trial-way they could not understand or believe—the cruel necessity of His betrayal, and the crucifixion in a world of sin, which Jesus saw must needs be the cup which it was the Father's will not to let pass from Him—all this was not enough to set His heart at strife with the way which to-day, and to-morrow, and the day following, He must walk, to make Him cease to call God's ordained hour, "My hour," or to go, eager and strong, to meet it. "Howbeit I must go on My way to-day and to-morrow, and the day following: for it cannot be that a prophet perish out of Jerusalem." In this obedience unto death the will of God which is to be done on earth and the will of man are one and the same pure will. (*Newman Smyth, D.D.*)

Ver. 34. O Jerusalem, Jerusalem.—*The Saviour's sorrow over lost men :*—I. WORDS LIKE THESE, SPOKEN AT SUCH A MOMENT, LET US SEE, AS FAR AS WORDS CAN DO, INTO THE INNERMOST OF JESUS' HEART. They are a wonderful expression of His deep-seated desire to save from ruin the worst of men, to save the unwilling, to save to the very last. 1. If ever excess of guilt could have alienated the Saviour and steeled Him against mercy, it must have been Jerusalem's. Her privileges had been surpassing. 2. But if sinners' sins cannot destroy Christ's willingness to save them, neither can their unwillingness to be saved. You thrust the outstretched arms away: they are stretched out still. You say, "I will not": He still says, "I will." He would that you would; prays you to turn; waits for your turning; grieves that you will not; but watches to welcome with joy the first poor timid tokens of your heart's relenting. Thus He maintains His Divine supremacy of love; offering to the spiritual universe the stupendous contrast of a willing God and an unwilling sinner. 3. Refusal, then, does not overbear this extraordinary desire of God to save us. Neither can delay out-weary it. On the contrary, time only tests to the utmost the sincerity of the Divine mercy. The perseverance of the Saviour is the measure of His love. II. In the next place, THIS LANGUAGE OF THE DEPARTING SAVIOUR TELLS US HOW HE BLESSES THOSE WHO WILL BE GATHERED. Strong love like His is gentle as it is strong. Only let the mighty Lover, who made you, gather you to Himself, and you will see how He will cradle you like a mother. I read it in these words, that, when He gathers men, He gathers them to His heart. They are a cry of love. Love seeks to have the loved one near, and is ever reaching forth and calling out to draw unto itself for the joy of having what it loves. Let me say it reverently: it is the deep desire of God in our Lord Jesus Christ to bring the most impure and evil of us all into as close a relation to Himself as can be. Let us remember, the place of nearness is the place of safety. To be under the shadow of wings meant in Hebrew ears to be where mercy reigned through blood-shedding, and a gracious covenanted God guarded His faithful people. It means the same thing here. For shelter from the doom, which, for their national sins, had already sent its forewarning signs over the political horizon, Jesus called His fellow-citizens to Himself. For shelter against impending judgment overhanging every sinful soul, He calls us to repentance and to faith. It is not safety alone that by this image the Lord offers us in His tenderness. Have you not seen how, when it is night and the sky over all has spread out wings of darkness to gather all things to rest; and in the soft still gloom the airs are hushed and the birds are dumb and the beasts make no stir, but all things sleep, down to the very flowers which shut their little cups and hang their leaves in dewy rest; have you not seen how then the brood is gathered by the hen to sleep upon her breast, and be curtained over with her wings? Who does not know how they pillow there upon the down, cherished by her body's warmth, till morning light? It is not I, it is the Lord, who says that it is so with His saved people. The soul that comes to Him finds in Him rest as well as shelter. Rest for the laden conscience in His blood; rest for the weary will in His powerful spirit; rest for the sad heart in being loved by His love and cherished in an infinite Divine comfort. III. So far I have spoken of what He would have done had the Jerusalemites gathered at His call; WHAT HE WILL DO IF WE GATHER TO HIM. Fain would I linger here; but my text forces me to a contrast from which my soul shrinks. Its words give deeper insight still into the Redeemer's heart. Underneath the joy of salvation it touches a fount of tears. It is, in truth, His last wail of sorrow over men who would not be saved. Remember, these are

funeral words. Israel's day is done ; Israel's hope is dead ; Israel's doom is sealed.
All the toil is ended; and no fruit. Farewell to mercy, for her God deserts her
temple. Farewell! It is just? I know it is, most just. They have deserved it?
Yes, with a thousandfold deserving. So have we all, and not one of us can blame
the righteousness which condemns. But, men and brethren, love weeps when
justice smites. The Lamb sorrows in His wrath. And it only makes justice the
more awful when you see that it has so much of pity in it and so little of poor
personal triumph or ungenerous readiness, that the Judge yearns and wails over
the soul He dooms. (*J. O. Dykes, D.D.*)   *The hen and chickens* :—The maternal
love and courage of birds have been celebrated in the literature of all nations.
Even the Mussulman admires it; witness the Moslem story of the white dove.
One came before Mohammed with two fledglings tied up in a cloth, which he had
taken from the wood. The mother dove had bravely followed. Mohammed commanded that the cloth should be opened; on which the dove flew down, and covered
her trembling offspring with her wings. Then the prophet directed that the mother
and her young should be restored unhurt to the nest in the wood, and took the
opportunity to teach a good lesson—

> " From Allah's self cometh this wondrous love ;
>   Yea, and I swear by Him who sent me here,
> He is more tender than a nursing dove,
>   More pitiful to men than she to these."

To appreciate the feeling of Jesus Christ for Jerusalem, we must remember how
complete was His knowledge of its sin. Let it not be thought strange that the
will of the people of Jerusalem should be allowed to resist and defeat the mercy of
the Son of God. The whole history of the nation was one of often-repeated resistance to the will of Jehovah, and rejection of His grace. The Lord desired to save,
but never would force salvation on any nation or any creature. Indeed, a forced
salvation would be futile, and mercy received against one's will could do no good.
The illustration used by our Lord implied that danger was at hand. Observe a hen
in the open field, happy with her chickens running about her, picking and chirping
in the sunshine. Suddenly a hawk appears in the air, or some mischievous animal
comes slyly over the ground. On the instant the hen calls her brood to her, covers
them with her wings, and is ready for their defence. Timid enough at other times,
she is brave for her chickens, and will die rather than let one of them be lost. So
the Lord Jesus, perceiving the danger which hovered over Jerusalem long before the
Jews were aware of it, was willing to cover and save them. So also is it in every
age and every nation. He who is the Saviour of the world sees the approaching
perdition of ungodly men, and is willing to deliver them. Those who come to Him
He will in no wise cast out. What a simple way of salvation! And how sure and
perfect the defence! When lambs are startled, they run to the ewes ; the kids to
the she-goats. Among the fiercest animals, the young run to their mothers for
protection, and these will guard their offspring at whatever peril to themselves.
But no quadruped, wild or tame, can cover her young so completely as a bird can
do with her folding wings. Therefore is this last the apt illustration of the
sufficiency of Christ to save. Those who trust in Him are completely covered by
His righteousness and strength. On this wise has Divine salvation always been
revealed. The Psalms frequently refer to the favour and protection of Jehovah as
the shadow of outstretched wings (Psa. xvii. 8; xxxvi. 7; lvii. 1; lxi. 4; lxiii. 7;
xci. 4). Our Redeemer's lament over Jerusalem shows what His heart is toward
all mankind. It is a grief to Him to have His offer of salvation slighted, a joy to
have it embraced. How unhappy the mother-bird while any of her brood continue
astray and heedless of her call! What manner of persons Christians ought to be!
What joy of faith, what restfulness of love should be under the covert of His
wings! What nearness, too, to one another, and what obligation to brotherly
kindness! The brood are packed very closely under the hen. (*D. Fraser, D.D.*)
Willingness to save :—I. Now, first, observe THE MANIFESTATION OF GOD TO ISRAEL
WHICH THIS VERSE BRINGS OUT BEFORE OUR VIEW. 1. We observe God's sovereignty
manifested in the choice of Israel. "O Jerusalem, Jerusalem." Why, we ask,
should Jerusalem be singled out from all other nations of the earth? Why should
the people of Israel receive God's special teaching, and be made examples of His
peculiar mercies? The Bible tells us that God dealt with Israel as He did not
deal with any other nation on the face of the earth—that He gave them special

instruction, that He communicated unto them special advantages, that their advantages were many every way, that is, in every point of view, but chiefly, because not to the Assyrians, not to the Egyptians, not to any other remarkable nation of antiquity, but to the Jews were committed the oracles of God. We can only account for this by God's sovereignty. 2. We notice also the manifestation of God's grace in the messages which He sent to this highly favoured people—"O Jerusalem, Jerusalem, thou that killest the prophets, and stonest them which are sent unto thee." God's prophets, God's messengers, those who were specially inspired or taught by His Holy Spirit, who alone can give understanding of the counsels of God, were sent to Israel. Why? Can we trace anything in their history which made them in a special manner deserving of such a favour as this? Nothing of the kind. Their whole history is a history of God's lovingkindness and man's ingratitude. 3. Observe, again, the mercy of God's character manifested in His dealings towards them. It was not one prophet, but many, that God sent; not one messenger, but various messengers—and one after another the messengers and prophets were ill-treated. 4. I notice, further, God's love—the love of God's character in His dealings with them. For what was His revealed purpose towards the children of Israel when He sent to them the prophets, and gave them instruction as to His will? It was to gather their children together as a hen gathereth her chickens under her wings!—to gather them together, to be unto them protection and safety. 5. Further, God's unchangeableness was manifested in His dealings with Israel. Observe the language of the Saviour, "How often would I have gathered thy children!" It was not one or two manifestations of God's grace which Israel had received, but many. Every repetition of His mercy is a proof of His unchangeableness. 6. And yet there is a solemn view of this subject, for the verse immediately following the text speaks of God's justice in His dealing with Israel. "Behold your house is left unto you desolate." 7. And then observe, further, God's faithfulness in the final issue of His dealings with Israel. "For I say unto you, ye shall not see Me henceforth, till ye shall say, Blessed is He that cometh in the name of the Lord." There are representatives of Israel after the flesh who shall occupy that favoured position. They shall receive the Saviour whom their forefathers rejected. And thus is it that God has, as it were, concentrated the rays of light which manifest His own character, in order that they may fall upon this single point—His willingness to save the sinful, the unworthy, the lost, and the undone. II. But now, to pass from this, what is the special instruction which we ourselves, to whom the oracles of God are come, may derive from what we have read and examined, concerning our Lord's willingness with reference to guilty Israel? We may learn, Christian brethren, WHAT WE HAVE TO DO WITH THE PURPOSES, WITH THE MESSAGES, AND WITH THE SALVATION OF GOD. 1. Learn what we have to do with the purposes of God. Observe, it was God's sovereign purpose, with which His creatures could not interfere, to choose Jerusalem—to choose, that is, the nation of Israel, as a nation honoured and privileged above all other nations. We may be sure of His willingness to save, because even His sovereignty is revealed so as to set forth in prominence this willingness. 2. What have we to do, then, with the messages of God? "How shall we escape, if we neglect so great salvation?" 3. What, then, have we to do with God's salvation, but to regard it as set forth to us in connection with our Lord and Saviour Jesus Christ? Observe, He speaks in the text as One who is able to save. He claims the attributes of Deity when He says, "How often would *I* have gathered thy children together!" The Man Christ Jesus, in the midst of His humiliation, speaks with the authority of God. But not only is He able to save, but willing. (*W. Cadman, M.A.*) *Choice may become habit :*—It is most necessary that the "instinct of migration" shall not be resisted, for such resistance means the loss of power to emigrate. In a recent article in a scientific paper upon the "Everglades of Florida," we read that so enfeebled have the birds that there resort become through failure to use their wings in flight that now they find it almost impossible to rise when pressed hard by their enemies. Even so is it with human souls. The "will not" becomes the "cannot." There is a process of deterioration that ends at last in death. Slaves of choice become slaves of habit. (*W. W. Wells.*) *The moorhen and her young :*—An angler, in Hampton Court Park, disturbed a moorhen who had just hatched, and watched her anxiety and manœuvres to draw away her young. She would go a short distance, utter a cry, return, and seemed to lead the way for her brood to follow. Having driven her away, that he might have a better opportunity of watching her young ones, she never ceased calling them : and they made towards her, skulking amongst the rushes till they came to the other side of the pond. They had only just left the shell, and had, probably, never heard the cry of their mother before. *Divine magnanimity :*—When Socrates was sentenced by the Athenian judges, the executioner wept as he handed him the fatal hemlock to drink. Christ knew the judges and rulers of Jerusalem would condemn Him to death, yet He weeps over them. In the former case, the executioner weeps over the executed, here the case is reversed. Truly, Socrates displayed the character of a philosopher, but Jesus Christ that of a God.